Basic Equivalents and Substitutions

A MORE COMPLETE LIST WILL BE FOUND ON PAGES 33-35.

Almonds, shelled	¼ pound	1 cup
in shell	1 pound	¼ pound nutmeats
Apples, raw, unpared	1 pound	3 cups, pared and sliced
Baking powder	1 teaspoon	¼ teaspoon baking soda plus ½ cup buttermilk or sour milk (reduce other liquid in recipe by ½ cup)
Beans, dried	1 pound	6 cups cooked
Bread, loaf	1 pound	12 to 16 slices
	1 slice	⅓ cup dry crumbs
Butter	1 stick	½ cup; ¼ pound; 8 tablespoons
	1 cup	1 cup margarine; ¾ cup chicken fat
Cabbage, raw	1 pound	4 cups shredded
Catsup or chili sauce in cooking	1 cup	1 can (8 ounces) tomato sauce plus ½ cup sugar, 2 tablespoons vinegar
Chocolate	1 square	1 ounce
		1 tablespoon, melted
		4 tablespoons, grated
		3 tablespoons cocoa plus 1 tablespoon butter or margarine, *or*
		4 tablespoons cocoa plus ½ tablespoon fat
Coffee	1 pound	40 to 50 servings
Corn meal, uncooked	1 pound	3 cups
	1 cup	4 cups cooked
Cornstarch	1 tablespoon	2 tablespoons flour; 1 tablespoon potato flour; 4 teaspoons quick-cooking tapioca
Cream, heavy	1 cup	2 cups whipped
	1 cup	⅓ cup butter plus ¾ cup milk
Cream sauce	1½ cups	1 can condensed cream-style soup plus ¼ cup liquid
Eggs, whole	1 cup	5 large eggs
whole	1 pound	9 medium eggs
yolks	1 cup	12 large yolks
whites	1 cup	8 to 10 large whites
in sauces, custards	1 egg	2 yolks
Flour, all-purpose	1 pound	4 cups
	1 ounce	4 tablespoons
	1 cup, sifted	1 cup instantized
	1 cup, sifted	1 cup plus 2 tablespoons cake flour
Garlic	1 medium clove	⅛ teaspoon garlic powder
Herbs, fresh, chopped	1 tablespoon	1 teaspoon dried
Lemon	1	2½ to 3½ tablespoons juice; 2 teaspoons rind
Macaroni	1 pound	9 cups cooked
Milk, whole	1 cup	½ cup evaporated milk plus ½ cup water
	1 cup	1 cup reconstituted nonfat dry milk plus 2 teaspoons butter
Milk, skim	1 cup	3 to 4 tablespoons dry nonfat milk solids plus 1 cup water
Milk, sour	1 cup	1 tablespoon lemon juice or vinegar plus milk to make 1 cup
Mushrooms, fresh	1 pound	6 to 8 ounces canned
Mustard, dry	1 teaspoon	1 tablespoon prepared
Noodles	1 pound	9 cups cooked
Orange	1 medium	5 to 6 tablespoons juice, 2 to 3 tablespoons grated rind
Peas in the pod	1 pound	1 cup shelled
Pecans, in shell	1 pound	⅓ pound shelled
Rice, uncooked	1 pound	2½ cups uncooked, 8 cups cooked
Raisins, seedless	1 cup	6 ounces
Salt, table	1 ounce	1½ tablespoons
coarse	1 ounce	2 tablespoons
Spaghetti, uncooked	1 pound	10 cups cooked
Sugar, brown	1 pound	2¼ cups, firmly packed
granulated brown	1 pound	3¾ cups
confectioners'	1 pound	4½ to 5 cups, sifted
granulated white	1 pound	2¼ cups
substitutions	1 cup granulated white	1 cup brown sugar, firmly packed, *or* 1⅓ cups granulated brown sugar
Tapioca	2 teaspoons	1 tablespoon flour (for thickening)
Tea	1 pound	120 servings
Yeast	1 cake	1 package active dry yeast

P9-BYT-526

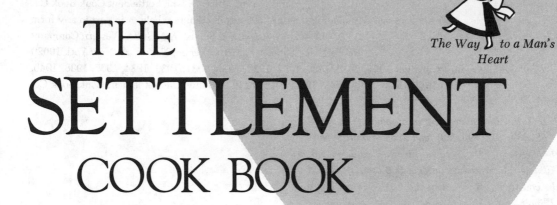

THE SETTLEMENT COOK BOOK

The Way to a Man's Heart

TREASURED RECIPES
OF SEVEN DECADES

THE FAMOUS ALL-PURPOSE
COOK BOOK FOR BEGINNER
AND EXPERT

THIRD EDITION / NEWLY REVISED

SIMON AND SCHUSTER · NEW YORK

Copyright © 1965, 1976 by The Settlement Cook Book Co.
All rights reserved, including the right of reproduction in whole or in part in any form
Published by Simon and Schuster, A Gulf+Western Company
Rockefeller Center, 630 Fifth Avenue, New York, New York 10020
Previous editions copyright 1901, 1915, 1920, 1922, 1924, 1930, 1931, 1933, 1934, 1936, 1938, 1940,
1941, 1943, 1944, 1945, 1947, 1949, 1951, 1954 by The Settlement Cook Book Co.

*The charts and drawings which appear on pages 265, 266, 267,
269, 284, 288, 289, 292, 293, 296, and 297 are reproduced
through the courtesy of the National Livestock and Meat Board,
Chicago, Illinois. The drawings on page 306 are reproduced
through the courtesy of the Poultry and Egg National Board,
Chicago, Illinois.*

Designed by Helen Barrow
Manufactured in the United States of America
Printed by The Murray Printing Company
Bound by The Book Press

1 2 3 4 5 6 7 8 9 10

Library of Congress Cataloging in Publication Data

Main entry under title:

The Settlement cook book.

   Includes index.
   1. Cookery, American.
TX715.S495   1975   641.5   76-21350
ISBN 0-671-22087-X

CONTENTS

PREFACE

THIS *thirty-third edition of* The Settlement Cook Book *retains most of the old favorites that have pleased so many users over the years. We have deleted recipes only when we felt we had a more desirable substitute or when old recipes included ingredients that are now difficult to obtain. The recipes we have added reflect some of the changes in today's society—simplified entertaining, more versatile use of leftovers, renewed interest in bread making, and an emphasis on low-cost high-protein main dishes. Because we believe that this newest edition of the* Settlement *is the best ever since our first little book appeared in 1901, we would like to tell old friends and new a little about our exciting history and growth.*

A Look at the Past

The Settlement *is unique among the basic cook books, in the way it began and in the way it has developed as a nonprofit, philanthropic organization. It all started in Milwaukee, Wisconsin, around the turn of the century. At that time there were vast migrations of people from Europe seeking freedom and a better life, and Milwaukee received its share of these newcomers. To help them learn about American life and American ways, classes in English and citizenship, sewing and cooking were organized and held in a neighborhood house called "The Settlement." Mrs. Simon Kander, an enthusiastic Settlement volunteer, was in charge of the cooking classes. She regretted that the eager students had to spend so much time laboriously copying down instructions and recipes from the blackboard. Then she had a brilliant idea. Why not print the lessons and recipes?*

Her volunteer ladies' committee thoroughly approved of the plan. But the conservative gentlemen of the Settlement board refused to authorize the $18 required. They suggested the ladies have the work done on their own, and laughingly offered to "share in any profits from your little venture."

The ladies were undaunted, and with the help of a friendly printer, advertisements were solicited to defray expenses, and the financial crisis was solved. In fact, a more ambitious book became possible. Mrs. Kander collected treasured recipes from the committee and their friends (many of them noted Milwaukee hostesses) as well as favorite European dishes of the students and their families, even recipes from noted chefs in this country and abroad.

Mrs. Kander was an accomplished cook, yet her students were not. She realized that a "pinch" of this or that must be converted into accurate measurements, and the recipes expressed in the simplest and clearest language. Perhaps her greatest contribution—and a principle that continues to be observed—was her insistence that every recipe be tested not once but many times by committee members in their own kitchens. (Mr. Kander once ordered her to "cut that pancake out of the bill of fare for at least a week"; how many other long-suffering families deserve our thanks.)

Finally, in April 1901 one thousand copies of a slim 174-page book appeared: The Way to a Man's Heart . . . The Settlement Cook Book. *Nobody dreamed it would eventually sell over a million and three-quarters copies in all its revised and expanded editions to date.*

The little book was a hit from the start. It was divided about equally between simple recipes for beginning cooks and more elaborate recipes for experienced cooks. Seemingly it pleased both groups, and copies of the first edition that were not needed for the cooking classes were quickly sold by a Milwaukee merchant at fifty cents apiece. The demand for more copies led to another edition in 1903. It must have given Mrs. Kander and her committee great satisfaction when proceeds from the sale of the first two editions were graciously accepted by the board toward a new Settlement House. In 1909 the cook book was able to provide the site for the new building. By this time the ladies, looking to the future, had formed the Settlement Cook Book Company, a philanthropic corporation expressly concerned with educational and recreational projects.

Over the years, our cook book has benefited our community in many ways. We assisted in the establishment of the first nursery school in Milwaukee. We have contributed scholarship aid to students. The Settlement House and its successor have received financial help for over seventy years. And the general community has benefited from contributions to many undertakings. We are proud to be a part of this nonprofit organization, and we think of those of you who use our cook book as our partners in these undertakings.

A Look at the Present

As The Settlement Cook Book *became an institution in hundreds of thousands of American homes, new ideas and new recipes were added and the book became bigger and more comprehensive.*

When we prepared for our present updating, we asked ourselves how we could make the Settlement even better and still preserve its essential character. Here is what we have done:

1. Added new recipes more in keeping with the lighter, less elaborate meals that are served these days.

2. Included new information on nutrition needs for all age groups.

We knew, however, that in spite of all the exciting new developments in cooking, you would still want to find the recipes that have earned our cook book its enduring popularity. True, it takes time and effort to bake kuchen and torten and fresh bread and tarts and strudels—but how worthwhile the effort is, perhaps especially so in today's speeded-up world. You'll find all the old favorites here in other categories, too: hearty soups, grandmother's hot puddings, old-fashioned pickles and preserves, and main-course dishes that have appeared in every edition of the book since 1901. In this new edition we have retained information often unobtainable elsewhere: how to pasteurize milk, make soap, light a coal stove or a campfire. It's not often needed, but it's a lifesaver when it is.

We hope this new edition combines the best of the old and the new, and that our book will continue to help the women of America find "The Way to a Man's Heart."

THE SETTLEMENT COOK BOOK COMPANY
MILWAUKEE, WISCONSIN
July 1976

1
MENUS

Based on Specialties of
THE SETTLEMENT COOK BOOK

The purpose of this special section is to give some idea of the wide range of new and traditional recipes in *The Settlement Cook Book*. By many loyal users the *Settlement* is valued chiefly for its "heirloom" dishes—rich simmered soups, old-fashioned stews with dumplings, hot puddings to highlight a simple meal, and wonderful baking recipes from breads to kuchen to torten to pastries.

This newest and most up-to-date edition of *The Settlement Cook Book* has made every effort to retain the best of the old recipes and to add new ones that are interesting, easy to prepare, and attuned to today's simpler, more informal approach to mealtime and entertaining. Barbecue and casserole dishes, appetizers for cocktail parties, snacks for the teen-age crowd, are some examples of the categories in which new recipes have been added.

Our hope is that this new edition of the *Settlement* combines the best of the old with the new, and that the following menus will inspire the cook to roam freely through the book creating her own favorite combinations of dishes.

The useful information that every cook needs to consult from time to time—on weights and measures, substitutions and equivalents —will be found beginning on page 32.

CASSEROLE DISHES

Preparing a main dish in advance for heating in the oven at dinnertime is such a convenience that casserole recipes have become favorites of modern cooks. Casserole dishes lend themselves equally well to family dinners and buffet entertaining. The listing that follows includes a variety of dishes from simple to elaborate.

A casserole dish is commonly defined as one that contains two or more elements such as rice or pasta in combination with meat or fish plus a sauce or gravy. Exceptions are constantly being created, however, to fulfill the demand for this popular method of cooking and serving.

If casseroles are made in advance and refrigerated, the heating or baking time should be increased.

A recommended method is to place the casserole in a cold oven, turn on heat, and begin timing when the indicated temperature is reached.

If placed in a preheated oven, reduce the indicated temperature 25° and bake 15 minutes longer.

Many casseroles make a complete meal with the addition of a salad.

The following table indicates:

Economy
One dish
Quick mixing
Leftovers
Company (buffet suppers especially)

CASSEROLE RECIPES

E	O	Q	L	C	RECIPE NAME	PAGE
√					Eggs and Rice	181
√	√				Bean Casserole	184
√					Baked Dried Lima Beans	184
√	√				Lima Bean and Vegetable Casserole	184
√	√				Cheese Sandwich Casserole (1)	231
√				√	Cheese and Bacon Sandwich Casserole	231
		√		√	Cheese and Tuna Sandwich Casserole	231
		√			Cheese Sandwich Casserole (2)	231
				√	Fish Casserole	239
		√		√	Salmon Casserole	240
	√	√			Fish and Vegetable Casserole	241

E	O	Q	L	C	RECIPE NAME	PAGE
				√	Fish and Cheese in Casserole	242
		√			Tuna or Salmon and Rice	244
	√			√	Tuna and Asparagus Casserole	244
√					Scalloped Tuna with Potatoes	244
	√	√			Scalloped Tuna with Noodles	244
	√			√	Tuna Tetrazzini	245
	√				Creole Codfish	245
		√		√	Scalloped Oysters and Clams	247
	√			√	Crab Meat Tetrazzini	248
				√	Crab Meat-Potato Casserole	249
		√		√	Baked Seafood Newburg	249
				√	Lobster-Mushroom Casserole	251
	√			√	Lobster Mornay	252
		√		√	Scalloped Oysters	254
				√	Shrimp and Rice Casserole	256
	√	√		√	Shrimp Creole in Casserole	256
				√	Shrimp-Mushroom-Artichoke Casserole	256
				√	Beef Casserole with Red Wine	274
	√				Beef Casserole Stew	274
√	√	√		√	Oriental Beef Casserole	279
√	√				Seamen's Beef	280
√	√	√			Meat-Cabbage Casserole	282
	√			√	Creole Veal Chops	285

E	O	Q	L	C	RECIPE NAME	PAGE
				√	Squabs en Casserole	322
	√		√	√	Noodles à la Neapolitan	336
		√	√	√	Vienna Noodles	336
√		√			Scalloped Noodles	336
				√	Scalloped Noodles and Prunes	336
√				√	Noodles and Apples	336
				√	Noodle Pudding	337
	√			√	Lasagne	337
				√	Macaroni with Mushrooms	338
√					Baked Macaroni and Cheese	338
				√	Macaroni and Oysters	338
√					Macaroni Pudding	338
√					Baked Macaroni with Chipped Beef	339
√	√				Southern Spaghetti	339
	√			√	Spaghetti Casserole	340
				√	Green Bean and Egg Casserole	413
√	√				Bean Sprout Casserole	413
				√	Brussels Sprouts and Chestnuts in Brown Sauce	414
				√	Carrot Pudding	417
√					Escalloped Corn	419
		√			Corn Pudding	419
	√			√	Eggplant-Zucchini Casserole	420
				√	Eggplant Casserole	421

E	O	Q	L	C	RECIPE NAME	PAGE
		√		√	Rice and Mushroom Casserole	422
√		√		√	Green Peas and Rice	424
√		√			Creamy Scalloped Potatoes	427
√		√			Scalloped Potatoes	427
		√			Scalloped Potatoes and Onions	427
			√		Potato Pudding	428
				√	Scalloped Sweet Potatoes with Apples or Oranges	429
				√	Scalloped Sweet Potatoes Creole	430
				√	Sweet Potato Casserole	430
				√	Orange Sweet Potato Puff	430
				√	Prosnos (Spinach Casserole)	432
		√			Zucchini and Rice	435

DAILY MEAL PLANNING
AND YOUR BUDGET

The main purpose of The Settlement Cook Book *since it first appeared in 1901 has been to help the housewife prepare meals that are satisfying, nutritious and economical. For daily nutrition needs, see Chapter 25. Budgeting the food dollar wisely means taking many factors into consideration.*

- Economy does not necessarily mean restricting the choice of foods. Fresh asparagus and fresh strawberries at the height of their season can be excellent buys, while these same foods out of season would be luxury purchases.
- Weekly "special" sales of meats and vegetables at your food market can provide a variety of economical bases for meal planning, even including foods usually considered high-priced, such as steaks, chops and roasts. A roast that can be served hot, then cold, then in a casserole dish or in lunchbox sandwiches can obviously have its original cost spread over several meals.
- Buying fresh foods in quantity for freezing, canning and preserving is economical and convenient.
- Processed and prepared foods usually save time rather than money, but for a small family convenience and quality may outweigh the cost. Sale purchases of frozen and canned vegetables frequently make them a better value than fresh produce.
- Low-budget foods such as pasta, rice, dried beans and peas make good bases for nourishing main dishes, and they make the meat or other high-quality protein in combination dishes go further.
- The trend to lighter meals and fewer courses does not mean that a rich dessert should never be a part of family meal planning. Served in reasonable portions and preceded by a light first course such as soup or salad, an old-fashioned pudding, cake or pastry can be enjoyed and the budget and calorie balance still maintained.

Typical Economy Menus

Chili Con Carne with Wine, 279
Corn Rye Bread, 69
Salad of Seasonal Greens
Economy Cake, 107,
with Preserved Fruit, chapter 23

• • •

Hamburger-Vegetable Soup, 397
French Bread, 67
Combination Salad
Cornstarch Pudding, 197

• • •

Stuffed Peppers with Corn, 425
Tomato Aspic, 367
Rolls
Two-Egg Sponge Cake, 118

• • •

Lima Bean and Vegetable Casserole, 184
Green Salad
Corn Bread, 84
Fruit in Season

• • •

Cheese and Tomato Rarebit, 233
Green Bean Salad, 359
Economy Cocoa Cake, 110

• • •

Refried Beans, 183
Tomato and Onion Salad, 359
Bread Sticks, 74
Jellied Fruit Dessert, 201

• • •

Cabbage and Sausages, 416
Mashed Potatoes with Onions, 426
Prune Pudding, 193

. . .

Potato Pancakes, 96
Baked Apple Sauce, 260   Sour Cream
Sugar Gingerbread, 113

. . .

Egg and Sardine Appetizer, 45
Macaroni with Tomatoes and Mushrooms, 338
Golden Glow Salad, 369, *with*
Three-Minute Mayonnaise, 374
Quick One-Egg Cake, 107

. . .

Dried Pea Soup, 396, *with* Baked Croutons, 406
Stuffed Pear Salad, 366
Fruit Salad Dressing with Honey, 378

. . .

Spareribs and Sauerkraut, 295
Hot Potato Salad, 360
Apple Tapioca, 198

. . .

*Look for other economy recipes in the following
categories:*

Stews (*See* Index)
Chopped Meat (*see Beef*)
Chicken combination dishes
Leftover Meats, 302-305
Leftover Chicken or Turkey, 317
Canned fish, especially tuna and salmon
Egg and cheese dishes, chapter 11
Pasta, chapter 16
Soups, chapter 21
Desserts, chapter 10, especially puddings, baked
    fruit desserts, gelatin desserts and fruit ices

MEATLESS MENUS

Meals for the Lenten season, or for those who prefer to omit meat from the diet for other reasons, are suggested here.

Hot vegetable platter: Harvard Beets, 414
Asparagus, 412, *with* Hollandaise, 388
Sautéed Mushrooms, 421
Chopped Spinach, 431
Saratoga Potato Chips, 428
Old-Fashioned Rice Pudding, 187

• • •

Vegetarian Loaf, 185
Shoe-String Potatoes, 428
Broiled Tomatoes, 433
Tossed Green Salad, 357
Baked Apples with Almonds, 260

• • •

Black Bean Soup, 399
Tomato and Onion Salad, 359
Oatmeal Muffins, 89
Pistachio Mousse, 213, *with* Pecan Fingers, 158

• • •

Broiled Mushrooms on Toast, 421
Salmon Fondue, 243
Tomato Salad, 358
Apple Pie, 345

• • •

Fish Soup, 404
Bean Sprout Casserole, 413
Vegetable Salad, 359
Cranberry Pudding, 189

• • •

Gazpacho, 399
Tomato-Cheese Pie, 232
Asparagus Salad, 359
Brown Betty, 192

• • •

Cheese Sandwich Casserole, 231
Ratatouille, 434
Pineapple Salad, 366
Marble Cake, 107

• • •

Avocado Pineapple, 364
French Dressing, 373
Green Beans, 412
Gingerbread with Whipped Cream, 113

• • •

Spicy Tomato Juice Cocktail, 44
Blintzes with Cheese Filling, 94
Thick Sour Cream
Strawberry Lemon Preserves, 439

• • •

Grapefruit and Lime Cocktail, 44
Egg Cutlets, 222, *with* Tomato Sauce, 390
Pumpernickel, 69
Fruit Tarts, 351

• • •

Selected Meatless Dishes

Apple Fritters, 101
Avocado Pineapple Salad, 364
Baked Seafood Newburg, 249
Carrot Soufflé, 417
Cheese Waffles, 97, *with* Spiced Honey Butter, 98
Clam Chowder, 404
Corn Ring with Crab, 419
Crab Meat Salad, 363
Deviled Crab Meat, 248
French Cheese Soufflé, 232
French Pancakes, 93
Macaroni with Mushrooms, 338
Macaroni Pudding, 338
Noodle Pudding with Apples and Nuts, 188
Potato Soup, 399
Red Snapper Marguery, 239
Rice and Mushroom Casserole, 422
Salmon with Horseradish Sauce, 239
Shrimp Pie, 255
Shrimp and Pineapple Salad, 364
Sour Cream Griddle Cakes, 92
Spanish Omelet, 226
Swiss Fondue, 231
Tuna Pie, 244

SUGGESTIONS FOR LOW-CALORIE MEALS

Americans are increasingly aware of the importance of maintaining correct weight for the sake of vitality, appearance and longevity. Diets and eating fads come and go, but the best plan is to follow sound nutritional principles and to eat moderately. *Basic nutritional needs and recommended daily allowances will be found in chapter 25.*

To lose weight it is necessary to cut caloric intake. This can be done by reducing the amount of food consumed and by avoiding, as much as possible, those foods that are high in calories, particularly carbohydrates (sugars and starches). Foods high in protein and vitamins are essential. To these add foods low in calories from the following categories for a diet that is varied and satisfying. *See also the calorie chart on page 483.*

Broiled or boiled foods are preferable to those that are fried or prepared with sauces.

Lemon juice, vinegar, onion and herbs in any desired combination are excellent on salads. Avoid oil or cream salad dressings.

Lemon juice and herbs are excellent on boiled or broiled fish or seafood.

Refer to the Herb Chart, pages 490-491, for variety.

MAIN DISH SUGGESTIONS

Meat and Poultry

Moderate portions of meat or poultry, prepared by boiling, roasting, or grilling, are recommended.

Boiled Beef, 276
Brisket of Beef with Cabbage, 277
Broiled Flank Steak, 271
Broiled Liver, 300
Broiled Sweetbreads, 47
Grilled Pepper Steak, 328
Hamburgers, 279
Jellied Meat Loaf, 371
Lamb Chops and Tomatoes, 290
Oven-Barbecued Chicken, 309
Stewed Chicken, 309
Stuffed Peppers with Beef, 425
Texas Red Hots, 327

Fish and Seafood

Lemon juice, Mustard Sauce, 389, and Lemon Fish Baste, 332, can be used moderately.

Cold Pike with Lemon Sauce, 238
Grilled Shrimp, 333
Oysters and Mushrooms, 253
Pickled Herring, 246
Salmon Salad, 363
Seafood Aspic, 372
Shrimp and Cucumber Salad, 364 (*marinate shrimp in lemon juice*)

Eggs

Eggs have high protein content and are substitutes for meat. Today with the availability of non-stick pans which require no butter or other fat, fried and scrambled eggs can be part of a diet.

Creole Eggs, 224
Eggs à la Tarcat, 222
Omelet with Herbs, 225
Venetian Eggs, 225

Salads

Serve either as an accompaniment to a meat or fish dish—or, in larger portions, many of these salads are a satisfactory main course. Use Dieter's Salad Dressing, 374, or lemon as the dressing.

Asparagus and Pepper Salad, 359
Celery Root Salad, 360
Crescent Honeydew Melon Salad, 365
Golden Glow Salad, 369
Green Bean Salad, 359
Molded Cucumber Salad, 369
Summer Salad, 358
Tomato and Onion Salad, 359

Vegetables

Most vegetables are low in calories, and excellent sources of vitamins needed for nutritional purposes. Avoid corn, lima beans, peas and potatoes.

Served raw, the following make good appetizers: carrots, celery, cucumber, lettuce, radish, tomato.

OTHER TIPS

Appetizers

Combine fruits, such as grapefruit, cantaloupe, fresh pineapple, apples, in a fruit cocktail.

Also recommended are any of the following juices: grapefruit, clam, sauerkraut and tomato.

Seafoods, served in small portions.

Clear soups such as chicken broth, bouillon.

Desserts

Fresh or stewed fruits of the low-calorie variety (use sugar substitutes in cooking), gelatins with fruit flavoring (page 201), or a slice of cheese.

MENU SUGGESTIONS

Tomato Juice, 480
Broiled Chicken, 308
Asparagus, 412
Tossed Green Salad, 357
Berries

• • •

Boiled Shrimp, 255
Individual Combination Salad, 357
Spinach, 431
Grapefruit, 259

• • •

Broiled Halibut Steak, 237
Broccoli, 414
Wilted Cucumbers, 358
Honeydew Melon

• • •

Scrambled Eggs, 224
Broiled Tomatoes, 433
Celery Root Salad, 360
Baked Bananas, 261

• • •

MENUS WITH A FOREIGN TOUCH

International flavors are increasingly popular in American cooking. They have always been a part of the Settlement, with its heritage of European recipes. The present edition offers a greater variety of foreign-inspired recipes than ever before.

Meat balls are a global dish. Here are recipes with a variety of accents and with suggested main-course accompaniments:

Meat Balls Cantonese, 280
Chinese Rice, 180
Cole Slaw, 358, *made with* Chinese Cabbage

• • •

Meat Balls Stroganoff, 280
Buckwheat Groats (Kasha), 179
Yellow Tomato and Beet Salad, 360

• • •

Swedish Meat Balls, 281
Scalloped Noodles, 336
Cucumber Salad with Sour Cream, 358

• • •

German Meat Balls (Koenigsberger Klops), 281
Vienna Noodles, 336
Hot German Potato Salad, 360

• • •

Italian Meat Balls, 281
Boiled Spaghetti, 339
Green Bean Salad, 359, *with* Lorenzo Dressing, 373

• • •

Sauerbraten, 273
Potato Dumplings, 103
Celery Root Salad, 360
Apple Kuchen, 352

• • •

Hungarian Goulash, 286
Fried Green Peppers, 425
Tossed Green Salad, 357
Strudel, 354

• • •

Chicken Marengo, 312
Duchesse Potatoes, 427
Green Peas French Style, 424
Raspberry Bombe Glacé, 215

• • •

Mexican Veal Cutlet with Noodles, 286
Avocado Pineapple Salad, 364
Cornsticks, 84
Mocha Layer Cake, 119

• • •

Antipasto, 359
Tamale Loaf, 278
Italian Bread
Biscuit Tortoni, 214

• • •

Oriental Beef and Vegetables, 272
Chinese Fried Rice, 182
Green Salad
Japanese Fruit Cake, 114

• • •

Moussaka, 291
Orange, Grapefruit and Avocado Salad, 365
Macaroon Custard Meringue, 200

• • •

Baked Fish à la Maurice, 239
Green Peas French Style, 424
Lyonnaise Potatoes, 428
Combination Salad
Chocolate Eclairs, 140

• • •

Thai Sour Soup, 396
Thai Pork and Crisp Noodles, 295
Chili Peppers
Ambrosia, 260

CHAFING DISH, FONDUE AND ELECTRIC SKILLET MEALS

The electric skillet is one of the most useful and versatile modern appliances. It will cook foods at high heat, keep them warm at low heat, and can be used to cook at the table. Chafing dishes have some of the same advantages but cannot be controlled so precisely. The same recipes are in general adaptable to both types of pans. They suggest menus that are light and informal, suitable for brunch, lunch, or late supper.

Sukiyaki, 271
Boiled Rice, 180
Pineapple Milk Sherbet, 211
Almond Sticks, 151

• • •

Fondue Bourguignonne, 271
with assorted Sauce Dips, 272
French Bread, 67
Baked Pears, 263

• • •

Veal Stroganoff, 304
Vienna Noodles, 336
Hard Rolls, 73
Green Bean Salad, 359
Jellied Fruit Dessert, 202

MAIN DISH SUGGESTIONS

Meat and Poultry

Chicken Livers and Mushrooms, 318
Creamed Turkey Stew, 320
Sherried Chicken, 310
Skillet Roast Beef Hash, 303
Pork Chop Suey, 294

Fish and Seafood

Buttered Lobster Chunks, 250
Lobster à la Thackeray, 251

Lobster Newburg, 250
Lobster Tails Cantonese, 252
Polynesian Fish Balls, 243
Oyster Rarebit, 254
Oysters Poulette, 253
Tuna à la King, 244
Creole Seafood in Cream, 257
Shrimp Wiggle, 255

Eggs

Curried Eggs, 222
Venetian Eggs, 225

Cheese

Beer Rarebit, 233
Cheese and Tomato Rarebit, 233
English Monkey, 233
Rinktum-Dity, 233
Swiss Fondue, 231
Welsh Rarebit, 233

Pancakes

Blintzes, 94
Buttermilk Griddle Cakes, 92

Desserts

Almond Dessert Omelet, 227
Crêpes Suzette, 95
Fruit Fritters, 102
Norwegian Pancakes, 93

PICNIC AND
LUNCHBOX SUGGESTIONS

Foods planned for an outdoor picnic or for school-box lunches should be those which keep well, pack easily, and are simple to eat. With the availability of plastic containers, aluminum foil and plastic wrap, waxed sandwich bags, Thermos flasks, and special containers to keep food hot or cold, meals can be as elaborate as desired.

Check to be sure that all the needed utensils are included: paper plates, napkins, paper cups, forks, knives, can opener, spoons, salt and pepper, tablecloth—also an insect repellent for summer picnics.

Sandwiches

Sandwich Butters, 379-380
Sandwich Fillings, 380-385
  (*Make with fillings which will not wilt or soak into bread. If a garnish such as lettuce or tomato is required, pack separately and add when ready to eat.*)
Cold sliced meats and poultry: chicken, turkey, roast beef, meat loaf, pot roast, corned beef, tongue, salami, bologna—add mayonnaise or mustard as desired.

Cooked Meats and Poultry

  (*Cool and pack, to be sliced or carved when ready to eat.*) Most popular are:
Roast Chicken, 307, *or* Turkey, 319
Brisket of Beef, 276
Pot Roast, 272
Meat Loaf, 278
Fried Chicken, 308
Ham, 296

Salads

(*Pack in plastic covered containers so that juices will not run.*)
Chicken Salad, 362
Cole Slaw, 358
Creamy Potato Salad, 360
Salmon Salad, 363, *or* Tuna Salad, 363
Egg Salad, 362

Miscellaneous

Nuts, olives, potato chips, crackers, and bread and butter (*if main course is not sandwiches*)
Pickles, 450-455
Catsups, 455
Mayonnaise, 374
Relishes, 456-458
Hard-Cooked Eggs, 221
Deviled Eggs, 45
Cheese, 228, sliced or cubed

Fruits and Vegetables

Fresh fruits of all kinds are suitable. Wash before packing. Tender-skinned fruits such as peaches and apricots can be protected by wrapping individually in paper towels.

Canned fruits can be taken in the can, to be opened when ready to serve. Serve in paper cups.

Raw vegetables such as carrots, celery, radishes and cucumbers should be cleaned, cut into bite-size pieces, if necessary, chilled and wrapped in plastic or foil. Cooked vegetables can form the base of salads (page 359), to be served cold.

Dessert and Beverages

Cakes are best sliced before packing, and those with soft icings should be avoided. Plastic boxes for transporting a whole cake or for individual pieces of cake or pie are obtainable.
Cookies should be placed in a container to avoid crumbling.
Cupcakes should be individually wrapped.

• • •

Bottled sodas, beer and milk should be chilled in advance and carried in insulated bags or other containers which keep foods cold.
Fruit drinks, like lemonade, should be prepared at home and packed into containers with tight lids, or in Thermos bottles or jugs.
Hot beverages (coffee, tea) can be packed in Thermos bottles.
Ice and ice cubes can be included in insulated containers, and will keep for many hours. Ice can be used in drinks or to help keep foods cold.

FOR CHILDREN AND TEEN-AGERS: SPECIAL OCCASION PARTIES

Child's Birthday

Deviled Hamburgers, 279
French Fried Potatoes, 428
Birthday Candlesticks, 138
Chocolate Pretzels, 158
Peppermint Stick Ice Cream, 207
Pineappleade, 54

• • •

Valentine's Day

Texas Red Hots, 327   Rolls, 73
Saratoga Potato Chips, 428
Piccalilli, 457
Heart-shaped Filled Cookies, 153
Cherry Charlotte Russe, 137
Hot Fruit Punch, 57

• • •

Fourth of July

Skewered Ham 'n' Sweets, 331
Pineapple Slaw, 358
Wax Bean Salad, 359
Brownies, 165
Watermelon
Fresh Fruit Lemonade Punch, 55

• • •

Sweet Sixteen

Ham and Olive Dip, 37, *served with crackers*
Sweet and Sour Meat Balls, 283
in Noodle-Cheese Ring, 336
Tomato and Onion Salad, 359
Angel Food Surprise, 137
Moonlight Punch, 56

• • •

Graduation

Assorted Fancy Sandwiches, 382-383
Cold Shrimp Platter, 255
Cabbage Rose Salad, 358
Parker House Rolls, 75
Chocolate Marshmallow Balls, 177
Maraschino Cherry Cake, 114
Fruit Punch with Lemon Ice, 55

• • •

Saturday Night Menus

Snack Mix, 41
Pizza, 385   Green Salad, 357
Lady Fingers, 129
Maple Ice Cream Fizz, 209

• • •

Rich Griddle Cakes, 91, *with* Maple Syrup, 98
Viennese Coffee, 50
Salt-Water Taffy, 171

• • •

Sloppy Joes, 282
Sweet Pickles, 451, *and* Cole Slaw, 358
Quick Fudge, 169   Lemon Ice, 210

• • •

Italian Bread Boat, 385
Assorted Fresh Fruits
Buttermilk Doughnuts, 99
Cider-Grape Punch, 55

• • •

Hot Turkey Sandwiches, 384
Candied Cranberries, 262
Corn Relish, 456
Chocolate Eclairs, 140
Ginger Punch, 55

HOLIDAY MENUS

Through the year a variety of holidays offers the imaginative cook an opportunity to serve a special-occasion menu that points up the day in an interesting way. Browsing through the book will suggest many more possibilities than these.

New Year Open House

Quick Cheese Sticks, 43
Snacks in Bacon Blankets, 42
Pecan Tidbits, 41
Japanese Fruit Cake, 114
Cinnamon Stars, 153
Frozen Eggnog, 215
Hot Buttered Rum, 63

• • •

Washington's Birthday

Select any company dinner (pages 29-31) and be sure to include one of these dishes!
Cherry Pudding, 193
Cherry Kuchen, 353
Cherry Strudel, 355
Bing Cherry Ring, 370
Canned Cherry Pie, 345
Duckling with Cherries, 320

• • •

Saint Patrick's Day

Cream of Spinach Soup, 402
Baked Pork Chops with Apples, 294
Stuffed Onions, 423   O'Brien Potatoes, 428
Shamrock Salad, 358   Clover Leaf Rolls, 75
Mint Fruit Ice, 210   Irish Coffee, 64

• • •

Easter

Baked Ham, 296
Boiled New Potatoes, 425
Brussels Sprouts and Chestnuts, 414
Salad of Spring Greens, 356
Rhubarb Pie, 346

• • •

Passover

Salted Almonds   Wine   Matzos
Charocis for Seder, 444, *and quartered hard-cooked egg, slice of horseradish root, sprig of parsley, radishes, watercress, served with salt water*
Chicken Soup, 394, *with* Matzos Balls, 408
Gefillte Fish, 242
Roast Chicken, 307
Butter-simmered Carrots, 417   Cauliflower, 417
Half an Avocado *with* French Dressing, 373
Potato Pudding for Passover, 194
Stuffed Prunes, 176   Nuts and Raisins

• • •

Fourth of July

Barbecued Pot Roast, 329
French Bread, 67
Foil Roasted Corn, 334
Pineapple Slaw, 358
Watermelon, 260

• • •

Thanksgiving

Cream of Oyster Soup, 403
Roast Turkey in Foil, 319
with Almond Stuffing, 324
and Giblet Gravy, 307
Cherry Cranberries, 262
Mashed Potatoes, 426
Boiled Onions, 423
Baked Stuffed Acorn Squash, 432
Pumpkin Pie, 350

• • •

Christmas Eve Tree-Trimming Snack

Mulled Cider, 56
Frothy Cocoa, 52
Christmas Spice Cookies, 153

• • •

Christmas Dinner

Consommé, 394, *with* Egg Custard, 410
Roast Goose, 321
Apple Sauce, 260
Orange Sweet Potato Puff, 430
Eggplant-Zucchini Casserole, 420
Mince Pie, 346
Grant Thomas Pudding, 193
Nuts   Mints

BRUNCH

Brunch—a combination of late breakfast and lunch—is usually served in a relaxed manner on weekends and holidays. It can be a simple family meal, or a fairly elaborate one if there are a number of guests to be served. Buffet service—letting the guests help themselves—is convenient for brunch, and permits the use of chafing dishes and electric skillets for on-the-spot cooking and serving. See Chafing Dish, Fondue, and Electric Skillet Meals, page 15, and Buffet Entertaining, page 24, for additional menu suggestions. Important for brunch: lots of hot, freshly made coffee.

Platter of Assorted Fresh Fruit
Platter of Assorted Cheese (*see* Chart, 228)
Apple Fritters, 101, *with* Pork Sausages, 302
Maple Syrup

• • •

Ambrosia, 260
Crisp Bacon, 298
Gingerbread Waffles, 98, *with* Cream Cheese
Hard Sauce, 219, *and* Coffee Sauce, 218

• • •

Grapefruit Cocktail, 44
Broiled Ham, 297
with Hawaiian Style Barbecue Sauce, 327
Sour Cream Griddle Cakes, 92
with Cherry Conserve, 444

• • •

Baked Oranges, 262 (*serve chilled*)
Creamed Chicken in Avocado, 317
Broiled Mushrooms, 421
Corn Bread, 84
Linzer Torte, 130

• • •

Sauerkraut Juice Cocktail, 44
Eggs Benedict, 223
Baked Peaches with Brandy Sauce, 263
Almond Crescents, 159

• • •

Rhubarb with Berries, 263
Chicken Livers, 318, *with* Scrambled Eggs, 224
Popovers, 90, *with* Cream Cheese and
Assorted Jams

• • •

Borsht, 394
Shad Roe and Cucumber Salad, 364
Asparagus with Hot Mayonnaise, 412
Rye Yeast Rolls, 73
Chocolate Sponge, 190, *with* Vanilla Sauce, 216

• • •

Melon in Season, 259
Soufflé Omelet, 226, *filled with*
Sweetbreads with Mushrooms
French Bread, 67
Orange Marmalade, 443

• • •

Minted Fruit Juice Cocktail, 44
Mixed Grill of Lamb Chops, 289, *and*
Chicken Livers, 318
Broiled Tomatoes, 433
Rice Muffins, 89, *with* Assorted Jellies

• • •

Cranberry Juice Cocktail, 44
Cold Pike with Lemon Sauce, 238
Salt Sticks, 74
Rich Bundt Kuchen, 78

• • •

Fresh Strawberries and Sour Cream
Cheese, Leek and Ham Pie, 232
Orange Toast, 72

• • •

Berries
Prosnos, 432
Broiled Tomatoes, 433
English Muffins, 76
Marmalade or Jelly

•   •   •

Grapefruit, 259
German Pancake, 96
with lemon and Maple Syrup, 98
Pork Sausages, 302

•   •   •

Tomato Juice, 480
Shrimp Pie, 255
Coffee Cake

•   •   •

Drinks for Brunch

When brunch is the equivalent of a weekend luncheon party, aperitifs (see page 60) or cocktails are frequently served before the meal. A popular cocktail for such an occasion is a Bloody Mary or a Screwdriver, vodka cocktails. Other drinks that are notable for their smoothness, hence especially acceptable at midday, are Clover Leaf, Orange Blossom, Pink Lady and Alexander cocktails, and Egg Milk Punch, Fizz or Flip. In cold weather a most agreeable hot pre-brunch drink is a Tom and Jerry. Other suggestions for alcoholic and non-alcoholic drinks—including alternates for tea and coffee—will be found in chapter 3, Beverages, page 49.

INFORMAL ENTERTAINING: TEA AND COFFEE PARTIES

Tea parties and "coffees" in the morning, late afternoon or evening are a pleasant way of getting together with friends. It's the easiest form of entertaining for a small informal gathering. A large afternoon tea or reception, however, may be quite formal, with the hostess's best linen, china and silver on display, a tea service at one end of the dining table and an alternate beverage—coffee, chocolate or punch—at the other. Help may be available to pass the assortment of hot and cold finger foods, cake and cookies, or the guests may help themselves. At a large affair, the hostess will ask one or two friends to "pour," leaving herself free to greet and introduce her guests.

Planning a menu: formal afternoon teas should include dainty tea sandwiches, cakes and cookies. If desired, a hot finger food or two, and tea breads and coffee cakes, sliced thin in small, easily managed portions, may also be served. The variety of cookies and cakes will depend on the wishes of the hostess and often on her baking skills.

With varying degrees of informality, the menu can be simplified to the point where it may consist of nothing more than a tempting home-baked coffee cake enjoyed with a couple of friends over morning coffee or shared with neighbors as an evening snack. "Come for dessert and coffee' is also an easy way to extend hospitality after lunch, dinner or supper.

The informal approach to entertaining applies to club meetings, bridge parties, and all those occasions where a formal meal is not required and the variety and selection of the food depends on the hostess's choice and imagination. The important thing is the spirit of friendly hospitality!

Beverages

Tea with Preserved Fruit or Rum, 50
Tea Orangeade, 54
Coffee for 40 People, 50
Viennese Coffee, 50
Iced Coffolate, 52
Raspberry Shrub, 54
Champagne Sherbet Punch, 57
Hot Fruit Punch, 57

Tea Breads and Coffee Cakes

Apple Muffins, 90
Apricot Nut Bread, 85
Swedish Tea Ring, 78
Almond Coffee Cake, 117
Caramel Tea Rolls, 81
Danish Pastry, 78
Short-Cut Coffee Cake, 77

Sandwiches

See To Prepare and Serve Fancy Sandwiches, 382-383
Pinwheel Sandwiches, 383
    with Blue Cheese and Nut Filling, 380
Checkerboard Sandwiches, 383
    or
Ribbon Sandwiches, 383
    filled with
        Olive Butter, 379, *or* Watercress Cheese Spread, 380, *or* Mushroom Filling, 382, *or* Foie Gras, 381, *or* Tuna Fish Filling, 381, *or* Cherry and Pineapple Filling, 382

Hot Appetizers

Cheese Puffs, 39
Crab Meat Canapés, 40
Rolled Toast with Mushrooms, 42
Asparagus in Rolled Sticks, 42
Cream Cheese Balls, 42
Cheddar Cheese Sticks, 43

Cookies and Small Cakes

Meringue-Topped Butter Cookies, 152
Honey Lebkuchen, 154
Springerle, 156
Peanut Icebox Cookies, 159
Curled Wafers, 162
Praline Kisses, 162
Chewy Brownies, 165
Petits Fours, 138, with Iced Cooked Fondant, 172
Ginger Cup Cakes, 141, with Brandy Frosting, 144
Nut Drop Cakes, 139

Candies and Confections

Cakes

COCKTAIL PARTIES

The Liquor

Consult page 59 for guidance on the amount of liquor to buy, sizes and types of glasses, and other necessary equipment. The most popular cocktails include the martini, page 61, Manhattan, page 61, Rob Roy, page 62, and Scotch Mist, page 62, as well as the rum cocktails—Daiquiri, page 60, and Bacardi, page 60—and the vodka cocktails—Bloody Mary, page 63, and Screwdriver, page 62. Even more popular than cocktails, however, are straight drinks "on the rocks." This usually means a 2-ounce jigger of Scotch, bourbon, rye or blended whiskey served with several ice cubes in an Old-fashioned glass; a small amount of water or soda may be added.

Instead of cocktails or straight drinks, a midwinter cocktail party might feature a bowl of eggnog or a hot wine punch; a summer party might star a champagne fruit punch or mint juleps. A wide assortment of alcoholic and non-alcoholic drinks will be found in Chapter 3. Thoughtful hosts will provide various alternatives for guests who do not drink alcoholic beverages—fruit juices, soft drinks, tea or coffee.

The Food

Cocktail-party food may be as simple as bowls of nuts or potato chips or it may be as elaborate as a smörgåsbord (see page 47). In any case, it should be easy to serve and to eat, and should demand a minimum of attention from the hostess during the party. The secret of a successful cocktail party, as of all successful entertaining, is this: prepare carefully in advance and then be free to enjoy your party and your guests.

Planning a Menu

See page 36, introducing the chapter on Appetizers, for a range of cocktail-party appetizer suggestions. Browsing throughout this chapter will suggest a variety of foods to be served. Chapter 19, Sandwiches and Sandwich Fillings, offers further suggestions. The sandwich spreads may be served with crackers. Almost any sandwich, served in small dainty portions, is suitable cocktail-party food. Main-dish chapters on meat, poultry and seafood present possibilities. Foods such as meat balls, smoked or pickled fish, shrimps, or oysters, when served in tiny portions and speared with toothpicks, are easily handled finger foods.

A simple cocktail party might be planned around such selections as these:

Cheese and Sherry Dip, 37, *with potato chips*
Celery Stalks Stuffed with Crab Meat, 41
Deviled Almonds, 41

• • •

Anchovy Butter Canapés, 38
Sour Cream and Dry Soup Dip, 37,
with crisp vegetables
Snack Mix, 41   Deviled Eggs, 45

• • •

For a larger crowd, add to either of the above:

Chicken Liver Spread, 38
with crackers or small rye-bread rounds
Sauerbraten Meat Balls, 43
(*served hot in chafing dish*)

• • •

When help is available to prepare and pass hot appetizers, include some of these:

Shrimp Tempura with Dipping Sauce, 257
Chicken Livers and Mushrooms, 318
Oysters in Blankets, 42
Rolled Toast with Sardines, 42
Fondue Bourguignonne, 271
Cheese Puffs, 39
Polynesian Fish Balls, 243
Lobster Croquettes, 252
miniature size, served on toothpicks
Fried Butterfly Shrimp, 255
with Zippy Seafood Cocktail Sauce, 45

• • •

Another possibility is to serve as the main cocktail food a cold roast turkey or ham accompanied by appropriate breads and crackers. Small thin slices of the meat or fowl should be cut in advance so that the guests may serve themselves. Crisp vegetables in bite-size portions accompanied by a dip or seasoned mayonnaise are a good complement.

To turn a cocktail party into a cocktail supper, hot main dishes and desserts from Buffet Entertaining, page 24, may be introduced at the appropriate time during the party.

WEDDING MENUS

Although many weddings are catered, the old-fashioned home wedding party still takes place when space and circumstances permit. The menu will depend upon the season of the year, on the time of day and on the number of guests invited.

Wedding Breakfast

Cocktails, 59-63; Champagne Punch, 57
Fried Chicken, 308
Maître d'Hôtel Potato Balls, 427
Green Asparagus, 412
with Hollandaise Sauce, 388
Tossed Green Salad, 357
Bride's Cake (White Cake), 108
Groom's Cake (Wedding), 116
Coffee   Candies (*see pages 168-178*)

• • •

Wedding Reception

Fancy Sandwiches, 382-383
Deviled Olives, 41   Stuffed Celery, 41
Chicken and Sweetbread Salad, 362
Assorted Ice Creams (*see pages 204-208*)
Wedding Cake, 116
Strawberry Froth Punch, 58
Champagne   Cocktails   Coffee
Candies

• • •

Wedding Dinner

Seasonal Fruit
Cream of Mushroom Soup, 402
Lincoln House Fish Balls, 46
Filet Mignon, 270, *and* Sautéed Potato Balls, 427
Cauliflower, 417, *with* Hollandaise, 388,
surrounded by Stuffed Tomatoes, 433, *and*
Green Beans with Almonds, 412
Parker House Rolls, 75
Avocado Rings *filled with* Melon Balls,
French Dressing, 373
Ice Cream
Wedding Cake, 116   Champagne   Coffee

• • •

Wedding Dinner

Shrimp, 255, *with* Thousand Island Dressing, 376
Broiled Chicken, 308, *with border of*
Baked Pickled Peaches, 458
and Cranberry Ring, 370
Carrot Pudding, 417, *filled with*
Sautéed Mushrooms, 421, *surrounded by*
Broccoli, 414, *with* Hollandaise, 388
Crescent Rolls, 75   Pêche Melba, 208
Wedding Cake, 116   Champagne   Coffee

COMPANY DINNERS

The most important aspect of company dinners is planning. Whether the guests number two or ten or twenty-two—if your dining table can accommodate that number on festive occasions—careful planning of the menu, shopping list, preparation, cooking and serving is essential if hosts and guests are to enjoy themselves. Suggestions for planning and serving will be found in chapter 26. The menus suggested here are for "sit-down" meals at a dining table, where the guests are served either by the host or hostess at the table or by a waitress or waitresses who pass the food, or by a combination of these services.

Company Dinners Informally Served without Help

When the hostess (or host, if he likes to cook) prepares, cooks and serves dinner, the following considerations are important:

1) Choose a menu that is easy to prepare. This will vary with the experience and talents of the cook, but these should not be overtaxed so that the cook-hostess is tired or nervous about the success of her efforts. Elaborate dishes should be practiced on the family in advance.

2) Cook and prepare in advance as much as possible. Reduce last-minute duties to a minimum. Guests much prefer a hostess's presence to her absence in the kitchen adding fancy touches to the meal.

3) Simplify service in all possible ways. Offering appetizers in the living room with drinks eliminates the need for serving and removing a first course at the table. While the guests are finishing their drinks, the hostess can dish up the main course and have it on the table as she seats her guests. The hostess (or host) may serve the entire main course, or she may serve the main dish and the guests may help themselves to the accompaniments.

The hostess should decide in advance whether she wishes help in clearing the table after the main course. Less confusion is created if no more than one guest assists the hostess. A serving cart beside the hostess, the lower shelf of which may be used to hold the dishes to be cleared, is one solution to the problem of graceful service without help. The dessert and dessert plates may be brought in on the upper shelf of this serving cart, or be placed on an adjoining buffet. Wine is served by the host (see page 58 for wine service).

A Typical Informal Company Dinner

Tangy Sunday Night Cheese Spread, 38,
with crackers
Deviled Almonds, 41

———

Chicken Rosé, 310
Green Peas and Rice, 424
Pineapple and Cucumber Salad Ring, 366
Clover Leaf Rolls, 75
(*bake in advance, warm to serve*)
Wine: *if desired, a rosé to complement
the chicken*

———

Almond Torte, 124
Rum Sauce, 217
Coffee, 49
Cordials, 64, *if desired*

Other Suggested Informal Company Dinner Menus

Seasoned Sour Cream Dip, 37, *with crackers*
Veal Fricassee, 286
Baking Powder Dumplings, 102
Buttered Green Beans, 412
Chocolate Pudding Cake, 188

• • •

Pickled Herring Canapés, 39
Beef Stroganoff, 271
Noodle Ring, 335
Tossed Green Salad, 357
with French Dressing, 373
Black Raspberry Sherbet, 212
with Praline Kisses, 162

• • •

Celery Stalks Stuffed with Crab Meat, 41
Beef Birds, 275
Potatoes Anna, 426   Chopped Spinach, 431
Apple Pandowdy (*Dimpes Dampes*), 191

• • •

Broiled Mushrooms, 47
Baked Pork Chops with Apples, 294
Sweet Potato Casserole, 430
Spinach Salad, 358, *with* French Dressing, 373
Maple Mousse, 213, *in* Meringue Torte, 131

Company Dinners Informally Served with Help

When a waitress is on hand to help serve dinner, the menu and service can be more flexible than when the hostess must do it all herself. Sometimes the waitress is also the cook, or shares the cooking responsibility with the hostess. However, one waitress cannot serve more than four to six guests individually. The host or hostess often prefers to serve the main course with the assistance of the waitress (see page 493).

The chief advantage of help is that it permits the hostess to be with her guests instead of in the kitchen before dinner, and it relieves her of the responsibility for clearing the table between courses. It permits the serving of a first course at the table. Many well-organized hostesses, however, manage such menus as the following without help, and some count on willing younger members of the family to assist with table clearing and other duties.

A Typical Informal Company Dinner—with Help

Cheddar Cheese Sticks, 43
(*served with drinks in living room*)

———

Crab Meat Cocktail, 46, *with*
Zippy Seafood Cocktail Sauce, 45
Crown Roast of Lamb, 289
with Potato Balls, 427, *and* Mint Jelly, 448
or Mint Sauce, 391
Sautéed Zucchini, 434
Cucumber Salad with Sour Cream, 358
Cushion Rolls, 73
Caramelized Apple Pie, 345

———

Coffee, 49
(*demitasse in living room with liqueurs, if desired*)
Coffee Candied Nuts, 174
or other homemade confections may be passed at this time. See chapter 8, Candies and Confections.

———

Suggested Wine: *a Chablis, Rhine or dry Sauternes may be served throughout the meal.*

Other Suggested Menus for Informal Company Dinners—with Help

Smoked Salmon Canapés, 39
Baked Steak and Vegetables, 270
Hashed Brown Potatoes, 428
Clover Leaf Rolls, 75
Romaine Salad, 356
with Vinaigrette Dressing, 374
Vanilla Ice Cream *with* Burnt Almond Sauce, 216

• • •

Egg and Tomato Appetizer, 45
Beef Tongue à la Jardinière, 301
Rice and Mushroom Casserole, 422
Steamed Caramel Pudding
with Lady Fingers, 129
and Caramel Sauce, 216

• • •

Sweet and Sour Pot Roast, 273
Potato Pancakes, 96
Red Cabbage with Wine, 416
Apple Sauce, 260
Peanut Butter Chiffon Pie, 351

• • •

Borsht, 394
Stuffed Roasted Cornish Hens, 322
Orange, Grapefruit and Avocado Salad, 365
Blueberry Pudding, 192, *with* Hard Sauce, 219

• • •

Company Dinners Formally Served

Formal service is rare these days, but there are occasions when it is necessary or desirable. The rules for formal service and table setting will be found in chapter 26. The planning of a formal dinner is not fundamentally different from a less formal one, except that more courses are usually served. The trend to lighter, simpler meals is observed, however, even in the most formal circumstances. It is now quite correct to serve a formal meal of no more than three courses. The following menus can all be shortened and adapted to less formal occasions.

A Typical Company Dinner— Formally Served

Shrimp Cocktail with Besetti Sauce, 45
Chicken Broth, 394
with Miniature Almond Dumplings, 407
Rib Roast of Beef, 269
with Yorkshire Pudding, 269
Braised Celery, 418
surrounded by Broiled Tomatoes, 433
Watercress and Belgian Endive Salad, 357
with French Dressing, 373
(served as a separate course with
Brie or Bel Paese cheese, 228-229, and crackers)
Strawberry Mousse, 213
Demitasse
Wines: *Burgundy or Bordeaux with beef*
Champagne, if desired, with dessert
Brandy or other liqueurs with coffee

Other Suggested Menus for Company Dinners—Formally Served

Crab Meat Canapés, 40
Roast Fillet of Beef with Vegetables, 269
Asparagus Salad, 359
with Sour Cream Boiled Mayonnaise, 375
Macaroon Ice Cream, 206

• • •

Melon Cocktail, 44
Oyster Bisque, 403
Filet Mignon with Artichoke, 271
and Béarnaise Sauce, 389
Puffed Potatoes (Pommes Soufflés), 429
Queen of Trifles, 136

• • •

Consommé, 394, *with* Fried Croutons, 406
Stuffed Suprèmes of Chicken, 311
Wild Rice, 180
Black-Eyed Susan Salad, 366
Lalla Rookh Cream, 215

• • •

Stuffed Tomato with Crab Meat and Caviar, 361
Duckling à l'Orange, 320
Sweet Potato Puffs, 430
Tossed Green Salad, 357
Crème de Menthe Ice, 210
Petits Fours, 138

USEFUL INFORMATION
FOR THE COOK

Before you begin to cook, read the recipe through. Check to make sure that you have all the necessary ingredients in the house. Assemble them, along with the utensils you will need to use. If you lack an ingredient, check the table of equivalents and substitutions (page 33) for possible alternatives. Do all preliminary preparation of separate ingredients, such as peeling, chopping and precooking.

COOKING TERMS USED
IN THE RECIPES
IN THIS BOOK

BAKE: Cook by dry heat in an oven; or, as applied to pancakes, on a griddle.

BARBECUE: Cook over an open fire on a spit, or in an oven, usually basting with a savory sauce.

BASTE: Moisten food as it cooks, with sauce, pan drippings, or fat.

BLANCH: Cook in, or simply cover with, boiling water for a few minutes, in order to make food easy to peel, or as a preliminary to freezing (vegetables), or in order to precook food before further preparation.

BOIL: Cook in boiling liquid in which bubbles rise vigorously to the surface. The boiling point of water is 212° F. at sea level.

BRAISE: Cook covered in a small amount of liquid, in the oven or on top of the range.

BROIL: Cook by exposure to direct heat under the broiler of a gas or electric range, in an electric broiler, or over an open fire.

CREAM: Blend ingredients with a spoon or fork or in an electric beater until softened and creamy. Used principally to describe the combining of butter and sugar for a cake.

DICE: Cut in small cubes about ¼ inch in size.

DOT: Scatter small amounts of specified ingredients—usually butter—on top of food.

DREDGE: Cover with a coating of flour, crumbs or cornmeal.

FOLD: Blend beaten egg white or whipped cream into a thicker, heavier mixture, using a gentle under-and-over motion that does not break down the air bubbles.

FRICASSEE: Stew pieces of fowl or meat and serve with thickened sauce.

FRY OR PAN-FRY: Cook in hot fat in a frying pan or skillet. To deep-fry requires using enough fat to cover the food completely.

GRILL: *see* BROIL.

MARINATE: Soak in a liquid containing an acid such as lemon juice, vinegar or wine, plus seasonings and sometimes oil. Used to flavor and tenderize meat, fish and poultry.

PARBOIL: Precook until partially done. See BLANCH.

POACH: Cook eggs, fish, chicken, fruit and other delicate foods in hot liquid at a temperature below the boiling point.

PUREE: Reduce food to smooth, uniform consistency by pressing it through a sieve or food mill or potato ricer or by whirling it in an electric blender.

ROAST: Cook by dry heat in an oven; or on a spit in an oven, or over charcoal, or in an electric rotisserie.

SAUTÉ: Cook in small amount of hot fat.

SCALD: Heat liquid, usually milk, to temperature just below the boiling point.

SCORE: Mark with a sharp knife or with a fork to make decorative lines.

SEAR: Brown quickly at high temperature.

SIMMER: Cook slowly, just below the boiling point.

STEAM: Cook over boiling water, in steam, without letting the water touch the food, which is contained in a colander, or in a mold on a rack. Sometimes means cooking in the top of a double boiler over boiling water; or in a very small amount of boiling water in a saucepan.

EQUIVALENTS AND SUBSTITUTIONS FOR COMMON FOODS

Almonds, shelled	¼ pound	1 cup
chopped, blanched	1 ounce	⅓ cup
in shell	1 pound	¼ pound nutmeats
Apples, raw, unpared	1 pound	3 cups, pared and sliced
Baking powder	1 teaspoon	¼ teaspoon baking soda plus ½ cup buttermilk or sour milk (reduce other liquid in recipe by ½ cup)
Beans, dried	1 pound	6 cups cooked
Bread, loaf	1 pound	12 to 16 slices
	1 slice	⅓ cup dry crumbs
Butter	1 stick	½ cup; ¼ pound; 8 tablespoons
	1 cup	1 cup margarine; ¾ cup chicken fat
Cabbage, raw	1 pound	4 cups shredded
Catsup or chili sauce in cooking	1 cup	1 can (8 ounces) tomato sauce plus ½ cup sugar, 2 tablespoons vinegar
Clams, raw, in shell	2 dozen	4 cups shucked
Chocolate	1 square	1 ounce
		1 tablespoon, melted
		4 tablespoons, grated
		3 tablespoons cocoa plus 1 tablespoon butter or margarine
		or
		4 tablespoons cocoa plus ½ tablespoon fat
Cocoa	1 pound	50 servings
Coffee	1 pound	40 to 50 servings
Coffee, instant	2 ounces	25 to 30 servings
Corn on the cob	12 ears	3 cups kernels
Corn meal, uncooked	1 pound	3 cups
	1 cup	4 cups cooked
Cornstarch	1 tablespoon	2 tablespoons flour; 1 tablespoon potato flour; 4 teaspoons quick-cooking tapioca
Cranberries	1 quart	6 to 7 cups sauce
Cream, heavy	1 cup	2 cups whipped
	1 cup	⅓ cup butter plus ¾ cup milk
Cream sauce	1½ cups	1 can condensed cream-style soup plus ¼ cup liquid
Eggs, whole	1 cup	5 large eggs
whole	1 pound	9 medium eggs
yolks	1 cup	12 large yolks
whites	1 cup	8 to 10 large whites
in sauces and custards	1 egg	2 yolks
Flour, all-purpose	1 pound	4 cups
	1 ounce	4 tablespoons
	1 cup, sifted	1 cup instantized
	1 cup, sifted	1 cup plus 2 tablespoons cake flour
	1 cup, sifted	1 cup rice flour or rye flour
	1 cup, sifted	½ cup flour plus ½ cup corn meal or whole-wheat flour
Garlic	1 medium clove	⅛ teaspoon garlic powder
Herbs	1 tablespoon fresh, chopped	1 teaspoon dried
Lemon	1	2½ to 3½ tablespoons juice; 2 teaspoons rind
Macaroni	1 pound	4 cups uncooked, 9 cups cooked

Meat, ground	1 pound	2 cups
Milk, whole	1 cup	½ cup evaporated milk plus ½ cup water
	1 cup	1 cup reconstituted nonfat dry milk plus 2 teaspoons butter
Milk, skim	1 cup	3 to 4 tablespoons dry nonfat milk solids plus 1 cup water
Milk, sour	1 cup	1 tablespoon lemon juice or vinegar plus milk to make 1 cup
Milk, for whipped topping	2½ cups topping	⅔ cup evaporated milk or 1 cup instant nonfat dry milk plus ½ cup water
Mushrooms, fresh	1 pound	6 to 8 ounces canned
Mustard, dry	1 teaspoon	1 tablespoon prepared
Noodles	1 pound	6 cups uncooked, 9 cups cooked
Nuts, ground	1 cup	3¾ ounces
Orange	1 medium	5 to 6 tablespoons juice, 2 to 3 tablespoons grated rind
Peanuts, in shell	1 pound	⅔ pound shelled
Peas in the pod	1 pound	1 cup
Pecans, in shell	1 pound	⅓ pound shelled
Rice, uncooked	1 pound	2½ cups uncooked, 8 cups cooked
Raisins, seedless	1 cup	6 ounces
Salt, table	1 ounce	1½ tablespoons
coarse	1 ounce	2 tablespoons
Spaghetti, uncooked	1 pound	10 cups cooked
Sugar, brown	1 pound	2¼ cups, firmly packed
granulated brown	1 pound	3¾ cups
confectioners'	1 pound	4½ to 5 cups, sifted
granulated white	1 pound	2¼ cups
substitutions	1 cup granulated white	1 cup brown sugar, firmly packed *or* 1⅓ cups granulated brown sugar *or* 1 cup honey less 3 tablespoons liquid in recipe *or* 2 cups corn syrup less ¼ cup liquid in recipe *or* 1 cup molasses less ¼ cup liquid in recipe
Tapioca	1½ tablespoons quick-cooking	4 tablespoons regular tapioca, soaked
	2 teaspoons	1 tablespoon flour (for thickening)
Tea	1 pound	120 servings
Yeast	1 cake	1 package active dry yeast
	1 package	2 teaspoons active dry yeast

TO MEASURE INGREDIENTS

Accurate measurement is essential to insure uniform results.

All measurements are level unless otherwise indicated.

Metal measuring cups are available in sets of 1-cup, ½-cup, ⅓-cup and ¼-cup sizes. Glass measuring cups, marked off in quarter and third cups, may be obtained in 1-cup, 2-cup and 1-quart sizes. Cups with a spout are best for measuring liquids; flat-surfaced measures are best for dry ingredients.

Measuring spoons come in sets of 1 tablespoon, 1 teaspoon, ½ teaspoon and ¼ teaspoon.

To Measure Dry Ingredients

Spoon lightly into flat-surfaced measuring cup. Do not press or shake down porous materials such as flour. Fill to overflowing, then level off excess with straight edge of knife. If fractional measuring spoons are not available: for ½ teaspoon divide 1 teaspoon through the middle lengthwise; for ¼ teaspoon divide the half crosswise; for ⅛ teaspoon divide the quarter crosswise.

To Measure Butter or Fat

PRINT BUTTER *or* MARGARINE: 1 pound butter equals 2 cups; 1 stick of butter is ½ cup; 1 inch of a stick equals 2 tablespoons.

BULK BUTTER *or* SHORTENING: Measure one cup of cold water into a glass measuring cup, then pour off the same amount of water as fat required. For example, to measure ¼ cup of fat, fill cup to 1-cup level with cold water, pour off ¼ cup of water, then add fat until 1-cup level is reached. The fat added will measure ¼ cup.

TO CUT THROUGH BRICK BUTTER: Cover the blade of the knife with waxed paper; or dip knife into very hot water; or saw through butter with a string.

STANDARD WEIGHTS AND MEASURES

A dash	8 drops
1 teaspoon	60 drops
1 tablespoon	3 teaspoons
1 ounce	2 tablespoons
¼ cup	4 tablespoons
⅓ cup	5⅓ tablespoons
½ cup	8 tablespoons
1 cup	16 tablespoons or 8 fluid ounces or ½ pint
1 pint	2 cups
1 pound	16 ounces
1 quart	2 pints
1 gallon	4 quarts
1 peck	8 quarts
1 bushel	4 pecks
1 dram	1/16 ounce
1 gram	1/30 ounce
1 kilo	2.20 pounds
1 liter	1 quart (approximate)
1 meter	39.37 inches

METRIC EQUIVALENTS

Linear

1 inch	2.54 centimeters
1 foot	30.48 centimeters
1 yard	91.44 centimeters
1 meter	39.37 inches

Liquid Volume

1 teaspoon	1⅓ fluid drams
1 tablespoon	4 fluid drams
1 cup	.236 liters
1 quart	.946 liters (approximately equal)
1 gallon	3.785 liters

Weights

1 gram	.035 ounces
1 kilogram	2.205 pounds
1 pound	453.6 grams

Temperatures

FAHRENHEIT		CELSIUS*
32°	freezing	0°
212°	boiling	100°
300°		149°
350°		176.6°
400°		204.5°
450°		232.3°

* Accepted in 1948 by international agreement as name for former Centigrade scale.

APPROXIMATE WEIGHTS AND MEASURES OF RAW FRUITS AND VEGETABLES

15 pounds potatoes	1 peck
3½ to 4 pounds spinach	1 peck
7½ pounds peas in pods	1 peck
50 pounds tomatoes (approximate)	1 bushel
50 pounds plums	1 bushel
48 pounds pears	1 bushel
48 pounds peaches	1 bushel
44 pounds apples	1 bushel

2
APPETIZERS

DIPS · SPREADS · CANAPES · FINGER FOODS · FIRST-COURSE APPETIZERS
· SMORGASBORD

Once the first course of a meal, appetizers now often serve as the spread set out with welcoming drinks, for a nibble or a buffet.

Appetizers can be simple or intricate, but they must always be tasty and appetite-stimulating, and easy to eat. The smart hostess will keep the makings of favorite appetizers on hand for unexpected guests. Before a party, many appetizers may be prepared in advance, and stored in the freezer or refrigerator. At the table, a cold appetizer may be put at each place just before guests are seated, to simplify serving.

In addition to foods prepared specifically as appetizers, many other dishes are appealing to serve as snacks, "pick-ups" or first courses. Remember to serve them in small portions that will not be too filling. Tiny meatballs or fish balls cooked in savory sauce may be served from a chafing dish, or kept warm over a candle-warmer or electric warming tray; or try hot sausage, cooked and cut in bite-sized pieces, then heated in dry white wine. Shellfish, hot or cold, may be served with cocktail sauce for dipping. Such simple foods as meat loaf, ham or steak, cut in small cubes and served on thin-cut buttered bread, are good appetizers, as are Spareribs Chinese Style, cut into individual ribs and served warm.

In planning appetizers for a party, select some which may be prepared well in advance. Arrange the cold ones on serving dishes, and cover with clear wrap or foil, to keep fresh. A few smaller dishes, which can be replaced as they are emptied, are more manageable than one large one. Hot ap-

petizers may be prepared and placed on the broiling or heating pans in advance, ready to finish as needed.

Very effective parties have been served with just two great appetizers, one hot and one cold. If a wider variety is offered, include some crunchy and some smooth, some bland and some sharp.

DIPS

Dips are easy to prepare from ingredients on hand, simple to serve, and they can be made in an endless variety of flavors and combinations. Use attractive trays or baskets to arrange crackers, thin bread squares or rectangles, potato chips or "puffs" to be used as dippers. Arrange crisp vegetable or shellfish dippers on a flat bowl or in a large bowl of ice.

FOODS TO BE DIPPED
Crackers, potato chips, toast sticks.

Vegetables such as celery, cucumber or carrot sticks, or small flowerets of raw cauliflower, raw sliced mushrooms, radishes or tiny tomatoes in season, or zucchini cut in strips.

Seafood such as cooked shrimp or fried oysters, slices of lobster tail.

BASE FOR DIPS
Sour cream or cream cheese, separately or combined to make mixture of desired consistency. For potato chip dippers, which break easily, make dip consistency thinner than for vegetable dippers or sturdy crackers.

TO MAKE DIPS, COMBINE BASE WITH:

CHEESE
Cheddar, grated
Parmesan, grated

SEAFOOD
Shrimp, chopped
Clams, minced
Smoked Salmon, minced
Caviar
Crab Meat

MEAT
Deviled Ham
Tongue, minced
Frankfurters, chopped
Dried Beef, chopped
Bacon, fried and crumbled

DRY SOUPS (commercially packaged)

Onion	Leek
Mushroom	Tomato

RELISHES
Chopped Olives
Pepper Relish

SEASONINGS
Worcestershire Sauce
Tabasco Sauce (sparingly)
Basil
Dill Weed
Thyme
Chives

COCKTAIL SAUSAGE DIP

Make Cheese Sauce, page 386. Add Burgundy or claret to taste. Keep sauce warm in chafing dish or over candle warmer. Serve as a dip with hot cocktail sausages or tiny meat balls.

HAM AND OLIVE DIP

1 package (8 ounces) cream cheese
1 small can chopped ripe olives
1 small can (2¼ ounces) deviled ham
1 teaspoon Worcestershire sauce
cream

Soften the cream cheese. Stir in the other ingredients. The amount of cream used will vary with the consistency desired. If the dip is to be used with potato chips which might break easily, add slightly more cream.

If using as a spread or as a filling for small cream puffs, add only about 1 tablespoon cream.

GUACAMOLE

3 ripe avocados
1 tomato, finely chopped
½ teaspoon Worcestershire sauce
3 tablespoons lemon juice
1 tablespoon grated onion
½ teaspoon salt

Peel and mash avocados. Combine with remaining ingredients. Cover bowl with plastic wrap to prevent dip from darkening. Chill.

CHEESE AND SHERRY DIP

1 package (3 ounces) cream cheese
1 small can (2¼ ounces) deviled ham
¼ cup dry sherry
1 cup small-curd cottage cheese
few drops Tabasco sauce
salt
parsley flakes

Soften cream cheese; add remaining ingredients except the parsley. Beat until smooth. Place in bowl; garnish with parsley.

Chapter 20 on Sauces offers many recipes suitable for use as a hot cocktail dip.

SPREADS

Savory spreads may be presented in a bowl, along with thin toast, crackers, or rounds of French bread, on buffet or coffee table where guests help themselves. For individual servings, mound spreads on crackers or crisp toast, and garnish. Almost any savory sandwich spread can be used as an appetizer spread.

CAMEMBERT SPREAD

Beat thoroughly ½ pound Camembert cheese with 2 tablespoons butter, ½ teaspoon paprika, 3 or 4 dashes of Tabasco and 3 drops of Worcestershire sauce; beat until smooth.

CAMEMBERT-ROQUEFORT SPREAD

½ pound Camembert cheese
¼ pound Roquefort cheese
¼ pound butter
garlic
paprika
chopped parsley

Place cheese and butter into a bowl which has been rubbed with garlic and blend well. Mold and chill. Unmold, sprinkle with paprika and chopped parsley.

CHEDDAR CHEESE SPREAD

Grate ¼ pound Cheddar cheese, season with ¼ teaspoon salt, a little paprika, ½ teaspoon mustard. Add 1 tablespoon each of butter and cream and stir until smooth.

PIMIENTO CREAM CHEESE

Mash a 3-ounce package of cream cheese, season with salt and a tablespoon of finely chopped pimiento; stir with a little cream until smooth.

TANGY SUNDAY NIGHT CHEESE

Cream thoroughly equal parts of cream cheese and butter. Add salt to taste, paprika, and 1 teaspoon each finely minced parsley, capers, pickles, olives, green pepper. If desired, flavor with anchovy paste.

ROQUEFORT SPREAD

⅛ pound Roquefort cheese
¼ pound cream cheese
1 tablespoon butter
1 tablespoon lemon juice
1 teaspoon salt
½ teaspoon chives, cut fine

Mash the cheese, stir with other ingredients until smooth.

WATER CRESS CREAM CHEESE

Mash a 3-ounce package of cream cheese, season with salt, add 1 tablespoon each of cream and finely chopped water cress.

POTTED CHEDDAR CHEESE

1 tablespoon butter
¼ pound Cheddar cheese, cut fine or grated
⅛ teaspoon cayenne pepper
¼ cup cream
yolk of 1 egg

Melt the butter, add cheese and pepper. Stir until cheese melts. Add cream to beaten yolk, pour into cheese mixture and cook, stirring constantly, until thick and smooth. Pour into small jars, store in refrigerator.

POTTED SNAPPY CHEESE

1 pound snappy cheese
2 teaspoons salt
1 teaspoon prepared mustard
speck of cayenne
½ cup diluted vinegar
1 tablespoon oil

Grate cheese. Add dry ingredients and vinegar; beat until blended. Add oil to make a smooth paste. Fill into jars, store in refrigerator.

CHICKEN LIVER SPREAD

Sauté a dozen chicken livers in hot fat with an onion until tender. Smooth to a paste, add salt, cayenne, butter and anchovy paste to taste.

SMOKED FISH SPREAD

1½ pounds smoked fish
2 teaspoons minced onion
2 teaspoons finely chopped celery
1 clove garlic, minced
2 tablespoons finely chopped sweet pickle
1¼ cups mayonnaise
1 tablespoon mustard
2 tablespoons chopped parsley
dash Worcestershire sauce

Remove skin and bones from fish and flake well. Mix all ingredients together and chill 1 hour before serving.

Many of the Sandwich Fillings and Sandwich Butters in chapter 19 make excellent spreads for appetizers.

CANAPES

Cold canapés can be prepared well in advance of serving time. To keep the bread or cracker bases fresh, spread them with a thin layer of butter before adding the filling. Arrange the prepared canapés on serving trays, insert toothpicks to hold the wrapping away from the canapés, and cover with plastic wrap or foil. Chill until serving time.

Cold

ANCHOVY BUTTER CANAPES

Spread triangle-shaped toasted bread with Anchovy Butter. Along one side sprinkle chopped whites of hard-cooked eggs; on second side, chopped yolks; on the third side, minced pickles. Place stuffed olive in center.

CAVIAR WITH EGG

Cut slices of hard-cooked eggs; take out the yolk, fill its place with caviar. Serve on thin slices of buttered brown bread, arranging the yolks, riced, as a border.

CAVIAR WITH ONIONS

Blend 1 part of caviar with ¼ part mayonnaise. Mix and spread on buttered bread or toast; sprinkle with grated or chopped onions.

CAVIAR WITH POTATO CHIPS

Chill one 3-ounce can caviar, season with lemon juice. Spread on large potato chips. Garnish with border of cream cheese.

CHICKEN LIVER CANAPES

Sauté a dozen chicken livers in hot fat with an onion until tender. Smooth to a paste, add salt, cayenne, butter and anchovy paste to taste. Spread on toast. Calf's liver may be used in place of chicken livers.

CHICKEN LIVER AND MUSHROOM CANAPES

Cook chicken livers slowly in hot chicken fat a few minutes. Drain and mash through sieve. Chop fresh or dried mushrooms fine and sauté. Mix with the liver, add lemon and onion juice, salt and pepper to taste. Spread on pieces of buttered toast.

PICKLED HERRING CANAPES

Chop ½ pound pickled herring tidbits and cream with 4 tablespoons butter. Add parsley and spread on fresh rye bread or toast. Separate hard-cooked egg, chop white fine and rice the yolks. Decorate with the egg.

PICKLED HERRING TIDBIT CANAPES

Bone and mash ½ pound pickled herring tidbits and add 2 tablespoons cream cheese, 2 tablespoons sweet butter, a little grated onion, a pinch of cayenne pepper. Spread on toast rounds or triangles.

SARDINE CANAPES

Mix equal parts of yolks of hard-cooked eggs and sardines, a little lemon juice, spread on toast. Top with riced whites, mix with chopped parsley.

Or to sardines and whites of hard-cooked eggs and pickle, minced fine, add a little Worcestershire sauce. Spread on buttered toast.

HARLEQUIN CANAPE

Use square loaf of rye bread. Remove crusts. Cut loaf lengthwise into slices ½ inch thick. Spread each slice thickly with creamed butter and mayonnaise. With large kitchen knife mark lines lengthwise on slice through butter and mayonnaise. These lines should be ½ inch apart and form 9 spaces. Put sandwich fillings of contrasting colors between lines, spreading lightly. In center space put smoked salmon, ground fine. On both sides of salmon put finely chopped, hard-cooked egg whites. In next spaces, riced yolks of eggs. Then sardine paste. Decorate space at either end by pressing softened cream cheese through pastry tube. Cut each slice crosswise into inch strips. Arrange slices on oblong platters, close together.

RAINBOW CANAPE WHEEL

Use large, round rye bread loaf. Remove lower crust. Cut thin round slice from bottom of loaf in one piece and spread thickly with butter and mayonnaise. Place this slice of bread on serving platter and decorate in distinct circles with a variety of sandwich mixtures. Mark without cutting a circle in center with tumbler. Spread caviar over this center. For second circle use 5-inch plate as a marker, spreading yolks of hard-cooked eggs, riced, in space. For third ring use minced ham; fourth, white of hard-cooked eggs; fifth, stuffed olives; sixth, yolk and white of hard-cooked egg, mixed; each variety chopped fine. Remove crust. Cut in small wedges to serve.

FILLED CREAM PUFFS

Fill tiny Cream Puffs with chicken or seafood salad, or well-seasoned sandwich spread.

SMOKED SALMON CANAPES

Spread toasted bread with butter, place thin round of smoked salmon on top; border with hard-cooked eggs minced with parsley.

TARTARE CANAPE

Season freshly ground beef with salt and onion juice. Spread on rye bread toast rounds; or omit onion juice and top with slice of onion.

Hot Canapes

Hot canapés may be prepared ahead, and refrigerated on the baking or broiling pan, covered, until time to heat and serve.

CHEESE AND OLIVE CANAPE

> 1 cup chopped ripe olives
> ½ cup scallions, sliced thin
> 1½ cups grated Cheddar cheese
> ½ cup mayonnaise
> ½ teaspoon salt
> ½ teaspoon curry powder

Mix ingredients. Spread on toasted rounds of bread. Broil until mixture is thoroughly heated and cheese is melted.

CHEESE PUFFS

> unsliced whole wheat bread or thin-sliced sandwich bread
> butter
> ½ pound aged Cheddar cheese
> ½ teaspoon baking powder
> 2 eggs, separated

Cut bread into ⅓-inch slices, then into 2-inch rounds and toast lightly on one side. When cool, spread the untoasted side well with creamed butter. Grate cheese, add baking powder, mix lightly with beaten yolks of eggs, then fold in the stiffly beaten whites. Spread a thick layer of this mixture on buttered side of toast, piling it higher in center. Place in broiler. When puffed and light brown, serve.

CHUTNEY CHEESE PUFFS

Prepare toast and cheese puff mixture, as above. Fry 4 slices bacon until crisp; chop and mix with 4 teaspoons prepared chutney. Place on toast, cover with cheese puff mixture, proceed as above.

PIQUANT PUFFS

1 egg white
1 cup highly seasoned mayonnaise
any crisp crackers

Beat egg white until stiff. Fold mayonnaise in gently, pile lightly onto crackers. Toast under broiler 1 minute or until delicately browned.

MINCED CLAM CANAPES

1 large can minced clams
8 ounces cream cheese
2 tablespoons lemon juice
garlic to taste

Drain clams; combine with other ingredients. Garlic powder is most easily used. Spread on rounds of toast. Sprinkle with paprika. Toast under broiler until thoroughly heated and slightly browned.

CHINESE SHRIMP BALLS

1 pound uncooked shrimp
6 water chestnuts
1 egg
1 teaspoon salt
½ teaspoon sugar
1 teaspoon cornstarch
oil for deep frying

Shell and devein shrimp. Mince shrimp and water chestnuts. Combine with remaining ingredients. Drop by heaping teaspoons into hot oil, 375° F. When balls turn pink, remove from oil and drain well. May be made in advance and reheated in oven.

CHUTNEY AND CHEESE CANAPES

Toast rounds of bread on one side; cover the other side with chutney, sprinkle with grated Cheddar cheese. Broil a few minutes until cheese is melted and serve at once.

CRAB MEAT OR LOBSTER CANAPES

Season chopped crab or lobster meat with salt, cayenne and a few drops of lemon juice. Moisten with Thick White Sauce. Spread on rounds of toast. Sprinkle with cheese and brown in oven.

SARDINE AND ANCHOVY CANAPES

1½ tablespoons butter
1 tablespoon anchovy paste
1 tablespoon flour
½ cup white wine
1 can skinless and boneless sardines (8 ounces)
4 slices toast (buttered)

Melt butter. Add anchovy paste, mixing to smooth paste. Add flour, stirring constantly, and cook until mixture bubbles. Add wine gradually, then sardines, heating slowly and taking care not to break sardines. Place sardines on toast, add sauce. Serve very hot.

TOMATO, CHEESE AND ANCHOVY CANAPES

Spread rounds of toasted bread with butter and anchovy paste. Place thin slice of tomato on top, sprinkle with grated Cheddar cheese; place under broiler until cheese is melted and serve hot; garnish with sprigs of parsley or a coiled anchovy.

TOMATO AND CHEESE CANAPES

Cut white bread into small rounds with cookie cutter. Toast one side, butter untoasted side. Cut slices of small firm tomatoes ¼-inch thick. Place on buttered side; flavor with salt and speck of grated onion. Pile grated Cheddar cheese on tomato and broil until cheese is melted.

FINGER FOODS

The simplest of all hors d'oeuvres to serve are the kinds picked up in the fingers to eat. Only two rules govern these—they must be small enough to swallow in one or two bites, and they must leave the fingers reasonably clean, or be simply speared with a pick. Anything goes for small cocktail spears, from simple wooden toothpicks, through frilled toothpicks, polished bamboo or mahogany, even sterling or vermeil. Or try edible picks: thin pretzel sticks or carrot slivers. You may offer a few of several kinds of cold tidbits, or an impressive quantity of one great favorite. For variety, spear the cold tidbits into a grapefruit or large red apple or loaf of bread, to make a "porcupine."

Cold

SNACK MIX

1½ cups ready-to-eat oat cereal
1½ cups bite-size shredded rice biscuits
1½ cups bite-size shredded wheat biscuits
1 cup salted peanuts
2 cups slim pretzel sticks
½ cup butter or margarine
4 teaspoons Worcestershire sauce
½ to 1 teaspoon garlic salt
1 teaspoon onion salt
1 teaspoon celery salt

Mix cereals, peanuts and pretzel sticks broken into small pieces in a large roasting pan. Heat butter until melted; stir in Worcestershire sauce and seasonings. Pour over cereal mixture and mix well. Bake in a moderately slow oven, 300° F., stirring every 10 minutes or so for about 30 minutes, until lightly browned. Cool before serving. Store in an airtight container. Yield: 2 quarts.

DEVILED ALMONDS, PECANS OR CHESTNUTS

Fry only until golden brown ½ pound blanched almonds, pecans or sliced chestnuts in about 1½ tablespoons butter. Stir constantly in heavy skillet over low heat to prevent burning. Season with salt, paprika, Worcestershire sauce and a dash of Tabasco sauce. Toss until coated. Serve cold.

SALTED NUTS

Place blanched nuts in shallow pan, in hot oven, 400° F., or in skillet on range. To ½ pound or 2 cups blanched nuts, use 1 teaspoon butter or oil. Stir frequently until a light brown. Sprinkle with salt.

Or fry a few at a time in deep hot oil in a small saucepan. Drain. Place on unglazed paper. Sprinkle with salt.

PECAN TIDBITS

Put 2 large halves of pecans together with anchovy paste, or with cream cheese mixed with anchovy paste.

DRIED BEEF SNACKS

3 ounces cream cheese
1 teaspoon prepared horseradish
1 teaspoon grated onion
pepper
sliced dried beef

Mix first four ingredients well. Spread on slices of drief beef. If slices of beef are small, use more than one slice to each roll. Roll up tight like jelly roll. Chill. Cut in ½-inch pieces and pierce with toothpicks.

SMOKED SALMON SNACKS

3 ounces cream cheese
1 teaspoon prepared horseradish
1 teaspon grated onion
pepper
sliced smoked salmon

Follow direction for Dried Beef Snacks, above.

SMOKED SALMON AND CAVIAR CORNUCOPIA

Roll thin slices of salmon into cone shape. Rice hard-cooked egg; mix with caviar. Season with lemon or onion juice and fill cones.

ASPARAGUS AND DRIED BEEF STICKS

Drain a can of asparagus tips. Trim slices of dried beef or cooked ham the length of asparagus tip. Spread slices with mayonnaise. Place one stalk on each slice. Roll up tightly, fasten roll with toothpicks.

CHEESE AND LETTUCE

Mix and cream well 3 parts of Roquefort cheese with 1 part of cream cheese. Chill. Wrap small portions in small, crisp lettuce leaves. Hold together with toothpicks.

STUFFED CELERY STALKS

WITH CHEESE

Wash tender celery stalks in cold water to crisp. Mix Roquefort cheese with a little cream cheese. Fill celery with mixture. Slice crosswise if desired.

Or stuff 1-inch pieces of celery stalks with cottage cheese, insert thin half slices of red radishes, red edge up, at equal distances.

WITH CRAB MEAT

Flake a 6-ounce can of crab meat. Add 1 tablespoon lemon juice and 3 tablespoons mayonnaise. Fill celery with mixture.

Celery may also be stuffed with any desired Appetizer Spread (see page 37) or Sandwich Filling (see chapter 19).

DEVILED OLIVES

Spread very small stuffed olives with cream cheese flavored with horseradish. Roll in finely chopped dried beef. Serve on toothpicks.

Browsing through the chapters on Fish and Seafood, as well as the one on Meat, Poultry and Game, may provide inspiration for unusual appetizers.

STUFFED OLIVES

1 pint of large, pitted olives
Pimiento Cream Cheese Spread, page 38

Fill olives with Spread. Pierce each with a toothpick.

See also recipes for Deviled Eggs, Boiled Shrimp, Popcorn.

Hot

Hot pick-up tidbits should be prepared in small batches, as needed. If necessary, they may be kept warm in a table warmer, but they taste best hot from oven or broiler. Fried appetizers may be fried ahead, and reheated in the oven or broiler just before serving.

FRANKFURTER SNACKS

Cut a frankfurter crosswise into ¾-inch lengths. Cut each piece slightly apart lengthwise, spread opening with prepared mustard and place a thin slice of pickle between. Hold together with a toothpick.

BROILED COCKTAIL FRANKS

Place Sterno lamp in hollowed-out center of a cabbage. Insert cocktail franks on toothpicks into outside of cabbage. Guests broil their own over flame.

SNACKS IN BACON BLANKETS

DEVILED OLIVES

Press ½ pecan nut meat into a pitted olive. Fold a thin slice of bacon around each olive, fasten with toothpick, brown slowly in frying pan and serve very hot, with any cocktail.

SHAD ROE

Cut parboiled roe in small pieces; wrap each piece in thin slice of bacon. Broil until crisp.

SHRIMP

Wrap shrimp in bacon as above.

CHICKEN LIVERS

Sauté in butter. Prepare as above.

CRACKER

Wrap a long thin cracker with thin slice of bacon, letting edges of slice overlap slightly. Broil until bacon is crisp.

ROLLED TOAST WITH SARDINES

Cut fresh wheat bread into ¼-inch slices. Butter. Spread with Sardine Paste. Remove crusts. Roll up tight and toast under broiler or cut in ½-inch slices crosswise and toast on both sides.

ROLLED TOAST WITH MUSHROOMS

Chop fresh mushrooms very fine. Sauté in butter 10 minutes; let cool and add mayonnaise and speck of grated onion to taste. Spread very fresh, thin slices of white bread with butter and chopped mushrooms. Remove crusts. Roll, toast in broiler and serve hot.

ASPARAGUS IN ROLLED STICKS

Slice fresh bread in ¼-inch slices, spread with creamed butter, or with anchovy paste. Remove crusts. Roll one stalk asparagus in bread, wrap in waxed paper, chill for 24 hours. Remove paper. Toast in hot oven and serve at once.

OYSTERS IN BLANKETS

12 firm oysters
red pepper
12 slices bacon (thin)
chopped parsley

Drain oysters and wipe dry and lay each oyster on a thin slice of bacon. Add a little red pepper. sprinkle with chopped parsley, fold bacon around oyster, fasten with a wooden toothpick. Brown slowly in a frying pan and serve hot with cocktails.

CREAM CHEESE BALLS

1 cup cream cheese
½ cup fine grated bread crumbs
5 drops Worcestershire sauce
1 egg, well beaten

Mix well and roll into small balls; place in wire basket, and just before serving, fry a delicate brown in deep, hot fat.

CHEDDAR CHEESE BALLS

1 cup grated Cheddar cheese
1 teaspoon flour
1 white of egg
½ teaspoon salt and pepper

Mix seasoning and flour with grated cheese, then fold into the stiffly beaten white of egg. Shape as desired. Fry in deep, hot fat.

FISH CAKES (FRIED)

1 cup cold boiled fish, shredded
1 cup cold mashed potatoes
salt, pepper
celery salt
1 egg, beaten
flour

Mix fish and potatoes, season with salt and pepper, add beaten egg, shape into small balls, dredge in flour, fry until browned on both sides. Or fry in deep fat.

SAUERBRATEN MEAT BALLS

1½ pounds ground beef
1 egg
1½ teaspoons salt
¼ teaspoon pepper
¼ cup fine dry bread crumbs
½ cup milk
2 tablespoons butter
1 cup water
2 tablespoons vinegar
2 tablespoons catsup
1 tablespoon brown sugar
8 peppercorns
1 bay leaf, crumbled
½ teaspoon salt
½ cup raisins (optional)
6 gingersnaps, crushed

Combine the first 6 ingredients, shape tiny meat balls. Brown in butter, shaking occasionally to brown evenly. While meat balls are browning, mix remaining ingredients. When meat is well browned, add sauce mixture. Bring to a boil over medium heat. Cover the skillet, reduce the heat, and simmer for 30 minutes. Stir gently once or twice during the time that the meat balls are simmering. Keep hot over a table warmer and serve with toothpicks.

Cocktail pastries, warm from the oven, can be served without a spread. Simply stack in a basket and pass with before-dinner drinks or juices. Fine with salads and soups, too.

CHEDDAR CHEESE STICKS

2 tablespoons butter
⅔ cup flour
1 cup fresh bread crumbs
1 cup grated Cheddar cheese
¼ teaspoon salt
⅛ teaspoon white pepper
pinch of cayenne
2 tablespoons milk

Cream butter, add flour, crumbs, cheese and seasonings. Mix thoroughly, then add milk. Roll and cut in strips ¼ inch wide and 6 inches long. Bake until brown in a moderate oven, 325° F.

QUICK CHEESE STICKS

¼ pound butter, creamed
1⅜ cups bread flour
½ pound aged Cheddar cheese, grated
salt and paprika
white pepper

Mix ingredients well, add a few grains white pepper. Spread on cookie sheet, then cut in 3-inch pieces. Bake at 475° F. about 10 minutes, or until light brown.

PARMESAN CHEESE STICKS

4 cups flour
2 teaspoons baking powder
1 teaspoon salt
1½ cups butter
2 yolks of eggs
2 cups milk
1 pound grated cheese, Parmesan or Edam

Mix dry ingredients, cut in butter, add eggs and milk. Roll; sprinkle one-half of the cheese over one-half of dough, fold, press edges together, fold again; roll ¼-inch thick. Sprinkle with rest of cheese and proceed as before. Cut in strips ¼ inch × 5 inches. Bake 8 minutes in a hot oven, 425° F.

FIRST-COURSE APPETIZERS

A first-course appetizer, served at the table, should be a refreshing introduction, whetting the appetite for the meal itself, or providing an interlude between the hors d'oeuvres and the dinner.

Fruit Cocktails

Fruit cocktails for a first course should not be oversweetened, and they are usually made of combinations of fruit, including some tart ones.

FRUIT COCKTAIL SAUCE

Boil 1 cup sugar and ½ cup water gently for 5 minutes. Cool and dilute with equal amount of ginger ale. Or, use juices from canned or fresh fruits or berries. Lemon or orange juice may be added. Or, use the syrup of maraschino or mint cherries. Wine, grape juice or ginger ale may be used. Serve over fruit cocktail.

LEMON FRUIT COCKTAIL SAUCE

Mix lemon juice with confectioners' sugar to the consistency of a sauce.

WINE FRUIT COCKTAIL SAUCE

Mix ½ cup sugar, ⅓ cup sherry, and 2 tablespoons Madeira or lemon juice.

AVOCADO FRUIT COCKTAIL

Combine cut-up avocado, pineapple, persimmons. Add Fruit Cocktail Sauce above. Serve ice cold in glasses.

FRUIT COCKTAIL WITH FRUIT ICE

Take equal parts of fresh diced pineapple and strawberries or any other fruit in season. Place tablespoon of orange, lemon or pineapple ice, in cocktail glass, fill with fruit. Decorate with mint leaves.

GRAPEFRUIT COCKTAIL

Sprinkle grapefruit sections with pomegranate seeds. Add grapefruit juice and serve ice cold.

GRAPEFRUIT AND LIME COCKTAIL

To 2 cups of grapefruit pulp with juice add ¾ cup sugar and juice of 2 limes. Mix well and chill 2 or 3 hours. Serve ice cold.

MELON COCKTAIL

Cut any variety of melon lengthwise in sections or slices and serve ice cold garnished with red or dark grapes.

ORANGE-BERRY COCKTAIL

Line cocktail glass with orange sections. Place a mound of fresh berries or white grapes in the center. Add Wine Fruit Cocktail Sauce.

PINEAPPLE AND GRAPEFRUIT COCKTAIL

Take equal parts of diced pineapple, grapefruit pulp and stoned white cherries. Place in cocktail glass. Sweeten with Wine Fruit Cocktail Sauce, above. Sprinkle with bits of mint or maraschino cherries.

WATERMELON COCKTAIL

Cut watermelon into cubes or balls; chill. Place 5 or 6 balls in each cocktail glass and pour ice-cold ginger ale over them. Cantaloupe, casaba or honeydew may be used, or they may be combined.

PINEAPPLE ON TOASTED RUSK

On a slice of rusk, place a thick slice of pineapple, over this sprinkle grated cheese. Lay strips of thinly sliced bacon on top, broil.

CHAROCIS FOR SEDER

6 or 7 apples
½ pound pecans or almonds
½ teaspoon cinnamon
sugar to taste
wine

Pare and grate the apples. Chop the nuts very fine. Blend apples, nuts, cinnamon, sugar and enough wine to bind all together or to the desired consistency.

CRANBERRY JUICE COCKTAIL

1 quart cranberries
1 quart boiling water
¾ cup sugar
¼ cup lemon juice
¼ cup orange juice
¼ teaspoon salt

Cook cranberries in water until soft. Strain. Add the remaining ingredients, bring to boiling point. Chill before serving.

FRUIT JUICE COCKTAIL

Mix the sweetened juice of fresh or canned fruit or berries with wine, carbonated water, or ginger ale. Serve chilled.

MINTED FRUIT JUICE COCKTAIL

Boil 1 cup water, 1 cup sugar for 5 minutes with 2 tablespoons chopped fresh mint. Strain. Use to sweeten and flavor fruit juices. Add lemon juice or orange juice to taste. Serve cold, garnished with sprig of mint.

PINEAPPLE JUICE COCKTAIL

Mix pineapple juice, fresh or canned, with orange or lemon juice.

Vegetable Juice Cocktails

SAUERKRAUT JUICE COCKTAIL

To 1 pint sauerkraut juice, add 2 tablespoons lemon juice, ¼ teaspoon caraway seed and ½ cup finely diced raw apple.

SPICY TOMATO JUICE COCKTAIL

4 cups tomato juice
¾ teaspoon salt
3 tablespoons lemon juice
3 teaspoons sugar
1 teaspoon grated horseradish
1 teaspoon Worcestershire sauce

Mix, chill, serve ice cold.

TOMATO JUICE COCKTAIL

2 cups tomato juice
¾ teaspoon salt
2 teaspoons sugar
1 tablespoon lemon juice

Mix, chill, serve.

Egg Appetizers

EGG AND CAVIAR APPETIZER

4 hard-cooked eggs
1 tablespoon caviar
salt and paprika to taste
Boiled Celery Root, page 418

Cook eggs, and while hot put through ricer. Mix with caviar, season, press in small buttered mold, chill for several hours. Cut in slices. Serve on slice of Boiled Celery Root. Top with mayonnaise.

DEVILED EGGS

4 hard-cooked eggs
¼ teaspoon salt
½ teaspoon dry mustard
⅛ teaspoon cayenne pepper
1 teaspoon vinegar
1 tablespoon melted butter

Cool eggs, remove shell and cut each in half, lengthwise. Remove yolks and rub them smooth; mix thoroughly with the rest of the ingredients or with mayonnaise. Fill each half white of egg with this mixture.

Or, add 4 boned anchovies, pounded smooth and strained. Or, add ¼ cup of chopped chicken, veal, ham or tongue.

EGG AND HAM APPETIZER

5 hard-cooked eggs
1 teaspoon chives, chopped
salt
paprika
mayonnaise
½ pound boiled ham

Separate yolks and whites of eggs. Mash the yolks, add chives, salt and paprika and mix to a smooth paste with mayonnaise. Grind ham and whites of eggs, mix all together and form into balls size of a walnut, serve with mayonnaise.

EGG AND SARDINE

Place slice of hard-cooked egg on a slice of fresh, buttered rye bread. Place half of a boned sardine on top of egg.

EGG, SARDINE, AND TOMATO

Cut rounds of bread, toast, and place on round a slice of tomato; on this put a boned sardine, then a slice of egg and over this mayonnaise.

EGG AND TOMATO APPETIZER

3 eggs
¼ teaspoon salt
¼ teaspoon paprika
onion juice
3 large, firm tomatoes
Gargoyle Sauce, page 376

Hard cook eggs; while warm, rice or chop them. Add salt, paprika, and a few drops of onion juice. Pack tightly into small buttered molds; chill 4 to 5 hours. Remove from mold, cut into ½-inch slices. Place thick slices of tomato on lettuce, add slice of egg; cover with Gargoyle Sauce.

Seafood Cocktails

Any cold, cooked seafood or fish may be served with a spicy sauce as a first course appetizer. White-fleshed fish such as halibut or haddock may be poached and used for cocktails instead of, or in a mixture with, crab, lobster, or shrimp.

BESETTI SAUCE

1 teaspoon dry mustard
2 tablespoons tarragon vinegar
juice of ½ lemon
1 teaspoon prepared horseradish
1 cup chili sauce
1 cup whipped cream
1 tablespoon mayonnaise
½ teaspoon Worcestershire sauce

Mix the mustard in the vinegar. Add other ingredients and mix well. Serve with seafood.

FAST COCKTAIL SAUCE

Add prepared horseradish to catsup or chili sauce to taste.

COCKTAIL SAUCE FOR SEAFOODS

½ cup tomato catsup
2 teaspoons prepared mustard
2 tablespoons lemon juice
1 tablespoon Worcestershire sauce

Mix and serve ice cold over any seafood. Let stand 15 minutes. Add a few drops Tabasco sauce and horseradish.

ZIPPY SEAFOOD COCKTAIL SAUCE

¾ cup catsup
3 tablespoons vinegar
1 teaspoon Worcestershire sauce
3 tablespoons wine
cayenne and salt to taste
juice of 1 lemon

Mix and serve cold with any seafood.

Other sauces for seafood cocktails include Russian Dressing and Thousand Island Dressing. For these and other salad dressings, see chapter 18.

CLAM COCKTAIL

Arrange small clams on the half shell on finely chopped ice. Serve with a thick wedge of lemon on the side and place a small dish of horseradish or cocktail sauce in center.

CRAB MEAT COCKTAIL

Shred crab meat, remove cartilage, serve with any seafood cocktail sauce. Lobster or tuna fish may be used in place of crab meat.

OYSTER COCKTAIL

Place 5 or 6 small oysters in each glass, cover with seafood cocktail sauce. Serve ice cold. Use oysters alone or combine with any other seafood.

See recipe for Oysters on Half Shell.

STEAMED CLAMS

Scrub shells of steamer clams to remove all sand. Place flat in a kettle, add ½ cup boiling water. Cover and steam over low heat until shells are partly open—about 5 to 10 minutes. Serve with melted butter.

SHRIMP AND AVOCADO COCKTAIL

Place slices of avocado in cocktail glasses. Sprinkle with salt and lemon juice; add whole cooked shrimp. Serve with any seafood cocktail sauce.

Fish Appetizers

Small portions of fish cooked with a savory sauce to be served hot or cold, make excellent appetizers for a more elaborate meal. For a formal dinner, a small fish course is served between soup and meat. See chapter 12, Fish and Seafood.

HERRING APPETIZER

Serve pickled herring, plain or with cream sauce, with fresh rye bread. Garnish with sliced onions, if desired.

LINCOLN HOUSE FISH BALLS

2 pounds trout
1 pound each pike and pickerel
1 teaspoon salt
pepper to taste
½-inch slice bread
½ pound carrots
½ pound onions
1 bunch celery
2 eggs, beaten
1 cup water

Scale fish, wash, and salt for several hours. Remove heads and skin. Scrape off flesh and set it aside. Wrap heads and bones in skin, place in kettle. Cover with water, add salt and pepper, and all the vegetables but 1 carrot, ½ onion, and heart of celery; let boil slowly while preparing fish balls.

Soak bread, press dry. Put fish, rest of vegetables and bread through grinder into chopping bowl. Gradually, while chopping, add the eggs and water. Dip hands in cold water, shape mixture into balls, drop into the boiling fish broth. Cover, cook 2 hours very slowly; uncover, cook ½ hour longer. Cool slightly, remove balls carefully. Strain liquid and pour over fish.

Can be served hot or cold; liquid jells when cold.

MOLDED SARDINE APPETIZER

2 large cans boneless, skinless sardines
¼ pound butter, softened
1 cup pimiento olives
lemon juice and paprika

Mash sardines with fork, add butter. Mix and season. Pack into small molds. Chill until firm. Unmold. Cover with sliced olives. Serve with sliced lemon and toast points.

SARDINES IN TOMATO ASPIC

Make Tomato Aspic, page 367. Place sardines (or use herring tidbits) in bottom of mold. Add a thin layer of aspic, chill until set. Add remaining aspic. Chill until firm. Unmold, serve on rounds of Boiled Celery Root, page 418.

SARDINE COCKTAIL

Skin, bone and cut sardines in pieces. Serve cold in glasses with cocktail sauce for seafood.

SAUTEED SHRIMP

2 pounds shelled and deveined shrimp
⅓ cup olive oil
½ cup dry vermouth
2 cloves garlic, crushed
¾ teaspoon salt
½ teaspoon pepper
3 tablespoons chopped parsley
3 tablespoons lemon juice

Sauté shrimp quickly in hot oil until lightly golden. Add vermouth, garlic, salt and pepper. Cook until liquid is almost gone. Sprinkle with parsley and lemon juice.

SWEET AND SOUR FISH

3½ pounds pike, trout or other fish
1 cup hot fish liquid
¼ pound gingersnaps
½ cup brown sugar
¼ cup vinegar
¼ cup seeded raisins
½ teaspoon onion juice
1 lemon, sliced and seeded

Clean, slice and salt fish and let stand overnight or several hours. Cook, following recipe for Boiled

Fish. Drain and bone, reserving 1 cup of the fish liquid. Mix fish liquid with the rest of the ingredients and cook until smooth and thick. Pour while hot over fish. Serve cold.

Miscellaneous Appetizers

GOOSE LIVER APPETIZER

    bread rounds
    butter
    tomatoes
    salt and pepper to taste
    goose liver
    hard-cooked eggs

Toast bread; butter lightly. Place a thick slice of tomato on top of this; season with salt and pepper. On top of this place slice of fried goose liver. Decorate top with yolk and white of egg, chopped separately.

BROILED SWEETBREADS

    1 pound sweetbreads
    salt and pepper
    Maître d'Hotel Butter, page 391

Parboil sweetbreads (page 298), split crosswise; sprinkle with salt and pepper and broil 5 minutes. Serve with Maître d'Hôtel Butter.

SWEETBREADS WITH MUSHROOMS

    1 cup cream
    1 tablespoon butter
    salt and pepper to taste
    2 egg yolks
    1½ cups Boiled Sweetbreads, diced, page 298
    1 cup Sautéed Mushrooms, page 421

Heat cream in a saucepan, add butter, pepper, salt and beaten yolks stirred with a little of the cream. Cook until thick, stirring constantly, add sweetbreads and mushrooms, and serve at once on buttered toast.

ARTICHOKE LEAVES AND SHRIMP

Boil artichokes (page 412) and separate leaves. Cover with boiled, chilled shrimp, top with mayonnaise or chili sauce.

ARTICHOKES VINAIGRETTE

Serve Boiled Artichokes chilled, with French dressing. Or, serve hot with melted butter.

BROILED MUSHROOMS

    1 pound mushrooms
    ¼ teaspoon salt
    ⅛ teaspoon pepper
    2 tablespoons butter

Wash mushrooms, remove stems and reserve for soup or sauce. Place caps in a buttered broiler and broil 5 minutes, under-side down. Turn, put a small piece of butter in each cap, sprinkle with salt and pepper and serve as soon as butter is melted. Serve on rounds of well-buttered toast.

CELERIAC VINAIGRETTE

Cook Celeriac (page 418), slice into julienne sticks, and serve cold, with French dressing.

CUCUMBER APPETIZER

Peel a large, firm cucumber, cut into 1-inch slices, scoop out center. Put each piece on a thick slice of tomato and fill center with riced yolk of hard-cooked eggs and caviar, mixed with mayonnaise.

VEGETABLE COCKTAILS

    2 tablespoons vinegar
    ½ cup chili sauce
    1 teaspoon salt
    1 teaspoon grated horseradish
    2 teaspoons sugar
    1 teaspoon finely chopped parsley
    1 teaspoon finely chopped green pepper
    dash of pepper
    dash of paprika
    a few drops of onion juice

Mix in order given; chill. Serve over cut-up cold cooked vegetables.

SMORGASBORD

This Scandinavian specialty is deservedly popular as a modern way of entertaining, particularly for large groups, since it reduces last-minute service to a minimum. Platters should be prepared in advance and covered with foil or plastic wrap until serving time. The size of the spread depends upon the use for which it is intended. It may be small and simple for before-dinner service, elaborate and elegant for a cocktail party, or lavish and generous, with emphasis on hearty dishes, when it is to serve as a meal.

The basic ingredients of the smörgåsbord are always fish, meat, cheese, salads, and relishes, a few hot dishes, always including meat balls, baked beans, and boiled potatoes, and usually dark-grained Scandinavian breads.

Fish for smörgåsbord may include pickled and brined herring and anchovies in all the many available styles. Smoked eel, salmon, carp and similar delicacies are available at specialty shops, and smoked oysters, mussels and clams come in cans and jars and are more generally distributed. Fresh boiled shrimp and lobster, with dill-flavored sauces, are popular. The cold meats may include roast pork, beef, and tongue or ham, or cold cuts as desired. Meat and fish are frequently incorporated into salad mixtures, as well. An aspic salad is usually selected, in addition to simple greens, pickled beets, celery hearts, radishes, green onions, canned artichokes, and other salad vegetables. Tiny meat balls in a tart creamy sauce and fish balls are the traditional hot dishes, but any savory meat or fish may be substituted.

Scandinavian lingonberry jelly, or American cranberry sauce or jelly, which it resembles, is always served on the smörgåsbord.

When the smörgåsbord is the entire meal, guests should be invited to come to the table three times: the first time, they fill their plates with fish and suitable accompaniments. On successive trips, they choose from the meats, cheeses, and salads, and the hot dishes. Foods are arranged on the smörgåsbord table in groups, in the sequence in which they are eaten, with an eye toward beauty in the arrangement and garnishing of the platters.

Beer is the usual accompaniment for smörgåsbord; hot coffee should follow with the dessert.

QUICK REFERENCE GUIDE TO USEFUL INFORMATION IN THIS BOOK

3
BEVERAGES

COFFEE · TEA · CHOCOLATE · MILK · FRUIT DRINKS · PUNCHES
· EGGNOGS · WINES · COCKTAILS

A beverage includes all drinks from a glass of water to breakfast coffee, from milk to a festive punch, from an aperitif to blazing Café Brûlot.

COFFEE

Choosing coffee depends upon personal flavor preference; blends vary widely from very mild to strong. Dark-roasted coffees are preferred for demitasse and espresso-type drinks.

Basic grinds of coffee	Use in
Regular grind	Percolator or pot
Drip	Drip or vacuum-style coffee maker
Fine	Vacuum-style coffee maker
Instant	Stir into hot or cold water

BASIC PROPORTIONS TO MAKE COFFEE

FOR ONE SERVING (5½ ounces is average)
¾ cup water (6 ounces)
2 level tablespoons coffee
(Plastic coffee measure in general use equals 2 level tablespoons.)

FOR FOUR SERVINGS
3 cups water
8 level tablespoons coffee

FOR EIGHT SERVINGS
6 cups water
16 level tablespoons coffee

If you use unusually large or small cups, check the liquid content and adjust the above proportions accordingly.

If using automatic coffee makers, follow the manufacturer's instructions.

DRIP COFFEE

Scald coffeepot with very hot water. Place fine drip grind coffee in filter cup of coffeepot. Add the boiling water gradually and allow it to filter or drip.

PERCOLATED COFFEE

When using a percolator, put freshly boiled or cold water in bottom and regular grind coffee in top compartment. Cover coffeepot. Place over heat, "perc" 5 to 10 minutes, counting from the time that the water begins to bubble up in the glass top. The percolator should never be less than half full.

VACUUM-STYLE COFFEE

Measure fresh cold water into lower bowl. Put on heat. Put filter in upper bowl, fill with extra-fine grind coffee. When water boils, reduce heat, insert upper bowl with slight twist. Let most of water rise to upper bowl. Stir thoroughly, let stand 3 minutes on heat. Remove from heat, let stand until brew returns to lower bowl.

BOILED COFFEE

6 measures regular grind coffee
6 tablespoons egg water
5 cups boiling water
1 cup cold water

Scald coffeepot; mix coffee with Egg Water (below), place in pot, add boiling water and let boil 3 minutes. Add cold water and let stand where it will keep hot, but not boil.

TO CLEAR BOILED COFFEE

EGG SHELLS

May be washed, saved and used for clearing coffee. Three egg shells will clear eight cups of boiled coffee.

EGG WATER

1 egg
1 cup cold water
pinch salt

Wash and break egg in large cup or pint jar, beating constantly while pouring on 1 cup cold water. Cover and place in refrigerator for future use. For each cup of coffee use 1 tablespoon of the egg water.

COFFEE FOR 40 PEOPLE

1 pound coffee
1 egg
10 quarts freshly boiling water

Mix the coffee, finely ground, with the egg and enough cold water to thoroughly moisten it. Place in thin bag and drop in the boiling water. Boil 10 minutes, let stand 10 minutes.

CAFFE ESPRESSO

Brew coffee double strength, serve in demitasse cups or 4-ounce glasses, with sugar and a twist of lemon peel. Serve after dinner.

CAPPUCINO

Brew coffee double strength, serve in cups with an equal volume of hot, but not boiled milk. Top with whipped cream, grated orange rind. Serve with pastries.

CAFE AU LAIT

Pour equal parts of freshly brewed regular coffee and hot, but not boiled, milk into a cup simultaneously, so that the mixture froths. Serve at breakfast.

VIENNESE COFFEE

Top hot, freshly brewed regular coffee with a generous spoonful of whipped cream. Serve as dessert, with pastry.

ICED COFFEE

Serve iced coffee with cream and sugar, if desired; or with sweetened whipped cream; or with vanilla or coffee ice cream, as dessert and beverage combined.

QUICK EXTRA-STRENGTH METHOD

Make hot coffee extra-strength by using two-thirds the amount of water to the usual amount of coffee. Pour over ice cubes in tall glasses. The extra-strong coffee allows for dilution from the melting ice.

COFFEE ICE CUBE METHOD

Brew extra breakfast coffee and freeze into coffee ice cubes. Then make iced coffee any time by pouring regular-strength coffee over the cubes.

ICED INSTANT COFFEE

Mix twice the usual amount of instant coffee with a little cold water in each glass. Add ice cubes, fill glass with cold water and stir thoroughly.

COFFEE CONCENTRATE

1 pound ground coffee
7 to 7½ cups cold water

Soak coffee in cold water for 12 to 24 hours. Filter. Store in glass jar in refrigerator.

For hot coffee, add boiling water to approximately 1½ tablespoons of concentrate per cup. Decrease or increase the amount of concentrate depending upon your preference.

For iced coffee use the same proportions of coffee and cold water as for hot coffee.

TEA

TO MAKE TEA

Heat an earthen or china teapot by rinsing it with boiling water. Then put in one teaspoon tea, or one tea bag, for each cup of water.

Pour freshly boiled water directly on the tea leaves or tea bags and steep 3 to 5 minutes. Serve with sugar, milk, or lemon, if desired.

TO SERVE TEA

WITH LEMON OR ORANGE

Serve tea hot, allowing a slice of lemon or orange to each cup, adding a few cloves, if desired.

WITH PRESERVED FRUIT OR RUM

Serve tea hot, allowing 1 teaspoon of rum, preserved fruit, strawberry, raspberry, cherry or pineapple preserves to each cup.

WITH SUGAR

Cubes of sugar may be flavored with lemon or

orange and packed and stored in jars to be used later, to flavor and sweeten the tea. Wash rind of lemon or orange and wipe dry, then rub over all sides of sugar.

WITH CANDY

Serve tea hot, sweeten with hard sugar candies, as lemon, clove or cinnamon drops, or with rock candy.

RUSSIAN TEA

    1 tablespoon tea leaves
    1 cup boiling water
    cube sugar
    lemon slices
    1 teaspoon preserved cherries, strawberries or rasp-
        berries

The water is kept hot in a samovar or urn. A strong tea is steeped in an earthenware teapot by pouring the cup of boiling water over the tea; let stand 3 minutes. In serving, pour into each cup ¼ to ½ cup of tea. Fill with hot water from samovar or urn and serve with sugar, thin slice of lemon, or preserves. Makes 2 to 4 cups.

ICED TEA

Make tea, as above, using only ¾ cup water to 1 teaspoon tea or 1 tea bag. Strain into glasses ¾ full of cracked ice. Serve with lemon and sugar. Or make tea usual strength, strain into a pitcher, and chill. Serve with ice, lemon, and sugar.

For suggested foods to serve at a "coffee" or afternoon tea party, see ideas in chapter 1, Menus. Or check index under Coffee Cakes, Kuchen, Tea Breads, Muffins, as well as Cakes, Cookies, Pies.

CHOCOLATE

CHOCOLATE SYRUP FOR DRINKS

    2 cups sugar
    1 quart water
    4 squares (4 ounces) unsweetened chocolate
    ½ teaspoon salt
    2 tablespoons cornstarch
    2 tablespoons cold water
    2 teaspoons vanilla

Boil sugar and water 5 minutes; add chocolate, salt and the cornstarch dissolved in cold water. Stir until smooth, cook 3 minutes. Cool, add vanilla, store in jar in refrigerator. Use 2 tablespoons to a glass of milk when ready to serve. Serve with or without sweetened whipped cream or ice cream. Makes 4 cups.

CHOCOLATE

    3 cups milk
    1½ ounces unsweetened chocolate
    4 tablespoons sugar
    few grains salt
    1 cup boiling water
    1 teaspoon vanilla

Scald milk; melt chocolate in small saucepan over hot water; add sugar, and salt and stir in boiling water gradually. Boil 5 minutes; add scalded milk. Add vanilla. Beat with egg beater and serve hot. Or chill and serve with ice.

   If sweet chocolate is used, omit the sugar. Makes 4 cups.

RUSSIAN CHOCOLATE

Follow recipe above, using ½ cup milk and ½ cup cream in place of milk. Then add 2 cups hot, strong coffee just before serving, and beat well with rotary beater. Makes 6 cups.

ICED CHOCOLATE WITH EGG

    4 tablespoons chocolate syrup
    1 egg
    fine ice
    ¾ cup milk

Combine ingredients in a bowl, beat thoroughly with rotary beater. Or pour into jar, cover, and shake thoroughly.

CHOCOLATE EGG MALTED MILK

    1 tablespoon malted milk
    1 tablespoon boiling water
    1 egg, beaten
    2 tablespoons chocolate syrup
    ½ cup milk
    2 tablespoons vanilla ice cream
    whipped cream

Stir malted milk with boiling water to a smooth paste. Add to egg; add syrup and milk, beating all the time; pour over the ice cream in glass and top with whipped cream.

RUSSIAN CHOCOLATE WITH COFFEE

    chocolate syrup
    chilled strong coffee
    coffee ice cubes
    vanilla ice cream
    whipped cream

Put 2 or 3 tablespoons chocolate syrup in a glass. Fill glass with coffee and coffee cubes. Add a scoop of ice cream and top with whipped cream.

ICED COFFOLATE

1 tablespoon cornstarch
2 squares unsweetened chocolate
½ teaspoon cinnamon
¼ cup sugar
2 cups hot strong coffee
2 cups scalded milk

Dissolve cornstarch in a little cold water and cook in double boiler with chocolate, cinnamon, sugar, and the coffee until thick; add milk, cook 15 minutes, stirring. Chill. Serve ice cold, topped with whipped cream. Makes 1 quart.

COCOA

2 teaspoons cocoa
2 scant teaspoons sugar
1 cup boiling water
1 cup milk
½ teaspoon vanilla

Put the cocoa, sugar and boiling water into a saucepan. Boil 1 minute, add milk and heat. Do not boil. Add vanilla. Makes 2 cups.

FROTHY COCOA

1 cup boiling water
2 tablespoons cocoa
2 tablespoons sugar
1 teaspoon cornstarch
few grains salt
3 cups milk
½ teaspoon vanilla
whipped cream

Stir the boiling water gradually onto the mixed dry ingredients, in a saucepan, let boil 5 minutes, stirring constantly. Heat milk in double boiler, add the cocoa mixture and vanilla. Beat with egg beater until foamy, serve hot, with a tablespoon of whipped cream on top of each cup. Or place 1 marshmallow in each cup and fill. Makes 4 cups.

COCOA BASE

½ cup cocoa
1¼ cups sugar
2 cups boiling water
few grains salt
1 teaspoon vanilla

Put the cocoa and sugar into a saucepan, pour on the boiling water gradually, stirring until cocoa is thoroughly dissolved. Boil until thick, stirring constantly; add salt and vanilla. Cover and keep in a cool place. When wanted, add 1 tablespoon of the paste to 1 cup hot milk or milk and water mixed. Stir until dissolved. Yield: base for 20 cups of cocoa.

ICED COCOA

Add 2 tablespoons Cocoa Base, above, to 1 glass ice-cold milk. Stir, top with whipped cream or ice cream, if desired.

MILK

Milk is one of the most important foods, containing well-balanced protein, carbohydrate, fat and mineral content as well as most of the essential vitamins.

FRESH, SWEET MILK is usually pasteurized before bottling, in order to destroy harmful bacteria, and Vitamin D is generally added.

HOMOGENIZED MILK is pasteurized milk with the fat globules broken and dispersed so that they remain stable. In homogenized milk, the cream cannot rise to the top of the bottle.

SKIM MILK is milk from which most of the fat has been removed.

NONFAT MILK is guaranteed to contain no more than 0.1% milk fat.

CERTIFIED MILK is not pasteurized, but it is produced and bottled under special conditions with extra-strict sanitation controls.

EVAPORATED MILK is pure whole milk with much of the water taken out and nothing added. It is homogenized and may or may not be irradiated, that is, enriched with Vitamin D. Evaporated milk mixed with an equal amount of water can be used in any recipe calling for milk.

EVAPORATED SKIM MILK is skim milk from which much of the water and fat have been removed.

SWEETENED CONDENSED MILK is pure whole milk with much of the water taken out and sugar added. Sweetened condensed milk may be used instead of milk and sugar, in coffee or chocolate drinks, for instance, and many recipes specifically require it.

NONFAT DRY MILK and WHOLE DRY MILK (*Powdered*) are made from skim and whole milk respectively, with just the water removed. When water is added according to the package directions, the resultant fluid can be used in any recipes calling for milk.

BUTTERMILK is the liquid that remains when butter has been churned. Cultured buttermilk is made by introducing a culture of lactic acid bacteria into skimmed or partially skimmed milk.

CULTURED MILK is whole milk, with lactic acid bacteria added.

YOGURT is made by fermenting whole or partially skimmed milk with a special bacteria, to produce a tart custardy mixture thick enough to eat with a spoon.

SOUR MILK can be made by adding one tablespoon lemon juice or vinegar to one cup of sweet milk.

WHEY is the watery part of the milk that, while souring, separates from the curd, or solid part.

CREAM is the fat that rises to the top of the milk.

HALF AND HALF is a mixture of milk and cream, about 10% milk fat.

LIGHT CREAM also called table cream or coffee cream, contains about 20% fat.

HEAVY CREAM contains not less than 36% butter fat. This is the cream usually whipped. See Whipping Cream.

SOUR CREAM is light cream to which a bacterial culture has been added.

HALF AND HALF SOUR CREAM is made by adding the same bacterial culture to a mixture of milk and cream containing about 10% milk fat. Both sour cream and half and half sour cream are used as dessert or salad toppings, in cooking and in baking.

TO PASTEURIZE MILK

Fill sterilized bottles or jars nearly full of milk, cork them with sterilized cotton, place on a rack in a pail and fill with cold water so that the water may be as high outside the jars as the milk is inside, place the pail over the fire and heat until small bubbles appear around the top of the milk (about 145° F.); decrease the heat and allow the bottles to stand there 30 minutes; then reduce the temperature as quickly as possible. When milk is cold remove the bottles from the water and keep in a cold place.

TO BOIL MILK

Bring to the boiling point. Remove from heat, cool as quickly as possible.

TO SCALD MILK

Heat milk over very low heat, or over hot water in double boiler, until small bubbles form around the edge of pan.

HOT MALTED MILK

1 tablespoon malted milk powder
boiling water
hot milk (or water)

PLAIN

Place malted milk powder in cup, mix to a smooth paste with a little boiling water. Fill cup with hot milk or water, stirring all the time. Season with salt and pepper or a little celery salt.

WITH CHOCOLATE

Mix 1 tablespoon cocoa with malted milk powder as above, add sugar and cinnamon.

WITH SOUP

Add ¼ cup chicken or beef broth to malted milk paste, fill cup with hot water.

HOT MALTED MILK WITH EGG

2 tablespoons malted milk
boiling water
1 egg
2/3 cup hot milk or water
few drops vanilla, or grated nutmeg

Mix malted milk in cup to smooth paste with a little boiling water. Beat egg until light, add to malted milk, add hot milk and flavoring, stir until smooth and serve.

FRUIT DRINKS

Fruit Syrups

An endless variety of drinks may be made by using as a foundation fruit syrup and juices. These may be purchased or made in the home, bottled and kept for future use. Syrups left over from canned or pickled fruits may be used.

GINGER SYRUP

Pour 1 quart of water over ½ cup of ground ginger root, let stand undisturbed 48 hours. Pour off water into kettle carefully, leaving sediment undisturbed; measure water, add an equal amount of sugar, boil 10 minutes. Pour into hot sterilized jars and seal. Use as flavoring with fruit juices.

LEMON SYRUP

6 lemons, grated rind
12 lemons, juice
2 quarts boiling water
1 pound sugar

Add grated rind of lemons to juice and let stand overnight. Pour water over sugar, stir until sugar is dissolved; boil 5 minutes. Cool, add lemon juice. Bottle and seal. Serve with equal amount of water. Makes 2½ quarts.

ORANGE SYRUP

Follow directions for making Lemon Syrup, in above recipe, substituting orange juice and rind, adding a little lemon for flavor.

RASPBERRY SYRUP

2 quarts raspberries
2 pounds sugar
2 cups water

Wash berries, mash, and strain through jelly bag. Boil sugar and water to soft-ball stage, 234° F. Slowly add fruit juice, boil again. Skim; pour into hot sterilized jars and seal.

Or, use strawberries, or black raspberries and currants, or cherries, currants and raspberries, or loganberries.

SPICED SYRUP

1 tablespoon each, whole cloves, allspice, cinnamon
4 pounds sugar
2 quarts water

Tie spices in a bag. Place sugar and water in kettle, let boil 5 minutes or until clear; add spices, cook until syrup is well flavored, then pour into hot sterilized bottles or jars, and seal. Use with fruit juices for flavoring drinks. Makes 2 quarts.

In addition to their use for fruit drinks, the preceding syrups add extra flavor to cooked fruits and fruit cocktails when added just before serving. They are also recommended as a topping for ice cream and sherbet.

SUGAR SYRUP OR BAR SYRUP

1 cup water
1 cup sugar

Boil sugar and water 3 minutes, until sugar is dissolved. Cool, bottle, and store to use in sweetening drinks.

Fruit Drinks

FRESH FRUIT LEMONADE

1 lemon, juice
1½ cups water
4 tablespoons sugar

Add the sugar to lemon juice and water and stir until dissolved. Add crushed ice if desired. Makes 1 drink.

LEMONADE

Fill glasses with equal parts Lemon Syrup, above, and cold water. Add ice.

PICNIC LEMONADE

Sweeten juice of 12 lemons with 1 pound of sugar. Add grated rind of 2 lemons, put in quart jar and seal. When ready to serve, add 4 quarts of ice water. Makes 4½ quarts.

LIMEADE

4 tablespoons sugar
1 lime, juice
1½ cups cold water

Add sugar to liquid. Stir until dissolved. Add crushed ice.

ORANGE JUICE

Chill and wash orange. Cut in half crosswise. Remove seeds. Extract juice and strain. Makes about ⅓ cup.

FRESH FRUIT ORANGEADE

2 oranges, juice
½ lemon, juice
1½ cups water
4 tablespoons sugar

Add sugar to liquid. Stir until dissolved.

ORANGEADE

Fill glasses with equal parts of Orange Syrup and cold water. Add ice.

TEA ORANGEADE

½ cup sugar
1 cup water
grated rind of orange
3 tablespoons lemon juice
2 cups orange juice
2 cups strong tea

Boil sugar, water and orange rind five minutes. Chill, add fruit juices and strained tea. Chill. Makes 4 drinks.

ORANGE FREEZE

juice of 1 orange
scoop of orange ice
carbonated water to fill glass

Pour orange juice over orange ice in tall glass. Add soda water, stir to blend. Serve with straw and long-handled spoon. Makes 1 drink.

PINEAPPLEADE

½ cup pineapple juice
½ lime or lemon, juice
2 tablespoons sugar
½ glass cracked ice

Mix well and serve. Makes 1 drink.

RASPBERRY SHRUB

4 quarts raspberries
1 quart vinegar
sugar

Mash red or black raspberries and cover with the vinegar. Let stand overnight or longer; strain. To each pint of juice, add 1 pound sugar, boil 20 minutes; then put in sterilized bottles, seal, and keep in a cool place. Use 2 tablespoons to a glass of water. Makes 1 gallon.

RASPBERRYADE

1 pint Raspberry Syrup, page 54
4 pints water

Place ice in pitcher or bowl, add syrup and water, stir until well mixed and serve. Will make 20 punch servings.

FLAVORED ICE CUBES

Put partition in tray. Fill with finely cut canned fruits or fruit juices. Or use ginger ale or root beer. Freeze from 4 to 8 hours.

FOR DECORATION

Add vegetable coloring to water. Or place a maraschino cherry, candied cherry, cranberry, or any other decoration in each compartment. Freeze. Serve in any fruit beverage.

PUNCHES

Punches—drink-blends combining tart and sweet flavors with varied bases and mixes—are customarily made in large quantities. They are served from a punch bowl with generous capacity, and simplify serving a large party. Lacking a silver or glass punch bowl, you can cover the outside of a large mixing bowl or similar vessel with foil, flowers, or ribbons, for a novel and attractive effect. The base of a punch and its sweetener may be made in advance. Sparkling beverages and ice are added just before serving. All punch ingredients should be chilled, and the punch is best served over a large block of ice, which melts more slowly and dilutes punch less than ice cubes. To make a decorative ice ring for a punch bowl, freeze colorful fruits in ½ inch of water in any cake pan or ring mold that fits the bowl. Fill the mold with water and freeze solid.

Fruit Punches

FRUIT PUNCH FOUNDATION

1 cup sugar
1 quart water
½ cup lemon juice
1 cup orange juice
grated rind of ½ an orange
grated rind of 1 lemon

Cook sugar and water for 5 minutes, cool, add juices and grated rinds. Makes 5½ cups punch base. Add any of the following:

GINGER PUNCH

1 quart ginger ale; ¼ cup preserved ginger, cut fine.

CHERRY TEA PUNCH

1 quart tea; ½ cup maraschino cherries, cut fine.

PINEAPPLE PUNCH

1 cup grated pineapple; 1 quart carbonated water.

RASPBERRY PUNCH

1 pint raspberry juice; 1 pint carbonated water.

CURRANT MINT PUNCH

1 glass of currant jelly dissolved in 1 cup hot water. Chill, and add ¼ cup mint, finely minced, 2 cups water. Garnish with mint sprays.

GRAPE-GINGER PUNCH

1 quart grape juice, 1 quart ginger ale, 1 quart carbonated water.

LOGANBERRY PUNCH

½ pint loganberry syrup, 1½ pints water, 1 quart ginger ale.

GRAPEFRUIT PUNCH

1 quart grapefruit juice, 1 quart ginger ale.

DOUBLE-BERRY PUNCH

Strained, sweetened juice of 1 quart strawberries and 1 quart raspberries, 1 quart carbonated water.

CIDER-GRAPE PUNCH

1 quart cider, 1 quart grape juice, 1 quart ginger ale.

FRUIT PUNCH WITH LEMON ICE

Add 1 quart Lemon Ice and 3 quarts ginger ale to any of the Fruit Punch Combinations, above.

FRUIT PUNCH WITH ORANGE ICE

1 cup crushed pineapple
½ cup maraschino cherries
2 quarts orange soda
1 quart carbonated water
1 pint Orange Ice, page 211

Combine, stir lightly. Makes 1 gallon.

FRESH FRUIT LEMONADE PUNCH

6 pounds sugar
5 dozen lemons, juice
1 dozen oranges, sliced
1 can (1 pound, 4 ounces) diced pineapple or a fresh pineapple
6 gallons water
ice

If pineapple is fresh, add 1 more pound of sugar. Mix sugar with fruit and juice, bring to boil and let stand to cool. Add water and ice and serve. Makes 150 servings.

CRANBERRY PUNCH

    1 quart cranberries
    4 cups water
    2 cups sugar
    juice of 2 lemons
    juice of 2 oranges
    2 quarts carbonated water

Cook cranberries in water until soft. Strain through jelly bag, add sugar, bring to boiling point, add lemon and orange juice, skim and cool. Place in punch bowl with ice. Pour in carbonated water and serve.

SPARKLING FRUIT PUNCH

    4 oranges, juice
    2 lemons, juice
    1 can (1 pint) pineapple juice
    1 small bottle maraschino cherries
    2 quarts sparkling white grape juice

Place fruit juices and cherries in punch bowl over cake of ice, add sparkling grape juice, serve in tall, hollow-stemmed glasses. Makes 3 quarts.

LOUISIANA TUTTI-FRUTTI

    1 cup sugar
    3 cups water
    1 cup pineapple, diced
    2 sliced bananas
    ½ cup maraschino cherries
    6 oranges, juice
    6 lemons, juice
    2 quarts carbonated water

Boil sugar and water for 5 minutes, cool; add fruit and juices. Pour into punch bowl over cake of ice. Add carbonated water and serve.

STRAWBERRY FRUIT PUNCH

    1 cup water
    2 cups sugar
    1 cup strong tea
    2 cups strawberry syrup (see Raspberry Syrup, page 54)
    juice of 5 lemons
    juice of 5 oranges
    1 can (1 pound, 4 ounces) crushed pineapple
    1 cup maraschino cherries, drained
    2 quarts carbonated water

Boil water and sugar for 5 minutes, add tea, strawberry syrup, lemon juice, orange juice and pineapple; let stand ½ hour. Strain, add soda and cherries. Makes 50 servings.

MOONLIGHT PUNCH

    1 quart Lemon Ice, page 210
    1 pint white grape juice
    1 pint pineapple juice
    2 cups sugar
    1 quart carbonated water

Place Lemon Ice in punch bowl. Stir in fruit juices mixed with sugar. Pour in carbonated water. Serve in punch glasses.

TEA PUNCH

    1 tablespoon tea leaves
    1 pint boiling water
    2 cups sugar
    1 lemon, juice
    1 orange, juice
    1 quart carbonated water

Place tea in large heatproof pitcher, pour on boiling water, cover well, steep 5 minutes and strain. Add sugar, fruit juices, and crushed mint leaves, if desired. Chill, add ice and chilled soda. Makes 1½ quarts.

WISCONSIN PUNCH

    2 cups sugar
    1 quart water
    3 quarts grape juice
    12 lemons, juice
    3 oranges, juice
    2-pound can pineapple juice
    3 quarts carbonated water

Boil sugar and water to a syrup, cool, add fruit juices. Pour into punch bowl over cake of ice, add soda. Makes 80 servings.

MULLED CIDER

    1 teaspoon whole allspice
    6 cloves
    1-inch stick cinnamon
    1 cup brown sugar
    2 quarts cider
    a little grated nutmeg

Add allspice, cloves, cinnamon and sugar to cider, place in kettle and let simmer for 15 minutes, and serve hot in punch glasses. Add nutmeg. Makes 2 quarts.

Menus for weddings and other festive occasions
will be found in chapter 1.

HOT FRUIT PUNCH

2 cups sugar
2 quarts water
2 lemons, juice and rind
1-inch stick cinnamon
½ teaspoon whole cloves
1 quart any fruit juice

Boil sugar, water, lemon rind and spices for 5 minutes and strain. Add juices, boil 5 minutes and serve hot in punch glasses. Makes 3 quarts.

HOT SPICED LEMONADE

1 quart cold water
½ cup sugar
½ teaspoon whole cloves
2-inch cinnamon stick
½ teaspoon allspice
1 quart boiling water
4 lemons, juice
1 lemon, sliced

Bring water, sugar and spices gradually to a boil. Simmer for 5 minutes and strain. When ready to use, add boiling water and lemon juice. Serve hot in punch glasses with a slice of lemon in each glass. Also good served ice cold. Makes 2 quarts.

Wine Punches

CHAMPAGNE PUNCH

½ cup sugar
2 lemons, sliced
2 oranges, sliced
pineapple slices
½ pint brandy
¼ pint maraschino juice
½ cup maraschino cherries
3 pints champagne

Dissolve sugar in a little water. Mix all except champagne and cherries. Pour into punch bowl with large piece of ice and add the cherries and chilled champagne.

CHAMPAGNE SHERBET PUNCH

1 quart Lemon Ice, page 210
1 pint carbonated water
1 quart domestic champagne

Place Lemon Ice in punch bowl, stir in soda and champagne and, when melted, serve.

SPARKLING WINE PUNCH

1 quart Lemon Ice, page 210
1 pint Rhine wine
1 quart carbonated water
1 pint champagne

Place Lemon Ice in punch bowl. Stir in the wine and, just before serving, the thoroughly chilled soda and champagne.

MOCK CHAMPAGNE PUNCH

Follow Sparkling Wine Punch, above, omitting champagne.

CLARET CUP

3 pints claret
½ cup curaçao
3 lemons, juice
½ cup sugar
1 bunch fresh mint
1 orange, finely sliced
12 strawberries
4 slices pineapple
1 pint carbonated water

Mix all ingredients except carbonated water; chill and, just before serving, add the chilled soda.

LEMON GINGER PUNCH

2 quarts ginger ale
1 bottle white wine
1 quart Lemon Ice, page 210

Mix ginger ale and wine. Add the Lemon Ice. When nearly melted, serve.

SANGRIA

2 small or 1 large orange
1 small apple
1 lemon
1 bottle (4/5 quart) red wine
⅓ cup sugar, approximately
¼ cup brandy
3 cups club soda

Slice oranges crosswise and quarter slices. Core and slice apple. Cut lemon in ½-inch pieces. Combine all ingredients in large pitcher, adjusting sugar to taste. Add ice to chill thoroughly.

MOSELLE PUNCH

1 pound sugar
2 quarts fresh pineapple, chopped
4 bottles Moselle wine
ice
1 quart champagne, chilled
1 quart carbonated water, chilled

Sugar the chopped pineapple, pour 1 bottle Moselle over and let stand, covered, 3 days to ripen. Add 1 bottle of Moselle to the fruit each day. Pour into punch bowl, add a large piece of ice and the chilled champagne and soda. Will serve 25 people.

STRAWBERRY FROTH PUNCH

2 quarts strawberries
2 pounds sugar
juice of 2 oranges
1 lemon, juice
ice water
1 cup champagne
2 whites of eggs

Crush the berries with the sugar. Let stand 2 hours; strain through cheese cloth. Add orange and lemon juice, and chill. When ready to serve, add an equal measure of ice water, the champagne, and the whites of eggs beaten stiff. Place in punch bowl with ice block.

WASHINGTON PUNCH

1 cup sugar
2 cups diced pineapple
½ bottle Moselle wine
2 bottles Rhine wine
1 bottle claret wine
2 cups pineapple, sliced
large piece of ice in bowl
1 quart champagne

Sprinkle the sugar over diced pineapple, add the half bottle of Moselle and let stand 24 hours. Strain, add the Rhine wine and the claret wine and the sliced pineapple. Pour over ice and just before serving, add champagne. Serve from punch bowl.

EGGNOGS

VIRGINIA EGGNOG

6 eggs, separated
1¼ cups sugar
1½ quarts cream
1 pint rye whiskey
1 jigger of rum
nutmeg

Beat yolks with 1 cup sugar. Add cream and whiskey and rum alternately. Season with ground nutmeg. Beat the whites of the eggs stiff, add ¼ cup sugar. Drop this on top of mixture in bowl. Dust top with nutmeg. Chill.

KENTUCKY EGGNOG

3 dozen eggs, separated
3 cups sugar
1 pint whiskey
1 pint rum
1 pint gin
1 pint brandy
1 gallon heavy cream

Beat yolks of eggs until very light; beat whites stiff. Add 1 cup of sugar to the whites and beat well. Add the remaining sugar to the yolks and beat until thick and lemon colored. Combine the mixtures lightly; slowly add the whiskey. Whip the cream; add it to the above mixture alternately with the rum, gin, and brandy. If mixture is too thick, thin to desired consistency with rich milk. Beating makes it smooth and prevents separating. Yields 80 servings.

WINE SERVICE

A glass of wine can make even the simplest meal taste better. Choosing wine is very personal; one should always serve and drink the wine that pleases him most. However, the experience of others has taught us certain facts about the relationship between wines and food from which we can benefit.

The "rules" for choosing wine are simple. Fish, seafood, and light meats taste best when they are accompanied by a light, white, dry (non-sweet) wine that enhances their flavor without overpowering them. Hearty red meats such as beef and game need the full flavored, heavy-bodied red wines. Some wines, notably rosé and champagne, are used with any food. Sweet wines are reserved for use with desserts, fruits and nuts. Flavored wines such as vermouth, and fortified wines such as sherry, have an appetizing quality that makes them especially good at the beginning of a meal. If the menu is an elaborate one, and more than one wine is to be served, the rule is to proceed from the lightest, driest wine to the richest and heaviest.

The "rules" for wine service are few, but they should be observed if wine is to give the greatest possible pleasure.

Champagne, rosé, and white wines should be served chilled; red wines and sweet dessert wines have greater aroma and flavor when they are at cool room temperature, about 60° F.

An all-purpose wine glass can take the place of the different sizes and shapes once thought necessary. It should be tulip-shaped, and have a capacity of 8 ounces. Wine glasses should be filled no more than half with white wine, no more than one-third with red wines.

You can have a selection of 8 or 12 wines on hand from which to choose by storing in an inexpensive metal or wooden wine rack that holds the bottles on a slant. This keeps the cork from drying out and shrinking, which would admit air to the bottle and spoil the wine. The custom of having the host first pour a little wine into his own glass to taste before serving others should be observed. It can prevent the embarrassment of offering a "corky" wine to guests.

Some wines deposit a sediment which should not be disturbed. All wines should be handled gently.

The wine designations below are the familiar European names but good domestic versions of each of these is available, in a price range to suit every purse.

Guide to the Right Wines to Serve with Foods

WITH	SERVE
Appetizers, Soup	Dry Sherry, Dry Vermouth
Fish and Seafood, Chicken, Lamb, Veal	*White Dinner Wines*: Chablis, Sauternes, Rhine Wine
Beef, Game, Game Birds, Cheese Dishes, Ham, Pork	*Red Dinner Wines*: Claret, Burgundy, Chianti, Bordeaux
Dessert	*Sweet Wines*: Port, Tokay, Muscatel, Madeira, Cream Sherry
Everything	Champagne, Rosé, Sparkling Rosé

COCKTAILS AND MIXED DRINKS

When you serve cocktails in your home, your objective should be to mix them accurately and serve them properly, with the best liquors and mixers you can afford. Standard recipes for favorite cocktails follow.

Necessary equipment includes:

GLASSES

Cocktail glasses, 3-4 ounces
Old-Fashioned glasses, 7-8 ounces
Liqueur or cordial glasses, 1 ounce
Highball glasses, 8-9 ounces
Sherry glasses, 2-3 ounces
Sour or Delmonico glasses, 3-5 ounces
Collins glasses, 14 ounces
Champagne glasses

BAR EQUIPMENT

Mixing glass
Cocktail shaker
Strainer
Jigger (1½-ounce measure)
Jigger (2-ounce measure)
Pony (1-ounce measure)
Measuring teaspoons or bar spoon
Sharp knife
Lemon squeezer
Bottle opener
Corkscrew
Ice bucket, tongs

HOW MUCH LIQUOR TO BUY

Cocktails served in standard cocktail glasses, without ice, contain 1½ to 2 ounces liquor: a fifth of liquor will make 16-17 cocktails, a quart will make 21 cocktails. Tall drinks, served over ice cubes, are customarily made with 2 ounces of liquor. A fifth of liquor makes 12 tall drinks, a quart makes 16.

BASIC BAR SUPPLIES

WHISKEY: blended, Scotch, rye, bourbon, Canadian
GIN
VODKA
RUM: light, dark
VERMOUTH: sweet, dry
SHERRY, dry or cream

MIXERS AND FLAVORING AGENTS

Bitters (Angostura)
Grenadine
Carbonated water
Ginger ale
Quinine water
Limes and lemons, peel and juice
Maraschino cherries
Olives, cocktail onions
Sweetened lime juice

ABOUT ICE

In general, you need crushed ice for drinks you mix in a cocktail shaker or blender; cubes for drinks you stir; big blocks or chunks of ice for a punchbowl (these melt more slowly, dilute punch less).

In buying ice cubes, or making them ahead for storage in the freezer, count on 3 ice cubes for every drink you plan to serve.

Drinks will have added appeal when they are well chilled, and this means chilling glasses, too. You can shake a cube or some crushed ice in each glass before filling, or place wet glasses on a tray in the refrigerator to frost ahead of time.

For appropriate foods to serve with cocktails, see the preceding chapter on Appetizers, starting on page 36.

APERITIFS

Most popular of the cocktail wines, or aperitifs, are vermouth and sherry, but any of the many flavored wines may be served in a cocktail glass, over ice cubes in an Old-Fashioned glass, with a twist of lemon peel, or with soda and ice in a tall glass as a refreshing before-dinner drink.

ALEXANDER COCKTAIL

1 ounce heavy cream
1 ounce crème de cacao
1 ounce gin or brandy

Half fill shaker with cracked ice, add cream and liquors, shake well, strain into cocktail glass. Makes 1.

BACARDI

2 ounces light rum
1 tablespoon lemon or lime juice
½ teaspoon sugar
dash grenadine

Half fill shaker with cracked ice, add ingredients, shake well, strain into cocktail glass. Makes 1 drink.

BRONX

2 ounces gin
½ ounce dry vermouth
1 ounce orange juice

Half fill shaker with cracked ice, add all ingredients, shake well, strain into cocktail glass. Makes 1 drink.

CHAMPAGNE COCKTAIL

1 sugar cube
dash of bitters
champagne, chilled
twist of lemon peel

Put sugar into champagne glass, saturate with bitters. Add ice cube, fill with champagne. Twist peel over glass and drop it in. Makes 1 drink.

CLOVER LEAF

1½ ounces gin
2 strawberries, crushed and sweetened
juice of ½ lime
white of 1 egg
maraschino cherry garnish

Half fill cocktail shaker with crushed ice. Add ingredients, shake well. Strain into cocktail glass, garnish with cherry. Makes 1 drink.

DAIQUIRI

2 ounces white rum
1 ounce sweetened lime juice

Half fill shaker with cracked ice, add rum and sweetened lime juice, shake well, strain into cocktail glass. For Frozen Daiquiri, blend with crushed ice in electric blender until frothy, serve unstrained in champagne glass, with a short straw. Makes 1 drink.

DUBONNET COCKTAIL

1 ounce gin
1 ounce Dubonnet

Half fill mixing glass with ice, add gin and Dubonnet, stir well. Strain into chilled cocktail glass. Makes 1 drink.

FLIP

1 teaspoon sugar
2 ounces cognac, port, sherry or rum
1 egg
nutmeg

Half fill shaker with cracked ice, add ingredients, shake well, strain into Delmonico glass, or use ¾ cup fine crushed ice, whirl in electric blender. Makes 1 drink. This is an after-dinner cocktail.

GIMLET

2 ounces gin or vodka
½ ounce sweetened lime juice

Half fill cocktail shaker with crushed ice, and gin and lime juice, shake well. Strain into cocktail glass, add dash of soda. Makes 1 drink.

KIEWERT

juice of ½ lemon
¾ tablespoon Amer Picon
2¼ tablespoons grenadine

Half fill cocktail shaker with crushed ice, add all ingredients, shake well, strain into cocktail glass. Makes 1 drink.

MAIDEN'S PRAYER

⅛ part orange juice
⅛ part lemon juice
⅜ part cointreau
⅜ part gin

Half fill mixing glass with ice, add juice, cointreau, and gin, stir well. Strain into cocktail glass. Makes 1 drink.

MANHATTAN

2 ounces whiskey (blend, bourbon, Scotch, or rye)
1 ounce sweet vermouth
dash of bitters
maraschino cherry for garnish

Half fill mixing glass with ice, add ingredients except cherry, stir. Strain into cocktail glass over cherry. Makes 1 drink.

DRY MANHATTAN

2 ounces whiskey
½ ounce dry vermouth
dash of bitters
twist of lemon peel

Half fill mixing glass with ice, add ingredients except lemon, stir. Strain into chilled cocktail glass, twist peel over glass and drop it in. Makes 1 drink.

PERFECT MANHATTAN

2 ounces whiskey
¼ ounce sweet vermouth
¼ ounce dry vermouth
twist of lemon peel

Half fill mixing glass with ice, add ingredients except lemon, stir. Strain into chilled cocktail glass, twist peel over glass and drop it in. Makes 1 drink.

MARTINI

2 ounces gin
½ ounce dry vermouth
green olive
twist of lemon peel

Half fill mixing glass with ice, pour gin and vermouth over it, stir. Strain into a cocktail glass. Garnish with olive and lemon twist, to taste. Makes 1 drink. There is considerable variation in vermouth proportion in martinis, ranging from 3 to 8 parts gin to one part vermouth.

DRY MARTINI

A very dry martini may contain only a very small proportion of vermouth, as little as a few drops or even a spray.

GIBSON

A martini garnished only with a cocktail onion becomes a Gibson.

VODKA MARTINI

Any martini may be made with vodka instead of gin.

SWEET MARTINI

2 ounces gin
1 ounce sweet vermouth
dash dry vermouth or bitters

Half fill mixing glass with ice, add vermouth, gin and bitters, stir well. Strain into cocktail glass, with lemon twist or olive. Makes 1 drink.

MARTINI ON THE ROCKS

Any martini may be served in an Old-Fashioned glass, over ice cubes.

OLD-FASHIONED

1 cube sugar
dash of bitters
1 teaspoon water
2 ounces rye, bourbon, Scotch
cherry, orange slice, twist of lemon peel, for garnish

Put sugar in Old-Fashioned glass. Dash with bitters, add water, crush sugar. Add whiskey, stir gently, add ice cubes. Garnish with cherry and orange, twist lemon peel over glass and drop it in. Makes 1 drink.

ORANGE BLOSSOM

1½ ounces orange juice
1½ ounces gin

Half fill cocktail shaker with crushed ice, add orange juice and gin, shake well. Strain into chilled cocktail glass. Makes 1 drink.

PINK LADY

3 ounces gin
1 ounce apple brandy
½ tablespoon lime juice
1 tablespoon grenadine
1 egg white

Half fill cocktail shaker with crushed ice, add all ingredients, shake well. Strain into chilled cocktail glasses. Makes 2 drinks.

PRESIDENTE

1/6 part curaçao
1/6 part French vermouth
2/3 part Bacardi rum

Half fill mixing glass with crushed ice, add curaçao, vermouth and rum, stir well. Strain into chilled cocktail glass. Garnish with twist of orange peel.

ROB ROY

2 ounces Scotch whiskey
½ ounce sweet vermouth
dash of bitters
stemmed cherry for garnish

Half fill mixing glass with ice, whiskey, vermouth, and bitters, and stir well. Strain into chilled cocktail glasses, add cherry. Makes 1 drink.

SCOTCH MIST

2 ounces Scotch whiskey
twist of lemon peel

Half fill an Old-Fashioned glass with crushed ice, add Scotch. Twist lemon peel over glass and drop it in.

SCREWDRIVER

1½ ounces vodka
1½ ounces orange juice

Half fill cocktail shaker with ice, add vodka and orange juice, stir well. Strain into cocktail glass. Makes 1 drink.

SIDECAR

2 ounces brandy
1 ounce cointreau
1 ounce lemon juice

Half fill cocktail shaker with ice, add brandy, cointreau, and lemon juice, and shake well. Strain into cocktail glass. Makes 1 drink.

SOUR

2 ounces bourbon, rye, Scotch, or other liquor
juice of ½ lemon
½ teaspoon sugar
fruit garnish

Half fill cocktail shaker with crushed ice, add liquor, lemon juice and sugar, shake vigorously. Strain into sour glass, garnish with cherry and orange slice, pineapple stick, to taste. Makes 1 drink.

STINGER

2 ounces cognac
1 ounce white crème de menthe

Half fill cocktail shaker with ice, add cognac and crème de menthe, and shake well. Strain into cocktail glass. Makes 1 after-dinner drink.

Long Drinks

Long drinks, or coolers, are sometimes served before dinner, but more often as odd-hour refreshment, especially in the summertime.

COBBLER

4 ounces of any wine, claret, Burgundy, port, Rhine wine, or sauternes
1 ounce cognac, rum, bourbon, whiskey
1 ounce curaçao-orange liqueur
fruit and mint leaf garnish, if desired

Fill tall glass with finely crushed ice, add liquors, stir gently. Garnish to taste. Makes 1 drink.

COLLINS

juice of 1 lemon
1 teaspoon sugar
2 ounces gin, rum, or whiskey
carbonated water

Combine lemon juice and sugar in a Collins glass, stir to dissolve sugar. Add gin and ice, fill with soda. Garnish with cherry, if desired.

FIZZ

juice of ½ lemon
1 teaspoon sugar
2 ounces gin, brandy, sloe gin, rum, or whiskey
carbonated water
mint for garnish

Half fill cocktail shaker with crushed ice, add lemon juice, sugar, and liquor, shake well. Strain into highball glass over ice cubes. Fill glass with soda, garnish with sprig of mint:

HIGHBALL

2 ounces Scotch, bourbon, rye, brandy, rum, gin
carbonated water, ginger ale, or cola

Pour liquor over ice in a highball glass, add water, soda, or ginger ale or lemon-lime soda, to fill. Favorite combinations: rye and ginger ale or lemon and lime soda; Scotch and soda; brandy and soda; gin and ginger ale.

RICKEY

½ lime
2 ounces gin, sloe gin, brandy, Scotch, whiskey
carbonated water

Squeeze lime juice into a highball glass, drop shell in. Add ice and liquor, fill with soda. A *buck* is a rickey made with ginger ale instead of soda.

TONIC

¼ lime
2 ounces gin or vodka
quinine water

Squeeze lime juice into a highball glass, drop shell in. Add ice and liquor, fill with quinine water.

BLOODY MARY

2 ounces vodka
4 ounces tomato juice
1 tablespoon lemon juice
dash Worcestershire sauce
salt, pepper

Stir all ingredients well in Old-Fashioned or high-ball glass, add ice.

CUBA LIBRE

½ lime
2 ounces golden rum
cola

Squeeze lime into highball glass, drop in shell. Add rum and ice, fill with cola.

EGG MILK PUNCH

1 egg
1 tablespoon sugar
½ cup crushed ice
1 ounce rum
2 ounces brandy
1/3 cup milk
nutmeg for garnish

Combine in cocktail shaker, shake well, strain into highball glass. Sprinkle with nutmeg.

FRENCH 75

1 tablespoon lemon juice
2 ounces gin
1 teaspoon powdered sugar
champagne

Stir lemon juice, gin and sugar in highball glass. Add ice, fill with chilled champagne.

GOLDEN FIZZ

1 egg yolk
1 tablespoon sugar
1 teaspoon lemon juice
2 ounces gin
½ cup crushed ice
carbonated water

Combine all except soda in cocktail shaker, shake well, strain into tall glass. Fill with soda.

MERRY WIDOW FIZZ

1 egg white
1 teaspoon sugar
juice of ½ lemon
juice of ½ orange
2 ounces sloe gin
½ cup crushed ice
carbonated water

Combine all except soda in cocktail shaker, shake well. Strain into highball glass. Fill with soda.

MINT JULEP

5 or 6 fresh mint leaves
1 teaspoon sugar
4 ounces bourbon
mint for garnish

Use a silver julep cup, or a highball glass. Crush mint leaves and sugar together in the glass, add bourbon, fill with ice. Stir until glass frosts, add more crushed ice. Garnish with more mint. If glass has no handle, wrap in cocktail napkin.

PLANTER'S PUNCH

½ lime
2 teaspoons sugar
4 ounces dark rum
orange slice, lemon slice, pineapple stick, cherry, mint

Squeeze lime into highball glass, add sugar, stir. Add rum, fill glass with finely cracked ice. Garnish to taste.

Hot Drinks

MULLED WINE (GLUEHWEIN)

1 quart claret
1 cup water
2 cups sugar
½ teaspoon whole cloves
1 teaspoon cinnamon sticks
1 lemon, sliced thin

Boil all together for 15 minutes. Strain, serve hot. Makes 6 drinks.

HOT BUTTERED RUM

1 sugar cube
pinches clove, allspice
2 ounces rum
boiling water
1 pat butter (½ ounce)

Put sugar, spices, and rum in mug, add boiling water. Float butter on top.

TOM AND JERRY

1 egg yolk
1 teaspoon sugar (brown or maple)
½ teaspoon allspice
2 ounces white or golden rum
1 egg white, beaten stiff
1 ounce brandy
hot milk or boiling water
nutmeg

Beat egg yolks until pale, add sugar, spice, and rum, beat well. Combine with egg white, add brandy. Pour batter into two warmed mugs, add milk or boiling water to fill. Sprinkle with nutmeg. Makes 2 drinks.

SCOTCH SLING

2 ounces Scotch whiskey
1 cube sugar
twist of lemon peel
boiling water
nutmeg for garnish

Put whiskey, sugar, and lemon into Old-Fashioned glass, set teaspoon in glass. Add water to fill as desired. Sprinkle with nutmeg.

PUNCH IMPERIAL

1 pound sugar
1 sliced pineapple
juice of 4 lemons
grated rind of 1 lemon
4 oranges, cut in pieces
grated rind of 1 orange
½ cup maraschino cherries
1 stick cinnamon, broken up
1 vanilla bean, 4 inches
1 pint boiling water
1 bottle red wine
½ bottle rum
1 bottle champagne, or carbonated water and claret

Sprinkle sugar over fruit and juice. Boil spices with water for 5 minutes. Remove spices; add sugared fruit, wine, and rum. Cover and heat. Add champagne, serve at once.

Hot drinks are particularly suitable for cold-weather entertaining. Serve in punch cups, mugs, or in a glass wrapped in a cocktail napkin.

IRISH COFFEE

1 cup hot black coffee
sugar to taste
2 ounces Irish whiskey
heaping tablespoon whipped cream

Warm large stemmed goblet, put spoon into glass, add hot coffee. Sweeten to taste, add Irish whiskey. Top with whipped cream, serve at once.

CAFE BRULOT

peel of ½ orange, in 5 or 6 pieces
2 sticks cinnamon, 4 inches long, broken
10 cloves
6 ounces cognac
7 sugar cubes
2½ cups hot, strong black coffee

Put orange peel, spices, cognac and sugar into metal bowl. Set over warmer. Fill a silver tablespoon with more cognac, and warm the cognac by holding a match beneath the spoon. Set the cognac aflame and pour it into the bowl. Stir for 2 minutes with ladle. Add hot coffee, ladle at once into demitasse cups. Serves 6.

CAFE ROYALE

Pour freshly brewed hot coffee into dinner cup Gently pour 1 tablespoon cognac over surface of coffee. Put sugar cube in teaspoon, fill spoon with cognac, hold close to hot coffee to warm the brandy. Set the brandy on fire, lower the flaming sugar cube into the coffee, stir gently until the flame burns out.

After-Dinner Drinks

CORDIALS

After a company dinner, a tray of brandies, cordials and liqueurs may be served with extra-strong coffee. Some guests may prefer a cordial, coffee, and a chocolate candy to a more conventional dessert. The coffee is usually served in demitasses, small cups, with sugar, but no cream. After-dinner brandy is served in a snifter, a round-bottomed glass that can be warmed by holding it in the hand. Sweet liqueurs and cordials may be sipped from small glasses, or they may be served frappé.

COFFEE LIQUEUR

2 cups water
2 cups sugar
2 ounces instant coffee
2 vanilla beans, chopped
1 bottle (4/5 quart) vodka

Bring water and sugar to boil. Cool. Add coffee, chopped vanilla beans and vodka. Pour into glass bottles. Seal. Store for about 3 weeks. Strain.

CORDIALS FRAPPES

Fill a cocktail glass with finely crushed ice. Add 2 ounces of crème de menthe, curaçao, benedictine, anisette, chartreuse, or any desired liqueur or cordial, and serve with two short straws.

POUSSE CAFE

Use a pousse café glass, or a slender cordial or liqueur glass. Fill the glass with successive layers of liqueurs, in the order given. Pour the liqueurs very slowly and carefully from the tip of a spoon, to prevent them from mixing. Since the liqueurs have different specific gravities, they tend to remain separate, and give the effect of vari-colored layers.

Crème de cacao, maraschino, orange curaçao, white crème de menthe, Parfait Amour, cognac.

Or: crème de café, apricotine or vanille, green crème de menthe.

Or: grenadine, anisette, crème d'Yvette, chartreuse, cognac.

4
BREADS

YEAST BREADS – Loaves, Rolls, Coffee Cakes, Kuchen • QUICK BREADS – Hot Breads,
Tea Breads, Biscuits, Muffins, Popovers • GRIDDLE CAKES • PANCAKES
• WAFFLES • DOUGHNUTS • FRITTERS • DUMPLINGS

For the beginning cook, the great variety of breads that can be made sometimes causes confusion. In general, YEAST BREADS include all the standard types of *loaves* made with white, whole wheat, rye, and flours of other grains. The basic dough can be shaped and seasoned to produce a variety of *rolls,* and, in sweetened form, yeast dough is used to make *coffee cakes* or *Kuchen* (their German name).

QUICK BREADS are those using baking powder or soda as a leavening agent instead of yeast. Some coffee cakes are to be found in this category, but the sweetened quick breads are more often known as "*tea breads,*" and they are generally in loaf rather than ring form. The general term "hot breads" usually means quick breads—in the form of *biscuits, muffins, popovers,* and certain loaf breads, such as *buttermilk bread* and *Boston brown bread,* as well as *corn bread* and *spoon bread.*

The basic ingredients that make a quick bread when baked, become a *griddle cake* or a *waffle* when cooked in the appropriate manner, or a *doughnut* or a *fritter* when fried in deep fat, or a *dumpling* when cooked in soup or stew. For this reason, *griddle cakes, doughnuts* and *dumplings* are to be found in this section—following the quick breads.

YEAST BREADS

A good loaf of bread should be rounded at the top and light in weight; the crust should be smooth, golden brown, tender and crisp. When cut, the crumb should show a fine grain, tiny even holes; be moist and elastic and spring back to shape when pressed; it should taste slightly sweet.

INGREDIENTS FOR DOUGH

FLOUR: Sift flour before using. For white bread, use all-purpose flour.

ENRICHED FLOUR is wheat flour which contains added vitamins and minerals. It can be used in any recipe calling for flour with no difference in method or taste.

SALT AND SUGAR: Sugar in limited amounts quickens the action of the yeast; salt will retard the action of yeast.

POTATO WATER helps keep bread moist and also hastens the rising. To make 1 cup potato water, wash and peel 1 or 2 potatoes, cover with boiling water, and when thoroughly cooked, drain off and save potato water. Mash potato fine, and add to potato water.

SHORTENING: Butter, margarine, emulsified vegetable shortenings, meat fat, or vegetable oil.

LIQUID: Use water, milk, skim milk, whey, potato or rice water alone or mixed with water. Milk should be scalded and cooled to lukewarm (98°-105° F.) before adding yeast.

YEAST: There are two types used in home baking: compressed fresh or cake yeast, and active dry granulated yeast. Both are living substances, and must be activated in warm liquid. One package dry yeast may be used in place of 1 cake of yeast. Dissolve contents of package of dry yeast in ¼ cup water that feels warm to the touch (110° F.), somewhat warmer than the liquid for cake yeast. Then follow any recipe using yeast. Cake yeast is perishable and must be kept in the refrigerator. Dry yeast will keep for several months on the pantry shelf; check package for expiration date.

One package active dry yeast contains 2 teaspoons yeast.

GENERAL RULES FOR MAKING BREAD

TO MIX

There are several methods of mixing bread dough.
Straight dough method: All the flour is added to make a stiff dough.
Sponge dough method: A sponge is made first with liquids, yeast and part of the flour and allowed to rise. The rest of the flour is added later to make a stiff dough.
Mixer method: Blend yeast with other dry ingredients using one-half of the flour. Heat liquid ingredients and shortening until warm (120° to 130° F.). If your recipe does not include water, substitute ¼ cup of water for ¼ cup of liquid in recipe for each package of yeast used. Water is necessary for the yeast to dissolve properly. Add liquid to dry ingredients, then add egg and blend mixture at low speed until moistened. Beat 3 minutes at medium speed. By hand stir in rest of flour and any other ingredients such as fruit or nuts. Knead dough as for any other recipe.

TO PROOF YEAST

Mix yeast with water. Allow to stand 3 to 5 minutes to be certain that the yeast is active. Bubbles will begin to appear on the surface. Water temperature: active dry yeast (110° to 115° F.), compressed yeast (85° F.).

TO KNEAD

Toss dough on a floured board. Fold edges of dough toward center, press down and away with palm of hand, turning dough around and around as you knead until it no longer sticks to hand or board; handle dough lightly. Dough is ready when smooth and elastic, full of blisters and, when pressed with fingers, it springs back.

TO RAISE

Grease bowl lightly. Place dough in bowl and turn dough so that all of it is lightly greased. Cover bowl. Let dough rise at room temperature, 70° to 80° F., free from drafts. An unheated oven provides an excellent place. When dough has doubled, punch down, and if time permits, let it rise again. To test if doubled in bulk: poke fingers into the dough; if the dent remains, the dough is ready.

TO SHAPE LOAVES

Roll out dough, roll it up like a jelly roll, pinch ends to seal. Place seam side down in pan. The standard bread or loaf pans are 5 inches x 9 inches and 4½ inches x 8½ inches. Do not fill pans more than half full. Cover lightly. Allow dough to rise almost to top of pan.

TO BAKE

Bake as directed. To test whether loaf is done, rap top with knuckles. The loaf should sound hollow.
To cool loaves: Remove loaves from pans and place on racks until cool. If soft crusts are desired, lightly cover loaves during cooling.

BASIC BREADS

Variations to basic white bread:

Substitute whole wheat or rye flour for one-half of the all-purpose flour.

Corn meal or oatmeal may be substituted for one-third to one-half of the all-purpose flour.

WHITE BREAD

1 package active dry yeast
¼ cup warm water
1¾ cups scalded water, potato water, or milk
2 tablespoons shortening
2 tablespoons sugar
1 tablespoon salt
6 to 6½ cups flour

Dissolve yeast in warm water. Pour rest of liquid over shortening, sugar, and salt. Cool to lukewarm. Add dissolved yeast and half the flour, and beat well. Add remaining flour gradually. Toss onto a floured board and knead until smooth and elastic.

Put dough into greased bowl, cover, and let rise. Proceed as in General Rules above. Makes 2 loaves.

WHITE BREAD (SPONGE METHOD)

1 package active dry yeast
1 cup scalded water or potato water, cooled to warm temperature
1 teaspoon sugar
2 cups flour
1 cup scalded milk
2 tablespoons shortening
1 tablespoon salt
1 tablespoon sugar
4 cups flour

TO MAKE THE SPONGE

Dissolve the yeast in warm water with 1 teaspoon sugar, beat in 2 cups flour to make smooth batter. Cover and let rise in a warm place until doubled in bulk. *To make the dough,* pour the milk over the shortening, salt, and 1 tablespoon sugar. Cool to lukewarm, add to the sponge. Stir in remaining 4 cups flour gradually. Toss dough on lightly floured board and knead until smooth and elastic. Place in greased bowl, let rise. Proceed as in General Rules, page 66. Makes 2 loaves.

FRENCH BREAD

Follow either recipe for White Bread, above, omitting sugar and shortening. Divide dough into 4 equal parts and shape into long, narrow loaves. Place on greased pans, far apart. Slash ⅛ inch deep through top of loaf, lengthwise. Brush with beaten egg white mixed with water. When doubled in bulk, bake in hot oven, 400° F., for first 15 minutes, then 350° F., until crisp and well browned.

CHEESE BREAD

1 package active dry yeast
¼ cup warm water
1¾ cups warm milk or water
2 tablespoons sugar
1 tablespoon salt
5½ to 6 cups flour
1½ cups sharp Cheddar cheese, grated
¼ cup grated Parmesan cheese

Dissolve yeast in ¼ cup warm water. Add liquid, sugar, salt, and gradually mix in flour. Knead dough thoroughly. Let rise until doubled in bulk. Punch down dough, knead in cheeses. Shape into 2 loaves. Grease pans well. Bake at 350° F. for 45 minutes.

CHEDDAR CHEESE BREAD

1 package active dry yeast
¼ cup warm water
½ cup boiling water
1½ teaspoons salt
¼ cup sugar
3 tablespoons shortening
½ cup evaporated milk
2 eggs, beaten
3½ cups flour
1 cup sharp Cheddar cheese, grated

Dissolve yeast in warm water. Pour boiling water over salt, sugar and shortening. Stir; add milk, yeast and eggs. Add half the flour; beat. Add rest of flour and beat again. Let rise until doubled in bulk, add cheese and beat again. Place in greased loaf pan, let rise until doubled in bulk. Bake at 400° F. for 20 to 25 minutes. Excellent toasted. Makes 1 loaf.

SABBATH TWISTS (CHOLLA) (1)

3 packages active dry yeast
1⅓ cups warm water
1 tablespoon sugar
1 tablespoon salt
3 tablespoons shortening, softened
3 eggs
5 cups flour
1 egg yolk
poppy seed

Dissolve yeast in warm water. Add sugar, salt, shortening, eggs, stirring well. Gradually add flour. Knead on lightly floured board. Let rise in greased bowl until doubled in bulk. Punch down. Divide dough into 6 equal parts. Roll each part between palms of hands into a strip which is fatter in center. Braid 3 strips being sure to press ends together. Place on buttered baking sheet. Let rise until almost doubled in bulk. Mix egg yolk with a little water. Brush loaves with egg, sprinkle with poppy seed. Bake at 400° F. for 40 minutes. Makes 2 loaves.

SABBATH TWISTS (CHOLLA) (2)

2 cups hot water
1 tablespoon salt
1 tablespoon sugar
2 tablespoons vegetable oil
1 package active dry yeast
¼ cup warm water
2 eggs, beaten
8 cups flour

Pour water over salt, sugar and oil in mixing bowl. When lukewarm, add yeast dissolved in warm water, add eggs and flour gradually. Mix and stir, then knead until smooth and elastic. Cover, set aside in a warm place until doubled in bulk. Cut down dough, divide in half. Put one-half on board, cut into 4 equal parts, roll each 1½ inches thick, twisting 3 into a braid; fasten ends well and place in floured bread pan. Cut remaining ¼ into 3 parts, roll each part ½ inch thick, braid and lay on top of braid in pan. Let rise until doubled in bulk. Make second cholla. Brush with beaten yolk of egg and sprinkle with poppy seed. Bake in hot oven 1 hour, 400° F., 15 minutes, then at 350° F. For hard crust, cool unwrapped.

FINNISH RYE BREAD

1 package active dry yeast
¼ cup warm water
½ cup dark corn syrup
1 tablespoon grated orange peel
1½ teaspoons salt
2 teaspoons caraway seed
2 cups buttermilk
3 cups rye flour
3 to 3½ cups all-purpose flour
1 tablespoon corn syrup

Dissolve yeast in warm water. Mix syrup, peel, salt, caraway seed and buttermilk. Heat only until warm. Add to yeast. Gradually add the flours. When all of the flour has been mixed well into the dough, let rest for 15 minutes before kneading on a floured board. Place in a greased bowl, turning the dough so that all sides are greased. Let rise until doubled in bulk. Punch down and divide into two parts. Shape each half into a ball. Place on greased baking sheet. Let rise until almost doubled in bulk. Brush with glaze made of 1 tablespoon corn syrup and 4 tablespoons water. During the baking, brush twice with same glaze and again immediately upon removing from the oven. Bake at 350° F. for 45 to 50 minutes. Cool on racks.

DARK BREAD

⅜ cup corn meal
¾ cup cold water
¾ cup boiling water
1 tablespoon shortening
1 tablespoon salt
2½ tablespoons brown sugar or molasses
1½ teaspoons caraway seed
1 tablespoon cocoa
1 tablespoon instant coffee
2 packages active dry yeast
¼ cup warm water
2 cups rye flour (dark preferably)
1½ cups whole wheat flour
1½ cups wheat flour
1 egg white

Mix corn meal in cold water. Add to boiling water, and cook, stirring constantly, until thick. Remove from heat; stir in shortening, salt, sugar, caraway seed, cocoa and coffee. Dissolve yeast in warm water. Add to corn meal mixture. Gradually add the flours. When thoroughly mixed, knead on floured board. Place in greased bowl and let rise until doubled in bulk. Punch down. Shape into loaves, place in greased pans, and permit to double in bulk. Brush tops with egg white beaten lightly with a little cold water. Bake at 375° F. for 50 to 60 minutes. Makes 2 loaves.

Free form: If desired to shape round loaves or cocktail-size loaf, sprinkle baking sheet lightly with corn meal, place loaf on baking sheet. For cocktail or snack-size loaf, cut baking time slightly.

RAISIN BREAD (BARCHES)

1 package active dry yeast
¼ cup warm water
1¾ cups scalded milk or water
⅓ cup butter or fat
½ cup sugar
1 teaspoon salt
1 egg, beaten
¼ cup raisins
8 cups flour
½ teaspoon powdered anise

Dissolve yeast in warm water. Set aside in warm place. Pour hot milk or water over butter, sugar and salt in a mixing bowl and when lukewarm, add the yeast and the egg. Mix and knead well on bread board with the rest of the ingredients, using more flour if necessary until smooth and elastic. Return to bowl, cover closely and set in a warm place until doubled in bulk. Form into plain loaves or divide dough into 4 parts, roll into long strands and with 3 of the strands, make a braid. Place in a large pan. Fold the remaining strand double, twist like a rope and lay lengthwise down the center of bread. Brush with beaten yolk of egg, sprinkle with poppy seed, if desired; let rise until double in bulk. Bake in a moderately hot oven (375° F.) 1 hour, until well browned. Makes 1 large loaf, or 2 smaller ones.

MILWAUKEE RYE BREAD

1½ packages active dry yeast
2 cups hot potato water
1 tablespoon salt
4 cups rye flour
2 cups wheat flour
1 cup riced potatoes, solidly packed
1 teaspoon caraway seed

Dissolve yeast in ¼ cup of the warm liquid. Add remaining liquid. Stir in rest of ingredients, knead until smooth and elastic. Let rise in warm place until doubled. Form into loaves, place in pans, let rise. When doubled in bulk, brush top with water, bake in a moderately hot oven (375° F.) 1 hour or longer. Makes 2 loaves.

CORN-RYE BREAD

1½ cups cold water
¾ cup corn meal
1½ cups boiling water
1½ tablespoons salt
1 tablespoon sugar
2 tablespoons shortening
2 cups mashed potatoes
¼ cup lukewarm water
1 package active dry yeast
6 cups rye flour
2 cups wheat flour
1 tablespoon caraway seed

Stir the cold water and corn meal until smooth; add the boiling water and cook, stirring constantly, for about 2 minutes. Add salt, sugar and shortening and let stand until lukewarm. Add potatoes and the yeast dissolved in the lukewarm water, and then the rye and wheat flour and caraway seed. Mix and knead to a smooth, stiff dough, using wheat flour or corn flour on the board. Cover, set aside in warm place until doubled in bulk. Shape into 3 or 4 loaves, place in greased pans. Let rise to top of pans, bake 1 hour or longer in a moderately hot oven (375° F.).

PUMPERNICKEL

Follow directions for Corn-Rye Bread above, using rye graham meal in place of the rye flour. Make smaller loaves and bake thoroughly.

SOUR DOUGH FOR RYE BREAD

Reserve 1 cup rye dough, above, set in warm place to ferment overnight. Stir down, store in refrigerator. Use ½ cup sour dough instead of 1 package yeast in recipe for any rye bread.

NORWEGIAN RYE BREAD

1 cup graham flour
¼ cup brown sugar
3 cups rye flour
1 tablespoon salt
hot water
1 package active dry yeast
1 cup warm water
flour

Mix dry ingredients. Pour and beat in as much hot water as flour will take up, making stiff batter.

Cover, let stand until lukewarm. Add the yeast, dissolved in warm water, and just enough flour to knead. Let stand till doubled in bulk. Shape into loaves; when doubled in bulk, bake in moderately hot oven (375° F.) 1¼ hours.

Be certain to read the General Rules for Making Bread on page 66.

VARIETY BREADS

COMBINATION BREAD

1 tablespoon shortening
1 tablespoon salt
2 tablespoons sugar
1 cup rolled oats
1 cup corn meal
2 cups boiling water
2 packages active dry yeast
½ cup lukewarm water
1 cup rye flour
1 cup whole wheat flour
1¾ cups white flour

Add shortening, salt, sugar, rolled oats and corn meal to boiling water, let stand 1 hour. Add yeast dissolved in the warm water, then add rye, whole wheat and white flour. Beat thoroughly, knead, place in bowl, cover and let rise. When doubled in bulk, knead, shape into 2 loaves; let rise until doubled in bulk and bake in a moderately hot oven (375° F.) about 45 minutes.

GLUTEN BREAD

1 package active dry yeast
¼ cup warm water
about 6 cups of gluten flour
3 cups hot milk or water
½ teaspoon salt
2 tablespoons melted butter
2 tablespoons sugar, if desired
1 egg

Dissolve yeast in warm water. Heat milk to lukewarm, add with 2 cups of flour to yeast to make a sponge. Let stand in warm place. When doubled in bulk, add salt, butter, sugar, if used, the beaten egg and enough gluten flour to make a stiff dough. Knead until smooth and elastic. Shape into loaves. Let rise until doubled in bulk. Bake about 1 hour in moderate oven (350° F.).

WHOLE WHEAT BREAD

1½ packages active dry yeast
2 cups warm water
2 tablespoons molasses
1 tablespoon salt
3¾ cups whole wheat flour

Dissolve yeast in ½ cup of warm water; stir in molasses. Add salt, flour and 1 cup of the water. Mix well. Add more water, if necessary, so that the dough is sticky. Place in well-greased pan. Let rise by about one-half of its volume. Bake at 450° F. for 45 to 55 minutes. If a crisper crust is desired, remove loaf from pan and place loaf on oven rack for additional 5 minutes. Makes 1 loaf.

GRAHAM BATTER BREAD

¾ package active dry yeast
1½ cups warm water
3 cups graham flour, unsifted
1 cup wheat flour
1 teaspoon salt
2 tablespoons butter
½ cup molasses, or ¼ cup sugar

Dissolve the yeast with a little of the warm water, mix the rest of water with other ingredients in the order given and add to yeast. Add, if necessary, more wheat flour to make a soft dough. Cover bowl and set in warm place. When doubled in bulk, beat and pour into bread pans, filling them half full. Let rise until nearly to top of pan; bake in a moderate oven (350° F.) for about 45 minutes. Makes 2 loaves.

OATMEAL BREAD

1½ cups rolled oats
2 cups boiling water
2 teaspoons salt
¼ cup sugar or ½ cup molasses
1 package active dry yeast
¼ cup lukewarm water
4½ to 5 cups wheat flour

Grind the rolled oats if a finer texture is desired. Pour the boiling water over the oats, salt and sugar and let stand until lukewarm. Add yeast dissolved in ¼ cup warm water and gradually beat in the flour. Knead it to a smooth dough. Let rise until doubled in bulk. Toss on floured board, shape into 2 loaves and place in greased bread pans. Let rise again until double and bake in a moderate oven, 350° F., from 45 to 60 minutes.

WHOLE WHEAT HEALTH BREAD

1 package active dry yeast
1 cup warm water or milk
1 cup boiling water
1 tablespoon salt
1 tablespoon sugar
2 tablespoons shortening
2 cups wheat flour
4 cups whole wheat flour

Dissolve yeast in warm water. Pour 1 cup boiling water on the salt, sugar, and shortening; when luke-warm, add the yeast, stir in the wheat flour, then add the whole wheat flour gradually; mix to a stiff dough and knead until smooth, adding more wheat flour if necessary. Let rise in a warm place until doubled in bulk. Shape into 2 loaves and place in greased and floured pans. Let rise again until double its bulk and bake at 350° F. for 45 minutes or until bread shrinks from pan. For variety, use 3 cups of whole wheat flour and 3 cups of wheat flour, or 1 cup bran or rye flour with 3 cups of whole wheat flour and 2 cups of wheat flour.

BACON-HERB BREAD

2 packages active dry yeast
¼ cup warm water
¼ cup brown sugar, firmly packed
1 tablespoon onion powder
2 teaspoons salt
1 tablespoon marjoram leaves
2 eggs
2 cups warm milk
¼ cup shortening, softened
4 cups wheat flour
2 cups whole wheat flour
⅓ cup crisp bacon, crumbled, or imitation bacon bits

Dissolve yeast in warm water; add brown sugar and allow to stand a few minutes. Add all other ingredients except the flours and bacon. Mix well. Gradually add flours. Turn onto floured board and add bacon bits as you knead. Place in greased bowl, let rise until doubled in bulk. Punch down. Shape into loaves; let rise until doubled again. Bake at 425° F. for 30 to 35 minutes. Makes 2 loaves.

ROUND HERB LOAF

1 package active dry yeast
¼ cup warm water
1¼ cups warm milk
2 tablespoons oil
1 egg
2 tablespoons sugar
1½ teaspoons salt
3 cups flour
⅓ cup melted butter
2 tablespoons grated Parmesan cheese
1 tablespoon sesame seed
½ teaspoon garlic salt
½ teaspoon paprika

Grease a 2-quart casserole. Dissolve yeast in warm water. Let stand a few minutes. Add milk, oil, egg, sugar and salt, mixing well. Gradually add flour. Knead briefly on a lightly floured board. Let rise until doubled in bulk. Punch down dough.

Pinch off walnut-size balls of dough, dip in melted butter. Place in 1 layer in casserole. Mix cheese, sesame seed, garlic salt and paprika. Sprinkle one-half of this mixture over the layer of dough. Proceed in the same manner with the rest of the dough, pour remaining butter over dough, sprinkle with the rest of the herb mixture. Let rise until almost doubled. Bake at 400° F. for 25 to 30 minutes. Cool in casserole for 5 to 10 minutes. Serve warm.

COTTAGE CHEESE-HERB BREAD

1 package active dry yeast
¼ cup lukewarm water
1 cup cream-style cottage cheese
1 tablespoon butter
1 egg
2 tablespoons sugar
1 teaspoon salt
¼ teaspoon baking soda
1 teaspoon instant minced onion
2 teaspoons dill seed
2¼ cups flour

Mix yeast and water and let stand. Heat cottage cheese and butter together until lukewarm. Add yeast mixture and remaining ingredients and mix well. Knead briefly. Put in bowl, cover, and let rise until double. Place in 1½-quart greased casserole or divide into two small loaf pans and let rise again. Sprinkle with 1 teaspoon salt and bake at 350° F. for 40 minutes for the casserole or 30 minutes for tins.

PUMPKIN BREAD

3 cups sifted all-purpose flour
½ teaspoon baking powder
1 teaspoon baking soda
1 teaspoon ground nutmeg
1 teaspoon ground cloves
1 teaspoon ground cinnamon
½ teaspoon salt
3 cups sugar
1 cup vegetable oil
3 eggs
1 16-ounce can pumpkin
1 cup coarsely chopped dark seedless raisins
1 cup chopped walnuts

Heat oven to 350° F. Grease a 10-inch fluted, tube baking pan with unsalted shortening and dust lightly with flour. In a medium-sized bowl sift together flour, baking powder, baking soda, nutmeg, cloves, cinnamon and salt. In a large mixing bowl place sugar, oil and eggs; stir until well blended. Stir pumpkin into egg mixture. Gradually add sifted dry ingredients to egg mixture, stirring well after each addition. Fold raisins and nuts into batter. Pour batter into prepared pan and bake 1 hour and 15 to 20 minutes, or until a cake tester inserted into center comes out clean. Cool on a wire rack for 10 minutes before removing from pan. Then cool completely on a rack. Makes 1 round loaf.

SPICY SPIRAL LOAF

2 packages active dry yeast
1 cup warm water
1 cup warm milk
¼ cup oil
2 tablespoons sugar
1 tablespoon salt
6 cups flour

FILLING

1 can (8 ounces) pitted black olives
1 2-ounce jar pimiento
2 tablespoons catsup
2 garlic cloves, minced, or ¼ teaspoon garlic powder
½ teaspoon salt

Dissolve yeast in warm water. Add milk, oil, sugar and salt. Gradually add flour. When thoroughly blended, knead well on lightly floured board. For filling: Place all ingredients in an electric blender, or chop olives and pimiento very fine, mix with catsup, garlic and salt. When dough has doubled in bulk, divide in half. Roll each piece into a rectangle 7 inches x 14 inches. Spread filling over the dough almost to the edge. Roll from narrow side being careful to seal edges as you roll. Place seam side down in greased pan. Brush top with oil. Let rise until doubled in bulk. Bake at 400° F. for 30 to 40 minutes. If tops are browning too rapidly, cover pans lightly with foil for the last 15 minutes. Makes 2 loaves.

ZUCCHINI BREAD

3 cups flour
1 teaspoon salt
1 teaspoon baking soda
¼ teaspoon baking powder
3 teaspoons cinnamon
3 eggs
2 cups sugar
1 cup oil
2 cups grated raw zucchini
2 teaspoons vanilla
1 cup chopped walnuts

Combine flour, salt, baking soda, baking powder and cinnamon. Beat eggs until light. Stir in sugar, oil, zucchini and vanilla. Add dry ingredients and then the nuts. Pour into greased pans. Bake in 350° F. oven for 1 hour. Makes 2 loaves.

TOAST

Toast is made from any sliced bread. It should be crisp, golden brown, and freshly made. Bread cut into triangles, fingers, or other fancy shapes and toasted is used for garnishing.

In Automatic Toaster: Follow manufacturer's directions.

In Broiler: Preheat broiler for 5 minutes. Place bread in pan on rack 2-3 inches from heat. Brown on one side, turn and brown other side.

BUTTERED TOAST

Make any toast, as above, and butter immediately. Or, butter one side of bread generously. Use broiler method for toasting. Toast buttered side first; turn and brown other side.

MELBA TOAST

Cut bread as thin as possible. Arrange in pan, place in slow oven (325° F.) and let dry out until crisp. Remove pieces as they brown.

TOASTED BREAD LOAF

Remove crust from top and sides of a small loaf of white bread. With a very sharp knife, cut thin slices down to but not through the bottom crust. Spread seasoned, creamed butter between slices and over top, sides and ends. Place in pan and toast in a very slow oven about 45 minutes or until golden brown. Serve whole.

CINNAMON TOAST

Toast ¼-inch slices of bread on both sides quickly. Spread with butter, sprinkle with a mixture of ½ cup granulated or brown sugar and 1 teaspoon cinnamon. Broil until sugar melts and forms a crust. Serve hot.

CINNAMON-GLAZED TOAST

Melt 3 tablespoons butter in skillet over low heat. Add 1 teaspoon cinnamon and ½ cup sugar. Stir constantly; cook for about 1 minute after the mixture begins to bubble. Spread on one side of toasted bread. Place under broiler until a glossy crust is formed.

BUTTERSCOTCH TOAST

Use brown sugar, free from lumps, in place of the granulated sugar in recipe for Cinnamon-Glazed Toast, above.

MAPLE TOAST

Scrape soft maple sugar and use in place of the sugar and cinnamon mixture in Cinnamon Toast recipe above.

MILK TOAST

    2 cups milk
    2 teaspoons butter
    ½ teaspoon salt
    4 slices bread

Heat milk, butter and salt almost to the boiling point. Toast bread. Serve toast in hot bowls with the hot milk, or butter the dry hot toast, sprinkle with sugar and cinnamon, add ½ teaspoon salt to 1 cup of hot milk, and pour it over the toast. Serve hot.

FRENCH TOAST

    2 eggs
    ½ teaspoon salt
    ⅔ cup milk
    6 slices day-old bread
    butter

Beat eggs lightly, with salt and milk. Dip bread into mixture, fry on both sides in hot butter.

Or, bake dipped toast on buttered pan at 500° F. until top browns; turn, continue to bake until brown on other side.

MATZOS FRENCH TOAST

    4 matzos (unleavened bread)
    6 eggs
    ½ tablespoon salt
    2 tablespoons fat, or olive oil
    sugar and cinnamon
    lemon, grated rind

Beat eggs very light, add salt. Heat the fat in a skillet. Break matzos into large, equal pieces. Dip each piece in the egg mixture and fry a light brown on both sides. Serve hot, sprinkled with sugar, cinnamon, and a little lemon rind.

ORANGE TOAST

    6 slices of bread
    butter
    grated rind of 1 orange
    ⅔ cup sugar
    juice of 1 orange

Toast bread quickly so it will not harden. Butter well. Mix grated orange rind and sugar. Moisten with the juice. Spread mixture on the buttered toast and place under broiler for a few minutes until the coating begins to sizzle. Serve at once.

ZWIEBACK

1 package active dry yeast
¼ cup warm water
¼ cup milk
¼ cup sugar
¼ cup melted butter
½ teaspoon salt
½ teaspoon powdered anise
3 eggs
flour

Dissolve yeast in warm water. Scald the milk, cool to lukewarm, add to the yeast. Add the sugar, butter, salt, anise, and the eggs unbeaten, and enough flour to handle. Let rise until doubled in bulk. Make into 3-inch oblong rolls, place close together in a buttered pan in rows 2 inches apart. Let rise again and bake 20 minutes at 400° F. When cold, cut in ½-inch slices and brown evenly in the oven.

HARD ROLLS

Hard, crusty rolls can be shaped with any bread dough. The secret of the crisp crust is a little water brushed on the rolls before baking. Serve rolls hot, or cool them uncovered to maintain the crispness.

CUSHION ROLLS (SEMMEL)

Follow recipe for White Bread, page 66, or French Bread, page 67. After first rising, pinch off small pieces of dough. Knead into rounds 1 inch high, 3 inches wide. Set 2 inches apart on a shallow pan; let rise slightly. Dip handle of knife in flour, press across center of each roll, rolling knife handle back and forth to make a deep crease through the middle of each. Let rise until doubled in bulk; brush top with egg yolk beaten with 1 tablespoon cold water. Bake 20 minutes at 400° F., or until crisp and golden brown. Yield: 16 to 24 rolls.

DOUBLETONS

Proceed as above through first rising. Form into smaller balls, set together in pairs; place 2 inches apart. When well risen, place a thin rolled strip of dough across the top of each pair. Brush with slightly beaten egg yolk mixed with 1 tablespoon cold water. Let rise until doubled in bulk and bake 20 minutes at 400° F. or until crisp and golden brown.

DINNER ROLLS

Proceed as above through first rising. Form dough into rounds 1 inch high and 2 inches wide. Place rolls close together, in rows set 2 inches apart. Through center top of rolls all along the row, make a ¼-inch deep cut. Brush with slightly beaten egg yolk mixed with 1 tablespoon cold water. Let rise again and bake 20 minutes at 400° F. until crisp and brown.

POPPY SEED HORNS OR CRESCENTS

Follow recipe for White Bread, page 66, or Kuchen, page 76. When dough has doubled in bulk, toss on floured baking board and roll into a round sheet ¼ inch thick. Spread with melted butter, then cut from center to outer edge in wedge-shaped pieces like pie. Roll, stretching a little, from the wide side to the point. Shape into long straight rolls, or into crescents or half moons. Place on greased pans 2 inches apart; brush with beaten yolk to which 1 tablespoon cold water has been added and sprinkle tops of horns with poppy seed. Set in warm place to rise until doubled in bulk. Bake in hot oven 20 minutes at 400° F. or until brown and crusty.

RYE YEAST ROLLS

Follow recipe for Milwaukee Rye Bread, page 68. After first rising, shape dough into loaves 1½ inches by 3 inches. Place far apart on floured pan, brush tops with slightly beaten white of egg mixed with a little cold water, and sprinkle with caraway seeds and salt. Let rise and bake in a hot oven 25 minutes at 400° F., or until crust is brown and crisp.

CARAWAY RYE ROLLS

2 packages active dry yeast
2¼ cups warm water
2 cups medium rye flour
3 tablespoons sugar
1 tablespoon salt
2 tablespoons caraway seed
2 tablespoons shortening, softened
3½ to 4 cups wheat flour
1 egg white
caraway seed
coarse salt

Dissolve yeast in water in large bowl. Let stand a few minutes. Stir in rye flour, sugar, salt, caraway seed and shortening. Gradually add wheat flour. Turn onto lightly floured board; knead until smooth. Place in greased bowl, cover, let rise until doubled in bulk. Punch down. Roll the dough into 24 balls; flatten slightly. Place on greased baking sheet. After 15 minutes, slash tops of rolls. Brush with egg white, sprinkle with caraway seeds and coarse salt. Let rise until doubled in bulk. Bake at 400 ° F. for 18 to 25 minutes.

BATTER DILL ROLLS

2½ cups flour
2 tablespoons sugar
½ teaspoon salt
1 tablespoon instant minced onion
2 teaspoons dill seed
2 tablespoons butter
1 cup drained small-curd cottage cheese, heated to lukewarm
½ cup warm water
2 packages active dry yeast
1 egg
butter
coarse salt

Grease muffin pans. Will yield 24 2-inch muffins. Blend first seven ingredients with fork or pastry blender. Mix water and yeast in a small bowl; let stand a few minutes. Mix in the egg. Add yeast mixture to flour mixture. Beat thoroughly. Cover. Let rise until doubled in bulk. Beat down dough. Fill muffin cups half full. Tap pans on table to settle batter. Let rise until batter touches top of muffin pans. Bake at 350° F. for 20 to 30 minutes. Remove muffins and cool on rack. Brush with soft butter and sprinkle with coarse salt.

VIENNA ROLLS

Follow recipe for White Bread, page 66, or Kuchen, page 76. After first rising, shape dough in 2- by 5-inch rolls, tapering at the ends. Place 1 inch apart on shallow pan. Let rise until doubled in bulk. Slash tops diagonally with sharp knife. Brush with egg white and water mixed. Bake about 30 minutes at 350° F.

BREAD STICKS

1 package active dry yeast
¼ cup warm water
¼ cup butter
1½ tablespoons sugar
½ teaspoon salt
¾ cup scalded milk
1 egg, separated
3¾ cups flour

Dissolve yeast in warm water. Add butter, sugar and salt to milk; when lukewarm, add yeast, white of egg well beaten, and flour. Knead, let rise until doubled in bulk, roll and shape the size of a lead pencil. Place in floured pan, far apart, brush tops with beaten yolk of egg and sprinkle with poppy seed, sesame seed or coarse salt (if desired). Let rise and bake in hot oven (400° F.) until brown and crisp.

BAGELS (PRETZEL ROLLS)

Make dough for Bread Sticks, above; let rise. Pinch off small pieces, roll with palm into strips the width of a finger and twice the length, tapering at ends. Shape into rings or pretzels, pinching ends well together. Let stand on floured board, only until they begin to rise.

Fill large, shallow pan half full of water; when very hot, but not boiling, drop rings in carefully, one at a time. Cook under the boiling point until they hold their shape; then turn with skimmer and continue to cook. They must be light and keep their shape when handled. If desired, sprinkle with salt and caraway seed. Place in hot oven (400° F.) on thin, ungreased baking sheet and bake until crisp and golden brown, first on one side, then on the other.

SALT STICKS

Follow directions for Bread Sticks, or make dough for Milwaukee Rye Bread, page 68, and proceed as for Bread Sticks. Before baking, brush with yolk or white of egg, beaten slightly, sprinkle well with salt and caraway seed. Bake in hot oven (400° F.) until brown and crisp.

SWEET BREAD STICKS

Follow directions for Bread Sticks, above, adding ¼ cup sugar. Before baking, brush with melted butter, sprinkle with sugar, cinnamon and chopped almonds. Bake in hot oven (400° F.) until crisp and golden brown.

SOFT ROLLS

The dough for soft rolls is richer, sweeter, and lighter than the dough used for bread. It frequently contains eggs, as well as butter and sugar. Soft roll dough may also be used to make breakfast buns.

DOUGH FOR SOFT ROLLS

4 tablespoons butter
2 tablespoons sugar
1 teaspoon salt
2 cups scalded milk
1 package active dry yeast
¼ cup warm water
1 egg
5½ cups flour

Add butter, sugar and salt to milk. When lukewarm, add yeast dissolved in lukewarm water. Add egg, slightly beaten. Stir in the flour gradually and form into a soft dough; add only enough more flour to knead. (Two large, freshly cooked and riced potatoes may be added before the final addition of flour.) Cover and let rise in a warm place until doubled in bulk. Toss gently on floured board, handle as little as possible. Shape according to choice.

Use above instructions for the various soft rolls in the following recipes. The baking method is described in Bowknots, below.

BOWKNOTS

Pinch off pieces of dough; roll with palm into strips ½ inch thick, 7 inches long. Tie each strip into a knot. Let rise until doubled in bulk. Bake in a hot oven, 400° F., 15 or 20 minutes, until lightly browned. Remove from oven and brush tops with melted butter.

BRAIDED ROLLS

Pinch off 3 pieces of dough; roll with the palm to make each the width of a finger and twice as long. Lay side by side, pinch top ends together and braid loosely. Press bottom ends together. Let rise until doubled in bulk. Bake like Bowknots, above.

BUTTERFLIES

Roll dough ¼ inch thick and 6 inches wide. Brush with melted butter. Roll like jelly roll, cut into 2-inch slices. Press knife handle across rolled side of each piece. Let rise until doubled in bulk. Bake like Bowknots, above.

CLOVER LEAF ROLLS

Grease muffin pans. Roll dough into 1-inch balls, dip into melted butter, place 3 in each cup. Let rise until doubled in bulk. Bake like Bowknots, above.

CRESCENT ROLLS

Roll dough ¼ inch thick in 9- or 10-inch rounds. Spread with melted butter, cut in pie-shaped wedges. Beginning at the wide end, roll to the point. Draw ends around into crescents. Let rise until doubled in bulk. Bake like Bowknots, above.

FAN TANS OR LEAFLETS

Roll dough ¼ inch thick, spread with melted butter, cut into 1-inch strips. Pile 8 strips one on top of the other, cut into 1½-inch lengths. Stand on end in greased muffin pans. Let rise until doubled in bulk. Bake like Bowknots, above.

FINGER ROLLS

Roll dough size and shape of finger. Place close together on well-greased pan, brushing melted butter between sides of rolls, or place in special grooved pans. Let rise until doubled in bulk. Bake like Bowknots, above.

MOUND ROLLS

Roll dough thin and cut with small biscuit cutter. Lay two biscuits one on top of the other in a pan and stand in a warm place to rise. Brush with sugar and water before placing in oven. Bake about 20 minutes in a moderately hot oven (375° F).

PARKER HOUSE ROLLS

Pat or roll dough ⅓ inch thick, cut into rounds 2½ inches across. Brush well with melted butter. Fold over double so edges meet, or dip handle of knife in flour and make a crease through the middle. Press edges together at crease to keep shape. Place in rows close together in greased pans. Let rise until doubled in bulk. Bake like Bowknots, above.

EVER-READY REFRIGERATOR ROLLS

1 package active dry yeast
¼ cup warm water
¾ cup milk
½ cup butter
¼ cup sugar
1 teaspoon salt
2 eggs, slightly beaten
4 cups flour

Dissolve yeast in warm water. Scald milk in large saucepan. Add butter, sugar and salt; when lukewarm, add dissolved yeast, eggs, and the flour gradually, and mix well. Add more flour if necessary. Toss on floured board and knead until smooth and elastic. Place dough in bowl. Let rise in warm room until double in bulk. Cut down. Cover tightly and put in refrigerator for 24 hours. When ready to use, pinch off the desired portion, shape into any of the preceding shapes. Place in greased pans, let rise several hours until doubled in bulk. Bake in a hot oven (425° F.) for 10 to 20 minutes or until done. Put the rest of the dough back in the refrigerator and use as wanted within a week.

REFRIGERATOR-POTATO ROLLS

2 packages active dry yeast
½ cup warm water
3½ cups hot milk or water
1 cup mashed potatoes
1 scant cup sugar
1 cup shortening
1 teaspoon salt
11 cups flour

Dissolve yeast in warm water. Combine next 5 ingredients in large mixing bowl. Stir until dissolved. Let stand until lukewarm. Add dissolved yeast. Stir in enough flour to make a thick batter. Let rise until light. Mix to a soft dough, adding more flour and beat until smooth and elastic. Place dough in bowl. Then proceed as in Ever-Ready Refrigerator Rolls, page 75. Makes 7 to 8 doz. rolls.

PLAIN ROLLS

Roll dough 1 inch thick and cut with biscuit cutter, or cut off small pieces, fold sides under until top of roll is round and smooth. For crusty rolls, place far apart; for soft rolls, place close together on greased tin. Let rise until doubled in bulk. Bake like Bowknots, page 75.

TEA ROLLS

1 package active dry yeast
¼ cup warm water
¾ cup milk
1½ cups flour
¼ cup sugar
1½ teaspoons salt
2 eggs
⅓ cup butter
flour

Dissolve yeast in warm water. Scald milk; when lukewarm add dissolved yeast and 1½ cups flour. Beat thoroughly, cover and let rise until light. Add sugar, salt, eggs, butter, enough more flour to knead. Let rise until doubled in bulk. Shape into balls or small finger rolls; place in buttered pans close together; when doubled in bulk, bake in a hot oven (400° F.). For crusty rolls, set far apart. If desired, brush tops while hot with ¼ cup confectioners sugar mixed with 2 tablespoons rum.

ENGLISH MUFFINS

1 package active dry yeast
¼ cup warm water
3 tablespoons butter
1 teaspoon salt
1½ cups hot milk
4 cups flour

Dissolve yeast in warm water. Add butter and salt to milk. Cool to lukewarm, add dissolved yeast. Stir in the flour, beat well, let rise in a warm place for several hours or until light and spongy.

Grease inside of 12 large muffin rings and place on well-floured board. Fill each ring ½ full of the batter, let stand until it just begins to rise. Heat griddle, grease if necessary. Place muffins with rings on griddle, using pancake turner. Let bake slowly about 15 minutes or until slightly brown; turn on other side with pancake turner, let bake slowly until done. When cool, and ready to serve, split, brush cut side well with melted butter, and then toast until golden brown. Or place filled rings on well-greased baking sheet and bake in hot oven, 400° F., until golden brown.

COFFEE CAKES AND KUCHEN

A sweetened yeast bread served with coffee is a pleasant informal way of entertaining, or a family treat on weekends. Recipes for such coffee cakes have originated in many lands, especially in Scandinavian and German-speaking countries. The German word for coffee cake, *Kuchen*, is found often in this section of our book because many of the recipes are of German origin, contributed by the good cooks of Milwaukee.

Since the procedures for making these yeast-dough coffee cakes resemble those of bread-making, the General Rules for Making Bread, page 66, may prove helpful.

Kuchen doughs are more easily handled if chilled. When time permits this step, decrease flour by one-quarter to one-half cup. Let rise in warm room until doubled in bulk, then cut through with knife. Put dough in greased bowl large enough to allow for rising, grease top, and cover tightly. Chill for 24 hours. When ready to use, form into any desired shapes and add desired topping. Let rise slowly until doubled in bulk and bake.

PLAIN KUCHEN DOUGH

1 package active dry yeast
¼ cup warm water
1¾ cups scalded milk
½ cup butter
¾ cup sugar
1 teaspoon salt
dash of nutmeg
grated rind of ½ lemon
6 cups flour
1 egg or yolks of 2

Dissolve the yeast in warm water. To the scalded milk add the butter, sugar, salt, a little nutmeg and lemon. When lukewarm, add 1 beaten egg or the beaten yolks of 2 eggs; stir in the yeast and only enough flour to knead. Knead dough until smooth and elastic. Cover tightly and let rise until doubled in bulk. Cut dough down, form into desired shape and bake in a moderately hot oven (375° F.) until browned.

PLAIN COFFEE KUCHEN

Make Plain Kuchen Dough, above, or Rich or Sweet Kuchen Dough, below. After first rising, spread ½ inch thick in shallow buttered pan. Cover and let rise again. Melt 2 tablespoons butter, spread over dough, sprinkle with sugar, cinnamon and chopped nuts or with Crumb Topping (Streusel). Bake 15 to 20 minutes in a moderate oven, 350° F.

RICH KUCHEN DOUGH

    1 package active dry yeast
    ¼ cup warm water
    1 cup butter
    ½ cup sugar
    3 eggs
    1 teaspoon salt
    grated rind of ½ lemon
    1 cup warm milk
    4 to 5½ cups flour

Dissolve yeast in warm water. Cream butter and sugar; add eggs, one at a time, salt, lemon rind, the dissolved yeast, warm milk and the flour. Knead until smooth and elastic. Cover and let rise in a warm place, until doubled in bulk. Toss on board, form into any desired shape; let rise again and bake in a moderately hot oven (375° F.) until browned.

SWEET KUCHEN DOUGH

    1 package active dry yeast
    ¼ cup warm water
    1¾ cups lukewarm milk
    8 cups flour
    1 cup butter, softened
    1 cup sugar
    4 eggs
    1 teaspoon salt
    grated rind of ½ lemon

Dissolve yeast in warm water. Add the milk and 1 cup of the flour and set aside to rise in a warm place. Cream the butter, add the sugar and the eggs, one at a time, stirring well after each addition; then add salt, lemon rind, the rest of the flour

and yeast mixture, alternately. Mix well and knead until the dough is smooth and elastic. Let rise in a warm place until doubled in bulk. Cut dough down and form into any desired shapes; let rise again and bake in moderately hot oven (375° F.) until browned.

SHORT-CUT COFFEE CAKE

    2 cups sifted flour
    ¼ cup sugar
    3 teaspoons baking powder
    ¾ teaspoon salt
    ¼ cup butter
    ½ package active dry yeast
    ¼ cup lukewarm water
    ½ cup milk
    1 egg, beaten

Preheat oven to 375° F., a moderate oven. Sift dry ingredients twice. Cut in butter with fork until fine as cornmeal. Dissolve yeast in lukewarm water, add milk and egg, combine with flour mixture. Beat well. Let stand in buttered and floured shallow 8-inch square pan ½ hour. Cover with Crumb Topping (Streusel). Bake 30 to 40 minutes.

COFFEE CAKE RING (YEAST KRANTZ)

Prepare Rich Kuchen Dough, above, add ¼ cup raisins; let rise in warm place until doubled in bulk. Divide into 3 or 4 parts, roll each part into a long strand; braid the strands. Form in a circle, or twist the braid to resemble the figure 8. Place in greased baking pan. Let rise again in a warm place and bake in a moderately hot oven, 375° F., ½ hour or until well browned. Brush with beaten egg and sugar, sprinkle with a few chopped almonds. Return to oven to brown nuts slightly.

KUCHEN ROLL OR RING (GUGELHOPF)

    Kuchen Dough, plain or sweet, pages 76, 77
    ¼ cup melted butter
    sugar and cinnamon
    ¼ cup seeded raisins

Roll ½ recipe of Kuchen Dough ½ inch thick on floured board; brush well with melted butter, sprinkle well with sugar, a little cinnamon, add the raisins. Begin at one end and roll into a long cylinder. Place in a well-greased long pan or round form with tube in center. Let rise until doubled in bulk and bake in a moderate oven, 350° F., until thoroughly done, 45 minutes to 1 hour.

1 package active dry yeast = 1 cake compressed yeast

KUCHEN ROLL VARIATIONS:

NUT, SPICE OR POPPY SEED

In Kuchen Roll recipe, page 77, instead of the filling of sugar, cinnamon and raisins, use Almond Paste Filling, Nut Paste Filling, Walnut Filling, Gingerbread Filling, or Poppy Seed Filling.

SWEDISH TEA RING

Use one third of the recipe for Kuchen Dough, page 76. When doubled in bulk, cut down and roll into an oblong sheet ⅓ inch thick. Brush with butter. Sprinkle with ¼ cup each of raisins and blanched, chopped almonds. Roll like jelly roll, place on a large baking pan, bring ends together and pinch to form ring. With scissors, cut through ring from edge nearly to center, making a cut every 1½ inches, turning each division upward to show raisins and nuts. Let rise until doubled in bulk. Brush with milk. Sprinkle with nuts, bake ½ hour at 350° F., until brown.

BUNDT KUCHEN (KUCHEN RING DOUGH)

PART 1
1 package active dry yeast
¼ cup warm water
¾ cup lukewarm milk
1 cup flour

Dissolve yeast in warm water. Add milk and flour. Mix well and let rise in warm place.

PART 2
½ cup butter
1 cup sugar
4 eggs
grated rind of lemon
a little grated nutmeg
2¼ cups flour

Cream butter, add the sugar, eggs, one at a time, lemon rind, nutmeg. Add yeast sponge (Part 1), and remaining flour. Grease a fluted pan with center tube (a Bundt form) with soft butter. Decorate bottom with blanched almonds. Place dough in pan, let rise until very light, bake 45 to 60 minutes in a moderate oven (350° F.)

RICH BUNDT KUCHEN

2 packages active dry yeast
½ cup warm water
½ cup lukewarm milk
4 cups flour
1 cup butter
1 cup sugar
8 eggs, separated
grated rind of 1 lemon
⅛ teaspoon salt

Proceed as in Bundt Kuchen, above, but separate the eggs and add the beaten whites last.

ICEBOX BUNDT KUCHEN

PART 1
1 package active dry yeast
¼ cup warm water
¾ cup lukewarm milk
1 cup flour

Dissolve yeast in warm water. Add milk and flour. Mix well and let rise in warm place.

PART 2
1 cup butter
½ cup sugar
grated rind of 1 lemon
3 yolks of eggs
1 teaspoon salt
3 cups flour

Cream butter, add sugar. Add grated lemon rind, salt and the egg yolks, one at a time. Beat until very light. Gradually add the ingredients that have been prepared in Part 1, alternately with the flour. Cover, place in refrigerator overnight. Remove dough from refrigerator. Roll ½-inch thick. Spread with Almond Paste, below.

PART 3—ALMOND PASTE FILLING
3 egg whites
¾ cup sugar
1 cup grated almonds
¾ teaspoon cinnamon

Beat egg whites stiff; add sugar, almonds and cinnamon.

After spreading on dough, above, roll like Jelly Roll. Work quickly to keep dough cool. Place in greased Bundt form. Let rise 3 to 4 hours in a cool place. Bake 1 hour at 350° F.

Toppings and fillings for coffee cakes and kuchen will be found on page 83.

DANISH PASTRY (KRINGLE)

2 cups flour
2 tablespoons sugar
½ teaspoon salt
½ cup butter
½ cup milk
2 egg yolks
1 package dry granular yeast
¼ cup warm water
1 egg white

Combine dry ingredients; cut in butter with pastry blender or two knives. Combine egg yolks and milk. Dissolve the yeast in the warm water. Add the liquids to the flour mixture and mix thoroughly. Cover bowl tightly and chill for at least 2 hours. Do not store for more than 48 hours. Divide the dough into 2 parts. Leave one in the refrigerator while shaping the first. Roll on well-floured pastry cloth or board into a 6- × 18-inch rectangle. Spread the center strip of the dough with half the egg white, beaten stiff but not dry. Cover with nuts, dates, raisins or coffee cake filling. Fold the ends of the dough over the filling. Then fold the sides over to make an envelope. Place on a buttered cookie sheet. This may be shaped as an oval or a horseshoe, or left as is. Repeat with second part. Cover and let rise until light, 30 to 45 minutes. Bake at 375° F. for 20 to 30 minutes, or until golden brown. While hot, spread with Confectioners Sugar Icing.

FRENCH COFFEE CAKE (SAVARIN)

2 packages active dry yeast
½ cup warm water
⅓ cup lukewarm milk
4 cups flour
1 cup butter
1 cup sugar
5 eggs
1 teaspoon salt
grated rind of 1 lemon
SYRUP
1 cup sugar
½ cup water
¼ cup rum

Dissolve yeast in water; add milk, 1 cup of flour and let dough rise. Cream butter and sugar. Add 3 eggs, one at a time, yolks of 2 remaining eggs, lemon, salt, the yeast mixture, remaining flour, ¼ cup seedless raisins, if desired, and 2 egg whites, beaten stiff. Beat until smooth and light. Butter two 10-inch ring forms, sprinkle with chopped almonds, add dough. Let rise nearly to the top of the forms. Bake about ½ hour in a moderately hot oven, first 15 minutes at 375° F., then 15 minutes at 350° F. When baked, turn out forms.

Boil 1 cup sugar with ½ cup water for 5 minutes, add ¼ cup rum. Pour syrup into empty forms. Return Kuchen to forms; let stand until it absorbs the syrup. Remove from forms and baste with any remaining syrup.

The General Rules for Making Bread, page 66, will be especially helpful to those cooks who have limited experience in baking. They apply to the baking of coffee cakes as well.

STOLLEN

2 packages active dry yeast
½ cup warm water
1½ cups lukewarm milk
8 cups flour
1 pound butter, softened
1 cup sugar
4 whole eggs
grated rind of 1 lemon
1 teaspoon salt
½ teaspoon nutmeg
½ cup each orange peel and citron, cut fine
¾ pound raisins
½ cup flour
½ pound chopped almonds, optional
¼ cup rum

Dissolve yeast in warm water. Add milk, and stir in 1 cup flour. Let rise. Cream butter with sugar, add eggs, one at a time, and beat well. Add lemon rind and salt; combine the two mixtures, add remaining 7 cups flour and nutmeg. Knead until smooth and elastic. Sprinkle additional ½ cup flour over the dried fruits. Mix and add to the dough with nuts and rum. Let rise until double its bulk. Toss on floured board. Divide into three or more loaves. Roll out slightly, spread top with melted butter, press down the center, and fold over double. Brush melted butter over top, let rise until double and bake in a moderate oven, 350° F., about 45 minutes. When slightly cool, cover with Confectioners Sugar Icing.

CHOCOLATE YEAST CAKE

3 cups flour
1 package active dry yeast
1 cup brown sugar, firmly packed
1 cup granulated sugar
1 teaspoon soda
½ teaspoon salt
2 squares unsweetened chocolate
1¼ cups milk
¼ cup water
1 cup shortening
3 eggs
1 teaspoon vanilla

In large mixer bowl combine all dry ingredients, including yeast. Melt chocolate. Combine and heat milk, water and shortening to about 120° F. Add liquid, eggs, chocolate and vanilla to the dry ingredients. Beat at lowest speed until moistened; beat 2 minutes at medium speed. Grease only the bottom of a 13 inch x 9 inch pan. Pour batter into pan, cover, and let rise for 30 minutes. You will not notice much change in volume. Bake at 350° F. for 45 to 50 minutes. Remove from pan and cool completely. Frost with Brown Butter Frosting.

SPICE YEAST CAKE

3 cups flour
1 package active dry yeast
1 cup brown sugar, firmly packed
1 cup granulated sugar
1 teaspoon soda
½ teaspoon salt
1 teaspoon cinnamon
½ teaspoon nutmeg
¼ teaspoon ginger
1¼ cups milk
¼ cup water
3 eggs
1 cup shortening, softened

In large mixer bowl combine all of the dry ingredients, including the yeast. Combine and heat milk and water to about 120° F. Add liquid, eggs and shortening to dry ingredients. Mix at lowest speed until moistened; beat for 2 minutes at medium speed. Grease only the bottom of a 13 inch x 9 inch pan. Pour batter into pan, cover, and let rise for 30 minutes. You will not notice much change in volume. Bake at 350° F. for 45 to 50 minutes. Cool completely. Frost with Brown Butter Brandy Frosting.

SWEET ROLLS

Sweet rolls of many sorts may be made with a rich Kuchen dough or from special sweet dough recipes, which follow. To stock your freezer with pastries you can serve within minutes, simply bake the rolls until they are fully risen, but only very lightly browned. Wrap for freezing. To serve, finish baking, glaze with simple confectioners icing, if desired, and serve fresh from the oven.

BUTTER HORNS

Make Rich Kuchen Dough, page 77. Let rise in warm place. Cut in 10 pieces, roll on floured board, making each ¼ inch thick, in 9-inch rounds. Spread with softened butter, then with Nut Paste Filling or with Almond Paste Filling softened with sugar and cream. Cut each round in 4 pie-shaped sections. Roll from wide end to opposite point. Form into crescent shape. Place on greased tin, point-side down, let rise again until light, about 2 hours. Bake in a hot oven at 350° F. to 400° F. about 20 minutes. While warm, ice with Confectioners Sugar Glaze, flavored with almond. Makes 40 butter horns.

SCHNECKEN (CINNAMON ROLLS)

Make any Kuchen Dough. Let rise. Roll on floured board until dough is ¼ inch thick in an oblong sheet about 9 inches wide. Brush well with melted butter. Sprinkle with sugar, cinnamon, half a cup of raisins. Roll like jelly roll. Cut into inch pieces. Brush sides with melted butter. Place close together cut side down in shallow, buttered pan. Brush tops with butter, sprinkle with sugar and cinnamon; let rise until light, bake about 25 minutes at 350° F. to 400° F.

CARAMEL SKILLET ROLLS

Prepare Cinnamon Rolls, above. Place 3 tablespoons melted butter in heavy skillet, cover with thick layer of brown sugar and 2 tablespoons of water. Cook 1 minute. Sprinkle with broken pecan meats or sliced almonds. Place rolls, sides brushed with melted butter, close together, cut side down in pan. Let rise until doubled in size. Bake at 350° F. to 400° F. about ½ hour. Invert pan, remove rolls at once.

CURRANT BUNS

Prepare any Kuchen Dough, pages 76-77, adding currants when kneading first time. After first rising, shape into smooth balls. Place close together in lightly greased tin. Brush tops with butter. Cover. Let rise again until fully 2½ times original size. Bake about 20 minutes in moderately hot oven, 375° F. to 400° F. Brush tops with ½ cup milk sweetened with 1 tablespoon of sugar and bake for 2 minutes longer.

HOT CROSS BUNS

Prepare like Currant Buns, above. When half risen in pans, cut two gashes at right angles across tops of buns. Let rise until 2½ times original bulk, then bake like Currant Buns. While still warm, fill gashes with Confectioners Sugar Glaze.

JAM THIMBLE BUNS

Roll a piece of any raised Kuchen Dough 1-inch thick on floured board, cut with biscuit cutter, and place close together in a buttered pan. Let rise until very light. Dip fingers in flour and make a cavity in center of each biscuit, and drop in a bit of jelly or preserves. Bake 15 to 20 minutes at 375° F. to 400° F.

PRUNE BUNS BOHEMIAN (KOLATCHEN)

Make any Kuchen Dough, pages 76–77. Add a bit cinnamon, mace and 1 teaspoon anise seed, well pounded. Let rise till very light, roll ½ inch thick. Cut in 3-inch rounds, place on a well-buttered pan, pressing down the center of each round. Place 1 tablespoon Prune Filling or jam in center of each cake. When well risen, brush with stiffly beaten egg white; sprinkle with confectioners sugar. Bake in moderately hot oven, 375° F. to 400° F.

PECAN ROLLS (HONEY BUNS)

Kuchen Dough, Sweet or Rich, page 77
soft butter
sugar and cinnamon
½ cup seedless raisins
chopped nuts, optional
½ cup melted butter
½ cup honey, warmed
¾ cup brown sugar
¼ pound pecan nut meats

After first rising, roll dough out on floured board into oblong sheet ¼ inch thick. Spread well with butter, sprinkle with sugar and cinnamon and raisins (or blueberries in season, rolled in sugar, cinnamon and a little flour). Add chopped nuts if desired. Roll as for Jelly Roll, pinching seam to seal. Cut into 1-inch slices. Place 1 teaspoon melted butter and 1 teaspoon warmed honey in bottom of each section of muffin pans, cover with 3 tablespoons brown sugar. Press 5 pecan halves, rounded side down, on sugar in each section. Place cut rolls, cut side down, on this. Cover, let rise until more than doubled in bulk. Bake about 15 minutes in hot oven, 400° F., then reduce heat to 325° F. and bake 10 minutes longer. Let cool 1 minute, then invert pan, remove rolls, replace any pecans if necessary and let cool, glazed side up. Will make 3 dozen rolls.

CARAMEL TEA ROLLS

Follow recipe for Pecan Rolls, above, but cut in ⅓-inch slices. Place on buttered cookie tin, flat side down, and cover each roll well with brown sugar and chopped nuts. Let rise until doubled in bulk, bake in moderate oven, 350° F., 20 minutes or until brown.

PURIM CAKES (HAMAN POCKETS)

After first rising, roll out any Kuchen Dough, pages 76–77, to ¼ inch thickness, cut into 4-inch rounds, brush with oil, spread Poppy Seed Filling, page 83, or Cheese Filling, page 94, on each round. Fold 3 sides to meet over filling, pinch together to make a three-cornered cake. Brush top with warm honey, let rise, and bake in a moderately hot oven, 400° F., until golden brown.

See the variety of toppings and fillings for sweet rolls and coffee cakes on pages 82-83.

KIPFEL (TURNOVERS)

Make Pastry, page 341, or Cookie Dough, page 342, or Kuchen Dough, page 76. Roll on floured board until ¼ inch thick. If using Kuchen Dough, wait until after first rising to roll out. Cut into 3-inch squares, place 1 tablespoon of jam or of any desired Kuchen Filling, page 83, in center of each square. Lift the corners of each square over the filling and pinch together on top and at corners to keep in juice; or wet top edges of the squares, take hold of one corner and fold and pinch it to the opposite corner, forming a three-cornered pie; or place filling on lower half of square, fold over the other half, pinch the edges well together.

Place on greased pan, let rise; bake in a moderately hot oven, 400° F., until well done and browned.

BOHEMIAN COFFEE BUNS

1 package active dry yeast
¼ cup warm water
3 cups flour
¾ cup butter
2 eggs, separated
¼ cup cream
1 cup sugar
¼ pound almonds, blanched and ground fine

Dissolve yeast in water; add 1 tablespoon flour. Let stand until light and spongy. Cream butter well, add yolks, cream, dissolved yeast and remaining flour. Mix and beat until smooth. Roll dough very thin into oblong sheet. Cut in 2½-inch squares. Spread teaspoon Filling (below) in center of each square. Fold over in oblong or three-cornered shapes, pinching edge well together. Place in pan, let stand 1 hour, bake 10 minutes at 400° F. While warm, spread with Confectioners Sugar Icing flavored with lemon and vanilla.

FILLING

Beat egg whites stiff, add sugar, almonds, mix well.

NUT HORNS

4 cups flour
1 teaspoon salt
1 package active dry yeast
1¼ cups shortening
3 egg yolks, beaten
¾ cup sour cream
1 teaspoon vanilla

Sift flour and salt; blend in yeast and shortening with pastry blender. Mix yolks, sour cream and vanilla. Add flour mixture and mix again. Divide dough into 8 parts. Roll each part into a ball, wrap in waxed paper, and chill thoroughly. Sprinkle board and roller with confectioners sugar. Roll each ball in a 10- to 12-inch circle; cut in 12 wedges. Spread each wedge with 1 teaspoon of Nut Paste Filling, page 83. Roll each wedge from wide end to the point. Bake in hot oven, 400° F., for 12 to 15 minutes, until browned.

SCHNECKEN (SNAILS)

1 package active dry yeast
¼ cup warm water
1 cup butter
5 egg yolks
¾ cup lukewarm cream
3 cups flour
¼ cup sugar
1 cup almonds, chopped

Dissolve the yeast in water. Cream butter, add yolks one at a time, the cream, the yeast and the flour. Beat until dough leaves the bowl. Chill thoroughly. Dredge board with the sugar and almonds. Roll dough very thin. Roll like jelly roll and cut in ½-inch slices. Place in greased pan, cut side down. Set in warm place to rise slowly. Bake light brown in hot oven, 400° F. Watch carefully.

KOLATCHEN (SOUR CREAM BUNS)

1 package active dry yeast
¼ cup warm water
½ cup butter
5 egg yolks
2 tablespoons sugar
grated rind of 1 lemon
1 cup thick sour cream
3 cups flour
raisins or cherries
2 egg whites

Dissolve yeast in warm water. Cream the butter, add egg yolks, sugar, lemon rind, sour cream and the yeast. Stir well and add the flour; mix and drop from teaspoon on well-greased pans. Let rise in a warm place until doubled in bulk. Place a raisin or cherry on the top of each cake, spread with beaten white of egg, sprinkle with sugar and bake 15 to 20 minutes at 375° F. to 400° F.

SOUR CREAM KIPFEL (CRESCENTS)

1 package active dry yeast
¼ cup warm water
4 cups flour
1 teaspoon salt
1¼ cups butter or shortening
3 egg yolks
½ cup sour cream
2 teaspoons vanilla

Dissolve yeast in warm water. Sift flour and salt. Add dissolved yeast. Cut shortening into flour mixture, mix thoroughly. Add egg yolks beaten light, sour cream and vanilla. Chill. Dredge board with confectioners sugar. Pinch off pieces of dough. Roll out very thin. Cut into squares. Place 1 teaspoon filling (below) on dough. Roll toward the center into crescents or fold. Bake at 375° F. for about ½ hour. Frost with Confectioners Sugar Icing while warm.

FILLING

Three egg whites beaten stiff, to which ¾ cup of sugar, 1 cup crushed wheat flakes or cornflakes, and 1 teaspoon vanilla have been added.

WALNUT CRESCENTS (KIPFEL)

1 package active dry yeast
¼ cup warm water
4 cups flour
½ cup sugar
1 teaspoon vanilla
¼ cup cream or milk
5 egg yolks
1½ cups butter

Dissolve yeast in warm water. Add 2 tablespoons of flour, let rise. Add the sugar, vanilla and cream to the beaten yolks. Blend the butter and remaining flour, combine the three mixtures, add more flour if necessary. Roll the dough quite thin, cut into small squares, place a small portion of filling in each square. Roll, beginning at one corner, and form into crescent shapes. Let rise 2 or more hours, bake 20 minutes at 400° F., then reduce to 325° F. and bake until done.

FILLING

1 pound chopped walnuts, the juice of 1 lemon, and ½ cup sugar. Or grind the nuts, add cream to make a paste, ½ cup sugar and ½ teaspoon vanilla.

COFFEE CAKE FILLINGS AND TOPPINGS

Many fillings for coffee cakes are obtainable in cans, ready to use. Almond paste and almond paste filling mixture, prune and apricot fillings, and various fruit fillings and preserves may be kept on hand ready to use. These fillings may be combined with home made doughs or used to fill refrigerator yeast rolls, sold in tubes in the dairy cases of food markets, to make home-baked coffee cakes in a hurry.

ALMOND PASTE FILLING

3 tablespoons butter
½ cup sugar
½ cup almonds, blanched
grated rind of ½ lemon
1 egg, slightly beaten

Cream butter and sugar, add grated almonds, lemon rind and only enough egg to make a paste.

NUT PASTE FILLING

3 egg whites
1 cup sugar
1½ cups grated nuts
1 teaspoon vanilla

Beat egg whites stiff; add sugar gradually. Fold in the nuts and vanilla.

WALNUT FILLING

2 cups grated walnuts
¼ cup sugar
¼ cup syrup or honey

Mix nuts and sugar, add enough syrup or honey to make a paste.

GINGERBREAD FILLING

5½ cups flour
2 cups molasses
2 tablespoons butter or goose fat
1 tablespoon soda
1 cup warm water

Place flour in bowl; make cavity in center. Add molasses, butter or goose fat, and soda dissolved in the warm water. Mix well and beat thoroughly about 20 minutes. Pour into buttered bread pans and bake in a moderately hot oven, 400° F., about 1 hour. Will keep for months in a dry place. When dry, grate and use as a filling for Spice Kuchen.

POPPY SEED FILLING

1 cup black poppy seed
1 cup milk
2 tablespoons butter
2 tablespoons honey or syrup
½ cup chopped almonds
grated rind of ½ lemon
1 tablespoon chopped citron
¼ cup seedless raisins
¼ cup sugar
1 tart apple, grated

Grind poppy seed and boil with milk and all other ingredients but apple, until thick. If not sweet enough, add more sugar. When cool, add apple or ¼ cup currant or raspberry jelly or jam.

PRUNE FILLING FOR PIE OR KUCHEN

1 pound prunes, boiled
½ cup sugar
1 tablespoon lemon juice

Stone and rub boiled prunes through colander. Mix well with juice, sugar and lemon. Use to fill turnovers (Kipfel) or coffee cakes, or as a filling for two-crust or open-faced pies.

CRUMB TOPPING (STREUSEL)

½ cup flour
2 to 4 tablespoons butter
5 or 6 tablespoons sugar
½ teaspoon cinnamon
almonds

Mix first 4 ingredients by rubbing well with the finger tips, until small crumbs are formed. Add a few chopped or pounded almonds. Sprinkle over any coffee cake that has been brushed with melted butter.

NUT CUSTARD GLAZE

1 egg yolk
3 tablespoons cream
sugar and cinnamon
2 tablespoons almonds, sliced or ground

Beat the yolk slightly, add the cream, mix well, spread over top of Kuchen, sprinkle thickly with sugar and cinnamon, and add the almonds. Let rise and bake. Use also with fruit kuchen, dripping it over the fresh fruit before baking.

CUSTARD GLAZE

2 eggs, well beaten
½ cup sugar
1 teaspoon vanilla
2 tablespoons milk or cream

Mix well and use as above.

APRICOT GLAZE

¼ cup sugar
¼ pound dried apricots
1 cup water

Add sugar to apricots and water and cook gently until tender and thick. Strain through fine sieve. Bottle while hot. When ready to use, dilute with water. Use to glaze coffee cakes, or to glaze open fruit pies or tarts.

QUICK BREADS

Hot Breads and Tea Breads

Quick breads are so called because they are made with baking powder or baking soda, and do not require the time that yeast breads need to rise before they are baked. The leavening action of the baking powder or soda takes place while the quick breads are baking. Some of the breads which follow are served hot, with a meal; others are sliced to serve either warm or cold with butter, cream cheese and preserves at tea, or to make into dainty sandwiches.

HOT BREADS

BUTTERMILK BREAD

4 cups flour
¼ teaspoon salt
1 teaspoon sugar
1 teaspoon baking soda
2 teaspoons cream of tartar
1 egg, beaten
1½ cups buttermilk

Sift the dry ingredients, add the rest and mix well. Place in well-buttered loaf pan and bake in a moderate oven, 350° F., 35 minutes.

BUTTERMILK GRAHAM BREAD

2 cups graham flour
1 cup wheat flour
½ teaspoon salt
1 teaspoon baking soda
1 tablespoon sugar
1 tablespoon butter, melted
1 egg, beaten
1½ cups buttermilk or sour milk
½ cup nut meats, cut up

Mix the dry ingredients, add the rest and stir well. Place in well-buttered loaf pan and bake in a moderate oven, 350° F., 35 minutes.

BOSTON BROWN BREAD

1 cup rye meal
1 cup corn meal
1 cup graham flour
1 teaspoon salt
¾ cup molasses
2 cups sour milk with ¾ tablespoon baking soda, or 1¾ cups sweet milk with 5 teaspoons baking powder

Mix and sift dry ingredients; add molasses and milk, stir until well mixed. Fill greased molds or 1-pound food cans ⅔ full; cover with foil and steam. Large mold 2½ hours; small molds, 1 hour.

TO STEAM

If ordinary kettle is used, place molds on rack, add warm water to half the height of mold. Cover kettle tightly, let water gradually come to boiling point, boil gently, adding more boiling water when necessary.

GRAHAM BROWN BREAD

1 egg
½ cup sugar
½ cup molasses
1 cup sour milk
2 teaspoons baking soda
1 teaspoon salt
2¾ cups graham flour

Beat egg slightly, add rest of ingredients. Mix well. Steam two hours in greased molds or 1-pound food cans, tightly covered.

BRAN BREAD

4 teaspoons soda
2 teaspoons salt
4 cups white flour
4 cups bran flour
1 cup molasses
4 cups milk

Sift the soda and salt with the white flour, add bran and mix well. Add molasses and milk. Add nuts or raisins or both as desired. Place in 3 greased loaf pans and bake 1 hour in moderate oven at about 350° F.

CORN BREAD

1¼ cups flour
¾ cup corn meal
4 tablespoons sugar
3 teaspoons baking powder
1 teaspoon salt
1 cup milk
1 egg, beaten
3 tablespoons butter, melted

Sift the dry ingredients. Add milk, egg and butter. Beat well and bake in an 8-inch greased pan in a hot oven, 400° F., 30 to 40 minutes.

CORN STICKS

Pour above batter into hot, greased corn-stick pans. Bake in hot oven, 425° F., 15 to 20 minutes.

SOUTHERN SPOON CORN BREAD

1 cup corn meal
2 cups boiling water
1 tablespoon shortening
2 eggs, well beaten
1 teaspoon salt
2 cups milk
2½ teaspoons baking powder

Scald corn meal with water, stir thoroughly, then cool. Add melted shortening, eggs, salt and milk. Add baking powder. The batter should be quite thin. Pour into greased baking dish and bake from 30 to 40 minutes in moderate oven 350° F. Leave in dish, serve with spoon.

TEA BREADS

WHITE NUT BREAD

2½ cups flour
4 teaspoons bak___ ____
½ c__ ____
½ te_____ ___
½ cu_ ___ _____ ____
1 egg
1 cup ___

Mix dry _____ add nuts, add egg to milk and com____ the 2 mixtures. Place in greased bread pan ___ ____ stand 20 minutes; bake in moderate oven, 350___ for 1 hour or until well done.

BROWN N__ _____

1½ cups g___ flour
¾ cup whe__ flour
1½ teaspo___ baking soda
½ teaspoon ____
1½ cups sou_ milk
⅓ cup dark ____ molasses
¼ cup broke_ walnuts

Mix dry ingred____, add milk to molasses and stir into dry ingred____. Add nut meats last. Place in greased bread pan and bake at 325° F. 1 hour.

Most baked goods—and especially breads, rolls and coffee cakes—freeze very well. The wise cook will often bake in double quantity and freeze some things for future use. Most baked goods thaw in one hour at room temperature. Thawing can be hastened by placing the food in a moderate oven, and it is usually desirable to serve it warm. Partially baked rolls or coffee cakes may be frozen and the baking finished before serving. See introduction to Sweet Rolls, page 80.

PEANUT BUTTER BREAD

2 cups flour
4 teaspoons baking powder
1 teaspoon salt
¼ cup sugar
1¼ cups milk
⅔ cup peanut butter

Sift flour, baking powder, salt and sugar together. Add milk to peanut butter, blend well and add to dry ingredients; beat thoroughly. Bake in greased loaf pan in moderate oven, 350° F., 45 to 50 minutes. Best when a day old.

APRICOT NUT BREAD

½ cup dried apricots
1 egg
1 cup granulated sugar
_ tablespoons melted butter
_ cups flour
_ teaspoon salt
_ teaspoons baking powder
_ teaspoon baking soda
_ cup strained orange juice
_ cup water
1 cup chopped nut meats

Wash and grind apricots. Beat egg until light, stir in sugar and mix well. Stir in butter. Sift rest of dry ingredients. Add alternately with the orange juice and water to the sugar mixture. Add nuts and apricots. Mix well. Pour into greased bread pan. Bake in moderate oven, 350° F., for 1 hour.

BANANA BREAD

2 cups sifted flour
2 teaspoons baking powder
½ teaspoon baking soda
½ teaspoon salt
¼ cup butter
½ cup sugar
2 eggs
2 medium ripe bananas
½ cup sour milk or buttermilk

Sift flour, baking powder, soda and salt. Cream butter and sugar, add eggs, mashed bananas, milk, and add alternately to the flour mixture. When well blended pour into a greased bread pan, and bake at 350° F. for 1 hour.

Tea breads are usually served sliced thin and buttered. This type of bread freezes well and slices most easily when cold.

DATE BREAD

1 cup hot water
1 cup dates, pitted and cut up
1 egg, beaten
½ cup white or brown sugar
1½ cups flour
1 teaspoon baking powder
1 teaspoon soda
1 teaspoon salt
½ cup pecans, cut in pieces

Pour hot water over dates. Let stand until cool. Beat egg, add sugar, then add date mixture. Sift dry ingredients, stir well with date mixture. Add nuts last, stirring well. Place in buttered bread pan and bake at 350° F. 1 hour. Let cool in pan.

ORANGE AND NUT BREAD

2 cups white flour
2 cups whole wheat flour
4 teaspoons baking powder
2 teaspoons salt
½ cup sugar
½ cup each candied orange peel and pecan meats, cut fine
1 egg, well beaten
2 cups milk

Mix dry ingredients well, add candied orange peel and nuts. Add milk to egg and combine the two mixtures. Stir until smooth, then beat well. Pour into two greased bread pans and bake in a moderate oven, 350° F., 45 minutes.

PRUNE, DATE, OR RAISIN BREAD

1 cup prunes, dates or raisins
2½ cups graham or 1 cup wheat and 1½ cups graham flour
¼ cup sugar
1 teaspoon salt
4 teaspoons baking powder
1 cup milk
1 tablespoon shortening

Wash prunes, soak several hours, drain, stone, chop. Chop dates, if used. Mix dry ingredients, add milk, beat well; add fruit and melted shortening. Put in greased bread pan; let stand 25 minutes in warm place. Bake in moderate oven, 350° F., 1 hour.

To freshen stale bread or rolls, put into paper bag, wet outside of bag, and heat in the oven until bag is dry.

BISCUITS

BAKING POWDER BISCUITS

2 cups flour
4 teaspoons baking powder
1 teaspoon salt
2½ tablespoons shortening
¾ cup milk or water

Sift the dry ingredients together. In a mixing bowl, blend the shortening into the flour. Make a well in the center. Into this pour all the milk at once. Stir only until all the flour is moistened. Toss on a lightly floured board, knead for 20 seconds, pat or roll ½ inch thick. Cut into rounds, place in pan, and bake in very hot oven, 450° F., 10 to 15 minutes. Yield, about 2 dozen 1½-inch biscuits.

DROP BISCUITS

Follow recipe for Baking Powder Biscuits, above, using 1 cup milk to make a softer dough. Drop by spoonfuls on greased pan or in greased muffin pans, and bake in very hot oven, 450° F., 10 to 15 minutes.

NEW ENGLAND TEA BISCUITS

Follow recipe for Baking Powder Biscuits, above, doubling the amount of shortening. Press cube of sugar dipped in orange juice or a little orange marmalade, on top of each biscuit. Bake in hot oven, 400° F., 10 to 15 minutes.

SANDWICH BISCUITS

Roll Baking Powder Biscuit dough, above, ¼ inch thick. Cut with small biscuit cutter. Spread half the rounds with creamed butter and thickly with chopped cooked meat. Cover with remaining rounds. Press together and brush tops and sides with milk. Bake in a very hot oven, 475° F., 10 to 12 minutes.

CHEESE BISCUITS

2 cups flour
4 teaspoons baking powder
1 teaspoon salt
2 tablespoons shortening
¾ to 1 cup milk
¾ cup grated Cheddar cheese

Sift dry ingredients together. Blend shortening into flour mixture with fork, stir in the milk quickly and add the cheese. Place on floured board, roll gently about ½ inch thick. Cut into rounds, place in a greased pan and bake in a hot oven, 400° F., 10 to 15 minutes.

Or roll out dough, dot with butter, sprinkle with grated cheese, roll up as for jelly roll, cut in 1-inch slices. Bake cut side down.

CHEESE WHIRLS

1½ cups flour
3 tablespoons baking powder
½ teaspoon salt
paprika
3 tablespoons shortening
½ cup milk
¾ cup grated cheese
2 pimientos, chopped

Toss flour, baking powder, salt and paprika to blend. Cut in shortening until mixture is like cornmeal. Add milk, stir to make firm dough. Knead on floured board for 30 seconds. Roll out in sheet 8" × 12", sprinkle with grated cheese and chopped pimiento. Roll like jelly roll, cut into 8 slices, flatten slightly and bake in very hot oven, 450° F., about 30 minutes or until browned.

IRISH POTATO CAKES

2 cups flour
4 teaspoons baking powder
1 teaspoon salt
1 tablespoon butter
1 teaspoon caraway seed
2 cups mashed potatoes
½ cup milk

Mix dry ingredients, blend in butter, add caraway seed, mashed potatoes and lastly the milk. Roll about as thick as biscuits and cut in squares. Brown slowly in a small amount of fat in heavy skillet over low heat. Split and spread with butter. Serve hot.

POTATO BISCUITS

1 cup flour
3 teaspoons baking powder
1 teaspoon salt
2 tablespoons shortening
1 cup mashed potato
½ cup water or milk (about)

Sift together flour, baking powder and salt. Blend in the shortening. Add potato and mix thoroughly. Then add enough liquid to make a soft dough. Roll the dough lightly to about ½ inch in thickness. Cut into biscuits and bake 12 to 15 minutes in hot oven, 400° F.

QUICK CINNAMON ROLLS

2 cups flour
3 teaspoons baking powder
⅛ teaspoon salt
2 tablespoons butter
⅔ cup milk
melted butter
½ cup raisins, chopped fine, or currants
2 tablespoons citron, chopped fine
2 tablespoons sugar
⅛ teaspoon cinnamon

Mix first 5 ingredients as for Baking Powder Biscuits. Roll ¼ inch thick, brush with melted butter and sprinkle with the raisins, citron, sugar and cinnamon. Roll like a jelly roll. Cut in slices ¾ inch thick. Place in buttered tins cut side down and bake 10 to 15 minutes in a hot oven, 400° F. Or, butter a skillet, spread well with brown sugar, place rolls in skillet and bake. Serve caramel side up.

QUICK ORANGE ROLLS

2 cups flour
3 teaspoons baking powder
⅛ teaspoon salt
2 tablespoons butter
¾ cup milk
melted butter
1 cup orange juice
2 tablespoons grated orange rind
4 tablespoons butter
⅔ cup sugar

Mix first five ingredients as for Baking Powder Biscuits. Roll ¼ inch thick, brush with melted butter. Roll like a jelly roll; cut in ¾-inch slices. Boil the orange juice, grated orange rind, butter, and sugar for 3 minutes. Pour this into a skillet or baking dish. Place rolls, cut side down, into dish. Bake in hot oven, 400° F., for 25 to 30 minutes. Remove from pan while still hot. Serve orange side up.

QUICK PARKER HOUSE ROLLS

4 cups flour
1 teaspoon salt
6 teaspoons baking powder
2 tablespoons melted shortening
1½ cups milk

Sift flour, salt and baking powder. Add shortening to milk, combine with dry ingredients, mix quickly until blended. Knead lightly on floured board and roll out ½ inch thick. Cut with biscuit cutter. Crease each circle with back of knife at one side of center. Butter the small section and fold, pinch edges together. Place 1 inch apart in greased pan. Allow to stand 10 minutes in warm place. Brush each with melted butter and bake in hot oven, 450° F., 15 to 20 minutes.

SCONES

    2 cups flour
    4 teaspoons baking powder
    2 teaspoons sugar
    ½ teaspoon salt
    4 tablespoons butter
    2 eggs
    ⅓ cup cream

Sift dry ingredients. Cut in butter with fork or blender. Add well-beaten eggs and cream. Toss on floured board, pat or roll to ¾-inch thickness. Cut in diamonds about 2 inches across, brush with white of egg, sprinkle with brown sugar and cinnamon. Bake on greased pan in hot oven, 425° F., for 15 minutes. Serve hot.

GRIDDLE SCONES

    2 cups flour
    1 teaspoon cream of tartar
    ½ teaspoon salt
    ½ teaspoon soda
    ¼ cup shortening
    ½ cup buttermilk

Mix flour with cream of tartar, salt, and soda; add shortening, mix with fork or blender. Add buttermilk. When thoroughly mixed, roll ½ inch thick, cut into squares, bake on griddle browning on both sides. Serve hot or cold.

SHORTCAKE BISCUIT

    2 cups flour
    4 teaspoons baking powder
    ½ teaspoon salt
    2 tablespoons sugar
    ½ cup shortening
    ¾ cup milk

Mix dry ingredients, work in shortening with fork or blender, add milk quickly. Toss on floured board; pat, roll, cut with large biscuit cutter or roll to fit 2 pans and bake in a very hot oven, 450° F., 12 to 15 minutes. If desired, omit sugar. Split biscuits and fill with crushed sweetened berries or other fruits. Top with whipped cream. Or may be shaped as individual baking powder biscuits and served as hot bread.

SOUR MILK OR SODA BISCUITS

    2 cups flour
    ½ teaspoon soda
    1 teaspoon baking powder
    1 teaspoon salt
    2 tablespoons shortening
    ¾ cup thick sour cream or sour milk

Mix dry ingredients. Work in the shortening with a fork, add liquid; mix quickly. Pat, roll out and cut into biscuits or drop by spoonfuls on greased pan or in greased muffin pans. Bake in a hot oven, 400° F., for 10 to 15 minutes.

SWEET POTATO BISCUITS

    ¾ cup mashed sweet potato
    ⅔ cup milk
    4 tablespoons melted butter
    1¼ cups flour
    4 teaspoons baking powder
    1 tablespoon sugar
    ½ teaspoon salt

Mix sweet potato, milk and butter. Add remaining ingredients, mixed, to make soft dough and fill greased muffin pans. Bake in hot oven, 450° F., about 15 minutes.

MUFFINS

GENERAL RULES FOR MUFFINS

Combine eggs and liquid ingredients well. Mix dry ingredients well. Then combine the two, but stir only until the dry ingredients are moistened. The batter will be lumpy. Add berries, nuts, or other special ingredients last. Bake in greased muffin pans, filled ⅔ full. Or use muffin pans lined with paper baking cups to eliminate greasing. Bake muffins in a hot oven, 400°-425° F., until well risen and browned, about 20 minutes.

PLAIN MUFFINS

    2 cups flour
    1 teaspoon salt
    4 teaspoons baking powder
    2 tablespoons sugar
    1 cup milk
    1 egg
    3 tablespoons melted shortening

Sift dry ingredients. Mix milk, beaten egg and shortening. Combine the 2 mixtures. Stir only until the flour mixture is moistened. Pour into well-greased muffin tins. Bake 15 to 20 minutes in hot oven, about 425° F.

BRAN MUFFINS

2 tablespoons shortening
¼ cup sugar or molasses
1 egg
1 cup bran
¾ cup milk
1 cup flour
2½ teaspoons baking powder
½ teaspoon salt

Cream shortening; stir in sugar or molasses. Add egg, bran and milk. Let stand until most of the moisture is absorbed. Sift remaining dry ingredients and stir into the bran mixture only until flour is moistened. Bake in greased muffin pans in hot oven, 400° F., for about 30 minutes.

CORN MEAL MUFFINS

¼ cup butter
½ cup sugar
2 eggs
1 cup milk
2 cups flour
1 cup corn meal
4 teaspoons baking powder
¾ teaspoon salt

Cream the butter and sugar. Add eggs beaten until light-colored and thick. Add the milk alternately with the sifted dry ingredients. Beat thoroughly. Place in well-greased muffin pans and bake about 20 minutes at 400° F.

CORN PONE

1¾ cups boiling water
2 cups corn meal
1 teaspoon salt
2 teaspoons fat

Pour the boiling water over other ingredients. Beat well. When cool, form into thin cakes and bake 30 minutes in a hot oven, 400° F., until crisp. Serve with butter or gravy.

OATMEAL MUFFINS

2 tablespoons butter
1 cup milk, scalded
¾ cup oatmeal, uncooked
1 egg, well beaten
3 tablespoons sugar
1½ cups flour
4 teaspoons baking powder
½ teaspoon salt

Melt the butter in the hot milk. Add the oatmeal and let stand for 3 minutes. Add egg and sifted dry ingredients, mixing just enough to moisten. Bake in greased muffin pans at 400° F. for 20 to 25 minutes.

POTATO FLOUR MUFFINS

4 eggs, separated
¼ teaspoon salt
1 tablespoon sugar
½ cup potato flour
1 teaspoon baking powder
2 tablespoons ice water

Beat egg whites stiff. Beat yolks, add salt and sugar, and fold into whites. Sift flour and baking powder twice and beat thoroughly into eggs. Add ice water. Bake in greased muffin pans in hot oven, 400° F., 15 to 20 minutes.

RICE MUFFINS

¼ cup sugar
¾ cup cooked rice
1 egg
2 tablespoons melted shortening
1 cup milk
5 teaspoons baking powder
1 teaspoon salt
2¼ cups flour

Mix sugar, rice, egg, shortening, and milk. Sift remaining dry ingredients and add to the rice mixture. Fill greased muffin pans ⅔ full; bake in hot oven, 425° F., for 30 minutes.

SALLY LUNN

¼ cup soft shortening
⅓ cup sugar
2 eggs, separated
2 cups flour
4 teaspoons baking powder
1 teaspoon salt
¾ cup milk

Cream shortening and sugar. Add unbeaten yolks into first mixture and beat until light, thick and lemon-colored. Sift rest of dry ingredients and add to mixture with milk. Fold in stiffly beaten egg whites. Fill greased muffin pans ¾ full and bake in hot oven, 400° F., 25 minutes. May also be baked in a loaf pan.

SOUR CREAM MUFFINS

1¾ cups flour
2 teaspoons baking powder
2 tablespoons sugar
½ teaspoon salt
1 egg
1 cup sour cream
½ teaspoon soda
1 tablespoon water

Sift first 4 ingredients. Beat egg very well, add cream, then soda mixed with water and add to dry ingredients. Mix only until moistened. Fill greased muffin tins two-thirds full and bake about 20 minutes at 425° F.

SOUR CREAM CORN MUFFINS

1¼ cups corn meal
¾ cup flour
2 tablespoons sugar
3 teaspoons baking powder
½ teaspoon salt
1 egg
¾ cup milk
½ cup sour cream

Preheat oven to 425° F. Sift together the dry ingredients. Add egg, milk and sour cream. Mix lightly but thoroughly. Place in greased muffin pans. Bake for 15 to 20 minutes. Yield: 12 medium muffins.

Sweet Tea Muffins

APPLE MUFFINS

2 cups flour
¾ teaspoon salt
2 teaspoons baking powder
4 tablespoons sugar
2 tablespoons butter
1 cup finely chopped apples
1 egg, beaten
½ cup milk
12 apple slices
½ teaspoon cinnamon

Mix flour, salt, baking powder and half of the sugar. Blend in the butter with a fork. Add chopped apples, mix. Add egg with the milk. Drop by spoonfuls into greased muffin pans. Place one slice of apple on each muffin, mix remaining sugar with the cinnamon, sprinkle this over top and bake in a hot oven, 400° F., about 20 minutes.

BLUEBERRY MUFFINS

2 cups flour
1 cup washed blueberries
¼ cup butter
¼ cup sugar
1 egg, well beaten
4 teaspoons baking powder
½ teaspoon salt
1 cup milk

Mix ¼ cup of flour with blueberries. Cream butter and sugar, add egg. Sift baking powder, salt, and remaining flour. Add the dry ingredients alternately with the milk; add floured berries last. Bake in greased muffin pans for 25 minutes at 425° F.

If canned blueberries are used, use 1¼ cups. Wash berries gently, drain well. Do not flour berries. Fold berries gently into batter.

HONEY AND NUT BRAN MUFFINS

1 cup flour
¼ to ½ teaspoon soda
½ teaspoon salt
2 cups bran
½ cup honey
1 tablespoon melted butter
1½ cups milk
¾ cup walnuts, chopped fine

Sift together flour, soda and salt and mix with the bran, add other ingredients. Bake in greased muffin pans in hot oven, 425° F., for 25 to 30 minutes.

TWIN MOUNTAIN MUFFINS

¼ cup butter
¼ cup sugar
1 egg
1 cup milk
2 cups flour
4 teaspoons baking powder
½ teaspoon salt

Cream the butter; add the sugar gradually; then alternately the egg beaten and mixed with the milk and the sifted dry ingredients. Bake in greased muffin pans at 400° F. about 25 minutes.

DATE MUFFINS

Add ¼ pound finely chopped dates to creamed butter and sugar in the above recipe.

CHOCOLATE MUFFINS

Add 1 to 2 squares melted unsweetened chocolate to the butter and sugar mixture in the above recipe.

POPOVERS

PLAIN POPOVERS

1 cup flour
¼ teaspoon salt
2 eggs
1 cup milk
1 tablespoon butter, melted

Sift flour and salt. Beat eggs with rotary beater, add milk, butter and sift in flour, beating only enough to make a smooth batter. Fill iron popover pans or muffin pans, previously heated and greased, one-third full. Bake in very hot oven, 450° F., 30 minutes, then at 350° F. for 15 minutes or until well-risen, browned, and crusty. Do not open oven door for first 30 minutes.

RYE POPOVERS

¾ cup rye flour
¼ cup wheat flour
¼ teaspoon salt
1 teaspoon sugar
2 eggs
1 cup milk

Sift dry ingredients. Beat the eggs and add milk and stir gradually into the flour mixture to make a smooth batter. Beat until full of air bubbles. Fill hot greased popover or muffin pans ⅔ full of the mixture. Bake in very hot oven, 450° F., 20 minutes. Reduce heat to 350° F. and bake 20 minutes or until crisp.

CHEESE POPOVERS

1 egg
⅜ teaspoon salt
1 cup milk
1 cup flour
¼ pound Cheddar cheese, grated

Beat the egg slightly, add salt and milk and stir gradually into flour to make a smooth batter. Beat until full of air bubbles. Have popover or muffin pans hot and well greased. Into each, drop a rounded teaspoon of this batter. Spread with a teaspoon of cheese, and cover with another teaspoon of batter. Bake in a very hot oven (450° F.) about 20 minutes. Reduce heat to 350° F. and bake 20 minutes longer or until well browned.

GLUTEN POPOVERS

2 eggs
2 cups water
2 cups gluten flour
1 teaspoon salt

Beat eggs, add water, and pour gradually into flour and salt mixed. Stir until smooth, beating well. Pour into hot greased popover or muffin pans, ⅔ full, and bake in a very hot oven, 450° F., for 20 minutes. Reduce heat to 350° F. and bake 20 minutes longer or until well browned and crusty.

GRIDDLE CAKES, PANCAKES AND WAFFLES

Any of these hot cakes may be served as main courses at luncheon or supper, and pancakes and waffles are used as desserts, as well.

Griddle cake batters are thick enough to hold their shape, so that they can be poured from a pitcher or the tip of a spoon to make perfect round cakes. Pancake batters are thinner, and take the shape of the skillet. Waffles should be baked on an electric waffle iron, according to the manufacturer's directions.

GRIDDLE CAKES

TO BAKE GRIDDLE CAKES

Heat a griddle or skillet and test temperature by sprinkling with a few drops of water. If water disappears at once, the griddle is too hot. If it flattens out and boils, the griddle is not hot enough. If the drops bounce, the griddle is ready for use. Brush lightly with fat, using a pastry brush. Pour batter in uniform amounts from a pitcher, or from tip of a large spoon. When cakes are full of bubbles turn with a pancake turner and brown other side. Turn only once.

LIGHT GRIDDLE CAKES

1 cup flour
2 teaspoons baking powder
¼ teaspoon salt
1 egg, beaten
1 cup milk
1 teaspoon melted butter

Sift the dry ingredients. Add the egg and milk and stir gradually to make a smooth batter; add shortening. Bake as directed at left.

RICH GRIDDLE CAKES

3 cups flour
1½ teaspoons baking powder
1 teaspoon salt
¼ cup sugar
1 egg
2 cups milk
2 tablespoons melted butter

Mix batter and bake as above.

BUTTERMILK GRIDDLE CAKES

1 cup flour
1 teaspoon baking powder
½ teaspoon soda
⅛ teaspoon salt
1 cup buttermilk
1 tablespoon shortening
1 egg

Mix dry ingredients. Add milk and melted shortening to egg. Combine the mixtures. Stir until smooth and bake on hot griddle.

SOUR MILK GRIDDLE CAKES

2½ cups flour
½ teaspoon salt
1¼ teaspoons soda
2 cups sour milk
2 tablespoons oil or melted butter
1 egg

Mix dry ingredients. Add milk, shortening and the egg. Drop by spoonfuls on a hot, greased griddle. Brown well on both sides.

Sour Cream may be substituted for sour milk; omit butter.

SOUR CREAM GRIDDLE CAKES

1 teaspoon baking soda
1 cup sour cream
2 eggs
½ cup flour
2 tablespoons cottage cheese

Mix baking soda and sour cream. Beat eggs, add sour cream to eggs, stir in flour. Add cottage cheese. Bake on greased griddle.

BREAD CRUMB OR CEREAL GRIDDLE CAKES

1½ cups fine bread crumbs or cookie crumbs,
    or 1 cup of cooked cereal
1½ cups hot milk
2 tablespoons shortening
2 eggs
½ cup flour
½ teaspoon salt
3½ teaspoons baking powder

Mix in the order given. One cup of any cooked cereal may be used instead of bread crumbs. Bake on hot, greased griddle. Serves 6.

BUCKWHEAT CAKES

½ package active dry yeast
4 cups lukewarm water
1 teaspoon sugar
½ cup flour
1 teaspoon salt
3¼ cups buckwheat flour
2 tablespoons molasses

Dissolve the yeast in ¼ cup warm water with 1 teaspoon sugar; add to the rest of the water and mix with the flour, salt and buckwheat to make a thin batter. Let rise overnight. Next morning, add molasses and bake on a hot, greased griddle. Serves 8. Or use prepared buckwheat pancake flour and follow directions on package.

COMBINATION HOT CAKES

1 tablespoon shortening
1 tablespoon sugar
2 eggs
½ teaspoon salt
1 teaspoon soda
2½ cups sour milk or buttermilk
1 cup wheat flour
1 cup barley flour
1 cup corn flour

Cream shortening and sugar. Add eggs well beaten, salt, and the soda dissolved in the sour milk. Mix the flours well and stir in gradually to make a smooth batter. Bake on a hot, greased griddle. Serves 8.

YEAST GRIDDLE CAKES

2 cups lukewarm milk and 1 cup water mixed
1 cup wheat flour
1 cup barley flour
1 cup corn flour
1 teaspoon salt
1 package active dry yeast
1 teaspoon soda
2 eggs
3 tablespoons syrup
2 tablespoons melted shortening

If cakes are to be used for breakfast, mix all but ¼ cup of the liquid the night before with the wheat; barley and corn flours and salt, adding yeast dissolved in the reserved ¼ cup of the liquid. In the morning add soda, eggs, syrup and shortening. Let rise 15 minutes and bake on hot, greased griddle.

CORN MEAL GRIDDLE CAKES

1 cup flour
1 cup corn meal
1 tablespoon baking powder
1½ teaspoons salt
1 or 2 eggs
2 cups milk

Mix the dry ingredients. Beat egg well, add the milk, and combine the 2 mixtures. A tablespoon of molasses may be added to the batter. Bake on greased griddle. Serves 6.

Or, 1 teaspoon soda and 2 cups sour milk may be used in place of the baking powder and sweet milk.

CORN MEAL AND RICE GRIDDLE CAKES

½ cup corn meal
½ cup flour
2 teaspoons baking powder
½ teaspoon salt
1 cup cooked rice
2 eggs, separated
1 cup milk

Mix dry ingredients and rice. To the beaten yolks add milk. Combine the mixtures, and fold in whites beaten stiff. Bake on hot, greased griddle. Serves 4.

RICE GRIDDLE CAKES

2 cups flour
3 teaspoons baking powder
2 cups hot boiled rice
1 teaspoon salt
2 cups milk
2 eggs, separated

Mix the dry ingredients and the rice. Add milk to beaten yolks. Combine the two mixtures and lastly fold in the beaten whites. Bake on hot, greased griddle. Serves 6.

SCOTCH PANCAKES

2 cups flour
3 tablespoons sugar
½ teaspoon salt
1 teaspoon soda
1 teaspoon cream of tartar
2 tablespoons shortening
1 cup sour milk
2 eggs, beaten light

Mix dry ingredients; cut in the shortening. Add sour milk and beat well; add eggs. Only a small amount of the batter should be used for each pancake. Bake on hot, greased griddle. Serves 6.

PANCAKES

SOUFFLE PANCAKE

2 or 3 eggs, separated
½ teaspoon salt
¼ cup flour or cornstarch
1 cup milk

Stir yolks with the salt and flour, until smooth, add milk gradually, then fold in the beaten whites. Heat skillet, add 2 tablespoons butter and when hot, pour in pancake. Turn to brown on both sides or finish baking in oven. Serve with jelly.

BAKED PANCAKE

2 eggs
¾ cup flour
½ teaspoon salt
1 cup milk
2 tablespoons shortening

Beat eggs, add flour, salt, and milk; blend well. Heat skillet in oven, add shortening. When shortening is melted, pour in egg mixture. Bake in hot oven, 425° F., for 15 minutes, reduce heat to 325° F. and continue baking until pancake is brown. Serve on hot platter with confectioners sugar and lemon slices or juice. Serves 4.

FRENCH PANCAKES

1 cup flour
½ teaspoon salt
1½ cups milk
3 eggs, well beaten

Sift flour and salt, add milk and eggs, beat all together very well. Batter should be as thick as heavy cream. Heat small skillet; grease lightly; pour in a little batter, tilt pan back and forth, so batter will spread all over bottom; when brown, turn and brown on other side. Spread each pancake with jelly or cottage cheese and roll up and dust with confectioners sugar. Serve hot. Serves 4.

Pancakes may be browned on one side, desired filling placed on browned side, pancakes rolled and set aside. When ready to serve, brown lightly.

CHICKEN IN PANCAKES

See page 317.

RUSSIAN PANCAKES

Make batter for French Pancakes. Drop from tip of tablespoon on hot, well-greased griddle to form small thin pancakes. Brown on both sides. Serve hot with thick sour cream and Russian caviar.

NORWEGIAN PANCAKES

Make French Pancakes in 10-inch skillet, but do not roll. Pile 6 or 8 pancakes on serving plate, spreading jelly or butter and scraped maple sugar between them. Or spread with Caramel Fudge Frosting. Cut into pie-shaped wedges. Serve hot.

See rules for determining proper temperature for griddle or skillet under the baking instructions on page 91.

BOHEMIAN PANCAKES

½ package active dry yeast
¼ cup lukewarm water
1¼ cups flour
1 tablespoon sugar
½ teaspoon salt
grated rind of ½ lemon
2 eggs, well beaten
¾ cup lukewarm milk
Prune Filling, page 83

Dissolve yeast in warm water, mix flour, sugar, salt, and lemon rind. Add well-beaten eggs, the milk, and mix well; add yeast. Beat thoroughly; let rise in a warm place until very light. Lift the dough by spoonfuls carefully from the top of the mixture so as not to disturb the remainder. Spread on griddle with back of spoon. Bake slowly so that they will rise again; turn and bake on the other side. These pancakes are served cold. Place on large platter or on individual plates. Spread top of pancakes with a thick layer of Prune Filling, cover generously with grated gingersnaps, and spread with sweetened whipped cream. Or, cover with sour cream and riced, dry cottage cheese. Makes 10 pancakes.

PANCAKE DESSERT

grated rind of 2 oranges
2 tablespoons sugar
½ pound maple sugar or light brown sugar
2 tablespoons butter
French Pancakes, page 93
candied fruits

Mix orange rind and sugar. Melt maple sugar and butter in top of double boiler and keep hot. Make French Pancakes in 10-inch skillet. As each is baked, stack in deep dish in oven and sprinkle each pancake with orange and sugar mixture. Pour hot syrup over pancakes, garnish with candied fruits. Serve hot.

BLINTZES

1 cup milk
4 eggs, well-beaten
1 cup flour
1 teaspoon salt

Add milk to eggs; stir in the flour and salt gradually until smooth. Heat heavy 6-inch skillet, grease lightly. Pour only enough batter to make a very thin pancake, tipping pan from side to side until batter covers bottom of pan. Bake on one side only until it blisters; toss on board fried side up. When a number have been fried in this manner, place rounded tablespoon of desired filling, below, in center of each pancake. Fold over both sides and roll into envelope shape. Proceed in this manner until all the batter has been used. To complete: before serving, fry envelopes on both sides or bake until golden brown. Serve hot with sugar and cinnamon or with sour cream and jam.

CHEESE FILLING

1½ pounds dry cottage cheese
2 yolks, beaten
1 tablespoon melted butter
1 tablespoon sugar

Press cheese through colander; salt to taste, add rest of ingredients.

POTATO FILLING

2½ cups mashed potatoes
1 egg
salt and pepper
melted butter
1 small, grated onion, optional

Combine mashed potatoes, egg, salt and pepper. Fry onion in butter until soft but not brown and add to potato mixture. Fill as described above and fry or bake. Serve with sour cream.

BLINTZ CASSEROLE

12 cheese blintzes, not fried
¼ cup melted shortening
5 eggs
1½ cups half-and-half (or non-dairy) sour cream
¼ cup sugar
2 tablespoons lemon or orange juice

Preheat oven to 350° F. Place blintzes in a layer in a well-greased baking dish. Beat or blend remaining ingredients until frothy. Pour over blintzes. Bake for 50 minutes. Serve with jam or fruit.

KNISHES

½ cup flour
2 tablespoons vegetable oil
3 tablespoons water
pinch of salt

Put half the flour into a mixing bowl and stir in oil with a fork. Add water and salt and mix until the mixture forms a dough. Toss on a floured board, work in remaining flour, and knead until the dough is smooth and elastic. Cover and chill for 1 hour or longer. Roll the dough out on a board as thin as possible. Pull and stretch it into a long rectangle. Cut into 3-inch circles. Put a tablespoon of filling, below, on each circle. Draw the edges of the circle together over the filling and pinch together to seal. Brush with chicken fat. Bake on a greased baking sheet in a moderate oven, 350° F., about 45 minutes, until dough is well browned. Or: roll and stretch dough and spread with filling. Roll up and cut the roll into 1½ inch slices. Lay slices cut-side down on a greased baking sheet and flatten lightly. Brush with fat and bake as above.

FILLINGS FOR KNISHES

Potato Filling: Mash 5 freshly boiled potatoes and mix with ⅓ cup ground crisp cracklings made with chicken according to the recipe for Goose Grieben, page 321. Season with salt and a generous amount of pepper, to taste. Or use chicken fat, about ⅓ cup. An egg may be added, if desired, and a small onion finely chopped and cooked until just translucent in the chicken fat. Fillings for blintzes, above, may be substituted.

Chicken Filling: Crumble 2 matzos and soak until soft in ¼ cup chicken gravy or chicken soup. Combine with 1 cup finely chopped chicken. Season well with salt, pepper, and cayenne, and add enough chicken fat to make a soft mixture.

CREPES

    3 eggs, well beaten
    1½ cups milk
    1 cup flour
    ½ teaspoon salt
    2 tablespoons melted butter

Combine eggs and milk. Add flour and salt and last the melted butter. Beat until smooth. Batter can be mixed in blender. Cover and place in refrigerator for 1 to 2 hours.

Heat a 6-inch greased skillet, add 1 tablespoon of batter. Tip skillet from side to side until batter covers the bottom of the skillet. Brown crêpes on both sides. Keep hot. Place desired filling in center and roll. Add sauce.

SUGGESTED CREPES FILLINGS

Deviled Crab Meat, page 248
Creamed Crab or Lobster, page 249
Oysters & Mushrooms, page 253
Creamed Spinach, page 431
Ratatouille, page 434
Creamed Chicken or Turkey, page 317
Chicken Hash, page 315
Beef Casserole with Red Wine (Leftover), page 274
Chipped Beef in Brown Sauce, page 277

SUGGESTED CREPES SAUCES

Thin Basic White Sauce, page 386
Cheese Sauce, page 386
Mornay Sauce, page 387
Mushroom Cream Sauce, page 387

A dash of wine added to the sauce adds flavor. Parmesan cheese sprinkled lightly over the top also enhances the flavor.

CREPES SUZETTE

    1 cup flour
    ⅛ cup confectioners sugar
    ¼ teaspoon salt
    2 eggs, separated
    1 cup milk
    grated rind of 1 lemon

Sift dry ingredients. Beat yolks, add milk, dry ingredients, lemon rind, and lastly the stiffly beaten egg whites. Heat a 6-inch greased skillet, add 1 tablespoon batter. Tip skillet from side to side until batter covers the bottom of the skillet. Brown pancakes on both sides and roll. Keep pancakes hot. Serve with one of the Suzette sauces below.

SUZETTE SAUCE FLAMBE

    ½ cup unsalted butter
    3 tablespoons confectioners sugar
    juice of 1 orange
    2 tablespoons grenadine
    1 tablespoon cognac
    1 tablespoon rum
    1 tablespoon Cointreau

Melt butter in a chafing dish, then add sugar and allow to cook a few minutes. Add orange juice and grenadine, stirring constantly. Then add the rolled pancakes, turning each in the sauce till well covered. Then add the liqueurs, light with a match, and turn pancakes, in flaming sauce, until the flame burns out.

SUZETTE SAUCE

    ½ cup unsalted butter
    2 cups confectioners sugar
    1 medium orange, juice and rind
    2 tablespoons grenadine and 1 tablespoon each
        cognac, rum, Cointreau, or 3 tablespoons rum

Cream the butter, add the sugar gradually. Add remaining ingredients. Dissolve sauce over hot water. Add the rolled pancakes one at a time, turning to cover thoroughly with the sauce.

Pancakes, blintzes and crêpes are international favorites and among the most versatile of foods. Don't limit them to breakfast; serve them as a main dish for lunch or supper, rolled around savory fillings (a good way to use leftovers) and heated in a sauce. Serve them as dessert after a light meal of soup or salad. Pancakes freeze well, filled or unfilled.

GERMAN PANCAKE

3 eggs
½ teaspoon salt
½ cup flour
½ cup milk
2 tablespoons butter

Preheat oven to 450° F. Beat eggs until very light, add salt and flour, and then the milk, beating all the time. Spread bottom and sides of a 10-inch cold skillet thickly with butter. Pour in the egg batter, and bake 20 minutes; reduce the heat to 350° F. and continue baking until crisp and brown. Place on hot platter and serve with confectioners sugar and lemon juice. Serves 4.

SOUR CREAM POTATO PANCAKES

4 large potatoes or 2 cups raw, grated potatoes
½ cup sour cream or ½ cup hot milk
½ teaspoon salt
2 eggs, separated

Grate the potatoes, place in a colander, set over a bowl and drain. When the starch has settled in bottom of bowl discard top liquid. Place drained potatoes in a mixing bowl, add starch, cream or hot milk, and salt. Beat yolks well; add to potato mixture; fold in the stiffly beaten whites. Drop by spoonfuls on a hot, well-greased skillet. Brown slowly on both sides. Serve with apple sauce. Serves 4.

POTATO PANCAKES

4 large potatoes or 2 cups raw grated potatoes
2 eggs
⅛ teaspoon baking powder
1½ teaspoons salt
1 tablespoon flour, bread crumbs or matzo meal
dash of pepper

Peel potatoes, grate, drain. Beat eggs well and mix with the rest of the ingredients. Drop by spoonfuls on a hot, well-greased skillet. Brown on both sides. Serve with applesauce. Serves 4.

BAKED POTATO PANCAKES

Mix as above. Heat a generous amount of fat in skillet, add potato batter; bake in hot oven, 400° F., for 25 minutes.

MATZOS PANCAKES

3 matzos, broken
2 whole eggs
1 teaspoon salt
pepper
goose fat or butter

Cover matzos with boiling water. Let stand 15 minutes. Squeeze water from matzos; add well-beaten eggs, salt, and a little pepper. Heat fat in a skillet; drop mixtures by spoonfuls and fry until well-browned. Serve with syrup or jelly.

MATZO MEAL PANCAKES

½ cup matzo meal
1 teaspoon salt
1 tablespoon sugar
2 eggs, separated
1 cup milk or water

Mix dry ingredients. Beat egg yolks, add milk and combine the two mixtures, let stand a half hour. Fold in the stiffly beaten egg whites. Heat griddle and grease. Pour cakes on the griddle from the tip of a large spoon. When cakes are full of bubbles, and brown on one side, brown the other side. Serve with sugar or pancake syrup.

MATZO MEAL-PUFF PANCAKES

¼ cup matzo meal
¼ cup water
1 teaspoon salt
4 eggs, separated
2 tablespoons fat

Pour water on matzo meal, add salt. Beat the egg yolks very light, add to meal mixture, let stand 5 minutes. Beat egg whites very stiff, fold lightly into the yolk mixture. Drop mixture by spoonfuls in small cakes on hot, greased skillet. Turn when brown and brown on other side. Serve with sugar, jelly or preserves.

To grease a griddle or skillet between pancakes, it is convenient to keep melted butter or other fat in a cup and brush griddle with a pastry brush.

WAFFLES

Waffles may be served with bacon or ham and syrup, or used as a base for creamed chicken and similar mixtures, or they may be served with ice cream or whipped cream for dessert.

Follow the manufacturer's directions to temper a new waffle iron. After the first use, it is rarely necessary to grease the hot iron except when the batter used is very low in fat.

NOTE: Sour milk or cream makes a more tender waffle than sweet milk. If sour milk or cream or buttermilk is used, use ½ teaspoon soda for each cup of liquid. Overbeating will toughen waffles.

Waffles are a favorite dish with most children and teenagers. See chapter 1, Menus for additional suggestions for dishes to please the young set.

PLAIN WAFFLES

2 cups flour
2 teaspoons baking powder
2 tablespoons sugar
½ teaspoon salt
2 eggs, separated
2 cups milk
4 to 6 tablespoons melted butter

Sift dry ingredients twice. Beat egg whites until stiff but not dry. Set aside. Beat egg yolks, add milk and mix with dry ingredients only enough to blend them. Add melted butter. Fold in the beaten egg whites last. Bake in electric waffle iron. Serve with any syrup or sauce. Makes 6 waffles.

SOYBEAN WAFFLES

Make Plain Waffles, above, using 2 cups soybean flour in place of white flour; add 1 teaspoon baking powder.

PECAN OR ENGLISH WALNUT WAFFLES

Make Plain Waffles as above, adding ¾ cup nut meats, broken in pieces. Or a few nut meats may be placed on batter before closing the waffle iron.

SOUR CREAM WAFFLES

1¼ cups flour
1 teaspoon baking powder
1 teaspoon soda
½ teaspoon salt
3 eggs, separated
2 cups sour cream
3 tablespoons butter, melted

Follow directions for Plain Waffles above.

CHOCOLATE WAFFLES

4 tablespoons shortening
10 tablespoons sugar
2 ounces chocolate, melted
3 eggs, separated
1¼ cups milk
1½ cups flour
3 teaspoons baking powder
¼ teaspoon salt
½ teaspoon vanilla

Cream shortening and add sugar. Add chocolate, and well-beaten egg yolks. Add milk alternately with the flour sifted with the baking powder and salt. Add vanilla and lastly, beaten whites. Bake. Serve with butter and confectioners sugar. Makes 6 waffles.

SPONGE CAKE WAFFLES

4 egg yolks
1 cup sugar
¼ cup water
1 teaspoon lemon juice or grated rind of ½ orange
1 cup cake flour
½ teaspoon salt
4 egg whites

Beat yolks until a light yellow color, add sugar and beat again. Add water and flavoring. Fold in flour and salt, then the stiffly beaten egg whites.

Grease iron before baking each waffle. Bake about 3 minutes. Waffle iron should be only moderately hot.

CHEESE WAFFLES

2 cups flour
2 teaspoons baking powder
1 teaspoon salt
2 tablespoons sugar
1 cup grated Cheddar cheese
2 eggs, separated
1½ cups milk
¼ cup melted butter

Sift dry ingredients and add cheese. Stir in the beaten yolks, milk, and butter. Lastly fold in stiffly beaten whites. Bake in hot waffle iron. Makes 6 waffles.

CORN MEAL WAFFLES

2 cups cake flour
2 cups yellow corn meal
6 teaspoons baking powder
2 teaspoons salt
3 tablespoons sugar
4 eggs, separated
2 cups milk
½ cup melted butter

Sift dry ingredients; beat egg yolks well, add milk and butter. Combine the two mixtures. Fold in stiffly beaten whites. Bake in hot waffle iron. Makes 12 waffles.

WHIPPED CREAM WAFFLES

⅔ cup flour
⅓ cup sugar
1 teaspoon baking powder
⅓ teaspoon salt
2 eggs, separated
1 cup heavy cream, whipped
1 tablespoon melted butter

Sift dry ingredients; beat egg yolks well. Combine egg yolks, whipped cream, and butter. Combine the two mixtures; lastly fold in the stiffly beaten whites. Bake in hot waffle iron. Serve with honey. Makes 6 waffles.

GINGERBREAD WAFFLES

3 eggs
¼ cup sugar
½ cup molasses
1 cup sour milk
1½ cups flour
1 teaspoon ginger
½ teaspoon salt
1 teaspoon soda
1 teaspoon baking powder
⅓ cup melted shortening

Beat eggs until light. Add sugar, molasses, sour milk and remaining dry ingredients sifted together. Stir until smooth, then add shortening. Bake. Serve with butter and confectioners sugar. Makes 6 waffles. For a more spicy waffle, add cinnamon and cloves.

SAUCES FOR PANCAKES AND WAFFLES

For best flavor, heat syrup for pancakes and waffles before serving.

BROWN SUGAR SYRUP

1 cup brown sugar
1 cup white sugar
1 cup water

Bring to a boil, stirring until clear. Serve warm.

MAPLE SYRUP

2 cups maple sugar, broken up
⅔ cup boiling water

Stir until sugar melts, boil until clear. Serve warm.

ORANGE HARD SAUCE

Cream ⅓ cup butter with 1 cup confectioners sugar. Add 2 teaspoons orange juice and ¼ cup finely chopped, candied orange peel.

BROWN SUGAR HARD SAUCE

1 cup brown sugar
3 tablespoons butter

Blend well together, beating with fork.

HONEY BUTTER

To ½ cup honey, strained, add ¼ cup butter. Blend by creaming.

SPICED HONEY BUTTER

To the foregoing recipe, add ½ teaspoon cinnamon.

CURRANT JELLY SAUCE

Combine a 6-ounce glass of currant jelly with ½ cup boiling water. Mix well and heat; add 2 teaspoons finely grated fresh orange rind.

GENERAL RULES FOR DEEP FRYING

Equipment: An electric deep-fat fryer with thermostatic control is the preferred equipment. An electric skillet can serve the same purpose if the foods to be fried are not too large. Lacking an electrically controlled fryer, a deep heavy pan can be used, preferably together with a deep-fat thermometer.

If a thermometer is not available, the temperature of the fat may be tested by the length of time it takes a cube of soft white bread to turn golden brown. Test several cubes at one time. The bread will brown in 30 seconds when the temperature is 375° F., in 35 seconds when the temperature is 350° F.

Deep-Frying Chart

FOODS TO BE DEEP-FRIED	TEMPERATURE	RECOMMENDED TIME
Doughnuts	360°-375° F.	3 minutes
Fritters	375° F.	3-5 minutes
Croquettes	375° F.	2-3 minutes
French-fried		
-potatoes	375° F.	6-8 minutes
-onions	375° F.	2-3 minutes
Chicken	350° F.	10-15 minutes
Fish fillets	375° F.	2-3 minutes
Whole fish	350° F.	5-8 minutes
Shrimp— raw or cooked	350°-375° F.	2-3 minutes
Oysters, clams	350°-375° F.	2-3 minutes

Fat: Vegetable fats or bland vegetable oils are best for deep frying. They heat quickly, are nearly odorless, and do not burn readily, as butter or margarine will do.

Procedure: Put fat or oil in the pan to a depth which would cover the food, but 3 or 4 inches lower than the rim of the pan. Heat to the desired temperature and add the food, which will float in the hot fat. Care should be taken not to lower the temperature of the fat too suddenly by the addition of large amounts of cold food. (If the temperature is too low the food will absorb fat; if it is too high the food will brown too quickly.) When cooked for the required length of time (see chart below or individual recipe) remove food with perforated spoon or frying basket and drain on both sides on paper towelling.

To Clarify and Reuse Fat: Cook a few thick slices of raw potato in the hot fat until brown and well done, discard potato, and strain fat through several thicknesses of muslin or double cheesecloth. Cover and store in a cool place.

DOUGHNUTS

The general rules for deep-frying are to be found opposite, because doughnuts, unlike other foods which are often deep-fried, cannot be cooked by any other method. Croquettes, for example, may be baked; fritters may be sautéed; fish may be cooked in many different ways. Recipes for deep-frying these and other foods will be found throughout the book, but for the cook who is new to this quick and popular method of cooking, the following basic rules can be helpful.

TO FRY DOUGHNUTS

Heat 3 or 4 inches of fat to a temperature of 360° F. to 375° F., the hotter temperature for yeast-raised doughs. Cook a few doughnuts at a time, turning them often until they are evenly browned on both sides. Drain on crumpled paper towels. To coat with sugar, mix sugar and cinnamon or other spices in a paper bag and shake the doughnuts in it, a few at a time.

PLAIN DOUGHNUTS

    2 cups flour
    ½ cup sugar
    1 teaspoon salt
    3 teaspoons baking powder
    ¼ teaspoon cinnamon
    dash of grated nutmeg
    2 tablespoons melted butter
    ½ cup milk
    1 egg, beaten

Sift dry ingredients, add butter. Add the milk to the egg and combine the mixtures. Knead lightly. Roll lightly or pat on well-floured board ¼-inch thick; cut with doughnut cutter and fry as directed above. Drain.

SOUR CREAM DOUGHNUTS

    3 eggs
    1 cup sugar
    1 teaspoon baking soda
    1 cup sour cream
    4 cups flour
    dash of grated nutmeg
    1 teaspoon salt

Beat eggs, add sugar gradually. Add soda to cream. Combine the two mixtures and add the flour, nutmeg and salt. If dough is chilled before being rolled out, reduce flour by ½ cup. Roll ¼-inch thick as above; cut and fry. Dust with confectioners sugar.

BUTTERMILK DOUGHNUTS

    2 eggs
    1¼ cups sugar
    2 tablespoons melted shortening
    1 cup buttermilk
    ½ teaspoon salt
    1 teaspoon grated nutmeg
    1 teaspoon soda
    2 teaspoons baking powder
    about 4 cups flour

Beat eggs, add sugar and shortening; add milk. Mix rest of the dry ingredients, combine the two mixtures. If dough is chilled before being rolled out, reduce flour by ½ cup. Knead slightly, roll ¼-inch thick, cut and fry. Dust with confectioners sugar.

BRAZIL NUT DOUGHNUTS

    3½ cups sifted flour
    4 teaspoons baking powder
    1 teaspoon salt
    ¼ teaspoon nutmeg
    ¼ teaspoon cinnamon
    ¾ cup sliced Brazil nuts
    1 cup sugar
    2 eggs, beaten
    2 tablespoons melted shortening
    1 cup milk

Sift together flour, baking powder, salt and spices. Add nuts. Add sugar gradually to the eggs. Add to the egg mixture the shortening and dry ingredients alternately with the milk, stirring lightly. This is a very soft dough. Add more flour if necessary. Roll ¼-inch thick on floured board. Cut with floured cutter. Fry as directed.

DOUGHNUT DROPS

2 eggs
¼ cup sugar
1 teaspoon salt
2 tablespoons melted shortening
⅛ cup milk
1½ cups flour
4 teaspoons baking powder

Beat eggs until light, add sugar, salt, shortening and milk. Mix flour and baking powder and combine the two mixtures. Drop by tablespoons into deep, hot fat, and fry until browned. Sprinkle with confectioners sugar. Add 1 square melted unsweetened chocolate to mixture for variety.

ORANGE DOUGHNUT DROPS

½ cup sugar
2 eggs, beaten
½ teaspoon salt
2 teaspoons baking powder
2 cups flour
½ cup orange juice
grated rind of 1 orange
½ cup sweet cream

Mix in order given. Drop by teaspoonfuls into deep, hot fat and fry until brown. Dip spoon into hot fat before each spoonful. Sprinkle with confectioners sugar if desired.

KRINGLES

1 egg, beaten
1 tablespoon sugar
1 teaspoon butter
¼ teaspoon salt
1 tablespoon cream
1 teaspoon lemon juice
1 cup flour (about)

Mix butter, salt and sugar with the egg. Add the cream and lemon juice and flour to make a stiff dough. Roll on a floured board very thin, cut in pieces 3 inches long by 2 inches wide. Make four 1-inch gashes crosswise at equal intervals on each piece. Gather up dough by running fork in and out of gashes, lower on fork into deep, hot fat. Fry until light brown, drain and sprinkle with confectioners sugar.

FRIED RIPPLES (HESTERLISTE)

3 eggs, well beaten
5 tablespoons melted butter
1 cup sugar
2 cups milk
2 teaspoons baking powder
8 cups flour

Mix as above. Roll as thin as pie crust. Cut into strips, and slash as in above recipe and fry in deep, hot fat. Sprinkle with sugar. Makes large quantity.

FRENCH CRULLERS (SPRITZ KRAPFEN)

1 tablespoon butter
2 cups water
2 cups flour
4 tablespoons sugar
rind of 1 lemon, grated
4 eggs

Add butter to water and when boiling, add all of the flour and stir vigorously to make a smooth paste. Remove from heat, add sugar and lemon rind and the unbeaten eggs, one at a time, beating constantly between each addition of eggs. Drop by spoonfuls or through Spritz Krapfen or large star-tipped pastry tube into deep, hot fat and fry until brown. Serve with White Wine Sauce, or frost with Confectioners Sugar Glaze.

RYE FRIED CAKES

¾ cup rye meal
¾ cup wheat flour
2 teaspoons baking powder
1 tablespoon sugar
1 teaspoon salt
1 egg
½ cup milk

Mix in order given, drop from tablespoon into deep, hot fat. Fry until cakes are brown and will not stick when pierced with a fork.

Yeast-Raised Doughnuts

Use recipe for Kuchen Dough, page 76. The doughnuts in the following recipes require a slightly higher cooking temperature. See instructions: To Fry Doughnuts, page 99.

RAISED DOUGHNUTS

Make Kuchen Dough, let rise until doubled in bulk, then roll into a thin sheet, and cut into rings. Let stand until nearly doubled in bulk, then fry in deep, hot fat. Drain on paper, and roll in confectioners sugar.

FILLED DOUGHNUTS (BERLINER PFANNKUCHEN)

Make Kuchen Dough. After first rising, roll ½ inch thick, cut into rounds with biscuit cutter. Place a teaspoon of preserves or a stewed prune in the center of ½ of them. Brush edges with white of egg and cover with plain rounds. Press edges to seal. Place on well-floured board, let rise until very light and fry in deep, hot fat, 360° F., turning once, until brown. When done they will have a white strip around center. Sprinkle with confectioners sugar.

RAISED CRULLERS

Make Plain Kuchen Dough. After first rising, roll ½ inch thick. Cut in strips 8 inches long, ¾ inch wide. Put on board; cover and let rise. Twist ends, turning hands in opposite directions. Fry in deep, hot fat.

ROSETTES (SWEDISH WAFERS)

1 egg
1 teaspoon confectioners sugar
¼ teaspoon salt
2 cups milk
2¼ cups flour

Beat egg very slightly, add sugar and salt. Add milk and flour alternately, beating until smooth. Put rosette mold in deep, hot fat; when well-heated remove from fat, dip bottom into batter, never allowing batter to run over the top of mold. Dip into the fat and fry until the rosettes are crisp and brown. Slip rosette off. Wipe iron occasionally to remove extra fat. Drain on unglazed paper. Serve hot or cold. Sprinkle with confectioners sugar, or, put filling or jam or fresh fruit between 2 of the rosettes and garnish with whipped cream, or fill with creamed chicken or salad, or serve plain with any salad. Yield: 60 wafers which will keep for a week or more if stored in air-tight container.

SWEDISH TIMBALE CASES

¾ cup flour
½ teaspoon salt
1 teaspoon sugar
½ cup milk
1 egg, beaten
1 tablespoon olive oil

Mix dry ingredients, add milk and egg gradually, then oil. Heat timbale iron in deep, hot fat. Dip hot iron into batter to ¾ depth of the mold. Then immerse iron in the deep, hot fat again; the mixture will rise to top of iron. When crisp and brown, it may be slipped off easily. If the cases are not crisp, the batter is too thick and must be diluted with milk.

Fill cases with creamed chicken, sweetbreads, fish, oysters or peas.

FRITTERS

Like pancakes and waffles, fruit fritters may be served as main courses at luncheon and supper, or as desserts. Fritters may be sautéed in butter, but they are better deep-fried in hot fat.

TO FRY FRITTERS

Heat fat in a heavy pan to a temperature of 350° to 360° F. Test temperature with a deep-fat thermometer, or by browning a cube of soft white bread in the fat in 35 seconds. Dip prepared fruit in batter, using a fork or slotted skimmer; drain off excess batter. Fry fritters until golden brown; those made with uncooked fruit should take about 5 minutes, with cooked or canned fruit about 4 minutes. Drain on paper towels. Serve hot, sprinkle with confectioners sugar if desired.

FRITTER BATTER

1⅓ cups flour
2 teaspoons baking powder
¼ teaspoon salt
⅔ cup milk
1 egg, well beaten

Mix and sift dry ingredients, gradually add milk and the egg. Fry as above.

RICH FRITTER BATTER

1 egg, separated
1 tablespoon melted butter
⅛ teaspoon salt
¼ cup water or milk
½ cup flour

Beat egg yolk, add the butter and salt and half the liquid, and stir in the flour to make a smooth dough. Add the remainder of liquid gradually to make a batter, and fold in the stiffly beaten egg white. Fry as above.

APPLE FRITTERS

2 large, tart apples
Fritter Batter, above
sugar and cinnamon

Core, pare and cut apples in ⅓-inch slices. Sprinkle with sugar and cinnamon. Dip pieces in Fritter Batter. Fry in deep, hot fat. Serve hot.

PINEAPPLE FRITTERS

Cover slices of fresh pineapple with a little sugar and let stand 1 hour. Or use sliced, canned pineapple, thoroughly drained. Dip prepared slices in Fritter Batter, above, and fry in deep, hot fat. Drain on paper and sprinkle with confectioners sugar.

CHERRY FRITTERS

1 cup flour
½ teaspoon salt
1 teaspoon baking powder
1 egg
1 tablespoon melted butter
⅛ cup milk
¾ cup drained sour cherries
2 tablespoons sugar

Mix dry ingredients. Beat egg, add melted butter. Combine with milk, add to the dry ingredients. Fold in the cherries. Drop by teaspoonfuls into deep, hot fat. Fry 4 or more minutes until browned. Drain and dust with sugar.

Serve with Fruit Juice Sauce made of cherry juice. Add fresh or canned cherries to sauce, if desired.

CRUSHED PINEAPPLE FRITTERS

1 cup flour
1 teaspoon baking powder
¼ teaspoon salt
2 tablespoons sugar
¼ teaspoon nutmeg
¼ teaspoon cinnamon
1 egg, beaten
⅓ cup milk
1 tablespoon melted shortening
1 tablespoon lemon juice
1 cup crushed pineapple, drained

Sift dry ingredients; mix egg and milk and shortening. Stir the liquid into the dry ingredients and beat until smooth. Add the lemon juice and pineapple. Drop by teaspoonfuls into deep, hot fat. Turn when they come to the surface. Fry until brown, remove from fat, drain on unglazed paper. Dust with confectioners sugar.

QUEEN FRITTERS

¼ cup butter
½ cup boiling milk or water
½ cup flour
pinch of salt
2 eggs
fruit preserves
2 tablespoons confectioners sugar

Heat butter and water to boiling point, add flour and salt, and stir until mixture leaves sides of saucepan. Remove from heat, add eggs, one at a time, beating constantly. Drop by spoonfuls in deep fat and fry until well puffed and browned. Drain, make an opening, fill with preserves and sprinkle with confectioners sugar.

FRUIT FRITTERS

Fresh peaches, apricots, oranges or pears may be cut in slices or in larger pieces, dipped in batter and fried as other fritters. Drained canned fruits may also be used.

See Instructions for Deep Frying on page 101.

DUMPLINGS

General Rules

Mix ingredients, following individual recipes, and test by dropping one dumpling into rapidly boiling, salted water. If it does not hold together, more flour must be added, just enough so that dumplings will keep their shape. Cook by dropping into a large kettle of rapidly boiling, salted water (one teaspoon salt to each quart of water), and boil until they rise to the top. Cover closely, and simmer gently a few minutes longer, or until inside is thoroughly cooked. Test one by pulling apart with 2 forks; when dry and spongy inside, the dumplings are done.

TO COOK DUMPLINGS IN STEW

15 minutes before serving, drop dumplings by spoonful into simmering stew, cover, and cook recommended number of minutes without lifting lid. Test for doneness.

GARNISHES FOR DUMPLINGS

Onions, cut fine and fried in butter; cracker or dry gingerbread crumbs; grated Cheddar cheese or cottage cheese with salt and pepper; or chopped walnuts.

PLAIN DUMPLINGS (SPATZEN)

1 egg
1 teaspoon salt
½ cup water or milk
1½ cups flour

Beat egg well, add salt and water and stir into flour to make a smooth batter. Test for right amount of flour (see General Rules, above). Drop by spoonfuls into large kettle of boiling, salted water, cover closely, and cook 10 minutes without lifting cover. Test for doneness. Drain in colander. Serve with melted butter or meat gravy.

BAKING POWDER DUMPLINGS

2 cups flour
4 teaspoons baking powder
½ teaspoon salt
1 scant cup milk or water

Mix the dry ingredients, stir in the milk or water gradually to make a soft dough. Drop by spoonful into boiling salted water or simmering stew. Cover tightly, cook 10 to 15 minutes before lifting cover. Test for doneness. Drain. Serve at once.

YEAST DUMPLINGS

½ package active dry yeast
1 cup warm water
2 cups flour
1 teaspoon sugar
2 eggs, beaten
1 teaspoon salt

Crumble yeast in warm water; add to the rest of the ingredients, knead well to a smooth dough and set aside in a warm place to rise. When light, turn out on floured board and mold into large, round dumplings. Cover with a cloth and let rise in a warm place again. Drop dumplings carefully into salted, boiling water (1 teaspoon salt to 1 quart water), and boil 10 to 20 minutes, in a closely covered kettle until they test done.

Remove each dumpling separately with a perforated skimmer; place on large, warm platter and serve covered with browned butter and sugar or any stewed fruit.

BREAD DUMPLINGS

2 tablespoons shortening
1 tablespoon chopped onion
2 cups white bread, soaked
1 teaspoon salt
2 eggs, beaten
½ cup cracker crumbs
1 teaspoon chopped parsley
paprika, nutmeg, and ginger

Heat fat, add onion; when just beginning to brown add bread, squeezed dry, and salt, stirring occasionally until fat is absorbed. Cool. Add eggs and cracker crumbs, parsley and seasonings. Mix well and form into small balls. Drop into salted boiling water or soup and simmer 10 to 15 minutes, or until done.

SPONGE DUMPLINGS

½ cup butter
1 cup flour
1 cup milk
4 eggs, separated
1 teaspoon salt
½ teaspoon nutmeg
1 tablespoon dry farina

Melt half of butter, mix well with the flour. Heat milk and while hot, stir butter and flour mixture into it gradually to a smooth paste that cleans the bottom of pan; put paste aside to cool. Cream remaining butter, add the egg yolks one at a time, the seasoning, then the paste. Blend well, add farina, and fold in the egg whites, beaten stiff. Drop from teaspoon into salted, boiling water. Cook 8 minutes or until done. Drain and garnish with bread crumbs and butter.

CRACKER DUMPLINGS

6 tablespoons fat or butter
3 eggs, beaten
¾ to 1 cup fine cracker crumbs or matzo meal
1½ teaspoons salt
nutmeg or other flavoring

Cream the fat or butter, add eggs, salt, crumbs, and nutmeg, onion juice or any other flavoring. Mix and shape into small balls. Drop into salted boiling water, simmer for 10 to 15 minutes or until done. Drain, serve with butter or gravy.

POTATO DUMPLINGS

3½ cups boiled, riced potatoes
2 eggs
1½ teaspoons salt
1 cup flour, or ½ cup flour and ½ cup cracker meal
grated nutmeg, optional

Cool potatoes. Add the eggs, salt, flour and seasoning. Mix and knead lightly until smooth. Try boiling 1 dumpling and if it falls apart, add more flour. Shape into 1 long, thick roll; cut in small pieces, and roll each piece into a dumpling. Cook in rapidly boiling, salted water until they rise to the top, then simmer a few minutes longer until cooked through to center. Drain, pour browned butter over them.

POTATO DUMPLINGS WITH CROUTONS

Add ½ cup croutons to Boiled Potato Dumplings, above, mixing well through the dough. Roll into egg-shaped balls. Cook as directed.

FARINA POTATO DUMPLINGS

Add ½ cup farina, and reduce flour to 1 scant cup in Boiled Potato Dumplings, above.

MATZO MEAL POTATO DUMPLINGS

Use ¾ cup matzo meal in place of flour in Boiled Potato Dumplings, above.

RAW POTATO DUMPLINGS

½ cup grated raw potatoes
2 tablespoons fat or butter
1 tablespoon onion, chopped
3½ cups boiled potatoes, riced and cooled
½ tablespoon salt
2 eggs, lightly beaten
¾ cup flour or ½ cup matzo meal

Drain raw potatoes well. Heat fat or butter in frying pan, add onion; when golden brown, add drained raw potato. Cook until it forms a paste; cool, add riced potatoes, salt, eggs and flour. Stir until smooth. Roll into balls or drop from teaspoon into boiling, salted water. Cook like Boiled Potato Dumplings, page 103.

LIVER BALLS

½ pound butter
4 unbeaten eggs
¾ pound calf's, steer or chicken liver, ground
1 tablespoon salt
few grains of pepper
few grains of nutmeg
2 tablespoons minced parsley
2¼ cups hard, dry bread crumbs

Cream butter well, add eggs one at a time, the liver, seasoning and bread crumbs. Mix thoroughly. Form into small balls for soup, larger balls for dumplings. Drop into boiling soup or salted water. Cook 10 to 20 minutes, depending on size. Test for doneness. Serve in soup or drained with any desired sauce.

LIVER DUMPLINGS

½ pound calf's liver or chicken livers
1 cup cracker or bread crumbs
1 cup milk or water
1 egg
1 teaspoon salt
½ teaspoon grated onion
⅛ teaspoon pepper
grated lemon rind

Skin the liver and remove tough fiber. Chop fine. Cook crumbs and water to a paste. Remove from heat, add egg, liver and seasonings and shape into small balls. Drop into boiling soup 10 minutes before serving. Test for doneness. The cooked heart and tender parts of gizzard of chicken may also be used either with or to replace liver.

MATZOS DUMPLINGS (MATZOS KLOESE)

6 matzos
2 tablespoons chicken or goose fat
½ onion
3 eggs
about ½ cup matzo meal
½ teaspoon chopped parsley
salt, pepper
nutmeg
1 onion

Soak the matzos in water and squeeze dry. Heat fat in a skillet, add ½ onion, cut very fine, and fry a golden brown; add the soaked matzos, stirring occasionally so that mixture will not stick to the pan. Cool, season, add the eggs and the matzo meal. Let stand 1 hour, shape into balls.

Drop in salted, boiling water and cook 15 minutes; drain and fry brown in hot fat or butter with 1 onion, cut fine and browned.

FILLED MATZOS DUMPLINGS

Make Matzos Dumplings mixture above. Stuff each dumpling with a cooked, pitted prune, roll until round. Drop in salted, boiling water (1 teaspoon salt to 1 quart water), cook 10 to 15 minutes. Heat fat, add an onion, cut fine, brown, and pour over the boiled dumplings.

PLUM OR APRICOT DUMPLINGS

Follow recipe for Yeast Dumplings or Potato Dumplings, both above. When dough is smooth, pat into flat, round cakes, about 2½ inches in diameter. In each, place a sweet, blue freestone plum, the pit removed, or a pitted apricot, with the space filled with sugar and cinnamon. Fold dough over and roll into a round dumpling. Cook, closely covered, in boiling, salted water for 10 minutes. Test for doneness. Drain. Serve with sugar, cinnamon, and melted butter.

5
CAKES AND SMALL CAKES

BUTTER CAKES · SPONGE CAKES · CAKE ROLLS · PASSOVER CAKES
· TORTEN · ICEBOX CAKES · PETIT FOURS · ECLAIRS · CUPCAKES

GENERAL RULES

All ingredients should be at room temperature for best results. Before starting to bake, assemble all materials. Use a round-bottom mixing bowl large enough to hold all ingredients for the final beating and folding. All measurements are level.

Flour: All purpose flour is meant unless cake flour is specified. If cake flour is called for, all-purpose flour may be used if 2 tablespoons are removed from each cup of flour and 1½ tablespoons of cornstarch are substituted.

Baking Powder: One teaspoon "double-acting" baking powder equals 1½ teaspoons of tartrate baking powder.

Chocolate should be melted over hot water. Where chocolate is called for, always use unsweetened baking chocolate unless "sweet chocolate" is mentioned.

Brown sugar must always be measured by packing solidly. To keep brown sugar soft, store in a closed container with bread or in refrigerator.

To Mix Cakes

Cakes are mixed by stirring, beating, and cutting or folding.

TO STIR

Let the spoon touch the sides and bottom of the bowl and move it round and round quickly.

TO BEAT

Tip the bowl to one side. Bring wire whisk, spoon or fork quickly into the mixture and through it and turn it over and over, scraping the sides well each time it goes in. Beat hard and quickly, taking long strokes, folding in as much air as possible. Or use rotary or electric beater.

TO CUT OR FOLD

To combine mixtures lightly, cut down through the base batter with a rubber spatula or side of a spoon. Fold it by lifting the mixture up from the bottom of the bowl and over the top of the batter. Turn bowl slightly after each stroke, folding as lightly as possible until blended.

TO CREAM BUTTER

Take butter or other shortening from refrigerator, let stand at room temperature until soft. With spoon, rub or work against sides of bowl until light and smooth.

TO ADD SUGAR

Add sugar gradually to creamed butter, stirring well until light and fluffy.

Adding Ingredients

WHOLE EGGS

Drop into butter-sugar mixture one at a time and beat until well blended.

YOLKS

Beat with rotary beater until thick and lemon-colored. Pour into butter-sugar mixture, stirring until smooth.

TO BEAT WHITES

Use a rotary beater or wire whisk and beat in mixing bowl until whites stand up in peaks but are still shiny. Do not overbeat.

DRY INGREDIENTS

Sift flour and sugar once before measuring. Add baking powder, baking soda, spices or cocoa if quantity is small, and sift again. Dry ingredients must be *dry*. Do not wash nuts or raisins. Blanch almonds day before using and dry in oven. Nuts and raisins should be sprinkled with flour and added last.

MILK OR OTHER LIQUIDS

Should be added a little at a time, alternately with the dry ingredients, and mixed only until blended.

Important Notes

METHOD

Flour and milk are added alternately to butter mixture, beginning and ending with the flour which must be thoroughly incorporated. Then fold in beaten egg whites gently, until no whites show.

WITH ELECTRIC BEATER

Cream butter and sugar together at medium speed. Add whole eggs or egg yolks, one at a time, still beating at medium speed. High speed may be used to beat this mixture until light and fluffy. Add flour and milk alternately, in small amounts, combining at lowest beating speed and mixing only until blended. Overbeating after flour is added makes cakes dry, coarse, and prevents rising. Beat about ½ time required for hand beating. Scrape sides of bowl often with rubber spatula. *Fold in stiffly beaten egg whites by hand.*

TO PREPARE PANS FOR BAKING

Rub pan with shortening. Sprinkle lightly with flour, and shake pan to coat lightly, then tap upsidedown to shake out excess flour. For some cakes, pans should be lined with a round of paper or aluminum foil, cut to fit the bottom of the pan. For cakes containing large amounts of fruit, the sides of the pan may be lined, also. Angel food cakes and sponge cakes are baked in ungreased pans.

TO FILL CAKE PANS

Fill cake pans ⅔ full. For tube pans, bring batter well along edges and tube, leaving a slight depression in center. Level sponge and angel food cakes with a spatula; butter cakes may be leveled by gently shaking the pan.

TO REMOVE CAKE FROM PANS

When done, remove from oven, let stand 10 minutes. Loosen sides and invert on wire cake rack so air can circulate under cake. Remove cake from pan and let stand until cool. Angel food and sponge cake should be inverted in pan and allowed to hang on inverted funnel until cool. This stretches the cake and prevents settling.

CAKE RECIPE ADJUSTMENT GUIDE FOR HIGH ALTITUDES

NOTE: When two amounts are given, the smaller adjustment should be tried first; then if recipe still needs adjustment, the larger amount should be used the next time.

ADJUSTMENT	3000 FEET	5000 FEET	7000 FEET
BAKING POWDER: reduce for each teaspoon in recipe	Less ⅛ teaspoon	Less ⅛ to ¼ teaspoon	Less ¼ teaspoon
SUGAR: Decrease for each cup in recipe	Less 0 to 1 tablespoon	Less 0 to 2 tablespoons	Less 1 to 3 tablespoons
LIQUID: Increase for each cup in recipe	Add 1 to 2 tablespoons	Add 2 to 4 tablespoons	Add 3 to 4 tablespoons

Baking

Accurate baking temperatures are important for success. Many ovens have an automatic thermostat to regulate heat. For ovens lacking automatic controls, an inexpensive oven thermometer can be very useful. Some recipes give only a descriptive term, rather than the exact temperature; the equivalents of these are as follows:

Description	Temperature
very slow	250°
slow	300°
moderately slow	325°
moderate	350°
moderately hot	375°
hot	400°
very hot	450°
extremely hot	500°

Always preheat oven to indicated temperature **before** placing cake in oven. If baking in glass, bake at 15° F. lower temperature than indicated in recipe.

Place cake in center of middle shelf, for an even heat. Do not move or jar. Crowding the oven and allowing the pans to touch oven walls interferes with heat distribution and causes burning or uneven baking.

TEST FOR DONENESS

Cake is done when it rises and is brown, shrinks

from the sides of the pan, and springs back when lightly pressed with a finger, or when a wire cake tester or a toothpick inserted in the center comes out dry.

BUTTER CAKES

QUICK ONE-EGG CAKE

¾ cup sugar
1½ cups sifted flour
¼ teaspoon salt
2 teaspoons baking powder
¼ cup melted shortening
1 egg, beaten
¾ cup milk
1 teaspoon flavoring

Preheat oven to 375° F., a moderately hot oven. Sift dry ingredients into mixing bowl. Drop egg into shortening, add milk and flavoring. Combine the two mixtures. Blend. Pour into greased and floured 9-inch round pan, bake about 20 minutes. Frost. Or bake in shallow 9-inch square pan. Frost and mark into squares.

QUICK TWO-EGG CAKE

1¾ cups flour
1 tablespoon baking powder
½ cup softened butter
1 cup sugar
2 eggs
½ cup and 1 tablespoon milk
¼ teaspoon salt
1 teaspoon vanilla

Preheat oven to 375° F., a moderately hot oven. Sift flour and baking powder, add remaining ingredients and beat until light and smooth. Bake in two greased 8-inch layer pans for 20 minutes.

QUICK ONE-BOWL DATE CAKE

⅓ cup soft butter
1⅓ cups brown sugar
2 eggs
½ cup milk
1¾ cups flour
3 teaspoons baking powder
½ teaspoon cinnamon
½ teaspoon grated nutmeg
½ pound dates, figs or raisins, finely chopped

Preheat oven to 325° F., a moderately slow oven. Combine all ingredients in a bowl. Beat thoroughly for 3 or 4 minutes. Bake in 9-inch pan lined with waxed paper, 35 to 40 minutes.

Leftover cake crumbs may be used as topping on coffee cake, or used to thicken fruit pies.

ECONOMY CAKE

2 to 4 tablespoons butter
1 cup sugar
1 egg
¾ cup water or milk
2 cups flour
3 teaspoons baking powder
½ teaspoon vanilla or grated rind of ½ lemon

Preheat oven to 350° F., a moderate oven. Cream the butter, add the sugar gradually, then the egg, and beat well. Add the liquid alternately with the flour and baking powder sifted together 3 times. Add flavoring. Beat thoroughly and bake in greased and floured 9-inch square pan or two 8-inch layer pans, about 25 minutes. Fill or frost as desired.

GOLD CAKE

½ cup butter
1 cup sugar
4 egg yolks
1 teaspoon vanilla
½ cup milk
2 cups cake flour
3 teaspoons baking powder

Preheat oven to 350° F., a moderate oven. Cream butter well, add sugar, continue beating, add yolks beaten light, vanilla, mix thoroughly, then add milk alternately with the flour and baking powder mixed. Beat, place in greased and floured 9-inch square pan or two 8-inch layers. Bake 35 to 45 minutes.

MARBLE CAKE

¾ cup butter
2 cups sugar
4 eggs
3 cups cake flour
4 teaspoons baking powder
1 cup milk
¼ pound unsweetened chocolate, grated
1 teaspoon cinnamon
½ teaspoon ground cloves
½ teaspoon vanilla

Preheat oven to 350° F., a moderate oven. Cream butter, add sugar and stir well, add eggs, one at a time, beating constantly, then add the flour (mixed with the baking powder) and the milk alternately and stir until smooth. Put ⅓ of the dough in another bowl, mixing well with chocolate, spices and flavoring.

Into a greased and floured 9-inch tube pan, place alternate layers of white and dark dough. Bake 45 minutes.

POUND CAKE

1 pound cake flour
1 pound butter
1 pound sugar
1 pound eggs in shell (9 or 10 eggs)
2 tablespoons vanilla or brandy

Preheat oven to 300° F., a slow oven. Sift flour, weigh it, and sift again. Cream butter well, add sugar gradually and cream until light and fluffy. Add eggs, two at a time, and beat well after each addition. Add flavoring. Add flour gradually and beat until smooth. Line three bread loaf pans with waxed paper. Pour mixture into pans and bake about 1 hour and 15 minutes.

SAND TORTE

1 cup butter
1 cup sugar
6 eggs, separated
1 cup flour
1 cup cornstarch
2 teaspoons baking powder
½ lemon, juice and rind
1½ tablespoons rum or brandy

Preheat oven to 350° F., a moderate oven. Cream butter and sugar very well, add beaten yolks. Sift flour, cornstarch and baking powder; add to the mixture with the lemon juice and flavorings; fold the stiffly beaten whites well into the batter. Bake in a greased and floured 9-inch tube pan for 45 minutes.

BUTTERMILK CAKE

2 cups cake flour
⅔ teaspoon salt
2 teaspoons baking powder
⅔ teaspoon soda
1 cup buttermilk
½ cup shortening
1¼ cups sugar
2 eggs, separated
1½ teaspoons vanilla

Preheat oven to 350° F., a moderate oven. Sift flour. Add salt and baking powder and sift again. Add soda to buttermilk and allow to stand while cake is being mixed. Cream shortening, add sugar and beat until fluffy. Add yolks, well beaten, and vanilla. Add the flour mixture alternately with the buttermilk, continue beating. Fold in the stiffly beaten egg whites. Pour into two greased and floured 9-inch layer cake pans. Bake about 30 minutes. Frost with Caramel Frosting.

White Cakes

White Cakes are butter cakes using only the egg whites; they differ from whole-egg cakes not only in color, but also in texture; they are less rich and tend to be fluffy rather than moist and firm.

QUICK ONE-BOWL WHITE CAKE

½ cup butter, softened
1 cup sugar
2 egg whites, unbeaten
¾ cup milk
1½ cups cake flour
2 teaspoons baking powder
1 teaspoon vanilla
⅛ teaspoon salt

Preheat oven to 350° F., a moderate oven. Put all ingredients in a bowl and beat vigorously for several minutes until perfectly smooth. Bake in two greased and floured 8-inch layer pans for ½ hour. Fill and frost with Sour Cream Caramel Frosting.

WHITE CAKE

½ cup butter
1 cup sugar
2 cups cake flour
3 teaspoons baking powder
⅔ cup milk
½ teaspoon almond extract
grated rind of 1 lemon
3 egg whites

Preheat oven to 350° F., a moderate oven. Cream butter, add sugar and continue beating. Sift flour once, measure, sift with baking powder 3 times, add to the butter mixture, alternately with the milk, beat thoroughly until smooth, add flavoring. Carefully fold in the egg whites, beaten stiff but not dry. Butter and flour a 12 x 8-inch pan. Put the batter into the pan and bake about 1 hour. Or bake in two greased and floured 9-inch layer pans at 375° F., 25 to 30 minutes.

Cake Frostings and Fillings will be found on pages 142 to 150.

Any type of cake may be frozen. It is best to freeze cakes BEFORE filling and frosting. For general directions on wrapping and freezing baked goods, see chapter 24.

SILVER CAKE

3 cups cake flour
3½ teaspoons baking powder
½ cup butter
½ cup milk and ½ cup water, mixed
1½ cups sugar
½ teaspoon vanilla extract
4 egg whites, stiffly beaten

Preheat oven to 375° F., a moderately hot oven. Sift flour once, measure; add baking powder and sift together 3 times; cut butter into small pieces and blend with flour with pastry blender; add milk and water mixture, sugar and flavoring and beat until smooth. Fold in egg whites and bake in greased and floured 9 by 13-inch pan from 25 to 30 minutes. Spread with Quick Caramel Frosting, or cover with whipped cream and coconut.

FLUFFY CAKE

    2½ cups sifted cake flour
    3 teaspoons baking powder
    ¼ teaspoon cream of tartar
    ½ cup butter or other shortening
    1½ cups sugar
    ½ cup milk or orange juice
    1 teaspoon vanilla
    6 egg whites, stiffly beaten

Preheat oven to 375° F., a moderately hot oven. Sift flour once, measure, add baking powder and cream of tartar and sift 3 times. Cream butter thoroughly, add sugar gradually, creaming together until light and fluffy. Add flour mixture alternately with milk or orange juice, a small amount at a time, beginning and ending with the flour. Beat after each addition until smooth. Add vanilla; fold in egg whites. Bake in two greased 9-inch layer pans for 30 minutes. Put layers together with Nut and Fruit Meringue Filling; cover top and sides with Four-Minute Frosting.

LADY BALTIMORE CAKE

Bake White Cake in two layers. Fill with Nut and Fruit Meringue Filling. Frost with Meringue Frosting.

COCONUT LAYER CAKE

Bake White Cake in two layers. Spread Seven-Minute Frosting between layers and over top; sprinkle generously with grated coconut.

DELICATE COCONUT CAKE

    1 cup sugar
    ¼ cup butter
    ½ teaspoon almond flavoring
    ½ teaspoon lemon flavoring
    ½ teaspoon salt
    2 cups cake flour
    3 teaspoons baking powder
    ⅔ cup milk
    3 egg whites
    ½ cup coconut

Preheat oven to 350° F., a moderate oven. Cream together the sugar and butter and add the flavoring. Sift together the dry ingredients and add

them alternately with the milk to the first mixture. Fold in the egg whites, beaten stiff; add the coconut. Stir well. Place in a greased and floured 9½-by 12-inch pan; sprinkle with additional shredded coconut and a few chopped almonds, if desired, and bake for 45 minutes.

Chocolate Cakes

QUICK ONE-BOWL COCOA CAKE

    6 tablespoons cocoa
    2 cups flour
    1½ cups sugar
    1 teaspoon soda
    1 teaspoon baking powder
    ⅛ teaspoon salt
    2 eggs
    ¾ cup butter, melted
    1 cup cold water

Preheat oven to 350° F., a moderate oven. Sift first six ingredients into mixing bowl. Add the rest all at once. Beat well. Bake in two greased and floured 8-inch layer pans for 40 minutes. Use Chocolate Butter Frosting or Mocha Icing between layers and on top.

COCOA CAKE

    ¾ cup cocoa
    ¾ cup sugar
    1 egg yolk
    ½ cup milk

Cook until thick, then cool. Reserve the egg white for the following:

    ½ cup butter
    1 cup sugar
    1 whole egg
    1 egg yolk
    2 cups flour
    1 teaspoon baking powder
    1 cup sour cream
    1 teaspoon baking soda
    1 teaspoon vanilla
    2 egg whites

Preheat oven to 350° F., a moderate oven. Cream butter and sugar well. Add 1 whole egg and 1 yolk. Mix thoroughly. Sift flour, measure and sift three times with baking powder. Add flour gradually, alternating with sour cream well mixed with the soda. Add cocoa mixture. Stir well, add vanilla, then fold in the 2 stiffly beaten egg whites. Bake 20 to 30 minutes in two well-greased and floured 9-inch layer pans. Fill and frost with Chocolate Butter Cream Frosting.

ECONOMY COCOA CAKE

1 cup sugar
2 tablespoons butter
3 tablespoons cocoa
1 egg
2 cups flour, scant
½ teaspoon baking powder
1 cup sour milk
1 teaspoon baking soda

Preheat oven to 350° F., a moderate oven. Cream butter and sugar with the cocoa, add the egg; add flour mixed with baking powder, alternately, with the milk mixed with the baking soda. Bake in two greased and floured 9-inch layer pans for 25 minutes. Put Chocolate Butter Frosting between layers and on top.

CHOCOLATE CAKE

2 cups cake flour
2 cups sugar
⅛ teaspoon salt
½ cup butter
1¼ cups water
4 squares unsweetened chocolate
3 eggs
1 teaspoon vanilla
2 teaspoons baking powder

Preheat oven to 325° F., a moderately slow oven. Sift flour, sugar and salt, add butter, mixing with finger tips or pastry blender to the consistency of corn meal. Boil water and chocolate. Cool and add to butter mixture. Beat very well. Chill thoroughly. Add eggs, well beaten, vanilla and lastly the baking powder. Bake in two well-greased and floured 9-inch layer pans from 35 to 40 minutes. Fill and frost with Chocolate Butter Frosting.

QUICK CHOCOLATE CAKE (SPANISH BUN)

2 squares unsweetened chocolate
½ cup butter
1 cup sugar
½ cup milk
2 eggs
1 teaspoon vanilla
¾ cup flour
2 teaspoons baking powder
1 teaspoon cinnamon
¼ teaspoon ground cloves

Preheat oven to 375° F., a moderately hot oven. Melt chocolate and butter over hot water, put in mixing bowl. Add sugar, milk, eggs, vanilla, flour sifted with the baking powder and spices. Do not stir until all ingredients are in, then beat hard for several minutes until smooth. Bake in two greased and floured 9-inch layer pans from 15 to 20 minutes. Fill and frost with Chocolate Caramel Filling. If desired, cinnamon and cloves may be omitted.

DEVIL'S FOOD CAKE

1 cup sugar
½ cup milk
4 squares unsweetened chocolate
1 egg yolk, beaten
1 teaspoon vanilla
½ cup butter
1 cup sugar
2 whole eggs
2 cups flour
2 teaspoons baking powder
½ cup milk

Preheat oven to 350° F., a moderate oven. Cook first three ingredients in double boiler until melted. Pour gradually onto egg yolk and cook until it coats the spoon. Cool, add vanilla. Cream butter and sugar, add whole eggs, one at a time, flour sifted with baking powder, and milk alternately. Mix well with chocolate mixture and bake in two well-greased and floured 9-inch pans for 25 minutes. Fill and frost with Chocolate Butter Frosting.

OLD-FASHIONED DEVIL'S FOOD CAKE

2 squares unsweetened chocolate
3 tablespoons water
1¼ cups sugar
½ cup butter
1 cup sour milk or buttermilk
1 teaspoon baking soda
1 egg yolk
2 scant cups flour

Preheat oven to 350° F., a moderate oven. Melt the chocolate, water and sugar in double boiler; when dissolved add the butter. Stir well. Set aside to cool. Mix buttermilk, baking soda and beaten yolk, add the melted chocolate mixture and then the flour. Bake in two well-greased and floured 9-inch layer pans for 25 minutes. Frost as desired.

MOCHA DEVIL'S FOOD CAKE

¼ cup butter
1 cup sugar
2 eggs, well beaten
1½ cups flour
1½ teaspoons baking powder
½ teaspoon salt
½ cup thick, sour milk
½ cup boiling coffee
2 squares unsweetened chocolate, melted, or
    4 tablespoons cocoa
1 teaspoon soda
1 teaspoon vanilla

Preheat oven to 350° F., a moderate oven. Cream butter, add sugar gradually, beat until very light. Add eggs. Beat thoroughly. Add flour mixed with baking powder and salt, alternately with the sour milk, a small amount at a time. Pour boiling coffee over melted chocolate or cocoa and mix quickly. To this add the soda and stir until cool. Then add to cake batter. Add vanilla and mix thoroughly. Bake in two well-greased and floured 9-inch layer cake pans for about 25 minutes. Fill and frost with Chocolate or Marshmallow Frosting.

FUDGE CAKE

    1¾ cups cake flour
    1 teaspoon baking powder
    1 teaspoon soda
    1 teaspoon salt
    ½ cup butter
    1½ cups sugar
    2 eggs
    2½ tablespoons vinegar
    1 cup milk
    3 squares unsweetened chocolate, melted

Preheat oven to 350° F., a moderate oven. Sift flour, baking powder, soda and salt. Cream butter, add sugar gradually and continue creaming. Add eggs one at a time and beat until fluffy. Add vinegar. Add the flour mixture alternately with the milk, and last the melted chocolate. Bake in two well-greased and floured 9-inch layer pans, for about 45 minutes. Fill and frost with Fluffy Chocolate Frosting.

RED CAKE

    ½ cup shortening
    1½ cups sugar
    2 eggs
    2 ounces red food coloring
    2 tablespoons cocoa
    1 teaspoon salt
    1 cup buttermilk
    2¼ cups cake flour
    1 teaspoon vanilla
    1 tablespoon vinegar
    1 teaspoon baking soda

Preheat oven to 350° F., a moderate oven. Cream shortening, sugar and eggs. Combine coloring and cocoa, mixing well. Add cocoa mixture to creamed shortening. Add salt, buttermilk, flour and vanilla, beating constantly. Mix vinegar and baking soda. Stir, *do not beat*, the vinegar mixture into the batter. Bake in two 9-inch greased and floured cake pans for 30 to 35 minutes. Cool. When the cake is thoroughly cool, cut each layer in half to form 4 thin layers. Put the following filling between the layers and on top of the cake.

FILLING

    5 tablespoons flour
    1 cup milk
    1 cup granulated sugar
    1 cup vegetable shortening
    1 teaspoon vanilla

Cook flour and milk until thick; set aside until cold. Cream sugar and shortening with vanilla until fluffy. Add to the flour mixture and stir, do not beat, until mixed.

Cakes with Fruit, Nuts, Spice

ALMOND OR FILBERT CAKE

    1 cup sugar
    ½ cup butter
    ½ cup milk
    1 teaspoon lemon or vanilla extract
    2 eggs, separated
    1½ cups flour
    ½ teaspoon baking powder
    ½ teaspoon cream of tartar
    1 teaspoon salt
    ¼ cup finely ground nuts
    ½ teaspoon soda dissolved in
        2 teaspoons water

Preheat oven to 350° F., a moderate oven. Cream butter and sugar well. Add milk and flavoring to well-beaten yolks. Sift dry ingredients. Add egg and flour mixture alternately to the creamed mixture. Add nuts, then the soda, stirring well. Fold in stiffly beaten egg whites. Bake in buttered and floured 8-inch square pan about 50 minutes. Frost with 1½ cups confectioners sugar creamed with 1 tablespoon butter, 1 teaspoon vanilla and 2 tablespoons strong black coffee.

APPLESAUCE CAKE

    ½ cup butter
    1 cup sugar
    1 egg
    1 teaspoon vanilla
    1 cup dates (sliced fine)
    1½ cups applesauce
    1 cup nuts, chopped coarse
    1 cup raisins, chopped
    ½ teaspoon cinnamon
    ¼ teaspoon ground cloves
    2 cups flour
    2 teaspoons soda

Preheat oven to 350° F., a moderate oven. Cream butter and sugar, add egg, well beaten, and the vanilla; add the rest of the ingredients; blend. Bake in a well-buttered loaf pan, for 1 hour.

BANANA CAKE

½ cup butter
1¼ cups sugar
2 eggs
1 teaspoon soda
4 tablespoons sour cream
1 cup banana pulp, mashed
1½ cups cake flour
¼ teaspoon salt
1 teaspoon vanilla

Preheat oven to 350° F., a moderate oven. Cream butter and sugar, add eggs, very lightly beaten, and the soda, dissolved in the sour cream. Beat well; then add the bananas, flour, salt and vanilla. Mix well. Bake in well-greased and floured 8-inch square or 9-inch tube pan for 35 to 45 minutes. Frost with Lemon Butter Frosting or Coffee Frosting.

BROWN SUGAR LOAF CAKE

½ cup butter
2 cups light brown sugar
4 egg yolks
1 egg white
½ teaspoon baking soda or 3 teaspoons baking powder
1 cup milk, sweet or sour
¾ cup chopped walnuts
2⅔ cups cake flour
salt
1 teaspoon cinnamon
½ teaspoon ground cloves
1 teaspoon vanilla

Preheat oven to 350° F., a moderate oven. Cream the butter and the sugar. Add the yolks one at a time, then the egg white. Beat well. *Use baking soda with sour milk or baking powder with sweet milk.* Sprinkle nuts with some of the flour, add a little salt. Mix the rest of the dry ingredients. Add alternately with the milk. Fold in nuts and vanilla last. If dough is too thick, add 2 tablespoons water. Bake in greased loaf pan 45 minutes.

Cake Frosting and Fillings will be found on pages 142 to 150.

CHERRY UPSIDE-DOWN CAKE

½ cup butter
1⅛ cups sugar
1 teaspoon vanilla
2 cups cake flour
¼ teaspoon salt
2 teaspoons baking powder
⅔ cup water
3 egg whites

Preheat oven to moderate temperature, 350° F. Cream butter and sugar, add vanilla. Sift flour with salt and 1½ teaspoons baking powder and add alternately with the water to the butter mixture, beating well after each addition. Beat the remaining baking powder with the egg whites until stiff. Fold whites into mixture. Divide batter into two greased and floured 9-inch layer pans.

SAUCE

1 can (1 pound, 4 ounces) pitted sour cherries
1 cup sugar
1 teaspoon red food coloring

Drain cherries well. Measure ¾ cup of juice. Add water if needed to make up the difference. Combine juice, cherries, sugar and coloring. Heat to the boiling point. Pour hot cherry sauce over cake batter.

Bake for 35 minutes. Cool for 3 minutes. Turn upside down. Place layers using sauce as both filling and topping. Serve with whipped cream.

DATE AND WALNUT LAYER CAKE

¾ pound dates
1 cup hot water
2 tablespoons butter
1 cup sugar
1 egg
¼ teaspoon salt
1½ cups flour
1 teaspoon soda
½ pound walnut meats, chopped

Preheat oven to 350° F., a moderate oven. Stone dates and chop. Soak in hot water; cool. Cream butter and sugar, add egg and salt. Add date mixture and stir; sift flour and soda, add walnuts. Mix all together, beat well. Bake in two well-greased and floured 9-inch layer pans for 40 minutes. Serve with sweetened whipped cream.

DATE CAKE

¾ pound dates
1 cup hot water
½ cup butter
1 cup sugar
2 eggs
¼ teaspoon salt
1½ cups flour
1 teaspoon baking soda

Follow directions for Date and Walnut Layer Cake, above.

To freshen stale cake, sprinkle with water or wine, enclose in brown paper bag and heat in moderate oven. Or cover cake with applesauce or another fruit mixture and heat in moderate oven. Serve warm as fruit pudding.

DATE AND WALNUT LOAF CAKE

    1 pound stoned dates
    1 pound English walnut meats
    1 cup cake flour
    ½ teaspoon salt
    4 teaspoons baking powder
    1 cup granulated sugar
    4 eggs, separated
    1 teaspoon vanilla

Preheat oven to 325° F., a moderately slow oven. Leave dates and nuts whole; place in mixing bowl, sift the flour, salt, and baking powder over them. Mix carefully, add sugar and mix again. Beat yolks until light and thick, add vanilla and stir into dry ingredients. Fold in the stiffly beaten whites until well blended. Bake in a shallow loaf pan lined with buttered paper, for 1 hour.

For best results in making cakes:

- *Assemble all ingredients beforehand.*
- *Preheat oven to desired temperature.*
- *Read the General Rules on pages 105-107.*

GINGERBREAD

    ½ cup currants
    3 cups flour
    2 teaspoons baking soda
    1 cup sour or buttermilk
    1 cup molasses
    2 teaspoons ginger
    1 teaspoon spices (cinnamon and clove)
    ½ cup butter
    1 cup sugar
    1 egg

Preheat oven to a moderate temperature, 350° F. Roll the currants in ½ cup of the flour. Mix baking soda and milk and add to molasses. Sift remaining dry ingredients except sugar. Cream butter and sugar, add egg. Fold in the dry ingredients and the fruit. Pour into greased and floured 8 x 12-inch pan and bake 30 to 45 minutes. Serve with whipped cream, if desired.

SUGAR GINGERBREAD

    ¼ cup butter
    1 cup sugar
    1 egg
    1½ cups flour
    ¼ teaspoon baking soda
    ½ teaspoon cream of tartar
    ¼ teaspoon cinnamon
    ¼ teaspoon ginger
    ⅛ teaspoon nutmeg
    ½ cup milk

Preheat oven to 375° F., a moderately hot oven. Cream butter and sugar, add egg. Sift dry ingre-dients, combine the two mixtures, and stir in the milk. Bake in greased and floured 8-inch square pan for 20 to 25 minutes. Sprinkle with sugar.

GRAHAM CRACKER CAKE

    ½ cup butter
    1 cup sugar
    3 eggs, separated
    ½ cup flour
    2 teaspoons baking powder
    ½ pound graham cracker crumbs
    1 cup milk
    1 teaspoon vanilla

Preheat oven to 350° F., a moderate oven. Cream butter and sugar, add yolks one at a time and beat well. Mix flour, baking powder and crumbs, add-ing alternately with the milk to the first mixture. Add vanilla, then fold in stiffly beaten egg whites. Bake in two well-greased and floured 9-inch layer pans for 30 minutes. Fill with Pecan Filling to which the grated rind and juice of ½ lemon have been added. Frost with Coffee Butter Frosting.

COCONUT GRAHAM CRACKER CAKE

    2 tablespoons butter
    1 cup sugar
    4 eggs, separated
    1 cup milk
    1 teaspoon vanilla
    ½ cup shredded coconut
    2 teaspoons baking powder
    2 cups graham cracker crumbs

Preheat oven to 350° F., a moderate oven. Cream butter and sugar, add well-beaten yolks, milk and vanilla, alternately, with coconut, baking powder, and crackers rolled fine. Fold in stiffly beaten whites. Bake in two well-greased 9-inch layer pans, about 30 minutes. Put Lemon-Flavored But-ter Frosting between the layers and on top of cake; sprinkle with coconut.

HICKORY NUT CAKE

    ½ cup butter
    1 cup sugar
    ½ cup milk
    1½ cups flour
    3 egg whites, beaten stiff
    ¾ cup chopped hickory nuts
    1 teaspoon cream of tartar
    ½ teaspoon baking soda dissolved in
        1 teaspoon milk

Preheat oven to 350° F., a moderate oven. Cream butter and sugar, add milk and flour, alternately; add eggs and nuts and beat until smooth; add cream of tartar and the dissolved baking soda. Beat. Bake in greased and floured 9-inch square pan for 45 minutes.

JAPANESE FRUIT CAKE

1 cup butter
2 cups sugar
4 eggs
1 teaspoon vanilla
3 cups flour
½ teaspoon salt
3 teaspoons baking powder
1 cup milk
1 teaspoon cinnamon
1 teaspoon allspice
1 teaspoon ground cloves
1 cup raisins (optional)

Preheat oven to 350° F., a moderate oven. Cream butter and sugar until light. Beat eggs until light; add gradually to butter mixture, add vanilla and beat well. Combine flour, salt and baking powder. Add alternately with the milk to the butter mixture. Put half of the batter into 2 greased and floured 8-inch layer cake pans. Add the spices and raisins to the remaining batter. Put this batter into 2 greased and floured 8-inch layer cake pans. Bake for 20 to 25 minutes.

FILLING

2 tablespoons flour
juice of 3 oranges
juice of 3 lemons
1 cup sugar
1 can (13½ ounces) crushed pineapple
1 cup grated coconut
1 cup pecans (optional)

Mix flour with a little juice; add remaining ingredients. Boil slowly until mixture is thick. Cool. Spread between layers of the cake, alternating the plain and spiced layers.

MARASCHINO CHERRY CAKE

8-ounce bottle maraschino cherries, cut up, and
    juice
milk
3¼ cups flour
¼ pound walnuts or pecans, broken in pieces
1 cup butter
2 cups sugar
4 eggs, separated
2 teaspoons baking powder
1 teaspoon baking soda

Preheat oven to 350° F., a moderate oven. Pour cherry juice into cup and fill with milk to measure 1 cup. Sift ¼ cup flour over cherries and nuts. Cream butter and sugar well, adding yolks one at a time, beating well. Add cherries and nuts. Sift baking powder, baking soda and 3 cups flour and add alternately with liquid to butter mixture. Fold

in beaten egg whites. Bake in greased and floured 9-inch fluted tube form 1 hour.

MARASCHINO CHERRY CHOCOLATE CAKE

1¾ cups flour
1 teaspoon baking soda
½ cup butter
1 cup sugar
1 egg, well beaten
1 square unsweetened chocolate, melted
½ cup broken nut meats
4-ounce bottle maraschino cherries, cut up, and
    juice
1 cup sour milk or cream

Preheat oven to 375° F., a moderately hot oven. Sift flour and baking soda. Cream butter well, add sugar and continue stirring. Add egg, melted chocolate, nuts, cherries, and cherry juice, stirring after each, then add flour mixture and milk alternately. Bake in greased and floured 9 by 12-inch pan for ½ hour. Frost with Chocolate Frosting.

ORANGEADE CAKE

¾ cup butter
1 cup sugar
2 eggs
2¼ cups flour
1 teaspoon baking powder
1 teaspoon baking soda
1 cup sour milk or cream
½ cup seedless raisins (optional)
1 cup pecans, chopped
grated rind of 2 oranges
1 cup orange juice
½ cup sugar

Preheat oven to 350° F., a moderate oven. Cream butter well, add 1 cup sugar gradually. Beat until light and fluffy. Add eggs one at a time, beating well. Sift 2 cups flour, baking powder and baking soda. Add alternately with milk to the butter mixture. Mix rest of flour with raisins, nuts and grated rind, add to dough and stir until smooth. Bake 1 hour in a greased and floured 9-inch tube pan. When done, immediately pour over it orange juice mixed with ½ cup sugar. Let stand in pan until cool.

PECAN CAKE

½ cup butter
1 cup medium brown sugar
2 eggs, separated
1½ cups cake flour
2 teaspoons baking powder
¼ teaspoon salt
¾ cup milk
1 teaspoon vanilla
¾ cup chopped pecans

Preheat oven to 350° F., a moderate oven. Cream butter and sugar until light and fluffy. Add yolks one at a time, beating well. Stir in flour sifted and mixed with baking powder and salt, alternately with the milk. Add vanilla and nuts and fold in stiffly beaten egg whites. Bake in two greased and floured 9-inch layer pans for 20 to 25 minutes. Fill and frost with Caramel Frosting.

PINEAPPLE CAKE

½ cup butter
1½ cups sugar
1 teaspoon vanilla
1 cup crushed canned pineapple
2½ cups cake flour
¼ cup water
3 teaspoons baking powder
⅛ teaspoon salt
3 egg whites

Preheat oven to 350° F., a moderate oven. Cream butter and sugar. Add vanilla and pineapple; add gradually 2 cups flour alternately with ¼ cup of water; then add remaining flour with baking powder and salt, and stir only until smooth. Fold in the egg whites, beaten stiff. Bake in two 9-inch greased and floured layer cake pans, 25 to 30 minutes. Cool and ice with Four-Minute Icing, piling it generously.

PINEAPPLE UPSIDE-DOWN CAKE

½ cup butter
2 cups brown sugar
1 can (1-pound, 14-ounce) sliced pineapple
walnut meats
candied cherries
4 eggs, separated
1 cup sugar
1 cup flour
1 teaspoon baking powder

Preheat oven to 350° F., a moderate oven. Melt butter in a heavy 10-inch skillet; cover with brown sugar, spreading it evenly. Place 1 slice of pineapple in center on top of sugar; cut rest of the slices in half; arrange these in a circle around the center slice like the spokes of a wheel, rounded edges facing the same way. Fill spaces with walnut meats and candied cherries. Cover with Sponge Cake batter: Beat yolks and sugar until light; sift flour and baking powder and fold into egg mixture ⅓ cup at a time. Fold in stiffly beaten whites. Bake about 30 minutes. Turn upside down. Serve with whipped cream.

Any canned fruit may be substituted for the pineapple.

CARAMEL UPSIDE-DOWN CAKE

Follow recipe above, using ½ cup chopped nut meats instead of fruit.

POPPY SEED CAKE

¾ cup poppy seed
¾ cup warm milk
1½ cups sugar
¾ cup butter
3 cups flour
3 teaspoons baking powder
5 egg whites

Preheat oven to 350° F., a moderate oven. Soak poppy seed in warm milk for several hours. Cream sugar and butter thoroughly; add poppy seed mixture and cream again; add flour mixed and sifted with baking powder; then add egg whites, beaten stiff. Bake in three greased and floured 9-inch layers about 25 minutes.

FILLING

2 tablespoons cornstarch
1½ tablespoons milk
4 egg yolks
½ cup sugar
1½ cups hot milk
vanilla
⅓ cup chopped nuts

Mix cornstarch in cold milk and cook in top of double boiler until smooth. Add yolks and sugar. Add hot milk gradually, and cook over hot water until custard coats the spoon, stirring constantly. When cool, add flavoring and nut meats.

Fill cake and cover with Chocolate Butter Frosting or Caramel Frosting.

PRUNE CAKE

½ cup butter
1 cup sugar
2 eggs
¾ cup thick sour cream
1½ cups flour
1½ tablespoons cornstarch
2 teaspoons baking powder
1 teaspoon baking soda
1 teaspoon each, cinnamon and ground cloves
1 cup stewed prune pulp
2 tablespoons prune juice

Preheat oven to 350° F., a moderate oven. Cream butter and sugar well, add eggs and sour cream. Mix dry ingredients, combine the two mixtures, adding prune juice and pulp. Bake in two well-greased and floured 9-inch layer pans for 25 minutes. Spread Cream Cheese Frosting between layers and over top.

FRUIT OR WEDDING CAKE

1 pound candied pineapple rings
1 pound each dates and figs
4 cups flour
1 teaspoon baking soda
2 teaspoons cinnamon
1 teaspoon ground cloves
1 teaspoon grated nutmeg
2 cups butter
2 cups brown sugar
12 eggs, beaten separately
½ cup molasses
½ cup fruit juice, wine, rum, or brandy
2 pounds seeded raisins
1 pound sultana raisins
¼ pound each candied orange, lemon rind and
   citron, cut fine
1 pound candied cherries
½ pound almonds, blanched
½ pound pecans, unbroken
brandy

Cut each ring of pineapple in 2 slices, then in half crosswise. Remove stem end from figs, cut in half lengthwise. Stone and cut dates, and mix with 1 cup of flour. Mix the rest of the flour with baking soda and spices. Cream butter, add sugar, then the well-beaten egg yolks and stir well. Add the flour mixture alternately with the molasses and fruit juice. Gently fold in the beaten whites, then the dates and gradually the raisins. Line 4 bread loaf pans with waxed paper. Put in a layer of batter, add a layer of pineapple down center, fill spaces and sides lightly with citron, orange, lemon rind, cherries and nuts; another layer of batter, then a layer of figs, the rest of the fruit and nuts and top with remaining batter. *Or cut up all fruit and mix through batter, adding beaten whites last.* Have pans ⅔ full. Set pans in slow oven, 300° F., in pan filled with 1 inch hot water. Bake ½ hour, cover with waxed paper, bake 2 hours longer, remove pans from water and bake ½ hour more. Remove from pans. Remove paper. Wrap in cloth moistened with brandy. Store in tightly covered tin box. Or bake in a very slow oven 4 to 5 hours (from 200° F. to 250° F.).

SPICE CAKE

⅔ cup currants or raisins
½ cup walnut meats, chopped
2½ cups flour
½ cup butter
2 cups sugar
3 eggs
3 teaspoons baking powder
½ teaspoon each, ground cloves, cinnamon, ginger
1 cup cream

Preheat oven to moderate temperature, 350° F. Mix the raisins and nuts with ½ cup of the flour. Cream the butter and sugar, add the eggs, one at a time. Mix remaining dry ingredients. Add cream and dry ingredients alternately to the butter mixture. Add raisins and nuts. Bake in two greased, floured 8-inch square pans for 30 to 40 minutes.

WHITE FRUIT CAKE

⅔ cup butter
1¾ cups sifted flour
½ teaspoon baking soda
1¼ cups confectioners sugar
6 egg whites, beaten stiff
2 tablespoons lemon juice
⅔ cup candied cherries
½ cup candied pineapple
½ cup sultana raisins
⅛ cup blanched pistachio nuts

Preheat oven to 325° F., a moderately slow oven. Cream butter well, gradually add flour mixed with baking soda. Beat sugar into beaten whites, combine the two mixtures, add lemon juice and fruit and nuts, cut fine and sprinkled lightly with additional flour. Stir well and bake in bread loaf pan lined with buttered paper about 1 hour.

Coffee Cakes

BLITZ KUCHEN (CRUMB CAKE)

1 cup butter
1 cup sugar
grated rind of 1 lemon
   or 1 teaspoon vanilla
4 eggs, unbeaten
2 cups flour
2 teaspoons baking powder

Preheat oven to 350° F., a moderate oven. Cream butter and sugar, add lemon rind or vanilla and the eggs, one at a time (reserving 1 egg white). Beat well, then add flour and baking powder mixed. Stir well, pour into a buttered oblong shallow pan, 8 x 12 inches. Spread with the reserved egg white, cover with Streusel and bake ½ hour until browned.

BAKING POWDER COFFEE CAKE
(BUNDT KUCHEN)

3 cups cake flour
2½ teaspoons baking powder
2 cups granulated sugar
1 cup butter, cut into pieces
4 eggs
1 cup milk
1 teaspoon grated orange or lemon rind
1 teaspoon vanilla

Preheat oven to 350° F., a moderate oven. Sift cake flour, measure. Mix first four ingredients together with knife or pastry blender until crumbly. Then add 4 eggs, one at a time, and beat well after each addition; then add milk, lemon or orange rind and vanilla. Pour into a well-buttered 9 or 10-inch tube form and bake for about 1 hour. Leave in pan until cold, about 1 hour.

ALMOND COFFEE CAKE
(ALMOND BUNDT KUCHEN)

 10 blanched almonds
 1 cup butter
 1½ cups sugar
 7 eggs
 1½ teaspoons grated rind of lemon and orange, mixed
 juice of ½ orange
 1 tablespoon rum
 1 teaspoon vanilla
 5 cups flour
 4 teaspoons baking powder
 ¾ cup milk

Preheat oven to 350° F., a moderate oven. Place almonds in the bottom of a well-greased bundt form (a deep, round, fluted cake pan with tube in center). Cream butter and sugar well together, add eggs, one at a time, beating constantly, add grated rind, juice and flavoring. Mix flour and baking powder and stir in alternately with the milk. Pour the cake mixture into pan and bake 45 minutes or until well browned.

See chapter 3, Beverages, for coffee and tea variations to serve with coffee cake.

EASY COFFEE CAKE (BUFFETEN KUCHEN)

 ¼ cup butter
 1½ cups sugar
 2 eggs, separated
 grated rind of 1 lemon
 2¼ cups flour
 4 teaspoons baking powder
 1 cup milk
 sugar and cinnamon
 chopped or sliced almonds

Preheat oven to 350° F., a moderate oven. Cream butter and sugar, add yolks of eggs and the lemon rind, stirring constantly. Mix flour and baking powder, add to the butter mixture, alternately with the milk, and fold in the stiffly beaten whites of eggs. Place in well-greased 8- by 12-inch coffee cake pan, sprinkle with sugar, cinnamon and a few almonds, sliced fine or chopped. Bake about ½ hour, or until well browned.

QUICK COFFEE CAKE

 1½ cups flour
 1 teaspoon baking powder
 ¼ cup soft butter
 1 cup sugar
 2 eggs, separated
 ½ cup milk
 ⅛ teaspoon nutmeg or ½ teaspoon flavoring extract
 melted butter
 sugar, cinnamon, slivered almonds

Preheat oven to 350° F., a moderate oven. Mix and sift flour and baking powder. Cream butter and sugar, add beaten yolks, then flour mixture and milk alternately, flavoring and stiffly beaten whites last. Pour into well-greased and floured 9-inch square pan, spread with melted butter, sprinkle with sugar, cinnamon and almonds. Bake about 30 minutes.

See pages 76-80 for other coffee cakes and kuchen.

Cream Cakes

BASIC CREAM CAKE

 ¾ cup sugar
 1½ cups sifted flour
 2 teaspoons baking powder
 2 eggs
 ⅔ cup cream
 1 teaspoon flavoring

Preheat oven to 350° F., a moderate oven. Sift dry ingredients; add eggs, cream, and flavoring; beat well. Bake in greased and floured 8-inch square pan for 45 minutes. If desired, split cake into layers, and fill and frost with sweetened whipped cream. Sprinkle with freshly grated coconut.

WHIPPED CREAM CAKE

 1 cup heavy cream
 1 cup sugar
 2 eggs
 1 teaspoon vanilla
 1½ cups cake flour
 2 teaspoons baking powder
 salt

Preheat oven to 375° F., a moderately hot oven. Whip the cream until slightly thickened but not stiff enough to hold a peak. Fold in the sugar, then the beaten eggs and the vanilla. Add the flour which has been sifted with the baking powder and pinch of salt. Mix only until smooth. Place in two greased and floured 8-inch layer cake pans and bake for 25 minutes. Cool. Fill and frost with Seven-Minute Boiled Icing or with 1 cup of heavy cream, whipped. Sprinkle with coconut.

SOUR CREAM CAKE

1 cup sugar
2 eggs
1 teaspoon lemon flavoring
⅛ teaspoon baking soda
1 cup sour cream
1¾ cups flour
½ teaspoon salt
1 teaspoon baking powder

Preheat oven to 350° F., a moderate oven. Beat sugar and eggs until very light, add the flavoring. Stir baking soda in sour cream and add alternately to the egg mixture, with the flour mixed and sifted with the salt and baking powder. Bake in two greased, floured 8-inch layer pans for 25 minutes.

SOUR CREAM COFFEE CAKE

½ cup shortening
¾ cup sugar
1 teaspoon vanilla
3 eggs
2 cups sifted flour
1 teaspoon baking powder
1 teaspoon baking soda
1 cup sour cream
6 tablespoons butter, softened
1 cup firmly packed brown sugar
2 teaspoons cinnamon
1 cup chopped nuts

Preheat oven to 350° F., a moderate oven. Grease a 10-inch tube pan or a 9″ x 9″ x 2″ pan. Cream shortening and sugar until light; add vanilla. Beat in eggs one at a time. Sift flour, baking powder and baking soda. Add to creamed shortening mixture alternately with the sour cream. Place half of batter in pan. Combine the softened butter with the brown sugar, cinnamon and nuts. Sprinkle the batter with about half this mixture. Add the remaining batter and top with the rest of the brown sugar mixture. Bake 50 to 60 minutes. Cool cake in pan for about 10 minutes before removing it.

CHOCOLATE LAYER CAKE WITH SOUR CREAM

yolks of 4 eggs
1⅓ cups sugar
2 squares unsweetened chocolate
1 cup thick sour cream
1 teaspoon baking soda
pinch of salt
1½ cups flour
flavoring extract
whites of 3 eggs

Preheat oven to 350° F., a moderate oven. Beat the yolks and sugar until very light. Melt the chocolate in part of the cream; cool and add it to the rest of the cream. Sift the baking soda, salt, and flour and add alternately with the cream mixture to the yolks and sugar. Add desired flavoring and fold in the whites, beaten stiff but not dry. Put batter into two greased and floured 8-inch square layer pans. Bake for 30 minutes. When cool, fill and ice with Meringue Frosting or Chocolate Nut Filling.

SPONGE CAKES

Sponge cakes contain no butter or shortening, and are made light with the yolks and whites of eggs. Whole eggs, or egg yolks, are beaten well with the sugar. It is advisable to use cake flour. Sift once, measure and resift. Flour is folded in very lightly and carefully, and the egg whites, beaten stiff, are folded in last. Sponge cakes should be inverted and cooled completely in the pan before they are removed. They are usually baked in an ungreased tube pan, but may also be baked in layer pans lined with waxed paper.

FOUR-EGG SPONGE CAKE

3 teaspoons baking powder
1½ cups cake flour
4 eggs, separated
1 cup sugar
1 teaspoon vanilla
¾ cup water

Preheat oven to 325° F., a moderately slow oven. Sift baking powder with ½ cup of the flour. Beat yolks until light and thick, add sugar gradually and continue beating. Add flavoring, then the water and the cup of flour alternately, then the baking powder mixture and lastly fold in the stiffly beaten whites of eggs. Bake in ungreased 9-inch tube pan from 40 to 50 minutes. Invert pan; when cool, remove cake.

TWO-EGG SPONGE CAKE

2 eggs, separated
1 cup sugar
⅜ cup hot water
¼ teaspoon lemon juice
1 cup cake flour
1½ teaspoons baking powder
¼ teaspoon salt

Preheat oven to 325° F., a moderately slow oven. Beat yolks until thick and lemon-colored, add half the sugar gradually, add water and lemon juice and beat. Whip egg whites until stiff but not dry, adding remaining sugar gradually. Combine mixtures. Fold in flour mixed and sifted with baking powder and salt. Bake in greased 9-inch layer pans for 35 minutes.

HOT WATER SPONGE CAKE

4 eggs
1½ cups sugar
½ teaspoon salt
1 teaspoon almond extract
2 cups cake flour
3 teaspoons baking powder
¾ cup boiling water

Preheat oven to 350° F., a moderate oven. Beat eggs, adding sugar gradually until very light and smooth. Add salt and flavoring. Fold in sifted flour and baking powder and add boiling water. Mix lightly, but thoroughly; do not beat. Pour into an ungreased 9-inch tube pan and bake about 50 minutes. Invert pan; when cool, remove cake.

GOLDEN SPONGE CAKE

¼ teaspoon salt
6 egg yolks
1 cup sugar
1 teaspoon lemon extract
½ cup boiling water
1½ cups cake flour
2 teaspoons baking powder

Preheat oven to 325° F., a moderately slow oven. Add salt to egg yolks and beat until very light. Gradually add sugar to yolks, beating all the time. Add flavoring. Stir in hot water. Sift flour and baking powder and fold into batter. Bake in 2 greased 9-inch layer cake pans for ½ hour. Fill layers with Lemon Filling, using 2 egg yolks, and spread Butter Frosting on top, adding 1 extra yolk to recipe.

COFFEE SPONGE CAKE

Substitute ½ cup strong coffee for water in Golden Sponge Cake, above, and use Mocha Filling and Butter Frosting. Proceed as above.

SWEDISH LAYER CAKE

5 egg whites
½ teaspoon cream of tartar
1 cup sugar
¼ cup cocoa
½ teaspoon vanilla
½ cup flour

Preheat oven to 350° F., a moderate oven. Beat egg whites until foamy, add cream of tartar, sugar and cocoa and beat until very stiff; add vanilla, fold in flour and bake in 2 greased 8-inch layer pans about 30 minutes. Put Marshmallow Filling between layers and on top. Sprinkle with chopped pistachio nuts and candied cherries.

Cake Frostings and Fillings will be found on pages 142 to 150.

IMPERIAL SUNSHINE CAKE

1½ cups sugar
½ cup water
6 eggs, beaten separately
1 teaspoon flavoring
1 cup cake flour
½ teaspoon cream of tartar

Preheat oven to 325° F., a moderately slow oven. Boil sugar and water until it threads when dropped from the end of a spoon. Pour gradually in a fine stream on the stiffly beaten egg whites, beating constantly until cool. Add the yolks, well beaten, and flavoring. Sift flour with the cream of tartar, fold in gradually, continue to beat. Bake in a 10-inch ungreased tube pan about 50 minutes. Invert to cool, remove from pan.

MOCHA LAYER CAKE

6 eggs, separated
1 cup sugar
1 tablespoon instant coffee
1 cup flour
1 teaspoon baking powder

Preheat oven to 350° F., a moderate oven. Beat yolks until thick and lemon-colored, add sugar gradually and continue beating. Add coffee and lightly fold in the whites beaten stiff but not dry. When the whites are partially mixed with the yolk mixture, carefully fold in flour sifted with the baking powder. Bake in two greased and floured 9-inch layer pans for 30 minutes.

FILLING

Use sweetened whipped cream, flavored with 1 tablespoon instant coffee between layers; ice with Mocha Icing.

ORANGE CAKE

5 egg yolks
1½ cups sugar
½ cup hot water
juice of 1 orange
grated rind of 1 orange
2 cups cake flour
2 teaspoons baking powder
3 egg whites

Preheat oven to 375° F. Beat yolks light, add sugar, beat until light. Then add water, orange juice and orange rind and the flour, sifted 3 times with the baking powder. Fold in egg whites beaten stiff but not dry. Bake in three greased 9-inch layer pans for 30 minutes.

Spread Orange Custard Filling between layers and cover with Orange Butter Frosting.

ORANGE PUFF CAKE

6 eggs, separated
2 cups sugar
½ cup orange juice
grated rind of 1 orange
½ cup boiling water
2 cups cake flour
2 teaspoons baking powder

Preheat oven to 325° F., a moderately slow oven. Beat yolks well, add 1 cup sugar and beat until light. Add orange juice and rind, then water, the flour mixed and sifted with baking powder. Beat egg whites, gradually add the remaining sugar and beat until stiff, then add yolk mixture. Bake in a 10-inch ungreased tube pan for 20 minutes. Increase heat to 350° F. Bake 1¼ hours in all.

Ice with 2 tablespoons butter, creamed with 1 cup confectioners sugar, ⅓ cup of orange juice, and the grated rind of half an orange.

ORANGE SPONGE CAKE

8 eggs, separated
¼ teaspoon salt
1 teaspoon cream of tartar
1⅓ cups sugar
grated rind of 1 orange
¼ cup orange juice
1 cup and 2 level tablespoons cake flour

Preheat oven to 325° F., a moderately slow oven. Beat egg whites and salt until foamy, add cream of tartar, beat until stiff, but not dry. Add ⅔ cup of sugar gradually, beating well after each addition. Beat the yolks of the eggs very thick, add remaining sugar, orange rind and juice. Fold the two mixtures together and fold in flour. Bake for 1 hour in an unbuttered 10-inch angel cake pan. Invert until cool. Split cake twice, making 3 layers.

FILLING

¾ cup sugar
juice and rind of 1 orange
3 tablespoons flour
1 egg
1 cup heavy cream

Mix ingredients except cream and cook in a double boiler until custard coats the spoon, stirring constantly. Cool. Fold in cream, whipped stiff.

FROSTING

4 tablespoons butter
1 egg yolk
2 cups confectioners sugar
1 tablespoon heavy cream
2 tablespoons orange juice
⅓ cup pistachio nuts, chopped

Cream butter and egg yolk. Gradually add sugar and cream. Mix, add orange juice. Spread on cake, sprinkle with nuts.

PINEAPPLE FLUFF CAKE

1½ cups cake flour
1 teaspoon baking powder
6 eggs, separated
¼ teaspoon salt
1½ cups sugar
1 tablespoon lemon juice
½ cup pineapple juice

Preheat oven to 325° F., a moderately slow oven. Sift flour; measure. Then sift with baking powder. Beat egg whites and salt until stiff but not dry, then beat in ¾ cup sugar gradually. Beat until stiff. Beat egg yolks well, add remaining sugar gradually, and beat until light. Stir in juices and the flour mixture. Fold this into the beaten whites. Bake in 10-inch ungreased tube pan 1 hour. Invert until cake cools. If desired, split and fill with Pineapple Marshmallow Filling. Frost as desired.

Any type of cake may be frozen. It is best to wrap layers separately, and fill and frost after thawing. For general directions on wrapping, freezing and thawing baked goods, see chapter 24. For directions on frosting and filling cakes, see chapter 6.

SUNSHINE CAKE

1 cup cake flour
6 eggs, separated
pinch of salt
1 cup sugar
1 lemon, grated rind
1 teaspoon vanilla
⅛ teaspoon cream of tartar

Preheat oven to 325° F., a moderately slow oven. Sift flour, measure; then sift 4 times. Beat yolks and salt with rotary egg beater until light-colored and thick; gradually beat in one half of the sugar and the lemon rind and vanilla. Beat whites until frothy, add cream of tartar. Beat until stiff enough to hold up in peaks but not dry. Beat in remaining sugar. Cut and fold some of white mixture into yolk mixture; fold and cut into yolk mixture the flour and salt; then the rest of the white mixture. Place in an ungreased 10-inch tube pan. Bake about 1 hour. Invert pan. When cool, remove cake.

For best results in making cakes:

- *Assemble all ingredients beforehand.*
- *Preheat oven to desired temperature.*
- *Read the General Rules on pages 105-107.*

EASY SUNSHINE CAKE

  6 eggs, separated
  ¼ cup water
  1 cup sugar
  ½ teaspoon lemon extract
  ½ teaspoon vanilla
  1 cup cake flour
  pinch of salt
  ½ teaspoon cream of tartar

Preheat oven to 325° F., a moderately slow oven. Beat yolks, water, sugar and flavorings until very light, fold in flour. Add a little salt to egg whites, beat until foamy, add cream of tartar, beat until stiff enough to hold up in peaks, but not dry, then fold carefully into other mixture. Place in ungreased 10-inch tube pan; bake 1 hour. Invert pan; when cool, remove.

RICH SUNSHINE CAKE

  8 eggs, separated
  1⅛ cups sugar
  ⅛ cup water
  2 teaspoons vanilla
  1⅛ cups cake flour
  pinch of salt
  ¾ teaspoon cream of tartar

Preheat oven to a moderate temperature, 350° F. Beat yolks, sugar, water, and vanilla until thick and light. Add flour. Beat egg whites and salt until foamy; add cream of tartar and continue beating until whites are stiff. Fold whites into the yolk mixture. Place batter in ungreased 10-inch tube pan, cover with brown paper. Bake for 15 minutes, remove paper, and bake 45 minutes longer. Invert pan until cake is cool.

Have egg whites at room temperature to attain maximum volume when beaten.

Angel Food

Like sponge cakes, angel food cakes are made without shortening. They are made light with beaten egg whites, which must be beaten until stiff, but not dry. The flour and sugar must be folded in very lightly, to avoid letting the air escape. Angel food cakes should be baked in an ungreased tube pan. To test for doneness, press top of cake with finger. If it springs back without leaving a dent, it is done. Invert over a rack until completely cold, about 1 hour. Loosen the sides of the cake with a spatula and remove. Cut angel food with a cake breaker or two forks, not with a knife.

ANGEL FOOD CAKE

  1½ cups egg whites (12 or 13 eggs)
  1¼ teaspoons cream of tartar
  ½ teaspoon salt
  1½ cups granulated sugar
  1¼ teaspoons flavoring
  1 cup plus 2 tablespoons cake flour

Preheat oven to 375° F., a moderately hot oven. Beat egg whites. Add cream of tartar and salt when eggs are frothy. Beat until a point of the egg whites will just stand upright. Gradually beat in 1 cup of the sugar, which has been sifted twice. Fold in the flavoring. Sift flour once before measuring, sift 3 times with remaining sugar. Fold in flour gradually. Pour into ungreased 10-inch tube pan and bake 30-35 minutes. Test for doneness. Bake longer if necessary. Invert pan until cake is entirely cold.

EASY ANGEL FOOD CAKE

  1¼ cups granulated sugar
  1 cup confectioners sugar
  1¼ cups cake flour
  ¼ teaspoon salt
  1½ cups egg whites (12 or 13 eggs)
  1 teaspoon cream of tartar
  1 tablespoon lemon juice or vanilla

Preheat oven to 350° F., a moderate oven. Sift sugars and flour together several times. Add salt to whites and beat until foamy. Add cream of tartar and continue to beat only until stiff enough to fold. Do not overbeat. Fold in flour mixture gradually. Add flavoring and pour into an ungreased 10-inch tube pan. Bake about 50 minutes. Invert pan until cake is cold.

IMPERIAL ANGEL FOOD CAKE

  1½ cups granulated sugar
  4 tablespoons water
  1 cup egg whites (8 or 9)
  1 teaspoon almond extract
  1 cup cake flour
  1 teaspoon cream of tartar
  ¼ teaspoon salt

Preheat oven to 325° F., a moderately slow oven. Boil sugar and water together until it threads. Pour gradually in a fine stream on the stiffly beaten whites of eggs, beating constantly, add flavoring and beat until cool. Mix and sift flour, cream of tartar and salt several times and gradually fold into the egg mixture. Turn into ungreased 10-inch tube pan. Bake about 50 minutes. Invert pan, cool, and remove cake.

See next page for angel food cake variations.

VARIATIONS

CHOCOLATE ANGEL CAKE

Substitute ¼ cup of cocoa for ¼ cup of flour in Angel Food Cake, above.

MARBLE ANGEL CAKE

Make ½ recipe Angel Food Cake and ½ recipe Chocolate Angel Cake, above. Put by tablespoons in pan, alternating chocolate and plain batters.

FRUIT ANGEL CAKE

Sprinkle thin slices of fruit and nuts (cherries, pineapple, pistachio, walnuts, pecans) through the batter of Angel Food Cake.

DAFFODIL CAKE

Mix stiffly beaten egg whites, cream of tartar, salt, and all the sugar of Angel Food Cake, above. Divide mixture in half. Add ¾ cup flour and 6 well-beaten yolks to one part, and ½ cup flour and flavoring to the other. Alternate batters when placing in pan.

ANGEL CAKE INDIANS

Bake an Angel Food or Sunshine Cake; pull the cake apart with a fork in irregular pieces about 2 inches in size; take each piece on a fork and dip in hot Chocolate Icing and let cool on a platter.

Chiffon Cakes

Chiffon cakes are sponge-like cakes made with oil. The method of combining the ingredients is different from that of sponge cake and should be followed precisely.

GOLDEN CHIFFON CAKE

    2 cups flour
    1½ cups sugar
    1 teaspoon salt
    3 teaspoons baking powder
    ½ cup vegetable oil
    7 eggs, separated
    ¾ cup cold water
    2 teaspoons vanilla
    grated rind of 1 lemon
    ½ teaspoon cream of tartar

Preheat oven to 325° F., a moderately slow oven. Sift flour, sugar, salt, and baking powder. Add oil, egg yolks, water, vanilla, and lemon rind, and beat until smooth and light. Beat whites frothy, add cream of tartar, continue to beat until stiff but not dry. Fold yolk mixture into the whites only until blended. Pour into ungreased 10-inch tube pan; bake for 55 minutes. Increase heat to 350° F. and bake for 10 minutes more. Invert pan until cake is cool.

ORANGE CHIFFON CAKE

    2¼ cups cake flour
    1½ cups sugar
    3 teaspoons baking powder
    1 teaspoon salt
    ½ cup vegetable oil
    5 egg yolks
    3 tablespoons grated orange rind
    ¾ cup orange juice
    1 cup egg whites (8 or 9 eggs)
    ½ teaspoon cream of tartar

Preheat oven to 325° F., a moderately slow oven. Sift flour, sugar, baking powder, and salt. Add oil, egg yolks, rind, and juice and beat until smooth and thick. Beat whites and cream of tartar until stiff but not dry. Fold yolk mixture into the whites only until blended. Pour into ungreased 10-inch tube pan; bake for 55 minutes. Increase heat to 350° F. and bake for 10 minutes. Invert pan until cake is cool.

BANANA CHIFFON CAKE

Substitute 1 cup of mashed bananas for the water and vanilla in Golden Chiffon Cake.

CAKE ROLLS

Do not overbake cake rolls. The paper on which the roll is baked is difficult to remove if cake is overbaked.

A cake roll is more easily rolled when warm. If it is not to be filled immediately, it should be rolled without filling and cooled. Unroll, fill with any desired filling or ice cream and reroll when ready to serve.

JELLY ROLL

    ¾ cup cake flour
    ¾ teaspoon baking powder
    ¼ teaspoon salt
    4 eggs
    ¾ cup sifted sugar
    1 teaspoon vanilla
    1 teaspoon confectioners sugar
    1 cup jelly

Preheat oven to 400° F., a hot oven. Sift flour, baking powder, and salt. Beat eggs, place over bowl of hot water, and add sugar gradually to eggs, beating until thick and light. Remove bowl from hot water, fold in flour mixture and vanilla. Pour batter into 10- by 15-inch pan lined with greased or waxed paper. Bake for 10 minutes. Turn on towel dusted with confectioners sugar. Remove paper, cut off crusty edges, spread with jelly and roll. Rolls also may be filled with any cake filling.

SPONGE JELLY ROLL

5 eggs, separated
1 cup sugar
grated rind of 1 lemon
2 tablespoons lemon juice
1 cup flour
confectioners sugar
1 cup jelly

Preheat oven to 375° F., a moderate oven. Beat yolks well, add sugar, beat until thick; add lemon rind and juice. Then add alternately the stiffly beaten whites and flour. Pour batter, not more than ¼ inch deep, into 10- by 15-inch pan lined with greased or waxed paper. Bake 12 to 15 minutes. Turn on towel dusted with confectioners sugar. Remove paper. Beat jelly with fork and spread on cake. Trim off crusty edges and roll while warm.

CHOCOLATE SPONGE ROLL

1¼ cups flour
2 teaspoons baking powder
¼ teaspoon salt
2 eggs
1 cup sugar
¼ cup hot water
1 teaspoon vanilla
2 tablespoons shortening
2 squares unsweetened chocolate, melted
confectioners sugar

Preheat oven to 375° F., a moderately hot oven. Sift flour, baking powder, and salt 3 times. Beat eggs and sugar until light, add hot water. Stir in vanilla, melted shortening, and melted chocolate. Fold in flour mixture as lightly as possible. Pour into a 10- by 15-inch pan lined with greased or waxed paper and bake 15 minutes. Turn out on towel dusted with confectioners sugar, remove paper, trim edges, and roll. When cool, unroll and fill with Fluffy Chocolate Frosting.

CHOCOLATE ROLL

5 eggs, separated
½ cup confectioners sugar
2 tablespoons cocoa
granulated sugar
1 cup heavy cream, whipped

Preheat oven to 425° F., a hot oven. Beat yolks and sugar until very light and thick. Add cocoa and stiffly beaten whites. Spread in a 10- by 15-inch pan greased and lined with waxed paper. Bake 5 minutes. Turn out on cloth sprinkled with granulated sugar. Remove paper. Roll while hot. Just before serving, unroll and spread with sweetened whipped cream or ice cream. Reroll, cover

with Fudge Frosting. Decorate with pistachio nuts.

COCOA ROLL

5 eggs, separated
1 cup sugar
¼ cup cocoa
¼ cup flour
1 teaspoon vanilla
confectioners sugar
1 cup heavy cream, whipped

Preheat oven to 350° F., a moderate oven. Beat yolks slightly, add sugar, and beat until light and thick. Add cocoa, flour, and vanilla, and lastly fold in the stiffly beaten whites. Grease a 10- by 15-inch shallow pan and line with waxed paper. Spread batter in pan; bake 10 to 15 minutes. Turn out on towel dusted with confectioners sugar, remove paper, and roll. Before serving, unroll and spread with sweetened whipped cream or with ice cream; reroll. Cover with Fudge Frosting.

WALNUT ROLL

6 egg yolks, beaten
½ cup sugar
1 cup walnuts, chopped
6 egg whites, beaten
confectioners sugar
heavy cream, whipped

Preheat oven to 350° F., a moderate oven. Beat the yolks well with the sugar; add nuts and lastly the stiffly beaten whites. Grease a 10- by 15-inch shallow pan and line with waxed paper. Spread batter in pan and bake 15 to 20 minutes. Turn out on a towel sprinkled with confectioners sugar, remove paper. Roll while hot. When cold, unroll, spread with sweetened whipped cream or ice cream. Roll again and serve with Caramel Sauce.

PASSOVER CAKES

Cakes for Passover are made with special flours, and no leavening is used except eggs.

POTATO FLOUR CAKE

9 eggs
1¾ cups sugar
½ lemon, grated rind and juice
1 scant cup potato flour

Preheat oven to 350° F., a moderate oven. Separate the eggs. Beat the whites of 7 eggs stiff but not dry. To the well-beaten yolks of 9 eggs and the whites of 2, add the sugar and the lemon juice and rind. Beat thoroughly, add the potato flour, and beat again. Fold in beaten whites carefully, and bake in ungreased 10-inch tube pan, 40 to 50 minutes. Invert pan until cake is cool.

MATZO-LEMON SPONGE CAKE

8 eggs, separated
1½ cups sugar
salt
½ lemon, grated rind and juice
1 cup sifted matzo cake meal

Preheat oven to 350° F., a moderate oven. Beat yolks until light, add sugar and beat again; then add a pinch of salt, the lemon juice and rind, then the matzo cake meal and lastly fold in the whites beaten until stiff but not dry. Bake in 10-inch ungreased spring form 45 minutes. Invert pan until cake is cool. If desired, split in two layers.

Serve with sweetened strawberries between the layers. Spread whipped cream, flavored and sweetened, over top and sides.

MATZO SPONGE CAKE

9 eggs, separated
1¼ cups sugar
¾ cup matzo cake meal
1 teaspoon vanilla

Preheat oven to 350° F., a moderate oven. Beat whites until stiff. Beat yolks and sugar until light. Fold beaten whites into the yolks, then fold in the cake meal and flavoring. Bake in ungreased 10-inch tube pan for 40 minutes. Invert pan until cake is cool.

MATZO SPICE SPONGE CAKE

12 eggs, separated
2 cups sugar
1½ teaspoons cinnamon
¼ teaspoon ground cloves
⅛ cup wine
1 cup chopped, blanched almonds
1½ cups matzo cake meal

Preheat oven to 325° F., a moderately slow oven. Beat egg yolks and sugar until very light; add spices, wine, nuts, and cake meal. Fold in stiffly beaten egg whites. Bake in large ungreased 10-inch tube pan about 1 hour. Invert pan until cake is cool.

MATZO SPONGE ROLL

4 eggs, separated
½ cup sugar
½ cup matzo cake meal

Preheat oven to 375° F., a moderately hot oven. Beat yolks well, add sugar, and sifted cake meal, and fold in the stiffly beaten whites. Spread on greased paper in a 10- by 15-inch shallow pan. Bake 10 minutes. Turn out on a sugared towel, remove the paper, spread with Lemon Fluff Filling or with jam. Roll.

TORTEN

GENERAL RULES

Torten are cakes in which ground nuts or crumbs are usually used instead of flour. They generally contain no shortening.

Most of the following recipes are for 9-inch spring forms.

The spring form should be greased and sprinkled lightly with flour. Spring forms are available with plain, tubed and Mary Ann shell inserts.

For Frosting: *Any nut torte in this chapter may be spread with chilled whipped currant jelly and sprinkled with toasted, slivered almonds.*

ALMOND TORTE

8 eggs, separated
1½ cups sugar
pinch salt
grated rind of 1 lemon
2½ cups almonds, blanched and grated
¼ cup bread crumbs

Beat yolks with sugar and salt; add lemon rind, fold in stiffly beaten whites, the almonds, and lastly the bread crumbs. Bake in greased and floured 9-inch spring form in a moderate oven, 350° F., from 45 minutes to 1 hour. Serve with Rum Sauce or cover with whipped cream.

JELLY-FILLED ALMOND TORTE

8 eggs, separated
1 cup sugar
½ pound almonds, grated
½ cup dry bread crumbs
juice and grated rind of 1 lemon
2 teaspoons flour
½ teaspoon baking powder
raspberry jelly

Preheat oven to 350° F., a moderate oven. Beat the yolks with the sugar until light. Add the almonds, bread crumbs and lemon juice and rind. Then fold in lightly the stiffly beaten whites, and the flour and baking powder mixed. Bake in a greased and floured 9-inch spring form for 1 hour. Allow cake to cool, then cut into two layers and fill with 1 cup raspberry jelly and 1 cup chopped walnuts. Spread top and sides with icing below.

RUM ICING

2 cups confectioners sugar
4 tablespoons heavy cream
2 tablespoons rum

Stir ingredients until smooth. Spread on cake. Decorate with walnut halves if desired.

ANGEL TORTE

2 cups almonds
½ pound dates
5 eggs, separated
¾ cup confectioners sugar
2 teaspoons baking powder
heavy cream, whipped

Preheat oven to 350° F., a moderate oven. Blanch almonds, reserving a few to decorate the top. Grind the nuts. Stone dates, pour boiling water over them, drain and mash to a smooth paste. Beat the yolks and gradually add the sugar and date pulp. Stir almonds lightly into the cake mixture. Fold the baking powder into the stiffly beaten whites and fold whites into the date mixture. Bake in a well-greased and floured 9-inch spring form for about 45 minutes. When cool, cut in 2 layers and spread layers and top with whipped cream. Sprinkle with the remaining almonds, sliced.

APPLESAUCE CHOCOLATE TORTE

1 cup bread crumbs
1½ teaspoons baking powder
6 eggs, separated
1 cup sugar
5 teaspoons cocoa
½ cup applesauce

Preheat oven to 350° F., a moderate oven. Mix bread crumbs and baking powder. Beat yolks until thick and lemon-colored. Add sugar and beat well. Add cocoa, then applesauce and bread crumbs, stirring well. Fold in stiffly beaten egg whites last. Bake in three greased and floured 8-inch layer pans about 20 minutes. Fill and frost with Hungarian Chocolate Frosting.

APRICOT MERINGUE TORTE

1 cup sifted flour
1 teaspoon sugar
½ cup softened butter
1 egg yolk
1 jar (12 ounces) apricot jam
1 can (1 pound 13 ounces) peeled apricot halves
4 egg whites
¼ cup blanched, sliced almonds

Preheat oven to 400° F., a hot oven. Mix flour and sugar; add gradually to the butter, stirring after each addition. Add egg yolk and mix well. Spread mixture on bottom of ungreased 9-inch spring form. Bake at 400° for 18-20 minutes. Cool slightly in pan. Spread ½ of the jam over the baked layer. Drain apricots well. Place apricots on jam layer. Beat egg whites until stiff. Fold in remaining apricot preserves. Spread over apricot halves; sprinkle with almonds. Bake at 350° for 25 minutes or until meringue is lightly browned. Cool before removing sides of pan.

BLUEBERRY MERINGUE TORTE

Rich Egg Pastry, page 342
bread crumbs
1 quart blueberries
¼ cup sugar
cinnamon
2 tablespoons lemon juice
1 egg yolk
3 tablespoons cream
4 egg whites
¼ cup sugar

Preheat oven to 400° F., a hot oven. Line bottom and sides of a spring form with Rich Egg Pastry. Sprinkle with bread crumbs, add blueberries, sprinkle with sugar and cinnamon and lemon juice. Over all, drizzle the egg yolk beaten with the cream. Bake for 15 minutes. Reduce heat to 325° F. and bake until crust is well browned. Beat egg whites until stiff, add sugar, spread over Torte, return to oven. Bake 15 minutes at 300° F.

CARROT TORTE

1 pound carrots, peeled
8 eggs, separated
2 cups sugar
rind of 1 large orange
1 tablespoon orange juice
1 pound almonds, blanched and grated

Preheat oven to 325° F., a moderately slow oven. Cook the carrots, chill, and grate. Beat the yolks until light and thick. Add sugar gradually, then orange rind and juice, carrots, nuts; mix well. Fold in the stiffly beaten whites. Bake in a greased and floured 9-inch spring form for 45 to 50 minutes. Chill for several hours, cover with sweetened whipped cream and serve.

CHEESE TORTE

1 cup butter
1 cup sugar
10 eggs, separated
½ pound dry cottage cheese (riced)
½ pound almonds, blanched and grated
5 tablespoons bread crumbs
juice and grated rind of 1 lemon

Preheat oven to 350° F., a moderate oven. Cream butter, add sugar and continue creaming. Add the well-beaten egg yolks, stirring constantly. Gradually add the cheese, the remaining ingredients and the stiffly beaten egg whites last. Bake in a buttered 10-inch spring form until well set, about 1 hour. Let stand in oven with door open. When cool, ice with Chocolate Butter Frosting.

CHERRY CREAM TORTE

Preheat oven to 350° F., a moderate oven. This recipe is made in four steps which follow below.

1. *RICH PASTRY*

Line a 10-inch spring form with Rich Egg Pastry.

2. *ALMOND PASTE*

½ pound shelled almonds
¾ cup sugar
grated rind of 1 lemon
4 egg whites

Grind almonds without blanching, add sugar, lemon rind and mix well. Fold in the stiffly beaten egg whites. Place mixture on top of dough.

3. *CHERRY FILLING*

Drain 3 cups canned pitted cherries and place on top of almond paste.

4. *CREAM CUSTARD*

2 cups cream
3 tablespoons sugar
10 egg yolks, well beaten
10 egg whites, beaten stiff

Heat the cream and the sugar in top of double boiler; when hot, pour very gradually onto the well-beaten yolks. Return to double boiler, cook slowly, stirring constantly until the mixture coats the spoon. Fold in the beaten egg whites and pour over the cherries. Bake for 1 hour.

CHERRY-FILLED TORTE

Preheat oven to 400° F., a hot oven. Make Rich Egg Pastry. Cover bottom and sides of a greased 9-inch spring form. Bake for 10 minutes. Remove torte and reduce oven temperature to 350° F. Place 3 cups drained canned sweetened cherries in torte. Cover with sponge made as follows:

6 eggs, separated
½ cup sugar
¼ pound grated, blanched almonds
grated rind of 1 lemon

Beat the yolks and sugar until light; add almonds and lemon rind. Fold in the stiffly beaten whites. Bake for ¾ to 1 hour.

CHERRY TORTE

1 cup drained, pitted, canned cherries
¾ cup zwieback crumbs
4 eggs, separated
2 cups sugar
¼ cup hot cherry juice
¼ cup chopped nut meats
1 teaspoon cinnamon

Preheat oven to 350° F., a moderate oven. Mix cherries with ¼ cup crumbs. Set aside. Beat yolks and sugar until lemon-colored. Add cherry juice,

stir well, add ½ cup crumbs, continue beating until smooth. Add nuts and cinnamon, then the crumbed cherries and lastly fold in the stiffly beaten whites. Place in a greased 9-inch spring form sprinkled with additional crumbs. Bake for 40 to 50 minutes. Serve with whipped cream.

CHESTNUT TORTE

1½ pounds chestnuts
milk
8 egg yolks
½ cup sugar
1 teaspoon bread crumbs
2 ounces grated almonds
1 tablespoon maraschino syrup or brandy
8 egg whites, beaten stiff

Preheat oven to 350° F., a moderate oven. Shell Chestnuts, page 418, then boil in a little milk until tender; put through ricer. Beat yolks and sugar until light, add crumbs, nuts, and other ingredients, the beaten egg whites last. Bake in a greased and floured 9-inch spring form for 45 minutes.

CHOCOLATE TORTE

9 eggs, separated
1 pound confectioners sugar
1 teaspoon vanilla
½ pound sweet chocolate, melted
½ pound almonds, ground
¼ cup sliced, toasted almonds (for decorating)

Preheat oven to 325° F., a moderately slow oven. Beat yolks, sugar, and vanilla until light; add melted chocolate and ground almonds, and fold in the stiffly beaten whites. Bake in a greased and floured 9-inch spring form for about 1 hour. Cover with Chocolate Butter Frosting. Stick sliced almonds on end in the frosting.

CHOCOLATE POTATO TORTE

1½ cups cake flour
¼ teaspoon ground cloves
1 teaspoon cinnamon
1 cup butter
2 cups sugar
4 eggs, separated
½ cup cream
1 cup freshly cooked, riced potatoes
1 cup grated almonds
4 squares unsweetened chocolate, grated
1 teaspoon vanilla
grated rind of 1 lemon
2 teaspoons baking powder

Preheat oven to 325° F., a moderately slow oven. Sift and mix flour and spices. Cream the butter and sugar, add one egg yolk at a time, then the rest of the ingredients, lastly the beaten whites.

Bake in greased and floured 9-inch spring form for 1½ hours. Spread Chocolate Icing on top.

CHOCOLATE WALNUT TORTE

2 cups shelled walnuts or almonds
¼ cup grated unsweetened chocolate
9 eggs, separated
1 cup sugar
½ cup fine cracker crumbs

Preheat oven to 350° F., a moderate oven. Chop the nuts, reserving ⅓ cup for decorating. Mix the nuts and chocolate. Beat the yolks and sugar until light. Then mix with the nuts, chocolate, and crumbs, and stir well. Lastly add the stiffly beaten whites. Bake in a greased and floured 9-inch spring form for 45 minutes. Frost with Fudge Frosting and sprinkle with remaining nuts.

COFFEE CREME TORTE

8 eggs, separated
½ pound confectioners sugar
½ pound blanched almonds, grated
2 tablespoons instant coffee
1 teaspoon vanilla

Preheat oven to 350° F., a moderate oven. Beat yolks until thick. Add sugar and the remaining ingredients, the stiffly beaten whites last. Bake in 2 greased and floured 9-inch layer pans for about 30 minutes.

COFFEE CREME

¾ cup butter
1 cup confectioners sugar
4 egg yolks
1 tablespoon instant coffee

Cream butter, add sugar, eggs one at a time, and coffee. Fill and frost torte. Decorate with small chocolate wafers and candied cherries. Refrigerate. Cut with a knife dipped in hot water.

DAISY TORTE

10 eggs, separated
1 cup sugar
¾ cup grated sweet chocolate
¾ cup almonds, grated
1 teaspoon brandy
1 cup dry wheat bread crumbs
½ teaspoon cinnamon
½ teaspoon ground cloves
1 teaspoon baking powder
1 lemon, juice and grated rind

Preheat oven to 350° F., a moderate oven. Beat yolks and sugar until light. Add the remaining ingredients, the stiffly beaten whites last. Bake in 3 greased and floured 9-inch layer cake pans for 30 minutes. Fill with Almond Custard Filling. Cover top and sides with Chocolate Icing. Decorate with blanched almonds and candied orange peel.

DATE TORTE

16 dates
2 tablespoons lemon juice, or 4 tablespoons wine or brandy
2 tablespoons almonds, chopped
2 tablespoons citron, cut fine
9 eggs (2 whole, 7 separated)
1¾ cups sugar
¼ cup grated unsweetened chocolate
1 teaspoon cinnamon
1 teaspoon allspice
1¼ cups cracker crumbs
½ teaspoon baking powder

Preheat oven to 350° F., a moderate oven. Mash the dates to a smooth paste with the lemon juice or wine or brandy. Add almonds and citron. Beat together two whole eggs and seven yolks, add sugar, beat again. Stir in the dates, chocolate, spices, cracker crumbs, and baking powder. Finally fold in the beaten egg whites. Bake in a greased and floured 10-inch spring form 40 to 60 minutes.

DATE AND WALNUT CAKE TORTE

1 cup sugar
4 eggs, beaten light
1 cup cake flour
2 teaspoons baking powder
¼ teaspoon salt
1 cup broken walnut meats
1 cup dates, cut up
½ teaspoon vanilla

Preheat oven to 325° F., a moderately slow oven. Add the sugar gradually to the beaten eggs. Then add ¾ cup flour mixed and sifted with the baking powder and salt. Mix nuts and dates with the remaining flour and cut and fold into the egg mixture; add flavoring. Bake in a greased and floured 9-inch spring form for 45 minutes to 1 hour. Cool and serve with whipped cream.

DATE AND WALNUT TORTE

2 eggs
1 cup sugar
2 tablespoons cream
2 tablespoons flour
1 teaspoon baking powder
1 cup walnuts, chopped
¼ teaspoon vanilla
1 cup dates, cut fine

Preheat oven to 325° F., a moderately slow oven. Beat eggs very light, add sugar and cream and continue beating, add flour mixed with the baking powder and lastly, the nuts, vanilla and dates. Bake in a greased and floured 8-inch square pan for about 1 hour. Serve with whipped cream.

DOBOS TORTE (SEVEN-LAYER CAKE)

1 cup flour
¼ teaspoon salt
7 eggs, separated
1 cup confectioners sugar

Preheat oven to 375° F., a moderately hot oven. Sift flour once, measure, add salt, sift four times. Beat egg yolks until thick, add sugar gradually, beat well. Fold in flour. Beat whites until stiff enough to hold up in peaks, but not dry, and fold in lightly. This will make seven layers. Line bottoms of 4 shallow 8- or 9-inch cake tins, or dobos torte set, with heavy paper. Grease paper. Spread batter evenly into four pans for the first baking, reserving enough batter for the three remaining layers. Bake about 8 minutes. Remove at once from pans, strip off the paper, cool, fill as follows:

DOBOS FILLING

½ pound sweet chocolate
3 tablespoons cold water
3 eggs
1½ cups sugar
½ pound butter
1 teaspoon vanilla

Melt chocolate with water in double boiler. Mix eggs and sugar, add to chocolate, cook until thick, stirring constantly. Remove from heat, add butter, stir until melted, and add vanilla. Beat until cool and stiff enough to spread. Spread between layers, over top and sides. To keep layers in place, put several toothpicks through top layers, until filling sets. Chill for 24 hours.

FARINA TORTE

6 egg yolks
1 cup sugar
1 cup grated almonds
1 cup farina
1 teaspoon baking powder
6 egg whites, beaten stiff

Preheat oven to 350° F., a moderate oven. Beat yolks and sugar until very light; add the remaining ingredients in order. Bake in a greased and floured 9-inch spring form for 40 minutes.

FILBERT TORTE

8 egg yolks
1½ cups confectioners sugar
½ cup bread crumbs
grated rind of 1 lemon
juice of ½ lemon
½ pound grated filberts or hazelnuts
8 egg whites, beaten stiff

Preheat oven to 325° F., a moderately slow oven. Beat yolks and sugar until very light, add bread crumbs and the rest of the ingredients in order, the beaten whites last. Bake in a greased and floured 9-inch spring form for 40 to 45 minutes. Cover with Nut and Fruit Meringue Filling. Decorate with additional nuts.

Or, bake in two layers; place fresh strawberries, or sweetened whipped cream, between layers and on top of cake.

HAZELNUT COFFEE TORTE

11 eggs, separated
1 pound confectioners sugar
1 pound ground hazelnuts
1 teaspoon instant coffee

Preheat oven to 350° F., a moderate oven. Beat yolks well, add sugar gradually, beating all the time. Then add the nuts, the coffee, and lastly fold in the stiffly beaten whites. Bake in a greased and floured 12-inch spring form for 50 to 60 minutes. Dust with confectioners sugar.

HAZELNUT TORTE

12 eggs, separated
2 cups confectioners sugar
1 lemon, juice and grated rind
3 cups grated hazelnuts, unblanched
¾ cup cracker crumbs

Preheat oven to 350° F., a moderate oven. Beat yolks and sugar well together. Add the lemon, nuts and cracker crumbs, and the beaten whites last. Place in a greased and floured 9-inch spring form. Bake 45 minutes to 1 hour. Cut into two layers. Spread Lemon Butter Frosting between layers and on top.

Almonds may be used instead of hazelnuts, if desired.

HIMMEL TORTE

1½ cups butter
¼ cup sugar
4 egg yolks
grated rind of 1 lemon
4 cups flour
1 egg white
¼ cup sugar
1 teaspoon cinnamon
½ cup chopped almonds

Preheat oven to 450° F., a very hot oven. Cream the butter and ¼ cup sugar well; stir in the yolks one at a time, blending well. Add the lemon rind and flour. Pat dough in 3 greased 7- by 11-inch pans. Mix egg white, ¼ cup sugar, cinnamon, and chopped almonds, spread on dough. Bake for 10 to 12 minutes, reduce heat to 350° F. and bake until well browned, 10-20 minutes longer. When torte is cold, spread raspberry jam and part of the following Crème Filling between the layers; and spread the rest of the Crème over the top.

CRÈME FILLING

1 tablespoon cornstarch
¼ cup sugar
2 cups thick sour cream
2 egg yolks
½ teaspoon vanilla

Mix cornstarch with sugar, add sour cream and cook in double boiler, stirring constantly until it coats the spoon. Pour gradually onto 2 well-beaten yolks. Reheat for 1 minute. Add vanilla.

LADY FINGER TORTE

6 egg yolks
1½ cups sugar
1 cup lady finger crumbs
2 tablespoons brandy or 1 tablespoon lemon juice
1 cup blanched, grated almonds
5 egg whites, beaten stiff

Preheat oven to 325° F., a moderately slow oven. Beat yolks and sugar until lemon-colored. Add the rest of the ingredients, the beaten whites last. Bake in two greased and floured 9-inch layer pans for 40 minutes. Spread Pecan Filling between layers.

LADY FINGER ALMOND TORTE

10 eggs, separated
1½ cups sugar
1 teaspoon vanilla
¾ pound unblanched almonds, grated
1 cup crumbled lady fingers
1 teaspoon baking powder

Preheat oven to 350° F., a moderate oven. Beat the yolks and sugar until very light; add vanilla, almonds, lady fingers mixed with baking powder. Fold in the whites of the eggs, beaten stiff. Place in greased and floured 10-inch spring form and bake 1¼ hours. Keep 2 days before using; then the day before using, cut across into 4 layers and put Almond Custard Filling between layers. Chill until served.

LADY FINGER APPLE TORTE

4 eggs, separated
¾ cup sugar
3 apples, pared and grated
1 cup lady finger or sponge cake crumbs
juice and grated rind of ½ lemon
¼ cup chopped almonds

Preheat oven to 350° F., a moderate oven. Beat yolks and sugar until light, add apples, crumbs, lemon juice and rind, and lastly fold in the stiffly beaten whites. Place in a greased and floured 8-inch spring form, sprinkle with almonds, pressing them into mixture with the back of spoon. Bake 20 to 25 minutes. Leave torte on bottom of spring form. Serve with cream.

LEMON TORTE

Rich Egg Pastry, page 342
½ pound butter
½ pound confectioners sugar
grated rind of 1 lemon
juice of 2 lemons
6 eggs

Preheat oven to 400° F., a hot oven. Line bottom and sides of a greased 9-inch spring form with Rich Egg Pastry. Cream butter and sugar, add lemon rind and juice and stir well. Beat the eggs until thick and lemon-colored. Combine the mixtures lightly and place on dough. Place in oven immediately and bake ½ hour. Serve from bottom tin of spring form.

LEMONADE TORTE

1½ cups sugar
¼ pound almonds, chopped
1½ cups wheat bread crumbs
¼ teaspoon baking powder
¼ teaspoon cinnamon
grated rind of 1 lemon
6 egg whites
1 cup lemonade

Preheat oven to 350° F., a moderate oven. Mix the first 6 ingredients and fold in the stiffly beaten whites. Bake in a greased and floured 9-inch spring form about 1 hour. While cake is hot, pour 1 cup lemonade gradually over the top. Let torte stand in pan until cool.

TO MAKE LEMONADE

Squeeze the juice of 1 lemon, add hot water to fill 1 cup, and stir in 1 tablespoon sugar.

LEMON VELVET TORTE

butter
15 graham crackers
½ cup butter, melted
6 eggs, separated
salt
juice of 2 lemons
grated rind of 1 lemon
1 15-ounce can sweetened condensed milk
½ teaspoon cream of tartar
½ cup sugar

Preheat oven to 350° F., a moderate oven. Spread sides and bottom of spring form well with softened butter. Roll crackers fine, mix with melted butter and pat evenly into pan to form the crust. Beat egg yolks well, add pinch of salt, lemon juice and rind, and very gradually the milk, beating constantly. Beat egg whites until foamy, add cream of tartar, beat until stiff and fold 5 tablespoons into lemon mixture. Put into spring form. Make meringue of remaining beaten egg whites, adding sugar; spread over top. Bake 15 minutes; cool, put in refrigerator overnight.

LINZER TORTE

1 cup butter
1 cup sugar
3 eggs, separated
1 lemon, grated rind and juice
1 tablespoon brandy
½ pound almonds, chopped fine
2 cups flour, sifted 3 times
1 teaspoon baking powder
12-ounce jar of jam or preserves

Preheat oven to 350° F., a moderate oven. Cream butter and sugar well. Add yolks, flavoring, and almonds. Add flour mixed with baking powder and fold in the stiffly beaten whites. Roll out or pat ⅔ of the dough in a greased and floured 9-inch spring form having the dough a little thicker on the bottom than the sides. Fill with jam. Roll remaining dough, cut in strips and place crisscross on top. Bake for 40 minutes. Before serving, fill hollows on top with jam.

MACAROON JAM TORTE

Rich Egg Pastry, page 342
½ pound confectioners sugar
7 whites of eggs
¾ pound almonds, blanched and ground
juice and grated rind of 1 lemon
cherry or gooseberry preserves

Preheat oven to 350° F., a moderate oven. Line a greased 9-inch spring form with Rich Egg Pastry. Combine the sifted sugar and the unbeaten whites in the top of a double boiler for 5 minutes, and heat stirring constantly. Cool. Combine with almonds and lemon. Spread preserves on top of dough. Fill with macaroon mixture. Bake ¾ hour.

MACAROON TORTE

Rich Egg Pastry, page 342
14 egg whites
2 cups confectioners sugar
1 teaspoon vanilla
1 pound blanched and grated almonds

Preheat oven to 325° F., a moderately slow oven. Line sides and bottom of spring form with Rich Egg Pastry. Beat egg whites very stiff, add sugar and beat again until stiff and dry, add vanilla and fold in the grated almonds.

Place the nut mixture in the dough-lined spring form and bake 1 hour; serve with whipped cream.

MARZIPAN TORTE PASTRY

½ cup butter
2 cups flour
2 tablespoons sugar
2 egg yolks
2 tablespoons water

Blend butter into flour and sugar, add egg yolks and water and mix well. Chill thoroughly. Roll out dough and line a greased 9-inch spring form. Reserve a small quantity of dough for strips for the top.

FILLING

1 pound almonds, blanched and grated
1 pound confectioners sugar
½ teaspoon salt
juice of 2 lemons
8 egg whites

Preheat oven to 325° F., a moderately slow oven. Heat almonds, sugar, salt, and lemon juice in a double boiler stirring until well blended. Cool. Add the stiffly beaten whites. Put the mixture on the dough, place strips of crust over the top. Bake 1 hour. Dust with confectioners sugar and decorate with candied cherries.

MATZO MEAL ALMOND TORTE

5 eggs, separated
1 cup sugar
1 cup almonds, ground without blanching
½ cup matzo meal
1 teaspoon baking powder
1 teaspoon cinnamon
¼ teaspoon ground cloves
1 tablespoon lemon juice or brandy

Preheat oven to 350° F., a moderate oven. Beat yolks and sugar until light; add the rest of the ingredients in order, the stiffly beaten whites last. Bake in a greased and floured 8-inch spring form for 1 hour.

CHOCOLATE MATZO MEAL TORTE

4 egg yolks, beaten
½ cup sugar
¼ pound almonds, blanched and grated
¼ pound raisins
⅛ cup matzo cake meal
¼ pound sweet chocolate, grated, or ½ cup cocoa
¼ cup wine
juice of 1 orange
4 egg whites

Preheat oven to 350° F., a moderate oven. Beat yolks and sugar until very light, add grated almonds, raisins, matzo cake meal, chocolate, wine, orange juice, and fold in the stiffly beaten whites. Bake in a greased and floured 8-inch spring form for 1 hour.

MERINGUE TORTE (SCHAUM TORTE)

6 egg whites
2 cups sugar
1 teaspoon vanilla
1 teaspoon vinegar

Preheat oven to 275° F., a slow oven. Beat whites until stiff enough to hold up in peaks; beat in 2 tablespoons sugar at a time, 3 times, beating thoroughly each time. Add vanilla, vinegar, and the rest of the sugar, beating all the time. Grease and flour a 9-inch spring form and fill with about ⅔ of the mixture. On a greased and floured tin, form a circle of small kisses with the rest of the mixture. Bake about 1 hour.

HIGH TEMPERATURE METHOD

Bake at 450° F., a hot oven, for 7 minutes. Turn off heat and leave torte in oven for 3 hours.

Before serving fill with whipped cream or ice cream and berries and decorate the top with the circle of kisses.

COFFEE SCHAUM TORTE

Follow recipe for Meringue Torte, above, but put all of the mixture into the spring form. Cover baked meringue with mounds of coffee ice cream. Serve with Coffee Sauce to which ½ cup whipped cream and ½ cup toasted, sliced almonds have been added.

MATZO MEAL APPLE TORTE

8 eggs, separated
¼ teaspoon salt
¾ cup sugar
1 cup matzo meal
1 teaspoon cinnamon
1 tablespoon orange juice
¼ cup almonds or other nuts
8 apples, pared and grated

Preheat oven to 350° F., a moderate oven. Beat whites with salt until very stiff; add sugar gradually, then beaten yolks. Mix and add dry ingredients, then orange juice and nuts, lastly apples. Bake in greased and floured 9-inch spring form 1 to 1¼ hours. Serve with Wine Sauce.

ORANGE TORTE

8 eggs, separated
1 cup sugar
½ pound grated almonds
2 tablespoons bread crumbs
grated rind and juice of 2 small oranges

Preheat oven to 350° F., a moderate oven. Beat yolks and sugar until very light; add other ingredients, the stiffly beaten egg whites last. Bake in 2 greased and floured layer cake pans for ½ hour. When cold, spread jelly between layers. **Spread Orange Butter Frosting** over top of torte and decorate with orange sections and candied cherries.

LEMON ANGEL PIE

4 egg whites
1 teaspoon cream of tartar
1 cup sugar
½ teaspoon vanilla
4 egg yolks
juice and grated rind of 1½ lemons
½ cup sugar
1 cup heavy cream, whipped
coconut

Make meringue of first four ingredients, as in Meringue Torte, above. Put mixture into greased spring form or deep 9-inch pie plate. Bake and cool, set aside. For filling, beat egg yolks until thick and lemon-colored. Add lemon juice and rind and then ½ cup sugar. Cook in double boiler until thick. Chill. Cover meringue with a layer of whipped cream, add lemon custard, top with whipped cream; sprinkle with freshly grated coconut. Chill for 24 hours.

For maximum lightness and volume in beating eggs:

- *Have eggs at room temperature.*
- *Be sure beater and bowl are free of grease.*
- *Separate eggs carefully, removing even the smallest amount of yolk from the whites (half an eggshell is convenient for this purpose).*

MERINGUE CAKE (MUSHKAZUNGE)

7 egg whites, unbeaten
1 cup plus 2 tablespoons sugar
½ teaspoon cinnamon
grated rind of ½ lemon
½ pound unblanched almonds, grated

Preheat oven to 350° F., a moderate oven. Beat whites until stiff enough to hold a soft peak. Gradually beat in sugar. Add cinnamon and lemon rind. Fold in grated nuts. Spread in a greased shallow pan, 9 x 13 inches. Bake for 20 minutes.

POPPY SEED TORTE

Rich Egg Pastry, page 342
bread crumbs
6 eggs, separated
¾ cup sugar
1 cup ground poppy seed
grated rind of lemon
2 tablespoons raisins, cut
1 tablespoon citron, cut fine
1 teaspoon vanilla
¼ cup ground almonds

Preheat oven to 350° F., a moderate oven. Line a 9-inch spring form with Rich Egg Pastry, sprinkle with bread crumbs. Beat yolks and sugar until light, add the rest of the ingredients, the stiffly beaten whites last. Fill the form and bake about 1 hour or until well set.

CHOCOLATE POPPY SEED TORTE

1¼ cups ground poppy seed
¾ pound grated almonds
1½ teaspoons cinnamon
1½ ounces grated sweet chocolate
1½ teaspoons baking powder
18 eggs, separated
1¼ cups sugar
¼ cup brandy
1 lemon, grated rind and juice

Preheat oven to 350° F., a moderate oven. Mix poppy seed, almonds, cinnamon, chocolate, and baking powder. Beat yolks and sugar until very light. Add brandy, lemon rind and juice, and dry ingredients. Fold in stiffly beaten whites. Bake in a very large greased and floured spring form until well set.

PRUNE TORTE

Rich Egg Pastry, page 342
1 pound prunes
2 egg whites
¼ cup sugar
grated rind of 1 lemon
1 cup chopped nuts

Preheat oven to 400° F., a hot oven. Line bottom and sides of a greased 9-inch spring form with Rich Egg Pastry. Cook prunes, drain, stone and chop fine. Beat the whites very stiff, add sugar, lemon rind, and fold in the prunes. Fill spring form; sprinkle the chopped nuts on top. Bake 25 to 30 minutes.

Many of these Torten are "heirloom" recipes that have been in all editions of the SETTLEMENT COOK BOOK *since the early 1900s.*

BLITZ TORTE (QUICK MERINGUE TORTE)

½ cup butter
½ cup sugar
4 egg yolks
1 teaspoon vanilla
3 tablespoons milk
1 cup cake flour
1 teaspoon baking powder

Preheat oven to 350° F., a moderate oven. Cream the butter and sugar. Beat egg yolks light and add to butter and sugar; add vanilla, milk, and flour sifted with baking powder. Mix well. Spread the mixture in 2 greased 8-inch layer cake pans.

TOPPING

4 whites of eggs
1 cup sugar
½ cup almonds, sliced
1 tablespoon sugar
½ teaspoon cinnamon

Beat the whites stiff and dry, add sugar gradually, and spread on the unbaked mixture in both pans. Sprinkle layers with almonds, sugar and cinnamon. Bake about 30 minutes. When cool, fill with Sour Cream Filling or Vanilla Custard Filling, using lemon or orange flavoring.

REGENTS TORTE

3 eggs, separated
1¼ cups sugar
½ pound almonds, blanched and grated
raspberry or currant jelly

Preheat oven to 350° F., a moderate oven. Beat the yolks with ½ cup sugar until very light; add half the almonds. Bake in a very small, well-greased spring form for ½ hour. When partially cool, spread with jelly and cover with meringue made by beating the whites very light, and adding the rest of the sugar and the almonds. Brown meringue in 375° F. oven.

RYE BREAD TORTE (BROD TORTE)

5 eggs, separated
1 cup sugar
1 cup rye or wheat bread crumbs
½ lemon, juice and grated rind, or
2 tablespoons wine
1 cup almonds, blanched and grated
1½ teaspoons baking powder

Preheat oven to 350° F., a moderate oven. Beat the yolks and sugar until very light. Soak the crumbs in the lemon juice or wine; mix all ingredients, the stiffly beaten whites last. Bake in 2 greased and floured 9-inch layer pans for 45 minutes. Fill with Walnut Filling.

BRANDY RYE BREAD TORTE

6 eggs, separated
1 cup sugar
¾ cup rye bread crumbs
1 cup grated almonds
½ cup cooked, riced potatoes
¼ teaspoon cinnamon
¼ cup brandy or wine

Preheat oven to 350° F., a moderate oven. Beat yolks and sugar until very light. Add the rest of the ingredients, the stiffly beaten egg whites last. Bake in a greased and floured 9-inch spring form for 1 hour.

CHOCOLATE RYE BREAD TORTE

10 eggs, separated
2 cups sugar
1¾ cups toasted rye bread crumbs
1 cup grated unsweetened chocolate
½ teaspoon cinnamon
¼ cup chopped almonds
2 tablespoons chopped citron
¼ cup preserved fruit
¼ cup fruit juice or red wine
2 teaspoons baking powder

Preheat oven to 350° F., a moderate oven. Beat the yolks and sugar until very light. Add the remaining ingredients gradually, the stiffly beaten egg whites last. Bake in a greased and floured 12-inch spring form for 1 hour.

SCHAUM TORTE PIE

3 egg whites
1 cup sugar
1 quart well-drained fruit (whole strawberries, blueberries, or pitted sour cherries)
baked pie shell, page 341

Beat whites until foamy; add sugar and beat until very thick and marshmallowy. Fold in the fruit, heap in pie shell, and bake for 45 minutes in a very slow oven, 250° F.

STRAWBERRY SHORTCAKE TORTE

9 egg whites
1½ cups sugar
1 teaspoon vanilla
¾ cup blanched and ground almonds
1 quart strawberries, cut and sugared
2 cups heavy cream, whipped

Preheat oven to 325° F., a moderately slow oven. Beat whites stiff and dry. Add sugar gradually, beating constantly; add flavoring and, lastly, fold in the nuts. Spread evenly in 2 greased and floured cake pans with removable bottoms. Bake 25 to 30 minutes. When cool, put cut and sugared strawberries and whipped cream between layers and on top.

VIENNA TORTE

7 eggs, separated
1¼ cups sugar
1 cup flour
¼ cup cornstarch
2 teaspoons baking powder
pinch of salt

Preheat oven to 350° F., a moderate oven. Beat whites until frothy. Add ½ cup sugar gradually, beat until stiff. Beat yolks until thick, add rest of sugar gradually and beat. Combine the two mixtures. Sift the flour with cornstarch, baking powder and salt and fold in carefully. Pour into 4 greased and floured 8-inch layer cake pans. Bake about 20 minutes. Cool.

FILLING

Heat 1¼ cups milk in double boiler. Mix ⅓ cup flour and ⅓ cup sugar and ¼ cup cold milk. Add to heated milk and stir until thick, then cover and cook 15 minutes. When cool, add 1 cup melted butter, mix well, then add 1 teaspoon vanilla and 1 cup confectioners sugar. Spread this between the four layers and on top and sides. Cover well with chopped nuts.

For high-altitude baking, see the cake-recipe adjustment guide, page 106.

For general directions on freezing cakes and other baked goods, see chapter 24. Recommended keeping period for frozen cakes is 3 months.

WALNUT TORTE

6 eggs, separated
1 cup sugar
¼ pound grated walnuts
1¼ cups grated lady fingers
2 tablespoons flour
1 teaspoon baking powder
½ lemon, juice and grated rind

Preheat oven to 350° F., a moderate oven. Beat the yolks and sugar until light; add the other ingredients in the order given, mixing baking powder with flour and lastly folding in the stiffly beaten whites. Bake in greased and floured 9-inch layer pans for 30 minutes. Place Custard Filling or Walnut Filling between layers. Cover sides and top of torte with Chocolate Butter Frosting.

ZWIEBACK TORTE

6 eggs, separated
¾ cup sugar
¼ pound almonds, grated
juice and grated rind of ½ lemon
¼ pound zwieback, crushed
½ teaspoon cinnamon
½ teaspoon ground cloves
2 teaspoons baking powder

Preheat oven to 350° F., a moderate oven. Beat yolks and sugar until very light. Add the remaining ingredients, and the stiffly beaten egg whites last. Bake in a greased and floured 9-inch spring form for about 40 minutes. Sprinkle with 2 tablespoons brandy or maraschino syrup and bake 5 minutes longer.

CHOCOLATE ZWIEBACK TORTE

¾ cup zwieback crumbs
1 teaspoon baking powder
6 eggs, separated
1 cup sugar
1 cup grated unsweetened chocolate
1 cup almonds, grated
1 teaspoon cinnamon
1 teaspoon ground cloves

Preheat the oven to 325° F., a moderately slow oven. Mix the zwieback and baking powder. Beat yolks and sugar until very light, add other ingredients, the stiffly beaten whites last. Bake in 2 greased and floured 9-inch layer cake pans for 45 minutes. Spread raspberry jelly between the layers and cover with Chocolate Butter Frosting.

ICEBOX CAKES
AND
CAKE DESSERTS

GENERAL RULES FOR LAYERED ICEBOX CAKES

Line the bottom and sides of a spring form pan with split lady fingers (or fingers of sponge or angel food cake). Trim if necessary, to fit, and arrange rounded side toward the pan. Add a layer of prepared filling (see recipes), cover with lady fingers, and repeat to fill mold. The last layer should be lady fingers, arranged like the spokes of a wheel. Chill overnight, until very firm. Remove the sides from the pan and put the cake on the serving platter without removing the pan bottom. Garnish with sweetened, flavored whipped cream, and decorate with pistachio nuts or candied cherries.

CHOCOLATE ICEBOX CAKE

2 squares unsweetened chocolate
½ cup granulated sugar
¼ cup water
4 eggs, separated
1 cup butter
1 cup confectioners sugar
2½ dozen lady fingers, split

Cook chocolate, granulated sugar and water in double boiler; when smooth, gradually add the well-beaten yolks; cook until thick and smooth, stirring constantly. Cool. Cream butter and confectioners sugar well, add the egg mixture, stir well, and fold in the stiffly beaten whites. Line cake form with lady fingers and follow directions in General Rules.

SWEET CHOCOLATE ICEBOX CAKE

½ pound sweet chocolate
4 tablespoons sugar
4 tablespoons water
5 eggs, separated
30 lady fingers, split
1 cup whipped cream

Melt chocolate in double boiler, add sugar and the egg yolks beaten with the water. Cook slowly until thick and smooth, stirring constantly. When cool, fold in the stiffly beaten whites. Line cake form with lady fingers and follow directions in General Rules.

DELMONICO DESSERT

Spanish Cream, page 204
12 candied cherries
12 macaroons moistened in sherry
Whipped Cream Sauce, page 218
¼ pound candied fruit, chopped
Sponge Cake, page 118
sherry
¼ pound blanched almonds
heavy cream, whipped

Make Spanish Cream and pour ½ inch into **large** melon mold. Chill. When it begins to harden, place a candied cherry on each moistened macaroon and line mold, cherry side down, pressing gently against mold. Pour in rest of Spanish Cream, then spread with Whipped Cream Sauce, sprinkled with candied fruit. Cut a 1-inch slice of Sponge Cake, baked the day before, to fit the cover of the mold. Place cake in cover, prick with fork and moisten well with sherry. Cut **almonds** lengthwise and stick halfway into the cake at frequent intervals. Place cover, with cake, over filled mold, pressing almonds down into the whipped cream layer. Let chill and set. Unmold and serve with a border of whipped cream. Serves 12 to 15.

LEMON-FILLED ICEBOX CAKE

3 eggs, separated
¼ cup granulated sugar
1 tablespoon cornstarch
¼ cup milk
juice of 1 lemon
grated rind of ½ lemon
½ cup butter
1 cup confectioners sugar
3 dozen lady fingers, split
1 cup heavy cream, whipped

In a double boiler, place the well-beaten yolks, the granulated sugar and cornstarch mixed with the milk; cook until thick and smooth, stirring constantly. Remove from heat, add lemon juice and rind and cool. Cream butter and confectioners sugar well, add to the egg mixture. Fold in the stiffly beaten egg whites. Line spring form with lady fingers and follow directions in General Rules.

ORANGE ICEBOX CAKE

Follow recipe for Lemon-Filled Icebox Cake, using juice and grated rind of 1 orange and only the grated rind of 1 lemon.

MARSHMALLOW ICEBOX PUDDING

½ pound marshmallows
¼ cup milk
1 cup heavy cream, whipped
1 tablespoon rum
½ cup broken walnut meats
½ cup chopped candied cherries
8 to 12 lady fingers

Cut marshmallows in pieces, add the milk and cook over hot water until dissolved. Remove from heat, stir well and when cool, fold in the whipped cream. Add rum and fold in the nuts and cherries. Place in a mold that has been dipped in cold water and lined with split lady fingers. Chill for 8 or more hours. Unmold and serve surrounded with fresh fruit if desired or serve with Rum Sauce.

MOCHA ICEBOX CAKE

1 cup hot milk
3 tablespoons instant coffee
2 tablespoons cornstarch
⅛ teaspoon salt
½ cup sugar
3 eggs, separated
1 teaspoon vanilla
30 lady fingers

Pour the hot milk over coffee and let it stand for 10 minutes. Mix cornstarch, salt and sugar in double boiler, add the yolks, well beaten, and stir in the coffee mixture. Cook slowly until thick and smooth; while still warm, add vanilla and fold in stiffly-beaten egg whites. Line bottom and sides of a spring form with lady fingers and follow General Rules.

ALMOND OR PECAN ICEBOX CAKE

18 lady fingers
30 macaroons
1 cup butter
1⅛ cup confectioners sugar
3 whole eggs
3 eggs, separated
½ pound blanched, grated almonds or pecans
2 cups heavy cream, whipped
candied cherries or pistachio nuts
¼ cup confectioners sugar
vanilla

Cut ends off lady fingers. Separate and place lady fingers close together on sides of 9-inch spring form, the rounded side toward the pan. Lay the macaroons close together on bottom, flat side down and fill in the small spaces with the lady finger ends. Cream butter and sugar, add 3 whole eggs, one at a time, and stir well. Add the yolks of the other 3 eggs, well-beaten, then the nuts, and lastly fold in the 3 beaten whites. Cover the macaroons with half of mixture, add another layer of macaroons, then the rest of the mixture. Chill for 30 hours. When ready to serve, remove rim of cake pan, leaving cake on pan bottom; cover top with the whipped cream, adding confectioners sugar and vanilla; decorate with candied cherries or chopped pistachio nuts.

PORCUPINE ICEBOX CAKE

1 cup butter
6 yolks of eggs
6 tablespoons sugar
3 tablespoons instant coffee
6 tablespoons sherry
24 lady fingers
¼ pound almonds, blanched, sliced

Have butter and eggs at room temperature. Cream butter, add yolks one at a time and stir well, then add sugar, ½ the coffee and all the sherry, stirring constantly. With some of this coffee mixture cover a 10 by 4-inch space on a serving platter. Over this place split lady fingers moistened with a few additional drops of sherry. Cover with coffee mixture, then a layer of lady fingers moistened with additional liquid coffee. Alternate layers until all lady fingers have been placed. Cover entire cake with rest of coffee mixture and insert sliced and roasted almonds upright into top and sides. Chill for 12 to 24 hours.

QUEEN OF TRIFLES

½ pound almonds
1 pound macaroons
2 cups sherry
1 pound lady fingers
½ cup sugar
2 tablespoons flour
1 egg, well-beaten
2 cups hot milk
½ pound candied cherries, halved
4 cups heavy cream, whipped

Blanch and chop almonds, not too fine. Soak macaroons in the wine. Line a large glass bowl with split lady fingers. Make a custard mixture by mixing sugar and flour with the egg, add gradually to the hot milk and cook in double boiler until very thick, stirring constantly. Cool, add almonds, cherries, and ¾ of the whipped cream. Pour custard mixture over lady fingers; top with macaroons. Cover with remaining whipped cream. Decorate with cherries. Serves 12.

CHOCOLATE GRAHAM ICEBOX CAKE

Make double portion Chocolate Cornstarch Pudding. When cool, add 1 teaspoon vanilla. Put a layer of graham crackers in an 8-inch square pan. Pour half of pudding over crackers, then another layer of crackers and the remaining pudding. Chill for 12 hours, cut in squares and serve with whipped cream.

FROZEN VANILLA WAFER ICEBOX DESSERT

1 cup vanilla wafer crumbs
3 eggs, separated
2 tablespoons lemon juice
1 tablespoon grated lemon rind
⅛ teaspoon salt
½ cup sugar
1 cup heavy cream or 1 can (8 ounces) evaporated milk, beaten stiff

Line a greased refrigerator tray with waxed paper. Sprinkle with ½ cup cookie crumbs. Beat egg yolks until lemon-colored. Add lemon juice, rind, salt and sugar. Cook in double boiler, stirring constantly, until mixture coats a spoon. Cool. Beat egg whites until stiff. Fold into first mixture. Fold in stiffly beaten cream or evaporated milk (To whip evaporated milk, chill well or freeze to mushy stage before whipping.) Pour into tray. Top with remaining crumbs. Freeze in freezing compartment of refrigerator for several hours. Serves 8.

CHOCOLATE MARSHMALLOW ICEBOX DESSERT

Graham Cracker Shell, page 343
20 marshmallows
½ cup milk
2 squares unsweetened chocolate, grated
¾ cup broken nut meats
1 cup heavy cream, whipped

Line a pie pan with Graham Cracker Crumb Crust, reserve some crumbs. Melt marshmallows in the milk in a double boiler. Cool, add the chocolate and the nut meats. Fold in the whipped cream. Fill shell. Sprinkle top with remaining crumbs. Chill.

CHOCOLATE CHARLOTTE RUSSE

2 envelopes unflavored gelatin
¼ cup cold water
2 squares unsweetened chocolate, grated
2 cups milk
1 cup sugar
1 teaspoon vanilla
2 cups heavy cream
12 lady fingers

Soak gelatin in cold water 5 minutes. Melt chocolate in double boiler, add milk and sugar, cook 5 minutes or until smooth, add gelatin and stir until dissolved. When cold, add vanilla. Beat cream until very stiff, gradually add the chocolate and gelatin mixture. Line a quart mold with split lady fingers, and fill with custard mixture. Chill for an hour or more. Unmold and serve with whipped cream and, if desired, sprinkle with bits of candied cherries, and pistachio nuts.

ANGEL CHARLOTTE RUSSE

1 envelope unflavored gelatin
¼ cup cold water
¼ cup boiling water
1 cup sugar
2 cups heavy cream, whipped
¼ pound blanched almonds, chopped
6 crushed, dry macaroons
12 marshmallows, cut up
2 tablespoons chopped, candied cherries
2 tablespoons vanilla or sherry

Soak gelatin in cold water, dissolve in boiling water, and add sugar. When mixture is cold, add whipped cream, almonds, macaroons, marshmallows and candied cherries. Add flavoring. Pour into a wet mold, and chill until firm. Unmold and serve.

CHERRY CHARLOTTE RUSSE

2 envelopes unflavored gelatin
½ cup cold water
2 cups heavy cream
¼ cup confectioners sugar
1 teaspoon vanilla
1 pint maraschino cherries and juice
12 lady fingers

Soak gelatin in cold water 5 minutes, place over hot water and stir until dissolved. Beat the cream until very stiff; gradually add sugar, vanilla, the dissolved gelatin and the syrup from the cherries, beating all the time. When the mixture begins to thicken stir in the chopped cherries and, if desired, ½ cup chopped nuts. Pour into a mold lined with split lady fingers, and chill until firm.

ORANGE OR STRAWBERRY
CHARLOTTE RUSSE

2 envelopes unflavored gelatin
⅓ cup cold water
⅓ cup boiling water
1 cup sugar
3 tablespoons lemon juice
1 cup fruit juice and pulp
3 egg whites
1 cup heavy cream, whipped
orange sections or whole strawberries

Soak the gelatin in cold water, then dissolve in boiling water. Add sugar, cool; add lemon juice, fruit juice and pulp. When cold, beat until frothy; add stiffly beaten whites and fold in cream. Line a mold with sections of orange or fresh, ripe strawberries. Pour in the mixture and chill until firm.

DESSERT IN CAKE SHELL

Cut slice from top of Sponge or Angel Cake; scoop out the inside of the remaining cake, leaving a ¾-inch wall; fill with Angel Charlotte Russe, replace top of cake, cover with whipped cream and garnish with candied cherries and blanched almonds. Or fill cake shell with any thick pudding mixture. Replace top of cake. Chill until firm. Top with whipped cream.

ANGEL FOOD SURPRISE

Angel Food Cake, page 121
3 cups heavy cream
6 tablespoons sugar
6 tablespoons cocoa
⅛ teaspoon salt
⅔ cup toasted almonds, chopped

Combine cream, sugar, cocoa and salt and chill for 1 hour or more. Whip mixture until stiff. Place cake with the larger surface at bottom on a large serving plate. Cut entire top from cake about 1-inch down. Lift off this top layer. Scoop out the inside of the remaining cake, leaving 1-inch wall on bottom and sides. Fill with one-third of the cream mixture to which one-half of the nuts have been added. Replace top, spread remaining cream over top and sides. Sprinkle with remaining nuts. Chill until served.

FILLED SUNSHINE CAKE

Make Sunshine Cake in spring form. Cut a ½-inch slice off the top. Scoop out the inside of the remaining cake, leaving 1-inch wall at bottom and sides. Fill with the following, mixed in order given:

1 cup heavy cream, whipped
1 egg white, beaten stiff
1 teaspoon cocoa
1 teaspoon vanilla
½ cup almonds, chopped fine
1 cup cake crumbs from the scooped-out cake, above

Cover with cut-off slice of cake and frost with Chocolate Butter Frosting, chill and serve.

RUSSIAN TORTE

Angel Food Cake, page 121
2 tablespoons granulated gelatin
¼ cup cold water
1 cup confectioners sugar
⅛ teaspoon salt
2 tablespoons instant coffee
8 egg yolks
2 cups heavy cream, whipped
1 teaspoon vanilla
½ cup chopped almonds, roasted

Make Angel Food Cake. Cut in two, the bottom layer a little thicker than the top. Soak gelatin in the water about 5 minutes. Put over boiling water to dissolve. Add confectioners sugar, salt, coffee, and set aside until mixture begins to jell. In the meantime, beat egg yolks well, add the whipped cream, and vanilla. Combine the two mixtures *before* the gelatin sets. Beat thoroughly. Spread between layers and over top of cake. Sprinkle with blanched almonds. Chill until set.

To beat egg whites, have whites, bowl and beater at room temperature.

To whip cream, chill cream, bowl and beater. To whip evaporated milk, chill in refrigerator tray until edges are frozen; beat in chilled bowl. Add lemon juice (2 tablespoons to a 14-ounce can) and sugar, if desired.

VENETIAN TORTE

Imperial Sunshine Cake, page 119
Almond Brittle, page 174
Basic Butter Frosting, page 143
2 squares unsweetened chocolate, melted
1 teaspoon instant coffee

Bake Imperial Sunshine Cake, in large spring form. When cold, cut into four layers. Make Almond Brittle, cool, put through coarse grinder. Make Basic Butter Frosting. To one-half of this frosting, add melted chocolate. To the rest add the coffee. Place the chocolate frosting between layers, and the coffee frosting over top. Sprinkle ground Almond Brittle over top and sides.

PYRAMID ICEBOX CAKE

Bake Sponge Cake in flat, oblong pan about 30 minutes at 325° F. When cold, cut lengthwise into 6 strips.

FILLING

1 cup butter
1 cup confectioners sugar
2 tablespons strong coffee or
    1 tablespoon instant coffee
2 egg yolks, well beaten
2 cups heavy cream, whipped

Cream butter and sugar well; add flavoring and egg yolks and beat until light. Fold in cream and place in refrigerator until needed.

TO ARRANGE CAKE

Place 3 strips on oblong platter, leaving ⅓ inch space between strips. Spread filling in spaces, and over top. Lay 2 strips along filled spaces, and spread filling in space between strips and over top; then place remaining strip along filled space in center, and cover entire cake with filling. Stud with ¼ cup almonds, blanched, split and toasted. Chill for 24 hours.

CAKE BASKETS

Make Sponge or Cup Cakes in muffin tins. When cold, cut off tops and carefully hollow out inside with cookie cutter and knife. Fill with fresh sweetened berries, ice cream or whipped cream. Make handle from strip of lemon or orange rind, or angelica, sliding the ends between filling and cake walls.

DESSERTS IN MARY ANN CAKE SHELLS

Mix any Sponge Cake. Bake in moderately slow oven, 325° F., about 45 minutes in Mary Ann Shell insert. Fill with ice cream, cover with any ice cream sauce, or with prepared fresh fruits topped with whipped cream or ice cream.

BIRTHDAY CANDLESTICKS

Make a candlestick base for each serving from circle of sliced loaf cake, ¾ inch thick. Cover cake with soft icing or sweetened whipped cream. Place half a banana cut crosswise, upright in center to represent the candle and stick a small wax candle in top of banana. Form handle of candlestick with lemon or orange rind slices. Light the candle and serve.

PINEAPPLE OR STRAWBERRY MERINGUE DESSERT

Bake Sponge Cake in shallow pan. Cover with drained, crushed pineapple or fresh strawberries, and Meringue. Bake a few minutes to delicate brown.

SMALL CAKES

The most elegant small cakes are made from a large sheet of plain cake; the large cake is cut into decorative shapes and each small cake is individually iced and decorated.

Other small cakes are made by dropping cake batter from a spoon to form a mound on a baking sheet; or by forcing the batter through a pastry tube; or by baking in special small pans.

PETITS FOURS (SMALL DECORATED CAKES)

sheet cake
jelly
Cooked Fondant, page 172
pistachio nuts
candied cherries, candied orange peel, candied
    lime peel, candied pineapple
candied rose petals, candied violets, candied mint
    leaves

Cut a sheet cake into small circles, diamonds, or squares about 1½ inches in diameter. Any sponge or butter cake or chiffon cake batter may be baked in a large, shallow pan for this purpose; a cake baked in a 13 x 9 x 2-inch pan will yield about 46 petits fours. Melt Fondant Icing of various colors and flavors over hot water, and keep it warm. To seal edges, brush cut sides of cake with jelly. Fix cakes on a fork and dip into icing; drain and invert on a rack over waxed paper to dry. Decorate each cake to taste with fruits and nuts. Pistachio nuts, cut lengthwise, can be used for leaves, and candied fruits for flowers. Or use candied flowers or leaves. Fix the decorations with a little warm fondant, let harden. *Put each cake in a little paper case, if desired.*

FILLED PETITS FOURS

Cut out cake shapes, above, from any frosted cake before icing with fondant and decorating. Or hollow out the cakes, fill with whipped cream, almond paste, or a custard filling, and sandwich in pairs; ice and decorate to taste.

COCONUT SNOWBALLS

Make Angel Food Cake; bake in ungreased angel food tin. Make Meringue Frosting. Cool cake, remove from pan, cut in 1½-inch cubes. Place on fork, dip into frosting, cover on all sides; roll in freshly grated coconut, place on waxed paper until set. Serve same day.

SMALL FROSTED CAKES

Bake Angel, Sponge or Sunshine Cakes in pans 1½ inches deep. Cover with any of the frostings as directed:

MARSHMALLOW FROSTING

Set marshmallows on cake about 1 inch apart in 3 or 4 rows, sprinkle with 3 tablespoons sugar and ½ teaspoon cinnamon. Place in moderate oven until marshmallow melts somewhat, cut cake into squares, a marshmallow on each square.

CHOCOLATE FROSTING

Frost cake with Chocolate Glaze, and while soft, cut into squares, place half a walnut on each.

MOCHA FROSTING

Let cake cool, cut into squares, cover with soft Coffee Icing. Sprinkle with finely chopped and blanched pistachio nuts, roasted almonds, or peanuts or with dried and rolled macaroons.

Cake Frostings and Fillings will be found on pages 142 to 150.

CHOCOLATE POTATO DROP CAKES

⅓ cup shortening
1 cup sugar
2 eggs, separated
2 squares unsweetened chocolate, grated
1 cup hot, riced potato
1 cup flour
3 teaspoons baking powder
½ teaspoon salt
⅓ cup raisins

Preheat oven to 350° F., a moderate oven. Cream shortening and sugar; add egg yolks, chocolate, and potato. Sift flour with baking powder and salt and add to mixture. Add raisins. Fold in **stiffly** beaten whites. Chopped nuts may be added. Drop small portions on greased cookie sheets. Bake for 15 minutes.

NUT DROP CAKES

2 tablespoons butter
¼ cup sugar
1 egg, well beaten
½ teaspoon lemon juice
½ cup flour
1 teaspoon baking powder
¼ teaspoon salt
2 tablespoons milk
⅛ cup chopped nuts

Cream butter and sugar, add egg and lemon juice. Beat well. Sift dry ingredients, add alternately with the milk to first mixture; then add nuts. Drop on greased cookie sheet 1 inch apart. Bake in moderate oven, 350° F., 15 minutes.

LADY FINGERS

3 eggs, separated
⅓ cup confectioners sugar
¼ teaspoon vanilla
3 tablespoons hot water
½ cup flour
¼ teaspoon salt
1 teaspoon baking powder

Beat egg whites until foamy. Beat in sugar gradually and continue beating until stiff. Fold in egg yolks, beaten until thick; add vanilla and hot water. Fold in flour sifted with salt and baking powder. Put into lady finger tins, sprinkle with confectioners sugar and bake 8 to 10 minutes in moderate oven, 350° F. Remove from tins while hot. Brush the flat surface of half the cakes with egg white and sandwich in pairs.

Or, press batter through a tube in portions 1 inch wide by 5 inches long on a cookie sheet covered with waxed paper.

SPONGE DROPS

Make Lady Fingers, above. Drop from teaspoon. Bake for 10 to 12 minutes in moderate oven. Put together with jelly.

OTHELLOS

Force Lady Finger mixture, above, through a tube onto a cookie sheet covered with brown paper, in 1½-inch rounds. When baked, spread the flat side of half of the cakes with Vanilla Custard Filling. Press together in pairs and dip in Chocolate Frosting. Let dry on waxed paper.

PROFITEROLES

Fill Tiny Cream Puffs with ice cream and either freeze until serving time or serve at once, with warm chocolate sauce. Makes 6 servings.

CHOCOLATE ECLAIRS

Force mixture for Cream Puffs, below, through pastry tube, 2 inches apart, on greased cookie sheets, in oblong shapes, 4 by 1½ inches. When baked and cool, fill with any custard filling; ice with Chocolate Icing. Makes 12 eclairs.

CREAM PUFFS

½ cup butter
1 cup water
1 cup flour
4 eggs, unbeaten

Heat butter and water. When mixture is boiling, add flour all at once and stir vigorously until mixture no longer sticks to sides of pan. Remove from heat; cool slightly; add eggs one at a time, beating after each addition. Drop by heaping tablespoons onto a well-greased cookie sheet, 2 inches apart, and bake in very hot oven, 450° F., 20 minutes. Reduce heat to 325° F., and bake about 20 minutes longer. Remove from baking sheet and cool. When ready to serve, cut open on one side, and fill with whipped cream or any desired filling.

TINY CREAM PUFFS

Drop Cream Puff Mixture, above, from teaspoon or force through pastry tube onto greased cookie sheets in 1 to 1½-inch mounds. When baked and cool, slit one side, fill with any custard filling. Ice tops with any of a variety of colored and flavored frostings.

CUPCAKES

Any cake batter may be baked in greased cupcake pans, or in pans lined with paper baking cups de-signed especially for this purpose. Increase baking temperature to 375° and reduce baking time to about 20 minutes, depending on the size of the cakes.

VANILLA CUPCAKES

1 cup sugar
2 cups flour
¼ teaspoon salt
3 teaspoons baking powder
¼ cup shortening
1 cup milk
1 egg, well beaten
1 teaspoon vanilla

Preheat oven to 375° F., a moderately hot oven. Sift dry ingredients together; add melted shortening to the milk, egg and flavoring mixed together. Combine mixtures well. Bake in greased muffin pans for 20 minutes. Yields 24 medium cupcakes.

COCOA CUPCAKES

3 tablespoons shortening
1 cup sugar
1 egg, well beaten
1 teaspoon vanilla
½ cup milk
1½ cups flour
3 teaspoons baking powder
⅓ cup cocoa

Preheat oven to 375° F., a moderately hot oven. Cream shortening and sugar; add egg and vanilla. To the mixture add the milk and sifted dry ingredients alternately. Bake in greased muffin pans for 20 minutes. Yields 18 medium cupcakes.

CHOCOLATE CUPCAKES

½ cup shortening
1 cup brown sugar
1 egg
1 square melted unsweetened chocolate
½ cup sour milk
1½ cups flour
1 teaspoon soda

Preheat oven to 350° F., a moderate oven. Cream shortening and sugar; add egg and chocolate. Add milk alternately with the flour and soda mixed. Bake in greased muffin pans for 20 to 25 minutes. Yields 18 medium cupcakes.

Cupcakes and other small cakes may be frozen. It is best to freeze them unfrosted, and to frost them after thawing. For general directions on wrapping and freezing baked goods, see chapter 24.

RAISIN CUPCAKES

1 cup raisins
1½ cups flour
⅛ cup shortening
1 cup sugar
1 egg, well beaten
½ cup milk
3 teaspoons baking powder
½ teaspoon vanilla

Preheat oven to 350° F., a moderate oven. Mix raisins with ¼ cup of the flour. Cream shortening and sugar; stir in egg. Add milk, and flour sifted with the baking powder. Mix well, add vanilla and floured raisins. Bake in greased muffin pans about 20 minutes. Yields 18 medium cupcakes.

GINGER CUPCAKES

¼ cup butter
¼ cup brown sugar
1 egg
1½ cups flour
½ teaspoon cinnamon
¼ teaspoon ground cloves
1 tablespoon ginger
1 teaspoon soda
½ cup molasses
½ cup boiling water

Cream butter and add sugar gradually, then add the egg. Mix and sift dry ingredients and add alternately with molasses and hot water, mixed. Bake in greased muffin pans, 350° F., for about 20 minutes.

PEANUT BUTTER CUPCAKES

½ cup butter
1½ cups brown sugar
½ cup peanut butter
1 teaspoon vanilla
2 eggs, beaten
1½ cups cake flour
½ teaspoon salt
2 teaspoons baking powder
⅔ cup milk

Preheat oven to 350° F., a moderate oven. Cream butter, sugar, and peanut butter. Add vanilla and eggs, beating well. Sift flour, salt, and baking powder; add to egg mixture alternately with the milk. Bake in greased muffin pans about 30 minutes. Frost with any Chocolate Frosting. Yields about 20 cupcakes.

PECAN CUPCAKES

½ cup flour
⅛ teaspoon salt
¼ teaspoon baking powder
1 cup brown sugar
2 eggs, slightly beaten
1 cup broken pecan meats

Mix and sift the first 3 ingredients. Add sugar to eggs, then the pecans sprinkled with flour, then the flour mixture. Bake in small greased muffin pans in moderately slow oven at 325° F. for about 20 minutes.

DELICATE CAKES

½ cup milk
2 tablespoons butter
1 cup sugar
1 cup flour
1 teaspoon baking powder
¼ teaspoon salt
4 egg whites
½ teaspoon cream of tartar
1 teaspoon vanilla or almond extract
currant jelly
coconut, shredded

Preheat oven to 350° F., a moderate oven. Scald milk and butter. Add sugar and stir until dissolved. Add flour sifted with baking powder and salt and mix thoroughly. Beat egg whites until foamy, add cream of tartar, beat until whites stand up in peaks but are not dry. Fold into batter and add vanilla. Pour into greased and floured muffin pans and bake for about 25 minutes. When cool, dip each cake into well-beaten currant jelly and roll in coconut, or frost with Coconut or Maple Frosting. Makes twenty 2-inch cakes.

6
CAKE FROSTINGS AND FILLINGS

UNCOOKED ICINGS AND FROSTINGS • BOILED FROSTINGS
• FUDGE FROSTINGS • BASIC FILLINGS • FRUIT AND NUT FILLINGS

Frostings, icings and fillings keep cakes moist, and add greatly to their flavor and appearance.

GENERAL RULES

A cake should be cold and free from crumbs before it is frosted. Cover the cake plate with 2 strips of waxed paper to protect it from drippings. The paper may be withdrawn after the cake is frosted. When frosting layer cake, invert one layer, spread filling evenly over flat surface, then place flat surface of second layer on top and frost by heaping frosting in center and with spatula, spreading over top and sides. Spatula may be dipped in hot water if the frosting thickens.

To prevent layers from slipping, insert several toothpicks and remove when cake is frosted.

Flavorings for Frostings and Cakes

VANILLA SUGAR

Cut fresh vanilla bean into inch pieces. Place in small jar of confectioners sugar and use instead of plain sugar in frostings and in cakes.

CARAMEL SYRUP

    1 cup sugar
    ½ cup boiling water

Melt sugar in heavy skillet, stirring occasionally until sugar becomes a light-brown liquid. Add water slowly. Simmer 5 to 10 minutes. Cool and bottle. Use to color and flavor cakes and frostings.

RUM FLAVORING

    1 ounce medium-bodied New England rum
    1 ounce Jamaica rum
    1 ounce arrack
    1 ounce vanilla

Mix and bottle and use to flavor cakes or torten.

UNCOOKED ICINGS

Recipes containing 1 cup of confectioners sugar will ice the top of one 8- to 9-inch cake.

CONFECTIONERS SUGAR GLAZE

    2 tablespoons hot water, or milk or light cream
    ¼ teaspoon vanilla, lemon, or other extracts, or
        1 teaspoon lemon juice or rum
    1 cup confectioners sugar

Stir the liquid into the sugar, adding more, a few drops at a time, as needed. The icing is of the proper consistency when it coats the spoon.

CONFECTIONERS SUGAR ICING

    ½ teaspoon butter
    2 tablespoons hot milk
    1½ cups confectioners sugar
    ½ teaspoon vanilla

Add butter to hot milk; add sugar slowly to make right consistency to spread; add vanilla. Spread on top and sides of cake.

CHOCOLATE ICING

1 square chocolate, unsweetened
6 tablespoons boiling water
⅛ teaspoon vanilla extract
1¾ cups confectioners sugar

Melt chocolate in top of double boiler, add boiling water and stir until smooth; add vanilla and the sugar; stir until mixture is smooth. Or dissolve ⅓ cup cocoa in the boiling water. A little cinnamon may be added.

COFFEE OR MOCHA ICING

3 tablespoons hot strong coffee
3 tablespoons dry cocoa
½ teaspoon vanilla
1⅓ cups confectioners sugar

Add coffee to cocoa, stir until smooth, add vanilla and enough sugar to reach spreading consistency.

LEMON ICING

grated rind of ½ lemon
1 tablespoon lemon juice
1 tablespoon boiling water
1 cup confectioners sugar

Add lemon rind to juice and water, stir into the sugar, a little at a time, until thick enough to spread.

ORANGE ICING

1 egg yolk
2 cups confectioners sugar
2 tablespoons orange juice
1 teaspoon lemon juice
grated rind of 1 orange

Add yolk to sugar, mix well; add the rest.

FRUIT JUICE ICING

1 teaspoon lemon juice
2 tablespoons fresh fruit juice or fruit syrup
1½ cups confectioners sugar

Add lemon juice and strained fruit juice (strawberries, cherries or grapes) to the sugar, a little at a time, until thin enough to spread.

CHOCOLATE GLAZE

Melt 2 squares sweet or semi-sweet chocolate with ½ teaspoon butter. When cool, spread thin coating over Marshmallow Frosting.

ROYAL ICING

2 cups confectioners sugar
1 egg white, unbeaten
1 teaspoon lemon juice
dash of salt

Add sugar gradually to egg white, work together well with wooden spoon until smooth and shiny, add lemon juice and salt; stir well. Use for decorative icing.

GLACE

2 egg whites
1½ cups confectioners sugar
1 teaspoon lemon juice
⅛ teaspoon cream of tartar

Beat whites until frothy. Add half the sugar gradually, beating until well blended. Add lemon juice, cream of tartar, then remaining sugar. Beat until thick. Spread on top and sides of cake.

UNCOOKED FROSTINGS

Frostings differ from icings in being richer and more substantial. They are usually made with butter, sometimes with eggs or cream cheese. Frostings may be used as a filling between cake layers, as well as to cover the top and sides of cakes.

BASIC BUTTER FROSTING

2 tablespoons butter
1 cup confectioners sugar
2 tablespoons milk, cream, sherry, rum or brandy
½ teaspoon vanilla

Cream butter and sugar well, add the flavoring and liquid until mixture spreads well.

CARAMEL BUTTER FROSTING

½ cup butter
2 cups brown sugar
¼ teaspoon vanilla
heavy cream

Cream butter, add sugar gradually and mix very well, add vanilla and only enough cream to obtain desired consistency.

CHOCOLATE BUTTER FROSTING

2 tablespoons butter
1 cup confectioners sugar
½ teaspoon vanilla
1 square unsweetened chocolate melted over boiling water, or ¼ cup cocoa

Proceed as for Basic Butter Frosting.

COFFEE BUTTER FROSTING

2 tablespoons butter
1 cup confectioners sugar
2 tablespoons strong, hot coffee
1 teaspoon cocoa (dry)
½ teaspoon vanilla

Proceed as for Basic Butter Frosting.

ORANGE OR LEMON BUTTER FROSTING

2 tablespoons butter
1 cup confectioners sugar
1 tablespoon milk or water
1 tablespoon orange or lemon juice and a little grated rind

Proceed as for Basic Butter Frosting, above.

BROWN BUTTER FROSTING

¼ cup shortening
2 cups confectioners sugar
3 to 4 tablespoons milk
½ teaspoon vanilla

Melt shortening until golden brown. Add to powdered sugar, milk and vanilla. Mix until desired consistency.

BROWN BUTTER BRANDY FROSTING

¼ cup shortening
2 cups confectioners sugar
2 tablespoons milk
2 tablespoons brandy

Melt shortening until golden brown. Add to confectioners sugar, milk and brandy. Mix to desired consistency.

FLUFFY CHOCOLATE FROSTING

2 cups confectioners sugar
½ cup milk
2 eggs
¼ teaspoon salt
½ teaspoon vanilla
4 squares unsweetened chocolate
6 tablespoons butter

Blend sugar, milk, eggs, salt and vanilla in a bowl over ice water. Melt chocolate and butter together. Add while warm to first mixture and beat until desired consistency.

CREAM CHEESE FROSTING

3 ounces cream cheese
1 tablespoon warm milk
2½ cups confectioners sugar
1 teaspoon vanilla

Mash cheese with milk. Add sugar, gradually, and vanilla. Beat until creamy. Any other desired flavoring may be substituted for the vanilla.

Tips for successful cake frosting:
- *Place strips of wax paper under the edges of the cake; remove after cake has been frosted.*
- *Cool cake and brush crumbs from it before frosting.*
- *Fill layers and frost sides before frosting top of cake.*

CREAM CHEESE CHOCOLATE FROSTING

3 ounces cream cheese
¼ cup milk
2 squares unsweetened chocolate, melted
2½ cups confectioners sugar
1 teaspoon vanilla
dash of salt

Mash cheese, add the rest gradually. Beat until smooth.

HUNGARIAN CHOCOLATE FROSTING

2 eggs
1 cup confectioners sugar
4 squares unsweetened chocolate, melted
¼ cup butter, softened
½ teaspoon vanilla
pinch salt

Combine all ingredients and beat well.

MOCHA BUTTER FROSTING

1 cup butter
1 egg yolk, beaten
2½ cups confectioners sugar
1 square unsweetened chocolate, melted over hot water
1 teaspoon instant coffee
1 teaspoon vanilla

Cream butter; stir in beaten yolk, the sugar, chocolate, coffee and vanilla.

BRANDY FROSTING

grated rind of 1 orange
grated rind of 1 lemon
1 tablespoon brandy
1 tablespoon orange juice
1 teaspoon lemon juice
2 egg yolks
2 cups confectioners sugar
¼ pound almonds, grated

Add grated orange and lemon rind to brandy. Let stand 15 minutes. Strain. Add 1 tablespoon orange juice, 1 teaspoon lemon juice. Stir gradually into eggs beaten with sugar. Fold in nuts.

BROILED COCONUT FROSTING

3 tablespoons melted butter
5 tablespoons brown sugar
2 tablespoons light cream
½ cup shredded coconut (dry)

Mix all ingredients. Spread on warm cake before removing cake from pan. Broil until sugar is melted and bubbles. This takes only a few minutes, and should be watched carefully, as it burns easily.

BOILED FROSTINGS

MERINGUE FROSTING

    1 cup sugar
    ½ cup water
    2 egg whites
    ½ teaspoon flavoring extract

Boil sugar and water over low heat until syrup spins a thread; pour very slowly onto stiffly beaten whites and beat until smooth and stiff enough to spread. Add flavoring. Spread on cake.

CHOCOLATE MERINGUE FROSTING

Substitute brown sugar in above recipe; add 1½ ounces grated unsweetened chocolate, or ¼ cup cocoa, proceed as above.

FOUR-MINUTE FROSTING

    1 cup sugar
    ¼ teaspoon salt
    3 tablespoons cold water
    ½ teaspoon cream of tartar
    3 unbeaten egg whites
    1 teaspoon vanilla

Put all ingredients in bowl. Set bowl over hot water and beat 4 minutes until fluffy. Any flavoring may be added.

SEVEN-MINUTE FROSTING

    1 egg white, unbeaten
    3 tablespoons cold water
    ⅞ cup granulated sugar
    ¼ teaspoon cream of tartar
    ½ teaspoon vanilla

Place all ingredients except vanilla in top of double boiler. Beat with rotary beater until thoroughly mixed. Place over rapidly boiling water, beat constantly until frosting stands in peaks. Add vanilla. Put pan over cold water, beat until cool. Spread on top and sides of cake. For filling and frosting two 9-inch layers, double the quantities. For variety add 4 tablespoons flavored gelatin with sugar.

COCONUT FROSTING

Make Seven-Minute Frosting, or Meringue Frosting, sprinkle shredded coconut thickly over the cake while the frosting is still soft.

TO FRESHEN COCONUT

To 1 cup dry shredded coconut add ¼ cup of milk. Cook in double boiler until milk is absorbed, let stand covered until ready to use.

MAPLE FROSTING

    1 cup maple syrup
    2 egg whites

Boil syrup until it spins a thread; add very slowly to stiffly beaten whites of eggs, beating constantly until stiff enough to spread.

BROWN SUGAR MARSHMALLOW FROSTING

    2 cups brown sugar
    1 cup granulated sugar
    ¾ cup water
    ½ teaspoon vanilla
    5 marshmallows
    2 egg whites

Cook sugar and water over low heat until it spins a thread. Add vanilla and marshmallows. Beat until marshmallows are dissolved. Pour gradually onto the stiffly beaten whites, beating constantly.

MARSHMALLOW FROSTING

    1⅓ cups sugar
    ½ cup water
    6 marshmallows
    3 egg whites
    ⅛ teaspoon salt
    1 teaspoon vanilla

Boil sugar and water without stirring until syrup spins a thread; melt marshmallows in syrup; pour slowly over stiffly beaten egg whites, beating constantly; add flavoring and spread very thickly.

ORANGE OR LEMON-FLUFF FROSTING

    juice and rind of 2 oranges or 1 lemon
    1 cup confectioners sugar
    2 egg whites, beaten stiff

Boil juice and grated rind with sugar until syrup spins a thread. Pour slowly onto whites, beating constantly until almost cool, then spread between layers of sponge or Angel Food cake.

ORNAMENTAL FROSTING

Make Meringue Frosting, and when stiff enough to spread, put over boiling water, stirring continually until icing grates slightly on bottom of bowl. Spread some on cake, force rest through pastry tube to make decorative designs.

SEA FOAM FROSTING

    2 egg whites
    ¾ cup light brown sugar
    ⅓ cup corn syrup
    2 tablespoons water
    ¼ teaspoon cream of tartar
    ¼ teaspoon salt
    1 teaspoon vanilla

Cook all ingredients except vanilla in a double boiler, beating constantly, until mixture stands in peaks. Remove from heat, add vanilla, beat until thick enough to spread.

Frostings Without Sugar

CORN SYRUP FROSTING

2 egg whites
1 cup light corn syrup
1 teaspoon vanilla

Pour egg whites and syrup into deep mixing bowl. Beat with electric beater at medium speed until mixed, then continue for about 15 minutes until stiff. Add vanilla. Will fill and frost 2 large layers.

CHOCOLATE MOLASSES FROSTING

Use 2 egg whites, 1 cup molasses and 2 squares melted unsweetened chocolate. Proceed as in the above recipe.

WHIPPED-CHOCOLATE FROSTING

2 squares unsweetened chocolate
½ cup light cream
1 teaspoon vanilla
2 egg whites, beaten stiff
1½ to 2 cups confectioners sugar

Cook chocolate and cream over boiling water until smooth; cool, add vanilla. Beat whites, add sugar and continue beating until stiff enough to cut. Combine the two mixtures, beat well.

COOKED FUDGE FROSTINGS

BROWN BEAUTY FROSTING

2 cups brown sugar
⅔ cup water
1 square unsweetened chocolate
¾ cup butter

Boil sugar and water until it spins a thread. Melt chocolate with the butter, then mix it with the syrup. Beat until thick enough to spread.

CREAMY CHOCOLATE FROSTING

¼ cup water
¾ cup sugar
1 square unsweetened chocolate
2 egg yolks

Boil water and sugar to a thick syrup, add the chocolate, pour syrup over the beaten yolks, stirring constantly. Beat until thick enough to spread.

CHOCOLATE NUT FROSTING

1½ cups brown sugar
¾ cup light cream
½ cup butter
2 squares unsweetened chocolate, melted
¾ cup chopped nut meats

Boil sugar, cream and butter until thick; stir until cool; then add melted chocolate and nuts; spread between layers.

CHOCOLATE CARAMEL FROSTING

1¼ cups brown sugar
3 squares unsweetened chocolate, grated
½ cup milk
2 tablespoons butter
1 teaspoon vanilla

Cook sugar, chocolate and milk until smooth, add butter, and vanilla; cool, spread between two layers of cake.

FUDGE FROSTING

2 squares unsweetened chocolate
½ cup milk or light cream
1½ cups sugar
2 tablespoons butter
1 teaspoon vanilla

Melt chocolate over low heat, add milk and sugar, boil until a few drops form a soft ball in cold water. Add butter and vanilla. Let stand undisturbed a few minutes, then beat until thick enough to spread. If too thick, stir in a little cream.

CHOCOLATE BRANDY FROSTING

3 cups confectioners sugar
5 tablespoons butter
2 tablespoons light cream
3 tablespoons brandy
3 tablespoons strong coffee
½ cup grated, sweet chocolate

Combine all ingredients in double boiler and cook, stirring until well blended. If necessary, add cream until thin enough to spread.

CARAMEL FROSTING

2 tablespoons granulated sugar
6 tablespoons butter
¾ cup brown sugar
6 tablespoons light cream or evaporated milk
1½ cups confectioners sugar

Melt granulated sugar in heavy skillet, add butter and brown sugar; stir until dissolved; add cream, a spoonful at a time, stirring well. Boil 1 minute. Remove from heat and add confectioners sugar. Beat well until frosting has lost its gloss.

QUICK CARAMEL FROSTING

3 tablespoons milk
1 cup brown sugar
3 tablespoons butter
¾ cup confectioners sugar

Bring milk and sugar to boil, add butter. When slightly cool, add confectioners sugar until stiff enough to spread.

CARAMEL ECONOMY FROSTING

1½ cups sugar
½ cup brown sugar
¾ cup evaporated milk
1 tablespoon butter
½ teaspoon vanilla

Boil sugar and milk for 5 minutes or to soft-ball stage, cool slightly, then add butter and vanilla. Beat until thick enough to spread.

CARAMEL FUDGE FROSTING

1½ cups brown sugar
¾ cup light cream or milk
2 tablespoons butter
½ teaspoon vanilla

Cook sugar with cream or milk until it forms a soft ball when dropped in cold water, add butter and vanilla, remove from heat and beat until of right consistency to spread.

SOUR CREAM CARAMEL FROSTING

1¼ cups brown sugar
¾ cup granulated sugar
¾ cup sour cream
1 teaspoon butter

Mix sugar and cream, let stand until dissolved, about ½ hour or longer. Add butter and boil 5 minutes or to the soft-ball stage. Beat and spread on cake.

FILLINGS

UNCOOKED FILLINGS

CHANTILLY CREAM FILLING

¾ cup heavy cream
¼ cup confectioners sugar
1 egg white
½ teaspoon vanilla

Place chilled cream in ice-cold bowl and beat until stiff. Add sugar, white of egg beaten stiff, and vanilla: After cake or pastries are filled, keep cool until ready to serve.

WHIPPED CREAM FILLING

1 cup heavy cream
¼ cup confectioners sugar
½ teaspoon vanilla

Beat cream until it begins to thicken; add sugar gradually, add flavoring; continue to beat until cream holds its shape when the beater is raised.

WHIPPED CREAM FILLING WITH PINEAPPLE AND NUTS

1 egg yolk, beaten
2 tablespoons confectioners sugar
½ cup heavy cream, whipped
½ cup chopped nuts
½ cup chopped pineapple

Fold yolk and sugar into cream, add nuts and pineapple.

WHIPPED CREAM FILLING WITH NUT BRITTLE

Peanut or Walnut Brittle, page 174
1 cup heavy cream, whipped
1 teaspoon vanilla

Make Peanut or Walnut Brittle. When cold, break in small pieces, put through grinder and mix lightly with the whipped cream and flavoring.

COOKED FILLINGS

VANILLA CUSTARD FILLING

1 tablespoon cornstarch
½ cup sugar
1 cup scalded milk
2 egg yolks
½ teaspoon vanilla

Mix cornstarch and sugar, add the hot milk and pour gradually on the slightly beaten egg yolks. Cook in double boiler, stirring constantly until thickened. Cool and flavor with the vanilla.

ALMOND CUSTARD FILLING

Prepare like Vanilla Custard Filling and when cool add 1 cup blanched, chopped almonds.

COFFEE CUSTARD FILLING

Prepare like Vanilla Custard Filling, substituting 1½ tablespoons instant coffee for the vanilla.

CHOCOLATE CUSTARD FILLING

Add 2 squares unsweetened chocolate, melted, to any custard filling in preceding recipes.

BUTTER CUSTARD FILLING

2½ cups milk
½ cup sugar
½ cup flour
¼ teaspoon salt
2 teaspoons vanilla
1 cup butter

Heat milk in double boiler. Stir hot milk gradually into the sugar, flour and salt mixed. Return to boiler, cook about 10 minutes, stirring constantly. Cool, add vanilla. Cream butter, add the custard gradually, stirring until smooth.

CARAMEL FILLING

1 cup sugar
1½ cups hot milk
⅛ cup flour
1 egg yolk, beaten
½ teaspoon vanilla

Melt ½ of the sugar in heavy skillet, stir in hot milk very gradually. Mix remaining sugar with flour, stir into hot mixture. Cook until mixture thickens, pour onto yolk, stirring constantly; add vanilla, spread between layers.

CHOCOLATE FILLING

½ cup sugar
1 tablespoon cornstarch
2 squares unsweetened chocolate, grated
½ cup milk
vanilla

Mix dry ingredients, stir in the milk, cook in double boiler until thick, stirring constantly; when cool, add vanilla to taste.

CREAM CUSTARD FILLING

¾ cup sugar
⅛ cup flour
⅛ teaspoon salt
2 cups milk or light cream, scalded
2 eggs
1 teaspoon vanilla

Mix dry ingredients, add the milk and pour gradually on the slightly beaten eggs. Cook in double boiler, stirring constantly until thickened; cool and flavor.

ORANGE CUSTARD FILLING

½ cup sugar
2 tablespoons flour
1 teaspoon grated orange rind
¼ cup orange juice
½ teaspoon lemon juice
1 teaspoon butter
1 egg, slightly beaten
speck of salt

Mix in order given, beat well, cook in double boiler about 15 minutes, stirring constantly until thick; when cool, spread between two 8-inch layers.

LEMON CUSTARD FILLING

Use the grated rind of 2 lemons, ¼ cup lemon juice and 1 cup sugar in place of the orange rind and juice, and proceed as in Orange Custard Filling, above.

LEMON CORNSTARCH FILLING

½ cup sugar
2 tablespoons cornstarch
¼ teaspoon salt
2 egg yolks
¾ cup water
⅓ cup lemon juice
1 tablespoon butter
1 teaspoon grated lemon rind

Put sugar, cornstarch and salt in double boiler. Mix slightly beaten egg yolks with water and lemon juice. Add to sugar mixture. Cook over boiling water about 15 minutes, stirring constantly. Add butter and lemon rind. Cool, then spread between layers.

GOLDEN SOUR CREAM FILLING

1 cup thick sour cream
1 cup sugar
5 egg yolks, beaten
1 teaspoon almond extract

Heat cream with sugar until dissolved and pour in a steady stream on yolks, stirring constantly. Cook in double boiler, continue stirring until thick and smooth. Cool slightly, flavor and, if desired, add 1 cup chopped nut meats.

SOUR CREAM FILLING

1 egg yolk
2 tablespoons sugar
1 tablespoon cornstarch
1 cup thick sour cream
½ teaspoon lemon or vanilla extract

Beat yolk slightly, add sugar and cornstarch mixed, stir in the cream; cook in double boiler until mixture coats the spoon. Add flavoring. If desired, add 1 cup chopped nuts.

FRUIT AND NUT FILLINGS

APPLE-LEMON FILLING

¾ cup sugar
1 tablespoon flour
3 tablespoons lemon juice
1 tablespoon cold water
1 egg
speck of salt
1 apple, pared and grated

Mix sugar and flour in saucepan; add lemon juice, cold water, beaten egg, salt and apple. Boil 2 minutes, stirring constantly. Cool before spreading.

FIG FILLING

¼ pound chopped figs
½ cup sugar
2 tablespoons cornstarch
½ cup boiling water
1½ tablespoons lemon juice
grated rind of ½ orange

Cook figs in small amount of water in double boiler until soft. Mix sugar and cornstarch in a double boiler, add the boiling water, stir until smooth and thick. Add the cooked figs, lemon juice and orange rind.

FIG MERINGUE FILLING

To Meringue Frosting, add ¼ pound chopped figs steamed in small amount of water until soft.

FIG PASTE FILLING

1 pound figs, chopped fine
1 cup sugar
½ cup water
2 egg whites
¼ cup confectioners sugar
vanilla to taste

Boil figs, sugar and water slowly to a smooth paste, about 15 minutes. Set aside to cool. Beat whites until stiff, add confectioners sugar and flavoring, and combine the two mixtures.

NUT AND FRUIT MERINGUE FILLING

To Meringue Frosting, add ½ cup each of chopped candied cherries and pineapple, or ½ cup each of chopped raisins and nuts.

PECAN FILLING

1 tablespoon cornstarch
1 cup milk, heated
2 egg yolks
½ cup sugar
½ cup pecans, chopped fine

Dissolve cornstarch in the milk, and cook in double boiler until smooth; beat yolks and sugar until very light; pour hot milk mixture gradually over yolks; return to boiler and cook until mixture coats the spoon, stirring constantly; when cool, add nut meats.

PINEAPPLE MARSHMALLOW FILLING

1 can (8¾ ounces) crushed pineapple
½ pound marshmallows
½ cup raisins, chopped
½ cup pecans, chopped

Drain pineapple, melt marshmallows over hot water. Combine all ingredients.

PRUNE FILLING

1 cup cooked, stoned prunes
⅛ cup orange marmalade
⅛ cup nuts, chopped fine
1 teaspoon lemon juice

Chop prunes and mix with remaining ingredients; spread between layers of cake.

RAISIN FILLING

1 cup raisins, chopped
⅛ cup sugar
1 cup light corn syrup
1 cup water
1 egg, slightly beaten
½ teaspoon lemon extract

Cook raisins, sugar, syrup and water until raisins are soft. Remove from heat, add egg, cook over water until thick, stirring constantly. Flavor, cool, and spread.

STRAWBERRY CREAM FILLING

1 cup heavy cream
½ cup sugar
1 egg white, stiffly beaten
½ cup strawberries, mashed

Whip cream until stiff, fold in sugar, egg white, and the mashed strawberries.

WALNUT FILLING

2 egg yolks, beaten
½ cup sugar
¾ cup milk
½ teaspoon vanilla or rum flavoring
1 pound chopped walnuts

Mix eggs and sugar, add milk, cook in double boiler until thick. Cool, add vanilla or rum, and the nuts. Spread between layers of Walnut Torte.

WHIPPED JAM FILLING

1 egg white
1 cup jelly or jam

Beat with electric beater until stiff enough to spread.

WHIPPED FRUIT FILLING

1½ cups pared, grated apple, peach or
    mashed berries
1½ cups sugar
2 egg whites
grated rind of 1 lemon

Mix all together. Beat until very stiff. Use between layers and on top of layer cake or as a filling for Schaum Torte.

QUICK REFERENCE GUIDE TO USEFUL INFORMATION IN THIS BOOK

7
COOKIES

**ROLLED COOKIES · MOLDED COOKIES · REFRIGERATOR COOKIES
· DROP COOKIES · KISSES AND MACAROONS · BAR COOKIES**

A full cookie jar is a sign of a hospitable household —and homemade cookies may be of any kind from the plainest to the most elaborate.

Certain basic rules and techniques apply to all cookie baking: Follow recipes accurately. Unless otherwise directed, always grease cookie sheets lightly. It is more efficient to work with two or more of these large, shallow pans, so that some of the cookies can be in the oven while others are being shaped and arranged on the extra baking sheets. Remove the baked cookies to a rack to cool in a single layer.

Clean the baking sheet with a paper towel, grease again, and begin to shape the next batch.

Baking times given for cookies cannot be absolutely accurate, but it is important not to overbake cookies. Soft cookies are done when they are firm and spring back from the pressure of a finger. Crisp cookies are done when they are very lightly and evenly browned. Cookies keep very well if they are properly packed: soft cookies should be stored in an airtight container, and crisp cookies in a jar that permits air to enter. If the crisp cookies get soft they may be crisped in the oven. A piece of apple or potato packed with soft cookies helps to keep them moist and chewy.

ROLLED COOKIES

Cookie dough that is to be rolled out should be well chilled for easier handling. Otherwise it be-

comes necessary to add more flour to make a stiffer dough, and this results in a tough cookie. With a rolling pin dusted with flour, roll the chilled dough out on a lightly floured board, half or one-third at a time. The thinner you roll it, the crisper the cookie. Soft cookies are always thick. Cut the dough into squares, diamonds, or bars with a floured knife. Or cut fancy shapes with a floured cookie cutter, making the cuts close together. The trimmings may be rerolled, but they are not so delicate.

For special occasions, patterns may be cut from cardboard, laid on the dough, and the shape cut out with a sharp knife.

ALMOND STICKS

1 cup sugar
½ pound almonds, grated
1 cup butter
2 whole eggs
grated rind of 1 lemon
2 cups flour
1 egg yolk

Reserve ¼ cup each of sugar and nuts for decorating. Cream butter, add rest of sugar, eggs, rest of almonds, lemon rind and flour. Chill. Roll thin and cut in strips or squares. Brush with yolk, sprinkle with reserved nuts and sugar and bake on greased cookie sheet in a moderate oven, 350° F., for 10 to 12 minutes.

BUTTER COOKIES (MUERBE)

1 pound butter
1 cup sugar
2 eggs, separated
½ lemon, rind and juice, or 2 tablespoons brandy
6 cups flour
1 teaspoon baking powder
1 cup almonds, chopped fine

Cream butter, add sugar, then the egg yolks, slightly beaten; add grated lemon rind and juice or brandy, and flour mixed with the baking powder. Chill dough several hours, then roll; cut cookies into desired shapes, brush with egg whites; sprinkle with sugar and chopped almonds. Bake on greased cookie sheets in a moderate oven, 350° F., 10 to 15 minutes.

EGG BUTTER COOKIES

1 pound butter
1½ cups sugar
rind and juice of ¼ lemon
3 hard-cooked egg yolks
6 cups flour
3 eggs, beaten
1 egg white
chopped almonds
sugar and cinnamon

Cream butter and sugar, add lemon juice, grated rind and cooked yolks rubbed through sieve. Add flour and beaten eggs alternately. Roll ⅛-inch thick, brush with egg whites. Cut into desired shapes. Sprinkle with chopped almonds mixed with sugar and cinnamon. Bake on greased cookie sheets in a moderate oven, 350° F., 10 to 15 minutes.

MERINGUE-TOPPED BUTTER COOKIES

1 cup butter
4 egg yolks
2 cups flour
1 teaspoon baking powder
4 egg whites, beaten stiff
1 cup sugar
½ pound blanched almonds, grated
1 lemon, rind and juice
confectioners sugar

Cream butter and yolks well. Sift flour and baking powder; combine the two mixtures. Chill thoroughly. Roll thin, cut into rounds. Cover cookies with this meringue: Beat egg whites until frothy. Gradually add sugar. Beat until whites stand up in peaks. Fold in almonds and grated lemon rind and juice. Bake on greased cookie sheets in a moderate oven, 350° F., for 15 minutes. Cool, dust with confectioners sugar.

CARDAMOM COOKIES

1 cup butter
1 cup sugar
2 eggs
4 cups flour
1 teaspoon cardamom seed, crushed
grated rind of 1 lemon

Cream butter and sugar; add other ingredients. Roll very thin on floured board; cut and bake in a hot oven, 400° F., for 10 to 12 minutes.

CHOCOLATE COOKIES

½ cup butter
1½ cups sugar
1 egg
¼ teaspoon salt
2 squares unsweetened chocolate, melted
2½ cups flour
2 teaspoons baking powder
¼ cup milk

Cream butter and sugar; add well-beaten egg, salt and chocolate. Beat well. Sift flour with baking powder and add, alternately, with milk. Beat again. Chill several hours, roll very thin, shape with a small cutter, bake on greased cookie sheets in a moderate oven, 350° F., 10 minutes.

CHOCOLATE ALMOND COOKIES

¼ pound almonds (unblanched)
½ pound sweet chocolate
1 cup butter
1 cup sugar
2 eggs
½ teaspoon cinnamon
¼ teaspoon cloves
3 tablespoons milk
4 cups flour
1 teaspoon baking powder
1 egg white

Grate the chocolate and almonds. Cream butter, add sugar, eggs, one at a time, spices, milk, flour and baking powder. Mix well, roll, cut in rounds, place on greased cookie sheets; brush with egg white and sprinkle with sugar. Bake in a moderate oven, 350° F., for 10 minutes.

MANDELCHEN

2 cups grated almonds
½ cup sugar
butter

Blanch almonds. Dry overnight. Grind fine, add sugar and enough butter to knead into a very stiff paste. Roll very thin, cut in small rounds, place on baking sheets, and bake at 350° F. for 20 minutes. Roll in grated almonds and confectioners sugar.

CHOCOLATE STICKS

4 eggs
1 pound brown sugar
½ teaspoon cinnamon
¼ teaspoon each allspice and cloves
¼ pound sweet chocolate, grated
1 cup almonds
2 ounces citron
3 cups flour
1 teaspoon baking powder

Beat eggs and sugar until light, add the spices and the chocolate. Blanch almonds and chop, cut citron fine; mix with the flour and baking powder and combine the two mixtures. Roll on floured board, cut into strips 3½ inches long, bake on greased cookie sheets, in a moderate oven, 350° F., 10 to 15 minutes.

CHRISTMAS SPICE COOKIES

2 cups brown sugar
½ cup syrup or honey
¼ cup butter
1 teaspoon cinnamon
½ teaspoon cloves
⅛ teaspoon nutmeg
2 ounces citron, ground very fine
2½ cups flour
1 tablespoon baking powder
1 egg
juice and rind of ½ lemon
2 tablespoons milk

Add sugar to syrup and cook until sugar is dissolved. Add butter, cool. Add spices to flour. Mix all ingredients and add additional flour to handle, if necessary. Roll ⅛-inch thick and cut into desired shapes. Bake on greased baking sheets in moderate oven, 350° F., 8 to 10 minutes.

CINNAMON STARS

6 egg whites
1 pound confectioners sugar
rind of 1 lemon
1 teaspoon cinnamon
1 pound grated almonds

Beat whites until stiff. Fold in sugar and lemon rind. Set aside ¼ of mixture. To the remainder add cinnamon and almonds, mixing well. Roll on board, using more sugar if necessary to prevent sticking; cut into star shapes, place on each cookie a small portion of the mixture set aside. Bake in a moderate oven, 300° F., on greased cookie sheets until crusty, about 20 minutes.

FIG COOKIES

½ cup butter
1 cup brown sugar
2 eggs, beaten
1 teaspoon baking soda
2 tablespoons sour cream
½ teaspoon cinnamon
1 cup chopped figs
2 cups flour

Cream butter with sugar, add eggs, soda dissolved in sour cream, the cinnamon and figs. Add flour. Roll out, and cut into desired shapes and bake on greased cookie sheets at 350° F. for 10 minutes.

FRUIT-FILLED COOKIES

Preheat oven to 375° F., a moderate oven. Prepare dough for Sugar Cookies, and cut into rounds. Place a teaspoonful of the following filling on half the rounds, and cover with remaining rounds, pinching edges well together.

FILLING

1 cup raisins
1 cup dates, cut fine
1 cup sugar
1 cup cold water
1 tablespoon flour
½ cup chopped nuts

Mix ingredients and boil until thick, stirring constantly. Cool. Bake on greased cookie sheets for 8 to 10 minutes.

HEART-SHAPED FILLED COOKIES

1½ cups butter
¾ cup sugar
3 cups flour
1 teaspoon cloves
1 teaspoon cinnamon

Cream butter and sugar. Add flour mixed with cloves and cinnamon. Roll out. Cut into hearts. Bake on greased cookie sheets in hot oven, 400° F., for 6 to 8 minutes. When done, put together in pairs with raspberry jelly between layers. Frost with Confectioners Sugar Glaze.

JELLY-FILLED COOKIES

Make dough for Sugar Cookies, page 156, and roll. Cut half the dough into rounds, the remainder with a doughnut cutter. Place doughnut-shaped cookie over plain round; fill center with jelly. Bake on greased cookie sheets in a moderate oven, 350° F., for 10 to 12 minutes.

GINGER CREAMS

1 cup butter
1 cup sugar
2 eggs
1 cup dark molasses
4 cups flour
1 teaspoon baking soda
2 teaspoons cinnamon
2 teaspoons ginger
1 cup sour cream
1 teaspoon cream of tartar

Cream butter, add sugar and cream well. Add beaten eggs, molasses, flour mixed and sifted with soda and spices, alternately with sour cream and the cream of tartar. Chill. Roll out about ¼ inch thick. Cut with large round cookie cutter. Bake on greased cookie sheet in a moderate oven at 350° F. for 15 to 20 minutes. Frost with Confectioners Sugar Glaze.

GINGER SNAPS

¼ cup butter
¼ cup sugar
1 egg
¼ cup molasses
¼ tablespoon ginger
¼ teaspoon baking soda
1½ cups flour

Cream the butter and sugar; add egg and molasses. Then add the ginger, soda and flour. Roll very thin on a floured board, cut into desired shapes, and bake on greased cookie sheets in a moderate oven, 350° F., for 10 to 12 minutes.

See page 151 for general rules for making and storing all types of cookies. Cookies can also be frozen successfully. See directions for freezing baked goods, chapter 24.

GINGER WAFERS

½ cup butter
½ cup dark molasses
½ cup sugar
1 egg
2½ cups flour
¼ teaspoon baking soda
⅛ teaspoon salt
½ teaspoon cinnamon
¼ teaspoon cloves
½ teaspoon ginger

Heat butter and molasses in large saucepan until butter melts, stir in sugar. Cool to lukewarm, add egg and flour sifted with soda, salt and spices. Chill. Roll very thin. Cut into rounds. Bake on greased cookie sheets at 350° F. 10 to 15 minutes.

HERMITS

1 cup butter
1½ cups sugar
1 cup chopped raisins
3 eggs
3 cups flour
1 teaspoon cloves
1 teaspoon nutmeg
1 teaspoon baking soda

Cream butter and sugar well; add raisins and eggs, beating well. Sift the dry ingredients and add to the mixture. Roll thin, cut into bars, and bake on greased cookie sheet in a moderately slow oven, 325° F., for 15 minutes.

MOLASSES HERMITS

½ cup shortening
1 cup sugar
2 eggs, beaten
¼ teaspoon salt
½ cup molasses
2½ cups flour
2 teaspoons baking powder
1 teaspoon cinnamon
¼ teaspoon cloves
1 teaspoon nutmeg
1 cup raisins, chopped
2 tablespoons milk

Cream shortening and sugar; add eggs, salt, and molasses. Sift dry ingredients. Add dry ingredients, raisins, and milk, to first mixture. Roll on floured board, cut into bars or rounds, and bake on a greased cookie sheet in a moderate oven, 350° F., for 10 to 12 minutes.

HONEY LEBKUCHEN

½ ounce powdered carbonate of potassium (obtainable in pharmacies)
3 tablespoons rum or wine
1 teaspoon cinnamon
½ teaspoon cloves
6 cups flour
⅛ to ¼ pound citron, chopped
4 eggs
1 pound sugar
½ pound honey
¾ pound almonds, ground medium

Dissolve powdered carbonate of potassium in the wine. Sift the spices with the flour. Add the citron. Beat the eggs light, add the sugar, honey and almonds, and combine the wine, flour, and egg mixture. Roll on board ¼ inch thick and cut into 2- by 3-inch squares. Lay on greased cookie sheets; let stand in cool place over night. Bake at 325° F. for 25 minutes and frost with Confectioners Sugar Glaze.

LEBKUCHEN

4 whole eggs
1 pound light brown sugar
2 cups flour
1 teaspoon cinnamon
¼ pound almonds or pecans
2 ounces citron, cut fine

Beat eggs and sugar until light. Mix flour and cinnamon with finely chopped nuts and citron; combine the two mixtures. Bake in two greased 10- by 15-inch pans in a moderately hot oven, 375° F., for 25 minutes. Frost with Confectioners Sugar Glaze. Cut into strips.

CHOCOLATE LEBKUCHEN

7 eggs, separated
1 cup brown sugar
1 cup molasses
1 teaspoon cinnamon
1 teaspoon salt
½ teaspoon allspice
¼ teaspoon grated nutmeg
¼ pound orange peel, cut fine
¼ pound citron, cut fine
½ pound almonds, blanched, ground
½ pound chocolate, grated
2 cups confectioners sugar
a little lemon juice
2½ cups flour
1½ teaspoons baking powder

Reserve 3 egg whites for the frosting. Beat yolks and 4 whites together until very light, add sugar, beat. Stir in the rest of ingredients, the flour and baking powder mixed. Flour hands, spread dough 1½ inches thick in well-greased, 9 x 13-inch pans. Bake in moderate oven, 350° F., for 30 minutes. Ice with Glacé, cut into strips. Let stand 1 week before using.

CHOCOLATE LEMON COOKIES

1 cup butter
2 cups flour
2 eggs, well beaten
½ pound sweet chocolate, grated
1 cup sugar
½ teaspoon vanilla
grated rind of 1 lemon
1 egg, slightly beaten
almonds

Blend butter and flour well; add 2 eggs, chocolate, sugar, vanilla, and lemon rind. Roll thin; brush top with slightly beaten egg. Sprinkle with chopped almonds or place ½ almond on top of each cookie. Bake on greased cookie sheets in a moderate oven, 350° F., for 10 minutes.

MATZOS COOKIES

½ cup butter or fat
1 cup sugar
2 eggs
½ cup potato flour
½ cup matzos meal
½ cup ground almonds

Cream butter and sugar, add the rest. Roll thin on board sprinkled with potato flour and sugar, cut into desired shapes and bake on greased cookie sheets in a moderately hot oven, 375° F., for 10 to 12 minutes.

ORANGE COOKIES

¼ cup butter
1 cup sugar
grated rind of ½ orange
4 egg yolks, beaten
2 tablespoons orange juice
2 cups flour
2 teaspoons baking powder

Cream butter and sugar, add orange rind, yolks, orange juice and flour sifted with baking powder. Mix, roll, and cut into desired shapes. Bake 8 to 10 minutes on greased cookie sheets in a moderately hot oven, 375° F.

SOUR CREAM COOKIES

1 cup sugar
3 cups flour
1 teaspoon salt
1 teaspoon soda
1 teaspoon nutmeg
1 cup butter
2 eggs, well beaten
1 cup thick, sour cream

Sift the dry ingredients. Blend in the butter. Add eggs and sour cream gradually. Chill dough thoroughly. Roll out; cut with cookie cutter and bake on greased cookie sheets in a hot oven, 425° F., for 6 to 8 minutes.

SOUR MILK COOKIES

¼ cup butter
2 cups sugar
2 eggs
4 cups flour
1 teaspoon soda
1 cup sour milk

Cream butter and sugar, add eggs, mix well, add flour and soda mixed with sour milk. Chill. Roll very thin on well-floured board, sprinkle with sugar, press sugar lightly on dough with rolling pin. Cut into desired shapes, bake on greased cookie sheets in a moderately hot oven, 375° F., 6 to 8 minutes.

SPRINGERLE

2 eggs
½ pound sugar, sifted
2 cups flour (about)
1 to 2 teaspoons anise seed

Beat eggs and sugar until very light. Add sifted flour gradually, stirring all the time until dough is stiff. Roll out about ⅛-inch thick, press floured springerle board down very hard on dough to emboss the designs. Cut out the squares and let dry 10 hours on floured board at room temperature. Bake on greased cookie sheets sprinkled with anise seed, in moderately slow oven, 325° F., until pale golden.

SUGAR COOKIES

½ cup butter
1 cup sugar
1 egg, beaten
¼ cup milk
¼ teaspoon vanilla, nutmeg or any other flavoring
2 cups flour (about)
2 teaspoons baking powder

Cream the butter and sugar. Add the egg, milk and flavoring. Sift flour. Mix baking powder with 1 cup flour, combine mixtures, then add the rest of the flour. Chill. Roll on floured board ¼ inch thick. Cut into desired shapes. Sprinkle with sugar, cinnamon, chopped nuts. Bake in a moderately hot oven, 375° F., 8 to 10 minutes.

DATE PINWHEELS

Follow recipe for Sugar Cookies. Roll into one large, thin sheet, brush generously with melted butter. Sprinkle with chopped dates and walnuts, sugar and cinnamon. Roll like jelly roll. Cut into 1-inch slices. Bake on greased cookie sheet in a moderate oven, 375° F., for 20 minutes.

MOLDED COOKIES

These cookies need not be rolled and cut out; they are quickly shaped by rolling bits of dough between the palms to make balls, or against a floured board with the palm of the hand to make fingers or sticks. Or they may be forced through a cookie press fitted with tubes to make decorative shapes.

Crisp cookies should be kept in a cookie jar or container that is not airtight. They may be re-crisped in the oven.

CRISS-CROSS BROWN SUGAR COOKIES

½ cup butter
½ cup brown sugar
1 egg
2 cups flour
1½ teaspoons baking powder
1 egg white
¼ cup chopped nuts

Cream butter and sugar; stir in egg. Add flour mixed with baking powder. Mix to a smooth dough. Roll into small balls. Put on greased cookie sheet 1 inch apart. Flatten criss-cross style with a fork dipped in flour. Brush with egg white and sprinkle with chopped nuts. Bake in hot oven, 400° F., for 10 to 12 minutes.

CRISS-CROSS PEANUT BUTTER COOKIES

1 cup shortening
1 cup white sugar
1 cup brown sugar
2 eggs, well beaten
1 teaspoon vanilla
3 cups flour
½ teaspoon salt
1½ teaspoons baking powder
1 cup peanut butter

Cream shortening and sugar well. Add the eggs, vanilla, the flour sifted with the salt and baking powder, and then the peanut butter. Mix well and knead. Roll into balls about ¾ inch across. Place 1 inch apart on greased cookie sheets, flatten with a fork, criss-cross style. Bake at 400° F. from 5 to 10 minutes.

BUTTER BALLS

½ cup butter
¼ cup sugar
1 egg, separated
½ teaspoon vanilla
rind of ½ lemon and orange
1 tablespoon lemon juice
1 cup flour
½ cup filberts, ground fine, or cornflakes, rolled fine
12 candied cherries, cut up

Cream butter and sugar well. Add yolk and flavoring. Beat. Add flour, beat until very light. Cover bowl. Chill over night. Roll into tiny balls, about fifty. Dip balls into slightly beaten egg white. Roll in nuts. Place on greased cookie sheets 1 inch apart. Press bit of cherry on top of each. Bake 20 to 30 minutes at 350° F.

Moist cookies should be stored in an airtight container.

CLOVER LEAF COOKIES

½ pound butter
½ cup confectioners sugar
1 cup cake flour
½ pound ground almonds
2 teaspoons vanilla
maraschino cherries
angelica

Cream butter and sugar, add flour, almonds and vanilla. Roll in tiny balls, place three together with a bit of cherry in center and a strip of angelica for a stem. Bake on greased cookie sheet at 350° F., 15 or 20 minutes.

GINGER COOKIES

¾ cup butter
1 cup sugar
1 whole egg
¼ cup dark molasses
2 cups sifted flour
2 teaspoons baking soda
1 teaspoon cinnamon
1 teaspoon ginger
1 teaspoon cloves

Cream butter and sugar, add egg, molasses and the dry ingredients, sifted together. Form into balls the size of a small walnut, roll in granulated sugar, place 2 inches apart on greased cookie sheet. Bake at 350° F., 10 to 12 minutes.

HONEYNUTS (TEIGLACH)

4 cups flour
1 teaspoon baking powder
3 tablespoons oil
4 eggs
¾ pound honey
½ cup sugar
½ pound filbert nut meats
ginger

Mix and knead first 4 ingredients until smooth. Divide into four parts, roll each into a pencil-thick rope, and cut into ½-inch pieces. Boil honey and sugar, pour into baking pan, add pieces of dough, place in hot oven, 375° F. Do not stir until dough is well puffed and just beginning to brown, then add chopped nuts, and bake until brown, stirring occasionally. Take from oven, turn out onto wet board; cool slightly. Pat flat with hands dipped in cold water, sprinkle with a little ginger and put into refrigerator.

See chapter 3, Beverages, for coffee and tea variations to serve with cookies. See chapter 1 for menu suggestions for afternoon tea or coffee get-togethers.

MOLDED SUGAR COOKIES

1½ cups flour
½ teaspoon baking powder
¼ teaspoon cream of tartar
pinch of salt
½ cup shortening
1 cup sugar
1 egg
1 teaspoon vanilla
sugar and cinnamon

Sift flour, baking powder, cream of tartar and salt. Cream shortening. Add sugar gradually, beating until fluffy. Add egg. Beat well. Then gradually add the flour mixture and flavoring. Roll into small balls. Place 1 inch apart on greased cookie sheet. Flatten with the bottom of a glass. Sprinkle with sugar and cinnamon. Bake at 400° F. about 10 to 12 minutes.

PFEFFERNUESSE

2 cups corn syrup
2 cups dark molasses
1 cup shortening
rind and juice of 1 lemon
½ pound brown sugar
10 cups flour
1 teaspoon soda
2 teaspoons cinnamon
¼ pound citron, cut fine
¼ pound almonds, chopped fine
1 egg white

Warm syrup and molasses, add shortening and lemon juice and the remaining ingredients in order given, flour and soda mixed. Almonds and citron may be omitted. Roll into little balls, brush with white of egg, place on greased cookie sheet far apart, and bake until brown, 350° F. Roll in confectioners sugar. Will keep.

ALMOND PRETZELS

1 cup butter
1 cup sugar
2 egg yolks and
2 whole eggs
½ pound unblanched almonds, ground
2 cups flour

Cream butter and sugar, add eggs, almonds, and flour. Mix and knead into one big roll. Chill in refrigerator. Cut into pieces size of a walnut. Roll into ropes ½ inch thick with palm of hands and form into hearts, rings, crescents and pretzels. Bake on greased cookie sheet in a moderately slow oven, 325° F., for 20 minutes.

CHOCOLATE PRETZELS

1 cup butter
⅔ cup sugar
1 egg
2 squares unsweetened chocolate, melted
1½ cups flour
dash of cinnamon
1 teaspoon vanilla

Cream butter and sugar; add egg and remaining ingredients. Chill. Roll small pieces of dough the thickness of a pencil. Shape into pretzels. Place on greased cookie sheets. Sprinkle with nuts and bake at 375° F.

MARZIPAN COOKIES

1¼ pounds sweet almonds
5 cups confectioners sugar
2 egg whites, unbeaten

Blanch almonds, dry over night, grind very fine. Sift sugar over them, mix and knead to a stiff paste with the egg whites. Add more egg, if needed. Shape into a roll with hands, on board sprinkled with confectioners sugar. Cut off pieces the size of a walnut. Roll each piece ½ inch thick, form into rings, crescents, hearts, bow knots and pretzel shapes, and bake until slightly browned, in a moderately slow oven, 325° F.

PECAN FINGERS

1 cup butter
¾ cup confectioners sugar
2 cups pecans, coarsely chopped
1 teaspoon vanilla
2 cups flour
1 tablespoon ice water
⅛ teaspoon salt

Cream butter and sugar; add the remaining ingredients. Roll with palms of hands into finger lengths. Bake on greased cookie sheet in a moderate oven, 325° F., for 20 to 30 minutes. Roll in confectioners sugar while warm.

SPRITZ COOKIES

1 cup butter
1 cup sugar
1 egg or 2 egg yolks
1 teaspoon vanilla
2½ cups flour

Cream butter and sugar well; add egg, vanilla and flour. Shape by using a cookie press. Bake on an ungreased cookie sheet in a moderately hot oven, 375° F., for 15 minutes.

ALMOND BREAD SLICES

2 eggs, well beaten
½ cup sugar
juice and grated rind of ½ lemon
½ teaspoon vanilla
1⅔ cups flour
¼ cup almonds, blanched and split lengthwise
¼ cup oil or softened butter
2 teaspoons baking powder

Beat eggs and sugar until light. Add lemon, vanilla, and 1 cup of flour. Add almonds, shortening and rest of flour with baking powder. Knead and roll into 2 long loaves about 2 inches thick. Place on greased and floured pan and bake in a moderately slow oven, 325° F., for 20 to 30 minutes. While warm, cut into half-inch slices.

COCOA ALMOND BREAD SLICES

Stir 2 teaspoons cocoa into ¼ of the dough in recipe for Almond Bread Slices. Form into roll ½ inch thick. Pat remaining dough into sheet ½ inch thick. Roll this around the cocoa dough. Proceed as above.

GLORIFIED GRAHAM CRACKERS

Spread ¼ pound graham crackers with ¼ cup creamed butter mixed with ⅓ cup sugar and 1 teaspoon cinnamon. Cover with ½ cup ground nuts. Bake 5 minutes at 350° F.

Or, place marshmallow on graham crackers and place under broiler until brown.

REFRIGERATOR COOKIES

Refrigerator or icebox cookies are among the quickest to make; the dough is molded into oblongs or uniform rolls, and thoroughly chilled. The roll is then sliced with a gently sawing motion that does not distort the shape. Refrigerator cookie dough keeps well, and the cookies may be sliced and baked in small quantities, as needed.

RUM SLICES

4 egg whites
1 pound confectioners sugar
½ pound pecans, ground
½ pound walnuts, ground
1 teaspoon vanilla
rum

Beat egg whites until stiff, add sugar and nuts. Flavor with vanilla or rum. Form into rolls ¾ inch in diameter. Chill for 45 minutes. Cut into ½ inch slices. Bake on greased cookie sheet in moderate oven, 350° F., about 15 minutes. While still warm, ice with confectioners sugar moistened with enough rum to spread.

ALMOND CRESCENTS

1¼ cups flour
1 cup blanched almonds
     or 1 cup blanched Brazil nuts, finely grated
¼ cup confectioners sugar
½ cup butter, creamed
Vanilla Sugar, see below

Mix flour with nuts and confectioners sugar; add butter. Knead until well blended and smooth. If dough crumbles, add a little egg yolk. Form into roll 2 inches thick; chill well; cut crosswise into ½-inch slices and shape into crescents. Bake on greased cookie sheets in a moderately slow oven, 325° F., for 20 minutes. They must remain almost white. Dip in Vanilla Sugar while still hot.

VANILLA SUGAR

Break one vanilla bean in small pieces or grind fine in a nut grinder, shake well in jar or paper bag with 1 cup of confectioners or granulated sugar. Let stand 24 hours.

GINGER SNAPS

¼ cup boiling water
½ cup butter, softened
½ cup brown sugar
½ cup molasses
1 teaspoon soda
1 teaspoon salt
1 teaspoon ginger
3 cups flour

Add water to butter, add sugar, molasses and the remaining dry ingredients sifted together. Line refrigerator tray with waxed paper. Pack mixture in well. Press down with waxed paper until smooth on top. Chill. Slice thin and bake on a greased cookie sheet at 400° F. for 8 minutes.

OATMEAL CRISPS

1½ cups flour
1 teaspoon baking soda
1 cup butter
1 cup granulated sugar
1 cup brown sugar, sifted and packed
2 eggs, well beaten
1 teaspoon vanilla
3 cups quick cooking oats
½ cup chopped nut meats

Sift flour. Measure. Add soda and salt and sift again. Cream butter thoroughly, add sugar gradually. Cream until very light. Add eggs, vanilla, oats and nuts, mixing well after each. Add flour mixture, stirring well. Form into 4 rolls, about 2½ inches thick. Wrap in waxed paper. Chill thoroughly. Slice thin. Bake on greased cookie sheets at 400° F., about 10 minutes.

PEANUT OR ALMOND ICEBOX COOKIES

1 pound butter
1 cup sugar
1 cup brown sugar
3 eggs, well beaten
½ pound peanuts or almonds, chopped
5 cups flour
1 tablespoon cinnamon
2 teaspoons soda

Cream butter and sugar well; add eggs, chopped nuts, and dry ingredients. Shape into a roll 2 inches thick. Chill until firm. Cut in thin slices. Bake on a greased cookie sheet in a moderate oven, 350° F., for 10 minutes.

PIN WHEEL COOKIES

½ cup butter
½ cup sugar
1 egg yolk
1½ cups flour
1½ teaspoons baking powder
3 tablespoons milk
½ teaspoon vanilla
1 square unsweetened chocolate, melted

Cream butter and sugar; add egg yolk and beat well. Sift dry ingredients and add to mixture with milk and vanilla. Divide dough in half. Add chocolate to one part. Chill. Pat each into a thin, oblong sheet on waxed paper. Place chocolate dough over white dough. Roll tightly. Chill until firm. Slice thin. Bake on greased cookie sheet in a moderately hot oven, 375° F., for 10 minutes.

DROP COOKIES

The dough for drop cookies is soft, and cannot be rolled or molded. Scoop up a teaspoonful of the dough and scrape it from the spoon onto a greased baking sheet with another teaspoon or with a rubber spatula. Allow at least 2 inches between cookies, since they spread during baking.

ANISE COOKIES

  3 eggs (room temperature)
  1 cup sugar
  1½ to 2 cups cake flour
  ½ teaspoon baking powder
  1 tablespoon anise seed

Beat eggs very light, add sugar, continue stirring 45 minutes; gradually add flour sifted with baking powder, and anise seed, rolled fine. Stir again 10 minutes. Or in electric mixer: Beat eggs and sugar for 20 minutes at low speed, add other ingredients and beat for 3 minutes longer. Drop from teaspoon onto well-greased and floured cookie sheets, 1 inch apart. Let stand overnight or about 10 hours, at room temperature, to dry. Bake in a moderate oven, 350° F., 10 to 15 minutes.

DELICATE CHOCOLATE COOKIES

  ¾ cup butter
  1 cup confectioners sugar
  2 squares unsweetened chocolate
  1 egg, beaten
  2 cups cake flour
  1 teaspoon baking powder
  ¼ cup milk
  1 teaspoon vanilla

Cream butter and sugar; add melted chocolate and egg. Sift flour and baking powder and add to mixture. Add milk and vanilla. Drop by spoonfuls on greased cookie sheet. Bake in moderate oven, 350° F., for 8 to 10 minutes. When cool top with the following frosting:

  ¾ cup confectioners sugar
  1 teaspoon melted butter
  1 teaspoon vanilla
  light cream

Mix ingredients; add cream until mixture is thin enough to spread. Beat well.

DEVIL DOGS

  2 cups flour
  ½ cup cocoa
  ½ teaspoon salt
  1 cup sugar
  ½ teaspoon baking soda
  ½ teaspoon baking powder
  ½ cup vegetable shortening
  1 egg, beaten
  1 cup milk
  1 teaspoon vanilla

Sift dry ingredients. Add shortening, egg, milk and vanilla. Mix well. Drop by teaspoon onto greased cookie sheet. Bake at 425° F. for 5 minutes.

FILLING

  ⅓ cup evaporated milk
  ⅔ cup shortening
  ½ cup sugar
  ½ teaspoon vanilla

Mix all ingredients. Beat in an electric mixer at high speed for 5 minutes. Put 2 cookies together with a generous amount of filling.

Children like to help bake cookies, and it's an excellent introduction to baking for the young cook. Drop, bar and molded cookies are good ones for beginners to start with.

COCONUT DROPS

  4 eggs
  1 pound confectioners sugar
  1½ cups flour
  3 teaspoons baking powder
  ¼ pound coconut

Beat eggs until light, add sugar and beat again; add flour and baking powder mixed, and stir in the grated or shredded coconut. Drop by ½ teaspoonfuls on well-greased cookie sheet 3 inches apart, since they spread. Bake in a moderate oven, 350° F., from 10 to 15 minutes. Keep in covered jar.

LACE COOKIES

  ¼ cup butter
  2 cups brown sugar
  2 eggs, well beaten
  1 teaspoon vanilla
  1 teaspoon baking powder
  ½ cup flour
  ½ pound pecans, coarsely chopped

Cream butter and sugar; add eggs, beat well; add vanilla. Add baking powder to flour and mix with nuts and combine the two mixtures. Chill until firm. Drop by ½ teaspoonfuls 3 inches apart on greased and floured cookie sheet. Bake in hot oven at 400° F. about 8 minutes. Remove from pan when slightly cooled.

MOLASSES LACE COOKIES

  ½ cup molasses
  ½ cup sugar
  ½ cup butter
  1 cup flour
  ¼ teaspoon baking powder
  ½ teaspoon baking soda

Boil molasses, sugar, and butter for 1 minute. Remove from heat. Add remaining ingredients. Keep mixture over hot water. Drop ½ teaspoonfuls of mixture 3 inches apart on a greased cookie sheet. Bake in a moderately slow oven, 325° F., for 15 minutes. When slightly cool, remove from pan.

OATMEAL LACE COOKIES

½ cup melted butter
2½ cups rolled oats
1 cup brown sugar
2 teaspoons baking powder
1 egg, beaten

Melt butter, add to dry ingredients. Add egg, mix well. Drop from spoon 1 inch apart on greased cookie sheets. Bake 8 to 10 minutes at 350° F. Let stand 1 minute, remove from pan. Makes about 6 dozen.

NUT PATTIES

1 egg, beaten
1 cup sugar
1 cup chopped walnuts
5 tablespoons flour

Beat egg and sugar until very light; stir in chopped nuts, then add flour. Drop by teaspoonful on greased cookie sheets and bake in a moderately hot oven, 375° F., about 10 minutes.

OATMEAL COOKIES

1 cup butter
1 cup sugar
2 eggs, beaten
2 cups flour
2 cups oatmeal
1 teaspoon baking powder
½ teaspoon baking soda
¼ teaspoon salt
1 teaspoon cinnamon
1 cup chopped raisins or dates
1 cup chopped walnuts
¼ cup milk

Cream butter and sugar, add eggs; mix the dry ingredients, sprinkle over the raisins and nuts and combine the mixtures, adding milk. Drop by teaspoonfuls on a greased cookie sheet, 1 inch apart. Bake in moderate oven, 350° F., for 15 minutes.

SPICE COOKIES

5 eggs, beaten
1 pound brown sugar
2 teaspoons cinnamon
1 teaspoon ground cloves
1 teaspoon vanilla
1 teaspoon ginger
1 teaspoon baking soda
3 cups flour

Mix the ingredients in order, roll into small balls or drop by teaspoonfuls on greased cookie sheets, and bake in moderately hot oven, 375° F., 10 to 15 minutes.

RAISIN SPICE COOKIES

⅔ cup butter
1½ cups granulated or brown sugar
2 eggs
1 cup raisins, chopped
1 teaspoon cinnamon
½ teaspoon cloves
½ teaspoon mace
¼ teaspoon salt
2½ cups flour
3 tablespoons sour milk
1 teaspoon baking soda

Cream butter and sugar, add eggs, raisins, spices, salt, then add alternately flour and sour milk, in which soda has been dissolved. Drop by teaspoonfuls on greased cookie sheets, bake in a moderately hot oven, 375° F., for 10 to 15 minutes.

ROCKS

3¼ cups flour
1 cup raisins, cut up
1 cup walnuts, in pieces
1 cup butter
1½ cups brown sugar
3 eggs
1 teaspoon cinnamon
½ teaspoon salt
1 teaspoon baking soda, dissolved in 1½ tablespoons hot water

Sprinkle ½ cup of the flour over the fruit and nuts. Cream the butter and sugar; add the well-beaten eggs. Add the remaining ingredients, folding in the fruit and nuts last. Drop from teaspoon on greased cookie sheets, 1 inch apart. Bake in moderate oven, 350° F., for 15 minutes.

ROLLED WAFERS

¼ cup butter
½ cup confectioners sugar
¼ cup milk
⅞ cup flour
½ teaspoon vanilla
almonds, grated

Cream butter and sugar; add milk very slowly; then add flour and flavoring. Spread thin on a greased cookie sheet. Sprinkle with almonds. Mark in 3-inch squares and bake in a moderately slow oven, 325° F., for 15 minutes. Cut squares with a sharp knife, roll while warm over handle of a wooden spoon, or shape into cornucopias. Fill with whipped cream.

CURLED WAFERS

butter
3 egg whites
⅔ cup confectioners sugar
½ cup flour
¼ cup finely chopped toasted almonds

Spread 9- by 12-inch cookie sheets, or inverted baking pan, thickly with butter and place in refrigerator. Beat egg whites stiff but still shiny; add sugar gradually and beat until stiff. Fold in flour. Spread mixture with back of spoon over buttered pans as smooth and thin as possible. Sprinkle lightly with nuts toasted light brown without butter. Bake from 5 to 8 minutes at 400° F. until slightly brown. With sharp knife cut into long strips, loosen each carefully with spatula. Return for one moment to soften in hot oven, then roll each strip around handle of wooden spoon lengthwise and form into curls. May also be cut into 3-inch squares and shaped into cornucopias, or into 1½-inch squares.

SCOTCH CORNUCOPIAS

1 scant cup flour
⅔ cup sugar
1 tablespoon ginger
½ cup molasses
½ cup butter

Sift dry ingredients. Bring molasses to boiling point, add butter, then slowly add the flour mixture, stirring constantly. Drop by ½ teaspoons on greased cookie sheets, 2 inches apart. Bake in slow oven, 300° F., 10 minutes. Cool slightly, remove from pan, roll over handle of wooden spoon into cornucopias.

SHREWSBURY WAFERS

3 eggs
2 cups sugar
2 tablespoons melted butter
¾ teaspoon vanilla
1 teaspoon salt
1 cup shredded coconut
2 cups rolled oats

Beat eggs thoroughly, add sugar gradually, beating constantly, add butter, vanilla and salt. Stir in coconut and oats. Line shallow pans with greased waxed paper. Drop mixture on this by ½ teaspoonfuls 1 inch apart. Bake light brown about 8 minutes in a moderate oven, 350° F. Lift sheets of paper out of pan, cool partly, then remove wafers.

For tender cookies it is important to mix or handle the dough as little as possible after the flour has been added. Overhandling makes cookies tough.

KISSES AND MACAROONS

FILLED MERINGUES

6 egg whites
½ teaspoon salt
1½ cups granulated sugar
1 teaspoon lemon juice
1 teaspoon vanilla
ice cream

Beat the whites and salt until frothy. Gradually add ¾ cup of sugar. Beat until whites stand in peaks. Add lemon juice and vanilla, beat until stiff. Fold in the remaining sugar, 2 tablespoons at a time. Drop mixture from a tablespoon on a baking sheet lined with brown paper, to form rounds or ovals. Bake in a slow oven, 275° F., for 45 minutes. When cold, cut off the top of each meringue, fill with whipped cream or ice cream and replace top.

PRALINE KISSES

1 egg white
½ teaspoon salt
1 cup medium brown sugar
1 cup pecan nut meats

Beat the egg white until foamy. Add the salt. Continue beating, adding the sugar gradually until stiff. Fold in the nuts. Drop mixture from tip of spoon ½ inch apart on greased cookie sheets. Bake in a very slow oven, 250° F., for 45 minutes. Remove from pan when slightly cool.

CHOCOLATE KISSES

3 egg whites
½ cup sugar
2 squares unsweetened chocolate grated
½ teaspoon vanilla

Follow method for Praline Kisses.

COCOA KISSES

2 egg whites
1¼ cups sugar
2 tablespoons cocoa
¼ teaspoon cinnamon
¼ pound almonds, blanched and chopped

Follow method for Praline Kisses, folding in chopped nuts last.

COCONUT KISSES

2 egg whites
¼ pound confectioners sugar
¼ pound shredded coconut

Follow method for Praline Kisses, folding the shredded coconut in last.

HICKORY NUT KISSES

2 egg whites
⅔ cup sugar
1 cup chopped hickory nuts

Follow method for Praline Kisses.

PECAN KISSES

2 egg yolks
1 cup sugar
1 cup chopped pecans
2 egg whites

Beat yolks and sugar until light; add nuts and fold in the stiffly beaten whites. Bake like Praline Kisses.

DATE AND ALMOND KISSES

30 pitted dates
1 cup almonds
1 egg white
1 cup confectioners sugar

Chop dates; blanch almonds and cut into long strips. Beat egg white very stiff, add sugar, dates and almonds. Drop on greased cookie sheets from a teaspoon and bake in a slow oven, 300° F., from 25 to 30 minutes.

DATE AND WALNUT KISSES

4 egg whites, beaten stiff
1½ cups sugar
½ pound dates, in pieces
1 cup walnut meats, cut up

Beat eggs until frothy, gradually beat in sugar, beat until very stiff. Add dates and nuts, cut up, not chopped. Drop from teaspoon on greased cookie sheet and bake in a slow oven, 300° F., from 25 to 30 minutes.

CHOCOLATE PECAN KISSES

2 squares unsweetened chocolate
1 15-ounce can sweetened condensed milk
2 cups pecan meats

Cook chocolate and condensed milk in a double boiler until thick. Remove from heat, add pecans. Drop by teaspoonfuls on greased cookie sheets, bake in a moderate oven, 350° F., for 15 to 20 minutes.

COCONUT DROP KISSES

3 cups dried coconut
½ teaspoon vanilla
1 15-ounce can sweetened condensed milk
¼ teaspoon salt

Combine ingredients well. Drop by teaspoonfuls on a greased cookie sheet, 1 inch apart. Bake in a moderately hot oven, 375° F., for 15 minutes. Remove from pans while warm.

CHOCOLATE COCONUT DROP KISSES

Follow preceding recipe, adding 1 square unsweetened chocolate, melted, to ingredients.

MACAROONS

½ pound Almond Paste, page 83
1 cup sugar
4 egg whites

Blend Almond Paste and sugar. Gradually add unbeaten whites and stir until mixture is smooth. Drop from tip of spoon, an inch apart, on cookie sheet covered with brown paper. Bake 15 to 20 minutes in a slow oven, 300° F. To remove the cookies, cool slightly, moisten the back of the paper and peel the paper off.

ALMOND MACAROONS

4 egg whites, unbeaten
½ pound confectioners sugar
½ pound grated almonds

Cook eggs and sugar in top of double boiler for 10 minutes. Remove from heat, add nuts and mix thoroughly. Drop on greased cookie sheets and bake in a slow oven, 300° F., 30 minutes, or until crisp.

FILBERT MACAROONS

1¼ cups filberts, coarsely ground
⅛ teaspoon cinnamon
grated rind of ½ lemon
2 egg whites
⅔ cup sugar
2 tablespoons lemon juice

Mix nuts with cinnamon and lemon rind. Beat whites very stiff. Fold in sugar, lemon juice, and the filbert mixture. Drop on greased cookie sheets 1 inch apart. Bake in a very slow oven, 275° F., for 30 minutes. When slightly cool, remove from pans. Makes 30 macaroons.

GOLDEN FILBERT MACAROONS

4 egg yolks, unbeaten
½ pound confectioners sugar
1 teaspoon vanilla
¼ pound filbert nut meats

Mix egg yolks with sugar, add vanilla, then nuts, unblanched and ground fine. Chill dough, roll into 24 balls. Top each with whole filbert. Bake on greased cookie sheets in moderate oven, 300° F., ½ hour or until crisp.

BROWN SUGAR MACAROONS

1 cup light brown sugar
1¼ cups pecans, ground fine
1 egg white, unbeaten

Mix all together and roll into balls size of a hickory nut; place on greased cookie sheet 2 inches apart, bake at 300° F., 10 to 15 minutes.

CHOCOLATE MACAROONS

¼ cup grated almonds
½ cup sugar
2 squares unsweetened chocolate, grated
¼ teaspoon vanilla
2 egg whites

Mix almonds, sugar, and chocolate; add vanilla and fold in the stiffly beaten whites. Drop by teaspoon on cookie sheet lined with greased paper. Bake in a moderately slow oven, 325° F., for 15 to 20 minutes. Remove from paper while warm.

PISTACHIO MACAROONS

3 egg whites
1 cup sugar
¼ pound pistachio nuts
¼ pound almonds

Beat egg whites until frothy, beat in sugar gradually and beat until stiff. Fold in the nuts, blanched and ground fine. Drop from a teaspoon on greased cookie sheets and bake in a slow oven, 300° F., ½ hour or until crisp.

CORNFLAKE MACAROONS

2 egg whites
¾ cup sugar
2 cups cornflakes
½ cup nuts, chopped coarse
⅛ teaspoon salt
1 teaspoon vanilla

Beat egg whites until frothy, gradually beat in sugar and continue beating until stiff. Add remaining ingredients. Drop from teaspoon onto greased cookie sheet lined with waxed paper. Bake at 300° F., for 15 to 20 minutes. Remove from pan while warm. Makes about 3 dozen cookies.

COCONUT AND CORNFLAKE MACAROONS

3 cups cornflakes
1 cup dried coconut
½ cup sugar
2 eggs
½ teaspoon vanilla
½ cup corn syrup
¼ teaspoon salt

Combine all ingredients and place small mounds, the size of a walnut, on greased cookie sheet. Bake in a slow oven, 300° F., 30 minutes. Remove from pan while warm.

CHOCOLATE CORNFLAKE MACAROONS

1 pound milk chocolate
1 cup cornflakes
1 cup chopped nuts

Melt chocolate; when slightly cool, add other ingredients. Drop by teaspoonfuls on a greased cookie sheet and bake in a slow oven, 300° F., for 30 minutes. Remove from pan while warm.

BAR COOKIES

Bar cookies are baked in a single sheet, and cut up after baking. Brownies and similar cake-like cookies are baked in this manner, as are some rich cookies of the shortbread type.

BLACK WALNUT AND COCONUT BARS

½ cup butter
½ cup brown sugar
1 cup flour

Cream butter and sugar well. Blend in sifted flour and spread mixture in a greased 9-inch square pan. Bake in a moderately hot oven, 375° F., for 20 to 25 minutes. Add topping below.

TOPPING

2 tablespoons flour
½ teaspoon baking powder
¼ teaspoon salt
½ cup shredded coconut
1 cup black walnut meats
2 eggs, well beaten
1 cup brown sugar
1 teaspoon vanilla

Sift flour with baking powder and salt and mix with coconut and nuts. Beat eggs, add sugar and vanilla, and continue beating until mixture is fluffy. Combine two mixtures and pour batter over baked crust. Bake at 375° F. about 20 minutes. Cool slightly, and cut into oblong bars.

BISHOP'S BREAD

1 cup raisins
1 cup almonds, chopped
1¼ cups flour
3 eggs
1 cup sugar
2 teaspoons baking powder
salt

Sprinkle raisins and nuts with ¼ cup flour. Beat eggs and sugar until light. Add the rest of the flour sifted with the baking powder and a pinch of salt. Beat until light. Fold in nuts and raisins. Bake in greased pan in a moderate oven, 350° F., for 12 to 15 minutes. Cut into rectangles while warm. Sprinkle with additional sugar and finely chopped nuts.

Brownies and other moist cookies should be stored in an airtight container. A piece of apple or potato may be placed in the container to keep the cookies moist and chewy.

Most types of cookies freeze well. For directions on wrapping and freezing baked goods, see chapter 24.

BROWNIES

2 squares unsweetened chocolate or
      6 tablespoons cocoa
2 tablespoons butter
2 eggs, beaten light
1 cup sugar
1 teaspoon baking powder
1 cup flour
½ cup walnuts, chopped
1 teaspoon vanilla
¼ teaspoon salt

Melt chocolate and butter; beat eggs and sugar. Combine the mixtures, beating thoroughly; add remaining ingredients. Bake in a greased 8-inch square pan in a moderate oven, 350° F., for 35 minutes. Cut into squares before removing from pan.

CHEWY BROWNIES

½ cup butter
1 cup sugar
2 eggs
½ teaspoon vanilla
2 squares unsweetened chocolate, melted, or
      6 tablespoons cocoa
½ cup flour
1 cup chopped walnuts
¼ teaspoon salt

Cream butter and sugar well. Beat in eggs, one at a time. Add remaining ingredients. Bake in a greased 8-inch square pan in a moderate oven, 350° F., for 20 to 30 minutes. Cut in squares when cool.

CARAMEL SQUARES

1 cup brown sugar
¼ cup butter
1 egg
1 cup flour
1 teaspoon baking powder
¼ teaspoon salt
¼ cup nuts, chopped
½ teaspoon vanilla

Heat sugar and butter in a saucepan, stirring constantly until sugar is thoroughly dissolved. Do not boil. Let cool. Beat the egg well, stir in flour with baking powder, salt, then nuts and vanilla. Spread in a greased 9-inch square pan. Bake 20 minutes in a moderate oven, 350° F. Cut in squares and cool in pan.

CARD GINGERBREAD

⅓ cup butter
1 cup sugar
1 egg
1 teaspoon salt
2 cups flour less 2 tablespoons
3 teaspoons baking powder
1 teaspoon ginger
1½ cups milk

Cream the butter and sugar; add the egg, well beaten. Add the dry ingredients alternately with the milk. Mix again. Spread thin on greased 9 x 13-inch pan. Bake 15 minutes in a moderate oven, 350° F. Sprinkle with sugar, cut in squares before removing from pan.

CHOCOLATE TOFFEE BARS

1 cup butter
1 cup brown sugar
1 teaspoon vanilla
1 egg
2 cups flour
¼ teaspoon salt
½ pound milk chocolate, melted
½ cup ground nut meats

Cream butter and sugar light and fluffy. Add flavoring, well-beaten egg, and flour sifted with salt. Stir well. Spread on greased 9 x 13-inch pan. Bake at 350° F. about 25 minutes. Remove from oven, cover with melted chocolate. Sprinkle with nuts. Cut at once into bars.

Bar cookies may be served frosted or unfrosted. In addition to frostings and glazes suggested here, adventurous cooks are urged to experiment with those in chapter 6, Frostings and Fillings, pages 142 to 150.

DATE BARS

½ cup melted butter
1 cup sugar
2 eggs, well beaten
¾ cup flour
¼ teaspoon baking powder
⅛ teaspoon salt
1 cup nut meats, cut fine
1 cup dates, cut fine
confectioners sugar

Mix in order given. Spread in greased pan, 9 by 13 inches. Bake in moderate oven at 350° F. about 20 minutes. Cut into bars and roll in confectioners sugar while warm.

DATE-FILLED CORNFLAKE SQUARES

1 cup butter
1 cup sugar
3 cups cornflakes, crushed
3 cups flour
2 teaspoons baking powder
¼ teaspoon salt
½ cup water

Cream butter and sugar, add rest of ingredients and stir. Spread with date filling and proceed as in recipe above. Ice with Chocolate Icing.

DATE AND NUT STICKS

2 eggs
1 cup sugar
2 cups chopped pecans
1 pound chopped dates
¼ pound candied cherries, cut up
1 teaspoon vanilla
½ cup flour
1 teaspoon baking powder

Beat eggs and sugar well, add nuts, dates, cherries, and vanilla, then flour mixed with baking powder. Spread in 2 greased 8-inch pans and bake in moderate oven, 350° F., about 25 minutes. Cut in strips before cold.

DATE-FILLED OATMEAL SQUARES

1½ cups rolled oats
1¾ cups flour
½ teaspoon soda
½ teaspoon salt
1 cup walnut pieces (optional)
1 cup brown sugar
1 teaspoon cinnamon
1 cup butter, melted

Mix all ingredients well in order given. Pat half the mixture on bottom of a greased 9- by 13-inch pan. Spread with date filling.

FILLING

Boil 1 pound pitted dates, cut fine, with 1 cup of sugar, and ½ cup water until smooth. Add grated rind of 1 lemon and 1 orange. Cool.

Pat remaining dough over this filling. Bake in a moderately slow oven, 325° F., for 30 minutes. Cut while warm. Dust with confectioners sugar, or top with Confectioners Sugar Glaze.

HONEY BARS

⅔ cup strained honey
2 cups confectioners sugar
½ pound blanched almonds
2 cups flour
1 ounce citron, cut very fine
⅛ teaspoon grated nutmeg
⅛ teaspoon ground cloves
¼ cup lemon juice

Boil sugar and honey, add almonds cut in half lengthwise, and stir thoroughly. Add the rest of the ingredients and knead the dough well. Cover and chill overnight. Pat out ½-inch thick and bake in a greased shallow pan in a moderately hot oven, 375° F., for 20 minutes. Cut into strips 1 by 2 inches and frost with Confectioners Sugar Glaze.

HURRY-UP BUTTER COOKIES

1 cup unsalted butter
1 cup sugar
1 egg, separated
juice and grated rind of ½ lemon
2 cups flour, sifted
½ cup chopped nuts

Cream butter and sugar well, add egg yolk and continue beating, then add lemon and flour, mix thoroughly until well blended. Pat dough about ¼-inch thick in greased and floured 9-inch square pan. Brush with slightly beaten egg white, sprinkle with nuts. Bake in slow oven, 300° F., 20 to 30 minutes. Cut while hot into squares or 1½-inch strips.

CINNAMON HURRY-UP COOKIES

In place of the lemon, above, sift and mix 3 teaspoons cinnamon with the flour.

CHOCOLATE HURRY-UP COOKIES

Add 1 square of melted unsweetened chocolate in place of lemon.

PENUCHE STICKS

1 pound brown sugar
4 eggs
1 cup chopped pecans
2 cups flour
1 teaspoon baking powder
⅛ teaspoon salt
1 teaspoon vanilla

Cook sugar and eggs in double boiler, stirring constantly until smooth. Remove from heat. Add pecans, dry ingredients, and vanilla. Spread on a well-greased 9 x 13-inch pan. Bake in a moderately hot oven, 375° F., for 15 minutes. When cool, cut into strips.

QUICK TOFFEE BARS

    24 double graham crackers
    ½ pound butter
    1 cup brown sugar, packed
    nuts

Separate graham crackers and place on a greased jelly-roll pan. Combine butter and sugar in a saucepan. Bring to a boil and simmer for about 2 minutes or until it starts to thicken. Pour hot mixture over graham crackers; sprinkle with nuts. Bake at 350° F. for 13 to 15 minutes.

MAPLE MERINGUE SQUARES

    ½ cup butter
    1 cup granulated sugar
    2 eggs, separated
    1¼ cups cake flour
    1 teaspoon baking powder
    a few grains salt
    ½ teaspoon almond extract
    ½ cup finely chopped nuts
    2 cups brown sugar

Cream butter and granulated sugar, add egg yolks one at a time, then flour, baking powder and salt mixed, add flavoring. Mix. Spread ¼-inch layer on well-greased cookie sheets. Sprinkle with nuts. Beat egg whites frothy, beat in brown sugar. Spread meringue over nuts. Bake about ½ hour at 350° F. Cut in squares when cold.

SCOTCH SHORTBREAD

    1 cup butter
    ½ cup sugar
    4 cups flour

Cream butter and sugar well. Gradually add the flour, kneading until smooth. Line two 9-inch pie pans with waxed paper; pat dough about ½-inch thick into bottom of pans. Flute the edges; prick with a fork. Score in narrow wedges. Bake in a moderate oven, 350° F., for 25 to 30 minutes. Break in pieces to serve.

WALNUT STICKS

    2 eggs
    1 cup brown sugar
    ½ cup flour
    1 cup chopped walnuts
    pinch of salt

Beat eggs and sugar well; add flour, walnuts, and a pinch of salt. Bake in greased 8-inch square pan in a moderate oven, 350° F., for 15 to 20 minutes. Cut in finger-length strips.

QUICK REFERENCE GUIDE TO USEFUL INFORMATION IN THIS BOOK

8
CANDIES AND CONFECTIONS

FUDGE • CARAMELS • PULLED CANDIES • TOFFEES • FONDANTS
• DIPPED CANDIES • NUTS • BRITTLES • GLACEED AND CANDIED CONFECTIONS

General Rules

Use a smooth, round-bottomed pan with straight sides for candy cookery. If sugar crystals form on the side of the pan, wipe them off with a fork wrapped in wet cloth. Watch carefully and test frequently, removing the pan from the heat for each testing. Use fresh cold water for each test.

Temperatures and Tests for Candy

Temperature	Cold Water Test	Texture
230°–234° F.	thread	Little syrup dropped from spoon forms flexible thread.
234°–236° F. 238°–240° F.	soft ball	Ball flattens but does not ooze out when pressed between fingers.
242°–248° F.	firm ball	Ball firm, yet can be flattened a little.
250°–265° F.	hard ball	Ball very firm, yet plastic. Holds its shape.
270°–290° F.	crack stage	Ball pressed flat will be brittle under water, bend out of water.
300°–310° F.	hard-crack stage	Ball pressed will be brittle in and out of water.

A thermometer makes candy-making easier by indicating the exact temperature, and thus the concentration of the syrup. The concentration of the syrup determines whether the finished product is a soft and creamy fudge or a hard brittle. The thermometer should be immersed below the surface of the syrup, but it should not touch the bottom or sides of the pan. Hold the thermometer at eye level to read it accurately. Check the accuracy of thermometer by immersing it in boiling water—water boils at 212° F. at sea level. At higher altitudes candy cooks faster.

FUDGE

Do not stir fudge mixtures after the syrup has dissolved. Cool the fudge, without beating, to 110° F. (warm to the touch). Then beat it until it is glossy and begins to harden. Turn out at once into a buttered pan, let harden, and cut into squares. Nuts and fruits should be added just before pouring. Store fudge in a tightly covered container.

CHOCOLATE FUDGE

2 cups sugar, white, brown, or maple
2 teaspoons corn syrup
1 cup cream, milk, or water
2 squares unsweetened chocolate or ⅔ cup cocoa
½ teaspoon salt
2 tablespoons butter
1 teaspoon vanilla

Cook sugar, syrup, milk, chocolate, and salt over low heat; stir occasionally to prevent burning. Boil to a soft-ball stage, 234° F. Add butter and vanilla. Cool until lukewarm and beat until thick and creamy. Press into buttered pans. Mark into squares and cut.

NUT FUDGE

When fudge is thick and beaten until almost creamy, add 1 cup chopped nut meats and 1 tablespoon candied fruit, chopped. Form into balls, roll in chopped nut meats or grated bitter chocolate.

CREAM FUDGE

    4 cups sugar
    4 tablespoons light corn syrup
    2 heaping teaspoons cornstarch
    1⅓ cups undiluted evaporated milk
    2 tablespoons butter
    2 teaspoons vanilla

Cook first 4 ingredients to soft-ball stage, 238° F., stirring constantly. Add butter and vanilla; do not stir. Cool to lukewarm, then beat until candy loses its sheen; when thick enough to handle, knead and shape into rolls. When set, cut in pieces.

MEXICAN FUDGE

    3 cups sugar
    ¼ cup boiling water
    1 cup undiluted evaporated milk
    pinch of salt
    grated rind 1 orange
    4 tablespoons butter
    1 cup chopped nut meats

Put 1 cup sugar into heavy skillet and place over low heat, stirring constantly. When melted to a light brown add ¼ cup water. Boil until sugar is dissolved and syrup forms. Add remaining sugar, evaporated milk, and salt and cook until it reaches 242° F. (firm-ball stage). Add orange rind and remove from heat. Do not stir after removing from stove. Drop the butter on the candy and let stand until cool. Beat until the mixture starts to lose its sheen. Add the nuts. Knead and form into rolls. Cut into 1-inch pieces.

PENUCHE

    2 cups brown or maple sugar
    ¾ cup milk
    2 tablespoons butter
    1 teaspoon vanilla
    2 cups chopped nuts

Boil sugar and milk to the soft-ball stage, 236° F. Remove from heat; add butter, flavoring and nuts. Cool to lukewarm. Beat till creamy and thickened; press into a greased pan, and when firm, cut into squares.

QUICK FUDGE

    4 squares unsweetened chocolate
    ½ cup butter
    1 egg, beaten slightly
    1 pound confectioners sugar
    ¼ cup sweetened condensed milk
    1 teaspoon vanilla

Melt chocolate and butter in top of double boiler. Mix egg and sugar; add milk, and stir in the chocolate-butter mixture. Add vanilla. Turn into buttered pan, chill and cut into squares.

QUICK CREAM CHEESE FUDGE

    3 ounces cream cheese
    2 cups sifted confectioners sugar
    2 squares unsweetened chocolate, melted
    ¼ teaspoon vanilla
    dash of salt
    ½ cup chopped pecans

Cream the cheese until smooth; blend with sugar. Stir in the melted chocolate and mix well. Add vanilla, salt, and nuts. Press into a buttered pan. Chill until firm. Cut into squares.

PRALINES

    2 cups brown sugar
    1 cup cream
    2 cups pecan halves

Boil sugar and cream to soft-ball stage, 236° F. Remove from heat; add nuts, and stir until mixture begins to sugar. Drop by tablespoonfuls on waxed paper.

NEW ORLEANS PRALINES

    2 cups confectioners sugar
    1 cup maple syrup
    ½ cup cream
    2 cups pecan halves

Boil sugar, syrup and cream to the soft-ball stage, 236° F. Then beat until mixture begins to sugar. Add nuts and drop on waxed paper into 2-inch patties.

COCONUT CANDY

    2 teaspoons butter
    1½ cups sugar
    ½ cup milk
    ⅓ cup shredded sweetened coconut
    ½ teaspoon vanilla or lemon extract

Melt butter in saucepan; add sugar and milk and stir until sugar is dissolved. Boil 12 minutes or to soft-ball stage, 238° F., remove from heat, add coconut and vanilla, and beat until creamy and mixture begins to sugar slightly. Pour at once into a buttered pan and mark into squares.

SEA FOAM

2 cups sugar
½ cup light corn syrup
½ cup water
2 egg whites, beaten stiff
1 teaspoon vanilla
1 cup walnut meats

Boil sugar, syrup, and water to very hard-ball stage, 265° F. Pour slowly onto beaten egg whites, beating constantly. When very thick and creamy, add vanilla and nuts, broken in rather large pieces. Drop from spoon onto waxed paper.

TURKISH CANDY

Follow recipe for Sea Foam, and when stiff and creamy, add nuts, and place in small, deep, well-buttered pan. Cover with 2 squares melted unsweetened chocolate. When cold, cut into slices or squares.

MAPLE FLUFFS

1 cup maple sugar
½ cup brown sugar
½ cup water
¼ teaspoon cream of tartar
6 marshmallows, cut fine
1 egg white
candied cherries or nut meats

Boil first 4 ingredients in a saucepan to crack stage (288° F.), then add marshmallows; let stand 5 minutes, pour over stiffly beaten egg white, beating constantly. Beat until light, and when it begins to set, drop from teaspoon onto waxed paper. Place halved candied cherries or nut meats in center of each piece; cool.

CARAMELS

VANILLA CARAMELS

2 cups sugar
2 tablespoons butter
1 cup milk
1 teaspoon vanilla

Boil sugar, butter, and milk to firm-ball stage, 245° F. Do not stir after sugar is dissolved. Pour on buttered platter, cool, beat until creamy. Add vanilla and chopped nuts or cherries if desired. Press into buttered pans; when firm, cut into squares. Wrap in waxed paper.

CARAMEL COVERED MARSHMALLOWS

½ pound marshmallows
Vanilla, above, or Chocolate Caramels, below

Follow recipe for Vanilla or Chocolate Caramels. Soften caramel mixture in saucepan over boiling water. Place marshmallows on a 2-tined fork or candy dipper. Dip into caramel mixture until coated and then remove to waxed paper. Let stand until coating is hard.

CHOCOLATE CARAMELS

2 cups white sugar
1 cup brown sugar, packed
1 cup dark corn syrup
½ cup cream
½ cup butter
3 squares unsweetened chocolate
⅛ teaspoon salt
1 teaspoon vanilla

Place all ingredients except vanilla in a heavy saucepan. Cover and boil for 5 minutes. Uncover, boil to firm-ball stage, 247° F. Remove from heat, add vanilla; add 1 cup chopped nut meats if desired. Pour into buttered 10- by 6-inch pan. When cold, cut into 1-inch squares. Wrap in waxed paper.

COFFEE CREAM CARAMELS

2 cups evaporated milk
½ cup very strong coffee
2 cups sugar
2 cups light corn syrup
¼ teaspoon salt
½ cup butter
1 teaspoon vanilla

Add milk to coffee. Boil sugar, syrup, salt to firm-ball stage, 245° F. Add coffee mixture and butter very slowly, as boiling must not stop. Cook quickly and stir constantly to 242° F., firm-ball stage. Add vanilla; pour ¾-inch deep in buttered pans; cool. Mark in squares. Chill until very firm; remove from pan, cut into squares. Wrap in waxed paper.

VANILLA CREAM CARAMELS

3 cups cream, heated
2 cups sugar
2 cups light corn syrup
1 cup walnuts
1 teaspoon vanilla

Boil 1 cup cream with sugar and syrup to soft-ball stage, 238° F. Add 1 cup hot cream; boil again to soft-ball stage. Add third cup of hot cream and boil again to soft-ball stage. Remove from heat, stir in nuts and flavoring, and pour into well-buttered pans. When cold, cut into squares. Wrap in waxed paper.

PULLED CANDIES AND TOFFEES

WHITE TAFFY

2 cups sugar
⅔ cup water
4 tablespoons butter
2 teaspoons cream of tartar

Combine ingredients and boil to soft-crack stage, 272° F., stirring as needed to prevent scorching. Add any flavoring desired. Pour into well-buttered pan and when cool enough to handle, pull quickly and lightly with oiled finger tips. It should become porous. Stretch out on board to harden; cut into pieces.

SALT-WATER TAFFY

1¼ cups corn syrup
1 cup sugar
1 tablespoon water
1 teaspoon butter
1 tablespoon vinegar
½ teaspoon vanilla

Mix all ingredients. Boil until syrup reaches the crack stage, 272° F., stirring as needed to prevent scorching. Pour into buttered pan. As soon as it is cool enough to handle, pull until candy is light and porous. When cold, chop into pieces.

CINNAMON BALLS

Add ½ teaspoon essence of cinnamon to Salt-Water Taffy before it is pulled. Let it cool and roll into balls.

BUTTERCUPS

2 cups sugar
½ cup water
½ teaspoon cream of tartar
food coloring
1 teaspoon lemon extract
1 teaspoon vanilla
Fondant, page 172

Boil sugar, water, and cream of tartar without stirring to hard-ball stage, 260° F. Add a little yellow coloring, lemon extract and vanilla. When cool enough to handle, pull the candy on a floured board in a long sheet, about 2 inches wide. In center of this strip lay a roll of Fondant the full length of the strip. Wrap the yellow candy around the Fondant; bring the edges together and press firmly. When cool, cut with scissors into ½-inch pieces. Make in various colors and flavors.

DAISY CREAM CANDY

3 pounds sugar
2 cups water
6 ounces butter
½ tablespoon vanilla

Mix sugar and water, add butter and boil without stirring until it reaches 262° F., hard-ball stage. Pour quickly on ice-cold, buttered marble slab. Pour vanilla or other flavoring over the mixture. When slightly cooled, pull until white, glossy and porous. Cut into squares. Will be soft and creamy the next day. Store in airtight box.

MOLASSES CANDY

1 teaspoon butter
1 cup dark molasses
1 tablespoon water
½ cup sugar
¼ teaspoon soda

Melt the butter in a heavy skillet, add molasses, water and sugar, and stir until sugar is dissolved. Stir occasionally until nearly done, and then constantly. Boil until the spoon leaves a track in the bottom of pan while stirring, to hard-ball stage, 255° F. Stir well, add the soda, stir thoroughly, and pour in a very well-greased pan. When cool enough to handle, pull until light-colored and porous. Work candy with finger tips and thumbs; do not squeeze in the hands. When it begins to harden, stretch to the desired thickness, cut in small pieces with large shears. Cool on buttered plates.

ENGLISH TOFFEE

1¾ cups sugar
⅛ teaspoon cream of tartar
1 cup cream
½ cup butter
1 teaspoon rum

Place sugar with cream of tartar in a deep saucepan, rounded at the bottom; add cream, boil a few minutes, stirring with wooden spoon. Add butter, boil to soft-crack stage, 290° F., stirring all the time. Add 1 teaspoon rum or any fruit flavoring. Pour into buttered pan. Cut into squares while warm.

ALMOND TOFFEE

Make English Toffee, omitting rum. Add 6 tablespoons chopped almonds. Pour at once into greased pan.

To prevent sugar crystals from forming on sides of pan: Stir sugar and liquid over slow heat until sugar is dissolved; cover pan for the first 2 or 3 minutes of boiling.

STICK CANDY

2 cups sugar
½ cup light corn syrup
½ cup water
juice and rind of 1 lemon

Boil all ingredients without stirring to soft-crack stage, 285° F. Remove from heat.

FOR LEMON STICKS

Add 1 teaspoon lemon extract. Pour on a buttered platter. When cool enough, pull and roll into sticks and cut.

FOR PEPPERMINT STICKS

Add 1 teaspoon peppermint extract. Divide candy into two parts. To one part add a little red vegetable coloring. Pour on buttered platters; when cool enough, pull each and roll separately, then twist one around other; form into canes or sticks.

SOFT BUTTERSCOTCH

2 cups brown sugar
¼ cup butter
½ cup water

Put sugar, butter, and water in skillet; boil and stir until the spoon leaves a track in bottom of pan, or to hard-ball stage, 252° F. Pour ¼ inch deep in buttered pans. When cool, cut into squares.

HARD BUTTERSCOTCH

1 cup corn syrup
2 cups brown sugar
½ cup butter
¼ cup water
1 tablespoon vinegar
1 teaspoon vanilla

Boil until syrup dropped into cold water separates into hard thin cords (288° to 290° F.). Pour into buttered pan. When hard, break into pieces.

FONDANT AND DIPPED CANDIES

Fondant, sometimes called Stock Dough for Candy, is the base for many candies. It may be flavored and colored to taste, and shaped as desired; or used to coat fruits, nuts, other candies or small cakes; or mixed with chopped nuts or dried or candied fruits; or used as centers for chocolate-covered bonbons. Fondant should be allowed to ripen at least 1 hour before it is used to make candies. It improves with ripening overnight or longer.

COOKED FONDANT

2 cups sugar
⅔ cup cold water
⅛ teaspoon cream of tartar

Bring sugar and water to a boil, stirring only until sugar is completely dissolved. Add cream of tartar. Continue to boil until syrup reaches the soft-ball stage, 238° F. If any crystals form on sides of pan, wash off with damp cloth wrapped around fork. Pour onto a buttered marble slab or large platter to cool. When mixture is lukewarm, beat with a spatula or wooden spoon until it is white and creamy. Knead on slab until smooth. Cover with a damp towel and let rest for 1 hour. Knead again and store in an airtight jar in the refrigerator.

CREAM FONDANT, UNCOOKED

1½ pounds confectioners sugar
1 teaspoon vanilla
3 tablespoons cream
1 egg white

Mix ingredients and knead thoroughly. Mold to shape.

BUTTER FONDANT, UNCOOKED

1 egg white
4 tablespoons butter, creamed
¼ cup cold water
1 teaspoon flavoring
1 teaspoon cream of tartar
1¾ pounds confectioners sugar

Mix ingredients in order, knead thoroughly, and mold to shape.

PEPPERMINT, WINTERGREEN OR FRUIT PATTIES

Put Fondant in top of double boiler, soften over hot water. Flavor with a few drops of peppermint, wintergreen or fruit flavors. Add coloring. Drop from tip of spoon onto waxed paper.

NUT CREAMS

Add enough cream to a cup of Fondant to make it thin enough to beat. Beat until consistency of whipped cream; add a little flavoring and ½ cup nuts. Press flat on a buttered baking sheet and cut into squares.

Fondant is used to ice and decorate Petits Fours. See the recipe for these small decorated cakes on page 138. Fondant will keep for several months if refrigerated in an airtight container.

TUTTI-FRUTTI CREAMS

½ cup candied cherries
½ cup candied orange peel
¼ pound nut meats
½ cup raisins, seedless
½ cup coconut, shredded
2 cups Fondant, page 172, melted

Chop the fruit and nuts, add coconut and raisins and mix with Fondant. Mold in small patties.

FONDANT DIP

To dip bonbons, melt Fondant in a saucepan over hot water. Add coloring and flavor as desired. Stir as little as possible; add a little boiling water if mixture seems too thick, confectioners sugar if too thin. Remove pan from heat while dipping. A second saucepan of fondant may be melting in the hot water, to use alternately. Put centers—nuts, candied fruit, fondant shapes or other candies may be used—on a dipping fork (pronged or with a loop at the end), lower into fondant, lift out, drain off excess fondant, and invert candy on waxed paper over rack to cool. Stir the fondant as necessary between dippings to prevent crust from forming.

DIPPED FRESH STRAWBERRIES

1 quart fresh strawberries
1 cup Fondant, page 172

Do not hull berries. Dip berries, one at a time, halfway into Fondant, softened over hot water, holding the berry by the stem. Lift the berry out quickly, turning it round and round in the air a moment, tip upward, to dry; then invert berry, stand on tip on waxed paper. Place each berry in a paper bonbon cup. Serve within an hour. Cannot be stored.

CHOCOLATE DIP

Melt 1 pound semi-sweet or milk chocolate over boiling water. Let stand until it feels cool (85°). Add a little butter or cocoa butter if chocolate is too thick. Proceed as for Fondant Dip, above.

CHOCOLATE CREAM DIP

Fondant, page 172
4 ounces bitter, sweet or milk chocolate

Make cone-shaped forms of Fondant. Place on waxed paper to harden. Dip, one at a time, into Chocolate Dip and cover all sides. Set on waxed paper to harden.

CHOCOLATE-DIPPED CHERRIES

Maraschino cherries
Fondant, page 172
Chocolate Dip, page 173

Drain the Maraschino cherries, but not too dry. Melt Fondant in double boiler, and dip the cherries one at a time; drop on waxed paper and let stand in cool place just long enough to harden. Then dip into Chocolate Dip.

CHOCOLATE-COATED FUDGE

Follow recipe for any Fudge, pages 168-169, dip squares into Chocolate Dip, let harden on waxed paper.

DATE OR FIG CHOCOLATES

Remove stones from dates or cut figs in halves lengthwise. Press into uniform shape and coat with Chocolate Dip. Marshmallows may also be dipped.

CHOCOLATE-DIPPED GRAPES (ACORNS)

½ pound Malaga grapes
2 ounces semisweet or sweet chocolate
2 tablespoons granulated sugar

Wash grapes; leave small stem on each grape. Drain dry between towels. Melt chocolate. Let stand until slightly cool. Dip stem end of grapes, one at a time, into the chocolate to about ¼ the depth of the grapes, holding them by the other end with the fingers. Remove from chocolate quickly, invert to cool a moment, then roll the chocolate end in the sugar and place chocolate side down on waxed paper to harden.

If melted chocolate becomes rough or lumpy, add a little homogenized vegetable shortening and stir until it becomes smooth again.

MINT JELLIES

2 envelopes unflavored gelatin
1⅓ cups water
2 cups sugar
2 tablespoons lemon juice
green coloring
few drops oil of peppermint

Soak gelatin in ⅔ cup cold water 5 minutes. Place sugar and rest of water in a saucepan, and bring to a boil. Add dissolved gelatin, bring to the boiling point and boil slowly but steadily 20 minutes. Remove from heat, add rest of the ingredients. Pour the mixture into a shallow pan to about 1 inch in thickness, let stand for about 12 hours or until firm. Remove to board, cut in cubes, roll in confectioners sugar.

FRUIT JELLIES

Different varieties can be made by using fruit juices instead of water and different coloring, also by adding ½ cup chopped nut meats or candied fruits.

MARSHMALLOWS

2 envelopes unflavored gelatin
1¼ cups water
2 cups sugar
speck salt
oil of peppermint or wintergreen
food coloring
confectioners sugar

Soak gelatin in ½ cup cold water 5 minutes. Cook sugar and ¾ cup water in saucepan until it threads, pour onto dissolved gelatin, let stand until partially cooled. Add salt and, if desired, a few drops of oil of peppermint or wintergreen and a little green or red coloring. Beat until light and thick. Pour into pan thickly dusted with confectioners sugar and put in a cool place to set. Turn out, cut into squares and roll in confectioners sugar.

NUTS AND BRITTLES

To BLANCH NUTS: Pour boiling water over shelled nuts; let stand 5 minutes, or longer. Strain; put into cold water; slip off skins. Dry in oven before storing.

To CHOP: Use special nut chopper or chopping knife and bowl.

To GRIND: Use special nut grinder or electric blender.

To SLICE: Use very sharp, thin-bladed knife to avoid breaking nuts.

SUGAR-COATED (OR BURNT) ALMONDS

2 cups sugar
½ cup water
1 pound almonds, unblanched
1 teaspoon cinnamon
red food coloring

Boil sugar and water until thick and clear. Add almonds; stir with a wooden spoon until the nuts crackle. Reduce heat, stir until dry. Remove nuts, add just enough water to sugar in skillet to moisten. Add cinnamon and red coloring and boil until syrup spins a thread, 230° F. Add sugared nuts and stir until thoroughly coated and separated.

COFFEE CANDIED NUTS

1½ cups sugar
1 tablespoon corn syrup
½ cup strong coffee
2½ cups unbroken halves of nut meats

Cook first 3 ingredients to soft-ball stage, 240° F. Remove from heat and add nuts. Stir gently until creamy. Spread on greased cookie sheet; separate with fork. Cool.

ORANGE CANDIED NUTS

Substitute ½ cup orange juice for coffee in Coffee Candied Nuts. Add ¼ teaspoon ground cinnamon with the nut meats.

ALMOND OR PECAN BRITTLE

1 cup sugar
1 cup blanched almonds or pecans, coarsely chopped

Melt sugar in skillet to a light-brown syrup. Add nuts. Cook a few minutes, stirring constantly. Spread on a greased pan, cool, break into pieces.

PEANUT BRITTLE

2 cups sugar
½ to 1 cup shelled skinned peanuts, coarsely chopped

Heat sugar in a heavy skillet until it becomes a thin, light-brown syrup, stirring constantly. Pour over peanuts; spread on a buttered pan in a single layer. Mark into squares while still warm. When cool, break in pieces. Brazil, pecan or walnut meats, puffed rice, or puffed wheat may be used in place of the peanuts.

CREAMY NUT BRITTLE

1 cup sugar
⅓ cup water
⅛ teaspoon cream of tartar
1 tablespoon cream
1 tablespoon molasses
½ cup chopped nuts
¼ teaspoon soda

Cook sugar, water and cream of tartar to 280° F., soft-crack stage. Then add the cream and molasses and cook to 300° F., hard-crack stage. Add nut meats and soda, mixing quickly. Spread thin on well-buttered cookie sheet. When cool, break into pieces.

BUTTER CRUNCH

1½ cups butter
2 cups sugar
3 ounces milk chocolate, melted
½ cup chopped, toasted almonds

Cook butter and sugar slowly in a deep saucepan, rounded at the bottom, to the hard-crack stage, 300° F. Pour into large buttered pan. Cool. Brush with melted chocolate, then sprinkle with almonds. Chill. Lift from pan, brush other side with melted chocolate and sprinkle with almonds. Cool until chocolate hardens. Break into pieces.

TO CARAMELIZE SUGAR

Put sugar into a heavy skillet; heat in moderate oven or on range over low flame until melted. Turn into lightly buttered pan. When cold, break into pieces.

TO CRUSH

Put pieces of caramelized sugar through meat grinder, or roll with rolling pin and sift.

GLACEED AND CANDIED CONFECTIONS

GLACEED NUTS OR FRUITS

2 cups sugar
1 cup boiling water
⅛ teaspoon cream of tartar

Heat ingredients in a saucepan, stirring until sugar is dissolved. Then heat to the boiling point and let boil, without stirring, to hard-crack stage, 300° F. Place over pan of hot water to keep syrup from hardening. Then quickly dip fruits and nuts, a few at a time, in the hot syrup and remove them with fork or wire spoon to waxed paper. Glacéed fruits should only be attempted in cold, clear weather. Oranges and tangerines should be separated into sections and allowed to dry a few hours or overnight before dipping.

GLACEED PRUNES

Remove stones from prunes, fill cavity with nut meats. Follow recipe for Glacéed Nuts and Fruits.

MARRONS GLACES

2 cups chestnuts
1 pound sugar
1 cup water
¼ vanilla bean

Boil chestnuts for 20 minutes, peel the chestnuts whole, cover with fresh boiling water and a little sugar and cook until tender but not broken; drain.

Boil sugar, 1 cup water and vanilla bean, without stirring, until syrup reaches hard-crack stage, 300° F.; add chestnuts at once. Leave them in 5 minutes. Take out carefully with silver fork, place on warm sieve in warm place. Next day heat syrup, repeat dipping and drying processes. Place in tiny paper cases or, lifting carefully with a fork so they do not break, put them in a sterilized bottle or jar and cover with boiling syrup. Seal and store.

CANDIED CHERRIES

1 pound sugar
1 cup water
1 pound fresh cherries, pitted

Boil sugar and water until the sugar spins a thread, 232° F. Add cherries, let come to a boil; cool. Lift cherries with perforated spoon to platter. Boil syrup 5 minutes longer, pour over cherries. Cover with glass or cheesecloth, set in sun for several hours. Allow cherries to dry by turning onto a clean cloth spread over wire cake rack. Store in glass jars.

CANDIED ORANGE PEEL

peel of 1 orange
½ cup sugar
¼ cup hot water

Wipe orange, remove peel in quarters and cut in narrow strips. Place peel in saucepan, cover with cold water, let boil up once and drain. Repeat five times. Heat the sugar with the hot water, and when dissolved, add orange peel. Cook slowly until syrup is nearly evaporated, drain and roll the strips in granulated sugar.

CANDIED GRAPEFRUIT PEEL

Peel grapefruit, cut peel into sticks. Measure the peel. Proceed as for Candied Orange Peel, using an equal amount of sugar and half as much water.

CHOCOLATE-DIPPED CANDIED PEEL

Melt 2 squares of unsweetened chocolate in double boiler and keep over hot water. Prepare Candied Orange or Grapefruit Peel. Dip each in melted chocolate. Remove to waxed paper and let stand until dry.

Tips for successful candy making:
- *Use a heavy straight-sided pan large enough to accommodate 4 times the ingredients.*
- *Grease the inside of the pan to prevent syrup from boiling over.*

CRYSTALLIZED APPLE SLICES

    3 firm Jonathan apples
    1 cup sugar
    ½ cup water
    cinnamon or mint flavoring
    granulated sugar

Peel, quarter and core apples. Cut each quarter into three slices. Boil sugar and water for 5 minutes in a small saucepan. Syrup may be tinted red with cinnamon candies or green with mint flavoring. Drop 12 apple slices into boiling syrup and cook slowly until transparent. Remove from syrup to waxed paper. Add 2 tablespoons water to syrup after removing each dozen pieces. Repeat until all slices are cooked. Cool for 24 hours in a dry place. Roll in granulated sugar and repeat every 24 hours. After the third rolling, let stand until absolutely dry.

NUT-STUFFED DATES

Make a cut the entire length of each date and remove pits. Fill cavity with English walnuts, blanched almonds, pecans or a mixture of chopped nuts, and shape in original form. Roll in granulated sugar or confectioners sugar.

FONDANT-STUFFED DATES

Slit and stone dates, fill with Fondant, page 172, and insert in Fondant a pecan or half a walnut. Roll in granulated sugar.

GINGER-AND-NUT-STUFFED DATES

Remove the stones from dates. Chop together equal measures of preserved ginger and blanched nuts, chopped (hickory, pecans or almonds). Mix with Fondant or a paste of confectioners sugar and ginger syrup. Use only enough to hold the ingredients together. Fill the dates with this mixture and roll in granulated sugar.

STUFFED FIGS

Steam large dried figs until soft in small amount of water in double boiler. Cool, cut off stem end, open, stuff each fig with pecans or English walnuts and ½ marshmallow. Close, press into shape, roll in granulated sugar.

STUFFED GLAZED FIGS

    ½ pound large dried figs
    ½ cup orange juice
    2 tablespoons sugar
    1 teaspoon lemon juice
    Maraschino cherries, halved
    pecan meats, broken

Cook figs very slowly in sauce of orange juice, sugar and lemon juice, turning and basting until tender. Drain, cool. Open and stuff each fig with Maraschino cherries and pecan meats. Close, press into shape, and roll in granulated or confectioners sugar.

STUFFED PRUNES

Steam 1 pound of large prunes until plump. Cool. Remove stones. Fill cavity with Fondant and half a pecan or walnut. Let stand until partially dry. Roll in granulated sugar.

APRICOT BALLS

    1 pound dried apricots, ground fine
    2 cups sugar
    peel of ½ medium-sized orange, ground fine
    few drops lemon juice
    granulated sugar

Mix ingredients well. Boil about 10 minutes, stirring constantly to prevent burning. Spread on large platter and chill overnight or for several hours, as it is much easier to roll when cold. Shape into balls and roll in granulated sugar. Makes about 6 dozen.

Candy making is best not attempted in hot humid weather. Fudges, fondants and glacéed candies in particular are apt to become sticky and sugary. In damp weather, cook all candies 2 or 3 degrees higher than in dry cold weather.

DATE LOAF CANDY

    4 cups sugar
    1 cup milk
    2 tablespoons butter
    1 package pitted dates
    ½ teaspoon vanilla
    lemon or orange rind, grated
    1 cup chopped nuts

Cook sugar, milk and butter to soft-ball stage, 236° F. Add dates, cut fine. Cook 5 minutes longer. Cool and add flavoring. Beat a few minutes, then add the chopped nuts and rind and continue to beat until it thickens. Roll in waxed paper or place in a buttered loaf pan; slice when cold.

DATE SAUSAGE

    1 pound dates, stoned
    2 ounces candied ginger
    ½ cup walnuts
    confectioners sugar

Grind dates; add the ginger and walnuts, coarsely cut. Knead and roll into sausage 1½ inches thick, using confectioners sugar to prevent sticking. Cut in thin slices.

DATE AND WALNUT BONBONS

½ pound shelled walnuts
½ pound pitted dates
1 egg white
2 tablespoons sugar

Grind nuts and dates fine, knead and form into date-shaped bonbons. Chill overnight. Beat egg white slightly, add sugar, dip bonbons in mixture. Place on greased baking sheet, bake at 300° F. until crisp.

SPANISH SWEETS

¼ pound candied cherries
¼ pound raisins, seedless
¼ pound figs
¼ pound dates, pitted
¼ pound almonds
½ pound English walnut meats
¼ pound hickory nut or pecan meats

Mix all together and grind fine or chop. Sprinkle board with confectioners sugar, toss on the mixture, knead well. Cut into small squares. Will keep packed in layers between sheets of waxed paper.

CANDIED FRUIT AND NUT SLICES

½ pound mixed candied fruit
¼ pound raisins, seeded
¼ pound dates, pitted
1 cup pecan meats
2 tablespoons brandy
½ cup chocolate sprinkles

Mix first 5 ingredients and knead. Form into a roll and cover with chocolate sprinkles. Cut into slices.

CARAMEL APPLES

5 medium apples
1 cup sugar
¾ cup dark corn syrup
1 cup cream
2 tablespoons butter
1 teaspoon vanilla

Wash apples, remove stems, and stick skewers into stem end of apples. Cook sugar, syrup, cream, and butter to firm-ball stage, 245° F. Do not stir. Remove from heat; add vanilla. Dip apples into syrup; spoon syrup over apples to cover completely. Remove apples; hold skewer between palms of hands and spin for a moment to cool caramel. If desired, roll in coarsely chopped nuts. Place apples upright on waxed paper.

POPCORN

Heat 2 teaspoons oil in corn popper or in skillet with cover. Add ⅓ cup popcorn kernels, cover tightly. Shake over heat until kernels pop. Makes about 1 quart. Melt 2 tablespoons butter, pour over popcorn, sprinkle with salt, toss well, and serve.

CARAMELIZED POPCORN BALLS

3 quarts Popcorn, above
1 cup molasses
½ cup sugar
1 tablespoon butter
½ teaspoon salt

Place Popcorn in a large bowl. Cook molasses, sugar, butter and salt to crack stage, 270° F. Pour over Popcorn and stir. Dip hands in water or oil and roll lightly into balls.

CHOCOLATE BALLS

½ pound sweet chocolate
1 egg, unbeaten
2 tablespoons butter
chocolate sprinkles

Melt chocolate in double boiler, add egg, stir until smooth, then stir in butter. When cool, form into balls, roll quickly in chocolate sprinkles or chopped roasted almonds or pistachio nuts.

CHOCOLATE MARSHMALLOW BALLS

¼ pound sweet chocolate
½ pound unsweetened chocolate
¼ pound marshmallows, cut up
1 cup pecans, chopped
confectioners sugar

Melt chocolate in double boiler. Let cool a bit, then pour over the marshmallows and nuts and mix until marshmallows are dissolved. Set aside to cool. When almost firm, form into balls and roll in confectioners sugar.

CHOCOLATE SAUSAGE

½ pound sweet chocolate
1 egg, unbeaten
½ cup almonds, blanched and sliced
granulated sugar

Melt chocolate in double boiler; add egg, stir until smooth, add nuts. Spread on buttered plate. When cool, form into rolls, 1½ inches thick. Roll in sugar, let stand until firm. Slice.

NUT BARS

½ pound semisweet chocolate
¼ teaspoon salt
⅔ cup seeded raisins
⅔ cup chopped peanuts

Melt chocolate over hot water. Stir until smooth and nearly cool, then add salt, raisins cut fine, and the nuts. Mix well, spread in buttered shallow pan to ¼-inch depth. When set, cut into strips.

RUM OR BOURBON BALLS

½ pound vanilla wafers
1 cup pecans, finely chopped
2 teaspoons cocoa
½ cup light corn syrup
¼ cup rum or bourbon
confectioners sugar

Crush wafers very fine. Add nuts, cocoa, syrup and rum. Stir until well blended. Dust hands with confectioners sugar and roll mixture into balls the size of a walnut. Let stand for about 1 hour to dry partially. Then roll in confectioners sugar.

COCONUT PEANUT-BUTTER CANDY

1 cup shredded sweetened coconut
1 teaspoon vanilla
¼ cup peanut butter

Mix ingredients well to a paste. Shape into small balls and chill until very firm. If coconut is dry, soak in a little milk or water for 5 or 10 minutes, and if it is not sweet add 1 tablespoon syrup.

QUICK REFERENCE GUIDE TO USEFUL INFORMATION IN THIS BOOK

9
CEREALS, RICE, AND LEGUMES

CEREALS

BREAKFAST CEREALS should be kept tightly covered, in a dry place. Cooking directions are on the package labels. Precooked cereals are now available, and are used a great deal in the feeding of infants.

COOKED BREAKFAST CEREALS are served with cream, milk, or fruit, with or without sugar, or with butter and brown sugar.

CEREAL WITH FRUITS: add fruit, fresh or dried, cut up, to the cooked cereal just before serving.

COOKED CEREALS seasoned with butter, salt, pepper, and chopped parsley or other herbs, may be served as an accompaniment for meat or fish at dinner or luncheon.

BARLEY, TAPIOCA, SAGO

1 teaspoon salt
1 quart boiling water
½ cup barley, tapioca or sago

Add salt to the boiling water and gradually add grain; boil until tender from 1 to 2 or more hours, according to the grain; each kernel should be separate when done. Add more boiling water as needed. Use as a vegetable, or in soups.

BARLEY RING

1 cup diced celery root
½ cup diced carrots
2 quarts boiling water
2 teaspoons salt
1 cup barley

Cook diced vegetables in salted water. Drain, reserving both vegetables and liquid. Bring liquid to

a boil, add barley and cook, as above. Mix vegetables with barley, season to taste, and place in well-greased ring mold in pan of hot water. Bake ½ hour in moderate oven, 350° F.

BUCKWHEAT GROATS (KASHE)

1 onion, diced
2 tablespoons fat
1 teaspoon salt
a little paprika
2½ cups fine buckwheat groats
1 egg
2 cups boiling water

Fry onion in the fat. Mix salt, paprika, and groats with the egg. Place in a greased baking dish. Stir in as much water as it will absorb; add onion and fat; cover and bake in a moderately hot oven, 375° F., for 20 minutes or until tender. Serve with roast chicken gravy or any other meat gravy.

CORN MEAL MUSH

2 teaspoons salt
4 cups boiling water
1 cup corn meal

Add salt to boiling water in upper part of double boiler, place over heat, add the meal slowly, stirring constantly. Cover and steam over boiling water from 1 to 3 hours.

Or mix meal with 1 cup of cold water and add to 3 cups of boiling salted water; proceed as above.

Corn meal mush served with cottage cheese and sour cream is a delicious Romanian supper dish.

FRIED CORN MEAL MUSH

Put leftover mush into a loaf pan. When cold, cut into slices ½ inch thick. Dip each slice into flour. Melt ½ teaspoon butter in a skillet. Brown the floured slices until crisp on each side. Serve on a hot plate with syrup. If wanted crisp and dry, fry slowly.

HAGGIS (SCOTCH)

¼ pound liver
1 pound steel-cut oats
salt to taste
½ teaspoon white pepper
½ pound minced suet
1 onion

Parboil liver until cooked through. Chill and grate or mince. Mix with other ingredients, add water to make a stiff paste, tie in pudding cloth ¾ full or in a thoroughly cleaned sheep's paunch. Put in boiling water, boil 3 hours.

HOMINY GRITS

1 cup fine hominy
1 teaspoon salt
4 cups boiling water

Stir hominy slowly into salted boiling water. Cover and cook, stirring occasionally, until tender and thick, about 1 hour.

RICE

Many varieties of rice are available, some of them precooked or processed to cook very quickly. In using processed rice follow the directions on the package.

Various methods of cooking ordinary rice are given in this chapter. Whatever method is used, the grains of rice should be just cooked through, but not soft and mushy. To test rice, press a grain between the fingers, or bite into it: there should be no hard center. The grains should be separate and distinct. Let rice stand over hot water for a few minutes, uncovered, to dry. To keep rice hot, or to reheat it, put it over hot water, uncovered; or set it in a pan of hot water in a moderate oven. One cup raw rice makes about 3 cups cooked.

BOILED RICE

1 cup rice
4 cups boiling water
2 teaspoons salt

Wash rice. Sprinkle slowly into rapidly boiling, salted water so as not to check the boiling. Stir with fork. Boil rapidly 20 minutes or until grains seem soft when pressed between fingers. Drain in coarse strainer, pour boiling water through rice. Put over hot water, uncovered, 5 to 10 minutes so grains will be whole, dry and fluffy.

QUICK BOILED RICE

1 cup rice
2 cups cold water
1 teaspoon salt

Wash rice. Place ingredients in pan with tight-fitting cover. Bring to a vigorous boil. Reduce heat as low as possible. Cook for 15 minutes. Turn off heat. Leave rice covered for 5 minutes before removing lid.

CHINESE RICE

1 cup rice, washed
1¼ to 2 cups cold water
1 teaspoon salt

Put rice in pan with cold water just to cover. Add salt. Place over heat, bring quickly to boiling point, cover tightly, reduce heat; cook slowly 20 to 30 minutes, until grains are just tender, and all water is absorbed. Uncover and keep over heat until dry.

STEAMED RICE

1 cup rice
3 cups boiling water
1 teaspoon salt

Wash rice in cold water; drain. Put boiling, salted water in top of double boiler. Set over direct heat and gradually add rice. Boil 5 minutes. Place over hot water and steam, covered, 40 minutes or until water is absorbed and grains are tender. Uncover to dry. Suitable for molds or rings.

BROWN RICE

1 cup brown rice
4 cups boiling water
2 teaspoons salt

Brown rice is rice from which the outer coat of bran has not been entirely removed. Cook from 40 to 60 minutes, following the recipe for steamed or boiled rice.

WILD RICE

Wash in fresh water many times until free from grit. Boil or steam like brown rice, until just tender, 40 to 60 minutes. Lift with fork but do not stir. For Wild Rice Ring, follow directions for Brown Rice Ring.

RICE CROQUETTES

2 cups cold, cooked rice
2 or 3 tablespoons milk
2 tablespoons butter
½ teaspoon salt
dash of pepper
cayenne
2 tablespoons chopped parsley
2 eggs
bread crumbs

Place the rice in a double boiler, add the milk, butter, seasoning, parsley, and 1 beaten egg, and cook until thick. Chill and shape into cones or cylinders. Dip into the remaining egg beaten with 1 tablespoon water, then in dry bread crumbs. Let stand 30 minutes. Fry in deep hot fat, 375° F., until brown.

EGGS AND RICE

3 cups cooked rice
1 10½-ounce can cream of mushroom soup
½ cup water
½ cup milk
1 cup dry bread crumbs
3 tablespoons butter, melted
½ teaspoon garlic salt
½ teaspoon pepper
8 to 10 hard-cooked eggs

Combine rice, soup, water and milk. Heat. Place in bottom of greased casserole. Combine crumbs, butter and seasonings. Sprinkle half of this mixture over the rice. Slice the eggs and place them over the crumbs, pressing lightly so that the slices are not broken. Sprinkle with remaining crumbs. Cover and bake at 400° F. for 20 minutes.

ITALIAN RICE WITH CHICKEN LIVERS (RISOTTO)

2 tablespoons chicken fat
2 tablespoons chopped onion
1 teaspoon chopped parsley
¼ pound chicken livers
1 cup rice, washed
3 cups hot chicken soup
2 teaspoons salt
⅛ teaspoon Spanish saffron
3 tablespoons grated Romano cheese

Heat fat in top of double boiler over direct heat; add onion, parsley and livers, diced. Cook gently until browned, stirring constantly. Add rice, cook until light yellow; gradually add soup. Boil for 5 minutes, add salt and saffron, dissolved in a little hot soup and strained, stir, cover pan and cook over hot water 20 to 30 minutes or until rice is tender. Add cheese, mix lightly and serve hot with additional grated cheese.

CURRIED RICE

1 cup rice
3 cups hot chicken or veal broth
1 onion, chopped fine
2 tablespoons butter
2 teaspoons salt
2 teaspoons curry powder

Cover rice with cold water, bring quickly to boiling point, drain and rinse in cold water. Cook rice in the broth and when partly done, add the onion sautéed in butter, salt and the curry powder creamed with a little butter. Mix thoroughly, add more stock if needed, and finish cooking in a slow oven. Serve with hot chicken or veal.

MEXICAN RICE

1 cup rice
2 tablespoons butter
1 cup strained tomato or ½ cup tomato pulp
2 teaspoons salt
1 quart water or soup stock

Wash rice. Melt butter in skillet, add rice, cook until light brown, stirring constantly. Add tomato and salt, cook a few minutes. Add boiling water or soup stock, stir well, cook gently, without stirring, until rice is tender and liquid is absorbed. Decorate with sliced hard-cooked eggs.

RICE RING

Steam rice, add ¼ cup melted butter and mix lightly. Pack into a well-greased ring mold, set in a pan of hot water and bake in a moderate oven, 350° F., 30 minutes. When ready to serve, loosen edges and turn carefully onto serving dish.

BROWN RICE RING

1 cup brown rice, washed
4 cups boiling water
4 tablespoons butter
2 teaspoons salt

Cook brown rice in boiling water. Melt butter, add salt and mix with the rice. Butter a ring mold well, pack firmly with the rice, set in a pan half filled with hot water, bake in moderate oven, 350° F., 30 minutes. When ready to serve, loosen edges and turn carefully onto serving platter. Surround with creamed chicken, and place mushrooms in center.

SPANISH RICE

1 cup rice, washed
4 tablespoons fat
5 onions, chopped
1 clove garlic, minced
2 cups strained tomato
1 cup water
1 red or green pepper, chopped, or 1 canned
    pimiento
1 teaspoon paprika
2 teaspoons salt

Place rice in skillet with fat, add onion and the garlic. Cook 10 minutes, stirring often. Add remaining ingredients. Cover and cook slowly about 1 hour until rice is tender and liquid absorbed.

TURKISH RICE

¾ cup tomatoes, stewed and strained
1 cup brown soup stock, highly seasoned
½ cup washed rice
3 tablespoons butter

Put tomato and stock in the top of a double boiler over direct heat; bring to the boiling point. Place over hot water. Add rice and cook until rice is soft; stir in butter with a fork. Serve as vegetable or as border for curried or fricasseed meat.

RICE AND MUSHROOM RING

1 cup rice
1 pound mushrooms
2 tablespoons butter
2 teaspoons minced onion
1 clove garlic

Steam rice. Clean mushrooms, and chop. Sauté in butter with onions and garlic. Remove garlic; mix mushrooms and onions with steamed rice. Pack firmly into a buttered ring mold, set in pan of hot water, and bake in moderate oven, 350° F., 30 minutes.

CHINESE FRIED RICE

¼ cup vegetable oil
1½ cups cooked rice
⅔ cup slivered scallions
1 tablespoon soy sauce
salt and pepper to taste
fine strips cooked chicken or fine strips cooked pork
fried bean sprouts

Place oil in a wide skillet. Add rice, scallions, soy sauce, salt and pepper to taste. Cook over low heat, stirring lightly, until rice becomes lightly colored. Add chicken, pork, bean sprouts or any combination thereof.

SHRIMP FRIED RICE

4 cups cold cooked rice
2 eggs, well beaten
8 ounces cooked baby shrimp
peanut oil or other oil for frying
1 medium onion, sliced thin
4 tablespoons soy sauce
2 tablespoons sherry
¼ teaspoon garlic powder
⅛ teaspoon pepper

Add a little water to rice to loosen grains. Mix beaten eggs and shrimp in a bowl. In skillet or wok, heat oil and sauté onion until tender. Add shrimp and eggs and cook over medium heat, stirring constantly. Add rice and cook 2 minutes, stirring constantly. Add last four ingredients and continue cooking for 2 minutes, stirring lightly.

GREEN RICE RING

1 cup rice
4 eggs, separated
1 cup parsley, minced
1 green pepper, chopped fine
1 small onion, chopped fine
1 cup heavy cream, whipped
4-5 tablespoons Parmesan cheese
1 teaspoon salt
paprika

Boil rice. Add beaten yolks and remaining ingredients, adding whites beaten to a froth last. Cheese may be omitted. Pack firmly into a buttered ring mold, set mold in a pan of hot water in moderate oven, 350° F., and bake 45 minutes, or until set.

Rice Combination Dishes

RICE AND MUSHROOM CASSEROLE
See page 422.

SUKIYAKI
See page 271.

CHICKEN CHOP SUEY FOR 15
See page 313.

CHICKEN AND RICE
See page 313.

CASSEROLE OF RICE AND CHICKEN
See page 314.

GREEN PEAS AND RICE
See page 424.

DRIED LEGUMES

Dried Legumes—beans, peas, lentils—are an inexpensive source of protein. They may be served as a main dish, with a little meat or cheese added for extra flavor and nutritive value, or as a meat accompaniment.

Dried legumes, except the precooked variety, should be soaked for several hours before cooking. Or they may be brought to a boil, then soaked for 1 hour. Always cook slowly—rapid boiling causes skins to break. Add boiling water as needed to replenish liquid, and avoid stirring.

BOILED DRIED BEANS

1 quart dried beans
1 tablespoon salt
Brown Sauce, page 387, or Sweet and Sour Sauce, page 388

Wash beans. Soak overnight in cold water. Add salt, heat slowly, simmer until tender, adding hot water if necessary. Drain and reserve 1 cup of liquid. Make a Brown Sauce, or Sweet and Sour Sauce with the bean liquid; pour over the drained beans and serve hot.

BAKED BEANS

4 cups navy beans
1½ pounds brisket of beef or ½ pound fat salt pork
½ tablespoon mustard
1 tablespoon salt
3 tablespoons sugar
2 tablespoons molasses
1 cup boiling water

Wash beans, cover with cold water and soak overnight. Heat slowly and simmer until tender 1½ to 2 hours. Drain beans and put in pot with the brisket of beef. If pork is used, scald it, cut through rind in ½-inch strips, and bury in beans, leaving rind exposed. Mix mustard, salt, sugar, molasses and water and pour over beans. Add enough water to cover. Bake slowly, covered, in a slow oven at 300° F., 6 to 8 hours. Uncover pot the last hour so that pork will brown and be crisp.

QUICK BAKED BEANS

1 can (1 pound, 12 ounces) baked beans
⅓ cup sherry
2 tablespoons brown sugar
1 teaspoon dry mustard
1 teaspoon instant coffee

Combine all ingredients; heat on top of range or in casserole in a moderate oven.

PUREED DRIED BEANS

Cook beans until tender. Drain. Purée through strainer or in blender. Add salt, pepper, onion powder (optional) to taste. Melt butter in saucepan, add purée, and stir vigorously while heating.

REFRIED BEANS

1½ cups dry kidney beans
1 cup chopped onions
2 medium tomatoes, chopped
¼ teaspoon garlic salt
1 teaspoon chili powder
dash cayenne pepper
1 teaspoon salt
vegetable oil

Soak the beans overnight. Drain. Cook beans in 5 cups of water with one-half of the onions, one-half of the tomatoes, the garlic salt, chili powder and cayenne until beans are tender. Add salt. Heat oil in a large skillet. Sauté remaining onions until clear. Add remaining tomatoes and cook 2 to 3 minutes. Gradually mash the beans into the skillet. Mash only a small quantity at a time and mix well before adding more beans.

BEANS AND BARLEY

½ cup navy beans
1 quart boiling water
½ cup barley
2 teaspoons salt
fat soup stock

Soak navy beans in cold water overnight. Drain, add boiling water and cook gently until nearly tender but not broken, 1½ to 2 hours. Add barley and salt; cook slowly until barley is almost tender. Add fat soup stock as water evaporates. Season to taste and bake in medium oven about ½ hour or until dry but not browned.

BEAN LOAF

2 cups dried beans, cooked
1 egg, well beaten
2 tablespoons tomato catsup
1 cup bread crumbs
1 tablespoon chopped onion
salt and pepper to taste

Combine ingredients, shape into loaf, and bake 25 minutes. Serve with strips of broiled bacon on top (optional).

BEAN CASSEROLE

1½ cups cooked dried beans
1½ cups cooked or canned kernel corn
1 1-pound can tomatoes
1 teaspoon salt
1 teaspoon brown sugar
1 teaspoon minced onion
buttered crumbs or chopped nuts for topping

Combine first six ingredients. Place in greased casserole. Top with buttered crumbs or chopped nuts. Cover and bake at 350° F. for 40 to 50 minutes.

BAKED DRIED LIMA BEANS

1 pound lima beans
salt
paprika
2 tablespoons fat
2 tablespoons flour
salt pork, or back or neck of a fat chicken

Wash beans thoroughly, soak in lukewarm water to cover for 2 hours. Bring quickly to boiling; simmer 1 hour or until tender. Add salt and paprika. Heat fat in skillet, add flour, stir until brown. Drain liquid from beans and reserve. Add 1 cup liquid to flour mixture and cook, stirring, until smooth and thick. Add beans. Turn into casserole, bury salt pork or chicken in beans, and bake 1 hour. Add more bean liquid as necessary.

LIMA BEAN CASSEROLE

2 cups dried lima beans
6 cups water
½ teaspoon salt
1 can (10½ ounces) condensed tomato soup or sauce
6 to 8 small pork sausages

Soak lima beans several hours. Add salt, boil gently, uncovered, until tender, about 1 hour. Drain. Place in a well-greased casserole. Pour tomato soup over beans. Place sausages on top. Bake at 350° F. until sausages are brown, about 1 hour.

LIMA OR KIDNEY BEANS, MEXICAN STYLE

1 tablespoon fat
1 slice green pepper, chopped
1 slice onion, chopped
1 cup strained tomato
½ teaspoon salt
garlic, if desired
⅔ cup cooked dried beans
parsley, chopped

Melt fat, add chopped vegetables, cook a few minutes; add tomato, salt, and a little minced garlic, if desired. When mixture boils, add beans. Simmer 15 to 30 minutes. Just before serving, add chopped parsley. Serves 3 to 4.

LIMA BEAN AND VEGETABLE CASSEROLE

1 pound dried lima beans
½ cup chopped carrots
1 cup finely sliced celery
2 cups chopped tomatoes, fresh or canned
2 teaspoons salt
¼ teaspoon pepper
4 tablespoons shortening
1 clove garlic, minced
1 teaspoon dry mustard
1 teaspoon paprika
pinch of thyme
¼ cup dry white wine

Soak beans overnight. Drain. Place beans, carrots, celery, tomatoes, salt and pepper in a large saucepan. Add 3 cups water. Cover pan. Simmer for about 1 hour, stirring occasionally. Drain. Add remaining ingredients except the wine. Bake in a greased casserole, covered, at 300° F. for 2 to 2½ hours. Stir occasionally. Just before serving, stir in the wine.

DRIED GREEN PEAS

2 cups dried green peas
6 cups cold water
2 teaspoons salt
½ teaspoon sugar
few grains pepper
Brown Sauce, page 387

Wash the peas. Soak several hours in cold water. Add salt, sugar, pepper and simmer several hours or until tender. Add more hot water if necessary. Drain, reserving 1 cup liquid. Keep peas warm. Make Brown Sauce, using reserved liquid; pour sauce over the peas and serve.

PEA PUREE

2 cups dried peas
6 cups cold water
½ teaspoon sugar
1½ teaspoons salt
speck of white pepper
⅛ pound bacon or other smoked fat
1 large onion, diced

Wash the peas. Soak for several hours in cold water. Simmer until soft, stirring frequently. Rub peas through a strainer, add a little boiling water or soup stock, add seasoning and beat.

Put bacon or other smoked fat, cut in small cubes, in skillet; fry until light yellow, add onion, and continue cooking until golden brown. Pour the bacon and onion over purée before serving.

VEGETARIAN LOAF

1 cup dried peas, boiled
¾ cup dry bread crumbs
¼ cup walnuts, chopped
1 egg
1 teaspoon salt
⅛ teaspoon pepper
2 tablespoons butter, melted
¾ cup milk

Drain peas and rub through strainer. Add other ingredients, mix well and put in a small buttered loaf pan. Cover with foil and bake 40 minutes in a slow oven, 300° F.

SPLIT PEAS

2 cups split peas
1 quart cold water
1½ teaspoons salt
Brown Sauce, page 387

Wash peas. Place in pan with water and soak several hours. Simmer gently until soft, adding boiling water if necessary. Add salt. Make Brown Sauce, using 1 cup of the liquid from the peas. Add to the drained peas, cook slowly 5 or 10 minutes and serve hot. A piece of fat corned beef, some smoked sausage, or a ham bone cooked with the peas improves the flavor.

LENTILS

Lentils may be substituted for dried peas or beans in many of the preceding recipes. The recipe for Split Peas, above, is especially suitable for lentils.

LENTILS WITH TOMATO SAUCE

1½ cups lentils
1 tablespoon salt
1 cup tomato sauce
2 carrots, diced
1 clove garlic, minced
1 bay leaf
1 large onion, chopped
2 tablespoons shortening

Soak the lentils overnight. Drain. Add salt, tomato sauce, carrots, garlic and bay leaf to lentils. Cover with cold water. Simmer until tender. Sauté the onion in the shortening. Add the lentils with enough of the liquid so that the mixture is not dry. Heat thoroughly.

CHICK-PEA LOAF

2 cups celery, diced
2 cups cauliflower, diced
1 green pepper, diced
2 cups chick-peas, cooked
4 tablespoons flour
1 cup water
½ teaspoon soy sauce
½ teaspoon thyme
½ teaspoon marjoram

Steam vegetables only until tender. Mash chick-peas and vegetables. Mix flour with water until smooth. Add soy sauce, spices and flour mixture to vegetables. Place in greased loaf pan. Bake at 350° F. for 45 minutes.

10
DESSERTS AND DESSERT SAUCES

HOT PUDDINGS · BAKED FRUITS · PASSOVER DESSERTS · SOUFFLES
· BISCUIT DESSERTS · CORNSTARCH AND TAPIOCA PUDDINGS · CUSTARDS ·
GELATINS · ICE CREAMS · ICES · MOUSSES · FROZEN PUDDINGS
· HOT AND COLD SAUCES

GRANDMOTHER'S HOT PUDDINGS

These old-fashioned puddings are treasured heir-looms that come down to us from a day when hard physical labor and a need for thrift made a hearty, filling, hot dessert the best possible way to end a meal. Nowadays, we choose this kind of dessert to follow a light meal. Serve warm, except where otherwise noted.

Baked Puddings
BREAD PUDDING

2 eggs
2 cups milk
½ cup sugar
nutmeg or cinnamon
4 cups dry bread or cake in cubes
¼ cup raisins
almonds

Beat the eggs, add milk, sugar, and gratings of nutmeg or cinnamon if desired; pour liquid over the bread in a pudding dish, let stand until thoroughly soaked. Add raisins and almonds, if desired. Bake 20 minutes or until firm in a moderate oven, 350° F. Serve with milk, jelly or any pudding sauce.

BREAD PUDDING PUFFS
2 cups bread crumbs
4 cups milk
4 eggs, separated
1 cup sugar
1 lemon rind, grated
¼ cup almonds, chopped
butter
brown sugar

Soak bread crumbs in milk ½ hour. Beat yolks well with sugar, add soaked crumbs, lemon rind, almonds, and lastly the beaten whites. Place in individual molds generously greased with butter, and sprinkled with brown sugar. Bake in moderate oven ½ hour or until firm. Remove to dessert plates and serve with Jelly Sauce or Orange Sauce.

CHESTNUT CROQUETTES
1 cup mashed French chestnuts
2 tablespoons heavy cream
2 egg yolks
1 teaspoon sugar
¼ teaspoon vanilla
1 egg yolk, beaten
bread crumbs

Boil chestnuts, page 418, and mash. Mix first five ingredients in order given. Shape into balls, coat with egg and crumbs, and fry in deep hot fat, 375° F., until golden brown. Serve as dessert, sprinkled with powdered sugar.

MERINGUE BREAD PUDDING

3 eggs, separated
½ cup sugar
1 teaspoon vanilla
2 cups milk
1 cup bread cubes
1 cup stewed apples or orange marmalade

Beat yolks of eggs and 1 white, add sugar and vanilla; add milk, and stir until sugar is dissolved. Pour this custard over the bread and bake in a moderately slow oven, 325° F., until set; or, at 375° F. if set in pan of hot water. Cover with stewed apples, marmalade or any preserve or jelly. Beat remaining 2 whites frothy, beat in 2 tablespoons granulated sugar, and a few drops of vanilla; beat stiff. Spread meringue over the apples, and place in oven until a delicate brown. Serve hot with or without cream.

Rice for Puddings

Processed rice, which will not disintegrate to make a cream, is unsuitable for these rice pudding recipes. Use regular, unconverted long grain rice. Serve puddings warm or chilled, as desired.

OLD-FASHIONED RICE PUDDING

½ cup uncooked rice
½ cup sugar
½ teaspoon salt
4 cups milk

Mix ingredients. Bake 2 hours in a buttered baking dish, covered, at 325° F., until the rice has softened; uncover, brown slightly. Serve with milk and sugar.

RAISIN RICE PUDDING

2 cups cooked rice
2 cups milk
⅛ teaspoon salt
⅓ cup sugar
1 tablespoon butter
2 eggs, well beaten
rind of ½ lemon, grated
¼ cup raisins

Mix ingredients well. Bake 20 minutes in a moderate oven, 350° F., in buttered baking dish, with bread crumbs at the top and bottom. If desired, fruit may be added to the rice in layers.

RICE PUDDING (KUGEL)

1 cup rice
4 cups boiling water
1 teaspoon salt
4 eggs, beaten
¼ cup sugar
¼ pound raisins
¼ cup fat (chicken, goose or butter)

Cook the rice in the boiling, salted water 30 minutes or until nearly done. Mix drained rice with the rest of the ingredients and place in well-greased baking dish and bake in moderately slow oven, 325° F., until quite brown.

FARINA PUDDING

¼ cup farina
2 cups milk, scalded
1 tablespoon butter
½ cup sugar
salt
5 eggs, separated
rind of ½ lemon, grated

Pour farina into scalded milk, add butter, sugar and salt and cook for 5 minutes. Cool, add yolks, lemon rind and egg whites, beaten stiff. Bake in a moderate oven, 350° F., about 20 minutes or until puffed and golden; serve at once with any dessert sauce.

INDIAN PUDDING

6 cups milk, scalded
1 cup yellow corn meal
½ cup molasses
¼ cup sugar
1 teaspoon salt
1 teaspoon ginger or grated lemon rind
¼ teaspoon soda
2 eggs, slightly beaten

Pour milk slowly on the corn meal, cook in double boiler 20 minutes, add other ingredients. Pour into buttered baking dish and bake 3 hours in a very slow oven, 250° F. Serve warm with cream.

NOODLE PUDDING

4 eggs, separated
1 cup confectioners sugar
2 tablespoons grated almonds
½ pound fine noodles, cooked

Beat yolks light with the sugar, add almonds and drained noodles and lastly, stiffly beaten whites. Pour into a well-greased baking dish, set in a pan half-filled with boiling water and bake in moderate oven, 350° F., ½ hour.

NOODLE PUDDING WITH APPLES AND NUTS

½ pound broad noodles
2 tablespoons butter
3 eggs, separated
1 cup sugar
1½ teaspoons cinnamon
2 apples, sliced
¼ cup dried currants
½ cup chopped nuts

Boil noodles and drain. Heat butter in a skillet, add the noodles and cook just long enough to absorb the fat. Remove from heat, add beaten yolks, sugar, rest of ingredients and stiffly beaten whites. Place in well-greased baking dish and bake ½ hour in a moderate oven, 350° F. Serve hot with any dessert sauce.

NOODLE PUDDING SOUFFLE

3 eggs, separated
1 pound creamed cottage cheese
½ cup butter, melted
1 cup sour cream
2 tablespoons sugar
½ pound medium noodles, cooked
½ cup crushed cornflakes
2 tablespoons butter

Beat egg yolks; combine cottage cheese, melted butter, sour cream and sugar with beaten yolks. Fold in noodles and lastly the stiffly beaten egg whites. Place in greased 2-quart casserole, sprinkle top with cornflakes and dot with butter. Bake at 375° F. for 45 minutes.

CHOCOLATE PUDDING CAKE

1 cup flour
2 teaspoons baking powder
½ teaspoon salt
⅔ cup sugar
½ cup milk
1 square unsweetened chocolate, grated
½ cup chopped nuts
2 tablespoons melted butter
1 teaspoon vanilla

Sift flour, baking powder, salt and sugar into bowl. Add milk, chocolate, nuts, butter, vanilla, and blend well. Pour mixture into a greased baking dish.

TOPPING

¼ cup white sugar
½ cup brown sugar
3 squares unsweetened chocolate, grated, or
    3 tablespoons cocoa
¼ teaspoon salt
1 teaspoon vanilla
1 cup boiling water

Combine sugar, chocolate, salt and vanilla, and spread evenly over first mixture. Pour the boiling water over this but do not stir. Bake in a moderate oven, 350° F., for 1 hour, until the cake that rises to the top tests done. There will be a layer of fudge sauce beneath. Can be served warm or cold, with or without cream.

LEMON PUDDING CAKES

2 cups sugar
6 tablespoons flour
¼ teaspoon salt
4 tablespoons melted butter
⅔ cup lemon juice
grated lemon rind
6 eggs, separated
3 cups milk

Blend sugar, flour, salt, butter, lemon juice and rind. Beat yolks well, add milk and mix. Add flour mixture gradually, stirring well. Fold in stiffly beaten whites. Pour into greased custard cups and place in shallow pan of hot water. Bake in moderate oven, 350° F., about 45 minutes. When baked, each pudding will be part custard and part cake. Chill. Garnish with whipped cream. Serves 12.

COCONUT PUDDING

1 cup bread crumbs
1 cup grated coconut
4 cups hot milk
2 tablespoons melted butter
2 eggs, slightly beaten
4 tablespoons sugar
a little salt
grated rind of ½ lemon

Soak the crumbs and the coconut in the hot milk for 1 hour. Mix all ingredients. Place in greased baking dish and bake in moderate oven, 350° F., until well set and brown.

COTTAGE PUDDING

⅓ cup butter
⅔ cup sugar
2 eggs, separated
2 cups flour
3 teaspoons baking powder
¼ teaspoon salt
1 cup milk

Cream butter and sugar; add yolks, beaten until thick; sift flour, baking powder and salt. Add to mixture alternately with milk. Fold in beaten whites. Bake in a greased and floured 8 x 12-inch pan, at 350° F., for 30 to 45 minutes. Cut in squares and serve with Hard Sauce or Lemon Sauce.

CRANBERRY PUDDING

3 tablespoons shortening
1 cup sugar
1 egg, beaten
1 cup milk
2 cups flour
2 teaspoons baking powder
2 cups fresh cranberries

Cream shortening and sugar. Blend in egg and milk. Mix flour and baking powder and add to batter. Stir in cranberries. Bake in greased baking dish at 350° F. for 35 to 40 minutes. Serve warm with sauce.

SAUCE

⅔ cup butter
1⅓ cups sugar
1 cup cream

Combine ingredients and heat in double boiler. Serve warm.

Steamed Puddings

A steamer is a covered kettle fitted with a rack on which molds can rest above boiling water. The food cooks in steam without touching the boiling water. As the water boils away replenish it, but do not allow the boiling to stop.

TO STEAM PUDDINGS

Grease mold and fill ⅔ full to allow for rising. Grease cover and adjust tightly. Or cover tightly with greased aluminum foil or waxed paper. Puddings may also be steamed in the top of a double boiler, over hot water.

STEAMED BREAD PUDDING

2 cups bread cubes
1 teaspoon soda
1 cup buttermilk
½ cup sugar
1 egg
1 teaspoon mixed spices
½ cup seedless raisins
1 tablespoon butter

Sprinkle bread with soda; add buttermilk. Let stand until soaked. Mix well with rest of the ingredients. Put in greased mold and steam, as directed above, 1½ hours.

Hot and cold dessert sauces for the puddings in this chapter will be found beginning on page 216. Many of these old-fashioned desserts and sauces have been in one edition or another of the SETTLEMENT COOK BOOK *since the early 1900s.*

STEAMED CARAMEL-ALMOND PUDDING

6 tablespoons sugar
1 cup hot milk
¼ cup butter, melted
1 tablespoon flour
3 ounces ground almonds
6 eggs, separated

Melt the sugar in a skillet until light brown. Add milk very gradually, stirring constantly. Cool, add butter, flour, almonds, the well-beaten yolks, and lastly the stiffly beaten whites. Butter the form, sprinkle with a little sugar. Add pudding. Steam, as directed above, 1 hour. Serve with whipped cream.

STEAMED CARAMEL PUDDING WITH LADY FINGERS

1 cup brown sugar
2 cups cream
1 dozen dry lady fingers, grated
5 eggs, separated

Melt sugar, add cream, then grated lady fingers. Add beaten yolks and lastly, stiffly beaten whites. Put in tightly covered mold and steam 2 hours. Serve hot with Caramel Sauce.

STEAMED CHERRY ROLL

Biscuit Dough, page 86
2 tablespoons butter
1 quart cherries, pitted
1 cup sugar

Roll biscuit dough in oblong sheet ½ inch thick, spread lightly with butter and cherries; sprinkle with sugar, and if desired, add a little cinnamon. Roll, wet edges and pinch together. Wrap roll with cloth, or place on heavy plate, and steam on rack as directed above 1½ hours. Serve in slices with Hard Sauce.

STEAMED CHOCOLATE PUDDING

1 egg
1 cup sugar
1 square unsweetened chocolate, melted,
    or 3 tablespoons cocoa
½ cup milk
2 tablespoons melted butter
1 cup flour
4 teaspoons baking powder

Mix ingredients; put in greased mold and steam 1 hour. Serve with Vanilla Sauce or Hard Sauce.

CHOCOLATE SPONGE

    6 eggs, separated
    1 cup sugar
    cinnamon
    cloves
    1 cup semisweet chocolate, grated
    2 tablespoons bread crumbs
    1 teaspoon baking powder
    1 teaspoon vanilla

Beat yolks and sugar, add cinnamon and cloves, if desired, other ingredients, finally beaten egg whites. Steam 1½ hours in covered pudding mold. Serve hot with Hard Sauce or Vanilla Sauce.

CHOCOLATE ALMOND PUDDING

    10 eggs, separated
    1½ cups sugar
    ¾ cup grated chocolate
    2 teaspoons cinnamon
    ½ teaspoon cloves
    ¾ cup grated almonds
    ½ cup flour

Beat yolks until very light, add sugar, and beat again, add chocolate, spices, almonds and flour, stir well; gradually fold in the stiffly beaten whites. Place in large buttered pudding mold, cover, and steam 2 hours. Serve hot with sweetened whipped cream flavored with vanilla.

STEAMED DATE PUDDING

    1 pound stoned dates
    ½ pound suet
    ½ cup sugar
    1 scant teaspoon salt
    ½ cup milk
    1 cup flour
    1 teaspoon cinnamon
    1 teaspoon ginger
    1 cup of soft bread crumbs
    2 eggs, well beaten

Grind or chop dates and suet. Mix all ingredients well, adding the eggs last. Turn into well-buttered molds, and steam 2 hours, as directed above. Serve with Hard Sauce or Wine Sauce. Figs, raisins, currants, candied peel, prunes or nuts, alone or in combination, may replace dates.

STEAMED FIG PUDDING

    1 cup beef suet, chopped fine
    ½ pound dried figs, chopped fine
    2⅓ cups dry bread crumbs
    ½ cup milk
    2 eggs, well beaten
    1 cup sugar
    ¾ teaspoon salt

Chop suet, work until creamy, add figs. Soak bread in the milk, add eggs, sugar and salt. Combine the two mixtures, place in buttered mold, cover and steam 3 hours.

STEAMED OATMEAL DATE PUDDING

    ½ pound dates, chopped
    1 cup rolled oats
    2 eggs
    ½ cup molasses
    ⅔ cup water
    ½ teaspoon soda
    ¼ teaspoon salt
    ½ lemon, juice

Mix all ingredients and steam in buttered mold 3 hours. Serve with any preferred pudding sauce.

STEAMED PRUNE WHIP

    1 pound prunes
    ¾ cup sugar
    5 whites of eggs

Soak prunes 1 hour in water barely to cover. Boil until tender, stone and mash through a strainer. Add sugar to egg whites, beaten stiff. Blend with prunes. Pour into buttered mold. Cover and steam for 1 hour. Serve hot with whipped cream or Custard Sauce.

DOUBLE-BOILER PRUNE WHIP

    4 egg whites
    ¼ cup sugar
    1 jar (4¾ ounces) strained prunes

Beat egg whites until stiff. Add sugar gradually, then fold in prunes. Steam in the well-greased top of a double boiler, covered, over boiling water, for 1½ hours. Turn from pan and serve with whipped cream or Custard Sauce.

STEAMED RAISIN PUFF

    2 eggs, beaten
    ½ cup sugar
    3 tablespoons melted butter
    ½ cup milk
    1 cup flour
    2 teaspoons baking powder
    ½ cup chopped raisins

Mix in the order given. Drop into greased custard cups, cover the cups, and place on a rack. Steam 35 minutes. Serve with Lemon or Vanilla Sauce.

TO STEAM PUDDINGS: *Set filled molds on a rack in a deep kettle. Add boiling water to halfway up the sides of the molds. Cover tightly. Keep water boiling, add more, if necessary, as it boils away.*

ENGLISH PLUM PUDDING

1 cup flour
1 pound seeded raisins
¼ pound citron, orange and lemon peel, cut fine
¼ pound seedless raisins
½ cup chopped almonds
½ pound bread crumbs
½ cup sugar
1 teaspoon baking powder
1 teaspoon ground cinnamon
½ teaspoon ground allspice
½ teaspoon ground cloves
1 teaspoon salt
1 cup suet, chopped fine
3 eggs, beaten
1 cup molasses
1 cup pickled peach syrup or brandy

Sift flour over fruit and nuts and mix well. Mix rest of dry ingredients, add suet, eggs, molasses, syrup or brandy and then the floured fruit. Pour into buttered molds ⅔ full; cover. Steam from 4 to 8 hours, according to the size of mold. Keeps well. To reheat, steam ½ hour or more. Serve with Hard Sauce or Brandy Sauce. Or pour rum or brandy over pudding just before serving, light and send flaming to the table.

STEAMED SUET PUDDING

2 cups dry cake or cookie crumbs
½ teaspoon soda
1 teaspoon cinnamon
1 teaspoon cloves and nutmeg
1 teaspoon salt
½ cup finely chopped suet
1 cup milk
1 egg
½ cup molasses
1 cup raisins
½ cup shredded citron

Mix dry ingredients, add the suet, milk, egg and molasses. Fold in raisins and citron. Put in greased molds and steam 2 hours. To reheat, steam 1 hour. Serve hot with Vanilla Sauce or Hard Sauce.

STEAMED WHOLE WHEAT PUDDING

2 cups whole wheat flour
½ teaspoon soda
½ teaspoon salt
1 cup milk
½ cup molasses
1 cup stoned and chopped dates, raisins, or ripe berries

Mix ingredients in order given. Steam 2½ hours and serve with whipped cream or any plain pudding sauce.

1 cup of figs, stewed prunes or chopped apples or raisins may be substituted for fruit, above.

BAKED FRUIT DESSERTS

Baked fruit desserts are as delicious as fruit pie, and they have advantages for the cook, since they are much easier and quicker to prepare. Eat them warm for best flavor and texture, with or without a topping of sauce, ice cream, or whipped cream.

APPLE PANDOWDY (DIMPES DAMPES)

½ cup sugar
¼ teaspoon salt
2 cups flour
2 cups milk
1 cup butter, melted
1 quart apples, pared and sliced

Mix sugar, salt and flour and gradually add the milk to make a smooth batter. Grease a 13- x 9-inch baking pan well with some of the butter, add the remaining butter and the apples to the batter. Mix and pour into pan. Bake in a moderate oven, 350° F., 30 to 45 minutes until brown.

APPLE PUFF

2½ pounds apples
5 eggs, separated
¾ cup sugar
¼ cup each chopped almonds and currants
1 tablespoon brandy
⅛ teaspoon cinnamon

Grate the apples. Beat yolks and sugar until light, add the rest of the ingredients and fold in the beaten whites. Bake in greased spring form in moderate oven, 350° F., until well set. Serve with whipped cream.

APPLE SOUFFLE (AUFLAUF)

1 tablespoon butter
¼ cup brown sugar
4 apples

Butter baking dish. Sprinkle with brown sugar. Peel and slice apples; place in bottom of pudding dish in layers, until dish is about ⅓ full. Bake until partially soft. Remove from oven, cover apples with following batter:

2 eggs, separated
½ cup sugar
1½ tablespoons cold water
½ cup flour
½ teaspoon baking powder
½ teaspoon vanilla

Beat yolks with sugar; add water, flour mixed and sifted with baking powder, vanilla, and lastly, fold in beaten whites. Bake at 350° F. ½ hour or until brown. Serve hot with any desired sauce.

MACAROON SOUFFLE (AUFLAUF)

Line a buttered baking dish with macaroons or any stale cake. Cover this with fruit, pared and sliced, or raspberries, add sugar to taste. Cover with a sponge made of 6 yolks, 6 tablespoons sugar, 6 whites beaten stiff, and ¼ cup chopped almonds. Bake at 400° F. for 15 minutes. Serve hot.

APPLE CHARLOTTE

  2 quarts apples, diced
  1 cup sugar
  ¼ cup almonds, blanched and chopped
  1 teaspoon cinnamon
  1 cup seeded raisins
  ½ cup currants
  1 lemon, grated rind and juice
  ¼ cup of red or white wine
  Rich Egg Pastry, page 342

Line a well-greased baking dish with Rich Egg Pastry, ½ inch thick; mix ingredients and fill dish. Cover with Rich Egg Pastry, ¼ inch thick; bake 50 to 60 minutes in hot oven, 400° F.

APPLE STREUSEL

  6 apples (2 pounds)
  2 tablespoons granulated sugar
  ¼ teaspoon cinnamon
  ½ cup brown sugar
  1 cup flour
  ½ cup butter

Butter bottom and sides of an 8- x 12-inch pan generously. Peel and core apples and cut into eights. Place apples in pan in overlapping rows as close together as possible; mix granulated sugar and cinnamon and sprinkle over the apples. Add brown sugar to flour, cut in butter, and rub with finger tips to crumbs. Sprinkle over apples and pat to make a smooth surface. Bake for ½ hour in a hot oven, 425° F., until apples are tender. May be served with Hard Sauce or ice cream.

Applesauce may be substituted for the sliced apples and granulated sugar.

APPLE-MARSHMALLOW DESSERT

  6 apples
  ¼ cup seeded raisins
  ½ cup sugar
  20 marshmallows

Pare and slice apples. Place in baking dish, in layers with raisins and sugar. Cover, bake in moderate oven, 350° F., until apples are tender. Remove cover, place marshmallows over top of apples, and brown.

BROWN BETTY (SCALLOPED APPLES)

  2 tablespoons butter
  2 cups soft bread crumbs
  ½ cup sugar
  ¼ teaspoon cinnamon
  ¼ teaspoon nutmeg
  1 lemon, rind and juice
  3 cups apples, chopped
  ¼ cup water

Melt the butter and add the crumbs. Mix the sugar, spice and grated lemon rind. Put one quarter of the crumbs in the bottom of a buttered baking dish. Cover with half the apples. Sprinkle with half the sugar mixture; then add another quarter of the crumbs, the remainder of the apples, and the rest of the sugar mixture. Add the lemon juice and the water, and put the rest of the crumbs over the top. Cover, bake 45 minutes at 375° F., uncover and brown. Serve with plain or whipped cream. Crushed cornflakes may be used in place of bread crumbs.

SCALLOPED RHUBARB

  3 cups rhubarb, washed and cut into ½-inch slices
  2 cups soft bread crumbs
  1 cup sugar
  grated rind of 1 orange
  ¼ teaspoon cinnamon
  ¼ teaspoon nutmeg
  2 tablespoons butter
  ¼ cup water

Follow directions for Scalloped Apples, above. If rhubarb is old, strip off skin.

BLUEBERRY PUDDING

  1 quart blueberries
  ¼ cup flour
  4 cups hot milk
  2 cups bread crumbs
  ¼ cup sugar
  few grains salt
  2 tablespoons butter

Clean berries, sprinkle with flour, let stand ½ hour. Pour milk over crumbs, add sugar, salt and the berries. Put into greased baking dish, dot with butter, bake 45 minutes in a moderate oven, 350° F. Serve with Hard Sauce.

For hot and cold dessert sauces, see pages 216-220.

Stale cake, cookie crumbs or bread crumbs are the basis for many of the delicious desserts in this chapter.

CHERRY PUDDING

4 cups milk
2 cups bread crumbs
salt
3 tablespoons butter
4 eggs, slightly beaten
1½ cups sugar
1 quart sour cherries, pitted

Scald milk and pour over the bread crumbs; add a pinch of salt and the rest of the ingredients. Bake in a moderate oven, 350° F., 45 minutes, until set.

PRUNE PUDDING (PRUNE KUGEL)

5 whole wheat rolls
¾ pound suet, chopped fine
½ cup brown sugar
1 tablespoon molasses
1 teaspoon cinnamon
grated rind of 1 lemon
1 tablespoon water
salt
½ pound prunes, stewed

Soak rolls, squeeze dry. Mix rest of ingredients, except prunes, with the soaked bread to make a dough. Line a greased heavy casserole or baking dish with alternate layers of dough and stoned prunes. Bake 2 hours in moderately slow oven, 325° F., basting often with prune juice.

DRIED FRUIT PUDDING (HUTZLE, SNITZ, OR BIRNE KLOS)

1 loaf dry white bread
½ pound suet, chopped fine or ground
¾ cup brown sugar
2 eggs
½ teaspoon cinnamon
½ teaspoon cloves
½ teaspoon allspice
lemon peel, grated
½ teaspoon salt
2 to 3 tablespoons flour
2 teaspoons baking powder
1 pound dried pears or other dried fruit, cooked and spiced

Soak bread in water. Squeeze dry. Add to suet and work well with the hands. Add sugar, eggs, and seasonings; then add flour mixed with the baking powder, to make a large ball. Place in center of a large kettle or greased roaster, on a layer of cooked spiced dried fruit. Grease top of pudding and spoon remaining fruit and juice over it. Bake at 350° F. for 3 hours, adding more fruit juice if necessary.

GRANT THOMAS PUDDING

2 eggs, beaten
1 cup sugar
3 tablespoons flour
1 teaspoon baking powder
1 cup broken walnut meats
1 cup chopped figs

Beat eggs and sugar until very light, add flour, sifted 3 times with baking powder, and the remaining ingredients. Stir well and bake in greased, shallow pan in a slow oven, 300° F., 25 minutes. Serve hot or cold with whipped cream.

STEAMED KUCHEN (DAMPF NUDELN)

Make Kuchen Dough. Let rise. Roll on floured board ½ inch thick and cut into finger lengths. Place them not too close together in a tightly covered baking dish, with ¼ cup melted butter at the bottom. Let rise in a warm place; add a cup of cold water. Add ½ pound stewed and stoned prunes, cover and bake in a moderate oven, 350° F., until water has all evaporated. Remove the cover and brown the top. Serve with stewed prunes.

PASSOVER DESSERTS

The following desserts which use matzos and matzo meal instead of leavened bread and wheat flour are traditionally served during the Passover holiday. In many households they are favorite desserts throughout the year.

MATZOS FRITTERS (CRIMSEL)

2 matzos
½ tablespoon salt
3 eggs
½ cup sugar

Soak matzos in water and squeeze dry. Mix in the rest of the ingredients and stir well. Drop from teaspoon in hot, deep fat, and fry until browned. Serve warm with hot honey, stewed cherries, or stewed prunes.

MATZOS FRUIT FRITTERS (FRUIT CRIMSEL)

3 matzos, soaked and squeezed dry
2 tablespoons seeded raisins, chopped
2 tablespoons chopped almonds
3 egg yolks
¾ cup sugar
grated rind of 1 lemon
1 tablespoon lemon juice
3 whites, beaten stiff

Mix in the order given and drop from tablespoon into deep, hot fat. Serve hot with stewed prunes flavored with orange juice.

FILLED MATZOS FRITTERS

1½ matzos
1 tablespoon goose fat
¼ cup matzo meal, sifted
2 eggs
2 tablespoons sugar
⅛ teaspoon salt
strawberries, or stewed prunes, stoned
1 egg, beaten

Soak the matzos in cold water and press dry; heat the fat, add matzos, matzo meal, eggs, sugar and salt. Mix well and let stand 2 hours; form into oblong cakes. Place a prune or strawberry in the center of each cake and form into balls. Dip balls in beaten egg and fry in deep, hot fat until brown. Serve hot with Jelly Sauce.

MATZOS BATTER PUDDING

2 eggs
2 cups milk
1 cup matzo meal
⅔ cup brown sugar
4 tablespoons butter
grated rind of 1 lemon
1 tablespoon rum

Make a batter of the eggs, milk and matzo meal; add sugar, melted butter and lemon rind; add rum. Pour into a greased baking dish and steam for 1 hour or bake for 1½ hours in a moderate oven, 350° F.

MATZO APPLE PUDDING

⅔ cup sugar
4 eggs, separated
2 cups grated apples
grated rind of ½ lemon
½ cup matzo meal
4 tablespoons almonds, chopped

Stir sugar with the beaten yolks, add the apples, lemon rind and matzo meal. Fold in beaten whites. Place in greased spring form, sprinkle with almonds. Bake in moderate oven, 350° F., until brown.

MATZOS CHARLOTTE

2 matzos
1 tablespoon goose fat or butter
4 eggs, separated
pinch of salt
½ cup sugar
½ lemon, juice and grated rind

Soak the matzos in cold water and squeeze dry. Stir matzos with the goose fat, add beaten yolks, salt, sugar, and lemon. Fold in the beaten whites,

pour into a well-greased baking dish. Bake in moderate oven, 350° F., about ½ hour. Serve immediately with Jelly Sauce.

MATZOS CHARLOTTE WITH APPLES

2 matzos
¼ pound suet, chopped fine
2 cups apples, sliced fine
¼ cup sugar
3 egg yolks, beaten
2 tablespoons raisins, seeded
1 tablespoon almonds, blanched and grated
¼ teaspoon cinnamon
3 egg whites, beaten stiff

Soak matzos in water and squeeze dry; add the rest of the ingredients, fold in the beaten whites last. Bake in greased baking dish about 1 hour in moderate oven, 350° F.

POTATO PUDDING FOR PASSOVER

4 yolks, beaten
½ cup sugar
2 tablespoons almonds, blanched and grated
½ lemon, juice and rind
¼ pound cold, boiled potatoes, riced
¼ teaspoon salt
4 egg whites, beaten stiff

Mix in order given. Place in well-greased baking dish and set the dish in a pan half filled with boiling water. Bake in 350° F. oven for ½ hour. Serve with Wine Sauce.

DESSERT SOUFFLES

Soufflés are not difficult to make, providing a few rules are followed exactly. It is important that the egg whites be beaten until they are very stiff and glossy; when the bowl is inverted they should not slip. They should be folded into the soufflé base very gently, to retain all the air. A soufflé is baked when it is well-puffed and browned; some people prefer soufflés that are soft in the center, thus providing their own sauce. To make these French style soufflés, bake in a hot oven, 400° F. Soufflés begin to fall as soon as they are removed from the oven, and must be served at once.

To prepare the baking dish for the soufflé, butter generously, then sprinkle with sugar.

SOUFFLE TIP: *If a bit of yolk gets into a bowl of egg whites, use the edge of an eggshell to scoop it out. Even the smallest amount of yolk will prevent the egg whites from whipping properly.*

CHOCOLATE SOUFFLE

1 tablespoon butter
2 tablespoons flour
½ cup milk
2 tablespoons water
3 tablespoons sugar
1 square unsweetened chocolate
2 eggs, separated

Heat the butter, add the flour, then the milk and cook until smooth. Add the water and sugar to the chocolate, stir until melted. Mix it with the cream sauce. Cool, stir in the beaten yolks, fold in the whites. Bake in a greased baking dish set in a pan of hot water in moderately slow oven at 325° F. from 30 to 40 minutes until soufflé is puffed and well-browned. Serves 3.

SWEET CHOCOLATE SOUFFLE

6 egg yolks
1 cup sugar
1 cup grated semisweet chocolate
6 egg whites, beaten

Beat yolks and sugar until lemon-colored. Add chocolate. Fold in stiffly beaten whites. Bake in a greased baking dish, set in a pan of hot water, for 1 hour at 325° F. Serve with plain or whipped cream.

LEMON OR ORANGE SOUFFLE

6 egg yolks
1 cup sugar
juice and rind of 1 large lemon or
⅓ cup orange juice and 1 tablespoon lemon
juice
6 egg whites, beaten stiff

Follow soufflé directions above.

WALNUT SOUFFLE

Follow recipe for Sweet Chocolate Soufflé, but in place of the chocolate, use 1 cup finely-ground walnut meats. Serve with any dessert sauce.

CHESTNUT SOUFFLE

1 cup chestnuts, shelled
½ cup sugar
2 tablespoons flour
½ cup milk
3 egg whites

Boil chestnuts, drain and rice or mash. Mix sugar and flour, add chestnuts and milk gradually, cook 5 minutes, stirring constantly; fold in stiffly beaten whites. Fill buttered and sugared individual molds

¾ full. Set molds in a pan of hot water and bake in slow oven, 300° F., until firm. Serve with Vanilla Sauce or Wine Sauce.

MACAROON SOUFFLE

1 dozen macaroons
1 cup hot milk
3 eggs, separated
chopped candied fruit
whipped cream

Crumble the macaroons in the hot milk, add to the beaten egg yolks and cook over hot water until slightly thickened; fold in the stiffly beaten whites. Bake at 350° F. in a buttered mold, set in a pan of hot water, from 45 to 60 minutes until puffed and very well browned. Test with knife. When firm, turn from the mold, sprinkle with fruit and surround with sweetened whipped cream.

NUT SOUFFLE

3 egg yolks
3 tablespoons sugar
3 tablespoons flour
¼ teaspoon salt
1 cup milk
¾ cup finely ground pecans or hazelnuts
3 tablespoons melted butter
4 egg whites, beaten stiff

Beat yolks until thick, add sugar and stir well; add flour and salt. Heat milk and nuts in double boiler. Add egg mixture and cook until thick, stirring constantly. Add the butter. Cool. Fold in the whites. Pour into well-buttered and sugared mold or casserole. Set in a pan of hot water and bake in moderately slow oven, 325° F., for 1 hour or until puffed and well browned. Serve at once with Rum Sauce or Coffee Sauce.

APRICOT SOUFFLE

½ pound dried apricots
½ cup sugar
½ teaspoon lemon juice
5 egg whites
½ teaspoon baking powder

Cook fruit in water until soft and rub through strainer. Add sugar and cook 5 minutes or until the consistency of marmalade. Cool. Add cold fruit mixture and lemon juice gradually to whites beaten stiffly with baking powder. Place in greased baking dish and bake 30 to 40 minutes in a slow oven, 275° F. Serve cold with thin custard or cream. Prunes or dates may be substituted for the apricots.

ORANGE SOUFFLE OMELET

1 egg, separated
rind of ⅛ orange
1 tablespoon orange juice
2 tablespoons confectioners sugar

Beat the egg yolk, add the orange rind, juice, and sugar. Fold in the white, beaten stiff, and pour into heated buttered pan. Cook until set. Sprinkle with confectioners sugar. Serves one.

BAKED BISCUIT DESSERTS

BASIC DOUGH FOR SHORTCAKE BISCUIT

2 cups flour
4 teaspoons baking powder
½ teaspoon salt
2 tablespoons sugar
½ cup shortening
¾ cup milk

Mix dry ingredients, work in shortening with fork or pastry blender, add milk quickly. Toss on floured board. Pat, roll, cut with large biscuit cutter or roll to fit 2 pans and bake in a very hot oven, 450° F., 12 to 15 minutes. Split biscuits and serve warm, filled with cold sweetened fresh fruit (or frozen fruit) and cream, plain or whipped.

STRAWBERRY SHORTCAKE

Shortcake Biscuit dough, above
1 to 1½ quarts strawberries
cream

Bake Shortcake Biscuit. Sweeten strawberries to taste. Crush slightly and put between and on top of shortcake. Serve with cream, plain or whipped.

PEACH SHORTCAKE

Prepare as above, using sliced peaches in place of strawberries.

BLACKBERRY ROLL

Shortcake Biscuit dough, above
2 tablespoons butter, melted
1½ quarts blackberries
1 cup sugar
cinnamon

Roll dough ½ inch thick, spread with melted butter and ½ of the berries, cover with ½ of the sugar and cinnamon. Roll up like a jelly-roll and put into well-greased pan, surround with the rest of the berries and sugar. Bake in hot oven, 400° F., 20 minutes until crisp. Cut in slices and serve warm with sauce remaining in pan.

CHERRY COBBLER

1½ quarts cherries or 1 1-pound can sour cherries
1 cup water
1 cup sugar
Shortcake Biscuit dough, above

Stone cherries if necessary and cook with the water and sugar. Roll dough ¼ inch thick and cut into small rounds. Place cherries in buttered baking dish, lay biscuits on top, bake in hot oven, 400° F., until brown. Serve with Lemon or Vanilla Sauce if desired.

PEACH COBBLER

1 egg
⅔ cup sugar, to taste
2 cups or 1 1-pound can sliced peaches
butter
Shortcake Biscuit dough, above

Beat egg lightly, add sugar and peaches; pour this mixture into buttered baking dish, dot with butter, cover with dough rolled ½ inch thick, and bake in a hot oven, 400° F., until brown. Serve with Hard Sauce. Cherries may be used in this recipe in place of peaches.

APPLE DUMPLINGS, BAKED

Shortcake Biscuit dough, above
6 apples, peeled and cored
1 cup sugar
6 teaspoons butter
1 cup water

Roll dough ¼-inch thick, cut into 6-inch squares, place on each an apple filled with 1 tablespoon sugar and 1 teaspoon butter, bring up corners, twist and pinch together and place in a well-greased baking pan. Add syrup made by boiling water and the remaining sugar for 10 minutes. Bake in a hot oven, 400° F., about 45 minutes or omit syrup and bake until crisp. Serve hot with sauce in pan, or Brandy Sauce.

APPLE ROLY POLY

Make Shortcake Biscuit dough or Pie Dough. Roll ½ inch thick. Spread with chopped apples or jam, raisins, sugar, and cinnamon; roll like jelly roll. Place in a baking dish, spread with butter, and add syrup made by boiling 2 cups of water and 1½ cups of sugar for 10 minutes. Bake in a hot oven, 400° F., about 1½ hours or until brown. Baste often with the sauce in the pan. Serve hot. Or cut in slices and bake cut side down.

DUTCH APPLE CAKE

2 cups flour
3 teaspoons baking powder
½ teaspoon salt
2 tablespoons sugar
½ cup butter
1 egg
about ⅔ cup milk
4 sour apples
sugar and cinnamon

Mix and sift the dry ingredients, cut in butter, add milk with the well-beaten egg, and mix quickly. Spread dough in a shallow, greased 8 x 8-inch baking pan. Pare, core and slice the apples; press apples into dough in parallel rows. Sprinkle with sugar and cinnamon. Bake in a hot oven, 400° F., ½ hour. Serve hot with Lemon Sauce.

CORNSTARCH PUDDINGS

Cornstarch has twice the thickening power of flour, and is often used to make desserts thicken enough to mold. When used to thicken fruit juices or sauces, it has the added advantage of not adding a milky color to the clear juice. The cornstarch should be dissolved in a little cold water before it is added to the hot mixture. When it is thoroughly cooked, the mixture will be clear and thickened.

BLANC MANGE OR CORNSTARCH PUDDING

¼ cup cornstarch
2 tablespoons sugar
⅛ teaspoon salt
¼ cup cold milk
2 cups scalded milk
½ teaspoon vanilla
2 egg whites, beaten stiff

Mix cornstarch, sugar and salt. Stir in cold milk. Add to scalded milk, in double boiler. Cook 15 minutes, stirring constantly. Cool slightly. Add flavoring and fold in egg whites. Pour into mold and chill. Unmold and serve with pudding sauce if desired.

CHOCOLATE CORNSTARCH PUDDING

1 square unsweetened chocolate
½ cup sugar
2 cups milk
3 tablespoons cornstarch

Melt chocolate in double boiler, add the sugar gradually, add 1½ cups of milk. Heat thoroughly;

add cornstarch mixed with remaining milk. Cook for 15 minutes, pour into mold and chill. Unmold and serve with milk or cream.

MOLDED PRUNE PUDDING

½ pound prunes
1 cup cold water
1 cup sugar
½ lemon, grated rind and juice
1-inch cinnamon stick
1¾ cups boiling water
⅓ cup cornstarch

Wash prunes and soak 1 hour in cold water; simmer until soft; remove stones, add sugar, lemon rind, juice, cinnamon and boiling water, and simmer 15 minutes. Mix cornstarch with ⅓ cup cold water, add to prune mixture and cook 15 minutes. Remove cinnamon stick. Pour into mold and chill. Unmold and serve with plain or whipped cream.

BAKED PINEAPPLE PUDDING

½ cup sugar
2 tablespoons cornstarch
1 cup pineapple juice
1 cup water
juice of 1 lemon
2 eggs, separated
1 cup pineapple cubes, fresh or canned, drained
whipped cream

Mix sugar and cornstarch in double boiler, stir in pineapple juice, water and lemon juice; cook until smooth. Pour into the beaten yolks, mix well; cool, fold in the beaten whites, and then the pineapple cubes. Pour into a buttered baking dish; bake 20 minutes in slow oven, 300° F. When cool, top with whipped cream.

DANISH DESSERT (ROTHE GRUETZE)

4 cups red raspberries
4 cups red currants
4 cups cold water
1½ cups sugar
⅓ cup cornstarch

Boil berries and water; strain and add sugar. Add cornstarch dissolved in a little cold water. Cook until thickened, pour into custard cups. If a molded pudding is desired, use more cornstarch. Serve cold with whipped cream.

To prevent skin from forming on pudding desserts, stir cooked desserts while cooling. Or, place plastic or waxed paper, cut to fit, on the surface of the pudding.

PEACH SNOW

2 tablespoons cornstarch
2 tablespoons cold water
2 1-pound cans of peaches
2 egg whites, beaten stiff
½ cup heavy cream

Mix the cornstarch with 2 tablespoons of cold water. Stir the cornstarch mixture into the peach syrup and cook until smooth and clear; add the peaches, puréed, and cool. Fold in beaten whites and cream beaten stiff. Pour into a mold, chill until firm and cold.

TAPIOCA PUDDINGS

When tapioca is used to thicken a pudding, it results in an interesting texture because the tapioca swells and appears in tender, chewy droplets throughout the pudding. These recipes call for quick-cooking tapioca. When using the old-fashioned pearl tapioca, soak the tapioca for 1 hour in cold water before using. Tapioca is cooked when it is transparent.

TAPIOCA CREAM

⅓ cup quick-cooking tapioca
2 cups milk
2 eggs, separated
¼ teaspoon salt
⅓ cup sugar
1 teaspoon vanilla

Add tapioca to the milk and cook in double boiler until the tapioca is clear. Beat the yolks, add the salt, sugar and the hot milk mixture and cook until it thickens. Remove from the heat, cool, fold in the whites, beaten stiff. Flavor when cold. Or make Meringue from egg whites and brown in oven a few minutes.

APPLE TAPIOCA

⅓ cup quick-cooking tapioca
2½ cups boiling water
½ teaspoon salt
1½ pounds cooking apples
½ cup sugar
2 tablespoons butter

Add boiling water and salt to tapioca; cook in double boiler until clear. Core and pare apples, arrange whole in buttered baking dish, fill apples with sugar, add tapioca mixture, dot with butter and bake in moderate oven, 350° F., until apples are soft. Or, use sliced apples. Serve with sugar and cream.

CURRANT JELLY TAPIOCA PUDDING

½ cup quick-cooking tapioca
3 cups boiling water
½ teaspoon salt
1 tablespoon lemon juice
½ cup sugar
6-ounce jar currant jelly

Cook tapioca in boiling water 15 minutes. Add remaining ingredients. Pour into mold, chill and serve.

GOOSEBERRY TAPIOCA PUDDING

⅓ cup quick-cooking tapioca
2 cups boiling water
2 cups green gooseberries
1 cup sugar
1 tablespoon lemon juice

Cook tapioca in boiling water 15 minutes. Cook gooseberries and sugar until soft. Add lemon juice. Combine mixtures. Chill and serve with whipped cream.

CUSTARDS

General Rules

Eggs should be slightly beaten and thoroughly mixed with sugar and salt; add the hot milk slowly, stirring all the time. When custard is cooked in a double boiler, water in lower part should be kept below boiling point and should not touch upper part. When thickened, the custard coats a metal spoon. If custard curdles from overcooking, set in a pan of cold water and beat with a rotary beater until smooth. For baked custard, set the baking dish in a pan of hot water in the oven. Test for doneness by inserting a knife near, but not at, the center. The knife should come out clean. Custard continues to cook after it has been removed from the oven.

SOFT CUSTARD

3 egg yolks
¼ cup sugar
few grains salt
2 cups hot milk
½ teaspoon vanilla

Beat eggs slightly, add sugar and salt. Stir the milk in gradually. Place in double boiler over hot water, stir constantly until the mixture thickens and coats the spoon. Cool and add vanilla.

STIRRED CUSTARD

4 tablespoons sugar
1 tablespoon cornstarch
¼ teaspoon salt
1 egg or 2 egg yolks
2 cups milk, scalded
½ teaspoon desired flavoring

Mix sugar, cornstarch and salt; add egg or egg yolks, slightly beaten. Add scalded milk, stirring constantly. Cook in double boiler over hot water until custard thickens and coats the spoon. Cool and flavor.

SOFT CHOCOLATE CUSTARD

Follow Soft Custard or Stirred Custard recipe, above, melting 1 square unsweetened chocolate with the milk.

BAKED CUSTARD

2 eggs
pinch salt
4 tablespoons sugar
2 cups hot milk

Beat eggs slightly, add salt and sugar and stir until the sugar dissolves; pour milk gradually onto eggs, stirring constantly. If desired, add a little nutmeg or ½ teaspoon desired flavoring. Pour into buttered custard cups or a baking dish; place the cups in a pan of hot water. Bake in a moderate oven 30 to 45 minutes at 325° F. until the custards are firm in the center. Test with a knife; if the knife comes out clean, the custard is done.

CARAMEL CUSTARD

Melt ½ cup of granulated sugar in bottom of baking dish until brown, tilting dish until evenly coated, or use brown sugar. Then add custard mixture and bake as above.

COFFEE CUSTARD

2 tablespoons instant coffee
2 cups hot milk
3 eggs
4 tablespoons sugar
¼ teaspoon vanilla

Dissolve coffee in milk. Beat eggs with sugar; add milk mixture and flavoring and mix. Pour into small buttered custard cups, place cups in shallow pan of hot water. Bake in moderately slow oven, 325° F., until the custard is firm.

CARAMEL-FLAVORED CUSTARD

½ cup sugar
4 cups scalded milk
5 eggs
½ teaspoon salt
1 teaspoon vanilla

Heat sugar in a skillet on range, stir constantly until melted to a light brown syrup. Add 1 cup milk very gradually, stirring constantly, being careful that milk does not bubble up and over. As soon as sugar is melted add rest of milk; add mixture gradually to slightly beaten eggs; add ½ teaspoon salt and flavoring, then strain into buttered molds or custard cups. Place cups in a shallow pan of hot water and bake at 325° F., 30 to 45 minutes or until firm. Chill and serve with Caramel Sauce.

COCONUT CUSTARD

2 cups milk
½ cup sugar
3 eggs, separated
salt
½ cup cream
½ cup confectioners sugar
¾ cup coconut

Heat milk with sugar, and stir into the egg yolks beaten until light; add salt, cream, and cook until thick. Pour into a buttered baking dish. Beat the egg whites until frothy; beat in confectioners sugar, beat stiff. Fold in coconut. Spread over the top of custard and brown lightly in the oven at 375° F.

FLOATING ISLAND

4 cups milk
½ cup sugar
½ teaspoon salt
1 tablespoon cornstarch
3 eggs, separated
¼ teaspoon spice or ½ teaspoon flavoring
2 tablespoons sugar

Heat the milk. Mix sugar, salt, and cornstarch; add to slightly beaten yolks and 1 egg white. Pour the hot milk on the egg mixture and cook in a double boiler until it thickens, stirring constantly. When cool, stir in flavoring. Beat the 2 whites until frothy, beat in 2 tablespoons sugar, and beat stiff. Drop by spoonfuls on top of cold custard. Dot with jelly.

To separate eggs easily, crack the egg smartly against the rim of a bowl. Pass the yolk from one half-shell to the other, letting the egg white drain into the bowl. Or break the whole egg into a funnel and the white will drain off.

MACAROON CUSTARD MERINGUE

6 eggs, separated
3 to 4 tablespoons sugar
juice of ½ lemon
rind of 1 orange
1 teaspoon cornstarch
¾ cup white wine
1 dozen lady fingers
¾ pound macaroons
6 tablespoons confectioners sugar

Beat the yolks well. Add sugar, lemon juice, and orange rind. Dissolve the cornstarch in a little of the wine. Add cornstarch and rest of wine to yolks; cook in double boiler until thick.

Split 10 lady fingers and place on an oven-proof platter. Use 2 crumbled lady fingers to fill in between. Cover all with a layer of custard, a layer of macaroons, a layer of custard and of macaroons.

For the meringue, add 6 tablespoons confectioners sugar to the 6 stiffly beaten egg whites. Cover pudding entirely with meringue and bake in a moderately hot oven, 375° F., until brown.

MACAROON FRUIT PUDDING

1 pint raspberries or peaches
granulated sugar, to taste
6 eggs, separated
1 cup white wine
1 pound macaroons
6 tablespoons confectioners sugar

Sweeten the fruit as desired. Beat the yolks until light, stir in the wine gradually. Cook in double boiler, stirring constantly, until mixture coats the spoon. Sweeten with additional sugar if desired. Cool. In a greased baking dish place layers of macaroons, fruit, and custard alternately. Beat egg whites frothy, beat in confectioners sugar, beat stiff. Spread this meringue on the pudding. Brown lightly in 375° F. oven.

MISCELLANEOUS COLD DESSERTS

CHOCOLATE RENNET CUSTARD

1 square unsweetened chocolate
    or 3 tablespoons cocoa
2 cups fresh milk
½ cup sugar
1 rennet tablet dissolved in 1 tablespoon cold water

Melt chocolate or cocoa in ½ cup milk and boil 1 minute. Remove from heat, add rest of milk and the sugar. Heat until lukewarm and add the dissolved tablet. Stir quickly and pour into custard cups. Let stand at room temperature for 20 minutes or until firm. Chill.

RASPBERRY RENNET CUSTARD

2 cups milk
1 package raspberry rennet powder
½ cup heavy cream
sweetened whipped cream
fresh raspberries or raspberry jam

Heat milk only until lukewarm, add rennet powder, crush any lumps, stir 1 minute until dissolved. Pour into 4 to 6 sherbet glasses. Let stand at room temperature for 20 minutes until firm. Remove to cool place without jarring. Serve with sweetened whipped cream and top with fresh raspberries or raspberry jam.

APPLE SNOWBALLS

6 apples
20 marshmallows
1 cup sugar
1½ cups water
juice of 1 lemon
shredded coconut

Pare and core apples and put a marshmallow in center of each. Make sauce by boiling sugar, water, lemon juice and rest of marshmallows. Set apples in sauce, cover, and cook slowly until tender to avoid breaking apples. Remove from sauce, cool slightly and roll in shredded coconut.

CHESTNUT DESSERT

1 pound chestnuts
2 cups sugar
1 cup water
2 cups heavy cream, whipped
1 tablespoon maraschino syrup
    or 1 teaspoon vanilla

Blanch and shell fresh chestnuts. Boil in water to cover until nearly tender. Drain and put them into a syrup made by boiling sugar with water 10 minutes; boil until soft. Rice chestnuts, chill, and serve with whipped cream flavored with maraschino or vanilla.

SWISS RICE

1 teaspoon salt
½ cup sugar
3 to 3½ cups scalded milk
1 cup rice
½ teaspoon vanilla
2 cups heavy cream, whipped
raspberry or cherry juice

Add salt and sugar to milk. Add rice and cook in the top of a double boiler, over boiling water 30 to 45 minutes until tender. Add vanilla. When cool, fold in all but ½ cup of the whipped cream.

Mold as desired and chill. Unmold. Add enough fruit juice to the remaining whipped cream to color; use it to garnish the top.

CHOCOLATE RICE PUDDING

    4 cups milk
    ½ cup rice, uncooked
    ¼ teaspoon salt
    5 tablespoons sugar
    1 tablespoon butter
    1 square unsweetened chocolate, grated
    1 teaspoon vanilla

Heat milk in double boiler over hot water, add rice, salt, sugar, butter, chocolate and vanilla. Cook 2 hours. Serve with whipped cream.

ENGLISH FRUIT PUDDING

    7 or 8 slices of bread
    2 tablespoons butter
    1 quart blueberries, cooked, canned or frozen
    sugar to taste
    ¼ teaspoon salt

Remove the crusts from the bread and butter one side. Grease a round-bottomed bowl and line with ½ the bread buttered side up. Crush the berries with the sugar and salt and pour into the bowl. Cover with remaining bread. Weight well with a plate and chill for 24 hours. The bread will absorb the juice and the pudding may be unmolded. Serve with cream.

GELATIN DESSERTS

Use 1 envelope unflavored gelatin or 1 package flavored gelatin to set 2 cups of liquid. Unflavored gelatin must be softened in cold water, then heated to dissolve in water or fruit juice, over low heat or over hot water. If 2 tablespoons or more of sugar are stirred into dry unflavored gelatin it will dissolve simply by stirring with boiling liquid. Gelatin is dissolved when the liquid is completely clear and no granules are visible.

To USE FLAVORED GELATIN DESSERTS: Follow directions on the package.

FRUIT SHOULD BE ADDED to gelatin when it reaches the syrupy stage. Whipped cream or beaten egg white should not be folded in until the gelatin is firm enough to mound on a spoon.

To MOLD GELATIN: Rinse mold in cold water, or oil very lightly. Chill until dessert is very firmly set. Dip mold quickly into hot water, or wrap in hot wet cloth for a few seconds. Loosen edges with sharp knife. Invert on wet plate and slide to center.

To DECORATE A GELATIN MOLD WITH FRUIT OR NUTS: Chill gelatin until syrupy. Coat the mold with a thin layer of syrupy gelatin and chill in the refrigerator. Arrange the fruit on this and cover carefully with more syrupy gelatin, being careful not to disturb the arrangement. Chill until set. Add remaining gelatin mixture.

To PREPARE GELATIN IN LAYERS of contrasting color and flavor: Let first layer begin to jell, but not quite set, before adding the next layer.

To WHIP PREPARED GELATIN: Let chill until very thick, then beat with rotary beater until frothy and doubled in volume.

LEMON JELLY

    2 envelopes unflavored gelatin
    1 cup cold water
    2 cups boiling water
    ¾ cup sugar
    ½ cup lemon juice

Soak gelatin in cold water 5 minutes; dissolve in boiling water. Add sugar and lemon juice and stir until dissolved. Pour into wet mold. Chill.

LEMON SPONGE (SNOW PUDDING)

    1 envelope unflavored gelatin
    ¼ cup cold water
    1 cup boiling water
    1 cup sugar
    ¼ cup lemon juice
    3 egg whites

Soak gelatin in cold water 5 minutes, add boiling water, sugar and lemon juice, stir until dissolved. When mixture begins to thicken, fold in stiffly beaten egg whites, beat thoroughly and pour into wet mold. Serve with Custard Sauce.

ORANGE JELLY

    2 envelopes unflavored gelatin
    1 cup each cold water and boiling water
    1 cup sugar
    1½ cups orange juice
    3 tablespoons lemon juice

Soak gelatin in cold water 5 minutes; dissolve in boiling water. Add sugar. Stir well; add orange and lemon juice. Pour into wet mold. Chill until firm.

GRAPEFRUIT JELLY

Substitute grapefruit juice and pulp for orange and lemon juice in Orange Jelly, above.

GRAPE JUICE JELLY

Substitute grape juice for orange juice in Orange Jelly, above.

PINEAPPLE JELLY

2 envelopes unflavored gelatin
1 cup water
1½ cups pineapple juice, heated
1 cup boiling water
¾ cup sugar
few slices pineapple, or ½ cup shredded pineapple
3 tablespoons lemon juice

Only canned or cooked pineapple can be used. Soak gelatin in the cold water for 5 minutes. Add pineapple juice, boiling water, and sugar. Stir until dissolved. When gelatin begins to thicken, add the pineapple and the lemon juice. Pour into wet mold. Chill until firm.

COFFEE JELLY

2 envelopes unflavored gelatin
1 cup cold water
2½ cups clear strong coffee
⅔ cup sugar
whipped cream

Soak gelatin in cold water. Dissolve in strong coffee heated to boiling. Add sugar and stir well. Pour into wet mold. Chill until firm. Serve with whipped cream.

CHOCOLATE JELLY

2 envelopes unflavored gelatin
4 cups milk
1 cup sugar
⅛ teaspoon salt
2 squares unsweetened chocolate, melted
1 teaspoon vanilla

Soak gelatin in ½ cup milk about 5 minutes. Scald remaining milk with sugar and salt, add softened gelatin. Stir over low heat until gelatin is thoroughly dissolved. Add chocolate. Cool slightly, add vanilla and pour into wet mold. Chill until firm. Serve with whipped cream.

WINE JELLY

2 envelopes unflavored gelatin
½ cup cold water
2 cups boiling water
1 cup sugar
1 cup wine (Madeira, claret, sherry or port)
3 tablespoons lemon juice

Add cold water to gelatin and let stand 5 minutes to soften. Add boiling water, stir until dissolved; add sugar. When cool, add wine and lemon juice. Pour into wet molds. Chill until firm. Serve cold. If a winier-flavored dessert is desired, add more wine and less water; a good combination of wines is 1½ cups sherry and port.

EASTER EGG DESSERT

Fill ring mold with Wine Jelly, above. Wash 12 large raw eggs; make pin hole at small end, a larger hole at rounded end. Blow out contents and use these in another recipe. Rinse shells and place upright, small end down, in egg cartons. Fill with cold water through funnel. Let stand until needed. Make ½ recipe each of Orange Jelly, Grapefruit Jelly, and Chocolate Jelly, or use contrasting colors of prepared gelatin dessert mixes. When gelatin mixtures are thick and syrupy, empty water from shells and fill them, using a funnel. Set in refrigerator to harden overnight. To serve, unmold the ring on a large platter to form a nest. Roll shells with the palm against a table to crush them, and the Easter eggs will come out in perfect egg forms; place eggs in nest and serve cold with whipped cream.

JELLIED ORANGE WEDGES

Cut oranges in half. Remove pulp and juice without destroying the orange shell. Scrape clean; set shells in muffin tins. Fill cups with Orange Jelly, as it is beginning to thicken. Chill until firm, and when ready to serve, slice into wedges. Arrange in fruit dish or serve as a border around meat.

JELLIED FRUIT DESSERT

Make jelly of any desired flavor. When gelatin mixture begins to thicken, fold in slices of banana, or halves or slices of any fresh or canned, drained fruit or berries. Pour into shallow pan, chill until firm. Cut into 1- x 3-inch slices and serve with plain or whipped cream.

GELATIN CREAM DESSERTS

BAVARIAN CREAM

1 cup milk
2 eggs, separated
½ cup sugar
¼ teaspoon salt
1 envelope unflavored gelatin
¼ cup cold water
½ teaspoon almond extract
1 cup heavy cream, whipped

Heat milk in double boiler. Beat egg yolks, sugar and salt well. Add milk gradually, stirring constantly. Return to double boiler. Cook until mixture·thickens and coats the spoon. Add gelatin softened in cold water and stir until dissolved. Cool. When mixture begins to thicken, add flavoring, whipped cream and stiffly beaten egg whites. Pour into mold rinsed in cold water. Chill.

BUTTERSCOTCH BAVARIAN

Make Bavarian Cream, above, omitting the sugar. Heat ¾ cup brown sugar and 2 tablespoons butter until well blended and add to hot custard. Proceed as above.

BAVARIAN CHARLOTTE RUSSE

1 envelope unflavored gelatin
¼ cup cold water
5 egg yolks
½ cup sugar
½ cup hot milk
2 teaspoons vanilla
1 cup heavy cream, whipped
12 lady fingers

Soften the gelatin in the water a few minutes. Beat yolks and sugar until very light; add milk and the softened gelatin. Cook in double boiler until gelatin is dissolved and the mixture coats the spoon, stirring constantly; cool, add vanilla and fold in the whipped cream. Pour into a mold lined with lady fingers. Chill until firm. Unmold and serve with fresh fruit or with Chocolate or Caramel Sauce.

NESSELRODE PUDDING

5 eggs, separated
⅓ cup sugar
2 cups hot milk
2 envelopes unflavored gelatin
½ cup cold water
3 tablespoons blanched, chopped almonds
⅔ cup raisins
small piece of citron, cut fine
salt
1 teaspoon vanilla

Beat egg yolks with sugar, stir in the hot milk. Cook in double boiler until custard coats the spoon, stirring constantly. Dissolve gelatin in the cold water. Add to hot milk mixture and stir until dissolved; then add the almonds, raisins, citron and a little salt. Cool until the mixture is thick enough to mound on a spoon. Fold in the beaten whites and vanilla. Chill in a mold until firm. Unmold, serve with plain or whipped cream.

CARAMEL CREAM

1 envelope unflavored gelatin
¼ cup cold water
⅔ cup sugar
½ cup hot milk
1 teaspoon vanilla
2 cups heavy cream, whipped

Soak gelatin in cold water a few minutes. Melt and brown half the sugar in heavy skillet, and very gradually pour in the hot milk. Stir until smooth; add to the gelatin mixture. Stir until gelatin is dissolved, add the rest of the sugar. When mixture begins to thicken, fold in the whipped cream and vanilla. Pour into a wet mold. Chill until firm.

COFFEE CREAM

2 envelopes unflavored gelatin
¼ cup cold water
2 cups strong, hot coffee
1 cup sugar
½ teaspoon vanilla
2 cups heavy cream, whipped
chopped nuts

Soak gelatin in water 5 minutes, add coffee and sugar, and stir until gelatin is dissolved. Cool until mixture begins to thicken. Fold in 1 cup whipped cream and vanilla. Pour into a mold rinsed in cold water. Chill until firm. Unmold and serve with the rest of the whipped cream. Sprinkle with chopped nuts.

PRUNE CREAM

1 pound stewed prunes
2 envelopes unflavored gelatin
½ cup cold water
juice of 1 orange
juice of 1 lemon
rind of ½ orange, grated
rind of ½ lemon, grated
1 cup sugar
1 cup heavy cream
1 cup chopped almonds
macaroons

Stone prunes. Soak gelatin in cold water, add enough boiling water to hot prune liquid to make 2 cups, add to gelatin. When dissolved, add the orange and lemon juice and rinds, sugar, and prunes; cool and when mixture begins to thicken, fold in the stiffly whipped cream and the almonds. Pour into mold and chill until firm. Serve with additional whipped cream mixed with crushed macaroons.

SPANISH CREAM

2 envelopes unflavored gelatin
½ cup cold water
3 cups hot milk or cream
¾ cup sugar
3 eggs, separated
1 teaspoon vanilla or rum

Soak gelatin in cold water 5 minutes; dissolve in hot milk or cream; add sugar and stir. Pour hot liquid gradually on well-beaten yolks, beating constantly. Cook in double boiler until mixture coats the spoon. Cool. When mixture begins to thicken, fold in stiffly beaten whites and flavoring. Pour into wet mold. Chill until firm. Serve with Butterscotch Sauce or whipped cream.

Spanish Cream will form into a layer of custard at bottom with gelatin at top if egg whites are added while mixture is hot.

VANILLA CREAM PUDDING

1 envelope unflavored gelatin
¼ cup cold water
½ cup scalded milk
½ cup sugar
2 cups heavy cream, whipped
1 teaspoon vanilla

Soak gelatin in cold water 5 minutes and dissolve in hot milk; add sugar. Cool until mixture begins to thicken, add cream and vanilla. Turn into wet mold and chill. Serve covered with grated coconut and Butterscotch Sauce, or whole or crushed berries.

MACAROON DESSERT

1 pound macaroons
½ cup sherry or other wine
2 envelopes unflavored gelatin
1 cup cold water
2 cups hot milk
5 eggs, separated
1 cup sugar

Moisten macaroons with wine. Soak gelatin in cold water 5 minutes; add hot milk and stir until dissolved. Pour gradually on yolks beaten well with sugar. Cook in double boiler, stirring constantly, until thick. Cool until mixture mounds on a spoon; fold in stiffly beaten whites. Pour into wet mold lined with macaroons. Chill until firm. Unmold, serve with whipped cream.

MACAROON CHOCOLATE PUDDING

1 envelope unflavored gelatin
2 tablespoons cold water
¼ cup boiling water
2 cups heavy cream, whipped
¼ pound sweet chocolate, grated
6 macaroons

Dissolve gelatin in cold water, add the boiling water and stir until dissolved. When cold, add it to the whipped cream. Divide the cream in two parts and into one stir the grated chocolate, and into the other the broken macaroons. Put in a dish in layers and chill until firm.

STRAWBERRY OR RASPBERRY CREAM

1 quart fresh strawberries or raspberries
½ to 1 cup sugar
2 envelopes unflavored gelatin
¼ cup cold water
¼ cup boiling water
2 cups heavy cream, whipped

Wash berries, reserving 12 or more for decoration. Sugar the rest of the fruit, let stand several hours, and crush. Soften the gelatin in cold water 5 minutes, add the boiling water, stir until dissolved; cool and add the crushed fruit. When mixture begins to jell, fold in the whipped cream. Place in wet mold. Chill for 2 or more hours. Unmold, decorate top with the whole berries.

For Pineapple Cream use 2 cups canned crushed pineapple and 1 tablespoon lemon juice.

DANISH RICE PUDDING

½ cup uncooked rice
2 cups milk
1 teaspoon butter
¼ cup sugar
2 envelopes unflavored gelatin
¼ cup cold water
2 cups heavy cream, whipped
1 tablespoon maraschino syrup or sherry

Cook the first 4 ingredients in double boiler until perfectly smooth; then put through a ricer. Soak gelatin in the cold water, dissolve in double boiler over hot water, add the strained rice. Cool and fold in the cream and maraschino. Pour into wet mold and chill. Unmold, serve with fresh fruit or Chocolate Sauce.

ICE CREAMS AND FROZEN DESSERTS

Old-Fashioned Freezer Ice Creams

GENERAL RULES

When making ice cream in a manually operated churn, scald and then chill can, cover and dasher of freezer before using. Adjust can in tub, put in the thoroughly chilled mixture. Fill can not more than ¾ full. Adjust dasher; cover can. Pack with fine chopped ice and rock salt.

Use 3 parts ice to 1 part salt. Pack freezer ⅓

full of ice before adding salt, then add the salt and remaining ice in alternate layers to above level of ice cream in can.

Turn crank slowly at first for about 5 minutes or until mixture begins to stiffen; then as quickly as possible until it is very difficult to turn. Add more ice and salt if necessary, using the same proportion. Pour off salt water. Do not let it flow over top of can. Push down ice and salt, wipe top with cloth. Uncover and remove dasher, scrape ice cream from it back into can. Place heavy paper over top of can, put on cover and place a cork in the hole. Repack the freezer in the ice and salt, put ice on top, cover with burlap or newspaper, and let stand several hours to ripen.

To use an electric churn freezer, follow the manufacturer's directions for your particular appliance.

TO WHIP CREAM FOR ICE CREAM

Cream, bowl and beater must be cold. Pour heavy cream into straight-sided mixing bowl with rounded bottom and beat with rotary or electric beater until thick enough to mound softly on a spoon.

Cream doubles in bulk when whipped. It must not be beaten too long or it forms butter.

TO WHIP EVAPORATED MILK

Whipped evaporated milk is an inexpensive substitute for whipped cream. For successful whipping, the bowl and beater must be chilled, and the undiluted milk frozen to the mushy stage. Freeze the milk in the can or in a refrigerator tray. Proceed as for whipped cream. Evaporated milk doubles or triples in bulk with whipping. For a more stable product, add 2 tablespoons lemon juice to each cup of evaporated milk while whipping.

TO PREPARE FRUIT FOR ICE CREAM

Crush fruit, add sugar to taste; let stand until sugar is dissolved. Strain seedy fruits. Add to partially frozen cream and churn slowly for 1 minute to blend. Continue freezing until stiff.

FRENCH ICE CREAM

1 cup sugar
1 cup water
pinch of salt
3 egg yolks
1 teaspoon vanilla
2 cups heavy cream, whipped

Boil sugar and water slowly for 5 minutes to make a syrup. Add salt to eggs in top of double boiler, beat thoroughly, then gradually stir in the boiling syrup. Cook over boiling water 3 minutes, beating constantly. Place over cold water, beat until cold, add vanilla and cream, and freeze in churn freezer.

STRAWBERRY ICE CREAM

One quart mashed and sweetened strawberries may be added to French Ice Cream when partially frozen. Finish freezing.

VANILLA ICE CREAM

2 tablespoons flour or cornstarch
1 cup sugar
⅛ teaspoon salt
2 cups hot milk
2 eggs, separated
1 quart light cream
2 teaspoons vanilla

Mix flour or cornstarch, sugar and salt, and add the milk gradually. Cook over hot water 10 minutes, stirring occasionally. Stir into the well-beaten egg yolks very gradually. Cook until the custard coats the spoon. Cool, add cream, stiffly-beaten egg whites and flavoring. Strain and freeze in churn freezer.

ORANGE ICE CREAM

Make custard for Vanilla Ice Cream, omitting the vanilla and adding to the custard mixture the grated rind of 2 oranges and of ½ lemon. Cool the custard and add the juice of 4 oranges. Freeze as directed.

CARAMEL ICE CREAM

Make a custard for Vanilla Ice Cream. Melt 1 scant cup sugar to a brown liquid in a heavy skillet, and pour gradually into hot custard. Cool, add ½ teaspoon vanilla and 1 quart light cream, and freeze in churn freezer.

PEACH OR APRICOT ICE CREAM

Add 4 cups sweetened peach or apricot pulp and 1 teaspoon almond extract to partially frozen Vanilla or New York Ice Cream. Finish freezing.

BANANA ICE CREAM

Add 2 cups mashed bananas, mixed with ½ cup lemon juice, to partly frozen Vanilla or French Ice Cream. Finish freezing.

PAPAYA ICE CREAM

Add 4 cups mashed, ripe papayas to partially frozen Vanilla Ice Cream, finish freezing.

PISTACHIO ICE CREAM

4 ounces pistachio nuts
few drops of rose water
¼ cup sugar
¼ cup light cream
½ teaspoon almond extract
Vanilla Ice Cream, above
green food coloring

Blanch and shell pistachio nuts. Grind and mix with a few drops of rose water, add sugar, cream and almond extract; stir to a fine paste. Add to Vanilla Ice Cream. Tint pale green with food coloring, and freeze in churn freezer.

NEW YORK ICE CREAM

1 quart light cream
4 eggs, separated
1 cup sugar
2 teaspoons vanilla

Scald half the cream in the top of a double boiler over hot water. Beat yolks until thick, add sugar and beat again. Beat whites stiff, add to yolks, mix well, turn back into double boiler. Stir constantly until the custard coats the spoon. Cool, add the rest of cream and the flavoring, and freeze in churn freezer.

PHILADELPHIA ICE CREAM

1 quart light cream
1 cup sugar
1 teaspoon vanilla

Heat 1 cup of the cream, add sugar and dissolve. Cool, add flavoring and remaining cream. Freeze in churn freezer.

CHESTNUT ICE CREAM

3 cups chestnuts, shelled and peeled
1½ cups sugar
1½ cups water
6 egg yolks, well beaten
3 cups light cream
½ teaspoon vanilla
½ pound candied fruit, cut fine

Boil and rice chestnuts. Cook sugar and water 5 minutes. Add chestnuts, bring to boil. Stir syrup and chestnuts gradually into egg yolks. Stir until cold, add cream, vanilla, and candied fruit. Freeze in churn freezer.

OLD-FASHIONED CHOCOLATE ICE CREAM

1 cup sugar
1½ squares unsweetened chocolate, melted
　　or ¼ cup cocoa
¼ cup hot water
1 quart light cream
1 tablespoon vanilla

Add sugar to cocoa or chocolate; add the hot water gradually, stir smooth. Cool, add cream and flavoring, and freeze in churn freezer.

MACAROON ICE CREAM

12 dry macaroons
¼ teaspoon salt
¾ cup sugar
1 quart heavy cream
1 teaspoon almond extract
2 tablespoons maraschino liqueur

Crush macaroons fine. Mix with salt, sugar, and 1 cup cream. Heat thoroughly. Cool, add flavorings and remaining cream, whipped stiff, and freeze in churn freezer.

COFFEE ICE CREAM

4 egg yolks
1¼ cups sugar
¼ teaspoon salt
1 cup very strong coffee
1 quart light cream

Mix the slightly beaten yolks with the sugar and salt; stir in coffee and half the cream. Cook in double boiler until thick. Cool, add remaining cream and freeze in churn freezer.

MAPLE ICE CREAM

1 cup maple syrup
4 yolks of eggs
2 cups heavy cream, whipped
1 white of egg, whipped

Heat syrup to the boiling point and pour gradually on the well-beaten yolks. Cook in double boiler, stirring until custard coats spoon. Cool. Fold in whipped cream and egg white; freeze in churn freezer.

MOCHA ICE CREAM

½ pound sweet chocolate
1 quart light cream
¾ cup sugar
1 cup very strong coffee,
　　or 3 teaspoons instant coffee
6 egg yolks

Melt chocolate in 1 cup of cream in double boiler. Add sugar and coffee, stir well. Beat egg yolks with a little cream and add to chocolate mixture. Cook until thick, stirring constantly. Cool. Add remaining cream. Freeze in churn freezer.

RICH CHOCOLATE ICE CREAM

Make Mocha Ice Cream, above, substituting for the coffee 1 cup hot milk and 1 teaspoon vanilla.

PEPPERMINT STICK ICE CREAM

1 cup sugar
½ pound peppermint stick candy
2 cups milk or light cream
2 cups heavy cream, whipped

Add sugar and crushed candy to milk or light cream. Let stand several hours to dissolve. Add the whipped cream, then freeze in churn freezer.

QUICK CARAMEL ICE CREAM

¼ pound mixed caramels
3 cups heavy cream
¾ cup sugar
2 eggs

Melt caramels with ¼ cup of the cream. Add sugar to eggs, beat well and stir gradually into the melted candy. Fold in the rest of the cream, beaten slightly. Freeze in churn freezer.

Refrigerator Tray Ice Creams

GENERAL RULES

To produce a smooth ice cream in the refrigerator without churning, a thickened base is necessary. This base may be made with flour, cornstarch, eggs, tapioca, gelatin, junket or marshmallows, with whipped cream added.

Mix ingredients, place in tray of refrigerator, freeze to a mush, remove to a chilled bowl, beat until light and add whipped cream if called for in recipe. Then pour back into tray, return to refrigerator, and freeze until mixture holds its shape. Ice creams should be frozen at the fastest speed. Confectioners sugar should always be used in uncooked mixtures; granulated sugar only when cooked to a syrup or in a custard.

For smoother texture, use ⅓ corn syrup and ⅔ sugar, instead of sugar only. When whipped cream is called for, beat only until it mounds softly. To prevent separation, all ingredients should be about the same temperature when combined.

ICE CREAM WITH CUSTARD BASE

2 cups milk
⅔ cup sugar
2 tablespoons flour
pinch of salt
2 egg yolks
1½ teaspoons vanilla
2 cups heavy cream, whipped

Combine scalded milk, sugar, flour and pinch salt. Stir until smooth. Cook 10 minutes. Pour mixture over beaten egg yolks. Mix until smooth, add flavoring. Freeze to a mush in refrigerator tray. Remove to a chilled bowl and beat until light; fold in whipped cream. Return to refrigerator to freeze.

ICE CREAM WITH CREAM BASE

⅔ cup confectioners sugar
2 cups light cream
1½ teaspoons vanilla
½ cup heavy cream, whipped

Add sugar to light cream and stir until dissolved. Pour into freezing tray, freeze until mushy. Remove to chilled bowl and beat until light. Add vanilla. Fold in whipped cream. Return to freezing tray.

For variety, add 2 chocolate squares, unsweetened and melted, 1 teaspoon instant coffee, or 2 cups fruit pulp.

ICE CREAM WITH RENNET BASE

1 rennet tablet
1 tablespoon cold water
1 cup fresh milk, not soft curd
½ cup sugar
1¼ teaspoons vanilla
1 cup heavy cream, whipped

Crush tablet and dissolve in cold water. Heat milk, sugar and vanilla to lukewarm. Remove from heat. Add dissolved tablet and stir a few seconds. Pour at once into refrigerator tray. Let stand undisturbed at room temperature until firm. Then cool in refrigerator for ½ hour. Fold in the whipped cream. Then place in freezing compartment. When partly frozen, scrape from sides and bottom of tray. Stir; finish freezing.

MARSHMALLOW ICE CREAM

16 marshmallows
1 cup hot milk
1 teaspoon vanilla
1 cup heavy cream or evaporated milk

Cut marshmallows into small pieces with scissors dipped in water. Put marshmallows in hot milk and stir until dissolved. Add flavoring. Let stand until firm. Whip cream or evaporated milk and fold into the marshmallow mixture. Freeze.

CHOCOLATE-MARSHMALLOW ICE CREAM

Add 2 squares unsweetened chocolate, melted, to 1 cup hot milk and follow recipe above.

PINEAPPLE-MARSHMALLOW ICE CREAM

Add ⅔ cup of crushed pineapple to Vanilla-Marshmallow Ice Cream, above, before folding in the whipped cream.

COFFEE-MARSHMALLOW ICE CREAM

1 cup strong, black coffee
16 marshmallows
1 cup heavy cream or evaporated milk

Heat coffee to boiling point. Add marshmallows. Stir until dissolved. Cool, place in refrigerator until firm. Whip cream or evaporated milk until stiff. Combine mixtures, folding until blended. Place in tray and freeze.

MOCHA-MARSHMALLOW ICE CREAM

1 square unsweetened chocolate
1 cup strong coffee
16 marshmallows
1 cup heavy cream or evaporated milk, whipped
chopped nuts, optional

Melt chocolate over boiling water. Then combine with coffee and proceed as above.

CHOCOLATE CUSTARD ICE CREAM

½ cup sugar
¼ cup flour
1 square unsweetened chocolate
    or ¼ cup cocoa
3 eggs
2 cups heavy cream, whipped

Cook first four ingredients in double boiler until smooth and thick, stirring constantly. Cool. Add cream and freeze according to General Rules.

QUICK CHOCOLATE ICE CREAM

1 cup heavy cream, whipped
2 egg whites, beaten stiff
5½-ounce can chocolate syrup

Combine cream and eggs, add syrup. Freeze.

BANANA CUSTARD ICE CREAM

2 teaspoons cornstarch
½ cup confectioners sugar
¼ teaspoon salt
1 cup milk
1 egg, beaten
2 bananas, mashed
1 cup heavy cream, whipped
1½ teaspoons vanilla

Mix cornstarch, sugar and salt with milk. Add egg and beat well. Cook in double boiler until thickened. Cool. Add bananas. Mix well. Fold in whipped cream and flavoring. Freeze quickly.

CHOCOLATE COOKIE ICE CREAM

1 cup crushed chocolate cookies
1 teaspoon vanilla
¼ cup sugar
2 cups heavy cream, whipped

Combine all ingredients, freeze as directed in General Rules.

FRESH STRAWBERRY ICE CREAM

Wash and hull 4 cups berries, add ¾ cup sugar and let stand 1 hour; crush or strain. Follow Ice Cream with Cream Base recipe, omitting sugar and vanilla. When partially frozen, beat well and add berries and whipped cream; freeze.

Ice Cream Desserts

ICE CREAM BALLS

Scoop out ice cream in balls, roll in grated coconut, chopped nuts or macaroon crumbs.

FILLED MERINGUES

See page 162.

PECHE MELBA

Cover a ball of ice cream with half a fresh or canned peach, rounded side up. Top with Melba Sauce.

STRAWBERRIES ROMANOFF

1 cup heavy cream
1 pint Vanilla Ice Cream, page 205
juice of ½ lemon
2 ounces Cointreau
1 ounce rum
2 quarts strawberries, hulled

Whip cream. Combine with softened ice cream. Add lemon juice, Cointreau and rum. Pour over whole, chilled, sugared strawberries.

BANANA SPLIT

Cut banana in two, put ice cream in center, add cherry or raspberry syrup, top with chopped nuts.

ICE CREAM SANDWICHES

Place a slice of brick ice cream between 2 thin layers of sponge cake. Spread with raspberry or strawberry jam.

ICE CREAM FLOWER POTS

Wash and dry small ordinary flower pots. Line bottom and sides with foil or paper cups. Just before serving, fill with your choice of ice cream, cover with grated sweet chocolate, and stick a fresh flower in center of each pot.

PEACH MELBA ICE CREAM CAKE

Bake Angel Food or Sunshine Cake in ring mold;

fill center with ice cream, border with peaches. Cover with Melba Sauce.

BERRY SUNDAE CAKE

Fill center of cake ring, above, with ice cream balls; serve with sweetened crushed berries.

FUDGE MINT ICE CREAM CAKE

Fill center of cake ring with mint ice cream and serve with Hot Fudge Sauce.

JELLY ICE CREAM CAKE

Spread cake ring with jelly; sprinkle with cooled and crushed caramelized sugar. Fill center with ice cream balls.

BAKED ALASKA

6 egg whites
6 tablespoons confectioners sugar
¼ teaspoon vanilla
thin sheet sponge cake
2-quart brick of ice cream

Make a meringue by beating whites until foamy; add sugar gradually, beating constantly. Add vanilla, beat until glossy. Place sponge cake on board covered with brown paper. Put ice cream on cake, having cake extend ¼ inch beyond cream. Cover ice cream and cake completely with meringue. Place in broiler 4 inches below heat and brown meringue quickly. Slip from paper to serving dish and serve immediately.

ICE CREAM SUNDAES

Place ice cream in dessert glasses, cover with any of the following toppings.

BERRY TOPPING

Crushed strawberries or raspberries. Top with whipped cream.

CHERRY-MARSHMALLOW TOPPING

Crushed cherries, Marshmallow Sauce; sprinkle with coconut.

PINEAPPLE TOPPING

Crushed or preserved pineapple, whipped cream, cherry on top.

PEACH TOPPING

Sliced peaches, whipped cream, a cherry or chopped pecans.

MELBA TOPPING

Half peach, covered with strawberry or raspberry preserves, or Melba Sauce.

NUT TOPPING

Dried crushed macaroons or blanched chopped pistachio nuts, black walnuts, pecans or crushed nut brittle.

TROPICAL TOPPING

Fresh grated coconut and bits of maraschino cherries.

CHOCOLATE ICE CREAM SODA

2 tablespoons chocolate syrup
chocolate or vanilla ice cream
carbonated water
1 tablespoon whipped cream

Put chocolate syrup into a tall glass, add ice cream, and fill glass with carbonated water. Top with whipped cream.

ROOT BEER FLOAT

Place a scoop of vanilla ice cream in a tall glass. Pour ice-cold root beer over it and serve.

GINGER FLOAT

Fill tall glass ½ full with vanilla ice cream. Add ginger ale to fill glass. Serve at once.

COFFEE ICE CREAM FLOAT

Fill tall glass ½ full with vanilla ice cream. Add hot coffee to fill glass. Serve at once.

PINEAPPLE FLOAT

Place scoop of vanilla ice cream in tall glass; fill glass with pineapple juice.

MAPLE ICE CREAM FIZZ

2 tablespoons maple syrup
4 tablespoons light cream
cracked ice
1 scoop ice cream
carbonated water

Mix syrup and cream, add ½ glass cracked ice and shake well. Add the ice cream and fill glass with carbonated water.

FRUIT ICES AND SHERBETS

GENERAL RULES

The method for freezing fruit ices and sherbets in a manually operated churn freezer is the same as that for ice cream, pages 204–205.
See also the Rules for Refrigerator Tray Ices.

Churn Freezer Ices

LEMON ICE

4 cups water
1¾ cups sugar
1 egg white, beaten stiff
¾ cup lemon juice

Boil water and sugar 5 minutes to make a syrup. Cool, fold in egg white, add lemon juice and freeze in churn freezer.

CREME DE MENTHE ICE

1 cup sugar
4 cups water
⅓ cup crème de menthe
green vegetable coloring

Boil sugar and water for 10 minutes and add crème de menthe and coloring; freeze in churn freezer.

CRANBERRY FRAPPE

1 quart cranberries
4 cups water
2 cups sugar
½ cup lemon juice

Cook the berries in water 5 minutes or until they stop popping, strain; add sugar and bring to the boiling point. Cool, add lemon juice; freeze in churn freezer.

FRESH FRUIT ICE

4 cups water
2 cups sugar
2 cups fruit juice or crushed fruit, strained
lemon juice to taste
1 egg white, beaten stiff

Boil water and sugar for 5 minutes to make a syrup, cool, add fruit juice and lemon juice. Fold in egg white, and freeze in churn freezer.

MINT FRUIT ICE

2 cups water
2 cups sugar
1 large bunch of fresh mint, finely cut
6 lemons, juice
2 oranges, juice
grated rind of 1 lemon
green food coloring
1 egg white, beaten stiff

Boil water and sugar 5 minutes to make a syrup. Pour syrup over mint. Cover and steep for 1 hour. Then strain over the fruit juice and rind. Add coloring, if desired. Cool. Fold in egg white and freeze in churn freezer. If desired, 4 or 5 drops of oil of peppermint and ⅓ cup crème de menthe may be used in place of the fresh mint leaves and sugar. Decorate with sprigs of mint.

GRAPE FRAPPE

4 cups water
2 cups sugar
2 cups grape juice
¼ cup lemon juice
⅔ cup orange juice
1 egg white, beaten stiff

Make a syrup by boiling water and sugar 5 minutes; cool; add grape, lemon and orange juice; cool, add the egg white and freeze in churn freezer.

STRAWBERRY OR RASPBERRY ICE

1½ cups sugar
4 cups water
2 cups berry juice
1 tablespoon lemon juice

Boil sugar and water for 10 minutes; cool, add berry juice and lemon juice; strain and freeze in churn freezer.

PINEAPPLE ICE

1 cup sugar
2 cups water
1 can (8 ounces) crushed pineapple
2 lemons, juice
2 egg whites, beaten stiff

Boil sugar with water 5 minutes to make a syrup. Cool, add pineapple and the lemon juice. Freeze until slightly thickened, then fold in whites and finish freezing.

LEMON MILK SHERBET

1¾ cups sugar
grated rind of ½ lemon
½ cup lemon juice
1 quart milk or buttermilk

Mix in the order given and freeze in churn freezer.

BERRY MILK SHERBET

1 cup sugar
1 cup raspberry, strawberry or loganberry juice
1 tablespoon lemon juice
1 quart milk

Mix sugar, fruit juice and lemon juice and set aside until sugar is dissolved. Add the milk and freeze in churn freezer.

PINEAPPLE MILK SHERBET

1 cup sugar
1 can (1 pound, 4 ounces) crushed pineapple
juice of 1 lemon
1 quart milk

Add sugar to pineapple and lemon juice; add milk and freeze in churn freezer.

Refrigerator Tray Ices

GENERAL RULES

Freeze mixture in ice cube tray, setting refrigerator at coldest point, until mixture is mushy and almost frozen. Remove from tray to thoroughly chilled mixing bowl and beat until light. Fold stiffly beaten egg whites into the frozen mixture quickly to keep it from melting. Return to tray and finish freezing. If mixture separates while freezing, beat again in tray with fork or spoon until well blended.

APRICOT ICE

1 cup apricot juice
1 cup apricot pulp
¼ cup sugar
1 egg yolk

Mix juice, pulp, and sugar until smooth. Add very well-beaten egg yolk. Freeze as directed.

LEMON WATER ICE

¾ cup sugar
2 cups water
½ cup lemon juice
1/16 teaspoon salt
grated rind of 1 lemon

Cook sugar and water slowly for 10 minutes to form a syrup. Cool, add to strained fruit juice; add salt and grated rind, pour into tray and freeze as directed.

LIME WATER ICE

⅔ cup sugar
2 cups water
½ cup lime juice
green food coloring
2 egg whites, stiffly beaten
pinch of salt

Cook sugar and water slowly for 10 minutes. Add to strained lime juice. Cool. Add coloring. Pour into freezing tray and freeze firm. Remove to ice-cold bowl and beat until very light. Fold in beaten egg whites to which salt has been added. Return to refrigerator and finish freezing.

MELON COUPE

1½ cups water
¾ cup sugar
3 cups cantaloupe, pulp and juice
¼ cup lemon juice

Boil water and sugar 5 minutes to make a syrup. Cool and add cantaloupe pulp and juice, strained through sieve, lemon juice and freeze until firm. Beat well, finish freezing. Serve in glasses, top with whipped cream and melon balls.

ORANGE WATER ICE

½ cup sugar
1⅓ cups water
1 envelope unflavored gelatin
⅔ cup orange juice
2 tablespoons lemon juice
grated rind of 1 orange
pinch of salt

Cook sugar with ½ cup water 3 minutes. Add gelatin soaked 5 minutes in 3 tablespoons cold water. Let cool. Beat until thick, add orange and lemon juice, grated rind, rest of water and a pinch of salt. Freeze as directed.

ORANGE ICE

1 cup corn syrup
¼ cup sugar
1½ cups water
2 tablespoons grated orange rind
1 teaspoon grated lemon rind
1½ cups orange juice
2 tablespoons lemon juice
pinch of salt

Boil corn syrup, sugar and water together for 5 minutes. Add grated rind. Cool. Add fruit juices and salt. Freeze as directed.

STRAWBERRY SHERBET

1 quart strawberries
1½ cups sugar
2 tablespoons lemon juice
2 egg whites, stiffly beaten

Wash and hull berries and put through strainer. Mix juice and pulp with the sugar and lemon juice. Fold in egg whites. Place in freezing tray and when almost frozen, remove from tray to an ice-cold bowl and beat until smooth. Then freeze until firm.

RED OR BLACK RASPBERRY SHERBET

1 envelope unflavored gelatin
½ cup cold water
⅔ cup sugar
1 pint fresh berries
2 tablespoons lemon juice
2 stiffly beaten egg whites

Soak gelatin in cold water for 5 minutes. Add sugar to berries and crush. Heat slowly and simmer for 5 minutes. Strain, add gelatin and lemon juice. Cool. Freeze in refrigerator tray until mushy. Remove to cold bowl and beat until very light. Fold in stiffly beaten whites. Return to tray and freeze.

APRICOT SHERBET

½ cup water
1 cup apricot juice
¼ cup granulated sugar
1 cup apricot pulp
1½ tablespoons lemon juice
2 egg whites, beaten stiff
pinch of salt
½ cup cream, whipped

Cook water, apricot juice, sugar slowly to a syrup. Cool. Add apricot pulp and lemon juice. Freeze in refrigerator tray until firm. Remove to a cold bowl and beat until light. Add egg whites, salt and cream. Finish freezing.

ORANGE MILK SHERBET

2 cups milk
1 cup sugar
⅔ cup orange juice
juice of 1 lemon

Heat milk and sugar to near boiling point. Cool. Freeze in refrigerator tray until mushy. Remove to chilled bowl; add orange and lemon juice. Beat until fluffy. Return to tray and freeze.

Fruit sherbets made with gelatin keep well in a home freezer or refrigerator freezer compartment. Store, closely covered, in moisture- and vapor-proof container. Keep at 0° F. or below.

MOUSSES, PARFAITS AND FROZEN PUDDINGS

GENERAL RULES

These desserts may be made in molds by packing in 4 parts of ice to 1 of salt, or in the home freezer, or in refrigerator trays. They are all made with heavy cream, whipped stiff, combined with a thick, flavored base, then frozen without stirring.

The dessert will be much smoother if the cream is whipped only until it mounds softly on a spoon.

Use only crushed fruits; whole fruit is apt to crystallize.

All ingredients should be about the same temperature when combined to prevent separation, especially when folding mixtures into whipped cream.

TO PREPARE MOLDS

Fill mold to top. If mold has a lid, cover the filling with waxed paper, bringing the paper down over the sides. Adjust the lid. If the mold is to be buried in salt and ice, apply a thin coat of shortening to the outside of the seam, to seal the closing and prevent water from seeping in. If the mold has no lid, cover mold with a double thickness of aluminum foil, bringing the foil well down the sides, and tie securely with string.

TO UNMOLD

Dip mold into hot water almost to top edge. Remove cover, run knife around edges of cream, and invert on serving dish. If frozen mixture does not slip out at once, put hot, damp cloth on top of inverted mold.

VANILLA MOUSSE

1 cup heavy cream
¼ cup confectioners sugar
½ teaspoon vanilla
1 egg white, beaten stiff
¼ teaspoon salt

Whip cream. Add confectioners sugar and vanilla. Fold in stiffly beaten egg white to which salt has been added. Pour into refrigerator tray or mold, and freeze without stirring. Serve with chilled and crushed fruit, or with an ice cream sauce.

QUICK CHOCOLATE MOUSSE

2 cups heavy cream, whipped
1 can (5½ ounces) chocolate syrup

Mix. Freeze in refrigerator tray or mold.

CHOCOLATE CHIP MOUSSE

4 tablespoons flour
4 tablespoons sugar
⅛ teaspoon salt
2 cups milk
2 cups heavy cream, whipped
½ pound chocolate-coated molasses chips, crushed

Mix flour, sugar and salt. Add milk gradually. Cook until slightly thickened. Chill. Fold in cream and candy. Freeze in refrigerator tray or mold.

CINNAMON MOUSSE

1 cup sugar
¾ cup water
7 tablespoons red cinnamon candies
3 egg whites, beaten stiff
2 cups heavy cream, whipped

Boil sugar, water, and 4 tablespoons candies until syrup spins a thread. Beat syrup gradually into egg whites and continue beating until cool. Add remaining candies, finely crushed. Fold in the whipped cream. Freeze in refrigerator tray or mold.

MACAROON AND FRUIT MOUSSE

¼ cup confectioners sugar
¼ pound candied cherries
12 crushed macaroons
½ slice candied pineapple, cut fine
vanilla or maraschino syrup to taste
2 cups heavy cream, whipped

Fold all ingredients into whipped cream. Freeze in refrigerator tray or mold.

MAPLE MOUSSE

4 eggs, separated
1 cup maple syrup
1 teaspoon vanilla
2 cups heavy cream, whipped

Beat yolks until very light, add syrup and cook over boiling water until custard coats the spoon, stirring constantly. Place the dish in a pan of ice and stir until creamy; add vanilla, beaten whites, and whipped cream. Pour into refrigerator trays or mold. Freeze. Serve in Schaum Torte or Kisses.

PEANUT BRITTLE MOUSSE

1 pound peanut brittle
1 dozen macaroons
2 cups heavy cream, whipped

Chop the peanut brittle and macaroons together and mix with the whipped cream. Freeze in refrigerator trays or mold. Unmold onto platter, slice. Serve with whipped cream and candied cherries.

PRALINE MOUSSE

¾ cup almonds
1 cup granulated sugar
2 cups heavy cream
½ cup confectioners sugar
pinch of salt

Blanch almonds and toast them in a slow oven. Chop nuts. Place granulated sugar in small skillet; stir until it melts to a light brown syrup. Place chopped nuts on greased inverted dripping pan, pour hot syrup over quickly, cool, then break into small pieces. Beat cream until stiff, add confectioners sugar, salt and the broken almond pieces. Freeze in refrigerator trays or mold.

PISTACHIO MOUSSE

1 teaspoon vanilla
¼ cup confectioners sugar
1 teaspoon almond extract
few drops green coloring
½ cup chopped pistachio nuts
1 cup heavy cream, whipped

Fold all ingredients into whipped cream. Freeze. Makes 1 pint.

STRAWBERRY MOUSSE

1 quart strawberries
1⅛ cups confectioners sugar
2 cups heavy cream, whipped
¼ teaspoon salt
1 teaspoon vanilla

Wash and hull berries, add sugar, let stand 1 hour. Mash and strain. Add salt and vanilla to whipped cream. Fold into mashed strawberries. Freeze in two refrigerator trays or in a mold, without stirring. Other berries or fruits, mashed or cut in very small pieces, may be used.

Parfaits

Parfaits are usually served in tall glasses, and topped with whipped cream.

ANGEL PARFAIT

1 cup sugar
½ cup water
3 egg whites
½ teaspoon vanilla
2 cups heavy cream, whipped stiff
1 cup English walnuts, candied pineapple and cherries, chopped fine

Boil sugar and water until syrup spins a thread. Beat syrup slowly into stiffly beaten whites, beat until cool, add flavoring. When cold, fold in whipped cream, nuts, and fruit. Freeze in refrigerator tray or mold.

COFFEE PARFAIT

1 cup sugar
1 cup triple-strength coffee
3 eggs, separated
2 cups heavy cream

Cook sugar and coffee until syrup spins a thread; pour syrup slowly onto the beaten egg yolks and beat well. Pour mixture onto the stiffly beaten whites and blend. When cold, fold in the stiffly whipped cream. Freeze in refrigerator tray or mold.

PINEAPPLE PARFAIT

1 cup sugar
¼ cup water
6 egg yolks, well beaten
1 teaspoon almond extract
2 cups grated pineapple
2 cups heavy cream

Boil sugar and water 5 minutes, stir slowly into the beaten egg yolks. Cook in double boiler until mixture coats the spoon, stirring constantly. Chill, add extract and pineapple and fold in cream, whipped stiff. Freeze in refrigerator trays or mold.

BISCUIT TORTONI

6 eggs, separated
¾ cup sugar
2 dozen macaroons, crushed
2 tablespoons marachino
2 cups heavy cream, whipped

Beat yolks with sugar until thick and light. Add three-fourths of the macaroons, flavoring, egg whites, beaten stiff, and cream. Finely chopped candied fruits may be added. Pack into fluted paper cups; sprinkle with remaining macaroon crumbs. Arrange cups on tray, cover with foil, and freeze quickly.

HARLEQUIN PUDDING

4 cups heavy cream, whipped
½ cup confectioners sugar
½ cup strawberry jam
30 almonds, chopped
9 macaroons
2 squares unsweetened chocolate, melted
pistachio nuts, blanched and finely chopped

Sweeten whipped cream with confectioners sugar. Divide into 5 parts. Add jam to one; almonds to the second; macaroons dried and crushed to the third; chocolate to the fourth. Leave the last plain. Line melon mold with waxed paper, sprinkle bottom with the pistachio nuts. Arrange the whipped cream mixtures in the mold in layers. Freeze.

FROZEN CHOCOLATE PUDDING

1 cup sugar
⅛ teaspoon salt
4 tablespoons cornstarch
2 cups scalded milk
2 ounces unsweetened chocolate, melted, or ¼ cup cocoa
2 teaspoons vanilla
1 cup heavy cream, whipped

Mix sugar, salt and cornstarch, add the scalded milk gradually, and cook over hot water for 10 minutes, stirring constantly. Add the chocolate or cocoa and stir until well blended. Cool, add the vanilla and fold in the cream. Pour into a mold, or refrigerator trays. Freeze.

FROZEN SWEET CHOCOLATE PUDDING

½ cup hot water
½ cup sugar
¼ pound sweet chocolate
6 eggs, separated
2 cups heavy cream

Boil the water and sugar for 5 minutes to make a syrup. Add chocolate and stir until melted. Beat syrup gradually into the well-beaten yolks and beat until thick and cool. Fold in the stiffly beaten whites and fold in the whipped cream. Freeze in refrigerator trays or mold. Serves 10.

FROZEN CARAMEL PUDDING

1 cup corn syrup or sugar
2 cups scalded milk
4 tablespoons cornstarch
cold milk
1 cup sugar
1 cup heavy cream, whipped
½ teaspoon vanilla

Add the corn syrup to the scalded milk, stir in the cornstarch mixed with a little cold milk, cook over hot water for 10 minutes, stirring. Melt sugar in a heavy skillet until it is brown, and stir it very gradually into the hot custard. Cool, add whipped cream and flavoring. Freeze in refrigerator trays or pour into a mold.

FROZEN DIPLOMAT PUDDING

2 dozen lady fingers
orange juice or sherry wine to moisten the lady fingers
⅛ pound candied cherries
2 tablespoons maraschino
2 cups cream
6 egg yolks, beaten
1 cup sugar
vanilla
2 cups heavy cream, whipped

Separate lady fingers and sprinkle with orange juice. Cut the cherries in half and soak in maraschino, or use maraschino cherries.

In a double boiler, scald the cream, stir into egg yolks beaten with sugar. Return to double boiler and cook until thick, stirring constantly. Cool. Flavor with vanilla, add whipped cream and freeze in refrigerator trays. Remove to a bowl, beat until light. Fill mold with alternate layers of frozen cream, lady fingers and candied fruit, beginning with a decorative arrangement of lady fingers and cherries, and ending with cream. Cover with foil and freeze.

FROZEN COFFEE PUDDING

2 cups scalded milk
3 tablespoons instant coffee
4 tablespoons cornstarch
¾ cup sugar
1 cup heavy cream, whipped
½ teaspoon vanilla

Mix the scalded milk and coffee, pour gradually over the cornstarch mixed with the sugar and a little water. Cook over hot water until smooth and thick, stirring constantly. Cool, fold in whipped cream and vanilla. Freeze in refrigerator tray or in mold.

LALLA ROOKH CREAM

5 eggs, separated
1 cup sugar
1 cup light cream
2 envelopes unflavored gelatin
cold milk
2 tablespoons rum
2 cups heavy cream, whipped

Beat egg yolks, add sugar and light cream and cook over hot water, stirring until mixture coats the spoon. Add gelatin softened in a little cold milk, and stir until dissolved. Cool, add rum. Fold in egg whites, beaten stiff, and whipped cream. Freeze in refrigerator trays or mold. Unmold. Decorate with maraschino cherries and some of the cherry juice.

FROZEN NESSELRODE

1½ cups sugar
¾ cup water
4 egg yolks, beaten
1½ cups chestnuts, boiled and riced
½ pound candied fruit, cut fine
2 tablespoons maraschino
4 cups heavy cream, whipped

Boil sugar and water to a syrup. Beat gradually into beaten yolks. Cook until smooth and thick, stirring constantly. Cool and add chestnuts and the remaining ingredients. Freeze in refrigerator trays or mold.

FROZEN FIG PUDDING

½ pound figs, cut fine
¼ cup orange juice or wine
1 dozen lady fingers
2 cups heavy cream
½ cup confectioners sugar

Soak figs in orange juice or wine overnight, drain. Line bottom of a 4-cup loaf mold with split lady fingers, rounded sides down. Cover with ½ of the cream, whipped stiff and sweetened with confectioners sugar. On top of this spread the drained figs, then the rest of the sweetened whipped cream and a final layer of lady fingers. Cover with foil. Freeze.

FROZEN RUM PUDDING

2 eggs, separated
¼ cup rum
2 cups heavy cream, whipped
2 dozen lady fingers
½ pound marrons glacé, chopped fine

Beat egg yolks until light. Fold in whites, stiffly beaten, rum, and whipped cream. Line melon mold with split lady fingers; cover with layer of egg-rum-cream mixture and sprinkle with marrons. Repeat until the mold is filled, ending with lady fingers. Cover mold with foil and freeze. Decorate with whipped cream flavored with rum.

RASPBERRY BOMBE GLACE

Raspberry Ice, page 210
1 cup heavy cream, whipped
1 egg white, beaten stiff
¼ cup confectioners sugar
½ teaspoon vanilla

Line a 3-pint melon mold with Raspberry Ice. Fill the center with whipped cream combined lightly with the other ingredients. Cover with foil, freeze.

FROZEN EGGNOG

3 eggs, separated
1 cup sugar
1 cup heavy cream
3 tablespoons rum

Beat yolks until thick and lemon-colored, add ½ cup sugar and beat until creamy. Beat egg whites until stiff, add ½ cup sugar and continue beating. Whip cream until stiff enough to fold. Combine mixtures and add rum. Freeze. Serve in glasses; top with grated nutmeg.

DESSERT SAUCES

A well-chosen dessert sauce will transform the simplest dessert into a special treat. Choose a sauce, hot or cold, to complement and contrast the dessert; a tart, fruit-based sauce with a creamy rice pudding; a fluffy whipped cream sauce for plain cakes; a rich and nutty butterscotch sauce over warm spice cake; a buttery hard sauce for a steamed fruit pudding. A special group of sauces for ice cream is also included, to make even drugstore ice cream into a company dessert.

Sauces for Cakes and Puddings

CARAMEL SAUCE

1 cup sugar
1 cup boiling water

Spread sugar evenly in heavy skillet, place over heat, stir gently with a spoon, moving sugar constantly to the hottest part of pan until melted to a smooth, light brown syrup. Then very gradually add the boiling water and simmer for 5 to 10 minutes. The sugar may again become hard, but will melt in a few minutes. If too thick when cold, add a little hot water and boil again.

BURNT ALMOND SAUCE

Blanch ⅓ cup almonds. Place in pan in oven and roast until crisp and slightly browned. Chop fine and add to Caramel Sauce, above.

VANILLA SAUCE

2 tablespoons butter
2 tablespoons flour
1 cup boiling water
2 tablespoons sugar
1 teaspoon vanilla

Melt the butter, add flour and stir until it bubbles; add the boiling water and sugar, stirring constantly. Cook until smooth and well blended. Add vanilla and serve hot or cold.

CLEAR BUTTERSCOTCH SAUCE

4 tablespoons butter
1 cup brown sugar
1 teaspoon cornstarch
½ tablespoon vinegar
¼ cup water

Combine and boil ingredients until of desired consistency. Serve hot.

BUTTERSCOTCH NUT SAUCE

1 pound brown sugar
¼ cup butter
1 cup light cream
½ cup chopped nuts

Combine first 3 ingredients and cook in double boiler ½ hour. Add nut meats. Serve hot or cold.

BUTTERSCOTCH SAUCE

2 cups brown sugar
¼ pound butter
½ cup light cream

Mix well. Boil rapidly, without stirring, for 5 minutes. Serve hot or cold.

CHOCOLATE SAUCE

1½ tablespoons cornstarch
2 cups cold milk
2 squares unsweetened chocolate, grated
2 eggs, separated
⅔ cup confectioners sugar
1 teaspoon vanilla

Mix cornstarch with a little of the cold milk, add to rest of milk, cook in double boiler until thick, add chocolate and cook until melted. Beat egg whites stiff, add sugar, then yolks unbeaten. Add to cooked mixture. Cook 1 minute, stirring, let cool, add vanilla. Serve hot or cold.

EASY CHOCOLATE SAUCE

1 cup boiling water
pinch of salt
1 square unsweetened chocolate
½ cup sugar
1 teaspoon vanilla

Cook first 4 ingredients slowly until desired consistency. Just before serving, add 1 teaspoon of vanilla. Serve hot or cold.

CUSTARD SAUCE

3 egg yolks
½ cup sugar
⅛ teaspoon salt
2 cups scalded milk
½ teaspoon vanilla or rum

Beat eggs slightly, add sugar and salt; stir constantly while adding the hot milk gradually. Cook in a double boiler until mixture thickens; chill and flavor.

CREAMY FRUIT SAUCE

1 cup sugar
1 cup grated or mashed fruit
white of 1 egg

The pulp of any fresh or canned fruit or berries may be used. Beat the sugar, fruit and egg together until frothy.

MELBA SAUCE

¾ cup sugar
½ cup water
1 pint raspberries or strawberries

Boil sugar and water 10 minutes; cool and when ready to serve, add to chilled and crushed pulp and juice of berries.

Or mix ½ cup strawberry syrup, ½ cup raspberry syrup and 1 teaspoon cornstarch dissolved in a little cold water. Simmer 10 minutes and cool.

FRUIT JUICE SAUCE

½ cup sugar
1 tablespoon cornstarch
2 cups fruit juice

Mix sugar and cornstarch in saucepan, add fruit juice, cook until smooth and clear, stirring. Remove from heat, add lemon juice to taste.

LEMON SAUCE

1 cup sugar
2 tablespoons cornstarch
2 cups boiling water
1 lemon, rind and juice
2 tablespoons butter

Mix the sugar and cornstarch; add boiling water gradually, stirring constantly. Cook 8 to 10 minutes, add lemon juice, rind, and butter. Serve hot or cold.

QUICK BRANDY SAUCE

Follow recipe above. Omit lemon and substitute brandy or kirsch to taste and add a sprinkling of nutmeg.

ORANGE SAUCE

2 tablespoons butter
2 egg yolks
3 tablespoons sugar
4 tablespoons light cream
¼ cup orange juice

Cream butter in top of double boiler. Stir in egg yolks, sugar, and cream. Put over hot water, cook until thick. Add orange juice. Serve hot or cold.

Wine Sauces

BASIC WINE SAUCE

1½ cups sugar
½ cup water
1 teaspoon lemon or vanilla extract
3 tablespoons brandy or wine
1 tablespoon butter

Cook sugar and water for 5 minutes. Remove from heat, add flavorings and butter.

SABAYON SAUCE

2 eggs
¾ cup sugar
1 cup Rhine wine, sherry or Madeira
lemon slices and cinnamon stick

Beat eggs and sugar until light. Heat wine to the boiling point and pour slowly over the eggs; add lemon and cinnamon and cook over hot water until thick, stirring constantly. Serve at once.

WHITE WINE SAUCE

1 cup white wine
½ cup water
3 slices lemon
⅛ teaspoon cinnamon
¼ cup sugar
1 teaspoon cornstarch
4 yolks, beaten
4 whites, beaten stiff

Heat first five ingredients in double boiler for 15 minutes. Dissolve cornstarch with a little cold water and add to the hot wine mixture, stirring constantly until clear and thickened. Pour the hot wine mixture gradually over the beaten yolks, stirring constantly to avoid curdling. Return to saucepan, add half the beaten whites, heat through and continue beating. Top with remaining whites sweetened with sugar.

RUM BUTTER SAUCE

2 tablespoons butter
¾ cup confectioners sugar
1 egg, separated
2 tablespoons rum

Cream butter and sugar. Add beaten yolk. Cook over hot water until thick. Add rum gradually, stirring constantly. Blend with stiffly beaten white. Serve warm.

RUM SAUCE

2 eggs, separated
⅓ cup sugar
2 tablespoons rum

Beat yolks and sugar until thick. Add rum gradually. Fold into stiffly beaten whites.

SHERRY FLUFF SAUCE

2 egg yolks
½ cup sugar
¼ cup sherry
½ cup heavy cream, whipped

Beat egg yolks well, add sugar gradually, and beat until smooth and lemon-colored. Add sherry slowly, stirring constantly. Fold in whipped cream. Serve with sponge cake. Rum, to taste, may be substituted for sherry.

BRANDY BUTTER SAUCE

½ cup butter
1 cup sugar
1 egg, well beaten
1 teaspoon water
2 or 3 tablespoons brandy

Stir butter and sugar over hot water until melted, add egg mixed with water, stir until it thickens. Add brandy to taste.

BRANDY CREAM SAUCE

1 cup sugar
1 cup water
3 egg yolks
⅛ cup light cream
2 tablespoons brandy
pinch of salt
grated rind ½ orange

Cook sugar and water 5 minutes. Beat yolks, add cream, brandy, salt, and grated orange rind. Add syrup slowly, beat until thick.

FOAMY BRANDY SAUCE

¼ cup butter
½ cup sugar
2 eggs, separated
⅛ teaspoon salt
½ cup rich milk or light cream
1 tablespoon brandy
1 tablespoon rum

Cream butter and sugar well. Add well-beaten yolks and the salt. Add hot milk slowly and cook in double boiler until mixture coats the spoon. Remove from heat. Add brandy and rum and pour slowly over the stiffly beaten whites beating continually. Sprinkle with nutmeg if desired.

GOLDEN BRANDY SAUCE

3 eggs, separated
½ cup confectioners sugar
1 tablespoon brandy

Beat egg yolks, add sugar, brandy, and the whites beaten stiff.

Whipped Cream Sauces

BASIC WHIPPED CREAM SAUCE

1 egg, separated
1 cup confectioners sugar
1 teaspoon vanilla
2 cups heavy cream, whipped

Mix egg yolk and sugar; add stiffly beaten egg white and flavoring. Just before serving fold in the whipped cream.

WHIPPED BRANDY SAUCE

2 eggs, well beaten
½ cup sugar
1 tablespoon butter
1 cup heavy cream, whipped
1 tablespoon brandy

Mix eggs with sugar. Add butter and cook over hot water, stirring until thickened. When cold, beat in whipped cream. Flavor with brandy or as desired. Delicious served as sauce for ice cream.

COFFEE SAUCE

¼ cup sugar
few grains of salt
½ cup very strong coffee
2 eggs, slightly beaten
½ cup heavy cream, whipped

Add the sugar and a few grains of salt to hot coffee and pour very gradually on the slightly beaten eggs. Place in double boiler and cook, stirring constantly until mixture coats the spoon. Chill; when ready to serve, fold in the whipped cream.

CREAM FRUIT SAUCE

¾ cup fruit pulp
¾ cup heavy cream
sugar to taste

Drain fruit and mash, or rub fruit through sieve. Whip cream, fold in fruit pulp and sweeten to taste.

CREAM FRUIT JUICE SAUCE

2 teaspoons butter
2 teaspoons flour
1 cup fruit juice, hot
juice of ½ lemon
1 cup cream, whipped
sugar to taste

Melt butter in double boiler, add flour, and blend; add fruit juice and lemon juice. Stir constantly until it thickens. Chill; fold in sweetened whipped cream.

ORANGE CREAM SAUCE

½ cup sugar
1 orange, juice and rind
2 egg yolks, beaten
1 cup cream, whipped

Mix sugar, rind and juice of orange in double boiler. Cook until sugar is dissolved. Add yolks and cook until mixture is thickened, stirring constantly. Chill; when ready to use, fold in whipped cream.

STRAWBERRY CREAM SAUCE

1 cup strawberry pulp
1 cup cream, whipped
1 tablespoon maraschino syrup
sugar to taste

Mix. Serve cold over any pudding or sponge cake.

Hard Sauces

PLAIN HARD SAUCE

¼ cup butter
1 cup confectioners sugar
1 tablespoon rum
1 teaspoon vanilla

Cream the butter, add sugar gradually, and flavoring, adding more sugar if necessary for desired consistency.

CREAM CHEESE HARD SAUCE

1 (3 ounces) package cream cheese
3 cups confectioners sugar
3 tablespoons sherry
¼ teaspoon each cinnamon and nutmeg
¼ teaspoon salt

Soften the cream cheese; combine with the other ingredients. Sauce will be stiff. Chill thoroughly. Serve on hot mince pie or hot plum pudding.

STRAWBERRY HARD SAUCE

⅓ cup butter
1 cup confectioners sugar
⅔ cup strawberries

Cream the butter, add the sugar gradually; add the strawberries and beat until berries are well mashed. Add more sugar if necessary for desired consistency.

Jelly Sauces

JELLY SAUCE

¼ cup hot water
1 6-ounce glass tart jelly
1 tablespoon butter
1 tablespoon flour

Add hot water to jelly and melt very slowly. Heat butter in saucepan, add flour and gradually the hot jelly liquid. Cook until smooth and serve hot over any pudding.

Or the jelly may be melted with the hot water and served.

JAM OR MARMALADE SAUCE

Heat ¼ cup jam or marmalade, the juice of 1 lemon and ½ cup of water. Stir until dissolved and serve hot or cold.

Sauces for Ice Cream

CHOCOLATE SUNDAE SAUCE

2 cups sugar
4 cups water
4 squares unsweetened chocolate
pinch of salt
2 tablespoons cornstarch
2 teaspoons vanilla

Boil sugar and water 5 minutes to make a syrup; add chocolate, salt, and cornstarch dissolved in a little cold water. Cook slowly and stir until chocolate is melted and mixture is smooth (5 to 8 minutes). Cool; add vanilla. Keep in jar in refrigerator.

MILK CHOCOLATE FUDGE SAUCE

½ pound milk chocolate
½ cup hot milk

Melt chocolate in top of double boiler, stirring constantly. When thoroughly dissolved, add milk gradually and stir until smooth. Serve warm.

FLUFFY CHOCOLATE SAUCE

2 squares unsweetened chocolate
¾ cup confectioners sugar
¼ cup hot water
1 cup heavy cream, whipped
1 egg white, beaten stiff
1 teaspoon vanilla

Melt chocolate in double boiler; add sugar and water, cook until smooth. Cool. Fold in cream and egg white. Add flavoring.

CHOCOLATE MARSHMALLOW SAUCE

½ pound marshmallows
¼ pound semisweet chocolate
½ cup hot cream or milk

Cut marshmallows in pieces. Place in top of double boiler, add chocolate and the cream. Cook until dissolved, stirring until smooth. Serve hot.

MARSHMALLOW SUNDAE SAUCE

½ cup sugar
¼ cup water
12 marshmallows, cut in pieces
1 egg white, beaten stiff

Boil sugar and water about 5 minutes to make a syrup, add the marshmallows. Let stand 2 minutes without stirring. Then pour gradually onto beaten egg white, beating constantly until smooth and cool.

MARSHMALLOW MINT SAUCE

Add 1 drop oil of peppermint or ½ teaspoon peppermint extract to Marshmallow Sundae Sauce.

MARSHMALLOW MOCHA SAUCE

Add 1 teaspoon instant coffee to Chocolate Marshmallow Sauce, above.

CARAMEL SUNDAE SAUCE

½ cup cream
1 pound caramels

Heat ingredients in double boiler, stirring constantly until well blended. Serve hot.

MAPLE SUNDAE SAUCE

2 cups maple syrup
¼ cup butter

Boil syrup and butter until it forms a thread when dropped from spoon. Serve hot.

BUTTERSCOTCH SUNDAE SAUCE

1 cup light brown sugar
2 tablespoons corn syrup
¼ cup milk or cream
2 tablespoons butter

Cook sugar, syrup and milk to soft-ball stage, stirring constantly. Add butter. Serve hot.

FRUIT SUNDAE SAUCE

Cook 1 cup sugar and ½ cup water 5 minutes. Pour over 1½ cups halved or sliced strawberries. Cool and serve over ice cream. Sauce may be kept a few days after making. Any berries, whole, sliced or crushed, or peaches may be used.

STRAWBERRY WHIPPED CREAM SAUCE

Sprinkle ½ cup sugar over 1 cup crushed strawberries. Let stand about 1 hour. Put through a sieve and fold in 1 cup whipped cream.

CLARET SAUCE

2 cups sugar
½ cup hot water
½ cup claret

Heat the sugar with the water. Stir until dissolved and then boil without stirring until the syrup forms a soft ball in cold water. Remove from stove and add the claret. Cool.

QUICK REFERENCE GUIDE TO USEFUL INFORMATION IN THIS BOOK

11
EGG AND
CHEESE DISHES

EGGS

USES FOR EGGS

WHITES

Angel food and white cakes, kisses, torten, meringues, cake frostings and fillings.

YOLKS

Custards, mayonnaise, cooked salad dressing, noodles, soup garnishes, gold cakes, eggnogs.

General Rules

Eggs should be cooked over low heat; high heat toughens them. If they are cooked in water, the water should simmer below the boiling point. Water must not touch bottom of double-boiler top in preparing custards or sauces containing eggs.

A stale egg rises in water; fresh eggs are heavy and sink to the bottom.

SOFT-COOKED EGGS

HOT WATER METHOD

Eggs should be at room temperature. Lower eggs into water at the simmering point, simmer 2 minutes for opaque but barely firm whites, runny yolks; 3 minutes for opaque, firm whites, soft yolks; 4 to 5 minutes for firm, opaque whites, yolks that hold their shape.

COLD WATER METHOD

Cover eggs (right from the refrigerator, if necessary) with cold water, bring slowly to the simmering point. At this point, whites are opaque but soft, and yolks are runny. Simmer 2 minutes longer for firm whites, soft yolks; 3 to 4 minutes longer for firm, opaque whites, yolks that hold their shape.

CODDLED EGGS

Bring water to a boil in both top and bottom of a double boiler. Lower eggs at room temperature into water in top of double boiler, remove from heat, set top over bottom, cover, let stand 4 to 8 minutes. This method produces eggs of uniform "set" all through.

HARD-COOKED EGGS

Lower eggs into simmering water and simmer 15 minutes; or start eggs in cold water, and allow 21 minutes cooking time in all. Turn the eggs occasionally as they cook, to center the yolks. This is important when the eggs are to be split, sliced, or cut in wedges for garnishing. Plunge eggs at once into cold water to chill before peeling. This prevents formation of a green ring around the yolks. Roll egg lightly against table with palm of hand to crack the shell, and peel. New-laid eggs are not a good choice for hard-cooking, since they do not peel smoothly.

GOLDENROD TOAST

4 hard-cooked eggs
2 cups Medium White Sauce, page 386
6 to 8 slices toast
parsley

Separate the egg yolks and whites and chop the whites. Make a Medium White Sauce. Add the whites to the sauce. Heat thoroughly, and pour the mixture over the toast. Sprinkle with riced egg yolks and garnish with toast points and parsley.

CURRIED EGGS

2 tablespoons butter
2 tablespoons flour
1 teaspoon chopped onion
½ teaspoon curry powder
⅛ teaspoon pepper
¼ teaspoon salt
1 cup hot milk
6 hard-cooked eggs

Sauté onion in butter, add flour, seasonings, and the hot milk. Simmer, stirring constantly until thickened. Slice the eggs and reheat in the sauce. Serve on rice or garnish with fingers of fresh toast.

EGGS A LA TARCAT

6 hard-cooked eggs
¼ pound chopped ham
1 tablespoon onion, chopped
¼ teaspoon prepared mustard
1 teaspoon salt
dash of red pepper

Cut the eggs in half lengthwise. Remove the yolks. Mash the yolks with the rest of the ingredients and refill the whites with this mixture. Serve cold on lettuce leaves with mayonnaise.

MOLDED EGGS

6 hard-cooked eggs
½ teaspoon salt
¼ teaspoon dry mustard
2 tablespoons Pepper Relish, page 457
1 tablespoon mayonnaise
¼ cup Thousand Island Dressing, page 376

Grind or chop eggs, add seasonings, drained Pepper Relish, and mayonnaise. Pack in small cups and chill for several hours. Unmold. Serve on lettuce and top with Thousand Island Dressing.

EGGS AND MUSHROOMS

2 cups Medium White Sauce, page 386
½ pound Cheddar cheese, grated
8 hard-cooked eggs, sliced
½ pound fresh or 4-ounce can sautéed mushrooms

Combine White Sauce and grated cheese, heat until cheese melts. Add eggs and mushrooms and serve on toast or in patty shells. Shrimp, crab meat, or lobster may be added if desired.

EGGS AU GRATIN

6 hard-cooked eggs
¾ cup grated Cheddar cheese
2 cups Medium White Sauce, page 386
¼ cup dry bread crumbs

Place eggs, sliced in half, in greased casserole.

Sprinkle with half of the grated cheese; add White Sauce, or Tomato Sauce, cover with bread crumbs, and sprinkle with remaining cheese. Bake in moderate oven, 350° F., until brown. Garnish with parsley.

EGG CUTLETS

1 cup Thick White Sauce, page 386
½ teaspoon paprika
salt
1 teaspoon onion juice
6 hard-cooked eggs, chopped
1 tablespoon chopped parsley
flour
1 egg, slightly beaten
fine bread crumbs

Season White Sauce with onion juice, paprika and salt. Remove from heat and add the eggs and parsley.

Place on a buttered dish and chill. Dust the hands lightly with flour and shape spoonfuls of mixture in small cutlets; use as little flour as possible. Dip each cutlet into slightly beaten egg, then in fine bread crumbs. Let stand 30 minutes. Fry in hot, deep fat, 375° F., until golden brown. Drain. Serve with Tomato Sauce or Cream Sauce.

POACHED EGGS

TO POACH EGGS

Bring 1 quart of water to a boil in a shallow pan. Add 1 tablespoon vinegar and 1 teaspoon salt. Break eggs carefully, one at a time, into a saucer, then slip them into the hot water, off the heat. Cover the pan and set over very low heat for about 5 minutes, or until the whites are set and a film has formed over the yolks. Remove from pan with a skimmer, drain, and serve on hot buttered toast.

To POACH EGGS FRENCH STYLE, stir the water with a wooden spoon to form a deep vortex in the center, and carefully slip in the egg. The swirling water will keep the egg shape. Do one egg at a time and remove to warm water until wanted.

OR USE AN EGG POACHER, designed to fit over hot water like a double boiler insert. Butter the pockets, break one egg into each, cover, and cook until set.

POACHED EGGS AND CHEESE

6 eggs
½ teaspoon salt
¼ teaspoon paprika
6 tablespoons grated Cheddar cheese
6 teaspoons butter

Butter 6 ramekins and drop a whole egg in each;

add salt and paprika, 1 teaspoon butter and cover with 1 tablespoon of the cheese. Place ramekins in a pan of hot water (½ inch deep) and bake until the eggs are set. Place under broiler and brown quickly.

POACHED EGG MORNAY

Cut toast rounds and put a poached egg on each. Sprinkle with cheese. Pour Medium White Sauce over each egg. Garnish with parsley.

EGGS BENEDICT

2 English muffins
4 slices boiled ham
4 poached eggs
Hollandaise Sauce, page 388

Split and toast English muffins. Fry rounds of ham and place on buttered muffins. Slip poached egg on ham. Cover with Hollandaise Sauce. Garnish with olive and pickles.

POACHED EGG AND ANCHOVY BUTTER

Butter thin, round pieces of toast and spread lightly with anchovy butter. Top with a poached egg.

POACHED EGGS WITH LOBSTER OR MUSHROOMS

12 poached eggs
6 slices toast
2 cups boiled lobster or sautéed sliced mushrooms
Cream Sauce, page 386
½ cup grated cheese

Place 2 poached eggs on toast in each of six individual casseroles. Add lobster or mushrooms mixed with Cream Sauce, sprinkle with cheese, place in 350° F. oven until cheese is melted.

SHIRRED OR BAKED EGGS

TO SHIRR EGGS

Butter an egg shirrer or individual baking dish, sprinkle with fine bread crumbs seasoned with salt, pepper, and paprika if desired. Break 1 or 2 eggs into each (2 is the usual portion) and sprinkle with more bread crumbs. Bake in a moderate oven (350° F.) about 15 minutes, until whites are opaque and firm.

SHIRRED EGGS IN TOMATO SAUCE

1 cup Tomato Sauce, page 390
6 eggs

Put half the sauce into a buttered baking dish, or into 3 individual casseroles. Carefully add eggs, cover with remaining sauce. Bake in a moderate oven (350° F.) about 15 minutes, until whites are set. Serve in the baking dishes.

BAKED EGGS A LA COLUMBUS

Select green peppers of uniform size. Cut around the stem and remove the seeds and veins. Parboil for 5 minutes. Drain. Set the peppers in small muffin pans, break a fresh egg into each, add salt and pepper and bake in a moderate oven about 15 minutes, or until the egg is set. Serve on hot buttered toast. Cover with Tomato Sauce.

EGGS IN A NEST

Using 2 eggs for each serving, separate and beat whites until very stiff. Butter individual casseroles; sprinkle fine bread crumbs on bottom. Spoon equal amounts of beaten whites in dishes, make hollows and slip in the yolks. Season with salt and pepper. Set casseroles in pan of boiling water, cover and cook just until whites are firm; or bake uncovered in moderate oven, 325° F., about 15 minutes.

EGG TIMBALES

4 eggs
1 cup milk
dash of pepper
1 teaspoon chopped parsley

Beat the eggs until light and lemon-colored, add rest of the ingredients. Butter the timbale forms or custard cups, fill with mixture and bake in a pan half filled with hot water 30 to 45 minutes in moderate oven, 350° F. Serve with Tomato Sauce or Mushroom Sauce.

FRIED EGGS

Heat enough butter or bacon fat in a skillet to cover the bottom generously. Use a pan large enough to accommodate the eggs to be cooked, with a little room left over for basting and easy turning. When the fat is hot, gently break the eggs into the pan, one at a time, keeping them separated. Or slide them in from a saucer. Cook very slowly until the white is opaque. If desired, spoon the fat gently over the yolk during the cooking. Do not allow the bottom to become crusty; if the flavor of browned butter is liked, allow the butter to brown slightly before adding the eggs to the pan. These are "sunny side up." Fried eggs may be turned and cooked very briefly to set the yolk further, if desired.

BACON AND EGGS

Lay thin strips of bacon close together in cold skillet. Place over low heat, fry slowly until bacon is crisp and brown. Pour off fat as it accumulates. To keep edges from curling, press occasionally with spatula. Remove bacon from skillet, drain, and keep warm on hot platter. Fry eggs in bacon fat; serve with bacon.

HAM AND EGGS

Slice ham ¼ inch thick. Grease skillet very lightly, heat, brown ham quickly on both sides. If cooked too long, it will become hard and dry. Remove ham from skillet and keep hot. Fry eggs in same pan, adding more fat, if necessary.

SCRAMBLED EGGS

BASIC SCRAMBLED EGGS

3 eggs
3 tablespoons milk or water
½ teaspoon salt
dash pepper
1 tablespoon butter

Beat eggs slightly, with milk or water and seasoning. Melt butter in a 7- or 8-inch skillet, and when hot add eggs. Cook over low heat, stirring constantly, until thick and set, but still creamy and moist.

Or let eggs cook without stirring until partially set, then lift and stir with fork or spatula until mixture is set. Or cook until edges set, then with a fork or spatula draw the set edges quickly toward the center. Repeat until eggs are set but still creamy.

DOUBLE BOILER SCRAMBLED EGGS

Allow 1 tablespoon liquid for each egg and add seasonings to taste. This is an excellent method for preparing scrambled eggs for the whole family; 1½ to 2 eggs per serving is the usual portion. Melt 1 teaspoon butter per egg in the top of a double boiler. Put boiler over hot water and add eggs. Cook, stirring constantly to remove the cooked portion from the bottom of the pan, until the mixture is set.

SCRAMBLED EGGS WITH TOMATO SAUCE

5 eggs
½ teaspoon salt
⅛ teaspoon pepper
½ cup milk
2 tablespoons butter
½ cup Tomato Sauce, page 390

Beat eggs slightly with fork; add salt, pepper and milk. Heat skillet, melt butter, and add eggs. Cook until creamy, stirring and scraping carefully from bottom of pan. Stir in Tomato Sauce to which 1 tablespoon sliced cooked mushrooms and 1 tablespoon capers may be added. Serve hot on toast.

SCRAMBLED EGGS WITH MATZOS

3 matzos
3 whole eggs
salt
4 tablespoons fat or oil
4 tablespoons sugar, if desired

Break matzos in small pieces in a colander. Pour boiling water through them; drain quickly. They should be moist but not soggy. Beat eggs well, fold the matzos in lightly. Add salt to taste. Heat the fat in a skillet, add the egg mixture; add sugar if desired. Cook slowly, stirring from the bottom as egg sets. Continue to cook gently until eggs are set.

CREOLE EGGS

1 tablespoon chopped onion
1 tablespoon green peppers
1 tablespoon butter
1 4-ounce can mushrooms
1 tablespoon capers
1 cup tomato juice
6 eggs
toast

Simmer onions and peppers a few minutes in the butter, add the mushrooms, capers and tomato juice. Heat thoroughly. Beat the eggs well and cook with the other ingredients, stirring constantly until the eggs are set. Serve on toast.

SCRAMBLED EGGS AND CORN

1 can (1 pound) whole kernel corn,
    or 4 to 6 ears cooked corn
1 tablespoon butter
1 teaspoon salt
⅛ teaspoon pepper
4 eggs, beaten

Cut corn from cob, or drain canned corn. Melt butter in skillet, add corn and seasoning, heat well. Add the beaten eggs, stir, and cook gently until eggs are set. Serve at once.

EGGS WITH DRIED BEEF

½ pound dried beef, shredded
1 tablespoon fat or butter
3 eggs
¼ cup milk

If beef is too salty, cover with boiling water, drain and dry. Heat the fat in a skillet, add the meat, cook a few minutes. Add eggs beaten with milk, cook slowly, stirring constantly, until the eggs are set. Serve immediately.

To freeze egg yolks, egg whites or whole eggs, see directions in chapter 24, Freezing and Drying.

EGGS AND SAUSAGE

1 pound sausage
2 tablespoons fat
6 eggs, beaten
salt, pepper

Skin and slice cold, cooked sausage ½ inch thick. Place in skillet with hot fat; brown on both sides a few minutes and just before serving add the eggs and seasonings to taste. Cook, stirring, until the eggs are set; serve immediately.

VENETIAN EGGS

1 tablespoon butter
1 tablespoon chopped onion
1 cup canned tomatoes
small bay leaf
1 teaspoon salt
1 teaspoon sugar
speck paprika
3 eggs

Melt butter, add onion and sauté for a few minutes; add tomatoes, bay leaf, salt, sugar, paprika. When hot, add the eggs. When slightly cooked, break eggs with fork. Serve on toast.

BUCKINGHAM EGGS

5 slices toast
1 cup Thin White Sauce, page 386
5 eggs
5 tablespoons milk
½ teaspoon salt
2 tablespoons butter
4 tablespoons grated Swiss cheese

Arrange toast in shallow baking dish, cover with White Sauce. Beat eggs lightly with milk and salt. Heat butter in skillet, add eggs, and cook, stirring constantly, until mixture is creamy, but very soft. Pour eggs over toast, sprinkle with cheese. Bake in moderate oven (350° F.) until cheese melts.

OMELETS

An omelet is something like a fluffy pancake, except that it should be moist clear through. For best results, an omelet pan should not be used for other purposes. Keep omelet pan well-greased and wipe with paper towel after each using. Do not overbeat eggs.

Heat butter in pan, add beaten egg, and pull in from edges as egg sets, allowing the uncooked portion to run underneath. Shake pan as egg sets to prevent sticking. When set, fold and roll onto platter and serve immediately.

To fill a cooked omelet, put a few spoonfuls of filling on half the omelet, fold part over it and roll onto a platter. Or put the filling near the edge and roll the omelet around it. Serve at once; omelets begin to shrink when they are removed from the heat.

CREAMY OMELET

4 eggs
4 tablespoons milk or water
½ teaspoon salt
⅛ teaspoon pepper
1 tablespoon butter

Beat eggs slightly to combine yolks and whites, add liquid and seasoning. Melt butter in a hot 8- or 9-inch skillet over moderate heat, add eggs. As mixture cooks, draw edges to center to allow uncooked portion to run underneath. Omelet is done when it is just set. To brown the bottom, hold over heat briefly, shaking pan to prevent sticking. As soon as set and browned, tip the pan and fold one side of omelet; roll onto a hot platter and serve at once. Serves 2. Halve recipe to make individual omelet.

CHEESE OMELET

Follow directions for Creamy Omelet, adding ½ cup grated Cheddar cheese to the beaten egg. Sprinkle finished omelet with grated cheese. Serves 2.

OMELET WITH HERBS

Follow directions for Creamy Omelet, adding 1 generous tablespoon chopped fresh herbs—parsley, chives, tarragon or any desired combination. Serves 2.

ASPARAGUS OMELET

1 can (about 1 cup) asparagus, (or fresh-cooked)
1 cup Medium White Sauce, page 386
1 4-egg Creamy Omelet, above

Drain and dry asparagus. Combine with sauce, fill omelet. Pour remaining mixture over folded omelet on serving dish. Serves 4.

ASPARAGUS AND CHEESE OMELET

½ cup scallions, slivered
2 tablespoons butter
1 cup cooked or canned asparagus
4 eggs
⅓ cup milk
salt
⅓ cup grated cheese

Sauté scallions in butter until clear. Add asparagus, cut into 1-inch pieces, and heat thoroughly. Beat eggs, milk and salt. Add cheese. Pour over the asparagus and cook until the eggs are set. Serves 4.

CHICKEN OR SWEETBREAD OMELET

1 cup Medium White Sauce, page 386
1½ cups cooked chicken, diced or cooked sweetbreads, diced, or a mixture of the two
1 4-egg Creamy Omelet, above

Combine White Sauce and chicken or sweetbreads, or use a mixture of both. Use half the mixture to fill omelet, pour rest over the folded omelet on the serving platter. Serves 4.

GREEN BEAN AND EGG CASSEROLE

See page 413.

SOUFFLE OMELET
(FRENCH PUFFED OMELET)

3 eggs, separated
½ teaspoon salt
dash pepper
3 tablespoons hot water
1 tablespoon butter

Beat the yolks until thick; add salt, pepper, and water. Fold in whites, beaten stiff. Melt butter in an 8- or 9-inch skillet, add egg mixture. Cook over moderate heat without stirring until bottom sets. Test by lifting with a spatula. Transfer pan to the highest shelf of a moderate oven (350° F.) and bake until top is golden. Fill as desired and fold.

SPANISH OMELET

2 tablespoons butter
1 tablespoon onion, chopped
6 olives, chopped
½ green pepper, chopped fine
1¾ cups tomatoes
1 tablespoon sliced mushrooms
1 tablespoon capers
¼ teaspoon salt
few grains cayenne
Soufflé Omelet, above

Melt the butter in a skillet, add the onions, olives and green pepper and cook a few minutes, then add the tomatoes and cook until moisture has nearly evaporated. Add the rest of the ingredients. Prepare Soufflé Omelet. Before folding the omelet, place half of sauce on it, then fold and pour the rest of the sauce over and around. Serves 2.

ZUCCHINI OMELET

1 cup scallions, slivered
2 medium zucchini, sliced
2 tablespoons butter
1 medium tomato, chopped
1 clove crushed garlic
¼ teaspoon dill weed
salt and pepper to taste
4 eggs

Sauté scallions and zucchini in 2 tablespoons butter until zucchini slices are lightly browned on both sides. Add tomato and garlic and cook until most of the juice has cooked away. Add dill, salt and pepper. Beat eggs and pour over vegetables. Cook only until eggs are set. Serves 4.

OMELET WITH FLOUR

1 cup milk
2 tablespoons flour
½ teaspoon salt
3 eggs, beaten separately

Mix ¼ cup milk with the flour and salt until smooth, add the rest of the milk and the beaten yolks. Fold in whites, beaten dry. Pour into a hot buttered skillet and cook slowly on top of range 5 minutes. Place in a moderately slow oven, 325° F. and bake 20 minutes more until golden brown. Fold and serve on hot platter. Serves 2.

BREAD OMELET

2 tablespoons bread crumbs
2 tablespoons of milk
speck of salt
speck of pepper
1 egg, separated
½ teaspoon butter

Soak the bread crumbs in the milk for 15 minutes, then add the salt and pepper. Beat the yolk until light. Add the yolk to the bread and milk and fold in the beaten white. Pour in the heated buttered pan and cook until set. Fold. Serves 1.

EGGS WITH SMOKED BEEF, HAM
OR TONGUE

1 cup finely cut smoked beef, ham, or tongue
4 eggs, beaten light
1 tablespoon green pepper, chopped
salt, pepper
1 tablespoon shortening

Fold meat into eggs, add green pepper and seasonings. Heat shortening in an 8- or 9-inch skillet, add eggs and cook over low heat until bottom is brown. Turn to brown other side.

CHINESE PANCAKES (EGG FOO YUNG) (1)

1 cup cooked pork or chicken
1 cup bamboo shoots
¾ cup water chestnuts
6 eggs
1 tablespoon salt
½ cup oil

Cut meat in small strips, slice bamboo shoots fine and then into strips 2 inches long; peel chestnuts, slice fine and cut into strips 2 inches long. Place meat, bamboo shoots and water chestnuts, squeezed dry, in mixing bowl. Add eggs and beat all together lightly. Heat large iron skillet, add salt and then oil, and heat. Drop egg mixture into hot oil from tablespoon, to make individual pancakes. Brown on both sides and remove to a hot platter to keep warm.

SAUCE

1 tablespoon cornstarch
2 teaspoons cold water
1 cup hot soup stock
1 tablespoon soy sauce

Dissolve cornstarch in cold water. Add soup stock and soy sauce, and cook until clear and thickened. Pour hot sauce over pancakes, and serve.

EGG FOO YUNG (2)

6 eggs
1 teaspoon salt
2 cups bean sprouts
½ cup chopped onion
2 tablespoons chopped green pepper
oil for frying

Beat eggs well. Add remaining ingredients. Drop egg mixture from tablespoon into hot oil in skillet. Fry on both sides.

ALMOND DESSERT OMELET

½ cup almonds
4 eggs
4 tablespoons cream
pinch salt
1 tablespoon butter

Blanch, chop and pound almonds until smooth. Beat eggs slightly, add cream and salt. Melt butter in skillet; pour in the egg mixture. Cook gently until nearly set. Sprinkle with almonds and roll. Serve at once on hot platter; sprinkle with confectioners sugar and additional chopped nuts.

PROCESS CHEESES

PROCESS CHEESES are pasteurized, which means that the natural cheeses have been heated to halt ripening. Some pasteurized process cheeses are a blend of cheeses, sometimes with seasonings added. They melt easily, and are often used in cooking for this reason.

PROCESS CHEESE FOODS are made by adding non-fat dry milk or whey solids and water to process cheese.

PROCESS CHEESE SPREADS have more liquid added, for increased spreadability.

COLDPACK OR CLUB CHEESES are not pasteurized, but are blended into a uniform product and packed in rolls or links.

COLDPACK CHEESE FOODS are made by adding dairy solids and water to coldpack cheese, and are oftened sweetened and flavored as well. They are soft and spread easily.

NATURAL CHEESES

UNRIPENED SOFT CHEESES such as cottage cheese and cream cheese are very perishable and should be kept in the refrigerator and used within a few days.

RIPE CHEESES of all kinds keep well in the refrigerator, wrapped in foil or plastic over the original wrappings, if possible. However, these continue to ripen, even in the refrigerator, and should be used before they become too strong. The mold that sometimes forms on ripe cheese is not harmful, and can be scraped off.

HARD CHEESES such as Parmesan and Romano are best when freshly grated, but they can be grated in advance and stored in the refrigerator, in a tightly covered jar, until wanted for garnishing or flavoring cooked dishes. Dry ends of other cheeses, such as Swiss and Cheddar, may be grated (by hand or in an electric blender) and used the same way.

HOME-MADE COTTAGE CHEESE

Heat sour milk or buttermilk slowly until the whey rises to the top; pour off whey, put curd in a bag, and let drip 6 hours without squeezing it. Place curd in a bowl, and break it fine. Season with salt. Refrigerate. It is best when fresh.

BOILED CHEESE (KOCH KAESE)

1 quart cottage cheese
1 teaspoon salt
1 teaspoon caraway seeds
1 tablespoon butter
1½ cups water
1 egg yolk, beaten

Press cottage cheese until dry, add salt and caraway to taste. Put in earthen dish, cover well, set in a warm place. Stir with a fork every day for a week or until ripe and clear. Place butter and water in a skillet; when warm, add cheese and boil slowly 20 minutes, stirring constantly. Remove from heat, add egg yolk and beat until glossy. Pour into bowl or cups rinsed with cold water. Refrigerate. Serve when cold.

See Index for suggested uses for cottage cheese. It is an excellent source of protein, low in cost and in calories.

CHEESE

DESCRIPTIVE CHART OF NATURAL CHEESES
[*Courtesy of U.S. Government, Department of Agriculture*]

Soft, Unripened Varieties

KIND OR NAME	FLAVOR	BODY AND TEXTURE	COLOR	USES
Cottage, plain or creamed	Mild, acid.	Soft, curd particles of varying size.	White to creamy white.	Salads, with fruits, vegetables, sandwiches, dips, cheese cake.
Cream, plain	Mild, acid.	Soft and smooth.	White.	Salads, dips, sandwiches, snacks, cheese cake, desserts.
Neufchatel	Mild, acid.	Soft, smooth, similar to cream cheese but lower in milkfat.	White.	Salads, dips, sandwiches, snacks, cheese cake, desserts.
Ricotta	Sweet, nut-like.	Soft, moist or dry.	White.	Appetizers, salads, snacks, lasagne, ravioli, noodles and other cooked dishes, grating, desserts.

Firm, Unripened Varieties

KIND OR NAME	FLAVOR	BODY AND TEXTURE	COLOR	USES
Gjetost	Sweetish, caramel.	Firm, buttery consistency.	Golden brown.	Snacks, desserts, served with dark breads, crackers, biscuits or muffins.
Mysost (also called Primost)	Sweetish, caramel.	Firm, buttery consistency.	Light brown.	Snacks, desserts, served with dark breads.
Mozzarella (also called Scamorza)	Delicate, mild.	Slightly firm, plastic.	Creamy white.	Snacks, toasted sandwiches, cheeseburgers; for cooking, as in meat loaf, or topping for lasagne, pizza, and casseroles.

Soft, Ripened Varieties

KIND OR NAME	FLAVOR	BODY AND TEXTURE	COLOR	USES
Brie	Mild to pungent.	Soft, smooth when ripened.	Creamy yellow interior; edible thin brown and white crust.	Appetizers, sandwiches, snacks, good with crackers and fruit, dessert.
Camembert	Mild to pungent.	Soft, smooth; very soft when fully ripened.	Creamy yellow interior; edible thin white, or gray-white crust.	Appetizers, sandwiches, snacks, good with crackers, and fruit such as pears and apples, dessert.
Limburger	Highly pungent, very strong.	Soft, smooth when ripened; usually contains small irregular openings.	Creamy white interior; reddish yellow surface.	Appetizers, snacks, good with crackers, rye or other dark breads, dessert.

Semisoft, Ripened Varieties

KIND OR NAME	FLAVOR	BODY AND TEXTURE	COLOR	USES
Bel Paese	Mild to moderately robust.	Soft to medium firm, creamy.	Creamy yellow interior; slightly gray or brownish surface sometimes covered with yellow wax coating.	Appetizers, good with crackers, snacks, sandwiches, dessert.
Brick	Mild to moderately sharp.	Semisoft to medium firm, elastic, numerous small mechanical openings.	Creamy yellow.	Appetizers, sandwiches, snacks, dessert.
Muenster	Mild to mellow.	Semisoft, numerous small mechanical openings. Contains more moisture than brick.	Creamy white interior; yellow tan surface.	Appetizers, sandwiches, snacks, dessert.
Port du Salut	Mellow to robust.	Semisoft, smooth, buttery, small openings.	Creamy yellow.	Appetizers, snacks, served with raw fruit, dessert.

Firm, Ripened Varieties

KIND OR NAME	FLAVOR	BODY AND TEXTURE	COLOR	USES
Cheddar	Mild to very sharp.	Firm, smooth, some mechanical openings.	White to medium-yellow-orange.	Appetizers, sandwiches, sauces, on vegetables, for hot dishes, toasted sandwiches, grating, cheeseburgers, dessert.
Colby	Mild to mellow.	Softer and more open than Cheddar.	White to medium-yellow-orange.	Sandwiches, snacks, cheeseburgers.
Caciocavallo	Piquant, similar to Provolone but not smoked.	Firm, lower in milkfat and moisture than Provolone.	Light or white interior; clay or tan-colored surface.	Snacks, sandwiches, cooking, dessert; suitable for grating after prolonged curing.
Edam	Mellow, nut-like.	Semisoft to firm, smooth; small irregularly shaped or round holes; lower milkfat than Gouda.	Creamy yellow or medium yellow-orange interior; surface coated with red wax.	Appetizers, snacks, salads, sandwiches, seafood sauces, dessert.
Gouda	Mellow, nut-like.	Semisoft to firm, smooth; small irregularly shaped or round holes; higher milk fat than Edam.	Creamy yellow or medium yellow-orange interior; may or may not have red wax coating.	Appetizers, snacks, salads, sandwiches, seafood sauces, dessert.
Provolone	Mellow to sharp, smoky, salty.	Firm, smooth.	Light creamy interior; light brown or golden yellow surface.	Appetizers, sandwiches, snacks, soufflé, macaroni and spaghetti dishes, pizza, suitable for grating when fully cured and dried.
Swiss (also called Emmentaler)	Sweet, nut-like.	Firm, smooth with large round eyes.	Light yellow.	Sandwiches, snacks, sauces, fondue, cheeseburgers.

Very Hard, Ripened Varieties

KIND OR NAME	FLAVOR	BODY AND TEXTURE	COLOR	USES
Parmesan (also called Reggiano)	Sharp, piquant.	Very hard, granular, lower moisture and milkfat than Romano.	Creamy white.	Grated for seasoning in soups, or vegetables, spaghetti, ravioli, breads, popcorn; used extensively in pizza and lasagne.
Romano (also called Sardo Romano, Pecorino Romano)	Sharp, piquant.	Very hard granular.	Yellowish-white interior, greenish-black surface.	Seasoning in soups, casserole dishes, ravioli, sauces, breads, suitable for grating when cured for about one year.
Sap Sago	Sharp, pungent cloverlike.	Very hard.	Light green by addition of dried, powdered clover leaves.	Grated to flavor soups, meats, macaroni, spaghetti, hot vegetables; mixed with butter makes a good spread on crackers or bread.

Blue-Vein Mold-Ripened Varieties

KIND OR NAME	FLAVOR	BODY AND TEXTURE	COLOR	USES
Blue (spelled Bleu on imported cheese)	Tangy, peppery.	Semisoft, pasty, sometimes crumbly.	White interior, marbled or streaked with blue veins of mold.	Appetizers, salads, dips, salad dressing, sandwich spreads, good with crackers, dessert.
Gorgonzola	Tangy, peppery.	Semisoft, pasty, sometimes crumbly, lower moisture than Blue.	Creamy white interior, mottled or streaked with blue-green veins of mold. Clay-colored surface.	Appetizers, snacks, salads, dips, sandwich spread, good with crackers, dessert.
Roquefort	Sharp, slightly peppery.	Semisoft, pasty, sometimes crumbly.	White or creamy white interior, marbled or streaked with blue veins of mold.	Appetizers, snacks, salads, dips, sandwich spreads, good with crackers, dessert.
Stilton	Piquant, milder than Gorgonzola or Roquefort.	Semisoft, flaky; slightly more crumbly than Blue.	Creamy white interior, marbled or streaked with blue-green veins of mold.	Appetizers, snacks, salads, dessert.

QUICK BOILED CHEESE

4 ripe hand cheeses
2 tablespoons butter
1 cup milk
½ teaspoon caraway seed

Cut cheese and place in pan; add rest of the ingredients, place over low heat and bring to a boil. Pour into cups or bowl rinsed with cold water. Refrigerate. Serve when cold.

BOILED CHEESE WITH BAKING SODA

½ pound cottage cheese
1 tablespoon butter, softened
⅓ teaspoon salt
pinch of cayenne pepper
½ teaspoon caraway seed
1 egg
½ cup cream or milk
¼ teaspoon baking soda

Place cheese, butter and seasoning in saucepan. Add ½ teaspoon mustard, if desired. Stir in egg and then the cream or milk. Heat over low heat, add baking soda, bring to boil, stirring constantly until smooth. Pour into cups. Refrigerate. Serve when firm and cold.

CREAMED SEASONED COTTAGE CHEESE

1 pound cottage cheese
¾ teaspoon salt
2 tablespoons melted butter
2 tablespoons cream, sweet or sour
⅛ teaspoon paprika

If cheese is moist, press dry through cotton bag. If small curd is desired, rice through colander. Mix with other ingredients. If desired, add 1 teaspoon each grated onion, finely cut chives and caraway seed. Or serve with jelly or jam.

Or mix with ½ pint of sour or whipped cream and beat until very light.

HOT CHEESE DISHES

BAKED CHEESE FONDUE

2 cups soft bread crumbs
1 cup milk
¾ cup grated cheese
4 tablespoons butter
1 teaspoon salt
4 eggs, separated

Heat first 5 ingredients in double boiler until cheese is melted. Remove from heat and cool slightly. Add beaten yolks. Fold in beaten whites. Pour into buttered baking dish. Bake in moderate oven, 350° F., about 30 minutes, or until firm. Serve from baking dish.

SWISS FONDUE

clove garlic
2 cups white wine
1 pound cubed Swiss cheese
1 tablespoon flour
salt, pepper, nutmeg
2 tablespoons kirsch
1 loaf French bread

Rub heatproof casserole with garlic. Set on rack of chafing dish, over low heat, add wine, heat till first bubbles rise. Toss cheese with flour. Add cheese gradually, stir until melted. Repeat until all cheese is added and mixture is smooth. Add seasoning to taste. Add kirsch. Break or cut French bread into bite-sized chunks, each with a bit of crust. Each guest spears a bit of bread with a long-handled fork and dips into the fondue.

CHEESE SANDWICH CASSEROLE (1)

8 slices 2- to 3-day-old bread
2 cups grated Cheddar cheese
4 teaspoons butter
3 eggs
¾ cup instant nonfat dry milk
1¼ cups water
½ teaspoon Worcestershire sauce
¼ teaspoon salt
¼ teaspoon dry mustard
4 slices tomato

Cut crusts from bread. Butter 8-inch square baking dish; place 4 slices of bread in bottom and cover with 1 cup of cheese. Top with other four slices of bread; spread each slice with 1 teaspoon butter. Top with remaining cup of cheese.

Mix remaining ingredients, except the tomato, and beat well until very light and fluffy. Pour this mixture over cheese sandwiches. Let stand 15 minutes. Bake 40 minutes in 350° oven. Top each sandwich with a slice of tomato and bake 10 minutes longer. Serves 4.

Mixture can be placed in the refrigerator for several hours before baking. In this case, be sure to use a baking dish which can be placed directly in the oven from the refrigerator.

CHEESE AND BACON SANDWICH CASSEROLE

Follow directions for Cheese Sandwich Casserole but add 4 slices of bacon, cooked and crumbled, to each cheese layer.

CHEESE AND TUNA SANDWICH CASSEROLE

Follow directions for Cheese Sandwich Casserole but add ½ cup drained and flaked tuna to each cheese layer.

CHEESE SANDWICH CASSEROLE (2)

8 slices 2- to 3-day-old bread
6 tablespoons butter
¼ teaspoon garlic powder
½ pound sharp Cheddar cheese, grated
4 eggs
2 bouillon cubes
1½ cups water
½ cup white wine
½ teaspoon nutmeg (optional)

Cut bread slices in half. Combine butter and garlic. Spread butter on bread. Place layer of bread in greased 2-quart baking dish; sprinkle with half the cheese. Repeat with layer of bread and layer of cheese. Mix remaining ingredients and pour over bread and cheese. Refrigerate for 6 to 8 hours or overnight. Bake at 325° F. for 50 to 60 minutes. Let stand about 10 minutes before serving. Serves 4.

FRENCH CHEESE SOUFFLE

4 tablespoons butter
4 tablespoons flour
1 teaspoon salt
paprika
cayenne or Tabasco
1 cup milk
1 cup finely grated aged Cheddar cheese
4 eggs, separated

Melt butter in double boiler. Add flour and seasonings and blend well. Add milk and cook until thick. Add cheese and stir until melted. Cool and add egg yolks, well beaten. Fold gently into stiffly beaten egg whites. Pour mixture into a very well-greased 1½-quart casserole. Bake in a very hot oven, 475° F., for 10 minutes, then reduce heat to 400° F. and bake about 25 minutes longer. Serve at once.

CHEESE SOUFFLE

2 tablespoons butter
2 tablespoons flour
2 cups milk, scalded
½ teaspoon salt
¾ cup grated cheese
4 eggs, separated

Stir butter and flour in pan over very low heat. When mixture bubbles, add hot milk gradually. Season. Add cheese and cook until cheese melts, stirring constantly. Cool. When lukewarm, add beaten yolks, then fold in stiffly beaten whites. Pour into a buttered 2-quart baking dish. Set baking dish in a pan of hot water and bake in a moderate oven, 350° F., for 1 hour, or until soufflé is puffed and browned. Serve immediately.

CHEESE, LEEK AND HAM PIE

1 package (1⅞ ounce) dry cream of leek soup
2 cups milk
1 cup light cream
4 eggs
2½ cups grated Swiss cheese (½ pound)
1 teaspoon dry mustard
1 teaspoon salt
¼ teaspoon pepper
2 4½-ounce cans deviled ham
3 tablespoons dry bread crumbs
10-inch unbaked pie shell, page 341

Preheat oven to 375° F. Heat soup and milk over medium heat. Remove from heat, let cool slightly; stir in cream. Cool in refrigerator for about 20 minutes. Beat eggs into soup mixture. Add cheese, mustard, and seasonings. Mix ham and bread crumbs; sprinkle over bottom of pie shell. Pour in the filling. Bake for 50 minutes or until a knife inserted near the center of the pie comes out clean. Serve hot.

SWISS CHEESE PIE (QUICHE LORRAINE)

¼ pound bacon
1 large onion, diced
2 tablespoons butter
1 cup grated Swiss cheese
9-inch unbaked pie shell, page 341
4 eggs
¼ teaspoon salt
¼ teaspoon nutmeg
dash of cayenne pepper
2 cups milk

Fry bacon until crisp. Drain well and crumble. Sauté onion in butter. Sprinkle cheese over bottom of pie shell, place bacon and onions over this. Beat eggs and seasoning; add milk and mix well. Pour mixture into pie shell. Bake at 425° F. for 15 minutes; reduce heat to 300° F. and bake for 35 to 40 minutes longer. May be used as a luncheon dish or appetizer.

SWISS CHEESE TARTS

Line small muffin tins with pastry and proceed as for Swiss Cheese Pie, above. Cut baking time according to the size of the tins.

CHEESE AND BEEF QUICHE

½ pound ground beef
1 tablespoon vegetable oil
3 eggs
1½ cups milk
½ teaspoon salt
dash of pepper
½ cup green onions, sliced
1½ cups Cheddar or Swiss cheese, grated or diced
9-inch unbaked pie shell, page 341

Brown beef in skillet. Beat eggs lightly, add milk, salt and pepper. Mix well. Then add onions, cheese and beef. Place in pie shell. Bake at 375° F. for 35 to 40 minutes or until knife inserted in center comes out clean.

TOMATO-CHEESE PIE

3 or 4 firm tomatoes
½ teaspoon salt
1 cup shredded Cheddar cheese
2 tablespoons grated Parmesan cheese
9-inch unbaked pie shell, page 341
4 eggs
1½ cups milk
¼ teaspoon pepper
2 teaspoons minced onion
dash of cayenne pepper

Preheat oven to 350° F. Peel and core the tomatoes. Sprinkle with salt and let them stand for about 15 minutes. Drain. Sprinkle cheeses on bottom of pie shell. Cover with the tomatoes, sliced. Beat eggs with remaining ingredients. Pour over filling. Bake for 1 hour or until a knife inserted in the center comes out clean.

WELSH RAREBIT

1 tablespoon butter
½ pound Cheddar cheese
⅛ teaspoon salt
⅛ teaspoon mustard
speck of cayenne pepper
1 egg
¼ cup milk

Melt the butter in double boiler or chafing dish. Break the cheese into small pieces, and add with seasoning. When the cheese melts, add the egg, beaten with the milk, and stir until thick. Serve at once on toast or wafers.

BEER RAREBIT

1 pound Cheddar cheese
1 tablespoon melted butter
¼ teaspoon salt
¼ teaspoon paprika
½ teaspoon dry mustard
½ cup beer
1 teaspoon Worcestershire sauce

Place cheese, cut in small pieces, over hot water in double boiler or chafing dish with butter and seasoning. As cheese melts, add beer very gradually. Stir constantly until smooth. Add Worcestershire. Serve on toast or crackers.

CHEESE AND TOMATO RAREBIT

½ cup soft bread crumbs
½ pound grated Cheddar cheese
1 cup strained tomatoes
¼ teaspoon salt
⅛ teaspoon pepper

Place all ingredients in the top of a double boiler and cook over water until smooth, stirring constantly. Serve at once on hot toasted bread.

ENGLISH MONKEY

1 cup dry bread crumbs
1 cup milk
1 tablespoon butter
½ cup soft, mild cheese cut in small pieces
1 egg
½ teaspoon salt
few grains cayenne

Soak bread crumbs in milk 15 minutes. Melt the butter over water, add the cheese and when melted, add crumbs, egg slightly beaten and seasonings. Cook 3 minutes and serve on toasted crackers.

MOCK CRAB ON TOAST

2 tablespoons butter
½ pound Swiss cheese
1 tablespoon anchovy paste
½ teaspoon salt
½ teaspoon dry mustard
few grains cayenne pepper
½ cup light cream
2 egg yolks

Melt butter in double boiler, add cheese, anchovy paste and seasoning. Stir the yolks into the cream and add to the mixture, stirring constantly; when smooth, serve on toast.

RINKTUM-DITY

1 can tomatoes
1 cup grated Cheddar cheese
½ small grated onion
1 green pepper, chopped
1 teaspoon salt
2 tablespoons butter
2 eggs

Mix tomatoes, cheese, onion, pepper and salt. Melt the butter in double boiler, add the mixture, and when heated, add the eggs, well beaten. Cook until creamy, stirring constantly. Serve on toast.

HOT CHEESE ON TOAST

Grate cheese, moisten with cream, season with salt and cayenne pepper. Spread buttered bread or crackers with the mixture and place in the oven. Serve when cheese is melted.

12
FISH AND SEAFOOD

FISH

FRESH · CANNED · SALTED, PICKLED AND SMOKED

Fish is least expensive and most appealing when it is freshly caught, in season; but a wide variety of fish and seafood, deep-frozen soon after it is caught and packed for the frozen food cases, is always available nowadays. Because of its comparatively low cost, its high food value, generally low-calorie count and wide variety, fish should be served often. Fresh fish can be identified by its firm flesh, bright eyes, and red gills. Fish should be cleaned quickly, stored, covered, in the refrigerator, and used as soon as possible for best flavor.

PREPARING FISH FOR COOKING
In most cases, fish that is purchased will be ready to use, cleaned and scaled, skinned, boned or filleted. The fish man will be glad to prepare your choice of fresh fish for the cooking method you plan to use.

Fish Fillets are completely free from bones and skin; frozen fish comes in this form, and fresh fish markets always have fillets of such fish as flounder, haddock, and sole ready for sale.

To use commercially frozen fish, follow directions on the package; many of these products can be cooked in the frozen state, without thawing. To thaw home-frozen fish, let stand overnight in the refrigerator; then dry and cook at once. When the family fisherman brings home a catch of fresh fish, and the preparation must be done at home, follow this procedure:

TO SCALE AND CLEAN FISH
Lay fish on heavy paper. Use fishscaler, ordinary grater or knife. Hold the fish by the tail. Scrape

from tail end to head, slanting knife toward you to prevent scales from flying. Remove gills, cut through the skin of the abdomen; take out entrails. Wash thoroughly in cold water.

TO SKIN A FISH
Lay the fish flat and with a small sharp knife cut through the skin close to the fins down both sides of the back. Pull out the fins, and, if desired, cut off head. Loosen flesh close to skin on one side and strip off toward tail. Turn and skin the other side. Cut open, remove entrails.

TO REMOVE FISH SKIN, WHOLE
Scale fish if skin is to be used. Bend head backward and, beginning at the base of the head, separate flesh from skin with small sharp knife, working toward the tail. With care, skin may be pulled off like a glove, in one piece with the head attached. It can then be stuffed to restore its original shape, for Stuffed Fish, page 242.

TO BONE A FISH
Scale and clean the fish. Beginning just below the head, cut along the spine as close to the backbone as possible down to the tail. Push the flesh on that side away from the backbone with the back of the knife. Separate the backbone in the same manner from the remaining half of the fish. Pick out small bones remaining in the fish.
OR:
After gutting and washing the fish, cut close to fins on both sides of fish, pull out fins. On both sides of backbone make an incision from head to

tail. Separate flesh from backbone with back of knife. Remove backbone and bones attached to it. Pick out remaining bones carefully.

Fresh Fish and Seafood in Season

AVAILABLE ALL YEAR ROUND

Bluefish	Mackerel	Whitefish
Butterfish	Perch	Whiting
Cod	Red Snapper	Crabmeat
Flounder	Salmon	Lobster
Haddock	Sole	Scallops
Halibut	Swordfish	Shrimp
	Trout	

JUNE 1 TO DECEMBER 1

Bullheads
Catfish
Pickerel
Walleyed Pike

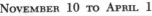

APRIL 1 TO JUNE 1

Shad

NOVEMBER 10 TO APRIL 1

Smelts

SEPTEMBER 1 TO MAY 1

Oysters

JUNE 1 TO AUGUST 1

Soft Shell Crabs

Fish Suitable for Boiling or Poaching

Cod	Muskellunge	Sole
Carp	Pickerel	Sea Bass
Halibut	Pike	Tilefish
Haddock	Pompano	Trout
Herring, fresh	Red Snapper	Weakfish
Mackerel, fresh	Salmon	Whitefish
Mackerel, salt	Sheepshead	

POACHING

Poaching is simmering fish in a liquid.

. . . Use a shallow fry pan, wide enough to hold fish without overlapping.

. . . Barely cover the fish with a liquid such as water seasoned with salt, herbs or spices, milk, or a mixture of either with wine.

. . . Put a lid on the pan and simmer the fish 5 to 10 minutes until just done.

. . . Serve poached fish as a main course or use it in casseroles or chilled and flaked in cold dishes.

BOILED OR POACHED FISH

3 pounds fish, cut in slices and sprinkled with salt
1 quart water
2 tablespoons vinegar
¼ teaspoon whole pepper
1 tablespoon onion, cut fine
1 tablespoon celery, cut fine
1 tablespoon carrot, cut fine

Clean and salt fish. Boil water, vinegar, pepper and vegetables for 5 minutes. Add the fish, a few slices at a time, and simmer just until the flesh is opaque and easily flakes and leaves the bones. Remove bones. Place fish on platter. Strain and reserve the fish stock, for sauce.

Boned fish fillets or whole fish, unboned, may be cooked in this manner. To remove a whole fish from the pan without breaking, wrap the fish in cheese cloth before cooking.

POACHED FISH FILLETS WITH CHEESE SAUCE

1½ cups milk
3 tablespoons sherry
½ teaspoon Worcestershire sauce
1 teaspoon salt
dash pepper
1½ pounds fish fillets
1½ tablespoons flour
5 ounces sharp Cheddar cheese, grated

Mix 1¼ cups of milk with the sherry, Worcestershire, salt and pepper in a skillet, and heat over low heat until it simmers. Add fish fillets, cover and poach until done. With a slotted spatula, carefully remove fish to a serving platter. Cover to keep warm. Combine ¼ cup milk and flour. Add to simmering liquid in pan and stir well with wire whisk. Add grated cheese and stir until cheese is melted and sauce is thick. Pour over fillets, sprinkle with paprika.

PICKLED FISH

5 pounds fish (salmon, whitefish, pike, or other suitable fish)
2 cups vinegar
2 cups water
salt to taste
20 peppercorns
18 allspice
5 bay leaves, broken up
5 sliced onions
4 slices lemon

Boil vinegar and water ½ hour with salt, pepper, allspice, bay leaves and 4 slices of onion. Add lemon slices, cook 5 minutes, then remove them. Simmer the fish in this liquid until you can pull out a fin. Cook only a few small fish or 2-inch slices of fish at one time. Pack fish into a half-gallon stone crock with one or more raw sliced onions between layers. Add the hot liquid with seasonings. Cover and refrigerate. In a few days the liquid will form a jelly around the fish. Will keep several weeks.

Sauces for Boiled or Poached Fish

Brown Sauce	Lemon Sauce
Cream Sauce	Parsley Sauce
Egg Sauce	Sharfe Sauce
Gingersnap Sauce	Sweet and Sour Sauce
Hollandaise Sauce	Tomato Sauce

Sauces will be found in chapter 20.

Fish Suitable for Broiling

Black Bass	Halibut steaks	Shad Roe
Bluefish	Mackerel, fresh	Sturgeon steaks
Bloater	Pike	Swordfish
Carp	Pompano	Tilefish
Cod	Porgy	Trout
steaks	Salmon steaks	Whitefish, fillet or
Flounder	Sea Bass steaks	steaks
Hake	Shad, whole or fillet	Whiting

BROILED FISH

Sprinkle fish with salt and pepper, spread with a little butter. Sprinkle skin side with flour. Place on well-greased broiler rack, flesh-side up, about 4 inches from the heat. Broil until flesh is firm, and delicately browned, basting occasionally. Whole fish and fish steaks should be turned and browned on both sides. Serve on hot platter. Spread with Parsley Butter, and garnish with parsley· and lemon slices.

Fish Suitable for Frying

Black Bass, sliced or fillet	Pickerel, steaks or fillet
Brook Trout	Pollock
Bullhead	Pompano, fillet
Butterfish	Porgy
Carp steaks	Red Snapper
Catfish	Salmon steaks
Cod steaks	Shad Roe
Flounder, fillet	Smelts
Haddock	Sole, fillet
Halibut	Swordfish
Herring	Trout
Pike steak or fillet	Whitefish, steaks or fillet
Perch	Whiting

FRIED FISH

PAN FRIED
Clean fish, sprinkle with salt and pepper, dip in flour, bread crumbs, or corn meal, and cook in skillet in ¼ inch hot fat. Shake the pan occasionally to prevent sticking. Brown both sides well.

DEEP FAT FRIED
Clean fish, wipe dry as possible, salt and pepper, dip in flour, crumbs, or corn meal, then in egg and again in crumbs. Let stand a few moments. Fry fillets golden brown in deep hot fat, 375° F., for 2-3 minutes. When a cube of white bread browns in 30 seconds, the fat is ready for frying small fish or fillets. Larger fish should be fried at 350° F., when bread cubes will brown in 35 seconds. Serve fried fish with Tartar Sauce or Hollandaise Sauce, or with melted butter and lemon juice, or with lemon wedges.

Fish Suitable for Baking

Black Bass	Mackerel, fresh	Shad
Bluefish	Mullet	Sole
Carp	Perch	Sturgeon
Cod	Pickerel	Swordfish
Flounder	Pike	Trout
Haddock	Red Snapper	Weakfish
Hake	Salmon, fresh	Whitefish
Halibut	Sea Bass	

BAKED WHOLE FISH

Fish should be scaled and cleaned, but skin and bones should not be removed. Sprinkle whole fish with salt and pepper. Fill with stuffing, below, and sew or skewer opening together. Brush with melted butter. Bake in greased pan in a moderate oven, 350° F., just until flesh separates easily from bone, allowing 12 to 15 minutes for each pound of fish. Baste every 10 minutes with butter and pan drippings. Serve with parsley and lemon slices.

STUFFING FOR BAKED FISH

½ cup bread crumbs
1 egg, lightly beaten
¼ cup melted butter
1 teaspoon chopped parsley
1 teaspoon chopped onion
1 teaspoon salt

Combine ingredients, and mix well. For moist stuffing use soft bread crumbs.

Fish Suitable for Planking

Bluefish	Striped Bass
Halibut steaks	Swordfish
Salmon	Trout
Shad	Whitefish

PLANKED FISH

Bone fish, page 234. Broil 5 minutes. Lay skin side down on a heated, well-oiled plank (hickory, oak or ash). Sprinkle with salt and paprika, brush with melted butter. Bake in hot oven 400° F., until fish is well browned, then reduce the heat to 325° F. Bake about 20 minutes. Arrange mashed potatoes, forced through pastry bag, around the edges; bake until potatoes are browned and fish flakes easily with a fork, about five minutes more. Add melted butter and sprinkle with minced parsley. Place plank on platter and serve.

HADDOCK FILLET

Cut the fish in serving portions, season with salt and pepper. Pour 2 cups of hot milk over fish, simmer until fish is opaque and flakes easily. Serve with melted butter and lemon juice, or any well-flavored fish sauce. Or broil or fry like other fish. May be dipped in French Dressing before cooking.

BROILED HALIBUT STEAK

Marinate 1-inch steaks in salad oil and lemon juice for ½ hour. Wipe dry and broil until flesh is white and firm, turning carefully when first side begins to brown. Before serving, spread with Parsley Butter.

BAKED HALIBUT STEAK

Marinate 3 pounds halibut steaks in juice of 2 lemons for 2 hours. Place strips of salt pork, 2 bay leaves, ½ teaspoon whole pepper and allspice and 2 or 3 cloves in pan. Lay the fish steaks over these. Sprinkle with salt, pepper, and 2 tablespoons melted butter. Bake about 20 minutes in a hot oven, 400° F., until flesh flakes easily. Serve with Tomato Sauce.

BAKED HALIBUT IN TOMATO SAUCE

1½ pounds halibut
1 cup Medium White Sauce, page 386
1 can (1 pound) tomatoes, sieved
salt, pepper
½ cup cracker crumbs
2 tablespoons butter, melted
½ cup grated cheese

Poach the fish, discard skin and bones, and flake fish into small pieces. Make White Sauce, add tomatoes and cook until smooth. Place fish in buttered ramekins in pan of hot water or in a baking dish; cover with the sauce, add salt, pepper, and cracker crumbs mixed with the butter; sprinkle with cheese. Bake 20 minutes in moderate oven, 350° F., until brown.

BAKED HALIBUT WITH CHEESE

2 pounds halibut
2 tablespoons lemon juice
4 tablespoons butter
4 tablespoons flour
2 cups hot milk
salt and pepper
¾ cup grated Cheddar cheese
3 tablespoons grated Parmesan cheese

Broil halibut steaks about 15 minutes, remove skin and bones, break into rather large pieces or leave whole and place in a buttered baking dish. Sprinkle with lemon juice. Melt butter in saucepan over low heat. Stir in flour. Gradually add milk and cook, stirring constantly, until thickened. Season with salt and pepper. Pour sauce over fish, cover with grated cheeses, and bake uncovered in moderate oven (350° F.) 20 minutes. Sprinkle with riced hard-cooked eggs before serving, if desired.

HALIBUT TIMBALES

½ pound halibut fillets
1 cup bread crumbs
½ cup milk
1 teaspoon salt
a dash of white pepper
5 egg whites

Grind raw fish. Heat bread crumbs with milk, stir to a smooth paste. Remove from heat, add the fish, salt and pepper; fold in stiffly beaten whites. Fill well-buttered individual molds, set in a pan of hot water in the oven, and bake at 350° F. for 20 minutes, until timbales are set and firm to the touch. Serve with Tartar Sauce, or Hollandaise Sauce.

HALIBUT AND SHRIMP NEWBURG

1½ pounds halibut
2 slices onion
2 cups Medium White Sauce, page 386
3 eggs, separated
½ teaspoon paprika
¼ cup sherry
1½ pounds shrimp, boiled

Cook halibut with onion in salted, boiling water until it flakes readily. Drain and shred. To 1 cup of the hot Medium White Sauce add the stiffly beaten whites, paprika and the shredded fish. Place in center of hot platter and keep warm. Add the wine to remaining White Sauce and pour gradually into the yolks, beaten with a little cold water. Add the shrimp, heat well, place around the halibut and serve at once.

HALIBUT SOUFFLE RING

1½ pounds halibut
salt
cayenne pepper
5 egg whites
1 cup heavy cream, whipped

Bone raw halibut, chop fine, add salt, cayenne. Fold in the stiffly beaten whites and the whipped cream. Pack in a greased mold and steam on a rack over hot water in a covered kettle 30 minutes; unmold. Serve garnished with Lobster Newburg.

HALIBUT SHRIMP RING

2 pounds halibut
3 tablespoons butter
2 tablespoons flour
½ cup cream or milk
1 teaspoon salt
4 eggs, separated
2 cups heavy cream, whipped
1 tablespoon chopped pimiento
1 pound shrimp
Hollandaise Sauce, page 388

Poach halibut, page 235. Remove skin and bones. Mince fish. Melt butter, add flour; when it bubbles, add ½ cup cream, stir until smooth, add salt and stir gradually into the well-beaten yolks. Stir in the minced fish. Cool, fold in stiffly beaten egg whites and whipped cream. Put in a well-greased ring mold dotted with bits of pimiento, and bake in a moderate oven, 350° F., in a pan of boiling water about ½ hour, or until well set. Unmold onto serving plater. Fill center with hot boiled shrimp in Hollandaise Sauce.

OVEN-FRIED PERCH FILLETS WITH TARTAR SAUCE

½ cup wheat germ
1 cup toasted bread crumbs (preferably whole wheat crumbs)
2 pounds ocean perch fillets
1 cup milk
4 tablespoons margarine or butter, melted
salt, pepper

Mix wheat germ and bread crumbs on piece of waxed paper. Dip fillets in milk, then press into crumb mixture. Place on flat pan, skin side down. Drip margarine or butter over top and sprinkle with salt and pepper. Bake at 500° F. for 10 minutes. Serve with Tartar Sauce, page 392.

Other sauces for fish will be found in chapter 20.

POACHED PIKE VELOUTE (SCHARFE PIKE)

3 pounds fillet of pike
1 cup hot fish stock
1 tablespoon butter
1 tablespoon flour
1 egg yolk

Clean and salt the fish and cook, following recipe for Boiled Fish. Reserve 1 cup of the fish stock. Melt the butter, add the flour and the hot fish stock. Remove from heat and pour very gradually into the beaten yolk. Pour while hot over the poached fish. Garnish with parsley. Any white-fleshed, freshwater fish may be prepared this way.

COLD PIKE WITH LEMON SAUCE (SCHARFE PIKE)

3 pounds pike
2 to 4 tablespoons sugar
1 lemon, juice and rind
2 egg yolks
1 cup hot fish stock
salt to taste
1 teaspoon chopped parsley

Poach pike, following recipe for Boiled Fish. Discard skin and bones and arrange fish on platter. Mix sugar, lemon juice and grated rind with well-beaten yolks and gradually add to it the strained fish stock. Cook until thick, stirring constantly. Add salt and parsley and pour over the fish. Serve cold. The sauce may be further thickened with 1 tablespoon cornstarch mixed with 2 tablespoons cold water.

SWEET AND SOUR FISH
See page 46.

PIKE À LA TARTARE

3½ pounds pike
yolks of 4 hard-cooked eggs
1 teaspoon dry mustard
1 tablespoon salad oil
¼ cup mayonnaise
1 tablespoon catsup
1 tablespoon confectioners sugar
1 tablespoon vinegar
1 cup strained fish liquid
whites of 4 hard-cooked eggs, chopped
1 teaspoon chopped parsley
1 tablespoon each, capers, pickles and onion, chopped
salt and pepper

Poach fish and bone. Leave it whole or cut in portions for serving. Mash the yolks with mustard and oil, add the rest of the ingredients. Season with salt and pepper to taste. Pour sauce over fish. Serve cold. Trout may be prepared this way.

FISH CASSEROLE

1½ pounds boned fish
3 anchovy fillets, chopped
1 tablespoon cornstarch
5 eggs, separated
1 cup cream
1 teaspoon salt
¼ teaspoon allspice
¼ teaspoon sugar

Grind the fish. Mix fish, anchovy, cornstarch, egg yolks, cream and seasonings. Beat egg whites until stiff and fold into the fish mixture. Place in well-greased casserole or ring mold. Set casserole in shallow pan of hot water. Bake at 350° F. for 1 hour or until lightly browned. Unmold. Serve with Mushroom Sauce.

BAKED FISH À LA MAURICE

1 green pepper, sliced
1 onion, sliced
1 tomato, sliced
1½ pounds fish fillets
¼ teaspoon salt
⅛ teaspoon pepper
¼ cup water (or tomato juice)
2 tablespoons butter
⅛ teaspoon paprika
1 cup yogurt

Place half of the vegetables in a greased baking dish. Season fish fillets with salt and pepper and arrange on top of vegetables. Cover with remaining vegetables. Add water or tomato juice, dot with butter and sprinkle with paprika. Bake at 350° F. 15 minutes or until almost done. Cover with yogurt and return to oven (under broiler if desired) until yogurt is bubbly and heated through. Serves 3 or 4.

RED SNAPPER MARGUERY

2 pounds red snapper
½ pound Cheddar cheese, grated
3 hard-cooked eggs, chopped
2 pounds shrimp, boiled and chopped
1 can (4 ounces) mushrooms
1 tablespoon chopped truffles, if available
2 cups Medium White Sauce, page 386

Poach fish. When cool enough to handle, remove skin and bones. Separate fish into large pieces. Put half the fish into a buttered casserole, cover with half the cheese, eggs, shrimp, mushrooms and

truffles. Repeat. Then cover with Medium White Sauce and bake about 30 minutes in moderate oven, about 350° F. Trout may be prepared this way.

RED SNAPPER WITH TOMATO SAUCE

3 pounds red snapper
salt and pepper to taste
2 onions, sliced
1 carrot, diced
2 stalks celery
few sprigs parsley
1 quart water
2 tablespoons butter
1 cup tomato purée
1 tablespoon flour
1 cup cream

Clean fish and season with salt and pepper. Place onions, carrot, celery and parsley in kettle with water. Boil 10 minutes, reduce heat, add fish, whole or in slices, and the butter and tomato puree. Simmer until flesh is firm and separates easily from bone. Remove skin and bones and transfer fish to platter. Strain liquid, add flour mixed with the cream, cook until smooth. Or omit cream, and thicken sauce by stirring gradually into the well-beaten yolks of 2 or 3 eggs. Pour over fish, garnish with chopped parsley and serve hot.

SALMON WITH HORSERADISH SAUCE

3 pounds fresh salmon
¼ cup melted butter
1 tablespoon parsley
½ pound horseradish root
2 cups heavy cream, whipped

Clean fish, and place in pan of simmering salt water (1 teaspoon salt to 1 quart water). Simmer ½ hour or until done. Lift out carefully, remove skin and bones, place fish on hot platter and pour the melted butter over it. Sprinkle with the parsley. Serve the following sauce in a separate bowl: Peel horseradish root, grate and mix well with the whipped cream. Serve cold or hot.

DILL BUTTER SALMON STEAKS

8 tablespoons butter or margarine
2 teaspoons dill seed
2 tablespoons lemon juice
4 teaspoons fresh chives and/or parsley
pinch pepper
4 salmon steaks (approximately 2 pounds)

Combine first five ingredients and chill at least several hours. Broil salmon steaks, basting with dabs of chilled mixture. Serve with remaining butter on top of steaks.

SALMON TIMBALES OR RING

1 pound fresh salmon fillets
¼ pound blanched almonds, chopped
⅛ teaspoon salt
1 pinch white pepper
1 teaspoon Worcestershire sauce
1 teaspoon onion juice
1 egg, separated
1 cup heavy cream, whipped

Grind the salmon very fine, add almonds, seasonings, the egg yolk and the white, beaten stiff. Fold in whipped cream; fill buttered timbale forms or a ring. Set the molds in pan half filled with hot water and bake in moderate oven, 350° F., 15 minutes for timbales, ½-¾ hour for ring, until set and firm to the touch. Unmold and serve with Cream Sauce.

SALMON CASSEROLE

4 ounces medium noodles
1 can (1 pound) salmon
1 can (10½ ounces) condensed tomato soup
1 cup grated Cheddar cheese
2 teaspoons lemon juice
1 tablespoon minced onion
1 teaspoon prepared mustard
2 teaspoons Worcestershire sauce
¾ cup cracker crumbs
2 tablespoons butter

Cook noodles; drain and flake salmon, reserving the liquid. Combine salmon liquid, soup, cheese, lemon juice, onion, mustard, and Worcestershire. Add noodles and salmon. Mix lightly. Place in greased casserole. Mix crumbs with melted butter and sprinkle on top. Bake in moderately hot oven, 375° F., for about 40 minutes until heated and crumbs are browned.

SALMON CROQUETTES

1 can (1 pound) salmon or 2 cups fresh cooked
    salmon
½ teaspoon salt
cayenne pepper
1 tablespoon chopped parsley
½ teaspoon grated onion
¼ cup cracker crumbs
1 egg, well beaten

Flake fish, removing any skin or bones. Add other ingredients and mix well. Shape into croquettes. Roll in bread or cracker crumbs. Beat one egg lightly with 1 tablespoon water. Dip croquettes in egg mixture, then again in crumbs. Let stand for 30 minutes. Fry in deep hot fat, 375° F., until golden brown. Drain on paper towels and serve hot with Tartar Sauce.

STUFFED SALMON

1 3-pound fresh or frozen dressed salmon or trout
    or 2 1½-pound fish
2 cups dry bread cubes
⅓ cup finely chopped onion
⅓ cup sour cream or yogurt
¼ cup chopped dill pickle
½ teaspoon paprika
½ teaspoon salt; pepper to taste
¼ cup salad oil

Thaw frozen fish. Combine bread cubes, onion, sour cream, pickle, paprika, salt, pepper. Sprinkle fish with salt and pepper. Place fish in well-greased shallow baking pan. Stuff fish loosely with mixture; brush fish with oil. Cover with foil and bake at 350° F. for 45 to 60 minutes.

BROILED SHAD

Clean and split a 3-pound shad. Spread with 1 tablespoon olive oil and sprinkle with a little salt and pepper. Let stand 1 hour. Put on well-greased pan in broiler, flesh side up. Brown well, then turn, broil slowly until flesh flakes easily. Spread with butter, add salt and pepper, reheat and serve.

BAKED SHAD

Clean and split a 3-pound shad. Place in a buttered pan. Sprinkle with salt and pepper, brush with melted butter and bake in a moderate oven, 350° F., for 15 minutes per pound.

SHAD ROE

Cook shad roe 15 minutes in simmering salted water to cover, with ½ tablespoon vinegar. Drain, cover with cold water, and let stand 5 minutes. Remove from water, place in buttered pan and cover with ¾ cup Tomato Sauce. Bake 20 minutes in hot oven, basting every 5 minutes. Place on platter, add more sauce.

BROILED

Parboil shad roe as above. Drain and dry. Brush with melted butter mixed with a few drops of lemon juice. Place in greased pan under broiler, broil slowly for about 15 minutes, then turn. Baste with butter. Serve with lemon quarters and Brown Butter.

FRIED

Parboil and drain roe, season with salt and pepper, dip in beaten egg, then in crumbs; fry golden brown in deep, hot fat.

Canned Shad Roe may be baked, broiled or fried like fresh roe.

Sauces for fish will be found in chapter 20, page 386.

SMELTS

SAUTEED

Clean smelts. If desired, leave on heads and tails. Sprinkle with salt and pepper, roll in flour. Fry in hot butter until brown. Serve with lemon.

DEEP-FRIED

Season with salt and pepper, roll in flour, dip in beaten egg, then in bread or cracker crumbs and fry in deep hot fat, 375° F., 5-8 minutes, until brown. Garnish with Parsley Butter.

BROILED

Brush cleaned smelts with melted butter and a few drops of lemon juice. Place in greased pan under broiler, and broil slowly for about 15 minutes, turning after one side is browned. Serve with Tartar Sauce.

FISH AND VEGETABLE CASSEROLE

    2 pounds fish fillets
    1 teaspoon salt
    ⅛ teaspoon pepper
    2 10-ounce packages mixed frozen vegetables
    ¾ cup milk
    3 tablespoons flour
    ½ cup grated cheese

Arrange fillets in bottom of greased casserole or baking dish. Sprinkle with salt and pepper. Spread vegetables over the fish. Gradually stir the milk into the flour until smooth. Pour liquid over the vegetables. Top with grated cheese. Bake at 375° F. for 45 to 50 minutes.

TILEFISH

Tilefish is bought either in steaks or in large pieces. To "boil" or poach, cover fish with boiling water, add 1 tablespoon vinegar, 1 small onion sliced, 2 tablespoons chopped parsley, 2 bay leaves, pepper and salt. Cook gently until flesh is opaque and flakes easily. Remove skin and bones. Serve with melted butter mixed with lemon juice and chopped parsley.

Broil tilefish steaks and serve with the same sauce.

BAKED TROUT WITH SALTED HERRING

    2- to 3-pound trout, split
    ½ cup butter, softened
    1 cup sour cream
    ¼ pound salted herring (sardellen)
    cayenne pepper
    cracker meal
    1 cup grated Cheddar cheese

Split a trout as for broiling and remove backbone. Place in a buttered baking dish, skin side down, cover with mixture of butter, sour cream, salted herring which have been soaked in water, drained, boned and chopped fine, cayenne pepper, and a little cracker meal; top with grated Cheddar cheese. Bake in a hot oven (400° F.) for ½ hour.

SALMON TROUT

    3½ pounds salmon trout
    2 or 3 egg yolks
    ½ cup cream
    1 tablespoon sherry

Cook fish as for Boiled Fish. Discard skin and bones. Place fish on platter. Strain the fish liquid. Beat yolks well, add cream. Pour the egg mixture gradually into the hot fish liquid, stirring constantly, then add the sherry. Pour sauce over the fish and serve immediately.

SALMON TROUT, CHAUD-FROID MAYONNAISE

    3 pounds salmon trout
    2 cups water
    2 lemons, juice
    2 tablespoons chopped almonds, blanched
    2 tablespoons seeded raisins
    2 tablespoons sugar
    1 teaspoon salt
    1 tablespoon cornstarch or 2 tablespoons flour
    4 egg yolks
    ¼ cup mayonnaise

Cook fish like Boiled Fish. Remove and discard skin and bones. Arrange fish on platter.

Boil water, lemon juice, chopped almonds and raisins until almonds are soft; gradually add the sugar, salt and cornstarch dissolved in a little cold water. Bring to a boil, stirring; add very gradually to the egg yolks, beaten with 1 tablespoon cold water. Cool, add mayonnaise, spoon over fish on platter. Serve cold, garnished with capers, olives or chopped pickles and hard-cooked eggs.

BAKED TROUT LOAF

    3 pounds trout fillets
    1 onion
    1 stalk celery
    ½ green pepper
    a little parsley
    ½ cup bread crumbs
    2 eggs
    pepper to taste
    1 cup water

Put first 5 ingredients through fine meat grinder. Add the rest and mix thoroughly. Put in well-buttered baking dish, dot top with butter, sprinkle with additional bread crumbs. Bake in hot oven, 400° F., about 1 hour.

BAKED TROUT

3½ pounds trout
1 can (1 pound) tomatoes
1 onion, cut fine
1 piece celery root
1 tablespoon flour
1 tablespoon butter
1 egg yolk
½ cup cream or evaporated milk
½ teaspoon Worcestershire sauce

Lay the cleaned fish in pan and add tomatoes, onion and celery. Sprinkle with flour, dot with butter, and bake in a moderate oven, 350° F., for ½ hour. Strain sauce, heat in double boiler, thicken with egg yolk mixed with the cream, add Worcestershire sauce. Pour over fish and serve immediately.

FISH BOIL

You will need a large kettle with a wire basket.

12 to 15 scrubbed medium-sized red potatoes, clipped at the ends but not peeled
1 cup salt
12 medium-sized onions, peeled
12 fish steaks or chunks, at least 1½ inches thick, approximately 8 to 10 ounces each (use whitefish, trout, salmon, halibut, haddock, pollock, red snapper, cod, king mackerel, grouper, sea bass, or rockfish)
optional seasonings (bay leaves, whole black pepper tied in cloth bag)
drawn butter; parsley; lemon wedges

Place potatoes and 8 quarts water in kettle with vents open or cover slightly ajar; bring to a boil. Add ½ cup salt and onions. Timing starts when water returns to boil. Cook for 20 minutes, regulating heat to produce a steady boil with cover still slightly open. Place fish in basket and lower into water. Add seasonings in cloth bag if used and another ½ cup salt. Cover and bring to gently rolling boil for approximately 12 minutes. To test for doneness, spear potato with a fork—it will penetrate easily if done. Fish is cooked when it flakes easily with a fork. Cooking time may vary a few minutes either way depending on the size of potatoes and thickness of fish. Lift out basket with fish; drain water off potatoes and onions. Serve with drawn butter, parsley and lemon wedges. Makes 12 servings.

To remove a fishy odor which may cling to the hands, rub hands with a cut lemon.

SCALLOPED FISH

2 pounds leftover cooked fish, flaked
1 cup bread crumbs
2 tablespoons butter, melted
Tomato Sauce, page 390
¼ cup slivered almonds
parsley

Butter baking dish or ramekins. Fill with alternate layers of fish and buttered crumbs. Cover with Tomato Sauce, sprinkle with almonds and additional crumbs. Bake 15 to 20 minutes in moderate oven, 350° F., until browned. Garnish with chopped parsley.

FISH AND CHEESE IN CASSEROLE

1½ pounds cooked fish
1 teaspoon Worcestershire sauce
½ cup soup stock
2 cups Medium Cream Sauce, page 386
¼ pound Parmesan cheese

Add the flaked fish, Worcestershire sauce, and soup stock to the cream sauce. Fill buttered casserole or ramekins. Sprinkle with grated Parmesan cheese and bake 20 minutes in a moderate oven, 350° F.

STUFFED WHOLE FISH (GEFILLTE FISH)

3 pounds white-fleshed fresh-water fish (pike, carp)
2 onions
1 slice of bread or ¼ cup matzo meal or crackers
salt and pepper
1 egg
1 cup cold water
¼ celery root or 1 stalk celery, cut up

Clean fish, remove skin whole, and bone fish. Grind 1 onion with flesh of fish. Add bread soaked in cold water and squeezed dry, or add cracker crumbs or matzo meal. Add salt, pepper, egg and 1 cup water, and mix thoroughly until smooth. Wash fish skin and fill with the mixture. Boil fish bones, remaining onion and celery for 20 minutes in water to cover. Sprinkle fish with salt and pepper and add to kettle. Simmer one hour or longer, until well done. Add water as necessary to prevent burning. Remove fish carefully to a platter, reduce broth until it is very thick, strain and pour it over fish. Serve hot or cold.

LINCOLN HOUSE FISH BALLS (GEFILLTE FISH)

See recipe on page 46 for this variation of stuffed fish made in small balls. A long-time favorite Settlement recipe, Lincoln House Fish Balls may be served as an appetizer or main course.

POLYNESIAN FISH BALLS

1 pound sole, flounder, or haddock fillets
1 can (5 ounces) water chestnuts
⅔ cup almonds
1 tablespoon chopped crystallized ginger
2 tablespoons cornstarch
2 tablespoons soy sauce
⅔ cup vegetable oil

Finely chop or grind fish, water chestnuts and almonds. Combine with ginger and cornstarch dissolved in soy sauce. Shape mixture into balls about 1 inch in diameter, pressing firmly. Heat oil in large skillet. Fry fish balls in oil, turning carefully to brown all sides. Just before serving, combine with the hot sauce:

SAUCE
1 can (13½ ounces) pineapple chunks
1 tablespoon soy sauce
½ cup vinegar
¾ cup sugar
3 tablespoons cornstarch
⅛ cup sauterne
½ cup celery, sliced thin
½ cup slivered scallions
1 large tomato, cut into wedges

Drain syrup from pineapple into a measuring cup. Add enough water to make one cup of liquid. Add to soy sauce and vinegar and heat to boiling. Mix sugar, cornstarch and wine; stir into the hot liquid. Cook, stirring constantly, until the sauce is clear and thickened. Add celery, scallions and pineapple chunks. Heat. Add tomato wedges.

See chapter 15, Outdoor Cooking, page 326, for additional recipes for fish and seafood—grilled, barbecued and skewered.

CANNED FISH

Canned fish of many kinds can be kept on the pantry shelf, ready to make nourishing, inexpensive, and delicious meals at a moment's notice. Tuna, salmon, and sardines are the most generally liked of these, and the first two are most suitable for main dishes. They may be substituted for other kinds of fish in many recipes where the fish is cooked before further preparation.

SWEET AND SOUR SALMON

1 can (1 pound) salmon
3 medium onions, sliced
1 teaspoon salt
3 tablespoons sugar
2 tablespoons flour
½ cup vinegar
2 egg yolks, beaten

Pick over salmon, removing skin and bones. Place salmon on serving platter. Cook onion slices in boiling water to cover until tender. Drain, reserving 1 cup of this liquid. Mix salt, sugar and flour; add vinegar and onion liquid. Cook a few minutes. Pour very gradually into egg yolks, stirring constantly. Reheat and pour over salmon and onion slices. Serve hot or cold.

CREAMED CANNED SALMON

Remove skin and bones from 1 cup canned salmon, flake and add 1 teaspoon lemon juice and 1 cup Medium White Sauce. Season and serve hot over toast points, noodles, rice. Or use as filling for patty shells, omelets, turnovers, etc.

SALMON FONDUE

2 tablespoons butter
3 tablespoons flour
1 can (7½ ounces) salmon
clam juice, chicken broth or milk
1 cup milk
1½ cups grated Swiss cheese
dash Tabasco
French bread

Melt butter in top of double boiler. Stir in flour. Drain salmon liquid into measuring cup and add clam juice, chicken broth or milk to measure ½ cup. Stir this liquid and milk into the butter-flour mixture and cook until smooth and thick, stirring constantly. Add cheese and stir until cheese is melted. Add the flaked salmon and the Tabasco. Heat for 5 minutes. Serve with French bread as a party dip, or over toast, noodles, or rice.

SALMON LOAF

1 can (7½ ounces) salmon
1 tablespoon butter
1 cup hot milk
1 cup bread crumbs
salt and pepper
2 eggs
Medium White Sauce, page 386

Remove skin and bones from salmon and mash fine. Melt butter in milk and add bread crumbs and seasonings. Combine with the fish. Add the well-beaten eggs. Pack into a buttered baking dish, place in pan of hot water, bake for 1 hour at 350° F.

Turn out onto platter and cover with Medium White Sauce, substituting the liquid from the salmon for an equal portion of the milk in making the sauce.

TUNA LOAF

Follow recipe for Salmon Loaf, above, using canned tuna in place of the salmon. Add ½ teaspoon each of chopped parsley and green pepper and a teaspoon of lemon juice. Bake in moderate oven 350° F., ½ hour. Serve hot or cold.

TUNA OR SALMON AND RICE

1 can (about 7 ounces) tuna or salmon
1 cup rice
1 cup Thin White Sauce, page 386
salt and pepper

Drain tuna or salmon, remove skin and bones and flake fish. Boil or steam rice. Make Thin White Sauce. Add seasoning. Line a buttered baking dish with a layer of the rice, spread the fish over this, cover with rice, add the White Sauce. Bake 15 minutes in a moderate oven, 350° F., until browned.

TUNA AND ASPARAGUS CASSEROLE

2 cans (6½ or 7 ounces each) tuna
2 packages frozen asparagus spears
½ cup chopped almonds
5 tablespoons butter
5 tablespoons flour
3 cups milk
1 teaspoon salt
¼ teaspoon pepper
dash of nutmeg
¼ cup sherry
paprika

Drain and flake tuna. Cook asparagus and drain. Place asparagus in bottom of buttered 11" x 7" baking dish. Cover with tuna. Brown almonds slightly in butter. Blend in flour; add milk and seasonings. Stir constantly until sauce is smooth and thick. Add sherry; pour sauce over tuna and asparagus. Sprinkle with paprika. Bake in a moderate oven, 350° F., for 25 to 30 minutes.

SCALLOPED TUNA WITH POTATOES

1 can (6½ or 7 ounces) tuna
2 cups Medium White Sauce, page 386
1 tablespoon Worcestershire sauce
salt and pepper
4 boiled potatoes, sliced
2 tablespoons chopped pimiento
1 tablespoon chopped parsley
1 cup crumbs
4 tablespoons melted butter

Drain tuna and flake. Add Worcestershire sauce and seasoning to white sauce. In a buttered baking dish put a layer of tuna and potato, sprinkle with pimiento and parsley, cover with white sauce. Repeat, topping with buttered crumbs. Bake in moderate oven, 350° F., until brown.

SCALLOPED TUNA WITH NOODLES

1 can (6½ or 7 ounces) tuna
1 can (10½ ounces) condensed mushroom soup
¼ cup water
1 tablespoon Worcestershire sauce
salt and pepper
2 cups cooked, drained noodles
1 cup crumbs
4 tablespoons melted butter

Drain tuna and flake. Combine mushroom soup, water, Worcestershire sauce and seasoning. In a buttered baking dish put a layer of tuna and noodles, cover with sauce. Repeat, topping with buttered crumbs. Bake in a moderate oven, 350° F., until brown.

TUNA À LA KING

2 cans (6½ to 7 ounces) tuna
2 cups Medium White Sauce, page 386
1 teaspoon Worcestershire sauce
¼ cup green pepper in strips
salt and pepper to taste
1 pimiento (canned), diced

Drain tuna and flake. Combine with white sauce and other ingredients. Heat thoroughly and serve.

If desired, add 1 can (4 ounces) mushrooms, including the liquid, ½ cup cream and ¼ cup sherry to sauce. Stir and then add 2 egg yolks, beaten with a little of the hot sauce.

TUNA PIE

3 tablespoons butter
½ cup sliced green pepper
2 slices onion
6 tablespoons flour
½ teaspoon salt
2 cups milk
2 cans (6½ to 7 ounces) tuna, drained and flaked
1 tablespoon lemon juice
Cheese Whirls, page 87

Melt butter, add green peppers and onion and cook until onion is golden brown. Add flour and salt and stir until well blended; add milk slowly, stirring constantly until thick and smooth. Add tuna and lemon juice; put in greased baking dish and cover with Cheese Whirls. Bake in a hot oven, 450° F., for about 30 minutes or until browned.

TUNA TETRAZZINI

4 ounces spaghetti
1 can (10½ ounces) condensed mushroom soup
1 can (4 ounces) sliced mushrooms
1 small onion, chopped
¼ cup diced pimiento
¼ cup diced green pepper (optional)
1¾ cups grated sharp Cheddar cheese
2 cans (7 ounces each) solid pack tuna
¼ cup dry sherry
salt and pepper

Break spaghetti in pieces and cook. Mix soup, ¼ cup liquid from mushrooms, mushrooms, onion, pimiento, green pepper, and 1¼ cups cheese. Add spaghetti, tuna broken in chunks, and sherry. Mix lightly; season with salt and pepper. Place in casserole and sprinkle with remaining cheese. Bake at 375° F. for 45 minutes until bubbly and browned.

TUNA FISH CROQUETTES

1 can (13 ounces) tuna, flaked
1¼ cups mashed potatoes
1 egg, lightly beaten
1 teaspoon chopped parsley
1 teaspoon lemon juice
salt, pepper, paprika, celery salt
bread or cracker crumbs

Combine ingredients, season to taste. Shape into desired forms, roll in bread or cracker crumbs. Beat one egg lightly with 1 tablespoon water. Dip croquettes in egg mixture, then again in crumbs. Let stand for 30 minutes. Fry in deep hot fat, 375° F., until golden brown. Serve with Cream Sauce.

Sauces for fish will be found in chapter 20, page 386.

SALTED, PICKLED AND SMOKED FISH

In buying smoked and salted fish, be sure to read the packer's directions to determine whether the fish has been pre-treated in any way, and revise the soaking and cooking times accordingly in following these recipes.

Ready-to-eat pickled herrings may be purchased at the dairy counter of many markets. The home-made pickled herrings given in this chapter keep for several weeks under refrigeration. When cream is added to the sauce, they should not be stored for longer than a week or two.

CREAMED CODFISH

Cut salt codfish in ¼-inch slices across the grain and soak in lukewarm water overnight, to draw out the salt and soften the fish. Drain. Simmer in fresh water for 10 minutes. Drain. Stir 1 cup hot Medium White Sauce into 1 beaten egg and add to fish just before serving. Garnish with hard-cooked eggs.

CODFISH BALLS

1 cup salt codfish
2½ cups potatoes
½ tablespoon butter
⅛ teaspoon pepper
1 egg, beaten

Soak the fish overnight in lukewarm water. Drain and shred, removing bones. Pare the potatoes and cut in pieces, cook fish and potatoes together in boiling water until the potatoes are soft. Drain, dry over heat, mash fine, add butter, seasoning and egg. Beat well, shape into balls. Test one codfish ball by dropping it into deep hot fat, 375° F. If it breaks apart, add a little more egg to the mixture. Fry balls until crisp and brown and drain on paper towels.

CREOLE CODFISH

1 cup salt codfish
4 boiled potatoes, sliced
2 pimientos
pepper
1 cup Tomato Sauce, page 390
buttered bread crumbs

Wash salt codfish in cold water. Cover with lukewarm water and let stand until soft; drain, bone and shred. Place alternate layers of sliced potatoes, fish, and pimientos cut in strips in a buttered baking dish. Season with pepper. Add Tomato Sauce, cover with buttered crumbs, and bake in a moderate oven, 350° F., until brown.

FINNAN HADDIE

Soak fish in cold water for several hours. Drain, cover with hot water and bake in a moderate oven, 350° F., about 30 minutes, until tender. Drain, spread with 2 tablespoons butter and serve.

CREAMED FINNAN HADDIE

Cover fish with cold water, bring slowly to the boiling point; boil 5 minutes, drain. Cover with milk. Bake at 350° F. 20 minutes. Make Medium White Sauce, using the liquid in which the fish was baked. Flake fish and reheat in the sauce.

FINNAN HADDIE IN CREAM

Cover fish with cold water, bring slowly to the boiling point, keep hot 25 minutes, drain and flake. To each cup of fish, add 1 tablespoon butter, 2 or 3 hard-cooked eggs, sliced thin, ½ cup heavy cream and a little chopped parsley. Heat gently.

BROILED FINNAN HADDIE

Soak fish overnight, drain, brush with butter and broil about 15 to 20 minutes, depending on the thickness of fish. Serve with melted butter and chopped parsley.

PICKLED HERRING (MARINATED HERRING)

    12 milter herring
    4 large onions, sliced
    2 lemons, sliced
    12 bay leaves
    2 tablespoons mustard seed
    2 tablespoons black peppercorns
    1 cup water
    2 cups vinegar
    3 tablespoons sugar
    1 large apple, grated (optional)

Soak herring in cold water overnight, drain and remove entrails, reserving the milt. If desired, skin and bone the fish, separating into two fillets. (See page 234.)

Place herring in crock in layers, with sliced onions and lemons, pieces of bay leaves, mustard seed and peppercorns.

Boil water, vinegar and sugar and set aside to cool. Mash the milt, add enough vinegar mixture to thin, strain through sieve, add the rest of the vinegar mixture and pour over herring to cover. A large apple, grated, may be added. Cover jar, let stand in refrigerator 4 to 6 days. Will keep a long while if refrigerated. Serve with boiled potatoes.

HERRING ROLLS (ROLLMOPS)

Soak, wash and bone herring as for Pickled Herring, above. Separate into two fillets. Spread with chopped onion and pickles, or with onions and bread crumbs and sprinkle with pepper. Roll and fasten with string or toothpick. Place in jar and cover with the vinegar and spice mixture for Pickled Herring.

PICKLED HERRING WITH SOUR CREAM

    6 milter herring
    juice of 2 lemons
    2 teaspoons sugar
    2 onions, sliced
    1 teaspoon white peppercorns
    1 lemon, sliced
    1 cup sour cream

Soak herring in water overnight. Clean, skin and bone. Cut herring into 1½-inch pieces. Mash the milt through a strainer with some of the lemon juice and the 2 teaspoons sugar. Place in glass jar or earthen dish, add onions, peppercorns, lemon slices, and strained milt with the remaining lemon juice, then add 1 cup sour cream. Let stand in refrigerator 48 hours before serving.

PICKLED HERRING FILLETS
IN CREAM SAUCE

    12 milter herring
    1 tablespoon sugar
    ¼ to ½ cup vinegar
    1 large onion, sliced
    8 whole bay leaves
    1 tablespoon peppercorns
    1 cup cream
    lemon juice

Soak herring overnight. Clean, skin, and remove fillets from bone. Mash the milt through a strainer, put into glass jar with sugar and a few tablespoons vinegar. Add herring, onion, bay leaves, peppercorns, and rest of vinegar. Let stand 3 to 4 days in refrigerator. Remove herring from jar. Combine cream with mixture in jar. Add enough vinegar or lemon juice to make a heavy sauce. Cover the fillets with the sauce and pack into glass jars. Seal. Will keep for a week or more in refrigerator after opening.

BAKED HERRING ROLLS

    6 herring
    2 tablespoons bread crumbs
    2 tablespoons butter
    1 tablespoon chopped parsley
    ½ lemon, juice
    salt and pepper to taste

Soak, wash and bone herring and divide into two fillets following directions in Pickled Herring, above. Mix the remaining ingredients to a smooth paste, adding hot water to soften. Spread on herring fillets, roll up and fasten with string or toothpick. Place in baking dish, cover with foil and bake in a moderate oven, 350° F., 10 to 15 minutes.

BROILED SMOKED HERRING

Soak fish in cold water overnight. Drain, add fresh water, boil 2 minutes, drain carefully and broil until tender. Top with 1 tablespoon melted butter and serve.

SALT HERRING

Soak herring overnight in cold water to draw out salt. Drain, rinse and serve with boiled potatoes.

Or, place in pan, cover with cold water, bring slowly to a boil and drain. Serve with boiled potatoes in jackets.

SALT MACKEREL

Soak mackerel overnight in cold water, skin side up, to remove salt. Drain, place mackerel in shallow pan, cover with water and simmer 10 to 15 minutes or until the flesh separates from the bone. Remove to platter, add hot melted butter or Medium White Sauce; serve with boiled potatoes.

BROILED SALT MACKEREL

Freshen the fish by soaking it overnight in cold water, skin side up. Drain and wipe dry, remove the head and tail, place on a buttered pan in broiler, and broil 10-15 minutes until a light brown. Dot with bits of butter and sprinkle with pepper, chopped parsley and a little lemon juice.

TO CURE AND SMOKE FISH

Scale, slit fish up the back, clean. Wipe with damp cloth (do not wash). For 20 pounds of fish, use 2 cups salt, 2 cups sugar, 1 ounce saltpeter. Mix together and rub well all over fish. Lay fish in stone crock one over another, with board on top pressed down with heavy weight. Let stand 5 days, then drain, wipe dry, stretch and fasten open with small sticks. Let stand in smokehouse 5 days or in a barrel over a smothered wood fire.

SEAFOOD

CRAB · CRAWFISH · FROGS' LEGS · LOBSTER · CLAMS · OYSTERS · SHRIMP

In addition to the crustaceans, such as shrimp, lobster and crab meat, and the bivalves (oysters, clams and scallops), this category also includes frogs' legs.

Hard-shell clams are opened like oysters and may be fried or served raw, on the half shell, with seafood cocktail sauce or lemon wedges and black pepper. Soft-shell clams are usually steamed open and eaten hot. Hard-shell clams are also chopped to make canned minced clams, and are used in chowders, both canned and homemade, because their flavor is stronger.

SCALLOPED OYSTERS AND CLAMS

1⅓ cups bread crumbs
salt and pepper
⅓ cup butter
1 tablespoon chopped parsley
1 tablespoon onion flakes
3 hard-cooked eggs, sliced
1 can (8 ounces) oysters
1 can (7½ ounces) minced clams
1 can condensed mushroom soup

Mix crumbs, seasoning, and butter. Reserve ⅓ cup of mixture for topping. Toss rest of crumbs with remaining ingredients and place in a shallow baking dish; sprinkle with topping. Bake in a hot oven, 400° F., for about 20 minutes until crumbs are browned.

See recipes on pages 45-46 for seafood appetizers. Leftover cold seafoods can also be used in salads.

CLAMS A LA ST. LOUIS

30 hard-shell clams
1 onion, finely chopped
2 tablespoons butter
1 tablespoon flour
salt and white pepper
½ teaspoon red pepper
½ teaspoon mustard
4 egg yolks
2 tablespoons cold water
12 mushrooms, sliced and sautéed
parsley and truffles, chopped

Split clams or steam open. Chop clams. Scrub and reserve half the shells. Fry the finely chopped onion in the butter, add flour, stir well, then add chopped clams and their liquid. Season with salt, white and red pepper and mustard. Cook for 10 minutes. Remove from heat, add egg yolks, slightly beaten with 2 tablespoons cold water. Pile mixture back into shells, garnish each with mushroom slice and sprinkle with parsley and truffles. Heat in moderate oven 5-10 minutes.

CRAB

Several varieties of crab are generally available in the market; canned, cooked and packed fresh or frozen in dairy-type cartons, and in the case of Alaska King Crab Legs, frozen in the shell or as solid meat.

Live hard-shell crabs are rarely available except in localities where they are caught. Soft-shells are sold at fish markets during their brief season.

Cooked crab meat usually contains membranes and bits of bone that have been overlooked by the packers, and the meat should be carefully examined to remove these.

FRIED SOFT-SHELL CRABS

If crabs have not been cleaned by the fish man, remove the sand bags. Raise apron, cut it away from crab, remove spongy substance surrounding apron. Wash and dry crab, season with salt and pepper; dip in crumbs, then in beaten egg, and again in crumbs; fry in deep, hot fat, 365° F., about 3 to 5 minutes. Serve immediately, with Tartar Sauce.

SAUTEED SOFT-SHELL CRABS

Prepare crabs as above, dip into seasoned flour, and sauté in a generous amount of butter until well browned on both sides. Serve with lemon wedges.

HARD-SHELL CRABS

Drop crabs, one at a time, in boiling water, adding 2 tablespoons salt for each quart water. Boil 20 to 25 minutes. Drain, wash carefully, remove claws, pull off hard shell and remove spongy part. Serve. To eat, crack claws with nutcracker and remove meat.

DEVILED CRAB MEAT

2 tablespoons butter
½ cup bread crumbs
1 cup cream
½ teaspoon dry mustard
2 cups cooked crab meat
2 egg yolks, beaten
salt and cayenne pepper
Tabasco, few drops

Mix the first 4 ingredients and heat over water; add the remaining ingredients. Heat thoroughly and serve on toast or in Rice or Noodle Ring.

DEVILED CRABS AU GRATIN

Divide Deviled Crab Meat, above, into individual shells or ramekins. Sprinkle with bread crumbs. Dot with butter, brown in oven or under the broiler.

FRENCH CRAB MEAT

2 tablespoons butter
2 tablespoons flour
1 cup chicken bouillon or light cream
2 egg yolks
1 cup crab meat
½ cup mushrooms
2 tablespoons sherry
salt and paprika to taste

Melt butter, add flour and when it bubbles, add the bouillon or cream and cook until thick and smooth. Beat yolks slightly, add a little of the hot sauce and gradually the remaining sauce. Add the crab meat and the mushrooms cut in pieces, wine and seasoning. Heat thoroughly and serve in heated patty shells or on toast. Or sprinkle with buttered bread crumbs and bake in ramekins or a casserole.

CRAB MEAT AND CHEESE

2 tablespoons butter
2 tablespoons flour
2 cups milk, scalded
¼ cup grated Cheddar cheese
¼ cup grated Parmesan cheese
½ cup butter
salt
cayenne pepper
2 cups crab meat

Melt 2 tablespoons butter, stir in flour, and cook for a few minutes, stirring. Gradually add milk and cook, stirring, until sauce is thick. Add cheese, stir over low heat until melted. Add ½ cup butter and beat well. Add seasoning. Place crab meat in a shallow, greased baking dish. Pour sauce over crab meat. Broil in moderate broiler, 350° F., for about 10 minutes. Lobster or lobster and shrimp may be substituted for or combined with the crab meat.

CRAB MEAT TETRAZZINI

1 package (½ pound) spaghetti
1 small onion, grated
3 tablespoons butter
1 can (6 ounces) mushrooms or
    ½ pound fresh mushrooms
1 can (10½ ounces) condensed tomato soup
1½ cups crab meat
½ pound sharp cheese, grated
1 can (18 ounces) tomato juice
salt
pepper

Boil spaghetti. Sauté onions in butter. If fresh mushrooms are used, sauté them at the same time. Combine soup, crab meat, spaghetti, onions, mushrooms, cheese, juice, and seasonings. Reserve enough cheese for topping. Pour into greased casserole, sprinkle with cheese. Bake in a moderate oven, 350° F., for 35 to 40 minutes.

CREAMED CRAB OR LOBSTER

    3 tablespoons butter
    3 tablespoons green pepper, finely chopped
       (optional)
    ¼ cup minced onion
    1 can (10½ ounces) condensed mushroom soup
    ½ cup sherry
    1½ cups cooked crab meat or lobster meat

Melt butter. Add green pepper and onion; sauté for 3 to 5 minutes. Add soup and wine and stir well. Add crab or lobster. Heat slowly. Serve with rice or heated Chinese Noodles. Crab meat and lobster may be combined if desired.

CRAB MEAT-POTATO CASSEROLE

Line a well-buttered baking dish with 2 cups well-seasoned mashed potatoes, place in hot oven, 400° F., until slightly browned. Fill with 2 cups crab meat, heated in 1 cup Medium White Sauce. Sprinkle with ½ cup cracker crumbs mixed with 2 tablespoons melted butter, and bake at 350° F. until crumbs are browned.

BAKED SEAFOOD NEWBURG

    2 cups Cream Sauce, page 386
    1 tablespoon minced onion
    ½ teaspoon dry mustard
    1 teaspoon minced parsley
    1 teaspoon Worcestershire sauce
    1 tablespoon lemon juice
    3 tablespoons sherry
    1 can (6½ or 7 ounces) tuna, oil packed
    1 can (4½ to 6½ ounces) shrimp
    1 can (5 to 6 ounces) crab meat
    ⅔ cups corn flakes or crushed potato chips
    3 tablespoons butter

Combine Cream Sauce, seasonings, lemon juice and sherry; mix well. Add oil from tuna, tuna broken into chunks, and drained shrimp and crab meat; mix lightly. Place in a greased baking dish. Mix crumbs and melted butter. Sprinkle in a border around edge of dish. Bake at 425° F. for about 20 minutes until mixture is bubbling hot.

SEAFOOD PANCAKE PIE

    French Pancakes, page 93
    cream cheese
    anchovy paste
    caviar
    crab meat or lobster
    Cream Sauce, page 386

Make pancakes in 10-inch skillet. Mix cream cheese with anchovy paste to taste. Spread alternate pancakes with cheese mixture and caviar, until 5 or 6 pancakes have been filled and stacked. Cover with lobster or crab meat heated in well-seasoned Cream Sauce. Keep warm in casserole in oven. Cut in wedges.

CRAWFISH

Crawfish, or crayfish, as they are sometimes called, are crustaceans that live in fresh water. They are closely related to shrimp, and are as large as the larger varieties of shrimp. They are not generally available except locally. Like lobster, they are cooked live, except that they should be washed and the intestinal vein removed before cooking.

BOILED CRAWFISH

Wash and devein the crawfish and plunge into boiling water, with 1 tablespoon salt and 1 tablespoon caraway seed or a generous bunch of fresh dill for each quart of water. Boil 10 to 15 minutes, until the shells are bright red. Cool in the cooking liquid and serve cold, with any cold seafood sauce.

FROGS' LEGS

SAUTEED FROGS' LEGS

Frogs' legs, which taste like very tender white chicken, are purchased skinned and ready to cook. Three pairs of legs make a serving. Wash them, dry them well, and dip in beaten egg and fine, seasoned cracker crumbs. Let the coating dry, then sauté in butter until browned. Serve with Tartar Sauce or lemon wedges.

FROGS' LEGS NEWBURG

    12 pairs frogs' legs
    1 lemon slice
    1 onion slice
    2 tablespoons butter
    ½ cup bouillon
    ½ cup Madeira
    salt, cayenne pepper
    1 cup cream
    3 egg yolks, lightly beaten

Simmer frogs' legs for 15 minutes in salted water to cover with lemon and onion. Drain. Melt butter, add bouillon, wine, and seasonings. Simmer 3 minutes. Combine cream and eggs, add slowly to hot mixture, stirring constantly until smooth. Pour over frogs' legs.

LOBSTER

Lobster may be purchased in three forms; live, frozen or as cooked lobster meat. In many markets the fish man will kill and split a live lobster, or even boil it, on order. Lobster should always be live until it is prepared for cooking, or it should be used as soon after it is killed as possible. Lobster meat is sold in dairy-type cartons, either frozen or fresh, and also in cans. Lobster tails, the meatiest portion of the rock lobster, are imported frozen from South Africa and elsewhere, and these are widely sold. Lobster tails may be used instead of regular lobster in many recipes.

TO BOIL LOBSTER

Plunge live lobsters, head first, into a large kettle of boiling salted water to cover. Use 2 tablespoons salt for each quart of water. Boil 15-20 minutes, depending on size. Serve hot in the shell, with melted butter, or refrigerate and serve cold with mayonnaise. Or remove meat, and use in recipes calling for cooked lobster meat.

TO OPEN BOILED LOBSTER

Break off claws. Separate large claws at joints, crack or cut shell, remove meat. Separate tail from body, draw out tail meat. Open the body through center of meat, take out intestinal vein. Hold body shell firmly, draw out the body, remove stomach. Pick out meat from body bones. The stomach and intestinal vein are not eaten.

To split lobster in half, cross large claws and hold with left hand. Draw a sharp pointed knife quickly through the undershell of the body lengthwise from head to tail. Crack claws slightly.

BROILED LIVE LOBSTER

Split the lobster and brush with melted butter or olive oil. Broil, meat side toward the heat, 15 to 20 minutes, depending on size of lobster. Season with salt and cayenne. Serve with melted butter.

BAKED LOBSTER

Split and clean a 2-pound live lobster. Place lobster in pan, flesh side up. Bake for 15 minutes in a hot oven, 450° F. Brush with melted butter, reduce heat to 350° F., bake 15 minutes longer. Serve with melted butter.

FROZEN LOBSTER TAILS

BOILED

Boil lobster tails in salted water to cover for 15 to 17 minutes, according to the size of the tail. Cut tails open lengthwise through thin undershell. Serve hot with lemon juice and melted butter; or chill and serve with desired salad dressing.

BROILED

Thaw Lobster Tails. Cut tails lengthwise through thin undershell. Spread halves so that they will lie flat, meat side up. Brush well with melted butter. Place about 4 inches below heating unit in broiler and broil at 400° F. for about 10-15 minutes, depending on size of tails. Brush with butter several times while broiling. Sprinkle with salt, pepper, and ginger. Serve with lemon and melted butter.

BUTTERED LOBSTER CHUNKS

1½ pounds cooked rock lobster tails
½ cup butter
1 tablespoon water
½ teaspoon salt
dash of pepper
½ teaspoon dry mustard
1 teaspoon lemon juice

Cut lobster meat in chunks. Simmer lobster, butter, and water in tightly covered pan for 10 minutes. Shake pan occasionally. Add seasonings and lemon juice. Serve with buttered noodles or brown rice.

STEWED LOBSTER

Cut cooked lobster meat into small pieces; place in a saucepan with enough milk or cream to moisten. Heat; add 1 teaspoon butter per serving and a little pepper. Cook only long enough to heat it, as longer cooking toughens it. Serve on toasted crackers.

LOBSTER NEWBURG

2 boiled lobsters
2 tablespoons butter
¼ teaspoon salt
¼ teaspoon red pepper
¼ teaspoon onion, grated
½ pound mushrooms
¼ cup sherry or Madeira
3 egg yolks
1 cup cream

Cut lobster meat in 1-inch pieces. Place butter, salt, pepper, grated onion and the mushrooms cut in small pieces in a saucepan or chafing dish and cook for 5 minutes; add the wine and cook 3 minutes. Place yolks of eggs in a bowl, add cream, beat well and add lobster. Combine mixtures and heat without boiling for 2 minutes or until well thickened. Serve immediately.

Recipes for grilled, barbecued and skewered seafood will be found in chapter 15, Outdoor Cooking, page 326.

LOBSTER À LA THACKERAY

meat of 2 boiled lobsters, cut in pieces
½ cup butter
¼ teaspoon salt
3 dashes cayenne pepper
1 tablespoon walnut catsup
1 teaspoon paprika

Put into chafing dish or saucepan, the green lobster liver or tomalley. Add butter, salt, cayenne, walnut catsup, and paprika. Cook 5 minutes, add lobster meat, heat and serve.

QUICK LOBSTER NEWBURG

Heat 2 cups Quick Newburg Sauce, page 390, over hot water. Add 2 cups cooked lobster meat, and heat only until lobster is heated through.

LOBSTER BORDELAISE

1 cup milk
1 tablespoon finely chopped carrot
1 small onion, chopped
2 tablespoons butter
2 tablespoons flour
salt, cayenne
1½ pounds cooked lobster meat, in chunks
¼ cup sherry

Bring milk almost to the boiling point with carrot and onion. Melt butter, add flour, and cook a minute or two, stirring. Gradually add hot milk and cook until sauce is smooth and thickened. Season to taste. Add lobster and heat gently. Just before serving, add sherry.

CREAMED LOBSTER

3 tablespoons butter
½ small onion, sliced
½ tablespoon green pepper, minced
1 tablespoon parsley, minced
1 tablespoon pimiento
1 cup mushrooms, chopped
2 tablespoons flour
2½ cups milk
2 cups diced boiled lobster
½ teaspoon salt
dash of cayenne
2 egg yolks, beaten
Patty Shells, page 343

Melt butter, add onion, pepper, parsley, pimiento and mushrooms, stir and cook 10 minutes. Sprinkle with flour, stir, gradually add 2 cups of milk, and cook 10 minutes, stirring until smooth and thick. Add lobster and seasonings, heat gently. Add remaining milk to beaten yolks, and just before serving, add to the lobster mixture. Heat without boiling and serve at once in heated Patty Shells.

LOBSTER-MUSHROOM CASSEROLE

2 cups Medium White Sauce, page 386
1 pound mushrooms, sautéed
2 pounds cooked lobster tails
1 egg yolk
¾ cup cream
butter
½ cup grated Parmesan cheese

Combine white sauce, sautéed mushrooms and diced lobster meat. Beat yolk and cream and stir gradually into lobster mixture. Pour into buttered casserole; dot with butter and sprinkle with cheese. Bake in a moderately hot oven, 375° F., for 20 minutes.

LOBSTER THERMIDOR

3 or 4 lobsters
2 tablespoons butter
1 teaspoon minced onion
¼ cup white wine
½ pound mushrooms, chopped fine
1 tablespoon tomato purée
2 cups Cream Sauce, page 386
grated Parmesan cheese

Boil lobsters, split in half, and pick out all meat, leaving main body shell intact. Dice meat into good-sized pieces. Heat butter in skillet. Add onion, lobster and wine. Cook 5 minutes, stirring constantly. Add mushrooms and tomato purée. Cook 5 minutes more. Fill shells, add Cream Sauce, sprinkle with cheese. Bake in very hot 450° F. oven until thoroughly heated and bubbly, or brown topping quickly under broiler, if desired.

LOBSTER FARCI

2 cups lobster meat
1 cup steamed mushrooms
½ small onion, grated
½ green pepper, chopped
2 tablespoons sherry
2 cups Medium White Sauce, page 386
cracker crumbs
butter

Dice lobster and mushrooms. Add with onion, green pepper and sherry to white sauce and cook 3 minutes. Fill ramekins or lobster shells, cover lightly with cracker crumbs and a little melted butter, and bake 15 minutes at 350° F.

LOBSTER MORNAY

1 pound cooked lobster meat or ½ pound lobster
    and ½ pound halibut or crab meat
salt, pepper, paprika
1 pound fresh mushrooms
2 cups spaghetti or noodles, cooked
2 cups Mornay Sauce, page 387
2 tablespoons butter

Cut seafood and fish in large pieces. Mix all ingredients, place in greased casserole, dot with butter. Bake in hot oven, 400° F., for about 20 minutes.

LOBSTER TAILS CANTONESE

3 pounds lobster tails
¼ cup salad oil
¼ teaspoon garlic powder
1 pound pork shoulder, ground
2 tablespoons cornstarch
⅓ cup cold water
¼ cup soy sauce
1 teaspoon salt
1 teaspoon sugar
½ teaspoon pepper
2¼ cups boiling water
2 eggs
½ cup slivered scallions

Cut lobster tails in two or more sections depending on the size. Heat oil in large skillet. Add garlic powder and pork; sauté for about 12 minutes, stirring occasionally. Mix cornstarch with cold water. Add cornstarch mixture, soy sauce, salt, sugar, pepper, and boiling water to pork. Simmer about 10 minutes or until clear. Add lobster, cover pan, and simmer for 8 to 10 minutes. Beat eggs lightly with a fork; blend with a little of the hot mixture. Stir eggs into lobster mixture: add scallions. Serve at once. This is appropriately served with rice. Serves 6.

LOBSTER CROQUETTES

2 cups cooked lobster meat, finely chopped
1 cup Thick White Sauce, page 386
½ teaspoon grated onion
1 teaspoon chopped parsley
salt
pepper
cayenne pepper
cracker crumbs
1 egg, beaten

Combine lobster, sauce, onion, parsley, and seasonings to taste. Cool thoroughly and shape into 8 "chops." Roll in bread or cracker crumbs. Beat one egg lightly with 1 tablespoon water. Dip croquettes in egg mixture, then again in crumbs. Let stand 30 minutes to dry. Cook in deep hot fat, 375° F., until golden brown. If fresh lobster is used, a piece of lobster claw may be inserted in the tail of the chop to represent the chop bone. Serve with lemon wedges and Tartar Sauce.

LOBSTER RISSOLES

1 cup cooked lobster meat, finely chopped
grated onion
salt, cayenne
3 hard-cooked egg yolks, riced
1 egg
1 tablespoon flour
2 tablespoons milk

If fresh lobster is used, mash the coral and add to the lobster meat, add onion and seasonings to taste, and riced egg yolks. Beat egg lightly, beat in flour and milk. Combine with lobster. Shape into balls and fry in deep hot fat, 375° F., until golden brown. Serve hot with Tartar Sauce or any seafood sauce.

OYSTERS

TO OPEN OYSTERS

Hold the oysters firmly against a towel on the table, large shell down. Insert a blunt-tipped, sturdy oyster knife between the shells and twist to force open. Sever the muscles that attach the oyster to the top and bottom shells. Pick out any bits of shell. Serve raw oysters in the deep shell, with cocktail sauce or lemon wedges and freshly ground pepper.

TO STEAM OYSTERS OPEN

When oysters are to be cooked, they may be steamed open. Put a small amount of water in the bottom of a large kettle, add the oysters, cover, and steam rapidly for just a few minutes, until the shells open. Strain the liquid before using it.

COOKED OYSTERS

When oysters are used in cooked dishes, it is important to avoid overcooking. Oysters are cooked when they swell, or plump slightly, and the edges curl. Overcooked oysters are tough and rubbery.

PANNED OYSTERS

Heat freshly opened oysters in their own liquor in the top pan of a chafing dish until they are plump and the edges begin to curl, shaking the pan or stirring to prevent sticking. Season with salt, pepper and a few tablespoons butter. Serve on buttered toast. Garnish with parsley.

PAN-BROILED OYSTERS

1 pint oysters
2 tablespoons butter
salt, pepper, cayenne
1 cup hot cream

Open oysters, drain and reserve liquor, and dry oysters on a towel. Melt butter in a skillet or the top pan or a chafing dish over direct heat. Add oysters, season, and cook, covered, until the oysters begin to plump up. Add hot cream and oyster liquor and cook, stirring occasionally, until the mixture is piping hot. Do not boil.

FRIED OYSTERS

24 large oysters, drained
1 cup bread crumbs
1 teaspoon salt
⅛ teaspoon pepper
1 egg

Dry oysters well. Roll in bread crumbs seasoned with salt and pepper. Let stand 15 minutes or more, then dip in beaten egg, roll in crumbs again, let stand 15 minutes or more in refrigerator to dry. Fry until golden brown in deep, hot fat, 350° F., 2-3 minutes. Drain on paper towels, serve on hot platter with lemon wedge.

OYSTERS, MANHATTAN STYLE

24 oysters in the shell
1½ tablespoons butter
½ teaspoon paprika
½ tablespoon salt
1 tablespoon parsley, finely chopped
3 strips bacon

Open oysters, and return to bottom shell. Cream the butter, add seasonings. Put a bit of this mixture on each oyster. Then cover each oyster with bits of bacon. Set shells on shallow baking pan, in a very hot oven, 450° F., for about 12 minutes or until bacon is crisp. Serve at once.

BROILED OYSTERS

1 pint freshly opened oysters
¼ cup melted butter
⅔ cup seasoned cracker crumbs
salt, pepper

Dry oysters between towels. Lift with fork by the tough muscle and dip in butter, then in cracker crumbs which have been seasoned with salt and pepper. Place in a buttered shallow pan and broil quickly until golden, turning once. Serve with Maître d'Hôtel Butter.

OYSTERS AND MUSHROOMS

12 large mushrooms
12 freshly opened large oysters
salt, pepper
butter
1 cup Brown Sauce, page 387
¼ cup cream

Wash mushrooms and remove stems. Chop stems for sauce. Sauté caps and stems separately.

Place mushroom caps in pan, hollow side up, place an oyster on each, season with salt, pepper, and brush with soft butter and broil until oysters are plump and browned; serve with Brown Sauce to which the chopped mushroom stems and cream have been added.

OYSTERS ROCKEFELLER

2 dozen large oysters
1 tablespoon chopped parsley
1 tablespoon green onion tops
¼ cup cooked spinach, chopped
juice of 1 lemon
salt, pepper, cayenne
½ cup butter
1 strip bacon, lightly cooked and chopped
rock salt

Open oysters and leave them on the bottom shell. Mix the parsley, onion tops, spinach, seasonings and lemon juice well with the butter. Put some of this mixture on top of each oyster. Top with bits of bacon. Set shells in heavy pie plate filled with heated rock salt and bake 5 minutes in a moderate oven, 350° F., until the oysters swell. Serve at once.

OYSTERS IN CRUST CASE

Cut ½-inch slice from top of a loaf of unsliced bread, remove soft bread, leaving a hollow container ½-inch thick. Brush inside with ½ cup melted butter. Bake in slow oven, 300° F., until crisp. Make well-seasoned Medium White Sauce, add 1 quart oysters, chopped; cook until oysters are plump and begin to curl. Turn into bread case, garnish with parsley and serve.

OYSTERS POULETTE

1 tablespoon butter
1 tablespoon flour
1 cup bouillon or chicken broth
salt, cayenne
juice of ½ lemon
4 egg yolks
1 cup cream
30 freshly opened oysters
chopped parsley

Melt butter, add flour, and cook, stirring. Gradually add bouillon and cook, stirring, until smooth. Add seasonings and lemon juice. Beat egg yolks with cream and add slowly. Cook over boiling water until thickened. Steam open 30 large oysters, page 252. Add oysters to sauce with the strained oyster liquor. Heat until edges curl. Garnish with chopped parsley.

OYSTER RAREBIT

1 cup freshly opened oysters
2 tablespoons butter
½ pound Cheddar cheese
¼ teaspoon salt
few grains cayenne pepper
2 eggs, lightly beaten

Cook oysters until plump in their own liquor; discard tough part. Melt butter, cheese and seasonings in chafing dish over hot water; as cheese melts, gradually add oyster liquor and eggs. Stir until thick and smooth, add oysters, heat gently. Serve at once on toast.

SCALLOPED OYSTERS

½ cup dry bread crumbs
1 cup cracker crumbs
½ cup melted butter
1 pint freshly opened oysters
salt
pepper
2 tablespoons oyster liquor
2 tablespoons cream or milk

Mix bread and cracker crumbs, stir in butter and put one third of the mixture in the bottom of a buttered, shallow baking dish; cover with half the oysters, sprinkle with salt and pepper; add 1 tablespoon each of oyster liquor and cream. Repeat, cover top with remaining crumbs. Bake 30 minutes in hot oven, 400° F.

OYSTERS BENEDICT

12 large panned oysters, page 252
12 slices boiled ham
6 English muffins
Hollandaise Sauce, page 388

Sauté oysters, fry ham. Split and toast English muffins. Place one slice of ham on each muffin half. Place sautéed oysters on ham. Cover with Hollandaise Sauce.

SCALLOPS

Scallops are a bivalve, like oysters and clams, but they are never sold in the shell in this country. The edible muscle is removed at the point of catch. The shells, which are sometimes very large, are used for ornamental purposes. Bay scallops, ½ to ¾ inch in diameter, are choice and expensive; sea scallops, which range from 1 to 1½ inches and larger, are slightly less delicate in flavor and texture. These are sometimes sliced before cooking.

SAUTEED SCALLOPS

Wash and dry scallops. Dip in seasoned flour. Melt butter in skillet. Add scallops and fry slowly until thoroughly cooked and golden brown. Serve with Tartar Sauce.

BROILED SCALLOPS

Wash and dry scallops, marinate in French dressing for 1 hour; roll in seasoned bread crumbs, brush with melted butter, broil until golden brown. Serve with melted butter and lemon juice.

FRIED SCALLOPS

Wash and dry scallops. Dip into milk or lightly beaten egg and dredge with fine, dry bread crumbs. Let them stand until the coating dries. Repeat. Fry in hot deep fat (350° F.) to a golden brown. Drain on paper toweling. Sprinkle with salt. Serve with Tartar Sauce and lemon wedges, or with a seafood cocktail sauce.

BAKED SCALLOPS
(COQUILLES SAINT-JACQUES)

1 pound scallops
1 cup dry white wine
few sprigs parsley, celery tops
onion slice
salt, pepper
¾ cup Mornay Sauce, page 387
¼ pound mushrooms, sautéed
grated Swiss cheese

Cover scallops in small pan with wine, add parsley, celery tops, onion, and salt and pepper, and simmer 5 minutes. Divide scallops among 4 individual ramekins or large scallop shells. Boil liquor to reduce it to half, strain, and combine with the Mornay Sauce. Add sautéed mushrooms. Divide sauce over scallops in ramekins. Sprinkle with cheese, bake in a hot oven (450° F.) until topping melts and browns.

SCALLOPS MARINARA

1½ pounds scallops
¼ cup oil
1 onion
1 green pepper
1 clove garlic
1 1-pound can tomatoes
1 8-ounce can tomato sauce
¼ cup dry white wine
1½ teaspoons salt
dash of pepper
2 bay leaves
2 tablespoons chopped parsley

If scallops are large, cut into bite-size pieces. Cook scallops in oil until tender, 5 to 7 minutes. Chop onion, pepper and garlic. Remove scallops from skillet and sauté onion mixture in same skillet for 3 to 5 minutes. Return scallops to pan, add other ingredients except parsley, and simmer until well blended. Remove bay leaves. When serving, top with parsley.

SHRIMP

Shrimp may be purchased fresh in the shell, or frozen, either in the shell or shelled and deveined. (Follow the packer's instructions in cooking frozen shrimp.) Canned shrimp, already cooked, is also available. Shrimp may be shelled and deveined before cooking, but the task is easier when the flesh is firmed by cooking.

BOILED SHRIMP

1 pound fresh shrimp
1½ quarts water
2 tablespoons salt
1 tablespoon caraway seed or pickling spice

Rinse shrimp and drain. Bring water to a boil with salt and spice. Add shrimp and boil about 7 minutes, just until the shells turn bright pink. Cool the shrimp in the liquid until they can be handled. Remove the shell by slitting the shell along the back and cut out the black intestinal vein. Reheat with any desired sauce, or chill and serve cold with seafood cocktail sauce.

COLD SHRIMP PLATTER

shredded lettuce
4 pounds Boiled Shrimp, above, shelled and deveined
4 tomatoes, sliced
4 hard-cooked eggs, sliced
sliced black olives
1¾ to 2 cups chili sauce
juice of ½ lemon
2 tablespoons chopped parsley
1 tablespoon chopped chives

Cover platter with shredded lettuce, pile shrimp in center. Surround with slices of tomato and place a slice of hard-cooked egg on each tomato slice and top with a slice of ripe olive. Combine the last four ingredients and pour over the shrimp.

ITALIAN SHRIMP

Heat cooked, shelled shrimp in Italian Tomato Sauce. Season well with salt and pepper and serve on hot boiled rice.

FRIED BUTTERFLY SHRIMP

1 pound large raw shrimp in shell
1 egg, slightly beaten
salt and pepper
1 cup cracker meal or flour
vegetable oil or fat

Wash, rinse and drain shrimp. Split along back, remove shell, leaving tail. Take out black intestinal vein. Chill thoroughly. Dip shrimp into seasoned egg, roll in flour or cracker meal and fry a few at a time in deep, hot fat, 350° F., 2-3 minutes, until golden. Splitting allows shrimp to curl. Serve hot with Cocktail Sauce or Chili Sauce.

Or shrimp may be shelled, deveined, breaded and fried without splitting.

SHRIMP PIE

¾ cup diced celery
2 medium onions, diced
2 tablespoons butter
1 pound cooked shrimp (fresh, frozen or canned)
1 tablespoon cornstarch
¼ cup lemon juice
2 eggs
¾ cup cooked rice
1 teaspoon salt
dash of pepper
1 unbaked 9-inch Pie Shell, page 341
1 green pepper, sliced (optional)

Sauté celery and onions in butter until lightly browned. Mix with shrimp. Mix cornstarch with lemon juice; beat eggs and mix with lemon juice mixture. Add rice, salt, and pepper. Put shrimp mixture into pie shell; pour egg mixture over the shrimp. Garnish with green pepper if desired. Bake in a moderate oven, 350° F., for 45 minutes, or until filling is set.

SHRIMP WIGGLE

4 tablespoons butter
2 tablespoons flour
½ teaspoon salt
paprika
1½ cups milk
1 cup cooked shrimp, cut up
1 cup canned peas, drained
Patty Shells, page 343

Melt the butter and add flour, salt and paprika; gradually add the milk and cook, stirring, until thick. Add shrimp and peas. Heat and serve in heated Patty Shells.

SHRIMP CREOLE IN CASSEROLE

2 pounds shrimp
1 can (6 ounces) mushrooms, drained
1 can (8½ ounces) peas, drained
1 cup canned tomatoes
3 cloves
1 bay leaf
2 tablespoons catsup
1 onion, chopped

Cook shrimp, shell, devein and dice. Combine with mushrooms, peas, tomatoes, cloves, bay leaf, catsup and onion. Bake in buttered casserole in moderate oven, 350° F., for ½ hour.

SHRIMP SPANISH IN CASSEROLE

2 egg yolks
salt and cayenne
grated onion
1 tablespoon light cream
1 tablespoon butter
1 tablespoon flour
1 cup hot soup stock
1 tablespoon catsup
2 tablespoons lemon juice
2 cups cooked shrimp, diced
1 cup buttered crumbs

Beat yolks with salt, cayenne, onion, and cream. Melt butter, add flour and stir over moderate heat for a moment. Gradually stir in stock, catsup and lemon juice and cook, stirring until smooth. Warm yolk mixture with a little sauce, combine. Add shrimp. Put into individual ramekins, cover with crumbs and bake 10 to 15 minutes in moderate oven, 350° F., until crumbs are browned.

SHRIMP FONDUE

5 slices bread
butter
2 pounds cooked shrimp
2 cups grated Cheddar cheese
salt and pepper
2 cups milk
4 eggs, slightly beaten
2-3 tablespoons sherry (optional)

Remove crusts from bread. Spread bread generously with butter. Cut bread into ½-inch cubes. Place a layer of cubes in the bottom of a buttered casserole; add a layer of shrimp and a layer of cheese. Sprinkle with salt and pepper. Repeat until all are used. Combine milk, eggs, and sherry; pour over the contents of the casserole. Set casserole in a pan of hot water and bake in a moderate oven, 350° F., for 50 to 60 minutes.

SHRIMP AND RICE CASSEROLE

3 cups cooked rice
2 cups cooked shrimp
2 cups milk
1 tablespoon butter
½ cup catsup
½ teaspoon Tabasco
1 teaspoon Worcestershire sauce
buttered crumbs

Combine all ingredients except crumbs. Pour into a greased casserole. Sprinkle with crumbs. Bake in a moderate oven, 350° F., for 30 minutes until crumbs are browned.

SHRIMP-STUFFED EGGPLANT

2 eggplants
½ cup chopped green onions
3 tablespoons butter
salt and pepper to taste
garlic (optional)
3 cups boiled shrimp
4 tablespoons bread crumbs

Parboil whole eggplants in salted water until tender but not soft. Cut in half lengthwise. Scrape out pulp leaving a ½-inch shell. Sauté onions in 2 tablespoons of butter until clear; add mashed eggplant and seasonings. Cut shrimp into bite-size pieces. Add shrimp and 2 tablespoons of bread crumbs to eggplant mixture. Refill shells with mixture, sprinkle with remaining crumbs, and dot with rest of butter. Bake in a shallow dish at 350° F. for 30 to 35 minutes until hot and browned on top.

SHRIMP-MUSHROOM-ARTICHOKE CASSEROLE

1 8-ounce can mushrooms
1½ pounds uncooked shrimp
    or 2 cups cooked shrimp
1 14-ounce can artichoke hearts
½ cup diced onion
¼ cup butter
½ cup sherry
1 tablespoon catsup
milk
¼ cup flour
¾ teaspoon salt
⅛ teaspoon pepper
1 teaspoon Worcestershire sauce
1 cup soft bread cubes
3 tablespoons butter, melted
paprika

Drain mushrooms and retain liquid. Boil uncooked shrimp; drain. Cut shrimp in half. If artichoke hearts are large, cut in half. Place shrimp, artichoke hearts and mushrooms in a greased casserole or baking dish. Sauté onions in butter until onions are transparent. Combine liquid from mushrooms, sherry, catsup, and enough milk to make 2 cups. Gradually add the flour to the sautéed onions, stirring constantly until thickened and smooth. Add salt, pepper, Worcestershire, and stir in liquid very gradually, stirring constantly until thickened and smooth. Pour sauce over the shrimp mixture. Top with bread cubes tossed in the melted butter. Sprinkle lightly with paprika. Bake at 375° F. for 30 minutes. If prepared in advance and refrigerated, bake at 350° F. for 45 minutes.

JAMBALAYA

2 tablespoons butter
2 medium onions, diced
1 tablespoon flour
2 cups water
1 can (1 pound) tomatoes
dash garlic powder
1 tablespoon chopped parsley
salt and pepper
1 cup uncooked rice
¼ teaspoon thyme
1 bay leaf
1 green pepper, chopped
2 cups cleaned and cooked shrimp
2 cups oysters

Melt butter in heavy skillet or kettle; add onions and sauté until browned. Add flour slowly and stir until browned. Add water, stirring constantly until a smooth paste is formed. Add all other ingredients except the seafood. Cover kettle and cook over low heat for about 15-20 minutes, until rice is tender. Add shrimp and oysters with the oyster liquor. Cover, heat thoroughly until edges of oysters are curled. Other fish or seafood may be added or substituted.

CREOLE SEAFOOD IN CREAM

1 tablespoon onion, finely chopped
1 tablespoon green pepper, cut fine
2 tablespoons butter
¾ can condensed tomato soup
1½ pounds shrimp, cooked
1 can (5 to 6 ounces) crab meat
1 tablespoon flour
1 cup cream

Sauté onion and pepper in butter. Add tomato soup, shrimp and crab meat and heat thoroughly. Add the flour blended with the cream. Cook until smooth. Serve with boiled noodles, garnished with browned bread crumbs.

MOLDED SEAFOOD SOUFFLE

GARNISHES

½ cup black olives, pitted and sliced
1 small can pimientos, in thin strips
1 cup picked-over crab or lobster meat

SOUFFLE MIXTURE

3 tablespoons butter
3 tablespoons flour
¼ teaspoon salt
1 cup hot milk or cream
3 eggs, separated
1 pound shrimp, cooked, shelled and chopped
1 pint oysters, drained, cut coarsely
1 pound sautéed mushrooms, drained and sliced

Prepare the garnishes first: slice the olives and cut the slices in half. Arrange in a greased fish-shaped mold to represent the fish scales. Use pimiento strips for fins. To make the eye, use the conical slice from the stem end of a large olive, skin side down, with a bit of pimiento in the center. Arrange the bright red pieces of crab or lobster in the head portion of the mold. Sprinkle the rest evenly over the rest of the mold.

Make the soufflé mixture: melt the butter, stir in the flour and salt, and cook for a few minutes. Slowly stir in the milk and cook, stirring, until the sauce is thick and smooth. Warm the beaten egg yolks with a little sauce and add to mixture. Cool slightly. Beat the egg whites stiff and fold in.

Fold one third of the soufflé mixture into the sliced shrimp and carefully spoon into the mold, being careful not to disturb the garnish. Repeat with oysters and mushrooms.

Put the mold into a pan of hot water and bake it in a moderate oven, 350° F., about 30 minutes, until the soufflé is firm and set. Loosen the edges, cover with a platter, and invert platter and mold together to unmold the "fish." Serve at once, with hot Sea Food Sauce, page 387, or Hollandaise Sauce, page 388.

SHRIMP TEMPURA

2 eggs, separated
1 cup water
1 cup cake flour
4 tablespoons cornstarch
1½ pounds shrimp, peeled and deveined

Beat egg yolks and water. Gradually beat in flour and cornstarch, and beat until smooth and light. Beat egg whites stiff, fold into batter. Dip shrimp into batter, drain off excess, and fry a few at a time in hot deep fat (375° F.) until richly golden. Drain on paper towels. Serve with dipping sauce, which follows.

DIPPING SAUCE FOR TEMPURA

¼ cup bouillon
¼ cup Sherry
¼ cup soy sauce
Japanese radish or horseradish, grated
ginger root, grated

Combine liquids and add grated horseradish (if using bottled, drain well) and ginger root to taste. Enough for 6 servings of Shrimp Tempura.

See pages 45–46 for seafood cocktails and appetizers.

Recipes for grilled, barbecued and skewered fish and seafood will be found on pages 332–333.

See chapter 20, page 386, for sauces suitable for fish and seafood.

QUICK REFERENCE GUIDE TO USEFUL INFORMATION IN THIS BOOK

13 FRUITS

FRESH • COOKED

FRESH FRUITS

Fruit, raw or cooked, is served as an appetizer, as a salad or luncheon main course, often with cottage cheese, as an accompaniment to a meat or poultry main dish, as snack or dessert.

A dessert that is always appropriate for any but the most formal dinner party is a selection of fresh fruits and cheeses. The fruit arrangement may serve as the centerpiece at dinner, and guests can help themselves to the fruit at the close of the meal, together with the cheeses, which are passed separately with crackers.

To Serve Fresh Fruit

PEACHES, apricots, plums, nectarines, and tangerines may be served whole, washed and chilled. Grapes are served in small bunches, or grape shears are provided. Pears, apples, and oranges are served with individual fruit knives to peel and slice the fruit.

GRAPEFRUIT HALVES

Cut grapefruit in half crosswise. Remove seeds with a sharp pointed knife. Separate pulp from pith all around the grapefruit. Loosen pulp from dividing membrane. Detach core from bottom, remove core and membrane in one piece. Sprinkle with sugar. Garnish with maraschino cherry.

GRAPEFRUIT SECTIONS

Peel grapefruit as you would an apple, removing the rind and all of the white pith. With a sharp knife, make a cut from the outside down to the core then up other side of each section and remove pulp of each section in one piece. Sprinkle with sugar if desired. Serve in sherbet glasses.

BANANAS are ripe and ready for eating when the skin is streaked with brown. Do not store bananas in the refrigerator. Serve bananas whole, or peel and slice them, and serve with sweet or sour cream and sugar.

STRAWBERRIES should be picked over without removing the hulls. Place berries in colander and dip in and out of a pan of cold water, changing water as necessary, until fruit is clean. Drain berries and serve with a bowl of confectioners sugar for dipping. The hull serves as a handle. Or hull the berries after washing and serve with sugar and sweet or sour cream.

OTHER BERRIES such as blueberries, raspberries, blackberries, and similar fruit should be picked over, discarding stems and leaves. Put fruit into a colander and dip in and out of a pan of cold water until fruit is clean. Drain and serve with sugar and sweet or sour cream, as desired.

ORANGES

Remove peel and white pith down to the juicy pulp. Serve fruit whole or sliced. Or cut in sections on both sides of each section of membrane, removing pulp. Arrange sections on plate in form of a daisy with mound of brown sugar in center.

LEMONS OR LIMES

Lemons are used raw as flavoring, cut in slices as garnish, in wedges when juice is to be extracted at the table. Limes are served in the same way.

MELONS

Cut melons in half, or in sections or slices, remove seeds and fibers. Serve ice cold with salt or sugar at the beginning of a meal, or fill with ice cream and serve as a dessert.

Or, the meaty portion may be cut into cubes or balls and served in the melon shells or in sherbet glasses.

WATERMELON

Chill a watermelon; cut into slices crosswise. Serve with or without the rind.

Or cut into cubes or balls and remove seeds. Sprinkle with chopped, fresh mint.

PAPAYA

Papaya is a southern fruit, a variety of melon. The ripe fruit is eaten flavored with lemon, lime or tart orange juice. Green papaya may be boiled as a vegetable, pickled or preserved.

PERSIMMONS

Wash soft, ripe persimmons. Serve whole or in halves. The fruit, cut in pieces, is also used for garnishing salads.

PINEAPPLE

Twist off leafy end. Cut pineapple in thick slices, crosswise. Put slice on board, cut around edge inside of peel. Cut away hard center core by making four straight cuts through the slice, close to the core, one on each side, thus #. Then cut sections in slices or dice. Or cut pineapple lengthwise in 4 or 6 sections. Cut away rind and core and cut out eyes. Sprinkle well with sugar, cover, let stand a few hours to ripen, and serve cold. Or, Boil 1 cup sugar and 1 cup water; pour this hot syrup over thin slices of peeled fresh pineapple. Keep covered until cool.

AMBROSIA

Cut a pineapple in 1-inch slices, then pare, core and dice. Pare 2 oranges and a grapefruit, separate sections from membrane. Sprinkle 1 cup sugar over all, add juice of a lemon; chill. Before serving, mix with fresh grated coconut.

COOKED FRUITS

APPLE SAUCE

2½ pounds cooking apples
1 cup water
½ cup sugar
1 tablespoon lemon juice
nutmeg or cinnamon

Wash, quarter and core cooking apples, add water barely to cover, cook until nearly soft, add sugar, lemon juice and nutmeg or cinnamon, if desired. Cook a few minutes longer, press through strainer. Cool.

BAKED APPLE SAUCE

Arrange 6 apples, pared, quartered and cored, in a baking dish, add ½ cup each of sugar and water. Cover and bake in a slow oven until apples are soft.

BAKED APPLES

Wash and core cooking apples. Leave peel on; or pare the top ⅓ of the skin; or cut a strip ½ inch wide around center of apple. Place in baking dish, fill center of each apple with sugar and cinnamon, place 1 teaspoon butter on each apple, and cover bottom of pan with cold water. Cover dish, place in moderately hot oven, 375° F., and bake 40 to 60 minutes, or until fruit is tender but not broken. When done, uncover; place a marshmallow on each apple and bake until the marshmallows brown.

BAKED APPLES WITH ALMONDS

Pare and core 6 tart apples. Place in a saucepan and pour syrup over them made by boiling 1 cup sugar with 1½ cups water for 5 minutes. Simmer until tender, turning the apples carefully. Remove from syrup. Cover the top part of each apple with blanched almonds. Pour syrup into a baking dish, arrange apples in dish, sprinkle with more sugar; bake in hot oven, 400° F., until nuts are browned. Chill. Serve with whipped cream.

SPICED APPLE RINGS

Core, pare and cut 6 apples in halves, crosswise or in thick slices. Boil 1 cup sugar with 1½ cups water for 5 minutes, adding 2 tablespoons red cinnamon candies. Place apples in covered baking dish, pour the red syrup over them. Cover dish and bake in oven or simmer, basting often, until apples are tender and pink. Serve as a border around meat or salad.

GLAZED BROILED APPLES

Wash and core cooking apples and pare halfway down from top. Put in shallow pan close together; fill centers with sugar. Cover with cold water ½ the depth of apples. Broil at 325° F. 4 inches under flame, basting occasionally, or bake in hot oven, 425° F. When almost soft, press top of apples crisscross with fork and baste often until slightly brown and glossy.

FRIED APPLE RINGS

Core and slice tart apples about ⅓ inch thick. Mix equal amounts of sugar and flour. Coat apple slices with this and fry in fat slowly until brown and tender. Use as a garnish for meat.

STEAMED APPLES

Wash, core and pare cooking apples; steam in the top of a double boiler until the apples are tender. Add sugar and cinnamon or nutmeg to taste.

POACHED APPLES

6 or 8 tart apples
1 cup sugar
1 cup water

Quarter, core and pare apples. Boil sugar and water to a syrup, add the apples to boiling syrup and cook, a few at a time, only until tender. Remove carefully. Pour syrup over the apples.

PINK APPLES

8 apples
1 cup sugar
grated rind of ½ lemon
juice of 1 orange
red vegetable coloring

Pare apples and cook in 2 inches of boiling water until soft, turning often. Remove apples. To the water add sugar, lemon rind, orange juice and a few drops of red vegetable coloring. Simmer liquid until reduced to 1 cup. Cool and pour over apples.

CABBAGE AND APPLES

See page 115.

ONIONS AND APPLES

See page 423.

SWEET POTATOES AND APPLES

See pages 429, 431.

PINK PEARS OR PINEAPPLES

Pink Pears or Pineapples are prepared like Pink Apples, above. If canned fruit is used, drain. Add coloring to syrup and cook as above.

BAKED APRICOTS AND RAISINS

½ pound dried apricots
1 cup seedless raisins
2 cups water
½ cup sugar
juice of 1 lemon
1 orange, peeled

Wash apricots and raisins. Add water and place in baking dish. Cover and bake 2½ hours at 325° F. Add sugar, lemon juice, and orange, cut in slices, and stir until sugar is dissolved. Chill.

BAKED BANANAS

Bake the bananas in their skins at 375° F., for about 20 minutes.

GLAZED BAKED BANANAS

Peel bananas. Arrange in shallow baking dish, sprinkle with lemon juice. Bake in a moderate oven, 375° F., 10 to 15 minutes. Sprinkle with confectioners sugar, and serve hot with meat course.

GINGER-SPICED CHERRIES

2 cans (1 pound each) pitted dark cherries
2 tablespoons cornstarch
1½ tablespoons lemon juice
¼ cup sugar
pinch of salt
2 tablespoons candied ginger

Drain and reserve cherry juice. Mix a small amount of cherry juice and cornstarch. Combine with the rest of the cherry juice, lemon juice, sugar, salt and the ginger sliced thin. Cook until clear and thickened; add cherries. Serve cold.

FRESH CRANBERRY RELISH

1 pound cranberries
1 large orange, seeded but not peeled
2 cups sugar

Grind or chop the cranberries and orange. Add sugar and mix thoroughly. Let stand several days before using. 1 cup crushed pineapple or 4 tart, red, unpared apples quartered, cored and ground may be added. Keeps well in the refrigerator or freezer. Serve with poultry or meat.

CRANBERRY SAUCE

2 cups water
2 cups sugar
4 cups cranberries

Boil water and sugar to a syrup about 10 minutes, add the washed cranberries. Cover and cook until cranberries pop open and are translucent. Serve cold with meat or poultry.

JELLIED CRANBERRY SAUCE

4 cups cranberries
2 cups water
2 cups sugar

Wash the cranberries. Cook in the water until they are soft and the skins pop open. Strain, add the sugar, and stir until the sugar is dissolved; boil 5 to 8 minutes, or until a drop jells on a cold plate; skim. Pour into individual wet molds or ring mold and cool.

See chapter 23 for instructions on how to make fruit preserves, jams, jellies and conserves. Chapter 24 gives instruction for freezing, canning and drying fruits.

APPLES IN CRANBERRY SAUCE

1 cup sugar
1 cup water
2 apples
1 cup cranberries

Boil sugar and water 3 minutes. Pare apples, cut into balls with cutter. Drop a few at a time in the boiling syrup, remove with skimmer when tender, but not broken. Place three balls in each individual mold. Wash and drain cranberries, add to hot syrup with apple trimmings. Boil until berries pop, about 5 minutes. Strain, pour over apples. Unmold. Serve as garnish for meat.

CANDIED CRANBERRIES

4 cups cranberries
1 cup water
2 cups sugar

Wash cranberries. Boil in water; when skins begin to burst, add sugar. Boil 5 minutes or until translucent.

CHERRY CRANBERRIES

4 cups cranberries
½ cup water
2 cups sugar

Prick each berry so that it will not burst. Add water to berries. When they begin to boil, cover with sugar and boil 5 minutes or until translucent.

BAKED CRANBERRIES

Place 1 quart cranberries in shallow baking dish with 1 cup water and 1 cup sugar; cover and bake in a slow oven, 300° F., 45 minutes; or bake without water in hot oven (400° F.) until mixture is thick and translucent.

BAKED CHERRY CRANBERRIES

4 cups cranberries
2 cups sugar
½ cup water

Prick each berry so that it will not burst. Boil sugar and water until sugar is dissolved. Add cranberries and bake 40 minutes in a slow oven at 300° F. Spread cranberries on waxed paper until almost dry, then roll in granulated sugar.

CRANBERRY COMPOTE

1 quart cranberries
2 cups preserved strawberries
1 cup sugar

Cover cranberries with water, bring to boil and cook, covered, for about 5 minutes. Then add strawberries and sugar and cook about 5 minutes longer. Serve cold.

GINGERED FIGS

1 pound dried figs
juice and grated rind of ½ lemon
1 large piece ginger root
sugar
1 tablespoon lemon juice

Wash figs and remove stems. Cover with cold water, and add lemon juice and rind, and ginger root. Simmer until the figs are puffed and soft. Remove figs. Measure juice and add one-half as much sugar; boil until thick and add 1 tablespoon lemon juice. Pour juice over figs. Serve cold with whipped cream, if desired.

BROILED GRAPEFRUIT

Cut grapefruit in half; cut out center core; loosen sections from membrane. Cover each half with 2 tablespoons brown sugar and ½ tablespoon butter, or sprinkle with granulated sugar and cinnamon to taste. Broil 15 minutes at 275° F., 3½ inches from flame. Serve hot.

BAKED KUMQUATS

1 quart kumquats
1½ cups sugar
1½ cups water

Wash kumquats well, cut a cross in blossom end; arrange in a baking dish. Bring sugar and water to a boil, pour over kumquats, cover and bake 1 hour in a slow oven, 300° F. Remove dish from oven, cool kumquats without removing cover. Transfer kumquats to serving dish, reduce syrup until very thick, pour over fruit. Serve chilled.

BAKED ORANGES

Grate rind of oranges slightly. Boil oranges 30 minutes; then cool. Cut slice off blossom end; remove core. Fill each orange with 1 teaspoon butter and 1 tablespoon brown sugar. Place in baking dish, add boiling water to about half way up fruit. Cover and bake at 375° F., 1½ hours. Remove oranges and serve hot or cold.

ORANGES IN ORANGE SYRUP

2 teaspoons grated orange rind
4 large navel oranges
¾ cup orange juice
¾ cup sugar
¼ cup lemon juice

Grate rind and peel oranges, being careful not to cut into fruit. Remove core with sharp knife, leaving fruit whole. Combine orange juice, sugar, lemon juice, and orange rind and boil for 5 minutes. Pour over the oranges. Chill.

SPICED ORANGE SLICES

3 oranges
1½ cups sugar
½ cup water
juice of 1 lemon
several sticks cinnamon

Wash oranges and cut into slices about ½-inch thick. Boil sugar, water, lemon juice and cinnamon to a syrup. Add orange slices and simmer slowly until rind is clear. Serve with meat.

FRESH PEACH OR PEAR COMPOTE

1½ cups sugar
1½ cups water
4 small pieces stick cinnamon
2 dozen peaches or 1 dozen pears

Boil sugar and water to a syrup, add the cinnamon; add the peeled and sliced fruit; simmer until tender. Serve cold with meat.

BAKED PEACHES WITH BRANDY SAUCE

2 No. 303 cans halved peaches
maple syrup
brandy

Pour maple syrup into canned peach halves. Bake in moderate oven until well heated. When ready to serve, pour heated brandy over them, ignite the brandy with a match, and bring to table flaming. Can be served with whipped cream.

SPICED DRIED PEACHES

1 pound dried peaches
water to cover
6 cloves
2 pieces cinnamon
2 pieces ginger root
½ cup sugar

Wash fruit and simmer with water and spices until nearly tender; add sugar; cook 5 minutes. Cool and serve. Other dried fruits may be prepared the same way.

BAKED PEARS

Wash pears. Remove blossom end. Place in baking pan, close together, stem end up. For each pear, combine 1 tablespoon boiling water, 1 teaspoon butter, 1 tablespoon sugar. Pour around pears. Cover. Bake 1 to 2 hours in moderately hot oven, 375° F., depending on variety of pear, until pears are tender. Baste occasionally. Or peel large pears, cut in half, place in shallow pan, and proceed as above.

FRIED PINEAPPLE

Drain canned pineapple slices or pear halves. Dip in flour. Sauté quickly in butter until browned. Serve as a garnish for roast meats.

STEWED PRUNES

½ pound prunes
3 slices lemon
¼ cup sugar

Wash the prunes and soak them in cold water to cover for 1 hour. Add lemon and cook slowly until tender. Add sugar and cook 5 minutes longer.

Dried apricots or any other dried fruit may be prepared the same way and mixed with the prunes.

PORK TENDERLOIN WITH PRUNES OR APRICOTS

See page 294.

BRISKET BAKED WITH PRUNES

See page 273.

RHUBARB SAUCE

Wash, cut off leaves and stem ends of rhubarb. Cut in ½-inch pieces. If the peel is tough, strip it off. Use about half as much sugar as fruit; or pour boiling water over the rhubarb, let stand 5 minutes, drain, and use less sugar. Place fruit and sugar in saucepan with just enough water to keep it from burning; cook until pieces are soft but not mushy. Flavor with grated rind of orange. Or, boil 2 cups sugar and 1 cup water to a syrup, add rhubarb, let boil a few minutes until tender.

BAKED RHUBARB

Place 2 cups sugar and 4 cups cleaned, sliced rhubarb in baking dish. Cover. Bake in moderate oven, 350° F., 45 minutes or until rhubarb is tender.

STEAMED RHUBARB

Cook 4 cups cleaned, sliced rhubarb and 2 cups sugar in double boiler about ½ hour, until rhubarb is tender.

RHUBARB WITH BERRIES

Use equal parts of rhubarb, cut in 1-inch pieces, and any fresh berries. Add sugar to taste. Let stand 1 hour or more. Place in saucepan, heat slowly until sugar is dissolved. Cook without stirring until rhubarb is tender. Cool and serve.

RHUBARB WITH PINEAPPLE

Use equal parts of rhubarb and fresh pineapple diced. Add about 2 cups sugar to 4 cups of fruit; proceed as above.

The syrup from fresh or canned fruits is served with the fruit; extra syrup may be used to sweeten beverages or fresh fruit mixtures, or in fruit sauces.

CANNED FRUIT COMPOTE

1 can fruit
wine
2 sticks cinnamon
3 slices lemon

Drain syrup from fruit and measure. Add an equal amount of wine. Boil wine, fruit syrup, cinnamon, and lemon for 10 minutes. Pour over fruit. Let stand 24 hours before serving. Serve cold with meat or as dessert.

SUGGESTED COMBINATIONS

—Pears with Rhine wine
—Pineapple, sour cherries with sweet port
—Peaches with sherry

FRUIT FREEZE

Place an unopened can of peaches, pineapple, pears or fruit cocktail in freezer or freezing compartment of refrigerator and freeze. When ready to serve, remove both ends of can and push frozen fruit out. Cut in slices and serve with sweetened whipped cream.

STEWED FRESH FRUIT

Boil 2 cups of water and 1 cup sugar to make a syrup; add cleaned and pared fruit. Cook gently until tender. Plums should not be peeled, but should be pierced before cooking.

QUICK REFERENCE GUIDE TO USEFUL INFORMATION IN THIS BOOK

14
MEAT AND POULTRY

MEAT

BEEF · VEAL · LAMB · PORK · VARIETY MEATS

General Rules

In buying meat it is important to select the right cut for the cooking method you prefer (see charts preceding each type of meat), keeping in mind that the edible portions of the cheapest cut are as high in nutritional value, and as good to eat, when properly prepared, as the most expensive cut.

Remove the market wrappings from fresh meat, wrap it loosely in moisture-proof paper and store in the coldest part of the refrigerator. Frozen meat should also be wrapped in freezer paper and stored in freezer compartment at 0° F. or lower until ready to defrost. Smoked meats should be stored in the refrigerator, as should canned hams, unless otherwise stated on the label. Leftover cooked meat should be closely covered before refrigerating.

Meat may be cooked in dry heat: roasted or baked in the oven or on the rotisserie, broiled, or pan-broiled in a hot skillet without fat. It may be cooked in moist heat, like pot roast or stews, which are braised in a covered kettle with a little liquid, either in the oven or on top of the range; or it may be simmered in water or stock. Thin cuts of tender meat may be cooked in a small amount of fat, a process called pan-frying or sautéeing. In deep-frying, the meat is cooked quickly in fat deep enough to cover it completely.

To cook frozen meat roasts without defrosting, increase the cooking time by one-third to one-half. The extra time needed to cook frozen steaks, chops, and hamburgers, depends upon the thickness and size of the meat.

Carving Meat

Meat looks better and goes farther when carved correctly. Always let meat stand to set the juices before attempting to carve it—about 20 minutes in a warm place for roasts, about 5 minutes for steaks. Use a wooden carving board or heated platter large enough to accommodate the meat easily. Have an extra heated plate at hand to hold the slices as they are removed from the meat. In addition to a sharp heavy-bladed carving knife and a two-pronged carving fork, two other implements are useful: a long, flexible knife for thin slicing, and a smaller version of the large carving knife to use on small birds and steaks. Meat is generally carved across the grain; when a piece of meat has more than one grain, like brisket, it may be carved in more than one direction.

RIB ROASTS WITH BONE

Separate the backbone from the ribs and remove it. Put the roast on the board large side down. With the left hand, force the fork in between the rib bones. Cut slices from the fat side to the bone and detach them from the rib with the point of the knife.

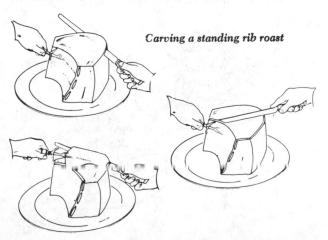

Carving a standing rib roast

BONELESS AND ROLLED ROASTS

Lay meat on the board large side down. Insert fork into left side of meat and slice from right to left across the top. Fillet of beef and similar long, narrow roasts may be sliced like a loaf of bread.

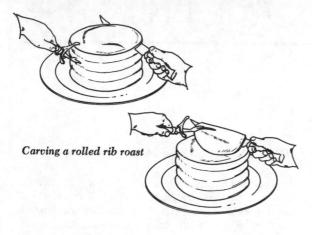

Carving a rolled rib roast

POT ROASTS

Cut a thin pot roast like steak, a thick roast like rib roast or boneless roast.

LOIN ROASTS

Have the butcher separate the backbone from the ribs without detaching it. After roasting, remove the backbone. Slice down between the ribs to make chops.

STEAK

Cut out bone with the point of the knife. Cut slanting 1-inch slices right across the steak, including parts of each section, which vary in tenderness, with each serving.

CROWN ROAST

Slice down between the ribs to make chops.

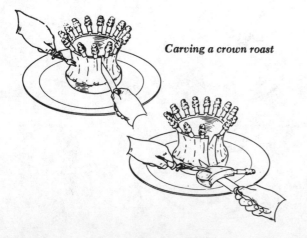

Carving a crown roast

WHOLE HAM

Balance ham on thin-meated side. If necessary, cut off a slice of meat to level it. Insert fork into butt end, near the top. Make a slanting cut down to the bone near the shank end, where the meaty part begins, and cut along the bone as far as possible. Make a straight cut to the left of the original cut, and lift out the wedge. Slice down to the bone on both sides of the wedge. Country-style hams, which are saltier than ordinary hams, should be thinly sliced.

FRESH HAM, LEG OF LAMB OR VEAL

These are carved like Whole Ham, above, without removing the wedge.

HALF LEG ROASTS, SHANK END

Cut the meatiest part of the leg away from the bone in one piece. Separate shank from rest of meat. Slice both boneless pieces.

HALF LEG ROASTS, BUTT END

Slice straight down to bone, then along the bone to release the slices.

Instructions for marinating will be found on page 327.

BEEF

There are two standards by which beef can be judged: the packer's own brand, and the U.S. Department of Agriculture grade. Of USDA stamped beef, the top grade, *Prime,* is sold principally to restaurants and hotels; the next two grades, *Choice* and *Good,* are most generally available in retail meat markets. *Good* has the least fat, is somewhat less juicy and tender, and is the least expensive of the three grades. Consult the listing that follows for cuts suitable to the various methods of cooking. Less tender cuts can be tenderized by marinating, by slow cooking in moist heat, or by using commercial tenderizers.

TO RENDER BEEF FAT

5 pounds beef fat, ground
cold water to cover

Place fat in a large heavy pan or in the bottom of a roasting pan. Add water to cover. Place over low heat on top of range or in a moderate oven, 350° F. Let try out until fat is clear and the sediment at the bottom is beginning to brown. Strain. When cool, cover and keep in a cool place.

BEEF CHART

RETAIL CUTS OF BEEF—WHERE THEY COME FROM AND HOW TO COOK THEM

CHUCK
Braise. Cook in Liquid

②③ Inside Chuck Roll

⑤⑥ Chuck Short Ribs

② Chuck Tender

③ Petite Steaks*

Blade ②③ Pot-roast or Steak

Arm ④⑤ Pot-roast or Steak

⑤ Boneless Shoulder Pot-roast or Steak

⑥ Boston Cut

RIB
Roast, Broil, Panbroil, Panfry

② Standing Rib Roast

② Rib Steak

② Rib Steak, Boneless

②→ Delmonico (Rib Eye) Roast or Steak

SHORT LOIN
Roast, Broil, Panbroil, Panfry

① Club Steak

② T-Bone Steak

③ Porterhouse Steak

①②③ Top Loin Steak

②③ Filet Mignon Tenderloin Steak
(also from Sirloin 1, 2, 3)

SIRLOIN
Roast, Broil, Panbroil, Panfry

① Pin Bone Sirloin Steak

② Flat Bone Sirloin Steak

③ Wedge Bone Sirloin Steak

①②③ Boneless Sirloin Steak

ROUND
Braise. Cook in Liquid

③ Round Steak

① Standing Rump*

③ Top Round Steak*

① Rolled Rump*

③ ← Outside (Bottom) Round Steak or Pot-roast →

③ Eye of Round

④ Heel of Round

FORE SHANK
Braise. Cook in Liquid

① Shank Cross Cuts

①② Beef for Stew
(also from other cuts)

BRISKET
Braise. Cook in Liquid

③ Fresh Brisket

③ Corned Brisket

SHORT PLATE
Braise. Cook in Liquid

① Short Ribs

①② Skirt Steak Fillets*

① Rolled Plate

② Plate Beef

GROUND BEEF
Roast, Broil, Panbroil, Panfry

Ground Beef
(Flank, Short Plate, Shank, Brisket, Rib, Chuck, Loin, Round)

Beef Patties

FLANK STEAK
Braise. Cook in Liquid

① Flank Steak*

① Flank Steak Fillets*

TIP (KNUCKLE)
Braise. Cook in Liquid

④② Tip Steak*

④② Sirloin Tip*

④② Cube Steak*

* May be roasted, broiled or fried from high quality meat.

RECOMMENDED COOKING METHOD	CUT OF BEEF
Roasting	Standing Rib Roast Newport Roast Rolled Rib Roast Standing Rump Roast Rolled Rump Roast Fillet or Tenderloin Sirloin Sirloin Tip
Broiling Pan Broiling Pan Frying	Porterhouse Steak Sirloin Steak Rib Steak T-Bone Steak Pinbone Sirloin Steak Top Round Steak Club Steak Fillet Steak Filet Mignon Flank Steak

RECOMMENDED COOKING METHOD	CUT OF BEEF
Braising Pot Roasting	Blade Pot Roast—Chuck Round Steak—Full Cut Standing Rump Arm Pot Roast—Chuck Top Round Steak Rolled Rump Boneless Chuck English Cut—Chuck Bottom Round Steak Heel of Round Brisket Plate Beef Short Ribs Flank Steak
Cooking in Liquid Stewing	Heel of Round Shank Cross Cuts Corned Beef Plate Beef Short Ribs

BEEF ROASTING CHART

Insert thermometer into thickest part of meat away from fat and bone. Use shorter time per pound for larger cuts; longer time for smaller cuts.

Plan to remove roasts from oven 20-30 minutes before serving time, so that meat may be carved more easily.

CUT OF BEEF	WEIGHT	OVEN TEMPERA-TURE	MEAT THERM. READING	COOKING TIME, MINUTES PER POUND
Standing Rib	4-8 pounds	325°	140 (rare) 160 (medium) 170 (well done)	18-20 22-25 27-30
Rolled Rib	4-6 pounds	325°	140 (rare) 160 (medium) 170 (well done)	28-30 32-35 37-40
Rolled Rump	4-6 pounds	325°	140 (rare) 160 (medium)	25-30 32-35
Rib Eye	4-6 pounds	325°	140 (rare) 160 (medium) 170 (well done)	18-20 20-22 22-25
Sirloin Tip	3-5 pounds	325°	140 (rare) 160 (medium)	30 35
Whole Fillet	4-5 pounds	425°	140 (rare)	10

See chapter 15, Outdoor Cooking, for recipes for
spit roasting, barbecuing and grilling.

Roast Beef and Steak Dishes

RIB ROAST OF BEEF

For a two- or three-rib Standing Rib Roast: Season with salt. Place in a roasting pan, fat side up, uncovered, and roast in a moderately slow oven, 325° F., following time on chart. No basting is necessary.

An alternate method is to place the roast in a hot oven, 500° F., from 20 to 30 minutes or until lightly browned, then reduce heat to 300° F. For rare meat allow 15 minutes to the pound, for medium 20 minutes, and about 30 minutes for well done. Baste occasionally with the fat in the pan.

For Rolled Rib Roast increase cooking period 10 minutes per pound.

GRAVY

Place 2 tablespoons of fat from pan in skillet, add 2 tablespoons of flour and stir until brown. Gradually add 1 cup or more soup stock or water. Cook 5 minutes, season and strain.

Roast Beef is traditionally served, in England, with Yorkshire Pudding, below.

YORKSHIRE PUDDING

1½ cups flour
¼ teaspoon baking powder
½ teaspoon salt
1¼ cups milk
2 eggs
⅛ cup beef drippings

Mix dry ingredients. Add milk gradually, then the eggs. Beat very well with rotary beater. Place hot drippings from roast beef in oblong pan; pour in batter ½ inch deep. Bake in moderate oven, 350° F., 20 to 30 minutes. For added flavor, Yorkshire Pudding may be cooked in the following manner: 20 to 30 minutes before Roast Beef is done, remove it from pan, and place directly on rack of oven. Under it place pan containing the pudding batter, to permit the beef juices to drip on the pudding while baking. Bake in moderate oven, 350° F., 20 to 30 minutes. Cut in squares, serve around Roast Beef.

ROAST FILLET OF BEEF

4-pound fillet of beef
strips of suet
salt and pepper
¼ cup butter
juice of 1 lemon
1 tablespoon Worcestershire sauce

Lard fillet with suet, or have butcher do it. Season with salt and pepper. Cover with melted butter and lemon juice. Let stand several hours. Place in hot oven, 400° F., add Worcestershire sauce and baste often. Roast from 30 to 45 minutes. Thicken gravy in pan as in Roast Beef.

ROAST FILLET OF BEEF WITH VEGETABLES

4-pound fillet of beef
salt and pepper
½ cup prepared mustard, if desired
¼ cup butter
Kitchen Bouquet
1 cup each hot cooked peas, carrots and Potato Balls, page 427

Season fillet with salt and pepper, spread with mustard. Fold thin end under and fasten with skewer or string. Dot with butter on upper side, or have butcher lard top with strips of suet. Place in roasting pan in hot oven, 400° F., for 30 to 40 minutes, basting often. Remove skewers or string, set fillet aside. Make gravy in pan as in Roast Beef, add Kitchen Bouquet, strain. Serve garnished with vegetables.

Or, when nearly done, add 1 cup of thick sour cream to fillet, simmer a few minutes. Serve on hot platter with the gravy and garnish with sautéed mushrooms.

STEAK BROILING CHART

| | TIME EACH SIDE IN MINUTES | | |
Thickness	RARE	MEDIUM	WELL DONE
¾"-1"	5	7	9
1½"	8	10	13
2"	15	18	20

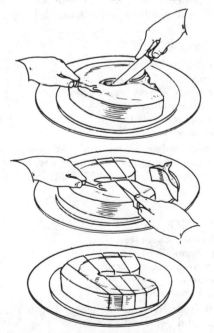

Carving a steak

To test a steak for doneness, with minimum loss of juices, slit the meat near the bone with the point of a sharp knife.

BROILED STEAK

If steak has thick edge of fat, slit outside edge at intervals, to prevent curling. Lay steak on rack in center of broiling oven, preheated to very hot, 3½ inches from source of heat. When steak is nicely browned on one side season with salt and pepper; turn and brown on the other side. Follow Steak Broiling Chart. Turn only once. When done, place on hot platter, season with salt and pepper, pour melted butter over steak, if desired, serve at once.

Steaks thinner than about ¾ inch, or very lean steaks like fillet, are not suitable for broiling; they should be sautéed quickly in a little butter or fat.

PAN-BROILED STEAK

Heat heavy skillet sizzling hot. Sear ¾- to 1-inch thick steak quickly on both sides. Reduce heat and turn often, pouring off fat so meat will broil, not fry. Cook only until medium rare. Place on hot platter, season with salt and pepper and spread with softened butter, if desired.

MINUTE STEAK

Minute steaks should be ¼-inch thick. Spread with softened butter. Add a few drops of lemon juice. Pan-broil in hot skillet 1 minute on each side.

BAKED STEAK

    Sirloin steak, 2 inches thick
    salt, pepper
    2 tablespoons Worcestershire sauce
    1 tablespoon walnut catsup
    3 tablespoons tomato catsup
    2 tablespoons butter

Season steak, place in pan, add Worcestershire, walnut catsup and tomato catsup; dot with butter. Bake in extremely hot oven, 500° F., for 30 minutes.

BAKED STEAK AND VEGETABLES

    4- to 5-pound sirloin steak
    1 large onion, sliced
    1 large green pepper, cut up
    1 cup catsup
    1 pound mushrooms, sautéed

Trim fat from steak. Chop onion. Clean pepper. Grind fat and pepper. Cover steak with a layer of onion, then of pepper. Pour catsup over all and top with chopped, sautéed mushrooms. Bake in hot oven, 400° F., from 30 to 45 minutes or longer if desired well done.

PEPPER STEAK

    3 tablespoons whole peppercorns
    3 pounds boneless sirloin steak
    2 tablespoons oil
    1 tablespoon butter
    ½ cup dry red wine
    2 tablespoons brandy
    1 teaspoon salt

Crush peppercorns with a rolling pin. Pat crushed peppercorns onto both sides of meat so that they stick. Heat oil in a large skillet. Over high heat brown each side of the meat for about 2 minutes. Reduce heat to medium and cook for 12 to 15 minutes depending upon your preference of rareness. Turn steak halfway through the cooking time. Remove steak to hot platter. Add butter, wine, brandy and salt to skillet. Bring to a boil and pour over the steak.

BEEFSTEAK AND ONIONS

Cook 4 or 5 sliced onions in 2 tablespoons fat in a covered skillet until soft and slightly browned. Season with salt and pepper. Serve on top of Broiled or Pan-Broiled Steak.

PLANKED STEAK

Broil a 1¼-inch thick porterhouse or sirloin for 4 minutes on each side. Butter a plank 1 inch larger than meat, place steak in center. Fill a pastry bag with mashed potatoes and pipe a border around the steak. Place in hot oven, 400° F., and bake until potatoes are browned. Spread steak with butter, season with salt and minced parsley.

FILET MIGNON

Cut a 3-pound beef tenderloin into fillets 2 inches thick. Flatten a little, season with salt and pepper. Pan-broil or sauté in a little butter or fat. Serve with melted butter or Béarnaise Sauce.

FILET MIGNON WITH BACON

Cut tenderloin of beef into 2-inch slices. Wrap around each a thin strip of bacon, and fasten with a wooden skewer. Broil under high heat 5 to 6 minutes on each side, until well browned. Serve on hot platter, season with salt and pepper, brush with butter and garnish with lemon slices and chopped parsley.

FILET MIGNON WITH ARTICHOKE

Pan-broil or sauté Filet Mignon, place on each a heated artichoke heart and a sautéed mushroom. Serve hot with Béarnaise Sauce.

FLANK STEAK WITH WINE SAUCE

¾ cup dry red wine
1 clove garlic, crushed (optional)
1 teaspoon salt
1 teaspoon pepper
¼ teaspoon dried dill
1 flank steak (about 1½ pounds)

Combine wine and seasonings; pour over the steak, cover, and let marinate in the refrigerator for 1 to 2 hours, turning meat several times. Remove meat from marinade, pat dry, broil or barbecue quickly until rare to medium rare. Cut diagonally across the grain of meat into thin slices. Add 1 tablespoon of butter to the remaining marinade, heat, and serve as a sauce with the steak.

BROILED FLANK STEAK

flank steak
mustard
Worcestershire sauce

Marinate flank steak in mustard and Worcestershire sauce for several hours; turn meat several times during this period. Broil 5 minutes on each side. Slice diagonally across the grain in thin slices.

See chapter 15, Outdoor Cooking, page 326, for grilled and barbecued steaks.

BEEF STROGANOFF

1½ pounds round steak
¼ cup flour
2 teaspoons salt
dash of pepper
2 tablespoons butter
1 pound fresh mushrooms or 1 can (6 ounces) mushroom caps
2 tablespoons catsup
1 cup consommé
1 tablespoon Worcestershire sauce
1 teaspoon dry mustard
½ cup sour cream

Cut round steak into 4 pieces. Place on waxed paper or board and pound flour mixed with salt and pepper into it with a mallet or the edge of a heavy saucer. Cut meat into ½-inch strips. Melt butter in heavy skillet; brown meat. Add all other ingredients except the sour cream. Simmer slowly until the meat is tender, adding more consommé if necessary. Cook about 1 hour. If desired, bring to table in chafing dish. Just before serving, stir in sour cream. Heat but do not boil. Serve with noodles or rice.

SUKIYAKI

2 pounds thinly sliced beef
   (sirloin tip or fillet)
3 tablespoons cooking oil
6 scallions, sliced, with part of the green tops
½ cup thinly sliced onions
½ cup bean curd (¾-inch squares)
6 ribs celery or Chinese cabbage, chopped
2 cups sliced mushrooms
1 pound spinach cut in 1-inch strips
2 cups bean sprouts

SAUCE
½ cup soy sauce
½ cup soup stock
1 teaspoon sugar
½ teaspoon monosodium glutamate

This is a dish to cook at the table, in an electric skillet or chafing dish.

Arrange meat and vegetables attractively on platter. Combine ingredients for sauce in small pitcher. All ingredients should be at room temperature.

Heat the oil over medium heat; cook the beef, turning frequently so that it does not brown, for about 3 minutes. Push the meat aside. Add the scallions, sauté until golden brown. Add the other vegetables one at a time, sprinkling each with a little sauce. Add bean sprouts last. Gently stir the meat with the rest of the ingredients and cook for about 4 minutes. Do not overcook. Serve immediately with boiled rice.

FONDUE BOURGUIGNONNE

This party dish is cooked at the table in a fondue pan or an electric skillet. Each guest impales a cube of sirloin or other tender beef on a long fork and cooks it to taste in oil or butter in the pan, then dips it into any one of an assortment of sauces.

Cut meat into ¾ inch cubes. Prepare clarified butter by melting ½ pound butter in a saucepan and pouring the clear liquid off the milky sediment that settles in the bottom of the pan. Heat the clarified butter in the fondue pan until it begins to brown. Spear piece of meat with fork, cook to taste in the hot butter, and dip into any one of these suggested sauces: mayonnaise with capers, herbs or curry; chutney with melted butter; mustard with catsup; bottled Chinese Duck Sauce or any favorite steak sauce.

BEEF TERIYAKI

2 pounds round steak
1 onion, sliced
1 teaspoon ground ginger
2 teaspoons sugar
½ cup soy sauce
½ cup orange juice
½ cup vegetable oil
1 clove garlic, chopped

Cut meat into very thin slices. If meat is well chilled or slightly frozen, it will slice easily. Place meat and onions in a shallow dish. Mix remaining ingredients and pour over the meat. Cover and refrigerate for at least 6 hours. Weave meat on skewers. Place on broiler pan so that meat is 4 inches from heat. Broil 5 minutes, turn, baste with the marinade, and broil other side of meat. Serve with hot rice.

ORIENTAL BEEF AND VEGETABLES

1½ pounds flank steak
1 green pepper
6 stalks celery
¼ cup vegetable oil
2 medium onions, sliced
1 6-ounce can water chestnuts
1 1-pound can tomatoes in purée
2 tablespoons cornstarch

MARINADE

⅓ cup soy sauce
1 clove garlic, minced
½ cup water

Mix the marinade. Cut beef into thin slices, cutting across the grain. Marinate beef for 30 minutes or more. Cut green pepper and celery into thin strips. Remove beef from marinade. Save marinade. Pat meat dry. In a wide skillet, brown the meat quickly in the oil. Push meat to one side; add onions, celery and water chestnuts. Cook about 2 minutes. Mix marinade, tomatoes and cornstarch. Add to meat, place green pepper strips on top, and cook until thickened, about 5 minutes.

Pot Roasts and Stews

See listing on page 268 for cuts suitable for pot roasts.

BASIC POT ROAST

2½ pounds of beef (chuck, rump, or flank steak)
2 tablespoons drippings
1 onion, chopped fine
½ cup boiling water
1 or 2 bay leaves
1 medium carrot, chopped
1 sliced celery root
1 cup canned tomatoes
salt and pepper
1 tablespoon flour

Season meat as desired. Heat the fat in a heavy saucepan or Dutch oven and brown the onion in it. Add the meat, brown on all sides. Add the boiling water, bay leaves, carrot and celery root. Cover tightly, simmer slowly about 2½ hours or until tender. Add a little more boiling water, if necessary, to prevent burning. One-half hour before serving add tomatoes and season to taste. Thicken gravy with 1 tablespoon flour mixed with a little cold water. Serve with Franconia Potatoes.

POT ROAST COOKED IN FOIL

4 pounds chuck roast
1 package dehydrated onion soup
1 cup sour cream

Spread meat with dehydrated soup mixture and sour cream. Place the meat on a double-thick square of heavy duty aluminum foil. Wrap with a double fold, and fold ends over to seal package, so that the juices will not escape. Bake at 300° F. for 3 to 3½ hours.

BEEF À LA MODE

3 pounds top round
clove of garlic, split
2 tablespoons beef fat (suet)
1 large onion, sliced
1 large or 2 medium carrots, chopped
½ cup chopped celery
salt and pepper
paprika
¾ cup tomato purée
1 thick slice rye bread

Rub meat with garlic. Heat beef fat until smoking hot in Dutch oven or a heavy pan with a close-fitting cover. Add sliced onion and when slightly cooked, add meat and brown thoroughly on all sides. Add chopped carrots, celery and seasonings. Cover tightly and cook slowly for 2½ hours. Then add tomato purée and the bread, crumbled, and cook until meat is tender and gravy smooth.

Instructions for freezing pot roast, either before or after cooking, will be found in chapter 24.

SWEET AND SOUR POT ROAST

6 medium onions, chopped
2 tablespoons fat
salt and pepper
3½ pounds beef rump, in thick slice
1 or 2 bay leaves
1 can (1 pound, 13 ounces) tomatoes
½ cup sugar
lemon juice

Fry the onions until golden brown in the fat; set aside. Season meat, brown on all sides in the fat, add bay leaf. Cover kettle tightly and let simmer for 2½-3 hours or until nearly tender, adding a little hot water if necessary to prevent scorching. Add fried onions, tomatoes, sugar and lemon juice to taste. Uncover and finish cooking in medium oven until gravy is thick and meat well browned.

TERIYAKI POT ROAST

3 to 4 pounds chuck or rump roast
1 tablespoon shortening
1 clove garlic, crushed
¼ cup soy sauce
¼ cup water
½ teaspoon ground ginger
2 onions, sliced
1 tablespoon cornstarch

Brown meat on all sides in the shortening. Add remaining ingredients except cornstarch to the roast. Cover and simmer until meat is tender, about 2½ hours. Soften cornstarch in a little cold water. Add to liquid in kettle. Stir constantly until thickened. Serve with the roast.

SAUERBRATEN

4 pounds beef, chuck, rump or round
salt and pepper
1 onion, sliced
3 bay leaves
1 teaspoon whole peppercorns
vinegar and water
salt and sugar
¼ cup brown sugar
¼ cup raisins
4 to 6 gingersnaps

Sprinkle meat well with salt and pepper and rub in thoroughly. Place with onions, bay leaves and peppercorns in a deep earthen dish. Heat water and vinegar (equal parts if vinegar is very strong), and add salt and sugar to taste. Pour hot over the meat to cover. Cover dish well, refrigerate, let stand 3 to 4 days, turning occasionally.

Put meat in kettle, add the onion slices and a little of the spiced vinegar, place in hot oven, 400° F., to brown. Cover tightly, reduce heat to moderately slow, and cook slowly about 3 hours, or until tender. Add more of the vinegar if necessary. Take out the meat, slice for serving and keep hot. Strain liquid in kettle, skim off fat. Melt ¼ cup brown sugar in an iron skillet, add the strained liquid very gradually, then the raisins and gingersnaps. Cook until thickened and smooth and pour hot sauce over meat.

Or follow method for marinating meat, and brown meat in 2 tablespoons fat in a Dutch oven. Add small amount of the spiced vinegar, cover tightly, simmer slowly until tender, adding the spiced vinegar from time to time until all has been used. When ready to serve, strain the liquid, thicken with flour to make a brown gravy, adding sour cream, if desired.

BRISKET AND CARROT STEW
(CARROT TSIMMES)

2 pounds brisket of beef
salt and pepper to taste
2 bunches of carrots
2 tablespoons fat
2 tablespoons flour

Season the meat and let stand several hours. Peel and dice carrots. Place in pan with meat, cover with boiling water and cook, covered, about 1 hour or until meat and carrots are tender. Heat the fat in a skillet, brown slightly, add the flour, and gradually 1 cup of the stock. Add to meat and carrots and simmer until carrots become browned, about 1 hour longer.

BRISKET BAKED WITH PRUNES
(POTATO AND PRUNE TSIMMES)

1 pound prunes
1 pound brisket of beef
salt and pepper
5 medium potatoes, Irish or sweet
½ cup sugar
small piece citric acid

Wash and soak prunes overnight in cold water. Place in pan with meat seasoned with salt and pepper. Cook slowly 1½ hours or until meat is nearly tender. Place meat and prunes on top of potatoes cut in small pieces. Add sugar and citric acid, cover and bake in oven, 375° F., until potatoes are done and all is browned, about 1 hour longer. Serve hot with gravy.

BEEF CASSEROLE WITH RED WINE

¼ cup all-purpose flour
½ cup fine dry bread crumbs
1½ pounds beef, cubed
¾ cup red wine
1 can (10½ ounces) condensed consommé
1 large onion, sliced
1 teaspoon salt
⅛ teaspoon pepper

Combine flour and crumbs; combine other ingredients. Blend all together and place in a casserole. Cover; bake in a slow oven, 300° F., for about 3 hours.

BEEF CASSEROLE STEW

2½ pounds beef, chuck or round
salt and pepper to taste
1 tablespoon flour
2 tablespoons beef drippings
1 small carrot, diced
1 small onion, sliced
1 cup strained tomatoes
1 bay leaf

Season meat, cut in pieces, dust with flour. Heat fat in a skillet and brown the meat in it on all sides. Place meat in casserole, add other ingredients, cover and simmer in a slow oven at 300° F. until tender, about 2½ hours. Serve hot with mashed or baked potatoes.

SWISS STEAK

3 pounds round steak, 1½ inches thick
1 garlic clove
¼ cup flour
2 teaspoons salt
⅛ teaspoon pepper
3 tablespoons fat
1 onion, sliced
2 cups hot tomato juice or boiling water

Put steak on board; cut garlic in half and rub over the meat. Pound the salt, pepper and flour into both sides of the meat with the edge of a heavy saucer or with a mallet. Cut into individual portions if desired. Melt fat in skillet, add onion, brown slightly, and set onion aside. Put meat into skillet, brown on both sides. Add hot tomato juice or water and onion. Cover and simmer 2 to 3 hours, or until tender.

See page 268 for list of cuts suitable for beef stew.

SWISS STEAK WITH TOMATOES

2 pounds round steak
garlic clove
salt and pepper
flour
¼ cup shortening
½ cup minced onion
1 cup chopped vegetables (carrots, peppers, and celery)
1 can (1 pound) stewed tomatoes, hot
1 cup stock, hot

Rub the steak with garlic. Pound in salt and pepper, and as much flour as the meat will hold, with the edge of a heavy saucer or with a mallet. Heat the shortening in a heavy casserole or Dutch oven. Sear one side of the meat, turn and add the vegetables, tomatoes and stock. Cover, and place in a moderate oven, 350° F. Cook for 2 hours or until tender.

OVEN BARBECUED SHORT RIBS

2-3 pounds beef short ribs
½ cup red wine
1 can (8 ounces) tomato sauce
2 tablespoons chopped onion
1½ teaspoons salt
2 tablespoons vinegar
1 tablespoon prepared mustard
dash of cayenne pepper

Rub hot Dutch oven with some of the fat from the short ribs; brown ribs slowly on all sides. Drain off fat. Combine other ingredients; pour over the ribs. Cover, bake in slow oven, 300° F., for 1½ to 2 hours, or until meat is tender.

ITALIAN MEAT ROLL
(BRACIOLA)

1½ pounds round steak or veal steak, ½ inch thick
½ pound sliced boiled ham
¼ pound chopped meat, pork and beef mixed
salt and pepper
6 hard-cooked eggs
Italian Tomato Sauce, page 390
oil or fat for frying

Spread steak (beef or veal) with fat. Lay ham evenly over steak. Spread chopped meat, pork and beef mixed, well seasoned with salt and pepper, over ham. Place eggs in a row down the center.

Form into one large roll and tie with string or fasten with toothpicks. Brown in hot fat in heavy kettle. Add Italian Tomato Sauce, and simmer 2 hours or until tender. Remove string. Serve hot or cold, sliced.

BEEF BIRDS (ROULADEN)

  1 pound round steak, ¼ inch thick
  salt, pepper
  1 tablespoon chopped fat bacon
  ¼ teaspoon prepared mustard
  1 teaspoon onion, chopped
  pinch paprika
  1 tablespoon chopped pickle
  flour
  2 tablespoons fat drippings
  1 bay leaf
  2 cups boiling water

Cut steak in 4 pieces. Flatten, sprinkle with salt and pepper, and spread with a mixture of bacon, mustard, onion, paprika and pickle. Roll each slice and fasten with string or toothpicks. Sprinkle with flour and brown in fat, add bay leaf and 1 cup boiling water, cover pan. Simmer 2½ to 3 hours or until tender, adding more water when necessary. Remove strings. Poultry dressing may be used as filling. A cup of sour cream may be added shortly before serving. Birds may be made with boneless veal cutlet the same way, except that veal will be done in 2 hours or less.

MOCK DUCK

  2 thin slices rump steak, or a flank steak
  1 teaspoon salt
  ⅛ teaspoon pepper
  ⅛ teaspoon ginger
  3 tablespoons fat drippings
  1 cup bread crumbs
  1 tablespoon grated onion
  1 teaspoon chopped parsley
  1 slice chopped boiled ham

Season steak with salt, pepper and ginger. Melt fat, add bread crumbs and the rest of the ingredients and spread evenly over half the steak. Cover with remaining steak and sew the edges together with coarse thread. Tie string around end of meat to resemble head of duck. Place the "duck" in skillet or heavy pan with a little fat. Brown, add 1 cup boiling water, cover and let simmer several hours or until tender. Remove strings, place "duck" in hot oven. Brown, basting often, and serve hot in its own sauce.

Or, in place of the bread filling, spread with 1 pound of chopped beef well seasoned with salt, pepper and paprika.

BEEF CURRY

  2 tablespoons oil
  1 tablespoon curry powder
  ½ clove garlic, chopped
  1 teaspoon salt
  ½ teaspoon pepper
  ¼ teaspoon ginger
  2 pounds beef, cubed
  3 onions, sliced thin
  3 tablespoons soy sauce
  1 cup bouillon
  2 tablespoons cornstarch
  ¼ cup cold water

In large skillet heat oil, stirring in curry powder. When hot, mash in garlic, add salt, pepper and ginger. When well mixed, add meat and onions. Stir until the onions are tender. Add soy sauce and bouillon. Cover and cook for 5 to 7 minutes. Soften cornstarch in cold water. Add to skillet and stir until liquid thickens. Serve with rice.

MOCK CHICKEN LEGS

  1 pound round steak
  1 pound boned veal cutlet or pork steak
  6-8 wooden skewers
  ¼ cup fat, melted
  ¼ cup flour or ¾ cup cracker crumbs
  2 teaspoons salt
  ½ teaspoon white pepper

Have meat cut about ⅜ inch thick. Pound well and cut each kind of meat into 1- or 1½-inch squares. Arrange skewers with 3 beef and 3 veal pieces, having top and bottom pieces somewhat smaller to represent drumsticks. Brush or roll in fat, then in flour or crumbs, season with salt and pepper. Brown in remaining fat. Cover pan tightly, cook slowly about 1½ hours, or until meat is tender, adding water if necessary.

BEEF STEW

  3½ pounds boneless beef
  ¼ cup flour
  salt and pepper
  ½ onion
  2 tablespoons beef drippings
  ¼ cup turnip, cut up
  ¼ cup carrots, cut up
  2 potatoes, diced
  Dumplings, page 102 and 407

Cut meat into small pieces. Dredge with flour, pepper, and salt; brown with the onion in the melted fat. Cover with water. Simmer 2 to 3 hours until the meat is almost tender. Add the vegetables. When done, thicken the gravy with 1 tablespoon flour mixed with a little cold water, season with pepper and salt. Add ½ cup tomato purée, if desired. Serve with Dumplings.

EASY BEEF STEW

    2 pounds beef, cubed
    flour
    2 tablespoons oil
    1 can (10½ ounces), condensed onion soup
    1 cup water
    ½ cup sherry
    salt and pepper
    1 package (9 or 10 ounces) frozen peas and carrots

Dredge meat with flour. Heat oil in heavy skillet or Dutch oven; brown meat on all sides. Add soup, water, sherry, salt and pepper. Cover and simmer until meat is tender. Stir frequently. If gravy becomes too thick, add a small amount of water as necessary. Shortly before serving, add cooked peas and carrots. Other vegetables may be used as desired.

OXTAIL STEW

Follow recipe for Easy Beef Stew, above, using oxtails.

BOILED BEEF

Boiled beef should not actually be boiled—it should be simmered in water kept just below the boiling point. Two methods of cooking meat in this fashion may be followed: if the meat is put on to cook in boiling water, the meat retains more of its flavor; if the meat is put on to cook in cold water, the broth will have more flavor, and the meat less.

ROASTED SOUP MEAT

    ¼ pound suet, diced
    1 clove garlic, chopped
    salt, pepper, ginger
    3 pounds rump roast or beef brisket
    ¼ cup diced onion
    ¼ cup diced celery
    ¼ cup diced carrot
    1 tablespoon flour

Mix suet, garlic, a generous amount of salt, and pepper and ginger to taste. Make deep gashes in the meat, about 2 inches apart. Pack the gashes tightly with the mixture. Put meat in a deep pan, add boiling water to cover, and simmer gently,

covered, for 1½ hours, adding more water to cover as needed. Add vegetables, cook 1 hour longer. When meat is tender, transfer it to a roasting pan. Season well with salt, pepper, and ginger, and brush with fat from top of soup. Add more fat to the roasting pan. Roast in a hot oven, 400° F., until meat is browned, basting often with fat and a little more soup. Place roast on serving plate. Add flour to pan drippings, stir until smooth; stir in 1 cup of the soup and cook until smooth and thickened. Skim fat from soup and serve as first course, with noodles or any desired soup garnish. The meat should be sliced and served with potatoes and vegetables as the main course of the meal.

BRISKET OF BEEF WITH SAUERKRAUT

    3 pounds brisket of beef
    water
    1 onion
    salt to taste
    2 pounds sauerkraut
    1 raw potato, grated
    1 apple, sliced
    1 tablespoon caraway seed

Wipe meat, place in large pan, add cold water to cover, bring to a boil and skim. Add onion and seasonings and continue to simmer until meat is tender, about 2 hours. Transfer the meat and one fourth of the liquid to another pan. The remaining liquid makes a strong broth to garnish with noodles and serve as soup. To the meat add the sauerkraut, potato, and apple. Sprinkle with caraway seed and simmer all together for 15 minutes.

BRISKET OF BEEF WITH BEANS

    1 pound dried navy or lima beans
    salt and pepper to taste
    2 pounds brisket of beef
    ¼ cup brown sugar
    ¼ cup molasses
    ½ teaspoon mustard
    2 tablespoons fat
    2 tablespoons flour
    1 cup bean liquid

Soak beans overnight in cold water. If quick cooking beans are used, no soaking is necessary. Season the meat and let stand 1 hour or longer. Drain beans, cover with fresh water and heat slowly. Add meat and simmer about 2½ hours, or until meat and beans are tender. Add sugar, molasses, and mustard. Heat the fat in a skillet, add flour and gradually a cup of hot bean liquid. Cook, stirring, until smooth. Pour this sauce over the meat and beans and cook until the beans are browned.

BRISKET OF BEEF WITH CABBAGE

2 or 3 pounds brisket of beef
1 head cabbage
1 small onion
2 tablespoons fat
2 tablespoons vinegar
2 tablespoons sugar

Cover meat with water and simmer until almost tender. Shred the cabbage, chop the onion, and brown in the fat. Add the cabbage and onion to the meat and simmer until tender. Add vinegar and sugar. If sauce is too watery, thicken with a sprinkling of flour and cook until smooth.

SWEET AND SOUR BOILED BEEF

3 pounds brisket of beef
salt and pepper
a little dill
1 bay leaf
1 onion, sliced
1 cup boiling water
juice of 1 lemon
3 tablespoons sugar

Place the meat in a pan adding salt, pepper, dill, bay leaf, the onion, sliced thin, and the boiling water. Simmer until meat is tender, about 2½ hours. Add lemon juice and sugar until sauce has the desired sweet and sour taste.

BOILED SHORT RIBS, SPANISH STYLE

Season short ribs of beef with salt and pepper, rub with garlic. Cover with boiling water, and a sliced onion. Simmer about 2 hours. Add 2 cups tomatoes, 1 teaspoon paprika and simmer 1 hour.

TO CORN OR PICKLE BEEF

10-pound piece of beef, brisket or rump
salt, white pepper, ginger, paprika, nutmeg, bay
    leaves, garlic
1 teaspoon saltpeter

Wash meat. Rub with salt, pepper and other spices. It should be well seasoned. Place meat in a large stone jar. Cover with water. Dissolve saltpeter in water and add. Cover with a plate and weight it down to keep meat submerged. Keep in a cool place, turning at least once a week. Leave in brine for 4 weeks. Add more salt during the process, if brine is not salty enough. Tongue may be prepared the same way.

BOILED CORNED BEEF

Rinse the corned beef well to wash off brine. If very salty, soak ½ hour in cold water; or bring to a boil, then drain. Place in large saucepan, cover with boiling water, and simmer 3 to 5 hours, or until tender. Remove from water and serve with Horseradish Sauce and Boiled Cabbage.

GLAZED CORNED BEEF

Cook corned beef, as above. Remove from liquid and place on a rack in an open roasting pan. Stud with cloves and pour ½ cup maple syrup over the meat. Bake in a moderate oven, 350° F., for 20 to 25 minutes or until the glaze has browned. Baste during the browning with additional maple syrup.

SHERRY-GLAZED CORNED BEEF

Stud cooked corned beef with cloves. Combine ½ cup sherry with ½ cup brown sugar and pour over meat. Brown corned beef in a moderate oven, 350° F., for 20 to 25 minutes, basting several times with the wine mixture.

NEW ENGLAND BOILED DINNER

4 pounds corned beef
3 large carrots
6 small parsnips
2 small turnips
1 small cabbage
6 medium onions
6 medium potatoes

Prepare as Boiled Corned Beef. Cook slowly 3 to 5 hours or until tender; 2 hours before serving, add carrots, parsnips, and turnips cut in quarters. Half an hour before serving add quartered cabbage, and whole onions and potatoes.

DRIED CHIPPED BEEF IN WHITE OR BROWN SAUCE

Cut dried beef into small pieces. If it is very dry or salty, pour boiling water over it, let stand 5 minutes and press dry in a strainer. Prepare Medium White Sauce or Brown Sauce, omitting the salt, and pour over the beef. Stir well and serve on toast or over baked potato. ½ pound dried beef is sufficient for 1 cup Brown or White Sauce.

Ground Beef and Meat Ball Dishes

BEEF LOAF

1 pound ground beef
1 teaspoon chopped onion
salt and pepper
¼ cup bread crumbs
½ cup cold water or tomato juice

Mix all the ingredients, form into a loaf. Lay strips of bacon over top. Place in a pan and bake in moderate oven, 350° F., about 1 hour. Serve with Brown Sauce or any desired sauce.

BEEF AND PORK MEAT LOAF

1½ pounds ground beef
½ pound ground pork
1½ teaspoons salt
½ teaspoon pepper
2 eggs, slightly beaten
1 medium onion, minced
1 stalk celery, minced
1 medium carrot, grated
½ cup cornflakes
2 tablespoons barbecue sauce

Have meat ground twice. Combine the beef and pork. Season with the salt and pepper. Add other ingredients, mix well and shape into a loaf. Bake in moderate oven, 350° F., for 1½ hours. Strips of bacon may be placed over the top before baking.

MEAT LOAF RING

2 pounds ground beef
1 pound ground shoulder pork
1 cup cracker crumbs
½ cup horseradish
3 tablespoons cream
2 small onions, grated
¼ cup minced green pepper
¼ cup catsup
2 teaspoons salt
2 eggs, separated

Mix all ingredients except egg whites. Fold in stiffly beaten whites, place in buttered ring mold and bake 1 hour at 350° F.

BEEF-MUSHROOM LOAF

½ pound fresh mushrooms, sliced,
    or 1 4-ounce can of mushrooms
1 medium onion, minced
3 tablespoons butter
1 cup bread crumbs
1½ cups milk
2 pounds ground beef
2 eggs, beaten
1 cup mashed potatoes
1½ teaspoons salt
½ teaspoon marjoram

Sauté mushrooms and onion in butter. Soak crumbs in milk. Mix all ingredients. Place in greased loaf pan or casserole. Bake at 350° F. for 1 hour. Serve with Hot Horseradish Sauce.

MEAT LOAF

1 pound beef
½ pound veal
small piece suet
1 egg
¼ cup chopped walnuts, optional
1 teaspoon salt
onion and celery salt
½ cup canned tomato
¼ pound bread
bacon
1 tablespoon fat

Grind meat and suet. Beat egg well, add meat, nuts, seasoning, tomato, and bread soaked in water and squeezed dry. Mix thoroughly, form into loaf, lay strips of bacon on top, place in roasting pan in which 1 tablespoon fat has been melted. Bake in a moderate oven, 350° F., for 1 hour.

TAMALE LOAF

1 clove garlic, minced
1 tablespoon butter
½ pound ground beef
1 tablespoon salt
1 cup corn meal
2 eggs
1 can (8 ounces) tomato sauce
1 can (1 pound) corn
1 tablespoon chili powder

Brown garlic or a little onion in butter; add meat and salt. Mix with remaining ingredients. Bake in loaf pan set in a pan of water for 1 hour in 350° F. oven. May be served sprinkled with additional chili powder if desired.

CHILI CON CARNE

1 pound beef, ground
1 onion, chopped
2 teaspoons fat
1 teaspoon chili powder
1 cup tomatoes
½ teaspoon paprika
salt to taste
1 cup water
1 can (1 pound) kidney beans
1 tablespoon flour

Brown the meat and onion in the hot fat, add chili powder, the tomato, paprika, salt, and water, and simmer for 10 minutes; add beans. Bring to a boil, add flour, blended with a little water, and cook a few minutes longer. Serve hot.

CHILI CON CARNE WITH WINE

1½ pounds lean beef, ground
1 large onion, chopped
1 clove garlic, chopped
2 tablespoons shortening
½ cup water
¾ cup red wine
1 beef bouillon cube
1 tablespoon cumin seed
1 tablespoon chili powder
2 teaspoons oregano
salt to taste
2 cans (1 pound each) red kidney beans

Sauté beef, onion and garlic in shortening until meat is lightly browned; stir meat with a fork so that it browns evenly and is broken into small pieces. Add water, wine, bouillon cube and seasonings. Simmer for about 40 minutes, stirring often. The mixture should still be moist but not juicy. Add kidney beans and their liquid; cover pan and simmer for 5 minutes to heat beans.

ORIENTAL BEEF CASSEROLE

1½ pounds ground beef
1 tablespoon shortening
2 medium green peppers
2 medium to large onions
½ cup uncooked rice
3 cups tomato juice
¼ cup soy sauce
¼ teaspoon garlic salt
¼ teaspoon ground ginger

Brown beef lightly in shortening. Slice peppers and onions. In the bottom of a large, greased casserole place half of the meat. Cover with half of the pepper rings and then with half of the onion slices. Sprinkle with the rice. Repeat the layers with the onion slices on top. Mix remaining ingredients and pour into casserole. Cover. Bake at 350° F. for 1 hour. If refrigerated after mixing, bake an additional 15 minutes.

HAMBURGERS

1 pound round steak, ground
3 tablespoons ice water
1 teaspoon salt
¼ teaspoon pepper

Mix lightly and shape in small patties, about ¾ inch thick. Grease skillet or broiler pan. Cook from 2 to 5 minutes on each side. Serve plain or with melted butter if desired.

DEVILED HAMBURGERS

2 pounds ground beef
6 tablespoons catsup
1 teaspoon Worcestershire sauce
2 teaspoons prepared mustard
2 teaspoons horseradish
1 tablespoon grated onion
1 teaspoon salt
¼ teaspoon pepper
½ cup dry bread crumbs

Mix ingredients thoroughly. Shape lightly into patties. Broil as above.

HAMBURGERS TERIYAKI

1½ pounds ground beef
1½ teaspoons cornstarch
¼ cup water
1 teaspoon ginger
⅛ teaspoon garlic powder
¼ cup soy sauce
1 8-ounce can sliced pineapple

Shape beef into 6 patties. Mix cornstarch with water. Add ginger, garlic, soy sauce and pineapple juice. Cook over low heat, stirring constantly, until thickened. Brush each patty generously with the sauce. Broil about 3 inches from the heat for 8 to 12 minutes, turning once. Place a pineapple slice on the top of each patty for the last 4 minutes of broiling. Serve remaining sauce with patties.

HAMBURGERS WITH BURGUNDY

1½ pounds ground lean beef
⅜ cup Burgundy wine
1 teaspoon seasoned salt
pepper to taste

Mix all ingredients and shape into patties. Prepare Burgundy Sauce, below.

BURGUNDY SAUCE

3 tablespoons butter
3 tablespoons soy sauce
3 tablespoons chopped chives or scallions
¼ cup Burgundy (or other red dinner wine)
cornstarch (optional)

Heat all ingredients except the cornstarch. If thickened sauce is desired, mix 1 teaspoon cornstarch with a little cold water; add to sauce. Cook until clear and thickened. Cook hamburgers as above, serve with sauce.

MOCK FILLET STEAK

1 pound round steak, chopped
bacon

Form chopped beef into flat rounds 1 inch thick; circle each round with a long, thin strip of bacon, to overlap at ends; fasten with toothpicks. Brown on both sides in hot skillet, then place in extremely hot oven, 500° F., until bacon is crisp. Sprinkle with salt and pepper.

MOCK STEAK (PAN-BROILED)

Pat and mold well-seasoned ground steak, 1 to 1½ inches thick. Place in greased skillet. Fry on both sides. Serve with fried onions.

SEAMEN'S BEEF

2 pounds ground beef
2 teaspoons salt
¼ teaspoon pepper
1 cup cold mashed potatoes
½ cup milk
1 egg
8 uncooked potatoes, sliced
2 large onions, sliced
2 cups beef bouillon

Mix beef, salt, pepper, mashed potatoes, milk and egg. Shape into patties. Brown patties on both sides in a skillet. In a greased casserole, place alternate layers of potatoes, onions and beef patties, beginning and ending with potatoes. Add bouillon. Bake at 350° F. for 50 to 60 minutes.

BASIC MEAT BALLS

1 pound ground beef
¼ cup fine dry bread crumbs
⅔ cup chopped onion
1 teaspoon salt
dash of pepper
⅔ cup evaporated milk
2 tablespoons butter

Combine the first 6 ingredients. Shape into 12 meat balls (a scant ¼ cup each) or 36 small meat balls, about 1 tablespoon each. Melt the butter in a skillet. Brown the meat balls in the butter. Serve with any of the variations given below. Meat balls may be made earlier in the day and heated slowly in the sauce.

The basic meat ball recipe can be used for hamburgers, meat loaf, or as filling in cabbage rolls or green peppers.

GROUND MEAT IN ACORN SQUASH

Split and parboil Acorn Squash until almost tender. Place in pan, fill with Basic Meat Ball mixture. Sprinkle with brown sugar, dot with butter, and bake at 400° F. 15 minutes or until meat is done.

MEAT BALLS STROGANOFF

Basic Meat Balls, preceding
1 can (4 ounces) sliced mushrooms
1 can (8 ounces) tomato sauce
⅛ cup flour
⅛ teaspoon pepper
¼ teaspoon garlic salt
1 cup evaporated milk
1 cup water
1 teaspoon Worcestershire sauce
2 tablespoons lemon juice

Prepare Basic Meat Balls. Drain mushrooms, saving liquid. After meat balls are browned, push to side of skillet, add mushrooms and brown over medium heat, stirring occasionally. Add enough water to the mushroom liquid to make ½ cup; pour this liquid and tomato sauce over the meat balls. Bring to a boil, cover skillet, reduce heat and simmer for 15 minutes. Remove from heat. Sprinkle in the flour a little at a time, stirring constantly to blend. Add pepper, garlic salt, evaporated milk, water and Worcestershire sauce in that order, stirring constantly. Return to low heat and cook until sauce is thickened, about 3 to 5 minutes. Add lemon juice and serve immediately with cooked rice or boiled noodles.

MEAT BALLS CANTONESE

Basic Meat Balls, preceding
1 can (1 pound) pineapple tidbits
1½ tablespoons cornstarch
2 tablespoons water
¼ cup vinegar
¼ cup sugar
2 teaspoons soy sauce
1 tablespoon butter
½ cup sliced green onions
½ cup green pepper rings cut ¼-inch wide
1 cup diced celery
1 large tomato, cut in wedges
¼ cup blanched almonds, toasted and salted

While meat balls are browning, drain the pineapple, saving juice. Mix the cornstarch with the water until smooth; add pineapple juice, vinegar, sugar and soy sauce. When meat balls are browned, add this mixture. Bring to a boil over medium heat. Cover skillet, reduce heat and simmer for 20 minutes. Add the butter and stir until melted. Add remaining ingredients except the almonds. Stir lightly. Cover the skillet and cook for 10 minutes over low heat. Just before serving, sprinkle with the toasted almonds. Serve with hot rice.

SWEDISH MEAT BALLS

Basic Meat Balls, page 280
2 beef bouillon cubes
1 cup boiling water
⅛ cup flour
½ teaspoon allspice
1 cup evaporated milk
½ cup water
1 tablespoon lemon juice

Prepare 36 or more small meat balls. While they are browning, dissolve bouillon cubes in 1 cup boiling water. After meat balls are browned, add bouillon. Bring to a boil, reduce the heat; cover the skillet and simmer for 15 minutes. Remove from the heat. Stir in the flour a little at a time. Add allspice and slowly stir in the evaporated milk and ½ cup water. Cook uncovered over low heat; stir occasionally. When the sauce is thickened (about 10 minutes), stir in lemon juice and serve immediately with buttered noodles.

EASY SWEDISH MEAT BALLS

2 pounds ground meat, beef, veal and pork
1 onion, grated
½ cup bread crumbs
salt, pepper
1 teaspoon Worcestershire sauce
2 eggs, beaten
4 tablespoons butter
2 cups stock or consommé
4 tablespoons flour
¼ cup sherry

Mix first six ingredients; shape into small balls. Brown in butter. Add stock, cover skillet and simmer for about 15 minutes. Remove the meat balls, keep warm. Thicken the gravy with the flour blended with a little cold water. Cook 5 minutes, add sherry. Reheat meat balls in gravy.

ITALIAN MEAT BALLS

1 pound beef, ground
1 pound pork, ground
1 onion, grated
½ cup bread crumbs
salt, pepper, nutmeg
2 eggs, well beaten
½ clove garlic, chopped fine
3 tablespoons grated Parmesan cheese
¼ teaspoon oregano
2 tablespoons butter
Italian Tomato Sauce, page 390

Mix all ingredients except butter and tomato sauce. Shape into balls. Brown the balls lightly in the butter. Place in a casserole, cover with the tomato sauce. Bake, covered, in a moderate oven, 350° F., for about 30 minutes.

GERMAN MEAT BALLS
(KOENIGSBERGER KLOPS)

1 pound beef, ground
1 pound pork, ground
1 onion, grated
⅛ cup bread crumbs
salt, pepper, nutmeg
5 egg whites, beaten stiff

Mix all ingredients, adding beaten egg whites last. Form into balls.

SAUCE

3 cups water
1 onion, cut fine
4 bay leaves
1 tablespoon sugar
1 teaspoon salt
½ teaspoon allspice and peppercorns, combined
¼ cup tarragon vinegar
1 tablespoon flour
5 egg yolks, beaten
1 lemon, sliced
capers

Boil first 6 ingredients 30 minutes. Strain; bring to boiling point, add meat balls and simmer 15 minutes. Remove meat balls to hot platter, keeping them hot. Add vinegar to liquid. Dissolve flour in small amount of cold water, add to beaten yolks. Add this thickening mixture gradually to seasoned liquid, stirring constantly until smooth and thick; pour over meat balls, and garnish with lemon slices and capers.

PORCUPINE MEAT BALLS

1 10½-ounce can condensed tomato soup
½ cup water
1½ pounds ground beef
½ cup uncooked rice
1 tablespoon minced onion
½ teaspoon allspice
1 teaspoon salt
¼ teaspoon pepper

Mix soup and water. Combine other ingredients and shape into small balls, 1 to 1½ inches in diameter. Bring liquid to a boil. Add meat balls. Cover pan and simmer for about 2 hours. Stir occasionally. If needed, add small quantities of water during cooking to prevent sticking.

SLOPPY JOES

½ cup minced onion
½ cup chopped green pepper
2 tablespoons butter
1½ pounds ground beef
½ cup chopped mushrooms
2-4 tablespoons chili sauce or catsup
salt to taste

Sauté the onion and green pepper in the butter until tender. Add the meat and cook until lightly browned, stirring with a fork. Add mushrooms, chili sauce and seasoning. Cook, uncovered, for five minutes. Serve on lightly toasted sandwich buns.

GROUND BEEF ON TOAST

Toast slices of bread on one side. Spread untoasted side thickly with well-seasoned ground round steak. Make small well in center and fill with catsup or chili sauce. Over this place 2 strips of bacon crosswise. Broil until bacon is cooked and meat is done.

BAKED STUFFED CABBAGE ROLLS

1 pound ground beef
1 cup cooked rice
½ cup bread crumbs
2 eggs
onion juice
1½ teaspoons salt
cabbage leaves
1½ cups tomato sauce

Mix first 6 ingredients. Cut out and discard hard center core of cabbage. Put cabbage in large pot. Pour boiling water over it, let stand until leaves are flexible and can easily be removed from the head. Fill each leaf with prepared mixture, roll up, and fasten with toothpicks. Sprinkle with salt and dredge with flour; brown in fat. Add tomato sauce, cover, and bake in a slow oven, 300° F., about 2 hours.

STUFFED CABBAGE ROLLS

8 large leaves of cabbage
1 pound lean beef, ground
salt and pepper, to taste
1 small onion, grated
½ cup cooked rice
2 cups tomatoes
1 onion, chopped
2 tablespoons vinegar
2 tablespoons sugar

Prepare cabbage leaves for stuffing as above. Season the meat with salt and pepper, add grated onion and rice. Roll a portion of the meat mixture in each leaf. Fasten with toothpicks. Place cabbage rolls folded sides down, with the rest of the ingredients in a Dutch oven. Add a little water and simmer for about 1 hour. Add additional sugar and vinegar if needed to adjust seasoning.

MEAT-CABBAGE CASSEROLE

1 head cabbage
2 tablespoons butter
2 tablespoons dark corn syrup
¼ teaspoon ground marjoram
2 teaspoons salt
1½ pounds ground beef
½ cup bread crumbs
½ cup milk
2 eggs, beaten

Shred cabbage. Cook in boiling water for 5 minutes. Drain. Add butter, syrup, marjoram and salt. In separate bowl mix beef, crumbs, milk and eggs. In a greased casserole place alternate layers of cabbage and beef, starting and ending with cabbage. Bake at 350° F. for 1 hour.

STUFFED PEPPERS WITH BEEF
See page 425.

SWEET AND SOUR MEAT BALLS

2 cups hot water
1 tablespoon matzo meal, or cracker crumbs
1 pound chopped beef
1 onion, grated
1 egg, beaten
salt and pepper
¼ cup raisins
¼ cup sugar
1 lemon, sliced
1 tablespoon fat
1 tablespoon potato flour

Pour ½ cup hot water over meal. Add next 4 ingredients and form into small balls. Place in saucepan with 1½ cups water, raisins, sugar and lemon. Cover. Cook slowly ½ hour, then add fat mixed with potato flour to thicken gravy, simmer a few minutes.

PASTIES (MEAT AND VEGETABLE TURNOVERS) (1)

Short Pastry, page 342
½ pound raw beef, finely minced
1 cup chopped onion
1 raw potato, diced fine
½ cup diced celery
salt, pepper
2 teaspoons butter

Divide pastry in half and roll each into a 9-inch round. Combine meat, vegetables and seasoning, and spread on half of each round, leaving a 1-inch margin. Sprinkle with salt and pepper. Fold pastry over to cover, press edges to seal well. Put the turnovers into a pie plate. Slash top crust of each, insert 1 teaspoon butter. Bake in a hot oven, 400° F., ½ hour, or until dough is browned; reduce heat to moderate, 350° F., and bake ½ hour longer. Pour a teaspoon of hot water into the openings occasionally to keep the filling moist.

PASTIES (2)

Substitute 1½ cups of any leftover meat in recipe above. If you have leftover gravy, use it instead of butter and hot water.

VEAL

Veal is the meat of the calf. It is very tender when it comes from a young animal up to 14 weeks of age, but much of the veal on the market is from older animals, and may require longer, moist cooking to make it tender. Since veal is naturally lean,

it is improved by cooking with added fat or liquid. Veal is always served well done.

VEAL CUTS

RECOMMENDED COOKING METHOD	CUT OF VEAL
Roasting	Arm Roast—Shoulder Blade Roast—Shoulder Rib Roast Standing Rump Center Cut of Leg Shank Half of Leg Rolled Shoulder Boneless Rump Breast Sirloin Roast Loin Roast
Pan Frying	Arm Steak—Shoulder Blade Steak—Shoulder Rib Chop Round Steak—Cutlet Sirloin Steak City Chicken Mock Chicken Legs Loin Chops Kidney Chops
Braising	Arm Roast—Shoulder Blade Roast—Shoulder Standing Rump Center Cut of Leg Shank Half of Leg Arm Steak—Shoulder Blade Steak—Shoulder Rib Chop Boneless Rump Round Steak—Cutlet Heel of Round Rolled Shoulder Breast Riblets Sirloin Roast Sirloin Steak Fore Shank City Chicken Mock Chicken Legs Loin Roast Loin Chop Kidney Chop
Cooking in Liquid Stewing	Heel of Round Riblets Boneless Stew Breast Fore Shank

VEAL CHART

RETAIL CUTS OF VEAL—WHERE THEY COME FROM AND HOW TO COOK THEM

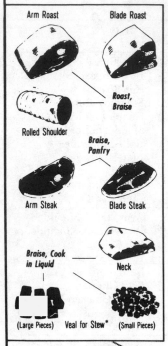

Arm Roast

Blade Roast

Roast, Braise

Rolled Shoulder

Braise, Panfry

Arm Steak

Blade Steak

Braise, Cook in Liquid

Neck

(Large Pieces) Veal for Stew* (Small Pieces)

Rib Roast

Roast

Crown Roast

Rib Chop

Braise, Panfry

Frenched Rib Chop

Loin Roast

Roast, Braise

Rolled Stuffed Loin

Loin Chop

Braise, Panfry

Kidney Chop

Sirloin Roast

Roast, Braise

Rolled Double Sirloin

Sirloin Steak

Braise, Panfry

Cube Steak*

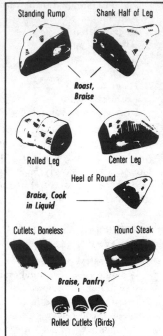

Standing Rump

Shank Half of Leg

Roast, Braise

Rolled Leg

Center Leg

Heel of Round

Braise, Cook in Liquid

Cutlets, Boneless

Round Steak

Braise, Panfry

Rolled Cutlets (Birds)

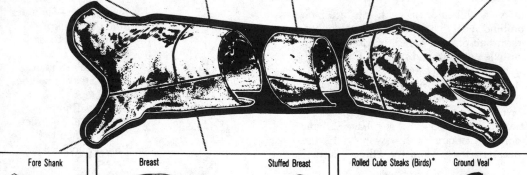

Fore Shank

Braise, Cook in Liquid

Brisket Rolls

Braise

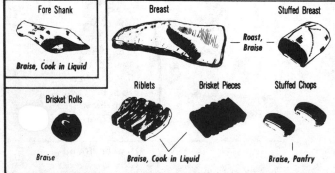

Breast

Stuffed Breast

Roast, Braise

Riblets

Brisket Pieces

Stuffed Chops

Braise, Cook in Liquid

Braise, Panfry

Rolled Cube Steaks (Birds)*

Ground Veal*

Patties*

Braise

Roast (Bake) Braise, Panfry

Mock Chicken Legs*

City Chicken*

Choplets*

Braise, Panfry

*VEAL FOR STEW, GRINDING OR CUBING MAY COME FROM ANY WHOLESALE CUT

VEAL ROASTING CHART

(Oven temperature is 325° F. for all cuts.)

WEIGHT	MEAT THERMOMETER READING	COOKING TIME MINUTES PER POUND
Leg	5-8 lbs.	170-180	35
Loin	4-6 lbs.	170-180	35-40
Rolled Shoulder	3-5 lbs.	170-180	40-45
Stuffed Breast			40-45
Shoulder	4-6 lbs.	170-180	35-40

ROAST VEAL

Choose leg, loin, rolled shoulder or bone-in shoulder. Dredge with salt and pepper, ginger and flour. Put in pan in moderately slow oven, 325° F., with 3 tablespoons of beef or poultry drippings. Roast, covered, according to chart, until very tender, basting often with pan drippings and water or stock. Uncover to brown, the last half hour of cooking time.

ROAST VEAL BREAST, STUFFED

Have the butcher make an opening on the underside of the veal breast or have him bone it. Stuff with Bread Stuffing, page 324, or Potato Stuffing, page 325, and sew up ends, or if boned veal is used, spread stuffing on flat side, roll and tie. Dredge with salt, pepper, ginger and flour; place in roasting pan with 2 tablespoons beef or poultry fat, an onion cut fine, and a little boiling water. Cover tightly, and roast at 325° F., about 3 hours. (See chart.) Uncover to brown the last half hour of cooking time.

Lamb breast may be prepared the same way.

See chart above for recommended oven temperatures for roasting veal.

BAKED VEAL CHOPS

4 veal chops
salt, pepper
flour
2 tablespoons butter
1 cup sour cream
1 egg yolk
2 tablespoons light cream

Season chops lightly with salt and pepper. Dip in flour. Fry chops slowly in butter until brown. Cover and bake in moderate oven, 350° F., for 30 minutes. Spoon sour cream over chops and bake

20 minutes more. Just before serving, stir sauce from pan into egg yolk beaten with a little cream.

CREOLE VEAL CHOPS

6 veal chops
1 clove garlic
salt and pepper
flour
1 cup finely sliced celery
1 onion, minced
4 tablespoons shortening
2 to 3 tablespoons catsup
1 cup tomato juice

Rub chops with garlic, salt and pepper; dredge with flour. Sauté the celery and onion in the shortening. Remove vegetables, increase the heat, and sear chops on both sides. Place chops, vegetables, catsup and tomato juice in a greased casserole. Cover. Bake at 350° F. for about 1 hour.

VEAL CUTLETS

Use slices of veal from the leg, cut ½ inch thick. Season with salt and pepper, dip in crumbs, let stand 15 minutes, then dip in egg mixed with 1 tablespoon water, then again in cracker or bread crumbs. Let stand 15 minutes. Brown on both sides, cover and finish cooking slowly about 30 minutes, or until tender, on top of range or in moderate oven, 350° F. Add a little hot water, if necessary, to prevent scorching.

VEAL BIRDS

See Beef Birds, page 275.

WIENER SCHNITZEL

Cut ½-inch thick veal steak in pieces for serving. Cook like Veal Cutlets, above. Sprinkle with lemon juice. Garnish each serving with lemon slices, capers, anchovy fillets, and a fried or poached egg.

PAPRIKA SCHNITZEL

1½ pounds veal cutlet
flour, salt, pepper
2 tablespoons fat
1 tablespoon paprika
3 onions, sliced
½ cup sour cream

Cut meat into serving pieces, dip in flour mixed with salt and pepper. Heat fat in skillet, stir in paprika. Cook onions in this until glassy. Add meat, cook until brown on both sides. Stir in sour cream, cover, and cook slowly until meat is tender.

POTTED VEAL CUTLET

veal cutlet or steak, 1½ inches thick
flour
ginger, dry mustard, salt, pepper, paprika
3 tablespoons fat
milk
2 tablespoons sour cream
onions, carrots, celery (optional)

Score meat, sprinkle with flour combined with seasonings, and pound well with mallet or edge of plate. Heat fat in small Dutch oven. Brown meat on both sides. Add milk to cover meat, and simmer, covered, 1 hour or until meat is tender. Add sour cream. Vegetables may be added with milk.

MEXICAN VEAL CUTLET WITH NOODLES

1 pound veal cutlet, cut thin
¼ cup flour
3 tablespoons shortening
1½ cups sliced onions
6 tablespoons chili sauce
1¼ cups bouillon
2 cups noodles, cooked
¾ cup condensed cream of chicken soup
grated Parmesan cheese

Cut meat into small serving pieces and dredge with flour. Heat shortening, brown meat quickly on both sides. Add onions, chili sauce, and heated bouillon. Reduce heat, cover the pan, and simmer about 30 minutes, until meat in tender. Arrange meat around rim of serving platter. Add noodles and soup to sauce, heat well, and pile in the center of the platter. Sprinkle with grated cheese.

VEAL SCALOPPINE

2½-3 pounds boneless veal cutlet, thinly sliced
flour
3 tablespoons butter
¾ cup chicken stock or ¼ cup stock and ¼ cup wine
(Marsala or other)
1 tablespoon butter

Pound the veal scallops very thin. Flour on one side. Heat the butter in a skillet. Sauté the meat for 3 minutes on each side, cooking the floured side first. Remove the meat from the skillet and keep it warm.

Add soup stock and wine to the skillet. Heat thoroughly. Add the tablespoon of butter. Pour the sauce over the hot cutlets. Serve at once.

VEAL PAPRIKA WITH WINE

3 tablespoons shortening
2 pounds boneless veal, cubed
3 tablespoons flour
1 cup hot water
½ cup white wine
1 can (6¾ ounces) mushrooms
2 tablespoons chopped parsley
1 onion, diced
1 teaspoon paprika
salt and pepper
1 cup sour cream

Heat shortening in heavy skillet. Add veal; brown well. Stir in flour. Add water and wine. Stir constantly until the mixture is thick and smooth. Add mushrooms, including liquid, parsley, onion, paprika, a dash of pepper and salt to taste. Cover and simmer 45 minutes to an hour. Stir frequently to prevent sticking. Stir in sour cream. Heat but do not boil. Serve with buttered noodles.

HUNGARIAN GOULASH

1 pound lean beef
1 pound lean veal
flour
1 tablespoon fat
1 large onion, diced
1 teaspoon salt
1 teaspoon paprika
1 cup strained tomatoes
8 peeled, small potatoes

Cut beef and veal into 1-inch cubes, roll in flour and brown in hot fat with the onions, salt and paprika. Add tomatoes. Cook 1 hour; add potatoes. Simmer, closely covered, until potatoes are done.

VEAL FRICASSEE

2 pounds boneless veal, cubed
1 small onion
2 stalks celery
1 carrot
salt, pepper
flour
3 tablespoons butter

Cook veal slowly until tender in boiling water to cover, along with onion, celery, carrot, salt and pepper. Remove meat. Season with salt and pepper, dredge with flour, brown in butter. Serve with Fricassee Sauce, made with the cooking stock, and Baking Powder Dumplings.

Meat can be browned in 3 tablespoons butter or fat before cooking it in the liquid.

VEAL CURRY

1 teaspoon sugar
¼ cup sliced onion
1 teaspoon curry powder
3 tablespoons fat
2 pounds boneless veal, cubed
1½ teaspoons salt
pepper, paprika, dry mustard
little grated lemon rind
1 quart boiling water
3 tablespoons flour
½ cup sour cream

Carmelize sugar in heavy kettle. Add onion, curry, fat, meat, seasonings and lemon rind. Add water gradually, then the flour mixed with a little cold water. Simmer 1½ hours or until meat is tender. Before serving add the cream. Serve with brown rice. If desired, omit curry and increase paprika and mustard to taste.

JELLIED VEAL LOAF (SULZ)

See page 371.

LAMB AND MUTTON

Lamb is the meat of the sheep under 1 year of age; it is firm-textured but tender, pink to dark red in color, and has a considerable amount of firm white fat. Mutton comes from sheep over 1 year of age; its texture is softer, it may be marbled with creamy-colored fat, and its flavor is distinctly stronger than that of lamb. Mutton is less popular, and thus less widely available than lamb in this country. Where it is sold in any substantial quantity, as in England, it is cheaper than lamb.

RECOMMENDED COOKING METHOD	CUT OF LAMB
Roasting	Square-Cut Shoulder Cushion Shoulder Breast Rib Roast—Rack Loin Roast Frenched Leg Rolled Shoulder American Leg Rolled Breast Crown Roast Rolled Loin Boneless Sirloin Roast
Broiling Pan Broiling Pan Frying	Shoulder Chops Rib Chops Loin Chops Saratoga Chops— Shoulder Patties English Chops Sirloin Chops
Braising	Breast Shoulder Chops Riblets Saratoga Chops— Shoulder Rolled Breast Neck Slices Shanks
Cooking in Liquid Stewing	Riblets Neck Slices Shanks

LAMB ROASTING CHART

(Oven temperature is 325° F. for all cuts.)

	WEIGHT	MEAT THERMOMETER READING	COOKING TIME MINUTES PER POUND
Leg	5-8 lbs.	165-170 (rare) 175-180 (medium)	25-30 30-35
Shoulder (cushion)	3-5 lbs.	175-180	30-35
Rolled Shoulder	3-5 lbs.	175-180	35-45
Crown Roast	4-6 lbs.	175-180	35-45

BROILING

	THICKNESS	MEDIUM	WELL DONE
Lamb Chops (Rib, Loin, Shoulder)	¾" 1½"	5 minutes* 9 minutes*	6-7 minutes* 11 minutes*

* Time per side

Mutton is cooked like lamb, and times given above apply also to mutton chops and roasts.

LAMB CHART

RETAIL CUTS OF LAMB—WHERE THEY COME FROM AND HOW TO COOK THEM

SHOULDER	NECK	RACK	LOIN	SIRLOIN	LEG

SHOULDER
Roast, Broil, Panbroil, Panfry

Square Shoulder · Arm Chop · Rolled Shoulder · Blade Chop · Cushion Shoulder · Saratoga Chops · Cubes for Kabobs*

NECK
Braise, Cook in Liquid

Neck Slices

RACK
Roast, Broil, Panbroil, Panfry

Rib Roast · Crown Roast · Rib Chops · Frenched Rib Chops

LOIN
Roast, Broil, Panbroil, Panfry

Loin Roast · Rolled Double Loin · English Chop · Loin Chops

SIRLOIN
Roast, Broil, Panbroil, Panfry

Sirloin Roast · Rolled Double Sirloin · Sirloin Chop

LEG
Roast, Broil, Panbroil, Panfry

Sirloin Half of Leg · Shank Half of Leg · Leg, Sirloin on · Leg Chop (Steak) · Leg, Sirloin off · Rolled Leg · American Leg · Combination Leg · Center Leg

FORE SHANK
Braise, Cook in Liquid

Fore Shank · Riblets

BREAST
Roast, Braise, Broil, Panbroil, Panfry, Cook in Liquid

Breast · Rolled Breast · Stuffed Breast · Ribs (for Barbecue, etc.) · Brisket Pieces · Stuffed Chops

HIND SHANK
Braise, Cook in Liquid

Hind Shank

GROUND OR CUBED LAMB
Roast, Broil, Panbroil, Panfry, Braise, Cook in Liquid

(Large Pieces) Lamb for Stew* (Small Pieces) · Cube Steak* · Ground Lamb* · Lamburgers*

*LAMB FOR STEW, GRINDING OR CUBING MAY COME FROM ANY WHOLESALE CUT

ROAST LEG OF LAMB

Make several incisions with a sharp knife through the skin and insert thin slice of garlic in each. Salt, pepper and dredge with flour. Place in roasting pan, fat side up, and roast in moderately slow oven, 325° F. Or roast in hot oven, 450° F., for about 30 minutes. If roast is lean, brush with butter or poultry fat. When lightly browned, reduce heat to 300° F., continue cooking uncovered, about 2 to 3 hours or 30 to 35 minutes a pound. Serve with Mint Sauce. May be boned and stuffed before roasting, if desired.

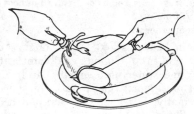

Carving a leg of lamb

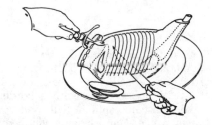

MUSTARD ROAST LEG OF LAMB

Make several incisions in the skin and insert thin slices of garlic. Sprinkle liberally with salt and pepper, spread with a heavy layer of yellow prepared mustard. Roast as above.

ROAST LEG OF LAMB WITH POTATOES

  leg of lamb
  salt
  pepper
  garlic
  ginger
  dry mustard
  2 tablespoons sugar
  ½ cup water
  ¼ cup vinegar
  potatoes, peeled

Season meat with salt, pepper, garlic, ginger and mustard. Bake uncovered at 450° F. for 30 min-

utes. Reduce heat to 350° F. Combine sugar, water and vinegar. Baste lamb with this mixture, adding more as needed. One hour before serving add potatoes. Cover roaster. The total baking time will depend upon the size of the leg of lamb; allow 30 minutes per pound.

ROAST LAMB

Follow as for Roast Veal, page 285.

CROWN ROAST OF LAMB

Sprinkle roast with salt and pepper, and place ribs down in an open roasting pan, so that the ends of the rib bones form a rack. Place in a very hot oven, 500° F., and sear until browned, about 20 minutes. Reduce heat to 300° F., a slow oven, and roast until done. Allow from 30 to 35 minutes per pound. Place on hot platter rib ends up. Garnish rib ends with paper frills, large grapes, or small round red radishes. Fill center of crown with mashed potatoes, potato balls, or peas.

STUFFED CROWN ROAST OF LAMB

The crown roast may be roasted upright, the center of the crown filled with dressing made from the ground trimmings mixed with bread stuffing. The rib ends are protected with foil caps or cubes of bread to prevent burning. Roast at 325° F., 35 to 45 minutes per pound.

BROILED LAMB CHOPS

Select chops of uniform thickness. Remove skin and extra fat. If desired, they may be boned, rolled and wrapped in a strip of bacon. Remove extra fat, follow directions for broiling. Season to taste.

PAN-BROILED LAMB CHOPS

Use rib, loin, or shoulder chops, cut 2 inches thick. Have skillet sizzling hot. Put in chops and cook 1 minute, turn and sear the other side; then cook slowly until done. Pour off extra fat so that chops will broil, not fry. Add salt and pepper. Serve hot, either plain, with peas, or with Tomato Sauce.

LAMB STEAKS

For lamb steaks, follow recipes for lamb chops.

LAMB CUTLETS

Salt and pepper meat, dredge with flour. Dip in beaten egg, then in bread or cracker crumbs; let stand 5 minutes. Fry in skillet with hot fat from 15 to 20 minutes, until browned on both sides.

STUFFED LAMB LOIN CHOPS

Have chops cut 2 inches thick. Remove outer skin. Slit largest part of chop and insert a mushroom. Tie with string, if necessary. Broil according to chart. Remove string, season with salt and pepper, and dot with butter before serving.

STUFFED LAMB RIB CHOPS

Have chops cut 2 inches thick. Remove bone and outer skin. Put a chicken liver or a slice of sausage near the long end of the chop and wrap the end around the filling to make a round, flat chop. Tie in shape with string. Broil according to chart. Remove strings. Season with salt and pepper, and dot with butter before serving.

BAKED STUFFED LAMB CHOPS

Prepare and stuff chops, as above. Broil in pan on rack, turning until well browned, about 10 minutes. Remove to a baking pan; add a little water, and bake at 350° F. about 20 minutes longer, or until tender, basting often. Brush with butter, remove to hot platter. Add Tomato or Chili Sauce to thickened gravy.

LAMB CHOPS AND TOMATOES

Brown thick lamb chops in a skillet; pour off fat. Add whole tomatoes, either fresh or canned. Cook, covered, for about 10 minutes. Just before serving, add 1 cup dry white wine, salt and pepper. Heat. Top each tomato with a bit of butter; serve.

LAMB STEW

Use neck or shoulder lamb, cut in pieces, for stew. Season pieces with salt and pepper. Brown in fat with chopped onion. Cover with boiling water; simmer 1 hour. Add small potatoes, carrots, onions and celery and simmer 1 hour longer. Serve hot on platter, garnish with parsley and Baking Powder Dumplings.

BRAISED LAMB BREAST

Cut lamb breast into serving pieces, season with salt and pepper, dust with flour, and brown in fat. Add a little water, cover tightly, and cook until tender. Add more water as needed.

LAMB WITH DILL

2 tablespoons fat
2 pounds lamb, cubed
2 teaspoons dill seed
salt
1 cup broth or soup stock
3 tablespoons flour
½ cup water
1 pound fresh mushrooms or 1 can (6 ounces)
    mushrooms
1 cup sour cream

Heat fat in heavy skillet. Brown lamb. Add dill seed, salt, and broth. Simmer until lamb is tender. Mix flour and water until smooth. Add to skillet, stir. Add mushrooms. Cook until thickened, stirring constantly. Stir in sour cream and heat, but do not boil. Serve with noodles, rice, or baked potatoes.

STEWED MUTTON

Remove the pink skin and extra fat. Cut in pieces, season, and cover with boiling water. Add a diced carrot and a sliced onion. Cook slowly until tender, about 2½ hours. Serve with a border of Baking Powder Biscuits, split in half, and cover all with Brown Sauce. Garnish with chopped parsley.

MUTTON WITH EGGPLANT

1 eggplant
½ pound raw mutton
salt and pepper, paprika
1 onion, chopped
1 teaspoon chopped parsley
Tomato Sauce, page 390

Peel a good-sized eggplant and chop. Put mutton through the food chopper and season. Add the chopped onion and parsley. Combine with eggplant and put mixture into a casserole, add Tomato Sauce, and bake in 300° F. oven about 1 hour.

To Tenderize Meat:
Less expensive cuts of lamb and other meats may be tenderized for broiling or barbecuing by the use of a commercial tenderizer or by marinating. See chapter 15, Outdoor Cooking, for marinades.

MOUSSAKA

1 large eggplant
1 pound ground lamb or beef
vegetable oil
2 medium onions, chopped
2 cloves garlic, minced
1 teaspoon salt
½ teaspoon thyme
½ teaspoon oregano
½ teaspoon nutmeg
2 tablespoons chopped parsley
1¼ cups canned tomatoes
½ cup white wine
2 egg whites
½ cup bread crumbs
2 tablespoons grated Parmesan cheese

Pare eggplant, cut into ½-inch slices, sprinkle with salt, and set aside for 30 minutes. Rinse and dry thoroughly. Brown meat in vegetable oil with onions and garlic. Drain off the fat. Add salt, seasonings, parsley, tomatoes and wine. Cover and cook slowly for 30 minutes. Cool. Mix in unbeaten egg whites and half of the crumbs. Brown the eggplant slices in vegetable oil. Sprinkle bottom of rectangular baking dish with remaining crumbs. Cover with the eggplant. Spoon meat mixture over the eggplant. Pour sauce, below, over this mixture. Top with cheese and bake at 350° F. for 45 minutes.

SAUCE

3 tablespoons butter
3 tablespoons flour
1½ cups milk
2 egg yolks
½ teaspoon salt
¼ teaspoon pepper

Melt butter. Add flour slowly, stirring constantly. Remove from heat. Slowly stir in the milk. Return to heat and stir until the sauce thickens. Beat egg yolks well. Gradually stir yolks, salt and pepper into the sauce. Blend well.

PORK, HAM AND BACON

The best quality fresh pork is pale pink in color, with white, firm fat.

Pork must always be cooked to the well done stage with no trace of pink showing; a meat thermometer will read 185° when the pork is cooked through.

PORK CUTS

RECOMMENDED COOKING METHOD	CUT OF MEAT
Roasting	Boston Butt—Shoulder Blade Loin Roast Loin Roast—Center Cut Sirloin Roast Fresh Picnic Shoulder Tenderloin Arm Roast—Shoulder Boneless Sirloin Roast Crown Roast Canadian Style Bacon Smoked Shoulder Butt
Baking	Whole Ham Half Ham—Butt or Shank End Smoked Picnic Shoulder Spareribs
Broiling	Center Ham Slice Sliced Bacon Jowl Bacon Square Canadian Style Bacon Smoked Shoulder Butt
Pan Broiling	Center Ham Slice Sliced Bacon Jowl Bacon Square Salt Pork—Side Canadian Style Bacon Smoked Shoulder Butt
Pan Frying	Blade Steak—Shoulder Loin Chops Tenderloin Center Ham Slice Sliced Bacon Rib Chops Jowl Bacon Square Salt Pork—Side Arm Steak—Shoulder Canadian Style Bacon Smoked Shoulder Butt
Braising	Blade Steak—Shoulder Loin Chops Tenderloin Rib Chops Arm Steak—Shoulder Hocks Spareribs

PORK CHART

RETAIL CUTS OF PORK—WHERE THEY COME FROM AND HOW TO COOK THEM

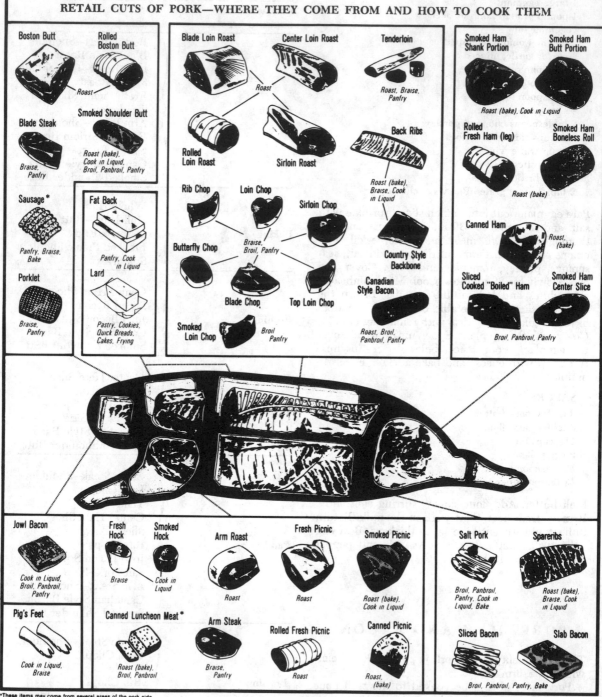

Boston Butt

Rolled Boston Butt

Roast

Smoked Shoulder Butt

Roast (bake), Cook in Liquid, Broil, Panbroil, Panfry

Blade Steak

Braise, Panfry

Sausage *

Panfry, Braise, Bake

Porklet

Braise, Panfry

Fat Back

Panfry, Cook in Liquid

Lard

Pastry, Cookies, Quick Breads, Cakes, Frying

Blade Loin Roast

Center Loin Roast

Tenderloin

Roast, Braise, Panfry

Roast

Rolled Loin Roast

Sirloin Roast

Back Ribs

Roast (bake), Braise, Cook in Liquid

Rib Chop

Loin Chop

Sirloin Chop

Butterfly Chop

Braise, Broil, Panfry

Country Style Backbone

Blade Chop

Top Loin Chop

Canadian Style Bacon

Smoked Loin Chop

Broil, Panfry

Roast, Broil, Panbroil, Panfry

Smoked Ham Shank Portion

Smoked Ham Butt Portion

Roast (bake), Cook in Liquid

Rolled Fresh Ham (leg)

Smoked Ham Boneless Roll

Roast (bake)

Canned Ham

Roast, (bake)

Sliced Cooked "Boiled" Ham

Smoked Ham Center Slice

Broil, Panbroil, Panfry

Jowl Bacon

Cook in Liquid, Broil, Panbroil, Panfry

Pig's Feet

Cook in Liquid, Braise

Fresh Hock

Braise

Smoked Hock

Cook in Liquid

Arm Roast

Roast

Fresh Picnic

Roast

Smoked Picnic

Roast (bake), Cook in Liquid

Canned Luncheon Meat *

Roast (bake), Broil, Panbroil

Arm Steak

Braise, Panfry

Rolled Fresh Picnic

Roast

Canned Picnic

Roast, (bake)

Salt Pork

Broil, Panbroil, Panfry, Cook in Liquid, Bake

Spareribs

Roast (bake), Braise, Cook in Liquid

Sliced Bacon

Slab Bacon

Broil, Panbroil, Panfry, Bake

*These items may come from several areas of the pork side.

NL56M9

RECOMMENDED COOKING METHOD	CUT OF MEAT
Cooking in Liquid Stewing	Half of Ham—Shank or Butt End Smoked Picnic Shoulder Jowl Bacon Square Salt Pork—Side Hocks Smoked Shoulder Butt Spareribs

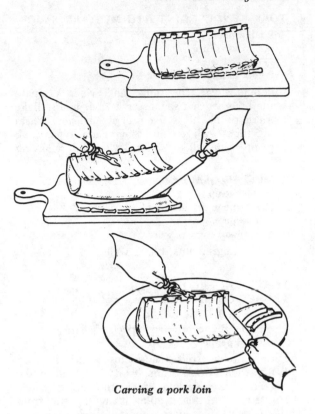

Carving a pork loin

SHERRY-GLAZED PORK

Roast pork according to chart. About ½ hour before cooking time is up, stud the meat with cloves. Pour over it a mixture of ½ cup sherry and ¼ cup brown sugar. Continue to cook until pork is cooked through and glazed, basting often with the pan drippings.

PORK TENDERLOIN

Choose a loin of pork and have the butcher cut out the boneless tenderloin. The ribs that remain can be used for spare ribs. Leave the tenderloin whole or have it split in half lengthwise. Roll in flour, season with salt and pepper. Melt butter in a skillet, add a chopped onion, and cook for a few minutes. Brown tenderloin on all sides in this mixture; add ½ cup sour cream, cover the pan, and simmer slowly until meat is tender and thoroughly cooked, about 1 hour in all. Baste often.

ROAST PORK

Rub pork loin, shoulder, or leg (fresh ham) with salt, pepper and ginger, and place in roaster, fat side up. Roast acording to chart until thoroughly cooked. Baste occasionally with the fat in the pan. A sliced onion may be placed on the roast. Serve with pan gravy. Any pork roast may be glazed like ham, or like pork tenderloin, below.

CROWN ROAST OF PORK

Prepare Crown Roast of Pork like Crown Roast of Lamb, page 289. Roast according to chart for roasting pork loin. Stuff, if desired, with Prune and Apple Stuffing, page 325.

PORK ROASTING CHART

(Oven temperature is 325° F. for all cuts.)

	WEIGHT	MEAT THERMOMETER READING	COOKING TIME MINUTES PER POUND
Loin	2-7 lbs.	185	35-45
Boston Butt (shoulder)	4-6 lbs.	185	45-50
Cushion Shoulder	5 lbs.	185	40-45
Leg (Fresh Ham)	5-6 lbs.	185	40-50
Crown Roast	6-7 lbs.	185	45-50

PORK TENDERLOIN WITH MUSTARD SAUCE

2 tablespoons brown sugar
¼ cup soy sauce
⅓ cup red wine
2 pork tenderloins, boned

Combine sugar, soy sauce and wine. Marinate tenderloins in this sauce for 1 to 2 hours. Bake tenderloins in 350° F. oven for about 1 hour. Baste 4 or 5 times with remaining marinade. When cool, cut into thin slices. Serve with the following sauce:

MUSTARD SAUCE
½ cup catsup
1 tablespoon dry mustard
1 tablespoon vinegar
½ teaspoon curry powder

Combine ingredients, blend well.

PORK TENDERLOIN WITH PRUNES OR APRICOTS

2 pork tenderloins, boned
½ pound prunes or dried apricots
salt and pepper

Have butcher split tenderloins lengthwise and flatten them. Cook prunes or apricots and purée. Spread one tenderloin flat in the roaster. Place fruit evenly on this, keeping it slightly away from the edge. Cover with other tenderloin. Secure edges with skewers so that the fruit will not ooze out. Sprinkle with salt and pepper. Roast at 350° F. for 1¼ to 1½ hours.

PAN-BROWNED PORK CHOPS

Wipe chops, sprinkle with salt and pepper, and brown in a hot skillet. Brown both sides well, cover the skillet, and cook slowly until meat is tender and very well done. Serve with slices of apple fried in the fat remaining in the pan.

PORK CHOPS WITH WINE

6 thick pork chops
2 teaspoons prepared mustard
salt and pepper
¼ teaspoon dried dill
brown sugar
6 thin lemon slices
1 cup dry white wine

Trim fat from pork chops; use a little of it to grease the skillet. Brown chops slowly on both sides; drain off any excess fat. Spread one side of chops with mustard, sprinkle each with seasonings and brown sugar. Place one lemon slice on each chop. Add wine, cover the skillet and cook slowly until tender, about 50 to 60 minutes. Remove chops and keep them warm; remove excess fat from the skillet, thicken the drippings with flour if desired, and spoon sauce over the meat.

BAKED PORK CHOPS WITH APPLES

Have pork chops cut 1½ inches thick. Sprinkle with salt and pepper. Cover each chop with half of an unpeeled apple, cut crosswise and cored, placing cut side on chop. Sprinkle apple with sugar, place in pan, in moderate oven, 350° F., and bake 40 to 50 minutes, basting often, until meat is well browned and thoroughly cooked. Serve hot with gravy slightly thickened with cornstarch, or a little sour cream.

CANTONESE PORK CHOPS

6 pork chops
1½ teaspoons salt
2 tablespoons shortening
1 cup chicken broth
½ cup pineapple juice
1 teaspoon soy sauce
⅛ teaspoon dry mustard
2 tablespoons cornstarch
1 cup canned pineapple chunks
½ cup chopped celery
1 tomato, cubed

Salt the chops. Brown slowly in shortening. Add 2 to 4 tablespoons of water, cover, and simmer until chops are very tender, about 40 minutes. Pour off fat. Combine broth, pineapple juice, soy sauce, mustard, and cornstarch. Simmer until smooth and thick, stirring constantly. Add remaining ingredients and simmer for 5 minutes. Reheat chops in this sauce; serve with steamed rice.

PORK CHOP SUEY

2½ pounds lean pork
2 tablespoons oil or fat
1 can (1 pound) bean sprouts
3 tablespoons cornstarch
2 teaspoons Chinese bead molasses
1 tablespoon salt
1 tablespoon soy sauce
3 cups onion, diced
3 tablespoons butter
3 cups celery, diced
1 cup Chinese water chestnuts

In advance, cut meat in small pieces, simmer slowly in fat until nearly tender. Drain liquid from sprouts and mix with cornstarch, molasses, salt and sauce. Add to meat and cook 15 minutes longer. Sauté onions in half the butter until glassy;

sauté celery in remaining butter until nearly tender. Add to meat. Just before serving, heat 5 minutes. Add bean sprouts. Cook 3 minutes, stirring. (If raw Chinese chestnuts are available, peel, slice thin and add with onion. If canned Chinese chestnuts are used, drain, slice and add to the meat with the celery.)

SWEET AND SOUR PORK

2 pounds boned pork
3 teaspoons soy sauce
½ teaspoon ground ginger
3 tablespoons flour
oil for frying
1 small onion, chopped
½ clove garlic, crushed
1 13½-ounce can pineapple chunks
1 tablespoon soy sauce
¼ cup vinegar
2 tablespoons sugar
½ cup slivered crystallized ginger
    or ½ teaspoon ground ginger
1 green pepper, cut in thin strips
2 tablespoons cornstarch

Cut pork into ½-inch cubes. Marinate in soy sauce and ground ginger for 15 minutes. Drain. Toss pork in flour until coated. Fry meat in hot oil, 375° F., for about 5 minutes or until golden brown. Sauté onions and garlic in a large skillet. Drain pineapple, reserving the juice. Add enough water to juice to make ¾ cup. Add soy sauce, vinegar, sugar and slivered ginger. Add this liquid to onions. Bring to the boiling point. Add green pepper and cook for 2 minutes. Soften cornstarch in 2 tablespoons cold water. Add to skillet, stirring until mixture thickens. Add pork and pineapple chunks. Heat slowly. Serve with rice.

THAI PORK AND CRISP NOODLES

1 pound ground pork
1 small onion, chopped
1 egg
salt and pepper
cooking oil
1 clove garlic
8 to 12 medium shrimp
4 to 6 scallions
½ cup mushrooms, sliced
1 to 1½ cups chicken broth
2 to 3 tablespoons soy sauce
½ teaspoon salt
⅛ teaspoon pepper
¼ teaspoon monosodium glutamate
1 tablespoon cornstarch
2 tablespoons water
2 3-ounce cans rice noodles

Combine pork, onion, egg, and salt and pepper to taste. Form into balls the size of walnuts. Heat oil in skillet; brown and cook meat balls until they are thoroughly cooked. Remove meat balls from pan. Quick-fry the garlic in same skillet; add shrimp and quick-fry. Do not overcook. Slice scallions lengthwise, including the green tops. Quick-fry scallions and mushrooms. Add chicken broth, soy sauce and seasonings. Dissolve the cornstarch in the water. Add to skillet and cook until thickened. Return meat balls to skillet and heat thoroughly over low to medium heat. Meanwhile heat the noodles in the oven. Serve the mixture over the crisp noodles. Chili peppers as a garnish are a Thai touch.

SPARERIBS AND SAUERKRAUT

2½ to 3 pounds spareribs
1 can (1 pound, 13 ounces) sauerkraut

Brown spareribs in a skillet. Transfer to a large kettle or Dutch oven, add sauerkraut, and cook covered 1 hour, until ribs are tender and very well done. Or bake in a moderately hot oven, 375° F., about 1 hour. If desired, ½ teaspoon caraway seeds, and 1 apple, pared, cored and grated, may be added.

HAM BAKING CHART

FOR UNCOOKED SMOKED HAMS
(Oven temperature is 325° F. for all cuts.)

WEIGHT	MEAT THERMOMETER READING	COOKING TIME MINUTES PER POUND
Whole Ham (Bone in) **8-20 pounds**	160	18-20
Whole Ham (Boned) **8-16 pounds**	160	18-20
Shank Half Ham or Butt portion (Bone in) **4-8 pounds**	160	35-40
Picnic (Bone in) **4-10 pounds**	170	35-40

FOR PRE-COOKED HAMS—TO HEAT BEFORE EATING

(Follow package directions, or the following chart. Oven temperature is 325° F. for all cuts.)

WEIGHT	MEAT THERMOMETER READING	COOKING TIME MINUTES PER POUND
Whole Ham (Bone in) 8-20 pounds	130	15
Whole Ham (Boned) 8-16 pounds	130	15
Shank Half Ham or Butt Portion (Bone in) 4-8 pounds	130	15-20
Picnic (Bone in) 4-10 pounds	130	25-35
Canadian Bacon	170	35-40

BROILING

	THICKNESS	TIME
Ham Slice, Uncooked	½"	8 min.
	1"	15-18 min.
	1½"	20-30 min.
Ham Slice, Pre-Cooked	½"	5 min.
	1"	10 min.

BAKED HAM

For tenderized commercial hams, follow directions on the wrapper. For regular hams, see chart for cooking time. Place ham thick side up on a rack in an open pan. Bake according to Ham Baking Chart. About 45 minutes before ham is done, remove from oven. Take off all rind except a collar around the shank bone. Score the fat to form diamonds. Moisten 1 cup brown sugar with fat drippings and 2 tablespoons flour, if desired, and rub over ham. Stud with cloves. Return to oven. Add 1 cup cider, or ginger ale, pineapple juice or wine to pan and baste ham often, increasing the heat to 400° F. for the last 20 minutes to brown the ham.

Bake half ham cut side down.

BAKED VIRGINIA OR KENTUCKY HAM

1 country-style smoked ham, 10 to 12 pounds
brown sugar
whole cloves

Soak ham for 12 hours in cold water. Drain and scrub thoroughly. Place in boiling water and simmer, covered, 25 minutes per pound. Let cool slightly. Lift from kettle and remove rind. Score fat in a diagonal pattern. Spread well with brown sugar and stud with cloves. Place in roasting pan and bake uncovered for 20-30 minutes at 375° F., basting with any desired liquid as above.

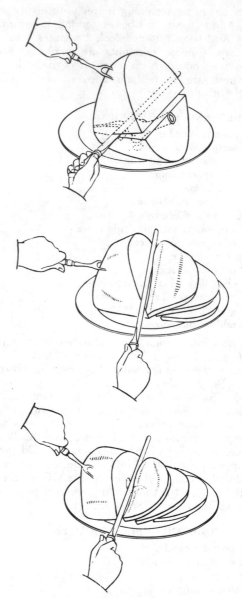

Carving a ham shank

BAKED COUNTRY HAM IN CRUST

Soak and scrub a country-style ham as above. Make a thick paste of rye flour and water and spread over the ham. Set on rack in pan. Bake in hot oven 400° F. to brown paste, then lower temperature, bake about 4 hours at 300° F. Make a hole in the paste and pour in a cup of hot cider and the pan drippings. Repeat twice if needed. Bake 1 hour longer, slit crust and remove it. Remove rind. Brush the fat with beaten yolk of egg,

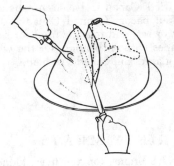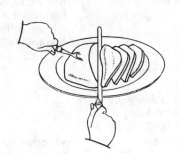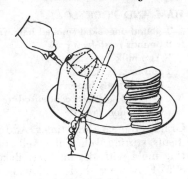

Carving butt end of a half ham

sprinkle with brown sugar and rye bread crumbs and brown. Save crust and use to keep leftover ham moist.

BOILED HAM

Simmer whole or half ham (uncooked) in boiling water to cover, allowing 40 minutes per pound, until tender. When ham is tender, the shank bone-end moves easily in its socket. Or reduce cooking time by half, drain the ham, cut off the rind and score and glaze as for Baked Ham, above. Bake 10 minutes per pound basting often. Half hams should be baked cut side down on a rack.

HAM SLICES

Ready-to-eat ham or boned canned ham may be substituted for uncooked ham in the recipes that follow. Reduce cooking time to about 30 minutes, just long enough to heat ham through and brown the glaze.

BAKED HAM SLICE
WITH ORANGE JUICE

   1 thick slice uncooked ham
   ⅓ cup brown sugar
   1 teaspoon whole cloves
   1 cup orange juice

Cover top of ham with sugar and stud with cloves. Pour orange juice around ham. Cover and bake in a moderately slow oven, 325° F. 1½ hours, or until ham is tender. Uncover for last 15 minutes.

BAKED HAM SLICE WITH FRUIT

   2-pound slice uncooked ham
   1 teaspoon ground cloves
   4 medium-sized tart apples, or 1 cup crushed
      pineapple, or 1 can (1 pound) sour cherries
   ⅓ cup brown sugar

Place ham in pan and sprinkle with cloves. Pare and cut apples in eighths, lay them around and over ham, sprinkle sugar over apples. Or add 1 cup pineapple; or omit cloves and add drained cherries with more sugar, to taste. Cover and bake at 325° F. for 1½ hours or until ham is tender. Uncover for last 15 minutes.

HAM AND SWEET POTATOES

   1 slice uncooked ham 1 inch thick
   6 medium sweet potatoes, cooked and peeled
   ¼ cup brown sugar
   nutmeg

Place ham in hot skillet, brown on both sides turning often. Remove from pan and place in covered dish. Set aside skillet with drippings. Bake ham in moderately slow oven, 325° F., 1½ hours or until tender. Quarter potatoes and place in the skillet with ham drippings. Sprinkle with sugar and nutmeg. Cook slowly on top of the range, turning often, until well browned. Serve meat on hot platter surrounded with the potatoes.

BROILED HAM

Snip fat edge of 2-inch thick slice of ham to keep it from curling. Broil on one side, then turn, cover with brown sugar, stud with cloves and broil until done, about 35 minutes altogether.

SCALLOPED HAM AND POTATOES

Brown slice uncooked ham ½ inch thick on both sides in skillet. Place in baking dish, add 2 cups raw sliced potatoes and 1½ cups milk; dot with butter. Cover and bake 1 hour in a moderately slow oven, 325° F. Uncover and bake ½ hour longer.

For pickles and relishes to serve with ham and other meats, see chapter 23, Preserving and Pickling.

HAM AND PORK LOAF

1 pound uncooked smoked ham, fat removed
2 pounds fresh lean pork
½ cup milk
1 cup bread crumbs
2 eggs, slightly beaten
1 can (10½ ounces) condensed tomato soup
1 small onion, grated

Grind the meat three times. Add remaining ingredients, stirring well. Fill a well-greased loaf pan or ring mold with the mixture. Bake for 2 hours at 375° F. Serve with the following sauce:

SAUCE

1 tablespoon butter
1 tablespoon flour
¼ cup sugar
1 teaspoon dry mustard
¼ cup vinegar
1½ cups tomato juice
1 egg, slightly beaten

Melt butter, add flour and stir well. Add remaining ingredients and cook, stirring, until thick. Serves 8.

HAM AND VEAL LOAF

1 pound cooked ground ham
½ pound ground veal
1 cup bread crumbs
1 tablespoon grated onion
½ cup chopped parsley
½ teaspoon salt

Mix ingredients well, adding 4 tablespoons water. Bake in loaf pan in a very hot oven, 450° F., for 10 minutes; reduce heat to 350° F. for 30 minutes. Or bake in ring mold and fill center with any desired cooked vegetables.

BACON

Place bacon slices in a cold skillet, cook slowly until crisp. Press fat from slices with broad knife to prevent curling. Turn occasionally. Pour off drippings while cooking. Drain slices on brown paper or paper toweling and serve.

Or place bacon in a hot skillet, reduce heat. Turn often to prevent curling until crisp and light brown.

Or place thin slices of bacon close together on rack over dripping pan. Broil 3 to 4 minutes per side, or bake in hot oven, 400° F., until crisp and brown.

CANADIAN-STYLE BACON

Canadian bacon, which is smoked boneless pork loin, has little fat. It should be sliced thin and broiled or pan-fried. Canadian bacon may be used like other cooked bacon. Canned Canadian-style bacon is ready to eat, and may be used for sandwiches or canapes without heating. Or the whole bacon may be glazed and baked like ham.

VARIETY MEATS

Sweetbreads, calf's brains, tongue, liver, kidneys, heart and tripe, are known collectively as Variety Meats. They may be expensive, like sweetbreads, or very inexpensive, like heart, but they are all high in nutritional values—especially liver. Variety meats are perishable, and should be carefully refrigerated and used soon after purchase.

Sweetbreads

Sweetbreads are the thymus glands of calf, steer, or lamb. Both kinds, the round heart sweetbreads and the longish throat sweetbreads, come in pairs. Everything except the thin covering membrane and the tubes and veins is edible. The meat is white, and so soft that sweetbreads should be chilled in cold water before and after parboiling to firm up the flesh. The cooked sweetbreads are then heated with a sauce or browned in the oven, under the broiler, or in melted butter. A pound of sweetbreads serves 4.

BOILED SWEETBREADS

1 pound sweetbreads
1 pint boiling water
½ teaspoon salt
1 tablespoon vinegar or lemon juice

Soak the sweetbreads in cold water for 20 minutes. Cook in boiling salted water with lemon juice or vinegar for 20 minutes. Plunge into cold water, remove and discard tubes and membranes. Slice, heat in Medium White Sauce, or Creole Sauce, pages 386, 388. Serve on toast, or with chicken, mushrooms or peas in Patty Shells; or wrap the sweetbreads in bacon and broil or pan-broil slowly until bacon is crisp.

BAKED SWEETBREADS

Prepare Sweetbreads as above, but leave them whole. Dip in melted butter, cover with crumbs, and bake in moderate oven, 350° F., 30 to 40 minutes, basting occasionally with butter.

SWEETBREADS WITH MUSHROOMS

2 tablespoons blanched almonds
1 cup canned or cooked mushrooms
2 tablespoons butter
2 tablespoons flour
½ cup milk, cream or mushroom liquid
½ cup chicken broth
2 cups diced cooked sweetbreads
salt, pepper and ginger
1 teaspoon chopped parsley

Chop the almonds, drain the mushrooms. Melt butter, add flour and gradually add the liquid. Cook until smooth, stirring constantly. Add all the other ingredients. Place in individual buttered ramekins, or in baking dish or casserole. Sprinkle with buttered crumbs and bake in moderate oven, 350° F., about ½ hour, until browned on top.

Diced cooked chicken may be substituted for sweetbreads in the above recipe.

FRIED SWEETBREADS

1 pound sweetbreads
¼ cup bread crumbs
½ teaspoon salt
⅛ teaspoon pepper
⅛ teaspoon ginger
1 egg

Prepare Sweetbreads as above. Roll in fine bread crumbs combined with seasonings, then dip in beaten egg and again in crumbs. Fry in deep, hot fat or sauté in skillet until brown on all sides.

SWEETBREADS BROILED IN CHILI SAUCE

1 pound sweetbreads
1 stalk celery
2 sprigs parsley
1 onion slice
juice of ½ lemon
½ cup chili sauce
6 tablespoons melted butter

Soak and cook Sweetbreads as above, adding celery, parsley, onion, and lemon juice to the cooking water. Plunge into cold water, drain sweetbreads, clean, place in shallow pan. Cover with chili sauce mixed with melted butter. Broil 15 minutes, turning occasionally. Fill the center of a rice ring with sautéed mushrooms and surround it with the broiled, sliced sweetbreads.

BRAISED SWEETBREADS

2 pounds sweetbreads
3 tablespoons butter
1 onion, chopped
1 cup sweetbread broth
salt, pepper, mustard

Prepare Sweetbreads as above. Melt butter in heavy skillet. In this, brown onion about 3 minutes, then remove. Cook sweetbreads in the butter until brown on all sides. Add reserved broth and seasonings to the skillet and bake in a moderate oven, 350° F., basting occasionally and adding more liquid as it cooks down until sweetbreads are cooked through. If gravy is desired, thicken liquid with 1 tablespoon flour dissolved in a little water. Flavor with 2 tablespoons sherry.

BROILED SWEETBREADS
See page 47.

Brains

Calf's brains are more expensive than beef and pork brains and they are more delicate in flavor and texture. All may be cooked the same way. Two calf's brains weigh about 1 pound, enough for 4 servings.

CALF'S BRAINS

Soak calf's brains in salted cold water to cover for 20 minutes. Cook slowly 20 minutes in boiling salted water with 1 tablespoon of vinegar added. Drain, plunge into cold water. Drain, remove membranes carefully. Cut into cubes or slices. Use like Sweetbreads, or add to scrambled eggs, or use in a Soufflé.

SWEET AND SOUR CALF'S BRAINS

Prepare brains as above, adding a few whole peppers and slices of celery root to the cooking liquid. Prepare Gingersnap Sauce, or Lemon Sauce, using stock in which brains were cooked. Pour over brains and serve cold.

Liver

Liver is recognized as a valuable source of iron, Vitamin A, and B vitamins. All kinds of liver have this same nutritional quality, from the expensive, delicately flavored veal and calf's liver to lamb, beef and inexpensive pork liver. Tender liver should be cooked very quickly in a little fat to the medium rare stage. Beef liver and pork liver, which are less tender, may need to be braised. Allow 1 pound of liver for 4 servings. Before cooking, remove the skin, and any veins that can be cut out without spoiling the appearance of the slice.

SAUTEED LIVER

1 pound calf's liver or baby beef liver, sliced
salt and pepper
2 tablespoons flour
2 tablespoons fat or butter

Wipe liver dry. Salt and pepper to taste, then dredge with the flour. Melt the fat and fry slices a few minutes on each side until brown. Reduce heat, cook a few minutes longer, to desired doneness. Liver has best flavor and texture when it is medium rare. Overcooking makes it tough and dry. If desired, serve liver with fried onions, or crisp bacon.

BROILED LIVER

Brush ⅓- to ½-inch slices of liver with melted fat. Place in flat pan and broil only 2 or 3 minutes on each side.

Or place in a greased skillet and pan-broil, allowing 2 or 3 minutes for each side.

CALF'S LIVER, POTTED

1 calf's liver, whole
2 tablespoons parsley, chopped
2 tablespoons celery, chopped
1 clove of garlic
salt and paprika to taste
2 tablespoons flour
3 tablespoons fat
1 onion, sliced

Wash the liver. Remove the skin. Cut 6 slits in the top, 1 inch wide and nearly to the depth of the liver and fill with the parsley and celery and, if desired, bits of garlic—all seasoned with salt and paprika. Tie string around liver, to keep in filling, making small grooves at side to hold the string in place. Dredge with flour. Place fat in heavy pan with close-fitting cover, add onion; when slightly browned add the prepared liver, brown, cover and simmer from ¾ to 1 hour until tender; overcooking will make it tough and dry. Add a little water, as necessary. If gravy is not thick enough, add more flour.

BAKED CALF'S LIVER

whole calf's liver
salt and pepper
2 tablespoons flour
2 tablespoons fat
2 onions, sliced

Wash, trim and skin calf's liver, sprinkle with salt, pepper and flour and place in an ovenproof skillet with fat and the onions. Spoon some of the fat over top of liver. Cover skillet closely and place in a hot oven, 400° F., for 15 minutes. Uncover,

reduce the heat to 325° F. and bake slowly 45 minutes to 1 hour, until tender and well browned.

LIVER AND DUMPLINGS

Dumplings, page 102
1½ pounds calf's liver
salt, pepper
flour
2 tablespoons fat
1 small onion, chopped
2 tablespoons flour
salt, paprika

Prepare Dumplings. Cut liver in pieces 1 inch thick, dredge with seasoned flour. Heat fat in skillet, add onion and brown lightly. Add liver, brown on both sides. Remove to hot platter. Surround with freshly made Dumplings. Stir 2 tablespoons flour into gravy in skillet, add 2 cups hot water, salt and paprika. Cook until thick and smooth and pour over liver and dumplings.

BRAISED PORK LIVER

1 pound pork liver in ½-inch slices
2 tablespoons flour
¾ teaspoon salt
⅛ teaspoon pepper
4 tablespoons fat
2 carrots, diced
4 potatoes, sliced
1 onion, diced
1 cup boiling water
1 cup tomato juice

Dip liver in seasoned flour. Brown on both sides in fat. Add vegetables, and liquid. Cover and simmer for 1½ hours or until tender.

LIVER PATTIES

Grind 1 pound raw beef liver with 3 slices of bacon and ½ small onion. Season with salt and pepper, add ½ cup flour. Form into patties or other small shapes and brown on both sides in butter or bacon fat.

Tongue

Beef or ox tongue is widely available in several forms: fresh, pickled, or smoked. Calf's tongues and lamb tongues are sold fresh; the calf's tongue is considered the choicer of the two. Allow 1 pound of tongue for 4 servings.

SMOKED BEEF TONGUE

1 smoked tongue
6 bay leaves
1 teaspoon whole pepper
1 teaspoon cloves
1 onion, sliced

Wash the tongue and if salty, soak in cold water overnight. Place in kettle with fresh water, add seasonings and simmer slowly until tender, from 3 to 5 hours. When the tongue is tender, the bone moves easily and the skin curls back at root. Slit and pull off the outer skin, cut off root, and let tongue cool in the stock. Discard skin and root. Tongue may be sliced cold or served hot with Sweet and Sour Sauce or Gingersnap Sauce.

BEEF TONGUE A LA JARDINIERE

Prepare fresh beef tongue, as above, but only boil for 2 hours. Reserve liquid. Skin and place in roasting pan on a layer of diced vegetables—carrots, turnips, celery, potatoes, peas, beans, button onions and tomatoes. Add some of the water in which the tongue was boiled; cover and bake slowly at 300° F. for 2 hours longer or until tender.

Remove tongue and vegetables. Thicken the gravy with browned flour. Place tongue on hot platter; surround with vegetables and add some of the gravy. Use remaining liquid from boiled tongue for soup, if desired.

CALF'S TONGUES

3 fresh calf's tongues
3 bay leaves
1 onion, sliced
1 teaspoon whole pepper
1 tablespoon salt
2 tablespoons prepared horseradish

Place tongues, bay leaves, onions, pepper and salt in kettle, cover with water. Cook slowly 20 minutes to the pound, until tongues are tender. Remove skin; cut tongues lengthwise. Strain liquid into a saucepan and add flour blended with a little cold water and the horseradish. Cook until smooth and thick, and serve sauce with tongue. Or, serve with Sweet and Sour Sauce or Gingersnap Sauce.

BRAISED CALF'S TONGUES

2 calf's tongues
vinegar
2 tablespoons hot oil
2 onions, sliced
2 carrots, sliced
1 cup beef stock
salt, pepper
2 tablespoons flour
½ cup milk or sour cream

Parboil calf's tongues for 20 minutes in salted water with a little vinegar. Drain and remove the skins. Brown tongues lightly in oil with the onion and carrots, stirring to prevent burning. Add beef stock and salt and pepper to taste. Cover pan and simmer gently for about 1 hour over moderate heat, or in a moderate oven, 350° F., until tongue is very tender. Add more stock if necessary. Remove tongue to platter. Blend flour with the milk and add to the pan. Cook, stirring, until sauce is thick and smooth. Season with salt, pepper and a dash of thyme, to taste.

Miscellaneous Variety Meats

KIDNEYS

Plunge 6 lamb or 4 veal kidneys in boiling water and remove skins. Soak in cold salted water 30 minutes. Remove and discard tubes and membranes, slice kidneys, season with salt and pepper. Heat 2 tablespoons fat, add 1 tablespoon chopped onion, fry 2 minutes, add kidneys, sauté for 5 minutes. Over-cooking toughens kidneys. Cover with Brown or Mushroom Sauce.

CALF'S HEART

Wash the heart, remove the veins and blood clots and stuff with ¼ recipe Bread Stuffing. Sprinkle heart with salt and pepper, dredge with flour and brown in 2 tablespoons fat. Place in deep pan, half cover with boiling water, cover closely and bake at 300° F. for 2 hours or until tender.

STUFFED DERMA (KISHKE)

3 foot piece of beef casing
1½ cups flour, or mixed flour and matzo meal
¾ cup rendered chicken fat
1 medium onion, chopped fine
salt, pepper, paprika
2 onions, sliced
1 cup boiling water

Wash and scrape the casing (the intestine of the beef). Sew one end of the tube. Blend flour, fat, and chopped onion. Season well with salt, pepper and paprika. Stuff casing lightly, to allow for expansion, and sew closed. Put sliced onions and boiling water into a baking pan. Lay kishke on onions, brush with more fat, and bake covered, in a moderate oven, about 2 hours, basting often.

HONEYCOMB TRIPE

Wash 1 pound fresh tripe carefully and cut into inch squares. Place in a saucepan with ¼ teaspoon each of salt, sugar, prepared mustard, and 2 cups water. Boil up and skim carefully. Simmer for 2 hours or until tender. Watch closely to prevent sticking and skim again if necessary. Stir in 1 tablespoon flour mixed with a little cold water, simmer ½ hour longer, season well and serve.

SAUSAGES

FRIED LIVER SAUSAGE

Fry sliced fresh liver sausage in 2 tablespoons fat until browned. Serve with sauerkraut and boiled potatoes, or with fried onions.

BOILED SAUSAGE

Place kielbasi or similar cooked smoked sausage in pan, add boiling water to cover, and simmer 5 to 10 minutes. Serve hot with Potato Salad.

FRIED PORK SAUSAGE

Prick sausage with a fork. Place in skillet with a little boiling water, cook until water is evaporated, and fry until brown and cooked through.

BAKED SAUSAGE

1½ pounds sausage meat
1 cup flour
3 teaspoons baking powder
½ teaspoon salt
3 tablespoons shortening
½ cup milk

Pat the meat into a shallow baking pan. Toss together the flour, baking powder and salt; cut in shortening until mixture looks like cornmeal. Add milk and stir to make a soft dough. Knead 5 or 6 times, and pat or roll into a sheet the size of the pan. Lay the dough on the sausage, mark in squares for serving, and bake in a hot oven, 450° F., 10 to 15 minutes, until biscuit topping is well browned and sausage is cooked through. Pour off excess fat.

CABBAGE AND SAUSAGES

See page 416.

GAME

VENISON

Venison always should be served rare. It may be stewed or braised. Prepare Venison Roast like Roast Lamb, allowing less time; Venison Cutlets like Veal Cutlets, or fried in skillet. Serve with Jelly Sauce, or Venison Jelly. Cook Saddle of Venison like Hasenpfeffer, below, or Beef à la Mode, or Sauerbraten. Venison Steak may be broiled like Broiled Beef Steak. Serve with Maître d'Hôtel Sauce.

RABBITS

Rabbits are cooked like chicken—stewed, fricasseed or roasted.

BELGIAN HARE FRICASSEE

Skin and remove the fine skin from the meat, or have hare cleaned by butcher. Cut in joints for serving, season and roll in flour. Try out several slices of fat salt pork; remove pork as soon as dry. Brown the joints of hare quickly in the hot pork fat. Cover closely and cook slowly until tender. Pour off the fat from the pan, and dissolve the brown bits that cling to pan in a very little water; pour this over the hare on the platter. Serve with gooseberry or any other tart jelly, or Horseradish Sauce.

HASENPFEFFER

Place rabbit meat in a jar and cover with equal parts vinegar and water, add sliced onion, salt, pepper, cloves and bay leaves. Allow this to marinate two days in refrigerator. Remove the meat and brown it thoroughly in hot butter, turning it often, and gradually add the sauce in which it was pickled, as much as is required to cover. Simmer a half hour or until tender. Before serving, add 1 cup thick sour cream.

LEFTOVER MEATS

Many classic favorites, such as roast beef hash and deviled beef bones are made from leftover meats. Leftover meats have endless uses, limited only by the imagination of the cook. It is often a real economy of time, as well as of money, to buy and cook more meat than is needed for a single meal, and to base another meal, more quickly prepared, on the "planned-over" meat.

TO STORE LEFTOVER MEAT

Remove cooked meat from bones as soon as possible, trim and discard fat and other inedible portions, and wrap the meat in moisture-proof paper to prevent drying. Use within a day or two—or wrap for freezing, in meal-sized portions, and freeze for storage up to 6 weeks.

SLICED LEFTOVER MEATS

Serve slices of cold meat with salads or hot vegetables. Or reheat lamb, veal, pork or pot-roasted beef in hot gravy, barbecue sauce, or other sauces.

LEFTOVER ROAST BEEF AND STEAK

Avoid recooking meats which should be served rare; let leftover rare roast beef and steak slices come to room temperature. At serving time, cover with very hot gravy and serve at once on warmed plates, or on toast as a hot sandwich.

BITS AND PIECES OF LEFTOVER MEAT

Leftover meat too small to slice may be cut into slivers or other uniform pieces and added to a mixed salad, to sauces or spaghetti or rice casseroles, or to stuffings for green peppers and other vegetables, or fillings for meat pies. The meat may be ground and used to make rissoles or croquettes, or a meat soufflé. Examples of these follow. Leftover lamb makes an excellent curry; veal may be heated in a sour cream sauce with mushrooms to make Veal Stroganoff, and pork makes an excellent Chinese-style dish when it is served in a sweet and sour sauce.

LEFTOVER STEW

This may be supplemented with freshly cooked vegetables, or served as a sauce for spaghetti or rice.

MEAT LOAF IN SOUR CREAM CRUST

    3 cups cooked ground meat
    2 tablespoons minced onion
    ½ cup shredded cheese
    1 4-ounce can sliced mushrooms
    milk

    CRUST

    2 cups flour
    1 teaspoon salt
    ¾ cup butter
    1 egg
    ½ cup sour cream

For crust: Mix flour and salt. Cut butter into flour until it resembles meal. Combine egg and sour cream and stir into flour mixture. Mix well. Divide the crust into two parts and roll each into a rectangle about 14 inches x 6 inches. Place one rectangle into a greased baking pan. Mix the meat, onion, cheese and mushrooms including the juice. Place the filling along the center of the dough in the pan. Cover with the other rectangle of dough, moistening edges in order to seal well. Prick the top with a fork. Brush with milk. Bake at 375° F. for 25 minutes or until the crust is browned.

ROAST BEEF WITH GRAVY

If not rare, cut cold roast beef in thin slices. Heat some of the gravy in skillet, add beef and reheat to the boiling point, on top of the range or in the oven. Serve at once.

SKILLET ROAST BEEF HASH

Combine 2 cups coarsely chopped leftover roast beef (or steak) with 3 cups chopped boiled potatoes. Season well with salt and pepper. Add 1 onion, minced fine, and ⅓ cup milk or cream or gravy, and toss to blend. Heat 2 tablespoons butter or meat drippings in a skillet. Add the hash, cook slowly until brown and crisp on the bottom, adding more fat if necessary. Fold like an omelet and serve.

BAKED ROAST BEEF HASH

Combine 2 cups chopped or cubed leftover roast beef or steak with 2 cups chopped boiled potatoes. Add 2 tablespoons tomato catsup and about ½ cup milk, cream, or gravy, to moisten well. Season well with salt and pepper and bake in a greased baking dish in a moderate oven, 350° F., until the mixture is hot and the top browned, about 30 minutes.

CORNED BEEF HASH

Substitute corned beef for the roast beef in either hash recipe, above.

RED FLANNEL HASH

    2 cups chopped corned beef
    6 boiled potatoes, chopped
    6 cooked beets, chopped
    1 onion, chopped
    ½ cup bouillon
    salt, pepper

Combine ingredients and season lightly with salt and generously with pepper. Pack into greased casserole and bake in a moderate oven, 350° F., about 30 minutes, until brown. Or brown slowly in skillet, in 3 tablespoons hot butter or fat, and fold like omelet to serve.

DEVILED ROAST BEEF BONES

Divide the ribs of a beef roast from which the meat has been carved. Sprinkle the ribs with wine vinegar, salt and pepper, roll in melted butter, mustard, and in fine dry bread crumbs. Broil slowly until the crumbs are browned. Serve with bottled steak sauce.

ROAST BEEF AND RICE CASSEROLE

Grind leftover roast beef and a very little of the fat, and season well with salt, pepper and minced onion. To 2 cups of ground beef add 1 cup Boiled Rice, and ⅔ cup condensed tomato soup. Bake in buttered casserole at 375° F. for 30 minutes, until hash is heated through and top is crusty. Serve with roast beef gravy heated with remaining tomato soup.

BEEFSTEAK WITH ONIONS

Slice onions thin. Place in skillet with a little fat and season with salt and pepper. Cover and brown slightly and put onions to one side. Place leftover steak in skillet, smother with the onions, cover tightly, and cook over low heat until steak is heated through. Serve with the onions spread on top.

VEAL STROGANOFF

2 tablespoons butter
1 tablespoon minced onion
1 tablespoon flour
1 cup chicken bouillon
1 can (4 ounces) mushrooms, with liquid
½ cup sour cream
2 cups leftover veal, in thin strips
salt, pepper

Melt butter in skillet, add onion, and cook until onion is tender but still crisp. Sprinkle with flour and stir over low heat for a few minutes. Add chicken bouillon and cook, stirring, until the sauce is thick and smooth. Stir in mushrooms and their liquid and sour cream, and heat without boiling. Add meat, and salt and pepper to taste. Heat without boiling. Serve with buttered noodles or rice.

LAMB CURRY

2 tablespoons butter
2 tablespoons chopped onion
1 tablespoon flour
1 teaspoon or more curry powder
2 cups chicken bouillon
2 cups leftover cooked lamb, in cubes
lemon juice, salt and pepper

Melt butter, brown onion very lightly. Stir in flour and curry powder and cook, stirring constantly, for a few minutes without browning. Stir in the chicken bouillon and cook until the sauce is thick and smooth. Add lamb, heat. Season with lemon juice, salt and pepper to taste. Serve with rice and chutney.

CHINESE SWEET AND SOUR PORK

1 green pepper
1 onion
2 carrots
¼ cup vegetable oil
1 can (8¾ ounces) pineapple tidbits
2 tablespoons wine vinegar
1 tablespoon cornstarch
1 tablespoon soy sauce
2 cups leftover pork, cubed

Clean and slice pepper, slice onion, cut carrots on the diagonal into very thin slices. Heat oil, add the raw vegetables and simmer slowly until vegetables are tender, but still crisp. Add pineapple, bring to boil. Stir vinegar, cornstarch and soy sauce together, add, and cook, stirring constantly, until sauce is clear and thick. Add pork, heat through. Serve with rice.

SCALLOPED MEAT

3 tablespoons fat
3 tablespoons flour
1½ teaspoons salt
¼ teaspoon pepper
1 small onion, chopped
1 tablespoon chopped parsley
1½ cups hot meat stock
2 cups bread or cracker crumbs
2 cups cold cooked meat

Melt fat over low heat, add flour, seasonings, onion, parsley and add ⅓ cup of the hot stock. Mix, then add the rest of the stock gradually. Line a baking dish with ½ of the crumbs. Pour sauce mixed with meat, cut in small pieces, into dish, cover with remaining crumbs and brown in 375° F. oven 20 minutes until heated through and crusty on top.

SHEPHERD'S PIE

Remove the bones, fat, and gristle from cold, cooked meat. Grind the meat, mix with ⅓ cup gravy for each cup of meat, ¼ teaspoon salt, a dash of pepper, 1 small chopped onion, and a little chopped parsley. Place in a buttered baking dish; spread mashed potatoes over the meat and bake in a moderate oven, 350° F., until potatoes are golden brown.

Or, cover with Potato Crust and bake until the crust is browned, about 15 minutes.

POTATO CRUST

2 cups flour
½ teaspoon salt
2 teaspoons baking powder
½ cup shortening
1 cup cold mashed potato
milk or water

Sift together the flour, salt and baking powder, cut in the shortening, add the potato, and lastly enough milk to form a soft dough. Roll on a floured board, cover pie, and slash. Bake as directed.

SURPRISE BALLS

seasoned mashed potatoes
lean cooked meat, chopped
butter or fat

Roll the potatoes into balls, hollow the top with a teaspoon. Season meat, fill the hollow and roll to cover. Place in greased pan with a little fat on the top of each ball, brown in the oven and serve hot.

BAKED MEAT CAKES (RISSOLES)

2 cups cooked meat
salt, pepper to taste
1 teaspoon chopped onion
1 cup bread crumbs
1 egg
meat stock or hot water

Cut the meat off the bones, remove fat, gristle, and skin; chop very fine; season with salt, pepper, chopped onion, and with celery salt if desired. Add bread crumbs, moisten with well-beaten egg and hot water or meat stock. Form into small cakes or a loaf. Put into shallow pans with a little beef drippings; bake in a moderate oven, 350° F., for about 30 minutes. Serve with Tomato Sauce, or a thickened gravy.

MINCED MEAT ON TOAST

Mince or dice leftover cold meat; season, add gravy or broth to moisten. Heat in a skillet. Serve hot on toast.

Meat Soufflés

Soufflés may be made with cooked beef, lamb, veal or pork, following the recipe below. Season to taste with Worcestershire sauce, Tabasco, or onion powder.

Other suggestions for using leftover meats and poultry will be found throughout the chapter on Salads, pages 356-378, and on pages 302-305.

HAM SOUFFLE

3 tablespoons butter
3 tablespoons flour
1 cup milk
3 egg yolks
1 cup finely ground cooked ham
salt, pepper, dry mustard or cayenne
4 egg whites

Melt butter, stir in flour, and cook a few minutes, stirring, without browning. Slowly add milk, and cook, stirring, until sauce is thick and smooth. Beat egg yolks, warm with a little sauce, and combine. Add ground ham, blend well. Season to taste with salt, if necessary, white pepper and spice. Beat egg whites stiff, fold in. Bake in 2 individual straight-sided soufflé dishes, or other baking dish, well greased, in a hot oven, 400° F., about 30 minutes, until soufflé is well puffed and browned. Serve at once. The soufflé may be sprinkled with grated cheese before baking, if desired. If other meat is substituted for the ham, the seasoning should be adjusted accordingly.

HAM AND CORNMEAL CAKE

4 tablespoons butter
½ cup brown sugar
8 slices canned pineapple
6 slices baked ham
Cornmeal Muffin batter, page 89
or 1 package (12 ounces) cornmeal muffin mix

Melt butter in 10-inch heavy skillet; sprinkle with the sugar. Arrange pineapple rings to cover the bottom. Over this place a layer of ham slices. Pour cornmeal muffin batter over the ham. Bake in a hot oven, 400° F., about 20 minutes, until the topping is well browned. Invert and serve with Mushroom Sauce.

JELLIED MEAT LOAF

See page 371.

POULTRY

CHICKEN • TURKEY • DUCK • GOOSE • GAME BIRDS • POULTRY STUFFINGS

You may buy poultry whole for roasting, cooking on the rotisserie, boiling or braising; split for broiling or barbecuing; cut up into serving-sized pieces for frying or sautéeing.

Most poultry is now sold eviscerated, completely pre-cleaned, ready for cooking or freezing.

The following directions for dressing and cleaning apply to whole, fresh-killed poultry or game.

HOW MUCH TO BUY

A small broiler, split, serves 2; larger broilers may be quartered to provide 4 servings. Fryers serve

3 to 4, as does an average duckling. In buying goose, allow 1 pound per serving. Plan on ¾ to 1 pound of turkey, dressed weight, per serving. A pound of boned turkey roll makes 3 to 4 servings.

TO DRESS AND CLEAN POULTRY

Singe by holding the chicken or other poultry over a flame. Cut off the head, turn back the skin, and cut the neck off quite close to body; take out windpipe and crop, cutting off close to the body.

Remove pinfeathers with the point of a knife. Remove oil bag from the tail.

If internal organs have not been removed, make an opening under one of the legs, or at the vent, and remove them carefully, leaving a strip of skin above the vent. Care must be taken that the gall bladder, which lies under the liver, is not broken; it must be carefully cut away from the liver. The lungs and the kidneys lying in the hollows of the backbone must be carefully removed. Cut off tip of heart and cut open to extract any blood. Cut gizzard, which has been removed with other internal organs, through to the inner coat, halfway around, take off the outer coat and throw the inner bag away. The gizzard, heart and liver constitute the giblets, and may be used in making gravies and dressings for poultry. Wash the giblets, put into cold water, heat quickly and cook until tender. The liver requires only a short time for cooking.

Scald feet with boiling water and pull off the skin and nails. Place in soup kettle with giblets and other meats for soup.

Wash chicken or other poultry thoroughly inside and out. Dry and season. Stuff and truss for roasting, or cut into pieces for stew or fricassee.

TO TRUSS POULTRY

Tuck end of skin of neck under at the back, and secure with poultry pin or skewer. Turn wings back under and secure tips against body. Tie drumsticks together, crossing thread under tail of bird and securing legs close to the body. Or, if flap of skin is slit at front of bird above tail cross legs and tuck them under this band of skin to secure.

TO DISJOINT UNCOOKED POULTRY

Use a sharp knife or poultry shears. Hold the leg away from the body and cut from the inside through cartilege at the joint to separate it from the body. Divide the drumstick from the thigh at the joint. Hold the wing away from the body and separate it from the body by cutting through at the joint. Separate the wishbone and the meat on it from the breast. Make a cut down either side of the backbone through the ribs. Remove the backbone. Divide the breast in half lengthwise, cutting from the inside. The neck, giblets, wings and backbone may be used to make stock for gravy, or they may be added to soup or stew.

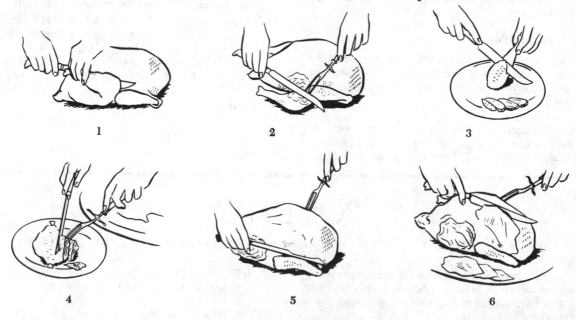

1   2   3

4   5   6

Carving roast chicken, capon or turkey

TO CARVE POULTRY

Place chicken, turkey or other fowl breast up on heated platter, with neck to left of carver. Bend leg away from body, cut between leg and body and divide at joint. Repeat with other leg. Cut off wings in same manner. Remove legs and wings to separate heated plate. Insert carving fork alongside the breastbone. Cut the breast meat in thin slices parallel to the breastbone, beginning above the wing and working up. Place the pieces neatly on one side of the platter. Divide legs at the joints, and, if fowl is large, slice legs and second joints. Separate the collarbone from the breast, slip the knife under the shoulder blade and turn it over. Cut and separate the breast from the back.

TO BONE POULTRY

Lay bird breast down on a board. With a small sharp knife split along backbone from neck to tail. Insert the knife between meat and bone and carefully work meat loose on one side to center of the breast. Repeat on other side. Sever the frame from the joints at drumstick and wings, and lift it out. Do not bone drumsticks or wings. Sew up the slit from backbone to neck. Turn the bird breast side up and fill with stuffing to restore natural shape. Stuff neck cavity. Close both openings with skewers and lace the body cavity securely. Truss and tie the legs. To carve boned poultry: remove the drum sticks and wings. Remove skewers. Beginning at one end, make diagonal slices toward center, cutting down through breast and stuffing.

GRAVY FOR ROAST POULTRY

Remove cooked poultry from pan and keep warm. Drain off all but 4 tablespoons fat. Add 4 tablespoons flour and cook until brown. Add 2 cups hot stock in which giblets, neck and tip of wings have been cooked. Cook 5 minutes, stirring in the brown bits that cling to the pan. Season with salt and pepper. Add the cooked giblets, chopped, and serve hot with poultry.

CHICKEN

Chickens are so plentiful that we welcome them on the menu frequently. There has also been a change in chicken style: most chickens that come to market now are BROILER-FRYERS, only nine weeks old. They weigh from 1½ to 3½ pounds and are usually tender and juicy. The ROASTER, marketed at 12 weeks, weighs between 3½ and 5 pounds. It costs more per pound and takes longer to cook. The STEWING HEN, fowl, or bro-hen —the names are used interchangeably—which is marketed at 1½ years, weighs from 4 to 6 pounds, and requires still longer cooking. Except in making chicken soup, many cooks feel that the stewing hen can be replaced by broiler-fryers. CAPONS, altered roosters, grow to as much as 7 pounds in weight, and are a luxury roast. Broiler-fryer parts are usually available, so that it is possible to buy only breasts, for a party meal, or only drumsticks for a picnic, only wings for a fricassee or grilling, or thrifty necks and backs for the soup pot. The broiler-fryer is the best all-around choice for every purpose from broiling or frying to roasting, cooking en casserole, and oven-baking.

Chicken has excellent value nutritionally; it is high in protein content, and lower in calories than most meats. In addition, the adaptability of chicken to all methods of cooking and seasoning, makes it deservedly popular.

RENDERED CHICKEN FAT

Wash fat, cut into small pieces, and put in small skillet or saucepan in ½ inch water. Cook over very low heat until most of fat is melted. Add ½ onion, diced, and continue to cook until fat pieces are crisp. Add salt to taste. Strain fat into jars, cover and store. To make crisp cracklings, cook a little longer, until brown. Drain on paper toweling, season with salt and pepper. Cracklings may be added to chopped liver and patés for interesting texture and flavor.

Duck, goose, or turkey fat may be rendered in the same way.

CHART FOR ROASTING STUFFED CHICKEN

CLASS	WEIGHT	TEMP.	HOURS
Broiler-fryer	1½ to 3 lbs.	375° F.	1 to 1½
Roaster	3½ to 6 lbs.	325° F.	2 to 3
Capon	5 to 7 lbs.	325° F.	2½ to 3½

ROAST CHICKEN OR CAPON

Preheat oven to temperature recommended on chart. Rinse bird with cold water, drain and pat dry. Rub inside cavity with salt, pepper, and ginger, or stuff as desired. Stuff neck skin lightly and/or fasten skin to back of chicken with skewer. Never stuff bird the day before. *If stuffing must be made ahead, be certain to refrigerate it separately from bird.* Stuff body cavity and close either with skewers, or by sewing with coarse thread. Tie the drumsticks together, crossing thread under tail of bird, or push drumsticks under band of skin at tail if this is intact. Roast bird on rack in open pan according to time recommended on chart, basting occasionally. Bird is done when thickest part of drumstick feels soft when pressed, and when the juices that run when the leg joint is pierced with a fork show no trace of pink.

ROTISSERIE ROASTING

Any bird that can be roasted can be spit-roasted, either over the barbecue or in an electric rotisserie. Since rotisserie equipment varies, it is best to follow the manufacturer's directions for your particular equipment. The bird or birds (two or three chickens or ducks may be rotisserie-roasted at the same time) must be tied securely and balanced on the spit so perfectly that the spit revolves uniformly throughout the cooking period. Cooking times given on the roasting charts for the various birds may be used as a guide, but a thermometer or other tests for doneness should also be used.

BOILED CHICKEN

Cut a stewing chicken in pieces, or leave it whole. Rub with salt, pepper, ginger. Let stand in refrigerator several hours or overnight. Place in pan, cover with boiling water, add onion, carrot, few stalks of celery, slice of lemon. Simmer 3 or 4 hours, until tender. Let cool in broth, chill broth and remove fat from top. Strain broth; remove chicken from bones and cut flesh in large chunks. Reheat in broth, or slice to serve cold; or remove skin and dice meat for Chicken à la King or salads.

OVEN-BROWNED BOILED CHICKEN

Prepare Boiled Chicken, above. Sprinkle with salt, paprika and ginger to taste and dredge well with flour. Heat 3 tablespoons chicken or other fat in a roasting pan, roll chicken in the melted fat; bake in hot oven 10 or 20 minutes, basting often, until well browned. If browned before ready to serve, reduce heat and cover closely, to keep meat juicy. Remove bird to platter. Add 1 cup of water to pan and cook a few minutes, stirring in the brown bits that cling to the pan.

BROILED CHICKEN

Split a small, broiler-fryer chicken (1½ pounds). Sprinkle with salt and pepper and rub well with soft butter. Place rack as far as possible from the heating unit of the broiler. Broil 30 to 40 minutes. Turn chicken several times so that it will brown evenly. Brush with butter and drippings. Serves 2.

FRIED CHICKEN

1 broiler-fryer (1½-2½ pounds), cut up
salt, pepper and ginger
flour
¼ cup butter, or poultry fat

Season chicken pieces with salt, pepper and ginger. Dredge with flour and fry in hot fat until brown. Cover, place over low heat or in slow oven, 300° F., 30 minutes or until tender. For crisp skin, remove cover for last 10 minutes. Serves 2.

CRISPY FRIED CHICKEN

1 broiler-fryer (1½-2 pounds)
salt, pepper
cracker crumbs
1 egg

Cut chicken in half or quarters and season with salt and pepper. Dip in cracker crumbs. Let stand 10 minutes, then dip in slightly-beaten egg and again in crumbs. Fry in deep, hot fat, or in a skillet with butter, until golden brown.

OVEN-FRIED CHICKEN

1 broiler-fryer (1½-2½ pounds) chicken
salt, pepper
¼ cup butter or poultry fat
bread crumbs

Cut chicken in half or quarters. Season, rub with softened fat, cover with fine bread crumbs, place in a pan and bake in hot oven, 400°F., ½ hour. Serves 2-4.

OVEN-FRIED CHICKEN À LA MARYLAND

Cut broiler-fryer chicken in serving pieces. Season with salt and pepper, dip in flour, lightly beaten egg, and crumbs. Let stand 45 minutes, then place in well-greased pan and bake 1 hour in moderate oven, 350° F., basting frequently with melted butter. Cover with 2 cups Medium White Sauce, omitting salt and seasoning with bouillon cubes.

BAKED CHICKEN

3 broiling chickens, split in halves
¾ cup butter
¾ cup dry white wine
1½ teaspoons salt
¼ teaspoon pepper
½ teaspoon tarragon
1 tablespoon cornstarch

Put chickens in a shallow baking pan, skin side up. Melt butter, add wine and seasonings. Pour a little of this over the chicken. Bake in a 325° F. oven for 1 hour or until tender, basting frequently with the sauce. When chicken is tender and brown, pour sauce from pan into a saucepan and heat to boiling. Mix cornstarch with a little cold water; add to sauce and boil for about 2 minutes, stirring constantly. Serve sauce with chicken.

OVEN-BARBECUED CHICKEN

1 3-pound broiler-fryer chicken, cut-up
3 tablespoons fat
¼ cup lemon juice
1 large onion, grated
2 tablespoons tomato paste
½ cup melted butter
1 tablespoon paprika
1 teaspoon salt
½ teaspoon pepper
1 tablespoon sugar

Brown the chicken pieces in hot fat. Combine the rest of the ingredients for the sauce. Place the chicken pieces in a baking dish; pour the sauce over them. Bake in a moderate oven, 350° F., for about 45 minutes. Baste frequently with the sauce.

STEWED CHICKEN

6 chicken feet, cleaned
veal bone, optional
salt, pepper
½ cup each of sliced onion and celery
1 stewing chicken

In a kettle large enough to hold the chicken, put the veal bone, chicken feet, seasoning and vegetables. Add 3 quarts cold water. Let cook about 1 hour; place the whole chicken, previously well seasoned, into the broth. Cover and simmer slowly until chicken is tender.

CHICKEN FRICASSEE

1 stewing chicken
½ cup each onion and celery, cut up
salt, pepper, ginger
3 tablespoons fat
4 tablespoons flour

Prepare Boiled Chicken with vegetables and seasonings, simmer until tender. Remove from broth. Melt fat in double boiler, add flour, stir well, and gradually add 2 cups chicken broth, stirring to prevent lumps. Add chicken, reheat.

CHICKEN FRICASSEE WITH BISCUITS OR DUMPLINGS

1 stewing chicken
salt, pepper
1 red pepper, seeded and sliced
1 sliced onion
½ clove garlic, minced
¼ cup diced celery
2 bay leaves

Season chicken with salt and pepper, add red pepper, onion, minced garlic, celery and bay leaves. Cover with boiling water and simmer until tender. Drain. Serve with Fricassee Sauce, page 387, made with stock, and Baking Powder Biscuits, page 86, or Farina Potato Dumplings, page 103.

CHICKEN PAPRIKA

2 broiler-fryer chickens, disjointed
1 teaspoon salt
¼ cup flour
1 tablespoon paprika
¼ cup butter or fat
1½ cups hot water or milk
2-3 tablespoons sour cream

Season chicken and roll in flour mixed with paprika. Heat fat in pan. Brown chicken in fat, add hot water or milk, cover and simmer 30 minutes, until tender. Just before serving, stir sour cream into gravy.

FILLETS OF CHICKEN

6 chicken breasts, split and boned
salt and paprika
cream
flour
½ cup butter
½ cup Madeira wine
thin ham slices
¼ pound mushrooms
Hollandaise Sauce, page 388

Sprinkle chicken fillets with salt and paprika, dip in cream, roll in flour, and brown lightly in butter. Place fillets in a greased pan; dot with butter, add wine. Cover with buttered paper and bake until tender in a hot oven, 400° F., basting with the hot fat. When ready to serve, place each fillet on a hot thin slice of fried ham, garnish with sautéed mushrooms and Hollandaise Sauce.

Chicken freezes well either cooked or uncooked. For instructions, see the sections on freezing poultry and freezing cooked foods in chapter 24, page 460.

CHICKEN ROSE

2 broiler-fryer chickens, cut in quarters
¼ teaspoon garlic salt
¼ teaspoon paprika
1½ tablespoons flour
3 tablespoons shortening
¼ teaspoon rosemary
¼ teaspoon basil
¾ cup rosé wine
¾ cup sour cream

Mix garlic salt, paprika and flour; dredge chicken in flour mixture. Brown chicken on both sides in the shortening. Add herbs and wine; cover pan and cook over low heat until chicken is tender, 25 to 30 minutes. Remove chicken, skim off excess fat; stir in sour cream. Replace chicken in sauce; reheat but do not boil.

SHERRIED CHICKEN

1 cup dry sherry
1 lemon
1 teaspoon salt
¼ cup peanut oil
2 broiler-fryer chickens, cut in pieces
flour, salt and pepper

Combine the sherry, juice of half the lemon, salt and oil. Pour this over the chicken and marinate the chicken for at least 2 hours in the refrigerator. Remove the chicken; save the marinade. Combine flour, salt and pepper and coat the chicken with this mixture. Brown the chicken in a little additional oil. Drain off any oil left in the pan. Slice the remaining half of the lemon very thin. Add lemon slices and marinade to the chicken; cover skillet, and simmer 20 to 25 minutes or until tender.

BRANDIED CHICKEN BREASTS

6 chicken breasts, boned
brandy
salt, pepper, marjoram
6 tablespoons butter
½ cup sherry
4 egg yolks
2 cups cream
salt, pepper, and nutmeg
grated Swiss cheese
buttered bread crumbs

Rub chicken breasts with brandy; let stand 10 to 15 minutes. Season with salt, pepper and marjoram. Sauté the chicken in the butter until done, 6 to 8 minutes on each side. Remove to heatproof dish and keep warm. Add sherry to chicken drippings in pan and simmer over low heat for 4 to 5 minutes. Beat egg yolks with cream. Pour this into the butter and sherry mixture, stirring constantly. Season with salt, pepper, and nutmeg. Cook until slightly thickened, stirring constantly. Pour the sauce over the chicken breasts. Sprinkle with grated cheese and bread crumbs. Place under the broiler just long enough to melt the cheese.

CHICKEN WITH MUSHROOMS

1 3-pound broiler-fryer chicken, cut up
2 teaspoons salt
paprika
¼ cup butter
1 small onion
1 pound fresh mushrooms, whole or sliced

Season chicken pieces. Heat butter in skillet, add sliced onion and chicken, and brown lightly. Cover and simmer 30 minutes, or until tender. Wash mushrooms well, cook in boiling salted water 5 minutes, then add to chicken and simmer 15 minutes longer.

CHICKEN EN CASSEROLE

1 3-pound broiler-fryer, cut up
salt, pepper and ginger
2 tablespoons flour
2 tablespoons fat
¼ cup strained tomatoes
onion, celery, carrot, optional

Season chicken pieces with salt, pepper and ginger to taste. Dredge with flour and fry in hot fat until brown. Add the strained tomatoes, and, if desired, a little onion and a piece of celery and carrot. Place in casserole, cover and put in slow oven or in Dutch oven over low heat. Simmer 45 minutes, or until tender.

CHICKEN À LA KING

3½ pounds broiler-fryer chicken, boiled
2 cups Medium White Sauce, page 386
1 cup chicken stock
1 cup sliced mushrooms
1 green pepper, sliced
3 tablespoons butter
¼ cup sherry
1 pimiento, cut up
salt, pepper and paprika to taste
2 egg yolks

In advance, remove chicken from bones, cut in small pieces. Make Medium White Sauce, using cream. Add chicken stock and cook, stirring constantly, until smooth. Cook mushrooms and green pepper in butter 5 minutes, stirring often. Add to sauce with sherry. Add chicken and pimiento and season with salt, pepper and paprika. Just before serving, reheat, beat egg yolks with a little water, add to sauce. Cook 1 minute.

Serve on toast or in patty shells, or on a deep platter, surrounded by cooked asparagus tips and green peppers stuffed with corn kernels.

CHICKEN À LA KING WITH SCALLOPED NOODLES

3 cups cooked broad noodles
Chicken à la King, above
1 pound mushrooms, sautéed
1 cup buttered bread crumbs

Fill a well-greased baking dish with alternate layers of noodles, Chicken à la King, and mushrooms, using noodles for top and bottom layers. Cover with crumbs and bake in moderate oven, 350° F., until the crumbs are browned.

STUFFED SUPREMES OF CHICKEN

6 chicken breasts with wings attached
Forcemeat, see below
½ cup poultry fat or butter
¼ cup Madeira wine
¼ pound mushrooms, sautéed

Remove skin from the chicken breasts. With a sharp knife cut through the flesh, close to the wishbone, along the breastbone and around the wing joint and remove the solid white breast meat. Reserve the smaller pieces, next to the bone, and the white meat of the wings for the Forcemeat. Cut an opening 3 inches long and 1 inch deep in the breast meat. Fill the pocket in the chicken breasts with Forcemeat. Close the opening and tie. Brown lightly in the hot fat and add the wine. Cover the pan, place in a hot oven, 400° F., and bake 15 minutes or until tender. Remove strings and serve with mushrooms and thin Cream Sauce, made with pan juices as part or all of liquid.

FORCEMEAT

Grind the leftover white meat, add half the quantity of bread, soaked in water and pressed dry, ½ teaspoon salt, a few drops of onion juice, a little pepper, 1 tablespoon soup stock, 1 egg and 6 mushrooms sliced fine. Blend well.

CHICKEN WITH ALMONDS

1 can (10½ ounces) cream of mushroom soup
1 can (10½ ounces) cream of chicken soup
1 can (10½ ounces) cream of celery soup
½ cup melted butter
½ cup slivered almonds
1¼ cups brown rice, uncooked
3 chicken breasts, boned and halved
¼ cup grated Parmesan cheese
¼ cup sautéed slivered almonds
parsley

Combine undiluted soups, melted butter and almonds. Set aside 1 cup of this mixture. Mix rice with the remainder of the mixture and pour into two-quart casserole or baking dish. Place chicken on top of soup-rice mixture. Bake in moderately slow oven, 325° F., for about 2 hours. Baste the chicken every 15 to 20 minutes with the reserved soup mixture. About 15 minutes before the end of the baking time, sprinkle the grated cheese over the chicken and allow it to brown. Before serving, garnish with ¼ cup sautéed almonds and parsley.

SPANISH CHICKEN

1 stewing chicken or 2 broiler-fryers, disjointed
salt, pepper and paprika to taste
¼ cup chicken fat or butter
1 Spanish onion, sliced
1 can (1 pound, 4 ounces) tomatoes
3 carrots, chopped fine
1 celery root or stalk, cut in small cubes
1 green pepper, seeded
1 can (6¾ ounces) mushrooms
1 can (8½ ounces) peas, drained

Season chicken pieces with salt, pepper and paprika. Heat fat, add onion and brown, add chicken, brown lightly, and cook very slowly, covered, about 1 hour for stewing chicken, about 15 minutes for broiler-fryers. Add tomatoes, carrots, celery and pepper, cover again and let cook until tender. Ten minutes before serving, add the mushrooms and peas. Season to taste.

CHICKEN CREOLE

Prepare Spanish Chicken, adding 1 cup rice with tomatoes, and omitting mushrooms and peas.

CHICKEN PERUVIAN

1 1-pound can tomatoes
1 frying chicken
3 medium onions, quartered lengthwise
salt and pepper
¼ cup catsup
¼ cup white wine or 2 tablespoons vinegar
2 tablespoons ground cumin
15 stuffed olives
⅓ cup almonds
¼ cup raisins

Combine first seven ingredients and simmer until chicken is very tender, about 1½ hours. Remove chicken and bone it. Discard skin and bones. Return chicken to liquid in which it was cooked. Add olives, almonds and raisins just before serving. Serve with rice.

CHICKEN MARENGO

1 thinly sliced onion
½ cup olive oil
2 frying chickens, quartered
½ cup dry white wine
1 crushed clove garlic
½ teaspoon thyme
1 bay leaf
1 tablespoon parsley flakes
1 cup chicken stock
2 cups canned tomatoes
16 to 20 small white onions
1 pound mushrooms, sliced
¼ cup butter
juice of 1 lemon
1 cup pitted black olives
1 jigger cognac

Sauté onion in olive oil. Remove onion; brown chicken on all sides in the same skillet. Add wine, garlic, thyme, bay leaf, parsley, stock and tomatoes. Cover and simmer for about 45 minutes, until chicken is tender. Remove chicken to a casserole. Strain the sauce and boil it for a few minutes to reduce it.

Sauté the small onions and mushrooms in the butter and lemon juice. Add with olives to casserole. Sprinkle with cognac. Add the sauce. Place in 350° F. oven until thoroughly heated. Serve with rice.

CHICKEN MONTEGO

3 tablespoons flour
1 teaspoon salt
⅛ teaspoon pepper
3 large chicken breasts, split
¼ cup shortening
4 ounces spaghetti twists or elbow macaroni
1 can (4 ounces) button mushrooms, drained
1 can condensed cream of celery soup
1 teaspoon marjoram
2 cups sour cream
1 can (1 pound) peas, drained
paprika

Mix flour and seasonings; roll chicken in this mixture. Brown in shortening; remove from pan. While chicken is browning, cook spaghetti. Brown the mushrooms in the skillet in which the chicken was browned. Add soup and marjoram and stir until smooth. Add sour cream. Put spaghetti in a shallow casserole; add peas and half the soup mixture; mix lightly. Place chicken breasts on top and cover with the remaining soup mixture. Cover and bake at 350° F. for 45 minutes. Remove cover and bake 15 minutes longer. Sprinkle chicken with paprika; serve.

CHICKEN JUBILEE

1 can pitted dark cherries
1 tablespoon minced onion
1 12-ounce bottle chili sauce
3 whole chicken breasts
¼ cup sherry

Drain cherries, saving the juice. Mix onion and chili sauce with the cherry juice. Season chicken and place in a large baking dish. Cover with one-half of the chili sauce mixture. Cover the baking pan. Bake at 350° F. for 1½ hours. During the baking, baste with the remaining sauce. Remove the cover and continue to bake for 15 minutes. Add cherries and sherry and heat through.

CHICKEN AND BROCCOLI CASSEROLE

1 5-pound chicken
1 teaspoon salt
6 tablespoons shortening
½ cup flour
1 cup milk
1 cup mayonnaise
1 teaspoon lemon juice
½ teaspoon curry powder
2 packages frozen broccoli

Half cover chicken with water, add salt, and simmer until tender. Remove chicken from bones in large pieces. Save broth in which chicken is cooked. Melt shortening, stir in flour until smooth, gradually add milk and 2 cups of chicken broth. Cook over low heat, stirring constantly, until thick and smooth. Remove from heat, add mayonnaise, lemon juice and curry powder. Mix well. Cook broccoli; place half of broccoli in bottom of shallow baking dish, place chicken in layer over broccoli. Pour sauce over chicken; place remaining broccoli on top. Bake at 400° F. for 20 minutes. If made in advance and refrigerated, heat at 350° F. for 30 minutes.

CHICKEN DIVAN

4 whole chicken breasts
2 10-ounce packages frozen broccoli spears
1 8-ounce package cream cheese
2 cups milk
1 teaspoon garlic salt
salt
½ cup grated Parmesan cheese

Boil or bake chicken breasts. Remove skin and bones. Leave breasts whole or cut in slices. Cook broccoli as directed on package and drain. Place broccoli in a large buttered baking dish. Heat cream cheese, milk and garlic salt over medium heat, stirring constantly until smooth. Salt to taste. Pour 1 cup of this sauce over the broccoli; sprinkle with half of the cheese. Place chicken on top.

Top with 1 cup of the sauce. Retain remaining sauce. Bake at 350° F. for 20 minutes. Top with remaining sauce and sprinkle with remaining cheese. Broil for 2 minutes until cheese is melted. Let stand for about 10 minutes before serving.

CHICKEN AND RICE

1 stewing chicken
salt, pepper
¼ cup chicken fat
1 medium onion, chopped
1 teaspoon paprika
1 cup rice, uncooked
1 teaspoon salt

Cut chicken into serving pieces. Season. Heat fat in heavy kettle, add onion, fry golden brown and set aside. Brown chicken in the fat. Add paprika and boiling water to cover. Simmer until almost tender. Combine rice, fried onion, 1 teaspoon salt and 3 cups of the chicken broth, more if necessary. Simmer until rice is nearly done, about 12 minutes; add the chicken and finish cooking in a slow oven, 300° F., ½ hour.

MEXICAN CHICKEN

1 3-pound broiler-fryer, cut up
3 tablespoons shortening
¾ cup blanched almonds
3 onions, diced
1-2 cloves garlic
3 tablespoons chopped parsley
1 can (1 pound, 4 ounces) tomatoes
salt and pepper
¾ cup sliced olives, green or ripe

Brown chicken pieces in shortening. Add remaining ingredients except the olives. Simmer, covered, until the chicken is tender. About 5 minutes before serving, add the olives.

BRUNSWICK STEW

1 pound brisket of beef
salt to taste
1 teaspoon paprika
¼ pound bacon, diced
1 medium onion, diced
4½-pound stewing chicken
2½ quarts water
2 cups fresh lima beans
2 cups fresh or canned corn
3 tomatoes, quartered
3 potatoes, diced

Sprinkle the meat with salt and paprika, let stand ½ hour. Fry bacon, add onion, cover, cook slightly.

Add meat and chicken cut into serving pieces, brown, add boiling water. Bring to the boiling point, reduce heat, cover and simmer 2 hours. Add rest of ingredients including 1 cup chopped okra, if desired, and cook 1 hour or until tender. Season to taste.

CHICKEN CHOP SUEY FOR 15

3½ to 4 pounds young chicken, raw
½ cup chicken fat, olive or peanut oil
½ pound lean pork, cubed
1 pound lean veal, cubed
2 tablespoons salt
1 pound Chinese water chestnuts, peeled (or use canned)
1 large bunch celery
½ can bamboo shoots
2 onions, chopped
1 can (8 ounces) mushrooms
1 can (1 pound) bean sprouts
¼ cup cornstarch
3 tablespoons water
¼ teaspoon pepper
soy sauce to taste

In advance, bone chicken and cut in thin strips. Heat fat in large kettle; add chicken, pork, veal, and salt; cover and simmer for 25 minutes or until tender. Add water if necessary. Cut chestnuts, celery, bamboo shoots, and onions into thin strips. Just before serving add with sliced mushrooms to the meat, cover, and cook 10 minutes. Add bean sprouts, drained, cornstarch dissolved in cold water, and seasoning. Cover and simmer 5 minutes; serve hot with rice.

CHOW MEIN (CHICKEN OR PORK)

1 cup water chestnuts
1 cup bamboo shoots
1 cup celery
2 green onions with tops
1 pound of raw boned chicken or raw pork
1 egg, beaten
⅓ cup oil
2 tablespoons cornstarch
2 tablespoons soy sauce
½ cup soup stock or water
1 can (3 ounces) Chinese fried noodles

In advance, slice chestnuts, bamboo shoots, celery, and onion into fine strips. Cut pork or chicken into strips 1½ inches long. Fry egg in small amount of oil, in skillet, remove to dish, cut in thin strips. Add remaining oil to skillet and sauté meat about 20 minutes, stirring occasionally. Add chestnuts, bamboo shoots, celery, and 1 tablespoon soy sauce. Cover, simmer very gently about 20 minutes, stirring occasionally. Just before serving, mix cornstarch with 1 tablespoon soy sauce and the soup stock or water. Add to the vegetables. Stir, add salt to taste, and cook 2 minutes. Serve over Chinese noodles, garnish with onion and egg strips.

CANTONESE CHICKEN

1 cup chopped celery
1 cup chopped onion
¾ cup slivered almonds
3 tablespoons butter
¼ teaspoon salt
4 cups cooked chicken, diced
2 tablespoons cornstarch
2½ cups pineapple juice
2 tablespoons soy sauce
2 teaspoons lemon juice
1 cup cooked julienne carrots
2 cups pineapple chunks
Chinese fried noodles

In advance, sauté celery, onions and almonds in butter. Add salt and chicken. Combine cornstarch with pineapple juice, soy sauce and lemon juice, and cook until thickened, stirring constantly. Just before serving, combine sauce and chicken mixture, heat, add carrots and pineapple chunks and heat through. Serve over Chinese noodles.

CHICKEN POT PIE

4 pounds chicken, cut up
2 celery tops
1 onion studded with 3 cloves
1 carrot, quartered
1 bay leaf
1 tablespoon salt
2 cups cooked mixed carrots and potatoes (in large pieces) and white onions
½ pound mushrooms
Baking Powder Biscuit dough, page 86

Put chicken, celery, onion, carrot, bay leaf and salt in pan. Add about 1 quart water, to cover. Bring to a boil, skim, and simmer, covered, until chicken is tender. Allow ½ hour to 45 minutes for broiler-fryers, 1 to 1½ hours for larger bird. Remove chicken to plate, discard bones and skin. Cut meat into large pieces, put into deep casserole. Add cooked vegetables and mushrooms. Add sauce, below, and cover with Biscuit Dough, rolled ¼ inch thick. Slash crust, bake pie in a hot oven (450° F.) about 20 minutes until crust is browned.

SAUCE

Melt 6 tablespoons fat or butter, stir in 6 tablespoons flour and cook, stirring, until mixture is richly golden in color. Reduce broth from cooking chicken to 3 cups and strain it gradually into the saucepan. Cook, stirring constantly, until the mixture is smooth and thick. Add salt and pepper to taste.

Rendered chicken fat (see page 307) may be used as a substitute for butter or oil in these recipes.

CHICKEN TETRAZZINI

2 stewing chickens, cooked
6 onions, sliced
1 bunch celery, sliced
1 pound mushrooms, sliced
1 green pepper, diced
1 can pimientos, diced
¼ pound butter
2 cans condensed tomato soup
1 teaspoon salt
1½ pounds spaghetti
grated Parmesan cheese

Remove chicken from bones and cut in bite-size pieces. Sauté onions, celery, mushrooms, pepper, and pimiento in the butter until tender. Add tomato soup and salt. Cook spaghetti in salted water and drain. Place chicken in center of casserole and surround with spaghetti. Pour sauce over all. Sprinkle with grated Parmesan and bake in moderate oven, 350° F., until topping browns.

The following recipes are excellent for using left-over chicken or turkey.

CASSEROLE OF RICE AND CHICKEN

2 cups cooked chicken
½ teaspoon salt
¼ teaspoon celery salt
⅛ teaspoon pepper
1 teaspoon chopped onion
1 egg
2 tablespoons cracker crumbs
1 cup stock or hot water
1 cup rice, cooked

Chop chicken very fine, add seasonings and onion, then the beaten egg, cracker crumbs, and enough stock or hot water to moisten. Line the bottom and sides of a greased mold or casserole ½ inch thick with cooked rice, pack in the meat mixture, cover with remaining rice packed firmly, then cover with foil and steam on a rack in a covered kettle, over boiling water, for 45 minutes. Loosen around the edge of mold, turn out on a hot platter and pour Tomato Sauce, page 390, around it. Garnish with parsley. May be served in the baking dish.

CHICKEN-GREEN BEAN CASSEROLE

1 can cream of mushroom soup
½ cup milk
1 teaspoon salt
1 can (14½ ounces) chop suey vegetables
3 cups cooked chicken, cut up
2 packages (9 ounces each) frozen green beans
⅛ cup chopped onion
1½ cups grated Cheddar cheese
1 can (3½ ounces) French fried onions

Blend soup, milk and salt. Drain chop suey vegetables. Fold in all the ingredients except the French fried onions. Place in 12″ x 7½″ x 2″ baking dish. Bake at 350° F. for 45 minutes. Top with French fried onions and bake 10 minutes longer.

CHICKEN HASH

4 cups cooked chicken, minced
½ cup diced celery
1 cup chicken broth
1 cup Medium White Sauce, page 386
2 egg yolks
1 teaspoon onion juice
½ cup sherry
1 teaspoon salt
¼ teaspoon pepper
¼ teaspoon paprika
1 tablespoon Worcestershire sauce

Heat chicken and celery in chicken broth. Prepare Medium White Sauce. Blend in egg yolks, onion juice, wine and seasonings, stirring constantly. Combine mixtures. Serve in patty shells or on toast.

CHICKEN CROQUETTES

3½ cups cooked chicken, very finely ground
2 cups Thick White Sauce, page 386
2 teaspoons lemon juice
1 tablespoon chopped parsley
salt, pepper
cayenne pepper
onion juice

Combine chicken and sauce, add lemon juice, parsley and seasonings and onion juice to taste. Spread mixture on platter to cool and become firm. Shape into cylinders, cones or any desired shapes. Roll in bread or cracker crumbs and let stand 5 minutes. Beat one egg lightly with 1 tablespoon water, dip croquettes in egg mixture and again in crumbs; let stand for 30 minutes. Fry in deep hot fat, 370° F., for about 2-3 minutes until golden brown and crusty. Drain on paper towels.

CHICKEN TIMBALES

3 cups cooked chicken
1 small onion, grated
1 teaspoon salt
1 pinch white pepper
3 slices dry white bread
3 eggs, separated
½ pound mushrooms, chopped and sautéed

Chop chicken, add onion, salt and pepper. Soak bread in cold water, squeeze dry and mash through colander. Combine with chicken, beaten egg yolks, mushrooms. Fold in the stiffly beaten whites. Butter small molds, fill with the mixture, place molds in pan of hot water. Cover and bake at 350° F. for ½ hour. Unmold and serve with Mushroom Sauce.

CHICKEN AND MACARONI

1 cup grated sharp Cheddar cheese
2 cups elbow macaroni, cooked
1 can (10½ ounces) mushroom soup
1 cup diced chicken or turkey
¾ cup milk
¼ cup chopped pimiento
¼ cup green pepper
¼ cup minced onion
salt and pepper to taste

Set aside ½ cup of the cheese. Mix remaining ingredients. Place in greased casserole. Sprinkle top with remaining cheese. Bake at 375° F. for 35 minutes. If made in advance and refrigerated, bake at 350° F. for 45 minutes.

CHICKEN-RICE CASSEROLE

1 package (10 ounces) frozen green beans
2½ cups chicken bouillon
¼ cup flour
½ cup sour cream
2 teaspoons curry powder
1 small onion, minced
2 cups diced chicken or turkey
1 can water chestnuts, sliced
2 cups cooked rice
⅓ cup dry bread crumbs
1 tablespoon melted butter

Cook green beans and drain. Stir bouillon gradually with flour until smooth. Add sour cream, curry powder and onion. Heat over low heat until thickened, stirring constantly. Add beans, chicken and water chestnuts. Grease casserole. Place in alternate layers the rice and the chicken mixture with chicken on top. Sprinkle with buttered crumbs. Bake at 350° F. for 25 to 30 minutes. If made in advance and refrigerated, bake at 325° F. for 40 to 45 minutes.

CHICKEN AND SWEET POTATO POT PIE

2 cups cooked chicken, diced
2 green peppers, thinly sliced
2 large onions, thinly sliced
⅓ cup parsley, minced
2 tablespoons butter
2 tablespoons flour
2 cups chicken broth
1 teaspoon grated orange peel
salt and pepper

CRUST

1 cup mashed sweet potatoes
¼ cup butter, melted
1 egg, beaten
1 tablespoon grated orange peel
2 tablespoons orange juice
1 cup flour
1 teaspoon baking powder
½ teaspoon salt

Grease casserole. Alternate layers of chicken, peppers, onions and parsley until all are used. Melt butter, blend in flour, gradually add broth, stirring constantly until thickened. Add peel and salt and pepper to taste. Pour over the contents of casserole.

For crust: Mix sweet potatoes, butter, egg, peel and orange juice. Combine flour, baking powder and salt. Add flour to potato mixture, stirring well. Roll crust and fit to top of casserole. Bake at 350° F. for 35 to 40 minutes.

CHICKEN (OR TURKEY) AND BROCCOLI BAKE

½ cup flour
1 cup milk
2 cups chicken broth
1 cup mayonnaise
1 teaspoon lemon juice
½ teaspoon curry powder
2 packages frozen broccoli (10 ounces)
2½ cups cubed cooked chicken or turkey
2 cups cornflakes or ½ cup packaged cornflake crumbs
1 tablespoon butter, melted

Blend flour and milk to make a smooth paste; stir in chicken broth. Cook until thickened, stirring constantly. Remove from heat. Stir in mayonnaise, lemon juice and curry powder. Cook broccoli according to package directions only until tender. Drain well. Cut broccoli stalks in half; arrange in 2-quart casserole. Cover broccoli with chicken; pour on sauce. Top with cornflake crumbs which have been mixed with the melted butter. Bake at 350° F. about 30 minutes or until thoroughly heated and crumbs are browned.

CHICKEN CASSEROLE

½ cup mayonnaise
½ teaspoon salt
dash of pepper
½ cup milk
1½ cups cooked or canned peas
2 cups diced cooked chicken
1 can (4 ounces) mushrooms
4 cups hot mashed potatoes
½ cup grated Cheddar cheese

Mix mayonnaise, salt, pepper and milk. Heat over low heat, stirring constantly. Add peas, chicken and mushrooms. Grease casserole. Put layer of mashed potatoes on bottom, cover with half of chicken mixture. Cover with a layer of potatoes, then the rest of the chicken mixture. Place the remaining potatoes in a ring around the edge of the casserole. Sprinkle cheese in center of ring. Bake at 350° F. for 15 minutes. If made in advance and refrigerated, bake at 325° F. for 25 to 30 minutes.

BAKED CHICKEN CASSEROLE

1 10-ounce package frozen peas
2 cups cooked chicken or turkey
1 cup celery, diced
1 5-ounce can water chestnuts, sliced
2 tablespoons chopped green pepper
1 tablespoon minced onion
1 tablespoon lemon juice
2 tablespoons white wine
½ teaspoon salt
½ cup milk
1 10½-ounce can cream of chicken soup
2 slices white bread, cubed
1 cup grated sharp cheese

Cook peas and drain. Combine peas, chicken, celery, water chestnuts, green pepper, onion, lemon juice, wine and salt. Place in a greased casserole. Heat milk and soup, stirring until smooth. Pour this sauce into the casserole. Sprinkle bread cubes on top. Bake at 375° F. for 20 minutes. Sprinkle cheese on top and return to oven for about 15 minutes or until the cheese is melted.

CHICKEN LOAF

2 eggs
½ cup milk
1 cup bread crumbs
2 cups cooked chicken, diced
1 cup peas, cooked or canned
1 cup diced cooked carrots
1 teaspoon minced onion
1 teaspoon minced parsley
salt
pepper

Beat eggs. Pour milk over crumbs and allow to stand for 2 to 3 minutes. Combine all ingredients. Pack in a buttered loaf pan. Bake at 350° F. for 45 minutes. Unmold. Serve with desired hot sauce.

CHICKEN OR TURKEY STROGANOFF

2 tablespoons slivered scallions
2 tablespoons butter
3 cups cooked chicken or turkey
1 4-ounce can sliced mushrooms
½ teaspoon salt
1 10½-ounce can cream of mushroom soup
¼ cup water
½ cup sour cream

Sauté scallions in butter. Add chicken and mushrooms, reserving the liquid from the mushrooms. Sauté chicken 2 to 3 minutes. Add salt, soup, mushroom liquid and water. Heat, stirring until smooth. Stir in sour cream, heat again, but do not boil. Serve with boiled noodles.

SPICY TURKEY

1 egg
½ teaspoon soy sauce
3 cups cooked turkey, cut in chunks
½ cup flour
2 tablespoons shortening
1 clove garlic, crushed
1 bunch scallions, cut in pieces
2 onions, cut in wedges or sliced
1 13¼-ounce can pineapple chunks
1 cup sugar
1 cup vinegar
2 tablespoons cornstarch
1 7-ounce package frozen Chinese pea pods
2 tablespoons catsup
2 teaspoons soy sauce

Beat egg with the ½ teaspoon soy sauce. Stir in turkey until pieces are coated. Let stand for 5 to 10 minutes. Coat turkey pieces with flour. Heat shortening in skillet, add turkey and stir lightly until all pieces are brown. Remove turkey and keep warm. If needed, add an additional tablespoon of shortening. Sauté garlic, scallions and onions. Drain pineapple chunks. Add enough water to pineapple juice to make 1 cup. Add juice/water mixture, sugar and vinegar to onions. Heat thoroughly. Mix cornstarch with ¼ cup cold water. Add to skillet and heat, stirring constantly until thickened. Reduce heat, add pea pods, catsup, and soy sauce and simmer until pods are tender. Add turkey and pineapple chunks, heat well. Serve with rice.

TURKEY LOAF

6 cups chopped turkey
½ cup dry bread crumbs
½ cup minced onion
½ cup chopped green pepper (optional)
½ cup chili sauce
1 cup mayonnaise
1 teaspoon salt
⅛ teaspoon pepper

Mix all ingredients well. Place in greased loaf pan. Bake at 350° F. for 30 minutes. If desired, serve with Mushroom or Brown Sauce.

TAMALE CASSEROLE

3 cups canned tomatoes
1½ cups corn meal
1 cup oil
1 to 2 tablespoons chili powder
2 teaspoons salt
2 to 3 cups cooked chicken, beef, or pork
1 11-ounce can kernel corn
1 8-ounce can pitted black olives

Chop or mash tomatoes. Mix corn meal, oil, chili powder and salt. Stir in remaining ingredients. Cook over low heat until thickened, stirring occasionally. Grease casserole. Add mixture, cover, and bake at 350° F. for 45 minutes.

CHICKEN IN PANCAKES

Fill freshly made French Pancakes, page 93, with diced Boiled Chicken, heated in well-seasoned Medium White Sauce. Roll. Place in buttered casserole. Spread each roll with sour cream and sprinkle with grated cheese. Bake at 400° F. until cheese is melted.

CREAMED CHICKEN IN POTATO BOAT

Scoop out baked Idaho potatoes leaving ½-inch shell; mash and season pulp and reserve it. Fill shell with cooked chicken or turkey heated in Cream Sauce. Press mashed potato through pastry tube to form border around filling. Bake in 400° F. oven until browned.

STUFFED PEPPERS WITH CHICKEN
See page 425.

CREAMED CHICKEN IN AVOCADO

Cut ripe avocados in half and remove stones. Fill with French Dressing to marinate ½ hour. Drain, fill with hot creamed chicken (or with seafood mixture). Top with buttered crumbs and brown in oven under broiler.

Chicken Buffet Dishes

PRESSED OR JELLIED CHICKEN

Cut up and season a 4-pound stewing chicken. Place in a kettle with 2 slices of onion, a little celery root, and a small carrot; cover with boiling water. Simmer until chicken is very tender. Remove chicken and take off meat in large pieces. Boil liquid until it is reduced to 1 cup. Strain the stock and skim off fat. Butter a large mold or individual molds; decorate bottom and sides with slices of hard-cooked eggs, grated raw carrot and chopped parsley. Season chicken to taste and pack carefully into molds. Add stock to fill the molds, chill until firm. In summer, soften 1 teaspoon gelatin in 1 tablespoon cold water and dissolve it in the boiling chicken broth.

JELLIED CHICKEN MOUSSE

3 egg yolks
1½ cups milk
1½ envelopes unflavored gelatin
¼ cup cold water
½ cup hot chicken broth
1 cup minced white meat of chicken
salt, pepper and paprika
1 cup heavy cream, whipped

Beat yolks, add milk and cook in double boiler until thick. Soften gelatin in cold water and dissolve it in the hot chicken broth. Add to the custard; then add the minced chicken. Season to taste and cool; fold in the whipped cream. Place in a ring mold; chill thoroughly. Serve on large platter; fill center of ring with fruit salad.

HOT CHICKEN MOUSSE

3 pounds cooked white meat of chicken
½ cup celery, chopped fine
½ cup mushrooms, chopped fine
1 teaspoon chopped parsley
salt, pepper, paprika
1 slice bread soaked in chicken broth and squeezed dry
¼ cup butter, creamed
3 egg yolks, well beaten
½ cup light cream
1 teaspoon lemon juice
1 tablespoon Worcestershire sauce
3 egg whites, stiffly beaten
bread crumbs

Grind the white meat of the chicken, not too fine. Add the rest of the ingredients except bread crumbs in order; mix well. Sprinkle a well-buttered mold with bread crumbs, pour in mixture,

set in pan and bake at 350° F. for 1½ hours. Unmold the mousse on a hot platter. Surround with pineapple slices that have been quickly fried in hot butter, and serve with Mushroom Sauce and hot biscuits.

Recipes for grilled and barbecued poultry will be found in chapter 15, Outdoor Cooking, page 326.

Chicken Livers

SAUTÉED CHICKEN LIVERS

1 pound chicken livers
½ teaspoon salt
⅛ teaspoon paprika
flour
1 onion, diced fine
3 tablespoons butter
½ cup soup stock

Cut each liver in half, season, and dredge well with flour. Sauté onion in butter until light brown. Add livers and brown evenly. Add soup stock, heat to boiling point. Serve on toast if desired.

CHICKEN LIVERS STUFFED IN TOMATOES

See page 433.

CHICKEN LIVER TIMBALES

12 chicken livers
¼ teaspoon chopped onion
1 tablespoon butter
½ teaspoon salt
speck red pepper
1 teaspoon chopped parsley
5 eggs, separated
1 tablespoon bread crumbs

Sauté the livers in onion and butter for 5 minutes. Rub through a sieve. Add seasonings, egg yolks and bread crumbs, and mix well. Beat the whites to a stiff froth and add to the mixture. Grease small molds, fill with mixture, sprinkle top with bread crumbs; bake in pan half filled with hot water ½ hour at 350° F. Unmold and serve hot with Mushroom Sauce.

CHICKEN LIVERS AND MUSHROOMS

4 slices bacon, cut small
½ pound chicken livers, cut in half
½ pound mushrooms, sliced
salt and pepper
2 teaspoons flour
½ cup light cream
toast

In advance, fry bacon in skillet; remove and drain. Sauté livers and mushrooms in bacon fat about 4 minutes. Season to taste. Stir in flour mixed with cream. Cook until smooth, add bacon, and serve on freshly made toast.

TURKEY

CHART FOR ROASTING STUFFED TURKEY

SIZE OF BIRD	OVEN TEMPERATURE	COOKING TIME
6 to 8 lbs.	325° F.	3 to 3½ hours
8 to 12 lbs.	325° F.	3½ to 4½ hours
12 to 16 lbs.	325° F.	4½ to 5 hours
16 to 20 lbs.	300° F.	5 to 6½ hours

CHART FOR ROASTING STUFFED TURKEY WRAPPED IN FOIL

6 to 8 lbs.	450° F.	1½ to 2 hours
8 to 12 lbs.	450° F.	2 to 2½ hours
12 to 16 lbs.	450° F.	3 to 3½ hours
16 to 20 lbs.	450° F.	3½ to 4 hours

For unstuffed birds, reduce cooking time by 20 minutes. Turkey roasted by either of the above methods is done when meat thermometer inserted in drumstick registers 185° F.

TO DEFROST FROZEN TURKEY

To defrost turkey for roasting, leave it in the refrigerator, in the original wrappings, for 2 to 4 days, allowing 24 hours for each 6 pounds of weight. Or defrost under running cold water or in a pan of cold water, for 6 to 8 hours. Or thaw at room temperature, allowing 1 hour per pound.

ROAST TURKEY

Preheat oven to 325° F. Rinse bird with cold water, drain and pat dry. Season with salt, pepper, ginger. Stuff if desired, and truss like chicken, page 307. Place turkey on rack in shallow roasting pan, breast side up. Brush skin with ½ cup melted butter or fat. To keep turkey moist, cover top with double thickness of cheesecloth, and baste occasionally. Remove cloth for last half hour of roasting. Roast according to time table. Turkey is done when thickest part of drumstick feels soft when pressed between fingers or when thermometer inserted in thickest part of drumstick (but not touching the bone) registers 185°. Remove strings and skewers and serve turkey garnished as desired.

ROAST TURKEY IN FOIL

Turkey of any size may be cooked at a high oven temperature wrapped in aluminum foil. This method is particularly suitable for cooking larger birds, weighing 16 to 24 pounds. Preheat oven to 450° F. and prepare turkey as for Roast Turkey, above. Place turkey in center of a foil strip long enough to meet on top of bird, plus 12 inches. If the standard 18-inch foil is not wide enough, splice two sheets of foil with a double fold pressed flat. Bring ends of foil together over breast of turkey and make double-fold to fasten above the bird. Bring sides of foil up high enough to prevent drippings from escaping into pan, but do not seal. Package should not be airtight. Place turkey breast up in shallow pan, but not on rack. Cook to within 30 to 40 minutes of the total time given in chart. Carefully open foil. Continue cooking until bird tests done, and is browned.

ROAST HALF-TURKEY

Rub cavity of uncooked half-turkey with salt or seasoning. Place cut-side down on rack in shallow pan. Brush with melted butter and cover with cloth as for whole turkey, basting as directed. Roast according to chart or use meat thermometer. If stuffing is desired, when turkey is half done, remove to a platter. Place a double thickness of well-greased aluminum foil on rack. Shape a mound of the dressing on the foil the shape of the cavity and put the turkey over it. Finish roasting.

BROILED TURKEY

4 to 6 pound turkey, split in half
½ lemon
melted butter
salt, pepper

Cut off wing tips or fold them back against the cut side of the bird. Rub with lemon, brush with butter, and sprinkle with salt and pepper. Lay on the broiling pan, skin side down. Broil as far as possible from the source of heat—about 8 to 10 inches away. The surface should begin to brown after about 20 minutes. Cook until browned, about 40 minutes in all. Turn skin side toward the heat and continue to broil until the skin is browned and crisp and the turkey cooked through, about 40 minutes longer. Baste occasionally with pan drippings and more butter, to keep surface moist. Test for doneness: the drumstick should be soft to the pressure of a finger, and the leg should move easily in the joint. If necessary, turn again and finish cooking. Divide into quarters for serving.

TURKEY ROLL

Boneless turkey roasts are usually purchased frozen. Let them thaw in their wrappings, 36 hours or longer in the refrigerator. To hasten thawing, leave under running cold water. After thawing remove wrapper, but leave strings in place.

Wipe the roast with a damp cloth and dry it. Sprinkle with salt and pepper, brush well with soft butter or other fat. Place on a rack in a shallow roasting pan and roast according to chart below. Baste often with fat and pan drippings. To test for doneness, insert a meat thermometer into the thickest part of the roll—the thermometer should register 175° F.

CHART FOR ROASTING BONELESS TURKEY ROLLS

SIZE OF ROLL	OVEN TEMPERATURE	COOKING TIME
3 to 5 lbs.	350° F.	2 to 2½ hours
5 to 7 lbs.	350° F.	2½ to 3½ hours
7 to 9 lbs.	350° F.	3¼ to 4 hours

CREAMED TURKEY STEW

⅛ cup butter
⅛ cup flour
1 cup cream
1¼ cups chicken or turkey broth
2 cups cooked turkey, diced
¼ cup sherry
1 cup each of the following cooked vegetables:
    peas, small onions, diced carrots; or two packages (10 ounces each) mixed frozen vegetables, cooked and drained
salt and pepper to taste
nutmeg

In advance, melt butter, stir in flour; stir in cream and broth. Cook until thickened, stirring constantly. Add other ingredients. Just before serving, heat thoroughly over low heat. Serve with noodles or rice.

For more leftover turkey recipes see pages 302 to 305, and 356 to 378, passim.

DUCK

ROAST DUCKLING

1 duckling, about 5 pounds
salt, pepper
curry or ginger
1 cup hot water or bouillon

Wipe the duckling inside and out and sprinkle it with seasonings to taste. If desired, the wings and legs may be tied together under the back, but trussing is not necessary, especially if the wing tips are cut off. Roast on a rack in a very hot oven, 450° F., for about 15 minutes, reduce heat to moderate, 350° F., and continue to roast about 20 minutes per pound, until tender. Pour off the fat as it accumulates and reserve for other uses. Baste the duckling often with water or bouillon and drippings. Remove duck to platter, pour off most of fat, and make pan gravy with drippings. Add the minced giblets and neck meat to the gravy.

ROASTED STUFFED DUCKLING

Trim off the neck and wing tips of the duckling and fill body cavity with Apple Prune Stuffing, page 325. Season and roast as above. Meanwhile, simmer the neck, wing tips and giblets in water to cover with a stalk of celery, half an onion, and salt and pepper. Use the stock to baste the duckling as it roasts, and to make pan gravy, using giblets as above.

DUCKLING A L'ORANGE

1 duckling, about 5 pounds
salt, pepper, ginger
1 orange, sliced with rind
1 onion, sliced
¼ cup honey
juice of 2 oranges
rind of 2 oranges
1 tablespoon flour

Wipe duckling inside and out, season with salt, pepper, and ginger. Stuff cavity with sliced orange and onion. Roast on a rack in a very hot oven, 450° F., about 20 minutes, reduce heat to moderate, 350° F., and continue to roast until tender, allowing about 20 minutes per pound. Pour off fat as it accumulates, and baste often with honey mixed with orange juice. Sliver the rind of 2 oranges and cover with water. Bring to a boil, simmer 10 minutes, drain. Spoon 2 tablespoons duck fat from the roasting pan over the peel, add flour, and cook a few minutes, stirring. Skim the fat from the roasting pan, measure the drippings, and add water to make 1½ cups liquid. Cook, stirring in the brown bits. Strain the liquid into the saucepan with the orange rind and flour, and cook, stirring, until the sauce is smooth and slightly thickened. A little red wine may be added, if desired. Arrange the duckling on a platter and garnish with sliced oranges. Spoon some of the sauce over the bird; serve the rest separately.

DUCKLING WITH CHERRIES

1 duckling, about 5 pounds
salt, pepper, ginger
2 cups white wine or apple juice
2 tablespoons flour
1 can (1 pound, 4 ounces) pitted bing cherries in syrup

Wipe the duckling inside and out and sprinkle with seasonings. Roast on a rack in a hot oven,

450° F., for 20 minutes. Reduce heat to moderate, 350° F., and continue to roast until tender, about 20 minutes per pound in all. Baste often with white wine or apple juice. Skim fat from pan drippings. Heat 2 tablespoons fat in a saucepan, add flour and stir until smooth. Stir in strained pan drippings and cook until smooth. Add cherries and syrup and heat. Spoon some of the sauce over the duckling on the platter and serve the rest separately.

Allow at least 1 pound of duck per person, as there is a rather large amount of fat and bone in relation to the amount of meat.

GOOSE

ROAST GOOSE

    goose, 12 to 14 pounds
    2 teaspoons salt
    1 teaspoon pepper
    2 teaspoons caraway seeds
    Apple Prune Stuffing, page 325

Wipe goose inside and out and sprinkle with salt, pepper, and caraway seeds. Stuff the cavity with Apple Prune Stuffing, or Bread Stuffing to which apples have been added. Place trussed bird on a rack in a shallow pan. Roast in a moderate oven (350° F.) about 3½ hours in all, draining off the fat as it accumulates. Baste bird occasionally with the pan drippings mixed with hot water. Test for doneness by pressing the flesh of the leg. The skin should be very crisp and brown. Make a pan gravy with the drippings.

FRICASSEED GOOSE (GAENSEKLEIN)

    back, wings, neck, gizzard and heart of goose
    salt, pepper, ginger
    a clove of garlic
    ½ onion, sliced
    a piece of celery root
    2 tablespoons fat
    2 tablespoons flour
    1 cup goose broth
    1 teaspoon chopped parsley

Season meat well with salt, pepper, ginger and, if desired, rub with garlic. Let stand overnight in refrigerator. Cover with boiling water, simmer several hours, add onion and celery, and continue to simmer until meat is tender. Strain the broth. Heat the fat, add flour and then the hot goose broth; cook, stirring constantly until smooth, season to taste. Add the goose pieces and reheat. Add parsley. Serve with Dumplings or Spatzen.

SMOKED GOOSE

    1 large goose
    clove of garlic, if desired
    1 tablespoon sugar
    ⅛ pound salt
    1 teaspoon saltpeter

Clean goose thoroughly. Remove wings, legs, skin and fat. Separate breast and back. Scrape the meat carefully from the bones of neck and back, discarding all tendons and tissues, and chop very fine. Fill neck skin with chopped goose and sew both ends with coarse thread. Season legs, breast and filled neck with salt. Rub well with garlic, sugar and saltpeter. Place in a stone jar. Cover with a cloth and put weights on top—to keep the meat under brine which will form. Let stand in a cool place for 7 days, turning occasionally. Take out of the brine, cover with gauze and cook in smoke oven. When done, serve cold, sliced thin.

GOOSE PRESERVED IN FAT (CONFIT D'OIE)

Separate breast, legs and thighs from rest of goose, salt and let stand in cool place overnight. Cut rest of bird and all fat into small pieces. Salt these and let stand as well.

To render the fat: the next morning, wash and drain the small pieces of goose and the fat, and place in deep kettle with several cups of cold water. Cover and let cook until water has evaporated and scraps are shriveled. Strain through a cloth the fat that remains in the kettle and discard the scraps.

Rinse and pat dry the breast, legs and thighs. Heat enough rendered fat to cover these, and cook pieces gently until tender and golden brown. Place meat in crock or jar. Strain fat again and cover goose with hot fat. Cool. Cover container with weighted plate. Keep in cool dry place.

BRAISED BREAST AND LEGS OF GOOSE

Brown the breast and legs of a goose in skillet in hot fat. Add a little boiling water, cover closely and simmer until tender, adding more water as needed. Serve hot with apple sauce.

GOOSE CRACKLINGS (GRIEBEN)

The fat skin of a goose cut into 1- to 1½-inch squares and fried with the rest of the fat when rendering is called Grieben. If chewy Grieben are desired, remove them as soon as the fat is clear and season with salt. If wanted crisp, leave them in the hot fat until well browned, season, and place in oven for a few minutes.

STUFFED GOOSE NECK

goose neck
Bread Stuffing, page 324
scraps of raw goose meat
1 onion, sliced

Remove skin from neck of goose. Tie the small end of the tube and stuff it with Bread Stuffing plus any scraps of raw goose meat, ground fine. Sew securely with coarse thread; place in a heavy pan, add a little water and the onion. Bake in a moderate oven, 350° F., basting occasionally, until crisp and brown. Serve hot.

CORNISH HENS

Cornish hens are small birds with an average weight of 1 to 1½ pounds whose flavor is a cross between chicken and game birds. They are usually served whole, one to a serving, but they may be cooked and served according to any of the recipes for chicken.

ROASTED CORNISH HENS

4 Cornish hens, about 1 pound each
½ lemon
salt, pepper
melted butter or fat
2 cups bouillon

Thaw hens, rub well with lemon and season with salt and pepper. Brush with butter and arrange on rack in open roasting pan. Roast in hot oven, 450° F., about 50 minutes. Baste frequently with pan drippings and bouillon. When done, the legs will move easily in the socket, and the flesh should feel soft. Thicken the drippings with a little flour, and serve as gravy.

STUFFED ROASTED CORNISH HENS

4 Cornish hens
salt, pepper
1 tablespoon butter or fat
½ onion, minced
¾ cup rice
2 cups bouillon
½ teaspoon thyme
butter or fat for basting

Thaw hens and season inside and out with salt and pepper. Melt fat, add onion and cook until golden. Add uncooked rice, stir over medium heat until colored; add bouillon, stir, cover, and cook until liquid is absorbed and rice is tender. Add thyme and salt and pepper to taste. Cool rice mixture and stuff hens. Roast in a moderate oven, 350° F., 1¼ to 1½ hours. Baste occasionally with pan drippings mixed with butter.

ROASTED SQUABS

Prepare Stuffing for Squabs, page 324. Loosen skin from breast from wishbone almost down to bottom of breastbone, to form a pocket. Fill pocket and neck with stuffing. Tie at the top. Or stuff body cavity as for other poultry. Fasten legs together at the back. Place squabs close together in a pan, spread tops with butter. Roast in very hot oven, 450° F., the first 5 minutes; reduce heat and roast ½ hour, or until tender, at 375° F., basting frequently. Make pan gravy, page 388, with the drippings. Add 2 tablespoons of sour cream, if desired.

BROILED SQUABS

Clean squabs, if necessary. Cut along the backbone with a small, sharp knife and split. Season with salt and pepper. Flatten breastbone and place bird on broiler, skin side toward the heat. Baste with butter. When brown, turn and broil 12 to 15 minutes until well done.

SQUABS EN CASSEROLE

6 squabs or pigeons
salt, pepper and paprika to taste
1 sprig parsley
½ carrot
1 onion
1 bay leaf
2 cups soup stock
1 tablespoon butter
1 tablespoon flour
12 mushrooms, sautéed
2 tablespoons sherry
1 tablespoon catsup

Season whole birds with salt, pepper and paprika. Stuff, if desired. Place in casserole, add parsley, vegetables, bay leaf and soup stock, cover and cook slowly 1 hour or longer on range or in a moderate oven, until tender and browned. Melt butter, add flour, and cook until light brown. Add the sauce from the birds; cook until smooth, remove from the fire and add mushrooms, sherry and catsup. Add sauce to birds; heat, and serve in the casserole.

GAME BIRDS

TO PLUCK WILD DUCK

⅜ pound or 1½ slabs paraffin
7 quarts boiling water

Melt paraffin in water. Dip duck in and out of boiling mixture 4 or 5 times. Cool from 3 to 5 minutes, or until paraffin has coated feathers. Then pluck. The feathers of game birds may also be loosened by plunging the birds into boiling water for about 10 seconds.

ROAST WILD DUCK

Clean duck well and draw. Season with salt, pepper, sprinkle with 1 tablespoon vinegar and place an onion inside. Let stand in refrigerator overnight. Remove onion. If duck is old or tough, first cook slowly in boiling water until tender. Season with salt and pepper, dredge with flour and place in roasting pan with 2 tablespoons fat. Roast in hot oven, 400° F., until browned, basting often. Serve with wild rice and currant jelly.

SPORTSMAN'S DUCK

Just before using, cut off wings, head and feet. Remove feathers. Singe over flame to burn off down. Draw, wash well and dry thoroughly. Season. Roast in extremely hot oven, 500° F., 18 to 20 minutes. The meat should be bright red. Serve with wild rice, stewed celery and currant jelly.

GUINEA HENS

Stuff and roast like chicken. Prepare guinea hen breasts like chicken breasts.

MUD HENS

Tie the necks of the hens, then make a slit over the breast, piercing only the skin. Pull the skin, plumage and all from the body of the fowl. Draw, wash thoroughly. Then let soak about 3 hours in water to which has been added a handful of salt and ½ cup vinegar. Wash again, and in each hen place a piece of onion and apple. Tie with cord so fowl retains its shape. Cover with cold water and boil about 10 minutes. Drain, add salt, pepper and paprika to taste and tie a piece of bacon on breast of each fowl. Heat 1 tablespoon butter in deep saucepan, place hens in this, breasts downward. Cover well and cook gently from 1½ to 2 hours or until tender. Add water to giblets and boil until reduced to ¾ cup of stock; gradually add this to the hens the last 15 minutes of cooking. Add 2 tablespoons thick sour cream to gravy just before serving. Serve hot.

ROAST PARTRIDGE

Pick, draw and wash the birds, wrap them with thin slices of bacon. Roast in pan 15 minutes in a hot oven, 400° F. Remove bacon, salt lightly, place in oven to brown. Serve with pan gravy or pour 1 cup of cream over top and sprinkle with bread crumbs, browned in butter.

BRAISED PHEASANT

Pick feathers, clean and singe, or skin. Wash, cut off wings and legs. Split back. Leave breast whole. Salt lightly. Brown pieces in butter. Add 2 cups water or cream and cover. Cook on range or roast in moderately slow oven, 325° F., adding more water or butter if necessary. Baste and turn often. For gravy, thicken liquid with 1 tablespoon flour and add 1 cup sour cream.

ROAST PHEASANT

Prepare birds as above, leaving wings and legs. Stuff body cavity and inside of neck, if desired, with Bread Stuffing. Roast like Roast Chicken, page 307, until tender.

QUAIL

Follow recipe for Broiled Squab, page 322. Allow 10 to 20 minutes for cooking young, tender birds. Serve on toast, with currant jelly. If the birds are tough, cook them like Squabs en Casserole, page 322.

POTTED QUAIL

Season birds well. Sauté in butter, turning often to brown all sides. Add hot water or soup stock and cook covered, basting frequently and adding more liquid as it evaporates. Cook in the oven or on top of the range. Thicken gravy with flour if desired, and add 2 or 3 tablespoons sour cream before serving. Place on individual toast points and garnish with currant jelly.

POULTRY STUFFINGS OR DRESSINGS

Small birds require about 1 cup stuffing per pound of weight; larger birds slightly less. Extra stuffing may be baked in a greased casserole alongside the bird, for about 1 hour. Fill the birds lightly because stuffing expands in cooking. Fill the body cavity, and the neck cavity as well, if desired, with the same or different stuffings. Ingredients for stuffings may be prepared ahead and chilled until needed, but they should be combined and packed into the bird just before roasting. Leftover cooked stuffing should be removed from bird and refrigerated separately, to prevent growth of harmful bacteria.

Most stuffings are based on bread, but rice or potatoes may be used. Bread for stuffing should be several days old. When the bread is soaked in milk or water before blending, the stuffing will be moist and compact; if the bread is simply tossed with fat, seasonings, and other ingredients, the stuffing will be crumbly.

BREAD STUFFING

4 cups dry bread cubes
1 teaspoon salt
⅛ teaspoon pepper
⅛ teaspoon ginger
¼ teaspoon poultry seasoning
1 teaspoon chopped parsley
2 tablespoons melted fat
1 egg
1 small onion, chopped fine

Soak bread in cold water and squeeze dry. Add seasoning and fat. Mix thoroughly, add the egg, slightly beaten, and the onion. Or, soak bread in cold water and squeeze dry. Heat fat in a skillet, add the soaked bread, stir until fat is absorbed. Season to taste, add the slightly beaten egg and the onion. Cool before filling the bird.

The liver, heart, and gizzard of the bird, cooked until tender and finely chopped, may be added to this dressing; or ¼ pound pork sausage, browned; or ¼ pound liver sausage.

SAVORY BREAD STUFFING

½ cup fat or butter
2 onions, chopped
1½ cups chopped celery
8 cups dry bread cubes
2 teaspoons salt
1 teaspoon pepper
1 teaspoon paprika
1 tablespoon poultry seasoning

Melt butter, add onions and celery, and cook a few minutes, stirring. Add bread and cook, stirring, until cubes begin to brown. Add seasonings, toss well with fork to mix. Cool and stuff 10-pound turkey.

CORN BREAD STUFFING

8 cups corn bread crumbs
¾ teaspoon poultry seasoning
salt, pepper
¾ cup melted butter or fat
1 onion, chopped
½ cup chopped celery
3 tablespoons chopped parsley

Combine crumbs, seasonings. Melt butter, add onion and cook until translucent. Toss with crumb mixture, add celery and parsley, stir over heat for a few minutes. Cool thoroughly before stuffing bird. Enough for a 6 to 10 pound bird.

OYSTER STUFFING FOR TURKEY

Follow recipe for Corn Bread Stuffing, above, and add a little oyster liquor and 12 or more large oysters coarsely chopped.

ALMOND STUFFING FOR TURKEY

4 cups bread crumbs
¾ cup milk
1 cup butter
3 eggs
2 cups diced celery
½ onion, grated
1 cup chopped almonds
½ teaspoon salt
¼ teaspoon pepper
¼ teaspoon ginger

Soak the bread crumbs in the milk. Soften the butter, and the well-beaten eggs; add other ingredients and mix well. 2 cups boiled chopped chestnuts may be used in place of the almonds.

CHESTNUT STUFFING FOR TURKEY

1 quart large chestnuts
¼ cup butter
1 teaspoon salt
1 egg
2 cups bread crumbs or hot mashed sweet potatoes
turkey liver, chopped fine

Blanch and shell chestnuts, page 418. Cook until tender in boiling salted water. Drain and rice. Add the rest of the ingredients and mix well. If desired, additional seasonings, such as onion or lemon juice and chopped parsley, may be added according to taste. If a moist dressing is preferred, add cream or stock.

ALMOND STUFFING FOR SQUABS

¼ cup white bread crumbs
½ cup milk, or milk and cream
2 tablespoons butter
1 egg, well beaten
pepper and salt
¼ cup almonds, blanched and chopped

Soak crumbs in milk, or milk and cream, mixed, add butter, creamed, add egg, season to taste, add almonds. Enough for 3 squabs.

LIVER STUFFING FOR SQUABS

2 tablespoons butter
2 eggs, well beaten
6 squab livers, lightly sautéed
salt and pepper
fresh bread crumbs

Cream butter; add eggs; add the livers, finely chopped, and the hearts if desired; season with salt and pepper and add enough bread crumbs to form a soft dressing that will drop from the spoon. For 6 squabs.

ORANGE STUFFING FOR SQUABS

To Bread Stuffing, page 324, add 2 tablespoons orange juice, grated rind of 1 orange, 1 tablespoon chopped parsley and seasoning to taste. Orange juice and rind may also be added to the pan gravy.

POTATO STUFFING

Add 2 cups of hot, mashed white or sweet potatoes to Bread Stuffing. Mix well and use to stuff a goose.

This stuffing is also suitable for veal or lamb breast.

BREAD STUFFING FOR GOOSE OR DUCK

4 cups of dry bread cubes
2 tablespoons fat
liver, gizzard and heart, cooked, chopped fine
¼ onion, chopped fine
¼ cup celery root, diced
½ cup strained tomatoes
1 teaspoon salt
⅛ teaspoon pepper
⅛ teaspoon ginger
⅛ teaspoon nutmeg
1 egg

Soak the bread in water and squeeze dry. Heat the fat in a skillet, add bread, brown slightly, add other ingredients and mix well.

APPLE STUFFING FOR GOOSE OR DUCK

To 10 tart apples, peeled and quartered, add 1 cup currants.

PRUNE AND APPLE STUFFING FOR DUCK OR GOOSE

¼ pound prunes
5 sour apples
1 cup bread crumbs
½ teaspoon poultry seasoning
½ teaspoon salt
dash of pepper

Follow directions for Stewed Prunes, page 263. Remove stones and cut in quarters. Peel, quarter and core the apples, and cook in a very small amount of water until half done. Add cooked and pitted prunes, the rest of the ingredients, and mix well.

STUFFING FOR GAME

1 slice wheat bread soaked in milk
2 hard rolls, crumbled
1 onion, chopped fine, with 3 or 4 slices of lightly cooked bacon
1 tablespoon butter, melted
3 eggs, beaten
1 piece orange rind
1 piece lemon rind
3 apples, cut in cubes
salt, pepper

Mix well.

QUICK REFERENCE GUIDE TO USEFUL INFORMATION IN THIS BOOK

15
OUTDOOR COOKING

CHARCOAL FIRES · MARINADES · SAUCES · GRILLING · BARBECUING
· SPIT ROASTING · SKEWER COOKING · CAMP FIRE COOKING

OUTDOOR COOKING

Cooking and eating outdoors is becoming more and more popular as an easy, friendly way to entertain guests, and for simplified family meals as well. Disposable paper or plastic plates, napkins, cups, and even flatwear are practical for informal outdoor meals.

All the cooking need not be done outdoors; sometimes the barbecue serves as a quick way to heat casseroles and other foods that were prepared indoors, or even just to keep them hot. Charcoal-grilled meats, poultry and fish are particularly flavorful, and when one of these is the main dish, it adds to the pleasure of the occasion to roast potatoes, corn on the cob, or other vegetables at the same time.

TO BUILD A CHARCOAL FIRE

All barbecue units from simple metal grills to elaborate chuck-wagons which include electrically driven spits and hoods, operate on the same principle. There must be a fire bed through which air can circulate and a grill on which to lay the food. Begin to lay the fire with crumpled paper; add dry twigs and set the paper aflame. When the twigs catch fire, cover them with a single layer of charcoal or charcoal briquettes. After 5 minutes, add a second layer of charcoal, and after 5 minutes more, a third layer.

The fire should cover an area just large enough to accommodate the food to be cooked, without crowding. Do not begin to cook until the coals have an ashy gray coat—about 30 to 45 minutes. Spread coals to uniform thickness.

To use commercial fire lighter: Pile charcoal on top of unlit twigs and paper, sprinkle well with lighter, let soak in for a minute or two, and ignite. The lighter fumes will burn off quickly, and the charcoal will catch more readily when this method is used. Charcoal fires continue to give off heat for a long time. If it is necessary to add more charcoal, add it around the edges of the fire.

EQUIPMENT FOR BARBECUING
Broiling basket or hinged broiler—for small fish or smaller cuts of meat.
Asbestos gloves
Tongs for turning meat (to avoid piercing it)
Long-handled fork and spatula-turner
Clothes sprinkler (handy for controlling flames caused by dripping fat)
Brush for basting.
Carving fork, knife, and board
Skillet
Small pan for basting sauce
Skewers

MARINADES

Marinades serve to tenderize and flavor meats and help to keep them moist as well. Most of the marinades that follow can be used as desired with poultry, steaks, chops, or roasts. The same marinade may be used as a basting sauce as well. Some marinades may also be served as a sauce with the meat.

GARLIC MARINADE

1 cup oil
2 cloves garlic

Soak garlic in oil overnight. Remove garlic. Marinate beef, veal, or lamb roasts, steaks or chops in the oil in a glass or china bowl for about 2 hours. Reserve leftover marinade (keeps well in the refrigerator).

SPICY LEMON MARINADE

1 cup oil
2 tablespoons lemon juice
1 tablespoon Worcestershire sauce

Combine ingredients and use as marinade for poultry and veal.

SWEET AND SOUR MARINADE

¼ cup oil
1 tablespoon vinegar
1 tablespoon lemon juice
3 tablespoons catsup

Combine ingredients, brush on poultry or any meat, let stand 2 hours.

WINE MARINADE

½ cup oil
¼ cup soy sauce
2 small onions, sliced
½ cup red wine

Combine ingredients and use to marinate cubes of beef, lamb or pork. Good with chicken and shrimp, if made with white wine instead of red.

HAWAIIAN STYLE BARBECUE SAUCE

3 tablespoons soy sauce
1 cup pineapple juice
1 teaspoon dry mustard
1 teaspoon garlic salt
½ teaspoon pepper
1 tablespoon brown sugar

Blend ingredients. Marinate pork chops, spareribs or chicken for 2 hours in this sauce. Use as a basting sauce. Heat remaining sauce and serve it hot with the meat.

FRANKFURTERS

Frankfurters are available in many sizes and shapes, with different seasonings; they may be made of all beef or of combinations of beef, veal, and pork. Serve barbecue-grilled franks on different kinds of rolls and breads, for variety and new interest.

GRILLED FRANKS

Broil on a hinged grill. Spear the franks on long forks or sticks for self-service.

STUFFED FRANKS

Cut long slit in frankfurter to make a pocket. Insert strip of Cheddar cheese. Wrap with bacon, secure with toothpicks. Broil until bacon is brown and crisp. Slit may be brushed with mustard before filling, and the frankfurter may be stuffed with a strip of pickle or fruit such as apple, banana, pineapple, or with drained baked beans.

BARBECUED FRANKS

Grill. Serve whole or cut in pieces with Barbecue Sauce as a dip.

Or dip frank into the barbecue sauce, grill on hinged broiler, basting often with more barbecue sauce, until crisp-skinned.

TEXAS RED HOTS (CHILI DOGS)

1 pound ground, lean beef
¼ cup fat
2 cups canned tomatoes
1 clove garlic
1-2 teaspoons chili powder
salt, pepper
1 cup chopped onion for garnish
12 frankfurters

Brown meat in fat, stirring with a fork. Add tomatoes, garlic, and chili, cover, and simmer 20 minutes. Add salt, pepper, more chili powder to taste. Spoon hot sauce over grilled franks on rolls, top with chopped onion.

HAMBURGERS

To Grill Hamburgers

Any hamburger mixture, page 279, may be broiled on the grill. The meat should be lightly shaped into patties of uniform thickness. Broil 3 inches from the coals, about 4 to 5 minutes each side for medium rare. Serve with garnishes to taste: catsup, chili steak sauce, mustard, pickles, sliced onion or tomato, or a barbecue sauce. For variety, serve hamburgers on toasted buns, toasted English muffins, French, Italian or rye bread.

GRILLED CHEESEBURGERS

Grill hamburgers as usual on one side, turn, top with a slice of Cheddar cheese. When bottom is browned, cheese will be melted.

GRILLED PIZZABURGERS

Grill hamburgers as usual on one side, turn, top with a slice of mozzarella cheese, a spoonful of spaghetti sauce, and a pinch of oregano. Serve on toasted English muffins.

GRILLED BURGUNDY BURGERS

1 pound lean ground beef
1 slice bread
¼ cup red wine
1 teaspoon salt
¼ teaspoon pepper
½ teaspoon minced onion

Break up meat with a fork. Crumble bread, soak in wine. Add rest of ingredients. Mix all together with a fork, shape into 4 patties. Brush with butter, grill as above, basting with sauce. Serve on slices of French bread with some of the basting sauce spooned over.

SAUCE
¼ cup butter, melted
2 tablespoons red wine
bit of garlic clove
salt, pepper, cayenne to taste

Combine ingredients.

GRILLED STEAKS AND CHOPS

To Barbecue Steaks and Chops

BEEF STEAKS

Choose tender steak 1 to 3 inches thick, well marbled, that is, streaked with fat. Less tender cuts, such as top round or rump roast, must be marinated or tenderized before broiling. Slash fat edge of steak to prevent curling. Rub grate with fat to prevent sticking. Grill 1-inch steak 2-3 inches from heat, 5 to 6 minutes each side, for medium rare; 2-inch steak takes 10-12 minutes each side. Or, sear steaks on both sides, raise grill, and cook to desired degree of doneness. To test, make small cut with sharp knife near bone.

GRILLED CHINESE STEAK

Brush steak on both sides with equal parts of honey, soy sauce, and sherry. Let stand 1 hour before grilling as usual.

GRILLED PEPPER STEAK

Crush ¼ cup peppercorns by pounding them in a paper bag. Press firmly into both sides of a 2-inch thick steak and grill as above.

GRILLED FLANK STEAK

2 tablespoons oil
2 tablespoons vinegar
½ clove garlic, mashed
¼ teaspoon freshly ground black pepper

Combine oil, vinegar and garlic; coat flank steak on both sides, sprinkle with pepper. Pierce with fork and pound with flat of heavy knife. Let stand 30 minutes. Grill 5 inches from coals, 5 minutes each side. Flank steak should be rare. Carve in thin diagonal slices.

GRILLED LAMB CHOPS AND STEAKS

Choose loin, rib, or shoulder chops, 1½ to 2 inches thick. Or have the butcher cut lamb steaks from the leg, about 2 inches thick. Marinate if desired, season, and grill on rack, 5 inches from the coals, about 7 to 8 minutes each side. This is for medium rare meat. Cook a little longer, if desired, but avoid overcooking.

GRILLED MARINATED LAMB CHOPS

6 lamb chops
½ cup oil
½ teaspoon garlic salt
1 tablespoon prepared yellow mustard

Brush chops on both sides with mixture of remaining ingredients. Let stand 1 hour before grilling as above.

MINTED LAMB CHOPS

6 loin lamb chops
2 tablespoons Worcestershire sauce
2 tablespoons butter
2 tablespoons lemon juice
2 tablespoons wine vinegar
black pepper
½ cup mint jelly

Trim excess fat from chops, but leave kidney, if present. Heat remaining ingredients, except jelly. Coat chops on both sides; let stand 30 minutes. Grill as above. Heat remaining marinade, add jelly, serve as sauce.

GRILLED PORK CHOPS

Choose chops or steaks about 1 inch thick. Trim off excess fat. Season with salt and pepper and grill slowly, about 8 inches from the heat, until the chops are cooked through. Pork must always be well done. The chops may be marinated if desired, and basted during cooking with the marinade.

When pork is on the barbecue, the plentiful fat drippings tend to catch fire; keep the sprinkler handy to douse the flames.

GRILLED HAWAIIAN PORK CHOPS

Hawaiian Style Barbecue Sauce, page 327
6 thick pork chops
6 slices canned pineapple
2 tablespoons brown sugar
powdered cloves

Prepare Hawaiian Style Barbecue Sauce and marinate chops for 2 hours. Cook chops 8 inches from heat, basting often and turning frequently, until they are browned and cooked through, but not dry. Lay pineapple slices on grill to heat. Brush with butter, sprinkle with brown sugar and cloves, continue to heat until sugar melts. Serve with chops. Sweet potatoes wrapped in foil and baked close to the coals are a good accompaniment.

GRILLED VEAL CHOPS OR CUTLETS

Veal, shoulder, rib or loin chops, or cutlets cut from the leg may be marinated and seasoned like lamb chops. Veal should always be cooked through for maximum tenderness. Grill thicker cuts 8 inches from the flame, thinner cuts 5 inches. Veal is a lean meat, and improves in flavor and tenderness when it is marinated and basted with the marinade during cooking. Use Garlic Marinade or Spicy Lemon Marinade, adding oregano to taste.

BARBECUING AND SPIT ROASTING

If you use an electrically turned spit or rotisserie, follow the manufacturer's directions for most efficient use of his particular product. It is important to adjust the meat or bird on the skewer so that it balances perfectly and will rotate smoothly and cook uniformly. Test the balance, and correct if necessary. Any holes made by the skewers in this trial and error procedure will be sealed during the cooking. Fix the spit in place and adjust the screws tightly. Put a pan under the meat to catch the drippings. If necessary, a pan may be made from a double thickness of foil. Baste roasts with fat during the first part of the cooking. Sweetened barbecue sauces burn easily and should be applied only for the last half or three quarters of an hour. Use a meat thermometer to make sure meat is at desired degree of doneness.

BARBECUED OR SPIT-ROASTED BEEF

Any beef roast—standing rib, sirloin, rump or tenderloin—can be roasted on a spit. If it has adequate fat cover, it needs no basting. The tenderloin or fillet will require either larding with suet or basting. Beef may be roasted on the rack, in a grill equipped with a cover. Leave the vent open. Roasts can be basted with any of the marinades. Internal temperature of beef roasts should be 140° F. for rare to 160° F. for medium. See chart, page 268, for cooking times.

BARBECUED POT ROAST

round bone pot roast 2½ inches thick
meat tenderizer
prepared mustard
coarse salt (such as Kosher salt)

MARINADE
¼ cup vinegar
¼ cup brown sugar
½ teaspoon Tabasco
¼ teaspoon oregano

Pierce meat with tines of fork and sprinkle generously with meat tenderizer. Place meat in marinade and let stand, refrigerated, for 5 to 6 hours. The roast will require 20 minutes cooking on each side.

ON COVERED GRILL
When coals are ready, spread mustard on one side of meat, sprinkle heavily with salt, and place salt side down directly on the coals. Cook for 20 minutes. Cover grill with vents open. Spread other side of meat as above and repeat. To serve: scrape salt and mustard covering from meat and slice thin.

ON UNCOVERED GRILL
Make paste of salt and mustard. Spread very thickly over the meat. Grill directly on coals for 20 minutes on each side. Meat is handled more easily if placed in a hand broiler. This prevents knocking off any of the coating until cooking is completed.

BARBECUED OR SPIT-ROASTED LAMB

Have butcher trim lamb leg for roasting; or have lamb shoulder boned and rolled, with as much of the fat removed as possible. Rub well with salt, pepper and garlic. Adjust on spit and roast according to chart on page 287, to the medium stage (170° F. on the meat thermometer) for juiciest results. Or to 175° F., medium, or 180° F., well done, if desired.

SPICY BARBECUED LAMB

1 cup oil
½ teaspoon garlic powder
4 tablespoons prepared yellow mustard
1 leg of lamb, trimmed for roasting

Blend marinade ingredients, coat lamb, let stand 6 to 8 hours or overnight, turning to season evenly. Adjust meat on spit and roast as above, basting with marinade occasionally.

GRILLED BONED LEG OF LAMB

boned leg of lamb
2 cups dry red wine
2 teaspoons salt
2 teaspoons poultry seasoning
3 cloves
1 teaspoon pepper
1 clove garlic, mashed

Unroll lamb and lay flat. Combine remaining ingredients in shallow platter. Marinate lamb for 24 hours, turning occasionally. Roll up and tie roast. Lay on grill about 5 inches from the coals. Cover with hood, roast, turning occasionally, 1½ hours, until done to taste.

BARBECUED SPARERIBS

Cut between ribs without separating them. Marinate 2 hours in any desired marinade. Lay on grill, bone side down at first, and cook 8 inches from the coals until very well done, 1½ hours or longer. Turn 4 or 5 times during the cooking, and baste often with marinade during the last 20 minutes. To serve, separate ribs. Ribs may be parboiled for 20 minutes to reduce outdoor cooking time; or they may be oven-roasted ahead of time, and finished on the barbecue, with frequent basting.

SPIT-ROASTED SPARERIBS

Marinate spareribs, and weave on rotisserie spit. Roast 8 inches from coals until very well done, 1½ hours or longer. Baste with marinade during last 20 minutes of cooking.

SWEET AND SPICY SPARERIBS

3 racks spareribs
¾ cup warmed honey
garlic salt
1 cup Basic Barbecue Sauce, page 390

Brush ribs with honey and sprinkle with garlic salt. Let stand several hours. Lay on grill, bone side down at first, 8 inches from coals. Cook until very well done, 1½ hours, turning often. Baste during last 45 minutes with Barbecue Sauce. Sweet and Spicy Spareribs may be cooked covered, or they may be spit-roasted.

SKEWER COOKING

Any foods suitable for grilling or broiling may be cut into uniform pieces and cooked on skewers over an outdoor grill, on a hibachi (Japanese charcoal grill) or in the broiler of a kitchen range. Foods should be chosen that take the same length of time to cook; or partly cooked foods may be combined with raw foods that cook quickly. Combinations should be chosen with an eye to harmony and contrast of flavors, colors, and textures. Many skewered foods should be marinated before cooking and basted with oil or butter during cooking for maximum flavor and juiciness.

Guests can assemble their own skewers for broiling, when a selection of the following foods, all suitable for broiling on a skewer, is set out for their choice.

MEATS: beef, lamb, veal, cut into uniform cubes or strips; ham, bacon, bologna, pork sausages, frankfurters, canned meats, luncheon meat; thin chicken slices; chicken livers.

SEAFOOD: fish fillets, scallops, shrimp, clams, oysters, lobster tails.

VEGETABLES: mushrooms, tomato wedges or cherry tomatoes, parboiled small onions or potatoes, raw onion wedges or slices, pieces of green pepper, eggplant, zucchini, parboiled or canned sweet potatoes, olives, gherkins.

FRUIT: pineapple chunks, apple or orange wedges, banana slices, canned apricots.

SHISH KEBAB

1 cup wine vinegar
½ teaspoon cinnamon
½ teaspoon cloves
1 onion, chopped
1 garlic clove, chopped
1 cup oil
2 pounds leg of lamb, in 1½-inch cubes
tomato wedges
mushrooms

Heat vinegar with spices; cool. Add onion, garlic and oil. Pour into bowl. Add lamb cubes, turn to coat, let stand 2 hours at room temperature, turning occasionally to season evenly. Thread lamb cubes on skewers alternately with vegetables, brush with marinade and broil 3 inches from heat until meat is crusty on the outside but medium rare inside.

SHASHLIK

1 cup oil
3 to 4 garlic cloves, grated
1 onion, grated
2 pounds leg of lamb, cut in 1½-inch cubes
salt
freshly ground pepper

Mix oil, garlic, and onion, pour into bowl. Turn lamb cubes in mixture to coat, cover, let stand overnight in refrigerator. About 2 hours before cooking, remove bowl from refrigerator, continue to marinate meat, turning occasionally. Thread on skewers, broil close to coals until lamb is crusty on outside but still pink inside. Season with salt and pepper to taste.

SKEWERED MINTED LAMB

1½ pounds boned lamb
1 teaspoon dried mint
½ cup dry red wine
¼ cup wine vinegar
1 clove garlic, crushed (optional)
1 teaspoon salt
¼ teaspoon pepper

Cut lamb into 1-inch cubes. Combine all other ingredients and pour mixture over lamb. Marinate for at least 1 hour, turning lamb once or twice to be sure that the meat is well coated. Remove the lamb from the marinade. Thread lamb on skewers; broil or barbecue, basting with the remaining marinade. Cooking time is about 20 minutes.

SKEWERED HAM 'N SWEETS

2 ham steaks, ¾-inch thick
6 sweet potatoes, cooked
1 can (1 pound, 13 ounces) pineapple chunks, drained
½ cup melted butter
¼ cup brown sugar

Cut ham into squares, thread on skewers alternately with chunks of sweet potatoes and pineapple, and roll in melted butter. Broil close to heat until potatoes are browned. Sprinkle all with brown sugar and remaining butter; broil until glazed.

TERIYAKI

3 pounds sirloin steak or raw chicken breasts
½ cup soy sauce
¼ cup sherry
¼ cup sugar
1 tablespoon slivered candied ginger or
    ½ teaspoon powdered ginger
2 garlic cloves, grated

Cut sirloin or chicken into very thin slices, across the grain. Combine remaining ingredients, marinate meat 1 hour at room temperature. Pleat on skewers and grill quickly, close to coals. Beef should be rare, but chicken cooked through. Baste with marinade during cooking.

GRILLED AND BARBECUED POULTRY

GRILLED BROILERS

Wipe and dry broilers, split in half. Rub with salt and pepper and brush generously with butter. Place bone side down on grill; turn to brown skin side. Baste about every 15 minutes with melted butter. Time: 30-45 minutes, according to the size of the chickens. Broilers may be marinated for several hours before cooking as above. Baste with marinade.

For barbecue sauces and marinades, see page 327.

BARBECUED WHOLE CHICKENS

Plump chickens can be spit-roasted. Season inside and out. Truss (page 307) carefully and balance on spit. Brush outside with melted butter or any barbecue sauce. Baste frequently. Time: 1 to 1½ hours, depending on size of chicken.

Barbecued chickens may also be stuffed with any desired stuffing. Sew up opening before trussing chicken on spit to prevent loss of stuffing. Roast an additional 15 minutes.

SPIT-ROASTED TURKEY

Small turkeys, weighing from 6 to 8 pounds, can be spit-roasted. They should not be stuffed for the rotisserie. Wipe, dry, and sprinkle inside and out with salt and pepper. Truss, page 307, and adjust on spit. Brush with melted butter or fat before cooking and occasionally during the roasting period. Baste with barbecue sauce only during last half hour. See chart, page 319, for timetable. A meat thermometer inserted into thickest part of breast should read 185° F., and the meat of drumstick should feel soft when pressed.

GRILLED TURKEY PARTS

Have the butcher cut up a 6- to 8-pound turkey: the drumsticks should be separated from the thighs and the wings from the breast. Have the breast cut into 4 pieces, the back in half. Marinate 2 hours at room temperature or overnight in the refrigerator in Hawaiian Style Barbecue Sauce or any desired marinade. Grill on a rack 8 inches from the coals, about 1½ hours, turning and basting often. Test for doneness by inserting a sharp knife into the drumstick near the bone. There should be no trace of pink showing. Or use a meat thermometer—the temperature should be 185° F. in the thickest part, the breast.

GRILLED CAPON

Capons may be grilled or spit-roasted like turkey but they cook in the same time as chicken of equal weight.

GRILLED CORNISH HENS

Whole or split Cornish hens should be cooked like broiler-fryers.

For other poultry recipes, see pages 305-323.

GRILLED AND BARBECUED FISH AND SEAFOOD

GRILLED FISH STEAKS

Choose steaks of salmon, halibut, haddock, swordfish, cut 1 inch thick. Brush on both sides with oil or melted butter and lemon juice, or with any fish basting sauce, to taste. Let stand ½ hour, if desired. Arrange on oiled grill, or on oiled hinged broiler with long handle, for easier turning. Grill about 15 minutes in all, turning often and basting frequently to keep fish moist. Fish is done when it flakes readily at the touch of a fork or toothpick. Do not overcook. Serve with basting sauce or lemon wedges.

GRILLED FISH FILLETS

Prepare like fish steaks, lay on oiled hinged broiler, and cook 5-6 inches from the coals until browned. Fillets cook very quickly, and should not be overcooked. Baste with butter and lemon juice or with barbecue sauce, and brown other side.

GRILLED WHOLE FISH

Clean fish, season inside and out with salt and pepper, and stuff if desired. Brush with butter or oil. Wrap in a double thickness of oiled aluminum foil if desired (stuffed fish should always be wrapped in foil to protect the stuffing) and grill 5 to 6 inches from the coals. Fish may be stuffed with sliced onions and celery tops and parsley, if desired, or with lemon slices for extra flavor. Whole fish takes 30 minutes to an hour or more to cook through.

FISH FILLETS IN FOIL

Fish fillets or steaks may be seasoned, wrapped in oiled foil, and grilled close to the coals. Sliced onion, green pepper, and tomato may be added to the packages, if desired.

BARBECUED TROUT

MARINADE

½ cup soy sauce
½ cup cooking sherry
1 tablespoon lime or lemon juice
¼ cup vegetable oil
1 clove garlic (crushed)

Put marinade ingredients into shaker and shake well.

1 large trout
¼ lemon wedge
herbs, if desired (such as parsley, basil or chives)

Brush trout cavity with juice from lemon wedge and sprinkle with herbs. Place in shallow pan and pour on marinade. Let stand 1 hour, turning once. Cook over hot coals on well-greased grill, turning once. Baste while cooking with strained marinade. Total cooking time is 5 to 8 minutes per side.

BARBECUE SAUCES FOR FISH

SPICY FISH BASTE

2 tablespoons butter, melted
3 tablespoons lemon juice
¼ cup water
6 tablespoons catsup
1 medium onion, grated
1 tablespoon Worcestershire sauce
1-2 tablespoons sugar to taste

Combine ingredients and use to baste fish. Serve with remaining sauce.

LEMON FISH BASTE

½ cup oil
1 tablespoon lemon juice
Dash of Tabasco (optional)

Combine ingredients and use to baste fish.

Barbecued Seafood

GRILLED WHOLE LOBSTER

Insert a sharp knife between the body and tail shells of the live lobster, and cut down to sever the spinal cord and kill the lobster. Lay on grill close to coals and grill 15 to 20 minutes, turning often. Split lengthwise, remove the stomach from behind the head and the black intestinal vein which runs from the stomach to the tip of the tail. Do not discard the green liver and the pink coral, or the roe. Serve lobster with melted butter and lemon.

GRILLED SPLIT LOBSTERS

Sever spinal cord as above and split lobsters lengthwise. Remove intestines and stomach. Brush with melted butter, season with salt and pepper. Broil, shell side down, 4 inches from coals, until meat is cooked through, about 12 minutes. Serve with melted butter and lemon.

GRILLED LOBSTER TAILS

Split frozen lobster tails, brush with butter, season with salt and pepper, and lay on grill shell side down and broil about 4 inches from heat about 30 minutes, until cooked. Serve with melted butter and lemon. Or thaw lobster tails before broiling and reduce cooking time to 10 to 15 minutes.

GRILLED SHRIMP

Split shrimp down the back through the shell and remove sand vein. Marinate for 2 hours in equal parts of soy sauce and white wine, or in Lemon Fish Baste. Lay on grill or in hinged broiler and broil, 3 inches from heat, about 5 minutes, until bright pink, turning occasionally. Serve with any seafood cocktail sauce.

GRILLED FROZEN "SCAMPI"

Melt ½ cup butter in small pan on grill, add ¼ cup white wine, 1 garlic clove, minced, and salt and pepper. Add 2 tablespoons chopped parsley. Dip large frozen shrimp into this sauce, lay in hinged broiler, and cook about 5 inches from coals just until pink and opaque. Turn and brush twice with more sauce.

GRILLED OYSTERS

Place unopened oysters on grill. Grill until shells open, 6-8 minutes. Serve with melted butter or any desired butter sauce.

BUTTER-GRILLED OYSTERS

Open oysters. Discard flat shell. Loosen oysters from deep shell. Replace in deep shell with butter or desired sauce. Grill, shell side down, for 8-10 minutes.

CLAMS ON THE GRILL

Hard-shelled clams may be roasted on the grill, like oysters, or they may be steamed open in a covered kettle. The thin-shelled clams called "steamers" are always cooked in the following manner. Wash clam shells thoroughly, and put into kettle with ½ cup water. Cover tightly and steam 5 minutes or longer, until clam shells open. Serve with melted butter for dipping, and cups of the clam broth for sipping.

GRILLED FROZEN KING CRAB LEGS

Split large frozen king crab legs, season, brush with butter, and grill, shell side down, just until heated through. These are pre-cooked, and do not require additional cooking.

Skewered Seafood and Fish

SKEWERED SHRIMP

Marinate shrimp 1 hour in Garlic Marinade or Spicy Lemon Marinade; thread on skewer with strip of bacon woven between. Broil until bacon is crisp, shrimp pink.

SKEWERED LOBSTER TAILS

Defrost lobster tails, remove meat, cut into chunks. Marinate in equal parts soy sauce, salad oil, and sherry, with garlic clove, salt and pepper to taste. Thread on skewer, broil until pink.

SKEWERED OYSTERS

Heat oysters in their own liquid until just plump. Wrap each in bacon, thread on skewers, grill until bacon is crisp.

SKEWERED FISH FILLETS

Marinate in equal parts oil and lemon juice, with salt and pepper to taste. Pleat on skewers. Broil until opaque and just beginning to brown. Brush with marinade during broiling.

SKEWERED SCALLOPS

Marinate like fish fillets, adding garlic to oil and lemon. Broil until opaque and cooked through. Brush with marinade during broiling. Or brush with melted butter, sprinkle with salt, pepper, and curry powder, thread on skewer and broil, brushing with butter occasionally, until just cooked through.

GRILLED VEGETABLES

POTATOES

Wrap medium-sized white baking potatoes or sweet potatoes in heavy-duty aluminum foil. Bake in coals, turning occasionally. Bake about 45 minutes, depending upon the size of potatoes.

For covered grill, wrap potatoes as above. Place on grill, cover, leaving the vents open, and bake for about 45 minutes.

Frozen French fried potatoes may be heated on the grill in aluminum foil.

GRILLED SCALLOPED POTATOES

For each serving, peel a medium-size potato, slice very thin, lay slices in overlapping layers on square of aluminum foil. Dot with 1 tablespoon butter, salt and pepper. Add 2 tablespoons milk. Seal package carefully with double-fold. Cook on grill, close to coals, about 15 minutes. Open package to test for tenderness, reseal for longer cooking.

HUSK-ROASTED CORN

Pull husks back carefully; remove silk. Twist husks tightly around ears. Soak in salted water for 30 minutes. Roast on grill for about 20 minutes, turning to roast evenly.

Or, if roasting on coals, wrap soaked corn in aluminum foil.

FOIL ROASTED CORN

Remove husks and silk. Brush corn generously with melted butter. Wrap in aluminum foil. Cook on coals for 10-15 minutes. Turn once or twice during cooking. If desired, a dash of garlic powder may be added to the butter.

GRILLED TOMATOES

Cut firm tomatoes in half crosswise. Brush cut side with melted butter; season. Broil in hand grill, cut side up.

GRILLED STUFFED TOMATOES

Cut firm tomatoes in half crosswise. Salt and pepper cut sides, place halves together again with a thin slice of onion between, secure with toothpicks. Wrap in foil. Cook on grill for 20 minutes.

GRILLED EGGPLANT

Cut eggplant into slices, soak in oil seasoned with salt, pepper and minced garlic. Grill until brown on both sides.

GRILLED GREEN PEPPER

Dip pepper strips into oil seasoned as for Broiled Eggplant, above. Lay on hinged broiler, grill until edges of strips brown lightly.

GRILLED MUSHROOMS

Dip mushrooms into butter, arrange on hinged grill, broil until browned and heated through. Sprinkle with salt, pepper, and oregano.

GRILLED ONIONS

Cut mild onions into thick slices, dip into butter, broil on hinged grill until brown on both sides. Sprinkle with salt, pepper, parsley or other herbs.

GRILLED FROZEN VEGETABLES

Open package of frozen vegetables. Sprinkle with salt and pepper and place pat of butter on top. Wrap in aluminum foil and seal carefully with a double fold on top. Wrap fairly loosely so that steam will form as vegetables defrost and cook.

Place package on grill, turning occasionally. Cook 10-15 minutes.

CAMP FIRE COOKING

TO BUILD A CAMP FIRE

If possible, select a hollow spot on the ground, or pile up stones along three sides to protect the fire from the wind. Start the fire with light chips and twigs; gradually add larger pieces of wood. When wood is reduced to a mass of glowing coals, the fire is ready for cooking.

Any of the recipes in this chapter can be adapted to camp cookery. The following recipes are especially for cooking over a camp fire.

TO GRILL RABBIT OR SQUIRREL

Clean and skin carefully. Cut off and throw away head and feet. Cut in two pieces through the back bone. Place on grill over coals until brown; turn and brown on other side. Sprinkle with salt and pepper; then cook slowly over the coals, turning occasionally, until tender.

TO GRILL GAME BIRDS

Pick, clean, sprinkle with salt and pepper and broil slowly over the coals.

TO BAKE BIRDS, FISH, SMALL GAME IN CLAY

Cut open, draw and wash them well. Cover with a thick layer of clay; place in the midst of a hot fire. Bake about 1 hour. Remove from fire, break open. The skin or feathers will stick to the clay.

TO STEW RABBITS

Skin, clean and joint. Season with salt and pepper. Place in kettle, cover with water, let come to a boil. Put fat in frying pan, add meat, simmer until done, adding boiling water when necessary. Or, boil slowly until tender.

Additional recipes for game will be found on page 302 and for game birds on pages 322–323.

16
PASTA

NOODLES · FILLED PASTA · MACARONI · SPAGHETTI

NOODLES

NOODLE DOUGH

- 2 cups flour
- ½ teaspoon salt
- 2 eggs, well beaten
- 2 tablespoons warm water

Sift flour and salt onto a pastry board, make a well in the center and add eggs and water. Work the flour into the egg mixture, adding more water if necessary to make a stiff but malleable dough. Knead on the board until smooth. Divide dough in half and let it rest for 30 minutes, covered. Roll out as thin as possible and cut into any desired shapes. Spread noodles on the board and let them dry well before using.

PACKAGED NOODLES

Commercially prepared noodles are available in all widths and may be used in any of the following recipes. Noodles gain approximately 50% bulk in cooking; one-half pound (8 ounces) of dry noodles yields about 4½ cups of boiled noodles. Follow instructions on package for cooking.

TO BOIL HOMEMADE NOODLES

Drop dried noodles in boiling, salted water and boil about 10 minutes, or until just tender. Drain well.

If noodles are to be used in rings or puddings, they should be boiled about 8 minutes. Drain in colander; rinse with cold water to prevent sticking together, and drain again.

TO FRY NOODLES

Brown fine noodles in butter in a skillet, until crisp; or fry them in deep hot fat and serve as a garnish on broad noodles.

CHINESE NOODLES (CHOW MEIN)

- 2 tablespoons oil
- 1 pound fine noodles

Sprinkle the oil over the dry noodles, place on rack of steamer, steam 15 minutes, lifting carefully with a fork to separate well. Spread on board, cool; fry until crisp and brown in deep, hot oil. Drain on brown paper.

NOODLE RING

- ½ pound broad noodles
- 2 tablespoons butter
- 1 cup browned bread crumbs or fried fine noodles

Boil noodles in salted water, drain in colander, pour cold water over them and drain. Mix with butter and place in a well-greased ring mold sprinkled with bread crumbs or fried noodles. Set in a pan of boiling water and bake in a slow oven, 300° F., about ¾ hour. Turn out on a hot platter and fill center with Sautéed Mushrooms, or Chicken à la King.

NOODLE-CUSTARD RING

- 2 cups noodles
- 3 eggs
- salt and pepper
- 1 tablespoon butter or chicken fat
- ¾ cup milk or cream

Cook fine or broad noodles in salted, boiling water, until tender. Place in colander, pour cold water over them and drain thoroughly. Beat eggs slightly, add salt and a little pepper, stir in the fat and the milk or cream. Grease medium-sized ring mold well, add the boiled noodles. Add the egg-milk mixture. Set in pan of hot water, place in moderate oven, 350° F., and bake without browning, 30 to 45 minutes, until the custard sets and a knife put into it comes out clean. When ready to serve, loosen edges with knife; turn out on a hot platter, fill center with creamed mushrooms or Chicken à la King.

NOODLE-CHEESE RING

½ pound noodles
4 eggs, separated
salt and pepper
1¼ cups grated cheese
1 tablespoon Worcestershire sauce
1 tablespoon catsup
1½ cups milk
1 tablespoon shortening

Cook fine or broad noodles in salted boiling water. Pour cold water over them; drain well. Beat egg yolks; add salt, pepper, cheese, Worcestershire sauce, catsup, milk. Fold in the stiffly beaten whites. Grease a ring mold, add the boiled noodles. Add the custard. Set in a pan of hot water, and bake in a moderate oven, 350° F., for 30 to 45 minutes. The ring is set if a knife inserted into it comes out clean. When ready to serve, loosen edges with a knife. Invert on hot platter.

NOODLES À LA NEAPOLITAN

½ pound broad noodles, boiled
2 cups chopped ham or dried beef or chicken cooked and seasoned
2 eggs
1 cup milk or cream
1 cup buttered bread or cracker crumbs

In a well-greased baking dish, place a layer of about one-third of the noodles, spread one-half the prepared meat over this, add another one-third of the noodles, the remainder of the meat and the rest of the noodles. Beat eggs well, add milk gradually and pour over the noodles and meat. Cover top with the crumbs and bake in a moderately slow oven, 325° F., about 30 minutes or until well browned

VIENNA NOODLES

½ pound noodles
½ cup cracker crumbs
½ pound cooked ham, chopped
¼ cup cream
2 tablespoons butter

Cook noodles in boiling, salted water until done. Drain and run cold water through them and drain in colander. Butter a baking dish, dust with cracker crumbs, add a layer of noodles, then the ham, then the rest of the noodles. Pour the cream over this, sprinkle with cracker crumbs and dot with butter. Bake ½ hour in moderate oven, 350° F., until brown.

SCALLOPED NOODLES

½ pound medium noodles
3 tablespoons butter
1 cup bread crumbs
¼ cup cracker crumbs

Cook noodles in boiling, salted water. Drain, and run cold water through them and drain again. Melt 2 tablespoons butter, add 1 cup bread crumbs, brown, then mix lightly through the boiled noodles. Butter a baking dish well, dust with part of the cracker crumbs. Place noodle mixture in dish, sprinkle rest of cracker crumbs over top and dot with butter. Bake ½ hour in moderate oven, 350° F.

SCALLOPED NOODLES AND PRUNES

6 ounces broad noodles
1 pound stewed prunes, with juice
sugar and cinnamon
2 tablespoons butter
1 cup buttered bread crumbs

Boil noodles until tender. Put in colander, pour cold water over noodles and drain. Stone prunes and sprinkle with sugar and cinnamon. In a well-greased baking dish place one-third of the noodles, bits of butter, add one-half of the prunes, then another layer of the noodles, butter, the remaining prunes, and the rest of the noodles. Add the prune juice, and spread crumbs over top. Bake 20-30 minutes in moderate oven, 350° F., until crumbs are brown.

NOODLES AND APPLES

2 cups broad noodles
4 apples
2 tablespoons butter
2 tablespoons fat
2 tablespoons sugar
salt, cinnamon

Boil noodles, rinse and drain. Wash, pare, and cut apples in eighths. Put melted shortening in a baking dish, add one-half the noodles, then the apples. Sprinkle with sugar, a speck of salt, and cinnamon, cover with remaining noodles. Bake covered at 350° F., for 10 minutes; remove cover and continue baking for 30 minutes, or until apples are soft and noodles browned.

NOODLE PUDDING (NOODLE KUGEL)

3 cups broad noodles
¾ cup fat (chicken, goose or butter)
4 eggs, well beaten
salt and pepper

Cook noodles in salted, boiling water 10 minutes. Drain; add fat and eggs. Place in well-greased pudding dish. Bake in a hot oven, 400° F., until top is well browned.

BAKED EGG BARLEY

2 tablespoons fat or butter
¼ cup onions, cut fine
2 cups uncooked Egg Barley, page 179
3 cups soup stock or boiling water with meat gravy
salt to taste

Heat the fat, add onions, fry until a golden brown, add the Egg Barley and brown. Place in baking dish, add hot soup stock to more than cover. Add salt. Bake in a moderate oven about 1 hour or until liquid has nearly evaporated and the egg barley stands out like beads and is soft. The onion may be omitted. Serve hot, with meat or poultry.

FILLED PASTA

MEAT RAVIOLI

Noodle Dough, page 335
1½ cups leftover chopped, cooked pot roast
½ cup chopped cooked spinach
¾ cup grated Parmesan or Romano cheese
¾ cup dry bread crumbs
½ pound pork sausage
2 eggs
salt, pepper
pot roast gravy for sauce

Make a double quantity of Noodle Dough. Let dough rest 30 minutes, divide in half, and roll as thin as possible. While preparing the filling, let dry on a cloth sprinkled with corn meal. Combine meat with remaining ingredients and blend well. Put filling by teaspoons on one sheet of dough, 2 inches apart. Cover with second sheet, pressing well between the mounds to seal the edges. Cut with a moistened pastry cutter. After ravioli has dried for 1 to 2 hours, drop into boiling salted water, cook 20 minutes or until dough is cooked through. Cut into edge of ravioli to test. Remove with skimmer to serving dish. Pour gravy over ravioli, sprinkle with grated cheese, and serve very hot. Or serve with melted butter, olive oil with a garlic clove heated in it, or any well-flavored tomato sauce.

CHEESE RAVIOLI

Fill ravioli, above, with a mixture of 1 pound ricotta cheese, 3 eggs, ½ cup grated Parmesan or Romano cheese, and salt and pepper to taste. Cook as above and serve with a sauce of melted butter and additional grated cheese; or with tomato sauce made without meat.

MEAT-FILLED NOODLES (KREPLACH OR PIEROGI)

Noodle Dough, page 335
1 pound cooked meat, chopped
2 teaspoons onion juice
1 egg
salt and pepper

Make a double quantity of Noodle Dough. Roll out very thin and spread on cloth to dry. Combine remaining ingredients. Cut the dough into 2-inch squares, place a teaspoon of meat mixture on every square, and then fold each to make a three-cornered shape, pressing edges well together. Drop into boiling soup, or salted water; cook 15 minutes. Drain, place on hot platter, and pour 2 tablespoons of hot fat over them. Garnish with browned cracker crumbs.

CHEESE-FILLED NOODLES (KREPLACH OR PIEROGI)

Noodle Dough, page 335
1 pound cottage cheese
1 egg
1 tablespoon sweet or sour cream, or melted butter
salt and pepper

Make a double quantity of Noodle Dough. Mix ingredients, and proceed as for Meat-Filled Noodles. If sweet kreplach are desired omit salt, pepper, cream. Add slightly beaten egg, sugar, grated rind of lemon or cinnamon to cottage cheese.

LASAGNE

1 pound ground beef
1 clove garlic, minced
2 tablespoons salad oil
1 can (1 pound 4 ounces) solid pack tomatoes
1 can (8 ounces) tomato sauce
1 teaspoon salt
½ teaspoon pepper
½ teaspoon oregano
½ pound lasagne noodles, cooked just tender
1 pound ricotta or dry cottage cheese
½ cup grated Parmesan cheese
½ pound mozzarella cheese, sliced

Brown beef and garlic in oil, stirring with a fork. Add tomatoes, first draining off half the juice; add tomato sauce and seasonings. Simmer for 30 minutes. Cook noodles, drain and rinse. Cover bottom of a large, greased baking dish with 1½ cups of beef mixture. Cover the beef mixture with single layer of noodles. Spread ½ the ricotta cheese on the noodles, sprinkle with ½ the Parmesan cheese and place over this ⅓ of mozzarella. Repeat. Top with remaining beef mixture and mozzarella. Bake in 350° F. oven for 45 minutes. Let stand 15 minutes after removing from oven. Cut into squares.

MACARONI

Macaroni and spaghetti come in scores of different shapes and sizes, which make it possible to have great variety in the pasta as well as in the sauce it is served with. Connoisseurs of pasta believe that the flavor changes with the shape, even when the dough is exactly the same; there are also many different doughs to choose from, including those made with eggs or spinach, which can be used interchangeably in the recipes that follow.

BOILED MACARONI

½ pound macaroni
2 quarts boiling water
2 teaspoons salt

Drop macaroni into the boiling salted water. Boil about 20 minutes, or until tender, or follow directions on package. Drain in colander. Serve hot with browned butter or any well-flavored sauce, and sprinkle with grated cheese.

MACARONI WITH MUSHROOMS

½ pound boiled macaroni
1 pound mushrooms, sautéed
1 cup Medium White Sauce, page 386
bread crumbs
butter

Arrange alternate layers of macaroni, mushrooms, and white sauce in a well-greased baking dish. Sprinkle with bread crumbs and dot with butter. Bake in a moderate oven, 350° F., for 30 minutes.

BAKED MACARONI AND CHEESE

Medium White Sauce, page 386
½ pound boiled macaroni
1 cup Cheddar cheese, grated
butter

Mix white sauce, macaroni, and ¾ cup of the cheese. Place in buttered baking dish, sprinkle top with remaining cheese and dot with butter. Bake for 15 minutes in a hot oven, 400° F.

WITH RED SAUCE
Use tomato sauce for the white sauce above.

MACARONI AND OYSTERS

1 pint oysters
2 cups boiled macaroni
1 cup Medium White Sauce, page 386
½ cup cracker crumbs
butter

Place drained oysters and macaroni in a well-greased baking dish. Cover with white sauce to which some of the oyster liquor has been added. Sprinkle with cracker crumbs and bits of butter. Bake until browned.

MACARONI WITH TOMATOES AND MUSHROOMS

1 tablespoon finely chopped dried mushrooms or ½ pound sautéed mushrooms
1 small onion, cut fine
1 tablespoon butter
3 tablespoons flour
1 cup beef or chicken soup
2 cups stewed tomatoes
salt and cayenne pepper
1 teaspoon parsley, chopped
½ pound macaroni, boiled
grated Parmesan or Cheddar cheese

If dried mushrooms are used, soak in warm water 1 or 2 hours, changing the water several times. Sauté the onion in butter; when slightly browned, add the flour, then the soup stock. Stir until smooth; add the tomatoes. Add mushrooms, season with salt and cayenne pepper, add the parsley and simmer 20 minutes.

Pour sauce over the hot boiled macaroni. Sprinkle with cheese.

MACARONI PUDDING

1 cup uncooked macaroni
1 cup cream
1 cup soft bread crumbs
¼ cup melted butter
1 canned pimiento, chopped
1 tablespoon chopped parsley
1 teaspoon onion juice
1 teaspoon salt
1 cup grated cheese
3 eggs, separated

Boil macaroni, drain and chop fine. Scald cream and pour over soft bread crumbs. Mix butter, pimiento, parsley, seasonings, cheese and well-beaten yolks. Add macaroni and crumb mixture. Mix well, fold in stiffly beaten whites. Pour into well-greased form and set form in pan of water, and bake in hot oven, 400° F., 1 hour. Serve with Mushroom Sauce.

BAKED MACARONI WITH CHIPPED BEEF

¼ pound dried beef, sliced
2 cups cooked macaroni
2 cups Medium White Sauce, page 386
¾ cup buttered crumbs

Soak beef for 10 minutes in hot water, drain and shred. Fill buttered baking dish with alternate layers of macaroni, beef, and white sauce, cover with buttered crumbs, bake in hot oven, 400° F., until crumbs are brown.

Fine noodles, ravioli and other pastas are also used as soup garnishes or in thick hearty soups served as a main dish. See pages 393-403 for soups to which pastas may be added as desired.

SPAGHETTI

BOILED SPAGHETTI

½ pound spaghetti
2 quarts boiling water
2 teaspoons salt
cold water

Drop spaghetti without breaking it into boiling, salted water. Boil only until cooked through—bite a strand to test it. Drain in colander, pour 1 cup cold water through it.

Serve with browned butter, sprinkle with grated cheese or add any well-seasoned sauce.

ITALIAN SAUCE FOR SPAGHETTI

4 onions, sliced
1 tablespoon bacon fat
½ cup water, warm
1 hot red pepper, diced
1 sweet red pepper or pimiento, diced
1 pound ground beef or pork or an equal mixture of both
2 small cloves garlic, minced
1 cup water
1 can (6 ounces) tomato paste
1 can (1 pound, 13 ounces) strained tomatoes
3 tablespoons brown sugar
¼ teaspoon red pepper
salt to taste

Fry onion in fat until golden brown. Add ½ cup water, peppers. When water has evaporated, add meat with garlic and cook, stirring with a fork, until meat is well browned. Add remaining ingredients. Simmer for 2 hours, stirring occasionally. Serve with strong grated Italian cheese.

SPAGHETTI AND MEAT BALLS

Beef Balls, page 280
Soup Stock, page 393
Italian Sauce, above
½ pound spaghetti, boiled
grated Parmesan cheese

Make Beef Balls and poach until done in boiling soup stock to cover. Add cooked meat balls to tomato sauce, simmer 30 minutes. Pour some of sauce over boiled spaghetti, surround with meat balls and remaining sauce. Sprinkle with grated cheese.

SPAGHETTI, SWEETBREADS AND MUSHROOMS

½ pound spaghetti
salt, pepper
1 pound sweetbreads
½ pound fresh mushrooms
¼ cup butter
1 tablespoon flour
½ cup milk or cream

Boil spaghetti. Drain and season with salt and pepper to taste, mix well. Pack into a well-buttered mold and keep hot. Boil the sweetbreads, page 298, and sauté the mushrooms in butter. To the butter in which the mushrooms were sautéed add the flour and when slightly browned, add the milk or cream. Stir over low heat until smooth. Turn spaghetti out of mold, surround with sweetbreads and add the mushroom sauce.

SOUTHERN SPAGHETTI

2 pounds spaghetti
½ pound bacon, diced
3 onions, sliced
1½ pounds chopped raw beef
2 green peppers, chopped
2 tablespoons chopped parsley
1 cup cooked kidney beans
1 cup cooked peas
1 can (10½ ounces) tomatoes
½ pound mushrooms, sliced
salt and pepper to taste
½ pound Cheddar cheese, grated

Boil spaghetti and rinse in cold water; drain. Place bacon in skillet, fry out fat; add onions, and fry to a golden brown. Add meat and vegetables and simmer a few minutes. Season to taste. In a large baking dish, alternate layers of spaghetti and meat mixture. Sprinkle the last layer of spaghetti with cheese. Bake in slow oven, 300° F., about 2 hours. Serves 15.

SPAGHETTI ITALIENNE

½ pound spaghetti
1 can (1 pound, 13 ounces) tomatoes
2 cloves of garlic, cut fine
4 bay leaves
2 peppercorns
salt to taste
¼ cup olive oil
¼ cup grated Parmesan cheese

Boil spaghetti. Sieve tomatoes, and place in sauce-pan with the seasonings and the oil. Simmer until well blended, strain and add to rinsed and drained spaghetti. Heat thoroughly. Serve sprinkled with grated cheese.

SPAGHETTI CHOP SUEY

2 pounds spaghetti
3 tablespoons fat
4 medium onions, sliced
½ clove garlic
¼ pound beef, chopped
¼ pound fresh pork, chopped
1 can (1 pound, 13 ounces) tomatoes
salt and cayenne to taste

Boil spaghetti. Fry onions and garlic until glazed; remove garlic, add meat and brown slightly. Add tomatoes, salt and cayenne and simmer for 20 minutes. Pour over the hot, drained spaghetti and serve.

SPAGHETTI CASSEROLE

2 (1 pound, 3 ounce) cans spaghetti
1 can (10½ ounces) condensed tomato soup
1 pound mushrooms, sautéed
2 teaspoons prepared mustard
½ teaspoon Worcestershire sauce
Beef Balls, page 280, or 2 pounds boiled shrimp, or
   1½ pounds sliced, boned chicken
½ pound Cheddar cheese, grated

Combine all ingredients, reserving ½ of the cheese for the top. Place in a buttered baking dish; sprinkle top with cheese. Bake in a moderate oven, 350° F., for 30 to 40 minutes.

STUFFED PEPPERS WITH SPAGHETTI

See page 425.

Other Pasta Combination Dishes

CHICKEN À LA KING

See page 310.

CHICKEN MONTEGO

See page 312.

CHICKEN TETRAZZINI

See page 314.

QUICK REFERENCE GUIDE TO USEFUL INFORMATION IN THIS BOOK

17
PASTRY

PIES · TARTS · FRUIT KUCHEN · STRUDEL

General Rules for Making Pastry

TO MIX

All ingredients should be chilled. Measure flour and salt into a chilled bowl. Work in the shortening quickly and lightly, rubbing it in with the finger tips, or cutting it in with a pastry blender, fork, or two knives held in the same hand, until the particles are the size of peas. Sprinkle with ice water, 1 tablespoon at a time, stirring it in with a fork, just until the particles are moistened and stick together. Cover the dough and chill for 30 minutes or longer before rolling.

TO ROLL PIE PASTRY

Dust a pastry board lightly with flour. Special boards covered with stockinet may be used, or a marble or formica counter top, or the dough may be rolled out between two sheets of waxed paper. Flatten the dough lightly. Roll it ⅛ to ¼ inch thick, from center to edges, with a lightly floured rolling pin, using short strokes, to make a round 1 inch larger than the pie pan.

Turn the dough often to keep it round. Do not turn it over, but lift from board occasionally. If the round splits at the edges, press together. Sprinkle board with flour as needed.

TWO-CRUST PIES

For a two-crust pie, divide the dough in two portions, one slightly larger than the other, and use the larger part for the bottom crust. Fit bottom crust loosely into an ungreased pie pan. Fill. Trim off overhanging dough. Moisten edges of dough with cold water or a little egg white. Fold top crust in half, adjust over filling,

open out; slash or prick top crust. Trim extra pastry ½ inch beyond rim. Fold edge of top crust under edge of lower crust and press with fingertips or fork to seal. Press edges with finger on one hand and pinch the dough between thumb and forefinger of other hand to flute the rim.

ONE-CRUST PIES

Fit bottom crust loosely into ungreased pie pan. Do not stretch the dough, but ease it into place to prevent shrinking. Trim edge ½ inch from pan. Fold edge under and flute rim, hooking points under pan edge to help hold shell in place during baking. Fill and bake as desired.

BAKED PIE SHELL

Proceed as above. Prick the shell well to prevent puffing. Bake in very hot oven (450° F.) 10-12 minutes. Cool and fill.

LATTICE TOP

Line pie plate with pastry, leaving 1 inch overhanging edge. Fill as desired. Roll remaining pastry into a round and cut into ½-inch strips, using a pastry wheel to make an attractive edge. Lay half the strips across the pie, 1 inch apart. Weave the cross strips over and under these, beginning at the center. Trim the ends of the strips; moisten edge of pastry with water, and fold edge of bottom crust over strips. Press to seal.

Many heirloom recipes are to be found in this chapter—especially among the Fruit Pies (page 345), Cheese Cakes (page 347), Fruit Kuchen (page 352) and Strudels (page 354).

PASTRY

SHORT PASTRY

2 cups flour
1 teaspoon salt
½ cup shortening
¼ cup butter
ice water

Have all materials ice-cold. Sift flour and salt. Blend the shortening and butter into the flour, add enough ice water, very slowly, to hold dough together. Chill half an hour or more. Roll ¼ to ⅛-inch thick and line pie plate.

FLAKY PASTRY

2 cups flour
1 cup shortening
1½ teaspoons salt
ice water

Follow directions above.

QUICK PASTRY

½ cup shortening
¼ cup cold water
1½ cups flour
½ teaspoon baking powder
½ teaspoon salt

Melt shortening, add water and mix with rest to a smooth dough. Chill before rolling on floured board. Shape and bake as under General Rules for Making Pastry.

CREAM CHEESE PASTRY

3 ounces cream cheese
½ cup butter
1 cup flour

Combine all to make a smooth dough. Chill. When ready to use, roll into desired shape for appetizers, tarts, or one-crust pies.

PEANUT BUTTER PIE CRUST

1 cup sifted flour
1 tablespoon sugar
½ teaspoon salt
¼ cup butter
¼ cup smooth or crunchy peanut butter
2 tablespoons water

Sift flour, sugar and salt; blend in butter and peanut butter. Sprinkle water over the mixture and mix with fork until the dough holds together. Press into a ball with hands; roll on lightly floured pastry cloth. Fit loosely into a 9-inch pan, make a tall fluted edge; prick dough with a fork. Bake at 425° for about 8 minutes. Excellent for chiffon pies.

EGG YOLK PASTRY

2 cups flour
1 tablespoon sugar
1 teaspoon salt
¾ cup shortening
1 egg yolk
1 tablespoon lemon juice
¼ cup milk

Sift dry ingredients, blend in shortening. Beat yolk, lemon juice, and milk with a fork. Stir egg mixture into dry ingredients. Place dough on floured cloth or board; invert bowl over it for 10 minutes. Roll.

FLOUR PASTE PIE CRUST

2 cups flour
½ teaspoon salt
¼ cup ice water
⅔ cup shortening

Sift flour and salt. Make paste of ⅓ cup of the flour and the water. Blend shortening into the remaining flour. Add paste. Stir well. Chill and roll.

COOKIE DOUGH FOR OPEN PIES

2½ cups flour
1 teaspoon baking powder
½ cup sugar
2 tablespoons butter
1 egg
½ cup milk

Mix dry ingredients and butter, add slightly beaten egg to milk and combine the two mixtures. Roll ¼ inch thick. Makes enough to line two pie plates or oblong pans. Use for open-faced fruit tarts or kuchen.

RICH EGG PASTRY (MUERBE TEIG)

1 cup butter
3 cups flour
2 egg yolks
¼ cup cold water
1 lemon
¼ cup sugar

Mix butter and flour. Beat egg yolks, add the water. Combine the mixtures, adding grated rind, juice of lemon and sugar. Pat into pan ¼ inch thick. Chill. Bake with desired filling.

Light tender pastry requires an experienced hand, and the beginning cook should not be discouraged if first attempts are not ideal. Minimum handling, chilled ingredients and as little liquid as possible are especially important.

GOLDEN EGG PASTRY (MUERBE TEIG)

   5 yolks of hard-cooked eggs
   1 raw egg
   1½ cups butter
   1 cup sugar
   3 cups flour
   3 tablespoons lemon juice

Rub the cooked yolks to a paste, add the raw egg. Cream butter, add sugar, cream well. Add egg mixture and flour alternately, and lemon juice. Pat dough ¼ inch thick onto pie plates. Chill. Bake with desired filling.

RAISED EGG PASTRY (MUERBE TEIG)

   ¾ cup flour
   1 teaspoon baking powder
   ¼ teaspoon salt
   2 tablespoons sugar
   2 tablespoons melted butter
   1 egg, beaten

Sift flour, baking powder and salt. Mix sugar with butter, add egg. Combine with flour. Pat very thin in bottom and sides of greased 8 x 12-inch pan. Chill several hours. Bake in hot oven, 400° F., for about 10 minutes; add desired fruit mixture under Fruit Pies. Continue baking until well browned.

PUFF PASTE (BLAETTER TEIG)

   1 pound butter
   1 pound cake flour
   1 cup ice water

Chill all utensils and ingredients. Wash the butter and divide into 3 parts and shape each into a thin oblong pat. Wrap 2 of these in waxed paper and place in refrigerator; work the other butter pat into the flour, with fork or pastry blender. Add ice water, using as little as possible to make a smooth paste; toss the paste on floured board, knead just enough to form a ball shape; pat and roll out ¼-inch thick, keeping paste a little wider than long and corners square; lay 1 pat of the butter on the paste, dredge very lightly with flour; fold over the paste so as to enclose the butter; roll up like a jelly roll; pat and roll out ¼ inch thick; chill. Add remaining butter and roll out as before. Fold as before and chill 30 minutes; roll out 4 or 5 times, with gentle strokes from center out. Paste should be ice cold, and the oven extremely hot, 500° F.; turn the pan frequently so that puff paste may rise evenly. When well risen, reduce the heat gradually to 350° F. and continue baking until lightly browned. Used for pies, patties, vol au vents, and tarts.

LARGE PATTY SHELL (VOL AU VENT)

Cut out two cardboard circles, one 7 and one 8 inches in diameter, to use as patterns. Roll out Puff Paste, above, and cut out two 8-inch circles with a sharp pointed knife. Lay one circle on a baking sheet covered with brown paper. Brush with ice water, and cover with a second circle. Lay the 7-inch cardboard pattern on top and cut through the second circle with a sharp knife. Bake in an extremely hot oven, 500° F., for 10 minutes, until well risen. Continue baking with oven at 350° F., until browned. The 7-inch lid may be removed and used as a lid after the vol au vent is filled.

Fill with Chicken à la King or other creamed mixtures.

For individual patty shells see below.

PUFF PASTE PATTY SHELLS

Roll Puff Paste, above, ⅓-inch thick. Cut into 3-inch rounds with a cookie cutter. With a smaller cutter, remove the centers from two-thirds of the rounds, thus forming rings. Fit two of these rings on each solid round and press lightly. Chill well before baking. Line baking sheet with brown paper. Bake shells in an extremely hot oven, 500° F., for 10 minutes, until well puffed, then at 350° F. for about 15 minutes, until brown. Bake half the cut-outs separately; these may be used as covers. The remaining cut-outs may be rerolled with the other scraps from the cutting, and filled with preserves or savory mixtures to make small sweet or cocktail turnovers.

PUFF PASTE TART SHELLS

Cut out rounds of Puff Paste, cover backs of muffin tins or custard cups, pleating edges to fit. Prick well and bake in an extremely hot oven, 500° F., until well risen, then at 350° F. until browned.

PUFF PASTE PIE SHELL

Roll half of Puff Paste ⅓-inch thick, in a round large enough to fit over the back of a pie plate. Trim excess; pleat edges to fit, and prick well. Bake like Puff Paste Tart Shells, above. Cool and fill.

CRUMB SHELLS

ZWIEBACK OR GRAHAM CRACKER SHELL

Blend 2 cups crumbs with 4 tablespoons confectioners sugar and ½ cup melted butter. Spread and press mixture on buttered sides and bottom of spring form. Chill for several hours before filling. For 8- or 9-inch pie pan use 1 cup crumbs, ¼ cup butter and 2 tablespoons sugar.

CHOCOLATE WAFER OR OTHER COOKIE CRUMB SHELLS

Spread softened butter thickly on sides and bottom of spring form and pat on 1½ cups fine cookie crumbs. Chill for several hours before filling. Reserve ¼ cup crumbs to sprinkle on the top of torte when filled.

CORNFLAKE SHELL

Blend 2 cups crushed cornflakes, ½ cup melted butter, 1 teaspoon cinnamon, and 4 tablespoons sugar. Reserve ¼ cup of mixture to garnish the filled pie. Spread remainder on sides and bottom of buttered spring form. Chill for several hours before filling.

GRAHAM CRACKER PEANUT BUTTER PIE SHELL

2 cups fine graham cracker crumbs
¼ cup sugar
¼ cup peanut butter, smooth or crunchy
2 tablespoons water

Mix crumbs and sugar; blend in peanut butter. Add water and knead gently. Press onto bottom and sides of buttered 9-inch pie pan. Chill thoroughly and fill with chiffon, cream, or ice cream fillings.

MATZOS PIE SHELL

2 matzos
1 tablespoon fat
¼ cup matzo meal
2 eggs
2 tablespoons sugar
⅛ teaspoon salt

Soak matzos in water and press dry; heat fat, add the soaked matzos and stir over low heat until dry. Add matzo meal, eggs, sugar and salt. Mix well and pat evenly against bottom and sides of pie plate, ¼-inch thick. Fill with any desired fruit filling and bake in moderate oven, 350° F., 30 to 40 minutes.

MERINGUE PIE SHELL

3 egg whites
1¾ cups confectioners sugar
1 tablespoon cornstarch

Beat egg whites until stiff. Add ¾ cup confectioners sugar gradually, in small amounts, beating after each addition until mixture holds stiff peaks when the beater is withdrawn. Mix the cornstarch and remaining sugar and fold gently into the egg-white mixture. Lay 9-inch round of brown paper on baking sheet. Cover with meringue, shaping hollow with back of spoon to make shell. Bake in a slow oven, 275° F., for 45 minutes. Cool, fill with fruit or any cream pie filling, cover with sweetened whipped cream.

PIE TOPPINGS

MATZOS PIE TOPPING

2 matzos
½ cup shortening
yolks of 2 hard-cooked eggs
1 cup sugar
1 teaspoon salt
2 raw eggs
grated rind of 1 lemon
¼ teaspoon nutmeg
1½ cups matzo meal

Soak the matzos in water for 10 minutes and squeeze dry. Cream shortening, add matzos and stir until thoroughly blended. Mash yolks of hard-cooked eggs with a fork, add to mixture, then add sugar, salt and well-beaten eggs. Add grated rind, nutmeg, and last the matzo meal, stirring the batter thoroughly as each ingredient is added. Use as topping for apple, prune, apricot or other fruit pie. Drop spoonfuls of batter, not too close together, on top of filling. Bake in moderate oven, 350° F., 30 to 40 minutes.

MERINGUE TOPPING

8-INCH PIES
2 egg whites
¼ teaspoon cream of tartar
4 tablespoons sugar

9-INCH PIES
3 egg whites
¼ teaspoon cream of tartar
6 tablespoons sugar

Beat egg whites with cream of tartar until frothy. Beat sugar in gradually, a little at a time. Continue beating until mixture is stiff and glossy, and sugar is dissolved. Swirl the meringue over the pie filling with a spatula, touching crust all around; lift spatula to form peaks. Bake in a moderately hot oven, 375° F., for 8-10 minutes until light brown, or bake at 300° F. for 15-20 minutes for a crisper meringue with less risk of "dew drops" of moisture forming on the meringue after it has cooled.

MARSHMALLOW MERINGUE TOPPING

3 egg whites
6 tablespoons sugar
5 marshmallows, cut up

Beat egg whites until thick, beat in sugar gradually. Fold marshmallows into meringue. Cover pie filling. Bake at 325° F. about 20 minutes.

FRUIT PIES

APPLE PIE

6 to 8 apples
½ cup sugar
1 tablespoon butter
cinnamon, nutmeg, or lemon juice

Pare, core and slice apples. Line a pie plate with pastry; fill with apples. Sprinkle with sugar, bits of butter and spices or lemon juice; slash and prick upper crust, adjust over filling and bake in hot oven from 45 minutes to 1 hour at 425° F., until crust is brown and fruit is soft.

APPLE MERINGUE PIE

2 eggs, separated
¾ cup sugar
4 large apples, chopped
¼ pound almonds, chopped
¼ cup raisins, seeded
1 lemon, juice and grated rind
Meringue Topping, page 344

Beat egg yolks with sugar, add apples, almonds, raisins and lemon; fold in beaten whites. Line a pie plate with Rich Egg Pastry. Place mixture on dough, dot with butter, and bake in hot oven, 400° F., for 20 to 25 minutes until crust is brown. Cover with Meringue Topping and brown lightly in oven.

CARAMELIZED APPLE PIE

¼ cup melted butter
½ cup brown sugar
1 teaspoon honey, heated
½ cup pecan nut meats, chopped

Place above ingredients in deep pie plate. Make pie crust, and divide into 2 parts. Roll out bottom crust, and spread over the sugar mixture and over the sides of the pie plate. Fill with apples as in Apple Pie, above, and cover with upper crust. Bake in hot oven, 400° F., 15 minutes; reduce heat to 325° F., and bake 20 to 30 minutes longer, until apples are tender and crust is brown. Cool. One-half hour before serving time, return to oven for a few moments to loosen caramel. Invert and serve caramel side up.

BERRY PIE

1 can (1 pound) berries
⅔ cup sugar
1½ tablespoons tapioca

Drain fruit. Mix tapioca and sugar with ¾ cup of the juice. Cook about 15 minutes until thick and clear. Add drained fruit and cool. 1 tablespoon lemon juice and a little cinnamon may be added. Line 8-inch pie plate with pastry, add filling, cover, and bake at 450° F. for about 20 minutes, then reduce heat to 375° F. and bake about 15 minutes longer, or until crust is brown.

CANNED CHERRY PIE

1 can (1 pound) tart red cherries, pitted
6 tablespoons sugar
2 tablespoons cornstarch
½ teaspoon salt
1 tablespoon butter

Line 8-inch pie plate with pastry. Drain cherries and place on unbaked crust. Sprinkle dry ingredients over fruit. Pour on cherry juice. Dot with butter. Cover with top crust, slashed or latticed. Bake at 475° F. 12 minutes. Reduce heat to 425° F. and bake about 40 minutes longer.

FRESH CHERRY PIE

1 quart sour cherries, pitted
1½ to 2 cups sugar
2 tablespoons cornstarch or flour

Line an 8-inch pie plate with pastry. Mix fruit with sugar and cornstarch. Fill crust. Cover with lattice crust. Bake in a hot oven at 450° F. for about 20 minutes, then reduce heat to 375° F. and bake about 15 minutes longer, until crust is browned.

CRANBERRY PIE

Make Cranberry Sauce, using 1 cup water. Add grated rind of ½ lemon, and ⅛ teaspoon cinnamon. Cool. Line a pie plate with pastry, fill with cooked cranberries and cover with a lattice crust. Bake at 450° F., until crust is brown.

CRANBERRY RAISIN PIE

1 cup cranberries
½ cup seeded raisins
1 teaspoon butter, melted
¾ cup sugar
1 tablespoon flour

Line small pie pan with pastry. Cut cranberries in halves, raisins in pieces. Combine with remaining ingredients, fill crust, cover with top crust, and slash. Bake in moderate oven, 350° F., for about 40 minutes.

CURRANT PIE

1 cup fresh, ripe currants
1 cup sugar
¼ cup flour
1 tablespoon water
2 egg yolks
Meringue Topping, page 344

Mix currants with sugar and flour, add water and the slightly beaten yolks. Pour into 8-inch pie pan lined with pastry and bake in moderate oven, 350° F., until set. Cover with Meringue Topping and return to oven to brown.

GOOSEBERRY PIE

1 pint fresh gooseberries
⅞ cup sugar
water if necessary

Line 8-inch pie plate with pastry. Remove stem endings from both ends of the berries. Put in saucepan with sugar and water and cook until softened. Cool. Fill pie, cover with top crust. Slash and bake in a hot oven, 450° F., about 25 minutes, until browned.

MINCE PIE

Line pie plate with pastry, fill with Mince Meat or Wine Mince Meat, below, or with commercially prepared mince meat. Cover with top crust, slash, and bake 30 to 35 minutes at 425° F. Reduce heat to 325° F. for 10 minutes more.

MINCE MEAT

3 pounds beef or venison, chopped
1½ pounds beef suet, chopped
6 pounds apples, chopped
3 pounds seedless raisins
2 pounds currants
1 pound citron, chopped fine
grated rind of ½ lemon and ½ orange
2 tablespoons ground cinnamon
1 tablespoon ground cloves
1 nutmeg, grated, or 1 tablespoon ground nutmeg
3 pounds brown sugar
1 quart boiled cider
1 quart molasses
salt to taste

Cook all together slowly for 2 hours and seal in sterilized glass jars.

WINE MINCE MEAT

2½ pounds fresh boiled tongue, skinned and chopped fine, or 2½ pounds beef rump, chopped
2 pounds sugar
rind of 1 orange, grated
1 nutmeg, grated
2 pounds raisins
½ pound suet
½ pound currants
1 pound citron, cut fine
1 teaspoon cloves or mace
1 tablespoon cinnamon
1 cup cider
1 quart dry wine
1 cup brandy

Mix first 10 ingredients. Put in a preserving kettle with cider and simmer about 2 hours; add wine and brandy; seal in sterilized glass jars. Chopped apples and pecan nut meats may be combined with mince meat before baking, to taste.

RAISIN PIE

2 cups raisins
1½ cups boiling water
½ cup sugar
2 tablespoons cornstarch
2 tablespoons lemon juice
grated rind of ½ lemon
juice of 1 orange
grated rind of ½ orange
1 cup chopped walnuts
½ teaspoon salt

Line 8-inch pie plate with pastry. Cook raisins in water 5 minutes. Mix sugar and cornstarch, add to the raisins and cook until thick, about 5 minutes. Remove from heat and stir in the remaining ingredients. Cool. Fill pie shell. Cover with top crust, slash and bake at 425° F., for 30 to 35 minutes.

RHUBARB PIE

3 cups rhubarb
2 tablespoons cornstarch
1 egg, slightly beaten
1½ cups sugar

Line a pie plate with pastry. Cut rhubarb in ¼-inch pieces; sprinkle with cornstarch. Add egg and sugar, mix well, turn into lined pie plate. Cover with top crust or lattice strips. Bake in a hot oven 30 minutes at 425° F., reduce heat to 325° F. for 15 to 20 minutes.

Mix equal parts rhubarb and sliced, fresh strawberries for variety.

CREAM AND CUSTARD PIES

BANANA CREAM PIE

⅛ cup sugar
4 tablespoons cornstarch
½ teaspoon salt
2 cups milk, scalded
3 egg yolks
1 teaspoon vanilla
3 sliced bananas
baked 9-inch pie shell

Mix sugar, cornstarch and salt. Add milk slowly, stirring constantly. Cook in double boiler until cornstarch is clear and begins to thicken. Beat egg yolks slightly. Add gradually to mixture. Cook about 2 minutes. Add vanilla. Cool. Put alternate layers of bananas and filling into baked pie shell. Cover with meringue or whipped cream.

BUTTERSCOTCH CREAM PIE

1 envelope unflavored gelatin
¼ cup cold water
¾ cup brown sugar
2 tablespoons butter
5 egg yolks, beaten
½ cup milk, scalded
1 teaspoon vanilla
1 cup heavy cream, whipped
8-inch crumb shell

Soak gelatin in water 5 minutes. Cook sugar and butter until blended. To yolks, add milk, sugar mixture and softened gelatin. Cook in double boiler until mixture coats spoon, stirring constantly. Cool, add vanilla and fold in whipped cream. Pour into prepared shell. Top with whipped cream or grated, dry macaroons.

BUTTERSCOTCH MERINGUE PIE

1½ cups water
1½ cups brown sugar
3 tablespoons cornstarch
2 tablespoons flour
½ teaspoon salt
2 tablespoons sugar
¼ cup cold water
2 egg yolks
½ tablespoon butter
1 teaspoon vanilla
baked 8-inch pie shell

Heat water and brown sugar in a double boiler. Mix cornstarch, flour, salt, sugar; add water to make a smooth paste. Add to the first mixture, and then cook over boiling water 15 minutes or until thick. Beat egg yolks slightly, stir carefully into cooked mixture; cook 5 minutes. Add butter and flavoring. Fill shell, cover with Meringue Topping.

OLD FASHIONED CHEESE PIE

Cookie Dough, page 342
1½ cups dry cottage cheese
pinch of salt
2 tablespoons flour
2 tablespoons cream
3 eggs, separated
¾ cup sugar
1 tablespoon butter, melted
¼ cup currants
½ teaspoon vanilla
grated rind of 1 lemon
¼ pound blanched almonds, cut fine

Line a pie plate with Cookie Dough.
Rub cheese through sieve, add pinch of salt, flour and cream, mix well. Beat yolks slightly, add sugar and butter, stir well and mix with the cheese mixture. Add currants, vanilla, lemon rind, and fold in the beaten whites. Place mixture on dough; top with nuts and bake 1 hour in a moderate oven, 350° F.

MERINGUE CHEESE PIE

1½ cups (¾ pound) creamed cottage cheese
½ cup sugar
3 eggs, separated
½ lemon, rind and juice
Graham Cracker Shell, page 343
¼ teaspoon cream of tartar
4 tablespoons sugar

Sieve or rice cheese; stir in sugar, egg yolks, one at a time, lemon rind and juice, and lastly fold in one stiffly beaten egg white. Pour mixture into crust. Bake in a moderate oven, 350° F. for 15 minutes, or until almost set. Beat remaining 2 egg whites with ¼ teaspoon cream of tartar until foamy. Then gradually beat in 4 tablespoons sugar and beat until meringue is stiff and glossy. Spread on pie and bake for 15 minutes at 300° F.

REFRIGERATOR CHEESE CAKE

mixture for Graham Cracker Shell, pages 343
2 envelopes unflavored gelatin
½ cup cold water
3 egg yolks, slightly beaten
1 cup sugar
pinch of salt
⅓ cup warm milk
1 pound dry cottage cheese, riced
juice and grated rind of 1 lemon
3 egg whites, beaten stiff
1 cup heavy cream, whipped

Line a buttered spring form with crumb mixture. Reserve ¼ cup for top. Soak gelatin in cold water 5 minutes. Cook yolks, sugar, salt and milk in a double boiler, stirring constantly until mixture coats the spoon. Add gelatin, stir until dissolved. Cool. When mixture begins to set, beat in cheese and flavoring. Fold in beaten egg whites and whipped cream. Pour mixture into spring form. Sprinkle with remaining crumbs. Chill for 4 to 5 hours. 1 cup crushed pineapple, ¼ cup nut meats or ¼ cup maraschino cherries may be added to filling.

CHEESE CAKE WITH ZWIEBACK CRUST
CRUST

6 ounces zwieback
1 cup sugar
1 teaspoon cinnamon
½ cup butter, melted

Preheat oven to 325° F., a moderately slow oven. Roll zwieback fine and mix with sugar, cinnamon and the melted butter. Set aside ¾ cup of the mixture to sprinkle over top. Butter a 9-inch spring form and press mixture on bottom and sides.

FILLING

6 eggs
1½ cups sugar
⅛ teaspoon salt
juice and grated rind of 1 lemon
1½ cups cream
2¼ pounds dry cottage cheese
⅜ cup flour
¼ cup pistachio nuts, chopped

Beat whole eggs with sugar until light; add salt and lemon. Stir in cream, add cheese and flour, and mix. Put through a sieve. Stir until smooth, pour into prepared form, sprinkle remaining zwieback mixture over top, add nuts and bake 1 hour or until set. Turn off heat, open oven door, let stand in oven 1 hour or until cooled. Remove rim of spring form, and place bottom with cake on serving plate.

For a smaller cake, use 1½ pounds cheese, 1 cup sugar, 4 eggs, 1 cup cream, pinch of salt, juice and rind of ½ lemon, ¼ cup flour, and ¼ cup pistachio nuts.

SOUR CREAM CHEESE CAKE

1¼ pounds dry cottage cheese
4 tablespoons cornstarch
5 egg yolks
1 cup sugar
2 cups thick, sour cream
5 egg whites, beaten stiff

Line spring form with Cookie Dough or Rich Egg Pastry, patted ¼ inch thick.

Put cheese through sieve or ricer and add cornstarch and a little salt. Stir in egg yolks, sugar and cream, beat until smooth. Fold in the beaten whites. Fill spring form; bake 1 hour at 350° F. or until well set and browned at bottom.

CREAM CHEESE CAKE

mixture for Zwieback or Graham Cracker Crust, pages 343
4 eggs
1 cup sugar
1 tablespoon lemon juice
4 8-ounce packages cream cheese, softened
2 cups sour cream
1 teaspoon vanilla
4 tablespoons of sugar

Line a spring form with the crumb mixture; reserve ¼ cup for topping. Preheat oven to 375° F., a moderately hot oven. Beat eggs, sugar, and lemon juice until light. Add the cheese and beat thoroughly. Pour filling into crust and bake for 20 minutes. Remove cake from oven; increase oven heat to 475° F., a very hot oven. Top cake with sour cream mixed with vanilla and sugar. Sprinkle with the remaining crumbs and bake 10 minutes

longer. Cool, and chill in refrigerator overnight before serving.

CHESS PIE

2 eggs
1½ tablespoons flour
⅔ cup brown sugar, firmly packed
½ teaspoon salt
1 cup pitted dates
1 cup walnut meats
1 teaspoon vanilla
1 cup heavy cream
½ cup seedless white raisins
9-inch unbaked pie shell

Beat eggs until thick and light. Mix flour, sugar and salt and add to eggs, beating constantly. Chop coarsely dates and nuts. Add these, vanilla, cream and raisins to the batter. Place in pie shell and bake in a moderate oven, 350° F., for 50 to 60 minutes, or until a knife inserted near the center of the pie comes out clean.

CHOCOLATE PIE

4 eggs, separated
1 cup sugar
1 teaspoon vanilla
¼ pound sweet chocolate, grated
3 tablespoons milk
9-inch pie shell, unbaked

Beat yolks slightly; add sugar and beat thoroughly. Add vanilla, chocolate and milk, and fold in stiffly beaten egg whites. Pour into deep 9-inch pie plate lined with pastry. Bake 15 minutes at 450° F., then 30 minutes at 325° F. Cool, cover with sweetened, whipped cream.

CHOCOLATE CUSTARD PIE

2 squares unsweetened chocolate
1 cup milk
salt
¼ cup cornstarch
1 tablespoon butter
3 eggs, separated
1 cup sugar
1 teaspoon vanilla
9-inch pie shell, lightly baked

Melt chocolate in double boiler, add milk, a speck of salt and cornstarch mixed with a little cold water, and cook until smooth and thick, stirring constantly; add butter. Mix the yolks and sugar and pour the hot mixture over them, stirring well; put back in double boiler and cook, stirring constantly, until mixture is very thick. Cool, add vanilla. Lastly, fold in the stiffly beaten whites. Fill shell with chocolate custard and bake at 300° F. for 30 minutes. Serve with whipped cream.

COCONUT CUSTARD PIE

3 eggs, separated
½ cup sugar
2 cups scalded milk
dash of salt
½ cup shredded coconut
8-inch pie shell, lightly baked

Beat egg yolks with the sugar, add milk gradually, salt, then the coconut and stiffly beaten whites. If desired, mix ½ tablespoon cornstarch with the sugar and use only 2 eggs. Fill shell and bake 30 minutes at 300° F.

COCOA PIE

⅓ cup cocoa
¼ cup cornstarch
dash of salt
½ cup sugar
2 cups hot water
1 teaspoon vanilla
baked 8-inch pie shell

Mix dry ingredients in double boiler, add water, stir and cook about 15 minutes or until thick and smooth; add vanilla. Fill prepared shell. Serve with whipped cream.

CUSTARD PIE

2 eggs
¼ cup sugar
a little grated nutmeg
speck salt
1½ cups milk, scalded
8-inch pie shell, lightly baked

Beat the eggs, add the sugar, nutmeg and salt. Stir in the scalded milk. Pour the mixture into the hot crust, which has been baked for 10 minutes in a hot oven, 450° F. Bake about 30 minutes longer at 300° F. until a knife inserted near center of custard will come out clean. Remove pie from oven at once; cool at room temperature.

LEMON MERINGUE PIE

1 cup sugar
¼ cup flour or cornstarch
1 cup boiling water
1 tablespoon butter
3 eggs, separated
grated rind of 1 lemon
¼ cup lemon juice
baked 9-inch pie shell

Mix sugar and flour, add the boiling water slowly and boil until clear, stirring constantly over low heat. Add butter and, gradually, the egg yolks, beaten lightly. Cook over boiling water until very thick, stirring constantly. Add lemon rind and juice. Cool. Use egg whites to make Meringue Topping. Fold half of meringue into filling mixture, fill shell. Cover with remaining meringue. Bake at 300° F. for 15 minutes.

LEMON SOUFFLÉ PIE

5 egg yolks
1 cup sugar
juice and grated rind of 2 lemons
5 egg whites
baked 9-inch pie shell
2 tablespoons sugar

Beat egg yolks until light, add sugar, lemon juice and grated rind. Cook in double boiler until thick and smooth, stirring constantly. Cool; fold in 3 of the whites, beaten stiff. Place mixture in pie shell. For the meringue, beat remaining whites until stiff, add 2 tablespoons sugar gradually. Spread over top; bake in slow oven, 300° F., until brown.

LEMON MARSHMALLOW MERINGUE PIE

½ cup cold water
7 tablespoons cornstarch
1½ cups hot water
1¼ cups sugar
3 egg yolks, slightly beaten
grated rind and juice of 2 lemons
1 tablespoon butter
baked 9-inch pie shell

Mix cold water and cornstarch. Combine hot water and sugar and bring to boil over direct heat. Add cornstarch paste and cook until mixture begins to thicken. Cook over hot water until thick and smooth, about 15 minutes. Add slowly to egg yolks and cook a few minutes longer. Add lemon rind and juice and butter. Cool and pour into pie shell. Cover with Marshmallow Meringue Topping, page 344.

PECAN PIE

8-inch pie shell, unbaked
1 cup pecan halves
3 eggs
½ cup sugar
1 cup dark corn syrup
¼ teaspoon salt
1 teaspoon vanilla
¼ cup melted butter

Make pastry shell with fluted edge. Spread nuts over bottom of shell. Beat eggs; add sugar, syrup, salt, vanilla, and butter. Pour filling over pecans. Bake 10 minutes in very hot oven, 450° F.; reduce heat to 350° F. and bake for 35 minutes longer.

Do's and Don'ts in Freezing Pies:
—*Add meringue to frozen pie before serving, brown unthawed in 325° F. oven.*
—*Don't freeze custard pies.*

PUMPKIN OR SQUASH PIE

⅔ cup brown sugar
½ teaspoon salt
1 teaspoon cinnamon
½ teaspoon ginger
½ teaspoon cloves
1½ cups canned or cooked, strained pumpkin or squash
2 eggs
½ teaspoon vanilla
grated lemon rind, if desired
½ cup milk
½ cup light cream
9-inch pie shell, unbaked

Mix sugar, salt and spices; add pumpkin, lightly beaten eggs, and the milk and cream gradually. If pumpkin is very moist, use less liquid. Brush shell with egg white. Add the filling, and bake in hot oven, 425° F., for 20 minutes. Reduce heat to 275° F. and bake 40 minutes longer; or until knife inserted near edge of custard comes out clean. Cool at room temperature.

FROZEN PUMPKIN PIE

6 egg yolks
1 cup granulated sugar
1¼ cups light brown sugar
2 teaspoons cinnamon
½ teaspoon nutmeg
¼ teaspoon each of allspice, ginger, cloves
¾ teaspoon salt
2½ cups light cream
2 cups pumpkin, canned or cooked
two baked 9-inch pie shells

Beat the egg yolks, add the sugar, spice and salt. Add 1 cup of the cream and cook in double boiler, stirring constantly until the custard coats the spoon. Add pumpkin and cool. Add the remaining cream and freeze. If frozen in a refrigerator tray, stir occasionally so the mixture will be smooth. Just before serving, fill the shells with the frozen mixture and cover thickly and completely with Meringue Topping. Place under the broiler; heat just long enough to brown the meringue.

STRAWBERRY CREAM PIE

1 cup sugar
2 quarts strawberries
1 tablespoon cornstarch
2 tablespoons cold water
2 cups heavy cream, whipped
baked 9-inch pie shell

Add sugar to berries. Let stand 1 hour. Strain. Dissolve cornstarch in cold water. Add to half of the berries and all of the juice and cook 15 minutes to thicken. Chill. Just before serving, spread whipped cream about ½ inch thick in baked pie shell. Put whole berries on top of cream and over this pour the thickened berries with juice. Decorate around edges with remaining cream.

STRAWBERRY MERINGUE PIE

unbaked 9-inch pie shell
1 quart strawberries
½ cup confectioners sugar
2 eggs, separated
½ cup granulated sugar
bread crumbs

Sprinkle pie shell with bread crumbs. Mix berries with confectioners sugar and fill pie shell. Cover with egg yolks, beaten well with granulated sugar. Bake in hot oven, 425° F., for 20 minutes, until shell is brown. Cover with Meringue Topping and return to oven until meringue is lightly browned.

CHIFFON PIES

CHOCOLATE CHIFFON PIE

1 envelope unflavored gelatin
¼ cup cold water
½ cup sugar
2 squares unsweetened chocolate
½ cup milk
½ cup strong coffee
½ teaspoon salt
1 teaspoon vanilla
1 cup heavy cream, whipped
baked 9-inch pie shell

Soak gelatin in water 5 minutes. Heat the sugar, chocolate, milk, coffee and salt in double boiler until well blended. Add the softened gelatin to this mixture, stirring thoroughly. Cool, add the vanilla. When the mixture begins to thicken, fold in the whipped cream. Fill shell. Chill. Before serving, garnish with whipped cream.

LEMON CHIFFON PIE

1 envelope unflavored gelatin
¼ cup cold water
4 eggs, separated
1 cup sugar
½ cup lemon juice
½ teaspoon salt
1 teaspoon grated lemon rind
baked 9-inch pie shell

Soak gelatin in cold water 5 minutes. To beaten yolks add ½ cup sugar, lemon juice and salt. Cook in double boiler until mixture coats spoon. Add rind and softened gelatin. Stir well. Cool. When mixture begins to thicken, fold in stiffly beaten whites to which remaining sugar has been added. Fill pie shell and chill. Top with a thin layer of whipped cream and serve.

ORANGE CHIFFON PIE

Follow recipe for Lemon Chiffon Pie, above, substituting ½ cup orange juice, 1 tablespoon grated orange rind and 1 tablespoon lemon juice for the lemon rind and the ½ cup of lemon juice.

STRAWBERRY CHIFFON PIE

1 envelope unflavored gelatin
¼ cup cold water
½ cup boiling water
1 cup sugar
1 cup strawberry pulp and juice
¼ teaspoon salt
½ cup heavy cream, whipped
2 egg whites
baked 9-inch pie shell

Soak gelatin in cold water 5 minutes. Combine the boiling water, ¾ cup sugar, strawberry pulp and juice, and salt. Add to softened gelatin and stir until dissolved. Cool. When gelatin mixture begins to thicken, fold in whipped cream. Beat egg whites until foamy. Add remaining sugar gradually, beating until stiff and glossy. Fold into strawberry mixture, pour into baked pie shell and chill. Serve garnished with whipped cream and whole strawberries.

FRUIT CHIFFON PIES

Pineapple, apricots, berries or any fresh fruit pulp and juice may be substituted for strawberries in preceding recipe.

PEANUT BUTTER CHIFFON PIE

1 envelope unflavored gelatin
⅔ cup cold water
2 eggs, separated
½ cup sugar
¼ teaspoon salt
⅔ cup smooth peanut butter
1 cup sour cream
baked 9-inch pie shell

Soften gelatin in cold water. Beat egg yolks, sugar and salt in top of double boiler, stir in gelatin and cook over boiling water, beating constantly with a rotary beater until mixture is thick and fluffy. Remove from heat and blend in peanut butter. Beat egg whites until stiff but not dry and fold whites and sour cream into the gelatin mixture. Pour into pie shell and chill until firm. Serve with sweetened whipped cream and shaved chocolate, if desired.

TARTS

TART SHELLS

Roll out any pastry dough. Cut out rounds 4 inches in diameter; fit over the backs of inverted muffin pans or custard cups. Pinch the edges to fit. Prick well and bake on a baking sheet in a very hot oven (475° F.) until browned. Or use individual tart pans, and fit the rounds in as you would for a large pie shell, pricking well and fluting the edges. Cool the tart shells and remove from the pans.

FRESH FRUIT TARTS

Shape tart shells with Cookie Dough for Open Pies. When cool, fill ⅔ full of Cream Custard Cake Filling. Arrange large strawberries or raspberries on filling, brush with melted currant jelly or Apricot Glaze. Add a second coat of glaze when the first has set. Decorate with sliced pistachio nuts, if desired.

ICE CREAM TARTS

Fill baked Tart Shells with ice cream; cover with very thick layer of Meringue Topping; broil at 350° F. until meringue is lightly browned, or bake at 400° F. about 5 minutes.

BANBURY TARTS

1 cup nuts, chopped
1 cup raisins, chopped
1 cup sugar
juice and grated rind of 1 lemon
1 egg
1 tablespoon butter
1 tablespoon water
6-8 unbaked tart shells

Mix ingredients together; fill tart shells and bake in a very hot oven, 450° F., until crust is brown, about 15 minutes.

MACAROON TARTS

6-8 lightly baked tart shells
jam or marmalade
3 egg whites
½ pound confectioners sugar
½ pound grated almonds

Half-fill tart shells with any desired jam. Beat the egg whites until frothy; add the confectioners sugar, beat until thick. Fold in the grated almonds. Dust your hands with confectioners sugar and roll and flatten egg-white mixture into strips. Cover tarts with a lattice of strips. Bake at 300° F. about 15 minutes. Cool in pans.

Pastry Miniatures

VIENNA TARTS

Make Cheese Pastry. Chill, roll out and cut into 3-inch squares. Put 1 teaspoon of preserves in center of each. Pick up corners, press together to form square turnovers. Bake in a very hot oven, 450° F., until browned.

RUSSIAN TEA CAKES

1 cup eggs, whites and yolks mixed
1 cup sugar
1 cup sour cream
4-6 cups flour
1½ cups butter
1 cup chopped almonds
sugar and cinnamon

Mix eggs, sugar and cream, and add enough flour to make a dough that can be handled. Roll out ¼-inch thick into a rectangle three times as long as wide. Spread half the butter thinly over the right-hand two-thirds of the dough. Fold the left-hand third over the buttered dough, then the right-hand third over this. Roll out and chill. Repeat with remaining butter. Chill well. Divide dough into 4 parts. Roll each part into a rectangle, as thin as possible, sprinkle with some of the chopped almonds, sugar and cinnamon, and roll. Cut in slices, sprinkle with the rest of the almonds, sugar and cinnamon. Bake cut-side down on a baking sheet in a hot oven (400° F.) until delicately browned.

APRICOT HORNS

DOUGH
1 pound butter
1 pound creamed cottage cheese
4 cups flour

FILLING
1 pound dried apricots
2 cups sugar

COATING
1½ cups ground almonds
1¼ cups granulated sugar
2 egg whites, slightly beaten
confectioners sugar

Blend dough ingredients. Roll dough in balls 1 inch in diameter. Chill thoroughly. Cook apricots in water to cover until soft. Add sugar and force through a sieve. Combine almonds and granulated sugar. Roll or flatten each ball into a 3-inch round. Work with only a few balls of dough at a time so that the others will remain cold. Place a teaspoon of the apricot filling in center of each round. Roll up and bend ends to shape of crescent. Dip into egg white and roll in nut mixture. Bake on greased cookie sheet at 375° F. for 12 minutes, or until lightly browned. Sprinkle with confectioners sugar.

LINZER TARTS

Roll pastry ⅛ inch thick. Shape with a fluted, round cutter dipped in flour. With a smaller cutter remove centers from half the pieces, leaving rings ½ inch wide. Brush the circles with cold water near the edge; fit on rings and press lightly. Chill. Bake 15 minutes in a very hot oven, 450° F. Brush with egg yolk beaten with 1 teaspoon water. Cool and fill with jam.

JAM TURNOVERS (SOUR CREAM KIPFEL)

1 cup butter
4 cups flour
¾ cup sour cream
2 eggs, separated
jam
2 tablespoons sugar
⅛ teaspoon cinnamon
¼ pound almonds, chopped

Cut butter into flour, add cream and egg yolks and chill thoroughly. Roll out and fold as in Puff Paste recipe, repeating 4 times. Roll thin, cut into 2-inch squares. Put a teaspoon of jam on each square, fold over the corners, press edges together. Spread top with the lightly beaten egg whites; sprinkle with sugar, cinnamon and chopped almonds. Bake in a hot oven, 400° F., for 15 to 20 minutes until brown.

FRUIT KUCHEN

Fruit Kuchen are open-faced fruit pies that differ from ordinary pies in that they are made with raised Kuchen Dough or with Rich Egg Pastry rather than with ordinary pie crust, and the fruit is covered with an egg custard mixture.

APPLE, OR OTHER FRUIT KUCHEN

Line a well-greased oblong pan with a very thin sheet of raised Kuchen Dough, or with Rich Egg Pastry. Core, pare and cut 4 or 5 apples in eighths. Lay them in parallel rows on top of the dough and sprinkle with sugar and cinnamon. Beat the yolk of an egg with 3 tablespoons cream, and drip around apples. Bake 20 or 30 minutes in hot oven, 425° F., until crust is well baked and apples are soft.

OR USE:

STRAWBERRIES, 1 quart, 2 eggs, 1 cup sugar.
BLUEBERRIES, 1 quart, 2 eggs, 3 tablespoons cream, ½ cup sugar.
PLUMS, 1 quart pitted, cut in half, 3 eggs, 1½ cups sugar.
CHERRIES, unsweetened, 1 can (1 pound, 4 ounces) 2 eggs, 1 cup sugar.
PEACHES, 1 quart, pared, halved, 1 egg yolk, 1 cup sugar.

SEEDLESS GRAPES, 1½ pounds, ¾ cup sugar, 2 tablespoons flour, 2 egg yolks.

APRICOT KUCHEN

    3 cups dried apricots
    water to cover
    1 cup sugar
    2 eggs, beaten
    ½ cup sugar
    2 tablespoons milk
    few drops almond extract
    Golden Egg Pastry, page 343

Cook apricots in water to cover until tender but not mushy; the liquid should be almost absorbed. Add sugar when fruit is nearly done. Cool. Line pan with Golden Egg Pastry. Fill with apricots. Beat eggs, add ½ cup sugar, milk and almond extract; mix well together, drizzle over fruit. Bake in a moderately hot oven, 375° F., for 20 minutes; reduce heat to moderately slow oven, 300° F., and bake 30 minutes longer, until browned.

CHERRY KUCHEN

    1 quart sour cherries, pitted
    Rich Egg Pastry, page 342
    bread crumbs
    ½ cup sugar
    cinnamon
    1 egg yolk
    3 tablespoons cream

Pit the cherries, reserving any juice. Place thin layer of Rich Egg Pastry in shallow pan; sprinkle with bread crumbs. Spread evenly with cherries. Sprinkle with sugar and cinnamon. Beat egg yolk well, add the cream and cherry juice and pour over cherries. Bake in a hot oven, 425° F., until crust is well browned. Add 1 cup pecans with fruit, if desired.

SOUR CREAM GRAPE KUCHEN

    Rich Egg Pastry, page 342
    3 eggs, separated
    1 cup sugar
    ½ cup sour cream
    1½ teaspoons cornstarch
    1 teaspoon vanilla
    1 teaspoon minute tapioca
    2 pounds seedless grapes
    ¼ pound blanched almonds, chopped

Line 9 x 12-inch pan with Rich Egg Pastry. Beat egg yolks with sugar; add sour cream, cornstarch and vanilla and blend well. Fold in the grapes and the stiffly-beaten egg whites. Sprinkle minute tapioca on the pastry. Add filling. Top with nuts. Bake in a moderately hot oven, 375° F., for 50 minutes.

BLUEBERRY KUCHEN

    Rich Egg Pastry, page 342
    2 cans (1 pound each) blueberries
    ¼ cup sugar
    1 tablespoon cornstarch
    1 teaspoon butter
    1 egg, slightly beaten
    1 tablespoon lemon juice

Line pan with Rich Egg Pastry. Drain berries, saving juice. Mix sugar and cornstarch; gradually add 1 cup of berry juice, butter and egg. Cook in double boiler until mixture coats the spoon. Add lemon juice. Spread berries on pastry, cover with custard. Bake in hot oven, 425° F., until crust is brown.

GRAPE KUCHEN

    Rich Egg Pastry, page 342
    1½ pounds seedless green grapes
    ¾ cup sugar
    2 tablespoons flour
    2 eggs, separated
    ¼ cup water
    ¼ cup sugar

Line pan with Rich Egg Pastry. Toss grapes with ¾ cup sugar and flour; fill crust. Beat egg yolks with water, drizzle over fruit. Bake in moderately hot oven, 325° F., ¾ of an hour. Beat egg whites stiff, beat in ¼ cup sugar and continue beating until meringue is stiff. Spread over fruit and return to oven to brown lightly.

PEACH OR PEAR KUCHEN

    Rich Egg Pastry, page 342
    1 quart canned peaches or pears
    3 eggs
    ½ cup sugar
    ½ cup cream or fruit juice

Line bottom and sides of a greased 9-inch spring form with Rich Egg Pastry. Drain fruit and place on pastry. Make custard by beating eggs well with sugar; add cream or fruit juice. Pour custard over fruit and bake in a hot oven, 400° F., for 10 minutes. Reduce heat to 350° F. and bake until custard is set. Cool, sprinkle with Ground Almond Brittle. Serve with whipped cream.

PRUNE KUCHEN

  Rich Egg Pastry, page 342
  1½ pounds prunes
  ½ cup sugar
  1 tablespoon cocoa
  vanilla to taste
  3 eggs, separated

Cook prunes, stone, rub through sieve, mix well with sugar, cocoa, flavoring and egg yolks. Fill pie plate lined with Rich Egg Pastry. Bake in hot oven, 425° F., until crust is brown. Cover with Meringue Topping made with the 3 egg whites. Return to oven and bake until lightly browned.

STRUDELS

STRUDEL DOUGH

  ¼ teaspoon salt
  1½ cups flour
  1 egg, slightly beaten
  ⅓ cup warm water
  ½ cup butter, melted

TO MIX AND KNEAD

Mix salt, flour and egg. Add the water, mix dough quickly with a knife, then knead on board, stretching it up and down to make it elastic, until it leaves the board clean. Toss on a small, well-floured board. Cover with a hot bowl and keep it warm ½ hour or longer.

TO STRETCH DOUGH

See that the room is free from drafts. Have materials for filling ready before stretching dough. Work quickly. Lay dough in center of a well-floured tablecloth on table about 30 by 48 inches. Flour dough. Roll into a long oval with rolling pin. Brush dough with ¼ cup of the melted butter. With hands under dough, palms down, pull and stretch the dough gradually all around the table, toward the edges, until it hangs over the table and is as thin as paper. Cut off dough that hangs over edge and drip ¼ cup more butter over surface of dough.

TO FILL, ROLL AND SHAPE

Sprinkle one of the following fillings indicated for each Strudel over ¾ of the greased, stretched dough, fold a little of the dough at one end over the filling. Hold the cloth at that end high with both hands and the Strudel will roll itself over and over, like a large jelly roll. Trim edges again.

Twist roll into greased pan 11 x 16 inches or cut into 3 strands and lay them side by side in pan.

TO BAKE STRUDEL

Brush top with more melted butter. Bake in hot oven, 400° F., ½ hour; reduce heat to 350° F. and bake ½ hour longer, or until brown and crisp, brushing well with butter from time to time during baking, using altogether about 1 cup melted butter for the strudel with its fillings.

APPLE STRUDEL

  Strudel Dough, preceding
  2 quarts cooking apples, cut fine
  1 cup seeded raisins
  ½ cup currants
  ¼ pound almonds, blanched and chopped
  1 cup sugar mixed with 1 teaspoon cinnamon
  ½ cup melted butter

Combine all ingredients except butter. As rapidly as possible, spread apple filling evenly over ¾ of the stretched, buttered Strudel Dough. Drip some melted butter over filling. Roll up, trim edges, then place in pan. Brush with rest of the butter from time to time while baking. Serve slightly warm.

ALMOND STRUDEL

  Strudel Dough, preceding
  4 egg yolks
  ½ cup sugar mixed with ¼ teaspoon cinnamon
  rind of 1 lemon
  1 tablespoon lemon juice
  ½ pound almonds, blanched, dried and ground
  ½ cup melted butter

Beat eggs, sugar and cinnamon until light; add lemon rind, juice and almonds. Spread evenly over ¾ of the buttered, stretched dough. Drip ½ of the melted butter over the filling. Roll, trim and bake, brushing top with the remaining butter.

CHEESE STRUDEL

  Strudel Dough, preceding
  2 pounds cottage cheese
  4 egg yolks, beaten
  2 tablespoons sour cream
  salt
  sugar
  2 egg whites, beaten stiff
  ½ cup melted butter

Rice the cheese, add egg yolks, cream, salt and sugar to taste. Fold in egg whites. Spread mixture over ¾ of the stretched buttered dough. Over this, drip ¼ cup melted butter. Roll and bake, brushing top with remaining melted butter.

CHEESE, NUT AND RAISIN STRUDEL

To the above ingredients add ¾ cup sugar, 1 cup ground almonds, ½ cup seeded raisins. Follow directions above.

CHERRY STRUDEL

Strudel Dough, page 354
½ cup bread, cracker or sponge cake crumbs
2 quarts sour cherries, fresh or canned
1½ cups sugar
½ cup melted butter

Sprinkle crumbs over the stretched dough, then the cherries, pitted and drained. Sprinkle with sugar and melted butter, roll and bake.

MARASCHINO CHERRY AND PINEAPPLE STRUDEL

Strudel Dough, page 354
½ cup melted butter
½ cup graham cracker crumbs
1½ cups sugar
1 teaspoon cinnamon
3½ cups fresh pineapple, diced
1 cup seeded raisins
1 cup walnuts, ground
½ cup maraschino cherries, cut fine

Mix crumbs, sugar and cinnamon and sprinkle over stretched and buttered dough. Spread fruit and nuts over ¾ of the dough evenly and drip half the melted butter over all. Roll, trim and bake, brushing top with remaining melted butter. If canned pineapple is used, drain well, reduce sugar to ¾ cup.

COCONUT, RAISIN AND CHERRY STRUDEL

Strudel Dough, page 354
1 egg white
⅛ pound shredded coconut
½ cup melted butter
¼ cup cracker crumbs
⅛ pound walnuts, ground
⅛ pound seedless raisins
juice of 1 orange
juice of 1 lemon
¾ cup sugar
½ cup preserves, drained, or
    ½ cup citron, chopped
½ cup maraschino cherries, cut fine

Stir egg white with coconut, prepare rest of the ingredients. Stretch Strudel Dough over tablecloth, brush with melted butter and sprinkle dough with the cracker crumbs, add nuts and raisins, mixed with the lemon and orange juice, then the remaining ingredients. Drip ¼ cup melted butter over all. Roll up quickly, place in pan and bake, first brushing top with remaining melted butter.

PRUNE AND APRICOT STRUDEL

Strudel Dough, page 354
1 cup stewed prunes, stoned
1 cup stewed dried apricots
½ cup melted butter
½ cup graham cracker crumbs
1½ cups sugar
1 cup seeded raisins
1 lemon, juice and rind

Drain prunes and apricots, cut fine. Drip half the butter over stretched Strudel Dough. Spread crumbs and sugar mixed, fruit and lemon, evenly, over ¾ of the dough. Roll, trim, and bake, basting often with remaining butter.

SOUR CREAM STRUDEL (RAHM STRUDEL)

Strudel Dough, page 354
1 quart thick sour cream
1 cup bread crumbs
2 cups granulated sugar
1 cup chopped almonds
1 cup raisins
1 teaspoon cinnamon
¼ cup melted butter

Spread stretched and buttered Strudel Dough with sour cream, sprinkle with bread crumbs and with remaining dry ingredients. Roll and put in well-buttered pan, brush top with melted butter. Bake, brushing often with butter.

CABBAGE STRUDEL

Strudel Dough, page 354
1 onion
½ cup butter or shortening, melted
1 quart cabbage, shredded and salted

Dice onion and sauté in ¼ cup shortening until tender. Add salted cabbage, well drained, and cook ½ hour longer. Spread mixture over ¾ of the stretched Strudel Dough, and drip remaining shortening over all. Roll Strudel, place in pan and bake. Sprinkle lightly with confectioners sugar and serve warm.

Many of these strudel recipes have been in one edition or another of the SETTLEMENT *for more than half a century, and several generations of cooks have learned the accomplishments of strudel-making from these pages.*

18
SALADS AND
SALAD DRESSINGS

GREEN SALADS · VEGETABLE SALADS · MAIN DISH SALADS · FRUIT SALADS
· MOLDED SALADS · SALAD DRESSINGS

A simple salad of greens or greens and other vegetables is becoming a regular part of every menu, in line with a growing trend toward lighter, yet nutritionally balanced meals. These salads, commonly called "green salads," are served with the main course, or between courses, or as a first course in California style.

Heartier salads, such as chicken salad, are served as a main course; others, including potato and macaroni salad, are part of the main course. A salad-appetizer like artichokes vinaigrette or tomato salad may introduce a meal. Molded salads frequently are a part of buffet or party menus. Fruit salads may serve as dessert.

Salad Dressings will be found on pages 373-378

GREEN SALADS

An increasing variety of salad greens which are available throughout the year makes it easy to add extra interest and appeal to salad bowls.

Choose a mixture of salad greens with an eye to contrast and harmony of texture and flavor; mix buttery leaves and crisp, sweet leaves with sharp and biting varieties.

CRISPHEAD is the correct name of the solid compact head lettuce usually called *Iceberg* or *Simpson* or *head lettuce*. This is the most widely used salad green. Since it transports well, it is usually available all year around, at reasonable prices.

LEAF LETTUCE, a loose head of long, frilly leaves, is mild and sweet in flavor, decorative in appearance. It is sold locally in season, and is the lettuce most often grown in home gardens.

BOSTON is the best-known variety of BUTTERHEAD lettuce. The head is round like Crisphead, but soft, loose, and light for its size. The leaves have a smooth, buttery texture, and a mild, sweet flavor.

BIBB or KENTUCKY LIMESTONE lettuce is the expensive, "gourmet" variety of Butterhead. The head is smaller, the color of the leaves dark, rich green shading toward pale green, the flavor sweet and nutty.

ROMAINE or Cos has long, stiff leaves, crisp texture and distinctive rich flavor. Romaine is widely available and inexpensive during the local growing seasons. This is the lettuce used for the famous Caesar Salad.

ESCAROLE has flat, lightly curled leaves that vary from dark green on the outside of the head to yellow-white in the middle. Its flavor varies from pleasantly biting to very bitter. Taste before deciding whether to use escarole as the main green in a salad of mixed greens, or only in small amounts, for contrasting flavor.

CHICORY, also called CURLY ENDIVE, comes in

large heads of decorative curly-edged leaves. Like escarole, the leaves may be too bitter to use in large quantities.

BELGIAN ENDIVE, sometimes called witloof or chicory, is a very small head of tightly packed, smooth, rather thick leaves, shaped like an elongated oval. Endive is sometimes cut into rings, sometimes served with the spear-shaped leaves separated from the head. The flavor is pleasantly bitter, the color pale green to white.

GREEN CABBAGE, either the tightly compact, smooth, round heads or the loose-leaved, wrinkled Savoy, is often shredded and used as a salad green and in slaws.

RED CABBAGE is used like green cabbage, as a colorful addition to the salad bowl, or for cole slaw. It is usually combined with the green for color contrast.

CHINESE CABBAGE, or CHINESE CELERY, grows in a celery-shaped stalk. It is tender, sweet-flavored, milder than green or red cabbage.

SPINACH leaves, very young and small, have a buttery texture, a mild unusual flavor and an attractive dark green color that make them an excellent addition to a mixed salad. A favorite wilted salad is made by adding a hot dressing to spinach leaves.

WATERCRESS has a sharp, lemony bite and tiny, rich green leaves that make it a most attractive garnish for the salad bowl. It is relatively expensive, but it is used in small quantities.

To Prepare Salad Greens

To crisp greens, wash thoroughly, dry and wrap in towel or put into closed container and refrigerate. To separate leaves of head lettuce, cut out the core in a cone-shaped wedge, and hold cut end under stream of cold water to loosen the leaves.

Discard any withered or darkened leaves, and very coarse leaves or centers before tearing the salad greens into pieces of a convenient size to eat with a fork. Avoid using a knife to cut salad greens unless the salad is to be served at once; knife-cut edges darken quickly.

For maximum crispness, do not add salad dressing until just before serving the salad.

Salad Vegetables

To add interest to an assortment of salad greens, add one or more of the following vegetables: radishes, tomatoes, scallions, celery, raw mushrooms, black or green olives, cucumbers, carrot slivers, cauliflower buds, green and red peppers. Certain cooked vegetables are a welcome addition to the salad bowl: green beans, green peas, zucchini, cauliflower, broccoli buds, potatoes.

TOSSED GREEN SALAD

Wash and dry any desired assortment of greens, above, and tear into pieces. If desired, add one fourth the amount of raw vegetables. At serving time, add 2 tablespoons salad dressing for each serving and toss well to mix. Allow about 1 cup salad per serving.

HEAD LETTUCE SALAD

Cut iceberg lettuce into wedges or crosswise slices, and serve at once with any desired salad dressing. A slice of tomato topped by a rolled anchovy is a good addition to Head Lettuce Salad.

INDIVIDUAL COMBINATION SALAD

Lay ½-inch thick slice of head lettuce on an individual salad plate or use shredded lettuce or lettuce leaves. Cover with a thick slice of peeled tomato, several cucumber slices, and sliced scallion. Garnish with bits of red or green pepper and with radish tulips. To make tulips, make 8 slices from the top of the radish to the stem, without cutting through, and soak the radishes in water until they spread into a flower shape.

BLUE CHEESE TOSSED SALAD

Tear any combination of salad greens into pieces. Rub a large wooden bowl with garlic. For each two servings of salad, add 2 tablespoons oil, 1 tablespoon granulated sugar, and a little salt. Add the greens, sprinkle with pepper, and toss with salad fork and spoon gently until greens are coated with oil. Add radishes, coarsely cut tomatoes, or other raw vegetables, to taste. Add 2 tablespoons coarsely crumbled blue cheese and 1 tablespoon lemon juice or tarragon vinegar. Adjust the seasoning with salt, pepper, and more sugar or lemon juice to taste.

CAESAR SALAD

    2 cups Croutons, page 406
    1 garlic clove
    2 heads romaine lettuce
    ¼ teaspoon dry mustard
    ¼ teaspoon black pepper
    ½ teaspoon salt
    4 ounces Parmesan or blue cheese
    6 to 8 anchovy fillets
    6 tablespoons olive oil
    juice of 2 medium lemons
    2 eggs

Prepare Croutons. Rub a wooden bowl with garlic.

Add the chilled romaine, torn into bite-size pieces; season with mustard, pepper, salt. Add the grated or crumbled cheese, the anchovies, olive oil and lemon juice. Boil 2 eggs for 1 minute—no more—and break them over the greens. Toss contents thoroughly but carefully. Add croutons, tossing just enough to mix. Must be served at once.

COLE SLAW

Remove outer leaves from medium-sized cabbage. Shred cabbage very fine. Mix with French Dressing or Sour Cream Dressing or mayonnaise to moisten generously. Chill before serving. Sliced green peppers and pimiento may be added.

Or, salt cabbage, let stand, press and drain and add Hot Salad Dressing.

PINEAPPLE SLAW

1 cup shredded cabbage
⅔ cup grated raw carrots
1 cup diced canned pineapple
Fluffy Cream Dressing, page 376
¼ cup walnuts or pecans

Mix the first three ingredients with salad dressing. Sprinkle with broken nuts.

CABBAGE ROSE SALAD

small solid cabbage
2 cups celery, diced or 2 cups boiled potatoes, sliced
Hot Salad Dressing, page 376
1 red pepper, shredded

Remove the outside leaves of the cabbage. Hollow out center with sharp knife. Place "cabbage bowl" in ice-cold water for one hour, drain and dry. Shred cut-out cabbage, mix with equal parts of celery or potatoes, moistened with Hot Salad Dressing, and refill cabbage. Turn back outer leaves of cabbage to resemble open rose, sprinkle thickly with shredded red peppers and serve cold. Or, fill "bowl" with any seafood and serve with mayonnaise.

CUCUMBER SALAD

Choose a firm, slim, long cucumber; peel lengthwise. Score the edges by drawing the tines of a fork down the length of the cucumber all around. Then slice crosswise in ⅛-inch slices not quite through so the cucumber will still look whole. Place in ice-cold water for several hours. When ready to serve, put in center of platter, sprinkle finely chopped green and red peppers and grated onion over the top and pour French Dressing over it. Surround with tomatoes and wedges of head lettuce.

CUCUMBER SALAD WITH SOUR CREAM

Choose long, firm, slim cucumbers. Pare. Cut crosswise in ⅛-inch slices. Drop into salted ice water 1 hour. Drain well. Beat ½ cup sour cream, 1 tablespoon lemon juice, 1 tablespoon vinegar, 1 tablespoon sugar, and ⅛ teaspoon salt. Mix dressing and cucumber. Chopped parsley and shredded onion may be added.

WILTED CUCUMBERS

1 cucumber
1 cup water
1 tablespoon salt
French Dressing, page 376

Pare cucumber if necessary and slice paper thin. Cover with cold, salted water. Let stand 10 minutes. Drain and rinse in cold water. Mix with French Dressing and let stand 10 minutes before serving.

WILTED LETTUCE

¾ pound leaf lettuce
Bacon Salad Dressing, page 373

Wash, drain and shred lettuce. Pour boiling water over it. Let stand 5 minutes until slightly wilted. Drain well. Add dressing.

SHAMROCK SALAD

Cut off stem of sweet green peppers, remove seeds. Fill with a mixture of cream or cottage cheese, bits of canned pimiento, olive and nuts. Chill thoroughly. When ready to serve, slice thin. Place a slice on a round of pineapple on ½-inch slice of Chinese cabbage. Serve with French Dressing.

SPINACH SALAD

Wash young, tender leaves of spinach carefully, drain, and crisp. Mix with French Dressing adding finely chopped crisp bacon if desired or mix with Bacon Salad Dressing.

SUMMER SALAD

1½ cups chopped cucumber
½ cup chopped green onion
½ cup diced celery
½ cup grated raw carrot

Mix all together and serve on lettuce with French Dressing.

TOMATO SALAD

Wash tomatoes, plunge in boiling water 1 minute, then in cold water; drain and remove skins; cool. Serve whole or sliced on lettuce with French Dressing or mayonnaise.

Salad dressings of all types will be found on pages 373-378.

TOMATO AND ONION SALAD

Cut 4 firm tomatoes in ¼-inch slices, and 1 medium Bermuda onion in thin slices. Place alternately in salad bowl. Cover with French or Tomato Soup Dressing.

VEGETABLE SALADS

Any desired combination of cooked vegetables may be used in a salad, or cooked vegetables may be added to a tossed green salad. For an attractive appetizer-salad, cook whole green beans or asparagus until just tender, cover with French Dressing while vegetables are still warm, and serve chilled. For best flavor, cook the different kinds of vegetables for a mixed salad separately, until tender but still crisp. Drain well, cover with dressing, and marinate in the refrigerator until chilled. A few thin rings of raw, sliced onion may be added to any cooked vegetable salad before marinating. Vegetable salads are ideal for buffet service.

Vegetable salads are especially suitable to serve at picnics or outdoor barbecues. Extra dressing may be added just before serving.

ANTIPASTO

1 small head cauliflower, broken into flowerets
1 green pepper, cut in strips
1 large carrot, sliced
1 large onion, sliced thin
4 stalks celery, chopped
1 5-ounce jar stuffed green olives
1 cup small button mushrooms
1 pound boiled, deveined shrimp (optional)
1 cup olive oil
1½ cups wine vinegar, lukewarm
5 tablespoons sugar
2 teaspoons salt
½ teaspoon pepper
1 tablespoon oregano
black olives
anchovies

Combine vegetables and shrimp. Combine olive oil, vinegar, sugar, salt, pepper and oregano and pour over vegetables. Toss until well blended. Cover and refrigerate for 12 hours. To serve: drain well. Garnish with black olives and anchovies.

ARTICHOKE SALAD

Boil artichokes, page 412, from 30 to 40 minutes, until the leaves may be easily pulled out. Chill.

Serve whole with mayonnaise, or French Dressing, served separately.

Or cut artichokes in half, remove thistle and fill centers with dressing.

Or use canned or frozen artichokes, following directions on label, and marinate in dressing.

ASPARAGUS SALAD

Drain cooked or canned asparagus; serve chilled on crisp lettuce with French Dressing or mayonnaise.

ASPARAGUS AND PEPPER SALAD

Drain stalks of canned asparagus. Cut green or red peppers in rings ⅓-inch wide. Place 3 or 4 stalks in each ring and serve chilled on lettuce leaves with French Dressing.

ASPARAGUS-EGG SALAD

Chop 1 tablespoon each of parsley, sweet red pepper and a hard-cooked egg for each serving. Mix and use as garnish for stalks of green or white asparagus; serve on lettuce leaves with French Dressing.

GREEN BEAN SALAD

1 pound green beans
2 tablespoons onions, chopped
2 tablespoons oil
2 tablespoons vinegar
1 tablespoon sugar
salt and paprika

Cook beans in boiling salted water until tender, drain and reserve ½ cup of the bean liquid. Mix beans and reserved liquid while hot with the rest of the ingredients and chill. Or mix cooked beans with French Dressing.

WAX BEAN SALAD

1 pound wax beans
2 eggs
2 tablespoons sugar
¼ cup tarragon or malt vinegar
½ pint sour cream
½ cup bean liquid, hot

Wash, string and slice beans. Cook until tender, drain and reserve liquid. Beat eggs well with the sugar, vinegar and sour cream. Add the hot bean liquid, beat constantly. Mix with the beans; store in the refrigerator. This will keep for several days.

BEETS, STUFFED WITH PEAS

Boil unpeeled medium-sized beets until tender; peel and cut a slice off the bottom so that they will stand upright, and scoop out carefully, keeping a ½-inch shell. When cold fill with cold cooked green peas and chopped celery; moisten with Boiled Dressing. Serve on lettuce leaves, and place a slice of hard-cooked egg on each portion.

YELLOW TOMATO AND BEET SALAD

In the center of a salad plate put shredded lettuce or sprigs of watercress. In a circle around it, lay alternate slices of cooked beet and yellow tomato overlapping each other. Sprinkle French Dressing lightly over all and serve with mayonnaise to which has been added 1 tablespoon chopped beet and 1 riced hard-cooked egg.

CELERY ROOT SALAD

3 or 4 celery roots or celeriac
1 teaspoon salt
⅛ teaspoon pepper
1 onion, sliced
vinegar

Scrub and peel small, firm roots. Boil in salted water for 2 hours or cook in steamer or pressure cooker until tender. Drain and slice; add salt, pepper, onion, and cover with vinegar diluted with equal amount of celery liquid or water. Serve warm or cold. Will keep if placed in covered jars.

CELERY ROOT IN SOUR CREAM

2 small celery roots
2 cups celery, diced
½ cup vinegar
¼ teaspoon pepper
1 teaspoon salt
¼ pound almonds, blanched
½ cup thick, sour cream

Scrub celery root well, peel and cook several hours until tender in salted water, or cook in pressure cooker. Slice; mix with the rest of the ingredients, adding the sour cream last. Serve cold.

GREEN PEA SALAD

1 can (1¼ cups) peas, drained
½ head lettuce, shredded
1 small onion, minced
2 medium tomatoes
2 hard-cooked eggs
Thousand Island Dressing, page 376

Combine peas, lettuce and onion. Slice tomatoes and eggs. Mix gently with the dressing, being careful not to break egg slices or tomatoes. Or garnish top of salad with tomato and egg slices.

Potato Salads

Moist, boiled, peeled potatoes are recommended for all potato salad recipes.

POTATO SALAD WITH MAYONNAISE

4 cups sliced boiled potatoes
1 medium onion, cut fine
½ tablespoon salt
1 cup celery, cut fine
1 cup mayonnaise
sliced cucumber

Mix the ingredients together lightly, season and serve cold.

CREAMY POTATO SALAD

6 cold, boiled potatoes
2 hard-cooked eggs
½ grated onion
1 teaspoon mustard
1 teaspoon salt
speck pepper
2 tablespoons vinegar
1 cup milk or cream
2 tablespoons butter

Cut potatoes in small cubes, add chopped egg whites and onion. Mash egg yolks, add mustard, salt and pepper. Mix thoroughly and add vinegar. Heat milk or cream to boiling point and pour slowly on egg mixture. Add butter. When butter is melted, pour mixture over potatoes. Cool and serve on lettuce with Boiled Salad Dressing.

HOT GERMAN POTATO SALAD

2 pounds potatoes
1 teaspoon salt
⅛ teaspoon pepper
1 teaspoon dry mustard
½ teaspoon sugar
½ teaspoon flour
½ cup water
½ cup vinegar
¼ pound bacon or fat smoked beef
or 2 tablespoons poultry fat or butter
1 medium onion, cut fine

Cook potatoes in boiling salted water until tender. Drain, peel, and while hot, cut into ⅛-inch slices; sprinkle with the salt, pepper, mustard, sugar and flour. Heat water and vinegar to boiling point. Place bacon or beef, sliced and chopped fine in skillet, fry light brown; add onions, brown slightly; add potatoes and the hot vinegar; heat through to absorb the vinegar and water; serve warm. If poultry fat or butter is used, the bits of fried bacon or beef may be omitted. If the salad is too dry, add a little hot water. It should have a glassy look without being lumpy or greasy.

HOT POTATO SALAD

To 1 quart hot, sliced potatoes add 1 medium

onion, chopped, and mix with Hot Salad Dressing. Garnish with parsley or chives.

MAIN DISH SALADS

A main dish salad for luncheon or supper has many advantages. It offers good nutrition without too many calories; it contains fresh fruits and vegetables, and it satisfies the appetite without surfeiting it. Also, these salads are simple to prepare ahead of time, or they may be quickly combined for serving. A salad menu may be rounded out with hot soup and dessert; or the salad may be served with hot biscuits, rolls or muffins.

The main dish salads given here fall into several categories; there are stuffed vegetable salads, chicken, meat, and seafood salads. Molded salads are often main dish salads; these follow in the next section.

Attractive Ways to Serve Salads

CUPS: Scoop out tomatoes, peppers, beets, oranges, lemons, apples, or avocados.

BOATS: Cut cucumbers or pineapple in half lengthwise. Scoop out center, leaving ½-inch wall.

BASKETS: Hollow cucumber as above, and for handle, cut slice of pepper, orange or lemon peel ½-inch thick.

TOMATO BASKETS: Use even-sized, firm tomatoes, one for each person. Cut ½-inch strip for handle, halfway down the center on the smooth flat side. Cut crosswise on both sides to the handle. Remove pulp.

Orange and lemon baskets are made like tomato baskets.

Stuffed Vegetable Salads

STUFFED AVOCADO SALAD

Just before serving, wash avocados, cut in half, and remove stones. Fill center with chicken or seafood salad, serve with French Dressing.

STUFFED TOMATOES WITH ANCHOVIES

6 tomatoes
1 dozen anchovies, in oil
2 slices boiled ham
½ green pepper
1 tablespoon pearl onions
1 tablespoon capers
2 hard-cooked eggs, chopped

Scoop out 6 tomatoes and chill. Chop the tomato pulp with anchovies, ham, and pepper; then add onions and capers, fill the tomatoes; cover with the eggs. Serve on lettuce with French Dressing.

STUFFED TOMATOES WITH ASPARAGUS

1 large green pepper
4 firm, red tomatoes
lettuce
1 can (1 pound) asparagus tips

Wash and cut the pepper into slices, crosswise, to form ¼-inch rings. Discard pith and seeds. Pierce tomatoes at stem with fork, dip into boiling water, lift out, peel, chill and cut in half, crosswise. Place on lettuce, cut side up. Lay 4 or 5 asparagus tips side by side in center of each tomato half. Slit pepper rings and place across the top of asparagus to meet the sides of the tomato, thus forming a handle to the tomato basket. Serve cold with French Dressing or Gargoyle Sauce.

STUFFED TOMATOES WITH CRAB MEAT AND CAVIAR

Stuff peeled, halved tomatoes with equal parts of shredded crab meat and caviar, cover with mayonnaise.

STUFFED TOMATOES WITH CUCUMBERS

6 ripe tomatoes
2 cucumbers
salt and pepper
1 cup Sour Cream Salad Dressing, page 375
finely chopped parsley
lettuce

Dip tomatoes briefly into boiling water, lift out, peel. Cut a slice from the top of each; scoop out center. Peel and dice the cucumbers, season lightly and mix with at least half the dressing. Fill the tomato cups with this, and put another spoonful of the dressing on top. Sprinkle with finely chopped parsley and serve on lettuce.

STUFFED TOMATOES WITH HERRING

6 tomatoes
6 salted herring tidbits
1 small can caviar
2 hard-cooked eggs
½ green pepper
½ dill pickle

Scoop tomatoes and chill; mix above ingredients, chopped fine, with some of the tomato pulp. Fill tomatoes; cover with mayonnaise.

Attractive garnishes for salads, made of cream cheese and other ingredients, will be found on page 372.

Chicken, Meat, and Egg Salads

CHICKEN SALAD

2 cups diced, cooked chicken
1 cup diced celery ·
French Dressing
mayonnaise

Mix chicken and celery. Marinate with French Dressing. Chill for several hours. Drain. Before serving, mix well with mayonnaise. Serve on crisp lettuce. Garnish with olives, slices of hard-cooked eggs.

CHICKEN AND SWEETBREAD SALAD

2 cups diced, cooked chicken
1 cup diced, cooked sweetbreads
1 cup celery, diced
1 cup mayonnaise

Chill ingredients, mix and serve on lettuce.

ELEGANT CHICKEN AND SWEETBREAD SALAD

To chicken, sweetbreads and celery in preceding recipe, add ½ cup pecan nut meats broken in pieces and 3 hard-cooked egg whites, diced. Mix with Boiled Dressing thinned with whipped cream. Serve in Jellied Fruit Salad Ring. Sprinkle with riced egg yolks.

CHEF'S SALAD

Wash, crisp and tear into pieces lettuce, endive, romaine, and cress. Add cucumbers, celery or radishes, cut in pieces. Chill. Place in salad bowl. Add 6 or 8 anchovies, drained and chopped. Arrange strips of Swiss cheese, cooked turkey, ham, tongue or chicken in heaps on the mixtures of greens. Garnish with hard-cooked eggs and tomato wedges. Toss the salad at the table with Celery French Dressing. The dressing may be seasoned with crumbled Roquefort or blue cheese, or with bottled walnut catsup or mushroom catsup to taste.

LIVER AND EGG SALAD

6 chicken livers
4 hard-cooked eggs, coarsely chopped
3 small onions, finely chopped
French Dressing
salt, pepper

Bake or sauté the livers and chop coarsely. Blend with eggs and onions and add French Dressing to moisten, and seasonings to taste. Serve in lettuce cups.

A thick slice of calf's liver, or any desired liver, may be used instead of chicken livers.

SWEETBREAD-CUCUMBER SALAD

¾ cup diced, cooked sweetbreads
1 cucumber, diced
French Dressing
¼ cup mayonnaise
2 tablespoons heavy cream
tomato wedges

Combine sweetbreads and cucumber, cover with French Dressing, chill 1 hour or longer. Drain, mix with mayonnaise and cream, arrange on lettuce. Use tomato garnish, serve with French Dressing.

HAM OR TONGUE SALAD

2 pounds cold boiled ham or tongue, chopped fine
½ teaspoon paprika
mayonnaise

Chop ham or tongue very fine. Sprinkle with paprika and mix with mayonnaise to moisten. Form into loaf; score top. Serve with radishes and potato chips. Chopped dill pickle or grated horseradish may be added. Serves 12.

WATER LILY SALAD

6 hard-cooked eggs
1 head lettuce or watercress
¼ cup green or stuffed olives
1 bunch red radishes
French Dressing
mayonnaise

Remove shells from hard-cooked eggs. Roll while warm to flatten ends so egg halves will stand. Slit the white at the half-way point with a sharp knife, making a uniform serrated edge around the center. Separate halves. Remove yolks, rice, season to taste. Refill whites, place far apart on shredded lettuce leaves, on a large platter. To represent buds, scatter olives or radishes. Surround platter with watercress and serve with French Dressing or mayonnaise.

EGG SALAD

4 hard-cooked eggs, chopped
½ cup chopped celery
1 teaspoon prepared mustard
¼ cup mayonnaise
salt and pepper

Mix all ingredients well; chill.

Fish and Seafood Salads

CRAB MEAT SALAD

1 pound crab meat, fresh or canned
4 hard-cooked eggs
½ cup almonds
2 cups heavy cream
1 cup mayonnaise
salt and paprika
lettuce
1 green pepper or pimiento

Pick over the crab meat and discard membranes. Chop egg whites. Blanch the almonds and cut into thin, lengthwise strips. Mix these ingredients. Whip the cream very stiff, fold into the mayonnaise, add salt and paprika. Add to crab mixture. Serve on crisp lettuce; garnish with strips of green pepper or pimiento and top with riced egg yolk.

FISH SALAD

2 pounds halibut, poached
2 cups mayonnaise
4 hard-cooked eggs, chopped
1 cup chow-chow pickle

Poach fish, page 235, cool and flake. Mix with mayonnaise, add eggs, and chow-chow. Serve cold on lettuce. Serves 12.

SALMON SALAD

1 can (1 pound) salmon
1 cup chopped celery
1 chopped green pepper
mayonnaise

Remove skin and bones from fish. Flake fish, add the celery and pepper. Add mayonnaise to moisten. Serve on lettuce, with more dressing. Garnish with radishes, tomato wedges, or olives.

TUNA SALAD

Substitute 2 cans tuna (6½ or 7 ounces each) for salmon in recipe preceding.

HERRING FILLET SALAD

Serve fillets of herring on lettuce on platter, garnished with hard-cooked eggs, slices of pickled beets and watercress. Or serve with sour cream and sliced onions.

HERRING SALAD WITH BEETS

½ dozen milter herring
1 cup vinegar
½ pound cold veal roast
2 heaping cupfuls apples
1½ cup beets, pickled
¼ cup onions
½ cup pickles
2 stalks celery
½ cup cold boiled potatoes
1 cup almonds
2 tablespoons horseradish
1 cup granulated sugar
4 hard-cooked eggs, sliced
2 tablespoons chopped parsley

Soak herring overnight, skin and take out all the bones. Rub the milt through a colander with some of the vinegar. Chop all ingredients but eggs, add milt and mix thoroughly. Decorate with hard-cooked eggs and parsley.

Or, heap salad on platter, rub yolks of eggs through a fine sieve and chop whites; decorate the mound of salad with alternate strips of white and yellow.

HERRING SALAD

4 hard-cooked eggs
vinegar
3 herrings
3 apples
3 boiled potatoes
½ cup mixed nuts
¼ cup chopped, cooked veal
1 pickle
1 small onion
pepper
¼ cup sugar
a few capers

Mash the egg yolks and mix with a little vinegar, chop the egg whites with the remaining ingredients and mix all together. Veal may be omitted.

LOBSTER SALAD

Cut cold, boiled lobster meat into small pieces. Marinate in French Dressing; serve on lettuce leaves; top with mayonnaise and garnish with lobster claws, olives, hard-cooked eggs and capers.

SHRIMP SALAD

2 pounds cooked, shelled shrimp
French Dressing
1 cup diced celery
½ cup mayonnaise
lettuce

Marinate the shrimp in the French Dressing for several hours. Add celery and mayonnaise. Serve on crisp lettuce.

SHRIMP AND CUCUMBER SALAD

Cut cooked, shelled shrimp in pieces and marinate in French Dressing to cover for several hours. Add an equal amount of chilled cubes of peeled cucumbers. Decorate with whole shrimp and sliced cucumber.

SHRIMP AND PINEAPPLE SALAD

6 slices pineapple
lettuce
1 large green pepper
1½ pounds boiled shrimp, chopped
French Dressing

Place slice of pineapple on lettuce; on top of this place ½-inch ring of green pepper. Fill center of pepper with shrimp. Cover with French Dressing, and serve cold.

SHAD ROE AND CUCUMBER SALAD

1 shad roe
1 slice onion
1 bay leaf
1 tablespoon vinegar
French Dressing
2 fresh cucumbers
mayonnaise
lettuce

Simmer shad roe 20 minutes in salted water with onion, bay leaf, and vinegar. Cool, cut in cubes and marinate in French Dressing; add one cucumber, peeled and diced, and mayonnaise to moisten. Place salad on lettuce leaves; garnish with the other cucumber, sliced.

FRUIT SALADS

Some fruit salads are suitable for serving as an appetizer first course, or to accompany the main course. Others make an excellent main course for a light luncheon or supper, or can be served as dessert, without lettuce or other greens, in smaller portions. Choose the dressing accordingly; the same salad can often serve as entrée or dessert, depending on whether it is dressed with a spicy French dressing or a sweet mayonnaise dressing with whipped cream folded into it.

FANCY FRUIT SALAD

head lettuce
pineapple slices
grapefruit, in sections
red apples, or persimmons
peaches, halves
maraschino cherries

Arrange a ¼-inch slice of head lettuce cut crosswise on each serving plate. Or use shredded lettuce. Place pineapple on lettuce and top with alternate sections of grapefruit and red-skinned apples or persimmons. In center place peach, cut side down. Place cherry on top of peach. Serve cold with desired fruit salad dressing. Or alternate fruits on shredded lettuce.

TROPICAL FRUIT SALAD

Arrange unbroken sections of grapefruit with half that quantity of orange sections and pineapple cut in strips. Serve ice cold with Grape Juice or Wine Dressing.

FRUIT SALAD IN ORANGE CUPS

3 oranges
½ pound grapes
½ cup pineapple, chopped
sugar to taste
juice of 1 lemon
3 bananas

Cut the oranges in half crosswise, remove pulp and membrane, reserve the shells. Remove seeds from grapes. Mix orange pulp, grapes, and pineapple, sprinkle with sugar, add lemon juice, and chill for several hours. Before serving add sliced bananas, and walnut meats if desired. Fill orange shells with mixture. Serve with any fruit salad dressing.

AVOCADO SALAD

Wash avocado. Cut in half. Remove stone. With a small vegetable cutter scoop out balls. Spread the remaining pulp evenly. Fill the shells almost to the top with grapefruit sections or pineapple pieces; then place the avocado balls over this. Surround each half with watercress or shredded lettuce. Serve with French Dressing or Lemon Cream Dressing.

AVOCADO PINEAPPLE SALAD

1 avocado
2 slices pineapple, fresh or canned
lettuce
1 teaspoon salt
¼ teaspoon paprika
2 tablespoons lemon juice
1 teaspoon lime juice

Peel avocado and cut pulp in small pieces. Cut

pineapple in cubes. Arrange on crisp lettuce. Mix the rest of ingredients and pour over fruit.

Or cut the avocado in half, pare, remove stone, fill center with pineapple and pour French Dressing over all.

BANANA SALAD

Peel bananas, cut in half lengthwise, roll in lemon juice. Serve on lettuce, cover with mayonnaise, to which whipped cream has been added. Sprinkle with chopped nuts.

BUTTERFLY SALAD

 pineapple slices
 lettuce
 ⅛ pound candied fruit, cut fine
 ⅛ pound pistachio nuts
 asparagus tips
 Fruit Salad French Dressing, page 378

For each serving arrange on shredded lettuce a slice of canned pineapple, cut in half, the rounded edges together. Sprinkle with bits of candied fruit and pistachio nuts. Place asparagus tips sprinkled with paprika in center of pineapple for the body and serve with dressing.

Or, sprinkle wings with chopped green and red peppers or with parsley and canned pimiento, chopped fine, and mold cottage cheese to form head and body. Use blossom end of cloves for eyes and sprinkle with paprika.

CANDLESTICK SALAD

Place a slice of canned pineapple on lettuce on each plate for base of candlestick. Place half a banana cut crosswise in the center of pineapple to form candle; half of a cherry placed on top of banana represents the flame. Make handle for the candlestick with a slice of lemon rind. Serve with desired dressing.

GRAPEFRUIT AND MÁLAGA GRAPE SALAD

Peel grapefruit, carefully remove the pulp in sections and place in measuring cup. Combine with half this measure of Málaga grapes, halved and seeded. Serve cold in center of any molded gelatin ring, with mayonnaise to which whipped cream has been added.

MELON SALAD

Cut melon in half; remove seeds. Scoop pulp into balls, or cut in 1-inch slices leaving shell intact. Different varieties of melon may be combined. Refill scooped-out shells with melon balls. Garnish with berries or cherries. Place on lettuce and serve with any fruit salad dressing. Or, marinate melon balls for several hours in lemon juice or sherry; serve in shells.

BUNCH OF GRAPES SALAD

 8 canned pear halves
 2 packages cream cheese
 ¼ cup mayonnaise
 1 or 2 bunches green grapes
 1 head lettuce

Drain pears well. Cover rounded side with cheese, mashed and moistened with mayonnaise. Cut grapes in halves, seed them; press grapes close together on the covered pears. Chill thoroughly. Serve on grape leaves or crisp lettuce leaves, with any desired dressing.

CRESCENT HONEYDEW MELON SALAD

Cut honeydew melon lengthwise into 6 crescents. Decorate with watermelon balls, dark cherries, berries. Garnish with a sprig of fresh mint leaves frosted with confectioners sugar. Serve with wedge of lemon and any fruit salad dressing.

ORANGE SALAD

 6 oranges
 ½ cup grapefruit juice
 lettuce
 ¼ cup pecan nuts
 ¼ cup pineapple cubes
 ¼ cup strawberries, cut up, or maraschino cherries
 Lemon Cream Dressing, page 070

Peel oranges; remove membranes. Sprinkle with grapefruit juice, chill. Serve on lettuce; place the nuts and cut-up fruits on top. Serve with Lemon Cream Dressing.

ORANGE, GRAPEFRUIT AND AVOCADO SALAD

Arrange orange and grapefruit sections, alternately with avocados, pared and sliced, on lettuce. Make the following dressing: grind to a powder or pound to a paste 1 tablespoon each of pecans and blanched almonds. Add ½ teaspoon each salt and paprika and beat well with 2 tablespoons each of lemon juice and oil. Cover fruit and avocado with dressing. Decorate with pomegranate seeds.

PEACH SALAD

Arrange halves of large peaches, hollow side up, on lettuce or endive. Chop hearts of celery and almonds; moisten with mayonnaise and fill cavity of each peach. Cover, if desired, with another half peach, top with mayonnaise and over this a soft cranberry jelly.

GINGER PEAR SALAD

Fill centers of canned pear halves with preserved

ginger cut fine, or with chopped walnuts, celery and apple or with cream cheese balls rolled in chopped nuts. Place on crisp lettuce. Surround with whipped cream garnished with thin slices of preserved ginger.

STUFFED PEAR SALAD

Fill centers of canned pear halves with moistened and seasoned cream cheese. Place the two halves together to form a whole pear. Stand upright on lettuce leaves, surrounded with watercress. Serve with any desired fruit salad dressing.

PORCUPINE PEAR SALAD

Drain large, whole, canned pears, cover with Grape Juice or Wine Fruit Salad Dressing, chill for several hours. When ready to serve, stick 2 cloves to represent eyes, one on each side near stem end; to represent quills, stick browned, blanched almonds cut into strips at equal distances over top and sides. Place on crisp lettuce; serve with more dressing.

PINEAPPLE BASKETS FOR SALAD DRESSING

Trim the leafy stalk at the top of a fresh pineapple, leaving the handsomest leaves intact. Make two cuts halfway down through the pineapple, one on each side of the stalk. Then cut crosswise from each side to the end of the first cuts, and remove the wedges. Scoop out the fruit pulp, leaving a thickish handle and a hollow basket. Fill basket with Pineapple Cream Dressing. Arrange basket in center of platter; surround with cut-up fruit mixture including the pineapple pulp.

PINEAPPLE BOATS

Take off the leafy stalk of a large, fresh pineapple by twisting back and forth, then set it aside. Cut the pineapple once lengthwise, and each half again into two or three lengthwise parts, according to size of pineapple and number of persons served. Cut and scoop out meat carefully in cubes, leaving the hollow shell intact. Chill. When ready to serve, mix pineapple cubes with French Dressing. Fill boats with the mixture. Place the leafy stalk upright in center of large platter. Arrange boats around it. Place Cheese Bonbons on crisp lettuce leaves between the boats.

PINEAPPLE SALAD

Arrange pineapple slices on lettuce leaves. Arrange 5 thick strips of pimiento on top of pineapple from center to represent a flower; fill center with riced cream or cottage cheese; sprinkle with paprika. Serve cold with French Dressing.

PINEAPPLE AND TOMATO SALAD

On top of a slice of canned pineapple, place half of a small, peeled tomato, rounded side up. Fill pastry tube with cream cheese mixed with a little cream and decorate the base of the tomato. Garnish with watercress. Serve with French Dressing.

PINEAPPLE AND CUCUMBER SALAD

Mix 2 cups diced pineapple and 2 cups finely diced cucumber with mayonnaise. Serve on crisp lettuce and decorate with chopped red and green pepper.

STUFFED PRUNE SALAD

    1 pound large prunes
    ¼ pound pecan nut meats
    1 head lettuce
    mayonnaise

Soak large prunes overnight in warm water or wine to cover. Bring slowly to a boil; drain, remove pits, stuff with 2 or 3 nuts. Or, fill with seasoned cream cheese. Chill. Serve on lettuce with mayonnaise or French Dressing.

BLACK-EYED SUSAN SALAD

Arrange orange or grapefruit sections like petals on individual salad plates. Fill centers with chopped dates and walnuts. Serve with French Dressing.

WALDORF SALAD

    2 cups celery, diced
    2 cups apples, diced, but not peeled
    mayonnaise
    1 cup pecan and walnut meats, broken
    lettuce

Mix diced celery and apple with mayonnaise. Fold in the nuts. Serve on lettuce.

MOLDED GELATIN SALADS

Salads may be molded with aspic jelly made with stock; or with tomato aspic made with tomato juice and gelatin; or with prepared tomato aspic or gelatin mixtures which are already flavored.

Rinse mold with cold water before putting in gelatin mixtures. See General Rules for Making Gelatin on page 201.

If mold is to be decorated, pour in dissolved gelatin to a depth of ½ inch and chill. Chill the remaining gelatin until it begins to thicken. When gelatin in the mold is set, place fruits, vegetables, etc., in desired position in the mold. Cover decorations with a little of the thickened gelatin. Mix desired filling with the remaining gelatin and fill mold carefully. Chill until ready to use.

Basic Rings and Molds for Salads

ASPIC JELLY

4 cups Clear Soup Stock, page 393
3 envelopes gelatin, unflavored
1 cup cold water
½ cup sherry

Heat clarified fish or meat stock and adjust seasoning to taste, if necessary, with salt, pepper, celery seed or lemon peel. Strain and cool. Skim fat from top. Heat stock to boiling again. Soften gelatin in cold water, add hot soup and stir over low heat until gelatin dissolves. Add wine. Pour into wet or lightly greased pans or molds and chill until firm. This aspic may be molded or cut into shapes to use as a garnish, or chopped or stirred with a fork, or it may be used to mold other ingredients for a salad.

SALAD BASE WITH UNFLAVORED GELATIN

2 envelopes gelatin, unflavored
1 cup cold water
2 cups boiling water
juice of 1 lemon
1 teaspoon salt
½ cup sugar
¼ cup vinegar

Soak gelatin in cold water 5 minutes. Add 2 cups boiling water, stir until dissolved; add the rest of ingredients. Cool. When gelatin begins to thicken and is syrupy, add 3 cups of any salad mixture, below. Turn into mold and chill until firm. Unmold and serve with desired dressing. Any fruit syrup or sweet pickle syrup may be used in place of 1 cup water.

SALAD BASE WITH FLAVORED GELATIN

Pour 1 cup boiling water over 1 package flavored gelatin dessert mixture. Stir until dissolved. Add 1 cup cold water. Or, use 1 cup boiling water and 1 cup fruit juice or wine and water. Chill. When jelly begins to thicken, add desired salad mixture. Pour into mold. Chill until firm. Unmold to serve, garnish as desired, and serve with dressing.

QUICK TOMATO ASPIC

Combine 2 envelopes unflavored gelatin softened in ½ cup cold tomato juice or vegetable juice cocktail with 3½ cups well-seasoned hot tomato juice or vegetable juice cocktail. Stir over low heat until gelatin is dissolved. Pour into ring mold or into flat pan and chill until set. Unmold to serve or cut into squares. Serve on lettuce leaves with mayonnaise, or with meat salads.

TOMATO ASPIC

2 cans tomatoes or 8 medium tomatoes
2 small onions, chopped fine
6 cloves
1 bay leaf
1 teaspoon salt
¼ teaspoon pepper
2 envelopes unflavored gelatin
½ cup cold water
grated rind and juice of 1 lemon
2 tablespoons vinegar

Boil tomatoes, onions and spices until tomatoes are soft; strain. Or use canned tomato soup. Measure 2½ cups; reheat to the boiling point. Soften the gelatin in ½ cup water for a few minutes; then add the boiling tomato soup, lemon and vinegar and stir over low heat until gelatin is dissolved. Pour into small molds or ring mold. Chill until firm. Serve on lettuce leaves with mayonnaise, or fill with chicken or other salad.

MAYONNAISE RING

1 envelope unflavored gelatin
¼ cup cold water
juice of 1 lemon
½ cup boiling water
1 cup mayonnaise
1 teaspoon chopped pimiento
1 teaspoon tarragon vinegar
1 teaspoon Worcestershire sauce
1 teaspoon grated onion
1 cup heavy cream

Soak the gelatin in the cold water. Add lemon juice and boiling water and stir over low heat until the gelatin is dissolved. Combine mayonnaise, pimiento, vinegar, Worcestershire sauce, and onion; add gelatin. When cold, fold in the stiffly beaten cream. Pour into moistened mold, chill until firm. Fill with any desired salad mixture.

MINT RING

2 envelopes unflavored gelatin
½ cup cold water
2½ cups boiling water
½ cup mint leaves
½ cup sugar
½ cup lemon juice
green vegetable coloring
⅛ teaspoon salt

Soak gelatin in cold water 5 minutes. Pour boiling water over mint leaves, let stand covered 5 minutes, strain. Reheat water to the boiling point and pour over gelatin; add sugar; stir until dissolved. Add lemon juice, coloring, salt. Pour into ring mold, chill until firm. Serve with mayonnaise in center and surround with any desired fruit salad.

GRAPEFRUIT RING

2 envelopes unflavored gelatin
½ cup cold water
1 cup boiling water
1½ cups sugar
salt
2 cups grapefruit juice
½ cup lime juice

Soak gelatin in cold water 5 minutes. Add boiling water, sugar and a little salt and stir until thoroughly dissolved. Cool, add fruit juices. Pour in ring mold. Set aside for several hours to chill until set. Serve with Lemon Cream Dressing in center, surround with any desired fruit salad.

Or, use ½ cup orange juice and ¼ cup lemon juice in place of lime.

CHEESE RING

½ pound Cheddar or cottage cheese
salt and paprika
1 envelope unflavored gelatin
¼ cup cold water
2 teaspoons chives or green peppers, chopped
2 cups cream, whipped

Grate the Cheddar cheese or sieve the cottage cheese until smooth. Use either one, or half of each kind. Season to taste. Soak gelatin in cold water. Dissolve over hot water. Cool. Combine all ingredients and beat until light. Pour into ring mold and chill. Remove from mold, serve with mayonnaise and any desired fruit salad.

CHEDDAR CREAM CHEESE RING

1 envelope unflavored gelatin
¼ cup cold water
6 ounces cream cheese
1 cup heavy cream, whipped
½ cup Cheddar cheese
salt, paprika

Soak gelatin in the cold water and dissolve over boiling water. Moisten cream cheese with a little cream and stir until smooth. Add Cheddar cheese, bits of green and red peppers, or candied cherries, whipped cream and gelatin. Season and turn into ring mold. Chill until firm. Fill ring with any fruit salad, and serve with Blackstone Salad Dressing.

TOMATO-COTTAGE CHEESE RING

Rice 1½ pounds dry cottage cheese (pot cheese), season well with salt and paprika and place in the bottom of a ring mold. Make Tomato Aspic, cool slightly and pour it over the cheese; chill. Serve on lettuce; garnish with hard-cooked eggs cut in lengthwise sections. Place a bowl of mayonnaise in center of ring.

TOMATO-CREAM CHEESE RING

2 envelopes unflavored gelatin
½ cup cold water
2½ cups tomato soup
6 ounces cream cheese
salt
1 cup heavy cream

Soak gelatin in cold water 5 minutes. Dissolve in 1 cup boiling soup. Soften the cheese with 1½ cups cold soup. Combine the two mixtures. Season with salt to taste. Cool and when it begins to thicken, fold in the cream, whipped stiff. Pour into ring mold and chill until firm. When ready to serve, remove to platter and fill with Chicken Salad.

FROZEN CHEESE RING

12 ounces cream cheese
2 cups milk
salt and paprika
1 cup heavy cream, whipped

In top of double boiler, mash cheese and gradually stir in the milk. Place over boiling water, and stir until the mixture is smooth and thick as mayonnaise. Remove from heat. Add salt and paprika to taste, stir until cool; add the whipped cream. Place in a ring mold and freeze until firm. Serve with Thousand Island Dressing and surround with pineapple slices and peach halves.

HORSERADISH AND CHEESE RING

2 cups boiling water
1 package lime-flavored gelatin
12 ounces cottage cheese
1 teaspoon salt
4 tablespoons prepared horseradish
1 tablespoon mayonnaise
1 teaspoon grated onion

Pour boiling water over gelatin and stir to dissolve. Put cheese through strainer, add salt to taste. When gelatin mixture is cool, add cheese and other ingredients. Beat well with rotary beater. A little green coloring may be added. When slightly thick, put into mold. Unmold and serve surrounded with seafood.

SOUR CREAM RING

2 envelopes unflavored gelatin
½ cup cold water
½ cup boiling water
4 cups thick sour cream
3 tablespoons vinegar
3 tablespoons sugar
1 cucumber, diced
4 tablespoons chives, cut

Soak gelatin in cold water, add boiling water, stir over low heat until dissolved. When cool, add rest of ingredients. Put in ring mold, chill until firm. Serve with any fruit salad dressing or any fruit salad.

FROZEN CHEESE FOR SALADS

    6 ounces cream cheese
    1 cup heavy cream, whipped
    ½ cup chopped olives
    ¼ cup chopped pimientos
    1 teaspoon lemon juice
    salt and cayenne pepper
    1 envelope unflavored gelatin
    ¼ cup cold water

Mash cheese, add the whipped cream, olives, pimientos, lemon juice and seasonings. Soften gelatin in cold water and dissolve over hot water. Add cheese mixture, put into mold rinsed in cold water, and freeze. Serve with salad.

Molded Vegetable Salads

MOLDED BEET SALAD

    1 package lemon-flavored gelatin
    1 cup boiling water
    1 can (1 pound) diced beets
    ⅛ teaspoon salt
    1 tablespoon vinegar
    1 cup celery, diced
    1 small onion, minced
    2 teaspoons prepared horseradish

Dissolve gelatin in boiling water; add juice drained from the beets. When gelatin thickens and is syrupy, add remaining ingredients. Pour into mold and chill until firm.

MOLDED CELERY, CABBAGE AND PEPPER SALAD

Combine 2 cups of diced celery, 1 cup shredded cabbage and 1 canned sweet red pepper, finely cut. Add to Gelatin Salad Base and mold as directed.

MOLDED RED AND WHITE CABBAGE SALAD

Prepare Salad Base with Unflavored Gelatin. Mix 1½ cups shredded red cabbage with ½ of the cooled mixture. Put in bottom of mold and chill until almost set. Mix 1½ cups of white, shredded cabbage with the rest of the gelatin; pour over first layer and chill until set.

MOLDED CUCUMBER SALAD

Pare and dice 2 cups cucumber; add 1 cup diced celery, 1 green pepper, cut fine. Mix with Gelatin Salad Base. Add green vegetable coloring.

FROZEN VEGETABLE SALAD

    1 tablespoon chopped onion
    ¼ cup chopped pimiento
    ¼ cup chopped green peppers
    3 cups tomatoes
    1 envelope unflavored gelatin
    3 tablespoons cold water
    3 tablespoons vinegar
    1 tablespoon lemon juice
    1 teaspoon horseradish
    ¾ teaspoon salt
    few grains red pepper

Combine first 4 ingredients and simmer 5 minutes. Soak gelatin in cold water, add to hot mixture, and stir to dissolve. Add vinegar, lemon juice, grated horseradish, salt and pepper. Place in molds. Chill until firm. Serve on lettuce and top with mayonnaise.

GOLDEN GLOW SALAD

    1 cup boiling water
    1 package lemon-flavored gelatin
    1 cup canned pineapple juice
    2 cups grated raw carrots
    1 cup drained crushed pineapple

Pour 1 cup boiling water over gelatin. Stir until dissolved. Add pineapple juice. Cool and when it begins to thicken, add the carrots and pineapple and pour into a mold. Chill until firm. Serve with mayonnaise. Surround with watermelon balls and pitted black cherries.

PINEAPPLE AND CUCUMBER SALAD RING

    Salad Base with Unflavored Gelatin, page 367
    ½ teaspoon green vegetable coloring
    1 cup chopped cucumber
    2 cups crushed canned pineapple
    bits of pimiento

Prepare Gelatin Salad Base. Color green. When it begins to thicken, add cucumber, pineapple and pimiento. Pour into ring mold. Chill until firm. Serve on platter with a bowl of Lemon Cream Fruit Salad Dressing in the center and surround with pears, peaches or pineapple.

Molded Fruit Salads

JELLIED FRUIT SALADS

Make Salad Base with Flavored Gelatin, page 367, and just when it begins to thicken, add any drained berries or fruit, or fruit combination. Fill molds and chill until firm. Serve on lettuce with salad dressing.

MOLDED APPLE OR CHERRY, CELERY AND NUT SALAD

1 cup apples, diced, or 2-pound can pitted white

cherries, 1 cup celery, cut in small pieces, ½ cup broken nut meats. Drain cherries, use syrup with water to dissolve gelatin, following instructions for Salad Base with Unflavored Gelatin. Chill until mixture begins to thicken; add fruit, celery, nuts.

AVOCADO RING

1 cup boiling water
1 package lime- or lemon-flavored gelatin
1 cup mayonnaise
3 tablespoons lemon juice
1 teaspoon salt
1 cup mashed avocado
1 cup heavy cream, whipped, or
    1 cup sour cream

Pour boiling water over gelatin, stir until dissolved. Let thicken, then add other ingredients. Pour into large ring mold. Chill until firm. Serve on lettuce surrounded with grapefruit sections and Stuffed Prunes, and any desired salad dressing.

BING CHERRY RING

4 envelopes unflavored gelatin
3 cups orange juice
2 cans (1 pound, 13 ounces each) pitted bing
    cherries
walnuts
2 cups cherry juice
½ cup lemon juice
1 cup sugar
pinch of salt
1½ cups sherry
few drops red coloring

Soak gelatin in 1 cup orange juice. Drain cherrie reserving the juice. Stuff each cherry with ½ w nut. Heat cherry juice, the remaining orange jui lemon juice, sugar, and salt to the boiling po Add gelatin, stir until dissolved, add sherry and red coloring. Cool. When mixture thickens fold in cherries, place in large ring mold; chill until firm. Serves 12.

CRANBERRY RING

1 can crushed pineapple
1 package lemon-flavored gelatin
1 cup ground raw cranberries
grated orange rind
1 envelope unflavored gelatin

Drain pineapple, add enough water to pineapple juice to make 2 cups liquid. Boil. Pour over gelatin. Stir until dissolved, then add fruit and orange rind. Pour in mold and chill until firm.

Special dressings for fruit salads will be found on page 378. Mayonnaises, page 374, and cream dressings, page 377, are also appropriate to serve with fruit salads.

FROZEN FRUIT SALAD RING

2 cups mixed fruit
6 maraschino cherries, cut fine
1½ cups Boiled Dressing, page 375
1½ cups heavy cream, whipped

Drain and dice the fruit. Make Boiled Dressing, using fruit juice in place of the water. Cool, fold in the whipped cream and the fruit. Place in ring mold. Freeze until firm. Serve with Orange Cream Dressing and any desired fruit.

GINGER ALE SALAD RING

1 envelope unflavored gelatin
2 tablespoons cold water
⅓ cup boiling water
1 cup   er ale
¼ cup   n juice
2 t ble
fe
¼

. Add boiling
d ginger ale,
mixture begins
gredients. Place
erve with fruit
e substituted.

more water to cover; cove   until tender but not broken. Drai   2 cups of juice. Bring prune juice and sugar boil; remove from heat. Add gelatin softened in ¼ cup cold water and stir to dissolve. Pit the prunes. Arrange in large ring mold, add gelatin mixture and chill until firm. Pour Cheese Ring Mixture on firm prune gelatin. Chill until firm. Serve with Lemon Cream Dressing.

Molded Chicken and Meat Salads

CHICKEN SALAD RING

1 envelope unflavored gelatin
½ cup cold water
Cooked Cream Salad Dressing, page 377
1 cup heavy cream, whipped
2 cups diced, cooked chicken
1 cup diced celery

Soften gelatin in ½ cup cold water. Add to Cream Salad Dressing and heat gently, stirring until gelatin is dissolved. When cool, fold in whipped cream, chicken and celery. Pour into mold. Chill until firm. Serve with any fruit salad and mayonnaise.

MOLDED HAM OR TONGUE SALAD

Mix 2 cups of diced, cold boiled ham or tongue, 4 pimientos, cut fine, with ¼ cup chopped sweet pickles. Garnish with slices of hard-cooked eggs. Combine with Aspic Jelly. Chill until set. Serves 10.

MOLDED SWEETBREAD SALAD

Combine 2 cups cold, cooked sweetbreads, diced; ½ cup hard-cooked eggs, sliced; ½ cup sliced olives; capers; broken nut meats. Asparagus tips may be used, but they must be carefully placed in the jelly just as it thickens. Mix with Aspic Jelly. Chill until set. Serves 10.

MOLDED CHICKEN SALAD

Substitute chicken for sweetbreads in preceding recipe.

JELLIED MEAT LOAF

2 envelopes unflavored gelatin
¼ cup cold water
2 cups hot soup stock or diluted gravy
2 cups cooked chopped meat
1 teaspoon chopped onion
2 tablespoons chopped celery
a little green or red pepper

Soften gelatin in cold water 2 minutes and dissolve it in hot soup. Cool until mixture begins to thicken, add meat and vegetables. Place in mold and chill several hours until set. Remove from mold and cut into slices.

JELLIED VEAL LOAF (SULZ)

2 pounds veal shank or knuckle
1 small carrot
1 piece celery root
1 small onion
1 tablespoon chopped parsley
salt and pepper
2 quarts water
2 hard-cooked eggs

Place seasoned meat and vegetables in water in deep kettle. Boil slowly until meat falls from bones. Strain the stock. Chop meat and vegetables. Place in mold garnished with slices of egg. Boil the stock until reduced one-half and add to meat. Pour into a loaf pan and chill until firm. Serve in slices.

PRESSED OR JELLIED CHICKEN

See page 318.

JELLIED CHICKEN MOUSSE

See page 318.

Molded Fish and Seafood Salads

MOLDED FISH, CELERY AND OLIVE SALAD

Combine 2 cups cold cooked halibut, or a 1-pound can of red salmon, flaked, and 1 cup finely sliced stuffed olives, mixed with diced pickle or cucumber, celery, sweet red peppers, beets, 10 capers. Mix with Gelatin Salad Base and chill until set.

MOLDED FISH WITH CUCUMBER SAUCE

1½ pounds cold poached halibut
2 envelopes gelatin, unflavored
½ cup cold fish stock or water
1½ cups boiling fish stock
¾ cup mayonnaise
2 cups heavy cream, whipped

Follow recipe for Poached Fish. Bone halibut and cut or break into ½-inch pieces. Soak gelatin in the cold fish stock or water, add the boiling fish stock, and stir over low heat until dissolved. Chill. When mixture begins to thicken, add the mayonnaise. Beat with a rotary beater until frothy, then fold in the cream, and the halibut. Place in mold. Chill until firm. Serve with Cucumber Sauce.

LAYERED FISH MOLD

2 pounds halibut or red snapper
1 envelope unflavored gelatin
¼ cup cold water
juice of 1 lemon
1 cup boiling water (scant)
¼ cup port wine or sherry
1 tablespoon each of pimiento and pickles in thin slices
1 tablespoon capers
1 carrot and pickled beet, cut fine
1 cup Sour Cream Salad Dressing or mayonnaise

Poach fish, bone and flake. Soak gelatin in cold water a few minutes with lemon juice, then add the boiling water and wine, and stir until dissolved. Cool and when mixture begins to thicken, place a few tablespoons in mold, put in a layer of fish, a sprinkling of the mixed vegetables and spread over this a thin layer of Sour Cream Salad Dressing, or mayonnaise. Add a few spoonfuls of the gelatin mixture to cover. Continue until mold is nearly filled, with gelatin on top. Chill until firm.

SALMON SALAD MOLD

1 can (1 pound) salmon
½ tablespoon salt
1½ tablespoons sugar
1 teaspoon dry mustard
¾ cup scalded milk
1½ tablespoons melted butter
2 egg yolks, beaten
¼ cup hot vinegar
1 envelope unflavored gelatin
2 tablespoons cold water

Remove skin and bones from salmon; flake. Cook dry ingredients and milk in a double boiler for 5 minutes. Add the melted butter, the yolks beaten with 1 tablespoon water, and the hot vinegar. Stir and cook for 1 minute. Remove from heat. Add gelatin softened in 2 tablespoons cold water. Stir until dissolved, add the salmon; place in mold and chill until firm. Serve with Cucumber Sauce.

SEAFOOD ASPIC

2 envelopes unflavored gelatin
¾ cup cold soup stock
1 cup boiling soup stock
juice of 1 large lemon
½ cup chili sauce
salt to taste
2 chopped dill pickles or sweet pickles
1 pound cooked shrimp, lobster or crab meat, diced
1 cup celery, diced

Soften gelatin in cold soup or water, add boiling soup and stir until dissolved. Cool slightly, add lemon juice, chili sauce and salt. When it begins to thicken, add the remaining ingredients, pour into mold and chill until firm. Serve with mayonnaise.

SEAFOOD SALAD IN FISH MOLD

½ cup small ripe olives
1 small can pimientos
1 pound crab meat
1 pound shrimp
1 pound halibut
2 envelopes unflavored gelatin
¼ cup cold fish liquid
3 cups boiling fish liquid

Cut olives in thin slices, then in half circles and place in fish mold in spaces representing scales. Cut pimientos in fine long strips and fit into spaces for fins. Place bit of pimiento in center of stem end of slice of olive to represent eye of fish. Shred and bone crab meat; place bright red pieces about the head. Pile rest of the crab meat evenly over all.

Boil and shell shrimp, cut in ½-inch cubes; boil halibut, strain and reserve liquid; cut fish into small cubes. Fill the mold with alternate layers of shrimp and halibut, being careful not to disturb the decorations. Soak gelatin in cold fish liquid, add boiling liquid, stir until dissolved. Pour into mold. Chill until firm. Serve with Tartar Sauce as a salad or appetizer. If desired, use only crab and halibut or crab and shrimp.

Cheese Garnishes for Salads

WALNUT CREAMS

Season cream cheese with salt, pepper, and paprika. Roll 1 tablespoon into a ball; press half a walnut, large pecan, or filbert on top.

STUFFED DATES

Mash cream cheese, season with salt and paprika and moisten with a little cream. Slit dates, remove stones, and fill each cavity with cheese mixture, allowing it to show.

PECAN BALLS

3 ounces cream cheese
3 tablespoons butter
6 dashes Tabasco sauce
1 tablespoon cream
¼ teaspoon salt
chopped pecans

Mix ingredients well. Form into small balls and roll in chopped pecans.

STUFFED FIGS OR PRUNES

Slit steamed prunes, remove stones and proceed as for Stuffed Dates. Steam dried figs in double boiler, remove stems, cut in two equal parts, slit, and proceed as for Stuffed Dates.

CHEESE CARROTS

Grate ½ pound of fresh, yellow Cheddar cheese, season with paprika. Roll a heaping tablespoonful, and shape in form of carrot. Place a sprig of parsley in stem end and serve as a garnish with salad. Makes 15 carrots.

CHEESE CRAB APPLES

Grate ¼ pound American cheese. For each crab apple, take a heaping tablespoon of cheese. Roll and shape cheese to form the crab apple. Stick a clove at each end of crab apple, having head of clove show at one end, the stem at the other end. Sprinkle with paprika.

FIG AND NUT CREAM CHEESE

Mash ½ pound cream cheese, mix with ¼ pound chopped figs and ¼ pound chopped nuts, shape into loaf, chill several hours. Slice and serve on lettuce with any desired Salad Dressing, or form into balls and use as garnish.

VEGETABLE CREAM CHEESE

Mash 3 ounces cream cheese, season with salt and cayenne pepper, add 6 finely chopped olives, ½ pimiento chopped, and finely cut parsley; shape into loaf as above, or form into balls.

SALAD DRESSINGS

Salad dressings may be of a thin consistency, made by combining oil with vinegar or fruit juice; or they may be thick and creamy with the addition of eggs, cream, or cheese. Varied seasonings can accent the dressing, from sharp and tangy, for green salads or meats, fish or vegetable salads, to sweet for fruit and dessert salads.

An electric blender or mixer is useful for combining ingredients for creamy salad dressings and mayonnaises.

Flavored Vinegars for Salad Dressings

GARLIC VINEGAR

Add a clove of garlic to 1 pint cider vinegar. Let stand 8 days. Remove garlic and use the Garlic Vinegar in place of plain vinegar when making salad dressings. For Tarragon, Mint, Celery or Dill Vinegars, see page 437.

OIL AND VINEGAR DRESSINGS

FRENCH DRESSING

¼ teaspoon salt
⅛ teaspoon paprika
⅛ teaspoon white pepper
1½ tablespoons vinegar
1½ tablespoons lemon juice
6 tablespoons salad oil

Beat all ingredients with rotary beater until well blended. Serve cold and use to marinate boiled meats, vegetables and salads. If desired, add a few drops of onion juice, or rub salad bowl with slice of garlic or onion. Shake well before using.

GARLIC FRENCH DRESSING

⅛ cup sugar
⅛ teaspoon cayenne pepper
1 teaspoon paprika
1 teaspoon salt
¼ cup lemon juice
½ cup tarragon vinegar
1 cup olive or vegetable oil
⅔ cup catsup
1 medium onion, grated
1 clove garlic cut into 1 pieces

Combine ingredients in order given; shake well. Remove garlic before serving.

CELERY SEED FRENCH DRESSING

¼ cup sugar
1 teaspoon dry mustard
1 teaspoon paprika
1 teaspoon celery seed
1 teaspoon salt
5 tablespoons tarragon vinegar
3 tablespoons lemon juice
1 tablespoon grated onion
⅔ cup olive oil

Mix dry ingredients. Add vinegar and lemon juice, mixing thoroughly. Add onion, then olive oil gradually, stirring constantly. Shake well before using.

LORENZO DRESSING

⅔ cup olive oil
⅓ cup malt vinegar
1 teaspoon salt
dash of black pepper
½ cup chili sauce
1 cup chopped watercress

Stir all ingredients thoroughly. Chill and serve.

PAPRIKA TOMATO SOUP DRESSING

1 can condensed tomato soup
1 cup malt vinegar
1 cup oil
⅔ cup sugar
2 tablespoons prepared mustard
1 tablespoon salt
4 tablespoons paprika
½ teaspoon pepper

Mix in order given. Beat well with rotary beater. Keep refrigerated.

ROQUEFORT CHEESE SALAD DRESSING

¼ pound Roquefort cheese
4 tablespoons cream
4 tablespoons olive oil
salt
¼ teaspoon paprika
3 tablespoons lemon juice

Rub the cheese through a sieve, mix gradually with cream and olive oil, season, add lemon juice gradually, and mix until well blended.

VINAIGRETTE DRESSING

3 to 6 tablespons olive oil
3 tablespoons tarragon vinegar
1 hard-cooked egg, riced
paprika
1 teaspoon minced chives or
      ½ teaspoon onion juice
1 teaspoon salt
2 tablespoons chopped parsley
½ sweet red pepper, or canned pimiento, chopped

Combine ingredients and beat with rotary beater.

TOMATO SOUP DRESSING

1 can condensed tomato soup
½ cup tarragon vinegar
½ cup malt vinegar
2 teaspoons salt
½ teaspoon paprika
1 tablespoon Worcestershire sauce
½ cup oil
¼ cup sugar
½ teaspoon pepper
1 teaspoon mustard
1 clove of garlic
1 teaspoon grated onion

Mix thoroughly; shake well before using.

DIETER'S SALAD DRESSING

¼ teaspoon salt
¼ teaspoon mustard
⅛ teaspoon pepper
2 tablespoons sugar
1 tablespoon onion, chopped fine
2 tablespoons vinegar
2 tablespoons lemon juice

Mix all ingredients. Keep refrigerated.

MAYONNAISE AND COOKED DRESSINGS

THREE-MINUTE MAYONNAISE

1 teaspoon salt
¼ teaspoon dry mustard
speck of cayenne
1 teaspoon sugar
1 tablespoon lemon juice
1 tablespoon vinegar
1 egg, unbeaten
1 cup salad oil

Add lemon juice and vinegar to dry ingredients; mix. Add egg and ⅓ the oil, beat with rotary beater until mixture begins to thicken. Add another ⅓ cup of oil, beat 1 minute, add rest of the oil and beat 1 minute more.

MAYONNAISE

1 teaspoon dry mustard
1 teaspoon salt
1 teaspoon sugar
dash of cayenne pepper
2 egg yolks
1½ to 2 cups salad oil
1 tablespoon lemon juice
3 tablespoons tarragon vinegar

Have all ingredients and bowl cold. Put dry ingredients in mixing bowl. Add egg yolks, beat well with rotary beater. Pour in ¼ cup oil, drop by drop at first, then in a steady stream, beating constantly. Gradually add the lemon juice and vinegar and the remaining oil, beating between each addition until mixture is thoroughly blended and thick. Keep very cold.

If it should separate while mixing, beat a yolk of egg with 1 tablespoon of cold water and beat the separated mixture into it very slowly until thick.

LARGE QUANTITY MAYONNAISE
16 egg yolks
8 teaspoons dry mustard
6 teaspoons sugar
6 teaspoons salt
½ teaspoon cayenne
1 cup lemon juice
1 cup cider vinegar
1 gallon salad oil

Follow directions for Mayonnaise.

QUICK MAYONNAISE
PART 1
2 egg yolks, unbeaten
1½ teaspoons salt
1 teaspoon dry mustard
1 tablespoon sugar
few grains cayenne
2 tablespoons lemon juice
2 tablespoons tarragon vinegar
1 cup oil

Put above ingredients in mixing bowl, but do not stir.

PART 2
1 tablespoon butter
⅛ cup flour
1 cup boiling water

Melt butter, add flour, then add boiling water. Cook until thick and smooth, stirring constantly. Pour at once, piping hot, over ingredients in bowl. Beat rapidly with rotary beater until well blended.

MAYONNAISE WITH HARD-COOKED EGGS
3 hard-cooked egg yolks
1 teaspoon salt
⅛ teaspoon pepper
1 tablespoon sugar
1 raw egg yolk
1 teaspoon prepared mustard
1 teaspoon grated onion
juice of 1 lemon
2 tablespoons white vinegar
1 tablespoon oil

Mash and rub the cooked egg yolks until smooth, add the dry seasonings, then the raw yolk and the rest of the ingredients, except the oil; stir until smooth and add the oil, drop by drop, stirring constantly; keep chilled.

COOKED MAYONNAISE BASE
Measure equal amounts of egg yolks and vinegar.

Beat until smooth and cook over hot water until thick; pack in air-tight, sterilized glass jars. When ready to use, add salt, pepper, mustard, and onion juice and thin with cream. Add whipped cream for fruit salads.

BOILED MAYONNAISE DRESSING
2 tablespoons flour
2 tablespoons oil
⅛ cup vinegar
⅛ cup lemon juice
1 cup boiling water
2 egg yolks
½ teaspoon mustard
½ teaspoon salt
cayenne pepper
1 cup oil

Mix first four ingredients, add the boiling water. Boil 5 minutes, stirring constantly. Pour at once over the well-beaten yolks, stirring all the time. Add seasoning and cool. When cool, but not cold, beat in oil. Catsup, chili sauce, or whipped cream may be added before serving.

SOUR CREAM BOILED MAYONNAISE
1 teaspoon sugar
½ teaspoon salt
few grains cayenne pepper
½ teaspoon dry mustard
4 eggs
½ cup oil
2 tablespoons vinegar
1 tablespoon lemon juice
½ cup sour cream

Mix dry ingredients, add eggs, well beaten; stir well and cook in double boiler over boiling water; add alternately oil, vinegar and lemon, stirring constantly. When ready to serve, add cream.

BOILED DRESSING
3 tablespoons sugar
1 tablespoon flour
1 teaspoon salt
½ teaspoon dry mustard
⅛ teaspoon red pepper
1 tablespoon butter
½ cup vinegar
½ cup water
4 egg yolks

Mix the dry ingredients, then add the butter, vinegar and water; cook in double boiler until smooth. Beat the yolks. Add the hot mixture very gradually to the yolks, stirring constantly. Cook in double boiler until mixture thickens, stirring constantly. When ready to serve, add a little cream or lemon juice to thin it.

WITH OIL

If desired, beat in ½ cup oil with rotary beater. It will not separate.

TO PRESERVE BOILED DRESSING

Pack Boiled Dressing, above, in sterilized, air-tight containers, seal and store. Four times the recipe makes 3 pints.

Boiled dressings and mayonnaises do not freeze well, but they must be refrigerated unless packed as above.

FLUFFY CREAM DRESSING

    ½ cup sugar
    ½ teaspoon cornstarch
    ½ teaspoon mustard
    ¼ teaspoon salt
    ⅛ cup vinegar
    1 egg, slightly beaten
    1 cup heavy cream, whipped

Mix dry ingredients, add vinegar and egg, beat; cook slowly over boiling water until mixture coats the spoon. Before serving, add cream.

COOKED BUTTER CREAM DRESSING

    ½ teaspoon salt
    1 teaspoon flour
    1 teaspoon dry mustard
    1 teaspoon sugar
    2 tablespoons butter, melted
    2 egg yolks
    ¾ cup cream
    ¼ cup vinegar

Mix dry ingredients with the melted butter; beat yolks and cream. Combine the two mixtures, gradually add the vinegar. Cook in a double boiler until it thickens, stirring constantly.

HOT BACON DRESSING

    3 slices bacon
    ¼ cup vinegar
    ½ teaspoon salt
    1 teaspoon sugar

Cut bacon into small pieces. Cook slowly until crisp. Stir in vinegar and seasoning. Reheat and pour at once over lettuce, spinach or any salad greens.

HOT SALAD DRESSING

    2 teaspoons sugar
    ½ teaspoon salt
    ½ teaspoon mustard
    ⅛ teaspoon pepper
    ¼ cup vinegar
    ¼ cup water
    1 tablespoon butter
    1 teaspoon flour
    1 egg or egg yolk

Place the first 6 ingredients in saucepan and bring to a boil. Blend the butter and flour and gradually add to the boiling liquid bit by bit. Cook 5 minutes. Beat this gradually into the well-beaten yolk or whole egg. Mix while hot with cabbage or potatoes. 1 cup sweet or sour cream or buttermilk may be added.

Mayonnaise Variations

BLACKSTONE SALAD DRESSING

    1 cup mayonnaise
    ⅔ cup olive oil
    ⅛ cup vinegar
    3 tablespoons chili sauce
    3 pimientos
    1 tablespoon pearl onions
    ¼ teaspoon salt
    pepper to taste

Mix in the order given and serve cold over quartered head lettuce, tomatoes, etc.

THOUSAND ISLAND DRESSING

    2 tablespoons green peppers, cut fine
    2 tablespoons pimiento, cut fine
    1 teaspoon onion juice
    1 hard-cooked egg, chopped
    1 teaspoon Worcestershire sauce
    1 tablespoon catsup
    2 tablespoons chili sauce
    1 cup mayonnaise
    salt
    paprika
    ¾ cup whipped cream

Mix the first seven ingredients, add a little salt and paprika, blend thoroughly with the mayonnaise and fold in the cream. Serve cold.

GARGOYLE SAUCE

    1 cup mayonnaise
    1 teaspoon Worcestershire sauce
    3 tablespoons chili sauce
    ¼ teaspoon paprika
    1 teaspoon pearl onions
    ½ teaspoon chopped green peppers

Combine all ingredients, chill well, and serve with fish salads or tomato salads, or with seafood.

GREEN MOUSSELINE SAUCE

few sprigs tarragon
2 hard-cooked egg yolks
2 anchovy fillets
¼ cup Medium White Sauce, page 386
½ cup mayonnaise
1 teaspoon prepared mustard
¼ teaspoon onion juice
1 tablespoon chopped parsley
green vegetable coloring
¼ cup heavy cream, whipped

Soak the tarragon a few minutes in boiling water and drain. Pound or chop the tarragon with the yolks and anchovies and rub through a sieve. Add White Sauce, mayonnaise, seasoning, parsley and a little green coloring. Finally, fold in the cream. Serve cold with fish.

LINCOLN HOUSE SPECIAL DRESSING

Add ¾ cup Pepper Relish to 2 cups of mayonnaise; bottle and seal. Before using fold in few tablespoons of whipped cream.

RUSSIAN DRESSING

Mix equal parts of mayonnaise and chili sauce.

SHARP RUSSIAN DRESSING

1 tablespoon prepared mustard
3 tablespoons grated horseradish
3 tablespoons chili sauce
1 cup mayonnaise or French Dressing

Mix first three ingredients, stir into mayonnaise or French Dressing, and serve ice cold over head lettuce, cold vegetables or seafood.

CREAM SALAD DRESSINGS

UNCOOKED CREAM DRESSING

1 cup heavy sweet or sour cream
2 tablespoons lemon juice
2 tablespoons vinegar
1 tablespoon sugar
1 teaspoon salt
¼ teaspoon pepper
1 teaspoon prepared mustard, if desired

Beat cream with rotary beater until smooth, thick and light. Mix other ingredients together and gradually add to cream, beating all the while.

COOKED CREAM SALAD DRESSING

5 egg yolks, beaten
½ cup cream
⅛ teaspoon cayenne pepper
1½ teaspoon salt
1 teaspoon mustard
1 tablespoon flour
2 tablespoons sugar
¼ cup water
½ cup vinegar

Beat the yolks well and add cream. Mix the dry ingredients with water, add to the yolks and cream. Add vinegar. Cook in double boiler until smooth, stirring constantly.

HORSERADISH CREAM DRESSING

½ cup heavy cream
3 tablespoons vinegar
¼ teaspoon salt
few grains pepper
2 tablespoons grated horseradish

Beat cream until it begins to thicken, add vinegar gradually; continue beating until cream is stiff; add salt and pepper and fold in the horseradish.

CATSUP CREAM DRESSING

2 tablespoons olive oil
1 teaspoon salt
2 tablespoons sugar
2 tablespoons vinegar
½ cup tomato catsup
1 cup sour cream

Mix the oil, salt, sugar and vinegar together, then beat in the catsup and finally add the cream, beating it in gradually. Use for vegetables or fish salads.

EVAPORATED MILK DRESSING

⅓ cup vinegar
½ cup salad oil
⅔ cup evaporated milk
1 teaspoon dry mustard
½ teaspoon salt
few grains cayenne
1 egg yolk, unbeaten

Place ingredients in jar in the order named. Cover tightly and shake vigorously for two minutes. Chill.

DRESSINGS FOR FRUITS AND FRUIT SALADS

LEMON CREAM DRESSING

⅓ cup sugar
½ teaspoon salt
⅛ teaspoon paprika
2 eggs or 4 egg yolks, beaten
2 tablespoons lemon juice
⅓ cup water
2 tablespoons butter
1 cup heavy cream, whipped

Mix dry ingredients, add eggs, lemon juice and water, cook over boiling water, stirring constantly. Add butter, cook until thick; cool. When ready to use, add the whipped cream.

ORANGE OR PINEAPPLE DRESSING

Use ⅓ cup orange or pineapple juice in place of the water in recipe above.

FROZEN MAYONNAISE DRESSING

2 tablespoons lemon juice
1 cup mayonnaise
1 tablespoon confectioners sugar
1 cup heavy cream, whipped

Add lemon juice to mayonnaise. Fold sugar into whipped cream and combine the two mixtures. Place in mold and freeze until partially frozen but not hard.

FROZEN CHEESE DRESSING

½ cup soft cream cheese
1 cup heavy cream, whipped
½ cup mayonnaise
2 teaspoons lemon juice
¼ teaspoon salt
½ teaspoon paprika

Cream the cheese well. Fold in the whipped cream, the mayonnaise, lemon juice, and seasonings. Place in mold and freeze until partially frozen but not hard. Serve on fruit salad.

GRAPE JUICE OR WINE DRESSING

½ cup sugar
2 tablespoons lemon juice
⅛ cup grape juice or wine

Mix and serve ice-cold over fruit salad.

MAPLE SYRUP OR HONEY SALAD DRESSING

1 egg yolk
¼ cup maple syrup or honey
¾ cup heavy cream, whipped
juice of ½ lemon

Beat yolk well in double boiler. Add maple syrup or honey and cook for a minute until thick. Cool, fold in cream and add the lemon juice.

FRUIT SALAD FRENCH DRESSING

¼ cup olive oil
2 tablespoons grapefruit or orange juice
½ teaspoon salt
¼ teaspoon paprika
1 teaspoon confectioners sugar
2 tablespoons lemon juice

Mix in order given; chill. Shake well before serving.

FRUIT SALAD DRESSING WITH CHEESE

Mash 3 ounces of cream cheese. Mix and thin with cream. Add enough raspberry or strawberry jam to color. Pour chilled over fresh or canned peaches or pears.

Or, beat ½ cup of French Dressing into the cheese. Fold in ½ cup heavy cream, beaten stiff.

FRUIT SALAD DRESSING WITH HONEY

¼ cup honey
¼ cup lemon juice
¼ teaspoon paprika

Beat well and serve over orange, grapefruit, avocado or berries.

FRUIT SALAD DRESSING WITH BAR-LE-DUC

¼ cup Bar-le-Duc
1 cup mayonnaise
½ cup heavy cream, whipped

Beat Bar-le-Duc (currant jam) until smooth; add mayonnaise, then fold in whipped cream. Serve over any fruit salad.

19
SANDWICHES AND SANDWICH FILLINGS

A sandwich may be a snack, a meal main dish, or party fare, according to how you prepare it. Cold sandwiches go well with soup, dessert and beverage for an appetizing light meal. Hot sandwiches, which do not usually contain salad ingredients, can be served with juice and salad or a fruit relish, dessert and beverage.

Any bread may be used for sandwiches. A thin layer of butter helps to keep the bread from absorbing the filling. Cream the butter for easy spreading. Choose fillings that create interesting contrasts in flavor and texture.

Sandwiches may be prepared ahead. When making large quantities, stack the sandwiches between sheets of waxed paper, on platters or a cookie sheet, cover with a damp napkin, and store in refrigerator until wanted. For longer storage, sandwiches may be wrapped in foil, freezer bags, or freezer wraps and frozen. They may be wrapped individually, or several sandwiches may be separated with two pieces of freezer paper before wrapping, to prevent them from sticking together. Avoid freezing fillings which contain mayonnaise, fresh salad vegetables, cream cheese or hard-cooked eggs—none of these freeze well.

SANDWICH BUTTERS

Sandwich butters may be used to fill dainty party sandwiches, or as bases for canapés—butter keeps the base from getting soggy. They are also used instead of ordinary butter in making simple sandwiches from sliced meats, poultry, or cheese.

Let the butter stand at room temperature until it is soft, but not oily, then cream it with a fork for easy blending.

ANCHOVY BUTTER

Mix anchovy paste with an equal amount of softened butter, add a few drops of onion juice and lemon juice.

GREEN PEPPER BUTTER

Remove the seeds and white portion from 3 or 4 green peppers. Cook peppers in boiling water until soft; drain well; chop fine, drain again and rub through a sieve. Add pulp to ½ cup of softened butter.

OLIVE BUTTER

Grind ripe or stuffed olives and mix with an equal amount of softened butter.

ONION BUTTER

Mix ½ cup of finely minced young onions, with ½ cup softened butter.

PIMIENTO BUTTER

Drain 3 large pimientos and rub through a sieve. Work the pulp into ½ cup softened butter, season with salt to taste.

SHRIMP BUTTER

Clean and chop fine 1 pound of cooked or canned shrimps. Blend with 1 cup of softened butter. Purée in electric blender or rub through a sieve.

SMOKED SALMON BUTTER

Mince ¼ pound smoked salmon finely, mix with 1 cup of softened butter. Add a few drops of lemon juice and a dash of white pepper to taste.

SARDINE BUTTER

Remove bones and skins of sardines or use boneless and skinless variety. Mash well, blend with an equal amount of softened butter. Add lemon and onion juice to taste.

VEGETARIAN NUT BUTTER

¼ pound almonds
½ pound pecans
½ pound hazelnuts or filberts
½ pound roasted peanuts
¼ cup butter

Shell, blanch, and grind the nuts. Add butter and knead until firm. Pack tightly in jelly glasses and place in the refrigerator. When ready to use, dip glass in hot water. The mixture should slip out easily. Cut into slices.

CREAM CHEESE SPREADS

Cream cheese spreads may be used as the only filling for dainty sandwiches, or in combination with other fillings for lunchbox sandwiches. Sweet cream cheese spreads are popular with fruit breads or raisin or nut breads for light meals or snacks, and the savory mixtures make heartier sandwiches.

To soften the cream cheese, let it stand at room temperature for 30 minutes; then mash with a fork and blend with other ingredients.

BASIC CREAM CHEESE SPREAD

Blend softened cream cheese with milk, cream (plain or whipped), evaporated milk, or mayonnaise, to desired light consistency. Beat with a fork until smooth.

CLAM AND CREAM CHEESE SPREAD

Mix 1 can minced clams, drained, with 3 ounces of softened cream cheese. Season with Worcestershire sauce, a pinch of dry mustard, salt, and onion juice to taste. Add clam juice to thin spread, if desired.

OLIVE CREAM CHEESE SPREAD

Blend 8 ounces softened cream cheese with ½ cup of drained chopped olives, green, stuffed, or ripe.

WATERCRESS CHEESE SPREAD

Wash, drain and chop about 1 cup of watercress, and mix with 8 ounces softened cream cheese.

WATERCRESS AND NUT CREAM CHEESE SPREAD

Chop ½ cup of nuts, mix with finely minced watercress and 8 ounces of softened cream cheese until smooth.

PEPPER RELISH CREAM CHEESE SPREAD

Blend 8 ounces of softened cream cheese with ½ cup drained Pepper Relish. Mix until smooth.

PIMIENTO CREAM CHEESE SPREAD

Blend 8 ounces of softened cream cheese with ½ cup chopped, drained pimiento.

PINEAPPLE CREAM CHEESE SPREAD

Blend 8 ounces of softened cream cheese with ½ cup of drained crushed pineapple.

PRUNE SPREAD

½ pound cooked prunes
2 tablespoons softened butter
2 packages (3 ounces each) cream cheese
¼ cup chopped walnuts

Pit, chop, and drain juice from prunes. Combine with remaining ingredients.

CHEESE, EGG AND SEAFOOD FILLINGS

COTTAGE CHEESE FILLING

½ cup cottage cheese, riced
cream or milk
¼ cup pimientos or stuffed olives, chopped

Mix cheese to a smooth paste with a little cream or milk; then stir in the pimientos. ½ cup walnuts, chopped, may be added. Salt to taste.

BLUE CHEESE AND NUT FILLING

¼ pound blue cheese
¼ cup butter, softened
¼ pound walnut meats
salt and paprika

Crumble the cheese, mix with the butter; chop the nuts, combine. Season with salt and paprika.

CHEDDAR CHEESE AND ANCHOVY FILLING

2 tablespoons butter
¼ cup grated Cheddar cheese
1 teaspoon anchovy paste
1 teaspoon vinegar
salt, paprika, mustard

Soften the butter, add the cheese, anchovy paste and vinegar. Season and mix well.

EGG SALAD FILLING

4 hard-cooked eggs
3 tablespoons mayonnaise
salt and pepper to taste

Chop the hard-cooked eggs; season with salt and pepper, and moisten with mayonnaise.

EGG AND SARDINE FILLING

Use equal quantities of hard-cooked egg yolks and sardines, drained, skinned and boned. Season with salt, cayenne pepper and mustard. Mash until smooth and add lemon juice and olive oil to make a paste. If desired, mayonnaise can be used in place of the lemon juice and oil.

CAVIAR SPREAD

¼ pound caviar
2 tablespoons lemon juice
paprika
3 tablespoons olive oil

Combine caviar with lemon juice, a little paprika and olive oil. Blend.

CRAB MEAT FILLING

2 hard-cooked egg yolks
1 tablespoon melted butter
1 tablespoon lemon juice
½-pound can crab meat

Mash the yolks to a smooth paste with the butter. Add the lemon juice and the crab meat, chopped fine. Mix well.

SALMON FILLING

1 can (7¾ ounces) salmon, drained and flaked
1 hard-cooked egg, chopped
2 tablespoons French Dressing, page 373
2 tablespoons chopped green olives
lemon juice to taste
mayonnaise

Blend ingredients lightly, using enough mayonnaise to make a spreadable mixture, not too moist.

SEAFOOD FILLING

Chop any cooked seafood. Season with salt, pepper, prepared mustard and lemon juice; or moisten with any salad dressing.

TUNA FISH FILLING

1 can (6½ or 7 ounces) tuna, drained and flaked small
¼ cup minced celery
½ teaspoon lemon juice
1 tablespoon chili sauce
mayonnaise
salt, pepper

Blend ingredients, using just enough mayonnaise to make a spreadable mixture, not too moist. Season to taste.

MEAT AND POULTRY SANDWICHES

Appetizing sandwiches can be made with plain slices of cooked meat, cold cuts, or cooked poultry, alone or combined with cheese. Several thin slices are easier to eat than a single thick slice. The bread may be spread with butter or mayonnaise, or with a sandwich butter. Lettuce, watercress or other greens, or sliced tomato, may be added. Mustard and ketchup may be served on the side, for those who wish to add it.

FOIE GRAS

Slice whole foie gras, the canned goose liver, or pâté of foie gras, goose liver paste. Combine with thinly sliced cucumber or tomato to make sandwiches.

GOOSE MEAT SANDWICHES

Spread thin slices of fresh or toasted rye bread or rolls with goose fat. Fill with sliced cooked goose. Or mince the meat, add 1 or 2 pickles, or a little catsup, and use as filling. Slices of cold duck may also be used.

HAM OR SMOKED BEEF FILLING

½ pound cold boiled ham or smoked pickled beef
¼ cup mayonnaise
thin slices of bread

Chop the ham or smoked beef very fine, including the fat. Mix with mayonnaise.

LIVER PASTE

½ pound cooked liver
2 hard-cooked eggs
½ onion, grated
½ teaspoon salt
⅛ teaspoon pepper
½ cup poultry fat

Chicken or goose liver may be used to make liver paste, as well as calf's liver, steer liver, or pork liver. Sauté in fat until cooked through, or bake in moderate oven.

Put first five ingredients through a meat grinder several times until very fine, or puree in an electric blender. Mix well, adding fat to make a light paste.

LIVER PASTE WITH MUSHROOMS

½ pound raw sliced liver
2 tablespoons hot rendered chicken fat
½ cup mushrooms, chopped fine
lemon juice
onion juice
salt
pepper

Sauté liver in fat slowly until tender; grind. Sauté mushrooms in chicken fat. Mix liver and mushrooms. Add seasonings and more chicken fat if necessary to make a smooth paste.

Recipes for mayonnaises and other salad dressings suitable for sandwich fillings begin on page 374.

MOCK PÂTÉ DE FOIE GRAS FILLING

Remove casing from liver sausage, mash to a paste with mayonnaise. If desired, spread between thin slices of buttered rye bread.

MEAT SALAD SANDWICHES

Chop cooked meat or poultry, moisten with mayonnaise and season to taste. Chopped celery or green pepper may be added to taste. A little minced green onion adds interest to many meat and poultry sandwiches.

STEAK TARTARE

Season freshly ground round steak with salt, pepper and onion juice. Spread on toasted rye bread. Top with an onion ring. Drop a raw egg into the onion ring. Garnish with anchovies.

CHICKEN AND NUT FILLING

Chop cold chicken fine, moisten with a little salad dressing. Add some chopped nuts, a few drops of lemon juice and celery salt.

SWEETBREAD FILLING

Chop cold, cooked sweetbreads. Mix with mayonnaise, chopped celery and nut meats.

CLUB SANDWICHES

Butter 3 slices of fresh toast; on 1 slice place cold, sliced chicken and thin slices of fried bacon; on second slice mayonnaise and lettuce with sliced tomato on top. Cover with third slice, cut in fourths diagonally and decorate with pickles, red radishes and olives.

FRUIT AND VEGETABLE FILLINGS

AVOCADO OR ALLIGATOR PEAR FILLING

Peel a ripe avocado and mash with a fork. Sprinkle with salt and pepper, and season with lemon or lime juice. French dressing or mayonnaise may be added, if desired.

CHERRY AND PINEAPPLE FILLING

Pit and slice dark red cherries, drain; add an equal amount of crushed pineapple and ¼ cup finely chopped, blanched almonds; moisten with mayonnaise.

CUCUMBER FILLING

Pare and chop medium cucumber, season with grated onion and mix with mayonnaise. If desired, 4 hard-cooked eggs, finely chopped, may be added.

FRUIT AND NUT FILLING

  1 pound raisins or figs
  1 pound dates or prunes
  juice of 2 oranges
  juice of 2 lemons
  ½ pound pecan nut meats
  ½ pound English walnuts

Remove stems and stones of fruit; chop or grind fine. Moisten with fruit juices. Add nuts, chopped fine. Filling keeps well in refrigerator in airtight jars.

LETTUCE SANDWICHES

Wash and dry fresh, crisp lettuce leaves, place between thin slices of buttered bread spread with mayonnaise.

ONION SANDWICHES

Cut Bermuda onions into thin slices and sprinkle with salt and a few grains of sugar. Place between slices of rye bread, buttered, or spread with goose fat or chicken fat.

Or fry the onions in fat until tender, add salt and pepper. Serve on a slice of fresh or toasted rye bread.

HORSERADISH FILLING

  ¼ cup butter
  ¼ cup grated horseradish
  1 teaspoon lemon juice
  salt
  sugar

Cream butter with grated horseradish, lemon juice, and a little salt and sugar.

MUSHROOM FILLING

Prepare Sautéed Mushrooms. Cool, chop fine, season and mix with mayonnaise.

PEANUT BUTTER FILLING

Blend peanut butter with an equal amount of jelly, preserves or jam; or with an equal amount of Basic Cream Cheese Spread.

TO PREPARE AND SERVE FANCY SANDWICHES

BREAD AND BUTTER SANDWICHES

Spread slices of brown and white bread with softened butter. Top brown slices with white bread and white slices with brown bread. Cut sandwiches into quarters and arrange on platter alternating dark with light.

Cover fancy sandwiches with a damp cloth and plastic wrap to keep them fresh until served.

MOSAIC SANDWICHES

Remove crusts from one unsliced loaf each of white and dark bread and cut soft inner part into thin slices lengthwise. Spread half the slices with creamed butter and any desired sandwich filling. Cut out small shapes from remaining slices, using round or fancy cutter. Place dark cut-outs in spaces of white bread and white designs in spaces of dark bread. Cover each slice spread with filling with one two-color slice. Cut into desired shapes.

CHECKERBOARD SANDWICHES

Cut top crust from unsliced white and whole-wheat bread loaves. Cut 3 slices lengthwise and ½ inch thick from each loaf. Spread each slice well with creamed butter and any desired sandwich filling. Put together alternate slices of dark and white bread. Press slices well together, put in refrigerator, place plate on top of pile; when filling is firm, cut off crusts. Then cut each pile crosswise into ½-inch slices; spread cut sides thickly with creamed butter and sandwich filling, and put together so that the brown and the white slices alternate. Place in refrigerator again, under light weight, until butter is firm; then cut crosswise into thin slices. Arrange on platter to show checkerboard pattern.

PINWHEEL SANDWICHES

Remove crust from unsliced, very fresh bread. Cut lengthwise in slices as thin as possible. Flatten lightly with rolling pin. Spread evenly with softened butter and any well-seasoned, minced sandwich filling. Roll each slice tightly, wrap in foil or plastic. Chill, seam-side down, until firm. When ready to serve, cut in thin slices crosswise.

TOMATO RING SANDWICHES

With large biscuit cutter cut slices of bread in rounds. With smaller cutter remove inside of half of these, thus forming rings. Spread large rounds with softened butter. Cover with lettuce and mayonnaise; place ring over lettuce and fill center with slice of tomato, or with Tomato Aspic cut into rounds. Ring sandwiches may be made with any desired combination of fillings. The cut-out rounds may be spread and served separately.

RIBBON SANDWICHES

1 loaf firm bread, unsliced
½ cup butter, creamed
Green Pepper Butter, page 379
1 cucumber, peeled
salt, pepper
mayonnaise
Pimiento Butter, page 379
2 hard-cooked eggs, riced

Trim crust from bread. Cut bread lengthwise into 5 slices ½-inch thick. Spread each slice with creamed butter, the top and bottom slice on one side only, the middle slices on both sides. On the bottom slice spread the Green Pepper Butter. Chop the cucumber, season, drain, and mix with mayonnaise; spread on the next slice. Spread Pimiento Butter on the third slice; eggs mixed with mayonnaise and seasonings on the fourth slice. Cover with the last slice of bread, buttered side down. Wrap in waxed paper. Chill until firm. Cut crosswise into thin slices. Any desired spreads in contrasting colors may be used.

RIBBON SANDWICH LOAF

Follow directions for making Ribbon Sandwich, above. Proceed as above with the following fillings: 1st filling—boiled ham, tongue, or chicken, ground, or lobster, shrimp or salmon, mixed with mayonnaise; 2nd—Olive Butter, page 379; 3rd—chopped eggs with caviar; 4th—Cucumber Filling. Press slices firmly together, wrap in damp cloth and chill until firm. Place on serving platter several hours before serving. Cover top and sides with 1 3-ounce package of cream cheese blended with ½ pound of cottage cheese, well seasoned and mashed to a paste with cream or mayonnaise. Decorate top with nuts, olive slices or pimiento, or bits of red and green pepper or roses made of tinted cheese. To serve, cut slices ½ inch thick.

HOT SANDWICHES

Open-faced sandwiches may be made with hot sauce poured over filling on bread, or may be baked in the oven or toasted or grilled under the broiler. Closed sandwiches may be browned on an electric sandwich grill, or in a skillet. French-toasted sandwiches are dipped into an egg and milk batter, and browned in butter or shortening in a skillet.

MILWAUKEE SANDWICH

Butter 2 slices of white bread. Trim off crusts. Place a slice of white chicken meat on 1 slice of bread. Sprinkle with Roquefort cheese. Season with paprika. Cover with the other slice, toast on both sides. Garnish with parsley; serve hot.

BAKED MILWAUKEE SANDWICH

Place sliced white chicken on a slice of toast. Moisten with Cheese Sauce, top with second slice of toast. Put into individual casserole, cover with well-seasoned Cheese Sauce. Heat thoroughly. Serve in casserole. Serves 1.

FRENCH-TOASTED HAM SANDWICHES

½ pound cold boiled ham
prepared English mustard
8 slices day-old bread
2 eggs
¾ cup milk
2 tablespoons butter

Chop or grind the ham very fine and moisten with mustard. Spread between thin slices of bread and press firmly together. Beat the eggs slightly, add milk and beat again. Dip sandwich in this egg mixture and sauté in butter until a golden brown on both sides. Makes 4 servings. Serve with knife and fork.

BROILED CHEESE AND OLIVE SANDWICH

6 English muffins, split
1 cup chopped ripe olives
½ cup slivered green onions
1½ cups grated Cheddar cheese
½ cup mayonnaise
½ teaspoon salt
½ teaspoon curry or chili powder

Toast muffins. Combine other ingredients; spread muffins with mixture. Broil until the cheese melts.

FOR HOT APPETIZERS

Substitute small rounds of toast for English muffins. Proceed as above.

GRILLED CHEESE SANDWICH

Butter thin slices of bread very lightly, sprinkle generously with thick layer of grated American Cheddar or Swiss cheese; press 2 slices firmly together, cut in half and toast quickly. Serve at once.

BROILED CHEESE SANDWICH

Slice bread, toast 1 side; sprinkle untoasted side with a thick layer of grated American, Cheddar or Swiss cheese, seasoned with salt and cayenne. Place in shallow pan. Broil or bake until cheese is melted. Serve at once.

GRILLED CHEESE, TOMATO AND BACON SANDWICH

Toast slice of white bread on one side. Cover untoasted side with sliced Cheddar cheese. On top of this, place ¼-inch slice of tomato and 2 slices of partly cooked bacon, placed crisscross on tomato. Broil until bacon is crisp and brown.

HOT HAM AND ASPARAGUS SANDWICH WITH CHEESE SAUCE

Cover buttered slice of toast with a slice of fried boiled ham. On this place cooked or canned asparagus tips. Cover with hot Cheese Sauce.

HAM AND EGG SANDWICHES

2 tablespoons butter
4 eggs
¼ cup cold water
salt and pepper
¼ pound boiled ham, chopped
6 slices buttered toast

Melt butter in skillet. Beat eggs with water, salt and pepper. Pour into hot skillet, stir over low heat until set but creamy. Spread ham on toast and cover with eggs. Serve hot. Makes 3 servings.

HAMBURGER SANDWICH

Hamburgers, page 279
Fried Onions, page 423

Prepare and broil hamburgers. Place between toast or hamburger buns, topping with onions if desired. Or serve with catsup or relish.

HOT BACON AND PEANUT BUTTER SANDWICHES

Cut unsliced loaf of white bread lengthwise in ¼-inch slices. Toast on one side. Spread untoasted side with a thick layer of peanut butter. Sprinkle top with bacon which has been fried crisp and crumbled. Before serving put under broiler to heat thoroughly. Cut into strips and serve with cocktails.

HOT CREAMED SALMON SANDWICH

Prepare Creamed Canned Salmon, page 243. Spread between slices of toast. Cover with seasoned Medium White Sauce.

HOT MUSHROOM SANDWICHES

Chop Sautéed Mushrooms fine. Add ¾ cup Medium White Sauce. Spread between thin slices of bread. Press firmly together, cut in half crosswise or in finger-shaped pieces and toast under the broiler until lightly browned.

HOT ROLLED CHEESE SANDWICHES

Prepare bread as for Rolled Toast Sticks, page 406, spreading slices with Cheddar Cheese Spread, page 38. Roll sticks in grated cheese. Bake in shallow pan in hot oven, turning to brown evenly.

HOT TURKEY SANDWICHES

1 small can deviled ham
4 slices bread, toasted
slices cooked turkey
1 can (10½ ounces) condensed mushroom soup
3 tablespoons mayonnaise
¼ cup dry sherry
paprika

Spread ham on toast; top each slice of toast with

slices of turkey. Place in shallow baking pan. Combine condensed soup, mayonnaise and sherry; heat to boiling point. Spoon sauce over sandwiches. Bake in a hot oven, 400° F., for about 10 minutes. Sprinkle with paprika, serve at once. Serves 4.

REUBEN SANDWICHES

    18 slices dark rye bread
    Thousand Island Dressing
    12 slices Swiss cheese
    ½ cup sauerkraut
    24 slices corned beef
    butter

Spread one side of 12 slices of bread with dressing. Place one slice of cheese, 2 teaspoons sauerkraut, and 2 slices of corned beef on each slice of bread. Stack two of these slices and top with a plain slice of bread. Put sandwiches together with picks. Butter outside of bread. Grill sandwich until cheese is melted. Makes 6 sandwiches.

PIZZA

    1 package active dry yeast
    2 tablespoons warm water
    1 cup boiling water
    2 tablespoons shortening
    ½ teaspoon salt
    ½ teaspoon sugar
    3 cups sifted flour
    olive oil
    3 cups tomato sauce
    ½ lb. mozzarella cheese
    oregano
    Parmesan cheese

Soften yeast in warm water. Add boiling water to shortening, salt and sugar. Cool to lukewarm and add to yeast. Add most of flour and beat until smooth. Add remaining flour and knead. Set in greased bowl, covered, in warm place to double in bulk. Punch down dough, divide into two parts. Place each half in a 12-inch pizza pan or rimmed cookie sheet greased with olive oil. Press dough firmly into pan, being sure that it comes well up on the sides. Brush with olive oil. Spread with tomato sauce and cover with thin slices of mozzarella cheese. Sprinkle generously with oregano and grated Parmesan. Bake in a hot oven, 450° F., until the crust is blistered and well-browned and the cheese melted, about ½ hour.

For variety, any of the following ingredients may be added to the filling for pizza: cooked, sliced Italian sausages, lightly sautéed mushrooms, anchovies.

Provolone or other good melting cheeses may be used instead of mozzarella cheese.

ITALIAN BREAD BOAT

    1 loaf (1 pound) Italian or French bread
    ½ cup milk
    1 egg
    salt, pepper, garlic
    1½ cups meat, fish, poultry, diced
    1½ cups diced celery
    ⅛ cup diced olives, green or ripe
    ½ cup mayonnaise
    2 hard-cooked eggs, sliced

Cut top crust off bread and reserve for cover. Scoop out soft crumbs. Mark boat and crust into desired number of servings cutting almost to the bottom crust. Soften removed bread crumbs in milk. Blend in raw egg and seasonings. Add desired meat or poultry and other ingredients. Mix well. Fill cavity of boat, top with egg slices. Replace crust cover. Brush outside of loaf with melted butter. Wrap in aluminum foil and bake at 425° F. for 30 to 40 minutes. Serve hot.

SANDWICH GRILL
Follow the manufacturers' directions for using the sandwich grill: most grills require 5 minutes pre-heating time.

Spread outside of sandwiches with softened butter, to prevent sticking. Grilled sandwiches should be served with a knife and fork.

Fillings for Grilled Sandwiches

BRICK CHEESE AND HAM
Slice of brick cheese, covered with thinly sliced sweet sour pickles, covered with slice of ham.

BRICK CHEESE AND TOMATOES
Slices of brick cheese, covered with slices of tomato, sprinkled with chopped green pepper.

SWEETBREAD AND CHEESE
Slices of cooked sweetbread between slices of Cheddar cheese.

CHICKEN AND MUSHROOMS
Sautéed sliced fresh mushrooms between slices of cooked chicken.

CHICKEN SALAD
Finely minced, seasoned chicken and celery, mixed with mayonnaise.

ANCHOVY PASTE AND SARDINES
Sardines and sliced hard-cooked eggs between slices of bread spread with anchovy paste.

PEANUT BUTTER AND TOMATO
Put slices of tomato or pineapple between slices of bread spread with peanut butter.

20
SAUCES FOR FISH, MEAT AND VEGETABLES

A well-chosen sauce can improve the taste of many foods by adding a complementary flavor, along with desirable moisture and interesting texture contrast.

Many of the sauces given in this chapter are multipurpose; they can be used with everything from eggs and spaghetti to vegetables, fish, and meat, according to preference. Some of them are made with the liquid from the dish they are to accompany—pan gravy and fricassee sauce are examples of this. Other sauces require milk, bouillon, or fruit juices as bases, or melted butter, eggs, cream, wine, or jelly.

The basic white and brown sauces are frequently used and are referred to in many recipes in this book.

WHITE SAUCES AND VARIATIONS

THIN BASIC WHITE SAUCE

1 cup hot milk
1 tablespoon butter
1 tablespoon flour
¼ teaspoon salt
⅛ teaspoon pepper

MEDIUM WHITE SAUCE

1 cup hot milk
2 tablespoons butter
2 tablespoons flour
¼ teaspoon salt
⅛ teaspoon pepper

THICK WHITE SAUCE

1 cup hot milk
3 tablespoons butter
3 tablespoons flour
¼ teaspoon salt
⅛ teaspoon pepper

Scald the milk. Melt the butter in a saucepan over low heat or in double boiler. Add flour, stirring constantly. Stir in the hot milk gradually and cook, stirring constantly, until the mixture thickens. If lumpy, beat well with rotary beater. Season and serve hot.

CREAM SAUCE

1 cup hot Medium White Sauce
2 egg yolks, beaten

Stir a few spoonfuls of the White Sauce gradually into the beaten yolks, then stir this into the remaining sauce and cook slowly, stirring constantly until thick. Or add a little cold water to the beaten yolks and stir slowly into the sauce. Serve at once, over cooked green peas, asparagus, fish, meat, or poultry.

CATSUP SAUCE

1 cup Medium White Sauce
3 tablespoons catsup

Mix White Sauce with the catsup and serve hot or cold over fish or meat.

CHEESE SAUCE

Add ½ cup of grated Cheddar cheese to 1 cup hot Medium White Sauce or Cream Sauce.

MORNAY SAUCE

Add ¼ cup each of grated Parmesan and Swiss cheese to 1 cup of hot Medium White Sauce. Stir until melted.

HORSERADISH SAUCE

Add 3 to 4 tablespoons prepared horseradish to Medium White Sauce or to Hollandaise Sauce. If desired, add tomato catsup to taste.

MUSHROOM CREAM SAUCE

½ pound mushrooms
1 cup Medium White Sauce
1 teaspoon chopped parsley

Cut thin slice from mushroom stems and peel thinly if discolored. Wash. Remove stems and slice for sauce; caps may be sautéed separately in a little butter, and used to garnish the dish. Or use mushrooms whole, sliced, or quartered. Sauté in a little butter. Make White Sauce, using mushroom liquid instead of part of the milk. Add mushrooms and parsley, and serve.

RAVIGOTE SAUCE

2 green onions
2 tablespoons butter
2 tablespoons tarragon vinegar
1 cup Thin White Sauce
1 tablespoon lemon juice
½ tablespoon parsley, chopped
½ tablespoon chives, chopped
salt and pepper to taste

Slice onions, add butter and vinegar. Cook until vinegar is reduced to half. Add remaining ingredients. If desired, tint green with food coloring. Serve hot with poultry and fish.

SEAFOOD SAUCE

garlic
Medium White Sauce
½ cup catsup
3 tablespoons Worcestershire sauce

Rub inside of saucepan well with garlic and make Medium White Sauce, using cream in place of milk. When smooth, add rest of the ingredients. Serve hot over lobster, shrimp, crab or oysters.

SOUR CREAM GRAVY

2 tablespoons butter
3 tablespoons flour
½ cup soup stock
1 cup sour cream
salt and pepper to taste

Melt butter in double boiler, add flour, stir in soup stock. Cook over hot water until thick, stirring occasionally. Then slowly add the sour cream. Season and serve hot.

FRICASSEE SAUCE

¼ cup chicken fat
¼ cup flour
1½ to 2 cups hot chicken stock
½ cup hot light cream
1 teaspoon salt
¼ teaspoon pepper

Heat fat in double boiler, add flour when it bubbles. Add soup stock at once, stir until thick, then add the cream and stir until smooth. Season to taste. Serve with chicken.

SARDINE SAUCE

4 to 6 sardines or salted herring bits
2 tablespoons butter
2 tablespoons flour
1 cup of fish or meat stock
juice of ½ lemon
½ cup white wine
salt and pepper
2 egg yolks

Soak the sardellen in cold water ½ hour, chop fine. Melt butter, add flour, then the hot stock, stir until smooth; add lemon, wine, and sardellen; cook slowly for 10 minutes; season with salt and pepper to taste and stir in very gradually the egg yolks beaten with a little cold water. Serve immediately with fish or meat.

BROWN SAUCE AND VARIATIONS

BROWN SAUCE

2 tablespoons butter or fat
1 small onion, chopped (optional)
2 tablespoons flour
1 cup meat, fish or vegetable stock
½ teaspoon salt
⅛ teaspoon pepper

Melt the butter or fat and, if desired, add onion, cook until brown. Add the flour, let brown; add liquid gradually, stirring constantly. Season. Cook 5 minutes, stirring often. Serve as gravy with meat, dumplings, mashed potatoes, etc.

ANCHOVY SAUCE

Season Brown Sauce, Drawn Butter Sauce, or Hollandaise Sauce with anchovy paste.

Or, skin and bone 3 or 4 anchovies, and mash until smooth. Add to the sauce, adding lemon juice to taste.

CAPER SAUCE

Add ¼ cup of capers, drained, to 1 cup Brown Sauce. Serve hot with tongue, calf's brains, sweetbreads, mutton or fish.

BROWN MUSHROOM SAUCE

1 cup Brown Sauce
1 can (6 ounces) sliced mushrooms or mushroom
    pieces, or 1 cup sliced fresh mushrooms sau-
    téed in butter
1 teaspoon chopped parsley

Make Brown Sauce, using mushroom liquid and beef bouillon as liquid. Add mushrooms, heat, add parsley.

CREOLE SAUCE

1½ cups Brown Sauce
2 tablespoons butter
2 tablespoons onion, chopped
2 tablespoons chopped green peppers
3 tablespoons canned tomatoes
¼ cup mushrooms
½ teaspoon salt
½ teaspoon paprika
1 teaspoon catsup
Kitchen Bouquet

Follow directions for Brown Sauce, increasing the amounts by half. Heat butter, add onion, fry lightly. Add the peppers, tomatoes and mushrooms and cook for a few minutes. Add vegetables to Brown Sauce with seasonings. Simmer 20 minutes. If desired, add ½ cup blanched, toasted almonds, sliced. Serve hot.

PIQUANT SAUCE

1 cup Brown Sauce
½ small onion, chopped fine
2 tablespoons lemon juice, vinegar, sherry or claret
1 tablespoon each of capers and pickles, chopped

Make Brown Sauce, add remaining ingredients. Serve hot with beef or fish.

PORT WINE SAUCE

Prepare 1 cup Brown Sauce; add ¼ cup currant jelly and 2 tablespoons port wine. Cook until jelly is dissolved and serve hot with venison.

SWEET AND SOUR BROWN SAUCE

2 tablespoons butter
2 tablespoons flour
½ teaspoon salt
¼ teaspoon pepper
1 cup hot vegetable liquid or soup stock
2 tablespoons vinegar
2 tablespoons sugar

Brown butter well, add flour and brown. Stir in liquid gradually; then seasoning. Add vinegar and sugar to taste. Cook until smooth. Serve hot with cooked string beans, carrots, soup meat, tongue or ham.

RICH SWEET AND SOUR SAUCE

½ cup sugar
1 tablespoon flour
1 cup boiling water or vegetable or soup stock
¼ cup vinegar
½ teaspoon salt
⅛ teaspoon pepper

Melt sugar in a hot skillet, stir in flour, and very gradually add the liquid, then the vinegar and seasoning. Cook, stirring, until smooth and blended. Serve as in preceding recipe.

BROWN EGG SAUCE

2 egg yolks, beaten
1 cup Brown Sauce
1 tablespoon vinegar or lemon juice

Follow recipe for Brown Sauce, using fish liquid from poached fish. Stir the hot sauce gradually into the beaten yolks, stirring constantly until thick. Remove from heat and add vinegar or lemon juice. Serve with fish.

RAISIN SAUCE

1 cup Brown Sauce
½ cup seeded raisins
sherry or Madeira to taste

Make Brown Sauce, using any desired fruit juice as liquid. Add raisins, simmer 10 minutes. Add wine to taste. Serve with ham or tongue.

PAN GRAVY

A pan gravy may be made for any roasted meat or poultry, or for any sautéed or pan-fried meat. Pour off the pan juices and skim off excess fat. Return 2 tablespoons fat to the roasting pan or skillet, or use butter; add 2 tablespoons flour and cook, stirring, until golden. Add the pan juices plus bouillon or water to make 1 cup liquid and cook, stirring in the brown bits that cling to the pan, until blended. Simmer 5 minutes, stirring often, and strain into a sauceboat. Add salt and pepper to taste.

HOLLANDAISE SAUCE
AND VARIATIONS

HOLLANDAISE SAUCE

2 tablespoons vinegar
¼ teaspoon white pepper
¼ cup water
1 cup butter
4 egg yolks
juice of ½ lemon
salt to taste

Boil vinegar, pepper and water until liquid is reduced to half. Divide butter into 3 parts; put 1 part into top of double boiler with egg yolks and lemon juice, place over boiling water, stir constantly with a wire whisk until butter is melted. Add second part of butter, and as sauce thickens, the third part. Add the vinegar water, cook 1 minute and add salt. Serve with vegetables and fish.

QUICK HOLLANDAISE SAUCE

    ½ cup butter
    2 or 3 egg yolks
    1 tablespoon lemon juice
    ¼ teaspoon salt
    a few grains cayenne pepper
    ½ cup boiling water

With a wooden spoon, cream the butter, add the yolks, one at a time. Beat well, add the lemon juice, salt and pepper. About 5 minutes before serving add the boiling water and stir rapidly. Cook mixture over hot water in double boiler, stirring constantly, until it thickens.

MOCK HOLLANDAISE SAUCE

    6 ounces cream cheese
    2 egg yolks
    2 tablespoons lemon juice
    salt

Soften the cream cheese. Add egg yolks one at a time, blending thoroughly after each. Add lemon juice and a dash of salt. Heat thoroughly in double boiler.

EASY HOLLANDAISE SAUCE

    3 tablespoons butter
    2 tablespoons flour
    1 cup hot water
    ½ teaspoon salt
    few grains cayenne pepper
    2 tablespoons lemon juice
    2 egg yolks

Melt butter in top of double boiler. Add flour and blend well. Add hot water gradually, and stir continuously until thickened and smooth. Add salt, cayenne and lemon juice, and place over hot but not boiling water, until ready to serve. Then pour mixture over well-beaten egg yolks, stir thoroughly, reheat quickly and serve at once.

BLENDER HOLLANDAISE SAUCE

    1 cup butter
    4 egg yolks
    ¼ teaspoon salt
    dash cayenne pepper
    2 tablespoons lemon juice

Heat butter just to bubbling. Meanwhile place other ingredients in electric blender. Cover, turn blender on high. Remove cover immediately and add hot butter in steady stream. May be stored, covered, in the refrigerator.

LEMON EGG SAUCE

    3 egg yolks
    1 whole egg
    2 lemons, juice
    2 cups fish liquid
    sugar to taste
    ¼ cup slivered almonds

Mix all ingredients, beat well, cook until thick over boiling water, stirring constantly. Serve at once with poached or steamed fish.

BEARNAISE SAUCE

    2 green onions
    2 tablespoons tarragon vinegar
    4 egg yolks
    4 tablespoons butter
    1 tablespoon soup stock
    1 teaspoon parsley, chopped fine
    ½ teaspoon salt
    ⅛ teaspoon paprika

Chop onions, add vinegar, simmer until reduced by half, strain and cool. Add yolks one at a time and stir. Cook slowly until smooth, stirring constantly; add butter, soup stock, parsley and seasoning. Serve hot with broiled meat or fish.

MUSTARD SAUCE

    2 whole eggs, and 1 egg yolk
    1 tablespoon dry mustard
    2 tablespoons vinegar
    ¼ cup olive oil
    ¼ teaspoon salt, pepper, paprika to taste
    light cream to thin

Beat eggs and egg yolk well, beat in seasonings and gradually add vinegar and oil, beating constantly. Cook over boiling water until thick, stirring constantly. Add cream to thin, if desired.

NEWBURG SAUCE

    2 tablespoons butter
    ¼ cup sherry or Madeira wine
    1 cup light cream
    3 egg yolks
    salt to taste
    ½ teaspoon paprika

Melt the butter, add the wine, and cook for 2 minutes. Add the cream, stir a few spoonfuls into the well-beaten yolks. Stir eggs into the rest of the sauce, add seasoning. Cook until thickened, stirring constantly. Serve at once. Use with fish or seafood.

QUICK NEWBURG SAUCE

4 or 5 egg yolks
3 tablespoons sherry
1 cup milk
1 cup light cream
salt and pepper to taste

Beat the yolks until very light, add the rest of the ingredients and cook over boiling water until thick and smooth, stirring constantly. Serve with fish or seafood.

LOBSTER OR SHRIMP SAUCE

Add ⅓ cup diced lobster or shrimp to any Hollandaise Sauce. Use for fish.

HOT HORSERADISH SAUCE

2½ cups soup stock
¼ cup fine dried bread crumbs
¼ cup sugar
salt to taste
juice of 1 lemon
⅛ cup almonds
1 cup fresh grated horseradish
2 egg yolks
1 tablespoon cold water

Add crumbs to soup stock, let boil a few minutes, add sugar, salt, lemon and almonds, blanched and chopped coarse. Just before serving, add horseradish; mix well, add the egg yolks mixed with a tablespoon of cold water. Stir constantly until smooth. Serve hot over pot roast, roast beef or fresh boiled tongue. For tongue, use tongue liquid in place of soup stock.

TOMATO SAUCES
AND VARIATIONS

TOMATO SAUCE

2 tablespoons butter
2 tablespoons flour
½ cup water
¼ teaspoon onion juice
1 cup strained tomato
1 teaspoon salt

Melt the butter, stir in the flour and cook without browning. Add the water gradually, stir well, add remaining ingredients, boil 5 minutes. Serve hot with macaroni, meat, eggs or fish.

ITALIAN TOMATO SAUCE

1 onion, chopped fine
1 clove garlic, chopped fine
1 tablespoon oil
1 quart stewed fresh tomatoes, sieved
salt and pepper to taste

Fry onion and garlic in oil until light brown, add tomatoes, simmer 30 minutes or until slightly thickened. Season to taste.

SPICY TOMATO SAUCE

1 can (1 pound) tomatoes or 1¾ cups stewed fresh tomatoes
2 slices onion
8 peppercorns
1 bay leaf
3 cloves
2 tablespoons butter or other fat
2 tablespoons flour
1 tablespoon sugar
¼ teaspoon salt

Cook tomatoes 15 minutes with the onion and spices. Strain. Melt the butter, add flour, sugar and hot strained tomatoes. Cook until thick. Season to taste. May be thickened with crumbled gingersnaps.

BASIC BARBECUE SAUCE

1 cup diced onion or 1 clove of garlic
2 tablespoons fat
1 cup chopped tomato
1 cup green pepper, diced
1 cup diced celery
2 tablespoons brown sugar
½ tablespoon dry mustard
2 cups stock from roast or soup, or water with bouillon cube
salt and pepper to taste
1 cup catsup

Fry the onion or garlic lightly in fat, add remaining ingredients, cook slowly 1 hour. Liquid should be reduced by about half and sauce should be well blended. Dip any meat in sauce before roasting, broiling indoors or out, or baste with sauce during roasting.

For other barbecue sauces and marinades, see chapter on Outdoor Cooking, page 326.

SPANISH CHILI SAUCE

10 red peppers, seed and pith removed
1 teaspoon salt
1 onion, chopped
1 clove of garlic, minced
½ teaspoon marjoram

Cook peppers until soft in boiling water to cover. Mash or press through colander. Add remaining ingredients. If a hotter sauce is desired, leave pith in the peppers.

SWEET AND SOUR SAUCES

GINGERSNAP SAUCE

4 to 6 large gingersnaps, crumbled
½ cup brown sugar
¼ cup vinegar
½ teaspoon onion juice
1 cup hot water or stock
1 lemon, sliced
¼ cup raisins

Mix all together and cook until smooth. Pour hot over cooked fish, meat, or tongue. Or chill and serve cold.

APPLESAUCE RELISH

1 can (1 pound, 13 ounces) applesauce
1 to 2 tablespoons horseradish
dash of nutmeg

Combine well and serve cold with hot meat, especially pork.

CURRANT JELLY SAUCE

½ lemon, diced
1 tablespoon chopped citron
1 teaspoon butter
½ wineglass sherry
½ glass (about 4 ounces) currant jelly
salt and pepper

Heat all ingredients together, stir smooth, and serve hot with game.

MINT SAUCE

1 tablespoon confectioners sugar or ½ cup
    strained honey
½ cup cider vinegar
¼ cup chopped mint leaves

Dissolve sugar in vinegar. Pour over mint and let stand 30 minutes over low heat. If vinegar is strong, dilute with water to taste. Serve hot over hot lamb.

Or boil sugar and vinegar, add the mint leaves and let boil up once. Set aside and serve cold with lamb.

WINE SAUCE FOR MEAT OR GAME

Heat ½ cup raisins with ¼ cup port wine. Combine with 1 cup whole cranberry sauce. Serve warm.

RAISIN SAUCE

To 2 tablespoons butter or pan drippings add 2 tablespoons flour. Cook, stirring, until smooth. Add gradually 1 cup fruit juice. Bring to a boil. Add ½ cup seeded raisins. Simmer for 10 minutes. Sherry or Madeira may be added to taste. Serve with ham or tongue.

See other sweet and sour sauces under Barbecue Marinades in outdoor cooking chapter.

BUTTER SAUCES

PARSLEY BUTTER SAUCE

1 tablespoon butter
1 teaspoon minced parsley
1 teaspoon lemon juice
salt, pepper

Cream butter, add parsley, lemon juice, salt and pepper. Spread over hot broiled fish or steak.

ANCHOVY BUTTER SAUCE

Follow recipe for Parsley Butter Sauce, using anchovy paste instead of parsley.

MAITRE D'HOTEL BUTTER SAUCE

¼ cup butter
½ teaspoon salt
⅛ teaspoon pepper
¼ teaspoon finely chopped parsley
¾ tablespoon lemon juice

Cream butter. Add salt, pepper and parsley; stir in lemon juice, very slowly. Spread over hot broiled fish, steak, or sweetbreads.

LOBSTER BUTTER SAUCE

Put lobster coral in heavy bowl, pound with ¼ pound of butter, then rub through a very fine sieve. Season with salt and pepper.

DRAWN BUTTER SAUCE

8 tablespoons butter
4 tablespoons flour
2 cups boiling water, milk or fish stock
½ teaspoon salt
⅛ teaspoon pepper

Melt 4 tablespoons butter in a saucepan. Add flour and blend well. Add the liquid, stirring constantly, the remainder of the butter and the salt and pepper. Boil 5 minutes and serve hot.

MUSTARD BUTTER SAUCE

Melt ⅓ cup butter, stir in 2 tablespoons prepared mustard and 1 tablespoon of boiling water. Serve hot over fish.

MAYONNAISE AND CREAM SAUCES

TARTAR SAUCE

1 cup mayonnaise
1 tablespoon chopped capers
1 tablespoon tarragon vinegar
1 tablespoon chopped olives
1 tablespoon cucumber pickles

Combine mayonnaise with the rest of the ingredients. Serve cold with hot fish or cold meat. Add minced chives or onions if desired.

CUCUMBER CREAM SAUCE

1 fresh cucumber
½ cup heavy cream
¼ teaspoon salt
a few grains pepper
3 tablespoons vinegar or lemon juice

Pare, chop coarsely and chill cucumber. Whip the cream until stiff, add the salt and pepper and gradually the vinegar or lemon juice. When ready to serve, fold in the cucumber.

CUCUMBER MAYONNAISE

1 cup mayonnaise
1 teaspoon dry mustard
1 cup sour cream
2 cucumbers, chopped
1 drop green vegetable coloring
2 tablespoons chopped chives or parsley

Blend mayonnaise, mustard and sour cream thoroughly. Add chopped cucumbers, coloring, and blend again. Fold in parsley or chives.

WHIPPED HORSERADISH CREAM SAUCE

1 cup heavy cream
salt and white pepper
¾ cup grated horseradish root
1 tablespoon sugar
1 tablespoon vinegar or lemon juice

Whip cream stiff, gradually beat in rest of ingredients. If prepared horseradish is used, drain, season to taste.

FROZEN HORSERADISH CREAM

Make Whipped Horseradish Cream Sauce, above, and freeze until firm. Serve with cold meat platters. If desired, add 1 tablespoon chopped pistachio nuts and 2 tablespoons chili sauce.

CREAMY EGG SAUCE

6 hard-cooked eggs, diced
1 cup light cream
1 tablespoon butter
salt and paprika
4 tablespoons finely chopped parsley

Place the first 4 ingredients in top of double boiler. When thoroughly heated, add parsley and pour over cauliflower, asparagus or fish.

21
SOUPS AND GARNISHES

CLEAR · HEARTY · JELLIED · MEATLESS · CREAM · BISQUES
· CHOWDERS · WINE SOUPS · GARNISHES · DUMPLINGS

Good home-made soup has many uses. Clear broth cooked from bones and meat (or chicken or fish) and vegetable-seasoned water serves as a base for sauces and other dishes, or to start a full meal. Hearty soups are an economical and satisfying way to round out a light meal, or even to serve as the meal itself.

SOUP STOCK WILL KEEP for several days if refrigerated. The cake of fat which forms on top will exclude the air and should not be removed until stock is used. Save all remnants of meat, bones, trimmings, gristle, marrow bone, fat and gravies and add to leftover soup stock, cooking slowly.

STOCK may also be made from bouillon or meat cubes or bouillon pastes, dissolved in hot water, or canned clear soups.

DEHYDRATED SOUPS may be reconstituted as directed on package or with any liquid drained from cooked vegetables or meat.

CANNED SOUPS may be used alone or in combinations.

TO FLAVOR SOUP

Onions, celery, celery root, parsley root, and carrots are used. Celery seed may also be used. Use outside leaves of onion, if dark color is desired.

Celery leaves, stalks and roots can be dried in a slow oven, powdered and bottled for future use.

TO REMOVE FAT FROM SOUP

Chill until the fat rises to the top and forms a firm layer. Remove hardened fat. When there is no time for chilling, skim fat with a spoon or paper napkin.

TO CLEAR SOUP

To 1 quart of soup stock, add the white of 1 egg mixed with 1 teaspoon water. Add the crushed eggshell. Boil for 2 minutes, stirring constantly. Add 1 tablespoon of ice water, then let stand to settle. Strain through cheesecloth placed in strainer.

TO USE CANNED SOUP AS SAUCE

Add only ⅓ cup of water or milk to condensed soup.

CLEAR SOUPS

SOUP STOCK
2½ pounds beef plate or brisket
3 quarts cold water
1 tablespoon salt
¼ teaspoon pepper
a few dried onion peels
¼ cup each onion, carrot and celery, diced
½ cup tomato, raw or canned
chopped green or red pepper
1 teaspoon chopped parsley

Wipe meat; place in soup kettle with the cold water. Add seasonings. Bring slowly to the boiling point. If clear soup is preferred, skim now. Cover. Simmer 3 hours or longer, add all the vegetables, except parsley, and cook 1 hour longer, adding more hot water if necessary. Strain, cool, skim off the fat. Adjust seasonings, reheat, and just before serving, add the parsley.

Remove meat from soup when tender and serve with horseradish or mustard sauce.

CONSOMME

2 pounds chicken
1 pound veal bone
1 pound marrow bone
1 beef knuckle
1 pound lean beef (round)
6 quarts cold water
1 tablespoon salt
¼ teaspoon pepper
¼ teaspoon nutmeg, grated
⅓ cup each onion, celery, and carrots, cut up
1 tablespoon fat

Clean chicken if necessary, separate it at the joints, and place in soup kettle with the soup bones. Cut beef into small pieces and brown in hot skillet with the marrow from the marrow bones, and add to soup kettle. Add the cold water and seasonings. Heat quickly to the boiling point, skim if a clear soup is desired. Cover, let simmer slowly for 5 hours. Fry the vegetables in 1 tablespoon fat 5 minutes; add, and let boil 1 hour longer. Strain, season to taste. When cool, remove fat. Serve hot in cups with any soup garnish.

The chicken should be removed as soon as tender. It can be served with any well-flavored sauce or used for salads or croquettes.

BOUILLON

4 pounds lean beef
5 pounds shin bone
chicken leftovers
4 quarts water
1 tablespoon salt
1/16 teaspoon red pepper
a few dried onion peels
1 bay leaf
¼ cup celery, cut up
1 small onion, sliced
1 carrot, cut up
1 potato, cut up

Place meat and bone in soup kettle, add the cold water, let stand 1 hour. Season. Bring slowly to the boiling point. Cover closely and simmer 4 or more hours. Add vegetables, boil 1 hour longer.

Strain all through a sieve and season to taste; skim off fat. Serve hot.

CHICKEN SOUP OR BROTH

3- to 4-pound stewing chicken, cut up
10 chicken feet, scalded and skinned, nails removed
3 to 4 quarts water
1 tablespoon salt
2 stalks celery or ¼ cup celery root, diced
1 onion
¼ teaspoon pepper
⅛ teaspoon nutmeg

Cover chicken and chicken feet with water, add salt and bring to a boil. Cover; simmer slowly 3 or more hours, add the vegetables, boil 1 hour longer, strain, remove fat and add seasoning to taste. Remove the chicken when tender and use for salads, croquettes, or serve with Brown Sauce.

HEARTY SOUPS

Hearty soups, including the meat and vegetables from which they are made, are served in small portions to begin a meal, in larger portions as the first course of a simple meal, or in generous bowls as the main course of a meal. In this case, they are accompanied by fresh rye or French bread and butter. A vegetable or fruit salad and a dessert can round out the menu.

BORSHT (BEET SOUP)

½ of a 5-pound chicken
3 quarts boiling water
½ cup lima beans
1 can (1 pound) tomatoes, strained
5 or 6 large beets, peeled and cut in strips
2 onions, peeled and sliced
2 apples, peeled and sliced
2 potatoes, peeled and cut in cubes
1 small celery root, diced
1 teaspoon salt
⅛ teaspoon pepper
2 tablespoons sugar
½ teaspoon citric acid
3 egg yolks, well beaten

Place chicken, cut at joints, in water. Add vegetables, apples, salt and pepper and cook slowly, covered tightly, 2 to 3 hours. Then add sugar and citric acid (sour salt) to taste and boil 3 minutes. Remove from heat and stir about 1 pint of this soup into the yolks gradually, so it will not curdle. Mix all together. Serve a piece of chicken with each serving. Boiling water may be added if mixture is too thick.

MEAT BORSHT

6 medium beets
1½ pounds beef, brisket or flank
3 large onions
3 pints water
salt
¼ teaspoon citric acid
sugar and vinegar to taste

Wash, scrape and grate or grind beets. Put in a kettle. Add beef, onions, water, and a little salt to taste. Cover and cook until beets and meat are tender. Then add citric acid (sour salt), vinegar, and sugar to taste, and a few cooked prunes, if desired. Boil about 15 minutes.

(For Borsht without meat see Beet Soup, Meatless, page 399.)

KARELIAN BORSHT

4 to 6 medium beets
2 tablespoons butter
1 teaspoon salt
4 tablespoons flour
2 tablespoons vinegar
1 small head cabbage, white or red, shredded
1 bay leaf
1 clove garlic
2 carrots, sliced
1 tablespoon sugar
8 cups beef bouillon
½ pound spicy sausages
sour cream (optional)
lemon slices (optional)

Grate or grind beets and sauté in butter. Add salt, flour and vinegar, stirring until well blended. In a large kettle place the beets, cabbage, bay leaf, garlic, carrots, sugar and bouillon. Simmer at least 2 hours. If the liquid boils down too much, add water. Serve hot, topped with sausage slices. Sour cream and lemon toppings may be used if desired.

CABBAGE BORSHT

2 pounds cabbage, shredded coarsely
⅓ cup Kosher salt
½ teaspoon pepper
1 cup chopped onion
1½ pounds beef chuck, cubed
1 large soup bone
2 1-pound cans tomato purée
1 large potato, cubed
2 teaspoons sour salt (to taste)
1 cup sugar
2 cloves garlic, minced

Combine cabbage, salt, pepper, onion and 1½ quarts of water in a large kettle. Cover and bring to a boil. Add beef, soup bone, tomato purée.

Cover and simmer for 1 hour. Add potato; simmer, covered, for 40 minutes. Add sour salt and sugar; simmer 15 minutes. Add garlic and simmer 5 minutes. This soup can be frozen.

CHICKEN GUMBO SOUP

½ recipe Chicken Soup, page 394
¼ cup rice
1 cup canned or cooked okra
1 small onion, chopped
2 stalks celery, cut up
¼ cup strained tomato

Make ½ recipe of Chicken Soup. When chicken is nearly tender, remove from bones, cut into small pieces, and return to soup. Add rest of ingredients, simmer for 1 hour, season with salt and pepper to taste.

TURKEY, GOOSE, OR DUCK SOUP

bones of turkey, goose or duck
scraps of the meat
leftover stuffing
leftover gravy
cold water to cover
1 teaspoon salt
⅛ teaspoon pepper
1 onion, sliced
¼ cup celery, diced
¼ cup carrot, sliced

Use any leftover poultry, break the carcass in pieces, add stuffing and gravy. Put into kettle with remnants of the meat; cover with cold water, bring slowly to the boiling point. Cover kettle and simmer 4 or more hours; add rest of ingredients and boil ½ hour longer. If a stronger soup is desired, add 1 or 2 chicken bouillon cubes. Strain, remove fat. Serve hot with Dumplings, Pfarvel, Barley, or Green Kern (see soup garnishes at end of chapter).

GREEN KERN SOUP

2 cups green kern
2 cups boiling water
1 teaspoon salt
¼ cup celery, diced
2 quarts Soup Stock, page 393, or Chicken Soup, page 394
⅛ teaspoon pepper
1 cup rye croutons

Wash green kern in cold water, then cook in boiling salted water 2 hours or until tender. Add the celery. As water evaporates, add soup stock. If soup stock must be made, keep skimming it as it cooks and add the "top soup," strained, to the green kern along with the stock to the desired consistency. A slice of toasted rye bread boiled with the soup improves the flavor. Season to taste. Serve hot with croutons. If you prefer, dry and grind the green kern fine and cook until tender in the soup.

DRIED BEAN SOUP

To 1 pint Boiled Beans, page 183, add Brown Sauce, page 387, using 2 cups soup stock in place of water.

DRIED PEA SOUP

2 cups split peas
3 quarts cold water
smoked brisket of beef, ham bone or bacon or
    tongue or dried beef or sausage
¼ cup celery, diced
1 small onion, cut fine
2 tablespoons butter or fat
2 tablespoons flour
1 teaspoon sugar
2 teaspoons salt
¼ teaspoon pepper

Pick over and wash the peas. Soak them in cold water overnight, or for several hours; if quick-cooking peas are used, do not soak. Drain, place in soup kettle with the smoked beef, ham bone, or tongue or bacon; add the cold water. Cover. Boil slowly but steadily 4 hours or more. (Quick-cooking peas require shorter cooking time.) Add the celery and cook until the peas and meat are tender. Remove meat when tender and place on platter. Skim fat off the top of soup. Heat 2 tablespoons butter or fat in a skillet, add the onions and brown, add flour and gradually a cup of the soup. Add to the rest of soup. Season to taste and serve with croutons.

Or cook peas until tender, add sliced smoked sausage or dried beef, boil a few minutes, and serve hot in the soup. A slice of toasted rye bread may be boiled with the soup. If soup is too thick, thin with milk, cream or soup stock.

VEGETABLE SOUP WITH MEAT

2 pounds shin of beef, with meat
2 quarts cold water
2 teaspoons salt
½ green pepper, chopped
1 cup tomato
½ cup cabbage
1 small onion
½ small carrot
1 sprig parsley
1 piece celery root
½ cup peas
1 teaspoon sugar

Wipe the meat, cut it into small pieces. Put it with the bone and salt into the cold water. Cover and simmer 4 hours; then add the vegetables, cut fine, and the seasoning. Cook 1 hour longer, cool. When ready to use, remove fat. Heat and serve.

BEEF-CHICKEN SOUP

1 pound ground beef
1 tablespoon shortening
1 frying chicken
6 cups water
2 onions, minced
1 can tomatoes
1 teaspoon dill weed
salt
pepper
2 packages frozen mixed vegetables

Brown beef in shortening in a large kettle. In another kettle, boil chicken in water until tender. Remove skin and bones. Cut chicken into bite-size pieces and add to beef. Strain the liquid in which the chicken was cooked and add to meat. Add onions, tomatoes, dill weed, and salt and pepper to taste. Simmer for 30 to 40 minutes. Add vegetables and cook only until vegetables are tender.

THAI SOUR SOUP

1 large or 2 medium cucumbers
½ pound ground pork or bulk pork sausage
1 egg
½ to 1 clove garlic
salt and pepper to taste
3 to 4 cups chicken broth
1 teaspoon monosodium glutamate
2 tablespoons lemon juice
chili peppers (optional)

Peel cucumber and slice about ½ inch thick. Carefully remove seedy portion leaving the circles whole. Combine meat, egg, garlic and seasonings. Stuff meat into cucumber circles. Bring chicken broth to full boil, add monosodium glutamate and gradually add the lemon juice to taste. Add stuffed cucumbers and cook about 5 minutes. The pork should be well cooked but the cucumbers should not be mushy. For a native touch, chili peppers may be served with the soup.

FRENCH ONION SOUP

6 (1 pound) onions
3 tablespoons butter
1 quart Soup Stock, page 393
6 small slices toast
grated cheese, Swiss, American or Parmesan

Peel onions and cut into ⅛-inch slices. Cook slowly in butter until tender and slightly browned, stirring constantly. Add Soup Stock, heat to boiling point, boil 2 or 3 minutes. Pour the hot soup into cups or soup plates, float toast on top, covered with 1 tablespoon cheese. Serve with additional cheese if desired.

BEEF-VEGETABLE SOUP, SOUTHERN STYLE

4 to 5 pounds shoulder of beef, unboned
6 cups diced potatoes
4 cups diced sweet potatoes
4 cups sliced carrots
2 cups cabbage, medium cut
3 cups canned tomatoes
2½ cups or 1 pound dried lima beans
2 tablespoons celery seed
2 tablespoons salt
½ teaspoon pepper
9 quarts cold water

The soup bone must be free from splinters, as the soup is not strained. Put all ingredients into a large kettle. Cook covered, boiling rapidly, for 2 hours, then reduce heat and simmer uncovered 2 to 3 hours longer. About 15 minutes before serving, remove meat and bone. Cut meat into pieces and add to soup. May be used as main course. Serves about 10.

HAMBURGER-VEGETABLE SOUP

½ pound ground beef
2 tablespoons fat
1 cup canned tomatoes
½ cup diced carrots
½ cup diced celery
1 chopped onion
¼ cup chopped parsley
½ teaspoon pepper
1 cup diced potato
1½ cups water
1 teaspoon salt

Brown ground beef in fat. Add remaining ingredients and simmer until vegetables are tender. Serves 3 to 4.

CURRIED PEANUT SOUP

½ cup chopped carrots
½ cup chopped celery
½ cup minced onion
1 teaspoon curry powder
3 tablespoons shortening
2 tablespoons flour
3½ cups chicken broth
½ cup chunk-style peanut butter
2 tablespoons catsup
2 teaspoons Worcestershire sauce
1 cup cooked rice (optional)
chopped peanuts
sour cream

Sauté vegetables and curry in shortening until the onion is clear, stirring constantly. Stir in the flour. Very gradually add the chicken broth, stirring constantly. Add peanut butter, catsup and Worcestershire sauce. If adding rice, add at this point. Simmer for 5 minutes. Chopped peanuts and sour cream are served separately to be added to the soup at the table.

LENTIL OR LINSEN SOUP

2 cups lentils
3 quarts cold water
3 pounds brisket of beef, or 1 pound smoked sausage, or a ham bone
¼ cup celery, diced
1 small onion
salt and pepper
2 tablespoons flour
croutons

Wash lentils and prepare same as Dried Pea Soup, page 396. 1 cup of strained tomato improves the flavor.

MOCK TURTLE SOUP

1 calf's head
2 teaspons salt
¼ teaspoon pepper
1 medium onion
1 cup strained tomatoes
1 large carrot
2 tablespoons butter
2 tablespoons flour, browned
juice and rind of ½ lemon
¼ cup sherry

Cover calf's head with cold water. Bring to boiling point. Add salt, pepper and vegetables. Simmer for 3 hours. Strain. Dice head meat. Melt butter, add flour and ¼ cup soup or milk. Add this to soup. Add lemon and sherry. Serve with head meat and sliced eggs.

QUICK MOCK TURTLE SOUP

1 can tomato soup
1 can mock turtle soup
4 cups Soup Stock, page 393
½ teaspoon paprika
4 cloves
1 teaspoon salt
6 tablespoons Madeira wine
6 thin slices lemon
4 hard-cooked eggs

Boil soups and seasonings together. Remove from heat and add wine. Place lemon slices, white of eggs chopped fine and whole egg yolks in a tureen. Pour hot soup over them.

PEPPER POT SOUP

1 can concentrated pea soup
1 can concentrated tomato soup
1 can concentrated pepper pot soup
2 cups milk

Combine and heat thoroughly, stirring constantly.

MULLIGATAWNY SOUP

3 pounds chicken, cut up
¼ cup fat
2 sour apples, sliced
¼ cup onions, sliced
¼ cup celery, cut in cubes
¼ cup carrots, cut in cubes
½ green pepper, chopped fine
1 tablespoon flour
1 teaspoon curry powder
2 cloves
1 cup tomato
⅛ teaspoon mace
1 teaspoon chopped parsley
1 teaspoon sugar
salt and pepper
4 quarts cold water

Brown chicken, vegetables and apples in the fat; add flour and curry powder; stir. Add the rest of the ingredients and cook slowly until chicken is tender. Remove chicken and cut the meat in small pieces. Strain soup and rub vegetables through a sieve. Add chicken. Season and serve hot with boiled rice.

OXTAIL SOUP

2 oxtails, split
2 tablespoons fat
3 pounds lean beef
5 quarts cold water
1 tablespoon salt
1 large onion, diced
¼ cup celery root, diced
1 tablespoon chopped parsley
3 carrots, diced
2 tablespoons flour

Cut oxtails into small pieces and fry lightly in fat. Put meat and oxtails in kettle, add water and salt. Cover. Let cook slowly about 4 hours. Add vegetables, cook 1 hour longer. Strain. Heat 2 tablespoons of top fat in skillet, add flour, brown slowly, add 1 cup of soup and stir into the remaining stock. To darken, add Kitchen Bouquet.

Dumplings, noodles and other garnishes for soup will be found beginning on page 406 and continuing to page 410.

SCOTCH BROTH

1½ lbs. lamb
1 quart cold water
1 teaspoon salt
2 onions, diced
2 tablespoons rice or barley
2 potatoes, diced
½ cup each carrots and celery

Cut mutton into small pieces, place in soup kettle with water and salt. Cover. Cook slowly 4 or 5 hours. Strain, cool and remove fat. Add barley or rice and vegetables. Cook for 1 hour. Season.

JELLIED SOUPS

Cold jellied consommé and consommé flavored with tomato, Madrilène style, make refreshing warm-weather soups. These are easy to prepare at home, and also come in cans, ready to chill in the refrigerator until set. To serve, stir contents with a fork, fill chilled cups, garnish with lemon wedge and chopped parsley.

JELLIED CHICKEN BOUILLON

2 cups boiling Chicken Soup, page 394
1 envelope unflavored gelatin
¼ cup cold water
salt
chopped parsley

Make Chicken Soup, season well. Soak gelatin in cold water 5 minutes. Add soup and stir until dissolved. When slightly cool, add parsley. Chill. Stir lightly with a fork, and serve in bouillon cups.

JELLIED BOUILLON

Use Bouillon, page 394, in place of Chicken Soup. Garnish with horseradish and catsup, or whipped cream sprinkled with paprika.

JELLIED CONSOMME MADRILENE

2 cans beef bouillon
1 can chicken bouillon
1 can (8 ounces) tomato purée
2 egg whites, beaten
2 crushed eggshells
1 onion
1 small bunch parsley
salt and pepper to taste
2 envelopes unflavored gelatin
½ cup cold water

Boil first 8 ingredients for 10 minutes; add gelatin soaked in cold water, stir to dissolve. Let stand 5 minutes, strain. Pour into cups with a slice of hard-cooked egg in the bottom of cup. Chill until firm. Serve with slice of lemon on edge of cup, or with catsup or horseradish.

MEATLESS SOUPS

BEET SOUP, MEATLESS (MILCHIK BORSHT)

Cut 2 small beets in strips; cover with water and let cook until tender; add citric acid and a little sugar to make sweet and sour, and a little salt. Add ¾ cup sour cream. Serve cold. Or add sweet milk, gradually pour hot soup over 2 or more well-beaten yolks of eggs. Stir constantly and keep over the fire until thick and smooth. Serve cold.

BAKED BEAN SOUP

1 quart baked beans, or 2 cans (1 pound each) baked beans
1 medium onion, chopped
2 quarts water
3 tablespoons butter
3 tablespoons flour
salt and pepper to taste

Cook beans, water and onions until beans are very soft. Put through a strainer. Melt butter, add flour, and when bubbling add ⅔ cup of the liquid. Stir well; add the rest of the soup. Season with salt and pepper, reheat to boiling point and serve. 1 cup strained tomatoes may be added.

BLACK BEAN SOUP

2 cups black beans
2 tablespoons chopped onion
3 tablespoons butter
2 quarts cold water
2 stalks celery or celery root
2 teaspoons salt
⅛ teaspoon pepper
2 tablespoons flour
1 lemon
2 hard-cooked eggs

Soak beans overnight; drain and rinse thoroughly. Fry the onion in 2 tablespoons butter, add the beans, celery, and 2 quarts water. Cook slowly until the beans are soft, 3 or 4 hours, add more water as it boils away; rub through a strainer, add the seasonings and heat; heat the remaining butter in a saucepan, add the flour, stir in the hot soup very gradually; cut lemon and eggs in thin slices and serve in the soup. ¼ cup of sherry may be added immediately before serving.

GAZPACHO (1)

3 tomatoes
1 large green pepper
2 carrots
1 cucumber
1 cup water
½ teaspoon garlic powder
½ teaspoon pepper
¼ teaspoon basil
¼ teaspoon thyme
1 teaspoon onion powder
½ teaspoon salt
1 teaspoon lemon juice
½ teaspoon parsley flakes

Parboil tomatoes for 3 to 5 minutes. Peel. Grind all ingredients or combine in blender. Serve chilled.

GAZPACHO (2)

½ pound onions
6 tomatoes
½ cup red wine
1 tablespoon salad oil
1 tablespoon paprika
1 clove garlic
1 cucumber
2 black olives, sliced
salt and pepper
parsley, finely chopped

Peel onions and tomatoes. Grind or purée in blender. Add wine, oil, paprika and garlic. Simmer for about 10 minutes. Remove garlic. When cooled, add cucumber, sliced very thin, and the olives. Add salt and pepper to taste. Chill. Serve garnished with the chopped parsley.

POTATO SOUP

2 tablespoons butter
2 teaspoons chopped onions
2 teaspoons chopped celery
3 potatoes (cut small)
1 quart boiling water
½ teaspoon salt
⅛ teaspoon pepper
1 teaspoon caraway seed
2 teaspoons parsley, chopped
1 tablespoon flour

Heat 1 tablespoon butter, add the onions and celery, and simmer 10 minutes. Add potatoes, cover, and cook 2 minutes. Add the water and seasonings, boil 1 hour. Add more boiling water as it evaporates. Brown the flour and mix with remaining butter, add some potato liquid and cook. Combine and serve hot with croutons. Any cold cooked leftover vegetable may be added.

QUICK POTATO SOUP

3 cups diced potatoes
2 tablespoons butter
1 teaspoon salt
⅛ teaspoon pepper
½ small onion, chopped
1 teaspoon caraway seed
2 cups milk

Cook first 6 ingredients with enough water to cover until potatoes are tender. Add milk, heat but do not boil.

CORN CHOWDER

2 onions, sliced
3 tablespoons fat
2 tablespoons flour
2 cups water
4 potatoes, cut in slices
1 can (16 ounces) corn or 2 cups fresh corn, cooked
3 cups scalded milk
salt and pepper

Fry onion in fat, add flour, stirring often; add 2 cups water and potatoes. Cook until the potatoes are soft; add corn and milk, and cook 5 minutes. Season and serve.

TOMATO SOUP

1 can (1 pound, 13 ounces) or 1 quart fresh
     tomatoes
2 cups water
4 cloves
1 slice onion
2 teaspoons sugar
1 teaspoon salt
2 tablespoons butter
2 tablespoons flour

Cook the first 6 ingredients 20 minutes; strain, reheat. Melt butter, add flour, and the hot strained liquid. Stir until well blended.

MIXED VEGETABLE SOUP

⅓ cup carrots, diced
⅓ cup cabbage, cut up
1½ cups potato, diced
¼ cup onion, sliced
¼ cup string beans
½ cup peas
¼ cup celery
4 tablespoons butter
1½ quarts boiling water
1 teaspoon sugar
1 cup strained tomatoes
2 teaspoons salt
1 teaspoon chopped parsley

Wash, pare and cut vegetables. Heat butter, add onions and sauté until soft; add all vegetables but potatoes and tomatoes. Cook covered for 10 minutes. Add potatoes, cook 2 minutes longer, then add boiling water, sugar, salt and tomatoes and boil until all vegetables are tender. Before serving add parsley.

VEGETABLE LEEK SOUP

4 potatoes, peeled
salt
2 to 2½ quarts water
3 large leeks
2 tablespoons butter
1 can (1 pound) tomatoes

Cook potatoes in salted water until soft. Mash potatoes in the liquid. Cut up leeks, using both green and white parts. Sauté in butter, cooking slowly about 10 minutes. Add leeks and tomatoes to potatoes and cook for about ½ hour. Season to taste.

CREAM SOUPS

The soups grouped under this heading have milk as part or all of their liquid base, and are thickened with flour, cornstarch, or eggs. They are rich and filling, and should be served with a light meal.

ALMOND SOUP

½ lb. almonds
6 bitter almonds
3 tablespoons butter
3 tablespoons cornstarch
6 cups chicken or veal soup
salt and paprika
1 cup cream

Blanch almonds, and grind to consistency of coarse meal. Melt butter, add cornstarch, add 1 cup soup, and make a smooth sauce. Add the sauce and almonds to the remaining soup, cook for a few minutes, add seasoning of salt and paprika, and 1 cup cream. Serve in bouillon cups with whipped cream on top of a small, round cracker in each cup.

CREAM OF ASPARAGUS SOUP

Cook 1 pound of Asparagus, page 412. Reserve liquid in which asparagus was cooked. Prepare Thin White Sauce, page 386, double quantity, adding 1 cup asparagus liquid to milk. Combine with the cut asparagus and serve. Season with paprika.

CREAM OF ASPARAGUS SOUP WITH STOCK BASE

    1 pound green asparagus
    6 cups Soup Stock, page 393
    3 tablespoons butter
    3 tablespoons flour
    ½ cup cream or milk
    ½ teaspoon salt
    ½ cup whipping cream

Wash and drain asparagus. Boil in soup stock 5 minutes. Remove tips and set aside. Dice remaining stalks and boil 20 minutes; rub stalks and stock through a coarse sieve. Make a sauce with melted butter, flour and 1 cup of hot stock. Cook until smooth. Add to soup, then add hot cream and seasoning. Serve in bouillon cups garnished with whipped cream and asparagus tips.

CREAM OF CORN SOUP

    4 cups hot milk
    1 slice onion
    1 can (12 ounces) kernel corn
    2 cups water
    2 tablespoons butter
    2 tablespoons flour
    1 teaspoon salt
    ⅛ teaspoon white pepper

Heat the milk and onion, then remove onion. Chop the corn or rub through a sieve, and cook it with the water 20 minutes. Melt the butter, add the flour, and when bubbling, add first ⅔ cup, then the rest of the milk gradually; cook till slightly thickened. Add the corn, salt and pepper. Top with whipped cream sprinkled with popcorn.

BEER SOUP

    1 cup water
    1 pint beer
    salt and nutmeg
    2 eggs, separated
    1 tablespoon sugar
    1 tablespoon flour
    1 cup milk

Add water to beer, bring to a boil, season with salt and nutmeg if desired. Beat yolks well with sugar and the flour mixed, add milk, stir until smooth, stir all together in the hot beer mixture, bring almost to a boil. Fold in beaten whites and serve at once with toasted bread cubes.

CREAM OF CELERY SOUP

    3 stalks celery
    1 slice onion
    3 cups milk
    2 tablespoons butter
    2 tablespoons flour
    ¼ teaspoon pepper
    1 teaspoon salt
    1 cup cream

Cut celery into small pieces. Cook in double boiler with onion and milk for 20 minutes. Remove onion and celery; heat the butter, add flour and seasonings, and gradually the celery broth; add cream and celery; cook until smooth and slightly thickened.

QUICK CREAM OF CELERY SOUP

    2 cups celery, diced
    double recipe for Thin White Sauce, page 386
    salt, celery salt

Cook celery in small amount of water until tender. Drain. Reserve liquid and add to White Sauce. Then add cooked celery. Season and reheat.

CHEESE SOUP

    ½ cup finely chopped onions
    4 tablespoons butter
    4 tablespoons flour
    1½ tablespoons cornstarch
    4 cups Chicken Broth, page 394
    4 cups milk
    1 cup cooked chopped carrots
    1 cup cooked chopped celery
    ⅛ teaspoon paprika
    ½ pound Cheddar cheese, finely cut
    chopped parsley

Sauté onions in butter until tender and glassy. Add flour and cornstarch, blending well. Add stock and milk gradually, stirring constantly. When boiling, add carrots, celery, paprika and cheese. Cook over low heat until cheese is melted. Add salt, if necessary. Serve hot with finely chopped parsley.

—*Basic soup stocks, pages 393-394*
—*Hearty meat and vegetable soups, pages 394-398*
—*Meatless soups, pages 399-400*
—*Fish soups and chowders, pages 403-405*
—*Dumplings and other soup garnishes, pages 406-410*

FRESH CORN SOUP

6 ears sweet corn (2 cups raw pulp)
1 teaspoon salt
⅛ teaspoon white pepper
1 teaspoon sugar
2 cups milk or cream, heated
1 tablespoon butter
1 teaspoon flour

Grate the corn. Cover the cobs with cold water, and boil 30 minutes, then strain. To 1 pint of this corn liquid add the raw corn pulp, cook 15 minutes, add the seasoning and hot milk. Heat the butter, add the flour, and gradually the corn mixture; cook 5 minutes longer.

MILK SOUP

4 tablespoons butter
4 tablespoons flour
1 teaspoon salt
4 cups hot milk, or milk and vegetable water mixed

Brown the butter, add the flour and salt and add some of the hot milk, stirring all the time. Add the rest of the liquid. Season to taste. Serve with dumplings or other soup garnishes. Rye flour may be used in place of the wheat flour and one or two yolks of eggs slightly beaten may be added very gradually.

For Cream of Vegetable Soup add 1 cup of any cooked, sieved vegetable.

CREAM OF MUSHROOM SOUP

4 tablespoons butter
½ pound mushrooms
1 quart chicken or veal broth
2 tablespons flour
1 cup cream
salt and pepper

Melt half the butter in skillet, add mushrooms, chopped or ground, cover; simmer 5 minutes. Add to broth. Cook 5 minutes. Melt rest of the butter in saucepan, add flour. When it bubbles, stir in broth; add cream and seasoning. Top with whipped cream sprinkled with paprika.

CREAM OF SPINACH, LETTUCE OR WATERCRESS SOUP

1 pound spinach, cooked, or 2 heads lettuce, finely cut, or 1 bunch watercress, finely cut
1 quart Chicken Soup, page 394
2 cups Thin White Sauce, page 386

Drain, chop and rub spinach through sieve. Add soup, boil 10 minutes. Add White Sauce, salt and pepper to taste. Serve in bouillon cups. Top with whipped cream; sprinkle with paprika. Raw lettuce or watercress may be substituted for cooked, sieved spinach. Boil it with soup, rub through sieve.

CREAM OF POTATO SOUP

3 potatoes
4 cups milk
2 slices onion
3 tablespoons butter
2 tablespoons flour
1½ tablespoons salt
¼ teaspoon celery salt
⅛ teaspoon pepper
few grains cayenne
1 tablespoon chopped parsley

Cook the potatoes till very soft. Scald the milk and onion in a double boiler. Drain the potatoes; add the milk. Rub through a strainer. Melt the butter in the double boiler, add the flour, add the hot milk mixture, and seasonings, stirring constantly; cook 5 minutes. Add chopped parsley and serve hot.

CREAM OF TOMATO SOUP

1 slice onion
1 quart milk or milk and cream mixed
2 tablespoons butter
2 tablespoons flour
¼ teaspoon white pepper
1 teaspoon salt
2 cups tomatoes
2 teaspoons sugar

Briefly cook the onion with the milk. Heat butter in double boiler. Add flour, seasoning, ⅔ cup hot milk, then the rest of milk gradually. Cook the tomatoes and sugar, strain. Add very gradually to the white sauce, stirring constantly.

VICHYSSOISE

4 to 5 leeks
2 tablespoons butter
4 medium potatoes
4 cups broth, chicken or veal
1 stalk celery, minced
parsley, chopped
2 cups cream
salt, white pepper
Worcestershire sauce
chopped chives

Cut white part of leeks into thin slices. Sauté in butter slowly for 10 minutes. Add potatoes, peeled and sliced very thin, broth, celery and parsley. Cover and simmer for 30 minutes. Strain, add cream, salt, white pepper, a few drops of Worcestershire and the chopped chives. Stir well. Serve ice cold.

PEANUT BUTTER SOUPS
Blend 1 tablespoon of peanut butter per serving into any of the following cream soups—tomato, celery, or chicken.

FISH AND SEAFOOD BISQUES

These creamy fish and seafood soups make very elegant and rich first courses.

CRAB MEAT BISQUE
6½-ounce can crab meat
10½-ounce can each of concentrated tomato soup and pea soup
1 cup cream
¾ cup sherry

Clean the crab meat. Place soups and cream in a saucepan and heat, stirring constantly. Add crab meat, heat thoroughly. Just before serving add sherry gradually. Serve hot with crackers.

SEAFOOD BISQUE
Follow recipe for Crab Meat Bisque, above, using 1 pint oysters and 1 pound cooked shrimp in place of crab meat.

LOBSTER BISQUE
2 pounds boiled lobster
2 cups cold water or chicken broth
3 tablespoons butter
3 tablespoons flour
1½ teaspoons salt
a few grains cayenne
2 cups milk
1 cup cream, scalded

Remove the meat from lobster shell. Dice body meat. Chop claw and tail meat fine. Add water or broth to body bones and tough ends of claws, cut in pieces; bring slowly to boiling point and cook 20 minutes. Drain, reserve liquid. Heat butter, add flour and seasoning, and gradually the liquid. Stir until smooth. Scald milk and stir in gradually. Add lobster meat and cook slowly for 5 minutes, add cream and serve at once.

ROSY LOBSTER BISQUE
2 cups milk
½ cup chopped celery
¼ cup grated onion
½ teaspoon salt
1 pound lobster meat, cooked
1 tablespoon butter
1 can condensed tomato soup
½ cup heavy cream, whipped

Cook milk, celery, onion, and salt in double boiler for 15 minutes. Cut lobster into small pieces; sauté in butter, add soup, and heat thoroughly. When ready to serve, combine the mixtures, add the stiffly beaten cream, and heat. Do not boil.

CREAM OF OYSTER SOUP
1 pint oysters
¼ cup cold water
1 cup Thin White Sauce, page 386
Salt and pepper to taste

Put oysters in strainer over saucepan; pour cold water over oysters. Keep water and oyster liquor. Remove any bit of shell. Add oysters to liquid; heat slowly to the boiling point and cook until oysters are plump and edges curl (3 to 5 minutes). Add to White Sauce, season, stir until smooth. Serve with crackers.

OYSTER BISQUE
1 pint oysters
1 cup finely chopped celery
2 tablespoons butter
2 tablespoons flour
1 pint cream
salt, paprika
chopped parsley
sherry

Clean oysters, chop very fine. Strain and reserve liquid. Cook celery and butter in double boiler until tender. Blend in flour. Add cream and seasonings, stirring well. When ready to serve, add oysters, oyster liquid, parsley and sherry to taste. Heat thoroughly, but do not boil.

CREAM OF SALMON SOUP

   1 cup canned salmon
   2 tablespoons butter
   2 tablespoons flour
   1 teaspoon salt
   ⅛ teaspoon pepper
   4 cups scalded milk

Drain oil from the salmon, remove skin and bones, and rub salmon through a sieve. Heat the butter, add flour and seasoning, gradually add the milk and the strained salmon. Cook until smooth and slightly thickened.

CHOWDERS

Chowders are so full of fish and vegetables that they can be the main course of a family meal, as well as an introduction to any fish menu or light meal.

CLAM CHOWDER

   1 quart clams
   2-inch square fat salt pork
   1 sliced onion
   4 cups potatoes cut in dice ¾ inch square
   4 cups milk
   4 teaspoons butter
   ⅛ teaspoon pepper
   1 teaspoon salt
   8 soda crackers

Drain the clams and remove the pieces of shells. Retain the liquor. Cut the pork into fine pieces and fry slowly until crisp, add the onion, fry 5 minutes, add the cubed potatoes, clam liquor and enough water to cover. Cook until nearly tender, pour into a saucepan, and add the milk, butter, pepper and salt. When the potatoes are done, add clams, whole or cut up, and the crackers. Cook 3 minutes longer.

QUICK CLAM CHOWDER

   1 can concentrated clam chowder
   1 can concentrated chicken gumbo soup
   2 cups milk

Combine and heat thoroughly, stirring constantly.

OYSTER STEW

   1 pint oysters
   2 tablespoons butter
   2 cups scalded milk, cream, or cream and boiling
      water mixed
   ½ teaspoon salt
   paprika

Put oysters in strainer over saucepan; keep the oyster liquor, remove any bit of shell, then add oysters to strained liquor. Put butter and oysters in skillet, cook slowly until edges of oysters curl (3 to 5 minutes). Combine with milk or cream, add salt. Cook 1 minute. Sprinkle with paprika. Serve at once with crisped crackers.

FISH SOUP

   1 medium-large rutabaga, diced
   1 quart water
   1 quart diced, peeled potatoes
   2 teaspoons salt
   1 medium onion, sliced thin
   1 pound fish, such as walleye pike or other white-
      fleshed fish
   1 tablespoon lemon juice
   1 tablespoon flour
   1½ cups milk
   1 to 2 tablespoons butter or margarine
   parsley, chopped fine

Cook rutabaga in water until it can be pierced with a fork. Add potatoes, salt and onion. Simmer 15 minutes. Add fish and lemon juice and simmer 10 to 15 minutes more. Mix flour and milk well. Add to above mixture and simmer 5 minutes. To serve, put thin slices of butter or margarine on top and sprinkle with parsley. Serves 4.

MANHATTAN FISH CHOWDER

   1½ pounds raw halibut, flaked
   6 large potatoes, diced
   6 large tomatoes, cut up
   2 large onions, diced
   salt, pepper
   6 cups water
   ⅔ cup butter
   1 cup heavy cream

Mix first 4 ingredients. Add salt, pepper, and water. Cook 1 hour. Add the rest and heat gently for 5 minutes.

NEW ENGLAND FISH CHOWDER

   4 pounds cod or haddock
   4 cups water
   1 sliced onion
   1½-inch cube fat salt pork
   6 cups potato, cut in ¼-inch slices or ¼-inch cubes
   ¼ teaspoon pepper
   1½ tablespoons salt
   3 tablespoons butter
   4 cups scalded milk
   8 soda crackers

Skin and bone fish. Cook head and backbone in 2 cups cold water 20 minutes; strain. Fry onion in strained, tried-out pork, add potatoes, with 2 cups boiling water. Cook 5 minutes, add fish liquid and the raw fish cut in pieces. Cover and let simmer 10 minutes. Add the rest, soaking crackers in a little cold milk.

SEAFOOD GUMBO

2 small onions, chopped
2 tablespoons butter
1 can condensed chicken gumbo soup
1 can condensed tomato soup
1 can clam chowder
1 can condensed chicken bouillon
3 cups seafood, frozen or canned
½ pound okra
¼ cup sherry
rice

Sauté onions in butter. Combine soups and seafood. Heat to boiling point. Add onions and okra. The okra may be omitted, if desired. Simmer for 10 to 15 minutes. Add sherry. Serve with rice. Mound the rice in the center of each soup plate and surround with gumbo.

RUSSIAN CREAM OF HERRING SOUP

2 cups milk
2 cups water
1 small onion
Salt and pepper to taste
2 herring (previously soaked)

Place milk, water, onion and seasoning in a saucepan. Boil for 10 minutes, add herring cut in small pieces; cook until herring is tender.

WINE AND FRUIT SOUPS

These soups may be served at the start of a meal, as a main course with small tea sandwiches or wafers, or as a refreshing snack. They are also sometimes recommended as part of the invalid's soft or semi-solid diet.

WHITE WINE SOUP

2 cups white wine
2 tablespoons sugar
2 yolks of eggs
croutons

Boil wine and sugar and pour very gradually over yolks, beaten very light. Add croutons and serve at once.

CREAM WINE SOUP

1 cup white wine
½ cup cold water
7 cubes sugar
3 whole cloves
3 small sticks cinnamon
1 cup sweet cream
2 egg yolks, well beaten

Boil water, wine, sugar and spices 10 minutes. Heat the cream, pour it gradually while hot over the yolks and then pour in the strained wine, stirring constantly to prevent curdling.

RED WINE SOUP

1 cup red wine
½ cup water
2 tablespoons sugar
3 whole cloves
3 small sticks cinnamon
1 egg yolk, beaten

Boil wine, water, sugar and spices 10 minutes. Strain. Pour while still hot over beaten egg yolk. Serve hot or cold.

WINE SOUP WITH CHERRIES

2 tablespoons sago or tapioca
1 cup boiling water
1 quart cherries (pitted)
1 quart water
¼ cup sugar
1 cup claret
3 or 4 inches stick cinnamon
½ lemon, sliced fine
2 egg yolks, well beaten

Cook sago or tapioca in 1 cup boiling water until tender, adding more water if necessary. Boil rest of ingredients, except eggs, for 15 minutes; add the cooked sago, bring to a boil, and pour very gradually over the 2 well-beaten yolks. Serve chilled.

Strawberry, raspberry, currant, plum, rhubarb or any dried fruit alone or in combination may be prepared the same way, or without the wine.

DUMPLINGS, NOODLES AND OTHER SOUP GARNISHES

In addition to the various garnishes and dumplings listed here, soups are also garnished for serving with finely slivered vegetables, called "julienne," with chopped parsley or chives, with a little crisp dry cereal, or with a lemon slice or a dusting of paprika.

BREAD, TOAST AND WAFERS FOR SOUP GARNISH

BAKED CROUTONS

Cut dry bread into cubes, place in pan and brown in the oven; or butter the bread, cut into cubes and then brown the same way.

FRIED CROUTONS

Cook small cubes of dry bread in deep hot fat until brown, or brown them in a hot skillet with a little butter or fat.

CRISPED CRUSTS

Cut the crusts of bread into strips 1 inch wide, 5 inches long, ½ inch thick; toast in oven to a golden brown.

ROLLED TOAST STICKS

Remove end slice from a very fresh loaf of bread. Spread cut end of loaf generously with creamed butter. Cut off a very thin slice. Remove crusts, lay slice, buttered side up, on a damp cloth and, beginning at one corner of slice, roll to opposite corner, putting on an extra bit of butter at end to fasten well. Repeat. Place sticks in shallow pan, put under hot broiler and toast evenly.

SOUP STICKS

Cut dry bread in ⅓-inch slices, removing crusts, spread with butter, cut in ⅓-inch strips, brown in the oven.

CRISPED CRACKERS

Place crackers in pan in hot oven a few moments to heat through or spread with creamed butter and place in pan in a hot oven for a few moments, butter side up, until delicately browned.

PUFFED CRACKERS

Cover soda crackers with ice-cold water. Let stand 5 minutes. Remove crackers with perforated skimmer. Dot with butter, place in hot oven about 30 minutes until browned and puffed.

CARAWAY POTATO WAFERS

1 cup boiled potatoes, riced
½ cup creamed butter
1⅛ cups flour
1 egg, slightly beaten
1 tablespoon caraway seed

Work the first 4 ingredients lightly with fork to a smooth dough. Chill for ½ hour. Roll ⅛ inch thick, place in pan, brush top with egg mixed with milk, sprinkle plentifully with salt and caraway seed. Cut with hot knife into narrow strips 1 × 3 inches. Bake in oven at 350° F., for 5 minutes. Increase heat to 400° F. Bake until crisp and a delicate brown. Serve with soup or salad.

GLUTEN WAFERS

⅜ teaspoon salt
⅜ cup cream
1 cup gluten flour

Add the salt to cream, then add the flour. Knead until smooth. Roll very thin. Mark with a grater or prick with a fork. Cut into strips and place in greased and floured pan. Bake in a hot oven, 425° F., until light brown. Serve with soup or salad.

PUFFED WAFERS

1 cup flour
1 teaspoon salt
1 tablespoon butter
milk

Sift flour and salt together, cut in the butter, and add enough milk to make dough. Knead until smooth. Form small balls and roll each one into a thin wafer. Place in shallow greased and floured pan. Bake in hot oven, 425° F., until puffed.

DUMPLINGS
FOR SOUP

ALMOND DUMPLINGS (MANDEL KLOESE)

2 eggs, separated
salt and pepper
½ teaspoon chopped parsley
6 grated almonds
½ teaspoon baking powder
flour

Beat yolks very light; add seasoning, blanched and grated almonds, baking powder and enough flour to make a stiff batter. Add beaten whites. Test a teaspoonful in boiling water and if it boils apart, add more flour. Drop from teaspoon into boiling soup 10 minutes before serving.

BAKING POWDER DUMPLINGS

1 cup flour
2 teaspoons baking powder
¼ teaspoon salt
½ cup milk

Mix dry ingredients, stir in the milk and mix to smooth batter. Drop by teaspoonfuls into boiling soup; cover kettle, let boil 5 minutes and serve at once.

BREAD AND MEAT DUMPLINGS

1½ cups diced bread
water
1 egg, well beaten
¼ cup raw chopped calf's liver, beef, or chicken meat
1 teaspoon salt
pepper and ginger to taste
1 teaspoon chopped parsley
1 teaspoon chopped onion
1 tablespoon soup fat
bread or cracker crumbs

Soak the bread in water and squeeze dry. Add the rest of the ingredients. Shape into balls the size of a walnut and roll in bread or cracker crumbs. Drop into boiling soup, let cook 10 minutes and serve. Makes 20 dumplings.

CRACKER BALLS

2 tablespoons butter or fat
1 egg
½ teaspoon salt
nutmeg, ginger and pepper to taste
1 teaspoon chopped parsley
6 tablespoons cracker crumbs

Cream butter, add the egg, the seasoning, and enough crumbs to make a mixture that holds its shape. Form into small balls. Let stand ½ hour to swell. Drop into boiling soup 10 minutes before serving.

CRACKER-PARSLEY DUMPLINGS

½ cup cracker crumbs
½ cup hot water or soup
½ teaspoon salt
1/16 teaspoon pepper
1 teaspoon chopped parsley
1 egg, slightly beaten

Scald cracker crumbs with hot soup or water, add remaining ingredients. Cool. Drop with teaspoon into boiling soup 10 minutes before serving.

EGG DUMPLINGS (SPATZEN)

1 egg
½ teaspoon salt
¾ cup flour
⅓ cup water

Beat egg well, add salt, flour and water, stirring to a stiff, smooth batter. Drop by teaspoons into boiling soup 10 minutes before serving.

FARINA BALLS

1 tablespoon butter
1 cup hot milk
½ teaspoon salt
pepper
½ cup farina
2 eggs, separated

Put butter, milk and seasonings into double boiler; when hot, add farina and stir until thick and smooth. When cool add the yolks of the eggs and the whites beaten stiff. Season to taste and add ½ cup grated almonds, if desired. Roll size of marbles. Drop them in boiling soup 10 minutes before serving and let them boil up once or twice. Or form into larger dumplings and cook in salted water.

FRITTER BEANS

1 egg
¾ teaspoon salt
½ cup flour
2 tablespoons milk

Beat egg until light, add salt, flour and milk. Put through colander into hot, deep fat and fry until brown. Drain, pour the hot broth over them, and serve.

MACAROONS FOR SOUP

1 egg, separated
2 teaspoons flour or cracker crumbs
¼ cup grated almonds
½ teaspoon salt

Beat yolk well, add the flour or crumbs, the almonds, the salt, and lastly the beaten white. Drop tiny bits from end of spoon in deep hot fat. Remove with skimmer. Drain; add to soup immediately before serving.

MATZOS BALLS

1 cup boiling water
1 cup matzo meal
2 tablespoons chicken fat
1 egg, slightly beaten
1 teaspoon salt
pepper and nutmeg to taste
½ teaspoon chopped parsley

Pour boiling water over matzo meal, stir until water is absorbed, add fat, then egg and seasoning. Mix well. Chill thoroughly. Roll dough into balls the size of a walnut. If sticky, grease palms of hands or moisten with cold water occasionally. Drop into boiling soup 15 minutes before serving. Boil gently uncovered.

MATZOS DUMPLINGS (MATZOS KLOESE)

2 matzos
2 tablespoons fat
¼ onion, cut fine
1 teaspoon chopped parsley
1 teaspoon salt
⅛ teaspoon pepper
¼ teaspoon ginger
⅛ teaspoon nutmeg
2 eggs
about ¼ cup matzo meal

Soak the matzos a few minutes in cold water and then drain and squeeze dry. Heat the fat in a skillet, add the onion, fry to a golden brown, then add the soaked matzos, stir until mixture leaves the skillet clean, add seasoning, the egg slightly beaten, and just enough matzo meal to make a soft dough. Let stand several hours to swell. Shape into balls the size of a marble. Test one by dropping into boiling water or soup; if it boils apart, add more meal. Boil dumplings for 15 minutes.

Other recipes for dumplings to be served with meat and poultry as main course dishes will be found on pages 102-104. The soup dumplings here may, in larger sizes, serve the same purpose.

MATZOS ALMOND DUMPLINGS

3 eggs, separated
⅛ teaspoon nutmeg
⅛ teaspoon salt
½ teaspoon sugar
½ cup grated almonds
1 tablespoon poultry fat or butter
matzo or cracker meal

Beat the yolks very light, add seasoning, almonds, fat and enough matzo or cracker meal to make a stiff batter, fold in the beaten whites. Drop by teaspoonfuls into deep hot fat, fry light brown; try one, and if it does not hold together, add more meal; place in oven to keep warm and put in soup before serving.

SPONGE DUMPLINGS

½ teaspoon salt
⅛ teaspoon nutmeg, grated
1 cup water
1 cup flour
2 eggs

Add salt and nutmeg to water and bring to boiling point. Sift in flour all at once. Beat well until mixture forms a ball and leaves sides of saucepan. Cool slightly, add whole eggs, 1 at a time, beating well each time until mixture is smooth. Drop from teaspoon into boiling soup. Boil 5 minutes and serve.

RICH SPONGE DUMPLINGS

½ cup butter
1 cup milk
½ teaspoon salt
1 cup flour
3 eggs
2 egg yolks
1 tablespoon cornstarch

Melt butter, add milk and salt. When boiling, add flour all at once, and stir over heat until it forms a ball. When cool, add eggs, 1 at a time, and 2 yolks, beating well after each, add cornstarch, beat 5 minutes. Drop by spoonfuls into boiling soup. Cook about 10 minutes covered.

PARSLEY SPONGE DUMPLINGS

3 eggs, separated
1 cup soup stock
½ teaspoon chopped parsley
¼ teaspoon salt

Beat the yolks, add the soup stock, parsley and salt; add the beaten whites. Pour into a buttered cup and place in pan of hot water and steam until firm; cool, remove from cup and cut into small dumplings with a teaspoon. Or bake in small frying pan in a hot oven until browned and when cool cut into small triangles. Add to the boiling soup.

NOODLES FOR SOUP

EGG NOODLES FOR SOUP

1 egg
¼ teaspoon salt
⅔ cup flour (about)

Beat egg slightly, add salt and enough flour to make a stiff dough. Knead well, let stand, covered, ½ hour. Roll out very thin, spread on cloth to dry. The dough must not be the least bit sticky and not so dry that it will break or be brittle.

Fold into a tight roll, or cut into 3-inch strips, placing the strips all together, one on top of another. Now cut these long strips crosswise into very fine strips or threads; or for broad noodles, cut ⅓ to ½ inch wide. Toss them lightly with fingers to separate well, and spread them out on the board to dry. When thoroughly dry, put in covered jars for future use. Drop by handfuls into boiling soup 5 minutes before serving.

NOODLE PUFFS (FINGERHUETCHEN)

Prepare and roll dough as for Egg Noodles for Soup. Let stand until almost dry, fold dough in half and cut through this double thickness with a small floured cutter or thimble, pressing well so edges stick together. Fry in deep hot fat until brown. They should be puffed like little balls. Place in tureen, or put a few in each bouillon cup, and pour the hot broth over them.

BAKED NOODLE PUFFS

Beat 1 egg slightly, add ¼ teaspoon salt and gradually ½ cup flour; form into a soft smooth dough. Place on well-floured board, pat ¼ inch thick, cut with floured thimble or small cutter into tiny balls. Heat ¼ cup butter or chicken fat in pan, drop balls in carefully, not too close, as they swell. Place pan in medium oven, 325° F. When lightly browned on one side, turn with pancake turner and brown on the other side. Drain. Drop 5 or 6 balls in each plate, add the boiling soup. Yields about 100.

NOODLE SQUARES (PLAETZCHEN)

Prepare and roll dough as for Egg Noodles for Soup. When dough is no longer sticky, cut into 3-inch strips and place strips one on top of the other. Then cut crosswise into ⅓-inch strips, cut again in opposite direction to form ⅓-inch squares. Spread out to dry. Drop into boiling water, let boil 5 minutes and serve.

PANCAKE GARNISH

⅛ teaspoon salt
2 eggs
2 tablespoons matzo meal or ¼ cup potato flour

Add salt to eggs, beat slightly, stir in matzo meal or potato flour. Heat a little fat in skillet, pour in egg mixture; when cooked on one side turn on the other. Roll pancake and cut into noodles ⅛ inch wide. Drop into boiling soup before serving.

NOODLES PFARVEL

Take scraps of rolled noodle dough that are too brittle, or use leftover broken noodles. Crush on breadboard with rolling pin, into small bits (not to powder). Shake a little at a time through colander into mixing bowl, forming even grains. To 2 cupfuls add 1 egg, slightly beaten. Mix thoroughly, rub through colander again. Let stand until thoroughly dry. Store. Cook until tender in boiling soup.

MATZOS PFARVEL

With a rolling pin crush broken pieces of matzos into crumbs. Heat 1 tablespoon fat in skillet, add 2 eggs slightly beaten and the matzos crumbs. Stir well until the crumbs are well separated. Let stand for several hours until thoroughly dry. Serve in boiling soup.

ADDITIONAL SOUP GARNISHES

CHINESE EGG DROPS

Beat 1 egg well and pour gradually into boiling soup just before serving.

EGG DROPS (EINLAUF)

1 egg
⅛ teaspoon salt
3 tablespoons flour
¼ cup water
1 teaspoon chopped parsley

Beat egg, add the salt, flour and water, stir until smooth. Pour slowly from end of spoon into boiling soup. Cook 2 to 3 minutes and serve hot; add chopped parsley to the soup.

EGG FLUFF

Pour 2 quarts clear boiling soup into tureen over stiffly beaten whites of 3 eggs. Sprinkle with paprika. Serve a portion of fluff on each serving. Serves 10.

EGG CUSTARD

　2 egg yolks
　2 tablespoons milk
　few grains salt
　chopped parsley and paprika

Beat yolks slightly, add milk and salt, pour into a small buttered cup, sprinkle with parsley and paprika, place in pan of hot water and let cook until firm. Cool, remove from cup and cut in small pieces before adding to soup.

RICE OR BARLEY GARNISH

Wash ½ cup barley or rice in cold water. Cook in 1 quart boiling salted water until tender. Drain. Add to 2 quarts well-seasoned soup stock or tomato soup. Let cook a few minutes, stirring to separate grains.

QUICK REFERENCE GUIDE
TO USEFUL INFORMATION
IN THIS BOOK

22
VEGETABLES

FROM ARTICHOKES · TO ZUCCHINI

Fresh vegetables are always first choice, for flavor as well as for price, when they are in season and grown locally. At other times of the year, frozen and canned vegetables assure a wide and interesting source of the vitamins and minerals your family needs.

Buying and Storing Vegetables

Buy the freshest, most perfect, unblemished vegetables possible, always in small quantities that you can use within a day or two. Even vegetables from your own garden lose freshness rapidly, and should be picked just before cooking, if possible; or stored in the refrigerator if necessary. Prewashed, packed vegetables may be refrigerated in the plastic bags they are sold in. Potatoes and onions should be stored in a cool, airy, dry place. Sweet potatoes do not keep well—buy only what you plan to use at once. Salad greens should be washed and stored at once in refrigerator bags or the vegetable crisper (see Chapter 18).

Cooking Vegetables

Vegetables, possibly more than any other food, require proper cooking and seasoning to bring out their maximum appeal. To preserve vitamins and minerals, pare them as thinly as possible, using a floating-blade peeler, if possible. Don't soak vegetables, except as necessary for cleaning, and don't add soda to the cooking water. Soda may help retain color, but it destroys vitamins. Vegetables look and taste best when they are cooked until just

tender in a minimum amount of liquid. Heavy pots with close-fitting lids permit the use of the least possible amount of liquid. Pressure cooking and steaming are also good methods of cooking vegetables. Whatever the method used, it is important to avoid overcooking, which destroys flavor, color and texture. Any water left after cooking should be used in sauces, stews or soups. If additional water is necessary, add to remaining liquid.

Seasonings and sauces should bring out, not disguise, the flavor of vegetables; a little sugar, for instance, emphasizes the flavor of many vegetables without adding perceptible sweetness.

BASIC VEGETABLE SOUFFLE OR RING

3 tablespoons butter
3 tablespoons flour
¼ teaspoon salt
1 cup hot milk or cream
3 eggs, separated
1 cup cooked, mashed or finely chopped vegetable

Melt butter, add flour. When it bubbles, add milk gradually, and cook, stirring constantly until smooth. Pour gradually onto well-beaten yolks. Add vegetables. Season to taste. Cool. Fold in stiffly beaten whites, place in a buttered casserole or straight-sided soufflé dish. Set in a pan with hot water 1 inch deep, and bake at 350° F. 45 minutes, or until puffed and brown. May be baked in ring or mold. Loosen edges and turn carefully onto hot platter.

ARTICHOKES

3 large or 6 small artichokes
4 quarts boiling water
3 tablespoons salt
2 tablespoons vinegar

With a sharp knife or kitchen shears trim about an inch from the top of the artichoke. Add salt and vinegar to water. Cook artichokes 20 to 30 minutes, or until leaves pull out easily. Drain and cut each artichoke in half lengthwise; or serve whole, removing the white fuzzy fiber or "choke." Serve cold as a first course with French Dressing or Vinaigrette Sauce or filled with any salad mixture. Serve hot with melted butter or Hollandaise Sauce.

CREAMED ARTICHOKE HEARTS

Make 2 cups Medium Cream Sauce using ½ cup sauterne for part of the milk. Drain 2 cans of artichoke hearts packed in water. Heat vegetable in the sauce. Top with buttered crumbs before serving.

JERUSALEM ARTICHOKES

Jerusalem Artichokes look like small potatoes but are not mealy. Wash and scrape, soak 2 hours in cold water and a little vinegar. Drain. Cover with boiling salted water and boil until tender. Drain immediately or they will harden again. Or, boil with the skins on and when tender, peel. Serve with Medium White Sauce. Use instead of potatoes in Potato Salad.

GREEN ASPARAGUS

Select asparagus with tightly closed buds. Wash thoroughly. Snap off lower tough ends of stalks and peel if not young. Tie in bunches, stand in rapidly boiling, salted water to cover stalks in lower half of double boiler, leaving tips out of water. Cook for 5 minutes and then cover with inverted upper half of double boiler until stalks are tender, about 10 minutes. Or follow directions for pressure cooker. Serve with melted butter, or Hollandaise Sauce; or sprinkle with bread crumbs browned in hot butter or sliced, blanched and toasted almonds.

WHITE ASPARAGUS

Stalks must be white at tips. If pink they are apt to be bitter. Snap off tough ends. Cut away thick skin at lower end and peel rest of stalk very thin. Parboil, drain, add fresh, salted boiling water and cook rapidly until tender. Serve as above.

ASPARAGUS RING

2 cans (1 pound each) of asparagus, drained
3 tablespoons butter
3 tablespoons flour
½ teaspoon salt
dash of pepper
1 cup cream or milk, warm
3 eggs, separated

Cut the asparagus into 1-inch pieces. Heat the butter, add the flour, salt and a little pepper, stir until well blended, add the milk or cream gradually, stirring until smooth. Beat egg yolks, heat in sauce. Cool, fold in the stiffly beaten egg whites and finally, the asparagus. Pour into a well-greased ring mold, set in a pan of boiling water and bake in a moderate oven for ½ hour, or until set. Remove to hot platter, place cooked peas in center and serve with Cream Sauce.

ASPARAGUS GARNISHES

Serve asparagus in bundles of 5 or 6, with a strip of pimiento laid over them to simulate a ribbon; or make rings of orange or lemon rind or green pepper to hold the bundle. Or hollow out French rolls, cut into rings, toast. Use to hold asparagus.

ASPARAGUS WITH HOT MAYONNAISE

½ cup hot Medium White Sauce
1 cup hot mayonnaise
1 tablespoon lemon juice
2 pounds cooked asparagus

Combine first 3 ingredients in the order given and serve hot over asparagus.

Green and Wax Beans

Green beans and wax beans may be used interchangeably. Most varieties now sold do not have strings, so the name "string bean" is out of date. Fresh beans snap crisply when you bend them. If there are strings, they will not break when you trim the ends of the beans in preparation for cooking, and can be pulled off down the pod.

GREEN BEANS

Wash beans, remove strings if necessary, trim ends, and cut into 1-inch lengths or thin, slanting slices. Or leave beans whole. Place beans in rapidly boiling salted water to cover. Cover pan and cook until just tender (20 to 30 minutes). Drain and add salt, pepper and butter.

Serve with Brown Sauce or with blanched almonds, cut lengthwise and browned in butter; or with Sautéed Mushrooms.

GREEN BEANS AND TOMATOES

2 pounds green beans, cooked
2 tablespoons butter
2 tablespoons flour
1 teaspoon salt
¼ teaspoon pepper
1 teaspoon sugar
1 cup strained tomatoes

Reserve ½ cup liquid in which beans were cooked. Heat the butter, add the flour, seasoning, bean liquid and the strained tomatoes; cook until smooth and pour this sauce over the beans; serve hot.

SWEET AND SOUR BEANS

2 pounds green or wax beans, cooked
2 tablespoons butter
1 tablespoon flour
2 tablespoons sugar
2 tablespoons vinegar or lemon juice
salt and pepper to taste

Drain and save liquid in which the beans have been cooked. Add enough water to make one cup. Melt butter, add flour; add the liquid and seasonings to taste. Add the beans and serve hot.

GREEN BEAN AND EGG CASSEROLE

1 package (9 ounces) frozen green beans
¼ cup butter
¼ cup minced onion
¼ cup flour
2 cups milk, hot
2 teaspoons salt
dash of pepper
dash of thyme
1 tablespoon dried parsley
6 hard-cooked eggs
¼ cup dry bread crumbs
½ cup Swiss cheese, grated

Cook green beans and drain. Melt butter; sauté onions in butter until tender. Remove from heat, stir in the flour and gradually stir in the milk. Cook, stirring constantly until smooth and thick. Add seasonings and parsley. Grease a casserole and fill it with alternate layers of beans, sliced eggs, and sauce. Sprinkle with the crumbs mixed with grated cheese. Bake in a moderate oven, 350° F., for 20 to 25 minutes until hot and browned.

Other sauces to serve with vegetables will be found in chapter 20, pages 386-392.

CHICKEN GREEN BEAN CASSEROLE

See page 315.

GREEN LIMA BEANS

Cover 1 quart of shelled lima beans with boiling water. Add 1 teaspoon salt. Boil for 5 minutes, cover. Simmer until tender, 20-40 minutes, depending on age. Add 2 heaping tablespoons butter or heavy sweet cream.

BEAN SPROUTS

Bean sprouts may be used raw in salads, chopped in sandwich fillings, in cooked vegetables and in soups.

To grow fresh bean sprouts, soak four tablespoons of mung beans overnight in lukewarm water. Drain. Place in a crock, cover with plate and let stand in a warm place for 3 or 4 days until beans have sprouted. Then store in refrigerator. Use for Chop Suey. Canned bean sprouts are available, packed in water. Drain and use as directed.

CREOLE SPROUTS

3 stalks celery
½ cup minced onion
1 clove garlic
1 tablespoon oil
1 can (1 pound) stewed tomatoes
1 teaspoon salt
⅛ teaspoon pepper
2 bay leaves
2 cups bean sprouts

Chop celery fine. Sauté celery, onion and garlic in oil until celery and onion are tender. Remove garlic. Add tomatoes and seasonings. Simmer for 5 minutes. Remove bay leaves. Add bean sprouts, cover, and cook over low heat 8 to 10 minutes.

BEAN SPROUT CASSEROLE

2 cups bean sprouts
3 tablespoons chopped green pepper
1 cup whole kernel corn
2 cups White Sauce
salt and pepper to taste
buttered crumbs

Mix all ingredients except crumbs. Place in greased casserole. Top with crumbs. Bake at 350° F. for 25 minutes.

BEAN CURD SUKIYAKI

3 cups spinach
1 green pepper
oil
½ teaspoon powdered ginger
¼ cup scallions, chopped
2 cups bean curd (canned or fresh)
½ cup mushrooms, sliced
1 cup bean sprouts
1 cup Chinese cabbage, sliced
2 tablespoons water
2 tablespoons soy sauce

Chop spinach; core and chop green pepper. Heat oil and ginger in a skillet over medium heat. Sauté scallions. Mix in other vegetables. Combine water and soy sauce. Stir lightly into vegetables. Cover and cook over low heat for 5 to 7 minutes.

BEETS

Wash beets, cut off leaves, leaving 1-inch stem and root to preserve color. Cook in boiling water until tender. Young beets will cook in 1 hour, old beets from 1-1½ hours. When cooked, put them in a pan of cold water and rub off the skin. Beets may be cut in quarters, sliced, diced, or cut in thin strips and served hot with butter, salt, pepper and hot vinegar.

Beet tops, if fresh, may be prepared like spinach.

HARVARD BEETS

2 tablespoons butter
1 tablespoon flour
½ cup sugar
½ teaspoon salt
¼ cup vinegar, mixed with
¼ cup water or beet juice
2 cups boiled or 1 can (1 pound) beets, sliced

Melt butter in saucepan or double boiler. Add flour. Stir. Add sugar, salt and the liquid gradually. Cook until clear, stirring constantly. Add beets and heat thoroughly.

COLD PICKLED BEETS

1 quart cold, boiled beets
1 teaspoon salt
⅛ teaspoon pepper
1 pint mild vinegar

Slice the beets, place in a jar and cover with the seasoning and vinegar; add a little caraway seed, or raw onion slices if desired.

PANNED BEETS

Peel raw, young beets and slice thin. Put 2 table-spoons butter in a saucepan, add beets, salt and pepper, cover, and simmer for about 20 minutes, until tender.

BROCCOLI

Wash well, cut off tough ends of stalks. If thick, split lengthwise. Cook uncovered in small amount of water, for 5 minutes, then cover, and continue cooking until stalks are tender. Drain and serve with melted butter or Hollandaise Sauce.

BROCCOLI RING

Use cooked, chopped broccoli in place of spinach, in recipe for Spinach Ring.

BRUSSELS SPROUTS

Choose firm, compact heads of uniform size. Discard any wilted leaves. Cut the stalks close to the heads. Cut a shallow cross in the bottoms, and soak in cold salted water 10 minutes. Drain well and cook in small amount of salted, boiling water for 5 minutes. Then cover, cook just until tender, 5-20 minutes, depending on size. Drain; add 2 tablespoons butter to 1 quart Brussels sprouts, or serve with White Sauce or Hollandaise Sauce.

BRUSSELS SPROUTS AND CHESTNUTS

1 quart Brussels sprouts, cooked
1 pound Italian chestnuts
⅛ cup butter
pepper and salt

Boil the sprouts as directed and drain. Put the chestnuts in saucepan of cold water, and boil until the shells and skins may be easily removed. Butter a baking dish, put in a layer of sprouts, then one of chestnuts, dot with butter, sprinkle sparingly with pepper, and add a little salt if necessary. Continue in this way till all are used. Add enough boiling water to moisten, and bake 30 minutes in a moderate oven.

BRUSSELS SPROUTS AND CHESTNUTS IN BROWN SAUCE

1 quart Brussels sprouts
½ pound chestnuts
4 tablespoons butter
2 teaspoons sugar
1 tablespoon flour
1 teaspoon salt

Cook sprouts and chestnuts, as above. Brown 2 tablespoons butter, add sugar. Stir constantly until sugar melts. Add chestnuts. Cook until nuts are well browned.

Heat 2 tablespoons butter, add 1 tablespoon flour, brown slightly. Add 1 cup of the sprouts liquid and cook until smooth. Add the chestnuts and sprouts, heat through and serve.

TO COOK CABBAGES

Green cabbage, Savoy or curly cabbage, and Chinese, or stalk cabbage (celery cabbage), are all cooked the same way. Remove and discard the core of the round heads, and the root end of the stalk cabbage. Cut into wedges and cook, covered. Or cut into large or small shreds, and cook until wilted and just tender. Red cabbage takes longer to cook than the green and white varieties, and a little lemon juice or vinegar should be added to the cooking water to preserve its color.

BOILED CABBAGE

1 small cabbage
1 quart boiling water
1 teaspoon salt

Cut a young cabbage in eight pieces, discard the core and trim the limp outside leaves. Cook covered in water until tender. Drain and serve with Medium White Sauce. Or melt 2 tablespoons butter, add 1 tablespoon lemon juice, 1 teaspoon sugar and 2 tablespoons prepared horseradish. Serve over cabbage.

CABBAGE AU GRATIN

½ large cooked cabbage, chopped
¾ cup grated cheese
paprika and salt
2 cups Medium White Sauce
½ cup cracker crumbs
3 tablespoons melted butter

Put a layer of chopped cabbage into a buttered baking dish; sprinkle with grated cheese, paprika and salt. Cover with a layer of Medium White Sauce. Repeat the layers until all ingredients have been used. Cover with cracker crumbs mixed with butter. Bake in moderately hot oven, 350° F., until bubbling hot and well browned.

CHOPPED CABBAGE

2 tablespoons fat
1 onion, cut fine
1 quart cabbage, chopped
1 teaspoon salt
⅛ teaspoon pepper
2 tablespoons flour

Heat fat, add onion, brown, add cabbage; cover and steam for 10 minutes; barely cover with boiling water; add salt and pepper, and cook until tender. Sprinkle with flour, boil a little longer and serve hot. Savoy or curly cabbage may be prepared in the same way.

CABBAGE AND APPLES

1 medium head cabbage
3 tablespoons shortening or fat
2 tart apples, peeled and sliced
2 teaspoons caraway seed
2 teaspoons salt
½ teaspoon paprika
½ onion

Shred cabbage fine, soak 10 minutes in salt water. Drain, heat the fat, add cabbage, apples, caraway seed, salt, paprika and onion. Cover and cook slowly about 1 hour.

CELERY CABBAGE

Loosen inner leaves of a firm head of celery cabbage. Soak 15 minutes in cold salted water. Drain. Cook covered in small amount of boiling salted water until just tender. Drain. Serve with melted butter or Cream Sauce.

RED CABBAGE WITH CHESTNUTS

1 small red cabbage
1 cup boiling water
¼ cup vinegar
2 tablespoons shortening or fat
salt and pepper
1 tablespoon sugar
¼ cup raisins
1 cup chestnuts, cooked and peeled
1 tablespoon flour

Shred cabbage. Pour boiling water and vinegar over cabbage, let stand 10 minutes. Drain and reserve liquid.

Heat 2 tablespoons fat in skillet, add cabbage seasoned with salt and pepper, brown well, cover and simmer 10 minutes. Add sugar to reserved cabbage liquid, add raisins and chestnuts; cook until raisins are plump. Sprinkle flour over cabbage, combine with chestnuts, cook a few minutes; serve hot.

Suggestions for using raw cabbage in salads will be found on page 357. For cole slaw, see page 358.

SWEET AND SOUR CABBAGE

1 cabbage (red or white)
salt and pepper
2 tart apples, sliced
2 tablespoons shortening or fat
2 tablespoons flour
4 tablespoons brown sugar
2 tablespoons vinegar

Shred the cabbage fine, add salt and pepper to taste and the apples. Heat fat in large skillet, add cabbage and apples. Add boiling water to cover and cook until tender; sprinkle with flour, add sugar and vinegar. Simmer 10 minutes; serve hot with Potato Dumplings.

RED CABBAGE WITH WINE

1 head red cabbage, shredded
1 onion, chopped fine
4 tablespoons butter or drippings
1 grated tart apple
¼ cup vinegar
½ cup red wine
½ glass currant jelly
1 tablespoon honey
1 teaspoon salt
pepper
2 tablespoons stock
1 tablespoon cornstarch

Soak shredded cabbage 15 minutes in cold water, drain. Sauté onion in fat until golden brown; add cabbage and all ingredients except the cornstarch. Simmer the cabbage mixture until tender, stirring occasionally. Fifteen minutes before serving add cornstarch dissolved in 2 tablespoons water. Serve on platter; surround with sautéed chestnuts.

BAKED STUFFED CABBAGE ROLLS

See page 282.

STUFFED CABBAGE ROLLS

See page 282.

CABBAGE AND SAUSAGES

6 sausages
4 cups cabbage, finely shredded
½ teaspoon pepper
salt if necessary

Fry the sausages crisp and brown. Remove sausages and pour off all but 3 tablespoons of the fat. Put cabbage in pan, cover and cook until tender; add seasonings. Arrange on a hot dish and garnish with the sausages. Serve with mashed potatoes.

Sauerkraut

Sauerkraut, which is made by salting cabbage and allowing it to ferment, may be eaten raw or cooked before eating. Canned sauerkraut is cooked during the canning process, and is prepared in a shorter time than the raw variety, which is purchased in bulk or in plastic bags.

SAUERKRAUT

2 tablespoons shortening or fat
1 onion, diced
1 quart sauerkraut
1 raw potato, grated
1 teaspoon caraway seeds
boiling water or soup stock

Heat the fat in skillet. Cook onion until translucent, add kraut. Cook 5 minutes, add potato and caraway seeds. Cover with boiling soup or water. Cook slowly ½ hour, cover well, cook ½ hour longer on top of range or in oven. Brown sugar and a grated apple may be added if desired.

TOMATO CREAM SAUERKRAUT

1 cup thick sour cream
1 small can tomato paste
½ cup brown sugar
1 large can (1 pound, 13 ounces) sauerkraut

Blend sour cream, tomato paste, and sugar. Add sauerkraut and mix thoroughly. Bake in greased casserole in moderate oven, 350° F., for ½ hour.

SWEET AND SOUR SAUERKRAUT

¼ cup butter
1 large onion, chopped
3 tablespoons brown sugar
1 large can (1 pound, 13 ounces) sauerkraut

Brown butter; add onion and sauté for a few minutes. Add sugar and sauerkraut. Simmer until thoroughly heated.

Carrots

Small young carrots may be scrubbed and cooked whole. Older carrots must be scraped, or thinly peeled, and cut into uniform pieces for cooking.

BOILED CARROTS

1 quart carrots
boiling water
1 teaspoon salt

Cover carrots with boiling, salted water, cover pan, and cook until just tender. Drain and serve with melted butter or with Brown Sauce made with liquid drained from carrots.

BUTTER-SIMMERED CARROTS

    4 cups raw carrots
    1 tablespoon butter
    2 to 3 tablespoons sugar
    1 teaspoon salt

Wash, scrape and slice carrots lengthwise. Put into heavy saucepan with butter, sugar and salt. Cover closely and simmer until tender.

SWEET AND SOUR CARROTS

Serve diced, boiled carrots with Sweet and Sour Sauce made with 1 cup of the liquid in which the carrots were cooked.

CARROTS AND PEAS

    2 cups sliced carrots
    2 cups fresh or frozen peas
    salt, pepper, sugar to taste

Cook carrots in boiling salted water to cover until tender. Remove carrots and cook peas in same liquid. Drain and reserve liquid. Add water to make 1 cup liquid and proceed to make Brown Sauce. Add vegetables to sauce, reheat, and serve.

CARROTS AND CELERY

Boil carrots. Stew celery. Drain both, reserving liquid. Make Brown Sauce, using vegetable liquid. Add vegetables. Reheat, season to taste and cook a few minutes longer.

CARROT PUDDING

    1 cup shortening
    ½ cup brown sugar
    1 egg
    1¼ cups grated raw carrots
    juice and rind of ½ lemon
    1¼ cups flour
    1 teaspoon salt
    1 teaspoon baking powder
    ½ teaspoon soda

Cream shortening and sugar. Mix the egg, carrots, and lemon juice and add rind. Sift the dry ingredients and add. Bake in greased baking dish or ring mold in a moderately hot oven, 375° F., for 30 to 45 minutes.

BRISKET AND CARROT STEW (TSIMMES)
See page 273.

CARROT SOUFFLE

Wash, scrape and grate carrots to make 2 cups. Cook in 2 tablespoons of butter in heavy saucepan, closely covered, over low heat until tender. Drain and season with salt, pepper, paprika, onion juice and Worcestershire Sauce. Follow directions for Basic Vegetable Soufflés, page 411.

Cauliflower

Select cauliflower with unblemished white head and fresh green leaves. Or use the more delicately flavored blue variety. Cut off the greens, trim the stalk level with the flower, and soak, head down, in cold salted water for 30 minutes. Drain.

TO COOK CAULIFLOWER

Cook, covered, in boiling water until just tender but still crisp, about 20 minutes. Or break the raw cauliflower into small flowerets, and reduce cooking time by about half. Discard the hard center core. Serve with brown butter, Hollandaise Sauce, White Sauce, or Cheese Sauce.

CAULIFLOWER POLONAISE

Cook cauliflower, above, and to serve, sprinkle over it 2 tablespoons fine soft bread crumbs browned in ¼ cup butter. Serve hot.

CAULIFLOWER AU GRATIN

Cover separated flowerets of boiled cauliflower with Medium White or Cream Sauce in buttered baking dish, top with buttered crumbs and grated cheese. Bake in moderate oven, 350° F., until crumbs are brown.

FRIED CAULIFLOWER

Separate cauliflower into flowerets. Cook in boiling salted water 10 minutes. Cool. Drain thoroughly, dip in crumbs, well-beaten eggs and again in crumbs. Drop in deep hot fat and fry a delicate brown. Drain on brown paper, season. Serve with Cream Sauce or Cheese Sauce.

CREAMED CELERY

    1 bunch celery
    1 teaspoon salt
    1 cup Medium White Sauce

Wash, scrape and cut the celery stalks into pieces 1½ inches long. Cook, covered, in a small amount of rapidly boiling salted water until tender. Drain and serve with Medium White Sauce.

BRAISED CELERY

Wash, scrape and cut outer stalks of celery into 3-inch pieces. Dry thoroughly. Sauté slowly in 2 tablespoons butter in heavy skillet until browned. Add bouillon cube dissolved in ½ cup hot water, or ¾ cup soup stock, and simmer until liquid is almost absorbed.

CELERY IN WINE

Cut celery into short pieces. Combine equal parts of beef stock or bouillon and dry white wine. There should be enough liquid to cover the vegetables. Cook, covered, until the celery is tender. Serve hot with butter.

Celery cooked in this manner may be used as a salad vegetable. Allow celery to cool in the liquid.

CELERY AND CARROTS

See page 417.

CELERIAC OR CELERY ROOT

Scrub, peel, slice, and cook, covered in small amount of salted, boiling water for 1 hour, until tender. Drain. Serve with Medium White or Brown Sauce.

Or chill, cut into sticks, and serve as salad, with French Dressing.

CELERY ROOT RING

3 large celery roots
4 eggs, separated
½ to ¾ cup cream
salt, pepper, paprika

Wash and peel celery roots and cook in boiling salted water until tender. Mash, add beaten yolks, cream and seasoning to taste. Fold in stiffly beaten whites. Bake in buttered ring mold placed in pan of hot water in moderate oven, 350° F., ½ to ¾ hour. Fill the ring with shrimp or mixed seafood or vegetables.

CELERY ROOT SOUFFLE

Cook celery roots, above, until tender. Drain and put through coarse grinder. Add to Basic Vegetable Soufflé mixture. Bake in buttered ring mold in pan of water, in a moderately slow oven (325° F.), for 30 minutes, or until puffed and golden.

TO SHELL AND BLANCH CHESTNUTS

WATER METHOD

Cover chestnuts with boiling water and boil until shell and skin can be easily removed (about 20 minutes).

SKILLET METHOD

Make ½-inch slit on flat side of chestnuts with sharp knife. Put 1 pint chestnuts (approximately 17) and 1 teaspoon butter in heavy skillet. Place over heat, shaking constantly, until butter is melted. Let stand in 350° F. oven about 5 minutes, until outside shell and inner skin can be easily removed at the same time.

BOILED CHESTNUTS

1 pound chestnuts, shelled and blanched
1 cup soup stock
1 tablespoon brown sugar
2 tablespoons butter

Cover chestnuts with boiling, salted water and cook until tender. Drain. Add soup stock and sugar and simmer a few minutes. Add butter. Reduce liquid and serve with chestnuts.

CHESTNUT PUREE

1 pound chestnuts, shelled and blanched
hot milk
2 tablespoons butter
salt, pepper

Cover chestnuts with boiling salted water and cook until tender. Drain and mash or put through ricer. Add enough milk to make a purée, butter, and salt and pepper to taste. Beat until light and smooth.

CHESTNUTS AND PRUNES

2 cups prunes
¼ cup sugar
½ lemon, juice
2 cups cooked chestnuts

Stew prunes, add sugar, lemon juice and cinnamon if desired, then add chestnuts, simmer a few minutes and serve.

RED CABBAGE WITH CHESTNUTS

See page 415.

Corn

Fresh corn on the cob should have light green, moist husks and a brown silky tassel. The ears should be full of kernels, and the kernels so juicy that when you cut into one with a fingernail it bursts with milky juice. Do not husk corn until just before cooking, since it loses freshness rapidly. Golden and white varieties are equally delicious, but the white is more delicate in texture.

Canned kernel corn, packed in water, may be substituted for fresh corn cut from the cob. Cream-style corn is packed in a milky sauce, and is more restricted in use.

CORN ON THE COB

Remove husks and silk threads, drop ears in a large amount of rapidly boiling water with a little sugar and boil 2 to 5 minutes. Remove from water and serve with butter, salt and pepper.

CREAM-STYLE CORN

Grate corn from cobs; cook slowly 2 to 5 minutes in its own juice with butter, salt and pepper. Add a little milk if necessary.

CORN KERNELS

Cut the cooked corn from the cobs and serve heated with butter, salt and pepper.

BAKED CORN

Soak corn still in the husks in cold water for 10 minutes. Bake in 400° F. oven for 10 to 15 minutes. Remove husks.

TO SCORE CORN

Stand ear on end, run point of sharp knife down through each row of kernels. Scrape out pulp with back of knife.

CORN WITH GREEN PEPPERS

    3 cups corn kernels or 1 can (1 pound, 13 ounces)
        kernel corn
    3 tablespoons butter
    4 tablespoons cream
    3 tablespoons green peppers, chopped fine
    salt and pepper to taste

Simmer corn with butter, cream, green pepper and seasonings until liquid is almost absorbed.

CORN, STUFFED IN GREEN PEPPERS

See page 425.

ESCALLOPED CORN

    6 ears of cooked corn or 1 can (12 ounces) kernel
        corn
    1 teaspoon salt
    ⅛ teaspoon pepper
    2 tablespoons flour
    1 teaspoon sugar
    ¼ cup milk
    1 tablespoon butter
    1 cup bread crumbs

Cut fresh, boiled corn from the cob; or use canned corn, drained. Mix corn with the salt, pepper, flour, sugar, and milk. Melt the butter, mix with the bread crumbs and cover bottom of a baking dish with ½ the crumbs; add the corn mixture and cover with the rest of the crumbs. Bake in a moderate oven, 350° F., about 20 minutes, and serve hot.

CORN FRITTERS

    2 cups grated corn pulp
    ½ teaspoon salt
    a little pepper
    ½ teaspoon baking powder
    cracker crumbs

Add seasonings and baking powder to corn pulp. Add enough sifted cracker crumbs to hold the mixture together. Drop by spoonfuls into deep, hot fat and fry until brown.

PUFFY CORN FRITTERS

    1 can (1 pound) corn, or 2 cups fresh kernels
    2 eggs, separated
    ½ teaspoon salt
    3 tablespoons milk
    2 tablespoons flour

Scrape the corn off the cobs, or drain the canned corn. To the corn, add the beaten yolks and the rest of the ingredients. Fold in the beaten egg whites last. Drop by teaspoonfuls in deep, hot fat and fry until brown. Or drop on a hot, greased griddle or frying pan. Serve with hot syrup.

CORN PUDDING

    2 eggs
    1 can (1 pound) kernel corn, chopped
    1 teaspoon salt
    ⅛ teaspoon pepper
    1½ teaspoons melted butter
    2 cups hot milk

Beat eggs slightly, add rest of the ingredients and turn into a well-buttered baking dish. Set in a pan of hot water and bake in a moderate oven, 350° F., about 1 hour, until firm. Serve hot.

CREAM CORN PUDDING

    1½ cups cream-style corn
    1 egg, beaten
    1 tablespoon melted shortening
    ½ teaspoon salt
    dash of pepper
    ¼ cup milk

Mix all ingredients. Bake like Corn Pudding.

CORN RING WITH CRAB

    1 can (1 pound) kernel corn
    4 eggs, separated
    1 teaspoon salt
    white pepper
    cayenne
    paprika
    1 cup cream

Chop corn, add well-beaten egg yolks, salt, white pepper, cayenne and paprika to taste; add cream. Fold in stiffly beaten whites. Place in a well-buttered ring mold, set in a pan of hot water, and bake in a moderate oven, 350° F., ½ hour or until set. Remove to hot platter, fill center with Sautéed Mushrooms. Surround with Crab Meat in Creole Sauce.

CORN TIMBALES

cooked corn kernels
2 eggs, separated
1 teaspoon salt
⅛ teaspoon white pepper
1 tablespoon melted butter
1 teaspoon sugar
½ cup soft bread crumbs

Chop and mash enough corn to make 1 cup of pulp. Add well-beaten egg yolks, salt, pepper, butter, sugar and bread crumbs. Fold in the stiffly beaten whites. Mixture should be stiff enough to drop from the spoon. If too stiff, add cream; if too thin, add more crumbs. Fill well buttered custard cups or molds ⅔ full, cover with oiled brown paper. Set in pan of hot water. Bake in moderate oven, 350° F., about 20 minutes, or until puffed. Unmold and garnish with parsley.

For variety, add 3 canned pimientos, mashed fine, and 1 tablespoon catsup to corn.

SUCCOTASH (CORN AND LIMAS)

1 cup cooked corn kernels
1 cup cooked lima beans
salt
pepper
¼ cup milk
butter

Combine corn, beans, seasonings, milk, and butter and heat a few minutes. For variety, mix with Stewed Tomatoes.

Cucumbers

Cucumbers are usually served raw with salad dressing, or pickled in brine. Young cucumbers need not be peeled, but cucumbers with waxed skins, or tough skins, should be peeled before using.

FRENCH FRIED CUCUMBERS

Peel cucumbers, cut lengthwise in ⅓-inch slices, and dip into well-seasoned fine bread crumbs. Dip into beaten egg and again in crumbs. Drop into deep hot fat and fry until brown.

DANDELION GREENS

Select dandelion greens early in the spring while they are still very pale in color. Wash thoroughly, trim roots. Cook in ¼-inch boiling salted water. Cook covered 1 minute, or until wilted. Stir, continue to cook, covered, until tender. Drain, season with butter, salt, pepper and vinegar. Or serve raw as a salad.

GREENS

To cook greens such as collard, kale, mustard, or turnip:

If greens are young, cook like spinach.

If greens are older or meat is to be served with them, simmer the meat in just enough water to cover. When meat is tender, add greens and simmer until just tender. The length of time will depend upon the age of the greens. Test at the end of 30 minutes.

CURLY ENDIVE, KALE OR ESCAROLE

Prepare any of these greens for cooking as you would Spinach. Cook in a small amount of rapidly boiling salted water until just tender, from 15 to 25 minutes. Drain, chop, and season. Add butter, cream, or cream sauce. Or substitute any of these greens for the cabbage in the recipe for Chopped Cabbage.

FRIED EGGPLANT

Peel eggplant thinly and cut in very thin slices. Dredge with flour and brown slowly on both sides in butter or oil.

Or dip slices in cracker crumbs, beaten egg, and again in crumbs, and fry in hot deep fat.

BAKED STUFFED EGGPLANT

eggplant
2 tablespoons butter or fat
1 small onion, cut fine
2 tablespoons bread crumbs
salt and pepper to taste
1 egg yolk or ½ cup of condensed tomato soup

Parboil whole eggplant in salted water until tender, but not soft. Cut in half lengthwise. Scrape out the pulp, leaving a ½-inch shell. Retain half shells intact. Heat 1 tablespoon butter or fat; brown the onion in fat; then add mashed eggplant, bread crumbs, salt and pepper to taste and the egg or tomato soup. Mix well, refill shells, sprinkle with cracker crumbs, dot with butter, place in pan and bake in moderate oven, 350° F., until brown.

EGGPLANT-ZUCCHINI CASSEROLE

1 eggplant
2 zucchini
2 eggs, beaten
butter or shortening
3 ounces cream cheese, softened
12 ounces sliced cheese, Cheddar and/or jack

SAUCE

1 can condensed tomato soup
1 4-ounce can sliced mushrooms
1 1-pound can tomatoes
1 6-ounce can tomato paste
1 medium onion
2 teaspoons oregano
½ teaspoon basil
1 teaspoon salt

Grease large casserole. Mix all ingredients for sauce. Simmer for 5 minutes. Peel eggplant and slice ½ inch thick. Slice zucchini ½ inch thick. Dip vegetables in egg. Sauté for 4 to 5 minutes on each side. Place layer of eggplant in casserole, add layer of cream cheese, then layer of zucchini. Top with some of vegetable sauce. Continue layering, using sliced cheese instead of cream cheese on second layer. End with vegetable sauce. Top with sliced cheese. Bake at 350° F. for 45 to 50 minutes.

EGGPLANT CASSEROLE

1 eggplant
1 cup chopped celery
1 green pepper, sliced
4 tablespoons shortening
1 1-pound can tomatoes
salt and pepper
bread crumbs
grated cheese

Peel and dice eggplant. Boil eggplant and celery until tender. Drain. Sauté green pepper in shortening. Add tomatoes and seasonings to taste. Alternate layers of eggplant and tomato mixture in a greased casserole. Sprinkle with crumbs and cheese. Bake at 350° F. for 20 minutes or until thoroughly heated.

SHRIMP-STUFFED EGGPLANT

See page 256.

MOUSSAKA

See page 291.

MUTTON WITH EGGPLANT

See page 290.

KOHLRABI

1 quart kohlrabi
2 tablespoons fat or butter
2 tablespoons flour
salt and pepper

Wash, peel and cut the kohlrabi root in slices, and cook in rapidly boiling salted water 5 minutes, then cover and boil until tender. Cook the greens or tops in boiling, salted water only until tender, drain and chop very fine. Heat the butter or fat, add the flour, then the chopped greens and 1 cup water in which they were cooked. Add the kohlrabi, season and reheat. Kohlrabi may also be served raw, thinly sliced and salted.

Mushrooms

Mushrooms need be peeled only when the peels are brown and ragged. Fresh, cultivated mushrooms are naturally white. Stems may be cooked with the mushrooms, or reserved for use in soups and sauces. Small mushrooms are served whole or stemmed. Larger mushrooms, except when they are to be stuffed or broiled for garnish, may be sliced.

STEAMED MUSHROOMS

1 pound fresh mushrooms
2 tablespoons butter
¼ teaspoon salt

Wash the mushrooms well. Drain and dry. Trim a thin slice from stem end. Put in double boiler, add butter. Season. Cook 20 minutes.

SAUTEED MUSHROOMS

1 pound mushrooms
2 tablespoons butter
¼ teaspoon salt
toast

Wash mushrooms, cut thin slice from stem end. Drain. Slice if desired. Place in skillet with butter and seasoning. Cover, cook 20 minutes, tossing them, or dredge lightly with flour and add cream. Serve on slices of hot toast, or as a main course garnish.

BROILED MUSHROOMS

1 pound mushrooms
2 tablespoons butter
¼ teaspoon salt
⅛ teaspoon pepper

Wash mushrooms, remove stems and reserve for soup or sauce. Place caps in a buttered broiler and broil about 5 minutes, cap side up. Turn, put a small piece of butter in each cap, sprinkle with salt and pepper and broil until butter is melted. Keep mushrooms stem-side up, to hold in the juices.

Serve as luncheon main dish on rounds of well-buttered toast or in smaller portions as a vegetable.

BAKED MUSHROOMS

1 pound mushrooms
salt and pepper
2 tablespoons butter
⅔ cup light cream

Wash the mushrooms, remove stems and reserve for other uses. Place in buttered baking dish, cap side up. Sprinkle with salt and pepper, dot with butter and add the cream. Bake 10 minutes in hot oven, 425° F. Arrange mushrooms on toast, add cream from baking dish.

CHICKEN WITH MUSHROOMS

See page 310.

CHICKEN LIVER AND MUSHROOM CANAPES

See page 39.

SWEETBREADS WITH MUSHROOMS

See page 299.

MUSHROOMS AND SOUR CREAM

1 pound mushrooms
3 tablespoons butter
2 tablespoons water
1 cup sour cream
salt, paprika to taste

Wash mushrooms, and slice if desired. Place butter and water in skillet, and sauté mushrooms gently. When tender (about 15 minutes) add sour cream. Cook slowly, stirring occasionally, until sauce is of desired consistency (about 10 minutes). Season with salt and paprika.

MUSHROOM RING

1 pound fresh mushrooms or 2 cans (4 ounces each)
    mushrooms
2 tablespoons butter
1 cup light cream
4 tablespoons flour
4 egg yolks
4 egg whites
1 teaspoon salt

Chop mushrooms fine, sauté in butter. Blend cream and flour until smooth, add mushrooms, cook until thick; pour gradually into yolks and cook until the mixture coats the spoon; then fold in stiffly beaten whites. Pour into a well-buttered ring mold and set into a pan of hot water; bake uncovered in moderate oven, 350° F., 20 to 30 minutes. Unmold, serve at once. If desired, fill center with Brussels Sprouts, and surround with peas and carrots.

MUSHROOMS AND ONIONS IN WINE

1 pound mushrooms
16 very small onions
½ cup butter
2 tablespoons flour
4 tablespoons chopped parsley
½ bay leaf
6 tablespoons soup stock
¼ cup sherry

Wash mushrooms, and slice if desired. Sauté onions in butter for 5 minutes. Add mushrooms, stir well, and add remaining ingredients except the wine. Cook over low heat, stirring often until onions are tender. Stir in sherry and reheat.

RICE AND MUSHROOM CASSEROLE

3 onions, sliced
2 cups mushrooms, fresh or 2 4-ounce cans
¼ pound butter
1 can consommé
1 cup water
1 cup uncooked rice
salt and pepper

Sauté onions and sliced mushrooms in butter. Add consommé and water. Add rice and stir. Season. Bake in greased casserole, covered, in moderate oven, 350° F., 45 minutes to 1 hour.

OKRA

1 pound okra
2 cups boiling water
1 teaspoon salt
2 tablespoons butter

Wash okra, cut off stem ends. If pods are large, cut in ½-inch pieces; if small, leave whole. Cook uncovered in boiling salted water to cover for 5 minutes; cover the pan, cook about 5 minutes, or until tender. Drain, season, add butter and serve with rice.

OKRA CREOLE

1 pound cooked okra
1 onion, chopped
½ green pepper, sliced
garlic clove, chopped
2 tablespoons butter
1 cup strained tomatoes

Drain cooked okra. Brown onion, pepper, and garlic lightly in butter, add tomato and simmer 5 minutes. Add okra, reheat, serve hot.

Onions

The onions that are commonly available in the market are dried, with the exception of the scallions, or green onions. Very small onions, both white and yellow skinned, are used principally for pickling. White onions about the size of large walnuts are used for boiling. Yellow onions are the least expensive and most widely used. The large, red Spanish or Bermuda onions, which are milder and more delicate in flavor, are first choice for serving raw in salads, and as a garnish.

BAKED ONIONS

Select medium-sized onions, wipe but do not peel, and cut a cross into the root end. Place in baking dish, cut side down. Add 2 tablespoons melted butter, salt and pepper and a little water. Bake in a moderate oven, 350° F., until tender (30 minutes). Or slice onions ½-inch thick and bake as above.

BOILED ONIONS

Cut a cross at root end of medium-sized onions. Pour boiling water over them, let stand 2 minutes, drain and peel. Boil in covered saucepan in one inch of rapidly boiling salted water only until tender. Drain, add butter and salt to taste; or cover with Medium White Sauce.

Green onions (scallions) may be boiled a few minutes until tender, served on toast with melted butter or White Sauce.

ONIONS AU GRATIN

Peel and boil onions, as above, until nearly done. Drain, and place in a baking dish; make 1 cup Medium White Sauce and pour over the onions; add a layer of buttered cracker crumbs, and ½ cup grated cheese, and bake 20 minutes in moderate oven, 350° F.

STUFFED ONIONS

8 medium onions, peeled
1 cup cooked green peas
1 cup soft bread crumbs
salt and pepper
light cream or melted butter
1 cup Medium White Sauce
2 boiled carrots
1 egg, hard cooked
4 sprigs parsley

Parboil onions and remove and chop part of center, leaving the root end intact. Chop removed onion. Combine with peas, and ½ cup bread crumbs. Season with salt and pepper and moisten with cream or melted butter. Fill onions with the mixture. Place the stuffed onions close together in a buttered baking dish and cover with Medium White Sauce. Sprinkle with remaining crumbs mixed with carrot, egg and parsley all chopped fine. Bake in a moderate oven, 350° F., until browned.

ONIONS AND APPLES

¼ cup fat
4 cups onions, sliced
4 cups apples, quartered
2 teaspoons salt
2 tablespoons sugar

Heat fat in a skillet, add onions and apples. Cover and steam 10 minutes, stirring occasionally until apples are soft and onions tender and slightly browned. Add salt and sugar. Serve hot.

FRIED ONIONS

Peel and slice 4 or 5 onions. Heat 2 tablespoons fat in skillet, add onions, fry slowly until golden brown, stirring constantly.

FRENCH FRIED ONION RINGS

Peel and cut Bermuda onions in ¼-inch slices, separate into rings. Soak in cold milk for ½ hour, drain and dry. Dredge with flour and fry in deep, hot fat, a few at a time, until brown and crisp. Remove and drain on brown paper. Keep warm in moderate oven. Serve with roasts or steaks.

FRIED ONION RINGS

1 large Bermuda onion
1 cup flour
1½ teaspoons baking powder
½ teaspoon salt
1 egg
⅔ cup water
1 teaspoon lemon juice
1 teaspoon melted shortening

Slice onion and separate rings carefully. Mix remaining ingredients until just blended. Coat onion rings in batter and deep fry until brown and crisp. Drain and serve.

OYSTER PLANT OR SALSIFY

Wash oyster plant, scrape and put at once in cold water with a little vinegar to keep from discoloring. Cut ½-inch slices and cook covered, in small amount of boiling water until soft. Add salt. Drain and serve in Medium White Sauce.

Or cook, covered, in small amount of boiling

water until tender. Cut in 4 pieces lengthwise, dredge with seasoned flour and fry in hot butter or fat until browned.

PARSNIPS

Wash young parsnips, scrape, cut in pieces and cook, covered, in small amount of salted boiling water until tender, about 45 minutes. Drain, and serve with hot butter, Drawn Butter, or Medium White Sauce.

Or wash and cook, covered, in small amount of boiling salted water until tender about 45 minutes. Drain and plunge in cold water and slip off skins. Cut in slices lengthwise and fry in butter. Or mash and season with butter, salt and pepper. Or shape mashed parsnips into flat, round cakes, roll in flour, and fry in butter or other fat until crisp.

GREEN PEAS

3 pounds green peas in pods
2 tablespoons butter or fat
1 teaspoon salt
a little pepper
1 teaspoon sugar

Shell peas, and wash. Place in pan with butter, add a small quantity of boiling water and boil uncovered for 5 minutes. Then cover and simmer until tender. Season and serve. Or serve with Medium White Sauce made with vegetable liquid.

GREEN PEAS FRENCH STYLE

2 tablespoons butter
4 scallions, minced
½ cup shredded lettuce
½ teaspoon salt
2 teaspoons sugar
2 cups freshly shelled green peas (or 1 10-ounce package, frozen)
¼ cup boiling water

Melt butter, add scallions and cook a minute or two. Add remaining ingredients, cover pan, and simmer about 15 minutes, until peas are tender, and water has almost evaporated. Add more butter, if desired, and salt and sugar to taste.

GREEN PEAS AND RICE

3 cups green peas, fresh cooked or canned
¼ cup butter or other fat
1 cup raw rice
boiling water
½ teaspoon salt
2 tablespoons sugar

Drain the peas and reserve the liquid. Melt but-

ter in a skillet, add rice, and stir over moderate heat until grains are coated. Add the reserved pea liquid and boiling water to make 2 cups. Add seasonings, stir, bring to a boil, add peas and pour into baking dish. Bake in moderate oven, 350° F., until rice is tender and the liquid is absorbed, about 35 minutes.

PEA TIMBALES OR RING

1 can (1 pound) peas or 2 cups cooked peas
salt and pepper
2 eggs, separated
2 tablespoons melted butter

Drain and mash peas through a sieve. There should be 1 cup of pea pulp. Season to taste with salt and pepper, and onion juice if desired. Stir in the egg yolks, well beaten, and the butter. Fold in the stiffly beaten whites. Fill greased timbale molds or ring mold ⅔ full. Set in pan of hot water, bake in moderately hot oven, 325° F., until firm, 20 minutes for timbales, ½ hour for ring mold. Serve with 1 cup Cream Sauce to which ⅓ cup peas is added.

STUFFED PEPPERS ITALIENNE

2 dozen sweet green peppers
½ cup olive oil
1 pound each chopped beef and pork
salt, pepper
½ cup seedless raisins
½ cup pignon nuts
½ pound crackers, crushed
¼ pound Romano cheese, grated
3 hard-cooked eggs, chopped
Italian Tomato Sauce, page 390

Cut off stem end and remove seeds and veins from peppers. Heat 2 tablespoons oil in skillet, add meat, season with salt and pepper; when brown remove and mix with rest of ingredients, except peppers, oil and Tomato Sauce. Stuff peppers with meat mixture, replace tops, fasten with toothpicks. Heat oil, add peppers and fry until slightly brown. Add Italian Tomato Sauce, and heat through.

STUFFED PEPPERS

4 green peppers
1 pound ground beef
½ cup chopped onion
1 10½-ounce can tomato soup
1 cup cooked rice
1 teaspoon Worcestershire sauce
½ teaspoon salt
¼ teaspoon pepper
1 16-ounce can tomato sauce

Cut peppers in half, lengthwise; remove seeds. Cook in boiling salted water about 5 minutes. Drain. Combine beef, onion, ½ can of tomato soup, rice, Worcestershire sauce, salt and pepper. Spoon meat mixture into pepper cases and place in a shallow pan. Combine remaining soup with the tomato sauce. Pour over peppers. Cover and bake at 375° F. for 1 hour.

STUFFED PEPPERS WITH BEEF

    4 green peppers
    1 pound ground beef, uncooked
    1 egg
    1 chopped onion
    salt and pepper

Cut off stem end and remove seeds and veins from green peppers, boil 2 minutes, drain. Mix meat with egg, onion, and seasonings. Fill peppers with meat mixture. Place in pan, add a little water. Cover pan and simmer on top of range or in moderate oven, 350° F., about 30 minutes.

STUFFED PEPPERS WITH CHICKEN OR OTHER MEAT

    8 green peppers
    2 cups cooked chicken, ham, veal or lamb, chopped
    2 cups boiled rice
    1 cup strained tomatoes
    1 tablespoon grated onion
    2½ tablespoons butter
    2 tablespoons fresh bread crumbs
    ¾ cup meat stock

Remove stem end and seeds of peppers, boil 2 minutes, drain. Mix the next 4 ingredients, and fill peppers. Add butter to crumbs, spread over peppers, place in baking dish with stock, and bake in moderate oven, 350° F., for 25 minutes.

STUFFED PEPPERS WITH CORN

    6 green peppers
    2 cups cooked corn
    1 teaspoon salt
    ⅛ teaspoon pepper
    ½ cup grated cheese
    2 tablespoons butter

Cut off stem end and remove seeds from green peppers, boil 2 minutes, drain. Mix corn with rest of ingredients. Fill peppers with mixture. Bake in pan with a little water 20 minutes in moderate oven, 350° F.

STUFFED PEPPERS WITH SPAGHETTI

Fill pepper cases with Spaghetti, Tomato Sauce and Cheese, and bake as above.

FRIED GREEN PEPPERS

    6 sweet green peppers
    2 medium onions
    2 tablespoons fat
    ½ teaspoon salt

Remove stem end and seeds of peppers and cut in ¼-inch slices. Peel and slice onions. Heat fat in skillet, add onions, fry for a few minutes. Add peppers, season, cover, and simmer 10 to 15 minutes or until tender.

PLANTAIN (PLATANOS)

The plantain grows in the tropics and looks like a banana. It should be boiled, baked or deep fried (prepared as a fritter).

Potatoes

All-purpose potatoes are available all the year round, and are the least expensive to buy. They can be used satisfactorily for baking, boiling, mashing and salads. When they are available, and the expense is warranted, choose the long russet potatoes for baking and French frying—these are mealier and fluffier than any other variety. For boiling whole, new potatoes, either red- or white-skinned, are an excellent choice in season. These potatoes are also particularly good for salad, since they are moist, firm, and hold their shape well.

BOILED POTATOES

    6 medium potatoes
    1 quart boiling water
    1 tablespoon salt

Peel potatoes thinly, dropping each into cold water to prevent discoloring. Cook in boiling water to cover 20 to 30 minutes. When nearly done, add salt. Drain, shake pan gently over heat to dry.

If a tightly covered heavy pan is used, potatoes may be cooked in 1 to 1½ cups boiling water.

BOILED NEW POTATOES

Pare new potatoes. Cook until tender in boiling salted water to cover; drain. Add 2 tablespoons melted butter and 1 tablespoon chopped parsley, or, if desired, 1 teaspoon caraway seed, or chopped chives. Shake well over heat and serve hot. Or boil in jackets and serve peeled or unpeeled. May also be served with Medium White Sauce.

BOILED POTATOES WITH ONIONS

Pare potatoes and cut in half. Place in pan with water to half cover them. Add 2 peeled and sliced onions and boil covered until done. Drain. Add 1 tablespoon salt, shake gently over heat to dry.

CREAMED POTATOES

4 cold cooked potatoes
½ cup milk
2 tablespoons butter
dash pepper
½ teaspoon salt
1 tablespoon chopped parsley

Cut the potatoes into cubes or thin slices. Put into a double boiler with the milk and cook until nearly all the milk is absorbed. Add butter and seasoning, cook 5 minutes longer. Sprinkle with parsley.

Or heat the potatoes in Thin White Sauce.

MASHED POTATOES

6 medium potatoes
3 tablespoons butter
⅓ cup hot milk
1 teaspoon salt
white pepper

Peel and boil potatoes until tender, drain, and put through ricer or mash well. Add butter, milk, and seasonings to taste, and beat well. To make Whipped Potatoes, add more milk, to reach the desired lightness of consistency. Serve in a heated dish. Top with a pat of butter and sprinkle with paprika.

MASHED POTATOES WITH ONIONS

6 medium potatoes
1 onion, finely minced
2 tablespoons butter or other fat
salt, pepper

Prepare mashed potatoes, above. Cook onion in fat until golden, but not soft, and season to taste. Pour over mashed potatoes; or stir into mashed potatoes.

STEWED POTATOES

2 tablespoons butter
1 chopped onion
2 tablespoons flour
1½ cups water
salt and pepper to taste
6 to 8 medium potatoes, peeled
1 teaspoon chopped parsley

Melt butter, add chopped onion and flour; cook until brown. Add water, and salt and pepper to taste, stir; cook until smooth. Add whole potatoes. Cover. Simmer gently until tender and sprinkle with parsley.

It is not advisable to home-freeze white potatoes, either raw or cooked.

BAKED POTATOES

In choosing potatoes for baking, select those of uniform size and shape, for better appearance and equal cooking time. Scrub potatoes well. Dry and rub lightly with any desired fat. Pierce with a fork to let the steam escape. Place in hot oven, 400° F., not too close together. Bake 1 hour or until tender when pressed with a finger. Cut a 2-inch cross at the center broadside top. Press toward the center with both hands and the skin will burst open. Top with a small cube of butter and a dash of paprika.

Or serve with crumbled blue cheese, or Cheddar cheese, or sour cream and chives. Serve at once.

POTATOES ON THE HALF SHELL

6 baked potatoes
2 tablespoons butter
1 teaspoon salt
¼ cup hot milk
1 cup Cheddar cheese, grated

Cut baked potatoes in half lengthwise, scoop out the pulp. Mash, mix with the butter, salt, milk, and beat well. Return to the shells, brush top with melted butter, and sprinkle with the cheese if desired. Place in moderate oven (350° F.) and bake 5 to 10 minutes, until hot and lightly browned. Leftover baked potatoes can be prepared this way.

POTATOES ANNA

4 large raw potatoes
¼ pound butter
salt, pepper
paprika

Pare potatoes, cut in ⅛-inch slices crosswise. Drop into cold water. Drain and dry. Dip each slice into melted butter and line a buttered, heavy skillet with overlapping slices. There should be no more than three layers. Season well and dot with butter. Place in very hot oven, 450° F., for 10 minutes; reduce heat to 350° F. and bake until tender and browned, about 30 minutes longer. Invert on platter.

BOSTON BROWNED POTATOES

Peel and quarter 6 medium-sized potatoes. Place in a shallow baking dish with 4 tablespoons melted butter. Coat potatoes, season well with salt, pepper, and paprika, and bake 30 to 45 minutes in a hot oven, 400° F. Or add to roasting pan 1 hour before meat is done, and coat with drippings.

FRANCONIA POTATOES

Peel potatoes of uniform size. Boil about 10 minutes and drain. Put in pan with meat, while roasting about 1 hour before meat is done, and baste when meat is basted. Or place in another pan, and baste with drippings.

POTATOES AU GRATIN

    4 cups cold boiled potatoes
    1 teaspoon salt
    ¼ teaspoon pepper
    1 tablespoon chopped parsley
    ¼ pound grated Cheddar cheese
    1 cup Medium White Sauce
    1 cup buttered cracker crumbs

Cut the potatoes in slices and season with salt, pepper and parsley. Layer with cheese in buttered baking dish, add Medium White Sauce and cover with layer of crumbs and grated cheese. Bake in a slow oven, 300° F., until brown.

IRISH VEGETABLES

    potatoes
    milk
    butter
    cabbage
    celery
    leeks or small onions
    salt and pepper

Boil potatoes in salted water. Rice or mash potatoes and add milk and butter. Cook cabbage, celery and leeks until tender. Drain well. Add vegetables to potatoes, mixing lightly. If necessary, reheat. Season to taste. Serve with melted butter on top.

CREAMY SCALLOPED POTATOES

    4 cups raw sliced potatoes
    2 cups Medium White Sauce

Pare potatoes, cut into ½-inch slices. Butter a baking dish, place a layer of potatoes at the bottom, sprinkle with salt. Cover with white sauce. Repeat. Bake 1 hour or longer at 350° F., until potatoes are soft and top is browned.

SCALLOPED POTATOES

    4 large raw potatoes
    salt and paprika
    4 tablespoons butter
    flour
    milk

Pare potatoes, cut in ⅛-inch slices. Put potatoes in layers in a buttered baking dish. Sprinkle each layer very lightly with flour, salt and paprika.

Dot with 1 tablespoon butter. Repeat. Cover with milk. Bake in a moderate oven, 350° F., for 45 minutes, covered. Uncover and bake until tender and browned, about 15 minutes longer. Add 1 tablespoon grated cheese and a sprinkling of dry mustard to each layer for variety.

SCALLOPED POTATOES AND ONIONS

    6 medium potatoes
    3 large Bermuda onions
    2 cups Cream or Cheese Sauce, page 386

Pare potatoes; cut in ⅛-inch slices. Peel onions, slice thin. Place alternate layers of onions and potatoes in a greased casserole. Cover with Cream or Cheese Sauce. Bake in a moderate oven, 350° F., until tender.

OVEN-FRIED POTATOES

Allow 1 large potato for each serving. Pare; cut lengthwise as for French Fried Potatoes. Soak in salted, cold water 1 hour; drain and dry. Place side by side in a shallow pan. Cover with melted butter, 1 tablespoon for each potato. Bake in a very hot oven, 450° F., 20 to 30 minutes until brown on bottom, turn, and cook until crisp, tender and brown on other side. Sprinkle with salt.

SAUTEED POTATO BALLS

    6 medium potatoes
    4 tablespoons butter
    1 teaspoon salt
    1 teaspoon chopped parsley

Pare potatoes, cut into balls, and let stand in cold, salted water until wanted. Scraps may be used for soup or mashed potatoes. Heat butter in a saucepan, add the potato balls and salt, cover and cook slowly until tender, shaking pan often. When ready to serve, sprinkle with chopped parsley.

DUCHESSE POTATOES

To about 2 cups freshly cooked or left-over mashed potatoes, add beaten yolks of 2 eggs; form in balls, or flat cakes, arrange on a greased baking sheet, brush with lightly beaten egg white, and brown in hot oven, 400° F.

MAITRE D'HOTEL POTATO BALLS

Make potato balls as above; cook until tender in boiling water, drain, and toss with Maitre d'Hotel Sauce.

COUNTRY-FRIED POTATOES

Slice cold, boiled potatoes. Melt fat in skillet. Brown the potatoes on both sides. Season and serve hot.

POTATO PUDDING

2 cups mashed potatoes
2 tablespoons melted butter
2 eggs, well beaten
1 cup milk or cream
salt and pepper

Mix the potatoes and butter, add the eggs and the cream. Season. Beat well, place in greased baking dish and bake in a hot oven until brown.

PAN-FRIED RAW POTATOES

4 cups raw sliced potatoes
3 tablespoons fat
1 teaspoon salt
¼ teaspoon pepper

Peel potatoes and slice very thin and place directly into a pan of cold water. Let stand 20 minutes, drain and dry. Heat fat in skillet, add potatoes, season, cover tightly and cook over low heat 20 to 25 minutes until bottom layer of potatoes is brown. Turn and brown on other side. Chopped onion may be added.

LYONNAISE POTATOES

2 cups cold boiled potatoes
salt and pepper
2 tablespoons shortening
1 teaspoon chopped onion
2 tablespoons chopped parsley

Slice the potatoes, season with salt and pepper. Fry the onion in shortening until light brown, add the potatoes and brown on one side. Turn, brown on other side. Sprinkle with parsley.

HASHED BROWN POTATOES

Cube 3 cups cold boiled potatoes. Salt and pepper to taste. Heat ¼ cup fat in skillet, add potatoes, mix and stir until fat and potatoes are hot and well blended. Press and smooth down with spatula on half of skillet. Cook until bottom is well browned, then loosen from pan with a spatula. Cover skillet and invert so potatoes will rest on cover browned side up. Add more butter to skillet, slip potatoes onto skillet uncooked side down and cook until brown. Turn out onto serving plate.

POTATO CAKES

Mix 2 cups well-seasoned, cold, mashed potatoes with 1 beaten egg. Shape into ½-inch thick patties, dip in flour, brown on both sides in hot fat in skillet.

SARATOGA POTATO CHIPS

Pare potatoes and slice very thin and drop directly into a pan of cold salted water. Drain and dry between towels. Fry a few at a time in deep, hot fat (375° F.), until brown and crisp. Drain on brown paper. Sprinkle with salt and serve hot or cold.

SHOE-STRING POTATOES

Cut peeled potatoes into very thin strips and drop directly into a pan of cold, salted water. Let stand 1 hour. Drain and dry. Fry a few at a time in deep, hot fat (375° F.), until crisp and slightly brown. Drain and sprinkle with salt.

FRENCH FRIED POTATOES

Pare long, thin potatoes. Wash and cut lengthwise into strips. Soak in cold water. Drain, dry, and fry in deep, hot fat (375° F.), until tender, crisp and golden brown. Drain on brown paper. Sprinkle with salt.

O'BRIEN POTATOES

8 medium potatoes
1 small onion, chopped
2 tablespoons butter
3 canned pimientos, cut fine
1 green pepper, chopped fine
1 tablespoon chopped parsley

Pare potatoes and shape into balls with vegetable cutter or cut into cubes. Soak in cold water and drain well. Fry in deep, hot fat (375° F.), until brown and tender. Drain and sprinkle with salt. Fry onion in 2 tablespoons butter until golden brown; add pimientos and green pepper. Heat thoroughly; add the fried potatoes. Serve hot, sprinkled with finely chopped parsley.

POTATO PUFFS

2 cups boiled riced potatoes
1 cup sour cream
1 cup flour
½ teaspoon salt

Blend potatoes with sour cream, add enough flour to make a dough. Add salt and knead for a minute or two. Roll out very thin on a floured board, cut into rounds with a biscuit cutter, and fry until brown in deep hot fat (375° F.). Drain on un-glazed paper. Serve hot.

PUFFED POTATOES (POMMES SOUFFLES)
Peel and slice baking potatoes ⅛ inch thick. Soak in ice water, drain and dry. Half fill a skillet with fat (or use an electric frying pan) and heat to 350° F. Add just enough potato slices to fit without crowding, and remove pan from heat until temperature goes down to 250° F. Put skillet back on heat. The temperature should not go higher than 300° F. When slices begin to brown and swell, skim them out of the fat with a slotted spatula and spread on paper toweling to drain and cool. The first cooking takes from 6 to 10 minutes. When all slices are cooked, heat the fat to 400° F., add the potatoes a few at a time. They will immediately puff and come to the top. Turn them constantly until they are brown. Drain on paper toweling, sprinkle with salt, and serve hot.

POTATO CROQUETTES
   2 cups boiled potatoes, riced
   ⅛ teaspoon white pepper
   ¼ teaspoon celery salt
   2 tablespoons butter
   ½ teaspoon salt
   1 egg yolk
   1 teaspoon chopped parsley
   onion juice
   bread crumbs
   1 egg, beaten

Mix first 6 ingredients, and beat until light. Add chopped parsley and a few drops of onion juice. Shape into cones. Dip in bread crumbs, then in beaten egg, then in crumbs again. Fry in deep, hot fat (375° F.). Drain on unglazed paper.

CREAMED CHICKEN IN POTATO BOAT
See page 317.

Sweet Potatoes
Sweet Potatoes are yellow and dry, Yams are orange, moist, and sweeter in flavor, but their preparation is the same and they may be used interchangeably in the following recipes.

   In selecting potatoes for baking, choose those of uniform size and shape, for best appearance and uniform cooking time.

BAKED SWEET POTATOES
Scrub sweet potatoes; rub with shortening. Bake in a hot oven, 400° F., ¾ hour or until tender when pierced with a fork.

BOILED SWEET POTATOES
Boil potatoes in jackets. Cool and remove skins. Or, wash, pare, cut, and cook 20 minutes or until tender in boiling, salted water to cover.

CANDIED SWEET POTATOES
   6 medium-sized sweet potatoes
   ½ cup brown sugar
   2 tablespoons water
   4 tablespoons butter

Wash and pare potatoes. Cook 10 minutes in boiling, salted water. Drain, cut in halves, lengthwise, and put in a buttered pan. Make a syrup by boiling the sugar and water for 3 minutes; add butter. Baste potatoes with syrup, bake slowly, at 300° F., until tender.

GLAZED SWEET POTATOES
Peel raw sweet potatoes and slice about ½ inch thick. Place in very shallow baking dish. Dot potatoes with butter, top with brown sugar. Pour ½ cup water in the dish. Bake in moderate oven, 350° F. When glazed on one side, turn and continue baking until other side is glazed.

SWEET POTATOES, SOUTHERN STYLE
   4 boiled sweet potatoes
   ¼ pound butter
   ¼ cup brown sugar
   1 tablespoon water
   lemon juice

Peel boiled potatoes and quarter. Place in baking dish, dot with butter, sprinkle with the brown sugar, add the water and a little lemon juice. Brown in moderate oven, 350° F., and serve hot.

SCALLOPED SWEET POTATOES WITH APPLES OR ORANGES
   2 cups boiled sweet potatoes
   1½ cups sliced tart apples or 1 unpeeled orange, sliced
   ½ cup brown sugar
   4 teaspoons butter
   1 teaspoon salt

Slice potatoes ¼ inch thick. Put half the potatoes in a buttered baking dish, cover with half the fruit, sugar, butter and salt. Repeat, and bake in a moderate oven, 350° F., 1 hour.

SCALLOPED SWEET POTATOES CREOLE

    2 pounds sweet potatoes
    1 pound cooked, peeled chestnuts
    ½ cup brown sugar
    ¼ cup hot water
    ¼ cup butter
    1 cup buttered crumbs

Wash, pare, and slice potatoes. Boil 5 minutes and drain. Fill a well-buttered baking dish with alternate layers of potatoes and chestnuts, cut in large pieces. Boil brown sugar and hot water for 3 minutes, add butter, pour over the potatoes; sprinkle with bread crumbs and bake in moderate oven, 350° F., ¾ hour or until potatoes are tender.

SWEET POTATO PUFFS

    3 large sweet potatoes
    1 tablespoon butter
    cream to moisten
    ½ teaspoon salt
    nutmeg to taste
    1 egg
    water
    crushed cornflakes

Boil potatoes; peel, rice, mix with butter and cream. Season. Roll into balls. Dip in egg mixed with a little water. Coat with cornflakes. Bake in greased pan in moderate oven, 350° F., or fry in deep fat.

Or, substitute concentrated orange juice for cream to moisten.

SWEET POTATO CROQUETTES

    2 cups mashed sweet potatoes
    ⅛ teaspoon pepper
    2 tablespoons melted butter
    ½ teaspoon salt
    1 egg yolk
    1 teaspoon chopped parsley
    bread crumbs
    1 egg, beaten

Mix first four ingredients and beat until light; add the yolk and mix well. Rub through a strainer; add chopped parsley. Shape into balls, or shape to resemble pears. Before frying, stick one clove at blossom end, showing head of clove, and another clove at opposite point, the stem end showing. Dip in bread crumbs, in beaten egg, then in crumbs again. Fry in deep, hot fat. Drain on paper.

Sweet potatoes do not freeze especially well, but they can be frozen if precooked.

SWEET POTATO CASSEROLE

    3 pounds sweet potatoes
    ½ cup butter
    ¾ cup apple cider
    ¼ teaspoon nutmeg
    ¼ teaspoon cinnamon
    ½ teaspoon salt

Boil sweet potatoes, peel and mash. Add ⅓ cup butter, cider, and seasonings. Mix well. Place in greased baking dish, dot with remaining butter. Bake in moderately hot oven, 375° F., for 30 to 40 minutes.

ORANGE SWEET POTATO PUFF

    3 pounds sweet potatoes
    ⅛ cup melted butter
    1 cup sugar
    6 eggs, separated
    1 tablespoon grated lemon rind
    1 cup orange juice
    ¼ teaspoon cinnamon

Boil the potatoes, peel and mash. Add the butter and ¾ cup of sugar. Beat the egg yolks. Add yolks, lemon rind, orange juice, and cinnamon to the potatoes. Fold in the stiffly beaten whites. Pour into a well-greased pudding dish. Sprinkle top with the remaining sugar. Bake in a moderate oven, 350° F., for about 1 hour. Serves 8.

SWEET POTATOES ON HALF SHELL

    6 baked sweet potatoes
    2 tablespoons butter
    salt
    ¼ cup hot milk
    juice and grated rind of 1 orange
    marshmallows

Cut potatoes in half lengthwise, scoop out the pulp. Mash, mix with butter, a little salt, milk, orange juice and rind. Return to the shells, cover with marshmallows. Place in moderate oven and bake until marshmallows are melted. Or place mashed potato in scooped out orange shells.

MASHED SWEET POTATOES

Peel, boil and mash sweet potatoes. To every 2 cups add 2 tablespoons butter, ½ teaspoon salt and a little hot milk or cream. Beat until light.

SWEET POTATO RING

    8-10 medium sweet potatoes
    ½ cup melted butter
    1 cup brown sugar
    ¼ cup nut meats

Cook and mash sweet potatoes. Spread bottom and sides of medium ring mold with butter, sprinkle with sugar and nut meats, chill. Fill mold with potatoes. Set in a pan of hot water and bake in a moderate oven, 350° F., 45 minutes. Invert on serving plate.

SWEET POTATOES AND MARSHMALLOWS OR PINEAPPLE

2 pounds sweet potatoes or 1 can (1 pound, 7 ounces) sweet potatoes
¼ cup sugar or syrup
¼ cup butter
½ teaspoon salt
marshmallows or 1 can (1 pound, 4 ounces) pineapple

Boil potatoes until tender and peel. Or use canned potatoes. Mash, add sugar or syrup, butter, and salt, and mix well. Turn into greased baking dish, dot top with marshmallows or drained sliced pineapple, place in moderate oven, 350° F., until brown. Serve hot.

SWEET POTATOES IN APPLES

8 baking apples
2 cups mashed sweet potatoes
¼ cup melted butter
½ cup sugar

Peel apples and scoop out core, making large cavity. Stuff with mashed sweet potatoes, above, roll apples in butter and then in sugar. Bake slowly, 300° F., 1½ to 2 hours, basting until well glazed.

PUMPKINS

Pumpkins are baked, boiled or steamed like winter squash, and seasoned the same way, but require longer cooking.

TO KEEP PUMPKIN FRESH

When a whole pumpkin is more than is needed, cut extra pumpkin in desired pieces, and coat with paraffin.

A pound of raw pumpkin yields 1 cup cooked, mashed vegetable.

TO WASH SPINACH

Fresh spinach is sold loose and in plastic bags, in 1- and 2-pound sizes. Two pounds serves 3 to 4. Cut off and discard the roots and any withered leaves. Put the spinach into a large basin of lukewarm water and shake leaves to dislodge the sand, which will settle to the bottom. Lift out the greens and discard the water and sand. Repeat until the water is clear.

CHOPPED SPINACH

2 pounds spinach, washed
2 tablespoons butter or fat
1 teaspoon grated onion
2 tablespoons bread crumbs
½ teaspoon salt
⅛ teaspoon pepper
dash of nutmeg
1 cup soup stock or meat gravy

Put washed spinach into pot, add small amount of boiling water, cover, and cook until leaves are tender. Drain thoroughly and chop fine. Heat butter in skillet, add onion, crumbs and seasonings, and brown lightly. Add stock gradually, stirring constantly. Add spinach, heat. Serve garnished with lemon wedge and sliced hard-cooked egg, if desired.

CREAMED SPINACH

Cook and drain spinach as above. Add 1 cup Medium White Sauce, or 1 cup condensed mushroom soup and heat.

SPINACH ITALIAN STYLE

2 pounds spinach, washed
1 clove garlic, minced
3 tablespoons oil
1 can (6 ounces) tomato paste
salt and pepper to taste

Cook spinach, as above, until tender, drain, chop fine. Brown garlic in oil, add tomato paste and spinach. Cook 15 minutes. Season.

SPINACH RING

2 tablespoons butter
2 tablespoons flour
½ cup milk, warm
3 eggs, separated
1¾ cups cooked, drained, chopped spinach
salt and pepper

Heat butter in skillet, add flour and gradually stir in milk. Cook, stirring, until sauce is smooth and thick. Stir gradually into the well-beaten yolks. Add spinach and seasoning, grated onion and nutmeg if desired. Cool, fold in the stiffly beaten egg whites; pour into a well-greased ring, set in a pan half-filled with hot water, bake in moderate oven, 350° F., 30 minutes, or until set.

PROSNOS (SPINACH CASSEROLE)

1 10-ounce package chopped spinach, thawed
1 cup creamed cottage cheese
2 tablespoons butter, cut in small pieces
4 eggs, beaten
4 tablespoons flour
½ pound Cheddar cheese, diced

Combine all ingredients and place in greased 1½-quart casserole. Bake, uncovered, 1 hour at 350° F.

SWISS CHARD

The green, tender leaves are prepared like spinach. The mid-ribs may be cooked like celery.

Squash

The many varieties of squash fall into two categories: the watery, tender varieties which cook quickly—such as the yellow crookneck, the green zucchini that resembles cucumber, and the white scalloped cymling or pattypan, and the hard-shelled dark-green acorn and Hubbard, and the tan butternut, which must be peeled and freed from seeds and stringy pith before cooking.

BAKED ACORN SQUASH

Cut small acorn squash in two lengthwise. Remove seeds and strings. Parboil, then place in pan with just enough water to cover bottom. Into each half place 1 teaspoon butter and 1 tablespoon brown sugar. Bake in moderate oven, 350° F., until soft. If desired, remove baked pulp from shell, mash, season with butter, salt and pepper. Refill shells and serve.

BAKED STUFFED ACORN SQUASH

3 medium acorn squash
2 tablespoons butter or fat
½ onion, chopped
½ cup soaked bread
½ teaspoon salt
⅛ teaspoon pepper
1 egg, beaten
½ cup cracker crumbs
butter

Bake squash as above. Scoop out pulp, being careful not to break shells. Heat butter or fat in a skillet, add the onion, chopped fine, brown, add the soaked bread, mashed, and the squash. Cook 15 minutes, stirring occasionally. Remove from heat, add the salt, pepper, and egg. Fill shells; sprinkle with cracker crumbs and bits of butter, and return to oven to brown.

BAKED HUBBARD SQUASH

Cut squash in 3-inch squares, peel, discard seeds and strings, place in baking dish with ½ teaspoon butter, 1 teaspoon brown sugar, salt and pepper for each square. Bake 1 hour at 350° F. or until soft.

MASHED BUTTERNUT SQUASH

butternut squash, medium-sized
½ cup milk
1 tablespoon butter
salt and pepper

Wash, peel and discard stringy portions and seeds. Cut in quarters or 2-inch squares. Cook, covered, in a very small amount of salted water 20 minutes or until tender. Drain and mash. Add the milk, butter and seasoning.

GROUND MEAT IN ACORN SQUASH

See page 280.

CYMLING OR PATTY-PAN SQUASH

Wash and cook, covered, in very small amount of boiling salted water until tender. Drain. Serve with melted butter or Cheese Sauce.

CROOKNECK SQUASH

crookneck squash, diced or sliced
salt and pepper
2 tablespoons light cream,
    or 2 tablespoons butter

Crookneck squash are good only when young, fresh and tender. Wash, peel if necessary, and cut into quarters or small pieces. Cook, covered, in very small amount of boiling salted water 20 minutes or until tender. Drain, mash and add rest of the ingredients.

TO SKIN AND SEED TOMATOES

To remove the skin from tomatoes, dip them into boiling water for a minute. Then pierce the tomato through the stem end with a fork, and with a sharp knife slit and remove the skin. It will slip off easily.

To remove tomato seeds cut the tomatoes in half and scoop out the pulpy mass containing the seeds. If tomatoes are strained after cooking, it is not necessary to remove skins and seeds beforehand.

TOMATOES AND GREEN BEANS

See page 413.

STEWED TOMATOES

Cut peeled tomatoes in pieces and cook slowly 20 minutes, stirring occasionally. Season with butter, salt, pepper and a little sugar. If desired, add bread crumbs, cracker crumbs, or croutons. For variety, add to stewed tomatoes: cooked lima beans and celery, or cooked corn and green and red peppers.

TOMATOES WITH WINE

1 can (1 pound) tomatoes, solid pack
¼ cup chopped onion
½ teaspoon dried dill
1 teaspoon celery seed
salt
pepper
¼ cup rosé wine
Parmesan cheese

Combine all the ingredients except the cheese; simmer for 3 to 4 minutes. Top with grated Parmesan.

STUFFED TOMATOES

6 firm tomatoes
2 tablespoons butter
1 cup rye or white bread crumbs
1 small onion, grated
1 tablespoon chopped parsley
salt, pepper
2 egg yolks

Wash and dry tomatoes. Cut off tops. Remove pulp with small spoon, and rub through a fine sieve. Put butter in pan, add bread crumbs, cook a few minutes; add onion, parsley, salt and pepper, and the tomato pulp. Stir in the egg yolks, and fill the tomatoes with the mixture. Top with bread or cracker crumbs, dot with butter, and place in moderate oven, 350° F., on buttered tin and bake ½ hour. Serve hot.

STUFFED TOMATOES WITH CHICKEN LIVERS

8 firm tomatoes
salt and pepper to season
1 tablespoon butter
1 medium onion, chopped
6 fresh mushrooms
½ pound chicken livers
½ cup bread crumbs
parsley, chopped

Wash and dry tomatoes. Cut through top without detaching to serve as a cover. Scoop out pulp. Season inside with a little salt and pepper. Melt butter, add onion and fry for 3 minutes to brown. Add mushrooms and the chicken livers, chopped. Season. Cook for 3 minutes, stirring occasionally. Add pulp, bread crumbs, parsley. Cook 2 minutes longer. Cool. Stuff tomato shells with mixture, close covers, and bake at 350° F. in buttered baking dish for 20 minutes. Serve hot. Sausage meat or chicken may be used in place of livers.

FRIED TOMATOES

Wash, but do not peel 4 medium-sized, firm tomatoes. Cut crosswise into halves. Dip cut side into seasoned bread crumbs. Heat a tablespoon of butter in a skillet, add tomato halves, cut side down, brown slowly a few minutes. Turn and cook a few minutes longer.

BROILED TOMATOES

Prepare tomatoes as above. Season well. Dip cut side in crumbs. Dot with butter. Broil, cut side up, on rack 5 inches below heat until crumbs are brown.

TOMATO VERTIS

8 large, firm tomatoes
½ pound raw spinach
   or 2 10-ounce packages frozen chopped spinach
2 carrots
1 green pepper
1 medium onion
3 large stalks celery
3 sprigs parsley
3 tablespoons butter
1 egg, beaten
1 cup dry bread crumbs
milk
salt and pepper to taste
½ cup grated cheese

Scoop out tomatoes, reserving the pulp. Turn tomatoes upside down to drain. If using frozen spinach, thaw it and drain well. Chop all vegetables very fine, including the tomato pulp. Simmer vegetables in butter until slightly browned. Add egg, crumbs, and up to ½ cup milk. If the filling is quite moist, do not add more than ¼ cup milk. Add salt and pepper. Fill the tomatoes with vegetable mix. Sprinkle top with grated cheese. Place tomatoes in greased baking dish and bake at 400° F. for 20 minutes.

TOMATO RING

1 can (1 pound) tomatoes
1 bay leaf
1 teaspoon salt
6 peppercorns
1 slice onion
2 tablespoons butter
4 tablespoons flour
3 eggs, separated

Cook the first 5 ingredients 20 minutes. Strain. Melt butter, add flour, and gradually add 1 cup strained tomato mixture. Cook, stirring, until smooth; mix sauce into 3 well-beaten egg yolks and set aside to cool. Beat whites very stiff and fold into tomato mixture. Turn into a well-greased ring mold, set in a pan of hot water. Bake in a moderate oven, 350° F., 20 to 30 minutes. Remove from pan carefully.

If desired, fill center with Halibut à la Newburg, and surround the ring with Potato Balls.

TURNIPS OR RUTABAGAS

Wash, peel and cut into uniform pieces. Cook covered in small amount of boiling salted water 20 minutes, or until soft. Drain, rice or mash, season with butter, salt, a little sugar, and pepper, or mix with equal quantity of hot mashed potatoes.

Or, drain and add 1 cup Medium White Sauce or Brown Sauce.

Tops of young turnips can be cooked like spinach.

VEGETABLE STEW

1 large onion, sliced
2 tablespoons shortening
1 cup kernel corn
1 cup peas
2 sweet potatoes, sliced thin
3 carrots, sliced
3 stalks celery, sliced
2 tomatoes, quartered, or
    ¾ cup canned tomatoes
salt
pepper
1 bay leaf
1 to 2 teaspoons dill weed
1 cup bouillon
2 teaspoons cornstarch

In a large skillet, sauté the onion in 2 tablespoons shortening for about 5 minutes. If canned corn and peas are used, do not add at this point. If fresh, add with other vegetables to skillet. Add seasonings and bouillon, cover, and simmer only until vegetables are tender. If canned corn and peas are used, add at this point. Soften cornstarch in a little cold water. Add to vegetables. Heat until thickened.

RATATOUILLE

1 small eggplant, peeled
1 large green pepper
2 medium onions, sliced
2 cloves garlic, minced
¼ cup oil
2 zucchini, cut in ¼-inch slices
3 tomatoes, peeled and chopped
2 tablespoons chopped parsley
2 teaspoons salt
½ teaspoon basil
⅛ teaspoon pepper

Cut eggplant into 1-inch cubes. Cut green pepper into strips. Sauté onion and garlic in oil. Add other ingredients. Cover and simmer for 10 to 15 minutes. Remove cover and simmer for a few more minutes until the sauce thickens.

ZUCCHINI

Scrub zucchini well, trim ends. Slice and cook, covered, in a very small amount of salted water, and serve with butter.

Or sauté the slices in a little oil or butter until translucent, sprinkle with oregano.

Or cut the zucchini into desired shapes and cook according to the recipe for Fried Eggplant.

ZUCCHINI LASAGNE

1 pound ground beef
1 clove garlic, minced
2 tablespoons salad oil
1 can (1 pound 4 ounces) solid pack tomatoes
1 can (8 ounces) tomato sauce
1 teaspoon salt
½ teaspoon pepper
½ teaspoon oregano
3 medium zucchini, sliced thin
1 pound ricotta or dry cottage cheese
½ cup grated Parmesan cheese
½ pound mozzarella cheese, sliced

Brown beef and garlic in oil, stirring with a fork. Add tomatoes, first draining off half the juice; add tomato sauce and seasonings. Simmer for 30 minutes. Cover bottom of a large, greased baking dish with 1½ cups of beef mixture. Cover the beef mixture with single layer of thinly sliced zucchini.

Spread ½ the ricotta cheese on the zucchini, sprinkle with ½ the Parmesan cheese and place over this ⅓ the mozzarella. Repeat. Top with remaining beef mixture and mozzarella. Bake in 350° F. oven for 45 minutes. Let stand 15 minutes after removing from oven. Cut into squares.

ZUCCHINI AND ONIONS

    1 pound zucchini
    1 pound small onions, boiled
    1 1-pound can tomatoes
    3 bay leaves
    1 teaspoon basil
    dash of pepper
    2 bouillon cubes

Cut zucchini into chunks or quarters. Combine all ingredients. Simmer only until zucchini is tender, 15 to 20 minutes.

ZUCCHINI AND RICE

    1 pound zucchini
    ⅓ cup oil
    1 clove garlic, crushed
    2 cups cooked rice
    salt
    pepper
    2 tablespoons grated Parmesan cheese

Wash zucchini well. Do not peel. Slice thin and sauté in oil with garlic for 8 to 10 minutes. Mix zucchini and rice. Season to taste. Before serving, sprinkle top with Parmesan cheese.

QUICK REFERENCE GUIDE TO USEFUL INFORMATION IN THIS BOOK

23
PRESERVING AND PICKLING

FRUIT JUICES · VINEGARS · WINES · CORDIALS · PRESERVES · PICKLES · CATSUPS · RELISHES · PICKLED FRUIT

FRUIT JUICES

GRAPE JUICE

    10 pounds Concord grapes
    2 pounds sugar
    2 quarts water

Use well-ripened but not overripe grapes. Pick over and wash grapes. Place in kettle, cover with the water and let boil until the seeds are free. Strain while hot through cloth bag. Heat juice to boiling point and skim. Let boil up again and skim; then add sugar.

Heat to the boiling point; boil 1 minute. Pour into hot sterilized jars and seal. Or use self-sealing bottles. If ordinary bottles are used, do not fill too full. Immediately after filling, place corks over bottles very lightly at first; as they cool, push corks down; then cover with melted paraffin or sealing wax to make the seal airtight.

WHITE GRAPE JUICE

Select ripe, white Delaware or Tokay grapes. Proceed as above.

GRAPE JUICE, UNCOOKED

    2 cups Concord grapes
    1 cup sugar
    boiling water

Wash grapes, stem and place in 1-quart, hot, sterilized, airtight jar. Add 1 cup sugar. Fill to overflowing with boiling water. Seal at once, and shake until sugar is dissolved. Let stand 3 or 4 weeks before using. Sugar must be thoroughly dissolved or the juice will turn into wine.

CURRANT AND RASPBERRY JUICE

    4 quarts currants
    2 quarts red raspberries
    3 quarts water
    3 pounds sugar

Pick over and wash fruit. Place in preserving kettle, cover with the water and boil until soft. Strain through jelly bag. Measure, and to every quart of juice add 1 cup of sugar. Proceed as in Grape Juice.

CHERRY, PLUM, LOGANBERRY, AND PEACH JUICES

To preserve the juices of these and similar fruits, prepare the fruit as for Jelly, page 445, but use only 1 cup of sugar to each quart of juice. If transparent juice is not required, press the pulp to extract all liquid.

APPLE CIDER

Use fully ripened apples, free from decay. Wash

them thoroughly and remove all leaves. Crush the apples and extract the juice or cider, in a clean press. Place the juice in a large, open preserving kettle and boil it down until it is reduced one-half, skimming it often. Pour at once into hot sterilized jars, and seal; or, pour the fresh juice at once into jars, put the covers in place loosely, without the rubber, stand the jars on a rack in warm water to within a few inches of the top of the jars. Cover kettle and boil 1 hour. Or process in Live Steam, page 469. Remove jars, one at a time, put a rubber in place and seal at once.

VINEGARS

CIDER VINEGAR
Let Apple Cider, above, stand in an open jug from 4 to 6 weeks and it will turn to vinegar.

HEALTH VINEGAR
   3 gallons water
   3 pounds dark brown sugar
   2 cakes compressed yeast
   2 slices wheat toast

Boil water and sugar together until dissolved, put in 5-gallon crock and let cool until lukewarm. Spread toast with yeast. Float, yeast side down, in crock. When bread falls to bottom of crock, vinegar is ready to use (about 5 weeks). Strain and bottle.

TARRAGON VINEGAR
Fill wide-mouthed jar with leaves and stalks of fresh or dried tarragon. Cover with cider vinegar, let stand 3 weeks, in sun if possible. Strain. Use in mayonnaise, sharp sauces or salads.

GARLIC VINEGAR
Put 4 to 6 minced garlic cloves in 1 quart cider vinegar. Let stand 20 days. Strain and bottle.

DILL, CELERY, OR MINT VINEGAR
Fill jar with dill blossoms, or fresh celery leaves and tips, or sprigs of mint, cover with cider vinegar, let stand 3 weeks in sun, strain.

BEET VINEGAR (ROSEL)
Wash and stem red beets and place in a stone crock. Cover with cold water, put in a warm place and let stand for 3 or 4 weeks or until mixture becomes sour. This is used as a vinegar during Passover, and to make Beet Soup, Russian style.

HOME-MADE WINE

The producer of wine for home use is subject to the Internal Revenue laws of the United States and the laws of the state where the production is proposed. Up to 200 gallons of wines may be lawfully produced annually for home use exclusively, only after notice to the District Supervisor, Alcohol Tax Unit, Bureau of Internal Revenue, in the district where the wine is to be produced. The production of any larger quantity is illegal unless the producer has a lawful "bonded winery."

GRAPE WINE
   9 pounds Concord grapes
   4¾ pounds sugar

Wash and pick over the grapes and place with sugar in a 2-gallon jar. Fill with cold water. Cover with cheese cloth and keep in a warm place. Stir twice a week for 6 weeks. Strain and let stand 2 weeks longer to settle. Strain and bottle like Grape Juice, page 436.

DRY GRAPE WINE
Pick over, wash and stem grapes. Put in stone crock and crush. Let stand a week but stir every day. Squeeze the grapes and strain juice. To every gallon of juice use 2 pounds sugar. Boil sugar with just enough water to dissolve; add hot syrup to juice. Place in a crock big enough to allow bubbling. Let stand 24 hours. Pour into sterilized jugs; do not cork. Cover with a piece of cloth as wine will ferment. When fermentation stops, taste; if not sweet enough, add cold Sugar Syrup, page 460. Bottle.

CONCORD GRAPE WINE, LARGE QUANTITY
4 large (12-pound) baskets of grapes. Pick over, wash, and mash grapes and put into crock with 1 pound sugar; let stand, covered with cheesecloth for a week to 10 days; press grapes and put juice in crock with 10 pounds sugar; skim daily until it stops foaming—about 10 days; siphon into 5-gallon keg; make a syrup of 1 cup sugar to a quart of water, and add syrup to keep keg filled, so wine can work and overflow; after it stops working, put in bung with vent; then change to tight bung in March. Bottle in the autumn when keg is needed for next year's wine. Drip through filter paper before bottling.

RED BEET PORT WINE

5 pounds beets
1 gallon water
2½ pounds sugar
½ teaspoon ground pepper
1 ounce dry granular yeast
1 slice whole wheat toast

Wash beets well. Grind beets with skins on. Boil in water until tender. Strain through cloth. Add sugar and pepper to liquid. Boil 15 minutes, then pour into crock and cool. Spread yeast on toast. Place on top of jar, yeast side up. Let stand 12 days in a warm place at room temperature, then strain and bottle.

CURRANT, BLACKBERRY, ELDERBERRY OR RHUBARB WINES

Make like Grape Wine, using less sugar for Blackberry or Elderberry Wines.

GRAPEFRUIT WINE

1 gallon grapefruit juice
2 pounds sugar

Add sugar to juice and mix well. Put in gallon jug. Put jug in large, shallow pan to catch the overflow. Cover with double thickness of cheesecloth. Let stand 4 weeks at room temperature, undisturbed, until fermentation has stopped. Then strain through cheesecloth, being careful not to use the sediment that forms at the bottom of the jug. Strain again, this time with filter paper. Pour into sterilized bottles and cork. Keep in a dark place.

RAISIN WINE

2 pounds raisins, chopped
1 pound white loaf sugar
1 lemon, sliced
6 quarts boiling water

Combine ingredients in a stone jar, cover and stir every day for a week. Then strain, bottle and cork. Wine is ready to drink 10 or 12 days after bottling.

CORDIALS

PEACH BRANDY

Pare peaches but do not stone. Put a ½-inch layer of sugar into a wide-mouthed half-gallon jar; then a layer of peaches. Cover well with sugar, carefully filling all crevices. Repeat layers of sugar and peaches, with sugar on top. Seal, let stand 6 months to ripen. Drain and bottle liquid. Peaches may be served as dessert sauce.

BLACKBERRY OR ELDERBERRY CORDIAL

1 tablespoon each, whole allspice, cloves and
    1 piece stick cinnamon
8 quarts blackberries or elderberries
2 quarts cold water
4 pounds sugar
2 quarts whisky or brandy

Tie spices in a cloth bag. Pick over and wash berries. Place in preserving kettle, cover with water, boil until thoroughly soft; then strain. Measure, and to each quart of juice add 2 cups sugar. Add spice bag and boil 20 minutes. Let cool, and measure again. To each quart of syrup, add 1 pint of whisky. Bottle and cork tightly. Will keep; improves with age.

CHERRY BOUNCE

1 quart cherries
½ pound lump sugar
1 tablespoon allspice, cinnamon and cloves
    (heads removed)
1 pint whiskey

Wash cherries and pick off the stems. Fill a large-mouthed bottle alternately with a thick layer of cherries, a layer of sugar and a few of the whole spices. Repeat until the bottle is almost full. Then add whiskey to fill. Cork and let stand in a dark place for 2 months or more. The older it is, the better.

DANDELION WINE

1 gallon dandelion flowers
1 gallon boiling water
3 pounds sugar
3 oranges, cut in small pieces
3 lemons, cut in small pieces
1 ounce yeast

Pick dandelion flowers early in the morning, taking care not to have a particle of the bitter stem attached. Pour boiling water over the flowers and let stand 3 days. Strain and add the rest of the ingredients; let stand 3 weeks to ferment. Strain, bottle.

PRESERVES, JAMS, MARMALADES AND CONSERVES

Preserves, jams, marmalades and conserves are made by cooking fruits—and sometimes vegetables—with from ¾ to their full weight in sugar. They retain their best flavor and bright color if not more than from 2 to 4 cups are cooked at a time. Jams made with pectin require less boiling. They require extra sugar, but produce more jam and jelly. For Berry Juice, crush, heat, and strain the imperfect berries.

TO SAVE SUGAR IN PRESERVES, JAMS AND MARMALADES

In any recipes, up to ⅓ of the granulated sugar may be replaced with corn syrup. Up to ½ of the granulated sugar may be replaced with honey. This requires longer cooking. Substitutions should be made with care, since the sugar is a preservative as well as a sweetening agent.

TO PACK PRESERVES

Pour hot into hot, sterilized jars. Seal at once, with a thin layer of melted paraffin, or a sheet of flexible plastic wrap cut to cover the surface, or special jar cover. **In warm climate, or if storage conditions are poor, process 10-20 minutes in a water-bath, at simmering point, before sealing.** See Canning Methods, page 468.

PRESERVES

STRAWBERRY PRESERVES

Select large, sound strawberries. Wash and hull them carefully. Place in preserving kettle alternately 1 pound berries and from ¾ to 1 pound sugar. Let stand overnight. Bring to a boil and boil rapidly 10 to 12 minutes, or until the fruit is clear. Cover and let stand overnight. Pack in hot, sterilized jelly glasses or jars and seal.

STRAWBERRY LEMON PRESERVES

    1 quart strawberries
    4 cups sugar
    ½ cup unstrained lemon juice

Wash, drain and hull berries. In a large preserving kettle, arrange berries and sugar in layers of 1 cup strawberries and 1 cup sugar. Let stand overnight. With a slotted spoon, lift berries gently into colander, letting juice drain into preserving kettle. Set berries aside. Bring sugar and strawberry juice slowly to the boiling point, then boil rapidly for 3 minutes. Add berries and boil 2 minutes longer. Let stand overnight, drain berries again. Boil juice hard for 3 minutes. Add berries and lemon juice, bring to boiling point and boil 3 minutes. Pack in hot, sterilized jars or glasses. Seal at once.

SUNSHINE STRAWBERRIES

Use equal weights of sugar and strawberries. Put alternate layers of berries and sugar in the preserving kettle. Heat slowly to the boiling point. Skim carefully. Boil rapidly for 10 minutes. Pour on platters, cover with glass propped up about ¼ inch from platter. Let stand in full sunshine 2 or 3 days, until syrup has formed a jelly. After each day's sunning, turn the berries. Take in house at night. Without reheating, pack jelled preserves in hot, sterilized jars and seal.

SUNSHINE CURRANTS OR CHERRIES

Select large, firm red or white fruit, remove the stems, and proceed as for Sunshine Strawberries, above. Stone the cherries before weighing them.

GINGER APPLE PRESERVES

    1 quart tart apples
    2 cups water
    2 cups brown sugar
    1 lemon, juice and grated rind
    6 pieces ginger root

Wipe, pare, quarter, core and cut the apples into small cubes. Boil water, sugar and lemon juice 5 minutes or until clear, add the lemon rind and ginger root and cook slowly 2 or more hours until thick and brown. Pour into hot, sterilized jars and seal.

Homemade preserves and jellies make attractive and thrifty gifts.

BEET PRESERVES

4 pounds beets
3 pounds sugar
2 ounces green or dried ginger root
3 lemons, rind and juice
¼ pound blanched almonds

Wash and peel young beets, grind or slice very thin. Cover with water and cook until tender. Add sugar, ginger root, blanched and sliced fine, the lemon juice and grated rind. Cook gently until thick and clear, about 1 hour. When nearly done, add ground almonds. Pour into hot, sterilized glasses and seal.

CANTALOUPE PRESERVES

Cut firm, not too ripe, cantaloupe into inch slices. Remove rind, seeds and pith. Dice. For 1 pound fruit, use ¾ to 1 pound sugar. Add sugar to fruit. Cover and let stand several hours. Add whole stick cinnamon, thin slices of lemon, ginger root crushed. Heat slowly to boiling, then boil rapidly until cantaloupe is clear and tender. Seal in hot, sterilized jars.

CHERRY OR RASPBERRY PRESERVES

5 pounds cherries or raspberries
5 pounds sugar

Wash raspberries, or wash and stone the cherries. Place alternate layers of sugar and fruit in kettle; let stand overnight. Bring slowly to a boil and boil rapidly until thick and clear. Pour into hot, sterilized glasses and seal.

GROUND-CHERRY PRESERVES

Remove husks from ground-cherries. Make a syrup of 1½ cups sugar, 3 cups water and juice of 2 lemons. Boil 5 minutes; add enough cherries to come to top of syrup. Boil slowly until cherries are tender and clear, seal in hot, sterilized jars.

GRAPE PRESERVES

4 pounds Concord grapes
½ cup water
4 pounds sugar

Wash, drain, and remove stems from grapes. Heat grapes and water to the boiling point and cook until the seeds are free. Rub through a fine sieve or food mill. Discard skins and seeds. For each cup of fruit add 1 cup of sugar. Simmer for 30 minutes, stirring occasionally to prevent burning. Pour into hot, sterilized glasses and seal.

WHOLE PRESERVED KUMQUATS

1 quart kumquats
1½ cups sugar
1½ cups water

Wash kumquats thoroughly, cut two slight gashes at right angles across blossom end. Make a syrup of sugar and water. Cool, add kumquats, cover the skillet and cook very gently 1 hour or until clear. Do not remove cover until the fruit is cold. Put in jars, cover with syrup, and seal.

GINGER PEAR PRESERVES

8 pounds pears
4 pounds sugar
¼ pound Canton ginger
4 lemons

Pare, quarter, core and remove the stems of the pears and cut into small slices. Add sugar, the ginger, cut fine, and the juice of the lemons. Cut the lemon rinds into long, thin strips; mix all together and let stand overnight. Cook slowly for 3 hours, or until thick and clear. Pour into hot, sterilized jars and seal.

PINEAPPLE AND PEAR PRESERVES

1½ cups sugar
¾ cup boiling water
1 pound pears
1 can (1 pound, 14 ounces) sliced pineapple

Boil sugar and water for 5 minutes. Cut pears in halves lengthwise, remove cores and skin. Cut pineapple slices into quarters. Add fruit to hot syrup, cook until tender and clear. Seal in hot, sterilized jars.

QUINCE PRESERVES

Wash, peel, core and cut quinces in ½-inch cubes. Add cold water to cover, boil until tender. Drain juice. Weigh fruit. For each pound of fruit use 1 pound of sugar. Boil juice and sugar 5 minutes, add fruit. Boil until fruit is clear and deep red. Pour into hot, sterilized jars and seal.

QUINCE AND SWEET APPLE PRESERVES

1 peck quinces
¼ peck sweet apples (Tolman)
½ peck pears
sugar

Wash quinces and apples, peel, core, and cut both in rings. Peel pears, cut in quarters and core. Cover cores and peels with cold water, boil thoroughly and strain. Boil the quinces in cold water until they can be pierced with a fork, remove carefully to platter. Weigh all the fruit, and for each pound of fruit, add ¾ pound sugar to liquid. Boil to a clear syrup. Add the fruit, boil slowly and steadily for 3 or 4 hours until a deep red color. Pour into hot, sterilized jars and seal.

RADISH PRESERVES (RUSSIAN STYLE)

1 quart black radishes
1 quart strained honey
1 ounce ginger root, cut up

Cut radishes in thin slices ¼ by 1 inch, or grate coarsely. Cook in boiling water 3 or 4 minutes. Drain and dry. Add honey and ginger and cook until mixture sheets from the side of a spoon (see page 445). Pour into hot, sterilized jelly glasses and seal. Serve mixed with sliced almonds.

RHUBARB AND FIG PRESERVES

½ pound figs
2 pounds rhubarb
2½ pounds sugar
2 lemons, juice and rind

Wash figs and rhubarb and cut into small pieces. Add sugar, lemon juice and grated rind, and stir often until juice is formed. Cook gently for 45 minutes, until thick and clear. Pour into hot, sterilized glasses and seal.

GREEN TOMATO PRESERVES

1 quart sliced green tomatoes
1 quart sugar
1 lemon, grated rind and pulp
1 stick cinnamon

Place tomatoes in skillet. Add sugar, lemon rind and pulp, and cinnamon. Let stand several hours to draw juice. Cook until tomatoes are thick and clear. Pour into hot, sterilized glasses and seal.

TOMATO PRESERVES

1 pound yellow pear tomatoes or red tomatoes
1 pound sugar
2 ounces Canton ginger, or a few pieces of
    ginger root
1 lemon, grated rind and juice

If yellow pear tomatoes are used, slice them. If red tomatoes are used, scald and peel. Cover with sugar and let stand overnight. Drain syrup into preserving kettle and boil until thick; skim. Add ginger, grated rind and juice of lemon, and tomato pulp. Cook until preserve is clear. Pour into hot, sterilized glasses and seal.

WATERMELON PRESERVES

Peel and discard the green rind of a watermelon that is not too ripe. Cut the white pulp into ½-inch cubes or strips, leaving as much of the firm, red meat as possible. To 4 cups of melon add 3 cups of sugar, 3 lemons (or 2 oranges and 1 lemon) sliced fine and seeded. Let boil slowly about 2 hours, until the rind is clear and the juice is thick. If desired, add 1 cup grated pineapple and cook 15 minutes longer. Pour into hot, sterilized jars and seal.

1-2-3 PRESERVE

1 pineapple
2 oranges
3 quarts strawberries
4 pounds sugar

Peel pineapple and cut into thin wedges. Slice oranges very thin. Wash and hull strawberries. Mix with sugar in preserving kettle, stir until sugar is dissolved. Boil for 1 hour and 15 minutes. Pour into hot, sterilized glasses and seal with paraffin.

UNCOOKED PRESERVES

An easy method of preserving small fruits, such as currants, strawberries, raspberries or gooseberries is as follows:

Wash and mash fruit thoroughly, or grind it. Measure equal weights of crushed fruit and sugar; mix, adding sugar gradually. Pack to overflowing in sterilized glasses. Seal.

CHERRY CURRANTS

Use 1¼ pounds sugar for each pound of berries. Crush berries thoroughly. Pack and seal as above.

PINEAPPLES

Slice, pare, and core pineapple: then grind or chop. Add an equal weight of sugar, let stand overnight. Pack and seal as above.

BAKED CRABAPPLE PRESERVES

2½ pounds crabapples
¼ cup water
2 pounds sugar

Wash, dry, and remove the blossom ends of large red crabapples. Pour water into bottom of a large casserole or covered baking dish. Add apples and sugar in alternate layers, the sugar on top. Cover. Bake 2 to 3 hours in a slow oven, 250° F., basting 3 or 4 times with the hot syrup. Pack in sterilized glasses and seal.

BAKED SECKEL PEAR PRESERVES

Prepare like Baked Crabapple Preserves. Flavor, if desired, with ginger or lemon juice.

BAKED QUINCE PRESERVES

Quinces may be wiped, cored, and quartered, and baked like Baked Crabapple Preserves, in a slow oven, 250° F., 3 or more hours until translucent.

BAKED CRANBERRY OR CHERRY PRESERVES

1 quart cranberries or sour cherries
4 cups sugar

Wash, drain, and prick large cranberries; or wash, stem, and stone large cherries. Grease a large casserole; add fruit and sugar alternately in layers, the sugar on top. Do not fill casserole too full. Bake in a slow oven, 250° F., for 2 hours; or in moderate oven, 350° F., for 1 hour. Baste several times. Pack in sterilized jars and seal.

APPLE BUTTER

1 peck apples
4 quarts water
2 quarts sweet cider
3 pounds sugar
3 teaspoons cinnamon
1½ teaspoons cloves

Wash the apples and cut into small pieces. Add the water; boil until the apples are soft; rub apples through a sieve or food mill, discard skin and seeds. Boil cider until it is reduced one-half; add hot apple pulp, sugar, and spices, and cook until thick enough to spread. Stir constantly to prevent scorching. Pour into hot, sterilized jars and seal.

JAMS

APRICOT JAM

Wash and pit apricots, slice into eighths. Weigh the fruit and to each pound of apricots add 1 pound of sugar. Let stand overnight. Crack apricot stones. Remove nut, blanch and slice. Cook fruit gently until thickened, about 20 to 25 minutes. Add some of the sliced nuts before pouring into hot, sterilized glasses. Seal.

DRIED APRICOT JAM

1 pound dried apricots
1 orange
1 cup seedless raisins
1½ cups sugar

Wash apricots, soak in cold water to cover for 1 hour. Measure ¾ cup of this water. Add the apricots and orange cut into small pieces, the raisins, and sugar. Cook slowly until thick, about 1 hour. Pour into hot, sterilized glasses and seal.

BLUEBERRY AND CRABAPPLE JAM

3 quarts crabapples
1 quart blueberries
6 pounds sugar

Cut crabapples in quarters, remove cores but do not pare; chop. Add enough water to almost cover, and cook 10 minutes. Add berries and sugar, cook until clear. Pour into hot, sterilized glasses; cool and seal with hot paraffin.

PEACH JAM

5 pounds peaches
3½ pounds sugar

Pare, remove pits, slice and weigh peaches. Mix with sugar. Place in preserving kettle with a few peach pits. Let come to a boil slowly, stirring until sugar is dissolved. Then cook rapidly for 30 minutes. Remove pits. When mixture jells, pour into hot, sterilized glasses. Seal with paraffin.

PLUM JAM

Wash plums. Remove the stones. If Damsons are used, cover stones with water and cook separately. Strain and add juice to plum pulp. Measure pulp and to each cup add from ¾ to 1 cup of sugar, depending on sweetness of fruit. Boil slowly, stirring constantly to prevent burning until jam is clear and thick. Pour into hot, sterilized glasses and seal.

STRAWBERRY-PINEAPPLE JAM

Pare, core, and chop pineapple. Use equal parts of pineapple and strawberries. To every 5 cups of fruit add 4 cups of sugar. Let stand several hours. Cook gently until thick and clear. Pour into hot, sterilized jars and seal.

STRAWBERRY-RHUBARB JAM

3 cups rhubarb
4 cups sugar
3 cups strawberries

Use tender red rhubarb. Trim off hard ends, wash, and without skinning cut into small pieces. Mix strawberries with rhubarb and sugar; let stand several hours. Cook until thick and clear. Pour into hot, sterilized glasses and seal.

FREEZER STRAWBERRY JAM

1 quart ripe strawberries
4 cups (1¾ pounds) sugar
2 tablespoons lemon juice
½ bottle liquid fruit pectin

Crush berries thoroughly. Place in a large bowl or pan. Add sugar, mix well and let stand. Mix lemon juice and fruit pectin together. Stir into the fruit mixture, continuing to stir until all sugar crystals are dissolved. Ladle quickly into jars. Cover at once with tight lids. When jam is set (may take up to 24 hours), store in freezer. If jam is to be used within 2 or 3 weeks, it may be stored in the refrigerator. Makes about 5 medium jars.

TOMATO-ORANGE JAM

    4 quarts yellow pear tomatoes
    5 oranges
    5 pounds sugar

Grind tomatoes and oranges. Mix with the sugar and boil until thick and clear. Pour into sterilized jelly glasses. Cool and cover with paraffin.

MARMALADES

CARROT MARMALADE

    3 pounds grated, raw carrots
    3 pounds sugar
    6 lemons, grated rind and juice
    ¼ pound grated almonds

Cover grated carrots with water and cook until tender. Press through a strainer. Add sugar, lemon rind and juice. Place in preserving kettle, cook gently about ½ hour, or until thick and clear. When nearly done, add almonds. Put into sterilized glasses and seal.

CITRUS MARMALADE

    2 grapefruit
    2 oranges
    2 lemons
    sugar

Wash fruit. Remove core and seeds of grapefruit. Remove thin, yellow rind and cut into fine strips. Discard the thick, white pith. Cut oranges and lemons into small pieces. Mix oranges, lemons, grapefruit pulp, and grapefruit rind. Add 3 times as much water as fruit and let stand overnight. Boil for 10 minutes. Remove from heat, cover, and let stand for 24 hours. Boil for 10 minutes; set aside again for 24 hours. The third day measure, add an equal amount of sugar, and boil 1 hour or until thick. Pour into sterilized glasses and seal.

ORANGE MARMALADE

    4 oranges
    1 lemon
    cold water
    sugar

Wash fruit, cut in half, remove seeds and stem end. Slice very thin or grind fine. For every cup of fruit add 1½ cups water. Let stand overnight. Pour into preserving kettle, cook slowly from 1 to 2 hours or until tender; again let stand overnight. For each cup of fruit, add 1 cup of sugar, and cook 20 minutes or until mixture sheets from the side of a spoon (see page 445). Pour into hot, sterilized glasses and seal.

GOLDEN CHIP MARMALADE

    6 pounds pumpkin
    2 ounces green ginger root
    4 lemons, sliced thin
    1 quart water
    6 cups sugar

Peel and seed pumpkin. Cut into balls or cubes. Add ginger root, lemon, and water; let stand overnight. Simmer until tender, add sugar and cook until mixture sheets from the side of a spoon (see page 445). Pour into hot, sterilized glasses and seal.

ORANGE-PEACH MARMALADE

    3 oranges
    9 peaches
    sugar

Wash oranges. Slice thin and cut into small pieces. Simmer until tender. Skin and pit peaches, slice, add to oranges. Measure, and to 4 cups fruit add 3 cups sugar. Simmer until thick and clear. Pack in sterilized glasses and seal.

PINEAPPLE-APRICOT MARMALADE

    1 large fresh pineapple, or 1 can
       (1 pound, 4 ounces), crushed
    3 pounds fresh or 1 pound dried apricots
    3 cups sugar

Pare, core, and cut pineapple in cubes; cut fresh apricots in halves, remove stones. If dried apricots are used, soak overnight, and use water and fruit. Do not drain the canned, crushed pineapple. Combine fruit, measure, and add ¾ cup sugar for each cup fruit. Cook until thick and clear. Pour into sterilized glasses and seal.

PINEAPPLE-GRAPEFRUIT MARMALADE

    1 pineapple
    1 grapefruit
    1 lemon
    sugar

Pare, core and shred the pineapple. Cut grapefruit and lemon in quarters, then in thin slices. Measure fruit and cover with water, 3 pints water to 1 pint of fruit. Set aside until next day. Boil 3 or more hours until rind is very tender. Set aside until next day. Measure and add an equal amount of sugar. Boil until a drop jells on a cold plate. Pour into sterilized glasses and seal.

CONSERVES

CHERRY CONSERVE

5 pounds ripe cherries
1½ pounds seedless raisins
5 pounds sugar
juice of 4 oranges
juice of 2 lemons

Wash, stem and pit the cherries. Wash raisins. Mix all ingredients and let stand overnight. Then boil slowly and steadily for several hours, or until thick and clear. Pour into hot, sterilized jars and seal.

CHERRY-PINEAPPLE CONSERVE

1 quart sour red cherries, pitted
1 cup grated pineapple
2 cups tart apples, diced
4 cups sugar

Mix all ingredients and cook slowly until mixture is thick and clear. Pour into hot, sterilized jars and seal.

CRANBERRY CONSERVE

1 quart cranberries, washed and picked over
1½ cups water
¼ pound raisins
1 orange, chopped
1½ pounds sugar
½ lb. walnuts, chopped

Boil cranberries with half the water until they burst. Add remaining ingredients, boil 25 minutes, pour in mold or glasses. Or combine all ingredients and boil until thick, adding nuts when nearly done.

GOOSEBERRY CONSERVE

3 pounds gooseberries
3 large oranges
3 pounds sugar
1 pound seeded raisins

Wash and stem berries. Grate the rind of the oranges, cut up pulp. Mix all ingredients and cook slowly until thick. Pack in hot, sterilized jars and seal.

GRAPE CONSERVE

8 pounds Concord grapes
3 or 4 oranges
2 lemons
1 pound seeded raisins or figs
sugar

Wash grapes and remove stems. Put in preserving kettle, add only a little water, simmer until the seeds are free; then press pulp through sieve, discarding skins and seeds. Add oranges and lemons, cut fine, and raisins or thinly-sliced figs. To 1 pound fruit, add 1 pound sugar. Boil until thick. Fill hot, sterilized jelly glasses and seal.

FOUR FRUIT CONSERVE

1 quart sour cherries, pitted
1 quart currants
1 quart raspberries
1 quart gooseberries
sugar

Clean fruit and weigh. For each pound of fruit add 1 scant pound of sugar. Cook fruit for 20 minutes, stirring to prevent burning. Add sugar and cook 5 to 10 minutes longer. Pour into hot, sterilized glasses. Seal.

PEACH-PINEAPPLE CONSERVE

3 pounds peaches
1 cup grated fresh pineapple, or canned, crushed pineapple
1 orange, cut up
sugar

Peel peaches, remove stones, add 2 cups of water and cook until soft. If fresh pineapple is used, cook with the peaches. Mash, or rub through coarse colander. Add canned pineapple, if used, with the finely cut orange, and cook until slightly thickened. Add three-quarters as much sugar as fruit mixture; cook until thick. Stir to prevent burning. Pour into sterilized jars and seal.

PEAR CONSERVE

1 peck pears
4 pounds sugar
1 pound raisins, seeded
1½ pounds walnut meats, broken
juice of 3 lemons
juice of 2 oranges

Pare, core and slice the pears in large pieces, crosswise; add sugar and let stand overnight. Drain the liquid into kettle and boil to a syrup, about 12 minutes; add pears and the rest of the ingredients. Cook slowly 1 hour until thick and clear. Pour into hot, sterilized jars and seal.

PEAR AND APPLE CONSERVE

9 hard pears
6 tart apples
1½ lemons, rind and juice
⅛ pound Canton ginger
1 cup water
sugar

Pare, quarter and core the pears. Pare apples, core and cut crosswise in ½-inch slices. Add the lemon juice to the water. Cut ginger into small pieces. For every pound of fruit use 1 pound of sugar. Boil sugar and water to a syrup, add the rest of the ingredients and boil ¾ hour or until thick and clear. Pack in hot, sterilized glasses and seal.

PLUM CONSERVE

3 pounds blue plums
1 pound seeded raisins
3 oranges, cut in small pieces
juice of 2 lemons
3 pounds sugar
1 pound walnut meats, broken

Wash the plums, remove the stones, and cut plums into small pieces. Mix with remaining ingredients. Cook until the fruit is thick and clear. Pack into hot, sterilized glasses and seal.

QUINCE CONSERVE

4 medium quinces
3 large tart apples
½ cup maraschino cherries
1 cup seeded raisins
¼ pound prunes, stoned
¼ pound dried figs, cut
1 quart water
4 cups sugar

Peel quinces and cut in thin slices. Peel, core and cut apples. Cut cherries fine. Mix all ingredients except sugar and cook slowly until quinces are tender. Add sugar, bring slowly to the boiling point. Cook until thick and clear. Pour into hot, sterilized jars and seal.

RHUBARB CONSERVE

3 cups rhubarb, cut up
3 cups sugar
3 oranges, juice and rind
1 lemon, juice and rind
½ pound almonds, chopped

Place rhubarb in skillet, add sugar, the grated rind and juice of the oranges and lemon. Cook 30 minutes. Add almonds. Cook 5 minutes longer. Pour into hot, sterilized jars and seal.

JELLY

GENERAL RULES

A good jelly is clear, bright in color. It should be tender and quivery, but firm enough to hold its shape.

TO PREPARE FRUIT

Use small quantities at one time:
2 pounds or 4 cups of prepared fruit will make about 2 cups juice; 2 cups fruit juice mixed with 1½ cups sugar makes about 2 cups jelly.

Larger fruit should be washed, stemmed, and cut into quarters. Add water to cover and cook until tender.

Berries, currants, grapes and other juicy fruits should be crushed with a spoon or masher. They need very little water, as mashing releases their own juices.

TO EXTRACT JUICE

Put cooked fruit into a jelly bag (see below), and let it drip for several hours or overnight. Do not squeeze the bag if a clear jelly is wanted. It is possible to make a second extraction, for a less clear jelly, after the first clear juice has been taken off. Add a small amount of water to the pulp remaining in the bag, reheat the mixture, return it to the bag and squeeze it through.

TO COOK JELLY

Cook in an enameled preserving kettle or pan. Measure the fruit juice. Allow ¾ to 1 cup sugar for each cup of juice, according to the amount of natural pectin in the fruit. (See Pectin, page 446.) Fruit with less pectin requires more sugar. Boil the juice rapidly for 5 minutes to reduce it slightly, add the sugar, and boil rapidly until the mixture reaches the jelly point (see below). Skim the froth from the jelly, pour at once into hot, sterilized glasses and seal (see following).

SUBSTITUTIONS FOR SUGAR IN JELLY

Substitutions must be made with care, since the sugar is a preservative as well as a sweetening agent. Up to half the sugar called for may be replaced with an equal measure of honey, or up to one-fourth the sugar with an equal measure of corn syrup. Adding these liquids instead of sugar increases the cooking time.

TO TEST "JELLY POINT"

A thermometer is the most reliable way to judge when the mixture has reached the jelly point, the point at which it will stiffen when it is cold. The thermometer should hang down the inside of the kettle, with the bulb completely covered with jelly, but it should not touch the bottom of the kettle.

The "jelly point" is reached at 8° F. above the boiling point of water in a given area; that is, at 220° F., in localities where water boils at 212° F.

"Jelly point" tests that can be used when a thermometer is not available include the "sheet test": when a spoon filled with jelly is tilted, two drops poured from the side of the spoon flow together and fall as one. Or, a few drops of jelly may be spooned onto a cold plate and quickly chilled. When a spoon drawn through this jelly leaves a track, it indicates that the rest will stiffen sufficiently when it is cold.

TO MAKE A JELLY BAG
Make a bag of cotton cloth or several thicknesses of cheesecloth. Place the cooked fruit in the bag and hang it over a bowl to catch juice as it drips. Or place the bag in a colander set into a bowl. Pour the fruit into the bag, gather the top ends of the bag and tie securely. Then lift the bag from the colander and hang it over a bowl.

TO FILL AND SEAL JELLY GLASSES
Wash glasses thoroughly, place in cold water, bring to boiling point gradually and boil 5 minutes. Keep hot. When ready to use, drain without handling the inside. Set glasses on a board or on hot, wet cloth and fill. To prevent cracking glasses, place sterilized spoon in glass. Pour in jelly at once, filling to ½ inch from top. Pour over the surface a tablespoon of melted paraffin. When cool and the paraffin is set, wipe off any jelly splashes around top and fill with melted paraffin. Protect the paraffin with a cover of metal or paper. Label glasses.

To melt paraffin break into small pieces and place over very low heat.

FRUIT SUITABLE FOR JELLY
Fruit should be fresh, just ripe, or a little underripe. Juicy fruits, currants, raspberries, should not be gathered after a rain. Currants, sour apples, crabapples, underripe grapes, quinces, wild cherries and green gooseberries contain ample amounts of natural pectin and make the best jellies.

WILD FRUITS FOR JELLY
Wild raspberries, blackberries, barberries, grapes, and beach plums all make good jellies. See General Rules. Failure in making these occurs because the fruit is not fresh, or because it is overripe.

PECTIN
Pectin is the natural substance in some fruit that, when heated and combined with fruit acid and sugar, causes the mixture to congeal or jell. All fruits do not contain this substance. The acid and pectin may be supplied by the addition of the juice of apples, plums, quince, etc., or homemade apple or commercial pectin.

To use commercial pectin, either liquid or powdered, follow the manufacturer's directions accurately for best results.

JELLIES

HOMEMADE APPLE PECTIN
4 pounds apples, skin and cores
9 cups water

Select tart, hard, ripe apples. Remove any bruised spots. Cut into thin slices. Add water. Place in large enamel kettle, bring quickly to boiling point. Cover, let boil rapidly 20 minutes. Let drip through 4 thicknesses of cheesecloth. When juice stops dripping, press pulp lightly with spoon, but do not squeeze bag. Set aside juice. Remove pulp from bag. Weigh or measure pulp and add to it an equal quantity of water. Boil again 20 minutes and strain. Pour the two extractions into a large, shallow pan so that liquid is not more than 2 inches deep. Boil rapidly 30 to 45 minutes, or until liquid is ½ inch deep or reduced to 1½ pints. If not wanted for immediate use, pour at once into hot, sterilized 4-ounce bottles and seal.

APPLE JELLY
Wash the apples and cut them into pieces without peeling them or removing the cores or seeds. Put fruit into kettle, add cold water to cover, and cook until very soft. Pour into jelly bag and let drip. Measure juice and an equal amount of sugar into a kettle, bring to a boil, and boil to the jelly point, see page 445. Flavor with vanilla or other extracts if desired. Pour hot jelly into hot, sterilized glasses; seal with paraffin.

THORN APPLE JELLY
Wash thorn apples, cut in halves, cover with water, boil until soft. Drip through jelly bag. Place juice in kettle, heat slowly, and skim. For each cup of apple juice, add 1 cup sugar. Boil to the jelly point, see page 445. Pour into hot, sterilized glasses. Seal with paraffin.

CRABAPPLE JELLY
8 quarts crabapples
4 quarts water
sugar

Select underripe crabapples. Wash, cut in half, but do not pare or core. Boil apples in water until soft. Mash, pour into jelly bag, and let drip. Do not squeeze. Measure juice and use equal amount of sugar. There should be about 3 quarts of juice. If desired, add a few rose geranium leaves. Boil juice 5 minutes, add sugar, and continue to boil to the jelly point, see page 445. Skim; pour into hot, sterilized glasses. Seal with paraffin.

Crabapple Sauce may be made by straining

the pulp left after the juice has dripped through. Add sugar and cinnamon or lemon juice to taste, and heat only long enough to dissolve the sugar.

CRABAPPLE-PLUM JELLY

¾ peck crabapples
¼ peck plums
sugar

Select underripe fruit. Wash, pick over, and cut in half, but do not pare or seed. Add water to cover. Boil until soft. Mash and pour into jelly bag to drip. Do not squeeze. Use equal measure of sugar and juice. Boil juice 5 minutes, add sugar and boil to jelly point, see page 445. Skim and pour into hot, sterilized glasses; seal with paraffin. Use pulp to make a sauce, as above.

CRABAPPLE-CRANBERRY JELLY

½ peck crabapples
2 quarts cranberries
sugar

Follow directions for Crabapple-Plum Jelly, above.

BERRY JELLY WITH PECTIN

2 quarts blackberries, boysenberries or dewberries
½ cup water
1 box powdered pectin
5 cups sugar (2¼ pounds)

Mash berries in preserving kettle. Add water; bring slowly to the boiling point. Boil rapidly for a few minutes until the berries are soft. Pour into a jelly bag and let drip. If berries are quite ripe and mild in flavor, add 1 teaspoon lemon juice to each cup of berry juice. Mix juice with pectin and stir over high heat until mixture boils hard. At once, stir in sugar. Bring to a full rolling boil, then boil hard 1 minute, stirring constantly. Remove jelly from heat; skim off foam with metal spoon. Pour into hot, sterilized glasses and seal with melted paraffin.

CHERRY JELLY

Unless the cherries are very tart and underripe they will not make stiff jelly. Combine them with other fruits, such as currants, or unripe gooseberries or add pectin and proceed according to manufacturer's directions.

CRANBERRY JELLY

Make Jellied Cranberry Sauce, page 261. Pour while hot into hot, sterilized glasses and seal with paraffin.

CURRANT JELLY

4 quarts currants
1 quart water
sugar

Pick over but do not stem underripe currants. Wash, put into kettle, add water, and boil until currants are nearly white. Strain through coarse strainer, then let juice drip through jelly bag. Measure juice, boil hard 5 minutes. Add 1 cup sugar for each cup juice, boil rapidly to the jelly point, see page 445. Skim and pour into hot sterilized jars. Seal with paraffin. Makes about 10 cups jelly.

CURRANT JELLY, COLD PROCESS

To make currant jelly by the cold process, follow the rule for Currant Jelly, preceding, as far as dissolving the sugar in the strained juice. Fill warm, sterilized glasses with this. Place the glasses on a board and put the board by a sunny window. Cover with sheets of glass and keep by the window until the jelly is set. The jelly will be more transparent if the juice is strained through a flannel bag. Jelly made by the cold process is more delicate than that made by the boiling, but it does not keep quite so well.

CURRANT JELLY WITHOUT COOKING

Wash and mash currants well, let stand overnight and strain. Place juice in stone jar and place in the coolest part of cellar for 24 hours. Remove scum from top, strain and to 1 pint of juice, add 1 pint sugar; stir until sugar is dissolved. Put in glasses and seal with paraffin. In 24 hours you will have a perfectly transparent jelly. No heat is required.

CURRANT-RASPBERRY JELLY

4 quarts currants
sugar
4 pints raspberries

The fruit should not be overripe nor gathered after a rain. Pick over the fruit, but leave stems on currants. Mash the fruit in a preserving kettle. Cook slowly until currants are nearly white. Strain. Take equal parts of sugar and juice. Boil over high heat to jelly point, see page 445. Skim, pour into glasses. Seal with paraffin.

BLACK CURRANT JELLY

Wash and pick over underripe fruit, cover with water, and boil until soft. Strain through coarse strainer, then let drip through jelly bag. Measure juice, bring to a boil; boil rapidly 5 minutes. Add 1 cup sugar for each cup juice, boil to the jelly point, see page 445. Skim and pour into hot sterilized jelly glasses; seal with paraffin.

BAR-LE-DUC (CURRANT JELLY)

1 pound large currants
¾ pound sugar

Wash and stem currants; add sugar and let stand overnight. Bring slowly to boiling point, stirring until sugar dissolves. Cook rapidly to jelly point, see page 445, about 30 minutes. Stir occasionally to prevent sticking. Pour into hot, sterilized jars; seal with paraffin.

CURRANT JELLY WITH CHERRIES

5 quarts currants
8 pounds sugar
2 quarts pitted cherries

Wash and mash currants with stems and cook slowly until very soft. Strain juice; there should be 2 quarts. Bring juice to a boil, add sugar; boil again and skim. Add cherries and cook slowly to the jelly point, see page 445. Pour hot into hot, sterilized jars; seal with paraffin.

ELDERBERRY JELLY

Take equal parts of elderberries and apples. Cover with water and boil. Mash, strain. To 1 cup juice, use 1 cup sugar. Boil juice, skim, add sugar. Boil to the jelly point, see page 445. Pour into hot, sterilized jelly glasses. Seal with paraffin.

GRAPE JELLY

A tart grape is best for this jelly. The sweet, ripe grapes contain too much sugar. Use half-ripe fruit. To 4 pounds grapes, crushed, use 2 cups water. Grape jelly may also be made without adding water to the grapes. To prevent crystallizing, add 1 cup tart apples, diced, to every quart of grapes before cooking.

Wash grapes, remove stems. Add water. Boil until the seeds are free. Press through colander, then strain through jelly bag. Measure ⅔ cup sugar to 1 cup of juice. When juice boils, add sugar and cook to the jelly point, see page 445. Pour into hot, sterilized glasses. Seal with paraffin.

SPICED GRAPE JELLY FOR VENISON

1 peck wild grapes or 12 pounds Concord grapes
1 quart vinegar
¼ cup whole cloves
¼ cup stick cinnamon
6 pounds sugar

Cook first 4 ingredients until grapes are soft. Strain through jelly bag. Boil juice 20 minutes. Add sugar, boil 5 minutes to the jelly point. Pour into hot sterilized glasses. Seal with paraffin.

GUAVA JELLY

1 quart guavas
sugar
lime or lemon juice

Use guavas that are still green; if ripe, add lime or lemon juice. Wash fruit, remove blossom and stems. Slice thin. Place in kettle with water barely to cover. Boil slowly until very soft. Drip through jelly bag. Measure; take equal parts of sugar and juice. Boil juice 10 minutes. Add sugar, boil mixture until it jells. Pour into sterilized glasses; cover with paraffin.

MINT JELLY

½ peck snow apples
sugar
½ cup fresh mint leaves
2 tablespoons lemon juice
green vegetable coloring

Wash apples, remove blossom ends, cut into quarters. Put into preserving kettle with cold water barely to cover. Cook slowly, covered, until apples are soft. Mash, drain off juice through jelly bag and measure it. Boil hard 5 minutes, then add 1 cup sugar for each cup juice measured. Bring to boil; boil 2 minutes and add mint leaves. Boil until mixture reaches jelly point, see page 445. Add lemon juice and green coloring to taste. Strain into hot, sterilized glasses; seal with paraffin.

PLUM JELLY

Use underripe, tart plums. Wash fruit, remove stems. Put into kettle, cover with water and simmer until plums are very soft. Drip juice through jelly bag and measure. Boil hard 5 minutes. Add 1 cup sugar for each cup juice measured, boil to the jelly point, see page 445. Pour into hot sterilized jars; seal with paraffin.

PEACH JELLY

2 cups peach juice
2 cups apple juice
juice of ½ lemon
3 cups sugar

The skins from peaches used for home-canning may be used to make juice for jelly. Cover with water, boil hard, and strain. Reduce to 2 cups. Add apple and lemon juice, bring to a boil. Add sugar, boil rapidly to the jelly point. Skim and pour into hot, sterilized jelly glasses. Seal with pariffin.

QUINCE JELLY

Rub the quinces with a coarse towel; cut out the blossom end. Wash the fruit, pare it, and cut into quarters. Cut out the cores (remove seeds) and put them into the preserving kettle. Have a large bowl half full of water; drop the perfect pieces of fruit into this bowl. Put the parings and imperfect parts, cut very fine, into the preserving kettle with the cores. Add a cup of water to every 2 cups of fruit and parings. Cook gently for 2 hours. Strain and finish like apple jelly. The perfect fruit may be made into preserves or canned.

PARADISE JELLY

10 medium quinces
20 medium sweet apples
1 quart cranberries
sugar

Peel and slice the quinces but do not core them. Slice apples, but do not peel or core. Place in preserving kettle with cranberries. Cover with water. Boil until very soft. Drain in jelly bag. Measure juice and use an equal measure of sugar. Boil 12 minutes; skim. Boil to the jelly point, see page 445. Pour into hot, sterilized glasses, seal with paraffin.

RASPBERRY-APPLE JELLY

¼ peck apples
5 pints red raspberries
sugar

Wash and quarter apples, cover with cold water and cook until very soft. Pick over berries, wash, place in kettle, mash. Currants may be added. Heat slowly to the boiling point and cook until soft. Place apples and berries together in bag and drain. Add 1 cup sugar for each cup of juice. Boil to the jelly point, see page 445. Skim, fill hot, sterilized glasses. Seal with paraffin.

BLACK RASPBERRY-CURRANT JELLY

2 quarts black raspberries
1 quart currants
2 cups water
sugar

Cook raspberries and currants with water for 20 minutes. Pour into jelly bag and let drip. Measure juice. Add an equal measure of sugar. Cook to the jelly point, see page 445. Pour into hot, sterilized glasses; seal with paraffin.

BLACK RASPBERRY JELLY

Wash the berries, measure, and to every quart of berries add ¼ cup water. If firm jelly is desired add 1 unpeeled tart apple, sliced, for every quart of berries. Heat slowly to the boiling point. Pour into a jelly bag and let drip. Boil the juice rapidly for 5 minutes, measure it, and add an equal amount of sugar. Continue to boil rapidly to the jelly point, see page 445. Pour into hot sterilized glasses and seal with paraffin.

BLACKBERRY JELLY

Follow the directions for Black Raspberry Jelly, above.

PICKLES, CATSUPS AND RELISHES

GENERAL RULES FOR PICKLES

Cucumbers for pickling must be fresh picked, not over 24 hours old. Dill is best when seeds are full grown, but not so ripe that the seeds fall off the stalk. Do not use iodized salt. Use a good, clear pickling vinegar (4 to 6% acetic acid).

Pickles will spoil if not kept completely under the brine. Use half as much brine as measure of cucumbers. To hasten dissolving of salt, mix with small amount of water, then add rest of the water.

BRINE

A salt brine is a solution of 1 cup salt to 5 cups water. A weak brine, 1 cup salt to 9 cups water, will cause quicker fermentation, but pickles kept in this brine will spoil in a few weeks, unless the scum that rises to top of jars is constantly skimmed off and the brine kept clear.

It is best, when all fermentation stops and the pickles are done, to remove them to jars, cover them with their own brine, or add fresh-cooled brine, and seal.

Pickles will shrivel if too much sugar or salt is added or if the vinegar is too strong. Pickles that are cured (salt, or dill pickles) may be made into sweet, sour or mixed pickles and will not shrivel.

PICKLES

SALTED CUCUMBERS FOR FUTURE USE

Cucumbers picked fresh from the vines every day may be preserved in strong salt brine for storing until they are made into sweet, sour, or mixed pickles. Leave from ¼- to ½-inch stems on cucumbers, wash carefully without removing the prickles; put them, as they are gathered, into a large stone crock. Make brine (following) to half fill the crock, which will completely cover the pickles. When ready to use, first soak the pickles in cold water until freshened.

BRINE

For every 2 quarts of water use 2 cups of salt. Boil, skim until clear, then cool.

SUMMER DILL PICKLES

    100 large cucumbers
    5 stalks dill
    bay leaves
    1 ounce black peppercorns
    grape or cherry leaves
    BRINE
    1 cup salt
    6 quarts water
    1 cup vinegar

Soak cucumbers in cold water overnight or 12 hours. Drain and dry. Fill a crock with alternate double layers of cucumbers, then 3 or 4 blossom ends of dill, a bay leaf and a teaspoon of whole black pepper; repeat, covering top layer well with dill and adding some cherry or grape leaves. Boil, salt and water, cool, and pour brine over the pickles to cover. Cover surface with cloth. Weight well with plate, to keep pickles under brine. Let stand in warm place to ferment for a week. Add 1 cup of vinegar if desired. Rinse off scum that rises and settles on the cloth, every day in warm weather and once or twice a week when cooler.

WINTER DILL PICKLES

    100 cucumbers, 4 inches long
    mustard seed
    horseradish root
    garlic
    dill

BRINE

    6 quarts water (24 cups)
    1 pint cider vinegar (2 cups)
    ¾ cup salt

Soak cucumbers overnight in cold water. Drain, wash and dry. Place 1 tablespoon mustard seed, a small piece of horseradish root and, if desired, a clove of garlic, in each 2-quart sterilized jar, add cucumbers and dill blossoms alternately until jar is filled. Boil water, vinegar and salt. Cover pickles and seal jars at once. If after a few days brine oozes out, wait until fermentation ceases, then open jars, add fresh brine to cover, and seal again.

CRISP DILL PICKLES

    100 cucumbers, 4 inches
    1 large bunch dill
    1 small horseradish root, diced
    BRINE
    10 quarts water
    1 cup salt
    ¾ cup vinegar
    alum, if desired

Scrub cucumbers. Soak in salt water overnight (1 cup salt to 4 quarts water). Drain and wipe dry. Place in 2-quart sterilized jars with layers of dill and small pieces of horseradish. Pour boiling water, salt and vinegar over pickles. Add a small piece of alum to each jar if desired. Seal at once.

TARRAGON PICKLES

    25 long, thin cucumbers
    1 bunch of dill (6 stalks)
    dried whole tarragon
    1 horseradish root, diced
    2 tablespoons white peppercorns
    12 bay leaves, dried
    2 quarts vinegar
    1 quart water
    1 cup salt
    ½ pound mustard seed

Soak pickles in cold water for 12 hours or overnight. Drain and wipe. In a crock, place a layer of pickles; over this layer place 2 or 3 blossom ends of dill, 3 or 4 ½-inch pieces of tarragon, a few small pieces of horseradish root, 1 tablespoon whole white pepper, and 3 or 4 bay leaves. Repeat layers until all these ingredients are used. Boil vinegar, water, and salt; beat until foamy, and pour over pickles to cover. Sew mustard seeds in a fairly large cloth bag; place bag on top of pickles. Cover with a plate and weight with a stone. Keep crock in cool, dry place; must stand 5 or 6 weeks.

SMALL DILL PICKLES

    thin cucumbers, 3 to 4 inches
    dill
    horseradish root
    small red peppers
    1 cup salt
    4 quarts water

Scrub pickles and place them upright in sterilized jars. Between the layers place a few blossom ends of dill, diced horseradish root and small pieces of red peppers. Add salt to water, pour over pickles to cover, and arrange stems of dill across top of jar to keep pickles under brine. Cover. Check daily for a week; if brine has oozed out, add more fresh brine to cover fully. After a week, seal jars.

EASY MUSTARD PICKLES

    small cucumbers
    1 cup salt
    2 cups sugar
    1 cup dry mustard
    2 quarts vinegar
    1 quart water

Soak cucumbers in cold water. Drain and dry. Mix dry ingredients, and add vinegar and water gradually. Pour over cucumbers to cover. If a large crock is used, fresh cucumbers and pickling brine may be added from day to day until crock is full. Then cover with plate and weight down. Ready for use in several weeks.

SWEET-SOUR PICKLES

    50 small cucumbers
    3 cups vinegar
    1 cup water
    2 cups sugar
    mixed pickling spices
    dill

Soak cucumbers overnight in cold water, adding ⅓ cup salt for every quart of water. Drain and dry. Boil vinegar, 1 cup water and sugar until clear, add cucumbers and simmer until they lose their grass-green color. Place 1 teaspoon spices and 6 stalks of dill in bottom of each jar, add pickles, cover with hot syrup, place additional dill on top. Seal.

SWEET PICKLES

    100 large cucumbers
    6 quarts water
    1 cup salt
    1 large bunch dill
    onion
    8 cups sugar
    4 cups cider vinegar

Wash and drain cucumbers. Boil water with salt and pour over them, add dill. Let stand overnight. Drain and dry. Cut into inch slices. Place in jars, adding 2 slices onion to each jar. Boil sugar and vinegar to make syrup. Cool, pour over pickles and seal.

SWEET-SOUR MUSTARD PICKLES

    300 2-inch cucumbers
    ⅔ cup salt to 1 quart water
    ½ gallon white vinegar
    4 tablespoons dry mustard
    ½ cup salt
    ½ cup mixed pickling spices
    1 whole ginger root, broken
    4 pounds sugar

Wash cucumbers, cover with water boiled with salt. Let stand overnight. Drain and dry. Layer in large crock. Mix vinegar, mustard, salt, spices, ginger root and 4 tablespoons sugar. Pour over pickles. Every day stir in ½ cup of sugar until the 4 pounds are used up. Bottle and seal.

SANDWICH PICKLES

    1 quart sliced cucumbers
    ¼ cup salt
    2 quarts water
    1 medium onion, sliced
    1 cup medium brown sugar
    1 teaspoon mustard seed
    ½ teaspoon celery seed
    1 tablespoon mixed pickling spices
    1 pint vinegar
    ¼ teaspoon turmeric

Use large green cucumbers. Scrub well. Cut off ends, but do not peel. Slice thin. Dissolve salt in water. Pour over pickles and onion. Let stand 3 hours. Drain. Add mustard, sugar and celery seed and the mixed spices, tied in a bag, to the vinegar, and bring to a boil. Add onions and cucumbers. Bring to boiling point again. Discard bag of spices. Add turmeric, stir. Pack with liquid to cover in sterilized jars; cool and seal.

For a small family, large-quantity recipes may be halved or even quartered.

SWEET DILL PICKLES

50 dill pickles
1 quart cider vinegar
6 pounds sugar
½ cup pickling spice

Drain pickles. Soak overnight in cold water. Drain. Cut in halves, lengthwise. Bring vinegar, sugar and spices, tied in a bag, to a boil. Add pickles, boil 2 minutes. Discard spices. Pack pickles in jars, fill with hot liquid and seal.

CELERY PICKLES (ICICLES)

25 six-inch cucumbers
1 bunch celery
medium onions, sliced
1 quart each, vinegar and water
2 cups sugar
½ cup salt

Cut cucumbers in quarters lengthwise. Cut celery stalks in 6-inch pieces. Pack cucumber wedges upright in sterilized jars; fill spaces between with celery stalks, and lay a thick slice of onion on top. Boil vinegar, water, sugar and salt until clear. Pour hot liquid over cucumbers and seal.

CHERRY LEAF PICKLES

25 six-inch cucumbers
2 quarts cherry leaves
3 tablespoons caraway seed
1 pint vinegar
3 pounds sugar
¼ cup mixed pickling spices

Place cucumbers in 2-gallon crock, alternately with cherry leaves and caraway seed, with cherry leaves on bottom and top. Cover with salt water, ½ cup salt to 1 gallon water. Cover with weight to keep pickles under brine. Let stand 14 days. Drain, cut in inch pieces. Drain in colander for 1 hour. Pack in quart jars. Boil vinegar and sugar with ¼ cup mixed spices tied in a bag. Discard bag. Pour boiling syrup over pickles. Seal.

SWEET DILL-OIL PICKLES

50 dill pickles, or 4 quarts, sliced
6 garlic cloves
½ cup olive oil
1 quart vinegar
½ cup white peppercorns
½ cup mixed pickling spices
6 pounds sugar

Drain brine from dill pickles, dry, cut crosswise in 1-inch pieces. Add remaining ingredients, and the mixed pickling spices tied in a bag. Boil 3 minutes. Transfer to a crock. Let stand 1 week, stirring every day. Then pack in jars, and seal.

SLICED OIL PICKLES

50 cucumbers, 3 inches long
2 medium onions
½ cup salt
1 quart vinegar
1 cup salad oil
½ ounce mustard seed
½ ounce celery seed
1 cup sugar

Slice cucumbers, without peeling, ⅛-inch thick. Slice onions. Sprinkle cucumbers and onions with salt and let stand 12 hours, drain. Add the rest of the ingredients, mix well. Set aside for a few hours. Pack in sterilized jars with liquid. Adjust rubbers, place covers on loosely. Put jars in hot water; simmer 15 minutes. Seal.

SACCHARIN PICKLES

2 teaspoons salt
1 quart small cucumbers
¼ teaspoon saccharin
1 teaspoon mixed pickling spices
alum, size of hazelnut
cider vinegar
water

Put 1 teaspoon salt in bottom of a 1-quart jar. Fill with half the cucumbers. Add ¼ teaspoon saccharin, then remaining cucumbers. Add 1 teaspoon salt and 1 teaspoon mixed spices, then the small piece of alum. Fill jar with ½ cider vinegar and ½ water. Seal.

RIPE CUCUMBER PICKLES

12 large ripe cucumbers
1 quart small white onions
salt
6 stalks dill
horseradish root
¼ cup mixed pickling spices
vinegar
water
1 tablespoon dry mustard
mustard seeds

Peel cucumbers, cut in halves lengthwise, scrape out seeds; cut cucumbers into pieces as desired. Peel onions, sprinkle with salt and let stand. Place cucumbers in salt water, 1 cup salt to 8 cups water. Let stand 5 or more hours; drain. In crock place alternate layers of cucumbers, onions, dill, and a few slices of horseradish root and mixed spices. Pour mixture of half vinegar and half water, mixed with mustard, over pickles. Cover pickles with bag filled with mustard seeds and let stand in warm place for 3 days. Place cover on crock; keep in cool, dry place.

NINE-DAY PICKLE RINGS

50 large cucumbers
1 tablespoon powdered alum
1 gallon water
3½ pounds sugar
3 pints vinegar
1 ounce celery seed
1 ounce allspice berries
1 ounce stick cinnamon

Wash cucumbers, cut in inch slices; remove centers with apple corer. Put in brine (1½ cups salt to 1 gallon water). Let stand 3 days. Drain. Mix alum with 1 gallon fresh water, add pickles; let stand 3 days. Drain and rinse. Cover with cold water; let stand 3 days. Drain, put in kettle. Cover with a syrup made by boiling sugar, vinegar and spices tied in a bag. Let stand overnight. Discard bag of spices. Next day, boil pickles in syrup for 3 minutes. Pour into hot sterilized jars, fill to overflowing and seal.

SWEET PICKLED RIPE CUCUMBERS
(SENF GURKEN)

1 dozen ripe cucumbers
3 pounds sugar
salt
1 quart vinegar
2 tablespoons mustard seeds
1 tablespoon cloves, heads removed
stick cinnamon

Peel cucumbers, cut in two, lengthwise, scrape out seeds, sprinkle with salt and let stand overnight. Drain and dry. Make a syrup by boiling sugar and vinegar. Add the mustard seed, cinnamon, and cloves, all tied in a bag. Boil cucumbers in this syrup only until they are glassy. They must remain crisp. Pack in sterilized jars and seal.

DILL BEANS

1 peck wax beans
2 large stalks dill
½ ounce black peppercorns
6 bay leaves
6 grape or cherry leaves
1 cup vinegar
4 quarts water
1 cup salt

Remove strings and cook beans in boiling salted water 5 to 7 minutes, allowing 1 teaspoon salt to each quart of boiling water. Drain and pack in layers in a crock. Add a few peppercorns, a little dill, some pieces of bay leaf; repeat, covering top layer well with dill and adding the grape or cherry leaves. Boil water and salt. Cool. Then follow recipe for Summer Dill Pickles.

PICKLED BEANS

1 peck wax beans
½ cup sugar
1 cup vinegar
boiling water

Remove strings and cut beans into 1-inch pieces; wash and cook in the boiling water to cover (with 1 teaspoon salt for each quart of water), until tender, but still crisp. Drain beans and reserve 2 quarts of the water in which they were cooked. Add the sugar and vinegar; heat, add beans and bring to a boil. Pour at once into the jars and seal. Use as a salad or sweet-sour vegetable.

SWEET PICKLED BEANS

1 peck of green beans
1 quart vinegar
1 quart water
1 pound sugar
1 tablespoon cloves
1 stick cinnamon (broken)

Wash the beans, string and cut. Boil in salt water (1 teaspoon to 1 quart of boiling water), until tender. Drain and dry; pack into sterilized jars. Boil the vinegar, 1 quart of fresh water, and the remaining ingredients for 15 minutes. Let cool, then pour into jars, and seal.

PICKLED BEETS

1 quart cold cooked beets
1 teaspoon salt
⅛ teaspoon pepper
1 teaspoon brown sugar
1 teaspoon caraway seed
1 pint vinegar

Peel and slice beets and place in crock in layers. Sprinkle with salt, pepper, sugar and caraway seed. Cover with vinegar. Pour into jars and seal.

SWEET PICKLED BEETS

2 quarts cold cooked beets
3 cups beet cooking liquid
1 cup sugar
2 cups vinegar
cloves
mace
2 teaspoons pickling spice

Peel and slice beets. Combine beet liquid with sugar and vinegar, a few cloves, and a little mace. Bring syrup to a boil, add beets and heat thoroughly. Put 1 teaspoon pickling spice into each quart jar; fill with pickled beets to overflowing, and seal. Makes 2 quarts.

PICKLED CARROTS

2 pounds carrots
¼ cup mixed spices
1 pint vinegar
4 cups sugar

Wash medium-sized carrots, cut in half lengthwise, then crosswise in 2-inch pieces. Cook in boiling salted water (2 teaspoons salt to 1 quart water) until tender but not broken. Drain and mix 1 pint cooking liquid with the vinegar, sugar and spices. Boil to a syrup, add carrots and simmer for several hours, until carrots are clear. Bottle while hot and seal.

PICKLED CABBAGE

4 quarts thinly sliced cabbage, red or white
4 teaspoons salt
½ teaspoon pepper
¼ cup mustard seed
¼ cup mixed pickling spices
1 cup sugar
2 quarts vinegar, not too strong

Select large, heavy cabbage, take off the outside leaves; cut in quarters and then in thin shreds, using cabbage cutter. Sprinkle the salt over cabbage, mix thoroughly, and let stand overnight. Drain slightly and add the pepper and mustard seed, mix and place in crock. Add sugar and pickle spices, tied in a bag, to the vinegar, bring slowly to boil and pour boiling hot over the cabbage to cover. If vinegar is strong, dilute with water. May be used cold, or when heated, as a vegetable, in place of sauerkraut. Will keep a long time.

PICKLED CAULIFLOWER

4 heads cauliflower
1 cup salt
¼ cup mixed pickling spices
2 quarts vinegar
2 cups sugar

Separate flowerets of cauliflower, salt them and let stand overnight. Place in colander, rinse with cold water and drain. Tie spices in thin bag, boil with vinegar and sugar; add cauliflower, boil a few minutes and fill wide-mouthed bottles or jars. Seal.

PICKLED ONIONS

4 quarts small white onions
1 cup salt
¼ cup mixed pickling spices
2 cups sugar
2 quarts vinegar

Pour boiling water over unpeeled onions to cover, let stand 2 minutes, drain, cover with cold water and peel. Let stand in salt and water to cover, overnight. Rinse in cold water and drain. Tie spices in bag and boil with sugar and vinegar. Remove spices, add onions, bring to a boil. Fill jars to overflowing and seal.

PICKLED RED PEPPERS

1 peck red peppers
1 quart vinegar
2 cups sugar

Wash peppers, remove stems and seeds, cover with boiling water, let stand 2 minutes, drain. Place in ice water, let stand 10 minutes, drain well and pack solidly in pint jars. Boil sugar and vinegar; pour over the peppers to cover. Seal. Use as a decoration for salads.

GREEN DILL TOMATOES

Select small, firm green tomatoes. Follow recipe for Winter or Summer Dill Pickles, using the green tomatoes in place of the cucumbers.

CHOW-CHOW (MUSTARD PICKLES)

1 quart very small cucumbers
1 quart large cucumbers, cut in cubes
1 quart green tomatoes, sliced
1 quart onions, sliced
1 quart small onions
1 quart cauliflower
4 green peppers, chopped
1 cup flour
1½ cups sugar
6 tablespoons mustard
1 teaspoon powdered turmeric
3 pints vinegar

Mix the first 7 ingredients, cover with salt water using 1 cup salt to 4 quarts water and let stand 24 hours. Bring slowly to a boil, cook 5 minutes. Drain. Mix the flour, sugar, mustard and turmeric to a smooth paste with 1 pint of the vinegar. Heat remaining vinegar in double boiler, add flour paste gradually. Cook until thick (do not boil), then add to the hot vegetables. Pack in sterilized jars, and seal.

Do's and Don't's for Pickling:

—*Soak pickles in pottery crock or glass or enamel container, never in metal.*

—*Cook in enamel-lined kettle, not in metal.*

—*Avoid corrosion by storing in glass jars with glass tops.*

MIXED PICKLES

    2 quarts tiny cucumbers
    2 quarts large cucumbers, cut into ¼-inch slices
    2 quarts small white onions
    1 quart string beans, cut up
    2 large cauliflowers, separated into flowerettes
    3 small red peppers
    1 large green pepper, sliced
    ½ cup horseradish root, diced
    ¼ pound yellow mustard seed
    1½ gallons cider vinegar
    5 pounds brown sugar
    1 teaspoon red pepper
    1 ounce turmeric

Mix first 7 ingredients, add salt water to cover, allowing 1½ cups salt to each 2 quarts water. Let stand 24 hours, drain. Put into crock. Boil the rest of ingredients and pour over vegetables, let stand 2 days. Pour into jars, seal.

Sauerkraut

OLD-FASHIONED SAUERKRAUT

    15 heads cabbage
    2½ pounds salt
    24 tart apples, if desired
    a wooden stamper
    a round board
    a small square of cloth
    a heavy stone
    an 8-gallon stone jar

Select large, heavy cabbages, remove and reserve outer leaves, cut in quarters, remove and discard core, and slice quarters very fine on large cabbage cutter. Into a large granite pan, place 5 pounds of the shredded cabbage, sprinkle with ¼ cup salt, mix thoroughly and then pack into the large crock; add, if desired, a cup of apples, cut fine. Pound and stamp down the cabbage with a wooden stamper, until the brine flows and covers the cabbage. Mix another 5 pounds of cabbage and ¼ cup salt, and pack into same crock, cover with 1 cup chopped apples and pound as before until covered with brine. Continue until all cabbage is used. Cover with cabbage leaves and a fitted square of cloth. Weight down with a board and stone to keep the contents under brine. Leave enough space in crock for the cabbage to swell or ferment without overflowing.

Put in warm place to ferment. In two weeks lift off stone and board and remove the scum, if any, carefully lifting up cloth, picking it up at the corners to catch all of the scum. Wash cloth, board, stone and sides of crock; cover again with cloth, board and stone; then remove to cool place. Sauerkraut is now ready to use. Remove scum and wash cloth, board and stone weekly as long as kraut lasts.

Or the fermented kraut may be packed in jars. Cover with the brine, heat thoroughly in a hot-water bath and seal. If there is not enough brine add ¼ cup salt mixed with 1 quart of water.

SAUERKRAUT IN GLASS JARS

Shave cabbage very fine. It takes about 2 pounds of cabbage to fill a 1-quart jar. Fill jar with cabbage, pressing down until about half full, add 1 teaspoon salt. Fill to shoulder of jar, packing very tightly. Add 1 teaspoon salt. Fill jar with cold water to overflowing. Adjust cover loosely. Let stand at room temperature for 9 days, adding more cold water each day as needed. Then screw cover tight. Sauerkraut is ready to use. Store for future use.

SALTED BEANS OR CORN

Green beans and corn may be preserved for winter use in stone jars by packing in salt or brine.

SALTED BEANS

Beans may be left whole or cut; blanch 3 minutes. Sprinkle a layer of salt at the bottom of the crock, then a layer of beans, then salt and repeat until the jar is full, making the top layer salt. Use 1 pound salt for 4 pounds beans. Place plate over top of beans, to press down well. Let stand overnight. If brine to cover has not formed in 24 hours, add 1 pound salt to 2 quarts water and pour enough of this brine over beans to cover well. Cover with cloth, then plate or board and a weight. Wash cloth if scum rises. When ready to use, soak beans overnight, drain, and cook like fresh beans.

SALTED CORN

Husk the ears of corn and remove the silk. Cook in boiling water for about 2 minutes. Cut corn from cob with a sharp knife. Weigh and pack in layers with salt, using 1 pound salt for every 4 pounds of corn. Proceed as for Salted Beans. When ready to use, soak overnight, then prepare like fresh corn.

CATSUPS

SPICED TOMATO CATSUP

    1 peck ripe tomatoes
    4 onions
    1 small clove of garlic
    2 red peppers, seeded
    2 tablespoons salt
    ¼ tablespoon cayenne pepper
    ¼ cup mixed cassia buds, whole allspice and
        stick cinnamon
    2 bay leaves
    ½ cup sugar
    1 pint vinegar

Boil first 6 ingredients until vegetables are soft, drain through colander and then through sieve. Tie mixed spices and bay leaves in bag. Add sugar and spices to strained vegetables. Boil rapidly 1½ hours, until thick or reduced by half. Stir often to prevent scorching. Remove spice bag, add vinegar, boil 10 minutes longer or until thick. Bottle while hot and seal.

TOMATO CATSUP

    30 tomatoes
    12 apples, peeled, sliced and cored
    5 green peppers, seeded
    10 onions
    3 cups sugar
    5 tablespoons salt
    1 teaspoon cinnamon
    ½ teaspoon Cayenne pepper
    1 quart vinegar

Cook first 4 ingredients until soft, strain through colander, then through sieve. Add the remaining ingredients; simmer for 1 hour until thick. Bottle while hot and seal.

CHILI SAUCE

    18 large tomatoes
    6 large onions
    2 tablespoons salt
    1 cup sugar
    1 pint vinegar

Scald, peel and chop tomatoes; peel onions, put through coarse grinder. Add salt, sugar and vinegar and boil 1 hour or longer, stirring often. Pour into hot, sterilized jars, and seal.

VEGETABLE CHILI SAUCE

    50 medium ripe tomatoes
    10 medium onions
    4 red sweet peppers, seeds removed
    1 large bunch celery
    1 quart vinegar
    1 tablespoon whole allspice
    1 teaspoon dry mustard
    1 tablespoon whole cloves and broken stick
        cinnamon
    3 cups brown sugar
    2 tablespoons salt
    1 nutmeg, grated

Scald, peel and chop the tomatoes. Chop all the vegetables. Add other ingredients except whole spices and boil 2½ hours. Tie whole spices in a bag, boil 15 minutes longer. Remove spice bag.

4 pecks of tomatoes = 1 bushel = 50 pounds.
Instructions for canning tomatoes and tomato products will be found in chapter 24.

RELISHES

SWEET BEET AND CABBAGE RELISH

    2 quarts boiled beets, peeled and chopped
    2 quarts cabbage, chopped
    1 cup horseradish, grated
    2 cups sugar
    2 teaspoons salt
    pepper to taste
    vinegar

Blend ingredients in gallon jar, add cold vinegar to cover, and store. Will keep well in cool place.

BEET RELISH

    3 cups chopped cold boiled beets
    ½ cup grated horseradish root
    ¼ teaspoon pepper
    1 teaspoon salt
    2 tablespoons sugar
    ¾ cup vinegar

Mix beets and horseradish, season with salt, pepper, and sugar. Add as much vinegar or vinegar and lemon juice as the horseradish and beets will absorb. Store in refrigerator in covered jar. Canned beets and bottled horseradish may be used.

ENGLISH CHUTNEY

    1 pound apples, chopped
    ¾ pound seedless raisins, chopped
    1 dozen ripe tomatoes, chopped
    2 red peppers, seeded and chopped
    6 small onions, chopped
    ¼ cup mint leaves, chopped
    1 ounce white mustard seed
    ¼ cup salt
    2 cups brown sugar
    1 quart vinegar, boiled and cooled

Mix ingredients. Cook slowly until thick and clear, fill small, sterilized jars, and seal.

CORN RELISH

    1 quart raw corn cut from the cob
    3 cups chopped cabbage
    1 cup chopped stalk celery
    2 red peppers, seeded
    2 green peppers, seeded
    1 onion
    1 cup sugar
    2 tablespoons salt
    3 tablespoons dry mustard
    3 cups vinegar

Grind or chop together the first 6 ingredients, add the rest of the ingredients, cook until corn is tender (about 15 minutes). Bottle and seal.

CONFETTI CORN RELISH

20 ears corn
1 medium head cabbage, core removed
4 green peppers
6 red peppers
4 onions
1 cup celery, chopped
½ cup salt
2 cups sugar
½ cup flour
½ teaspoon turmeric
4 tablespoons dry mustard
1 quart white vinegar

Cut corn from cob; grind rest of vegetables. Mix flour, turmeric, and mustard. Gradually stir in the vinegar; bring to a boil. Add the vegetables, the salt and sugar. Boil ½ hour; bottle and seal.

CUCUMBER RELISH

2 green cucumbers
2 cups celery, cut fine
1 tablespoon salt
1 cup vinegar
¼ cup sugar
few grains cayenne pepper
2 tablespoons horseradish
1 tablespoon onion, chopped
1 tablespoon green pepper, chopped
1 teaspoon pepper

Peel and chop cucumbers (about 1 pint), add celery. Sprinkle with salt and drain overnight in cheesecloth bag. Rinse well, drain. Add the remaining ingredients. This relish may be used immediately; or packed into sterilized jars and sealed.

Instructions for sterilizing jars will be found in chapter 24 in the section on canning, along with instructions on sealing, processing, and storing, which are equally applicable to pickles and relishes.

PEPPER RELISH

12 large red peppers
12 large green peppers
15 onions, peeled
vinegar
1 pint vinegar
3 tablespoons salt
3 cups sugar
3 tablespoons mustard seed

Remove seeds from peppers; chop or grind peppers and onions and cover with boiling water. Let stand 5 minutes; drain. Make a solution of 1 part vinegar and 2 parts water to cover. Add pepper mixture, bring to a boil, let stand 10 minutes; drain. Add 1 pint vinegar, salt, sugar, and mustard seed; boil 2 minutes; bottle and seal.

SPANISH PICKLE (PICCALILLI)

½ peck green tomatoes
1 dozen red peppers, seeded
1 dozen green peppers, seeded
1 medium head cabbage
10 large onions
3 tablespoons salt
3 cups sugar
3 cups vinegar
3 tablespoons mustard seed
1 teaspoon turmeric

Chop the first 5 ingredients, add the salt, let stand overnight. Drain. Mix with the rest of the ingredients and boil 20 minutes. Pour into jars and seal.

TOMATO RELISH

1 peck ripe tomatoes
2 cups chopped onions
2 cups chopped celery
2 quarts cider vinegar
4 red peppers, seeded, chopped fine
2 cups sugar
1 cup mustard seed
½ cup salt
1 teaspoon black pepper
1 teaspoon paprika

Peel and chop tomatoes and put in colander to drain; add rest of ingredients to tomato pulp, and fill to overflowing in sterilized jars; seal. Ready for use in 6 weeks.

GREEN TOMATO RELISH
(MOCK MINCE MEAT)

1 peck green tomatoes
1 tablespoon salt
4 pounds sugar
1 pound raisins, seeded
1 pound dried currants
1 cup vinegar
1 tablespoon cinnamon
½ tablespoon ground cloves
2 oranges, rind and juice
1 lemon, rind and juice

Wash the tomatoes and chop in small pieces. Place in colander, pour boiling water over them 3 times, draining well each time. Remove to preserving kettle, add salt, sugar, raisins and currants, well washed, and boil slowly until tender. Add vinegar and the remaining ingredients. Heat to boiling point. Bottle while hot and seal. Use as a relish or as a filling for pie.

TOMATO-PEPPER RELISH

1 peck ripe tomatoes
6 large onions, peeled
1 cup salt (scant)
8 red or green peppers, seeded
1 bunch celery, chopped
¼ cup celery seed
2 pounds sugar
5 cups cider vinegar

Chop tomatoes and put into colander. Chop onions and peppers. Place in bag with salt. Drain all overnight. Add celery, celery seed, to tomato pulp, onions, and peppers. Boil sugar and vinegar and let cool; pour cold over vegetables. Pack into sterilized jars and seal.

GREEN TOMATO PICKLE

1 peck green tomatoes, sliced
¾ cup salt
¼ peck onions, sliced
1 tablespoon white mustard seed
2 tablespoons stick cinnamon
2 tablespoons cloves, heads removed
½ gallon cider vinegar
2 pounds brown sugar
4 red peppers, chopped
2 stalks celery, cut up

Mix tomatoes with ½ cup salt and onions with ¼ cup salt. Let stand overnight, drain. Tie spices in a bag and place in a kettle with the vinegar and sugar; heat to the boiling point, add the other ingredients and simmer slowly for 20 minutes. Remove spice bag. Pack into sterilized jars and seal.

PREPARED HORSERADISH

Wash 1 pound horseradish root, cut or scrape off thick peel; grate. Mix well with white vinegar to cover. Add 3 tablespoons of sugar. Bottle and seal.

PICKLED, SPICED AND BRANDIED FRUIT

PICKLED CHERRIES

Pit 2 quarts sour cherries, put into stone jar, cover with vinegar, let stand 24 hours. Stir occasionally. Drain off vinegar. Measure same amount of sugar as cherries, and alternate in layers, sugar on top. Stir each day for 3 days until sugar is dissolved. Seal in sterilized jars.

PICKLED CRABAPPLES

9 pounds crabapples
6 pounds sugar
1½ quarts vinegar
1½ pints water
¼ cup broken cinnamon and cloves, mixed

Select sound, large crabapples. Do not remove stems or pare. Wash crabapples, mix with sugar, add vinegar and water; let stand overnight, covered. Drain off juices and to these add spices tied in a bag. Heat slowly; when clear, add apples; boil only until tender. Transfer apples into sterilized jars, using skimmer; place cover on jars. Boil syrup down, remove spices, pour boiling syrup over fruit to overflowing. Seal.

PICKLED APPLES

Pare, quarter, and core. Proceed as above.

SPICED GOOSEBERRIES

5 pounds underripe gooseberries
2 cups vinegar
4 pounds sugar
1 tablespoon cinnamon
½ tablespoon allspice
½ tablespoon cloves

Wash and stem the fruit. Bring vinegar, sugar and the ground spices to a boil. Add the berries and boil slowly 20 minutes. Pack into overflowing sterilized jars and seal.

PICKLED PEACHES

6 pounds peaches
3 pounds sugar
1 pint cider vinegar (dilute if strong)
⅛ cup cloves, heads removed
2 sticks cinnamon, broken up

Dip large clingstone peaches into scalding water and slip off skins. Boil sugar, vinegar, and spices, tied in a bag, about 12 minutes, or until clear. Add peaches, enough to fill 1 jar at a time; cook until tender. Lift out of kettle with skimmer, place in jar and cover to keep hot. When jars are full, cook syrup down a little. Pour boiling hot syrup over the peaches to overflowing. Cover and seal.

BAKED PICKLED PEACHES

8 pounds peaches
cloves
4 pounds sugar
1 pint cider vinegar
1 cup water
1 or 2 sticks cinnamon

Peel peaches, stick a clove in each. Mix other ingredients and pour into a large flat pan. Place peaches in the syrup, cover, and bake 3 hours at 300° F. Pack in sterilized jars, fill to overflowing, and seal.

PICKLED PLUMS

6 pounds plums
2 cups vinegar
3½ pounds sugar
1 tablespoon cinnamon
½ tablespoon allspice
½ tablespoon cloves

Remove stones from plums or prick with fork. Boil vinegar, sugar and spices, then add plums, boil slowly 30 minutes. Place in jars; fill jars with syrup to overflowing and seal.

PICKLED PEARS

10 pounds Seckel pears
4½ pounds sugar
1 cup water
3 cups vinegar
¼ cup broken stick cinnamon and cloves, mixed

Wash and peel pears, leaving stems on. Place in a crock alternately with layers of sugar. Cover with the water and vinegar. Let stand covered overnight. Drain and to the liquid add the spices tied in a bag. Heat slowly until syrup is clear, add the pears, boil until tender, but not soft, a few at a time. Place pears in sterilized jars, covering each jar. When jars are full, lift covers and pour the boiling syrup over fruit to overflowing and seal at once.

SWEET PICKLED WATERMELON RIND

7 pounds watermelon rind
water
½ teaspoon salt
½ teaspoon alum
2½ pounds granulated sugar
2½ pounds light brown sugar
1 quart vinegar
1 pint water
6 sticks cinnamon
1 tablespoon cloves
2 lemons, sliced

Pare green from rind and discard. Cut white into strips. Boil until tender and clear in water with ½ teaspoon salt and alum. Drain. Chill in ice water, drain and dry. Boil sugar, vinegar and 1 pint water to a light syrup, add spices in a bag, melon rind and lemon slices; boil until clear. Remove

spices, pack rind and syrup to overflowing in sterilized jars; seal. Let stand 4 weeks before using.

BRANDIED DRIED FRUITS

Dates, figs, apricots, prunes or any dried fruit may be brandied by covering in jar with 2 parts of strained honey to 1 part of brandy. Seal jars; let stand 4 weeks or more before using.

PICKLED CANNED FRUIT

1 cup sugar
syrup from can
¼ cup vinegar
1 3-inch stick cinnamon
1 teaspoon cloves, heads removed
1 can (1 pound, 13 ounces) peaches, pears or apricots

Boil sugar, syrups, vinegar and spices. Simmer until thick and clear, about 10 minutes. Pour hot syrup over fruit. Let stand 24 hours before using.

BRANDIED CHERRIES

5 cups sugar
2 cups water
5 pounds bing cherries
2 cups brandy

Boil the sugar and water 8 minutes, to a clear syrup; pour syrup over cherries and let stand overnight. Drain cherries, bring syrup slowly to the boiling point, add cherries, boil about 8 minutes. Lift out cherries with perforated skimmer, pack into hot, glass jars, and cover. Boil the syrup down until thick. Add the brandy, pour the syrup over the cherries to overflowing and seal.

BRANDIED PEACHES OR PEARS

9 pounds peaches or pears
9 pounds sugar
1 quart water
2 tablespoons stick cinnamon
2 tablespoons whole cloves, heads removed
3 pints brandy

Select large clingstone peaches or perfect pears. Peel and weigh fruit and adjust sugar to equal amount. Boil sugar and water with spices, tied in a bag, until clear; add fruit, a few pieces at a time, and boil until tender, but not soft. They must remain whole. Place fruit on platter to drain. Repeat until all fruit has been cooked. Let syrup boil until thick; cool, add brandy and stir well. Place fruit in sterilized jars, cover with the syrup to overflowing. Seal.

24
FREEZING, CANNING AND DRYING

FREEZING

General Rules

1. Frozen foods must be stored at 0° F. or lower.
2. Select foods of the best quality. Freezing does not improve them, but will retain the original quality and flavor.
3. Prepare, package, and freeze food immediately after picking or purchasing.
4. Food expands when frozen. Allow ½ inch head space in all containers.
5. Moisture- and vapor-proof packaging is essential.
6. Materials to be frozen should be placed in separate compartment for freezing or along bottom of shelf or along side walls of freezer. Do not stack packages until frozen.
7. Label and date all packages clearly. Use older packages first.
8. Do not refreeze foods that have been thawed.
9. In case of power failure, keep freezer doors closed. Fully loaded freezer will hold temperature for 2 days. If failure lasts longer, add dry ice on racks above food—25 pounds per 10 cubic feet.

FREEZING FRUITS

PACKAGING MATERIALS FOR FRUITS

Cartons, wide-mouthed jars, and plastic containers especially designed for freezing.

PREPARING FRUITS FOR FREEZING

Three methods are used to prepare fresh fruits for freezing. They may be packed covered in cold syrup of the designated strength; or with dry sugar, or without sweetening. Ascorbic acid is added to fruits which tend to darken after cutting, to retain light color; it may be dissolved in the syrup, or mixed with the sugar, or dissolved in water. Use ¾ teaspoon ascorbic acid for each quart of syrup, unless otherwise noted; or ¼ teaspoon per quart of fruit; or ¼ teaspoon per cup of sugar.

SUGAR SYRUP FOR FROZEN FRUITS

(Sugar listed is amount to be used per quart of water.)

Syrup	Sugar	Yield of Syrup
Light 30%	2 cups	5 cups
Medium Light 40%	3 cups	5½ cups
Medium Heavy 50%	4¾ cups	6½ cups
Heavy 60%	7 cups	7¾ cups

In any of the above syrups white corn syrup may be substituted for one quarter of the sugar.

See chart, pages 464-465.

TO STORE FROZEN FRUITS

Most fruits maintain high quality at 0° F. for 8 to 12 months. Citrus fruits and citrus juices should be used within 4 to 6 months. Unsweetened fruits lose quality faster than those packed in sugar or syrup.

TO THAW FRUITS

Leave fruit in sealed container to thaw. Frozen dessert fruits are best when slightly frosty. A 1-pound package will thaw in 6 to 8 hours in the refrigerator or in 2 to 4 hours at room temperature.

FREEZING VEGETABLES

General Rules

1. Process not more than 1 pound of vegetables at a time.
2. Place prepared vegetables in colander or wire basket.
3. Immerse colander or basket in large quantity of rapidly boiling water.
4. Cover kettle to bring water back to boil as quickly as possible.
5. As soon as water returns to boil, begin to time blanching. Time accurately.
6. After blanching, plunge immediately into cold running water or ice water to cool. It takes about as long to cool foods as to heat them.
7. Drain well and dry.
8. Pack and freeze immediately, allowing ½-inch head space.

PACKAGING MATERIALS FOR VEGETABLES

Plastic bags, cartons, wide-mouthed jars, and plastic containers especially designed for freezing.

TO STEAM VEGETABLES

Certain vegetables, among them mushrooms, pumpkins, sweet potatoes, and winter squash, may be steamed instead of blanched. Put a rack in a kettle or saucepan fitted with a tight lid. Put an inch or two of water in the bottom of the kettle; bring to a boil. Put vegetables in a colander or steaming basket in a single layer and cook covered, in the steam, for the designated time.

TO STORE FROZEN VEGETABLES

All vegetables except asparagus, corn, and green beans maintain high quality for 8 to 12 months. Asparagus should be used within 6 months; corn and green beans within 8 months.

TO COOK FROZEN VEGETABLES

(*Except corn on the cob and greens.*) Put the frozen vegetables into a small amount of rapidly boiling, salted water. Separate vegetables with fork to insure uniform cooking. Cook until tender.

CORN-ON-THE-COB: Thaw, cook in rapidly boiling salted water.

GREENS: Thaw partially before cooking in rapidly boiling, salted water.

See chart, page 467.

FREEZING MEAT

General Rules

Any high quality uncooked meat can be frozen satisfactorily. All meats should be cut into size and quantity convenient for family needs. If more than one cut is placed in packages, such as a number of chops or steaks, place two sheets of moisture- and vapor-proof paper between the layers for easy separation.

Do not season uncooked meats before freezing.

1. Wrap package tightly and seal. If package is uneven, protect wrapping by covering package with stockinette.
2. Label and date package clearly.
3. Freeze quickly.

PACKAGING MATERIALS FOR MEATS

Heavy aluminum foil
Heavy-weight freezer paper
Freezer-weight plastic wrap
Polyethylene bags
Stockinette
Freezer tape

To Use Frozen Meats

ROASTS

Thaw in wrapping. Roast immediately. Or roast frozen—allow 1½ times cooking time used for unfrozen meat.

STEAKS, CHOPS, AND HAMBURGER PATTIES

Broil 4 inches below heating unit; if still frozen increase prescribed broiling time by half.

GROUND BEEF AND VARIETY MEATS

Thaw completely and cook as fresh meat.

FREEZING POULTRY

PACKAGING MATERIALS

Use the same as those for meat.

TO PREPARE POULTRY FOR FREEZING

Any poultry can be frozen satisfactorily.
1. Poultry may be frozen whole or cut up.
2. Separate pieces with two sheets of moisture- and vapor-proof paper.
2. Pack giblets in moisture- and vapor-proof paper. They may be replaced, wrapped, in the cavity, if poultry is to be used within 3 months, or packed separately. It is advantageous to pack livers separately, for special uses.
4. Wrap tightly, seal. Label and date.
5. Do not stuff poultry before freezing.

TO USE FROZEN POULTRY

Thaw completely and use like fresh poultry. Poultry may be stewed or braised without thawing.

FREEZING FISH

PACKAGING MATERIALS

Use the same as those for meat and poultry.

TO PREPARE FISH FOR FREEZING

Fish, freshly caught, should be cleaned, scaled, and frozen as rapidly as possible.
1. Leave fish whole or cut into steaks or fillets. Immerse lean fish in salt solution, ⅓ cup salt to 2 quarts of water, for 30 seconds. Do not immerse fatty fish such as salmon or mackerel.
2. Wrap in moisture- and vapor-proof materials. Seal, label, and date.

TO PREPARE SHELLFISH

1. OYSTERS, CLAMS, AND SCALLOPS. Shell and wash in brine, 1 tablespoon salt to 1 quart of water. Drain, pack in moisture- and vapor-proof plastic containers. Label, date, freeze immediately.
2. SHRIMP. Clean, package, and freeze. Or cook, shell, package, and freeze.

TO USE FROZEN FISH

Thaw and prepare like fresh fish, or broil frozen.

RECOMMENDED STORAGE PERIODS

The recommended storage periods for home-frozen meats and fish held at 0° F. are given below. For best quality, use the shorter storage time.

PRODUCT	STORAGE PERIOD
Beef:	*(months)*
GROUND MEAT	2-3
ROASTS	8-12
STEAKS	8-12
Lamb:	
CHOPS	3-4
GROUND MEAT	2-3
ROASTS	8-12
Poultry:	
GAME BIRDS	8
CHICKENS	6
TURKEYS, DUCKS, GEESE	6
GIBLETS	3
Fish:	2-4
Shellfish:	
OYSTERS	1
CLAMS	3
SHRIMP	4
Pork, cured:	
BACON	Less than 1
HAM	1-2
Pork, fresh:	
CHOPS	3-4
ROASTS	4-8
SAUSAGE	1-2

Veal:	
CUTLETS, CHOPS	3-4
GROUND MEAT	2-3
ROASTS	4-8

FREEZING EGGS

PACKAGING MATERIALS

Use the same as those for fruits and vegetables.

Eggs may be frozen without shells, yolks and whites mixed together, or yolks only, or whites only. Package small quantities of eggs. Pack in one package only the amount that can be used at one time.

General Rules

Whites need no treatment other than packaging and labeling.
1. Prepare yolks by adding 1 teaspoon salt to 1 cup of yolks. Stir, but do not beat. If eggs are to be used for baking, substitute 1 tablespoon sugar or white corn syrup for salt. Package and label, noting on label whether sugar or salt has been added.
2. Prepare whole eggs by adding 1 teaspoon salt to 1 cup of eggs. If eggs are to be used for baking, substitute 1 tablespoon sugar or white corn syrup for salt. Stir thoroughly but do not beat. Package and label, noting on label whether sugar or salt has been added.

TO USE FROZEN EGGS

Thaw in refrigerator. Use as you would fresh eggs.
   1½ tablespoons white equal the white of 1 egg
   1 tablespoon yolk equals the yolk of 1 egg
   2½ tablespoons whole egg equals 1 egg.
   STORAGE PERIOD
Whites, yolks, or yolks and whites
mixed together   8-12 months

FREEZING BAKED GOODS

PACKAGING MATERIALS

Use any moisture- and vapor-proof materials, plus boxes to protect the cake or pie.

PIES

1. Freeze unbaked. Use disposable foil or paper pie plates. 2. Fruit and mince meat pies freeze successfully. 3. Chiffon Pies freeze well. Defrost in refrigerator for 1-1½ hours. 4. Do not freeze custard pies. 5. Unbaked pie shells or pie dough may be frozen.

TO BAKE FROZEN PIES

Remove wrapping. Bake like freshly made pie, at prescribed temperature. Slit crust when sufficiently thawed. Allow 10 to 12 minutes additional baking time at high control heat.

CAKES

Any type of cake may be baked and frozen. It is best to fill and frost cakes when ready to serve. Wrap cakes carefully and label. Thaw cakes in wrapping.

BAKED ROLLS, COOKIES, MUFFINS AND BREAD

Wrap in moisture- and vapor-proof material, seal, and label. May be thawed at room temperature, or placed in moderate oven to thaw and heat.

STORAGE PERIOD

Bread, Rolls, Cakes	3 months
Cup Cakes	2-4 months
Pies, unbaked	8 months
Biscuits, Muffins, Cookies	2-3 months

FREEZING SANDWICHES

Meat, fish, poultry, and peanut butter fillings freeze well. Spread bread generously with butter or margarine to edge of bread. Package sandwiches individually in moisture- and vapor-proof wrapping. Seal, label and freeze immediately. Keep only 2 to 3 weeks. Sandwiches will thaw in 5 to 6 hours in refrigerator, 2 to 3 hours at room temperature.

FILLINGS WHICH DO NOT FREEZE WELL
Raw vegetables
Salad greens
Whites of hard-cooked eggs
Cheese, unless combined with other foods
Jellies
Mayonnaise

FREEZING CANAPES OR HORS D'OEUVRES

Fancy party sandwiches and hors d'oeuvres can also be frozen. Although the fillings and spreads will be different from those used in lunch sandwiches, the rules for making, packaging, freezing, and storing are the same. Freeze in a single layer on baking sheets. Package in moisture- and vapor-proof materials, placing two pieces of paper between layers. Canapés which are to be broiled or toasted may be transferred from the freezer to the broiler or oven. Sandwiches, canapés, and hors d'oeuvres should be stored no longer than 1 month.

FREEZING COOKED FOODS

Cooked foods, either leftovers or foods cooked especially for the purpose, may be frozen for fu-

ture use. They should be used within 2 to 3 months. They may be wrapped in the containers in which they are to be heated and served, or in plastic freeze containers, cartons, or jars especially designed for freezing. It is economical of time and effort to make double or triple recipes of certain dishes, in order to freeze some for later use. The following dishes are particularly suitable.

Baked beans	Chicken à la King
Stews	Fried Chicken
Spaghetti Sauce and Meat Balls	Candied Sweet Potatoes
	French Fried Potatoes
Chili	French Toast
Soups and Stocks	Waffles
Meat pies and turnovers	Stuffed Peppers

Generally speaking, most cooked foods freeze well, with the following exceptions:

Cheese and crumb toppings for casseroles should not be added until just before reheating.

Mixtures containing hard-cooked egg white or potatoes—the egg whites get rubbery in consistency, and the potatoes become mushy.

General Rules

1. Foods cooked especially for freezing should be slightly undercooked, since they cook during the reheating process. This is especially true of combinations containing vegetables, pasta, or rice.
2. Cool the food to be frozen as quickly as possible by setting the pan of hot food in a pan of ice and water. Package and freeze, allowing ample head space.
3. Casseroles may be left temporarily frozen in the dish in which they were cooked, then turned out of the dish, and wrapped in moisture and vapor proof paper. At serving time, they can be refitted into the same dish, and heated in it.
4. Do not allow food to thaw before reheating.
5. Stews, creamed mixtures and the like are most easily heated in a double boiler over boiling water.
6. Casseroles should be heated in the oven, allowing ample time for them to heat thoroughly.
7. Fried foods may be heated in a moderately hot oven (400° F.) in a single layer, without a cover, to restore crispness.
8. Frozen waffles and sliced bread may be heated in a toaster.

STORAGE PERIOD FOR COOKED FOODS

Cooked foods remain at top quality for 2 to 3 months, and up to 6 months under ideal conditions (perfect wrapping, uniform 0° storage). After 6 months storage, the quality may decline, although the food is still safe.

FRUITS FOR FREEZING

FRUIT	PREPARATION	SUGAR OR SYRUP
Apples for Dessert	Peel and slice directly into syrup with ascorbic acid.	Pack in 40% syrup with ½ teaspoon ascorbic acid per quart.
Apples for Pie	Peel and slice directly into cold water with 1 teaspoon ascorbic acid for each quart of water. Steam in single layer 1½ to 2 minutes. Cool in cold water, drain.	Add ½ cup sugar for each quart of apple slices, stir.
Apricots for Dessert	Dip into boiling water, remove skins, cut in half and discard pits.	Pack in 40% syrup, with ¾ teaspoon ascorbic acid per quart.
Apricots for Pie	Peel and pit as above; sprinkle each quart fruit with solution of ¼ teaspoon ascorbic acid to ¼ cup cold water.	Add ½ cup sugar for each quart fruit; stir until dissolved.
Avocados	Peel and mash. Add ⅛ teaspoon ascorbic acid to each quart fruit.	Use no sugar.
Blackberries, Boysenberries, Dewberries, Loganberries FOR DESSERT FOR PIES	Wash and sort. Handle as little as possible. Wash and sort. Handle as little as possible.	Pack in 40-50% syrup. Use ¾ cup sugar for each quart berries.
Blueberries, Elderberries, Huckleberries DRY PACK FOR DESSERT	Sort and wipe clean. Wash and sort.	Freeze in single layer, then pack. Pack in 40% syrup, or use ¾ cup sugar for each quart berries.
Cherries, sour FOR DESSERT FOR PIES	Sort, stem, and wash. Drain and pit. Sort, stem, and wash. Drain and pit.	Pack in 60-65% syrup. Use ¾ cup sugar for each quart cherries.
Cherries, sweet	Prepare very quickly! Sort, stem, wash and drain. Remove pits.	Pack in 40% syrup, with ½ teaspoon ascorbic acid per quart.
Cranberries, whole UNSWEETENED SWEETENED	Stem and wash. Dry, pack into containers, seal and freeze. Stem and wash.	Use no sugar. Pack in 50% syrup.
Currants, whole UNSWEETENED SWEETENED	Stem and wash. Dry. Pack into containers, seal and freeze. Stem and wash.	Use no sugar. Pack in 50% syrup, or use ¾ cup sugar for each quart.
Figs	Sort, wash, cut off stems. Peel if desired, slice or leave whole. Or, prepare as above, pack into containers. Cover with water with ¾ teaspoon ascorbic acid for each quart.	Pack in 35% syrup with ¾ teaspoon ascorbic acid for each quart. Use no sugar.
Gooseberries FOR DESSERT FOR PIES OR PRESERVES	Sort, stem and wash. Sort, stem, and wash, and pack into containers.	Pack in 50% syrup. Use no sugar.

FRUITS FOR FREEZING
(Continued)

FRUIT	PREPARATION	SUGAR OR SYRUP
Grapefruit	Wash and peel, divide into sections, removing all membranes and seeds.	Pack in 40% syrup with ½ teaspoon ascorbic acid per quart.
Grapes	Wash and stem. Leave seedless grapes whole, cut other grapes in half, remove seeds.	Pack in 40% syrup.
Melon	Cut melon flesh into cubes, balls, or slices.	Pack in 30% syrup.
Nectarines	Sort, wash and pit fruit. Peel and cut up, if desired, and drop directly into container of syrup with ascorbic acid.	Pack in 40% syrup with ½ teaspoon ascorbic acid for each quart.
Oranges, see Grapefruit		
Peaches, halves and slices	Sort, wash, pit and peel. For best results, peel peaches without blanching.	Pack in 40% syrup with ½ teaspoon ascorbic acid for each quart. or Dissolve ¼ teaspoon ascorbic acid in ¼ cup cold water, sprinkle peaches. Pack with ⅔ cup sugar for each quart of fruit.
Pears	Wash, peel, cut in halves or quarters.	Heat pears in boiling 40% syrup for 1-2 minutes. Drain and cool. Pack with cold 40% syrup with ¾ teaspoon ascorbic acid for each quart.
Pineapple	Pare, remove core and eyes. Slice, dice, crush, or cut into wedges. Pack tightly. Seal and freeze without sugar, or in syrup pack.	Pack in 30% syrup made with pineapple juice if available.
Plums, Prunes	Wash, cut in halves or quarters.	Pack in 40-50% syrup with ½ teaspoon ascorbic acid for each quart syrup.
Raspberries	Select fully ripe, juicy berries. Sort, wash and dry. Freeze in a single layer and dry-pack.	Use ¾ cup sugar for each quart berries; or pack in 40% syrup.
Rhubarb	Choose firm, tender, well-colored stalks with few fibers. Wash, trim, cut into 1-2 inch pieces. Heat in boiling water for 1 minute, plunge into cold water.	Pack in 40% syrup.
Strawberries		
WHOLE, DRY PACK	Sort. Wipe clean. Do not hull.	Freeze in single layer; pack without sugar.
WHOLE, WATER PACK	Choose firm ripe berries. Sort, wash, and hull. Pack into containers.	Cover with water with 1 teaspoon ascorbic acid for each quart.
WHOLE, SWEETENED	Sort, wash and hull.	Use ¾ cup sugar for each quart of berries or pack in 50% syrup.
SLICED, SWEETENED	Sort, wash, hull and slice.	Use ¾ cup sugar for each quart of berries.

VEGETABLES FOR FREEZING

VEGETABLE	PREPARATION	BLANCHING TIME IN BOILING WATER
Asparagus	Sort according to thickness of stalk. Wash, snap off tough ends.	Small stalks; 2 minutes. Medium stalks; 3 minutes. Large stalks; 4 minutes.
Beans **Limas, shell**	Shell and blanch; sort according to size, or blanch in pods, shell after cooling.	Small beans or pods; 2 minutes. Medium beans or pods; 3 minutes. Large beans or pods; 4 minutes.
Snap, green or wax	Pick over stringless beans. Wash, remove ends. Cut in 1- 2 inch lengths or in julienne strips.	3 minutes.
Soybeans	Select, wash. Blanch in pods, cool, squeeze beans out of pods.	5 minutes, in pods.
Beets	Select beets not more than 3 inches across. Wash and sort according to size. Trim, leaving ½ inch stems. Cook until tender. Cool. Peel and cut into slices or cubes, pack and freeze.	Blanching time for small beets; 25-30 minutes. Medium beets; 45-50 minutes.
Broccoli	Select tight dark heads with tender stalks. Wash, peel stalks, and trim. If necessary to remove insects, soak for ½ hour in solution of 4 teaspoons salt to 1 gallon cold water. Split into flowerets 1½ inches across.	3 minutes or steam 5 minutes.
Brussels Sprouts	Trim, remove coarse outer leaves. Wash thoroughly. Sort for size.	Small heads; 3 minutes. Medium heads; 4 minutes. Large heads; 5 minutes.
Carrots	Wash and peel. Leave small carrots whole. Cut others into ¾ inch cubes, thin slices or lengthwise strips.	Whole small; 5 minutes. Diced or sliced; 2 minutes. Strips; 2 minutes.
Cauliflower	Break or cut into 1 inch pieces. If necessary to remove insects, soak for 30 minutes in a solution of salt and water—4 teaspoons salt to 1 gallon of water.	Blanch in salted water (4 teaspoons salt to each gallon of water) for 3 minutes.
Celery	Select crisp stalks, free from coarse strings. Wash thoroughly, trim and cut into 1 inch lengths.	3 minutes.
Corn: whole kernel, or cream style	Husk, remove silk, and wash. For whole kernel—cut kernels from cob at ⅔ the depth of the kernels. For cream style—cut kernels from cob at center of kernels. Scrape cob to remove juice and heart of kernel. Pack and freeze.	Blanch corn on cob as below. Then cut from cob.
Corn on the Cob	Husk, remove silk, wash and sort ears according to size.	Small ears (1 to 1¼" in diam.); 7 minutes. Medium ears (1¼-1½" in diam.); 9 minutes. Large ears (over 1½"); 11 minutes.

VEGETABLES FOR FREEZING
(*Continued*)

VEGETABLE	PREPARATION	BLANCHING TIME IN BOILING WATER
Greens: Beet Greens, Chard, Collards, Kale, Mustard, Spinach, Turnip	Select tender, young leaves. Wash thoroughly. Remove tough stems and imperfect leaves.	Beet greens, kale, chard, mustard, turnip greens; 2 minutes. Collards; 3 minutes. Spinach; 2 minutes. (very young, tender leaves; 1½ minutes.)
Kohlrabi	Select small to medium, young kohlrabi. Cut off tops and roots. Wash, peel, and leave whole or dice in ½ inch cubes.	Whole; 3 minutes. Cubes; 1 minute.
Mushrooms	Sort according to size. Wash in cold water, trim off ends of stems. If larger than 1 inch in diameter, quarter and slice. Dip for 5 minutes in solution of 1 teaspoon lemon juice or 1½ teaspoons citric acid for each pint of water.	Steam whole; 5 minutes. Caps or quarters; 3½ minutes. Slices; 3 minutes.
Okra	Select young, tender green pods. Cut off stems, but do not open pods. Leave whole or slice crosswise.	Small pods; 3 minutes. Large pods; 4 minutes.
Parsnips	Choose small to medium parsnips. Remove tops, wash and peel. Cut into ½ inch cubes or slices.	2 minutes.
Peas, field (blackeye)	Shell, and pick over, discarding hard peas.	2 minutes.
Peas, green	Shell. Discard hard peas.	1½ minutes.
Peppers, Green	Wash, cut out stems, cut in half, remove seeds. If desired, dice or cut in strips or rings. If peppers are to be used in salads, do not blanch.	Halves; 3 minutes. Strips; 2 minutes.
Peppers, hot	Wash and stem. Pack into small containers, leaving no head space.	No blanching.
Pimientos	To peel, first roast until skin begins to blacken in a hot oven (400° F.) 3 to 4 minutes. Rinse off charred skins in cold water. Drain and pack.	No blanching.
Pumpkin	Select mature pumpkin with fine texture, not stringy. Wash, remove seeds and fibers; dice.	Cook until soft in boiling water, steam, or cook until tender in a pressure cooker, or in the oven. Remove pulp from rind, purée, cool, and pack.
Rutabagas	Cut off tops, wash and peel, cut into ½ inch cubes.	2 minutes.
Squash, Summer	Wash, cut into ½ inch slices.	3 minutes.
Squash, Winter, mashed	Prepare like pumpkin.	
Sweet Potatoes	Peel, dip into solution of 1 tablespoon citric acid to each quart of water.	Cook until tender; drain. Roll in sugar if desired.
Sweet Potatoes, mashed	Cook as above; mash.	
Turnips	Wash, peel, dice.	2 minutes.

CANNING

General Rules

Fruits and vegetables selected for canning should be of excellent quality without bruises or blemishes, as fresh as possible, and underripe rather than overripe. Can each variety in season, when it is best and cheapest.

It is not necessary to can large quantities of food at a time. Two to three pounds of fruit or vegetables will fill a quart jar. For a small family, use pint jars.

There are three principal steps in canning: *preparing* the food, *packing* it in jars, and *processing* the jars of food in boiling water, by pressure or by steam.

PREPARATION

Instructions for preparing individual fruits and vegetables are given in the Fruit Canning Chart, page 472, and the Vegetable Canning Chart, page 474.

PACKING

RAW OR COLD PACK METHOD

Used for fruits, not advised for vegetables, except tomatoes.
1. Pack fruits raw into hot sterilized jars.
2. Pour hot syrup over fruit, or hot, salted tomato juice over tomatoes.
3. Allow ½ to 1 inch headspace at the top of each jar to allow for expansion during processing. Remove air bubbles by running a table knife around the inside of the jar. Add more liquid if needed to cover foods.
4. Adjust new scalded rubber rings and tops, wipe with a clean damp cloth, and seal jar according to type being used.
5. Process for length of time indicated on Fruit Canning Chart, page 472.

HOT PACK METHOD

Used for all low-acid vegetables. May also be used for fruits and tomatoes.
1. Precook fruits in syrup, vegetables in boiling water, in open kettle for length of time indicated in charts at the beginning of the chapter.
2. Pack while hot into hot, sterilized jars.
3. Allow ½ inch head space at top of jar if food is to be processed in water bath, 1 inch if processed in pressure cooker.
4. Remove air bubbles by running a table knife around the inside of the jar, and seal according to the type of jar being used.
5. Process for the length of time indicated on appropriate canning chart.

PROCESSING

Fruits and tomatoes may be processed:
—in a boiling water bath
—under pressure in a pressure canner or pressure cooker
—by steam in a pressure canner.

All other vegetables must be processed under pressure in a pressure canner or pressure cooker.

Oven processing is not recommended.

Pressure canning is the preferred method for processing all foods. At high altitudes, it is advised even for fruits and tomatoes, since water boils at decreasingly low temperatures as altitude increases.

ALTITUDE PROCESSING

For water bath, add 1 minute for each 1,000 feet above sea level if time is 20 or less, 2 minutes if time is longer. For a pressure cooker, increase pressure 1 pound for each 2,000 feet.

BOILING WATER BATH

Use a large kettle, a wash boiler, a lard can or a straight-sided pail. The vessel should have a close-fitting cover and a rack to raise the jars off the bottom and permit water to circulate around them. A rack may be made of perforated cake tins, wire broilers or cake coolers, or of thin pieces of wood nailed together. Wire baskets to fit individual jars may also be used. The vessel should be deep enough to permit an inch or two of water above the jars.
1. Have water in vessel hot for cold pack foods, boiling for hot pack foods.
2. Lower jars slowly into water. Be sure they are at least ½ inch apart. Cover container.
3. Count time required for processing (see Fruit Canning Chart, page 472) from when water comes to a rolling boil. If necessary add more boiling water during processing.
4. Remove jar from water, complete seal if necessary, cool upright on a cloth or rack, away from drafts.

PROCESSING IN CANNER

PRESSURE

For canning food in any quantity a pressure canner is necessary, and the manufacturer's directions for operating the canner should be followed. Pint jars may be processed in a pressure saucepan, adding 20 minutes to processing time.

1. Place 2 or 3 inches of water in bottom of pressure canner, to the level of the rack. Have water hot for cold pack foods, boiling for hot pack foods. If food is to be processed longer than one-half hour, a little more water is required.

2. Place filled jars on rack, not too close together. Cover canner.

3. Bring to specified pressure, then start counting the processing time indicated in charts, pages 473 and 474.

4. When processing period has been completed, turn off the heat. Do not open canner until pressure registers zero.

5. Wait two minutes, then open petcock gradually. Remove cover from canner, tilting so steam can escape away from face and hands.

6. Remove jars, complete seal if necessary, cool upright on cloth or rack, away from drafts.

STEAM PROCESSING IN CANNER

This method may be used for fruits, tomatoes and sauerkraut. *Not recommended for other vegetables.*

1. Arrange jars on rack in pressure canner, add hot water to shoulders of jars.

2. Cover canner, leaving the vent open. Bring water to a boil.

3. Count processing time from when steam pours steadily from open vent. Time requirements are the same as for Boiling Water Bath, Hot Pack (see Fruit Canning Chart, page 473).

EQUIPMENT

Jars, tops and rubber rings must be in perfect condition. Even the smallest flaw may cause the canned food to leak or spoil.

TO TEST BEFORE CANNING

Fill jars with water, adjust rubber ring and cover, and invert. If jar leaks it is imperfect. The tests following should also be observed.

JARS, AND VACUUM-SEAL DOME-LID JARS

Test by examining sealing surface. The top edge of jars must be smooth.

GLASS-TOP JARS

Fit top to jar. If top rocks when tapped, it should not be used on that jar. The upper clamp should not be too tight or too loose. Bend it until it goes into place with a light snap.

SCREW-TOP JARS

Use only enameled, lacquered, zinc porcelain-lined or glass-inset tops. Screw the top on tightly without the rubber. If thumb nail can be inserted between top and jar, the top is defective.

RUBBER RINGS

Buy new ones every year. Fold the ring and press tightly. Then turn it over and reverse, fold in same place. A perfect rubber will show no crease or break.

TO STERILIZE CANNING EQUIPMENT

Wash jars, covers and rubbers. Place jars on their sides in a pan of cold water, bring water to boil and boil 10 minutes. Covers, except the self-sealing type with sealing compound, may be sterilized with jars or separately. Let stand in hot water until time to fill. Lift with sterilized tongs or a skimmer and invert on towel to drain. Boil rubbers for 2 minutes only. Cups, spoons, and other utensils should be dipped into boiling water to sterilize. Check the manufacturer's instructions for using other types of jars and closures.

TESTING JARS AFTER CANNING

After processing, lift jars from canner one at a time and complete the seal at once if jars are not self-sealing type.

Place jars with freshly canned fruit or vegetables upright on a cloth or board with spaces between so they may cool quickly. Shield from drafts, to prevent their cracking. Tip jars to test seal. If jars leak, remove cover and examine. If cover is not perfect, use another which has been sterilized. In cold pack method, screw on loosely and process or sterilize again 10 minutes. If cover is perfect, and rubber imperfect, place new one on jar, replace cover, and sterilize 10 minutes. If rubber is bulged out, press rubber back in shape while hot, invert, and if jar leaks, place new rubber on jar and sterilize 10 minutes.

TO TEST FOR A PERFECT SEAL

Next day, or when jars are cold, test by turning the jar over in your hands. Or, if jar has a flat, metal lid, test it by tapping the center of the lid with a spoon. A clear, ringing sound means a good seal. Lid will also be curved slightly inward. In both Hot Pack and Cold Pack Methods, self-sealing caps are screwed tightly.

LABELING

When jars have been tested and are ready to be stored, wipe them with a wet cloth, dry, and label with name of product and date.

STORAGE

A cool, dark, dry place is best for storing canned goods. *Jars may be stored on shelves or in boxes in which jars were bought.* Place jars of berries on their sides for several days before storing, and turn them frequently. This keeps the berries from "floating."

FRUIT YIELD

Each of the following makes 1 quart canned fruit:

	Pounds
Apples	2½ to 3
Berries, except strawberries	1½ to 3
	(*1-2 qt. boxes*)
Cherries (canned unpitted)	2 to 2½
Peaches	2 to 3
Pears	2 to 3
Plums	1½ to 2½
Tomatoes	2½ to 3½

SYRUP FOR CANNING FRUIT

Use thin syrup for sweet fruit, medium syrup for moderately sweet fruit, thick syrup for sour fruit. Allow 1 cup of syrup for every quart of small fruit, 1½ cups of syrup for every quart of large fruit.

THIN SYRUP: 2 cups sugar, 4 cups water. Yield: 5 cups.

MEDIUM SYRUP: 4 cups sugar, 4 cups water. Yield: 5¾ cups.

THICK SYRUP: 8 cups sugar, 4 cups water. Yield: 6½ cups.

Stir sugar and water over low heat until sugar is dissolved. Heat slowly to the boiling point and boil gently without stirring from 1 to 5 minutes. Honey may be substituted for one-half of the sugar, corn syrup for one-third.

CANNING FRUIT WITHOUT SUGAR

Pick over, wash and cut up the large fruit. Pack fruit very tightly in hot jars, filling jars full. Put rubbers on jars. Set jars and covers on rack in canner or kettle. Add enough water to cover bottom of rack. Cover pan and heat water gradually to boiling point. Boil 20 minutes. Fruit will shrink. Use fruit in one jar to fill the other jars. Place hot covers on jars, screwing them not quite tight. Replace jars in kettle. Add boiling water to cover. Cover kettle and process for length of time indicated for Boiling Water Bath (Hot Pack) see chart, page 473. Fruit may be sweetened and used for jams, pies, puddings, sauces and salads.

TO PREVENT FRUIT DISCOLORING

Light-colored fruits such as apples, peaches and pears can be helped to retain their natural color by dropping them as they are prepared into cold water to which has been added 1 tablespoon each of salt and vinegar to each 2 quarts of water. Or ascorbic acid may be added to the water or to the syrup in which the fruit is packed. See product label for directions.

CANNING VEGETABLES

Most vegetables have a low-acid content. They require a higher processing temperature than fruits, and canning under pressure is the only method advised for any vegetables except tomatoes.

Some vegetables do not can well. Broccoli, Brussels sprouts, cabbage, cauliflower, rutabagas and turnips tend to discolor, and may develop a strong flavor.

Peas, lima beans and corn need 1 inch of head space at the top of the jar for expansion during cooking; other vegetables require only ½ inch.

Vegetables should be cleaned with special care for canning. Any dirt remaining on them may contain harmful bacteria and cause spoilage.

When home-canned low-acid foods are to be served, always boil them in an open pan for 10 to 15 minutes before tasting or serving.

VEGETABLE YIELD

Each of the following makes 1 quart canned vegetable:

	Pounds
Asparagus	2½ to 4½
Beans, lima, in pods	3 to 5
Beans, snap	1½ to 2½
Beets, without tops	2 to 3½
Carrots, without tops	2 to 3
Corn, sweet, in husks (*canned whole kernel style*)	3 to 6
Okra	1½
Peas, green, in pods	3 to 6
Pumpkin or winter squash	1½ to 3
Spinach and other greens	2 to 6
Squash, summer	2 to 4
Sweet potatoes	2 to 3

HOME CANNED TOMATO PULP

Wash tomatoes. Cut them up and boil 30 minutes. Rub pulp through a sieve, add 1 teaspoonful of salt to each quart and cook gently, until thick and reduced to one half of the original bulk, stirring constantly to prevent burning. Put into clean, hot glass jars. Process as for Hot Pack Method in Boiling Water Bath or pressure canner.

Use for making soups and sauces. When ready to use, add ⅔ of the amount of hot water.

HOME CANNED TOMATO JUICE

Cut tomatoes in quarters. Simmer ½ hour. Strain. To each quart of juice add 1 teaspoon salt. **Reheat** and pour boiling hot into hot sterilized jars; fill to overflowing, or leave ¼ inch head space. Process as above.

HOME CANNED YELLOW TOMATO JUICE

Use any yellow tomatoes, removing stems. Wash, core if large, and cut into thick slices. If pear-shaped, or small and round, cut in half. Proceed as above.

HOME CANNED TOMATO SOUP

  1 peck ripe tomatoes
  4 onions, sliced
  12 sprigs parsley
  2 bay leaves
  1 teaspoon peppercorns
  1 teaspoon celery seed
  1 teaspoon cloves, heads removed
  2 tablespoons salt
  1 tablespoon sugar

Wipe tomatoes and quarter. Tie spices in a bag. Combine all ingredients and heat very slowly; simmer for ½ hour. Strain, reheat and bring to the boiling point. Pour into sterilized air-tight jars to overflowing and process like Home Canned Tomato Pulp, preceding. Use for meat, fish or vegetable gravies or for soups.

HOME CANNED VEGETABLE SOUP

  1 quart carrots, diced
  1 quart onions, diced
  1 quart potatoes, diced
  2 quarts tomatoes
  1 quart green beans, sliced
  3 chopped green peppers
  1 quart wax beans, sliced
  1 quart celery, diced
  1 quart corn, cut from cob
  1 quart cauliflower, in pieces

Wash, pare and dice carrots, onions and potatoes. Scald tomatoes, dip in cold water, remove skins and slice. Cut beans in ½-inch pieces. Scald peppers, remove stems, seeds, and chop. Mix all vegetables, add boiling water to cover. Boil 5 minutes. Pack at once, hot as possible, into clean, hot jars. Adjust new scalded rubbers. Place a teaspoon of salt in each quart jar. Close covers tightly if self-sealing. Process 1 hour in pressure canner at 10 pounds pressure. Remove jars. When ready to serve, add, if desired, a tablespoon butter, a beef cube, or a little soup stock to each pint.

See canning charts, pages 474-475.

FRUIT	PREPARATION	COLD PACK METHOD
Apples	Pare, core and cut into halves, quarters, or smaller pieces.	Pack raw at once in clean hot jars. Cover with boiling hot thin syrup. Process at once.
Apple Sauce	See recipe, page 260.	
Raspberries Blackberries Blueberries Huckleberries	Pick over, wash and hull. Drain.	Pack raw in clean hot jars. Cover with boiling hot medium syrup. Process at once.
Strawberries	Pick over, wash and stem.	
Cherries	Wash, stem and remove pits.	Pack raw in clean hot jars. Cover with boiling hot syrup, using thick syrup for sour cherries, and medium for sweet. Process immediately.
Peaches Apricots Nectarines	Pour boiling water over until skins loosen. Dip in cold water, remove, peel. Cut in halves or slices. Remove pits.	Pack raw in clean hot jars. Cover with medium syrup, boiling hot. Process immediately.
Pineapples	Cut in thick slices, pare, cut in small slices to the core.	Pack raw in clean hot jars. Cover with medium syrup, boiling hot. Process immediately.
Pears	Wash, pare, if desired. Small pears may be canned whole or cut in halves or quarters.	Pack raw in clean hot jars. Cover with medium syrup, boiling hot. Process immediately.
Plums	Wash, stone if desired. If left whole, prick.	Pack raw in clean hot jars. Cover with medium syrup, boiling hot. Process immediately.
Rhubarb	Wash, cut into ½-inch pieces with sharp knife. Add ½ cup sugar to each qt. fruit. Let stand to draw out juices, bring to boil. or, Measure the rhubarb, place it in a baking dish and add ¼ as much sugar by measure as rhubarb. Cover and bake in the oven at 350° F. for 30 or 35 minutes or until the rhubarb is tender, but whole.	
Tomatoes	Pour boiling water over until skins loosen. Dip in cold water. Cut out stem core, slip off skins. Leave whole or cut in pieces.	Pack raw in clean hot jars. Cover with hot tomato juice. Add 1 teaspoon salt to each quart. Process immediately.

CHART

| HOT PACK METHOD | PROCESSING IN MINUTES
Boiling Water Bath (212° F.) | | | | In Pressure Canner at 5 Pounds Pressure |
| | Cold Pack | | Hot Pack | | |
	Pints	Quarts	Pints	Quarts	
Boil in thin syrup. Pack hot. Cover with syrup. Adjust covers. Process.	25	30	15	20	10
Pack at once as hot as possible into hot scalded jars. Process at once.			10	10	5
Precook berries in just enough medium syrup or fruit juice to prevent sticking to pan. Pack hot. Cover with hot syrup. Process.	10	15	10	15	10
To each quart add 1 cup of sugar. Let stand 5 to 6 hours in cool place. Heat slowly until sugar dissolves and berries are hot. Pack while hot into hot jars leaving ½ inch head space.			10	15	5
Or remove pits, add sugar as desired, bring to boil and pack. Process immediately.	20	25	10	15	10
Precook in medium syrup. Pack hot. Cover with hot syrup. Process at once.	25	30	15	20	10
Precook, as for Peaches.	25	30	15	20	10
Or if pears are hard or whole, cook for 4 to 8 minutes in boiling hot medium syrup. Pack hot in jars and cover with boiling syrup. Process immediately.	25	30	20	25	10
Or, put medium syrup in preserving kettle. Add plums, pitted. Let come to a boil. Pack at once into hot jars, leaving ½-inch space at top of jar. Process at once. For sour plums, use thick syrup.	25	30	20	25	10
Pack as hot as possible in hot jars. Process immediately.			10	10	5
Heat to boiling. Pack hot. Add 1 teaspoon salt to each quart.	35	45	10	15	15

VEGETABLE CANNING CHART

| VEGE-TABLE | PREPARATION | HOT PACK METHOD | PROCESSING IN MINUTES Pressure Canner at 10 Pounds Pressure | |
			½ Pints and Pints	1½ Pints and Quarts
Asparagus	Wash, remove tough ends, cut to fit jar, tie in bundles, or cut in half-inch lengths.	Place bundles in saucepan with boiling water over lower tough portion, cover tightly and boil 4 or 5 minutes. Place hot as possible in clean, sterile jars, tip end up. Add 1 teaspoon salt to each quart jar, and cover with boiling liquid. Seal tightly. Process at once. Or, place half-inch lengths in saucepan, cover with boiling water. Bring to boil and pack at once in clean, scalded jars. Add salt. Cover with boiling liquid. Process immediately.	25	30
Beans, Snap or Green	Wash stringless beans. Snap off tips and tails. Leave whole or cut in small pieces crosswise or lengthwise.	Place in saucepan with boiling water to cover. Boil 5 minutes. Pack hot in clean jars. Add 1 teaspoon salt to each quart. Cover with the hot liquid. Process immediately.	20	25
Beans, Lima	Shell and wash. Can only tender beans.	Put in preserving kettle. Cover with boiling water and when boiling, pack at once into clean jars. Add 1 teaspoon salt to each quart. Cover with hot liquid. Process at once.	40	50
Beets	Use baby beets only. Cook in boiling water until skins loosen. Remove skins.	Pack hot as possible in clean, sterile jars. Add 1 teaspoon salt to each quart of beets. Cover with boiling water. Process immediately.	30	35
Carrots	Use only young carrots. Remove tops, scrub. Cook in boiling water until skins loosen. Remove skins.	Pack hot as possible in clean, sterile jars. Add 1 teaspoon salt to each quart of carrots. Cover with boiling water. Process immediately.	25	30
Corn	Use only tender, young sweet corn. Remove husk and silk. Cut from cob.	Place in saucepan with boiling water to cover. Heat to boiling. Pack hot as possible in clean, sterile jars to within 1 inch of top. Add 1 teaspoon salt and 1 tablespoon sugar to each quart jar and process immediately.	55	85
Greens	Pick over, wash in several waters until free from sand. Cook only until wilted or steam, page 32.	Pack at once in clean, sterile jars. Add boiling water to cover and 1 teaspoon salt to a quart. Process immediately.	70	90
Peas	Use only tender, young peas. Shell and wash.	Place in saucepan with boiling water to cover. Heat to boiling. Pack hot as possible in clean, sterile jars. Add 1 teaspoon salt and 1 tablespoon sugar to each quart jar. Process immediately.	40	40
Pumpkin, Squash	Cut in half, then in strips. Remove stringy center and seeds.	Steam until tender, put through colander to remove rind and stringy fiber. If not hot, reheat. Pack hot as possible in clean, sterile jars. Add 1 teaspoon salt to each jar and process immediately.	65	80
Sweet Peppers	Leave skins on. Steam 5 minutes. Stem and seed.	Pack hot in ½-pint jars. Add ¼ teaspoon salt, boiling water. Seal. Process at once.	35	Not recommended
Sweet Potatoes	Boil or steam until skins come off easily, peel quickly. Cut into quarters.	Pack hot as possible in clean, sterile jars. Cover with fresh boiling water. Process immediately.	65	95

BOILING WATER BATH

VEGE-TABLE	PREPARATION	HOT PACK METHOD	½ Pints and Pints	1½ Pints and Quarts
Pimientos	Use whole, ripe Spanish peppers. Remove skins, as in recipe, page 467.	Pack hot in scalded ½-pint jars. Add ½ teaspoon salt. No water. Process at once.	45 min.	60 min.
Sauerkraut	Follow recipe, page 455. When fermented, pack and process.	Put sauerkraut in saucepan. Cover with its own brine. Heat to boiling. Pack in clean, scalded jars, adding salt water, if necessary, to cover. Close jars tight; process immediately.	30 min.	30 min.
Tomatoes	See Fruit Canning Chart, page 472.			

DRYING FRUITS AND VEGETABLES

OVEN DRYING

A very slow oven (never above 150° F.) may be used for drying. Spread foods on paper, platters, or metal sheets covered with cheesecloth. The oven door must be left open a few inches.

DRYING APPLES, PEARS OR QUINCES

Pare, core and cut the fruit in eighths, or core and slice in rings, ¼ inch thick. As soon as a small amount is ready, dip for a minute in salt water, 3 tablespoons salt to a gallon of water, to prevent discoloration. Drain and dry on cheesecloth. Spread on trays, dripping pans or platters, or spread cheesecloth on oven racks. Set thermostat at 150° F. with oven door propped open. The fruit will be done when it is so dry that it is impossible to press water out of the freshly cut ends, but not so dry that it will snap or crackle. This will take from 4 to 6 hours. Cool quickly. Store in paper bags, tie with string, and coat bags with melted paraffin, or use moisture-proof, plastic bags. Store in a tightly closed tin container. Pears and quinces may be steamed 10 minutes before drying.

TO COOK DRIED FRUIT

Soak 6 to 8 hours, or overnight, using 3 parts of water to 1 part fruit. Thinly sliced apples need only 2 hours' soaking.

DRYING MUSHROOMS

Mushrooms should not be peeled. Trim and slice as soon as possible after collecting. Cut the stems crosswise. They should be dried quickly. Spread on a board or paper and set in a sunny place, in a very slow (110°-140° F.) oven, or in a warm place, near the furnace for example. Rinse well in cold water before cooking.

MORELS

These mushrooms will dry without slicing; put a string through them and hang them up in the kitchen or any warm, dry place.

DRYING PEPPERS

Hang large whole peppers by their stems on strong string, so they will not touch each other, near a window to dry slowly and evenly.

DRYING SWEET CORN

Only very young and tender corn should be used for drying, and it should be prepared at once after gathering. Cook in boiling water 2 to 5 minutes, long enough to set the milk. Cut the kernels from the cob with a sharp knife, taking care not to cut off pieces of the cob. Spread thinly on trays, and place in oven to dry. Stir occasionally until dry, from 3 to 4 hours at 110° to 145° F.

TO COOK

Soak the corn for 2 to 4 hours in water, using 2 cups of water to 1 cup of corn. Cook in the water in which it was soaked until tender. Then season with butter, salt, pepper, and sugar.

DRYING PEAS AND BEANS

Allow the peas or beans to mature on the vines. Spread on plates or pans in a sunny room to dry. Stir frequently to prevent molding.

DRYING CELERY LEAVES, PARSLEY, ETC.

Celery tops, parsley, mint, sage, basil, chives and other herbs, onion tops, and cress are easily dried. Wash them well, drain and wipe off the water, place them on racks and dry slowly in the oven.

DRIED TOMATO PASTE

Use ripe, sound, fleshy tomatoes. Wash and cut in thick slices. Sprinkle well with salt, about 1 cup to a bushel. Let tomatoes stand for several hours in a colander. Boil until very soft. Cool and rub through a fine sieve. Place pulp in kettle and simmer until thick enough to hold its shape. Stir often to prevent burning. Spread the paste on a bread board, or similar hard wood scoring the mass a number of times to hasten the drying process. Place in the bright sun on a clear day, or in slightly warm oven. Work the mass frequently with a spatula to aid the drying. When dry, put in pans and allow it to stand for about 4 days. Then cut and roll in small egg-shaped portions. Dip these balls in oil, using olive oil or any other good salad oil. Place them in a stone jar and cover with heavy paper or cloth dipped in oil and salt. If they dry out too much, pour a little oil over them. Will keep indefinitely.

This paste is used in soups, sauces, with macaroni, etc. When ready to use, dissolve a small amount in boiling water.

FRUIT AND VEGETABLE DRYING CHART

Vegetables	Blanching Time (Minutes)	Drying Time (Hours)	Temperature Fahrenheit
Sweet Corn	5 to 10	3 to 4	110 to 145
Carrots	6	2½ to 3	110 to 150
Onions	5	2½ to 3	110 to 140
Pumpkin	3	3 to 4	110 to 140
Celery	3	3 to 4	110 to 140
Swiss Chard	3	3 to 4	110 to 140
Peppers		Dry thoroughly	110 to 145
Spinach	4 to 6	3	110 to 140
Tomatoes	To loosen skin		110 to 145

Fruits	Not Necessary to Blanch	Drying Time (Hours)	Temperature Fahrenheit
Plums	Cut in halves; remove pits.	4 to 6	110 to 145
Apricots	Cut in halves; remove pits.	4 to 6	110 to 150
Peaches	Cut in halves; remove pits.	4 to 6	110 to 150
Apples	Pare, core, slice, dip in salt water.	4 to 6	110 to 150
Quinces	Pare, core, slice, dip in salt water.	4 to 6	110 to 150
Pears	Pare, core, slice, dip in salt water.	4 to 6	110 to 150
Berries	Wash and drain.	6 to 8	110 to 140

25
FOOD AND YOUR
FAMILY'S HEALTH

DAILY NUTRITIONAL GUIDE

For nutrition purposes, foods can be divided into four basic groups. An adequate diet includes at least the minimum number of servings daily from each group. Adolescents, and men and women who do hard physical labor need extra portions, as do women during pregnancy and lactation. Children and adults past middle age need smaller portions but adequate amounts of protein.

THE BASIC-FOUR FOOD GROUPS

	Recommended Daily Amounts	Major Contribution
Milk and Milk Foods: Use fresh, canned, dried milk; cheeses; ice cream.	ADULTS—2 or more cups daily. CHILDREN—3 to 4 cups. TEENAGERS—4 or more cups. PREGNANT WOMEN—4 or more cups. NURSING MOTHERS—6 or more cups.	Principal source of calcium for bones and teeth; also, contains high quality protein, riboflavin, Vitamin A, other nutrients.
Meats and Variety Meats; Poultry; Fish and Shellfish; Eggs: Alternates are nuts, dried beans and peas, although these are less complete protein sources.	Two or more servings daily of 2 to 3 ounces, all edible—without fat or bones—of meat, poultry or fish; or 2 eggs.	Essential proteins to build, repair and regulate formation of all body tissues—muscles, organs, blood, skin and hair.
Vegetables and Fruits: Choose those especially rich in Vitamin A and Vitamin C.	Four or more servings including: One serving of a good source of Vitamin C (citrus fruits, berries) or two servings of a fair source (tomatoes, cabbage). One serving at least every other day of a good source of Vitamin A (deep green or yellow vegetables). A serving is ½ cup cooked vegetable or fruit or an ordinary portion—1 apple, banana or orange, or half a grapefruit.	Major sources of vitamins and minerals, particularly Vitamin C, for healthy tissues such as gums and muscles, and Vitamin A for growth, normal vision, healthy skin.
Breads and Cereals: Whole grain, enriched or restored breads and cereals are recommended. Alternates are pastas, rice.	Four or more servings each day, including one serving of cereal (or five servings if no cereal is included). A serving consists of 1 slice of bread or 6 ounces ready-to-eat cereal; or ½ to ¾ cup cooked cereal, pasta or rice.	Good source of B Vitamins, iron and protein; help release energy from foods, regulate appetite. Promote healthy skin and digestive tract, healthy nerves.

In addition, fats, oils, sugars, foods containing them, and other foods that satisfy the appetite and add variety to the diet, may be consumed in moderation so long as basic nutrition needs are satisfied and calorie allowances not exceeded.

The standard guide to food values needed daily is the following Recommended Daily Dietary Allowances, prepared by the Food and Nutrition Board of the National Research Council. It is intended for persons normally active in a temperate climate.

FOOD AND NUTRITION BOARD, NATIONAL ACADEMY OF SCIENCES—NATIONAL RESEARCH COUNCIL
RECOMMENDED DAILY DIETARY ALLOWANCES,[a] Revised 1974

Designed for the maintenance of good nutrition of practically all healthy people in the U.S.A.

	Age (Years)	Weight (kg)	Weight (lbs)	Height (cm)	Height (in)	Energy (kcal)[b]	Protein (g)	FAT-SOLUBLE VITAMINS				WATER-SOLUBLE VITAMINS							MINERALS					
								Vitamin A Activity (RE)[c]	Vitamin A Activity (IU)	Vitamin D (IU)	Vitamin E Activity[e] (IU)	Ascorbic Acid (mg)	Folacin[f] (µg)	Niacin (mg)	Riboflavin (mg)	Thiamin (mg)	Vitamin B6 (mg)	Vitamin B12 (µg)	Calcium (mg)	Phosphorus (mg)	Iodine (µg)	Iron (mg)	Magnesium (mg)	Zinc (mg)
Infants	0.0–0.5	6	14	60	24	kg × 117	kg × 2.2	420[d]	1,400	400	4	35	50	5	0.4	0.3	0.3	0.3	360	240	35	10	60	3
	0.5–1.0	9	20	71	28	kg × 108	kg × 2.0	400	2,000	400	5	35	50	8	0.6	0.5	0.4	0.3	540	400	45	15	70	5
Children	1–3	13	28	86	34	1,300	23	400	2,000	400	7	40	100	9	0.8	0.7	0.6	1.0	800	800	60	15	150	10
	4–6	20	44	110	44	1,800	30	500	2,500	400	9	40	200	12	1.1	0.9	0.9	1.5	800	800	80	10	200	10
	7–10	30	66	135	54	2,400	36	700	3,300	400	10	40	300	16	1.2	1.2	1.2	2.0	800	800	110	10	250	10
Males	11–14	44	97	158	63	2,800	44	1,000	5,000	400	12	45	400	18	1.5	1.4	1.6	3.0	1,200	1,200	130	18	350	15
	15–18	61	134	172	69	3,000	54	1,000	5,000	400	15	45	400	20	1.8	1.5	2.0	3.0	1,200	1,200	150	18	400	15
	19–22	67	147	172	69	3,000	54	1,000	5,000	400	15	45	400	20	1.8	1.5	2.0	3.0	800	800	140	10	350	15
	23–50	70	154	172	69	2,700	56	1,000	5,000	—	15	45	400	18	1.6	1.4	2.0	3.0	800	800	130	10	350	15
	51+	70	154	172	69	2,400	56	1,000	5,000	—	15	45	400	16	1.5	1.2	2.0	3.0	800	800	110	10	350	15
Females	11–14	44	97	155	62	2,400	44	800	4,000	400	12	45	400	16	1.3	1.2	1.6	3.0	1,200	1,200	115	18	300	15
	15–18	54	119	162	65	2,100	48	800	4,000	400	12	45	400	14	1.4	1.1	2.0	3.0	1,200	1,200	115	18	300	15
	19–22	58	128	162	65	2,100	46	800	4,000	400	12	45	400	14	1.4	1.1	2.0	3.0	800	800	100	18	300	15
	23–50	58	128	162	65	2,000	46	800	4,000	—	12	45	400	13	1.2	1.0	2.0	3.0	800	800	100	18	300	15
	51+	58	128	162	65	1,800	46	800	4,000	—	12	45	400	12	1.1	1.0	2.0	3.0	800	800	80	10	300	15
Pregnant						+300	+30	1,000	5,000	400	15	60	800	+2	+0.3	+0.3	2.5	4.0	1,200	1,200	125	18+[h]	450	20
Lactating						+500	+20	1,200	6,000	400	15	80	600	+4	+0.5	+0.3	2.5	4.0	1,200	1,200	150	18	450	25

a The allowances are intended to provide for individual variations among most normal persons as they live in the United States under usual environmental stresses. Diets should be based on a variety of common foods in order to provide other nutrients for which human requirements have been less well defined.

b Kilojoules (KJ) = 4.2 × kcal.

c Retinol equivalents.

d Assumed to be all as retinol in milk during the first six months of life. All subsequent intakes are assumed to be half as retinol and half as β-carotene when calculated from international units. As retinol equivalents, three-fourths are as retinol and one-fourth as β-carotene.

e Total vitamin E activity, estimated to be 80 percent as α-tocopherol and 20 percent other tocopherols.

f The folacin allowances refer to dietary sources as determined by **Lactobacillus casei** assay. Pure forms of folacin may be effective in doses less than one-fourth of the recommended dietary allowance.

g Although allowances are expressed as niacin, it is recognized that on the average 1 mg of niacin is derived from each 60 mg of dietary tryptophan.

h This increased requirement cannot be met by ordinary diets; therefore, the use of supplemental iron is recommended.

INFANT FEEDING

Sound eating habits begin in infancy. The infant child early comes to associate food with satisfaction, warmth and emotional well-being.

THE FIRST FEEDINGS

Usually a newborn is allowed to rest for the first 12 hours after birth. Then he is offered sweetened water. His first drink is prepared by measuring 3 ounces of water (6 tablespoons) into a bottle. Add one teaspoon of sugar and shake gently to dissolve. Put the nipple on and boil the entire bottle and contents for 10 to 20 minutes.

Cool the water in the bottle to a temperature that is comfortable when you shake a few drops on your wrist. This drink is given more as a "trial run" than because the baby will be thirsty. He may enjoy it, or not. If not, do not force him. One should never force a baby to drink anything.

At about 24 hours of age, a baby receives his first feeding of formula milk unless he is being breast fed, and thereafter he is fed every 3 or 4 hours for the first weeks. The amount of milk taken at the first few feedings does not matter. Do not try to make him eat more than he wants. Whether you are breast or bottle feeding, try to rest comfortably as you feed your baby and make this an enjoyable time for both of you.

THE FORMULAS

If you are not nursing your baby, or if you need a bottle for emergency feedings and do not have a doctor to help you plan the formula, the following sample formulas will be suitable for most babies.

	FIRST FORMULA		LATER FORMULAS	
Evaporated milk	6 ounces	10 ounces	13 ounces.	
Water (boiled)	10 ounces	15 ounces	19 ounces.	
Sugar or corn syrup	1½ tablespoons	2½ tablespoons	3 tablespoons.	

or

	FIRST FORMULA		LATER FORMULAS	
Fresh whole milk (boiled)	12 ounces	20 ounces	26 ounces.	
Water (boiled)	4 ounces	6 ounces	6 ounces.	
Sugar or corn syrup	1½ tablespoons	2½ tablespoons	3 tablespoons.	

For the first feedings, divide the formula into 8 bottles of 2 ounces each, or into 6 bottles of about 2½ ounces each. As soon as he drinks all the milk in the bottle at most feedings, increase the amount in each bottle by half an ounce to one ounce. When he begins to sleep through a nighttime feeding, prepare one less bottle and divide the extra formula among the other bottles. Soon, however, the baby will probably show—by more frequent hunger cries—that he is ready for an increase in the total amount of his feeding and in the milk proportion; change the formula to give him more. By the fifth or sixth day, he should be offered about 3 ounces at a feeding.

Shift gradually from one formula to the next, keeping the proportion of water to milk about the same as shown in the samples above. Do not increase the amount of sugar or corn syrup in a day's feeding to more than 3 level tablespoons unless your doctor advises it. Formulas may also be made with special preparations from the drugstore which need only the addition of water.

After the first week or two of life, your baby will probably take about 1 ounce of evaporated milk, or 1½ to 2 ounces of fresh milk (properly diluted with water) per pound of his weight. That is, a 10-pound baby will probably take about 10 ounces of evaporated milk, or 20 ounces of fresh whole milk daily.

After the baby begins to take solid food, gradually cut down on the water and sugar in his formula, until he is getting equal parts of evaporated milk and water with no sugar, or undiluted fresh whole milk, or skim milk if he is gaining weight too rapidly or has difficulty in digestion.

ADDITIONAL FOODS

By the time the baby is three months old, he should be receiving supplemental vitamin D and probably vitamin A and vitamin C in the form of orange juice or a substitute. The formula-fed baby should receive 2 to 4 ounces of orange juice or 4 or more ounces of tomato juice; the breast-fed baby may be given this much but does not require the additional vitamin C if his mother's intake is good.

SOLID FOOD

As early as six weeks, the baby may be ready to try solid food—strained fruit, cereal, or egg yolk. Begin with a teaspoon at a time, and mix food with formula to thin it. Most babies reject any solid food at first. Avoid making an issue of getting the food into the baby and try again the next day. Eventually he will learn to manage it and will like it. Increase his daily intake, little by little, until he is taking about 5 tablespoons of cereal, or 4 tablespoons of fruit. Introduce new kinds of cereal and fruit from time to time, to accustom him to a variety of flavors.

Soon after becoming accustomed to fruits, cereals and egg yolk, the baby will be ready to try strained vegetables and meats. Hard toast and zwieback should be introduced when the baby's first tooth appears. By the time the child is about nine months old, he should be eating three meals a day and beginning to share a number of simple foods from the family table.

SPECIAL RECIPES FOR INFANTS

VEGETABLE MEAT SOUP

¼ pound lamb shoulder or beef soup bone
3 pints water
2 tablespoons rice
1 tablespoon pearl barley
1 potato
2 carrots
1 onion
2 stalks celery
salt

Bring meat and water to a quick boil. Skim. Rinse rice and barley and add. Simmer 2 hours. Dice and add vegetables. Simmer 1 hour, add salt and strain.

This will keep 3 or 4 days if kept refrigerated and the entire quantity brought to a boil before each serving.

TOMATO JUICE

To prepare tomato juice, slice tomatoes and add very little water, boil 10 minutes and strain. Canned tomatoes, strained to remove the pulp and seeds, can be used.

BEEF JUICE

Cut ½ pound round steak into small squares. Broil until slightly brown. Squeeze out the juice into a warmed cup. Season with salt. Prepare only enough to serve; this does not keep well.

SCRAPED BEEF

Cut a piece of tender steak ½ inch thick. Lay it on a meat board and with a dull table knife or spoon scrape off the soft part from the tough, stringy fibers. Season the pulp with salt, make into little flat, round patties ½ inch thick, and broil them 2 minutes in the broiling oven or in a very hot frying pan.

GROUND BEEF PATTIES

Put beef, preferably top round, through the fine grinder. Season with salt. Mold lightly into patties and broil as above.

PRUNE PULP

Stew ½ pound prunes in 2 cups of water until quite soft and then rub them through a coarse sieve. Put this pulp back in the water in which the prunes were cooked, add one teaspoon sugar and boil for about ten minutes.

PRUNE JUICE

Wash thoroughly ½ pound of prunes, cover with cold water and soak overnight. In the morning, place on stove in same water, cook gently until tender; strain.

BARLEY WATER

Mix one level tablespoonful of Barley Flour (obtain from druggist) with a little cold water, making a paste. When perfectly smooth, add two cups of salted water. Boil in double boiler ½ hour. Add additional boiled water to make two cups. May be kept several days in refrigerator.

RICE WATER

Wash 1 heaping tablespoonful of rice, soak overnight, drain and add a pinch of salt. Cook in a double boiler for 3 or 4 hours or until the grains of rice are quite soft, adding water to keep the quantity up to two cups. Strain through muslin.

OAT WATER

Add 1 level tablespoonful of rolled, ground or crushed oatmeal to one pint of water, boil 3 hours in a double boiler, add enough water to make 2 cups and strain. Salt to taste.

OATMEAL GRUEL

½ cup oatmeal
1 teaspoon salt
3 cups boiling water
milk

Add the oatmeal and salt to the boiling water, and cook thoroughly in a double boiler. Strain and dilute with milk or cream.

CRACKER GRUEL

4 tablespoons powdered cracker crumbs
½ teaspoon salt
1 cup boiling water
1 cup milk

Bring to a boil and serve.

BABY'S SOFT CUSTARD

1 egg yolk
1 teaspoon sugar
few grains salt
1 teaspoon cool, boiled water
½ cup milk

Mix egg yolk, sugar and salt well. Add water and blend thoroughly. Bring milk to a boil. Add to egg mixture gradually, stirring constantly. Pour into top of small double boiler and cook over hot water, stirring constantly until mixture coats the spoon— about 3 minutes. Cool and store in refrigerator. Makes 3 to 4 portions.

CORNSTARCH PUDDING (BLANC MANGE)

1 to 1½ tablespoons cornstarch
2½ tablespoons sugar
few grains salt
¼ cup cold milk
¾ cup boiled milk
¼ teaspoon vanilla

Mix together cornstarch, sugar and salt. Add cold milk and blend well. Add boiled milk slowly, stirring constantly. Pour into double boiler and cook over boiling water, stirring constantly until smooth and thickened. Cover and cook for 15 minutes, stirring occasionally. Add vanilla. Pour into custard cups. Cool. Store in refrigerator. Makes 4 small portions. Use smaller quantity of cornstarch at first, gradually increasing the amount. Brown sugar may be used in place of granulated, using 1 or 2 additional teaspoons. For a child over 2 years, add 2 tablespoons cocoa and ½ tablespoon more sugar, for chocolate pudding.

APPLESAUCE

6 apples
1 cup cold water
1 teaspoon sugar

Pare 6 apples and cut them into quarters. Place them in a saucepan, add 1 cup cold water, and boil apples about 30 minutes. Strain, and sprinkle with 1 teaspoon of sugar before serving.

DIET FOR THE TODDLER AND PRESCHOOL CHILD

The year-old child sometimes prefers solid foods to liquids, and refuses milk, which can be given to him in thickened soups, custards, and other milk puddings. Dried skim milk can be added to cooked cereal or mashed potato. If, on the other hand, the older infant prefers liquids and refuses solid foods, the intake of milk may be cut to a pint a day for a short time, until he learns to eat other foods.

A good daily intake for a year-old child includes:

1 to 1½ pints of milk
2 or more kinds of fruit
(one a good source of vitamin C)
2 or more vegetables
lean meat, poultry or fish
1 egg
cereal and bread
butter or margarine
simple dessert
vitamin D source

One or two tablespoons of solid food make a serving at this age. His food should be in three meals and three snacks. From 18 months to two years, 1½ pints or more milk are taken daily. He will still need 300 to 400 units of vitamin D daily. Children in the preschool years continue in the same diet pattern but the variety of foods can be greater and quantities larger. The pulp of fresh fruits may be added. Orange sections may be given instead of juice. Crisp foods are introduced gradually: Bacon, raw celery, lettuce and strips of carrot are finger foods which toddlers enjoy.

FOOD FOR YOUNG SCHOOL CHILDREN

Daily meals for school-age children should include the following:

1. Milk at every meal, as a drink, if possible
2. Another protein-high food, such as meat, fish, poultry, cheese or an egg, in each meal
3. Raw fruit and raw vegetable—at least one serving at each meal. Include citrus fruit and juices and tomato juice as often as possible.
4. Cooked vegetables, at least two good servings daily, especially dark green and bright yellow vegetables.
5. Enriched or whole-grain cereals and breads, three or four servings
6. Mildly sweet desserts, of milk and eggs, or fruit, or a combination of these
7. A vitamin D preparation

FOOD FOR ADOLESCENTS

Adolescents need more than three meals a day, as they are in the period when their greatest growth is taking place. The basic food plan remains the same as for younger children, but extra foods are eaten as snacks. These additional foods should contribute to the overall nutritive needs of the adolescent, and should as often as possible include milk, protein foods and fruits and vegetables.

ADULT FOOD NEEDS

The young adult, 20 to 25 years old, needs much the same kinds of food as the adolescent, including milk, but smaller amounts of all these foods. When active growth stops, many adults also become less active physically, which means that still fewer calories are required in the daily diet.

The mature adult should cut down on the amounts of food consumed at meal times, and also on the quantity and frequency of snacks. With increasing years, the daily calorie intake needs to be still further reduced in order to avoid weight gain. However, it is of vital importance to the health and vitality of older people that their reduced calorie intake should not mean any reduction of the major food values, particularly proteins, vitamins and minerals, in their daily diet.

SPECIAL DIETS

HELP FOR WEIGHT WATCHERS

A gain in weight means that more food is being eaten than the body is using up as energy each day. Food is measured in terms of its energy value by calories. Each gain of 1 pound in weight means that approximately 3,500 calories have been eaten in excess of the body's needs, and the excess has been stored as fat. To lose a pound it is necessary to cut calories below the body's needs in order to use up the stored excess. It is best to plan on losing weight gradually. Many different special reducing diets have been suggested as temporary ways to lose weight. None of these work over a long period of time unless habits of eating are altered, first to lose weight, and then to maintain it at a sound level. Special reducing diets should be undertaken only after consultation with a physician. However, it is possible for anyone to eat the basic foods indicated as daily requirements and to maintain good health with as few as 1200 calories a day, which is low enough in most cases for a regular, gradual weight loss. The amounts of proteins, vitamins and minerals needed daily should be maintained while calories are reduced. This is best done through a diet including lean meats, poultry, fish or eggs, fruits and vegetables, and skim milk or low-calorie cheeses.

CALORIE CHART

The calorie values on the chart which follows are necessarily averages. They represent the most accurate generalization possible, according to government and other authoritative nutrition sources. The calorie count of foods may be arrived at by calculating the calories in the basic components. These consist of proteins and carbohydrates, generally calculated at 4 calories per gram, and fats, calculated at 9 calories per gram. Calories of wines or liquors are calculated on the basis of alcoholic content (½ the proof equals the percentage of alcohol) at 7 calories per gram. There are 28.3 grams to an ounce.

BREADS & CEREALS & PASTA	Calories
Baking powder biscuit—2½" diameter	140
Bran muffin—1 medium	106
Bread, rye—1 slice	55
Bread, white—1 slice	60
Bread, whole wheat—1 slice	55
Bread crumbs, fine—1 cup	345
Cornbread—2" square	140
Cornflakes—¾ cup	65
Cracker, graham—1 2½" cracker	14
Cracker, salted—1 2" cracker	17
Cracker, soda—1 2½" cracker	25
Cream of Wheat, cooked—¾ cup	129
Farina, cooked—1 cup	100
Flour—1 cup	400
Griddle cakes—1 4" diameter	60
Macaroni, cooked—1 cup	190
Macaroni and cheese—1 cup	470
Muffin—1 medium 2¾" diameter	140
Noodles—1 cup, cooked	200
Oatmeal, cooked—1 cup	130
Pizza, cheese—1 section, 5½" diameter	185
Popcorn (butter & salt)—1 cup	65
Puffed rice or wheat—1 cup	55
Rice, white or brown, cooked—1 cup	185
Roll, Parker House—1 average	115
Roll, white, hard—1 average	160
Rye wafer—2	45
Shredded Wheat—1 large biscuit	100
Spaghetti, plain, cooked—1 cup	155
Waffles—1 6" diameter	210

DAIRY PRODUCTS & EGGS	
Butter or margarine—1 pat	50
Butter or margarine—1 tablespoon	100
Buttermilk—1 cup	90
Cheese, Cheddar or American—1" cube	70
Cheese, Cottage—½ cup	120
Cheese, Cream—1 ounce	105
Cheese, Swiss—1 ounce	105
Chocolate milk drink—1 cup	190
Cream, coffee—2 tablespoons	60
Cream, heavy—2 tablespoons	110
Cream, sour—2 tablespoons	110
Egg, boiled—1 medium	80
Egg, fried with 1 tsp. fat—1 medium	113
Egg, scrambled—1 medium	110
Margarine—1 tablespoon	100
Milk, skim—1 cup	90
Milk, whole fresh—1 cup	160
Yogurt, plain—1 cup	120

FRUITS	
Apple—medium	70
Apple juice—1 cup	120
Apricots, canned, sweetened—4 halves with juice	105
Apricots, dried—4	39
Apricots, fresh—3 medium	55
Avocado—½ medium	185
Banana—1 medium	85
Blackberries—1 cup	85
Blueberries—1 cup	85
Cantaloupe—½ of 5" melon	60
Cherries, canned—½ cup	115
Cherries, fresh—½ cup	40
Cranberry sauce—2 tablespoons	50
Dates—3 or 4	85
Figs, dried—1 large	60
Figs, fresh—3 small	90
Fruit cocktail, canned—½ cup	97
Grapefruit—½ medium	55
Grapefruit juice, unsweetened—1 cup	95
Grape juice—1 cup	165
Grapes, green, seedless—1 cup	95
Grapes, Malaga or Tokay—1 cup	95
Honeydew melon—¼ medium melon	35
Lemon—1 medium	20
Nectarine—1 average	40
Orange—1 medium	75
Orange juice—1 cup	110

	Calories
Peaches, canned—2 halves with juice	90
Peaches, fresh—1 large	50
Pears, canned—2 halves with juice	90
Pears, fresh—1 medium	100
Pineapple, canned—1 slice with juice	90
Pineapple, fresh—1 cup, diced	75
Plum—1 medium, 2" diameter	25
Prune juice—1 cup	200
Prunes, dried—1 large	17
Prunes, stewed—4 medium with juice	75
Raisins, seedless—¼ cup	115
Raspberries, fresh—½ cup	35
Raspberries, frozen—½ cup	110
Rhubarb, stewed—½ cup, sweetened	192
Strawberries, fresh—1 cup	55
Strawberries, frozen—½ cup, sweetened	124
Tangerine—1 average	40
Watermelon—1 slice 4" x 8"	115

VEGETABLES	
Artichokes—1 medium	45
Asparagus—8 stalks	25
Baked beans with pork, canned—½ cup	160
Beans, dried, cooked—½ cup	100
Beans, green, cooked—½ cup	15
Beets—½ cup	25
Broccoli—⅔ cup or 1 large stalk	26
Brussels sprouts—6 or ½ cup	22
Cabbage—½ cup, chopped	12
Cabbage, cooked—½ cup	15
Carrots—1 medium, raw	20
Carrots, cooked—½ cup	22
Cauliflower, cooked—1 cup	25
Celery—2 medium stalks	10
Chickory or curly endive—10 small leaves	10
Coleslaw—1 cup	120
Corn, cream-style—½ cup	85
Corn, fresh—1 medium ear	70
Cucumber—½ medium	15
Green pepper, or red—1 medium	15
Kale, cooked—1 cup	30
Lettuce—¼ large head	15
Lima beans—½ cup	90
Mushrooms, canned—½ cup	20
Mushrooms, fresh—10 small	15
Okra—10 pods	30
Onion—1 2½" diameter	40
Onions, green (scallions)—5 medium	25
Parsley, chopped—1 tablespoon	1
Parsnips, cooked—1 cup	100
Peas, canned—½ cup	82
Peas, fresh cooked—½ cup	55
Potato, baked—1 average	90
Potato, boiled—1 average	90
Potato chips—10 large	115
Potato, sweet, baked—1 average	155
Potatoes, French fried—10 pieces	155
Potatoes, mashed, (milk and butter added),—1 cup	185
Radish—1 medium	1
Sauerkraut—1 cup	45
Spinach, cooked—½ cup	20
Squash, summer, cooked—½ cup	15
Squash, winter, cooked—½ cup	65
Tomato juice—1 cup	45
Tomatoes, canned—1 cup	50
Tomatoes, fresh—1 medium	35
Turnip greens, cooked—1 cup	25
Turnips, cooked—1 cup	35
Vegetable juice—1 cup	45
Water cress—1 bunch	10
Zucchini, cooked—1 cup	30

MEATS AND POULTRY	
Bacon, crisp—1 6" strip	50
Beef, corned—3 ounces	185
Beef, corned, hash—3 ounces	155
Beef, filet mignon—4 ounces	400
Beef, hamburger—1 large (4 ounces)	325

	Calories
Beef, rib roast—3 ounces	375
Beef, sirloin—3 ounces	330
Beef stew with vegetables—1 cup	210
Beef tongue—3 ounces	210
Bologna—4 x 1″ wedge	85
Chicken, fried, drumstick	90
Chicken, broiled—3 ounces meat	115
Chicken, fried—½ breast	155
Chicken pie—1 pie 4¼″ diameter	535
Chicken salad—½ cup	200
Chili con carne—1 cup canned (no beans)	510
Frankfurters—1 average	155
Ham, baked—3 ounces	245
Ham, boiled—3 ounces	201
Lamb, roast leg—3 ounces	235
Lamb chop, broiled—4 ounces	400
Liver, beef, fried—2 ounces	130
Pork chop, broiled—1 average, 3½ ounces	260
Pork roast—2 slices	310
Sausage, pork—4 ounces	540
Turkey, roasted—2 slices, 4½″ x 2½″ x ¼″	190
Veal chop, loin—1 medium (3 ounces)	185
Veal roast—3 ounces	230

FISH

	Calories
Clams, raw—3 ounces	65
Codfish, fillets in Spanish sauce—3 ounces	100
Crab cakes—1 large (3 ounces)	180
Crabmeat, canned—½ cup	112
Flounder, baked—3 ounces	195
Haddock, fried—3 ounces	140
Halibut, broiled—3 ounces	165
Lobster salad—3 ounces	105
Mackerel, broiled—3 ounces	200
Oysters, raw—6 medium	75
Oyster stew, with milk—1 cup	200
Salmon, canned—3 ounces	120
Salmon, fresh, baked—3 ounces	210
Sardines, canned—3 ounces	175
Shrimp, boiled—3 ounces	70
Shrimp, fried—3 ounces	200
Sole, fried—1 fillet, 3″ x 2″ x ¾″	200
Swordfish, broiled—3 ounces	150
Tuna fish, in oil—½ cup	224
Tuna fish, water packed—½ cup	135
Whitefish (baked)—average serving (3 ounces)	210

DESSERTS AND SWEETS

	Calories
Apple, baked, 2 tablespoons sugar—medium	200
Apple pie—1/6 of 9″ pie	400
Applesauce, unsweetened—½ cup	50
Applesauce, with sugar—½ cup	115
Blueberry pie—1/6 of 9″ pie	370
Brown Betty—½ cup	172
Cake, angel food—3″ slice	165
Cake, butter, with frosting—2″ square	370
Cake, chocolate with frosting—2″ slice	445
Cake, sponge—2″ slice	120
Caramel candy—1 ounce	115
Cherry pie—1/6 or a 9″ pie	414
Chocolate bar—1 ounce	150
Chocolate eclair—1 average size	320
Chocolate fudge—1″ square	115
Chocolate pie—1/6 of 9″ pie, no whipped cream	300
Cookies, sugar—1 3″ cookie	120
Cornstarch pudding, blanc mange—½ cup	135
Cornstarch pudding, chocolate—½ cup	220
Custard—½ cup	142
Custard pie—1/6 of 9″ pie	325
Doughnut, baking powder—1 average	125
Doughnut, yeast—1 average	130
Flavored gelatin dessert—½ cup	70
Gingerbread—2″ cube	175
Honey—1 tablespoon	65
Ice cream, chocolate—½ cup	180
Ice cream, vanilla—½ cup	145

	Calories
Jam or jelly—1 tablespoon	55
Lemon meringue pie—1/6 of 9″ pie	356
Maple syrup—1 tablespoon	55
Marmalade—1 tablespoon	55
Marshmallow—1 ounce	90
Mince pie—1/6 of 9″ pie	340
Molasses—1 tablespoon	50
Pumpkin pie—1/6 of 9″ pie	355
Sherbet—1 cup	260
Sugar, brown—1 tablespoon	45
Sugar, confectioners—1 tablespoon	30
Sugar, granulated—1 tablespoon	45

SOUPS

	Calories
Asparagus soup, cream of, canned—1 cup	110
Bean soup with pork, canned—1 cup	170
Bouillon—1 cup	30
Bouillon—1 cube, or powder package	5
Celery soup, cream of, canned—1 cup	122
Chicken noodle soup—1 cup	65
Clam chowder, Manhattan—1 cup	87
Consomme, canned—1 cup	30
Pea soup, green, canned—1 cup	130
Tomato soup, clear—1 cup	90
Tomato soup, cream, canned—1 cup	125
Vegetable soup (beef base)—1 cup	80

ALCOHOLIC BEVERAGES

	Calories
Beer—12 ounces	144
Bourbon—1½ ounces	120
Brandy—1 ounce	75
Champagne, 3½ ounces	90
Daiquiri cocktail—4 ounces	125
Gin—1½ ounces	107
Manhattan cocktail—4 ounces	167
Martini cocktail—4 ounces	145
Old-fashioned cocktail—4 ounces	185
Rum—1½ ounces	105
Rye whiskey—1½ ounces	120
Scotch whiskey—1½ ounces	105
Tom Collins	180

MISCELLANEOUS

	Calories
Catsup—1 tablespoon	15
Cocoa, all milk—1 cup	235
Coffee, black	none
Cola beverages, regular—8 ounces	95
Corn syrup—1 tablespoon	60
French dressing—1 tablespoon	60
Gelatin, unflavored—1 envelope dry	35
Ginger ale, regular—1 cup	70
Hollandaise sauce—1 tablespoon	60
Lard—1 tablespoon	125
Mayonnaise—1 tablespoon	110
Olive oil—1 tablespoon	125
Olive, green—1 large	5
Olive, ripe—1 large	8
Pickles, dill or sour—1 large	15
Pickles, sweet—2¾″ x ¾″	30
Popcorn, added oil and salt—1 cup	65
Pretzels—5 small sticks	20
Salad oil—1 tablespoon	125
Shortening, homogenized—1 tablespoon	110
Tapioca—1 tablespoon raw	35
Tartar sauce—1 tablespoon	100
Tea, clear, unsweetened	none
Vinegar—1 tablespoon	2
Yeast—1 ounce package or cake	25

NUTS

	Calories
Almonds—12-15 nuts	90
Brazil nuts—¼ cup	229
Cashew nuts—¼ cup	190
Coconut, dried—2 tablespoons	42
Coconut, moist—2 tablespoons	42
Peanut butter—1 tablespoon	95
Peanuts—¼ cup halves	210
Pecans—¼ cup halves	185
Walnuts—¼ cup halves	162

LOW FAT AND LOW CHOLESTEROL DIETS

The individual need for a fat-restricted diet must be determined by a physician. Such a need may result from overeating, with excess calories stored in the body as fat. Fats now account for 40% of the calories in the diet of many Americans, but doctors recommend a general lowering to about 25-30%. Fats have more than twice as many calories per gram as do proteins and carbohydrates. In addition to fats such as butter and margarine, oil and shortening, there are fats in the tissues of meats and poultry, and in foods such as egg yolks, milk and nuts, as well as in baked goods, sauces and other dishes.

A low-cholesterol diet must also be undertaken only upon the advice of a physician. Here a distinction is made between fats of different types: **Saturated** fats, which are generally solid at room temperature and are primarily of animal origin, and **polyunsaturated** fats, which are generally vegetable in origin and are liquid at room temperature.

When an excess of cholesterol in the body is revealed, doctors often recommend reducing or eliminating saturated fats from the diet, and substituting polyunsaturated fats for cooking and table use.

Foods low or lacking in saturated fat content:

Chicken
Cottage cheese (plain, not creamed)
Egg whites
Farmer cheese
Fish
Fruits
Gelatin (fruit flavored)
Grains and cereals (barley, corn meal, farina, oatmeal, rice, wheat flour)
Oils (corn, cottonseed, safflower, sunflower)
Nuts (except Brazil nuts and coconut)
Vegetables

Foods high in saturated fat content:

Butter
Butterscotch
Cakes and pastries
Caramels
Cheese
    (except skim milk cheese)
Chicken fat
Chocolate candies
Cocoa
Coconut and coconut oil
Egg yolks
Frankfurters and sausages
Fried foods
    (in solid fats)
Goose fat
Gravies and sauces
    (especially when thickened)
Ice cream
Lard
Margarine
    (ordinary kinds)
Meat
    (including luncheon meats)
Milk
    (whole)
Potato chips
Shortenings
    (hydrogenated)
Soups
    (creamed types)

ALLERGY DIETS

WHEAT-FREE, EGG-FREE OR MILK-FREE

Due to sensitivity to certain foods, special diets calling for the omission of particular ingredients are sometimes necessary. Wheat, eggs and milk present greater difficulty than less commonly used foods. Diets should be prescribed by a physician. The following suggestions may be helpful in carrying out his orders. **It is advisable that labels on prepared foods or ingredients be carefully read, to avoid foods not permitted.**

Wheat-Free Diets

The following flours and meals may be substituted for 1 cup wheat flour.

    ½ cup barley flour
    1 cup corn flour
    ¾ cup coarse corn meal
    1 scant cup fine corn meal
    ⅝ cup potato flour
    ⅞ cup rice flour
    1¼ cups rye flour
    1 cup rye meal
    1⅓ cups ground rolled oats
    ½ cup rye flour and ½ cup potato flour
    ⅔ cup rye flour and ⅓ cup potato flour
    ⅝ cup rice flour and ⅓ cup potato flour

Coarser meals and flours require more leavening. It is advisable to use 2½ teaspoons of baking powder to each cup of coarse flour. The above or any other combinations of flours permitted may be kept on hand, ready-mixed in the proper proportions. Flour combinations require at least 5 or 6 siftings, and longer, slower baking.

Egg-Free Diets

A standard recipe requiring leavening may be made egg-free by increasing the required amount of baking powder by 1 teaspoon for each egg omitted. Avoid baking powder containing egg white.

Milk-Free Diets

Persons sensitive to milk sometimes tolerate butter, and may be able to take dried, evaporated or hypoallergic milk. Cake pans may be greased with salad oil or other milk-free fats; or coated pans which do not require greasing may be used. Poultry fats and vegetable fats not churned in milk may often be used. Foods containing cheese, buttermilk, sour milk or sour cream should be avoided.

A few of the most commonly used wheat-, egg- or milk-free recipes are listed. Many hundreds of recipes in this book can be used without change, such as fruit and vegetable salads, with French Dressing, fruit gelatins, fresh and stewed fruits and water ices, while others may be adapted by substituting permitted ingredients, such as potato or rice flour for wheat flour, and cornflakes, riceflakes and crisp rye crumbs for bread crumbs.

Wheat-Free Recipes

Norwegian Rye Bread, page 69
Potato Flour Muffins, page 89
Corn Pone, page 89
Rye Yeast Rolls, page 73
Potato Flour Cake, page 123
Oatmeal Crisps, page 159
Oatmeal Lace Cookies, page 161
Coconut Drop Kisses, page 163

Milk-Free Recipes

Rye Yeast Rolls, page 73
Potato Biscuits, page 87
Sponge Cakes, pages 118-122
Buckwheat Cakes, page 92

Egg-Free Recipes

Old-Fashioned Rice Pudding, page 187
Scalloped Apples (Brown Betty), page 192
Prune Pudding, page 193
Apple Tapioca, page 198
Custards, pages 198-200
Honey Bars, page 166
Scotch Cornucopias, page 162
Mandelchen, page 152
Rolled Wafers, page 161
Scotch Shortbread, page 167

Wheat- Egg- Milk-Free Recipes

Chocolate Cornflake Macaroons, page 164
Rye Yeast Rolls, page 73
Apple Snow Balls, page 200

Grateful acknowledgment is made to the American Dietetic Association for permission to reprint part of the above material from "Allergy Recipes."

LOW-SUGAR, LOW-CARBOHYDRATE DIETS

Earlier editions of the *Settlement Cook Book* carried information on low-sugar, low-carbohydrate diets particularly aimed at diabetics. Such a diet should of course not be undertaken without a physician's advice, and the physician will provide all the information the patient needs on the foods to be included in the diet. Since information in this field is constantly being expanded and improved, it has been thought best not to include any specific lists of foods, but to suggest that diabetic patients use the index to this book to find interesting ways to prepare those foods which they are permitted to eat.

SODIUM-RESTRICTED DIETS (LOW SALT)

Some sodium is necessary for good health, and in the normal diet more than enough is obtained from food and beverages. When the doctor advises a restriction of sodium, salt and other ingredients containing sodium are omitted in cooking and, as a rule, foods lower in natural sodium are selected.

There is generally little sodium in fruit; somewhat more in vegetables. Some meats are fairly high in sodium. That portion of meat which is nearest the bone often has the highest sodium content. Salty or smoked meats must be avoided. Dairy products are very rich in sodium.

Foods to avoid include:

Canned vegetables and soups; examine label carefully.
Meat products such as sausage, ham, bacon
Baking powder
Most pickles, mustard, catsup, seasoned salts, bouillon cubes, soup mixes
Commercial breads

Salt substitutes are available, but should be used only with a doctor's recommendation. Many spices and herbs will season food so that the absence of salt will not be missed. Suggestions for seasoning with herbs and spices will be found in the charts on pages 489 and 490-491.

INVALID COOKERY

In preparing food for an invalid or convalescent the following points should be kept in mind:

The food should be served in the most pleasing manner possible. It should be served in small quantities, suit the digestive powers of the patient, and satisfy hunger or furnish needed strength and food values for body repair. In a severe illness the doctor prescribes the kind and amount of food to be given. In long and protracted illness, it is necessary to take nourishing food in small quantities at frequent intervals.

LIQUID DIET

Only fluid foods are used in this diet. It consists of the various beverages, milk, strained broths and soups, gruels, beef juice or extracts, fruit juices, and raw eggs in milk or broth. Suggestions:

Milk, page 52
Chocolate Egg Malted Milk, page 51
Coffee, page 49
Tea, page 50
Cocoa, page 52
Lemonade, page 54
Orangeade, page 54
Milk Punch, page 487
Eggnog, page 58
Fruit Juices, page 436
Barley Water, page 480
Rice Water, page 480
Bouillon, page 394
Consommé, page 394
Chicken Broth, page 394
Oatmeal Gruel, page 480
Cracker Gruel, page 480
Beef Tea, page 487
Strained Gruels, page 480

LIQUID DIET RECIPES

LIME WATER

Pour 2 quarts boiling water over an inch cube unslaked lime; stir thoroughly and let stand overnight; in the morning pour off the liquid that is clear and bottle for use. Keep in refrigerator.

ALBUMENIZED MILK

1 egg white
½ cup milk

Put egg white in a tumbler, add milk, cover tightly, and shake thoroughly until well mixed, or blend in electric blender.

MILK PUNCH

½ cup milk
1 teaspoon sugar
1 tablespoon sherry, whiskey, rum or brandy
a few gratings nutmeg

Mix ingredients, cover and shake well until frothy, or use electric blender.

EGGNOG

1 egg, separated
1 tablespoon sugar
⅛ teaspoon vanilla or
    1 tablespoon sherry, whiskey, rum or brandy
hot or cold milk
nutmeg

Beat yolk and sugar until very light, gradually add the flavoring or liquor, then add egg white, beaten stiff. Pour in a glass and add hot or cold milk. Grate the nutmeg on top.

ORANGE EGGNOG

1 egg, separated
2 tablespoons sugar
1 cup orange juice
½ cup cracked ice

Beat egg yolk and sugar until thick and lemon colored. Add orange juice, stirring constantly, and stiffly beaten egg white. Pour over cracked ice, stir and serve.

CITRUS NOG

1 egg yolk
2 oranges, juice
½ lemon, juice
2 teaspoons honey

Mix ingredients and beat thoroughly, or use electric blender.

PRUNE JUICE DRINK

½ cup prune juice
1 teaspoon lemon juice
Sugar
¾ cup milk

Mix juice with sugar. Add milk gradually. Shake well, or use blender.

LEMONADE OR ORANGEADE

2 tablespoons sugar
1 cup water
Juice of ½ lemon or orange

Combine and stir until dissolved. Or boil sugar and water to a syrup, cool, add juice. Serve hot or cold.

BEEF JUICE

Select ½ pound of beef steak from upper part of round, or the rump. Cut into small pieces. Broil or warm slightly 1 to 2 minutes to set free the juices, then squeeze out the juice by means of a press or lemon squeezer, into a slightly warmed cup. Salt, if necessary, and serve at once. Prepare only enough to serve, as it does not keep well.

SCRAPED BEEF TEA

Scrape ½ pound lean, juicy beef. Put both the scrapings and beef in top of double boiler, with cold water in the lower part, heat gradually, and keep it simmering 1 hour, or until the meat is white. Strain and press out the juice, season with salt to taste, and serve hot.

SHREDDED BEEF TEA

Shred ½ pound lean, juicy beef, and place it in top of a double boiler, with 1 cup of cold water and ½ teaspoon salt. Let it stand 1 hour. Then put boiling water in the lower part of boiler and cook 5 or 10 minutes, until the juice is brown. Strain and press meat to obtain all juice. Serve hot; salt to taste.

CAMBRIC TEA

Pour 1 cup boiling water over 1 teaspoon of tea or tea bag and let steep 3 minutes. Strain into glass or china container. Warm ⅔ cup of milk. Add 1 teaspoon of sugar and 1 teaspoon of the tea infusion. Stir to dissolve sugar.

SOFT OR SEMISOLID DIET

Included in this diet are all foods in the liquid diet and other semisolid or soft foods easily digested. Green vegetables and fresh fruits are omitted, as are solid meats and fish. However, fruit juices and certain puréed fruits, and strained soups made from vegetables, and meat jellies and custards are permitted. Even finely minced, creamed chicken and flaked, creamed fish are sometimes included. Suggestions:

SPECIAL RECIPES

SHREDDED WHEAT WITH MALTED MILK

Warm the biscuit in the oven. Pour 1 cup hot malted milk over it, letting the milk be absorbed.

LIVER SOUP

Add a quarter of a pound of finely ground raw liver to 1 cup of tomato soup or chicken broth. Season with onion if desired. Heat to cook liver.

RED WINE SOUP

1 cup red wine
½ cup water
2 tablespoons sugar
3 whole cloves
3 small sticks cinnamon
1 egg yolk

Boil wine, water and spices 10 minutes and pour boiling hot, gradually, over well-beaten egg yolk. Serve hot or cold.

CREAM WINE SOUP

1 cup white wine
½ cup cold water
7 lumps loaf sugar
3 whole cloves
3 small sticks cinnamon
1 cup sweet cream
2 egg yolks, well beaten

Boil wine, water, sugar and spices for 10 minutes. Heat the cream, pour it gradually while hot over the yolks and then pour in the strained wine mixture, stirring constantly to prevent curdling.

CHICKEN CUSTARD

4 egg yolks
⅛ teaspoon salt
1 cup cream
1 cup strong chicken soup

Beat yolks until thick and lemon colored, add salt, beat into the cream; stir in the hot soup. Pour in small custard cups, place the cups in a pan of hot water, bake 30-45 minutes at 325° F., until custards are firm in center.

RENNET CUSTARD

½ rennet tablet
½ tablespoon cold water
1 cup fresh milk (not canned or soft curd)
2 tablespoons sugar
½ teaspoon vanilla

Dissolve tablet in water. Heat milk until lukewarm, add sugar and flavoring; when sugar is dissolved, add dissolved tablet. Stir quickly, for a few seconds only. Turn into small molds, let stand at room temperature until firm. Then refrigerate.

When rennet powder is used, follow directions on package.

SPICE CHART

Spice	How to Identify	Seasoning Uses
Allspice	Small brown berries or dark brown powder	Fruits, cakes, cookies, beets, spinach, pickles, marinades, pot roast, stews, ketchup, fruit and pumpkin pie; mincemeat
Caraway	Crescent-shaped seeds, striped light and dark brown	Rye bread, rolls, crackers, cheese spreads, coleslaw, cabbage, cauliflower, onions, sauerkraut, pot roasts, pork
Cardamom	Small brown berries or light brown powder	Danish coffee cakes, custard, fruit cup, melon, baked apples, sweet potatoes, squash, pumpkin pies
Cayenne (or Red Pepper)	Orange-red powder	Deviled eggs, egg salad, seafood and barbecue sauces, melted cheese dishes, cheese spreads, fish salads
Celery Seed	Small seed, light to dark brown-green	Soups, meat loaf and stews, fish chowders and stews, coleslaw, pickles, cabbage, potatoes, tomatoes, rolls, stuffings, salads and salad dressing
Chili Powder	Red powder, a blend of ground chilies with other spices and herbs	Arroz con pollo, chili con carne, meat mixtures, shellfish, eggs, seafood cocktail sauces, relishes, French dressing
Cinnamon	Brown, bark-like sticks or rich brown powder	Cakes, cookies, desserts, fruit pies, hot beverages, sweet potatoes, pumpkin, carrots, pickled fruits
Cloves	Dark brown round-headed "nails" or deep brown powder	Smoked meats especially ham, pickled or preserved fruits, apple, mince, pumpkin pie, hot beverages, pickles, cream of tomato or pea soup
Curry Powder	Rich gold powder, a blend of turmeric and other spices	Curry sauces for eggs, meat, fish, shrimp, salted nuts, creamed vegetables, mayonnaise
Ginger	Greyish tan, dried, bulbous root, or light beige powder	Cookies, cakes, Indian puddings, fruits, poultry, pork, Chinese dishes, preserves, beets and carrots
Mixed Pickling Spice	Combination of whole spices and herb leaves	Boiled tongue, ham, corned beef, shrimp, marinades for lamb and beef, pickles, relishes
Mustard	Small brown seed or light yellow powder, or in ready-mixed sauce	Seed in pickles, salad dressing, marinades for meat and fish. Powder in sauces, cream cheese dishes, vegetables, Chinese mustard, deviled eggs. Ready mix for frankfurters, sauces as above.
Nutmeg	Filbert-sized brown "nut" for grating; or copper-colored powder	Cakes and cookies, stewed fruits, pumpkin pie, carrots, sweet potatoes, beans, egg nogs, custards
Paprika	Bright red powder	Hungarian goulash, chicken, veal stews, vegetables, gravy, cheese dishes, deviled eggs, chowders
Pepper, Black	Small black berries, coarsely crushed berries, or finely ground powder	Any non-sweet dish that needs sparkle. Add a speck to apple pie!
Pepper, Crushed Red	Bright orange-red flakes	Pizza, sausages, Italian specialties
Pepper, White	Small pale beige berries or white-beige powder	Use as above, where light color is desirable and less sharp flavor
Poppy Seed	Blue-gray seeds	Sprinkle on bread, rolls, coffee cake, pie crusts, noodles, salad dressings, cake fillings
Saffron	Threads or powder—wine-red	Adds exotic color and flavor to rice, bread, fish stews, Spanish dishes
Sesame	Cream-colored seeds	Sprinkle on rolls, breads, buns, cookies, candies, pie crust, salad dressing, fish, asparagus, beans, tomatoes.
Turmeric	Tan root or orange powder	Pickles, mustard, salad dressings, creamed eggs, fish, seafood. Adds color similar to saffron.

	Bay	Basil	Marjoram	Oregano
APPETIZERS	Tomato juice Pickling	Cheese spreads Tomato juice	Pâté Canapé butters	Pizza Tomato juice
SOUPS	Tomato Beef Chicken	Minestrone Tomato Pea	Spinach Clam Onion	Tomato Bean Onion Vegetable
FISH AND SHELLFISH	Court bouillon for poaching fish	Baked, or broiled fish Shrimp Salmon	Broiled, baked or creamed fish Steamed clams	Stuffings Lobster Creamed fish Shellfish
EGGS AND CHEESE		Scrambled Eggs Cheese Soufflé Spanish Omelet Rarebits	Rarebits Omelets Scrambled Eggs Cheese Soufflés	Boiled Eggs Baked Macaroni Cream and Cottage Cheese
MEAT	Pot roast Sauerbraten Smoked meats	Liver Roast pork Stews Meat pies	Sausage Veal Lamb Meat Loaf Chili	Roast Pork Veal Lamb Meat Loaf Chili
POULTRY, VENISON	Chicken Fricassee Roast duck All venison	Roast poultry Fricassees Goose Venison Stuffings	Creamed Chicken Stuffings Goose Venison	Stuffings Rabbit Venison Goose Turkey
VEGETABLES	Potatoes Carrots Beets	Eggplant Tomatoes Squash Onions	Zucchini Spinach Eggplant Cabbage	Beans Mushrooms Onions Tomatoes Broccoli
SALADS	Tomato Salad dressing	Seafood Greens Chicken Cucumber Potato	Mixed greens Chicken	Avocado Seafood Aspic Greens Bean
SAUCES	Sweet-sour Wine Tomato	Tomato Spaghetti	Sour cream Butter sauce for vegetables Cream sauces Gravies	Tomato Mushroom Spaghetti Barbecue

CHART

Rosemary	Sage	Savory	Tarragon	Thyme

Fruit cup	Cheese spreads	Vegetable juices	Vegetable juices
			Seafood cocktail
			   sauce
				Clam juice
				Sauerkraut juice
				Seafood cocktail
				   sauce

Turtle Chicken Pea Spinach	Fish chowder Tomato	Lentil Bean Chowder	Consommé Chicken Tomato	Borscht Clam chowder Vegetable

Broiled & boiled fish
Stuffings
	Clams
	Fish Stews
		Broiled baked fish
		Crab
			All Fish & Shellfish:
			   broiled, baked,
			   fried
				All Fish & Shellfish:
				   broiled, baked, fried
				Fish stews

Omelets Scrambled Eggs Deviled Eggs	Cottage, Cream or Cheddar Cheese	Omelets Scrambled Eggs Deviled Eggs	Omelets Scrambled Eggs Fried Eggs	Eggs: shirred, fried Cottage Cheese
Ham Loaf Stews Meat Loaf Broiled Meat	Pork Other Roasts Sausages Stuffings Meat Loaf	Baked Ham Pork Veal Spareribs	Roast Beef Steaks Chops Sweetbreads	Meat Loaf Veal kidneys Boiled meat
Game birds Poultry Venison Rabbit	Stuffings Rabbit Venison Goose Turkey	Poultry Venison Stuffings	Stuffings Stews Roast chicken & turkey	Game Birds Chicken Venison Stuffings Stews
Cauliflower Carrots Peas Beans	Onions Corn Peas Beans	Beans: green & limas Dried mushrooms Sauerkraut	Mushrooms Tomatoes Baked Potato	Onions Baked beans Asparagus Beets
Fruit		Vegetable Greens Egg	Flavor vinegar for salad dressings	Coleslaw Beet Chicken Mayonnaise

Cream sauce
Seafood sauces
Marinades
Barbecue sauces
  for Fish or
  Chicken
	Butter sauce for
	  vegetables
		Sauces for fish
		Barbecue
		Horseradish
			Mayonnaise
			Tartar
			Hollandaise
			Béarnaise
				Creole
				Tomato
				Curry
				Mustard

26
ENTERTAINING
GUESTS

A successful party depends as much upon a relaxed and charming hostess as it does on the food served. A simple meal of a few courses, served comfortably, with the guests unaware of the hostess's work, can often be as impressive and enjoyable as the elegant "formal" ceremonial dinner, so rarely served these days.

Entertaining today is primarily of an informal nature, but there are certain traditions and conventions about serving which are important to know. As important is the knowledge that these rules *can* and *should* be adapted to such considerations as the number of guests to be invited, the space available for entertaining, budget limitations and whether help is available. The type of meal and service will depend upon these factors. Suggestions for every type of luncheon or dinner party will be found in chapter 1.

PLANNING AHEAD

A few good rules to remember:

Simple well-cooked dishes with which the cook is familiar are preferable to experimental recipes never before attempted.

Dishes which can be cooked ahead of time and either frozen or refrigerated until needed are a great convenience.

Menu and marketing lists should be written out well in advance; supply of staples should be checked as well as the needs for the specific menu. Marketing should be done at least one day ahead to avoid the necessity for last-minute changes, should certain foods not be available.

Plan linen, china, silver and serving pieces to be used; see that all are clean and silver polished ahead of time.

Plan menus which do not complicate either use of oven or refrigerator storage. Foods to be cooked in the oven should require the same oven temperature. There should be ample space in the refrigerator to accommodate all cold dishes. Otherwise, change the menu to avoid such problems.

Do as much as possible in advance: table can be set; raw vegetables and salad can be washed and prepared in the morning; ice can be put in buckets. This is particularly helpful where the hostess must do all the planning, preparing, cooking and serving.

Make a timetable to determine in what order foods should be cooked. Start with the dish that takes the longest cooking time, then the next longest, and so on. Such a timetable will help all elements of the meal to be ready to serve properly cooked at the proper time.

If cocktails are planned, serve appetizers with them which do not have to be prepared at the last minute.

Meat and rolls can be kept hot in a slow oven (125° F.). Other foods can be warmed in a double boiler.

TYPE OF SERVICE

Most entertaining today falls into two general classifications: the "sit-down" meal which is served by help or by the hostess herself, and the buffet meal at which guests serve themselves and are then seated either at the dining table or at small tables scattered through the living-dining area.

The advantages of each are obvious. With fewer

guests and ample space, the sit-down meal at the table is most convenient and comfortable. Where there are many guests, and possibly limited space, the more informal buffet is preferable. The buffet has also become extremely popular for small groups since it generates a more relaxed and convivial atmosphere.

SETTINGS FOR THE TABLE

General Rules

LINENS

Cover the table with table pads or a silence cloth of felt or flannel. Over this spread a tablecloth, the middle crease up, dividing the table exactly in half and the edges hanging evenly all around the table. Lace tablecloths require no silence cloths, but would need trivets under hot dishes.

For breakfast, luncheon, supper or any dinner except the most formal kind, place mats (on heat-resistant mats for hot plates) may be used instead of a cloth.

DECORATIONS

The center decoration should not obstruct the view. It may be fruit or flowers. For formal occasions, two candelabra or four candlesticks are placed at each side of the centerpiece. Compote dishes, filled with nuts and candies may be placed toward the ends of the table.

For luncheons no candles are used. Small ornaments of glass or china are substituted if desired.

Place everything upon the table, as neatly and attractively as possible, and avoid crowding.

INDIVIDUAL COVERS

A cover consists of plates, glasses, silver and napkin to be used by one person. The covers should be one inch from the edge of the table, allowing about twenty-five inches between plates.

The actual settings and their variations are best shown and clearly explained in the diagrams which follow.

Basic Settings for Informal Lunch or Dinner

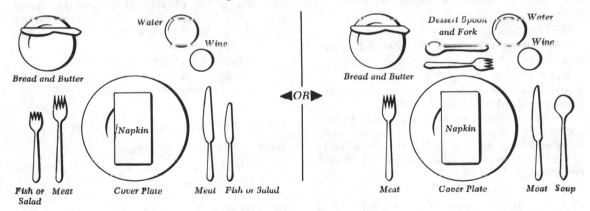

Formal Setting

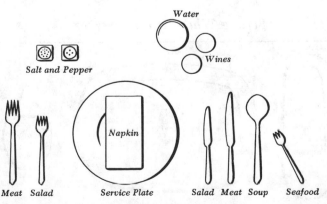

Heat china and silver dishes in which hot food is served by placing in warm oven, protected by pad or by rinsing in hot water. Chill dishes for salads and ices.

SILVER
Place at each side of the plate in the order in which it is used, commencing from the outside and continuing toward the plate, at right angles to the edge of the table.

KNIVES
Place at the right, sharp edges toward the plate.

FORKS
Tines are turned up and placed to the left of the plate.

SPOONS
Bowls are turned up and placed to the right of the knives. The cocktail spoon or fork is placed at the extreme right end. Other spoons are brought in with their respective courses.

Silver for the dessert course is not put on with the other silver at a formal dinner, nor are more than three forks laid. Additional silver is brought in with the dessert and coffee, either on the plate or placed, from a napkin or tray, at the right of the plate.

WATER GLASS
Place at the right, at or near the point of the knife. It should be only three-fourths full.

WINE GLASS
Place below and to the right of the water glass. It should be only three-fourths full.

See Wine section, page 58, for a description of appropriate wines to serve with various foods. Wine may be poured by host—first to himself, and to woman on his right—then passed to next male guest who does the same.

SERVICE PLATE
This plate should remain in place until it is exchanged for the plate of the first hot course. On the service plate is placed the plate containing the cocktail glass for fruit or shellfish, the appetizer, the bouillon cup or soup plate and the entrée.

BREAD AND BUTTER PLATE
Place directly above the forks, with the spreader straight across the top of the plate, handle to the right. At formal dinners no spreader is used and sometimes the bread and butter service is omitted entirely.

INDIVIDUAL SALT AND PEPPER
Where used, these may be placed above each plate or between each two covers. Ashtrays, cigarettes and matches are sometimes included as well.

NAPKIN
Place to the left of the forks with the fold at the top, the hemmed edges parallel with the forks and the table edge. At formal dinners, the napkins may be placed on service plate.

FINGER BOWLS
When used these are usually brought in before dessert, and placed at the left of the cover. Usually the finger bowl is half filled with tepid water, containing a thin slice of lemon or a few flower petals. It is brought in before the dessert course on a plate on which is first placed a doily and the dessert silver. It is set before each person, who removes the doily and finger bowl to the left, and the silver to the right.

SERVING TABLE OR SIDEBOARD
Use to hold all silver for serving and all extras which may be needed during a meal.

DIRECTIONS FOR SERVING

WHERE THERE IS NO MAID
All the food belonging to one course is placed on the table in platters or suitable dishes before the person who is to serve or on a nearby teacart or small table. The number of plates necessary may be in a pile directly in front of the server, or the

Setting Where Hostess Serves

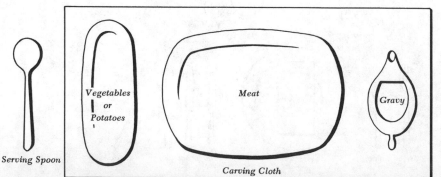

Serving Spoon — Vegetables or Potatoes — Meat — Gravy — Carving Cloth

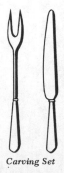

Carving Set

plates may be passed by each individual in rotation. Salad plates may be placed at the left or right of the cover for informal service.

INFORMAL SERVICE WHERE THERE IS A MAID

The table is set with a plate and silver for each person. The platter or dish containing the main course is placed before the host, who serves the first portion on the plate before him. While the host is carving, the waitress holds an empty plate in her left hand and stands to the left of the server. She removes the filled plate, places the empty plate before the server, and passes the plate with the food to the first person to be served, at the same time taking the empty plate from this place. She brings this empty plate back to the server, removes the second filled plate, replacing it with the empty plate, and continues in the same manner until everyone is served. The last empty plate is then set aside.

PLATTER SERVICE

By this method everything pertaining to a complete course is served from large platters.

Any number of guests may be served in this manner provided a proportionate amount of help is supplied in the kitchen and dining room. One waitress can easily serve from six to eight persons.

INDIVIDUAL SERVICE

A simple way of serving large seated groups is by individual service. Small portions of everything belonging to one complete course are artistically arranged on individual plates in the kitchen and served to each person.

FORMAL SERVICE

The host and hostess take no part in the service. No platters are put on the table. All serving is done from the pantry or serving table by waitresses. Four to six guests are assigned to one waitress. Each plate may be brought to the table with a portion of the main dish of the course, or the plates are set down empty and the food is served from platters from which the person helps himself. The waitress removes one plate with the right hand and places the plate for the next course with the left hand, the table never being without plates. Before serving the dessert, everything but the decorations is cleared away, then crumbs are removed from the cloth. After-dinner coffee may be served at the table or poured by the hostess in the living room.

ORDER FOR SERVICE

The host sits at the head of the table, the hostess directly opposite. The guest of honor, if a man, is seated at the right of the hostess; if a woman, at the right of the host. Serve the lady guest of honor first and continue toward the right. The next course should be served toward the left, that no side be always served last. At a formal dinner two waitresses serve, one from the hostess to the right, the other from the host to the right.

BUFFET TABLE SUGGESTIONS

A long narrow table, placed against one wall and covered with an appropriate cloth, is particularly

A Typical Buffet Setting

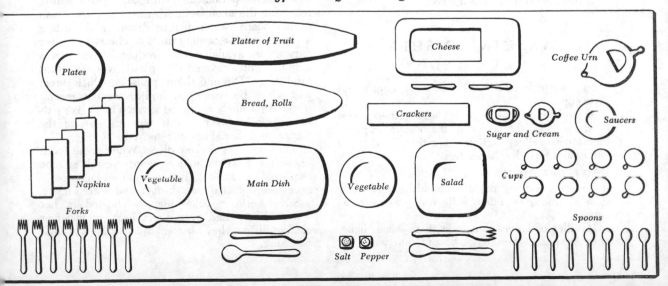

convenient for buffet service, although a round or square or oblong table can also be used. The principle to observe is to have plates available at one end, and then the main dish and accompaniments in the order in which you wish guests to serve themselves. The traffic should move in one direction only.

With the availability of electrical hot plates, chafing dishes, hot trays, the dishes you serve can be kept properly hot whether simple or elaborate. It is customary to avoid food which requires the use of a knife, although poultry, ham and other meats are often served and carved at the buffet in small, thin slices.

Dessert and coffee can be served from a sideboard, or from a rolling cart.

CLEARING THE TABLE

When the main course is finished, remove all dishes containing food first: the platters, vegetable dishes and smaller serving dishes, not taking the silver from them; next the individual cover, consisting of the large plates and the butter plates, then the sauce dishes, if any, and last of all the clean plates and silver not used.

Do not remove cutlery or silver from dishes at the table.

Do not pile dishes one upon the other.

Before serving the dessert, remove salts and peppers, relishes and all other dishes. Remove all crumbs with a folded napkin, brushing them on a plate or crumb tray.

After the meal is over and the family or guests have left the dining room, the table should be cleared of the last course.

Brush the crumbs from the cloth and remove it.

Brush the crumbs from the floor.

WASHING DISHES BY HAND

Scrape waste from dishes, rinse them; empty and rinse cups.

Arrange all articles of each kind together: plates by themselves, the largest at the bottom; cups by themselves; silver articles together, and steel knives and forks by themselves.

SOAKING DISHES

If possible, cooking utensils should be washed as soon as used, or filled with water as soon as emptied.

Handles of knives and forks, if of wood, bone, ivory or pearl, should not be put into water, as they are apt to split. They should be wiped first with a wet, then with a dry cloth.

Cold water should be used for soaking dishes which have been used for milk, eggs, fish and starchy foods; hot water, for dishes used for sugar substances and for sticky, gummy substances like gelatin. Greasy dishes of all kinds, including knives, are more easily cleaned if first wiped with soft paper.

TO WASH DISHES

Order: (1) glassware; (2) silver; (3) cups and saucers; (4) plates; (5) platters, vegetable dishes, etc.; (6) cooking utensils.

Have a pan half filled with hot water containing soap or detergent. Slip glasses and fine china in sideways, that the hot water will touch outside and inside at the same time, and thus avoid danger of cracking. If dishes are very greasy, add a little washing soda, or ammonia. Rinse all dishes in clean hot water, drain, wipe with clean, dry towels if necessary. If water is sufficiently hot, dishes will not require wiping.

DRAINING DISHES

As the dishes are washed and rinsed, place them in a dish drainer. For fine dishes and glassware, do not use drainer, but place on a folded dish cloth to avoid nicking.

CARE OF SILVER

Use silver often; sterling improves with use, and frequent use prevents the formation of tarnish. Polish silver periodically with good silver polish, following the manufacturer's directions, and wash in hot soapy water before drying and putting away. Tarnish-retarding storage chests for silver flatware are available. Less frequently used pieces may be tightly covered with plastic wrap to retard tarnishing. "Dip and shine" polishes, which direct that silver be soaked in liquid, are not recommended for finely engraved silver. The darker pattern areas in silver of this type are part of the design, and should not be removed.

Salt and eggs darken silver. When these foods are served in silver holders, empty vessels as soon as possible and clean silver in usual way at once. It is best to protect silver salt-dishes with glass liners.

Silver serving dishes may be heated in hot water. When used over direct heat, as in silver chafing dishes, they blacken and require thorough polishing.

27
MARKETING,
KITCHEN NEEDS
AND HOUSEKEEPING

EFFICIENT MARKETING

It pays to develop special skills in shopping for food, in order to get the best value for your money and to provide the best possible meals for your family. Modern food markets offer a broad selection of foods, and a wide variety of forms in which foods may be purchased.

Five simple rules are basic to efficient marketing:

1. Plan meals in advance—if possible, a week ahead, and buy with your advance needs in mind.
2. Keep the menus flexible enough to allow you to take advantage of special prices at the market.
3. Take advantage of seasonal plentiful foods in planning menus.
4. Keep your basic food supplies stocked, checking refrigerator, vegetable bin, cupboards and freezer before you begin to shop. See that the makings of an emergency meal and impromptu snack are on hand.
5. Read the label of foods you select. You will find ingredients of the contents listed in order of importance, along with description of the product and information on use.
6. Read the label for Recommended Daily Allowances.

When you shop, select your purchases in this order: canned goods, package goods, household supplies and other imperishables first; then dairy products, meat, fresh fruits and vegetables and frozen foods last, so that they will have the shortest possible wait before they reach their destination.

EMPTYING THE MARKET BASKET

As soon as you arrive home, unpack your purchases, sorting into groups: frozen foods to go directly into the freezer; meats and poultry to be unwrapped, then covered loosely for storage in refrigerator or prepared and re-wrapped for freezing; fruits and vegetables, separating those for refrigeration and those to be stored elsewhere; dairy products, assembled so that they may be carried easily to refrigerator and stored; packaged goods grouped for storage in respective cupboards.

Work with items which require freezing or refrigeration first. Remember that foods tend to lose moisture or take on other flavors in the refrigerator. Wrap foods for storage in plastic bags or wrappings, or tightly covered plastic or glass containers; store vegetables in a closed container or crisper.

The temperature of the refrigerator should be between 38° and 42° F. An accumulation of frost on the freezing coils can raise the temperature dangerously. Defrost as often as necessary to prevent this, especially in warm weather or when the refrigerator is being opened frequently. (In refrigerators equipped with automatic defrosters, check drip pan as indicated in manufacturer's directions.)

KITCHEN EQUIPMENT

In selecting pots and pans choose individual pieces according to the use to which they will be put, rather than a matched set of many different sizes. The following materials are readily available, and are useful for different purposes because of their varying basic qualities:

ALUMINUM PANS: Heavy, fine quality aluminum heats evenly, is satisfactory for general-purpose cooking, frying, sautéeing.

CAST-IRON PANS: Heavy, heat evenly for browning food or cooking in fat. Good for use over high heat.

COPPER PANS (*tin lined*): Heat quickly, give excellent results if used with care. Need polishing after use.

COPPER-CLAD OR COPPER-INTERLINED STAINLESS STEEL PANS: These conduct heat quickly yet evenly. Excellent for sauce-making, sautéeing, braising. Avoid high heat when using.

EARTHENWARE can be used top-range or in the oven, but it cracks easily and must be used over low heat, and guarded against sudden changes of temperature.

ENAMEL PANS: Light-weight, non-porous, excellent for boiling, as for pastas, boiled dinners, soup stocks, foods with acid content which should not be in contact with metal.

ENAMEL-COVERED IRON: Heavy, but excellent cooking tools, combining the qualities of iron and enamel.

GLASS OR CERAMIC MATERIALS: Heat quickly, excellent for boiling and braising; satisfactory for frying and baking, but temperatures should generally be reduced slightly, to compensate for faster heating. Some are made for both top-of-range and oven use; others are designed either for direct or indirect heat. Like enamel, good for acid foods.

NO-STICK COATED PANS are so finished that foods may be cooked without fat or liquid, without sticking. Lower temperature must be used for these, and wooden or plastic spatulas are recommended for stirring, to prevent scratching the no-stick finish.

PRESSURE COOKERS are designed to cook foods rapidly under steam pressure. These are available in plain or electric models. Good for high altitudes and, in large size, for canning.

CERTAIN SPECIALTIES are best made in pans specifically designed for their use. An omelet pan is best reserved for that purpose, and wiped clean with a paper towel between usings, so that the "finish" is preserved and eggs roll out easily. An enameled oval fish cooker with a steaming rack is excellent for poaching fish, or for steaming asparagus or artichokes.

BASIC PANS FOR TOP-RANGE COOKING

3 heavy skillets, 6, 8 and 12 inch sizes
1 kettle, about 6 quarts
double boiler, 1½ and 2 quart sizes
3 saucepans, 2-cup and 1 and 3 quart sizes
1 Dutch oven with cover (also for use in oven)
1 coffeepot
1 teakettle

BASIC PANS FOR THE OVEN

1 roaster, about 12-15 inches long, with rack and cover
2 casseroles, oven-to-table style, 1½ and 2 quart sizes
1 pie plate, 9 inch
1 muffin tin, 12 cups, about 3 inches in diameter
2 layer pans, 8-inch
1 square or round casserole or pan, 9-inch
1 tube pan with removable bottom, 9-inch
1 shallow-sided baking sheet
1 loaf pan, 9" by 5"
1 pan with removable sides (spring-form)

SMALL ELECTRICAL EQUIPMENT

Toaster
Mixer
Blender
Coffee maker
Waffle iron (optional)
Can opener (optional)
Skillet (optional)
Broiler (optional)

BASIC KITCHEN TOOLS

SPECIAL TOOLS FOR BAKING

flour sifter
rubber spatula
rolling pin
pastry blender
cooling rack

FOR FOOD PREPARATION

cutting board
4 knives: paring knife, bread knife, butcher knife or chopper, slicer
vegetable scrubbing brush
vegetable peeler
egg beater
grater
kitchen shears
juicer
can and jar openers
mixing bowls, 1 pint, 1 quart, 3 quart sizes
rubber spatula
timer

FOR USE AT THE RANGE

wooden spoons, 2 sizes
long-handled 2-tined fork
ladle
metal spatula
pancake turner
whisk

FOR USE AFTER COOKING
carving knife and fork
colander
food mill
potato masher

HOUSEKEEPING GUIDE

ORGANIZING A HOUSEKEEPING SCHEDULE

Make a schedule of essential housekeeping tasks, and use this as a guide to jobs to do every day, once a week, at the major change-over time in the spring and fall. Clean regularly; dirt and stains are easier to remove when fresh.

First, list your daily chores: general tidying, bed-making, top-dusting, sweeping and vacuuming, care of the bathroom and kitchen, meal preparation and dishwashing.

Make a second list of chores done on special days of the week: ideally, each room should be done thoroughly once a week, with work divided equally among the working days you allot to housekeeping. Weekly cleaning should include dusting of less accessible places—ledges, moldings, woodwork, picture frames, and mirrors, polishing furniture and floors, airing beds, dusting springs and mattresses, and changing linens. Plan for laundering as part of your weekly schedule.

Learn to dovetail jobs, so that two can be going at once. Let the washer run by itself while you do surface cleaning. Dovetail your own time and motions, too. For example, in making a bed, it is much faster to spread all the layers of the bed clothes at once, then tuck in one corner at a time, instead of walking around the bed three or four times to tuck in one layer at a time.

CARE AND CLEANING OF THE REFRIGERATOR AND FREEZER

Consult the manufacturer's booklet for hints on the care of your refrigerator. Generally speaking, the following suggestions apply to all models.

Automatic defrosters have a drip tray to collect water. The tray also collects spills, and should be washed often.

Nonautomatic-defrosting refrigerators should be defrosted as often as necessary to keep the freezing coils free of ice—more often in hot weather.

Empty the refrigerator regularly, once a week, or once every two weeks. Discard useless bits of food and consolidate small but edible amounts of food in small containers. Make note of leftovers for use in meals you are planning. Remove all the movable refrigerator parts and wash them in sudsy water. Wash refrigerator itself with a solution of 3 tablespoons baking soda in 1 quart warm water. Rinse and dry all thoroughly. Wash the rubber door seal with plain warm water and dry.

Freezer or freezer compartment should be defrosted and cleaned twice a year or more often, if ice has accumulated. Remove frozen foods and place in insulated bags, or cover with an insulating layer of several thicknesses of newspaper. Defrost the freezer. To hasten defrosting, put flat pans of boiling water on the shelves, changing them as necessary until the ice melts or softens and can be lifted out. Wash the interior with warm water and soda, like the refrigerator, rinse, and dry well. Clean and polish outside surfaces of refrigerators and freezers, including metal trim, with kitchen wax.

CARE OF THE RANGE

Consult the manufacturer's leaflet for special instructions covering care of your range. All ranges, whether gas or electric, require the same sort of cleaning care. (An exception is the new type of oven with automatic cleaning device.)

Wipe up spills and spatters on the surface with paper towels, at once, before they dry. As part of the regular cleaning routine after meals, wash burner trays with sponge or cloth.

Remove oven broiler pan immediately after use and rinse with hot water. Clean thoroughly with steel wool pads, rinse, and dry. Wipe broiler oven walls with sponge or cloth after each use. A strip of disposable foil may be laid directly on the broiler tray to reduce cleaning. Wipe oven walls and bottom after each use with sponge or cloth. Use oven cleaner to remove any baked-on spills.

Allow range to cool before cleaning thoroughly. If washed when hot, the enamel may crack.

Use mild soap or cleanser that will not scratch.

To prepare oven for cleaning, place a small dish of ammonia in the oven for several hours. This will loosen any crust and make cleaning easier. Commercial preparations are also widely available.

Periodically unscrew removable parts, soak in solution of 3 tablespoons baking soda to 1 quart hot water, and scrub clean. Rinse and dry well.

Clean and polish enamel and porcelain surfaces and bright metal trim with kitchen wax.

DIRECTIONS FOR USE OF THE GAS RANGE
CORRECT USE OF TOP BURNERS

Place cooking utensil over burner before lighting it.

Automatic top burners light at the turn of the burner control knob. Turn on full, then adjust it to give desired flame, or follow manufacturer's directions.

To light nonautomatic burners, turn knob on

full and immediately press pilot light or apply a lighted match.

CORRECT USE OF OVEN

Automatic oven burners light at the turn of the oven control knob.

For nonautomatic oven burners, turn oven-burner knob on full and immediately apply lighted match.

Set oven regulator at temperature indicated in recipe. The correct oven temperature is maintained by the regulator which automatically adjusts the oven-burner flame.

If preheating is indicated in the recipe, allow 10 minutes for oven to reach desired temperature. Many foods are satisfactory baked from a cold start.

After using, leave oven door closed until oven is cool.

CORRECT USE OF BROILER

Light as for oven, above.

Set temperature regulator for broiling, place rack about 3 inches from tip of flame and preheat broiler for 5 minutes, except for bacon.

Broil foods as indicated in recipes.

When the broiling compartment is under the oven, the broiler pan should be removed when oven is in use, or put on the lower rack.

EFFICIENT USE OF GAS

Do not light gas until you are ready to use it and turn it off when utensil is removed from flame or oven.

The top burner should be smaller than the cooking utensil.

Crowding the oven and allowing the pans to touch oven walls interferes with heat distribution and causes poor results.

Use the simmer burner whenever possible.

Do not use a stronger flame than is necessary; reduce it when boiling temperature is reached. If flame burns yellow and smoky, turn off gas a few seconds and light again. Flame should be blue.

USE OF A PORTABLE THERMOMETER

If range has no oven heat regulator, or a stationary thermometer, buy a good portable oven thermometer. Set upright on floor of a cold oven six inches back from door, at right or left side, according to best light. If low grate interferes, insert thermometer sideways through grate. Light oven and let heat slowly until the desired degree of heat is reached as indicated by the thermometer. Then reduce flame so it will remain at that point 3 or more minutes. Place food to be baked in the oven. The mixture, being cold, will cool the oven somewhat, so turn the gas a little higher and look at the thermometer after a few minutes, to see when it reaches the required heat. Then lower the flame, look into the oven occasionally and, if necessary, regulate the flame so that it remains at that degree until the bread, cake, pie, meat or other food is baked or roasted.

Wherever possible, in the recipes, the temperatures in degrees Fahrenheit have been inserted, but the following equivalents of the various degrees of heat may be found useful.

> 275-300° F. is a slow oven.
> 325-375° is a moderate oven.
> 400-450° F. is a hot oven.
> 450-500° F. is a very hot oven.

TANKED OR BOTTLED GAS FOR COUNTRY HOMES

Special gas stoves may be had for country use. The gas is stored in cylinders outside the home and piped in a manner similar to that of city gas.

DIRECTIONS FOR USE OF ELECTRIC RANGE

SURFACE UNITS

(1) Boiling. Turn switch to "high" until boiling point is reached, then turn immediately to "low" or "off" for remaining time required.

(2) Frying. Preheat frying pan on "high," keep frying temperature by turning to "low" or "medium."

(3) Deep Well, or Thrift Cooker. To be used for foods that require long-time cooking, such as soups, stews, vegetables, and beans—also for steaming. Keep covered and on "low" until ready to serve.

BROILER

Set control at "broil." Place food in broiler pan so that surface of food is about 2 to 5 inches below broiler unit. Leave oven door ajar during entire process.

OVEN

Crowding the oven and allowing the pans to touch oven walls or each other interferes with heat distribution and causes burning.

If broiler pan is in oven unit, remove when oven is in use. Do not use broiler pan for baking.

EMERGENCY HOUSEKEEPING AND IMPROVISING

WHEN ELECTRIC POWER FAILS

Check first whether a fuse has blown. Keep a reserve supply of each size of fuse used in your home on hand, for replacements. *Do not replace a fuse with a larger size.* A blown fuse has a break in the surface metal which conducts electricity, and sometimes also shows surface blackening. Simply unscrew and replace with a new fuse. A blown fuse is a signal of overloading or faulty electrical wiring. Check for the source of problem.

TO START A WOOD AND COAL FIRE

Plan to build the fire on a surface where air can circulate. To improvise a fire-site outdoors, dig a shallow hole in the ground, then make a base through which air can circulate by piling uneven rocks loosely. On a loose mound of twisted paper or twigs or bits of wood and bark, pile larger pieces of wood in a cone shape, or scatter with fine coal or charcoal. If stove with a firebox or a fireplace with a grate is used, have all drafts open. Ignite the paper, and as wood or coal settles down, add more wood or coal gradually. In using a firebox, add coal until the firebox is filled. When the blue flame of coal disappears, close the dampers, and open the dampers again when more coal is added. When the coal is red it is nearly burned out. To keep a fire several hours, shake out the ashes, fill with coal, close the dampers and partially open the slide above the fire. For continual use it is better to add a little fuel at a time, but not in the midst of baking. For soft coal, keep the chimney damper partially open to allow the soot and smoke to escape. Remove ashes every day.

A charcoal or wood fire is hottest when flames die down and gray ash shows.

TO COOK WITHOUT EQUIPMENT

Wrap food in leaves and place in fire, or impale on a spit made from a green twig.

TO KEEP FOODS COLD

Immerse in cold water (in a stream if possible) or wrap thickly in newspapers and keep wet. Or, in cold weather, hang a porous container outdoors, outside a window with easy access.

IF FOOD SCORCHES

Remove unburned portion to another pan, being careful not to pick up any scorched material. Add more liquid if necessary and finish cooking.

TO PICK UP BROKEN GLASS

Small pieces of broken glassware may be picked up from floor or other hard surfaces with dampened, absorbent cotton or paper towels.

TO MAKE SOAP

> **5 pounds lukewarm melted fat**
> **1 can (1 pound) lye**
> **1 quart cold water**
> **3 teaspoons borax**
> **1 teaspoon salt**
> **2 tablespoons sugar**
> **½ cup cold water**
> **¼ cup ammonia**

Fats that are not fit for food may be made into soap. Melt fat and strain through cheesecloth. Dissolve the lye in cold water and let stand until cool, then add the fat slowly, stirring constantly. Mix the other ingredients together and add to the first mixture. Stir the whole until thick and light colored. Pour into a pan lined with cloth. Mark into pieces of desired size before the soap becomes hard. When hard, break pieces apart and pile in such a way that soap may dry out well.

STAIN REMOVAL

Always try to deal with stains at once, for best results.

If a stain is of unknown origin, but seems nongreasy, soak it in cold water, then wash in warm suds. If it seems greasy, sponge with carbon tetrachloride or a similar dry-cleaning solvent, then wash.

Always try any chemicals used in stain removal on the inside of a hem or other inconspicuous place.

General laundering directions apply to stain removal as well—for instance, wool, rayon, and many synthetics cannot be washed in hot water or bleached with some types of household bleach. Combinations of fibers should be treated according to the most delicate fiber in the combination.

REMOVAL OF COMMON STAINS

STAINS	PRE-TREATMENT	TREATMENT	IF STAINS PERSIST
Adhesive Tape	Sponge with kerosene	Wash in hot suds	
Alcoholic Beverages	Soak or sponge with cool water	Wash in warm suds	Soak in weak solution of household bleach and wash again
Ballpoint Ink	Sponge with carbon tetrachloride	Wash in warm suds	
Blood	Sponge or soak in cold water	Wash in warm, not hot suds	Soak in weak solution of household bleach and wash again
Candle Wax	Scrape off excess wax, place fabric between white blotters and press with a hot iron	Wash in warm suds	Rub with cold turpentine, wash again in warm suds
Cheese	Scrape off excess, sponge with cool water	Wash in hot suds	
Chocolate or Cocoa	Wash in hot suds	Soak in weak solution of household bleach or hydrogen peroxide, wash again	
Cod-Liver Oil	Sponge with glycerine or carbon tetrachloride, rinse in warm water	Wash in warm suds	Old stains are almost impossible to remove
Coffee and Tea	Stretch fabric taut over a bowl, pour boiling water through stain from a height of 3 or 4 feet	Wash in hot suds	
Egg	Scrape off excess, soak in cool water	Wash in warm suds	
Fruits: Peach, pear, cherry and plum	Sponge with cool water and rub lightly with glycerine, let stand a few hours. Apply a few drops of vinegar, rinse	Wash in warm suds	
Berries, other fruits	Stretch fabric taut over a bowl, pour boiling water through stain from a height of 3 or 4 feet	Wash as usual	
Ink, washable		Wash in hot suds	
Ink, oil-based	Rub with glycerine	Wash in hot suds	
Lipstick	Rub with glycerine	Wash in hot suds	
Mayonnaise	Sponge with cold water, then sponge with warm suds	Wash as usual	
Meat Juices	Soak in cool water	Wash in hot suds	
Mildew	Wash in warm suds, dry in sun	Rub with lemon juice and salt, dry in sun. Wash again	
Milk or Cream	Sponge or soak with cool water	Wash in hot suds	
Mustard	Sponge with cool water, rub with warm glycerine	Wash in hot suds	
Paint	If fresh, wash in hot suds. If dry, sponge with turpentine or kerosene	Wash in hot suds	
Scorch		Wash in hot suds	Bleach in the sun, or dampen with hydrogen peroxide, dry in sun, then launder in hot suds

STAINS	PRE-TREATMENT	TREATMENT	IF STAIN PERSISTS
Shoe Polish **White liquid**	Sponge with cool water	Wash as usual	
Wax Types	Sponge thoroughly with suds	Wash as usual	Soak in household bleach, then launder again
Soft Drinks **Fresh**	Sponge with cool water or with a solution of equal parts of alcohol and water	Wash in hot suds	
Dry	Rub glycerine into the stain, let stand half an hour	Rinse with warm water. Wash in hot suds	
Stamping Ink	Soak in weak solution of household bleach	Wash in hot suds	
Tomato and **Tomato Catsup**	Sponge with cool water. Rub with glycerine, let stand half an hour	Wash in hot suds	

INDEX

THE SETTLEMENT COOK BOOK/CONTENTS

Important: For best results, read the general rules at the beginning of each chapter.

Most of the recipes in this book will serve from 4 to 6 persons, depending on the size of serving. Average single servings of common foods:

Meat, poultry, fish	4 ounces (¼ pound)
Vegetables and fruits	½ cup
Desserts, ice cream	½ cup
Pies	⅐ or ⅛ of a 9″ pie
Cakes	2″ wedge or cube

OVEN TEMPERATURES

250°	very slow
300°	slow
325°	moderately slow
350°	moderate
375°	moderately hot
400°	hot
450°	very hot
500°	extremely hot

STANDARD WEIGHTS AND MEASURES

A dash	8 drops
1 teaspoon	60 drops
1 tablespoon	3 teaspoons
1 ounce	2 tablespoons
¼ cup	4 tablespoons
⅓ cup	5⅓ tablespoons
½ cup	8 tablespoons
1 cup	16 tablespoons *or* 8 fluid ounces *or* ½ pint
1 pint	2 cups
1 pound	16 ounces
1 quart	2 pints
1 gallon	4 quarts
1 peck	8 quarts
1 bushel	4 pecks
1 dram	$\frac{1}{16}$ ounce
1 gram	$\frac{1}{30}$ ounce
1 kilo	2.20 pounds
1 liter	1 quart (approximate)
1 meter	39.37 inches